Life Insurance

The Prentice-Hall Series in Security and Insurance
Consulting Editor: Kenneth Black, Jr.

Eleventh Edition
Revised

LIFE
INSURANCE

Kenneth Black, Jr.
Regents' Professor of Insurance
College of Business Administration
Georgia State University

Harold D. Skipper, Jr.
Director, Center for Risk Management
and Insurance Research
College of Business Administration
Georgia State University

 Special Edition for The American College

PRENTICE HALL, ENGLEWOOD CLIFFS, NEW JERSEY 07632

Library of Congress Cataloging-in-Publication Data

Black, Kenneth.
  Life insurance.

  (The Prentice-Hall series in security and insurance)
  Incldues bibliographies and index.
  1. Insurance, Life. 2. Insurance, Health.
I. Skipper, Harold D., 1947- . II. Title.
III. Series.
HG8771.B55 1988   368.3'2   88-5799
ISBN 0-13-535980-5

Editorial/production supervision and
  interior design: Robert C. Walters
Cover design: Ben Santora
Manufacturing buyer: Harry P. Baisley

ISBN 0-13-539446-5

Prentice-Hall International (UK) Limited, *London*
Prentice-Hall of Australia Pty. Limited, *Sydney*
Prentice-Hall Canada Inc., *Toronto*
Prentice-Hall Hispanoamericana, S.A., *Mexico*
Prentice-Hall of India Private Limited, *New Delhi*
Prentice-Hall of Japan, Inc., *Tokyo*
Simon & Schuster Asia Pte. Ltd., *Singapore*
Editora Prentice-Hall do Brasil, Ltda., *Rio de Janeiro*

To

Kenneth Black, Sr., *and the memory of* Margaret Virginia Black

and

George W. Skipper, Jr., *and the memory of* Harold D. Skipper, Sr.

Solomon Stephen Huebner

Dr. Solomon Stephen Huebner was a distinguished Professor of Insurance at the Wharton School, University of Pennsylvania, and chairman of the Department of Insurance at that institution. He not only introduced the first university-level insurance courses in the United States but also wrote the first university-level insurance textbooks. Dr. Huebner wrote the first edition of this text, published in 1915, and since that time, succeeding editions have been in continuous use both at the university level and in professional designation programs. Through his strong leadership, he came to be known as the father of insurance education in the United States.

While at the University of Pennsylvania, Dr. Huebner was the moving force behind the establishment of both the American College and the American Institute for Property and Liability Underwriters. He served as the first president of the American College, using criteria of knowledge, character, and ethical practice to transform the distribution system of the life insurance business in the United States from the commercialism of the early twentieth century to the service-oriented professionalism a half century later. This earned him the accolade "the teacher who changed an industry."

The authors are pleased to have been able to perpetuate this great educator's text. He built bridges of knowledge and understanding. The authors had the opportunity to cross one of his many bridges, moving from student to teacher, through the S. S. Huebner Foundation for Insurance Education at the University of Pennsylvania. We are grateful for the privilege that has been afforded us and hope that throughout this volume we have maintained the high standards of excellence and professionalism to which Dr. Huebner's entire career was committed.

KENNETH BLACK, JR.
HAROLD D. SKIPPER, JR.

Contents

Preface

This book is a revision of its predecessors, the first of which was published in 1915, and contains the most substantive changes made to the volume within the last thirty years. We have endeavored to alter its emphasis on factual information about the life insurance industry, its products, and its operations to one that combines current information with its use in the life and health insurance marketplace. We have attempted to build on the earlier editions' strengths while reshaping the tone and emphasis to meet current educational and marketplace realities.

The turmoil experienced by the financial services industry within the past few years has called for a new, more detailed examination of life and health insurance and their uses and evaluations. We have attempted to respond to these new demands not only by completely updating and rewriting many chapters but also by giving more depth to the subjects to provide the basis for a deeper understanding by the college or university student as well as by the insurance or other financial professional.

A financial management perspective has been adopted to explain how life and health insurance products fit into a broad framework of financial planning. In this context, these products have both unique advantages and some disadvantages. We have endeavored to present a forthright appraisal of them and to suggest how they may be evaluated from both contractual and cost viewpoints. With an increasingly competitive marketplace, the student and advisor will need to be armed with an appreciation of the means of making fair comparisons and the shortcomings of comparison methods. Of more fundamental importance, however, are the principles upon which life and health insurance are based. For this reason, the volume contains an expanded treatment of life and health insurance fundamentals in Part I.

The discussion of the life insurance planning process builds on the traditional programming approach of earlier editions but extends the concept to cover both inflation and a dynamic approach. We believe current computer technology renders it within the grasp of students and practitioners alike.

Entire chapters have been devoted to the tax treatment of life insurance, to estate planning, and to the business uses of life insurance. While these areas are subject to rapid obsolescence, we nonetheless believe that their inclusion is desirable for those students and practitioners who have had little exposure to the topics elsewhere and for those who need an easy summary of the materials.

The institutional aspects of life insurance are dealt with in the later chapters of the book. They have been updated in all areas and, in many cases, completely rewritten. Some actuarial notations have been introduced into the discussion of the mathematical aspects of life insurance to permit a more complete understanding of this important material. Even with these additions, the mathematical section has been shortened and simplified.

We have made a special effort to produce a text that is logically developed and easily assimilated. It aims to bring together in an organized manner those facts, principles, and practices that will enable the student, practitioner, and layperson to gain a comprehensive understanding of life and health insurance and the legitimate ways they may and should be employed in the interest of personal, family, and business welfare. Special effort has been taken to make the presentation, as Einstein said, "as simple as possible, but not simpler."

Whether this revision accomplishes the mission we seek to achieve, can be judged only by its users. The authors invite critical comments in this regard.

ACKNOWLEDGMENTS

The authors benefited greatly from the constructive advice and criticism of many individuals. These include: Dr. John F. Adams; Mr. James B. Lockhart III, Alexander and Alexander Services, Inc.; Mr. Robert S. Seiler, Allstate Life Insurance Company; Dr. Burton T. Beam, Jr., Dr. Robert W. Cooper, Mr. Edward G. Graves, and Dr. John J. McFadden, The American College; Mr. John K. Booth, Mr. Daniel F. Case, Mr. Richard V. Minck, Mr. William Schreiner, Mr. Anthony T. Spano, and Dr. Kenneth M. Wright, American Council of Life Insurance; Mr. Charles E. Farr, Mr. Thomas J. Graf, Mr. Donald Lanning, and Mr. Larry Zimpleman, The Bankers Life; Mr. E. Paul Barnhart; Mr. William B. Harman, Jr., Davis and Harman; Mr. H. G. Allen, Equitable Variable Life Insurance Company; Mr. Charles Carroll and Mr. Robert L. Posnak, Ernst & Whinney; Mr. Charles Shephard, Georgia International Life Insurance Company; Mr. G. Clair Plank, Kansas City Life Insurance Company; Mr. James C. Brooks, Jr., and Mr. David A. Stonecipher, Life Insurance Company of Georgia; Mr. Samuel H. Turner, The Life Insurance Company of Virginia; Mr. Archer L. Edgar, Mr. Lucian J. Lombardi, and Dr. Walter H. Zultowski, Life Insurance Marketing and Research Association; Ms. Anne Heape, Life Office Management Association; Mr. Wayne L. Winters, The Life Underwriter Training Council; Mr. Richard A. Hemmings, Lord, Bissell & Brook; Mr. John W. Baker, Mixon-Baker Financial Services; Mr. David E. Scarlett and Mr. Robert J. Shlifer, Monarch Life Insurance Company; Mr. Solon P. Patterson, Montag and Caldwell; Mr. Ronald N. Nagler, Monumental Corporation; Mr. Stanfield Hill, MONY Financial Services; Mr. David M. Holland, Munich American Reassurance Company; Mr. Robert J. Myers; Mr. Peter F. Frenzer, Nationwide Insurance; Mr. Harry A. Woodman, Jr., New York Life Insurance Company; Mr. John J. Horrigan, Mr. Gerald A. Levy, and Mr. Ron McGinnity, North American Reassurance Company; Mr. William O. Goodwin, Mr. Richard L. Hall, and Mr. James J. Murphy, Northwestern Mutual Life Insurance Company; Mr. Jeffrey Cropsey, Ms. Katherine Mason, and Mr. Gary Rubinek, Peat, Marwick, Mitchell & Co.; Mr. Walter Campbell, Piedmont Capital Management; Mr. Jarrett L. Davis, Provident Life and Accident Insurance Company; Mr. Robert P. Walker, Provident National Assurance Company; Dr. J. Robert Ferrari, The Prudential Asset Management Company, Inc.; Mr. Walter N. Miller, Mr. Paul E. Sarnoff, and Mr. Richard A. Yorks, The Prudential Insurance Company of America; Kenneth Black, III, Roe, Martin and Neiman; Mr. Richard M. Drury, Scudder Insurance Asset Management; Mr. William M. Atkin, Security Mutual Life Insurance Company of New York; Mr. Edward Flicker and Mr. Stanley Miller, Office of Commissioner of Insurance, State of Georgia; Mr. Thomas Farmakis, Swiss Re Advisers, Inc.; Mr. William P. Perry and Mr. Julius Vogel, Tillinghast, Nelson and Warren; Mr. James Toner, The Toner Organization; Mr. Robert D. Thompson, Towers, Perrin, Forster & Crosby; Mr. F. Charles

McMains, Jr., Union Life Insurance Company; Mr. Greer F. Henderson, USLIFE Corporation; Mr. Frank V. Suozzo, USLIFE Corporation; Mr. Robert E. Carey, Veterans Administration; and Mr. Leland T. Waggoner, Virginia Life of New York.

Special acknowledgment is due Mr. Robert I. Damon of The Guardian Life Insurance Company of America for his preparation of the bulk of Chapters 16 and 17 on individual health insurance. We also wish to thank our undergraduate and graduate students who used drafts of these chapters in their coursework and who generously (yet tactfully) shared their suggestions and criticisms. We hope this "test by fire" has made the book a better educational tool. We are also indebted to several Georgia State University faculty including Mr. Robert W. Batten, Dr. Bruce D. Fielitz, Dr. John F. Newman, Dr. Bruce A. Palmer, Dr. Fred A. Tillman, and doctoral student Arthur Powell. Each of these persons read individual chapters and shared his criticism and judgment. A special note of thanks goes to Inbum Cheong for his computer assistance.

Finally, the authors would like to record their appreciation of Ms. Jonnie Bostic, Ms. Irene Cook, Ms. Nanette Embry, Ms. Judy Murray, and Ms. Jan Robson for their efforts and personal interest in helping with the many administrative duties associated with producing the manuscript.

Of course, none of those who reviewed the manuscript bears any responsibility for the deficiencies that may remain in the completed work.

KENNETH BLACK, JR.
HAROLD D. SKIPPER, JR.

Chapter 1

Life and Health Insurance in Personal Financial Planning

Life and health insurance have long been recognized as necessary and essential elements in an individual's or family's financial program. The late S. S. Huebner is generally credited with being the catalyst behind this recognition through his logical and forceful arguments regarding the "duty" of family breadwinners to insure their lives for the benefit of those financially dependent upon them.[1] He observed that in a modern society, a sense of family responsibility meant that life and health insurance would grow in importance. He argued that people's responsibility to themselves and their families included both the years of survival (and hence included savings accumulation) and the years after death.

He also was among the earliest proponents of the need for a broad-based effort to plan and coordinate individuals' overall financial affairs. His early recommendation that the individual or family unit should be established and run on a sound business basis is now widely accepted and underpins the study of personal financial planning.[2] Life and health insurance continue to occupy an important role in the financial planning process. This chapter provides an introduction to this process and highlights the means by which life and health insurance can assist in accomplishing one's financial plans.

PERSONAL FINANCIAL PLANNING[3]

Nature and Purpose

Although no universally accepted definition of personal financial planning exists, it can be considered as being the process whereby an individual's or family's overall financial objectives are used to develop and implement an integrated plan to accomplish the objectives. The essential elements of this financial planning concept are the identification of *overall* financial goals and objectives and then the development and implementation of an *integrated* plan to accomplish the

---

[1] See generally, Solomon S. Huebner, *The Economics of Life Insurance* (New York: D. Appleton and Company, 1930).

[2] *Ibid.*, pp. 14–17.

[3] This and the following sections draw on G. Victor Hallman and Jerry S. Rosenbloom, *Personal Financial Planning*, 3rd ed. (New York: McGraw-Hill Book Company, 1983), Chaps. 1 and 2; and C. Arthur Williams, Jr., and Richard M. Heins, *Risk Management and Insurance*, 5th ed. (New York: McGraw-Hill Book Company, 1985) Chaps. 1 and 9.

1

objectives. The idea is to focus on the individual's (or family's) objectives as the starting point in financial planning rather than starting with a particular financial instrument and determining how it may fit into a financial plan.

Most persons will use a variety of financial instruments to achieve their financial objectives. Thus such basic financial tools as life insurance, property and liability insurance, mutual funds, common stocks, bonds, annuities, savings accounts, wills, trusts, and real estate will prove to be essential elements of many soundly conceived financial plans.

Unfortunately, many persons either fail to plan or do not follow a consistent, logical pattern in carrying out their financial plan. Failure to plan is not only foolish but often costly. Human nature being what it is, however, it is easy for busy persons to procrastinate. Many believe that their assets or incomes are not sufficient to justify a financial plan or that the costs of planning services will be too high relative to the benefits. Others may fail to plan or follow seemingly erratic patterns in accomplishing financial objectives because planning involves consideration of such unpleasant events as death, disability, unemployment, old age, destruction of property, being subjected to a law suit, and so on.

Generally, these reasons, either alone or in combination, do not constitute valid objections to financial planning. This is not to suggest that the family earning $25,000 per year will utilize the same financial instruments or seek advice from the same financial advisors as a family earning $250,000 per year. However, each family should plan for death, disability, saving, and so on. Details vary, but the need for planning does not.

Within the financial planning process, it will be seen that life and health insurance prove to be valuable and flexible financial instruments. Moreover, for most persons, the life insurance agent has typically been the initiator of the financial planning process and, where the assets or income are substantial or the planning complex, will join other professionals, such as accountants, attorneys, tax consultants, trust officers and others, in carrying out the financial planning process.

The Process

The personal financial planning process might be considered a road map for accomplishing an individual's financial objectives. Of course, the process is not an end in itself. Rather, it is intended to provide an orderly, systematic approach to personal financial planning. The process involves six interrelated steps, which are discussed briefly below. Although the steps are presented as discrete actions to be taken, in fact, each step blends into and complements those that precede and follow.

Gather Information. The first step in the financial planning process is to assemble the relevant quantitative and qualitative information concerning the client. Relevant financial information varies from situation to situation but usually includes a listing of the individual's assets, liabilities, and net worth as well as information regarding the person's income and expenditures. Additionally, information is usually needed concerning the nature of the person's investments; life, health, and other insurance protection; employee benefits; tax situation; relevant estate planning documents such as wills and trusts; and inheritance prospects. This gathering of information about the client is usually accomplished with the aid of a fact-finding questionnaire or form, available from numerous sources.[4] The more complete the information gathered, the better equipped the financial planner will be to do a quality job.

In addition to the preceding quantitative information, qualitative information will be sought concerning such things as the individual's interests, life-style, attitudes and desires, family situation, health, and related information that will underlie the individual's goals and objectives. In fact, it is often at this stage that the financial advisor assists the individual in establishing his

---

[4]See, for example, *Fact Finder for Comprehensive Financial Planning,* 2nd ed. (Bryn Mawr, Pa.: The American College, 1984); and "Data Survey Form," in *Study Guide I: Introduction to Financial Planning* (Denver, Colo.: College for Financial Planning, 1984), Appendix A.

or her objectives—the second step in the financial planning process.

Establish Objectives. The process of setting goals and objectives is, in some ways, the most challenging aspect of the financial planning process. The competent financial planner is most helpful at this stage, for if an indivdual's goals and objectives are poorly formulated and conceived, any ensuing financial plan is likely to be faulty.

To aid the client in this endeavor, the advisor often must probe into aspects of the client's business and personal affairs and relationships that can be among an individual's most sensitive and confidential. This requires not only the necessity of establishing a keen bond of trust— and seeing to it that this trust bond is never broken—but it also involves the ability of the advisor to communicate and probe effectively and professionally.[5]

Analyze Information. The third step in the personal financial planning process is to analyze the quantitative and qualitative information gathered and to do so in light of the client's objectives. Insurance policies would be reviewed carefully, as would all other financial, tax, and legal documents that the planner was competent to examine. Other financial and legal advisors may need to be consulted and advice sought from them at this stage. Deficiencies in the client's existing financial arrangement would be revealed by this analysis and the groundwork laid for the next stage in the process.

Develop Plan. As the planner is reviewing and analyzing the information gathered, both individually and in consultation with the client and his or her other advisors, he or she will probably already be formulating mentally the elements of a proposed financial plan. The plan should represent a coordinated, integrated effort to resolve problems and to help the client achieve his or her objectives in light of current financial and other

constraints and limitations with appropriate consideration concerning future possibilities.

Implement Plan. With a proposed financial plan now available, the advisor would hold further discussions with the client to help him or her to understand how the plan can be implemented and how present financial and other constraints may affect the complete achievement of his or her earlier stated objectives. An outline plan showing implementation dates and types of actions to be taken and products to be purchased is often used. It is not unusual for the proposal to be modified in light of further goal clarification resulting from these continuing discussions. Implementation normally requires the services of other professionals, especially those in the legal and tax areas. Appropriate involvement of these professionals in the planning process will smooth the implementation process.

Monitor and Revise Plan. After the plan is implemented, it is essential to monitor the results to ascertain the extent to which results are compatible with initial expectations. If they are not, changes may be needed. In addition to the need for revisions occasioned by results deviating from expectations or projections, revisions will also be necessitated by the client's changing financial fortunes, family situation, and related goals and objectives.

It goes almost without saying that no plan is foolproof. Changes will occur. This should be expected. The need for the planner to stress this simple, yet important fact to the client is too often overlooked in the planning process.

THE ELEMENTS OF A PERSONAL FINANCIAL PLAN

Personal financial plans should be just that: personal. They should be tailored to the individual, with no two being exactly alike. Even so, almost all financial plans will have certain elements in common. This section presents an overview of the six common elements as well as an introduction to how life and health insurance can be useful in helping to accomplish an individual's objectives.

---

[5]See, generally, G. Hugh Russell and Kenneth Black, Jr., *Human Behavior in Business* (Englewood Cliffs, N.J.: Prentice-Hall, Inc., 1972), and especially Chaps. 4 and 5.

Establish Risk Management Plan

Nature of Personal Risk Management. Most financial planning experts agree that the most basic and usually the initial element of each individual's financial plan is the establishment and maintenance of a sound program of personal risk management. The practice of risk management has been defined as the identification, measurement, and treatment of exposures to potential losses.[6] Risk management is concerned with losses that arise from damage to or destruction of property, from liability, and from loss of health or life. Although historically, the business enterprise has been the chief focus of risk management attention, it is acknowledged that the individual and family should be organized and managed as one would a business. Hence the concept of *personal* risk management makes good financial sense.

As one authority on the subject has noted, in a sense, the practice of risk management is not an option. Individuals and families need merely to exist to face exposures to loss. Such exposures can be ignored altogether, but this is tantamount to selecting a risk management approach by default, and the approach selected often is not the best one. By properly managing one's exposures to loss, more acceptable results can be accomplished at minimum long-run costs.[7]

The Risk Management Process. Risk management involves the identification, measurement, and treatment of property, liability, and personal loss exposures. The risk management process tracks the six-step personal financial planning process.

1. *Gather information.* One must first gather information to permit loss exposure identification. Individuals, families, and businesses face three classes of losses: *property, liability,* and *personal.*

Direct property losses are those that occur because of damage to, destruction of, or disappearance of personal or real property. To illustrate: a building is destroyed by fire, interior walls to a home are defaced by vandals, an automobile is damaged in a collision, or jewelry is stolen while on a vacation.

Indirect property losses occur when an individual, family, or business suffers a reduction in income (revenues less expenses) because it loses use of property or when the value of property that is not damaged is lessened because of direct damage to other property. To illustrate: a family must live in a hotel until the fire damage to their home is repaired. The extra living expenses constitute an indirect loss to the family.

Liability loss exposures exist from "just living." One can be sued for numerous reasons, the most common cause being law suits related to automobile accidents.

Personal loss exposures arise from possibilities of death, illness or injury, and unemployment.[8] Such losses are associated with families, but businesses can and do suffer personal losses as well. For example, the death of a key employee in a small business could have a severe adverse financial impact on the welfare of the business.

Of the three classes of loss exposures discussed above—property, liability, and personal losses—this book deals only with the personal category.[9]

2. *Establish risk management objectives.* The second step in the risk management process is to establish objectives. These objectives should be consistent with and complement those established in connection with one's overall personal financial plan. In fact, the goals associated with the personal risk management program will probably already have been developed as a part of establishment of the personal financial goals. Often, the overall goal may be stated as simply the family's avoiding financial catastrophe as a result of any of the three loss exposure classifications.

---

[6]Williams and Heins, *Risk Management and Insurance,* p. 4.
[7]*Ibid.*

[8]Many authorities include old-age financial dependency (superannuation) as a personal loss exposure. Although this approach has merit, for purposes of this book, the area is shown as an element of personal financial planning separate from personal risk management. This treatment is justified because of the great importance of retirement planning.

[9]For a discussion on property and liability loss exposure treatment, see S. S. Huebner, Kenneth Black, Jr., and Robert S. Cline, *Property and Liability Insurance,* 3rd ed. (Englewood Cliffs, N.J.: Prentice-Hall, Inc. 1982).

3. *Analyze information.* The third step in the risk management process is to analyze the information gathered to permit estimation of the potential financial consequences of losses. This important step technically involves the determination of the probability or chance that a particular loss will occur and the impact that such a loss would have on the financial affairs of the individual, family, or business.

It is instructive to observe loss probabilities so that the planner may gain a better appreciation for the personal loss exposures facing his or her clients. As mentioned previously, primary personal loss exposures flow from the likelihoods of death, loss of health, and loss of job.

(a) Death. The major financial loss faced by most families as a result of death is loss of earning power, although death can also cause the family to incur additional expenses (e.g., funeral expenses or estate taxes). In measuring the financial consequences to a family (or a business) from the death of a major family income earner (or profit producer in the case of an entrepreneur), one of several techniques could be adopted. These are discussed in Chapters 12 to 15. All techniques attempt to place a dollar value on the financial loss suffered by the family (or business) and this value is often the basis upon which life insurance is purchased.

Table 1–1 shows the probability that persons of certain ages will die within the next year and will die prior to attainment of age 65. Clearly, the probability of death within the next year is small for persons during their working years. However, the likelihood of death prior to age 65 is not insignificant. Indeed, approximately one in five persons now between the ages of 20 and 40 will die prior to age 65. (Also, for many persons, death occurring after age 65 can create significant financial hardships, and death probabilities after age 65 are high.) This high probability, combined with the magnitude of the potential financial loss, suggests the need for meaningful risk management measures with respect to the financial consequences of death.

(b) Loss of health. Poor health, like death, may cause two types of losses: (1) loss of earnings and (2) extra expenses. If a person is totally disabled, the dollar value of the loss of earnings may be computed in a manner similar to that used in calculating the loss occasioned by death.

Unexpected extra expenses accompanying an injury, a sickness, or an impairment can take the form of hospital bills, surgical fees, drugs, or other medical expenses. Estimating the probability that a person will suffer a "morbidity condition" and the extent to which that condition will be disabling is extremely difficult because (1) morbidity, unlike mortality, cannot be defined exactly; (2) morbidity varies in seriousness as well as frequency; and (3) morbidity conditions are not reported on a regular basis to public authorities.

Even so, some information is available from insurance data. Table 1–2 shows the number of insured lives by gender and by age that are disabled per 1,000 lives exposed. The table also shows the number of disabled by durations of one,

TABLE 1-1. Probabilities of death within a year following birthday and prior to age 65

Age	Probability of Death Within a Year	Probability of Death Prior Age 65	Age	Probability of Death Within a Year	Probability of Death Prior Age 65
0	0.0132	0.23	35	0.0016	0.20
5	0.0004	0.22	40	0.0023	0.19
10	0.0002	0.22	45	0.0037	0.18
15	0.0007	0.22	50	0.0060	0.16
20	0.0013	0.22	55	0.0091	0.13
25	0.0014	0.21	60	0.0143	0.08
30	0.0013	0.21			

Source: Derived from *Vital Statistics of the United States, 1979,* Volume II, Part A, Section 6, Life Tables (Washington, D.C.: U.S. Department of Health and Human Services, Public Health Service, 1984), p. 11.

TABLE 1-2. Out of 1,000 lives, number disabled per year

| | Duration of Disablement | | | | | |
| | Male Lives | | | Female Lives | | |
Age	1 Month	3 Months	1 Year	1 Month	3 Months	1 Year
17	24	11	3	34	8	1
22	37	17	4	43	13	1
27	40	19	5	53	19	2
32	50	17	3	56	24	3
37	43	17	5	65	30	5
42	56	20	5	87	34	5
47	50	22	7	93	38	6
52	60	24	8	88	38	8
57	77	34	13	85	41	11
62	106	49	18	85	43	13
67	106	43	22	94	49	16
72	122	56	28	88	52	20

Source: E. Paul Barnhart, "The 1982 Disability Tables," *Transactions of the Society of Actuaries,* Vol. XXXV (1983), pp. 784–787.

three, and 12 months. For example, out of 1,000 females, all age 32, it is estimated that 56 will suffer a total disability that lasts at least one month, 24 will suffer a total disability of at least three months duration, and three will be disabled for at least one year.

By comparing the Table 1-2 figures to those in Table 1-1, it can be observed that the probability of an individual being totally disabled for three months or longer within the next year is greater than probabilities of death, although the increase in morbidity with age is not as great as the increasing death rate with age. The rates of disablement are for insured lives, and such experience is more favorable than that found in the population as a whole. Thus, the Table 1-2 figures understate the rates of disablement for the average person. It is clear that the chance of a serious disability is substantial.

According to the *National Health Survey,* on the average day in 1981, about 14 percent of the population had their activities limited to some degree by a chronic condition (defined as a condition that lasts at least three months). Almost 11 percent were limited in their major activity as a worker, homemaker, or student.

Personal health care expenditures for medical care in the United States in 1984 were $342 billion or over $1,394 per capita, of which 46 percent was spent for hospital care services,

22 percent for physicians' services, 9 percent for nursing home care, 8 percent for drugs and medical sundries, 7 percent for dentists' services, and 7 percent for all other medical care. Consumers of medical care paid about 28 percent of these expenses directly. Private health insurers paid about 31 percent, and government paid most of the remainder.[10]

National Health Survey data reveal that in 1981 hospital discharges per 100 persons were 14.2. The average stay was 7.4 days. The average person visited a physician almost five times within a year. Females visited their doctors more often than males, and older persons were more frequent visitors than younger persons. Dental visits were less frequent, with less than two per person per year.[11]

(c) Unemployment. Involuntary unemployment caused by economic factors is another threat to a person's earning power. The potential loss can be computed in a manner similar to that used for disability.

[10]*Health Care Financing Review,* Vol. 7 (Fall 1985), pp. 8, 9, and 16.
[11]National Center for Health Statistics, *Current Estimates from the Health Interview Survey, United States—1981,* U.S. Department of Health and Human Services, Public Health Service, series 10, no. 141 (October 1982), pp. 25, 28, and 30.

During 1985, monthly unemployment rates for the civilian labor force ranged from 7.4 to 6.9 percent. The March 1986 unemployment rate was 7.2 percent. Unemployment rates vary greatly over time. During 1983, the unemployment rate reached 11.4 percent. In 1933, about one-fourth of the labor force was unemployed in an average month. These data do not reveal the extent of partial unemployment.

One measure of the magnitude of unemployment loss is the duration of the unemployment. As one would expect, the average duration is related to the general state of the economy, but particular industries, areas, or persons can suffer substantial losses even when the economy is performing satisfactorily by most standards.

4. *Develop risk management plan.* Once exposures have been identified and measured, the various tools of risk management should be considered and a decision made with respect to the best combination of tools to be used. The tools include primarily (1) avoiding the risk altogether, (2) reducing the chance that a loss will occur or reducing the magnitude of a loss if it does occur, (3) transferring the financial consequences of a loss to some other party, and (4) retaining or bearing the risk internally. Examples of each category would be as follows: (1) **risk avoidance**—not purchasing a car for a college student, thus avoiding the liability and other exposures associated with such auto ownership; (2) **risk reduction**—wellness programs being adopted by employers or, from an individual's viewpont, exercising regularly and adopting proper eating habits, thus reducing the risk of having a heart attack;[12] (3) **risk transfer**—purchasing a medical expense policy from an insurance company, thereby transferring the financial consequences of incurring medical expenses because of loss of health; and (4) **risk retention**—retaining any disability income losses that would result from disability lasting three months or less.

5. *Implement risk management plan.* The fifth step in the risk management process is to implement the risk management plan. For the average family, this may be a matter as simple as purchasing an insurance policy. If the personal risk management program involves such things as risk reduction through better eating and exercise habits, however, a major personal commitment is required from the individuals concerned.

6. *Monitor and revise risk management plan.* The sixth and final step in the risk management process involves monitoring the entire risk management plan and revising it as circumstances dictate. This means that the family should be aware that possible exposures to loss can be eliminated (e.g., selling the beach house and eliminating the financial consequences to the family of its possible destruction), created (e.g., buying a mountain cottage), and altered (e.g., leasing of the newly owned mountain cottage creates new possibilities for incurring liability). This step in the risk management process can be viewed as ''completing of the circle'' in the sense that it represents a linkage with the first step in the process, that of loss exposure identification.

Uses of Life and Health Insurance in Personal Risk Management. Life and health insurance have little relevance with respect to the property and liability risk exposures of an individual, family, or business.[13] However, life and health insurance can and usually should be an element of the risk management program of the average individual or family with respect to personal risk exposures.

Life insurance is unique among private-sector financial instruments in its function of being able immediately to provide funds with which to help replace the financial losses arising from an individual's death.[14] Life insurance alone guarantees that for a relatively modest outlay, an individual's family or business will not have to

---

[12]Corporate wellness programs continue to grow in popularity. See, for example, Rosemary McConkey, Shawn M. Connors, and Clement R. Brown, "Investing in Health—An Alternative to the Cost of Illness," *The Journal of the American Society of CLU,* Vol. XXXIX (September 1985).

[13]An important exception is that of estate conservation in connection with estate planning. See Chapter 14.

[14] Government benefits are made available to qualified individuals under certain conditions. See Chapter 25.

suffer a major financial loss because of an individual's death. As will be discussed below, life insurance can be useful in other elements of a given individual's personal financial plan, although its function of providing protection against the adverse financial consequences of death undoubtedly is the best known.

Since it is not possible to eliminate the possibility of suffering a major sickness or injury, other means are required for dealing with the financial consequences that arise from loss of earnings and expenses that are occasioned by loss of health. In the vast majority of cases, health insurance is the method chosen and is essential in an individual's personal risk management plan. Most individuals need protection against both types of financial exposures: the risk of increased medical expenses and the risk of loss of earnings.

Such protection is usually provided by one's employer with limited protection provided to certain individuals through government plans. Even with such broad-based coverage, however, upon close examination many persons discover that they and their families are exposed to the adverse financial consequences in the event of loss of health to an extent that good risk management principles find unacceptable.

Establish Savings/Investment Program

The second element of most persons' financial plans involves the establishment and maintenance of a savings and investment program. For some persons, especially those just entering the work force, this element can seem distant or even illusory. Indeed, some families' incomes are such that their every dollar must be spent on current living expenses, with no surplus available for savings. Other persons, for various reasons—usually lack of discipline—spend all of their disposable incomes on current consumption even though their total current needs could be met reasonably within their current income level and, at the same time, leave sufficient funds to establish a savings and investment program.

Individuals want to accumulate wealth for a number of reasons, some of the more important of which are discussed below. Naturally, the relative importance of these reasons varies with individual circumstances and attitudes.

Emergency Fund. An emergency fund is usually needed to meet unexpected expenses that are not planned for in the family budget; to pay for "smaller" disability losses, medical expenses, and property losses that purposely are not covered by insurance; and to provide a financial cushion against such personal problems as prolonged unemployment.

The size of the needed emergency fund varies greatly and depends on such factors as family income, number of income earners, stability of employment, assets, debts, insurance deductibles, uncovered health and property insurance exposures, and the family's general attitudes toward risk and security. The size of the emergency fund can be expressed as so many months of a family income, such as three to six months.

By its very nature, the emergency fund should be invested conservatively. There should be almost complete security of principal, marketability, and liquidity, although, of course, a reasonable rate of return is a desired objective. Within these constraints, logical investment outlets for emergency funds have included regular savings accounts in banks and savings and loan associations and certain types of government securities and life insurance policies.

Education Fund. The cost of higher education in the United States has increased dramatically over the last few years, particularly at private colleges and universities, but also at the high school level. These high costs can result in a tremendous financial drain for a family with college-aged children, and as a predictable drain, it can be prepared for in advance.

An investment fund for educational needs often is a relatively long-term objective, and it is set up with the hope that the fund will not be needed in the meantime. Therefore, wider investment latitude is often justified than in the case of the emergency fund, with the result that a more attractive investment yield can often be obtained. Life insurance can be used as a vehicle for funding educational needs, at least in part. The cash value buildup in any cash value insurance policy can be tapped at the time of the need. In addition, a life insurance policy can ensure that the educational fund is completed even if the breadwinner of the family dies prematurely. Finally, some life insurance companies sell specific educational insurance policies, the purpose of which is to provide an amount of money at the time the child reaches college age.

General Investment Fund. Many persons desire to accumulate capital for general investment purposes. They want to obtain a better standard of living in the future, a second income in addition to the earnings from their employment or profession, greater financial security or a sense of personal self-reliance, the ability to retire early or to "take it easy" in their work in the future, or a capital fund to pass onto their children or grandchildren; or they may simply enjoy the investment process. In any event, individuals normally invest money for the purpose of maximizing their after-tax rates of return, consistent with their objectives and the investment constraints under which they must operate.

A wide variety of investment instruments exists for the purpose of accumulating capital. Generally, these instruments are classified as either fixed-dollar or variable-dollar investments. **Fixed-dollar investments** are those whose principal and/or income are contractually set in advance in terms of a specified or of a determinable number of dollars. **Variable-dollar investments** are those where neither the principal nor the income is contractually set in advance in terms of dollars. In other words, both the value and income of variable-dollar investments can change in dollar amount, either up or down, with changes in economic conditions.

Common fixed-dollar investments include bonds, savings accounts and certificates at banks and savings and loan associations, certificates of deposit, Treasury bills and notes, and other short-term investments, preferred stock, and most life insurance and annuity cash values.

Variable-dollar investments include home ownership, common stocks, mutual funds, certain tax-sheltered investments, ownership of business interests, commodities, fine arts, precious metals, and variable annuities and variable life insurance.

Retirement Fund. For many persons, the objective of providing for one's retirement is of extreme importance. Because of the importance and unique characteristics of retirement planning, this subject is dealt with as a separate element within the overall financial plan and is discussed below.

Provide for Retirement

Another element of most persons' financial plans is to make provision for their retirement. This element is typically of little concern to young working persons, with this concern increasing greatly in importance as one approaches retirement age. Although this element is a subset of the one discussed above, it is often of such great importance that it is segregated from the general investment program, especially since the financial instruments used to fund for retirement and the applicable tax laws are often designed for this specific purpose.

At advanced ages, although a person's earning power usually stops or is considerably reduced, expenses continue. The person may prepare for this retirement period by saving and investing during his or her earning career, but (1) saving is neither painless nor automatic, and the amounts needed may be very great, and (2) the necessary amount is indefinite because it depends on the length of the retirement period.

The probabilities that persons at selected ages will survive to age 65 are presented in Table 1–3. The table also indicates the average number of years that a person of each age will live beyond age 65. Consider the plight of a person now age 35. The chances are about four out of five that this person will live beyond age 65, his or her probable retirement age. The average person age 35 will live almost 11½ years beyond age 65. Therefore, if a 35-year-old is willing to be considered average, he or she will have to accumulate a sum which, invested at a reasonable

TABLE 1-3. Probability of survival to age 65 and average remaining life, 1979

Age	Probability of survival to Age 65	Average Remaining Lifetime, Years	Average Remaining Lifetime Beyond Age 65, Years
0	0.77	73.7	8.7
10	0.78	65.0	10.0
20	0.78	55.4	10.4
30	0.79	46.1	11.1
35	0.80	41.4	11.4
40	0.81	36.8	11.8
45	0.82	32.2	12.2
50	0.84	27.9	12.9
55	0.87	23.9	13.9
60	0.92	20.0	15.0

Source: Derived from *Vital Statistics of the United States, 1979*, Volume 11, Part A. Section 6, *Life Tables* (Washington, D.C.: U.S. Department of Health and Human Services, Public Health Service, 1984), p. 11.

rate of return, will produce enough income to meet his or her expenses over a period of 11.4 years. Of course, there is no way that a given individual knows whether he or she will live for exactly 11.4 years beyond age 65, for one year, or for 30 years.

As the person grows older, the average number of years that he or she can expect to live beyond age 65 increases. If a person knew that he or she would live to be 100 years old and that his or her earning power would end completely at age 65, that person would have to accumulate over $245,600 by retirement age, assuming expenses of $15,000 a year and a 5 percent return after taxes on the balance of the accumulated sum. Few persons will live this long, but some will, and their identity is unknown.

Unlike the probabilities associated with the other personal loss exposures, which have been declining over time, the probabilities associated with superannuation have been increasing. Much attention is now being devoted to this peril, particularly because of the increasing proportion of aged persons in the total population. In 1920, 40 percent of the population was under 20 years of age, 54 percent between 20 and 64, and 5 percent was aged 65 or more. In 1983, the corresponding percentages were 30 percent, 58 percent, and 12 percent.

Today, a person can plan for retirement in many ways. Some involve government programs, others rely primarily on private insurance or other personal savings and investment. Some involve tax advantages, others do not. This particular aspect of personal financial planning is discussed in more detail in Chapters 7, 14, 25, and 28. However, at this point it may be noted that typical sources of retirement income include some of the following: Social Security retirement benefits, other government benefits, employer-provided pension plans, individual retirement accounts and annuities, deferred profit-sharing and other employee benefit plans, nonqualified deferred compensation plans, investments in other assets owned by the individual, individually purchased fixed-dollar or variable-dollar annuities, and life insurance cash values. The entrepreneur will usually rely on his or her business to provide retirement funds, either through the sale of the business or by continuing to receive income from the business.

Minimize Taxes

Because most families in the United States pay taxes of various sorts, it is further understandable that the desire to minimize taxes is a logical and laudable element in personal financial planning. This means that the tax implications of most financial transactions at least must be considered, and in some cases, a decision regarding a particular transaction is greatly influenced by the tax treatment.

Individuals are subject to a variety of taxes. These include sales taxes, property taxes, Social Security taxes, federal income taxes, state and/or local income taxes, federal estate taxes, state inheritance and/or estate taxes, and federal gift taxes. The relative importance of these taxes varies considerably among families, depending on their circumstances and income levels. When engaging in tax planning, however, most persons are concerned primarily with income taxes, death taxes, and perhaps gift taxes.

It is doubtful that anyone would purchase life insurance or annuities solely to gain tax advantages. It is nonetheless true that certain tax advantages, which are justified as sound social policy, accrue to these products. The effect of these tax advantages can make them very attractive for certain purposes within a broad personal financial plan.[15] Briefly stated, these tax advantages are four in number:

1. Exemption, in general, from income taxation of life insurance proceeds paid upon death, even though the proceeds received may greatly exceed the premiums paid for the insurance
2. Exemption (in whole or in part) from state inheritance taxation of life insurance death proceeds payable to certain named beneficiaries
3. Tax deferral on the interest credited to qualified life insurance and annuity cash values
4. Imposition of a moderate federal income tax on annuity income payments involving a favorable rule taxing the interest earnings of the principal sum being liquidated

Establish Program for Heirs

Whether by design or default, all individuals have a ''plan'' as to how their assets will be distributed on their deaths. Either the individual prepares the plan, or failing that, the state law imposes a plan. A sound personal financial plan does not leave this element to chance or to the state law. It includes a conscientiously formulated and implemented program that comes into being upon the death of the individual, if not prior thereto.[16] The orderly and efficient transfer of property and the meeting of objectives established for one's heirs constitute the heart of this element of the plan.

Estate planning in the narrow sense of protecting an existing estate has three fundamental objectives: (1) reduction of the cost of estate transfer, (2) arrangement for the most economic method of paying transfer costs that cannot be eliminated, and (3) changes in the character of estate property so as to make wise use of assets. Estate planning also includes the disposition of business interests and the use of pension and profit-sharing plans and other devices for individuals to help them establish larger estates with tax-deferred dollars. Many techniques have been developed to achieve these objectives. Life insurance plays a vital role in a number of these techniques. The life insurance agent; the attorney, who prepares the necessary legal documents; the accountant, who gathers much of the needed information; and the trust officer, who is prepared to provide expert fiduciary services when needed, all make up the estate planning team. Each provides a service of a particular expertise.

Manage Family Cash Flow

The last element of the typical family's personal financial plan is management of the family's cash flow. In a sense, this element permeates all other elements and therefore logically should not be viewed as the "last" element but rather as providing the broad scheme that permits the accomplishment of all the other elements.

Managing family cash flow means establishing a budget wherein monthly (or more frequent) income and expenditure patterns are projected, together with the system for keeping track of and analyzing actual income and expenditures. Clearly, all of the elements of a person's financial plan discussed would fit into the budget/analysis process.

As one would suspect, life and health insurance can assist in the cash flow management process only in indirect ways. For example, premium payment modes often can be varied to suit a family's special income pattern, or policy loans can be used to overcome temporary cash flow shortages. Cash value life insurance policies can be arranged such that under appropriate conditions, premiums can be paid through policy loans or cash values where the need arises.

[15]See Chapter 13.
[16]See Chapter 14.

THE FINANCIAL PLANNING TEAM

As alluded to previously, the financial planning process usually relies on the advice and services of several professionals. Historically, the life insurance agent has been the catalyst for the initiation of the process for most persons. Many agents today are broadening the scope of their financial planning activities to serve the role not only as catalyst but as manager as well. Professionals in the securities, accounting, legal, and other areas increasingly are doing likewise.

Indeed, viewed from the standpoint of a team approach, comprehensive financial planning can be considered as the process that integrates and coordinates the expertise of specialized professionals in financial services for the benefit of the client.[17] In this team approach to the client's interest, each specialization assumes a definable and specific role in relation to the client's overall objectives. Their contributions of consultative advice and service and product implementation are more professional because they are directed toward satisfying needs and attaining objectives that have been clearly and comprehensively determined in the counseling sessions by the financial planner.

Comprehensive financial planners evolve and grow into their roles from a professional status that is nearly always initially grounded in a speciality—law, accounting, insurance, investments, and so on. As generalists they are distinguished from other specialists not so much by greater intelligence or technical competence as by their adoption and practice of the financial planning process and by their placing the client's interest first. The planning process itself thus becomes an *additional* specialized competence that the financial services professional brings to the service of client needs. It broadens knowledge, enables the professional to function as a peer of other specialists, and helps clients take fuller responsibility for their economic lives.

Clearly, the financial planning process demands both a comprehensive financial planner to direct it and a team of other specialized professionals in financial services. All teams and organizations are characterized by pecking orders, and on the financial planning team, the comprehensive financial planner who has the client's trust and confidence is the natural leader. In no sense, however, does this relationship belittle the positions of other specialists on the team. On the contrary, participation in a concerted planning effort for a client *enhances* the professionalism of specialists' contributions because their efforts are directed not only toward immediate problem solving, but also toward preventive strategies that contribute to the client's general well-being.

INTERRELATIONSHIP BETWEEN BUSINESS AND PERSONAL FINANCIAL PLANNING

The distinction between business financial planning and personal financial planning is essentially one of convenience, the chief difference being the entity for which the planning is performed. Even so, the principles, if not all the details, are identical.

For most persons, moreover, a close relationship exists between the home and the business or vocation in which they are engaged. Indeed, the owner of a business, generally speaking, conducts the business primarily for the purpose of supporting a home, thus showing that the welfare of the home and the welfare of the business can be so intimately related as to be inseparable.

Therefore, for purposes of this book, it should be understood that references to *personal* financial planning extend to *business* financial planning to the extent that an individual's personal financial affairs are influenced by or are derived from his or her business or vocation.

---

[17]This discussion draws from Dale S. Johnson, "Comprehensive Financial Planning: The Process and the Professionals," *The Journal of the American Society of Chartered Life Underwriters,* Vol. XXXVII (October 1983), pp. 47–48.

Chapter 2

Life and Health Insurance Fundamentals

PRINCIPLES OF INSURANCE

As discussed in Chapter 1, human beings are exposed to many serious perils, such as property losses from fire and windstorm, and personal losses from disability and death. Although it is impossible for the individual to predict or completely prevent their occurrence, it is possible to provide against their financial effects. The function of insurance in its various forms is to safeguard against such misfortunes by having the losses of the unfortunate few paid by the contributions of the many who are exposed to the same peril. This is the essence of insurance—the sharing of losses and the substitution of certainty for uncertainty. If the peril under consideration is that of death, the financial loss suffered can be reduced or even eliminated through life insurance. If the peril under consideration is disability, the financial loss can be indemnified through health insurance.

Insurance Defined

Insurance may be defined from two perspectives: that of society and that of the individual. From society's viewpoint, life or health insurance may be defined as a social device whereby individuals transfer the financial risk associated with loss of life or health to a group of persons, and which involves the accumulation of funds by the group from these individuals to meet the uncertain financial losses associated with loss of life or health. Note that this definition has two key elements. First, for insurance to exist there must be a *transfer* of the risk from the individual to the group. Second, there must exist a *sharing of losses* by the members of the group.

From the individual's point of view, life or health insurance may be defined as an agreement (insurance policy or certificate) whereby one party (the policyowner) pays a stipulated consideration (the premium) to the other party (the insurer) in return for which the insurer agrees to pay a defined amount of money if the person whose life is insured dies or suffers an illness or other disability during the term of the policy (or, in some cases, survives to a stated time). Note that the emphasis here is legal and financial.

Every insurance organization is a mechanism for distributing losses. This is true whether a group mutually insures each member of the group (mutual life insurance company), or an independent contractor (stock life insurance company) assumes the risk and pays the resulting losses.

Law of Large Numbers

To minimize the speculative element and reduce violent fluctuations in the year-to-year losses, it is necessary that the **law of large numbers** be applicable to the insurance operation. This basic principle, as applied to insurance, states that the greater the number of similar exposures (e.g., lives insured) to a peril (e.g., death), the less the observed loss experience will deviate from the expected loss experience. Risk and uncertainty diminish as the number of exposure units increases.

The law of large numbers does not suggest that losses to particular individuals will become more predictable. Rather, it states that the larger the group insured, the more predictable will be the loss experience for the group as a whole, other things being the same.

To insure a single life against death for $1,000 during a given year is clearly a gamble. If the number of persons insured is increased to 100, the element of uncertainty as to observed results is still present to a very large extent. If 500,000 lives of similar characteristics are combined into the same group, average year-to-year death rate fluctuations will probably vary by only a fraction of 1 percent. The company would thus be able to determine its anticipated death claims with a manageable degree of accuracy. *In theory,* if the number of lives insured by a company were so large as to make the application of the law of large numbers virtually perfect, and if no possibility of a catastrophe existed (e.g., war or epidemic), practically all uncertainty as to the accuracy of the estimated losses during a given period would be removed.

Nature of Perils Insured

Although all forms of insurance are alike in that they require a combination of many risks into a group, they are different with regard to the perils covered. A peril is a cause of loss, such as fire or windstorm with respect to property insurance or an automobile accident with respect to life and health insurance. In the nonlife forms of insurance, perils insured against may or may not happen, and in the great majority of cases, do not happen. In life insurance, the event against which protection is granted—death—is an uncertainty for one year, but the probability of death generally increases each year until it becomes a virtual certainty. If a life insurance policy is to protect an insured during the whole of his or her life, an adequate fund must be accumulated to meet a claim that is certain to occur.

In the case of health insurance, not everyone becomes disabled and the risk of disablement does not follow as consistent a pattern as the risk of dying. Under long-term health insurance contracts, however, the risk insured against increases over time, so it is necessary to accumulate an adequate fund to meet the relatively higher rates of claim that will develop as insureds in the group grow older.

Gambling and Insurance

Some persons allege that insurance is a gamble. One hears, "the insurance company is betting you won't have a loss. You're betting that you will." From the insured's point of view, insurance is the antithesis of gambling. Gambling creates a risk where none existed. Insurance transfers an already existing risk and through the pooling of similar loss exposures actually reduces risk. Insurance companies, of course, prefer that insureds not have losses. However, losses are inevitable and are planned for in insurers' rate structures.

PRICING INDIVIDUAL LIFE AND HEALTH INSURANCE

The foregoing insurance concepts and principles are fundamental to understanding how insurance functions in the broadest sense. This section provides an overview of how life and health insurance are priced. This section also explains, in a simplified manner, the interactions of the various elements involved in pricing life insurance.

Life and Health Insurance Pricing Objectives

Three life and health insurance pricing objectives are that rates should be (1) adequate, (2) equitable, and (3) not excessive.

Rate Adequacy. Above all else, it is essential to the sound operation of a life insurance company that rates be adequate in light of the benefits promised under the company's insurance products. Rate inadequacy can lead to severe financial problems, if not insolvency.

Rate adequacy means that for a given "block of policies," total payments collected now and in the future by the insurer plus the investment earnings attributable to any net retained funds should be at least sufficient to fund the current and future benefits promised plus cover related expenses. A "block of policies" constitutes all risks of the same type issued by a company under the same schedules of rates and values.

In practice, an insurer cannot know with certainty the degree of the rate adequacy until the final policy in the block has terminated. Because individually issued life insurance and many forms of health insurance are issued at rates and on terms and conditions that may be guaranteed for years to come, the issue of rate adequacy is especially important in establishing the initial premium levels. In fact, as shown below, life insurance companies conduct tests to ensure that rates charged are adequate (as well as equitable and not excessive).

Life insurance rates are not directly regulated to ensure adequacy. However, life insurance companies are required by state laws to establish certain minimum liabilities on their financial statements based on state-mandated assumptions.[1]

Rate Equity. Rates charged for life and health insurance should be equitable to policyowners. Equity means charging each individual insured an amount commensurate with the risk that the individual brings to the insurance process. Stated differently, there should exist no unfair subsidization of any class of insureds by any other class of insureds.

The achievement of equity is a goal to be sought. In an imperfect world, it cannot be attained absolutely. Concepts of equity must give way to practical realities. These include the fact that the larger the number of separate classifications of insureds, the greater the expense in administering the plan. Also, it is necessary to have a large enough group to permit reasonable prediction of losses within each classification. It simply is not possible to assess with exactness the precise degree of risk that each proposed insured brings to a group.

As discussed later, the pursuit of equity is one of the goals of underwriting. Life insurers strive toward equitable treatment of insureds by varying life insurance rates by such factors as age, sex, plan, health, and benefits provided. Generally, a greater degree of refinement in rate classes—and therefore more actuarial equity—exists for life insurance than for health insurance. **Actuarial equity** is sometimes in conflict with concepts of **social equity.** For example, some persons believe it to be socially unacceptable to charge different life and health insurance rates to otherwise identically situated men and women.[2]

Rates Not Excessive. Life and health insurance rates should not be excessive in relation to the benefits provided. If the rate adequacy criterion can be considered as establishing conceptually a minimum floor for rates, the "rates not excessive" criterion can be considered as establishing a ceiling.

Many states have defined excessiveness with respect to some health insurance policies. These states often provide that the insurer must reasonably expect to make (or actually pay) in claim payments at least a certain minimum percentage (e.g., 50 percent) of the premiums collected.

Only the state of Wisconsin actually specifies a maximum rate charge for individually issued life insurance. It is questionable whether the need exists for laws to specify what constitutes rate excessiveness in the United States. Since the country was founded on the private enterprise concept of competition, one would argue that rate ceilings should justifiably exist only with respect to those industries where competition did not function well enough as a restraint on excessive prices.

---

[1]See Chapter 20.

[2]See Chapter 23.

Although prices charged for life insurance do vary from company to company and with some companies, prices would be considered as relatively high, it is nonetheless true that competition today within the life insurance business is keener than in times past, thus largely militating against the possibility of excessive prices. Simply put, a life insurance company is not likely to sell much life insurance if the rates it charges or the interest rates it credits to policy cash values are not competitive. Indeed, competition has been so severe with respect to some products that some industry observers are concerned that the objective of rate adequacy has been ignored by some companies.

The Elements of Life and Health Insurance Pricing

A sound understanding of life and health insurance requires a sound understanding of the elements used in their pricing. The calculation of life and health insurance rates and values requires information and assumptions regarding six elements:

1. The probability of the event insured against occurring
2. The time value of money
3. The benefits promised
4. Expenses
5. Profits
6. Contingencies

Insurance pricing is based on the concept of loss sharing. Loss sharing, in turn, involves the accumulation of a fund from amounts paid by insureds to provide benefits to the unfortunate few who suffer loss. To establish the amount to be charged, the insurer must start with some idea as to the likelihood of losses for the group.

The likelihood of losses in life and health insurance (i.e., probabilities of loss of life and probabilities of loss of health) are shown by specially constructed tables—mortality and morbidity tables, respectively. These tables show incidences of death and loss of health for a given group of insureds over time—from birth to the death of the final persons in the group. These tables constitute the foundation upon which the expected costs of life and health insurance are based.

Persons purchasing life insurance are not the same age. On the average those insuring at the younger ages are less likely to die within the next year than those who purchase insurance at older ages. Equity therefore requires that the amounts charged be graded upward as the age at which the policy is issued increases. This is also true in health insurance, to the extent that the loss insured increases with increasing age.

Life and health insurance companies collect premiums in advance of providing the insurance coverage. In longer-term coverages, that portion of amounts collected but not needed immediately to cover expenses is invested and produces earnings that are used to supplement premium income to fund future expected benefits and ongoing expenses. In such cases, life and health insurers discount (lower) premiums in advance in recognition of the fact that they will earn interest on the accumulated funds.

Besides the recognition of the time value of money, premium computation must take into account the period of coverage, the level of coverage, as well as all other factors related to the benefits promised the insured under the contract, including the likelihood of policyowners voluntarily terminating their insurance policies.

Many types of insurance policies are on the market, some insuring against death or disability for a limited number of years only, whereas others cover the whole of life; some call for the payment of premiums for a stated number of years only, others for the entire duration of the contract; some have premiums that are fixed, others permit the policyowner to determine the level of premiums to be paid, within certain guidelines. Some promise the payment of policy benefits in one lump sum, others provide for payment in a fixed number of installments, and so on. The rates for each coverage configuration are determined not only with reference to estimated probabilities of death or disability, but also according to the nature of the benefits promised and the expected premium payment pattern.

These complex conditions cannot be gauged appropriately by companies unless they follow scientific principles in the computation of their rates. Life insurance typically provides a definite benefit amount in the event of death. Disability insurance typically promises a definite benefit in the event of disability. Other forms of health insurance provide benefits that are a function of medical expenses incurred because of a particular illness or injury. It is essential, therefore, that an accurate determination of the expected benefit cost be made and that an adequate amount be charged, equitable as to ages, sex, types of coverage and other relevant factors. This is especially important because, unlike most other types of insurance, life and some health insurance contracts can extend for a long period of time or even throughout life and cannot be canceled by the company.

Later chapters will discuss the pricing of life and health insurance in detail. The following discussion is intended to provide an overview of the pricing process for the pure risk component only, as well as the principles involved, to facilitate a study of the evaluation and use of individual life and health insurance.

Life and health insurance rates calculated to recognize (1) the probability of the event insured against occurring, (2) the time value of money, and (3) the benefits promised are referred to as **net rates.** They do not make allowance for the expenses the insurer incurs (e.g., selling, issuing, and maintaining the policy), nor do they make provision for unforeseen contingencies or for profits. It is essential, therefore, for the insurer to add to its net rate an additional amount to cover these necessary elements of its operation. When the amount for expenses is added to the net rate, the **gross rate**—the amount charged policyowners—is obtained. In computing net and gross rates, the company considers its objectives and its past experience for each factor involved. This procedure for deriving gross rates is followed in principle by many life insurance companies. It is used in this chapter since it illustrates well the concepts involved in life insurance pricing. However, a more common method of deriving a company's gross premium rate structure is for the insurer to select gross rates for pivotal ages (say, based on market and competitive considerations), and then "test" these selected rates against its objectives and expectations as to realistic future

experience. If the "test rate" does not produce the profit and other results desired, the rate (or the policy elements) will be changed and the test repeated. With this procedure, the insurer does not calculate a net rate and then add amounts to cover expenses, profits, and contingencies. Rather, the insurer simply selects a target gross rate to be tested. This amount, for example, may be the rate presently being charged by the company or it may be the rate being charged by selected competitors for similar coverage.[3]

Still another approach to establishing a gross premium rate structure is to calculate gross premium rates directly through the use of realistic interest assumptions, a realistic mortality table, realistic expense and lapse assumptions, and a specific provision for profit (or contribution to surplus). With cash values and a dividend scale assumed, the calculation of a gross premium rate structure can be carried out by solving a mathematical equation.

It is important to note that no matter how the "tentative" gross rate is derived, it is tested carefully under the company's anticipated future operating experience.

Life Insurance Rate Computation

The simplest form of life insurance protection is the yearly renewable term insurance plan. A brief explanation of this plan, as well as the single-premium, traditional level-premium, and flexible-premium plans, which are discussed hereafter, will serve to illustrate the preceding discussion of basic principles.

Yearly Renewable Term Life Insurance. Yearly renewable term (YRT) insurance provides insurance for a period of one year only, but guarantees the policyowner the right to renew (i.e., continue) the policy even if the insured suffers poor health or otherwise becomes uninsurable.[4] Each year's premium is used to pay the policy's share of mortality costs for that year. The renewal rate increases each year to reflect the annual rise in death rates as age advances.

[3]See Chapter 21.
[4]See Chapter 4.

The increasing probability of death may be seen in Table 2-1, which shows the annual male and female rates of mortality per 1,000 lives at various ages according to the **1980 Commissioners Standard Ordinary (CSO) Table of Mortality,** the standard as currently required by state regulatory authorities in certain circumstances for the valuation (measurement) of policy liabilities.[5] It should be noted that insurers, in practice, may use a different set of mortality rates that it judges to represent the realistic expectations of future mortality experience for insured risks.

TABLE 2-1. Rates of Mortality per 1,000 lives
(1980 CSO table)

Age	Rate of Mortality	
	Male	Female
10	0.73	0.68
20	1.90	1.05
30	1.73	1.38
40	3.02	2.42
50	6.71	4.96
60	16.08	9.47
70	39.51	22.11
80	98.84	65.99
90	221.77	190.75
99	1,000.00	1,000.00

Table 2-1 shows that the rate of dying generally increases with age at an increasing rate, rising ultimately to a certainty. It should also be observed that female mortality experience is more favorable than that of males at every age. As a result of these mortality differences, all life insurers vary their premium charges by age, and the vast majority also vary them by the gender of the insured, with females being charged lower rates for life insurance.[6]

An example will illustrate YRT rate derivation. The mortality rate for males, age 30, according to the *1980 CSO Table,* is 1.73 per 1,000. If 100,000 males age 30 are insured for $1,000 each, a company would expect to pay 173 death claims for a total payment of $173,000. Since 100,000 persons would be insured, the company would

have to collect $1.73 from each insured individual to accumulate a fund sufficient to meet the 173 death claims. This rate is the same as the death rate.

This illustration includes only the mortality charge since investment income as well as allowances for contingencies, expenses, and profits are ignored. To derive a net rate, it is necessary to consider investment earnings.

Assume that the insurer credits a 5 percent annual return on all policyowner accumulations. To simplify the analysis, assume also that payments by policyowners to the insurer are made at the beginning of the policy year (a realistic assumption) and that death claims are paid only at the end of the year (not a realistic assumption) and, therefore, the insurer has use of funds for a full year.

Ignoring other pricing components for now, it can be observed that the insurer need not now collect the full $173,000. In fact, the insurer need collect only $164,762. This amount, accumulated at 5 percent interest, will equal the $173,000 needed at the end of the year to honor all death claims ($164,762 ×1.05 = $173,000).

Thus the insurer need not charge each insured the full $1.73 per $1,000 of insurance. It can charge $1.65 per $1,000, relying on its investment income to contribute the additional needed $0.08 per $1,000.

To this net rate would be added an amount necessary to provide reasonable allowances to cover expenses, contingencies, and profit. To keep the analysis simple, these elements will continue to be ignored.

Since death rates increase with age, the rate that policyowners must be charged each year increases proportionately. As surviving members of a group of insureds continue to renew their insurance, year after year, the increasing rate causes some to question the advisability of continuing the insurance. As the increases become more burdensome, there is a tendency for those in good health to discontinue their coverage, whereas those in poor health have a strong incentive to continue to renew their policies even at the higher rate levels necessitated by advancing age. This tendency is known as **adverse selec-**

[5]See Chapter 20.

[6]The state of Montana prohibits the use of sex-distinct rates.

tion, and if life insurers did not anticipate this phenomenon, eventually it would result in a continuing group of insureds whose mortality experience would exceed that implicit within the rate schedule. Irrespective of the impact of adverse selection, the rates charged ultimately become prohibitive even for those in poor health. In view of the fact that adverse selection produces abnormally high mortality rates, the insurance process can break down; consequently, insurance companies usually place a limit on the period during which yearly renewable term insurance can be renewed or, alternatively, provide premium levels for later years that are high enough to cover the anticipated adverse selection.

The Single-Premium Plan. Another method of purchasing insurance is to pay for the policy with a single premium. In contrast to the yearly renewable net rate at age 30 of $1.65 (followed by a series of rates each of which increases annually), the net premium for a single premium whole life policy at age 30 is $150.45 for each $1,000 coverage. This amount, when increased by necessary allowances, pays for the contract in full.

The single-premium whole life plan involves the payment of the policy's entire future mortality charges in a single sum. Since the insurer will on average have use of these funds over an extended period of time, investment earnings constitute the major component from which benefits will be paid.

A highly simplified and admittedly unrealistic example will demonstrate the points made above. Assume that 100,000 males, all age 95, are interested in purchasing single-premium whole life policies whose face amounts are all $1,000. Assume further that the life insurer calculates its net rates based on the *1980 CSO Mortality Table* with interest at 5 percent per year.[7] A modified version of the *1980 CSO Mortality Table* is shown in Table 2-2.

Of the 100,000 males living at age 95, approximately 33,000 will die during the year, based on the probability of death of 0.330 (i.e., $100,000 \times 0.330 = 33,000$), which is taken from the *1980 CSO Table.* This means that 67,000 will have survived to age 96.

Of the 67,000 who survived, an estimated 25,795 will die during the next year, again based on the *1980 CSO Table* death probability of 0.385 (i.e., $67,000 \times 0.385 = 25,795$). Thus 41,205 of the original group of 100,000 are estimated to survive to age 97, of which an estimated 19,778 will die during the next year, and so on. Note that during age 99, all 7,328 of the survivors will be considered to have died.

From these data one can calculate the total amount of money the insurer must collect today to be able to honor all future death claims as they are incurred in this group. Table 2-3 illustrates the calculation.

Column 4 gives present value factors that convert a given amount to be paid in the future to its present-day equivalent, assuming a time value of money of 5 percent. For example, $1,000 to be paid in five years is equivalent to $783.50 today ($1,000 \times 0.7835$). Stated differently,

[7]The reader is reminded that actual rate computations usually involve the use of mortality tables based on current company or industry experience.

TABLE 2-2. Modified version of *1980 CSO Mortality Table*

(1) Age	(2) Number Living (Beginning of Year)	(3) Probability of Death (during the Year)	(4) Number Dying (during the Year)
95	100,000	0.330	33,000
96	67,000	0.385	25,795
97	41,205	0.480	19,778
98	21,427	0.658	14,099
99	7,328	1.000	7,328
100	0		

TABLE 2-3. Calculation of present value of claims
(males, age 95)

(1) Policy Year	(2) Number Dying during the Year	(3) Total Death Claims ($1,000×No. Dying) for the Year	(4) Present Value Factor at 5%	(5) Present Value Total Death Claims
1	33,000	$33,000,000	0.9524	$31,429,200
2	25,795	25,795,000	0.9070	23,396,065
3	19,778	19,778,000	0.8638	17,084,236
4	14,099	14,099,000	0.8227	11,599,247
5	7,328	7,328,000	0.7835	5,741,488
			Total present value	$89,250,236

$783.50 today will accumulate to $1,000 in five years if invested to earn 5 percent per year.

During the first policy year (i.e., during age 95), 33,000 insureds of the original group of 100,000 are estimated to die, so the insurer will have to pay out a total of $33,000,000 in death claims ($1,000 ×33,000 deaths) at the end of the first year. However, the insurer need have on hand today only $31,429,200 since this amount accumulated at 5 percent interest will equal $33,000,000 at the end of one year.[8]

During the second policy year, a total of $25,795,000 is estimated to be needed to honor the claims falling due during that year. However, those claims will not have to be paid for two years from the time of the issuance of the single premium policy. Thus the insurer need collect only $23,396,065 in advance ($25,795,000 × 0.9070) to have available $25,795,000 in two years.

The process is continued for the other three policy years, with the present value factor getting smaller (i.e., the discount being larger) the greater the time period involved. The result of this process is that the life insurer must collect $89,250,236 to be able to honor the $100,000,000 in claims as they occur; that is, the insurer need collect only $0.89 in premiums for each dollar of benefits to be paid out. The additional $0.11 is derived from investment income.

Since the initial number of insureds assumed was 100,000, this means that the insurer would charge a net single premium of $892.50

($89,250,236 divided by 100,000) to each insured for each $1,000 of whole life insurance protection. To this net premium would have to be added amounts to cover expenses, and so on, the result of which may yield a gross premium in excess of $1,000! No one would logically purchase insurance at such advanced ages since it is not economically feasible. As in the case of other risks insured, the administrative costs added to the value of the pure loss costs makes insurance practicable only when the probability of loss is relatively low. Good risk management would argue for avoiding merely exchanging dollars with the insurance company.

This calculation also demonstrates clearly that a life insurance policy for the whole of life can be viewed as a series of yearly renewable term insurances. Note that the column 3 figures shown in Table 2-2, if multiplied by the policy face amounts of $1,000, would represent the year-by-year mortality charges, thus giving the yearly renewable term costs without the interest factor.

Since all mortality charges with single-premium whole life insurance are prepaid, the life insurance company cannot consider the full premium earned when paid. As is clear from Table 2-3, the initial premium plus interest earned thereon will, in essence, be utilized over the policy period to meet the claims. At any point in time, the insurer must show a liability on its balance sheet equal to the value of the unused fund. This value represents the present value of the future benefits promised under the life insurance policies and is the policy reserve referred to earlier.

Table 2-4 illustrates how these policy reserves

[8]Remember that premiums were assumed to be paid in advance and death claims were assumed to be paid at the end of the year.

TABLE 2-4. Development of policy reserves for net-single-premium whole life policy

(1) Policy Year	(2) Number Living at Beginning of Year	(3) Fund Balance at Beginning of Policy Year	(4) Interest Earned on Fund (at 5%) during Policy Year [(3)×5%]	(5) Death Claims Paid at End of Policy Year (Table 2-3, Col. 3)	(6) Fund Balance at End of Policy Year [(3)+(4)-(5)]	(7) Fund Balance per Policy [(6)÷2 Next]]
1	100,000	$89,250,236	$4,462,512	$33,000,000	$60,712,747	$906
2	67,000	60,712,747	3,035,637	25,795,000	37,953,384	921
3	41,205	37,953,384	1,897,669	19,778,000	20,073,053	937
4	21,427	20,073,053	1,003,653	14,099,000	6,977,705	952
5	7,328	6,977,705	348,885	7,328,000	0[a]	—

[a]Actually equals minus $1,410 instead of $0. The cumulative effect of rounding causes this slight relative difference.

evolve for this block of policies. The initial fund of $89,250,236 is developed from each of the 100,000 insureds each age 95 paying a net single premium of $892.50 for $1,000 of insurance coverage. This fund earns interest (at 5 percent) of $4,462,512 during the first policy year. Death claims of $33,000,000 are paid at the end of the first year, resulting in a fund balance or aggregate policy reserve of $60,712,747 at the end of the first policy year.

Although policy reserves for a block of policies are an aggregate concept, the portion applicable to each policy can be calculated. This is found by dividing the aggregate reserve by the number of insureds surviving the first policy year, in this case 67,000, to yield a fund balance or reserve per policy. This first-year figure is $906.

At the beginning of the second policy year, the aggregate reserve liability is the same as the previous year's ending balance ($60,712,747).[9] This fund is credited with $3,035,637 in interest, and $25,795,000 is paid out in death claims at year-end. The aggregate reserve has therefore fallen to $37,953,384. This represents the present value of the future benefits promised under the remaining policies. Note that the reserve per policy has increased to $921 even though the aggregate reserve has declined.

The process above is continued through the third, fourth, and fifth policy years. The reader should note, again, that the aggregate policy reserve (column 6) continues to decline but the per policy reserve continues to build. This is understandable as the fund balance per policy must continue to grow since for a whole life policy, the payment of the death claim is a certainty. The per policy reserve must equal the policy face amount the instant before the final policies mature as a death claim at the end of age 99.

The last policy year deserves some comment. The number of insureds living at the beginning of this year is 7,328. Based on the mortality table used here, all of these remaining insureds are assumed to die during this year and the full $1,000 face amount per policy paid to the beneficiaries at year-end.

[9]This assumes that all surviving policyowners choose to continue their participation.

The beginning reserve is $6,977,705. Interest of $348,885 is credited to the reserve. The $7,328,000 in death claims is assumed paid even if, in reality, some insureds survived the period. The assumption within the premium computation is that all insureds died, so the insurer would pay the face amount on all policies even if all insureds did not die.

The aggregate reserve at the end of the fifth policy year (i.e., at age 100) would be exactly zero, were all rounding errors eliminated. In theory, the aggregate policy reserve balance the instant before the 7,328 claims were paid would, of course exactly equal the death claims and the per policy reserve would be $1,000 per policy.[10]

In the preceding example, it was assumed that all 100,000 insureds paid their net single premiums for their $1,000 of insurance coverage and made no effort to terminate their policies prior to death. In fact, policyowners regularly decide, for various reasons, that they would prefer voluntarily to terminate (other than by dying!) their insurance policies. In these situations, the question arises as to what, if anything, the terminating policyowner should be entitled in terms of a refund of all or a portion of the prepayments made toward future mortality charges. Should the policyowner be considered as having forfeited these prepayments, or should the insurer be required to provide some "nonforfeiture" benefit?

This important question has been settled by state law and, before that, by industry practice. Current law requires that all life insurance policies that involve *significant* prepayments of future mortality charges provide for a type of partial refund of these prepayments to the policyowner.[11] This refund is referred to as a life insurance policy's **cash surrender value** and is available to the policyowner upon termination of

[10]The reader is cautioned that the preceding examples as well as others in this chapter have purposely been simplified to illustrate the concepts involved and, in fact, do not represent actual insurance company practice. For example, minimum policy reserve standards are established by state law and may have little or no relationship to actual insurer results. The mortality and interest assumptions mandated by these laws only rarely coincide with those implicit within an insurer's gross premium rate structure—contrary to that shown in the example.

[11]What is "significant" is determined by law. See Chapter 20.

a life policy other than by death. This value is the "savings" element in every cash value insurance policy. This savings element is different from the policy reserve since the policy reserve is simply a pro rata share of the balance sheet representation of the company's future obligations to policyowners as a group. Cash surrender values are those amounts that are available to the policyowner upon policy surrender. More is said on this point later.[12]

The Level-Premium Plan. In general, the single-premium method of providing life insurance has not proven to be very popular (even for insureds less than 95 years old!) except in specialized situations.[13] The relatively large initial outlay required discourages most purchasers. The practical difficulties arising from the single-premium plan and the fact that the mortality rate increases with age have been solved through the use of the level-premium plan. The fundamental idea of the level-premium plan is that the company can agree to accept the same premium each year (a level premium), provided that the level premiums collected are the mathematical equivalent of the corresponding single premium. As a result, the level premiums paid in the early years of the contract will be more than sufficient to pay current death claims but alone will be less than adequate to meet death claims that occur in later years. Life insurance was thus one of the first products marketed on the installment plan.

For a particular class of policies, this results in the creation of a fund from the annual level premiums paid in the early policy years, when mortality rates are low, just as a fund is created in the case of single-premium policies. Naturally, the fund would be smaller under level-premium plans than under single-premium plans, since the former involves less of a pre-funding of future mortality charges. At any point in time, the fund, future interest, and future premiums together should be sufficient to enable the insurer to pay all death claims as they occur during the remain-

ing period of the coverage provided by the class of policies.

The principle of the level-premium plan may be applied to a life policy of any duration, from short-duration term policies to whole life policies. The level annual premium may amortize the single-premium cost of the insurance over the entire duration of the policy's coverage period or over any shorter period. For example, a whole life policy can have level premiums paid over the entire policy duration (i.e., the whole of life). Such a policy is referred to as an **ordinary life policy.** Whole life policies can have level premiums paid over any shorter period, such as 10, 15 or 20 years, or to a specified age, for example, to age 65. These policies are referred to as **10-, 15-,** and **20-payment whole life policies** and **life-paid-up-at-age-65 whole life policies,** respectively.

1. *Net-level-premium calculation.* A brief, if (again) unrealistic example will illustrate how level premiums are calculated. Recall that the life insurer would charge each of our 100,000 males all 95 years old a net single premium of $892.50 per $1,000 of insurance for whole life coverage. In total, the insurer needed to have collected $89,250,236 at date of issue.

If the 100,000 insureds preferred to pay premiums on an annual basis, how much must the insurer charge each insured such that the insurer would be indifferent as to whether an insured paid for the whole life coverage with a single premium or a level premium (i.e., so that the two systems of payment were actuarially equivalent)? This is the fundamental question for beginning the analysis. Again, for simplicity, the illustration will ignore all allowances for expenses, profits, and contingencies.

The problem can be solved using simple algebra. We know that the present value of the death claims equals $89,250,236. This is the amount that the insurer must collect, in total, as net *single* premiums. The insurer must therefore collect the mathematical equivalent in net *level* premiums if the insurer is to be indifferent as to method of premium payment. In other words, the present value of the net level premiums must be equal to the sum of the net single premiums,

---

[12]See Chapter 9. Terminating policyowners may be afforded several options as to how to utilize the policy's cash value.
[13]See Chapter 5.

both of which, in turn, must equal the present value of the future death claims.

Table 2–5 illustrates the necessary calculation. The net level annual premium being sought is an unknown quantity, labeled "P" in column 2. It will be collected from each survivor each year. A total of 236,960 of these net level premiums (or 236,960P) is to be collected (the sum of column 3). However, the value today of these premiums is 225,722P.

Note that the present value factors for column 4 of this table are different from those shown in column 4 of Table 2–3. This is because premiums (unlike claims) are assumed to be paid at the *beginning* of each year. Thus the present value of each dollar in premiums to be collected the *first* policy year *is* a dollar.

It was mentioned above that the insurer must collect in net level premiums an amount equal, in present value terms, to the amount it expects to pay out in death claims. Thus the present value of present and future net level premiums (225,722P) must equal the present value of future claims ($89,250,236). This is shown in Table 2–5. Dividing both sides of the equation by 225,722 yields the net level premium of $395.40. This would be the annualized equivalent of the single premium.[14]

The net level premium is considerably higher than one-fifth of the net single premium. This should not be surprising since prior to the payment of the series of death claims, the insurer has use of far less money under the level-premium plan than under the single-premium plan, and therefore interest income is not as large a factor in causing the premium to be lower. Also, note that the insurer will collect premiums only from those who survive. This odd-sounding statement is highly important, however, in explaining the level-premium concept. Under the single-premium plan, the life insurer collects a full premium from all insured individuals. With the level-premium plan the insurer does not collect a full annual premium from 100,000 persons each year. It collects only from those who survive, thus necessitating a higher premium than otherwise would be the case. In other words, *the level-premium plan discounts for both interest and mortality.*[15]

It can be demonstrated that the net level premium of $395.40 is exactly sufficient, when combined with interest, to pay all death claims and to end the last policy year with a balance of zero, as was illustrated in Table 2–4 with the net single premium.

[14]An alternative but mathematically identical procedure to derive net level premiums is followed in Chapter 19. This alternative procedure relies on expected value concepts rather than algebraic concepts.

[15]In practice, the level-premium method also considers probabilities of policy terminations by other than death. See Chapter 21.

TABLE 2-5. Illustrative net-level premium calculation

(1) Policy Year	(2) Net Level Premium to be Paid Annually by Each Survivor	(3) Number Living at the Beginning of Each Year	(4) Present Value Factor at 5%	(5) Present Value of Total Net Level Premiums [(2 × 3 × 4)]
1	P	100,000	1.0000	100,000P
2	P	67,000	0.9524	63,811P
3	P	41,205	0.9070	37,373P
4	P	21,427	0.8638	18,509P
5	P	7,328	0.8227	6,029P
			Total present value	225,722P

Since Present value of net level premiums (PVP): 225,722P
Present value of claims (Table 2–3) (PVC): $89,250,236

And   PVP = PVC
Then   225,722 P = $89,250,236
So   P = $395.40

2. *Net amount at risk.* Policy reserves *when stated on a per policy basis* can be considered as "vanishing" or ending on the death of the insured. As a result, the insurance company can be considered to have less than the policy's face amount at risk. Under this approach to the reserve, therefore, the actual amount of pure life insurance protection at any point can be viewed as the difference between the policy reserve at that point and the face amount of the contract. This difference is called the **net amount at risk.**

Figure 2-1 shows a whole life insurance policy of $1,000, which is payable on the death of the insured and may be purchased by a male age 30 with a net level premium of $8.43 payable annually until death. The increasing reserve and the declining net amount at risk reflected in this view of the life insurance contract are apparent.

For example, at age 65, the reserve is $460 and the net amount at risk is $540. Remember that the sum of the net amount at risk and the reserve equals the face amount of the policy ($1,000 in the example). For all whole life policies, the net amount at risk declines as the reserve increases.

The foregoing analysis can be interpreted as dividing a life insurance policy in two parts: a decreasing amount of term insurance and an increasing savings element, which, when combined, are always just equal to the face of the policy. This can be a helpful way of viewing traditional cash value insurance policies and is, in fact, an accurate way of viewing universal life policies, as discussed below.

The Flexible-Premium Plan. Many life insurers in the United States are now selling life insurance policies that permit the policyowner the flexibility of deciding the amount of premium that he or she would like to pay. Universal life (UL) policies are examples of such flexible-premium plans.[16]

UL policy cash values are a function of the level of the policyowner's past and present premium payments (and past and present expense and mortality charges) as well as interest credits. Unlike the situation with traditional forms of cash value insurance, the cash values of UL policies are not by-products of the leveling of premiums. Rather they flow directly from the structure of the policy itself.

[16]See Chapter 6.

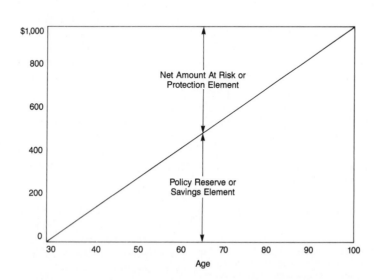

FIGURE 2-1. Proportion of protection (amount at risk) and reserve in a $1,000 ordinary life contract issued to male age 30 (1980 CSO Table, 5%).

Subject to company rules regarding minimums and maximums, the policyowner may pay whatever premium during a policy year that he or she wishes. From this premium may be subtracted an amount to cover the insurer's expenses and mortality charges. The balance remaining, plus the previous period's fund balance, then forms the policy's cash value.[17] Mortality charges are based on the policy's net amount at risk calculated using the cash value.[18] Interest at the company's current rates is then credited to the cash value for the year. This process is repeated on each premium due date, with the policyowner paying no premium if desired.

No illustration is made here concerning UL premium development since the policyowner "develops" his or her own premium payment schedule. Of course, if the premium currently paid plus the current cash values are insufficient to cover fully all current mortality and expense charges, the UL policy will terminate.

The Savings Aspect of Life Insurance

Many life insurance policies have cash values. Conceptually, all life insurance policy cash values can be derived in the same way and all evolve for the same basic reason—prefunding of future mortality. As a practical matter, however, policies are usually viewed in different ways. Thus with traditional forms of life insurance, the savings element is considered a by-product of the level-premium method of payment. With universal life and some other newer forms of life insurance policies, the savings element is usually considered to be a more integral part of a policy, specifically designed for building a savings fund from which mortality charges are withdrawn.

The Savings Aspect of Traditional Cash Value Insurance. Life insurance premiums tradi-

tionally have been computed by making assumptions regarding all elements impinging on the policy and deriving an indivisible premium to be charged for the policy. Much of the misunderstanding about traditional forms of cash value life insurance flows from ascribing to individual policies concepts that apply to insurance companies' financial operations. The "per policy" reserve referred to earlier is a prime example. If the policy reserve (a liability) is translated into a fund held on behalf of an individual policyowner, it is possible to look on the death benefit as a combination of that fund plus term insurance. This model, unless used carefully, can lead to false conclusions and to a general misunderstanding of the underlying realities of the life insurance business.

Economists and marketing personnel tend to view a level-premium whole life contract as a divisible contract providing financial protection to the insured's beneficiaries in case of death, with other contract benefits available, including cash surrender and loan values. A policyowner may discontinue the insurance and surrender the policy for its cash value. Alternatively, a policyowner may borrow from the insurer an amount up to the level of the cash value, at a contractually stated rate of interest, using the cash value as collateral. Despite these and other "living benefits," the whole life policy is, theoretically, an *indivisible* contract. It is not partly "protection" and partly "savings," with the premiums divisible among these components, as evidenced by the fact that the policyowner cannot withdraw the cash value *without giving up the insurance protection.* Even though the idea that the whole life contract is an indivisible entity is legally and actuarially correct, some companies and individuals continue to explain it as a combination of "term insurance protection" that decreases and "savings" that increase over a person's lifetime.

The Savings Aspect of Universal Life Insurance. During the late 1970s, a new form of life insurance—referred to as universal life (UL) insurance—was introduced in the United States. This new form has since captured a major share of new life insurance sales in the United States, with a 1986 market share of about one-third.

---

[17]A *surrender charge* may be levied against this cash value if the policy is terminated voluntarily.

[18]The careful reader will note that the net amount at risk used here is found by subtracting the *cash value* from the policy face amount, whereas the technical definition for the net amount at risk is the face amount less the individual policy reserve. Both definitions are used within the life insurance business.

The distinguishing features of universal life policies are their (1) flexibility and (2) transparency. UL policies are flexible in that they permit policyowners, within limits, to increase or decrease (even to zero) premium payments as they wish, and also, subject to certain constraints, to increase or decrease the face amount of the policy.

UL policies are said to be transparent in the sense that the three key elements of life insurance product pricing—mortality, interest, and expenses—are identified and disclosed. The level of the savings component of UL policies is a direct function of the level of the premium payments made by the policyowner. Other things being equal, the higher the premium payments, the higher will be the cash value.

With UL policies, the protection and savings components really are divisible and the methods used to derive each are apparent. The fact that one policy is technically indivisible and another is divisible does not change the fundamental nature of the policies. They simply constitute different ways of viewing the same thing.

Experience Participation in Life Insurance

A great proportion of the life insurance policies sold in the United States today provides that the policyowner will benefit (or suffer) from the favorable (or unfavorable) experience of the life insurance company. This "experience" is often based on the key elements of life insurance pricing: mortality, interest, and expense, profit, and contingency allowances. Thus if the life insurance company experiences or expects to experience (1) lower mortality, (2) greater investment earnings, or (3) lower expenses and taxes than the assumptions on which its premiums are based, the insurer may pass along to the blocks or classes of policyowners producing or expected to produce such favorable deviations the savings or a portion thereof accruing to the company. In other words, the policyowners can benefit in such favorable experience. Of course, the opposite may also occur.

Some life insurance is sold on a guaranteed cost basis, meaning that all policy elements (i.e., the premium, the face amount, and the cash values, if any) are guaranteed and will not vary with the experience of the company. Such policies are called **guaranteed-cost, nonparticipating policies** and can offer advantages and disadvantages to policyowners, as discussed more fully later. The chief drawback of such cash value policies is that in periods of high investment return, they offer no means of passing excess returns to the policyowners, with the result that they become viewed as expensive policies and may even be replaced. Premium adequacy for long-term, guaranteed-cost, nonparticipating policies requires a conservative approach, leading to higher premium levels than would be necessary if all elements were not guaranteed.

Past Experience. The oldest method of recognizing experience, policy **dividends,** reflects the insurer's *past* experience. Dividends are paid on those life insurance policies that base experience participation on cumulative deviations of operating experience relative to the mortality, interest, and expense assumptions built into the premium. Such policies are classified as **participating policies.**

Premiums for participating policies are usually—but not always—based on fairly conservative mortality, interest, and expense assumptions and include a specific allowance for some level of dividend payments, with the result that the payment of some level of dividends over the life of a policy by the company is reasonably assured. The actual amount to be paid is not known and is never guaranteed. If future results equal the assumptions implicit in the premium, the dividends *illustrated to be paid when the policy was issued* should be met. If future results are more favorable, dividends should be higher than were originally illustrated, and vice versa. The term "dividend" as used in life insurance should not be confused with the same term used to refer to earnings on shares of stock.

Dividends paid under participating life insurance policies usually are, at least in the early policy years, mainly a return to the policyowner of a portion of his or her premium payment. As pointed out, premiums for participating policies are usually calculated assuming a specific allowance for some level of dividend payments.

Historically, the dividend allowance included has been fairly conservative, with the result that most insurers selling participating life insurance policies have paid higher dividends than originally illustrated.[19] Today, however, many insurers illustrate dividends on a liberal basis, thus reducing the possibility of future paid dividends exceeding illustrated dividends.

Current and Expected Future Experience. Some life insurance policies permit policyowners to participate in *current* and *expected future* deviations of actual mortality, interest, and/or expense experience from that built into the premium. The premiums and values of such **current assumption policies,** like those of participating policies, are usually—but not always—based on fairly conservative mortality, interest, and expense assumptions, thus providing the company with reasonable assurance that *some* favorable deviations will occur. Again, like that of traditional participating policies, the extent of such favorable deviations is not known and is never guaranteed over the policy period.

These current assumption policies—also sometimes referred to as interest-sensitive policies— do not yet have a generally accepted label. These policies are not "participating" in the sense of reflecting past experience. Most are, in fact, classified in state law as nonparticipating policies, but without guarantees with respect to all policy elements. Universal life policies are examples of this type of policy.

Interaction among Life Insurance Pricing Elements

Earlier illustrations suggest that all a life insurance company needs to do to develop its gross premiums is to review its own experience carefully, calculate a net premium, and add allowances for expenses, profit, and contingencies. Although this can be a first step, many other facets enter into pricing in life insurance. For example, will the gross premium so developed be competitive? What proportion of the policyowners is expected voluntarily to terminate their policies, and when? What levels of cash value should be included (subject, of course, to state-imposed minimums)? What level of dividends should be included? How might inflation alter expected results? Are agent commissions sufficiently high to induce agents to sell the policy? The list of questions goes on and on, the answers to which may suggest the need for further thought and change.

A life insurance company's raw materials— its operating experience in terms of mortality, interest, and expenses and its philosophy regarding profits and contingencies— can be changed only so much. However, the elements derived from these raw materials can be altered and rearranged. For example, a company offering a participating policy could have a lower gross premium if it were willing to lower its schedule of policy dividends. A cash value higher than the required minimum necessitates a higher premium, other things being equal. Assuming a very competitive price and liberal comissions, company market support costs may be significantly reduced. The marketing system(s) employed may permit adjustments in either agent or market support compensation.

The point is that an interaction exists among the various life insurance policy pricing elements. This section briefly explores this interaction to help the reader to understand better how a life insurance company functions from the standpoint of income and disbursements.

The discussion can be considered as a microcosm of a life insurance company. It will focus on a simulated test of a single block of policies, even though a typical life insurance company will have many policy blocks. The reader is invited to notice, in particular, the sources of the company's income for this block of policies (i.e., premiums and investment income) and how they interact with the disbursements.

The Asset-Share Calculation. The testing of a tentative gross premium rate schedule and other policy elements is performed using the **asset-share calculation.** This really is a simulation of the anticipated operating experience for a block of policies using the best estimates of what the individual factors will be for each future policy year. The purpose of the asset-share calculation

---

[19]See Chapter 21 for more detail on dividends and their calculation.

is to determine, for a block of policies, the expected fund (per $1,000 of insurance) held by the company at the end of each policy year (usually the test is for a maximum of 20 or 30 years) after payment of death claims, expenses, dividends or other nonguaranteed benefits or credits, surrender values, and allowance for actual interest earnings. The accumulated fund at the end of each policy year is divided by the number of surviving and persisting policyowners (lives exposed) to produce each policy's "share of assets" or asset share.

Figure 2–2 shows in simplified fashion the mechanics of an asset-share calculation. Disbursements are netted against income. The balance represents the net addition to the insurer's assets. Of course, much of the accumulated assets will be required to fund future death claims, expenses, and so on. In other words, they are required to back policy reserves, and to the extent that the accumulated assets are not sufficient to do so, the insurer must, in essence, "loan" surplus to make good the deficit.

Asset-share calculations are made before the fact. Since future experience is not known, estimates must be made that are thought to be reasonable representations of future experience. An asset-share calculation seeks to determine whether the individual elements of a policy are well balanced and will produce acceptable results for both the insurance company and policyowners.

In the event that the asset shares produced by the tentative gross premiums are deficient in

light of company objectives, the premiums may be increased in some fashion or some specific benefit (i.e., dividends, cash values, etc.) or expense decreased. If the fund accumulation appears excessive, the premiums can be reduced or benefits increased. Naturally, for participating insurance or nonparticipating insurance that has one or more nonguaranteed elements, the available asset share may also be adjusted by modifying the tentative dividend scale or other nonguaranteed policy elements.

Illustrative Asset-Share Calculation. The process by which a gross premium rate structure is tested can be explained most effectively by means of an illustrative asset share calculation. Table 2–6 shows the results of such an asset share calculation. For purposes of this illustration, all assumptions have been simplified and are somewhat arbitrary.

The tentative gross premium rate being tested is $15.50 per $1,000 for a participating ordinary life policy issued to males, age 35. Column 3 shows the expected number of deaths each year based on an initial 100,000 insureds and on what the insurer believes to be the most reasonable expected future mortality experience. Column 4 provides the insurer's best estimate as to the number of insureds who will **lapse** (voluntarily terminate) their insurance policies each year.

The insurer's expected expenses over each of the next 20 years are listed in column 6, and columns 7 and 8 show cash values and illustrated dividends that the insurer is also testing. The cash values are the minimum permitted by law. The insurer could have higher cash values but no lower. The dividend scale can be changed as the insurer judges appropriate, depending on test results. As shown in column 8, this would be the dividends the insurer would illustrate on all sales materials and advertisements and would show in its rate book, in the absence of a change.

Column 9 shows the value of the total asset fund carried over from the previous year. In the first year, it is, of course, equal to zero. Yearly premium income figures are shown in column 10; total yearly expense disbursements in column 11; total yearly death claim payments in column 12;

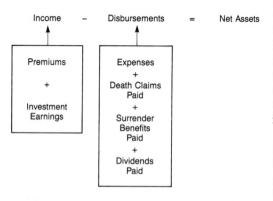

FIGURE 2-2. Insurance company funds flow.

TABLE 2-6. Asset-share calculation, $1,000 ordinary life issued at male age 35 ($15.50 rate per $1,000)

(1) Policy Year	(2) Number Paying Premiums at Beginning of Year	(3) Number Dying[a]	(4) Number Withdrawing[b]	(5) Number Alive at End of Year after Withdrawals [(2) − (3) − (4)]	(6) Expense Rate per $1,000	(7) Cash Value per $1,000 on Withdrawal[c]	(8) Dividend per $1,000
1	100,000	88	20,000	79,912	27.00	0.00	0.00
2	79,912	81	8,630	71,201	3.00	0.00	0.50
3	71,201	85	5,696	65,420	3.00	0.00	1.00
4	65,420	91	4,056	61,273	3.00	6.70	1.50
5	61,273	94	2,941	58,238	3.00	14.04	2.00
6	58,238	105	2,096	56,037	3.00	21.72	2.50
7	56,037	113	1,793	54,131	3.00	29.73	3.10
8	54,131	121	1,569	52,441	3.00	38.12	3.70
9	52,441	130	1,415	50,896	3.00	46.87	4.30
10	50,896	139	1,272	49,485	3.00	56.02	5.90
11	49,485	157	1,187	48,141	3.00	65.55	6.60
12	48,141	168	1,107	46,866	3.00	75.50	7.30
13	46,866	179	1,031	45,656	3.00	85.88	8.00
14	45,656	191	958	44,507	3.00	96.71	8.70
15	44,507	203	890	43,414	3.00	108.01	9.40
16	43,414	217	868	42,329	3.00	119.79	10.20
17	42,329	233	846	41,250	3.00	132.02	11.00
18	41,250	250	825	40,175	3.00	144.69	11.80
19	40,175	270	803	39,102	3.00	157.79	12.70
20	39,102	292	782	38,028	3.00	171.28	13.60

TABLE 2-6. (Continued)

Policy Year	(9) Fund at Beginning of Year [(16) Prior Year]	(10) Premium Income [($15.50)×(2)]	(11) Expense Disbursements [(2)×(6)]	(12) Death Claims [$1,000×(3)]	(13) Amount Paid on Surrender [(4)×(7)]	(14) Total Dividends Paid [(5)×(8)]
1	0	1,550,000	2,700,000	88,000	0	0
2	-1,345,460	1,238,636	239,736	81,000	0	35,601
3	-497,996	1,103,616	213,603	85,000	0	65,420
4	273,053	1,014,010	196,260	91,000	27,186	91,910
5	974,785	949,732	183,819	94,000	41,281	116,476
6	1,641,374	902,689	174,714	105,000	45,517	140,093
7	2,287,256	868,574	168,111	113,000	53,314	167,806
8	2,917,408	839,031	162,393	121,000	59,813	194,032
9	3,537,220	812,836	157,323	130,000	66,327	218,853
10	4,149,049	788,888	152,688	139,000	71,252	291,962
11	4,707,452	767,018	148,455	157,000	77,804	317,731
12	5,245,756	746,186	144,423	168,000	83,574	342,122
13	5,772,539	726,423	140,598	179,000	88,539	365,248
14	6,289,774	707,668	136,968	191,000	92,652	387,211
15	6,798,458	689,859	133,521	203,000	96,129	408,092
16	7,300,371	672,917	130,242	217,000	103,975	431,756
17	7,786,424	656,100	126,987	233,000	111,686	453,750
18	8,255,015	639,375	123,750	250,000	119,370	474,065
19	8,705,313	622,713	120,525	270,000	126,704	496,595
20	9,130,727	606,081	117,306	292,000	133,942	517,181

TABLE 2-6. (Continued)

Policy Year	(15) Interest Earned during Year {0.09 [(9)+(10) −(11)−½ (12)]}	(16) Fund at End of Year [(9)+(10)−(11)−(12) −(13)−(14)+(15)]	(17) Asset Share at End of Year: [(16)÷(5)]	(18) Reserve[d] at End of Year	(19) Surplus p $1,000 at E of Year [(17)−(18]
1	−107,460	−1,345,460	−16.84	7.63	−24.47
2	−34,835	−497,996	−6.99	15.61	−22.61
3	31,456	273,053	4.17	23.94	−19.76
4	94,077	974,785	15.91	32.60	−16.69
5	152,433	1,641,374	28.18	41.61	−13.43
6	208,516	2,287,256	40.82	50.97	−10.15
7	263,810	2,917,408	53.90	60.67	−6.77
8	318,019	3,537,220	67.45	70.73	−3.27
9	371,496	4,149,049	81.52	81.14	0.38
10	424,417	4,707,452	95.13	91.93	3.20
11	472,276	5,245,756	108.97	103.09	5.87
12	518,717	5,772,539	123.17	114.65	8.52
13	564,198	6,289,774	137.76	126.61	11.15
14	608,848	6,798,458	152.75	138.99	13.76
15	652,797	7,300,371	168.16	151.79	16.36
16	696,109	7,786,424	183.95	165.03	18.92
17	737,913	8,255,015	200.12	178.66	21.46
18	778,108	8,705,313	216.68	192.68	24.01
19	816,525	9,130,727	233.51	207.06	26.45
20	852,615	9,528,994	250.58	221.77	28.81

[a]Deaths based on select and ultimate experience mortality table. Deaths assumed to occur in middle of policy year on the average.
[b]Withdrawals based on Linton BA lapse rates. Assumed to occur on anniversary at end of policy year.
[c]Minimum required cash values; 7½ percent interest assumption.
[d]Net-level-premium reserves, 1980 CSO Table, 6%.

total yearly cash surrender value payouts in column 13; and total yearly dividend payments in column 14. Note that based on the minimum permissible cash values (shown in column 7), nothing would be paid to terminating policyowners until year 4.

Interest earned on net accumulated assets is shown in column 15 and the year-end fund balance is shown in column 16. Interest is earned (column 15) on the fund carried over from the previous year (column 9) plus premiums collected at the beginning of the year (column 10). However, from these two amounts one must subtract the expense disbursements (column 11)—assumed to be made at the beginning of each year—and one-half of the year's death claim payouts. Recall that the item of interest here is interest earned (or forgone) during the year on the funds on hand for the year. The assumption with respect to death claims is that they are paid out uniformly throughout the year. Therefore, the company has had use of only one-half of the funds, on average, throughout the year; hence the one-half factor applied to the column 12 figures.

The first two years' negative figures in both columns 15 and 16 indicate that the insurer has spent more money than it has received from premiums and interest earnings from this block of policies. Finally, the entire process translates into assets accumulated on a per $1,000 basis, as shown in column 17.

The asset share fund for this block of policies is analogous to an income-outgo account. Each year, premiums and interest earnings are credited to the account as income, and death claims, surrender and dividend payments, and expense disbursements are charged against the account. The account balance at the end of each year (column 16) is divided by the number of surviving (i.e, those who did not die) *and* persisting (i.e., those who did not terminate) policyowners (column 5) to obtain the pro rata share of the account for each surviving and persisting policyowner—the asset share (column 17). For example, at the end of the tenth year, $95.13 in assets is expected to have been accumulated for each of the 49,485 surviving and persisting policyowners.

A number of significant facts is shown by the asset-share study. First, the asset share is negative at the end of the first two policy years, reflecting the high first-year expenses involved in selling, underwriting, and issuing new business and the use of a level premium.

Comparisons of columns 7 and 17 show that the surrender values granted on withdrawal are greater than the asset share until the third policy year. This means that the company would suffer an operating loss on any policy in this class terminating prior to the third policy year. From the third year on, the company would experience a net gain on policies that are surrendered each year. Of course, future profits expected on such policies would be lost.

Column 18 shows the per policy reserve that is assumed to be set up for this block of policies. Column 19 shows the year by year net cumulative effect on the company's surplus. Although policy reserves are not segregated on a company's balance sheet on a per policy basis, they are shown on a per policy basis here to illustrate better the concepts involved. Thus, during the first policy year, a reserve of $7.63 per policy is established. This amount is greater than the increase in assets (−$16.84) which results from the first year's operations. As a result, surplus is lowered to the extent of the difference (a total of −$24.47). This "surplus strain" continues through the eighth policy year. From the ninth policy year on, this block of policies, under the anticipated operating conditions, is expected to contribute positively to surplus, having "repaid" fully the amounts "borrowed" from surplus in the early policy years. After the eighth policy year, the increase in the asset side of the balance sheet more than offsets the increase in the reserve liability and does so increasingly as the years pass.

This example shows results for a single year of issue. Blocks for other years of issue also would not result in positive figures for many years under the assumptions used here.

As pointed out above, if the findings of the asset-share study do not develop satisfactory results for the company in terms of its objectives, elements of the policy would be changed to achieve results judged acceptable in light of the company's objectives. The asset-share calculation also tests the effect of the proposed surrender values and dividend scale. Asset shares are also used to test premiums under "disaster" conditions (i.e., extremely unfavorable investment earnings, mortality or lapse experience, expense, inflation, etc.). The computer has facilitated asset share research, permitting prompt and economical analysis of the impact of proposed changes in any factor affecting the financial experience of a block of life insurance policies. It should be noted that historical asset-share research is a major input to product pricing, planning, and development.

Relation of Surrender Values, Reserves, and Asset Shares

Previous discussions have attempted to delineate surrender values, reserves, and asset shares. To summarize: The **cash surrender value** represents the amount made available, contractually, to a withdrawing policyowner who is terminating his or her policy. This value is intended to represent an equitable distributiuon of the pro rata share of the amount accumulated on behalf of the particular block of policies from which the policyowner is withdrawing.

The **policy reserve** is a more conservative value, representing the measure of the liability of the company for a given block of policies. Minimum liability values are mandated by regulation in the interest of solvency.[20]

The **asset share** is the pro rata share of the assets accumulated on the basis of the company's anticipated operating experience, on behalf of the block of policies to which the particular policy belongs. In the case of a historical asset share, the assets accumulated would be based on the company's actual operating experience.

The asset share is typically less than the reserve in the early years, due to the uneven incidence of expense outlay as compared with expense provision in premiums. The length of time it takes the asset share to exceed the reserve is a management decision reflecting how soon the company wishes to recover its excess first-year expenses. After the asset share equals the reserve, under most cash value policies, both continue to increase, but with the asset share normally growing at a slightly faster rate.

The surrender value is a more arbitrary value, reflecting the elements of expense incidence, competition, and the company's (and state lawmaker's) philosophy with regard to equity between persisting and withdrawing policyowners. In the early years, it usually lies somewhere between the asset share and the reserve.

[20]See Chapter 20.

Chapter 3

The Role and Importance of Life and Health Insurance

That life and health insurance are of great importance in countries throughout the world can be gleaned from Table 3–1. This table shows the ratio of life insurance in force to national income in selected countries. By this statistical measure, Japan leads all other nations shown. Canada ranks second, followed by the United States. Other countries in which life insurance in force equals or exceeds national income include the Netherlands, Sweden, New Zealand, Ireland, the United Kingdom, Australia, and France. It can be observed that, in general, the more economically developed a country, the greater the role of life insurance as an economic security device. Indeed, a United Nations' Committee recently formally recognized "that life insurance companies can play an important role in providing individual economic security and in national development efforts, including the mobilization of personal savings."[1]

This chapter presents an overview of the role that life insurance plays in the U.S. economy and society and attempts to provide some idea of its importance, both from the individual's perspective as well as that of society as a whole.

LIFE INSURERS AS FINANCIAL INSTITUTIONS

Life insurance companies today have grown to be major financial institutions and play a correspondingly important role as financial intermediaries. This section provides an idea of the role of life insurers as financial institutions in today's society.

Nature of Life Insurance Company Investment Activity

It was shown earlier that under the single-premium, level-premium, and flexible-premium plans of providing life insurance protection, the insurer, in effect, retains portions of the premiums paid during the early policy years and accumulates them, together with investment earnings on them, toward the payment of benefits in later years. As the rate of return on invested assets increases, other things being equal, the company can lower the premiums it charges for new or existing policies, increase the dividends or other nonguaranteed benefits it credits on existing policies, or both. Since premium rates and net costs are important

---

[1]*Resolution 21(X). Life Insurance in Developing Countries,* adopted at the 10th session of the Committee on Invisibles and Financing related to Trade, United Nations Conference on Trade and Development, December 1982.

TABLE 3-1. Ratio of life insurance in force to national income in selected countries
(Percent)

	1978	1983
Developed countries		
Australia	107	109
Belgium	48	51
Canada	162	177
Denmark	49	58
Finland	20	17
France	95	106[a]
West Germany	55	67
Iceland	8	11
Ireland	155	136
Italy	10	8
Japan	262	322
Netherlands	113	137
New Zealand	141	126
Norway	41	48
Spain	20	57
Sweden	123	127[a]
United Kingdon	100	116[a]
United States	148	170
Developing countries		
Brazil	16	24[a]
Fiji	53	53[a]
South Korea	19	89[a]
Pakistan	17	16
Peru	6	3
Philippines	23	22
Tanzania	3	5[a]
Thailand	6	10
Tunisia	10	12
Venezuela	NA	32
Zambia	NA	11

[a]Data for 1982.
Source: *Life Insurance Fact Book, 1984* and *1985 Update* (Washington, DC: American Council of Life Insurance) p. 102.

competitive considerations, the investment function is a significant factor in a company's competitive position. This investment activity establishes the life insurance business as a significant factor in the capital markets.

Sources of Investable Funds. In a life insurance company, investable funds arise from both insurance and investment operations. The cash flow from insurance operations arises out of the difference between cash receipts (premiums, annuity considerations, and other deposits) and cash disbursements (benefits and expenses). The cash flow from existing investments develops from current income (earnings from net interest, dividends,

and realized capital gains), maturities, prepayments, redemptions, calls, and sales.

There is a close relationship between these two sources of investable funds. Part of each premium payment becomes available for investment in the economy. In calculating premiums, anticipated investment earnings are taken into account, thereby reducing the price of life insurance.

In 1985, total income of all U.S. life companies was $234.0 billion; 66.6 percent was from premium receipts and 29.0 percent from investment earnings. The remaining 4.4 percent came from other sources. Table 3-2 provides life insurance company income data for selected years.

Magnitude of Investment Activity. The magnitude of life insurance company investment activity can best be illustrated by considering the figures in Table 3-3. On December 31, 1985, the assets of all U.S. life insurance companies approximated $825.9 billion, an increase during that year of $102.9 billion.

As large as the 1985 asset increase of $102.9 billion may seem, companies made investments far in excess of that figure during that year. In addition to the "rollover" (reinvestment at maturity) and purchases of Treasury bills and other short-term paper, investment decisions must be made on the return flows of funds from the sale or redemption of securities and mortgage-loan principal amortization and prepayments. For example, in 1981 (the latest year for which data are available), the gross amount of investments acquired came to $435.7 billion even though asset growth that year was only $46.6 billion.

Through life insurance company investment operations, another pooling arrangement is brought to bear. Millions of policyowners, contributing relatively small amounts of premiums annually, create a fund to be invested by professional investors. So invested, the funds provide the financial basis for more and better homes, utility systems, and schools, and for a more rapidly advancing technological base. All of this accrues at least indirectly to the benefit of the policyowner, just as the proceeds of the policy enhance the economic security of the policyowner and the beneficiary.

TABLE 3-2. Income of U.S. life insurance companies
(millions)

Year	Premium Receipts				Investment Income[b]	Other Income[c]	Total Income
	Life Insurance Premiums	Annuity Considerations	Health Insurance Premiums[a]	Total Premium Receipts			
1915	$ 776	$ 6	—	$ 782	$ 241	$ 20	$ 1,043
1930	3,416	101	—	3,517	891	186	4,594
1945	4,589	570	—	5,159	1,445	1,070	7,674
1960	11,998	1,341	$ 4,026	17,365	4,304	1,338	23,007
1970	21,679	3,721	11,367	36,767	10,144	2,143	49,054
1980	40,829	22,429	29,366	92,624	33,928	4,336	130,888
1985	60,127	53,899	41,837	155,863	67,952	10,212	234,027

[a]Includes some premiums for workers' compensation and auto and other liability insurance.

[b]Beginning with 1951, investment income is net of investment expenses.

[c]Beginning in 1975, "Other Income" includes commissions and expense allowance on reinsurance ceded. Considerations for supplementary contracts with and without life contingencies are included under "Other Income." Prior to 1947, the business of health departments was not included.

Source: 1986 Fact Book.

TABLE 3-3. Total admitted assets of U.S. life insurance companies
(millions)

Year	Amount
1900	$ 1,742
1910	3,876
1920	7,320
1930	18,880
1940	30,802
1950	64,020
1960	119,576
1965	158,884
1970	207,254
1975	289,304
1980	479,210
1981	525,803
1982	588,163
1983	654,948
1984	722,979
1985	825,901

Source: 1986 Fact Book

Types of Life Insurer Investments. Assets of life insurance companies, largely comprised of financial instruments, are used to back life and health insurance and annuity obligations and have been built up from policyowners' premiums and investment earnings. Table 3–4 shows the magnitude and distribution of assets of U.S life insurers. The largest component of life insurance company assets in 1985 was corporate debt

issues. Holdings of corporate debt increased from $254.1 billion to $296.8 billion, or 36.0 percent of total assets, by year-end 1985.

Mortgages, the second largest component of life insurance company assets increased from $156.7 billion to $171.8 billion during 1985. As a proportion of total assets these holdings were 20.8 percent in 1985, compared to 21.7 percent in 1984.

The third largest category, government securities, increased to represent 15.0 percent of total assets in 1985. Corporate stock holdings amounted to $77.5 billion, or 9.4 percent of total assets.

Life Insurance Company Investment Performance

The rate of return on invested assets is considered one of the basic criteria in measuring the investment performance of a life insurance company. The portfolio rate of return is the weighted average of investments made over time at different rates of return. This composite rate is a summary measure of past and current investment results. Table 3–5 illustrates the average net rate of return that has been earned by U.S. life insurance companies over the years. These rates exclude in-

TABLE 3-4. Distribution of assets of U.S. life insurance companies

Year	Government Securities	Corporate Securities		Mortgages	Real Estate	Policy Loans	Misc. Assets	Total
		Bonds	Stocks					
Amount (Millions $)								
1930	1,502	4,929	519	7,598	548	2,807	977	18,880
1940	8,447	8,645	605	5,972	2,065	3,091	1,977	30,802
1950	16,118	23,248	2,103	16,102	1,445	2,413	2,591	64,020
1960	11,815	46,740	4,981	41,771	3,765	5,231	5,273	119,576
1970	11,068	73,098	15,420	74,375	6,320	16,064	10,909	207,254
1980	33,015	179,603	47,366	131,080	15,033	41,411	31,702	472,210
1985	124,598	296,848	77,496	171,797	28,822	54,369	71,971	825,901
Percent								
1930	8.0	26.0	2.8	40.2	2.9	14.9	5.2	100.0
1940	27.5	28.1	2.0	19.4	6.7	10.0	6.3	100.0
1950	25.2	36.3	3.3	25.1	2.2	3.8	4.1	100.0
1960	9.9	39.1	4.2	34.9	3.1	4.4	4.4	100.0
1970	5.3	35.3	7.4	35.9	3.0	7.8	5.3	100.0
1980	6.9	37.5	9.9	27.4	3.1	8.6	6.6	100.0
1985	15.0	36.0	9.4	20.8	3.5	6.6	8.7	100.0

Source: *1986 Fact Book*

come tax and, importantly, capital gains and losses. For some companies, such gains and losses have a material effect on overall investment performance. Individual company performance, naturally, varies both above and below the average for the industry.

TABLE 3-5. Net rate of interest earned on invested funds, U.S. life insurance companies

Year	Rate[a](%)
1930	5.05
1940	3.45
1950	3.13
1960	4.11
1970	5.30
1975	6.36
1980	8.02
1981	8.57
1982	8.91
1983	8.96
1984	9.45
1985	9.63

[a]The net interest rate is calculated using industry aggregates and represents the ratio of (1) net investment income to (2) mean invested assets (including cash), less half the net investment income. Before 1940, some federal income taxes were deducted from net investment income; beginning with 1940, the rates are calculated before deducting any federal income taxes. The data include the assets and investment income of separate accounts.

Source: *1986 Fact Book.*

Since the rate of return is a weighted average of returns on investments made in different time periods, the rate is clearly influenced by the timing of cash flows with respect to market interest rates. The portfolio rate of return is determined by factors that in the short run are largely out of the control of present investment officers; for this reason, the rate of return on new investment is an additional and important criterion for measuring investment performance. During the past several years, yields on new investments were higher than portfolio rates of return.[2]

Life Insurance Companies in the Money and Capital Markets

Investments by life insurance companies in the money and capital markets of the United States are an important source of funds to the American economy. Net investments in U.S. capital markets by life insurance companies totaled $73.3 billion in 1985.

The leading financial institutions in the United States are commercial banks, savings and loan associations, life insurance companies, cor-

[2]See Chapter 9 for a discussion of the different ways that insurance companies allocate investment income among policies.

porate pension funds, non-life insurance companies, and mutual savings banks. Table 3–6 shows that commercial banks are the most significant of these as a source of funds in the U.S. money and capital markets.

The life insurance industry is obviously a significant factor in the capital markets. Its role is particularly significant in that despite relatively close regulation, life insurance companies are able to utilize a wider range of loan instruments than many other financial institutions. Despite a favorable rate of growth in life insurance in force since World War II, the relative rate of savings through life insurance has decreased. This has been caused by increased competition from other financial and nonfinancial institutions and is reflected within the life insurance industry by a shift to term insurance, both individual and group, which has little or no savings element.

LIFE AND HEALTH INSURANCE OWNERSHIP

Life Insurance Ownership

Life insurance in force in the United States reached a new high of $6,053.1 billion at the end of 1985, an increase of $553.1 billion, or 10.1 percent over year-end 1984. Some 154 million policyowners, or two out of three persons in the country, were insured by life insurance companies at the end of 1985.

If this were divided equally among all American families, each would have had $63,400 of protection at year-end 1985. Excluding families without life insurance, the average for insured families was about $74,600. Despite significant increases in the amount of coverage, protection for all families equalled only about 25 months of total disposable personal income per family at the end of 1985.

Participating life insurance accounted for $3,255.8 billion, or 45.6 percent of all life insurance in force with U.S. companies at the end of 1985. The remaining $3,880.0 billion, or 54.4 percent of life insurance in force, was nonparticipating either on a guaranteed or nonguaranteed cost basis.

Mutual life insurance companies, which have no stockholders and whose boards of directors are elected by their policyowners, provided $2,882.4 billion, or 40.4 percent, of total life insurance in force with U.S. life companies at the end of 1985. Stock life insurance companies, which are owned by their stockholders, accounted for $4,253.4 billion, or 59.6 percent, of total life insurance in force at the end of 1985. Mutual companies accounted for 52.6 percent of total group

TABLE 3-6 Sources of funds in the United States money and capital markets
(billions)

	1970	1975	1980	1984	1985
Life insurance companies	$ 9.0	$ 18.8	$ 33.6	$ 57.0	$ 73.3
Private non-life insurance company pension plans	6.6	25.1	48.3	22.3	36.5
State and local retirement funds	6.3	11.7	26.2	35.3	37.2
Savings and loan associations	11.9	34.8	46.2	123.4	62.3
Mutual savings banks	4.1	10.9	5.4	10.0	9.4
Commercial banking	35.7	29.5	100.6	181.6	196.7
Federal reserve banks	5.0	8.5	4.5	8.4	21.6
Federal loan agencies	10.4	11.6	45.6	73.2	101.6
Nonfinancial corporations	1.9	12.2	3.3	22.8	−5.0
Fire and casualty companies	4.8	6.6	13.0	5.8	11.0
Real estate investment trusts	1.9	−4.8	−0.7	0.8	2.3
Mutual funds[a]	1.6	0.2	17.9	69.6	102.0
Foreigners	11.2	10.8	28.6	43.2	80.4
Individual and others	7.3	44.4	70.9	182.8	291.7
	$117.7	$220.3	$443.4	$836.2	$1,021.0

[a]Includes money market funds of $0.7 billion in 1975, $14.9 billion in 1980, $38.0 billion in 1984, and $1.5 billion in 1985.
Source: *1986 Fact Book.*

life. Stock life companies provided 64.9 percent of the total industrial life insurance in force, and they also accounted for 77.2 percent of credit life in force.

The number of annuities in force with U.S. life insurance companies under individual and supplementary contracts totaled 10.5 million at the end of 1985. Individual annuities accounted for 10.0 million of this total. The growth was due largely to purchases of annuities for individual pension plans.

Health Insurance Ownership[3]

At the end of 1984, more than 188 million Americans were protected by one or more forms of private health insurance. These include over 193 million persons under 65—representing 83 percent of this age group, who have some form of health insurance. Nearly 15 million older persons—over one-half in the 65-and-older population—held private health insurance policies to supplement benefits available through Medicare.

Various forms of private health insurance coverage are available from several different types of insurers: insurance companies; hospital and medical service plans, such as Blue Cross and Blue Shield; group medical plans operating on a prepayment basis, such as health maintenance organizations; and others. Chapter 16 includes more information on the types and operations of health insurers.

Over 800 private insurance companies in the United States were writing individual and/or group health insurance covering nearly 107 million persons at year-end 1984. Policies issued by insurance companies provide for payment directly to the insured or if assigned by the insured, to the provider of services for reimbursement of expenses incurred. As mentioned earlier, health insurance coverage made available by insurance companies is generally divided into two categories: medical expense insurance and disability income insurance. Medical expense insurance is a "reimbursement type" of coverage that provides broad benefits that can cover virtually all expenses connected with medical care and related services. Disability income insurance provides periodic payments when the insured is unable to work as a result of sickness or injury.

Blue Cross and Blue Shield plans are nonprofit member plans that service statewide and other geographical areas, offering both individual and group coverage. Blue Cross plans provide hospital care benefits on essentially a "service type" basis, under which the organization, through a separate contract with member hospitals, reimburses the hospital for covered services provided to the insured. Blue Shield plans provide benefits for surgical and medical services performed by a physician. The typical Blue Shield plan provides benefits similar to those provided under the benefit provisions of hospital–surgical policies issued by insurance companies.

Health care coverage is also provided through health maintenance organizations (HMOs), which provide comprehensive health care services for their members for a fixed periodic payment. In such plans, a group of physicians, surgeons, dentists, or optometrists furnish needed care as specified in the contract to subscribers. From mid-1971 to January 1985, the number of operational HMOs increased from 33 to 377 and the number of subscribers increased from 3.6 million to 16.7 million.[4]

It is estimated that some 39 percent of the total 1983 insurance company group coverage is represented by Administrative Service Only (ASO) arrangements and Minimum Premium Plans (MPPs). Under these systems, corporations and other organizations establish self-funded health plans. Insurance companies or private organizations are paid a fee by the self-funding group to process the claims and benefits payments. These types of arrangements represented less than 5 percent of total insurance company group coverage prior to 1975.

---

[3]Data presented in this section are taken from *Source Book of Health Insurance Data, 1986 Update* (Washington, D.C.: Health Insurance Association of America), p. 4 and *Statistical Abstract of the United States* (1987), p. 44.

[4]See Chapter 16.

LIFE AND HEALTH INSURANCE BENEFIT PAYMENTS

Life Insurance and Annuity Benefit Payments

As Table 3-7 shows, Americans received $66.5 billion in payments from life insurance policies and annuities during 1985, a 10.1 percent increase over 1984. These payments, increasing steadily for many years, reflect the growing use of life insurance, not only in providing funds for the family whose breadwinner dies, but for family financial needs during the policyowner's lifetime.

Several factors affect the pattern of life in-surance benefit payments. Primary among them are the changes in the death rate among insured individuals and the growth of group life insurance and other term insurance policies that do not have cash values.

Another way of viewing life insurance bene-fit payments is to express payouts in terms of a single dollar. Of course, this composite dollar represents the business as a whole and will be dif-ferent for individual companies, depending on types of business written, age and type of com-pany, and many other factors. Table 3-8 sum-marizes this composite dollar of benefit payment.

TABLE 3-7. Life insurance and annuity benefit payments in the United States[a]
(millions)

| Year | Life Policyowners and Beneficiaries | | | | | | Annuity Payments | Grand Total |
	Death Payments	Matured Endowments	Disability Payments	Surrender Values	Policy Dividends	Total		
1940	$ 995	$269	$104	$ 652	$ 468	$ 2,488	$ 176	$ 2,664
1950	1,590	495	100	592	627	3,404	327	3,731
1960	3,346	673	124	1,663	1,512	7,288	830	8,118
1970	7,017	978	233	2,887	3,214	14,329	2,120	16,449
1980	12,884	908	592	6,678	6,785	27,847	10,195	38,042
1985	18,226	779	536	15,589	10,121	45,251	21,259	66,510

[a]Figures represent benefit payments under original policy contracts, including benefits that are left with the companies for future payment under supplementary contracts, but excluding payments from existing supplementary contracts. Annuity payments include death, surrender, disability, and dividend payments.
Source: *1986 Fact Book.*

TABLE 3-8. Life Insurance Company Dollar in Benefit Payments, 1985[a]
(U.S. Life Insurance Companies)

	Cents
Benefit payments and additions to funds for policyowners and beneficiaries	
Benefit payments in year	45.7
Additions to policy reserve funds	33.4
Additions to special reserves and surplus funds	1.9
	81.0
Operating expenses	
Commissions to agents	5.9
Home and field office expenses	9.0
	14.9
Taxes	2.7
Dividence to stockholders of stock life insurance companies	1.4[b]
	100.0

[a]Direct investment taxes (such as real estate) are excluded from taxes and are deducted, with other investment expenses, from investment income, Federal income taxes, however, are included in taxes.
[b]For stock companies only this ratio woud be 2.9 cents per dollar.
Source: *1986 Fact Book.*

Of the 1985 industry outgo dollar, 81.0 cents was assigned to meet current or future obligations. That included 45.7 cents paid in benefits to policyowners or to beneficiaries during the year, 33.4 cents added to policy reserves for future benefit payments, and 1.9 cents added to special reserves and surplus funds.

The outgo dollar also varies by major line of business. For the life insurance line, 54.7 percent of the income in 1983 (the latest year for which data are available) was needed for benefits and 20.6 percent was added to policy reserves for future benefit payments. The annuity line set aside 63.3 percent for contract reserves, while the health line needed 67.1 percent of income to pay claims and policy dividends.

Operating expenses based on industry aggregates declined from the previous year to 14.9 cents. This proportion had remained about the same for several decades. Its decline during the past seven years reflects the expansion of the annuity business and the fact that the annuities have lower sales expenses per dollar of income. Included in the 1985 figure were 9.0 cents for expenses of home and field offices and 5.9 cents for commissions to agents.

The expense share as measured by this analysis, applies to the entire life insurance business, not to any single company. The proportions vary widely among companies, depending on such factors as the types of coverage offered by a given company and its ratio of recently issued insurance to its total insurance force. Expenses are higher for new policies because the initial costs of issuing and selling a policy are higher than those of maintaining older policies. Agents' commissions are normally considerably higher in the first policy year than in subsequent years.

A total of 2.7 cents was used for taxes (not including taxes directly connected with investment, such as real estate taxes). On an overall dollar basis, stock dividends to shareholders amounted to 1.4 cents. For mutual life insurance companies, of course, this amounted to zero; for stock life companies, dividends to shareholders amounted to 2.3 cents of the outgo dollar.

The main reason individuals buy life insurance is to protect their dependents against financial hardship when the insured dies. During 1985, life insurance companies paid $18.2 billion to beneficiaries of insureds who died. Of this total, ordinary insurance policies accounted for 48.2 percent of the payments and provided $8.8 billion. Group life insurance payments to beneficiaries totaled nearly $8.3 billion. Group life insurance has grown as a proportion of total death payments, accounting for 45.4 percent of death payments in 1985, compared to 41.4 percent in 1975.

Analysis of death payments indicates that members of policyowners' immediate families are the beneficiaries of most of the proceeds from all types of life insurance. Most other payments go to relatives outside the immediate family, with small proportions going to estates and trusts, business firms and partners, and to educational, charitable, and other institutions.

Although the basic purpose of life insurance is to provide protection against the economic risks of death, most policies also generate important additional values for the individual policyowner. Payments to life insurance policyowners in 1985 totaled $27.1 billion, 59.7 percent of total life insurance benefit payments in the United States. They consisted of payments from matured endowments, surrender values, disability provisions, and policy dividends.

Matured endowments resulted in policyowners being paid $779 million during the year. Disability payments under life insurance policies totaled $536 million. Cash surrender values paid on policies terminated voluntarily during the year amounted to a record $15.6 billion, an increase of 5.8 percent over the previous year.

Dividends to policyowners accounted for 37.4 percent of all payments to life insurance policyowners in 1985. These policy dividends amounted to over 10.1 billion. Annuitants received $21.3 billion in payments and dividends in 1985, up 18.7 percent from the $17.9 billion paid in 1984.

Health Insurance Benefit Payments[5]

A total of $109 billion in health insurance benefits was paid by private insuring organizations in the United States in 1984, a 2.7 percent increase over 1983 and four times the amount paid 10 years earlier. The increase was because

[5]*Ibid,* pp. 19–22.

of the rising cost of medical care, expansion of benefits, and higher utilization. Of this amount, insurance companies paid out somewhat less than one-half.

Medical expense benefits, which include payments under hospital, surgical, physician's expense, and major medical insurance, totaled $96.0 billion in 1984, an increase of 2.3 percent over 1983, of which commercial insurers paid out somewhat less than one-half. Dental expense benefits for 1984 totaled $7.7 billion, with commercial insurers paying out about 64 percent.

Health insurance benefits are provided by private insurers in two ways: through indemnity payments or through service arrangements. Benefits by insurance companies are provided primarily through indemnity payments, whereby the insured person is paid a specified sum of money toward his or her covered expenses. (Payments can also be made directly to the provider of care through an assignment of benefits.) Blue Cross–Blue Shield and other plans usually make payments for covered services directly to the participating hospital or physician.

According to a report by the Social Security Administration, American workers suffered a $45.6 billion loss in earnings resulting from short-term, nonoccupational sickness or injury during calendar year 1983, an increase of 7.2 percent over the previous year. Benefits paid under programs providing protection against such income loss amounted to $16.4 billion, a 1.0 percent increase

over 1983. Insurance company plans provided $2.7 billion of benefits, 16.5 percent of the total.

Table 3–9 shows the aggregate amount of health insurance benefits as well as a breakout by category of benefit payments made by commercial insurance companies in the United States. The reader might note the relatively low level of benefit payments under disability income policies as compared to total benefit payouts. This relatively low benefit payout level is due in part to the far lower extent of coverage under disability income polices than with most other forms of health insurance.

INDIVIDUAL BENEFITS OF LIFE INSURANCE

Aside from the advantage of providing a measure of financial protection for individuals and families, life and health insurance also benefit policyowners in other important ways.[6] The policyowner, in other words, can be considered as a "beneficiary" under his or her own life and health insurance. A number of potential advantages deserves special mention in this respect. The extent to which they may be applicable to a particular individual varies as a function of each person's motivations, worries, fears, and so on.

[6]The advantages that follow were first taken from S. S. Huebner, *Economics of Life Insurance*, 3rd ed. (New York: Appleton-Century-Crofts, 1959), pp. 143–240. As presented here, they represent modifications of those originally postulated by Huebner.

TABLE 3.9 Health insurance benefit payments of insurance companies in the United States[a]
(millions)

Year	Grand Total	Group				Individual and Family Policies		
		Total	Medical Expense	Dental Expense	Disability Income	Total	Medical Expense	Disability Income
1950	$ 755	$ 438	NA	NA	NA	$ 317	NA	NA
1960	3,069	2,350	NA	NA	$ 541	719	$ 421	$ 298
1970	9,089	7,476	$ 6,043	$ 140	1,293	1,613	1,090	523
1975	16,470	14,191	11,607	599	1,985	2,279	1,557	722
1980	37,002	33,002	25,895	2,795	4,312	4,000	2,970	1,030
1984	57,338	51,244	42,424	4,913	3,907	6,094	4,841	1,253

[a]For 1975 and later, data include benefit payments in Puerto Rico and other U.S. territories and possessions. Insurance company benefit paymetns for 1975 and later include administrative service only agreements and minimum premium plans. Aggregates in prior years contained only a portion of these data. Figures do not add to totals in some cases, due to rounding. NA, not available.

Source: *Source Book of Health Insurance Data, 1986 Update*, p. 11.

Can Assist in Making Savings Possible

One occasionally hears those who argue that they prefer to save rather than purchase life insurance. Certainly, good savings habits should be encouraged but to do so involves time, resources, and willingness. A policy of savings can yield only a small amount at the start, whereas a policy of insurance guarantees the full face value or income benefit from its beginning and thus can hedge the policyowner against failure through early death or disabilty to have sufficient working time to save adequately through other channels. Thus, if one is able to save $1,000 annually, it would take nearly 16 years to accumulate a fund of $25,000, assuming that the accumulations are safely invested annually at 6 percent compound interest. Even at that, an individual's ability to accumulate such a savings fund is contingent upon his or her survival for the full period and may be defeated by death or disability before the savings have reached any appreciable sum. To depend entirely on saving as a means of providing for the future of the family could prove disastrous financially. It is generally accepted that the first requisite in providing for the future support of dependents is reasonable certainty. Life and health insurance (or a rich and sharing relative!) serve as a hedge against the possible failure to continue the annual accumulations to the savings fund because of early death or disability. Through life and health insurance, a fund of $25,000 can be assured in any case.

Experience has shown that many persons hold an overly optimistic view concerning their resolution and ability to continue a savings program. Most persons leave no estate worthy of mention. The habit of saving, as already stated, should be encouraged, but the facts suggest that accumulating savings and purchasing life insurance should not be considered as being mutually exclusive. Both should be practiced. If, because of limited financial resources, only one is possible, sound personal risk management principles would hold that the large potential loss should be covered first.

Can Furnish a Safe and Profitable Investment

In addition to guaranteeing an immediate estate, some life insurance policies contain a savings element that can reach large proportions in later policy years. Life insurance policies, beyond a certain minimum size, are admirably adapted as accumulation devices, for the reasons cited earlier. Of course, as in any marketplace, variations exist. Some policies and companies afford better value than others. As discussed in Chapter 10, the wise purchaser shops competitively for his or her insurance.

Life insurance (and annuities) can furnish a profitable and safe investment service, but life insurance policies also make it possible for the policyowner to arrange for the safeguarding of the policy death proceeds for the benefit of the beneficiaries. Too often funds provided heirs through life insurance death proceeds (and inheritances) are lost by the heir or beneficiary through speculation, unwise investments, or excessive, unnecessary expenditures. Sound financial planning suggests that such a contingency should be contemplated by the individual and can be discouraged or even prevented through judicious use of life insurance settlement options, trusts and various other means.

Can Encourage Thrift

Life insurance can constitute an excellent means of encouraging thrift for many persons. As mentioned earlier, many persons who might not otherwise save regularly, will, nevertheless, regularly pay premiums on a life insurance policy. If the policy is of the type that has a cash value, this can constitute a type of semicompulsory savings plan.

Can Minimize Worry and Increase Initiative

Writers have frequently asserted that life and health insurance can be regarded not so much as producers of wealth, but as mechanisms for distributing funds from the fortunate to the unfortunate. In reality, however, life and health insurance can be an important force in the production of wealth, in that they can relieve the policyowner of worry and increase his or her efficiency. Constant worry can inhibit productivity. To the extent that concern about the financial consequences of loss of life or health causes an individual uncertainty and worry, life and health insurance could help reduce this concern.

Can Afford Protection against Claims of Creditors

Most states have enacted exemption laws that protect life insurance cash values and/or death benefits from the claims of the insured's and/or beneficiary's creditors. Most frequently, the amount of such insurance exempt from creditor's claims is limited to some reasonable amount. In some states, the exemption relates to all policies, without respect to amount and without regard to policyowners' rights to change the beneficiary.

Can Furnish an Assured Income in the Form of Annuities

Life insurance can also prove valuable to those older persons who have succeeded in saving only a limited amount of capital, and who have no one to whom they particularly care to transfer this sum on death. Assume that a person aged 60 has accumulated $100,000 and that this represents the entire funds available to the individual in his or her retirement years. Because of the limited size of the fund, the owner will be obliged to invest it in a most careful manner. Current rates of return for such investments would probably not exceed 5 to 9 percent. Consequently, this individual's income will be limited to between $5,000 and $9,000 per year. Nor can he or she afford to take a portion of principal for living expenses, because this would reduce the available annual income in the future. The danger confronting this individual

is just the opposite of that facing the person who wants insurance against premature death. The latter wants insurance because it is not known how long he or she will live, while the former is confronted with the danger of living too long—that is, of outliving available income.

Just as the man or woman who felt that death or disability might intervene too soon could hedge against that risk, so can the owner of the $100,000 fund, who feels that the income is too limited or that he or she might outlive this income, hedge against those risks by buying an annuity. A life annuity is a contract under which an insurance company promises to pay the owner a certain guaranteed minimum income every year as long as the individual lives, with payment ceasing on death (unless a refund feature had been selected).[7] The life insurance company is able to liquidate both the capital sum and the interest thereon in making these payments. Applying the law of large numbers to the probabilities of survival, instead of probabilities of death, as in the case of life insurance, the insurer can further "discount" the cost of providing an annuity (i.e., guarantee a larger income payment) and, at the same time, guarantee that the annuitant will not outlive the payments.

LIFE INSURANCE AND SOCIETY

Life insurance companies have undertaken many programs and projects to demonstrate that besides performing the worthwhile function of risk bearing and risk transfer, they are also good corporate citizens. Some of the programs and projects have involved efforts to improve housing, to create jobs, to hire and train more handicapped and disadvantaged persons, to promote and support community services, and a host of other programs.

In a private enterprise economy, some would argue that life and health companies do

[7]See Chapter 7.

not need to perform functions outside those related directly to the insurers' main corporate objectives. Life insurance companies' social responsibility can be considered as being met, according to some, if they provide fairly priced, high-quality services to the public in an efficient manner. It is not the purpose of this volume to take sides in this debate. It is however, noteworthy that a recent study conducted by a United Nations' agency highlighted the broad economic and societal advantages that can accrue to a country by having a strong and efficient life insurance market.[8] This study, prepared for developing countries, can be useful in helping those of us who live and work in so-called developed countries to appreciate the too-often neglected importance of life insurance and life insurers to our own economy and well-being.

The study noted the classical advantages of life insurance:

> Life insurance can serve the interests of developing countries in numerous ways. Individual citizens who purchase life insurance policies provide their families with a measure of protection against the adverse financial consequences of premature death. This can provide individuals with a greater sense of security and can help minimize worry and distress both prior to and after the death of a family breadwinner. Life insurance can also serve as a vehicle through which individuals can save money for emergencies and for retirement.[9]

It is instructive to note the similarity between the above-listed advantages and those discussed earlier. The reference to developing countries could have just as easily been redirected toward developed countries.

In addition to the individual advantages noted above, the study noted that a strong and efficient life insurance market can aid in overall economic development. The following advantages were enumerated:[10]

1. Life insurance can contribute to social stability by permitting individuals to minimize financial stress and worry.
2. Life insurance can reduce the financial burden on the State [government] of caring for the aged and for those made financially destitute because of the death of a family breadwinner.
3. Through the accumulation from thousands of policyholders of small amounts of private savings, life insurers can accumulate sums to be invested in the public and private sectors. This can benefit an economy by creating a source of financing for new businesses, for new homeowners and for farmers and their equipment.
4. The life insurance business generates employment.
5. Life insurance can permit more favorable credit terms to borrowers—both individuals and businesses—and can decrease the risk of default. Life insurance can also minimize the financial disruption to business caused by the death of key employees and owners.
6. By making available a variety of employee benefit plans . . . , life insurance companies can promote better employee/employer relations and can provide low cost benefits to a broad spectrum of persons who may otherwise have been unable to obtain such protection.

The study introduction then notes: "Because of the foregoing reasons, the expansion and development of life insurance has been actively encouraged in many countries".[11]

It is clear, then, that life and health insurance and life insurance companies play a critical role in our, as well as other, societies, and that their importance will likely to continue to grow worldwide.

[8] *The Promotion of Life Insurance in Developing Countries,* The United Nations Conference on Trade and Development, Geneva, Switzerland, 1982.
[9] *Ibid.,* p. iii.

[10] *Ibid.,* pp. iii, 1-2.
[11] *Ibid.,* p. 2.

Chapter 4

Introduction to Life Insurance Products and Their Environment

This and the three succeeding chapters discuss the principal types of individual life insurance and annuity contracts that exist in the United States. This chapter begins with an examination of the general nature of recent life insurance product innovations, then provides an overview of the principal classes of life insurance. There follows a review of the nature and types of term life and endowment policies. Chapter 5 discusses the nature and the types of the various fixed premium whole life policies, including variable life and current assumption whole life. The various forms of flexible-premium life insurance policies, including universal life, are presented in Chapter 6. Annuities and some special life insurance policies are then discussed in Chapter 7.

RECENT LIFE INSURANCE PRODUCT INNOVATIONS

Before embarking on a presentation of the various types of life insurance policies, it will be instructive to review briefly the environmental influences causing recent innovations in life insurance product design as well as the general nature of these innovations.

Environmental Influences

No single catalyst has caused the changes that are taking place within the life insurance business and in product design. Rather, a number of interrelated forces are at work simultaneously, five of which are discussed below.

Economic Concerns. The high inflation rates of the 1970s and early 1980s, high budget deficits, and resulting high interest rates have caused existing and prospective policyowners to question whether traditional insurance products offer sufficient economic sensitivity and flexibility. Insurers began to witness a diversion of premium dollars as consumers perceived better financial opportunities through other savings and investment media. Cash flow problems were created for many insurers as dissatisfied policyowners either surrendered their policies or exercised their rights to obtain policy loans at below market rates (see below).

Inflation also caused insurance company operating expenses to rise at a time when premium income for many companies was static or even declining. Agency systems became more expensive to maintain and many companies began marketing their products through alternative means. These additional marketing systems brought further competition to the industry.

In times of significant economic uncertainty, many consumers seek shorter-term, liquid investments and avoid longer-term, fixed commitments. Traditional cash value life insurance products were often perceived as long-term, fixed commitments and, therefore, demand for them shrank.

The combination of these various economic factors resulted in pressure on insurers to develop new products which were intended to meet the needs of both insurers and policyowners.

Social Change.   Consumers today are better educated and more demanding. They are better able to discriminate ''good'' from ''poor'' value and increasingly are demanding a dollar's worth of benefit for each dollar spent. These heightened expectations have been spurred on by pressures on personal disposable income which have caused consumers to spend their dollars more carefully.

The net result is that existing and proposed policyowners began to examine more carefully the quality of existing or proposed policies and sometimes found them deficient in light of the new economic realities.[1] Their heightened expectations led them, quite naturally, to demand better value.

Government.   Recently, regulators and legislators have seemed to support more strongly the notion of less regulatory involvement and to support regulation that promotes competition in the marketplace.[2] This attitude and some concrete actions taken as a result of this attitude have created a more competitive environment generally, with the life insurance business experiencing these same pressures.

A controversial 1979 Federal Trade Commission (FTC) staff study on life insurance cost disclosure undoubtedly had a significant impact in terms of increasing consumer awareness about life insurance.[3] This report, which received wide publicity, was critical of existing life insurance cost disclosure requirements and of various life insurance products and pricing. The life insurance industry took strong exception to the report's findings and conclusions,[4] but this very controversary added to consumer awareness about life insurance and the need to shop carefully.

Another government-related cause of change relates to obsolete liability valuation and non-forfeiture laws.[5] These laws generally forced insurers to calculate reserves and cash values on overly conservative bases. As a result, gross premiums usually had to be higher than they really needed to be.[6] Consumers looking for low premium outlays tended, therefore, to avoid higher premium cash value policies and gravitated toward term policies that contained little or no savings element. The result, again, was pressure on insurers as surrenders of cash value products increased and lower profit margins on term insurance caused lower overall profitability.

Insurers responded by developing innovative ''indeterminate'' premium products (discussed later in chapter) that were designed to minimize reserve problems. Other short-term solutions also ensued, but the net effect of having these restrictive laws was that great pressure built to have the laws changed. This change was accomplished in every state between 1980 and 1985, with the result that insurers are now permitted much greater latitude in product pricing and innovation.

Another regulatory factor that has brought about pressures for product innovation relates to the emphasis by regulators on mandated cost disclosure in life insurance. As discussed in Chapter 10, the NAIC model cost disclosure regulations probably have caused consumers to become more aware of cost differences in life insurance and to shop more competitively. As mentioned above, the FTC report had an effect on consumer awareness as well.

---

[1]As a practical matter, it should be recognized that much of this ''increased consumer awareness'' was fostered by agents seeking to replace existing policies. Many agents probably took advantage of this situation to promote unjustified replacements. Many others performed a worthwhile consumer service by doing so.

[2]See, for example, Harold Skipper, Jr., ''The Homogenization of the Financial Services Community,'' *The Journal of the American Society of Chartered Life Underwriters,* Vol. XXXVI (January 1982), p. 32.

[3]FTC, *Life Insurance Disclosure* (Washington, D.C.: U.S. Government Printing Office, 1979). See Chapter 10.

[4]See Blake T. Newton, Jr., ''The Misleading Report on Life Insurance Cost Disclosure of the Federal Trade Commission Staff,'' *The Journal of the American Society of Chartered Life Underwriters,* Vol. XXXIII (October 1979), p. 12.

[5]See Chapter 20.

[6]See Chapter 21.

Finally, another factor causing change has been federal tax reform. The Deficit Reduction Act of 1984 included, for the first time, a general definition of "life insurnce" for purposes of qualifying for the favorable tax advantages afforded policyowners and beneficiaries.[7] High-savings forms of life insurance were restricted, with the result that most forms of endowment insurance no longer qualify as "life insurance" for tax purposes.

The Tax Reform Act of 1986 has had a major impact on life insurance product design and sales. The Act eliminated the tax advantages of several classes of investments while retaining traditional tax treatment for life insurance. As a result, life insurance policies are seen in an even more favorable light by many persons interested in tax-favored savings. Some insurers have been designing their products and marketing efforts to take advantage of this situation. This enhanced public awareness of the tax-favored status of life insurance runs the risk, however, of drawing undue attention to these tax advantages, with the result that pressures are built for repeal of what many believe to be favortism justified on sound public policy grounds.

Technology. Information and communication technology continue to make astounding progress. Many of these improvements have been adopted by the life insurance industry. Many of today's flexible products are economically feasible only because of the application of this new technology.

Competition. Consumer awareness as to life insurance cost differences has increased over the past decade. This has enhanced product competition. The news media seem more acutely aware of life insurance variations and find it to be a more exciting topic for discussion and analysis than in times past.

Insurance Company Reactions

The net effect of the environmental influences discussed above is that competition among financial service retailers is increasing, particularly in the middle- and upper-income markets with expectations for even more vigorous

competition ahead. This increased competition emanates from consumers—as discussed above—and within the life insurance business, from agents demanding lower-cost/higher-quality products and services for their customers.

In one sense, the old notion that "there isn't and can't be anything new in life insurance" is correct. The ingredients or basics of life insurance do not change. In another, very real sense, however, much is new.

Many consumers have "demanded" life insurance whose rates of return are in line with contemporary investment returns and that permits a rapid change in this rate of return to reflect marketplace realities.[8] Some have stated a preference for flexible premium payment schedules and the ability to alter other policy elements easily. Some have wanted life insurance policies "unbundled" to show more clearly the various pricing components. Some have demanded greater disclosure and more up-to-date policy information. These are just a few of the types of "requests" that today's marketplace has made of insurers.

Potentially Lower Cost Coverage. Life insurance coverage being offered today is *potentially* lower in cost than that offered in years past. This downward trend is attributable in large measure to the high investment returns earned by life insurers on money invested in the 1970s and 1980s and therefore was to be expected. However, there can be little doubt but that competition among life insurers (and agents), as well as between life insurers and other financial institutions, has put pressure on actuaries and insurer management to design and offer lower-cost policies. For example, prices of yearly renewable term life insurance, where investment returns have relatively little impact on premium levels, fell by an average of 32 percent from 1977 to 1982.[9] This decline was in the face of a 59 percent increase in the consumer price index over the same period.[10]

---

[7]See Chapter 13.

[8]"Marketplace realities" means that rates of return can fall as rapidly as they can increase, a danger often overlooked by consumers.

[9]*The Term Marketplace: Lapses and Other Issues* (Hartford, Conn.: Life Insurance Marketing and Research Association, Inc., 1983), p. 1.

[10]*Ibid*, p. 2.

Insurers have adopted several innovative approaches to be able to offer potentially lower cost insurance, three of which are mentioned here: (1) use of "indeterminate" premium payment patterns, (2) preferred risk classification systems, and (3) direct recognition of policy loan activity in policy benefits.

1. *Indeterminate premium plans.* Indeterminate premium life insurance policies are technically classified as nonparticipating policies but with nonguaranteed premiums. A dual-premium structure is utilized whereby a scale of guaranteed maximum premiums is contained in the contract but the insurance company reserves the right to, and typically does, charge lower premiums. The guaranteed maximum premium represents the "cap" on the current premium.

The lower current premium actually charged is subject to periodic change, but only on a class-wide basis. Changes may be made if anticipated future interest and mortality experience are expected to differ from that implicit in the current premium charged. Premiums can be raised or lowered by the company but can never exceed the guaranteed maximum. The indeterminate premium approach was first used with fixed-premium cash value life policies but has since been adapted to term life insurance policies and to flexible-premium forms.

2. *Preferred risk classification systems.* In an effort to offer lower-priced insurance, insurers have adopted various preferred risk classification systems. The most common is to use different premium rates for smokers and nonsmokers. A substantial body of evidence indicates that mortality experience for smokers is substantially higher than that for nonsmokers. Life insurers have seized on this finding to justify charging the two classes different rates.

Insurers have also provided lower rates for persons who were judged to be "superstandard" or "preferred risks." Preferred risks may be defined as nonsmokers whose health, life-style, and other characteristics are such as to suggest that they will exhibit mortality experience significantly better than average.

Additionally, some insurers offer products that permit insureds who demonstrate period-

ically that they are still in good health to pay lower-than-standard premiums. These "reentry" products are discussed later in this chapter.

3. *Direct recognition.* In an effort to refine life insurance pricing further and to be able to offer lower-cost insurance to select consumers, many companies now include in their insurance policies a provision that permits the company to recognize directly in its excess interest or dividend formula the extent of policy loan activity within the policy. Such provisions increase policy costs to those who take out policy loans (and decrease costs for those who do not).[11]

Policies being sold today therefore can offer the careful buyer unparalleled opportunities for procuring low-cost life insurance protection of all sorts. Life products today not only have generally lower "going-in" costs but also afford the policy-owner the opportunity to benefit from the insurer's future favorable experience. Participating life insurance has, of course, always had this as its distinguishing feature. However, nonparticipating policies are increasingly affording policyowners similar opportunities.

Increased Flexibilty. Life insurance products offered today permit policyowners unprecedented flexibility. Many policies provide that the face amount may be decreased or increased (often subject to insurability requirements) at any time. Increased flexibility in premium payment is permitted, with some policies allowing the owner to pay premiums as desired, subject to tax and procedural limitations.

Life insurance products have always been flexible financial tools in the hands of the knowledgeable planner. Many provisions within life insurance policies have ensured the policyowner of the ability to alter various dimensions of the policy.[12] Further flexibility was often accorded policyowners by allowing them by company practice to do that which they wished even if the contract provisions did not make allowance for the action.

However, even with these acknowledged contractual and extracontractual opportunities,

[11]See Chapter 9.
[12]See Chapter 9.

product flexibility today must be considered as superior to that which existed in the past. As stated earlier, pressure for this enhanced flexibility had emanated from several sources, but such flexibility has become feasible only because the technology to support such systems has also developed.

Greater Disclosure. Improved disclosure as to policy benefits and costs has been required by regulation in most states since the late 1970s. However, only in the 1980s did insurers begin to incorporate disclosure as a key element of policy design and operation.

This increased disclosure has two dimensions. First, some new products (e.g., universal life and current assumption whole life) disclose to the potential purchaser various elements that make up the product's pricing structure. This permits the prospect to see clearly the portion of each premium payment that is applied toward mortality and expense charges, and toward cash value buildup. The interest credited to cash value accumulations is also disclosed clearly in such products.[13]

In addition to disclosure of the elements of the pricing and benefit structures at the time of purchase, owners of such policies also receive, annually, up-to-date policy information. They are thus able to monitor actual policy financial results relative to those illustrated at time of purchase, and to compare such results against prevailing investment returns and other financial factors within the economy.

Increased Risk to Consumers. The purchaser of a life insurance policy today stands to benefit in some or all of the foregoing ways. However, the benefits of these new products are not without their price. For one, enhanced flexibility within a contract is more costly than would be the situation otherwise, even in the face of significant technological advances and lower unit costs of production.

Another highly important aspect of this "price" is that insurers cannot offer both lower-cost, interest-sensitive policies on the one hand

[13]However, the stated interest rate may not reflect accurately the policy's internal yield, as policy charges could be inflated to "subsidize" the interest credits. See Chapter 7.

and liberal long-term, fixed-dollar guarantees on the other. Many of today's life insurance products offer less liberal traditional insurance-type guarantees. Therefore, much of the investment, expense, and some of the mortality risk that traditionally has been borne almost exclusively by life insurers is shared increasingly by policyowners under these new products.

OVERVIEW OF TYPES OF LIFE INSURANCE

As suggested in Chapter 2, life insurance policies can be constructed and priced to fit a myriad of benefit and premium-payment patterns. Historically, however, traditional life insurance benefit patterns have fit into one or a combination of four classes:

1. Term life insurance
2. Endowment insurance
3. Whole life insurance
4. Annuities

This classification scheme remains valid today, although it is not always possible to determine, at the point of policy issuance, the exact class into which some newer types of policies fall. As discussed in more detail in Chapter 6, some of these newer forms permit the policyowner great flexibility effectively to alter the type of insurance during the policy term, thus allowing the policy to be classified as to form only at that particular point. For presentation purposes, these flexible forms of life insurance are discussed as if they were an additional classification even though all properly can be placed (at a given point in time) into one or a combination of the four traditional classes.

TERM LIFE INSURANCE

Since the 1950s there has been a continuing shift in volume of insurance sold toward term products. Term life insurance sales, as measured by face amount, accounted for only 34 percent of individual life insurance sold in 1955, but, by 1977, reached 50 percent. This proportion continued to rise, reaching a peak of 60 percent of market share in 1982. Market share declined for the first time in many decades in 1983, and had fallen to 38 percent in 1985. The primary cause of term life's declining market share is its growing competition from several new cash value life products, such as current assumption whole life, universal life, and variable life policies.

Nature of Term Insurance

Term life insurance furnishes life insurance protection for a limited number of years. The face amount of the policy is payable only if death occurs during the stipulated term and nothing is paid in case of survival. Term policies may be issued for a period as short as one year[14] but customarily provide protection up to age 65, 70, or beyond.

Term insurance compares more closely to property and liability insurance contracts than any other life insurance contract. If a building valued at $10,000 is insured for that amount under a five-year term policy, the company will pay this amount only in case of the total destruction of the building during the term. Similarly, if a person insures his or her life for $10,000 under a five-year term policy, the company will pay $10,000 only in case of the insured's death before the expiration of the five years; nothing is paid if death occurs after the expiration of the contract period.

Initial premium rates per $1,000 of coverage are lower for term life insurance than for other life products issued at the same age since the periods of protection are limited. However, premiums for term coverage can escalate rapidly as the duration of the policy lengthens.

Three features common to many term life policies deserve special attention before discussing specific term products. These are the renewability and convertibility features as well as the interaction that exists between a term policy's conversion and premium waiver features.

Renewabilty. Almost all one-year and five-year term policies and many 10-year and other-duration policies contain an option that permits the policyowner to "renew" the policy for a limited number of additional periods of protection. This option permits the policyowner, at the expiration of each term period, to continue the policy without reference to the insured's then insurability status. Usually, however, companies limit the age (generally to age 65 or 70) to which such term policies may be renewed.

The premium, although level for a given period, increases with each renewal and is based on the attained age of the insured at the time of renewal. The scale of guaranteed future rates is contained in the contract, although for some types of term insurance, the company may charge a rate lower than that stated by the policy.

As the premium rate increases with each renewal, mortality experience increasingly reflects selection against the company, as discussed in Chapter 2. Resistance to the higher premiums and lower-cost product opportunities cause many insureds in good health to fail to renew, whereas the majority of those in poor health will renew even in the face of higher premiums. The companies recognize this problem in their pricing structure or through other means, such as the dividend scales, by limiting renewability to stipulated maximum ages, or by product designs that encourage (or require) conversion.

From the policyowner's perspective, the term "renewability" means simply that the policy can be continued to the stipulated termination age. Renewal rates are fixed by contract and renewal is effected merely by the policyowner paying the billed premium. Therefore, renewable term policies can be viewed as increasing-premium, level-benefit term life insurance from the policyowner's perspective.

Convertibility. Most term insurance policies include a convertible feature. This feature permits the policyowner to exchange the term policy for a whole life or other cash value insurance contract *without evidence of insurability.* Often, the period during which conversion is allowed is shorter than the maximum duration of the policy.

The conversion privilege increases the flexibility of term life insurance. For example, at the

---

[14]So-called "preliminary" or "initial" term insurance is available for periods as short as one month, but a maximum of 11 months. This insurance is usually restricted to situations in which it is desired to have protection start immediately, with the policy having a formal effective date one or more months in the future.

time a term policy was purchased, a policyowner may not have definitely selected the type of policy best adapted to his or her needs. He or she may have preferred another type but because of budget constraints, decided on some form of low-premium term coverage. Following the issuance of the term policy, circumstances may have changed such as to enable the policyowner to purchase an adequate amount of other insurance. Or he or she may desire to utilize insurance as a means of accumulating funds rather than using it entirely for protection against death. If, therefore, an individual concludes that term insurance does not meet present and future needs, this conclusion could be implemented by exchanging the term contract for a type that conforms better to his or her needs.

A significant percentage of insureds become uninsurable or insurable only at higher than standard rates. Under such circumstances, a term policy that cannot be renewed may fail to protect the insured in the desired manner. If, however, the policy contains a conversion privilege, and if the time limit for making an exchange of the policy has not yet expired, it can be to the insured's advantage to exercise this privilege and thus protect against the possibility that insurance may expire before death occurs.

If the insured under a term policy is insurable at standard rates, little or no financial advantage may exist to exercising the conversion privilege over reentering the marketplace and shopping carefully. Although some insurers provide certain financial incentives to effect conversion, such as a limited credit toward the converted policy's first premium, most standard-classed insureds should view conversion in the same manner as they would a replacement of one policy with another (see Chapter 10).

Conversion often is permitted on an attained age or original age basis. The **attained-age method** of conversion involves the issuance of a whole life or other cash value policy of a form currently being issued at the date of conversion. The premium rate for the new policy is that required at the attained age of the insured and would be the same as that offered by the company to new insureds who could qualify for standard rates.

The **original-age method** involves a retroactive conversion, with the whole life or other cash value policy bearing the date and premium rate that would have been paid had the whole life or other cash value policy been taken out originally instead of the term policy. Most companies offering this option require that retroactive conversion take place within five years of the date of issue of the term contract. The policyowner is required to pay the difference between (1) the premiums (net of dividends or other credits) that would have been paid on the new policy if it had been issued at the same time as the original policy, and (2) the premiums actually paid for the term policy, with interest on the difference at a stipulated annual rate (e.g., 6 or 8 percent).

In making a choice between the two bases of conversion, it was said that the policyowner may prefer an original age conversion because he or she could obtain a lower premium rate and possibly more liberal contract provisions. However, with the trend toward lower premiums and better-valued products, it is far from clear that either potential benefit would necessarily materialize. Even if the premium rate for the original age conversion were less than the rate for current issues, it is questionable whether an original age conversion makes sound financial sense for most persons.

Interaction between Premium Waiver and Conversion Features. The majority of individual life insurance policies sold in the United States provides that if the insured becomes totally disabled (see Chapter 7) the insurer will waive (i.e., excuse) premium payments during the period of disability. This provision may be automatically included within the policy or, more commonly, it is offered as an additional benefit for a specified additional charge.

When this premium waiver (PW) feature is incorporated within a term policy, how the conversion feature interacts with the PW feature can be of great importance. There are three different provisions available in the market. First, some contracts provide that if the insured becomes totally disabled, premiums for the term policy will be waived, but if the policyowner wishes to exercise the conversion option during this period, the company will not waive the premiums on the newly converted policy. In other words, full premiums must be paid by the policyowner on the new policy. Second, other contracts permit the conversion *and* will waive premiums on the new policy. Clearly, this approach is more valuable to the policyowner than the former.

Third, some contracts provide for a waiver of the premium on the term policy and on the new policy but only if the conversion is delayed until the end of the period during which conversion is allowed. At that point an automatic conversion will take place *and* premiums on the new policy will be waived. This benefit provision falls between the two previously discussed provisions in terms of policyowner value.

Naturally, other things being equal, the more liberal the interaction of the PW and conversion features, the higher the additional premium for the PW feature should be, although actual pricing may not reflect this. This interaction can be a significant element of product evaluation, as can the definition of disability used in the provision.[15]

Types of Term Life Insurance Policies

Term life policies have traditionally been issued on either a participating or guaranteed-cost, nonparticipating basis. As alluded to earlier, this is changing as insurers seek ways of gaining a competitive edge. Term life insurance usually provides either a level or decreasing death benefit, with some increasing death benefit policy riders sold.

Level Face Amount Policies. The vast majority of term life insurance sold today provides for a level death benefit over the policy period. Premiums for such contracts either increase with age or remain level, with the former being the more common.

1. *Increasing premium contracts.* Term policies with level death benefits and increasing premiums are commonly referred to as contracts that are "renewable," with this term being synonomous with "increasing premium," as alluded to earlier. Thus, **yearly renewable term** (YRT)—also called **annual renewable term** (ART)—and **five-year renewable term** policies are increasing premium contracts. Some insurers offer renewable term policies of other durations, such as three, six, and

10 years. YRT policies are by far the most common form sold today with other-duration renewable term policies regaining popularity recently, as insurers have sought ways of minimizing the adverse effects of the high YRT lapse rates and low profitability on YRT business.

YRT product design has been of considerable interest, as intense price competition has centered around these products, although it is said to be lessening somewhat. The trend in YRT design over the past few years has been toward (1) even lower premium rates, (2) longer renewal periods (even to age 100), (3) a greater number of rate bands (e.g., banding rates at $100,000, $250,000, $500,000, and $1 million), and (4) differentiated pricing categories.

Differential pricing can be accomplished in several ways. One common method is through use of separate smoker/nonsmoker rates. In a recent study of 62 of the major writers of YRT, all but one offered either nonsmoker rates or a preferred risk category.[16]

YRT premium differences between smokers and nonsmokers can be substantial. Table 4–1 lists first year YRT smoker and nonsmoker premiums for several companies.

Another method used by several companies in an effort to develop more competitive YRT rates is through the sale of **select and ultimate term,** also known as **reentry term** and as **revertible term.** To understand better the mechanics of reentry term, it is necessary to understand that life insurers use three types of mortality tables:

TABLE 4-1. Selected companies' YRT smoker and nonsmoker premiums
($100,000, male, age 35)

Company	Premiums for:	
	Smoker	**Nonsmoker**
A	$204	$192
B	207	137
C	225	194
D	236	177
E	241	150
F	282	185
G	319	192

---

[15]See Chapter 9.

[16]"Indeterminate Premium Annual Renewable Term Policy Comparison," *Best's Review,* Vol. 86 (September 1985), pp. 84–85.

select, ultimate, and aggregate.[17] A **select** table reflects the mortality experience of newly insured lives only. These persons exhibit superior (i.e., low) mortality relative to others of their same age and sex, since to qualify for life insurance in the first place they must have been in reasonably good health and otherwise insurable at standard rates. This select period or "benefit of selection" usually lasts from five to 15 years.

An **ultimate** table reflects the mortality experience beyond the select years (i.e., it is of those who already have been insured for several years). The benefit of selection has faded from the mortality experience of the ultimate group. Thus, a select table represents very favorable initial experience, whereas an ultimate table excludes this experience and therefore exhibits higher mortality. An **aggregate** table includes data from both select and ultimate experience.

Traditional YRT premium scales are based on aggregate mortality experience. Select and ultimate term premiums are based on a select/ ultimate mortality split. This results in a scale of rates that varies not only by age—as with traditional YRT—but also by the duration since the insured last demonstrated insurability. It would therefore be common to find three or more persons of the same age and sex and otherwise identically situated paying different YRT premiums for the same coverage under the same policy form. The 30-year-old female, who just purchased a term policy using select and ultimate pricing would be paying one rate; another female, now age 30, who purchased the same policy type last year (say, at age 29 and now age 30) would be paying a somewhat higher rate; a third female who purchased her policy two years ago (at age 28 and who is now 30) would be paying a still higher rate; and so on through from two to 12 more such situations, depending on the select mortality table used as the basis for the rates. Even though each insured would now be age 30, the select/ultimate dichotomy leads to a premium schedule that permits the person most recently insured to pay the lowest rate.

The policy is also referred to as reentry term because an insured may be able to "reenter" the select group periodically—often every five

years—if the insured resubmits to the insurer satisfactory evidence of insurability at that time. For those insureds who fail to take advantage of the reentry provision or who fail to qualify for reentry because of insurability problems, ultimate rates are charged thereafter. These ultimate premiums are naturally considerably higher than the select premiums and higher than traditional "aggregate" YRT rates as well. A person who cannot qualify for select rates usually will be unable to qualify for a new policy based on aggregate rates and therefore must pay the higher ultimate rates.

Table 4–2 illustrates two companies' YRT products. Policy A is a traditional aggregate-based product and policy B is a select and ultimate product with a five-year reentry feature. The high level of the ultimate premiums is apparent and expected.

Besides reentry classifications, separate smoker and nonsmoker rates are common as are indeterminate premiums, each of which allows insurers the opportunity potentially to offer even lower prices. For example, in the study cited earlier, first-year current premiums per $1,000 for 47 indeterminate premium policies ranged from a low of $1.30 to a high of $2.78 for 35-year-old males. Whereas the premium level actually charged for indeterminate premium plans is set by the insurer on a *class* basis, the level of reentry premiums actually charged is a function of the *individual's* characteristics.

Many **graded-premium whole life** policies are, in effect, YRT policies that grade into level-premium whole life coverage at advanced ages (e.g., age 70). These policies are discussed in more detail in the following chapter.

It should be noted that the overall industry-wide mortality, lapse, and expense experience with YRT products seems to be poor, with many companies experiencing substantial losses. Keen competition is usually given as the reason for why the industry permitted itself to end up in this situation. Recently, however, many insurers have been revising product designs and raising underwriting standards in an effort to reverse these trends.[18]

[17]See Chapter 18.

[18]See, for example, James J. Marcus, "Term Insurance and Universal Life. . .One Expensive Lesson or Two," *Emphasis* (September 1983).

TABLE 4-2. Traditional YRT premiums and reentry YRT premiums
(male, age 35, nonsmoker)

Policy Year	Age	Face Amount	Policy A Aggregate Premiums	Policy B Premiums	
				Select (Reentry)	Ultimate (Maximum)
1	35	$100,000	$145	$111	$ 111
2	36	100,000	148	132	132
3	37	100,000	154	147	147
4	38	100,000	162	165	165
5	39	100,000	172	185	185
6	40	100,000	185	138	228
7	41	100,000	200	176	291
8	42	100,000	219	204	372
9	43	100,000	242	236	470
10	44	100,000	268	272	597
11	45	100,000	299	181	770
12	46	100,000	333	241	972
13	47	100,000	373	287	1,182
14	48	100,000	417	337	1,401
15	49	100,000	466	393	1,631
16	50	100,000	521	238	1,869
17	51	100,000	581	327	2,124
18	52	100,000	646	395	2,389
19	53	100,000	716	466	2,667
20	54	100,000	791	544	2,953

2. *Contracts with other premium patterns.* A minority of term life insurance sold in the United States has premium payment patterns that do not fit into the increasing premium category discussed above, although the face amount may still remain level. Some contracts provide for level premium payments during the contract term, while others provide for higher premiums in the first year than in subsequent years.

Level-premium term contracts may be written for a set number of years or to cover the working lifetime of an individual. Contracts of the first type include 10-year and 20-year level-premium, nonrenewable policies. Contracts of the second type, providing essentially the same protection, are (1) life-expectancy term and (2) term to age 65.

The **life-expectancy contract** provides protection for a number of years equal to the average life expectancy for a person of the proposed insured's age and sex, based on some specific mortality table. Although this contract is strictly a protection contract, the leveling of the premium over many years produces a cash value, which increases to a point and then declines to zero at the termination of the policy.

The **term-to-65 contract** provides protec-tion for a somewhat shorter period than does the life-expectancy policy and consequently has a slightly lower premium. The rationale of the policy is that it provides protection during the period of the individual's productive effort, since 65 is usually considered retirement age. As in the case of the life-expectancy contract, there is a cash value during the term of the policy. Neither of these contracts is very popular today. In fact, some companies have discontinued offering these long-term contracts altogether. The YRT market has become so competitive that premiums for such traditional contracts often are uncompetitive.

Some life insurance companies sell what might be most accurately described as **front-end-loaded term,** although they carry other names. These products have been designed by insurers principally to overcome one of the problems that has existed for agents in selling YRT and other low-premium term contracts: Commissions, ex-pressed as a percentage of premiums, are low on such contracts.

A few years ago, some insurers began designing what were basically 10-year and other-duration level-premium term policies but with a first-year premium that was higher than the other premiums, thus permitting higher agents' commissions and greater company profit. Obviously, however, the problem was to figure out how to sell the product to the public, especially since YRT prices were considerably lower in cost.

This marketing problem was solved by providing a modest endowment (maturity value) feature at the end of the 10-year period. This differentiated the product from common 10-year term and tended to obscure its higher cost. Companies purposely designed the endowment amount to be an exact multiple (usually two or three times) of the difference between the first- and second-year premium. This difference they called a "deposit" and they sold the endowment feature not as an endowment, but as being a return of the "deposit" doubled, or tripled, or any other relationship desired. At the end of this initial period, several options were (and are) typically made available to the policyowner: (1) renew for another term period at a higher premium; (2) continue the policy but as level premium decreasing term life insurance to age 100; or (3) convert to a form of whole life insurance.

This made for an attractive sales presentation that basically masked the high front-end load. The sales presentations also led to misleading and deceptive marketing practices that have been the cause of much regulatory attention.[19] Indeed, the name used for these policies—**"deposit" term**—was and is inherently misleading and has been outlawed in several states.

Variations on the 10-year pattern and the death benefit patterns are common. Other recent variations on the theme of "front-loaded term insurance" have combined high-first-year-premium or increasing-premium term policies with an annuity or mutual fund. They are sold as a package, with the net result that what can be an expensive term policy is submerged in the sales presentation presenting the two as a package.

In theory, front-loaded term policies should result in lower long-run costs than the more traditional forms of term insurance, other things being equal. This is because the high first-year premium

can cover most, if not all, of the high acquisition expenses, and importantly, those who terminate their policies during the initial period would have "paid their own way." Stated in terms of the Chapter 2 example, the asset share for terminating policies should be positive from policy year 1 and always be larger than the cash value (if any) paid on them. Lapse rates should be lower, with the result that the insurer should be able to offer the policy at a price lower than that of other term life products. This theoretical promise has not materialized in the marketplace, although a few insurers apparently are now designing products to achieve this objective rather than for purposes of a misleading sales presentation.

Non-level Face Amount Policies. A significant amount of term life insurance sold in the United States involves policies (or riders) whose face amounts decrease or increase with time. Decreasing term policies are commonly used to pay off an outstanding loan balance on the death of the debtor/insured, be it in connection with a home mortgage or a business or personal loan. Thus, **mortgage protection policies** provide for face amount decreases paralleling the projected decreases in the principal amount owed under a mortgage loan. Since the larger portion of each early mortgage loan payment is applied to pay interest, the initial decrease in a mortgage loan's outstanding balance is slight with later declines being substantial. Mortgage protection policies' death benefits track this pattern and are available to cover a variety of mortgage loan durations (e.g., 10, 15, 20, 25, or 30 years) and amortization schedules. They also provide for a conversion right. Level premiums are sometimes limited to a somewhat shorter period than the duration of the policy.

Term insurance that decreases by a set amount each year is also available. Such policies are for durations of from 10 to 30 years and often decrease by the same amount each month.

A type of decreasing term is available as a special type of coverage that is designed to ensure that premiums due on a life insurance policy sold on a juvenile's life will be paid even if the premium payor dies. In the latter case, the decreasing death benefit on the payor's life would

[19]For a description of this product and marketing practices associated with it, see Harold Skipper, "Perspectives on Partial Endowment Type ("Deposit Term") Life Insurance: Implications for Regulators, "*The Journal of the American Society of Chartered Life Underwriters,* Vol. XXXIII (July 1979).

be exactly sufficient to pay all premiums due until the insured's age 21 if the payor were to die before the juvenile attained this age.

Another type of decreasing term life insurance is designed to appeal to young men or women whose family responsibilities call for a monthly income to be paid to the surviving spouse (typically) until a certain age or for a set period of usually 10, 15, or 20 years from the date of policy issuance. This **family income policy,** which is also available as a rider to other forms of insurance, is often sold to protect the family during the child-rearing years. Of course, if the insured lives beyond the specified age or beyond the set number of years of issue, no further coverage is provided by this benefit.

Term insurance whose death benefits increase with time is also sold but virtually never as a separate policy. Insurers offer increasing term coverage as a cost-of-living (COL) rider to many policies. The COL riders provide for automatic increases in the policy death benefit in accordance with increases in the Consumer Price Index (CPI). The policyowner would be billed with the regular notice for the additional coverage. No evidence of insurability is required for these increases as long as the rider remains in force and is exercised fully each year. Declines in the CPI do not result in declines in amounts purchased. Rather the amount purchased in the preceding year is simply carried forward to the current year.

Another type of increasing term insurance is provided under the **return of premium features** (or riders) contained in some policies. This feature provides that if the insured dies within a set number of years from the policy issue date (e.g., 20 years), the death benefit will include not only the basic policy face amount but also an amount equal to the sum of all the premiums paid to that point. This benefit is provided by increasing term insurance whose death benefit exactly equals the sum of the premiums paid.

The feature can be useful in certain business situations (see Chapter 15), but also is sometimes included in an attempt to differentiate the underlying policy from other similar contracts (thus making comparisons difficult) and to make the proposed policy seem more attractive to a prospect.

Increasing term insurance is also sometimes

purchased through the use of policy dividends. This can be a valuable source of additional needed coverage and can render certain arrangements more flexible.[20]

Uses and Limitations of Term Insurance

Term life insurance has long been the subject of debate. There are those who advocate the use of term insurance to the virtual exclusion of cash value insurance, especially whole life insurance, and vice versa. Those providing advice regarding life insurance should understand the product's uses and limitations.

Term insurance can be useful for persons with low incomes and high insurance needs, often occurring because of family obligations. Good risk management principles suggest that the family unit should be protected against catastrophic losses. If the current income level does not permit the individual the option of purchasing whole life or other, higher-premium forms of cash value life insurance in sufficient amounts, the individual arguably has no choice but to purchase term if he or she is to provide adequate financial protection.

Moreover, those who have a career to establish and have a temporarily limited income arguably should use their resources primarily to establish their careers. Investment in the person for self-improvement during the early career development years clearly should have a very high priority.

Term life insurance can also prove useful for persons who have placed substantially all their resources in the assets of a new business that is still in its formative stages, and where death would result in serious loss to, if not destruction of, the invested capital. New enterprises are particularly speculative and become more settled only as time elapses. Term insurance can serve a useful purpose, because of its low early dollar outlay in the initial stages of such undertakings.

Many persons use term insurance as a supplement to an existing life insurance program during the child-rearing period. It has also been suggested that term insurance is particularly ap-

---

[20]See, for example, Chapter 15 under nonqualified deferred compensation.

propriate to use as a hedge against a financial loss already sustained and where a little time is required to repair the damage.

Term life insurance is naturally suited for ensuring that mortgage and other loans are paid off on the debtor/insured's death and as a vehicle for ensuring that educational or other desired funds will be available if death were to cut short the period needed for the provider/insured to earn the needed funds. Term insurance is also a natural for all situations that call for temporary income protection needs.

Term insurance can be the basis for one's permanent insurance program *if* the program is well conceived and well executed. A well-conceived program is one that recognizes the increasing premium nature of most term policies sold today and devises a plan either to accommodate these increasing premiums or to minimize their impact (e.g., by having a program for reducing the insurance needs over time). A well-conceived program realistically assesses the policyowner's willingness, ability, and commitment to follow through with the plan. A well-executed program is one that includes high-quality, reasonably priced coverage that provides the capability to adapt to changing circumstances. It involves the faithful execution, usually on an annual basis, of the program devised. For example, if the decision is made to save through other than life insurance policies but the individual fails to set aside the planned amounts regularly, the program could be judged to have failed in its mission.

ENDOWMENT INSURANCE

The amount of endowment insurance sold in the United States, relative to the other forms of life insurance has been declining steadily for several years. It accounted for approximately 9 percent of all policies sold in the United States in 1973 and only 1 percent by 1984. This percentage is likely to decline further because of recent tax-law changes that do not extend to most newly sold endowment policies the tax benefits available under other forms of cash value life insurance.[21]

[21]See Chapter 13 for a discussion of the 1984 tax-law amendments.

Even so, many endowment policies remain in force, and from the reader's perspective, an understanding of the concepts that underlie endowments is essential.

Nature of Endowment Insurance

Term policies provide for the payment of the full policy amount only in the event of death. Endowment policies, by contrast, provide not only for the payment of the face of the policy on the death of the insured during a fixed term of years, but also the payment of the full face amount at the end of the term if the insured is living. Whereas policies payable only in the event of death are purchased chiefly for the benefit of others, endowment policies, although affording protection to others against the death of the insured during the fixed term, usually pay to the insured if he or she survives the endowment period.

There are two ways of looking at endowment insurance: (1) the mathematical concept, and (2) the economic concept.

Mathematical Concept. There are two promises made by the company under endowment insurance: (1) to pay the face amount if the insured dies during the endowment period, and (2) to pay the face amount if the insured survives to the end of the endowment period. The first promise is identical with that made under a level term policy for an equivalent amount and period. The second introduces a new concept, the **pure endowment.** A pure endowment promises to pay the face amount *only* if the insured is living at the end of a specified period, nothing being paid in case of prior death. Pure endowment insurance is not sold as a separate contract by itself. It is said that few people are willing to risk the apparent loss of all premiums paid in the event of death before the end of the endowment period. Thus, to provide a death benefit during the endowment period, only term insurance for the same period need be added to the pure endowment. It can be seen that these two elements, (1) level term insurance and (2) a pure endowment, will together meet the two promises made under endowment insurance.

Economic Concept. Another analysis of endowment insurance, the economic concept, divides endowment insurance into two parts, **decreasing term insurance** and **increasing investment.** The investment part of the contract is viewed as a savings accumulation that is available to the insured through surrender of or loan against the policy. This increasing "investment" feature is supplemented by decreasing term insurance, which when added to the investment accumulation will equal the face amount payment under the policy. This is the same analogy discussed in Chapter 2 with respect to whole life insurance policies.

Insurance contracts have not always fit the increasing investment, decreasing term insurance model.[22] In the early days of the business, there were no nonforfeiture values under life insurance contracts. If an individual were forced to cease premium payments, no return of any sort was available as a matter of contract. The contract promised to pay in the event of the occurrence of death or survival to a certain age, but if the contract were discontinued prior to the occurrence of these contingencies, all premiums were considered fully earned, and the reserve or savings element was forfeited.[23]

Types of Endowment Policies

Many variations of endowment insurance exist. Such policies are for set durations of 10 to 30 or more years, and others are arranged to mature at certain ages, such as 60, 65, 70, or higher. Usually, contract premiums are due throughout the term, although limited payment plans, such as an endowment at age 65 paid up in 20 years were available.

Besides the standard contracts, other applications of the endowment principle are sometimes made. In the case of the **retirement income policy,** the amount payable upon survival is greater than the face amount, and the amount payable at death is the face amount or cash value, whichever is greater. The contract is popularly used in insured pension plans utilizing individual contracts.[24] A **semiendowment policy** pays upon survival only one-half the sum payable in the event of death during the endowment period. The so-called "**deposit**" **term policy** discussed earlier provides a small endowment amount as a maturity value. Also, various kinds of **juvenile endowment policies** have been issued by certain companies. These include endowments maturing at specified ages for educational purposes.

Since the company's liability under an endowment policy involves not only payment of its face upon death but also payment of the full amount of the policy upon survival of the term, it follows that the annual premium on such policies is much higher than that for whole life or term policies, except for the very long endowment periods, where the rate is only slightly higher than that charged on an ordinary life policy.

Uses and Limitations of Endowment Insurance

Endowment insurance was at one time considered as an effective vehicle for accumulating savings. However, even before the 1984 tax law changes effectively limited the endowment insurance market to various qualified retirement plans, endowment insurance was having great difficulty in competition against whole life and term insurance.

Endowment policies issued prior to 1985 continue to enjoy the same tax treatment as other life insurance policies.[25] Thus, existing endowment policies could provide reasonable customer value, especially for those in poor health. Endowments are still used in certain tax-qualified retirement plans, and the careful shopper in such circumstances can locate policies that provide good value.

[22]See *The Nature of Whole Life Contract* (New York: Institute of Life Insurance, 1974).

[23]Some companies did allow a cash value, but the policy usually contained no provision for them, so that the policyowner had no *right* to any surrender value. The values, when allowed, were small and generally were granted only if application was made within a short period after lapse. There was no *regulatory requirement* as to the allowance of a surrender value in any form until 1861, and no regulatory requirement for a *cash* surrender privilege until 1906.

[24]See Chapter 28.
[25]See Chapter 13.

Chapter 5

Whole Life
Insurance Policies

In contrast to term life insurance, whole life insurance provides insurance protection over one's entire lifetime. Whole life insurance has been the mainstay of the life insurance business for over a century and continues to be a significant component of new life insurance sales and an even larger component of life insurance in force.

For 1985, traditional whole life insurance comprised 13 percent (by face amount) of all new individual life insurance sales, with variable life contributing 1.5 percent to this share. This represents a decline for traditional whole life insurance from a 1981 market share of 40 percent.[1] This decline results primarily from a shift in sales from traditional whole life to universal life.

THE NATURE OF WHOLE LIFE INSURANCE

The essence of **whole life insurance** is that it provides for the payment of the face amount upon the death of the insured regardless of when death occurs. Its name describes its nature. It is insurance for the whole of life. As used in this text,

the name does not refer to any specific type of whole life policy—of which there are many—but rather is generic and is used to describe any type of life insurance that can be maintained in effect indefinitely. By this definition, universal life and other flexible-premium policies can function as whole life policies if they have sufficient cash value. However, they could provide protection for a limited period only. For discussion purposes, **flexible-premium** policies are distinguished from the **fixed-premium** policies of this chapter, and they are discussed separately in Chapter 6. By "fixed premium" we mean that the contract stipulates or the company decides the minimum premium level to be paid over the contract life, as opposed to the policyowner making the decision. This definition recognizes implicitly that premiums need not be "fixed" at the same level from year to year and that they need not be guaranteed.

Almost all whole life policies sold in the United States are based on mortality tables that assume that all insureds die by age 100. Since all insureds do not, in fact, die by age 100 but insurance companies price whole life insurance as if they do, it is only fair that the insurance company should pay the policy face amount to those

[1]*1986, Life Insurance Fact Book* (Washington, D.C.: American Council of Life Insurance), p. 13.

few persons who live to age 100—as if they had died. This is the reason that whole life policies are sometimes referred to as endowment-at-age-100 policies. Another, equally valid viewpoint is that they are also term-to-age-100 policies. This view is justified by noting that the actuarial technique used for pricing whole life is the same, in concept, as that used to price any term policy. The age 100 "endowment," referred to above, really is not an endowment in the usual sense but rather is paid by the insurer in recognition that the underlying reserve (and cash value) of the policy equals the policy face amount at age 100 and therefore there is no "pure" insurance protection beyond that point. Thus, the insurer should terminate the policy. Even if the company did not do so, the policyowner may surrender the policy for its cash value—which would equal the face amount.

The face amounts payable under whole life policies typically remain at a constant level throughout the duration of the policy unless the policy has a special provision permitting or causing changes (e.g., a cost-of-living rider). Also, through the use of dividends, participating policies' total death benefits can be increased over time.[2]

In most whole life insurance policies the premium remains at a constant level throughout the premium payment period. There are exceptions (e.g., graded-premium whole life) wherein the level of future premium changes is stated in and set by the contract. Also, with the advent of the indeterminate premium approach, many whole life policies' future premium levels are unknown except that the maximum possible premium level is set by contract and except that near-term premiums may be guaranteed.

All whole life polices involve some degree of prefunding of future mortality costs. The degree of prefunding is a function of the premium payment pattern and period. Because of this prefunding, all whole life policies have cash values and, as mentioned earlier, the cash value must build to the policy face amount, usually by age 100.[3]

Whole life policy cash values are available to the policyowner at any time by the policyowner's surrendering (canceling) the policy. Alternatively, cash values can be used in other ways, providing flexibility to the policyowner.[4] Whole life policies must, by law, contain cash value schedules that show for selected time periods the guaranteed minimum amounts that the policyowner could receive from the company on surrender of the policy.

Owners of whole life insurance policies do not have to surrender their policies to have access to accumulated policy savings. Policyowners normally can obtain a loan from the insurer under their policies for any amount up to that of the cash value. Interest is charged for this loan and the loan is deducted from the cash value if the policy is surrendered or from the face amount if the insured dies and a death claim is paid. Policy loans may be repaid at any time and are a source of policy flexibility.[5]

Most whole life insurance sold in the United States is participating, although a significant and increasing proportion is nonparticipating but with some nonguaranteed element. The amount of guaranteed-cost, nonpar whole life sold continues to decline. This decline is understandable, as companies cannot afford to guarantee liberal pricing assumptions for decades into the future. As a result, conservatively priced products providing such long-term guarantees do not compete well against those wherein the insurer does not guarantee every policy element.

The dividends paid under participating whole life policies can provide the policyowner with an additional source of flexibility, as they may be used in several ways.[6] Some insurers have restructured the use of dividend payments to develop new variations of whole life insurance, such as the "economatic" policy discussed below.

Insurance companies always provide a **dividend illustration** to prospective purchasers of participating policies. The illustration shows dividends that are expected to be paid under the particular policy under review if the mortality, expense, and

---

[2]See Chapter 9.
[3]Some policies endow at ages slightly less than 100 (e.g., at age 95). In general, any policy that matures at such a late age is, in effect, a whole life policy and is so considered here.

[4]See Chapter 9.
[5]See Chapter 9.
[6]See Chapter 9.

interest experience implicit in the current scale of illustrated dividends were to be the actual basis for all future dividends. The dividend illustration is usually based on the recent past mortality, expense, and interest experience of the company. There are important differences in the way that insurers allocate amounts to be paid out as dividends, and these differences can have a major impact on the level of the dividends illustrated as well on the dividends that are actually paid.[7]

As mentioned in Chapter 2, dividends are not and cannot be guaranteed. Actual dividends paid will equal those illustrated only if the experience basis used to determine future dividends is the same as that implicit in the illustration. Future experience rarely tracks past experience exactly, and never over an extended period. On the other hand, some insurers have "frozen" their dividend scales (i.e., pay dividends exactly as illustrated regardless of the developing experience). This practice treats dividends more as a series of nonguaranteed pure endowments and clearly is not in keeping with the principle of equity underpinning participating life insurance.[8]

The dividends that are actually paid under a participating policy are referred to as **historical dividends.** Over the past several years, these dividends have exceeded illustrated dividends for the vast majority of policies. This, of course, is as expected, since the last few decades have been a period of generally rising interest rates. For example, a 1965 dividend illustration would have been predicated on a company's pre-1965 experience. Actual dividends paid from 1965 to 1985 under a whole life policy should have been higher than illustrated since post-1965 experience, especially as to interest, would have been better than pre-1965 experience. In fact, this was the situation for most companies.

Table 5–1 shows illustrated versus historical dividends for three life insurers' participating ordinary life policies. Companies A and B paid dividends greater than illustrated and for both companies, dividends in later years were considerably higher than illustrated. This was caused primarily by the high investment returns the insurers had been earning by 1985.

Company C, on the other hand, obviously had some difficulties. One cannot deduce the cause of difficulties simply from viewing illustrated versus paid dividends. Either this insurer had particularly adverse experience with this block of policies, or management decided, for its own reasons, to pay significantly lower dividends than it should have based on the principle of equity underlying participating life insurance, or a combination of reasons applies.[9]

Some years ago, there were basically only two types of whole life insurance. One provided for level premium payments to be made for the whole of life (ordinary life) and the other provided for premium payments to be made for a limited period of time only (limited-payment whole life). Today, however, whole life policies vary not only by the duration of the premium payment period but also by other factors. For presentation purposes, they are broadly segregated as between those plans that provide insurance on the life of a single individual and those that cover more than one person.

TYPES OF WHOLE LIFE INSURANCE POLICIES: SINGLE INSURED

The Chapter 4 discussion regarding the changes that are taking place with respect to life insurance product development applies particularly to whole life policies. Some companies' policies have been perceived by many persons, rightly or wrongly, as providing inadequate value for money spent and as not being responsive enough to changing economic conditions. As a result of the pressures discussed earlier, many innovations have developed in whole life insurance pricing and policy provisions.

[7]See Chapters 6 and 9.

[8]Insurers selling participating life insurance can be considered as implicitly agreeing to distribute surplus accumulated on behalf of a block of policies in a fair manner and in appropriate quantities. See Chapter 9.

[9]The owner of a company C policy probably would not be aware that paid dividends were less than originally illustrated unless he or she had retained the 1965 illustration and had compared results with illustrations. Companies usually do not show on annual dividend notices the originally illustrated dividend.

TABLE 5-1. Illustrated versus paid dividends for three life insurers[a]
(1965 issues; per $1,000)

Year	Company A		Company B		Company C	
	Illustrated	Paid	Illustrated	Paid	Illustrated	Paid
1966	$ 0	$ 0	$ 2.27	$ 2.27	$ 0	$ 0
1967	2.11	2.19	2.61	2.66	2.06	2.06
1968	2.74	2.92	2.98	3.06	2.28	2.28
1969	3.40	3.64	3.39	3.55	2.50	2.51
1970	4.08	4.46	3.82	4.03	2.73	2.74
1971	4.76	5.23	4.24	4.33	2.97	2.98
1972	5.44	5.99	4.65	4.77	3.22	2.98
1973	6.11	6.73	5.06	5.19	3.48	2.98
1974	6.77	7.47	5.46	5.61	3.73	3.21
1975	7.46	8.23	5.86	6.03	3.99	3.49
1976	7.68	8.60	6.25	6.11	4.98	3.96
1977	7.90	9.02	6.69	6.57	5.98	4.91
1978	8.14	9.81	7.15	7.54	6.97	6.44
1979	8.37	10.59	7.62	8.07	7.97	7.48
1980	8.61	12.77	8.10	9.78	8.72	8.21
1981	8.85	13.71	8.57	12.15	9.45	8.50
1982	9.10	15.33	9.03	12.96	9.73	8.80
1983	9.34	16.99	9.49	15.85	10.00	9.07
1984	9.60	19.54	9.94	16.78	10.27	9.32
1985	9.83	21.51	10.43	17.68	10.54	9.59

Gross premiums per $1,000:

Company A $23.34
Company B $22.90
Company C $24.19

[a]Based on $10,000 ordinary life policies, male, age 35 in 1965.
Source: *Best's Flitcraft Compend* (Oldwick, N.J.: A.M. Best Co., 1985).

Because of the vast array of new whole life products and the even greater number of internal policy variations, the following discussion can only highlight the most important policies in terms of current interest. The classes discussed in this section provide coverage on a single individual's life.

Ordinary Life

Ordinary life policies provide whole life insurance with premiums payable for the whole of life. This oldest form of whole life goes by several names, including **straight life** and **continuous premium whole life,** and often the term "whole life" itself is used to denote ordinary life insurance. The term continuous-premium whole life is logically more descriptive than ordinary life but does not have much recognition.[10]

Ordinary life policies afford permanent protection at a relatively modest annual outlay since the mortality costs are spread over the entire policy period. Table 5–2 lists gross premiums charged for several otherwise similar participating and guaranteed-cost, nonparticipating life insurance policies. Premium levels vary significantly. The premium paid for any cash value policy, including whole life, is not a measure of the *cost* of the policy. A policy can have a relatively high premium yet

[10]A further problem with the term ordinary life is that it easily can be confused with the same term that is used to distinguish the broad classes of life insurance (i.e., group, credit life, industrial, and ordinary).

TABLE 5-2. Ordinary life gross premiums charged by selected companies
(age 35, male, $25,000 policy basis)

Type of Policy	Company	Gross Premiums per $1,000
Participating	A	$13.64
	B	14.31
	C	14.88
	D	16.16
	E	17.11
	F	17.90
	G	23.69
Guaranteed-cost nonpar	H	12.02
	I	12.33
	J	13.45
	K	13.52
	L	14.04
	M	18.05
	N	18.90

be low in cost by having large dividends, cash values, and/or excess interest credits.[11]

[11]See Chapter 10.

Ordinary life policy cash values normally increase at a fairly constant rate, reaching the policy face amount at age 100. (Reserves usually are more than cash values but exhibit a similar growth pattern.) Cash values in early policy years are typically low, since the high costs associated with policy sale and issuance are charged off in the first years. These high costs result from commissions paid to the salesperson, which often are 40 to 80 percent or more of the first-year premium, as well as underwriting and other administrative expenses.

Table 5–3 shows an illustration for a participating $100,000 ordinary life policy issued to a 35-year-old male nonsmoker. Dividends are shown both as being netted against the premium payment and as purchasing paid up additional insurance. Of course, only one option would be selected. The impact on early cash values of the front-end load is clear. The table shows that the guaranteed cash value at age 45 is to equal $12,854, and at age 50 it will be $22,074.

FIGURE 5-1. Terminal reserve values per $1,000, whole life insurance (male age 40), *1980 CSO Table*, 5% interest).

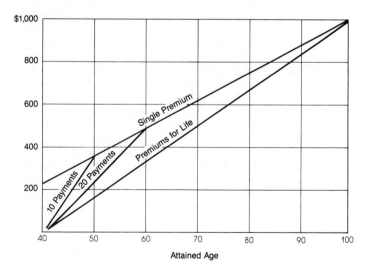

TABLE 5-3. Policy premiums and values for $100,000 ordinary life par policy
(age 35, male, non-smoker)

(1)	(2)	(3)	(4)	(5)	(6)	(7)	(8)
					If Dividends Used to Purchase Paid-Up Additions		
End of Year	Gross Premium	Illustrated Dividends (Year-End)[a]	Premium Less Dividend [(2)−(3) Prev.]	Guaranteed Cash Value	Paid-Up Additional Insurance Purchased	Total Cash Value[b]	Total Death Benefit (Year-End)[c]
1	$1,446	$ 3	$1,446	$ 0	$ 11	$ 3	$100,011
2	1,446	29	1,443	145	101	177	100,112
3	1,446	57	1,417	1,593	199	1,685	100,311
4	1,446	160	1,389	3,082	541	3,344	100,852
5	1,446	290	1,286	4,613	971	5,193	101,823
6	1,446	422	1,156	6,181	1,413	7,244	103,236
7	1,446	559	1,024	7,789	1,877	9,523	105,113
8	1,446	698	887	9,438	2,357	12,052	107,470
9	1,446	804	748	11,126	2,858	14,853	110,328
10	1,446	986	606	12,854	3,384	17,957	113,712
11	1,446	1,131	460	14,622	3,925	21,389	117,637
12	1,446	1,262	315	16,428	4,451	25,161	122,088
13	1,446	1,398	184	18,273	5,013	29,311	127,101
14	1,446	1,536	48	20,156	5,607	33,875	132,708
15	1,446	1,684	−90	22,074	6,239	38,889	138,947
16	1,446	1,849	−238	24,028	6,919	44,403	145,866
17	1,446	2,038	−403	26,014	7,638	50,459	153,504
18	1,446	2,223	−592	28,036	8,405	57,113	161,909
19	1,446	2,443	−777	30,091	9,237	64,426	171,146
20	1,446	2,681	−997	32,180	10,121	72,462	181,267

[a]Dividends assume no policy loans; loans will reduce dividends. Based on current dividend scale–1985 issue. Not an estimate or guarantee of future results. 8% loan provision.
[b]Column 5 plus cash value of paid up additional insurance.
[c]$100,000 plus sum of column 6.

Limited-Payment Whole Life Insurance

Under the terms of **limited-payment whole life** policies, the face of the policy is payable at death, but premiums are charged for a limited number of years only, after which the policy becomes **paid up** for its full face amount. The limitation may be expressed in terms of a *number* of years of premiums or the *age* to which annual premiums must be paid. A paid-up policy should not be confused with a **matured** policy. A policy is considered matured when the face amount becomes payable either as a death claim or because the policy cash value equals the face amount, as in an endowment policy. A paid-up policy is one that has not matured but on which no further premium payments are due.

Under limited-payment forms, premium payments may be fixed at almost any number of years—from 1 to 30, or even more. If premiums are limited to 20 years, for example, the policy is known as a **20-payment whole life** policy. The greater the number of premium payments, the more closely the contract resembles the ordinary life form.

Companies also make available contracts that limit premiums on the basis of age, such as to age 60, 65, 70, or even higher. The objective typically would be to permit the buyer to pay up the policy during his or her working lifetime. Thus, a policy that requires premiums to age 65 would be known as a **life-paid-up-at-65** (often abbreviated LP65) policy. It should be noted that a 30-payment life and an LP65 policy both issued at age 35 (and based on the same pricing assumption) would have the same premium, since actually, they are the same policy.

As limited-payment policies require the payment of premiums during a term that is less than the term of the contract, it follows that the annual level premium under this plan must be larger than that necessary when premium payments continue throughout the life of the policy. Theoretically, the premiums payable under a limited-payment policy would be the actuarial equivalent of the premiums payable for the entire lifetime of the insured under an ordinary life plan.[12]

Because of the higher premiums, limited-payment plans are not well adapted to those whose income is small and whose need for insurance protection is great. Furthermore, many persons who may be able to pay premiums may feel that an ordinary life policy will fit their needs better than a limited-payment contract, since they may be able to invest the difference in the premiums more profitably. For these and other reasons, sales of this class of whole life insurance are relatively small except in the juvenile and business insurance markets.

On the other hand, the disadvantage to the individual of higher premiums might be offset by the availability of larger values in the policy. The higher-premium policies have greater cash values (due to the greater prefunding of mortality charges) which are available for use in an emergency or at retirement. All limited-payment policies contain the same nonforfeiture options, dividend options, settlement options, and other features of the ordinary life insurance policy that provide flexibility for the policyowner.

The one-payment or **single-premium whole life** policy is the extreme form of limited-payment life insurance. Such policies have very substantial cash and loan values immediately and, of course, the policy is fully paid up from inception. Consequently, such contracts require a substantial outlay. The other extreme for whole life protection is represented by the ordinary life insurance policy, where premiums are payable until the maturity of the contract. Limited-payment contracts vary between these extremes. The five- and 10-pay life policies are closely allied to the single-premium policies, whereas a policy paid up at age 85 or beyond is, for all practical purposes, the equivalent of an ordinary life policy. All things remaining the same, as the number of premium payments increases, the annual premium, and consequently, the rate of growth of policy values, become correspondingly smaller.

Figure 5–1 shows terminal reserve values for various whole life insurance policies for a male age 40. The figure illustrates that the size of the reserve varies inversely with the length of the premium-paying period. Thus, the ordinary life plan, with payments for life, has the lowest level of reserves, and the single-premium plan, which involves only

[12]See Chapter 19.

one premium payment, has the highest. It should be noted, however, that after the premium payments cease under the 10-payment and 20-payment whole life plans, the reserves in each instance would equal those under the single-premium plan. This must be the case, since after any limited-payment period expires, the value to the company of future premiums is zero and *all* future mortality costs must be prefunded.

Indeterminate-Premium Whole Life Insurance

To increase their ability to compete effectively with participating products, some companies offer **indeterminate-premium whole life** policies. This concept, discussed in Chapter 4, applies to all forms of insurance but was first widely used and is still more prevalent with whole life.

The key to this dual-premium contract is a premium actually payable that is lower than the maximum premium. A significant *discount* off the maximum premium is guaranteed for the first few contract years. Annually thereafter, reductions are declared which may be larger or smaller than the initial discount. The policy is designed to reflect, through its premium structure, up-to-date expectations as to future experience.

Variable Life Insurance [13]

Variable life insurance (VLI) was first offered for sale to the general public in the United States in 1976. Its success was initially quite limited, with only the Equitable Life Assurance Society involved in pioneering efforts to market the product. Since that time, several insurers have begun offering VLI and, once again, much attention is devoted to new versions of VLI. VLI sales had a 1986 market share of 3 percent, representing a major increase from earlier years. Its market share is expected to continue to rise.

When VLI was introduced in this country—after being used successfully in the Netherlands, the United Kingdom, and Canada—it was thought of as a product that could help offset the adverse effects of inflation on life insurance policy values. Since it was believed that over the long term the investment experience of common stocks supporting the policies would increase with inflation, it was anticipated that VLI benefits would increase as the value of the underlying stocks did, thus providing a hedge against inflation. Even if this were true in the long run, short-term variations are inevitable, with inflation heading in one direction and investment performance in the other. Increasingly, VLI investment funds have moved away from common stocks only and, as mentioned below, a variety of investment media is now available, many of which are more stable in the short run.

Product Design. A variable life insurance policy is characterized as whole life insurance under which the death benefits and/or cash values vary to reflect the investment experience of a separate pool of assets (a **separate account**) supporting the reserves for such policies. Currently, most VLI policies are of a fixed-premium nature, similar to traditional insurance. A new verison of variable life, called variable universal life, is discussed in Chapter 6.

In VLI policies, premiums less an expense or sales load and a mortality charge are paid into a separate investment account. The policyowner may specify, within limits, where the cash value is to be invested. Several options are generally available. Most companies offer money market funds, common stock funds, and bond funds, as well as other types of funds. The policy death benefit ordinarily is directly related to the investment performance. However, regardless of the investment performance, there is a minimum amount below which the death benefit can never fall. Cash values also vary with the investment performance of the underlying funds but are not guaranteed. The cash value at any point in time is based on the market value of the assets backing the policy. *The VLI contract passes all investment risk to the policyowner. The insurer retains the expense and mortality risks.*

---

[13]This section draws on Gregory D. Jacobs, "Pricing Nontraditional Individual Life Products," *SOA Part 10 Study Note* (Itasca, Ill.: Society of Actuaries, 1984); Mary Jo Napoli, "Variable Annuities," *ibid.* (1985); and Frank L. Rainaldi, "Variable Life—An Investment Oriented Life Insurance Product with a Non-investment Alternative," *The Journal of the American Society of CLU,* Vol. 38 (January 1985).

The death benefit is composed of two parts. The first is a *guaranteed minimum death benefit* that corresponds to the basic plan of insurance underlying the VLI contract. The second part of the death benefit is *variable*. Any positive excess interest credits (i.e., the excess of the return on the underlying funds over the assumed investment return) is used to buy additional "pieces" of insurance. These additional units of VLI are generally purchased at net premium rates on a daily, monthly, or annual basis. If the excess interest credits are negative, prior variable units that have been credited will be "surrendered" and the death benefit lowered. In no event will the total policy death benefit fall below the minimum guaranteed death benefit.

The cash value of a VLI policy varies daily. However, unlike the variable insurance amounts, there is no guaranteed minimum. At any point in time, the actual cash value available is based on the market value of the policy's share of the separate account's underlying funds.

Variable life policies may be participating or nonparticipating. With participating VLI, the dividend is a function only of possible mortality and expense savings and includes no element of excess investment earnings. Excess investment earnings, less an asset management charge, are credited directly to the policy cash values.

VLI should be distinguished from index-linked life insurance, where death benefits vary with an outside index such as the Consumer Price Index (CPI) or the Standard and Poor's 500 Stock Price Index. Funds backing indexed policies are invested in the insurer's general account, just as with traditional forms of whole life insurance. Index-linked policies' cash values do not vary with the underlying investment performance.

Regulatory Developments. VLI is influenced by regulation on more fronts than most insurance products. Issuers of VLI must, as with all insurance products, comply with state insurance laws and regulations. Variable contracts and their issuers are also subject to federal securities laws and are regulated by the Securities and Exchange Commission (SEC).

1. *Federal securities regulation.* Federal securities regulation of VLI has its basis principally in three laws and related regulations. The SEC administers these laws. The three laws are the Investment Company Act of 1940, the Securities Act of 1933, and the Securities Exchange Act of 1934.

Entities that invest VLI policyowner assets in securities are "investment companies" as defined in the **Investment Company Act of 1940.** This act is the focal point of securities regulation for VLI. The Act regulates investment company management and operation. It sets ground rules concerning security owners, maximum sales charges, investment management of contributions, and distribution of periodic financial reports.

After extensive hearings and reversals of position, the SEC, in December 1976, promulgated Rule 6e-2, providing limited exemptions from the sections of the 1940 Act that require management accountability to contractholders, impose limitations on sales loads, and require issuers to offer refunds under certain circumstances. The rule, for example, sets out a definition and maximum for the "sales load"—currently 9 percent of premiums during the first 20 policy years, with some exceptions. This rule defines VLI as a policy that must:

1. Be funded by a life insurance company separate account.
2. Provide death benefits and cash values that vary to reflect investment experience.
3. Provide a minimum death benefit guarantee.
4. Have the mortality and expense risk borne by the company.

The **Securities Act of 1933** sets registration standards, financial standards, and disclosure standards for securities. A VLI policy is a "security." The main impact of this act upon VLI (and variable annuities—see Chapter 7) is the requirement that the potential purchaser be provided with a prospectus. This booklet includes the identity and nature of the insurer's business, the use to which the insurer will put the premiums, financial information on the insurer, the fees and expenses to be charged, and policyowner rights.

Whereas the 1933 Act deals principally with new securities issues, the **Securities Exchange Act of 1934** regulates the secondary securities market (i.e., the exchange of securities). Under the 1934

Act, the entity that distributes the VLI—the insurance company or a sales company—must usually register as a broker-dealer. The Act requires that *associated persons* pass an examination on the securities business. Associated persons include agents and many home and agency office employees. The 1934 Act regulates advertising, annual reports to shareholders, shareholder proxies, and financial reporting requirements.

The Maloney Act, an amendment to the Securities Exchange Act of 1934, made provision for the securities industry to form one or more bodies to regulate itself in accordance with the standards established by the Act. The National Association of Securities Dealers (NASD) was established for this purpose in 1939. All broker-dealers, including agents who sell VLI, must now register with the NASD and pass an examination.

2. *State insurance regulation.* VLI may be issued in all states, and all states make provision for separate accounts. Introduction of VLI in the states required legislative or regulatory authority. The basis for VLI regulations is the Model VLI Regulation adopted by the National Association of Insurance Commissioners.

The regulation establishes certain mandatory policy design characteristics and policy provisions. The regulation also covers the qualifications of a company to conduct a VLI business, operations of a VLI separate account, and reserve requirements.

Policy Provisions. In most other aspects (with some minor differences) the VLI policy operates in the same fashion as a traditional whole life insurance policy. Fixed premiums are payable on regular due dates, and if not paid, the policy lapses and goes under an option on lapse. Both reduced paid-up and extended term insurance on a fixed-dollar basis are available.

The policy may be reinstated subject to usual rules, except that the past-due premiums collected must not be less than 110 percent of the increase in cash value immediately available upon reinstatement. This condition is necessary because the reinstated policy reflects values assuming that the policy had never lapsed and thus would reflect

any favorable investment experience during the period of lapse.

Typically, loans up to 90 percent of the cash value may be taken at a fixed (8 percent) or a variable interest rate. Loans against policy cash values have the effect of creating an additional investment fund. Under this approach, variable benefits are affected, since the return reflected in benefits is a blend of the separate account investment return and the net return earned on any policy loan. An interesting characteristic of this provision is that it presents an opportunity for a policyowner to influence the variable benefits that emerge under the policies. In making a loan, the policyowner withdraws funds from the separate account and may make the policy less variable (up or down) while the policy loan is outstanding. This **direct recognition** feature was discussed in Chapter 4.

Illustrations of Death Benefits and Cash Values. Although it is relatively easy to describe how variable life insurance policy benefits will vary to reflect the investment experience of the underlying separate account, to describe the specific method of determining benefit variations is a challenge. To supplement the narrative descriptions in the policy and prospectus, illustrations of policy benefits (assuming hypothetical rates of return in the separate account) have been developed. Currently, applicable regulations permit illustrations based on (1) annual gross rates of return (after any tax charges and before other deductions) of 0, 4, 6, 8, 10, and 12 percent, and (2) the Standard & Poor's 500 Stock Price Index with dividends reinvested. Table 5–4 summarizes an illustration for a $100,000-level-face-amount policy issued to a male nonsmoker age 35.

The Appropriateness of VLI. Variable life insurance should be appealing to those who desire whole life insurance at a fixed, level premium and also the potential for important equity-type gains (and losses). Obviously, since the investment risk rests with the policyowner, VLI becomes riskier than the more traditional forms. As a result, it may not be appropriate as the centerpiece of many persons' insurance/savings programs. As

TABLE 5-4. Illustration of variable life policy values for $100,000 face amount
(male, age 35, nonsmoker; annual premium: $1,570)

Year	Death Benefit ($) Assuming Hypothetical Gross Annual Investment Return of:				Cash Surrender Value ($) Assuming Hypothetical Gross Annual Investment Return of:			
	0%	4%	8%	12%	0%	4%	8%	12%
1	100,000	100,000	100,064	100,135	379	397	418	438
2	100,000	100,000	100,278	100,591	1,506	1,590	1,680	1,771
3	100,000	100,000	100,642	101,380	2,680	2,879	3,092	3,312
4	100,000	100,000	101,153	102,508	3,703	4,064	4,455	4,874
5	100,000	100,000	101,814	104,000	4,870	5,444	6,077	6,773
10	100,000	100,000	107,519	117,746	10,322	12,755	15,799	19,605
15	100,000	100,000	117,238	144,059	15,081	20,693	28,743	40,323
20	100,000	100,000	131,170	187,013	18,877	28,931	45,550	73,231
30	100,000	100,000	173,150	349,955	23,683	45,744	94,741	206,022

discussed in Chapter 1, most sound financial plans have as one of their elements a savings program that is both highly liquid and relatively riskless. A VLI policy, at any point in time, may or may not meet this objective. Its cash value might be more appropriately considered as an element in one's long-term *investment* program.

Current Assumption Whole Life

Current assumption whole life (CAWL) insurance is one of the new, nontraditional policy types whose market share is growing rapidly and that holds out the potential for low-cost whole life insurance protection. The key elements in CAWL are the use of current interest rates in cash value determination and the use of an indeterminate premium structure. This has led to the product also being referred to as **interest-sensitive whole life** insurance. Since most such products also take account of current mortality and expense charges—as opposed to those guaranteed within the contract—the authors prefer the term "current assumption" to "interest sensitive." Also, traditional participating whole life policies are "interest sensitive" through dividend payments.

Figure 5–2 illustrates the funds flow pattern of a CAWL policy. The premium, determined in accordance with the procedure mentioned below, is paid to the insurer. Expense charges (if any) are then deducted. The contract sets out the maximum that can be charged, but companies often charge less. Many CAWL policies have no stated

expense charges; these are met from higher mortality charges and through a margin in the interest earnings.

The net amount remaining is added to the preceding year's accumulated fund balance to constitute a beginning-year balance. To this balance is added interest based on the insurer's current rate. As of early 1986, insurers were crediting rates in the range 8 to 11 percent. Guaranteed minimum rates were in the range 4 to 6 percent, with 4 and 4½ percent being most common.

Next, the mortality charges are assessed. These charges can be calculated based on the maximum permissible rates as set forth in the contract or, more often, on lower current rates. The rate is applied to the policy's net amount at risk (face amount less cash value).

Most contracts stipulate that surrender charges will be levied against the fund balance to arrive at the net surrender value. This value is never less than that required by the standard nonforfeiture law.

Product Design. CAWL products can be classified as falling into either a *low-premium* or a *high-premium* category. Each category of products has characteristics in common:

1. Use of an accumulation account, which is composed of the premium, less expense and mortality charges, and credited with interest based on current rates.

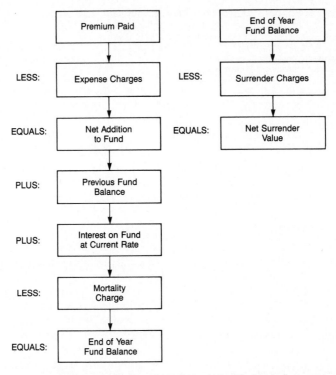

FIGURE 5-2. Current assumption whole life funds flow.

2. Use of a surrender charge, fixed at issue, which is deducted from the accumulation account to derive the policy's net surrender value.

3. Use of a fixed death benefit and maximum premium level at time of issue (on the low-premium version, either of these may be subject to change).

If there is a stated expense charge, it generally equals $20 to $50 per year. The surrender charge is usually expressed as some percentage of the first-year premium (often 100 percent) or of the accumulation account value. It usually grades down, as a percentage of the accumulation account, over a maximum of 15 to 20 years.

The low-premium version has several unique features. The initial (indeterminate) premium is very low by traditional ordinary life insurance standards. The policy contains a **redetermination provision.** This provision generally states that after the initial guarantee period, the company can redetermine the premium using the same or new assumptions as to future interest and/or mortality. The policy contains specific quantitative guarantees as to the minimum interest rate to be credited and the maximum mortality charge to be levied. The premium is then redetermined such that together with the existing accumulation account value, it will be able to maintain a level death benefit to the end of life if the new assumptions hold true. This will be recognized as a type of indeterminate premium structure.

If the new assumptions are the same as those used at time of issue or previous redetermination, the premiums and death benefits are guaranteed for another period of years. However, if the assumptions have changed since the last redetermination, the new redetermined premium may be higher or lower than previously.

If the new premium is lower than the previous premium, the policyowner often may elect one of three options:

1. Pay the new lower premium and maintain the previous death benefit.
2. Continue to pay the previous premium, maintain the previous death benefit, and have the difference in the two premiums added to the accumulation fund.
3. Continue to pay the previous premium and use the difference to pay for an increased death benefit, subject to evidence of insurability. (This option is not always available by contract.)

Typically, the contract will stipulate one of these as the **automatic option**—often option 2 above—but the policyowner may elect a change at any time.

If the new premium is higher than the previous premium, the policyowner also may elect one of three options.

1. Pay the new higher premium and maintain the previous death benefit.
2. Continue to pay the previous premium but lower the policy death benefit to that which the new premium will sustain.
3. Continue to pay the previous premium and maintain the previous death benefit. (This option is not always available and, when available, requires the accumulation fund to be at or above a certain level for at least the next five policy years.)

Contracts typically stipulate option 1 as automatic, but the policyowner may direct otherwise at any time.

The high-premium version also has several unique aspects. The premium is relatively high. An optional pay-up or **vanishing premium provision** is usually contained in the contract. This provision states that the policyowner may elect to cease paying premiums at a given point in time and essentially have a paid-up contract. The "point in time" is determined by comparing the accumulation account to a net single premium needed to pay up the contract but with the net single premium based on current interest rates and mortality costs. Once the accumulation account exceeds this net single premium, the contract is essentially paid up. This typically occurs between the fifth and ninth policy years for most such CAWL policies. It remains "paid up" *if and only if* the current interest and mortality levels are con-

tinued unchanged until maturity of the contract or are more favorable than the initial experience. This paid-up provision is not mandatory and the paid-up period is not guaranteed. The policy remains "paid up" as long as the accumulation account exceeds the minimum required cash value. Once it falls below this level, premiums are required or the standard nonforfeiture options apply.

The low-premium and high-premium versions are simply two different approaches applied to the same basic product. With the low-premium version, current assumptions as to interest, mortality, and expenses are used to lower the current premium charged. With the high-premium version, these favorable anticipated deviations result in a far more rapid increase in cash values, with the result that the policy can be paid up quickly, although the contract is not guaranteed to remain paid up. Therefore, the vanishing-premium version is not strictly comparable to the limited-payment whole life policies discussed previously.

Of course, variations in CAWL product design are found. For example, some insurers offer a death benefit equal to a level, stated face amount plus an additional amount equal to the accumulation fund balance. Some insurers make premium redeterminations every year or every three years instead of every five years. A few CAWL policies make adjustments based on interest alone and some index the policy's current interest rate to interest rates on money instruments, such as Treasury bills or certain bond indexes.

Policy Illustrations. Table 5–5 shows illustrated premiums and policy values based on one company's low-premium and high-premium CAWL policies. Note that the difference between the two premium levels is significant ($6.18 versus $13.00 per thousand) and that the charge for the low-premium version is considerably less than the premiums illustrated in Table 5–2 for ordinary life policies. Premiums are subject to a five-year redetermination period.

At current rates and assumptions, the high-premium policy would be tentatively paid up at the end of six policy years if the policy contained the vanishing premium provision. If premiums

TABLE 5-5. Illustrative premiums and values for two current assumption whole life policies
(age 35, male, nonsmoker)

Policy Year	Death Benefit	Low-Premium Version (per $1,000)			High-Premium Version (per $1,000)		
		Current Premium	Guaranteed Surrender Value	Projected Surrender Value	Current Premium	Guaranteed Surrender Value	Projected Surrender Value[a]
1	$100,000	$6.18	$ 0	$ 0	$13.00	$ 0	$ 0
2	100,000	6.18	1	1	13.00	0	6
3	100,000	6.18	6	6	13.00	4	21
4	100,000	6.18	12	12	13.00	16	36
5[a]	100,000	6.18	17	17	13.00	28	54
10[b]	100,000	6.18	46	49	13.00	97	175
15[b]	100,000	6.18	78	93	13.00	176	373
20[b]	100,000	6.18	112	144	13.00	261	678

[a]Assumes premiums continue to be paid each year and death benefit kept at initial amount.
[b]Premium to be paid for next five years is redetermined by company.

were stopped at that point, later duration surrender values would be less than those shown in Table 5-5.

Uses of CAWL. Compared with universal life (discussed in Chapter 6), current assumption whole life's level premium allows for easier company and policyowner administration. The level premium also gives the company greater control over the cash value buildup. The level premium/face amount combination may be more familiar to many persons than the universal life approach and therefore could be a more "comfortable" product. It is a blend of new and old.

Unlike universal life, the CAWL policy will lapse if the premium is not paid. This may provide some incentive for the policyowner to pay renewal premiums regularly and therefore could assist individuals who perceive themselves as not having the discipline to pay flexible premiums.

Other Forms of Whole Life Insurance

Five other forms of whole life insurance policies that insure a single life are covered here. The total market share of these five forms is not great but they can be important products to individual buyers and they are an important part of total sales of a number of companies.

Modified Life. A **modified life** policy is a whole life contract under which premiums are redistributed so that they are lower than an equivalent type of level-premium ordinary life policy during the first three or five years and higher thereafter. Thus, one company under a "modified 5" may set the premium during the first five years so that it will double thereafter. Other redistributions are also used. During the preliminary period, the premium is more than the equivalent level term premium for such a period, but less than the ordinary life premium at date of issue. Logically, after the preliminary period, the premium is somewhat larger than the ordinary life premium at the date of issue but less than the ordinary life premium at the insured's attained age at the end of the preliminary period. Regardless of the redistribution arrangement utilized, the company would receive the actuarial equivalent of the regular ordinary life premiums assuming, of course, that all underlying assumptions were equivalent.

"Economatic" Whole Life. Several mutual companies offer a type of participating whole life policy that uses dividends to provide some form of level constant coverage. The details, including the name given the plan, vary from company to company, but the purpose is basically the same: to provide a whole life participating policy with a low premium. Under these policies, dividends are earmarked. Under one approach, the face amount of a special ordinary life policy is reduced after a few years. However, dividends are used to

purchase deferred paid-up whole life additions such that at the time the policy face amount is to reduce, the paid-up additions fill the gap, with the result that the total death benefit is at least equal to the original face amount (based on illustrated dividends).

Under another approach the actual policy face amount may be 60 to 80 percent of the death benefit, but with the difference made up by the purchase of paid-up additions and term insurance in such proportions that the total death benefit is intended to remain equivalent to or greater than the initial policy death benefit. Under this approach it is hoped that paid-up additions eventually are sufficient to require no further purchase of term insurance.

A guarantee period is used in all such policies to ensure that the total death benefit during the early policy years does not fall below the original level even if dividends prove insufficient to meet the desired objective. With most companies, if dividends actually paid exceeded those needed to purchase the requisite amount of additional coverage, the excess would be used to purchase paid-up additions. If dividends paid were lower than illustrated, the majority of plans require that one-year term be purchased.

Indexed Whole Life Insurance. Several companies offer a whole life policy whose face amount increases with increases in the CPI. In general, these policies have been classified as to whether the policyowner or the company assumes the inflation risk. Under the approach where the *policyowner assumes the risk,* the death benefit increases each year in accordance with the CPI and the insurance company bills the policyowner each year for the new, higher amount of insurance. The company agrees, by contract, not to require evidence of insurability for these increases as long as each year's increase is accepted. If the policyowner declines one year to purchase the increase, no further automatic increases are permitted.

The approach under which the *insurer assumes the inflation risk* is similar in effect to the preceding approach, except that the premium charged initially by the insurer is loaded in anticipation of future face amount increases. Thus, increases in face amount do not alter the premium

level paid. Such policies often have a "cap" as to the maximum total increase permitted.[14]

Graded-Premium Whole Life. **Graded-premium whole life** (GPWL) policies, in existence for many years, have taken on a new wrinkle recently. The more traditional forms of GPWL provide that premiums begin at a 50 percent or lower level of those for a comparable ordinary life policy. Premiums increase annually for a period of from five to 20 years and remain level thereafter. Cash values evolve much more slowly than with ordinary life, often not appearing for five or more years. Policies may be participating or nonparticipating or may have indeterminate premiums.

Many of the newer forms of GPWL are more akin to yearly renewable term (YRT) policies than whole life insurance. These types of GPWL begin with premiums comparable to those charged for YRT (and sometimes lower), with YRT-type increases for periods ranging from 15 to 40 years. The premium levels off thereafter. Typically, no cash values evolve until well after the tenth policy year. For some policies, there are no cash values at policy year 20 or even by age 70 for a few. Such products appear as and compete with YRT and, from the buyer's perspective, should be considered as YRT policies that automatically convert to ordinary life at later ages. Premiums are often indeterminate and smoker/nonsmoker rates are typically used. A few companies also have reentry provisions.

Single-Premium Whole Life. **Single-premium whole life** (SPWL) plans have been available for decades. Historically, few persons purchased a whole life policy with a single premium, in large measure because of the exceedingly high outlay required relative to the face amount—often 40 to 50 percent or higher of the face amount at age 35.

Most SPWL sold today uses the current assumption approach discussed earlier with respect to level premiums. See Figure 5–2. The purchaser pays a (typically large) single premium to the insurer that credits current rates of interest to the fund value. Rather than mortality and

[14]Many companies also offer a cost-of-living rider similar in effect to that of indexed policies. See Chapter 7.

TABLE 5-6. Illustrative single-premium whole life policy values $100,000 single premium
(male, age 45)

Policy Year	Projected[a]			Guaranteed[b]	
	Fund Value	Cash Surrender Value	Death Benefit	Cash Surrender Value	Death Benefit
1	$100,000	$100,100	$349,584	$110,100	$349,584
2	121,000	111,320	349,584	111,320	349,584
3	133,100	123,783	349,584	123,783	349,584
4	146,410	137,625	349,584	129,646	349,584
5	161,051	152,998	349,584	135,715	349,584
6	177,156	170,069	349,584	141,978	349,584
7	194,871	189,025	349,584	148,426	349,584
8	214,358	210,071	366,553	155,043	349,584
9	235,794	233,436	386,703	161,812	349,584
10	259,374	259,374	407,217	168,723	349,584
15	417,724	417,724	559,751	195,675	349,584
Age 65	672,749	672,749	820,754	222,980	349,584

[a]Projected values are neither guarantees nor estimates but are based on the current interest rate of 10.0%. The death benefit is illustrated as increasing as from year 8 to ensure that the policy complies with the tax-law definition of life insurance.

[b]The minimum interest guarantee is 10.0% for the first three years and 6% thereafter. A one-time policy fee of $100 is charged in addition to the single premium.

expense charges being deducted annually from the cash value, they are netted against the interest credited to the fund. Thus, there appears to be no specific deduction for these charges in the fund accumulation. Additional first-year per policy expense charges might be levied against the premium.

Back-end surrender charges are typically used. Some insurers also include **bailout provisions,** which provide that if the credited interest rates fall below a certain level, the policyowner may surrender and incur no surrender charge.[15] The usual range of policy options is available, including policy loans. Insurers usually impose high (e.g., $10,000) minimum premiums. Table 5-6 gives values for one company's SPWL based on a premium of $100,000 and a current interest rate of 10 percent.

SPWL insurance can be useful for those individuals with the funds to purchase such coverage, although its appropriate usage is quite limited. Wealthy older persons often purchase it.

The Tax Reform Act of 1986 (TRA '86) has been the cause of much more interest in SPWL policies. The Act maintained the favorable tax treatment for life insurance cash value

accumulations while eliminating the favorable tax treatment of many other savings approaches. The tax-preferred status accorded life insurance redounds to the benefit of the SPWL purchaser. Thus, tax on interest earnings is deferred, if not avoided altogether. Death proceeds are tax free and can easily avoid the publicity and expense of probate.[16]

TYPES OF WHOLE LIFE POLICIES: MULTIPLE INSUREDS

The vast majority of life insurance sold in the United States is written on the life of one person. It is theoretically possible to write a life insurance policy on any number of lives and to construct it to pay on each person's death or on the death of the first, second, third, etc., or last of the group to die. In practice, two important plans have evolved: (1) the joint life policy and (2) the survivorship life policy.[17]

[16]See Chapter 13.

[17]Another type of multiple-insured policy, contingent life, is discussed in Lawrence L. Hoffman and Steven A. Smith, "The 'Next Death' Approach to Funding the Business Buy-Out," *Journal of the American Society of Chartered Life Underwriters,* Vol. XXXII, No. 1 (January 1978), pp. 21–30.

[15]But see Chapter 7.

Joint Life Insurance

Joint life insurance promises to pay the face amount of the policy on the death of one or two or more insureds covered by the contract. The policy is often used to insure both the husband and wife, with each being the beneficiary of the other. The policy pays only on the death of the *first* to die and is terminated at that time.

The survivor is without life insurance coverage under this policy. Contracts usually provide, however, that the survivor has the right to purchase a whole life policy on his or her life without providing evidence of insurability. Some contracts continue insurance temporarily and most provide that if both insureds die in a common disaster, the insurer will pay the face amount on each death. The importance of having a contingent beneficiary is clear.[18]

The premium for a given face amount would be smaller than the total premiums that would be paid for two individual ordinary life polices covering each individual. It should be noted that joint life coverage is also found under term and universal life plans.

Survivorship Life [19]

Survivorship life—also referred to as **second-to-die** and **last-to-die** insurance—insures two or more lives and pays the death proceeds upon the death of the second or last insured to die. Most survivorship policies are whole life, but some are term. They are available as either traditional or universal life insurance.

The survivorship policy is priced based on the probability of having to pay benefits at the death of someone *other than* the first to die. This is in contrast to joint life. Premiums are less than the cost of separate policies on each of the insureds. Premiums normally continue after the first death, but some products provide that premiums cease at the first death, or offer this feature as a rider.

The reserves required to be maintained by the insurance company are minimal when pay-ment of the face amount is contingent upon two deaths rather than one. However, when the first insured dies, the death benefit will become payable upon the occurrence of only one event and the reserve requirements for this contingency are much greater than the reserve required for two contingencies. Thus, both cash values and reserves increase substantially after the first death.

This product is attractive in estate planning situations where the unlimited marital deduction is used.[20] It also can be used in many business and family situations. It is particularly attractive in those situations where a business or family could survive financially after one death, but not after a second death.

One version of this product will insure as many as five lives, and at the time of issue, the policyowner can elect at which death(s) proceeds will be paid. Also, the face amount may be paid more than once. For example, assuming five insureds, the policyowner might select payment at the second, third and fifth deaths.

RECENT EFFORTS TO ENHANCE VALUE WITHIN EXISTING POLICIES

Because of the various competitive and other forces impinging on today's life insurance companies, they began witnessing record numbers of surrenders in the high inflation period of the late 1970s and early 1980s. Policyowners often purchased replacement life insurance and often the new policy was some form of fixed or flexible premium current assumption policy.

If the older policy was a guaranteed-cost, nonparticipating product, it had great difficulty competing with the new generation of products. These older products, which were priced on older, more conservative assumptions (by today's standards), did not make provision for the pass-through to policyowners of favorable experience.[21]

[18]See Chapter 9.

[19]This section draws on *Contemporary Life Insurnce Products* (Washington, D.C.: The Life Underwriter Training Council, 1985), pp. 27–28.

[20]See Chapter 13.

[21]One study found that older guaranteed-cost, nonpar ordinary life policies often could be appropriately replaced, even at the insured's increased age, with the newer *guaranteed-cost,* nonpar ordinary life products of the same company. See Harold Skipper, Jr., "Replacement Vulnerability of Older Nonparticipating Ordinary Life Policies," *The Journal of Risk and Insurance,* Vol. XLVII (December 1980).

These products were and are particularly susceptible to replacement.

In theory, older participating policies should be far more resistive to replacement if the insurer's experience is at least average and if the insurer distributes the accumulated surplus from such policies in a reasonable and equitable manner. Regrettably, not all insurers have met these two tests, with some even freezing dividend scales.

A problem with older whole life policies is that they often, by contract, permit the policyowner to exercise the loan option at interest rates well below prevailing market rates. Naturally, when a person can borrow money at below market rates and invest the proceeds at or above prevailing market rates, he or she is wise to do so, other things being the same. This process is called **disintermediation.** This is exactly what happened and, when combined with record numbers of policy surrenders, led to massive insurer cash outflows in the late 1970s and early 1980s. In fact, many life insurers actually experienced a negative cash flow for the first time since the great depression.

This meant that insurers had to liquidate bonds and other securities, usually at a significant price below par. This aggravated the problem further. In addition, and of great importance, many insurers were forced to forgo investing in contemporary, high-yielding assets since they needed the cash flow to fund not only the normal cash outflows, such as dividend payments, death claim payments, and expenses, but they also had to fund the greatly increased surrender value and policy loan outflows. When an insurer makes a policy loan at 5, 6, or 8 percent, it is "investing" its assets in that loan at that rate much as if it made a commercial mortgage loan. The critical difference, of course, is that the commercial loan might have earned as much as two or more times the rate of interest earned on policy loans.

As a result of these lost investment opportunities and the increased level of investments in policy loans—reaching 20 percent and higher of assets in some insurers—many companies' overall portfolio earnings rates did not grow as fast or to a level that they otherwise would have. Because of this, dividends paid on many participating policies were not competitive with excess interest and other credits on current assumption policies.

Companies were keenly aware of these problems and many undertook efforts to enhance the value of their existing older policies to render them less prone to surrender and replacement or to undertake other efforts to retain the policyowner as a client. These efforts generally fall into three categories:

1. Unilateral enhancements
2. Bilateral enhancements
3. Policy exchanges

Unilateral Enhancements[22]

Several insurance companies have made unilateral changes in certain classes of older policies, the intended effect of which is to enhance the value of the policy to its owner. Enhancements have been made with both participating and nonparticipating policies, although the exact extent of such activity is not known.

Some companies have unilaterally increased death benefits either on a permanent basis or on a year-to-year basis. One company, for example, provides an increase in the death benefit of pre-1974 issues of whole life policies equal to one-half of 1 percent of the policy face amount for each year the policy has been in force. This additional insurance is provided by one-year term additions at no additional charge to the policyowners.

Other companies have effected a permanent increase in policy face amount by changing the reserve (and usually cash value) interest assumptions underpinning the policies. There have been some tax advantages to insurers following this approach, and they are used to offset partially the cost of the enhancement. If the reserve/cash value bases are changed, it is possible that cash values per $1,000 face amount will be less, but the total policy cash value is usually greater after the change.

One company has instituted a unilateral enhancement of certain older participating policies by changing to a direct recognition dividend formula. Thus, policyowners who borrow heavily at

---

[22]This section draws from Charles C. McLeod, "Accentuating the Positive," *Best's Review,* Life/Health ed., Vol. 84 (March 1984).

low interest rates receive lower dividends. If little or no loan exists, dividends are higher, as discussed in Chapter 4.

Bilateral Enhancements

Several insurers have embarked on bilateral "update" programs for older policies. These programs have involved the insurer offering to change—usually improve—some benefit in the policy in return for the policyowner's agreement to change some aspect of the life insurance contract itself.

Many bilateral update programs have revolved around the policy loan clause. The first types were simply requests by some insurers to increase the guaranteed policy loan interest rate on certain older policies, in return for which the insurer would place the policy in a higher dividend classification. The amendment option typically was offered to those who owned policies that contained 5 and 6 percent loan clauses. The new loan rate was usually raised to 8 percent, although some companies have opted to introduce a variable-loan-rate clause.

Policyowners had the option of accepting or rejecting the offer, although questions arose about whether this resulted in a totally fair system.[23] Those who borrowed heavily were probably wise to reject the offer unless their marginal tax bracket was sufficiently high. High-bracket taxpayers could benefit from acceptance of the higher loan rate, by paying higher interest charges that were, at the time, tax deductible while receiving higher dividends that were tax-free.[24]

Another type of bilateral update program involes the direct recognition of policy loan activity within the policy's dividend formula. This is the approach discussed previously under "Unilateral Enhancements," except that unlike the company cited there, most other companies have perceived

the change to be of such significance as to warrant formal policyowner agreement.

Bilateral enhancements usually involve no change in premium or guaranteed cash values. The insurance coverage usually is not affected. Dividends are usually the only item changed besides the policy loan rate.

Policy Exchanges

Many—perhaps most—life insurance companies have addressed the problems of enhancement of older policies through exchanging old policies for new ones. This process may involve a formalized company plan and procedure for a systematic internal replacement program; it may involve revised procedures and plans to accommodate internal replacements that agents initiate but with no company sponsorship; or it may involve the insurer being totally "in the dark," with agents effecting internal replacements of their clients' policies. The net results from the policyowner's viewpoint can be the same.

Companies that have formalized exchange programs usually offer existing policyowners the opportunity to replace their older policies with newer versions under favorable terms or conditions. For example, many insurers will forgo or streamlime evidence of insurabilty requirements. Reduced loadings may be offered on the new policy or increased policy face amounts may be offered.

Insurers' older policies are a major source of profits. As the asset share calculation in Chapter 2 illustrated, policies' contributions to surplus (profit) typically increase over time. Thus, companies that undertake any meaningful enhancement programs usually forgo some current profit in hopes of future profit. This future profit may be expected to be realized through existing improved policies because of higher earnings from higher loan interest rates. Increased profits may be expected to arise from increased business that flows from an improved company image among agents and consumers. Tax savings might also offset partially current lost profits.

---

[23]See Joseph M. Belth, "Distribution of Surplus to Individual Life Insurance Policy Owners," *The Journal of Risk and Insurance,* Vol. XLV (June 1978), pp. 21–22.

[24]See Chapter 9. TRA '86 will phase out such consumer interest deductions. See Chapter 13.

Chapter 6

Flexible-Premium Life Insurance Policies

GENERAL NATURE OF FLEXIBLE-PREMIUM LIFE INSURANCE POLICIES

Traditional life insurance policies have certain features that improve their ability to adapt to changing circumstances. The nonforfeiture and policy loan provisions, the dividend options of participating policies, and the renewable and convertible features of term insurance are all good examples. Yet considerable rigidity exists in traditional life insurance products. It is usually not convenient to change either the face amount or the premium, except by lapsing or surrendering the old coverage and starting afresh.

Indeed, all life insurance policies sold in the United States prior to the 1970s were fixed premium contracts issued on either a participating or guaranteed-cost, nonparticipating basis. With the advent of enhanced computer technology, flexible premium policies became feasible.

The first major U.S. life insurance industry change in policy flexibility occurred during this period when the **adjustable life** (AL) policy was introduced in 1971. The policy permitted the policyowner to select whatever premium he or she wished, within limits, and later to "adjust" the premium and/or policy face amount, within limits.

The introduction of **universal life** (UL) in 1979 built on the strengths of adjustable life, but also provided true flexibility in premium payments, contemporary interest rates, and an "unbundling" of the savings and pure protection elements and associated pricing. Increased disclosure to the prospective purchaser and to the existing policyowner acompanied the introduction of UL.

Both AL and UL are fixed-dollar contracts in the sense that they contain traditional insurance-type guarantees as to minimum cash values and death benefits. The marriage of flexibility and transparency with the equity-based potential of variable life insurance (VLI) was to be expected. With the introduction of **variable universal life** by Life of Virginia and Acacia Mutual, almost simultaneously in early 1985, this is now reality.

These three types of life insurance policies are distinguishable from the fixed-premium contracts discussed in Chapters 4 and 5. Flexible-premium policies permit the policyowner, not the insurer, to decide, within limits, the premium level to be paid. As sold today, each also permits the policy death benefit to be adjusted.

ADJUSTABLE LIFE INSURANCE

Adjustable life (AL) combines elements of traditional, fixed-premium life insurance and the ability, within limits, to alter (i.e., adjust) the policy plan, premium payments, and face amount.

Nature of Adjustable Life[1]

At any point in time, adjustable life is a level-premium, level-death-benefit life insurance policy that can assume the form of any traditional term or whole life policy (within certain guidelines). It is thus a continuum of traditional level-premium life insurance—ranging from low-premium term through ordinary life to high-premium limited-payment whole life.

Adjustable life has all the usual features of level-premium cash value life insurance. It has cash and other nonforfeiture values (even in the term range), a policy loan provision, dividend options, a reinstatement provision, and settlement options. It can carry waiver of premium or accidental death benefit agreements, and the guaranteed insurability option.

The feature that distinguishes AL from other life insurance contracts is the provision that gives it its name. The **adjustment provisions,** which in essence are more fully developed versions of the typical change of plan provision, are the key to the AL concept. The policyowner can change the plan by requesting the insurer to change the policy configuration. Adjustments are made prospectively only, affecting the future but in no way amending the past. Premiums can be increased or decreased. The face amount of insurance can be increased (subject in most cases to evidence of insurability) or decreased. Some policies make allowance for an unscheduled or extra premium. Whenever any of these adjust-

ments occur, the plan of insurance will usually also change.

As one would expect, an increase in premium has the effect of increasing future cash values—and hence (1) lengthening the period of coverage if the policy is in the term portion of the adjustable life range, or (2) shortening the premium payment period if the policy is in the whole life range. A decrease in premium has exactly the opposite effect. Simultaneous changes in face and in premium are within AL capabilities, and the effect on future cash values and the future plan reflects both.

To illustrate the flexibilities, consider an adjustable life policy sold to a 25-year-old with an initial face amount of $25,000 and an initial premium of $200 per year. The initial plan may be term to age 60. Three years later $10,000 is added to the face and $100 to the premium, changing the insurance plan to term to age 63. Another three years later the policyowner finds that he or she can pay $575 per year, and his or her $35,000 AL policy now provides lifetime protection with premiums payable to age 84. At retirement the policyowner may want to reduce the premium outlay and may need less insurance. He or she finds that $30,000 of protection can now be carried for the whole of life for the original premium of $200 per year.

New Concept

The AL policy introduced a new concept to the life insurance business. The traditional approach to life insurance programming first determines the face amount and plan of insurance; then, by entering the ratebook at the insured's age, the premium is calculated. If the resulting premium is not consistent with premium-paying ability, adjustments to the face amount or a change to another insurance plan must be considered. If the original plan was a base policy with a term rider, a common adjustment to develop a satisfactory premium is to vary the term/whole life mix.

Under AL, the process is similar, but in a different order and with a different emphasis. Amount of insurance and premium can be estab-

[1]Minnesota Mutual pioneered this new product, issuing the first AL policies in 1971. The Bankers Life Company of Iowa entered the market in 1977. This section draws on Charles L. Trowbridge, "Adjustable Life—A New Solution to an Old Problem," *Journal of the American Society of Chartered Life Underwriters,* Vol. XXXI, No. 34 (October 1977), pp. 12–20.

lished first. Then the plan of insurance is forced out by entering a modified "ratebook" at the insured's age.

An appropriately priced and designed adjustable life policy could be viewed as the last and only policy needed. An increase in premium under an adjustable life policy is for many purposes treated as a new sale, but the existing policy is adjusted rather than a new one issued. A new table of nonforfeiture values is, of course, necessary—as is a statement of the new premium, the new amount, and the new plan. The policy usually is like any similar traditional policy between adjustment dates in that premiums are fixed and may not be skipped.

Other Features

The new concepts introduced by adjustable life had and continue to have some interesting "spin-offs." Among these are a cost-of-living agreement, certain aspects of lapse and reinstatement, and a new approach to substandard insurance.

The Cost-of-Living Agreement. The cost-of-living (COL) agreement, attached to most standard adjustable life policies without extra premium, waives evidence of insurability for limited face amount increases, essentially those that adjust the face for changes in the cost of living.

Normally, the additional insurance is associated with an increase in premium so calculated that the plan of insurance is unaffected. Unless the insurance company is notified to the contrary, the premium for the ensuing policy year will be billed on this basis. A 20 percent increase in face would add more than 20 percent to the premium, because of the higher age for the same plan.

The COL agreement is not unique to adjustable life. Similar provisions are offered by many companies for term, whole life, and UL. As with other changes, however, adjustable life handles the mechanics easily.

Lapse, Nonforfeiture, and Reinstatement. AL cash values are normally zero at the end of the first policy year, but cash values develop by the end of the second year, even in the low-premium versions that are technically term. Cash and reduced paid-up whole life coverage are the nonforfeiture options under one company's contract, and the reinstatement provisions are the familiar ones.

One other significant writer of adjustable life offers extended insurance as the automatic nonforfeiture option and has no explicit reduced-paid-up option. Reduced paid-up can, nonetheless, be accomplished by a reduction in face amount at the date of lapse. By judicious choice of the extended insurance amount, the protection period can be as long as one chooses (provided that sufficient value remains), even for the whole of life.

An interesting by-product of this extended term approach is the ease with which reinstatement can be accomplished. The reinstating policyowner need not pay back premiums with interest, as under more traditional policies, and he or she need not reinstate all the lapsed premiums. A resumption of the premium-paying status, possibly at a lower level that the policyowner can then afford, is all that is necessary. Evidence of insurability may be required.

Rated Adjustable Life. The payment of an extra premium is the normal requirement if a buyer of conventional life insurance is found to have a medical impairment, or if for any reason the policy must be issued on other than a standard basis. The agent finds that placing of the rated policy is often difficult, and the "not taken" rate is high.

The modifications necessary to issue an adjustable life policy on a substandard basis are conceptually simple. The mortality table normally used for cash value and reserve purposes is modified to recognize the degree of impairment. With this one exception, the cash value and plan calculations are performed in the usual manner. Dividend calculations are modified by the same technique. Should the insured's condition improve such that the rating can be removed, the adjustment routine will recalculate and upgrade the plan, unless the policyowner prefers to maintain the plan and lower the premium.

At some time after issue of a standard AL policy, the policyowner may apply for an increase in amount. Should he or she be rated for the increase, the adjusted policy will operate under a blend of two mortality tables—the standard table in proportion to the previous amount of insurance and a rated table in proportion to the increase.

This procedure is practical with current computer technology. There is but one policy under these circumstances. The policyowner receives credit for his or her original determination as standard—and is treated as substandard only with respect to the increase.

Old Concepts

As mentioned above, AL introduced some important new concepts, but at the same time, retained many aspects of traditional products. While the AL policyowner may alter (adjust) the level of premiums paid, premiums generally cannot be taken to zero without policy lapse. Therefore, AL policies require certain minimum annual premium payments, usually equivalent to that for a five-year term policy. This is not the case with UL policies. Also, any change in the level of premium payments ordinarily requires formal notification to the company and a redefining of the resultant plan.

Once a particular premium payment level is decided upon, that premium is due at future due dates *unless* the policyowner specifically requests a change. In this respect, AL is similar to fixed-premium policies. Of course, it is different in that the owner has the ability to alter the amount by negotiating a change. By contrast, UL policies require no implicit assumption regarding the level of future premium payments.

AL policies' cash values are calculated in the same manner as traditional cash value products. The traditional approach needs a specific level of future anticipated premiums, whereas the retrospective approach, as followed with current assumption whole life (CAWL) and UL policies, does not.

AL policies are "bundled" in the sense that their individual pricing elements are not shown separately and the pure protection and savings components are not segregated. This traditional approach is to be contrasted with that which exists under CAWL and UL policies, wherein the protection and savings elements and the accompanying pricing structures are "unbundled" and shown separately. Table 6–4, later in this chapter, sum-marizes these important similarities and differences.

UNIVERSAL LIFE INSURANCE

Perhaps no new life insurance product has been discussed, debated, and written about as much and as intensely as universal life (UL) insurance. UL has captured not only a major share of the life insurance marketplace—and in record time—but perhaps more important, it has captured the news media's and the public's attention and imagination.

It is perceived as responding to consumer demands for low-cost, flexible life insurance. UL policies offer great policyowner flexibility but, like all life insurance policies—both traditional and new—whether they are low-cost is a function of the manner in which the insurer has priced the product. Both of these important points are made clearer later in this chapter. First, however, it is worthwhile to develop an appreciation for the origins and growth of UL in the United States.

The Origins and Growth of Universal Life Insurance

The concepts upon which UL is based are as old as the concepts of level-premium payments and reserves, well over 100 years old. A key element, the use of the retrospective approach to cash value (and reserve) development, is analyzed and discussed, for example, in Spurgeon's 1922 authoritative book, *Life Contingencies,* long the standard for the study of this subject by U.S. actuarial students.[2] Jordan's 1952 and 1957 editions of *Life Contingencies* continued the treatment.[3]

It is said that the idea of universal life as a product was mentioned by H. L Riedner in 1946 and by Alfred N. Guertin in 1964.[4] Ken E. Polk's 1974 article in the *Transactions of the Society of Actuaries,* together with the accompanying

[2]See E. F. Spurgeon, *Life Contingencies* (London: Charles & Edwin Layton, 1922), pp. 96–97.

[3]See, e.g., C. W. Jordan, *Life Contingencies,* 2nd ed. (Chicago: The Society of Actuaries, 1957), Chap. 5.

[4]Stuart J. Kingston, "On Universal Life," *The National Underwriter,* Life/Health ed. (January 2, 1982), p. 25.

TABLE 6-1. Estimated universal life sales in the United States

Year	Planned Periodic Premiums (Millions)	UL as Percent of Total Individual Life Premium	Approx. Number of Companies Selling UL by Year-End
1981	116	2	25
1982	525	9	100
1983	1,320	18	200
1984	2,530	30	300
1985	3,650	38	350
1986 (prelim.)	3,400	35	375
1987 (proj.)	2,800	26	375

Source: Life Insurance Marketing and Research Association.

discussion papers, provided virtually all the formulas needed for developing a workable UL policy. Polk referred to his hypothetical policy as variable-premium life insurance.[5]

It seems, however, that principal credit for conceiving of UL as a product goes to George R. Dinney of Great-West Life, a Canadian insurer.[6] He appears to have conceived of the idea as early as 1962, although a written description of the product, which he dubbed the Universal Life Plan, apparently was made public only in 1971.[7]

James C. H. Anderson, president of the actuarial consulting firm of Tillinghast, Nelson and Warren, Inc., probably did more than anyone to publicize UL as a viable product and to cause serious thinking about the possible need and wisdom for developing such a product. His paper, "The Universal Life Insurance Policy,"[8] presented at the Seventh Pacific Insurance Conference in 1975, is considered by many to be the most important step along the road to UL.

In 1976, one insurer, American Agency Life, in fact, developed and sold a UL policy of the type described in Anderson's paper. Because of adverse

[5]Ken E. Polk, "Variable Premium Life Insurance," *Transactions of the Society of Actuaries,* Vol. XXVI (1974), pp. 449–465; and discussion, pp. 467–478.

[6]"Universal Life," *The Actuary,* Vol. 15, supplement (September 1981), p. 1 and J. Timothy Lynch, "Universal Life Insurance: A Primer," *The Journal of the American Society of Chartered Life Underwriters,* Vol. XXXVI (July 1982).

[7]Paper entitled "A Descent into the Maelstrom of the Insurance Future," presented in 1971 at the Canadian Institute of Actuaries.

[8]The paper was reproduced in the Tillinghast publication *Emphasis* (November 1975).

tax problems, the company soon discontinued sales. UL in its current form was not introduced and sold widely until its introduction by E. F. Hutton Life (then Life of California) in 1979. As of 1987, 375 companies sold UL. No life product in recent times has gained acceptance so rapidly.

The UL concept was at first not welcome by the life insurance business. It was perceived (and still is by some) as a threat to the orderly development of the industry and as not being in consumers' or agents' best interests. Today, few persons oppose UL. Most now see it simply as another, albeit highly important life product available for consumers. There are, however, still some concerns, some of which are addressed later in this chapter.

Universal life policy sales have had a meteoric rise since its introduction in 1979. Table 6-1 shows that from 1981, UL market share as a percentage of total individual premiums written grew from 2 percent to a high of 38 percent in 1985. The 1986 UL proportion decreased to 35 percent.

The number of companies estimated to be selling UL has increased from one in 1979 to an estimated 375 in 1987. Data from the Life Insurance Marketing and Research Association suggest that UL quickly has become the largest individual life product seller within those companies selling UL.

Because of UL sales growth, the "mix" of individual life insurance sales has undergone a shift, as highlighted in Table 6-2. It can be seen that traditional cash value policies'—mostly whole life's market share has declined the greatest,

TABLE 6-2. Changing mix of life insurance sold in the United States

	Percent of Total Individual Life Premiums[a]							
Product Type	1980	1981	1982	1983	1984	1985	1986 (prelim)	1987 (proj)
Traditional cash value	82	78	70	62	43	33	33	41
Universal life	—	2	9	18	30	38	35	26
Current assumption whole life	—	—	1	3	12	14	14	13
Variable life	—	1	2	2	3	3	3	4
Variable universal life	—	—	—	—	—	1	3	6
Term life	18	19	18	15	12	11	12	10

[a]Riders classified with base policy. Single premium whole life included at 10%.
Source: Life Insurance Marketing and Research Association.

with UL and current assumption whole life (CAWL) being used as an alternative cash value accumulation product.[9]

Term insurance's market share, as a percent of premiums, has also declined. Some of this decline is explained by the overall decline in term premiums, but the majority is due to a shift from term to UL and CAWL products. These products have allowed the life insurance industry to recapture part of consumers' savings that was lost through an increasing reliance on term life insurance by the public.

The Nature of Universal Life Insurance

Universal life insurance is a flexible-premium, adjustable-death-benefit life insurance policy. UL policies offer *flexible*, potentially *low-cost* coverage on a basis that permits product *transparency*. After making an initial premium payment of at least some required minimum, policyowners may thereafter pay whatever amounts and at whatever times they wish, or even skip premium payments as long as the cash value will cover policy charges, subject to company rules and the tax law.[10] Also, policyowners may raise—usually subject to evidence of insurability—or lower their policies' death benefits as they deem appropriate with a

[9]Not all of this market share decline can be attributed to UL sales. Much of it is no doubt due to many persons using flexible-premium deferred annuities and other investments along with term life insurance as a substitute for traditional cash value policies.

[10]See Chapter 13.

minimum of difficulty. These are the two key elements of UL **flexibility.**

UL policies offer the potential for **low-cost coverage.** Most UL policies provide for interest credits based on contemporary rates of interest subject to a specific guaranteed minimum rate. In addition, the current mortality charges associated with the pure insurance element can be low. UL policies expense components are often lower than those charged under traditional policy forms, but not always. Together these elements mean that UL policies are *capable* of affording policyowners low-cost coverage.

UL policies are **transparent** in their operation. The policyowner is able to see exactly how the policy operates internally. An illustration is provided to prospective purchasers describing how policy elements—premiums, death benefits, interest credits, mortality charges, expenses, cash values—interact. Each year the policyowner receives similar information in the form of an annual report, a sample of which is shown in Figure 6-1. Transparency *does not mean* that the policyowner can necessarily evaluate the adequacy of projected values; only that the policyowner will be able to see, after the fact, the disposition made of policy funds.

A key element of product transparency is that UL policies' cash values and pure insurance amounts are shown separately—they are **unbundled** or **decoupled.** The cash value changes each year in accordance with premium payments made, expenses related thereto, accompanying mortality charges, and interest credits. The net

FIGURE 6-1. Sample annual report for a universal life policy.

ABC Life Insurance Company
Universal Life Policy

Summary of Policy Activity for Year Ending: October 11, 1987
Policy Number: 000–000–00   Name of Insured: Mary Doe

Mary Doe   Benefits: Shown Below
200 Spring Street
Anytown, Anystate 10000

Month Ending	Premiums Received	Cost of Protection	Other Charges	Amount Needed to Repay Loan	Interest Credited	Month End Savings Element	Basic Death Benefit
11/11/86	$ 100.00	$ 25.51	$ 37.50	0.00	$ 19.70	$2,800.65	$75,000
12/11/86	0.00	25.50	30.00	0.00	20.24	2,767.39	75,000
01/11/87	200.00	25.50	45.00	$1,005.62	14.87	2,909.76	75,000
02/11/87	100.00	25.48	37.50	1,012.68	15.39	2,962.17	75,000
03/11/87	100.00	25.47	37.50	2,025.70	10.68	3,009.88	75,000
04/11/87	100.00	25.46	37.50	2,039.67	10.86	3,057.78	75,000
05/11/87	100.00	25.45	37.50	2,053.64	11.03	3,105.86	75,000
06/11/87	.00	25.44	30.00	2,067.61	11.21	3,061.63	75,000
07/11/87	200.00	25.45	45.00	2,081.58	11.44	3,202.62	75,000
08/11/87	100.00	25.42	37.50	2,095.55	11.83	3,251.53	75,000
09/11/87	.00	25.97	0.00	2,110.73	12.44	3,238.00	75,000
10/11/87	200.00	25.97	15.00	2,125.92	13.01	3,410.04	75,000
	1,200.00	306.62	390.00		162.70		

The first $1,000 of the Savings Element was credited with 4.50% guaranteed interest rate. The amount loaned was credited with 4.50%. The remaining amount of the savings element was credited with the current interest rate shown at the end of this statement.

*Includes mortality charge for base policy, and any rider or benefit shown above.

Please remember that the values illustrated in the table above would be reduced by the amount of your outstanding loan in the event of a claim.

In the event that you surrender this policy during the current year, a surrender fee of $371.25 will be deducted as provided by the policy.

Summary of Current Interest Rates for Year Ending   October 11, 1987

Month Ending	Effective Annual Current Interest Rate (%)
11/11/86	12.00
12/11/86	12.00
01/11/87	12.00
02/11/87	12.00
03/11/87	12.00
04/11/87	12.00
05/11/87	12.00
06/11/87	12.00
07/11/87	12.00
08/11/87	12.00
09/11/87	12.00
10/11/87	12.00

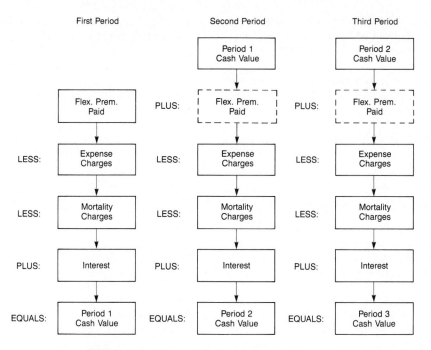

FIGURE 6-2. Universal life funds flow illustration.

amount at risk plus the cash value produces the total policy death benefit.

Figure 6–2 illustrates the operation of a typical UL policy. Similar to the operation of CAWL, UL policies differ in that neither the premium level nor the death benefit is fixed. Otherwise, the products are the same in concept. In fact, CAWL policies are sometimes referred to as fixed-premium UL policies.

Referring to Figure 6–2, the mechanics of a UL policy would be as follows: The policyowner pays a first premium of at least a certain required minimum amount (to cover initial expense and other charges). From this initial premium would be subtracted first-period expense charges, although many UL policies now sold have no identifiable front-end loadings.

Next, mortality charges based on the insured's attained age and the policy's net amount at risk and charges for any supplemental benefits (e.g., premium waiver) would be subtracted. The mortality charges are usually indeterminate, with the actual charge usually being less than the stated maximum rate contained within the policy.

After subtracting expense and mortality charges, the resulting fund is the initial policy cash value (not shown). This initial cash value will then be credited with interest, usually at new money rates, to arrive at the end-of-period cash value. Many UL policies levy high first-year surrender charges against the cash value of any terminating policy.

The second policy period (usually a month) begins with the previous period's ending cash value balance. To this amount the policyowner may add a further premium in an amount of his or her choosing. However, if the previous period's cash value is sufficient to cover the current expense and mortality charges, no premium need be paid. If the previous period's cash value is not sufficient, the policy will lapse in the absence of a further premium payment.

Expense and mortality charges would be subtracted from the sum of the previous period's ending cash value balance and any premium payment, to arrive at the second period initial cash value (not shown). Interest at the current rate would then be credited to this initial cash value to arrive at the end-of-period cash value for the second period.

The entire process would be repeated in the third, fourth, etc., periods. If the cash value at any time were not sufficient to sustain the policy, the policy would lapse without further premium payments. However, no further premium need be paid if the cash value is sufficient.

Universal Life Product Design

Numerous UL product design variations exist. This section does not attempt to address all of them. Rather, an effort is made to describe what seems to be the mainstream of product design.

Death Benefit Patterns. Universal life policies typically offer two death benefit patterns, from which the purchaser selects one. Of course, the pattern may be changed at any time, but in the absence of a request for a change, the pattern selected will be followed during the policy term.

The two patterns are usually labeled options A and B. **Option A** provides a level death benefit pattern and **option B** provides a pattern that varies directly with cash value variations.

Under option A the net amount at risk (NAR) is adjusted each policy period (usually monthly) such that the cash value and the NAR together always provide a constant death benefit. Thus, if the cash value increases over time, the NAR decreases by the same amount, and vice versa. This option can result in the same policy benefit pattern as that provided by traditional cash value policies.

Option B stipulates that the policy death benefit at any time will be equal to the sum of a stated, level NAR and the then cash value. Thus, if the cash value increases over time, the total policy death benefit increases exactly with the cash value increase.

Figure 6–3 illustrates these two death benefit patterns assuming that the cash value increases over time. It can be seen that with option A, the NAR decreases whereas with option B, it remains at a constant level.

The option A benefit pattern provides for a **corridor** of NAR as the cash value approaches the level death benefit amount. If this did not occur, the policy would effectively become an endowment and, of far greater importance, the policy would not qualify as life insurance under existing tax law. If a policy fails to meet the Internal Revenue Code (IRC) definition of life insurance, the policy is not accorded favorable tax treatment. Chapter 13 discusses the important details of this IRC definition.

Naturally, the greater the NAR, the higher will be the monthly mortality charges. Therefore, the option B pattern will result in a greater outlay for mortality charges.

Decreases in the policy death benefit can be made by policyowner request at any time. Since the insurer's NAR is lowered, no evidence of insurability is required for decreases. A lowering of the death benefit naturally also lowers the mortality charges, assuming no cash value withdrawal.

Increases in UL policy death benefits, other than those provided for automatically under option B or any cost-of-living rider, typically require evidence of insurability. Otherwise, those in poor health would increase policy death benefits (i.e., they would select against the company). Insurers often permit "minor" increases without evidence, but this is usually done extracontractually.

Naturally, increases in policy death benefits ordinarily result in higher monthly mortality charges since the NAR will be increased. Companies selling UL policies have minimum death benefit requirements that range from $25,000 (or even lower) to $100,000, depending upon age and policy form. Also, most will permit changes only where the change is greater than some minimum (e.g., $5,000).

Many companies permit policyowners to attach a cost-of-living (COL) rider to their UL policies, similar to that used with adjustable life policies. Such riders provide that the policy death benefit will be increased each year in accordance with the previous year's increase in the Consumer Price Index (CPI). Thus, if the CPI increased 4 percent, a $100,000 policy would increase next year automatically to $104,000. No evidence of insurability is required, with the monthly mortality charges simply reflecting the higher NAR.

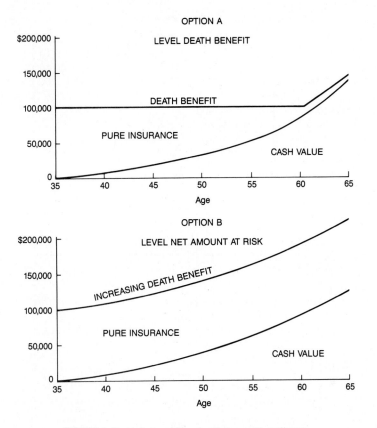

FIGURE 6-3. Universal life death benefit patterns.

Premium Payments. UL policyowners pay whatever premiums they desire and whenever they desire, subject to company rules regarding minimums and maximums. Most companies require only that the first premium be sufficient to cover the first-month expense and mortality charges, although most purchasers pay an amount well in excess of this minimum.

One of the potential disadvantages of UL is that policyowners might too easily allow their policies to lapse since there is no "forced" savings, that is, no "required" and billed premium, as is the situation with the products discussed in Chapters 4 and 5. To overcome this concern, at least partially, companies will bill for a *planned or target premium* in accordance with the stated preference of the policyowner.

Thus, the buyer might agree to a monthly preauthorized draft of his or her bank account. Alternatively, the insurer might send a "bill" to the policyowner for the planned premium. The amount of the automatic bank draft or "bill" would be set by the policyowner.

Figure 6-4 illustrates the flexible premium feature of UL policies. In this illustration, it is assumed that Diane, a 35-year-old female policyowner, decides to pay $1,000 per year into her UL policy. This she does for five years, at which time she needs a lower outlay because she is sending her son to college. Diane therefore pays nothing for the next five policy years, with the cash value continuing to build based on the current interest rate net of mortality and expense charges.

At the end of the five-year period, she

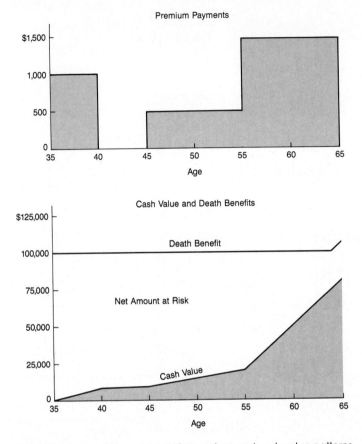

FIGURE 6-4. Illustrative universal life premium and cash value patterns.

resumes premium payments but at a lower level ($500), as she is undertaking an important and costly expansion of her business. At age 55, she decides to increase payments to $1,500 per year.

The option A death benefit pattern is assumed and the interest rate and expense and mortality scales are assumed to remain on their current bases, an admittedly unrealistic assumption. The initial $1,000 premium payment causes a constant rise in cash values to almost $5,000 by age 40. The cash values continue to build even with no premium payment to age 45, although the rate of growth is far lower, at which time the cash value is about $6,000. The $500 per year payments combined with current interest credits are more than enough to cover mortality and expense charges for the next 10 years, so the age 55 cash value is almost $22,000. The higher $1,500

premium causes a rapid buildup in cash values such that by age 65, they stand at somewhat greater than $79,000.

If payments were continued beyond that point, the combination of the payments and interest credits would cause the cash value to grow to over $140,000 by age 70. This would necessitate a death benefit increase to over $163,000 by that time.[11]

Naturally, any premium payment pattern could be assumed, subject only to company rules and the need to have a sufficient cash value to maintain the policy in force. If insufficient cash value exists to continue the policy, the policy-

[11]If the insurer used the maximum permissible charges and the guaranteed interest rate, this premium payment pattern would support the full $100,000 in force only until age 68, at which time the $1,500 premium would not be sufficient to sustain the coverage.

owner is provided a 30 (or 60)-day grace period in which to make a premium payment. Failure to do so results in the termination of coverage.

Policy Loadings. Figure 6-2 illustrated the nature of UL policy expense and other loading elements. UL policies have imposed identifiable loadings in one or both of two ways: (1) **front-end loads** and/or (2) **back-end loads.**

The front-load approach was the first used with UL. Many newer UL products rely more heavily or totally on back-end load—also called **surrender charges.** Some UL contracts are both back and front loaded, and a few have neither.

The loading charges of a UL policy rarely, if ever, track a company's actual incurred expenses. Usually, the amount actually charged is insufficient to cover initial expenses, especially on policies with little or no front-end loadings.

These excess first-year expenses, it is hoped, will be recouped through renewal expense charges, through high early surrender charges, through interest margins, and/or through mortality margins. Indeed, for policies with little or no front-end load, it would be incorrect to contend that the policy had no "loading." While "no load" policies of all types do not have *identifiable* loading elements, there is always a loading that must be charged somehow against the policy.

The margin between the actual investment earnings of the company and the rate it credits to UL policies is often an important source of income to cover excess expenses and to provide profits. Mortality margins can also be important, but usually less so than interest margins.

Most UL policies' first-year expense charges are higher than charges assessed on renewal. Both initial and renewal expense charges can be stated on a per policy and/or a per $1,000 face amount basis and as a percentage of premium. Some insurers use all three bases, while others use two, one, or none.

For example, one company's expense loading for the first policy year is composed of a flat $96 policy assessment plus a charge of $0.15 per $1,000 per month (i.e., $1.80 per $1,000 per year) plus a further charge of 10 percent of the premiums paid. Renewal expense charges are based solely on the 10 percent premium charge. This front-loaded policy has very low surrender charges.

Most companies assess a percentage premium charge, with the majority having the same first-year and renewal percentage. They typically fall within the range 2½ to 20 percent. Some insurers still assess a high first-year policy fee with little or none thereafter, although the trend seems to be to have the same policy fee for all years. Typical "high" first-year fees fall within the range $200 to $400, with the newer levels in the range $25 to $50 per year.

Companies seem to be discontinuing the use of fees based on each $1,000 face amount, with this trend being especially pronounced for renewal years. Many insurers now assess only a percentage of premium load.

For companies with low or no identifiable front-end loads, the back-end loads—surrender charges—tend to be high, although they cannot exceed those permitted by law. Surrender charges may be expressed as a percentage of the first-year premium (most common for policies with no front loads), as a loss of excess interest for one year, as a flat dollar assessment per $1,000 face amount (e.g. $10 per $1,000), as a flat dollar assessment (e.g., $25), or as an amount equal to unpaid first-year expense charges. Policies that emphasize front loads usually have low or no back loads. In any event, surrender charges are highest during the first few policy years and grade downward with duration, often decreasing yearly after the first five policy years or sooner, reaching zero in from 10 to 20 years.[12]

Mortality Charges. Each month mortality charges are deducted from UL cash values. The total monthly mortality charge is derived by multiplying the applicable rate by the policy's NAR. The maximum rates per $1,000 are stated in the contract for all ages and actual rates charged are guaranteed never to exceed these maximums. Most UL mortality charges are indeterminate, as mentioned previously, as well as differentiated between cigarette smokers and nonsmokers. Some

[12]Very high back-end-loaded policies can create a so-called "tontine effect." This effect results whenever death-related or lapse-related values are diminished currently so as to afford higher values later. In this case, high surrender charges can generate profits in early years to fund higher values in later years to those who persist.

insurers also use a reentry rate scale, whereby policyowners may pay a lower premium by periodically demonstrating to the insurer continued good health.[13]

Most insurers base their maximum mortality charges (printed in the policy) on those derived from the *1958 CSO mortality table,* a conservative, valuation table. Increasingly, insurers are adopting the *1980 CSO* table as the basis for their contractually guaranteed maximum rates. This valuation table, which has lower rates than the *1958 table,* is still conservative.[14] The level of the current and anticipated *actual* mortality charges is of greater importance than the level of the guaranteed rates because they are the ones actually charged.

Mortality rates actually charged by issuers of UL vary considerably. Table 6–3 lists mortality charges currently (1986) being levied by six companies for three different ages. These are *monthly* charges and therefore a difference of only a few dollars can sum to a large amount over time. One cannot conclude from these figures alone which of the various companies' policies is the best buy. Interest credits and loadings must also be factored into the analysis. For example, company F, with the highest mortality charges, has relatively low front-end loads and no surrender charges. Ob-

TABLE 6-3. Selected companies' current mortality charges per month for $100,000 UL policy
(male, nonsmoker)

Company	Age 25	Age 40	Age 55
A	$ 6.67	$14.43	$35.33
B	9.17	12.08	25.83
C	10.00	16.00	37.00
D	14.00	21.00	46.00
E	15.00	21.00	51.00
F	16.00	31.00	73.00

[13]See Chapter 4.

[14]It may be noted that the basis used for the guaranteed maximum mortality charges also serves as the basis for maximum premiums that can be paid into the policy (so-called "guideline premiums") and still maintain qualification as "life insurance" under the current tax law definition. See Chapter 13. Thus, maximum mortality charges based on the *1958 CSO* table will produce higher guideline premiums than will use of the *1980 CSO.* This has tended to discourage adoption of the *1980 table* as the basis for maximum mortality charges.

viously, its mortality charges implicitly include provisions for expense recovery.

Cash Values. The student will recall from Figure 6–2 that the cash value is simply the residual of each period's funds flow. It results from taking the previous period's ending cash value balance (if any), adding to it any premium paid, subtracting expense and mortality charges, then adding current interest credits to the resulting fund balance. The result is the end-of-period cash value. All items except the current interest credit have been discussed above.

UL policies guarantee to credit at least some minimum, contractually stated rate of interest to policy cash values. Guaranteed rates of 4 or 4½ percent are most commonly found, although a few contracts guarantee somewhat lower or higher rates. Although these rates may seem low by today's standards, they are reasonable long-term guarantees and potentially of great value to the policyowner.

Companies currently credit interest rates well in excess of their guaranteed rates. In 1987, current rates were commonly in the range of 6 to 10 percent, with some companies crediting as low as 5.5 percent and some as high as 11 percent. A downward trend in credited rates was in evidence, reflecting changing market conditions.

The first UL policies utilized a two-tiered interest approach wherein only the guaranteed rate was credited on the first $1,000 or so of cash values, with amounts in excess of $1,000 receiving the current rate. Most UL policies sold today do not make this distinction, crediting the entire cash value with the current rate, subject to a direct recognition feature.

Like all cash value policies, UL policies permit policyowners to obtain policy loans on the security of the policy's cash value. The direct recognition provision in UL policies is important in this regard. It provides that interest at the current rates will be credited only to that portion of the cash value that is not used to secure a policy loan. That portion backing any policy loan is usually credited only with the contractually guaranteed interest rate or sometimes a rate one or two percentage points below the policy loan interest rate.

Not all UL issuers use a direct recognition provision. A few credit the current interest rate on the entire cash value, irrespective of policy loan activity. If the UL policy contains the variable loan rate now permitted in most states, little need exists for a direct recognition provision.[15]

Most UL policies provide that the current interest rate will be determined by the company. Others are indexed, providing that the current interest rate will be set at a level slightly below that being credited on some external, well-recognized money instrument such as three-month or one-year Treasury bills.

Most nonindexed UL policies receive interest credits based on the companies' "new money" rate of return. As discussed in Chapter 2, this rate represents that which the company expects to earn on its new investments. Many insurers, by contrast, use a "portfolio" rate of return such as the company's investment income rate based in its entire asset portfolio, or the assets backing a block of such policies.

New money rates are more responsive to changing market interest rates. This can work for or against the policyowner. If market rates are generally rising, UL cash values credited with interest on this basis should be higher than those credited with portfolio rates during the period.

On the other hand, when market rates fall, portfolio rates could be—and at some point will be—higher than new money rates. In such circumstances, the portfolio-based UL policy should outperform its new money brother, other things being the same.

Most UL policies permit partial cash value surrenders, although the tax standpoint should be considered.[16] Usually, such surrenders must be for at least a minimum about (e.g., $500) and there often is a separate fee (e.g., $25) for processing the partial surrender. The policy death benefit is reduced by the exact amount of any partial surrender. If it were not, the company would be inviting adverse selection. Total policy surrender, as discussed previously, may involve a surrender charge.

Uses and Limitations of Universal Life Insurance

Just as the adjustable life policy offers the possibility of being the only life insurance policy a person needs over his or her lifetime, so does the universal life policy. Its flexibility in premium payments and death benefits renders it well suited as an individual's "life-cycle" policy.

Simplified "Life-Cycle" Illustration. Figure 6–5 provides a simplified "picture" of how this life-cycle approach could work. This illustration ignores inflation and takes a simplistic view of insurance planning.[17] It assumes that Larry Townsend, age 25, purchases a $50,000 UL policy using option A (level death benefit) and pays a premium of $500. The purpose of this policy is to pay off education debts incurred from his obtaining a law degree. This starting situation is depicted at point A.

At point B, Larry marries his long-time sweetheart, Sandra, and because of further obligations, believes the coverage amount under his UL policy should be increased to $75,000 (point B). At the same time, he increases the premium payment to $1,000. Cash values build slowly, as shown.

When Larry is 30, Sandra, who has been working, has a child, Emily (point C). Because this "life event" has major implications for Larry and Sandra, they increase the UL coverage amount to $200,000 but with no increase in premium. Larry again meets the insurability requirements. Sandra decides to remain home during Emily's formative years.

Two years after Emily's birth, at point D, Larry and Sandra withdraw $3,000 from the UL policy to help make a down payment on a new home. Such a cash withdrawal would normally reduce their death benefit by an equivalent amount, but they increase the coverage to maintain the previous amount. At this point, they also cease making premium payments to devote needed funds to the mortgage payment.

Two years later, they are able to resume some premium payment, to $500. Two years after

---

[15]See Chapter 9.

[16]See Chapter 13.

[17]But see Chapter 12.

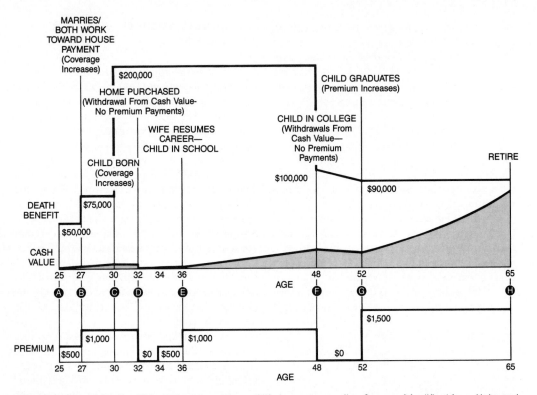

FIGURE 6-5. Hypothetical life cycle using universal life insurance policy. Source: Modified from *Universal Life Basics* (Indianapolis, Ind.: Pictorial Publishers, 1983), pp. 6–7D. Used with permission.

that point (point E), they are able to increase the payment to $1,000, as Sandra resumes outside employment.

Life continues merrily for the happy family and at Larry's age 48, Emily enters college (point F). They withdraw $2,500 per year for each of the next four years to help defray Emily's educational expenses, and they cease premium payments as well. They conclude that with the responsibilities of rearing Emily being essentially over, they can, simultaneously, decrease their total insurance amount to $100,000, although this amount will further decrease each year by the amount of the $2,500 withdrawals.

Four years later, Emily is graduated from college and goes into the world to seek her fortune, independent of Larry and Sandra. The happy couple is now able to resume premium payments, and with an eye toward accumulating a retirement fund, make premium payments of $1,500 per year until age 65, at which time (point H) they cease making premium payments and begin a system-

atic withdrawal program under their UL policy (and, of course, live happily ever after).

Notice that the single UL policy has served the needs of our hypothetical family well throughout their various "life cycles." The death benefit was altered as needed to suit the then current needs. Premium payments were similarly increased and decreased as financial circumstances dictated and the cash values were a source of needed cash throughout life. This simplified example illustrates the flexibility of UL.

Although only one insured is shown in this figure, on close analysis (see Chapter 12), significant amounts of insurance may be needed on Sandra's life also. A UL policy on her life could have been illustrated as easily as one on Larry's life, but for simplicity, only one insured is considered here.

UL can be used in countless other ways as well—as can most other cash value policies. A UL policy can be used in virtually every circumstance where a whole life policy could be used. Like whole

life, however, UL probably should not be purchased for short-term needs. Term will usually
prove superior in such situations.

Limitations on Illustrated Values. UL has
helped the life insurance business regain consumers' savings dollars. UL is undoubtedly flexible and its operations more transparent than
most life products. That it can prove to be low
cost is not questioned, but as with all life policies
that contain nonguaranteed elements, whether
it actually will be low cost can be determined only
over time. It will be necessary to examine how
insurers treat their UL policyowners in terms of
actual excess interest credits and actual mortality
and expense charges.

Moreover, some argue that UL flexibility,
especially with respect to premium payments,
could easily lead to poor persistency, with the
result that consumers lose money from early UL
policy terminations in the same way as they would
with early whole life policy terminations. Results
to date do not suggest that this concern is borne
out by facts. It remains largely a *potential* problem
at this stage.

There is concern that UL policy advertisements and sales aids place undue emphasis on
the current high-interest-rate credit to the exclusion of other potentially important elements, such
as expense loadings and mortality charges.

For example, a $100,000 option B UL policy
that credits 11 percent has a projected 20-year cash
value of $79,828 based on a 35-year-old male,
nonsmoker, paying $2,000 per year, while another
that credits 10 percent has a 20-year projected cash
value of $90,597.

Consider also that the following policies,
each of which advertises an 11 percent current
interest credit and is based on similar policy and
buyer profiles, show projected 10- and 20-year
cash surrender values as follows:

UL Policy	10-Year Projected Cash Value	20-Year Projected Cash Value
A	$20,528	$ 75,808
B	23,432	80,423
C	24,430	96,359
D	26,043	89,321
E	27,535	106,324
F	28,382	102,724

Of course, these differences are all explain-
able to anyone who examines each element of these
UL policies. To the great credit of these policies,
their transparency of operations permits this
examination—whereas such is not always easy
with other cash value products.

The concern does not rest with any deficiency related to transparency. Rather, it rests
with marketing approaches that place potentially
unwarranted emphasis on current interest rate
credits to the point that the average purchaser of
the UL policy may be misled as to the product's
value.

Another concern results from the practice
of projecting high interest rates for years and even
decades into the future. Such projections, unless
carefully explained, can mislead and distort product value. Although no one can know the "correct" rate to use for projections, everyone knows
that the current rate is not correct. Rates will
change.

The keys to avoiding deception—intended
or otherwise—are carefully prepared illustrations
and advertisements with appropriately worded
caveats, illustrations that show policy value results
using rates of interest between the guaranteed
and current rates, and, of greatest importance,
well-informed agents and other financial advisors
who very carefully guide the client through a
potentially misleading morass. Of course, these
concerns apply to other new money products, including participating whole life policies that use
new money dividend illustrations.

Another concern, again not just with UL
policies but with all interest-sensitive products,
including traditional participating whole life
policies, is that in competition today one finds that
the prospective purchaser is often shown noncom-
parable comparisons of two or more policies'
future values. This "apples and oranges" problem
has been alluded to earlier but warrants further
comment.

Historically, dividend illustrations under
participating policies were based on the company's average portfolio investment rate of return.
Companies were loath to pay dividends less than
those which were originally illustrated at the time
the policy was sold. As a result, illustrations based
on current portfolio average returns were conservative. In effect, the purchaser of such a policy

had reason to believe that these nonguaranteed illustrated dividends would, in fact, be paid—and probably at a level higher than illustrated.

Within the last few years, many companies selling participating insurance shifted to a new money or investment generation approach to investment income allocation within their dividend formulas. This was done at a time of rapidly rising interest rates, so the result was that dividends illustrated at new money rates were higher than those illustrated on portfolio rates since the portfolio rate is a weighted average of old and new investment returns. At this point, the two dividend illustrations became far less comparable.

The advent of nonparticipating new money products such as UL and CAWL which used not only current investment returns but also contained an element of *anticipated* favorable future results, including mortality and expenses, put further competitive pressure on illustrations. It was no longer sufficient in such a competitive environment, in the judgment of many companies, to illustrate dividends based on current and immediate past *actual* results—let alone portfolio results. It became necessary to build into dividend illustrations an element of anticipated future results, not very dissimilar from that which existed with the new money nonparticipating products. Such illustrations began to take on the look of projections.

In one sense, this rendered some traditional-looking participating products more comparable to interest-sensitive nonparticipating products. However, many companies base dividend illustrations and interest rates for UL and CAWL policies on portfolio rates.

Therefore, we are now faced with three sets of future value illustrations/projections: (1) portfolio average, (2) genuine investment generation method, and (3) new money with anticipated future projected experience. In a period of rising interest rates, the likelihood of actual results being as favorable as illustrated/ projected are: for (1) excellent to good; for (2) good to fair; and for (3) fair to unlikely. Yet each type of illustration is used in competition with the others. We are comparing "apples to oranges" when this is done. Moreover, for the first time, many dividend "illus-trations" are not in fact conservatively based with the result that it is to be expected that dividends actually payable under these policies in the future will be less than illustrated.

How the advisor factors these complex matters into his or her analysis is not easy. The financial analysis still must be conducted in many cases. However, the first step to an intelligent interpretation of results is to gain an understanding of the assumptions underpinning the numbers. Chapter 10 picks up further on these points.

VARIABLE UNIVERSAL LIFE INSURANCE

A next logical step in life insurance product evolution was to combine some of the flexible characteristics of universal life with the investment flexibility of variable life. This new product, **variable universal life,** must still be considered in its formative stages, but many believe that it will occupy an important portion of the total individual life market.

Variable universal life (VUL) products are also referred to as **universal life II** and **flexible-premium variable life.** Each refers to a variable life insurance (VLI) policy whose premium payment pattern is flexible and whose death benefits are adjustable.

VUL is subject to the same SEC and state regulations as VLI. Thus, under SEC interpretation of the laws discussed earlier, the VUL contract itself, the separate account, and the selling agent must all be registered.[18]

Some technical provisions of SEC regulation are being altered to accommodate the differences between the traditional fixed-premium VLI contract and the VUL contract. These relate primarily to relief from SEC-mandated sales load limitations—which had been based on actual premium payments and had been oriented exclusively toward front-end-loaded contracts.

At the state level, the adoption by the states of the NAIC **Variable Life Insurance Model Regulation** would eliminate the earlier model regulation's restrictive product design criteria. To date, about two-thirds of the states have

[18]See Chapter 5.

adopted a version of the regualtion, with more being added to the list monthly.

Nature of Variable Universal Life Insurance

VUL tracks the UL model in that the policyowner decides, within limits, the premium to be paid each period, if any. The policyowner also has the option of increasing or decreasing the policy death benefit at will, subject only to policy minimums and, with respect to death benefit increases, evidence of insurability requirements.

Unlike UL, the assets backing the VUL policy are maintained in one or more separate accounts. In this respect, VUL is identical to VLI. The cash values of VUL are subject to fluctuation just as VLI cash values and, like cash values of VLI, there also is no guarantee with respect to either a minimum rate of return or principal. In other words, cash values can decrease to zero.

The treatment of death benefits under most VUL policy designs differs from that under VLI, instead following the UL approach. VUL death benefits fluctuate with changes in the values of the underlying assets only under option B. With the option A death benefit pattern, the face amount remains constant unless changed by the policyowner. As a result, all variations in investment returns are reflected solely in the policy's cash values, with no part used to fund changes in the policy's net amount at risk.

Uses and Limitations of Variable Universal Life

VUL policies are both too new and too few in today's life insurance marketplace to permit a reasoned assessment of the products. They would seem to be potentially useful for those persons who desire to assume the investment risk themselves.

The policy runs the danger that if separate account investment results are not favorable, the policy's cash value could be reduced to zero, at which point the policy would lapse without further premium payments. This risk should be considered most carefully. One of the strengths of the life insurance industry historically has been its investment guarantees. Whether consumers in large quantities will be willing to forgo these guarantees remains to be seen.

VUL offers the same flexibility as UL but without the guarantee. Whether the product will be successful probably will depend on the extent to which separate account investment performance is superior to the current fixed-dollar investment returns credited to UL and other life insurance policies.

LIFE INSURANCE POLICY COMPARISON CHART

The great variety of life insurance products available in today's marketplace can cause bewilderment. However, the vast majority of individual life insurance sold today is of one or more of six product types.

These six types are listed in Table 6–4 in the order in which they were presented in this book. Beside each type is a summary of its basic features and a listing of its advantages and disadvantages, both to the buyer and to the seller. The table is intended to highlight key points only and is to be interpreted only with the corresponding area of the book that discusses the product. As with all such shorthand charts, countless exceptions to the general statements exist. Therefore, the chart must be used only with the greatest of caution and only as a reminder to the reader of essential product features.

TABLE 6-4. Life insurance policy comparison chart

Product	Death Benefit	Premium	Cash Value	CV and/or Dividends Use Current Interest?	Partial Surrenders Permitted?	Policy Elements
Annual renewable term	Fixed, level	Fixed, increasing	No cash value	N / A	N / A	Bundled
Participating ordinary life	Fixed, level	Fixed, level	Fixed with minimum interest rate guaranteed; excess through dividends	Yes	Yes, but through paid up additions only	Bundled
Current assumption whole life	Fixed, level	May change based on insurer's experience. CV has GTD min. % Maximum guaranteed but insurer may charge less	Minimum guaranteed interest; excess lowers premium or increases CV	Yes	Yes	Unbundled
Variable life	Guaranteed minimum; can increase based on investment performance	Fixed, level	Based on investment performance; not guaranteed	N / A	No	Bundled, but to some degree shown in prospectus
Adjustable life	Adjustable	Adjustable at option of policyowner	Varies depending on mix of premium and death benefits; fixed with minimum guaranteed interest; excess through dividends	Yes	Yes	Bundled
Universal life	Adjustable	Flexible at option of policyowner	Varies depending on face amount and premium; minimum guaranteed interest; excess increases CV	Yes	Yes	Unbundled

This table is an adaption of those published by the Life Insurance Marking and Research Association and by the Life Underwriter Training Council.

Direct Borrowing Recognition	Advantages		Disadvantages		Risks To Buyer
	To Buyer	**To Seller**	**To Buyer**	**To Seller**	
N/A	Low outlay, can purchase large amounts; buyer can develop outside investment program	May be easier to sell	Increasing outlay; buyer may not invest difference or may realize lower return	Low commission, little profit; high lapse rates	Increasing premium Can buyer earn more on investments than insurer?
Yes, with many policies	Familiar product; predictable; helps buyer discipline; interest, mortality and expense experience can be recognized	Same as buyer; traditional commissions; greater margins	Costly if lapsed early; lack of flexibility; can be more costly	Sales declining; can be difficult to compete	Failure to meet premium commitment
Yes	Take advantage of high current interest rates and improved mortality	Same as buyer; traditional W.L. commissions; responds to buy term invest difference	Premiums can increase or CV be lower than projected; buyer takes risk on high premium version, policy can become "unpaid" up.	If projections not met, can be negative client reaction	If assumptions change adversely, premiums can be higher than with traditional products or cash value can be lower than with traditional products
Yes	Take advantage of growth in economy	Responds to inflation objection; traditional W.L. commissions	Buyer must decide on underlying investments and monitor them for change; few guarantees	Needs securities license; older agents not used to selling. Rules of SEC could be troublesome	Investment risk is great Can be higher in cost than traditional products
Yes	Flexibility to adjust to changing needs; only one policy needed	Salable as only policy needed; commission comparable to traditional	If needs are known, and likely to change, other products may be more competitive; may be more costly per unit of protection	Servicing may be costly; renewal commissions less certain because of flexibility	Changes made by buyer to satisfy short-term needs may have an impact on the satisfaction of long-term goals
Yes	Same Adj. Life; also greater transparency and more flexibility	Consumer accepted; widely publicized, may be easier to sell	Flexibility places greater responsibility on buyer; buyer assumes greater investment and mortality risks	Generally, lower commissions; renewals uncertain; computer backup essential; readily lapsable	If assumptions change adversely, investment performance can affect satisfaction of long-term goals and cash value can be lower than with traditional products

Chapter 7

Annuity and Special-Purpose Benefits

ANNUITIES

The proportion of U.S. personal disposable income spent for annuities has been rising for several years even in the face of a decline in the proportion spent for life insurance. Clearly, annuities have become even more popular as accumulation instruments. This increased popularity reflects the maturing of the American population, leading to purchases of annuities to fund individual pension plans made possible by favorable federal pension legislation and to an increasing awareness of the tax-preferred status of annuities.

Nature of Annuities

In the broadest sense, an annuity is simply a series of periodic payments. An annuity contract, then, is an insurance policy that promises to make a series of payments for a fixed period or over someone's lifetime. If the payments are made with reference to life contingencies, the contract is known as a **life annuity.** Life annuities may be either **temporary** (payable for a fixed period or until the death of the annuitant, whichever is earlier) or **whole.** The term "life" in the title of an annuity simply indicates that payments are contingent upon the continued ex-

istence of one or more lives. In the following discussion, reference to life annuities will mean whole life annuities unless specifically indicated otherwise.

Liquidation, the Basic Mission of Annuities. Life insurance has as its principal mission the *creation* of a fund. The annuity, on the contrary, has as its basic function the systematic *liquidation* of a fund. In one sense, a life annuity may be described as the opposite of insurance protecting against death. In its pure form, a life annuity may be defined as a contract whereby for a cash consideration, one party (the insurer) agrees to pay the other (the annuitant) a stipulated sum (the annuity) periodically throughout life. The understanding is that the consideration paid for the annuity is fully earned by the insurer immediately upon the death of the annuitant. The purpose of the annuity is to protect against the possibility of outliving one's income—just the opposite of that confronting a person who desires life insurance as protection against the loss of income through premature death.

Each payment under an annuity may be considered to represent a combination of principal and interest income and a survivorship element. In theory, if a person exactly lives out his or her life expectancy, he or she would have neither gained nor lost through utilizing an annuity contract. If one outlives his or her life expectancy under the contract, the additional payments would be derived from the funds contributed by those who failed to survive to their expectancy. On the other hand, if one dies in advance of his or her life expectancy, the entire contributions would not have been recovered, with the excess providing income for those who outlived their expectancy. Since no one knows into which category he or she will fall, it is an equitable arrangement and can succeed, from the company's point of view, through the operation of the law of large numbers. Only a life insurance company can guarantee that a given sum can be scientifically liquidated in equal installments over the duration of a human life.

Despite the difference in function, annuities are simply another type of insurance and both life insurance and annuities are based on the same fundamental principles. Technically, the two types of contracts are closely related, since both employ the pooling technique, and premiums in each case are computed on the basis of probabilities of death and survival as reflected by a mortality table.

Classification of Annuities. Annuities may be classified in a number of ways. Here they will be classified as to the (1) number of lives, (2) method of premium payment, (3) time when income commences, (4) method of disposing of proceeds, and (5) units in which benefits are expressed. Figure 7–1 shows this classification schematically.

1. *Number of lives.* This classification involves simply the question of whether annuity payments are made with reference to a single life or more than one life. If the contract covers two or more lives, it is known generally as a **joint-**

FIGURE 7-1. Basis for annuity classification.

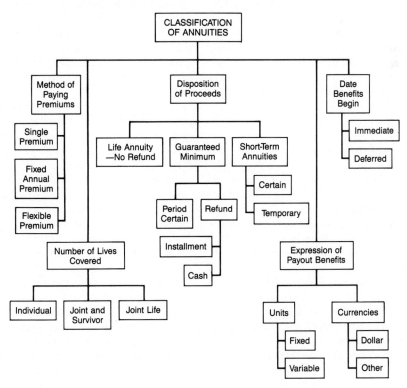

life annuity. The two most important types of joint-life contracts, the joint-life annuity and the joint and survivor annuity, are discussed later in this chapter.

2. *Method of premium payment.* Annuities may be purchased with *single premiums, fixed periodic premiums,* or *flexible periodic premiums.* Thus, a single-life annuity could be purchased with a lump sum accumulated through savings, inheritance, or other media, or an individual may choose to spread the payment over a specified period by paying periodic premiums.

3. *Time when income payments commence.* Annuities may also be classified as to whether the beginning point of income payments is deferred or immediate. An **immediate annuity** is one under which the first benefit payment is due one payment interval (monthly, annually, or other) from the date of purchase. The **deferred annuity,** on the other hand, may be purchased with either a single premium or a fixed or flexible periodic premium. Under a deferred life annuity, there must be a period longer than one benefit payment interval before benefit payments begin. The longer the deferred period, the more flexibility may be permitted in premium payments. Normally, a number of years elapses before benefit payments commence. The majority of individual deferred annuity contracts are sold on a flexible-premium basis.

4. *Disposition of proceeds.* Under this basis of classification, the method by which the annuity proceeds are distributed is considered, including whether there is a refund feature and the duration of the benefit payout period. This subject is discussed in the following section, regarding the nature of the insurer's obligation before and after the commencement of income payments.

5. *Units and currencies in which benefits are expressed.* Traditionally, annuity benefits have been expressed in fixed dollars. With the advent of the variable annuity (see below), the units in which payout benefits are expressed forms another basis of classification. Similarly, in recent years some

annuity benefits have been denominated in foreign currencies (see Figure 7–1).

Nature of Insurance Company's Obligation. This discussion is based on the classification of benefits payable in the event of death prior to or following the commencement of income payments under the contract—that is, during the accumulation period or the liquidation period.

1. *Accumulation period.* During the accumulation period of an annuity, the insurer is obligated to return all or a portion of the annuity cash value if the purchaser dies. Minimum required cash values are defined by law in most states but are equal to the contributions to date, less withdrawals and expenses, plus interest earnings. Some insurers also provide for a separate surrender charge, as discussed below.

2. *Liquidation period.* Regardless of the manner in which funds are accumulated, the amount of money necessary to provide a given amount and form of income starting at a stated age is the same, other things equal. Consequently, the following discussion of the nature of the company's obligation during the liquidation period is applicable to both immediate and deferred annuities, as well as to settlement options (discussed in Chapter 9).

Broadly, there are two classes of life annuity payouts: (1) **pure** and (2) **refund.** This discussion does not apply to **annuities certain,** where income payments are guaranteed and have no reference to life contingencies. The pure life annuity, frequently referred to as a **straight life annuity,** provides income payments that continue for as long as the annuitant lives, but *terminate upon the annuitant's death.* Upon the death of the annuitant, no matter how soon that may occur after the commencement of income, no refund is payable to the annuitant's estate or any beneficiary. Under this form of income, the entire purchase price is applied to provide income to the annuitant, no part of it paying for any refund benefit. Thus, the pure life annuity provides the maximum income per dollar of outlay. It should be pointed out, however, that at the younger ages, because of the high probability of survival, the difference in income between a pure life annuity and one with a refund feature is very small.

Regardless of questions of equity and technical soundness, most persons oppose placing a substantial sum of money into a contract that promises little or no return if they should die shortly after income payments commence. Therefore, companies permit annuitants to select options that have refund features if death occurs shortly after annuity payments have begun. In contrast to the pure life annuity, not all of the purchase price is used to provide income payments to the annuitant. Part of the purchase price is applied to meet the cost of guaranteeing a minimum amount of benefits, irrespective of whether the annuitant lives to receive them. Thus, for a given premium outlay, a smaller periodic income payment will be available under a refund life annuity than would be available under the pure life annuity form. The minimum benefit guarantee or refund feature may be stated either in terms of a guaranteed minimum number of payments or in terms of a refund of the purchase price (or some portion thereof) in the event of the annuitant's early death.

One class of life annuities with refund features is named, variously, "life annuity certain and continuous," "life annuity with installments certain," or "life annuity with minimum guaranteed return." This arrangement calls for a guaranteed number of monthly (or annual) payments to be made whether the annuitant lives or dies, with payments to continue for the whole of the annuitant's life if he or she should live beyond the guaranteed period. Contracts are usually written with payments guaranteed for 5, 10, 15, or 20 years. The size of the income payments from a given principal is smaller the longer the guarantee period.

There are two important forms of annuity incomes that promise to return all or a portion of the purchase price. The first form, the **installment refund annuity,** promises that if the annuitant dies before receiving income installments equal to the purchase price, the payments will be continued to a beneficiary until this amount has been paid. The second form, the **cash refund**

annuity, promises to pay, in a lump sum to the beneficiary, the difference, if any, between the purchase price of the annuity and the simple sum of the installment payments made prior to the death of the annuitant. The cash refund will provide somewhat less in absolute amount, since the insurance company loses the interest it would have earned had the balance been liquidated in installments. In either case, the payments to the annuitant continue as long as he or she lives, even after the guaranteed minimum benefits have been recovered.

It might be well at this point to compare the income that can be provided under some of the important forms of annuities for a given amount of principal sum. The figures in Table 7–1 are all based on the same rate basis. Variations are intended to show the impact that the form of annuity income and the age and sex (where permitted) of the annuitant have on the yield (in this case, monthly) available from a $1,000 principal sum.

It should be apparent from Table 7–1 that the cost of the refund feature is inconsequential at the younger ages but becomes quite expensive at the higher ages. It is not until about age 60 or 65 that any appreciable difference in income is given up to add a refund feature. Consequently, in general, it might be considered economically unsound to purchase a pure life annuity below age 60 or perhaps age 65.

Types of Annuity Contracts

There are actually a limited number of different annuity contracts, although individual company variations can be of great importance. Four categories of annuities are discussed below:

1. Flexible-premium deferred annuity
2. Single-premium deferred annuity
3. Joint and last-survivor annuity
4. Variable annuity

Flexible-Premium Deferred Annuity. The most significant individual annuity contract sold today is the **flexible-premium deferred annuity** (FPDA), also referred to as a **flexible-premium retirement annuity,** which is offered by a major-

TABLE 7-1. Immediate life annuity monthy incomes per $1,000
(nonparticipating)

Age Last Birthday	Pure		10 Years Certain and Continuous		Cash Refund	
	M	F	M	F	M	F
50	$ 5.00	$ 4.54	$4.91	$4.51	$4.68	$4.40
55	5.54	4.97	5.37	4.90	5.09	4.75
60	6.26	5.54	5.95	5.41	5.58	5.18
65	7.22	6.34	6.64	6.06	6.19	5.73
70	8.57	7.46	7.40	6.83	6.93	6.42
75	10.47	9.06	8.15	7.68	7.85	7.28
80	13.05	11.35	8.77	8.46	8.96	8.37

ity of companies. The contract provides for the accumulation of funds to be applied at some future time designated by the contract owner to supply an income for the annuitant.

The interest credited on annuity cash values is not taxable to the contract owner as long as it remains on deposit with the life insurance company. On liquidation, annuity payments are taxable as ordinary income to the extent that each payment represents previously untaxed income. Obviously, the tax-deferred nature of cash accumulations under annuities represents a significant privilege—especially for those in high marginal tax brackets—which is justified as an instrument for encouraging individuals to provide for their retirement needs. Tax-law changes made in 1982 and 1984 are intended to ensure that this privilege is not abused by imposing certain restrictions on withdrawals from annuities prior to retirement.[1]

FPDA contracts permit flexible contributions to be made as and when the owner desires, either monthly, yearly, or with some companies, as often or as infrequently as the owner desires. There is no set contribution amount or required payment frequency. Although a premium payment is not generally required each year for FPDA contracts, companies usually do establish a minimum acceptable payment level (e.g., $25 to $50) if a payment is to be made.

FPDA contracts have effectively supplanted an earlier product known as the **retirement annuity contract.** This contract provided for a fixed schedule of annual premiums and had high

loadings by today's standards. The product was not "unbundled," so that its internal functioning was not transparent. Few of these contracts are sold today.

The trend today is toward FPDA contracts that have little or no identifiable **front-end load,** just as is the case with the universal life (UL) policies. This has been brought about by the keen competition for consumers' savings dollars not only within the life insurance business but, more importantly, between the life insurance business and other financial institutions, such as banks, brokerage firms, savings and loan associations, and money market funds.

In a recent survey of 100 of the largest writers of FPDA, 49 had no identifiable front-end loads and an additional 35 had loads of under $50 per year. The other 16 companies' loads were expressed either as a percentage of each contribution (with the rate being higher for the first contract year) or as a percentage of the annuity fund balance.

In place of front loads, many insurers have adopted **back-end loads,** known as **surrender charges**—again analogous to the approach followed with UL and other policies. Provision is made within many FPDA contracts to assess a surrender charge whenever a cash withdrawal made in any year is in excess of a stipulated percentage (e.g., 10 percent) of the fund balance. If the withdrawal is less than the set percentage, no charge is levied.

The surrender charge percentage commonly decreases with duration. Thus, an insurer may provide that a surrender charge of 7 percent will be levied during the first contract year on all

[1]See Chapter 13 for details.

withdrawals in excess of 10 percent of the fund balance, with this rate decreasing 1 percent per year, thus grading to zero in contract year 8, and with no surrender charge thereafter. Surrender charge percentages and durations vary considerably, with some first-year charges as high as 25 percent but many with no surrender charges at all. Most fall within the range 6 to 10 percent for the first year. A few policies do not have either identifiable back-end or front-end loads.

FPDA contracts guarantee to credit interest at no lower than the contract guaranteed rate, which is usually within the range 3½ to 4½ percent. Although this percentage may seem low, it must be recognized that the guarantee is for the life of the annuitant and over a period of several decades, the guarantee could prove to be exceedingly valuable. For its part, the insurer would be foolish to guarantee high rates for such long durations. In any event, this type of long-term guarantee is not found in any other comparable savings media such as those offered by banks, savings and loan associations, or money market accounts.

The actual rate of interest credited at any time to the FPDA fund balance will be a function of the earnings rate of the insurer and its competitive position within the financial services marketplace. Currently, insurers are commonly crediting interest in the range 7 to 11 percent. These rates are subject to change by the insurer, and if the downward trend in interest rates (being experienced at the time this book was being written) continues, the preceding rates will decline.

Table 7-2 illustrates the operation of a hypothetical FPDA during the accumulation phase. This annuity credits 11 percent on the full premium payment; that is, it has no front-end load. It provides for a graded surrender charge of 7 percent in year 1 with a 1 percent per year decrease thereafter. The illustration shows both guaranteed (at 4 percent) and nonguaranteed projected values and the difference between the net surrender value and the cash value. A variable premium pattern is assumed. The reader should note that the cash values and surrender values are the same from contract year 8.

The amount of the retirement income provided by the FPDA is a function of the accumulated fund balance, the annuitant's sex (where permitted), and the age at which the contract

TABLE 7-2. Hypothetical flexible-premium deferred annuity accumulations

Contract Year	Premium Payment	Year-End Cash Values Based on:		Year-End Surrender Values Based on:	
		Guar. Rate (4%)	Current Rate (11%)	Guar. Rate (4%)	Current Rate (11%)
1	$ 2,000	$ 2,080	$ 2,220	$ 1,934	$ 2,065
2	2,000	3,923	4,684	3,688	4,403
3	1,000	5,120	6,309	4,864	5,994
4	1,000	6,365	8,114	6,110	7,789
5	500	7,139	9,561	6,925	9,274
6	0	7,425	10,613	7,277	10,401
7	0	7,722	11,780	7,645	11,662
8	0	8,031	13,076	8,031	13,076
9	10,000	18,752	25,614	18,752	25,614
10	5,000	24,702	33,982	24,702	33,982
11	0	25,690	37,720	25,690	37,720
12	0	26,718	41,869	26,718	41,869
13	300	28,099	46,808	28,099	46,808
14	493	29,735	52,504	29,735	52,504
15	0	30,925	58,279	30,925	58,279
16	2,000	34,242	66,910	34,242	66,910
17	0	35,611	74,270	35,611	74,270
18	5,000	42,236	87,989	42,236	87,989
19	8,000	52,245	106,548	52,245	106,548
20	15,000	69,935	134,919	69,935	134,919

owner elects to have payments commence. At that time, the usual range of benefit payout options is available with each providing for both a guaranteed minimum interest rate and a current rate.

As with UL policies, the purchaser of a FPDA can place undue emphasis on the stated current interest rate. The loading charges can be important. Thus, it is easily possible that a FPDA crediting 11.5 percent may not develop values as high as one crediting 11.0 percent because of the loading factor. In any event, one must exercise great prudence in interpreting results that show high interest rates (by historical standards) projected for many years or even decades into the future.

Single-Premium Deferred Annuity. The **single-premium deferred annuity** (SPDA), although in existence in theory and in reality with a few companies for many years, actually should be considered a new product because of the vastly increased number of insurers now selling the product and because of some features that distinguish the current version from its ancestors.

The SPDA is a model of simplicity. Its name is truly descriptive: It is a deferred annuity contract that is purchased with a single premium. As with the FPDA, a minimum stated rate of interest is guaranteed by contract to be paid throughout the duration of the contract, but most insurers pay competitive market rates. The rate actually credited is a function of the insurer's current investment earnings rate and its desired competitive posture in the market and is subject to change by the insurer.

The single premium is often unreduced by identifiable front-end loads. Provision is usually made for graded surrender charges, similar to those for FPDA, and for partial withdrawals with no surrender charges. SPDA contracts often have **bail-out provisions.** These provisions stipulate that if the interest rate actually credited to the SPDA fund falls below a set rate (often set at 1 to 3 percent below the current rate being credited), the contract owner may withdraw all funds without any surrender charge. This provision is valuable, but it should be noted that any such withdrawal could result in a tax surcharge,[2] and

if the insurer felt compelled to so reduce its credited interest rate, this probably would occur because overall market interest rates had fallen significantly, and therefore the contract owner may be hard-pressed to find comparable financial instruments in which to invest that credit a higher rate.

The sales of SPDA reached a peak in the early 1980s, were stable between 1982 and 1983, and have generally resumed growth since then. These 1982–1983 results were attributable to the 1982 and 1984 tax-law revisions, which discouraged the use of annuities for other than retirement-related purposes. Many wealthy persons were purchasing SPDAs simply to avoid having to pay income tax on the current earnings and would withdraw amounts from the annuity on a tax-free basis prior to retirement. Under previous tax law, withdrawals made before the annuity payouts actually began were treated as withdrawals of principal first and therefore were not subject to income tax to that extent.[3]

The SPDA can be an important element in a retirement program. As with all insurance contracts, it is important that the contract suit the needs of the client and that the insurer offering the product is reliable.

Joint and Last-Survivor Annuity. The **joint and last-survivor annuity** is finding increasing acceptance, primarily as an alternative income settlement form under individual life insurance and annuity contracts, and in private pension plans. It can be appealing since it provides that income payments continue for as long as *either* of two or more persons lives. Its most obvious use is for a husband and wife or other family relationships.

Since the annuity provides for payment until the *last* death among the covered lives, it will pay to a later date, on the average and is therefore, more expensive than other annuity forms. Stating it in another way, a given principal sum will provide less income under a joint and last-survivor form than under a single-life annuity form at either of the two ages.

The joint and survivorship form is usually offered on either a pure life basis or with a certain

---

[2] See Chapter 13.

[3] See Chapter 13.

number of installments guaranteed. In its usual form, the joint and last-survivor annuity continues the *same* income until the death of the *last survivor.* Most companies, however, offer a modified form that provides (assuming two covered lives) that the income will be reduced following the death of the first annuitant to two-thirds (or one-half, depending on the contract) of the original income. This contract (or option) is known as a **joint and two-thirds annuity** (or **joint and one-half**). Naturally, for a given amount of principal sum, the modified form will provide more income initially because of the later reduction.[4]

Another type of joint-life annuity is a contract that provides a specified amount of income for two or more persons named in the contract, with the income ceasing upon the *first* death among the covered lives. Although such a contract is relatively inexpensive, it has a very limited market.

The Variable Annuity.[5] **The variable annuity** contract provides benefits that vary directly with the investment experience of the assets that back the contract. Assets backing variable annuities, like those backing variable life policies, are maintained in a separate account and the investment results of this account are reflected directly in the variable annuity values. In contrast, the assets backing the products discussed earlier are those of the life insurer's general account.

The rationale for the creation of variable annuities was that they should offer, over the long run, protection against the debilitating effects of inflation on fixed incomes, such as that which would be provided by fixed annuities. The hope was and is that long-run returns on common stocks and other investments will keep pace with inflation—admittedly a hypothesis that remains to be proven.

Under a FPDA, SPDA, or other fixed (non-variable) annuities, the insurance company guarantees a minimum rate of interest to be credited

to the account during the accumulation period. In addition, a minimum amount of annuity payout per dollar accumulated is guaranteed. A variable annuity does not have these interest guarantees. The contract owner bears the investment risk and receives the return actually earned on invested assets, less charges assessed by the insurance company.

The general account of an insurance company is restricted by state laws to the type and quality of investments it may hold. Since these investments support liabilities for products with interest guarantees, they must offer safety of principal and a predictable income stream. Separate accounts have few, if any, investment restrictions. Income, gains, and losses on separate account assets are credited to or charged against the separate account. Income, gains, and losses on the rest of the company's business are kept apart from the separate account. Funds of variable annuity contract owners are held in the separate account, and the contract owners participate fully in the investment results.

State nonforfeiture laws require that most individual and certain group annuity contracts that allow contract owners the option of receiving a lump-sum settlement at some point in time (such as a stated contract maturity date or retirement) must allow a lump-sum settlement at *all* times. These laws and competitive pressures limit the amount by which the surrender value can be less than the full accumulated account value, as is evidenced from the discussion on FPDA.

1. *History of the variable annuity.* The College Retirement Equities Fund (CREF) provided the first variable annuity in the United States in 1952. The Arkansas and District of Columbia insurance departments were the first to regulate variable annuities. Three life insurance companies were organized in these states in the mid-1950s primarily to sell variable annuities: Participating Annuity Life Insurance Company (PALIC), founded in 1954 in Arkansas; Variable Annuity Life Insurance Company (VALIC), founded in 1955 in the District of Columbia; and Equity Annuity Life Insurance Company (EALIC), founded in 1956, also in D.C. The Prudential Insurance company was a pioneer in

---

[4]The joint and last-survivor form found in private pension plans commonly provides that the income is reduced *only* when the *employee* dies first.

[5]This area draws, in part, from Mary Jo Napoli, *"Variable Annuities," SOA Part 10 Study Note* (Itasca, Ill.: Society of Actuaries, 1985).

variable annuity research and worked with the state of New Jersey and the Securities and Exchange Commission (SEC) to develop a viable regulatory environment.

Companies temporarily stopped issuing variable annuities in 1959 when the Supreme Court ruled in a landmark decison, *SEC v. VALIC,* that variable annuities were subject to federal securities regulation.[6] The companies resumed issuing annuities after attaining the necessary registered status.

New state separate account and variable annuity statutes were enacted from the late 1950s to the early 1970s. During this time period the mortality and expense guarantees in variable annuities were improved.

2. *Nature of the variable annuity.* Variable annuity premiums paid to the insurance company are placed in a special "variable annuity account." Each year the premiums, after deduction for expenses, are applied to purchase accumulation units in the account, the number of units depending on the current value of a unit. Thus, if each unit, based on current investment results, is valued at $10, a premium of $100 after expenses will purchase 10 units the following year. If the value of a unit is changed, the level premium of $100 would purchase more or less than 10 units. This procedure would continue until the maturity of the contract. At that time, the accumulated total number of units credited may be applied, according to actuarial principles and based on the current valuation of a unit, to convert credited units to a retirement income of so many units, to be valued annually for the lifetime of the annuitant.

Instead of providing for the payment each month of a *fixed number of dollars,* the variable annuity may therefore, provide for the payment each month or year of the current value of a *fixed number of annuity units.* Thus, the dollar amount of each payment would depend on the dollar value of an annuity unit when the payment is made. The valuation assigned to a unit would depend upon the investment results of the special account. For example, if an annuitant were entitled to a pay-

[6]*Securities and Exchange Commission v. VALIC,* 359 U.S. 65 (1959).

ment of 100 annuity units each month, and the dollar values of an annuity unit for three consecutive months were $10.20, $9.90, and $10.10, the annuitant would receive an income for these months of $1,020.00, $990.00, and $1,010.00.

Variable annuities may be purchased on a FPDA, SPDA, or immediate annuity basis. In all cases, the usual range of payout options is available and product expenses and charges are identified.

3. *Regulation of variable annuities.* As a "security," variable annuities are subject to the same federal laws as variable life, as discussed in Chapter 5. Thus, requirements similar to or identical with those imposed on variable life insurance apply to variable annuities with respect to disclosure, sales loads, registration and financial standards, agent licensing, as well as others.

State laws and regulations on variable annuities are not uniform, although many states have followed the procedures included in the 1979 NAIC **Model Variable Annuity Regulation.** This regulation provides guidelines for separate account investments and requires that variable annuity contracts state clearly the essential elements of the procedure for determining the amount of the variable benefits. Other policy standards are laid down, including a requirement that annual status reports be mailed to the contract owner.

Uses and Limitations of Annuities

Annuities can be exceedingly useful in both the tax-qualified and nonqualified markets. The annuitant has the benefit of the high-quality investment management offered by insurers. This can be especially important for older persons who may desire to be freed of investment cares and management.

Annuitants (at retirement age) would enjoy monthly incomes equal to or significantly higher than those obtainable through the customary channels of conservative investment if they are willing to have the principal liquidated. Each year, the company would pay to the annuitant the current income on his or her investment plus a portion of the investment itself. If the buyer exercised care in the purchase decision, the net return on his or her annuity should prove competitive with other investments of comparable quality. When tax benefits are considered, the net return often will exceed that of comparable savings media.

The large income is certain, and the annuitant may spend it without fear. It will last as long as life lasts. In the absence of an annuity, there is always the danger of spending too much or too little. But with the annuity, the scale of spending is not only increased but is definite in amount.

Uses in Tax-Qualified Markets.   Annuities are used as funding vehicles for retirement plans established under various sections of the Internal Revenue Code (IRC) which allow contributions to be excluded from the taxable income of the employee, the employer, or both. These plans differ greatly and it is beyond the scope of this section to analyze comprehensively all of these features. Below are brief descriptions of the most common types of such plans. A more complete description of these appears in Chapter 28.

Annuities can be used to fund **pension** and **profit-sharing plans** qualified under IRC Section 401 for corporations and self-employed individuals. Annuities are also used with plans qualified under Section 403(b) of the IRC. These plans, commonly referred to as **TDA** (tax-deferred annuity) or **TSA** (tax-sheltered annuity) plans, are available to employees of public educational institutions and of certain tax-exempt organizations. Up to a specified limit, contributions to the plan, either by the employer or by the employee through a voluntary salary reduction agreement, are excludable from the employee's taxable income. Employees' rights under such plans are nonforfeitable and must be nontransferrable. Prior to enactment of the Tax Reform Act of 1986 (TRA '86), pre-retirement withdrawals could be made at any time without penalty. TRA '86 also made several changes with respect to TDA-backed loans, the effects of which are to curtail their availability. Such loans formerly were a source of flexibility for employees.

Annuities are also used to fund **public employee deferred compensation** plans. These plans are qualified under IRC Section 457 and may be established for persons who perform services for states, political subdivisions of states, agencies or instrumentalities of states or political subdivisions of states, and certain rural electric cooperatives.

For tax years after 1986, individuals who are not active participants in employer-sponsored retirements plans and those who are active participants but whose adjusted gross incomes do not exceed $25,000 (single return) or $40,000 (joint return) can make a contribution of up to $2,000 of earned compensation to an **Individual Retirement Account** (IRA). Interest credited to IRAs accrues on a tax deferred basis. Individuals not meeting the above qualification requirements still may contribute to an IRA but contributions are not tax deductible. Annuities can be used to fund IRAs.

Annuities can also be useful in a so-called **401(k) plan.** This is a type of profit-sharing plan established by an employer under which up to three types of contributions are permitted: employee contributions, employee contributions from after-tax income, and employee salary reduction ("elective") contributions. Neither employer nor elective contributions are included in the employee's taxable income. Further, the employer may deduct both of these from taxable income, up to a limit.

Uses in Nonqualified Markets.   Both annuities and life insurance policies have been used to fund "unfunded" **deferred compensation plans.** Under such arrangements, private employers enter into agreements under which an employee agrees to defer the receipt of current compensation until a later date. Employees may defer up to 100 percent of compensation, or the plans may be limited to providing benefits in excess of those permitted under tax-qualified plans. These plans generally are limited to a select group of highly compensated employees. These plans are not explicitly provided for in the Code, but are supported by case law and revenue rulings.

The employer owns and controls the deferred amounts. The employee has only a contractual right to a benefit at a later date. The term "unfunded" means that no funds are set aside in which the employee has a nonforfeitable right. However, as a practical matter most employers have informally funded such agreements through the purchase of annuity or life insurance contracts or other investments. The employee is not taxed on compensation deferred, but the employer does not receive a tax deduction until benefits are paid under the plan. In general, the employee must specify the time and manner for the payment of benefits before the deferred compensation is earned.[7] Prior to TRA '86, interest credited to such corporate-owned annuities was tax deferred. TRA '86 eliminated this treatment.

Individuals purchase thousands of annuities that are not related to employment nor qualified under any plan for deductibility of contributions. Such annuities have the important tax advantage of deferring tax on investment earnings while providing contemporary investment returns. Even though annuity benefits do not escape taxation wholly, the fact that tax is deferred for several years means that the contract owner—not the government—has the use of the money. The effect of this is that the great power of compounding at before-tax rates yields a significantly larger sum than would otherwise be the case. Moreover, even if that sum were subject to immediate and full taxation later, the net result remains strongly in favor of the tax-deferred instrument.

SPECIAL-PURPOSE LIFE INSURANCE POLICIES

In addition to the life insurance and annuity contracts already discussed, life insurance companies issue a wide variety of special policies and policy combinations. These special forms are based on the same principles already discussed, differing only in that they present a combination designed to serve a particular market segment. Most of these contracts were developed for merchandising purposes and do not offer the same flexibility as do the more common forms of contracts. The amount of insurance protection sold under these contracts is small in proportion to the total sold each year in the United States.

Family Policy or Rider

Most companies issue a policy or, more commonly, a rider that insures all or selected members of the family in one contract, commonly called a **family policy** or **family rider.** When issued as a policy, it provides whole life insurance on the father or the mother, designated as the principal insured, with a premium based on his or her age. Term insurance is generally provided on the wife and children or on the father and children where the wife is the principal insured. When coverage is issued as a rider, no underlying insurance is provided through the rider on the principal's insured's life. The policy to which the rider is attached provides the basic coverage, with the net result possibly being the same as the family policy.

Coverage on the spouse may be a stated amount or vary in amount with age and is usually term insurance. Insurance on the children is term for a fixed amount. All children living with the family are covered, even if adopted or born *after* the policy is issued. Coverage is afforded children over a few days old (e.g., 15 days) and under a stated age, usually 18. The children's term insurance coverage expires at a stated age, such as 18, 21, or 25, and is usually convertible to any whole life plan of insurance without evidence of insurability (and often for up to five times the amount of expiring term insurance). If the principal insured dies, the insurance on the spouse and children usually becomes paid up.

A unit of coverage under the policy may consist of $5,000 whole life on the principal insured, $1,000 or $1,500 whole life or term on the spouse, and $1,000 term on each child. When issued as a rider, a certain number of units of coverage on the spouse's life is purchased where a unit might provide $5,000 term to age 65 coverage on the spouse and $1,000 of term insurance on each child.

The premium does not change on the inclusion of additional children (i.e., via birth or adoption). The premium for the children's coverage is based on an average number of children, but in the event of the spouse's death prior to the insured's, the insurance is paid to his or her beneficiary.

---

[7]See Chapter 15 for details of deferred compensation plans.

Family Maintenance Policy or Rider

The **family maintenance policy** or rider is similar to the family income rider discusssed in Chapter 4. The distinguishing feature of the family maintenance policy or rider is that if the insured dies during a specified period (e.g., 20 years), income payments are payable for a full 20 years regardless of the point within the specified period at which the insured dies. In other respects, the family maintenance policy or rider provides the same benefits as the family income rider. Just as in the family income policy, if the insured dies after the specified period has expired, only the face amount of the underlying policy is payable.

The family maintenance policy is a combination of whole life insurance and level term insurance. Interest on the proceeds of the underlying whole life insurance serves to reduce the amount of term insurance necessary. Today, the family maintenance policy as such is sold by relatively few companies.

Reversionary Annuity

The **revisionary annuity** furnishes an income benefit. Also referred to as a survivorship annuity, the policy is life insurance combined with an annuity agreement. It provides that if the beneficiary should outlive the insured, the beneficiary will receive a *predetermined* income for life, regardless of his or her age at the insured's death. In the event the beneficiary predeceases the insured, however, the contract terminates and no further premiums or benefits are payable.

The size of a life income is normally a function of the age of the beneficiary at the death of the insured and cannot be known beforehand. The reversionary annuity, on the other hand, establishes a set amount prior to the insured's death. The policy premium, which is based on the joint probability of death of the insured and the beneficiary, would be relatively low if the policy were taken out when the insured is young and the beneficiary is old. For this reason, the policy can be attractive when a child desires to protect an aged parent or other aged relative.

A modified form of reversionary annuity, the **life income policy,** differs only in that a minimum number of payments is guaranteed

following the insured's death, irrespective of whether the beneficiary is alive to receive them. For the guaranteed benefits, the beneficiary may be changed, or a cash surrender value will be payable if the contract is discontinued.

Juvenile Insurance

Juvenile insurance is insurance written on the lives of children from the age of 1 day to 14 or 15 years of age, issued on the application of a parent or other person responsible for the support of the child. In the past, most companies and some states limited the amount of insurance that could be written on the lives of young children. This is less common today.

Most companies permit the purchase of any reasonable amount of life insurance on a child's life subject to underwriting requirements as to perceived need and adequacy of coverage on parent's and children's lives. Some companies will insure a child from the age of one day, but many require that the child be at least one month old. Because the insured under a juvenile policy is a minor, control of the policy is usually vested in the applicant (usually a parent) until the child attains age 18 or the prior death of the applicant. Many companies will issue regular polices to minors on their own application, provided that they are above the juvenile age limit set by the particular state involved.

Provision can be made in all forms of juvenile insurance for the waiver of premium payments in the event of the death or total disability of the person responsible for the payment of premiums (usually the parent). This **payor benefit,** when added to the juvenile policy, provides that premiums will be waived until the insured (the child) attains a specified age, usually 25, or the paid-up date of the contract, whichever is earlier, in the event the premium payor dies or becomes disabled. Evidence of insurability must be furnished by the premium payor before the clause can be attached to a contract.

Juvenile insurance is sold to provide funds (1) for last-illness and funeral expenses, (2) for college education, (3) to start a "permanent" insurance program for a child at a low premium rate, and (4) to assure that a child will have some life insurance even if he or she later becomes uninsurable. Whether any of these reasons is convincing to a parent or grandparent is a matter of judgment. It can be observed, however, that often inadequate insurance coverage exists on the parents' lives and that the primary objective should be to insure fully against loss of income brought about by the death of the breadwinners. The death of a child, as sad as it is, rarely causes major financial loss to the family and, in such circumstances, life insurance on a child's life is of questionable need at best.

Industrial Life Insurance

At one time, **industrial life insurance** was the backbone of the U.S. life insurance industry. It was originally designed for low-income families who could not afford the amounts of protection and premium payments associated with ordinary life and individual health insurance. Industrial life insurance policies are issued for small amounts, usually less than $1,000, and the premiums generally are paid weekly or monthly to an agent who calls at the policyowner's home. Total industrial life insurance coverage in the United States was $28.2 billion at the end of 1985, a *decrease of* $1.9 billion during the year. The average-size industrial life insurance policy in force as of 1985 was $640.[8]

Industrial insurance represented 0.5 percent of all legal reserve life insurance in force at the end of 1985, compared with 4.4 percent two decades before.[9] The relative decline in industrial insurance has been due largely to the fact that industrial life insurance was legislatively defined many years ago and that amounts of life insurance under $1,000 provide little economic security in today's environment and are quite costly per unit of coverage. Other important factors have been the rapid expansion of group insurance, the significant growth in the survivorship benefits under Social Security, and the adverse publicity given industrial insurance.

In recent years, industrial life insurance and **monthly debit ordinary** (MDO) have come to be known as **home service life insurance.** Both of these types of individual policies are serviced by agents who call at the policyowner's home to collect the premiums. The volume of home service insurance in force declined for the third year in a row. Total home service insurance in force at the end of 1985 was $147.6 billion, 2.1 percent of all life insurance in force with U.S. life companies.[10]

Comparison with Other Forms of Life Insurance. Although industrial life insurance is a modified form of ordinary, level-premium life insurance and is written by companies that also write ordinary life insurance, it has certain fundamental characteristics that distinguish it from all other forms of insurance. Two of these distinguishing characteristics—often, weekly payment of premiums and home collection —were mentioned above. These two characteristics account for the much higher cost of industrial insurance.

Another key difference is that the law with respect to industrial life insurance policy provisions is different from that applicable to other forms of individual insurance. In general, those provisions are intended to permit the insurer to recognize the need for simplified procedures and to avoid administrative complications. For example, industrial policies contain a **facility of payment** clause whereby if the beneficiary fails to make claim under a policy within a specific period (e.g., 30 or 60 days) after the death of the insured, as well as under other specified circumstances, the *insurer* may make payment to anyone who by blood or marriage or otherwise appears to be equitably entitled to the benefit. Other important differences also exist.[11]

Uses and Limitations of Industrial Insurance. Whether a given low-income person should purchase an industrial insurance policy is rapidly

[8]*1986 Life Insurance Fact Book,* (Washington, D.C.: American Council of Life Insurance), p. 33.

[9]*1986 Fact Book,* p. 34. Virtually all companies writing a significant volume of industrial life insurance also write ordinary insurance. Industrial agents write both forms of insurance and are usually referred to as **combination agents.** It is also quite common to refer to such companies as **combination companies.**

[10]*1986 Fact Book,* p. 14.

[11]See Robert A. Marshall and Eli A. Zubay, *The Debit System of Marketing Life and Health Insurance* (Englewood Cliffs, N.J.: Prentice-Hall, Inc., 1975).

becoming a moot question, as sales continue to dwindle and insurers continue to withdraw from writing this class of life insurance. The continuing decline of industrial insurance seems assured in view of inflation, the legislative definition of industrial life insurance, and numerous other factors.

Those who consider purchasing weekly-premium industrial insurance would be better off financially in purchasing an MDO or a regular ordinary policy. Under MDO policies, premiums are collected monthly, often at the policyowner's home. All other provisions of an MDO policy are the same as a "premium notice" ordinary policy.

Industrial insurance has been the focus of much public concern and debate.[12] Problems alleged to exist with industrial insurance have not been limited to the high cost of benefits compared to other forms of insurance but have also included high lapse rates, unfair contract provisions, overloading (the practice of selling to a person more policies than he or she can afford), churning of policies (the practice of repeatedly selling to a person new policies to replace old policies), misleading and high-pressure sales tactics, and exorbitant profits. While acknowledging that some problems exist, particularly with the industrial product, industry spokespersons nonetheless have forcefully defended the home service system of marketing.

That industrial life insurance is expensive cannot and is not denied. The underlying public policy question regarding this class of insurance is whether the expense factor in premiums is so high in relation to benefits provided that the sale of industrial policies should not be permitted. At least one state (New York) has effectively prohibited the sale of industrial life insurance because of this and other problems. The home service system of marketing should be distinguished, however, from the industrial product since regular ordinary life and health insurance and property and liability insurance products are also distributed through this system.[13]

[12]See, for example, Elizabeth D. Laporte, *Life Insurance Sold to the Poor: Industrial and Other Debit Products* (Washington, D. C.: Office of Policy Planning, Federal Trade Commission, January 1979). See also *Life Insurers Conference Response to the Elizabeth Laporte Report* (Richmond, Va.: Life Insurers Conference, March 1979).

[13]See Chapter 30.

OPTIONAL BENEFITS AND RIDERS

The practice of adding benefits to appropriate **riders** permits flexibility in adapting basic plans to individual needs. Several such common riders are discussed below.

Disability Benefit

It is quite common to attach riders to a life insurance contract that provide certain benefits in the event of total and permanent disability. The two most common disability benefits are (1) **waiver of premium** and (2) **disability income.** The definition of disability is exceedingly important and usually is the same for both waiver of premium and disability income benefits.

Definition of Disability. Under the disability clauses in life insurance policies, the risk covered pertains to total and permanent disability. Although phraseology varies greatly, the customary wording of the clause declares the policyowner to be entitled to the benefits promised when the insured's illness or injury results in his or her *total and permanent* disability.

As explained in more detail in Chapter 17, the word *total* proved difficult to interpret legally, and regardless of the exact language used, the interpretation given the clause by most companies today contemplates all cases where the insured is unable to pursue his or her own occupation or any job for which he or she is reasonably suited by education, training, and experience.

Similarly, there has been doubt as to the meaning of the word *permanent.* The problem, however, is usually settled by the companies themselves, in that the clause specifies that total disability lasting continuously for a stated waiting period shall be presumed to be permanent until recovery.

Waiver of Premium. Almost all companies offer a waiver-of-premium benefit. Sometimes the price for the benefit is included in the overall policy premium, but more often the waiver-of-premium provision is added to the life insurance contract for a small extra premium. It provides that in the event the insured becomes totally and permanently disabled before age 60 or 65, premiums on the contract will be waived during the continuance of disability beyond a specified waiting period, customarily six months. The operation of the contract continues just as if the policyowner were paying the premiums. Thus, dividends continue to be paid on participating policies, cash values (if any) continue to increase, loans may be secured, and so on.

It should be noted that all premiums are waived during disability, not just those falling due after the expiration of the waiting period. This is different from the case in disability income insurance and in most waiver-of-premium provisions in individual health insurance policies. Most companies require six months of continuous disability before the waiver-of-premium benefit takes effect. As long as disability commences during the period of coverage, all premiums and/or charges are waived while it continues, or as otherwise specified in the contract. Usually, there is a maximum age when a covered disability can start, frequently age 65, and there would be an automatic limitation if the policy is a limited pay plan or if it expires or matures prior to the customary age limitation.

Disability Income. Most companies providing disability income benefits by rider pay monthly 1 percent of the face of the policy ($10 per month per $1,000).[14] Many companies limit the maximum monthly income they will issue to some stated figure, such as $1,000, with a further limit on the amount the company will participate in within all companies. The latter limit may range up to $2,000 or more, with an additional limit frequently imposed, based on a percentage of net earned income. The majority consider six months' total disability as permanent and commence payments at the end of the sixth month. This is really the equivalent of a six-month elimination period with a one-month retroactive payment. Some companies impose a four-month waiting period, but the practice stated above is the most common.

Premiums on both the base policy and the

[14]At least two companies issue a $20 benefit, one of which reduces to $10 after age 60.

disability income rider are waived during a period of covered disability. Dividends are paid as usual, and in other respects the basic life contract continues as though no disability had occurred. Should the insured recover, income payments will cease, and premiums becoming due thereafter must be paid.

Accidental Death Benefit

An **accidental death benefit** clause or rider (sometimes called **double indemnity**) may be added to most life insurance contracts. It provides that double or triple the face amount of insurance is payable if the death of the insured is caused by an accident.

From an economic standpoint, there is no reason why double or triple the policy face amount should be paid in the event of death from accident, as compared with death from other causes. The loss to the family is equally great irrespective of cause of death. Moreover, the likelihood of an accidental death is, with respect to most persons, much less than the likelihood of death from other causes. The clause has value, of course, and its price is comparatively low, due to the relatively low probability of loss. This small premium, coupled with the belief by most persons that if they die soon, the cause of death will be an accident, are probably the main reasons for its appeal.

Definition of Accidental Death. A typical clause includes the following definition of accidental death: "Death resulting from bodily injury effected solely through external, violent, and accidental means independently and exclusively of all other causes, with death occurring within 90 days after such injury."

The expression *accidental means* insists that both the *cause* and *result* of the death must be accidental. For example, if death occurs as a result of the insured's intentionally jumping from a moving vehicle, the results may be accidental, but the means are not accidental. Death caused by others, such as muggers and robbers, although intentional as to such other person would be interpreted as accidental means under the clause. The original intention of such provisions was to limit the coverage to deaths that were purely and entirely accidental.

Exclusions. Certain causes of death (even where the causes and results are accidental) are excluded by the accidental death benefit provision. These exclusions fall into five classes: (1) deaths resulting from certain illegal activities; (2) deaths where an accident was involved but where illness, disease, or mental infirmity was also involved; (3) deaths from certain specified causes where considerable doubt may exist about the accidental character of the death; (4) deaths resulting from war; and (5) deaths resulting from aviation, except passenger travel on scheduled airlines. The rather numerous exclusions in the accidental death benefit clause indicate the practical difficulties inherent in this form of coverage.

Time and Age Limits. To be covered, a death must occur within 90 days of an accident. The purpose of this restriction is to assure, reasonably, that the accident is the sole cause of death. In general, the time limitations are enforced, although some serious problems can be created, with some courts holding that the 90-day requirement need not be strictly applied.

Accidental death coverage is usually limited to age 60, 65, or, in a few cases, 70. The majority of companies grade their premium charges by age at issue, and a number of companies now offer multiple indemnity (two, three, or more times the face amount) coverage.

Guaranteed Insurability Option

One of the problems faced by young individuals just starting their careers is a combination of limited income and a growing future need for life insurance protection as their life cycle evolves. This problem is highlighted in Chapter 12. The **guaranteed insurability option** (GIO) was developed to permit young individuals to be certain they would be able to purchase additional insurance as they grew older, regardless of their "insurability." This rider, also known as the **additional purchase option,** permits an insured to purchase additional amounts of insurance at stated intervals without providing evidence of insur-

ability. The usual rider gives the insured the *option* of purchasing additional insurance at three-year intervals provided that the insured has not attained a specified age, the most common being age 40. "Special" option dates may be provided for such life events as birth or adoption of a child and marriage.

In most cases, the amount of the additional insurance is limited to a multiple of the face amount of the basic policy or an amount stipulated in the policy for the additional purchase option, whichever is smaller. Although the maximum amount of each option was originally $10,000, a number of companies now offer up to $50,000 or more per option date. The option requires an extra premium that is based on the company's estimate of the extra mortality that will be experienced on policies issued without evidence of insurability. The premium is payable to the last option date and, for the insured, is the cost of insuring his or her insurability.

For purposes of illustration, assume that the owner/insured purchases a $10,000 ordinary life policy at age 21 and that the guaranteed insurability option is a part of the policy. Under this option, the company agrees to issue, without evidence of insurability, and on the owner/insured's request, an additional policy on his or her life at each option date. The customary option dates would occur at ages 25, 28, 31, 34, 37, and 40. So if the insured desires, he or she could add $10,000 insurance at each of these six dates, despite having become uninsurable. This could result in as much as $60,000 coverage in addition to the original policy of $10,000.

Although potentially beneficial, the GIO is not as flexible as one might like. It permits the exercise of the options at specified dates only, provides additional protection of relatively low amounts (for most companies), and requires the purchase of an additional insurance policy with attendant policy fees and front-end loads (although many companies now permit internal policy increases in face amounts via the GIO, such as with universal life policies). Although admittedly complex to devise, price, and administer, insurers could provide a useful service by devising a pure guaranteed insurability rider *and* policy with greater flexibility.

Cost-of-Living Rider

The cost-of-living (COL) rider has already been discussed in connection with increasing term life insurance (Chapter 4) and with flexible premium life insurance. It is, therefore, sufficient merely to recall that this feature can usually be added as a supplemental benefit to most forms of life insurance. It can be useful where one's needs for life insurance are expected to increase over time in approximately the same proportion as changes in the cost of living.

Although for many persons, the need for life insurance protection may increase, it will not normally increase in proportion to COL increases. This aspect should be examined carefully.

Other Insureds Rider

Another optional benefit that sometimes can be useful is a rider than provides life insurance coverage on additional insureds. This rider is most frequently used to insure other family members, usually the spouse and/or children. If the rider insures only the children, it is often referred to as a children's rider; otherwise, it is referred to as a family rider (see "Family Policy or Rider" earlier in this chapter).

Chapter 8

The Life Insurance Contract: I

INTRODUCTION

This and the following chapter are intended to provide a basic understanding of the life insurance contract as a legal document and to provide some basics relative to certain noncost aspects of life insurance evaluation. As will be seen, life insurance contracts are sound, flexible legal instruments.

Dual Nature of Cash Value Contracts

All cash value life insurance policies can be viewed as being made up of a savings or investment element and a complementary amount of pure life insurance, such that the total equals the policy death benefit.[1] Although the central purpose of the contract is insurance protection, the contract also provides auxiliary rights that are available to the policyowner if he or she wishes to alter the original arrangement. Many of these stem from the premium payment plan, wherein the policyowner pays more than the pure cost of current insurance protection to permit accumulation of a fund against the rising cost of mortality

[1]See Chapter 2.

in later years when the actual premium paid alone would be insufficient.

Within fixed-premium life insurance contracts, the so-called savings element is not caused by a desire to set aside savings as in a savings bank, but is rather a means of saving the insured from a loss of protection that would result if annual premiums reached impossibly high levels in later years. Notwithstanding the original intent, the presence of this savings element naturally led to increasing emphasis on the lifetime features of such policies.[2] The values built up *have* actually been "saved" by the policyowner. With the introduction of a nonforfeiture provision, the dual nature of the cash value life insurance contract emerged, and the so-called prematurity rights have continued to be enlarged and emphasized. Universal life policies, with their clearly separate cash value element, have simply heightened this awareness.

The contract provisions relating to nonforfeiture, assignment, and policy loans arise essentially because of the savings aspect of life insurance contracts. In addition, the savings element

[2]But see *The Nature of the Whole Life Contract* (New York: Institute of Life Insurance, June 1974). This concept of the dual nature of the whole life contract has led to consumer confusion.

may be applied under the settlement options to provide retirement income to the insured and/or other beneficiaries. The savings element in cash value life insurance permits individuals to save, within the limits of the premium payments provision, through their policies and utilize the investment services of the life insurance company. The point here is that although the basic purpose of the life insurance contract is to *provide a fund at the death of the insured,* the prematurity rights of the policy have become of increasing importance.

Statutory Control over Policy Provisions

Although there is no statutory standard policy, life insurance contract provisions are subject to considerable state control and regulation. This involves the requirements that (1) no policy form may be used until approved by the state insurance department, and (2) policies must contain certain standard provisions, as specified in the insurance law.[3] In general, the statutes do not prescribe the exact wording to be used for these standard provisions; rather, they stipulate that actual policy wording must be at least as favorable as that of the statute. Provisions more favorable to the insured may be and are used.

The standard provisions generally required by the various states include those relative to (1) the entire contract clause, (2) the incontestable clause, (3) the grace period, (4) reinstatement, (5) nonforfeiture provision, (6) policy loans, (7) annual dividends, (8) misstatement of age and sex, (9) settlement options, and (10) deferment of loan and cash value payments. These and other provisions are discussed below.

Individual states may have other relevant regulations that relate to the policy contract or its terms. New York, for example, expressly prohibits any exclusion from liability for death except for those set forth in the law.[4] Many states require that

each policy form be identified by a code number and that a brief description of the policy be placed at the bottom of the first page (e.g., "whole life with premiums payable for life").

Life and health insurance policies are required to be written in simplified language in two-thirds of the states, including New York. Most of these laws and regulations are based on the **Life and Health Insurance Policy Language Simplification Model Act** of the National Association of Insurance Commissioners (NAIC). The laws and regulations require that policy language meets a readability ease test,[5] and that policies be printed in a minimum type size, with an accompanying table of contents (or index).

Because of the expense of maintaining a different policy form for use in each state, companies attempt to produce contracts that meet the requirements of all or substantially all states in which they do business. Thus, in practice, a New York requirement will have an effect on policies issued in other states by New York–licensed companies. Occasionally, conflicting state requirements or company preferences will cause the use of special policy forms or modification by endorsing the regular forms in particular states.

A host of provisions make up life insurance contracts. Some are included to protect the policyowner (e.g., grace period to prevent inadvertant lapse), some are included to make the policy more flexible from the standpoint of the policyowner (e.g., clauses permitting a change of beneficiary), and some are included to protect the company (e.g., clauses excluding payment if the insured commits suicide within a certain time period).

Although some provisions can be viewed as protecting both the company and the policyowner, the discussion of contract provisions in this and the following chapter is organized on the foregoing pattern. It will also include a brief review of the law pertaining to the agent.

---

[3] Not every state requires standard provisions as a matter of law. For example, Missouri and Connecticut have no statutory required provisions, although Connecticut has adopted some standard provisions by regulation.

[4] Permissive exclusions: (1) war clause; (2) suicide clause, limited to two years; (3) aviation exclusion clause, unlimited; and (4) an occupational or residence exclusion, limited to two years. New York Law, §155(2).

[5] The Flesch readability test is usually used in these laws. The laws require policies to attain a certain minimum readability score. See Rudolph Franz Flesch, *The Art of Readable Writing with the Flesch Readability Formula,* 25th ed. (New York: Harper & Row, Publishers, Inc., 1974).

THE POLICY AS A CONTRACT

A life insurance policy is a contract and must therefore conform to the rules governing general contract law. Before examining these basic rules as they apply to life insurance contracts, it should be helpful to review the characteristics that distinguish insurance contracts from many others. These characteristics underlie the distinctive judicial interpretations accorded life insurance contracts.

Distinguishing Characteristics of Life Insurance Contracts

First, the insurance contract is one of the **utmost good faith**—that is, each party is entitled to rely in good faith upon the representations of the other and each is under an obligation not to attempt to deceive or withhold material information from the other. The rule of *caveat emptor*[6] does not generally apply. The company must depend to a great extent on the statements of prospective owners/insureds in assessing their acceptability for insurance, and the buyer must rely on the good faith of the insurer because the insurance contract is intricate and highly technical.

The life insurance contract is characterized as being one of **adhesion.** This means that its terms and provisions are fixed by the insurer and, with minor exceptions, must be accepted or rejected *en totale* by the prospective buyer. The fact that the contract is highly specialized and technical in nature also prevents it from being a bargaining contract. As a result, the courts have held that any ambiguities or unclear elements in the contract will be construed in favor of the party—the policyowner—not participating in the construction of the contract wording.

The life insurance contract is not a contract of indemnity, as are most other insurance contracts. Under a contract of indemnity, the insured is never entitled to profit by reason of the insurance. The insurer, at most, returns the insured to the same financial position that he or she would have been in had no loss occurred. Under a life insurance contract, the insurer promises to pay

a definite sum of money, which does not purport necessarily to represent a measure of the loss. It is a **valued policy.** The rules relating to the insurable interest discussed below reflect this characteristic.[7]

The contract is **conditional** in that the obligation of the insurer to pay a claim depends upon the performance of certain acts, such as the payment of premiums and the furnishing of proof of death.

In addition, the life insurance contract is **unilateral** in nature. Only one party, the insurer, gives a legally enforceable promise. The owner of the contract makes no promise to make premium payments, but if he or she chooses to pay them in a timely manner, the insurer is bound to accept them and meet its obligations under the contract.

Finally, the life insurance contract is classified as **aleatory,** as opposed to commutative. In a commutative contract, there is an exchange involving approximately equivalent values, whereas an aleatory contract involves the element of chance, and one party may receive more in value than the other. This important distinction is discussed further below.

Formation of the Life Insurance Contract

The agreement between a life insurance company and a person seeking insurance must meet all the requirements prescribed by law for the formation of a valid contract. For any contract to be valid, four requirements must be met: (1) there must be an agreement based on an offer made by one of the parties to the contract and the acceptance of that offer by the other party on the same terms; (2) the parties to the contract must be legally capable of making a contract; (3) there must be a valid consideration; and (4) the purpose of the agreement must be lawful.[8] A life

---

[6]"Let the buyer beware."

[7]It should be noted, however, that in cases where an individual is insured for business purposes, the extent of the applicant's possible loss in the event of the insured's death is a definite factor in assessing insurability.

[8]Some contracts have to be in a particular *form* to be binding on the parties. New York, Georgia, and many other states require life insurance contracts to be in writing. The states, also generally, require the filing of policy forms with their insurance departments for approval, so that for all practical purposes, policies have to be in writing in every state.

insurance policy is a contract and must therefore conform to these requirements.

Capacity of the Parties. The parties to a contract must have the legal capacity to contract. If the insurance company is licensed to transact business in the state under consideration, and otherwise complies with the state insurance code, its capacity to contract is clear. Where the insurer is incompetent by reason of noncompliance or incomplete compliance with the requirements of the state in which the contract is executed, the question of the validity of the contract and the respective rights of the parties has not been uniformly decided. In some states the contract may be void entirely. In others it may be voidable; that is, enforceable only at the option of the innocent party. In the majority of states, however, the execution of the contract is penalized rather than prohibited and remains binding on both parties. The policyowner is even able to sue a nonadmitted insurer in the state courts where the policyowner resides, under the so-called Long Arm Statute.[9]

In connection with the legal capacity of the applicant (proposed owner) to contract, no problem arises unless the applicant is (1) a minor, (2) intoxicated or under the influence of other drugs, (3) mentally incompetent, or (4) an enemy alien.

1. *Minors.* With few exceptions, the minimum age at which a person can enter into contracts (the so-called **age of majority**) is 18. However, laws are not uniform and there may be special age limitations in a particular jurisdiction. In some states, minors have the legal capacity to enter into contracts if they are married. In the absence of contrary state law, contracts made by minors are voidable at the option of the minor, except for the reasonable value of **necessaries.**[10]

Meanwhile, the other party, such as an insurance company, remains obligated to perform the contract. If the minor decides to void or repudiate the contract, the other party must return all of the consideration that has been paid. There is, of course, no problem in the case of juvenile insurance, where the application for insurance on the life of the minor is made by a competent adult.[11]

Although life insurance is not a necessary, it has important values to the insured and his or her family. To encourage insurance companies to provide insurance for older minors but without danger of later repudiation by them, many states have enacted statutes that give minors, older than a specified age, the legal capacity to contract for insurance. The specified ages range from 14 to 18, with 15 the most frequent age. Some of these statutes additionally limit the parties eligible to be named beneficiaries under life insurance policies issued to such minors to spouses or parents.

2. *Intoxicated persons.* A person under the influence of intoxicating liquor or drugs, to the extent that he or she is unable to understand the nature of the transaction in which he or she is engaged, lacks legal capacity. The effect is to make such contracts voidable and the individual, with some exceptions, may be able to repudiate the contract within a reasonable length of time after he or she recovers sufficiently to understand the consequences of the previous act.

3. *Mental incompetency.* Contracts made by an insane person are voidable and are treated in the same manner as are the contracts made by minors, provided that no guardian has been appointed. If a person has been declared legally insane and a guardian appointed, all contracts made by the ward are void. As in the case of minors, an insane person may be held liable for the reasonable value of necessaries.

4. *Enemy aliens.* Trading with enemy aliens in time of war is illegal, and no valid contract can be entered into during such a period. Contracts already in force between domestic citizens and enemy aliens are either suspended or terminated

---

[9]*McGee v. International Life Insurance Company,* 355 U.S. 220, 78 S. Ct. 199. 2 L.Ed.2d 223 (1957); *Vencedor Mfg. Co. v. Gougler Industries, Inc. et al.,* 557 F. 2d 886 (1977).

[10]This term refers not only to basic needs such as food, clothing, and shelter but also can include other, less obvious items that can be judged by a court as appropriate for a person under certain circumstances.

[11]See Chapter 7.

by declaration of war. Court decisions in regard to life insurance contracts under such conditions are not uniform.

Mutual Assent. As in the case of other contracts, there must be an offer and an acceptance before the life insurance contract is created. The process by which an insurance contract comes into being is somewhat different from other contracts. An applicant for insurance rarely comes to an insurance company seeking insurance. Instead, the applicant is usually first contacted by an insurance agent who solicits an application that is submitted to the insurance company.

The life insurance contract can be created either by payment of the first premium with the application or the application can be submitted without payment of a premium. The latter situation is merely an invitation to the insurance company to make an offer to insure. The insurer can make the offer by issuing the policy. The applicant can then accept the insurer's offer by paying the premium at the time the policy is delivered.

1. *Premium receipts.* There are three general categories of premium receipts providing some form of temporary coverage used by life insurance companies where the premium is paid with the application. The **approval type of conditional premium receipt** provides that insurance will be effective only after the application has been approved by the company. Thus, the period of protection—from the date of approval until the date the policy is issued or delivered—is typically minimal. The approval premium receipt is of interest primarily from a historical standpoint, having largely been replaced by the insurability premium receipt.

The **insurability type of conditional premium receipt** provides that the insurer is considered as having made an offer conditional upon the proposed insured's insurability, and the applicant accepts the conditional offer by payment of the premium. The insurance becomes effective as of the date of the conditional receipt or, if later, the time of the medical examination, provided that the proposed insured is found insurable. The delivery of the policy itself is not essential. Under

this arrangement, if the proposed insured died before the application and other information reached the company's home office and the proposed insured otherwise would have been insurable according to the company's normal standards, the claim would be paid. Insurers have paid many such claims. The purpose of this type of receipt is, of course, to provide protection, assuming that the proposed insured is insurable, between the date of the conditional receipt (or medical examination, if later) and the time of policy delivery.

The **binding premium receipt** provides insurance effective from the date the receipt is given. Usually, both the conditional and binding receipts stipulate a maximum amount that would be payable if death occurred during the period of coverage under the receipt. The coverage is provided for the lesser of a stipulated, fixed time period or until the insurance company renders an underwriting decision on the application.

Infrequently, the premium is paid with the application, but no receipt is issued. In such cases, no contract is in force until the policy is issued and delivered. Here the applicant is considered to have made an offer that he or she may withdraw at any time before acceptance by the company.

2. *Policy effective date.* In the absence of complications, the **effective date** of a policy is that mutually agreed upon by the company and the applicant. However, complications can arise, the effect of which can be to bring the "true" policy effective date into dispute.

In some cases, a policy may be backdated to "save age." **Backdating** means that premiums will be those for the earlier age and therefore lower. Backdating beyond six months typically is prohibited by state law. Backdating does not alter the effective date of the protection, but it does raise two important questions. First, when is the next premium due? Second, from what date do the incontestable and suicide periods run?[12] A few courts have held that a full year's coverage must be provided for the annual premium. However, the majority of the decisions have held that the **policy date** (i.e., the date appearing on the

[12]See *Lentin v. Continental Assurance Co.,* 412 Ill. 158, 105 N.E.2d 735, A.L.R.2d 463 (1952).

contract) determines the date on which subsequent premiums are due, even though this means that less than one full year's protection is granted during the first year.[13]

With regard to the suicide and incontestable clauses, the general rule is that the earlier of the effective date or the policy date establishes the point of measurement. Thus, with a backdated policy, the clauses generally run from the policy date. When the policy date is later than the effective date, the clauses are held to run from the effective date. When the clauses themselves specify a certain date, this date is usually recognized.

Consideration. In the life insurance contract, the consideration given by the applicant for the promises of the company consists of the statements in the application and the payment of the first premium. Premium payments subsequent to the first are not part of the legal consideration, but are simply conditions precedent that must be performed to keep the contract in existence.

The insurer may agree to accept a check, note, or, in the absence of a prohibitive statute, services in payment of the first premium. Although a check is customarily considered cash, payment by check is usually accepted only as conditional payment. This means that if a check is not paid when presented, there has been no payment and the insurer's promise is no longer binding, regardless of the good faith of the policyowner.

If an agent has company authority to deal in promissory premium notes, the note is adequate consideration. Thus, unless the note has a provision to the effect that the policy will be repudiated if the note is not honored at maturity, the premium is considered paid and constitutes adequate consideration for the contract. In such cases, the note is a separate transaction, and the company's action is limited to its rights on the note if it is not honored at maturity.[14]

[13]Robert E. Keeton, *Insurance Law, Basic Text* (St. Paul, Minn.: West Publishing Co., 1971) p. 331; John Appleman, *Insurance Law and Practice* (St. Paul, Minn.: West Publishing Co., 1980), §7953.

[14]There are conflicting decisions as to the effect of a forfeiture provision when it is included in only the policy or the note. Where the forfeiture provision is contained in both the policy and note, the provisions have uniformly been held valid and enforceable. See *ibid.,* §3281.

Legal Purpose. To be valid, a contract must be for a legal purpose and not contrary to public policy. For example, in most states, gambling transactions are illegal and, therefore, unenforceable at law. Gambling transactions and life insurance contracts are both aleatory in character, as contrasted to commutative contracts.

In a commutative agreement, an exchange of approximate equal values is intended. For example, in a real estate sale, the seller relinquishes ownership of property whose value is agreed to by the parties. In return, the buyer pays an amount equal to the agreed value. Opposed to the commutative agreement is the aleatory agreement. Each party to such an agreement recognizes that one of them may obtain more than the other, but each also recognizes the outcome is governed by chance. Gambling and wagering arrangements, which are frequently illegal, are aleatory. The insurance contract is also aleatory, yet is legal and universally recognized as conducive to the public good. The distinction between a contract of insurance and an illegal wagering contract is vitally important. One's purpose in entering a wager is, through chance, hopefully to gain at the expense of others. One's purpose in entering an insurance contract is to avoid loss—not to make a gain—and to transform uncertainty into certainty.[15] The requirement of an insurable interest in insurance takes the agreement out of the gambling category. This subject, so vital to insurance, is discussed in detail in a separate section below.

In addition to the fact that a life insurance contract will fail if there is no insurable interest on the part of the applicant in the insured, a contract may be illegal and against public policy for other reasons. As was mentioned earlier, a contract with an enemy alien is held to be against public policy and void. Also, a contract is illegal and void (and the insurer is relieved from paying the death claim) where it is negotiated with intent to murder.

[15]It should be noted that the combination of a large number of risks, and the law of large numbers removes, to a great extent, the speculation on the part of insurance companies. They are not gambling either. Also, when all policyowners are viewed as a group, there is an exchange of approximately equal value between the policyowners and the company.

Insurable Interest

A contract of life insurance must, according to law, be based on an interest in the continuance of the life of the insured by the applicant or beneficiary. Such an insurable interest may assume many forms and may have its origin in a variety of relationships.

In the absence of a valid insurable interest, life insurance policies are unenforceable at law.[16] In the first place, unless they are based on a valid insurable interest, they are wagers and void as against public policy or contrary to statutes prohibiting gambling. More important, such contracts would be an incentive to crime in that they could encourage the taking of human life. Most states have incorporated this interpretation into statutory law and provide that such contracts are "void unless the benefits are payable to the individual insured or his personal representative or to a person having, at the time of such contract, an insurable interest in the individual insured."[17] This doctrine evolved out of regard for public welfare rather than for the protection of insurance companies. The presence of insurable interest removes the insurance policy from the wagering category. Conversely, the absence of an insurable interest renders the policy a mere wager.

In discussing insurable interest in life insurance, it is important to recognize that there are three roles usually involved: (1) applicant, (2) insured, and (3) beneficiary. In many cases, the insured persons are also the applicants/owners and may even designate themselves (i.e., their estate) as beneficiaries. In this text, the word **applicant** is used to denote the person who makes the application for insurance and who is proposed to be the policyowner. In analyzing the question of what constitutes a valid insurable interest, it is helpful to examine the question from the standpoint of whether the policy is applied for by the insured on his or her own life or by someone other than the individual to be insured.

Insurable Interest in One's Own Life. A fundamental principle of law is that every person possesses an insurable interest to an unlimited extent in his or her own life, and that he or she may make the insurance payable to whomever he or she wishes.[18] In cases where the insurance is applied for by the person whose life is insured, courts have refused to require any specific relationship to exist between the amount of insurance and the value of the life on which it is taken. When the contract is taken without collusion and without intent to violate the laws prohibiting wagers, the natural love of life is held to constitute a sufficient insurable interest to support a policy for any amount. Although legally there is no limit to the amount of insurance that may be taken out by an individual on his or her own life, in practice, life insurance companies usually limit the amount that they will write on one life to a sum that is not unreasonably large relative to the insured's financial status and earning capacity.

Insurable Interest in Another Person's Life. Court decisions are not uniform with respect to circumstances where the applicant is not also the proposed insured. As a general rule, a person applying for insurance on the life of another must have an insurable interest in the other's life. It has been held, however, that if the beneficiary has such an interest, the person applying for the insurance need have none. But even where the interest exists, a policy obtained without the knowledge and consent of the insured is contrary to public policy and void.[19] Insurable interest may arise out of one or more of the following three classes of relationships.

1. *Insurable interest in family and marriage relationships.* Courts have generally held that certain close relationships create an insurable interest, even though the element of financial dependence is not necessarily present. Thus, the relationship of husband and wife is conclusively presumed to

---

[16] *Warnock v. Davis* 104 U.S. 775, 779, 1881; *Peoples Life Insurance Co. v. Whiteside,* 94 F.2d 409, (1938).

[17] Georgia Statutes, 1969, §56-2404.

[18] 44 Am. Jur. 2d, Insurance, §1729; *Bell v. Phillips et al.,* Tex., 152 F.2d 188 (1946).

[19] 44 Am. Jur. 2d, Insurance, §1741. Some states (e.g., Louisiana) permit either spouse to take insurance on the life of the other without the consent of the one insured. But see consequences where the husband took out over $1 million of term life insurance on his wife in *State v. Thompson* (Minn.), 139 N.W. 2d 490 (1966).

establish an insurable interest on behalf of either party in the other's life. Some courts have added the relationship of parent and child and of brother and sister, but have refused to extend it further. As regards other relationships, the courts have generally taken the position that the interest should be based upon a reasonable expectation of deriving pecuniary benefit from the continuance of the insured's life.

2. *Insurable interest in creditor–debtor relationships.* The rule is well settled that a creditor has an insurable interest in the life of his or her debtor, although the important question of an acceptable amount of insurance, as compared with the amount of debt, is not well settled. Where a creditor has paid the premiums for a policy insuring the debtor's life, the creditor's insurable interest, arguably, should not be limited solely to the face of the indebtedness. The creditor should be reimbursed for an amount equal to the debt, the premiums paid, and interest on both. The courts are not uniform concerning the validity of a policy where the amount of insurance exceeds the debt.

The rule adopted by the U.S. Supreme Court places an indefinite restriction upon the insurable interest of the creditor by providing that the relationship between the amount of insurance and the amount of the debt must not be so disproportionate as to make the policy take on the appearance of a wagering contract as distinguished from its legitimate purpose—security for the indebtedness. In *Cammack v. Lewis,* for example, the court declared a policy of $3,000 taken out by a creditor to secure a debt of $70 to be "a sheer wagering policy, without any claim to be considered as one meant to secure a debt."[20] The Supreme Court has made the relationship between the amount of the debt and the insurance amount an important factor to be considered but it has never defined this relationship precisely. Various theories were used by courts to make the insurance proceeds in excess of the debt payable to the estate of the debtor or other beneficiary designated by the debtor. Where the law was not explicit and the terms of the transaction not clear, the most popular theory for making such payments is that the creditor is the trustee for the benefit of the debtor's estate.[21]

A special class of life insurance for use in credit transactions has become commonplace, particularly since the 1930s. In the majority of jurisdictions, these **credit life policies** must be in the form of decreasing term (expiring when the loan is fully paid). If the loan is paid earlier, most of the statutes require a refund of unearned premium.

There is a basic conceptual difference between ordinary life insurance and credit life insurance. In credit life insurance, the debtor pays the premiums directly or indirectly and purchases the policy as part of the credit transaction. Normally, it will have no property value unless the insured dies. Although ostensibly for the benefit of the creditor, the policy is a form of special collateral and provides protection to the debtor/insured's estate. In the event of a prepayment of the debt, any unearned premiums should be the property of the debtor. Similarly, if the insured dies before the debt is discharged, any insurance in excess of the debt amount should be paid to the debtor's estate.

About 40 states have adopted the **NAIC Model Bill to Provide for the Regulation of Credit Life Insurance.** The Uniform Commercial Credit Code (UCCC) provisions relating to credit insurance, patterned on the NAIC Model Act, are in effect in 10 states.[22] These laws require certain disclosures to a debtor in connection with credit life insurance and a refund of unearned premiums. The courts are empowered and instructed to refuse to enforce contracts that are unconscionable.[23] The enforcement of these laws is generally left to state insurance departments.

Under current credit practices, premiums included in charges for loans must be disclosed to the debtor. The UCCC provides that credit life insurance cannot exceed the amount of the loan and also requires uniformity in premiums.[24] In most states the amount of insurance that is in ex-

---

[20]15 Wall. 244, 82 U.S. 647.

[21]See Appleman, *Insurance Law and Practice,* §§20 and 1311–1352, for current literature in this area.

[22]*Uniform Commercial Credit Code.*

[23]*UCCC,* Sec. 2–302; Sec. 4–202.

[24]*UCCC,* Sec. 4–202.

cess of the unpaid indebtedness is payable to a beneficiary other than the creditor, named by the debtor or to the debtor's estate.[25] As a practical matter, the language reflected in the statutes is largely a codification of current case law. In other words, courts examine the potential benefits to the debtor, the need for such insurance, the length of time the loan is in existence, the circumstances under which the assignment was made, elements of unconscionability, and other data relevant in determining the case.

3. *Insurable interest in other business relationships.* Numerous business relationships, other than that of creditor and debtor, can justify the purchase of insurance by one person on the life of another. Thus, an employer may insure the life of an employee and the employee the life of an employer; a partner the life of a copartner and the partnership the life of each partner; and a corporation the life of an officer. Similarly, a surety on a bond, although no default on the bond has occurred, has an insurable interest in the life of the principal. A corporation holding a property interest contingent upon another person's reaching a certain age may protect itself against the loss of the contingent right through the death of that person before attaining the prescribed age. The courts have even held that those furnishing funds for corporate enterprises have an insurable interest in the lives of the managers and promoters of the corporations. Certain stockholders have purchased life insurance on the lives of prominent financiers who were instrumental in financing and promoting the corporations whose stock they held.[26]

The Time and Continuity of Insurable Interest. In property insurance, the general rule is that insurable interest must exist at some time during the period of coverage and at the time of the loss. In other words, it is unnecessary to have an insurable interest at the time the property insurance contract is made. In life insurance, the insurable interest must exist at the inception of the contract. It will not thereafter be voided if the interest ceases unless the provisions of the policy are such as to bring about that result. The fact that insurable interest need exist ly at the inception of the contract is a corollary to the view that life insurance policies are not contracts of indemnity. This view is also reflected in the fact that when an insured is executed for a crime, the proceeds are payable to the appropriate beneficiary. Similarly, when a beneficiary murders the insured, the proceeds still must be paid out but, of course, to an innocent beneficiary.[27]

Governing Law

Generally speaking, the construction of the contract as to its validity will be governed by the law and usages of the place where the contract is made. This is held to be where the last and essential acts necessary to formation of a contract took place. It is possible that several jurisdictions' laws, including those of a foreign country, appear to apply but in a conflicting manner (conflict of laws), and the general rule becomes subject to special interpretation. Thus, where an insured was a citizen of Missouri and made application for insurance in Oklahoma to a Tennessee insurer, it was held that the state of domicile had a more significant relationship to the parties and therefore Missouri law applied.[28] Similarly, assignments and other matters relating to performance of the contracts are governed by the law of the place of performance, regardless of the place where the original contract was made.

The Application and Its Interpretation

An application for life insurance may be defined as the applicant's proposal to the insurer for protection and may be considered as the

---

[25]Georgia Statutes, 1969, §56-3306(2).

[26]George Richards, *The Law of Insurance,* 5th ed. (posthumous) by Warren Fredman (New York: Baker, Vaorhis & Co., Inc., 1952), pp. 398–401.

[27]This assumes that the beneficiary did not procure the policy with the intent to murder the insured.
[28]V.A.M.S. 375, 420, 376, 620; 36 O.S. 1971, §4024; *Moss v. National Life & Acc. Ins. Co.* (D.C. Mo. 1974), 385 F. Supp. (1921); *Mutual of Omaha Ins. Co. v. Russell* (C.A. Kan. 402 F.2d 339, 29 A.L.R.3d 753, certiorari denied 80 S.Ct. 1465, 394 U.S. 973, 22 L.Ed.2d 753 (1968) (flight policy issued to a Kansas citizen in Missouri and court applied Kansas law).

beginning of the policy contract. In this document, the proposed insured is required to give true answers to questions relating principally to his or her personal and family history, habits, total insurance already taken out, and other applications for insurance that either are pending or have been postponed or refused. The policy usually stipulates that insurance is granted in consideration of the application for the policy, which is declared to be a part of it, and generally contains a clause to the effect that the policy and the application (a copy of which is attached to the policy when issued) "constitute the entire contract between the parties." Most state laws require the annexation of applications to policies, on penalty of the company's being **estopped** (i.e., prevented) from using the applicant's incorrect statements to avoid payment under the policy.

Full Knowledge and Disclosure. In deciding whether to assume a given risk, the insurer relies in part on information furnished by the proposed insured. Consequently, the company is entitled to have all information that may have an influence on its decision to assume or not assume a given risk, especially given the highly aleatory nature of the life insurance contract. As a result, the applicant must act in good faith, and if the information given is false or incomplete, the insurer may be in a position to rescind or cancel the contract, although the incontestable clause may bar any such action (see below). Thus, either the failure of the proposed insured to disclose fully all pertinent information (doctrine of concealment) or the falsity of positive statements made by the proposed insured may be grounds for rescinding the contract (doctrines of warranties and representations).

1. *Concealment.* Courts have repeatedly stated that insurance policies are contracts involving the utmost good faith. In early cases, it was held that they were based upon chance and that the withholding of any essential facts by either party rendered the risk actually insured different from that intended. The validity of the policy therefore depended upon the full disclosure of all material information. The **test of the materiality** of a fact concealed (or misrepresented—see below) is

whether its knowledge by the company would have influenced its underwriting decision—that is, whether the company would have issued the insurance on the same terms, conditions, and premiums had it known the correct information. Whether a fact is material and should have been revealed is generally a question for a jury.

The doctrine of **concealment,** which was developed in connection with marine insurance, was primarily for the protection of the underwriter and at one time was applied to all branches of insurance, but as the business developed, the courts concluded that some relaxation of the rule should be made. With respect to life insurance, the question was thoroughly reviewed in the case of *Penn Mutual Life Insurance v. Mechanics' Savings Bank and Trust Company.*[29] In this case the court held that "no failure to disclose a fact material to the risk, not inquired about, will void the policy, unless such nondisclosure was with intent to conceal from the insurer a fact believed to be material; that is, unless the nondisclosure was fraudulent."[30]

2. *Warranties.* Closely associated with the common-law doctrines of concealment and representations is that of **warranty.**[31] Technically, a warranty must be absolutely and literally true, and a forfeiture will result if merely the falsehood of the statement can be shown, irrespective of its materiality. A company need prove only that a warranted statement is incorrect. The courts assume that the materiality of the thing warranted has been established and that all inquiry on the subject is precluded.

Because of the hardship and injustice that the technical enforcement of the common-law rule pertaining to warranties sometimes caused, and also largely because certain insurance companies took undue advantage of warranties in their policies, the vast majority of states passed statutes protecting insureds against technical avoidance of

[29]72 Fed. 413 (C.C.A.), 1986; *Blair v. National Security Insurance Co.,* 126 F.2d 955, 1942.

[30]*Ibid.,* 434, 441; *Haubner v. Aetna Life Ins. Co.,* 256 A.2d 414 (D.C. App. 1969) (insured has affirmative duty to disclose material information).

[31]Keeton, *Insurance Law, Basic Text,* pp. 320–323; for warranties, generally, see Appleman, *Insurance Law and Practice,* §§9401–9417; 27 A.L.R.3d 840.

life insurance contracts because of breech of war-ranties. These statutes differ widely in their wording but are similar to the New York statute, which provides in effect that all statements purporting to be made by the insured shall be deemed representations and not warranties.[32]

3. *Representations.* In general, a **representation** is a statement made to an insurer for the purpose of giving information or inducing it to accept a risk. A **misrepresentation** occurs when the information given is incorrect.

As a general rule, representations are construed liberally in favor of the insured and need be only substantially correct. The tendency of court decisions has been in the direction of protecting the insured by giving him or her the benefit of the doubt wherever possible. The rule formerly was that a material false representation rendered a policy voidable at the option of the company, even though there was no fraudulent intent on the part of the insured. This rule has been modified in certain states either by court decision or by statute. Thus, one court has stated that "a forfeiture does not follow where there has been no deliberate intent to deceive, and the known falsity of the answer is not affirmatively shown."[33] Intent is a state of mind and, in effect, some courts require that the insurer show not only that the representations in the application were false, but also that they were fraudulently made.[34] However, in those jurisdictions that provide that the misrepresentations have only to be material, a rescission is permitted without regard to intent or even knowledge.[35] Some state statutes provide that the policy will not be invalidated unless the misrepresentation is made with intent to deceive; others, that the misrepresentation must have con-tributed to the loss. The general purpose of such laws is to prevent a forfeiture of the policy unless the company has been deceived to its detriment.

Clearly the application of the law regarding representations varies widely. Thus, in many jurisdictions today, to void a policy the insurer must show that (1) the misrepresentation is material; (2) it was false; (3) the insured knew that it was false when he or she made it or made it recklessly without any knowledge of the truth; (4) the insured made the representation with intention that the insurer would act upon it; and (5) the insurer did act upon it.[36]

Presumption of Death—Disappearance

A well-settled rule of law is that when a person leaves his or her usual place of residence and is neither heard of nor known to be living for a term of seven years, the presumption of life ceases and that of death arises. Therefore, if an insured disappears for a period of seven years and the absence is unexplained, he or she is presumed to be dead, and the insurance company is required to pay the policy death proceeds. The only presumption, however, is that of the fact of death; there is none as to the time of death. But if evidence is presented that the absent person, within the seven years, encountered some specific peril, or within that period came within the range of some impending or immediate danger that might reasonably be expected to destroy life, the court or jury may infer that life ceased before the expiration of the seven years. In such cases, the insurer must pay the face of the policy plus interest thereon from the date of *proof* of death.

The insured is presumed to be alive until the end of the seven-year period. Therefore, if premiums are not paid, the beneficiary is not entitled to the proceeds unless it can be proven that death occurred before the due date of the next premium or unless the policy has remained in force under one of its nonforfeiture options. The time of death may become important in case a primary beneficiary dies during the seven-year period and there is a contingent beneficiary. In

---

[32]*New York Insurance Law,* §142(3); for representations, generally, see Appleman, *Insurance Law and Practice,* §§7291–7312; 27 A.L.R.3d 840.

[33]*Kuhns v. N.Y. Life Ins. Co., Appellant,* 297 Pa. 418, 423, 147 A.76 (1929); *Travellers Ins. Co. v. Heppenstall Co.,* 61 A.2d 809, 812 (Pa. 1948).

[34]*Russ v. Metropolitan Life Ins. Co.,* 270 A.2d 759, 112 N.J. Super. 265 (1970); *Kizirian v. United Benefit Life Ins. Co.,* Pa., 119 A.2d 47 (1956); *Evans v. Penn Mutual Life Ins. Co. of Philadelphia,* 322 Pa. 547, 186 A. 133 (1936).

[35]West's F.S.A., §627.409; *Garwood v. Equitable Life Ass. Soc.,* Fla., 299 So.2d 163 (1974).

[36]*West v. Farm Bureau Mut. Ins. Co. of Michigan,* 234 N.W.2d 485, 63 Mich. App. 279 (1975).

the absence of an agreement between the parties, a court may have to decide on the distribution of the policy proceeds.

Insuring Agreement

In the **insuring agreement,** the company agrees to pay the policy face amount immediately to the beneficiary upon receipt of written proof of the insured's death, subject to the provisions of the policy. An illustrative clause in simplified language contains the insurer's promise:

> If the insured dies while this policy is in force, we will pay the sum insured to the beneficiary, when we receive at our home office due proof of the insured's death, subject to the provisions of this policy.

The owner's consideration for this promise is, of course, the application and payment of the initial premium. The promise will continue in effect in accordance with the policy provisions as long as the required condition—payment of renewal premiums—is met.

THE LAW PERTAINING TO THE AGENT

Since life insurance is written almost exclusively by corporations, in most instances transacting business in many states, the agent is a necessary factor to the business' success. If the agent is to perform properly the duties connected with the solicitation of business, he or she must be given certain authority.

Overview

Agency is a relationship between two parties against all others. The **principal** creates the agency. Agency law classifies agents in accordance with the type of authority granted by the principal:

1. Actual or express
2. Implied
3. Apparent or perceived

Actual or **express authority** is that granted by the principal in some specific language or terms. It may involve wide or general authority or it may be limited to a narrow field or even to a specific act. **Implied authority** is that associated with certain duties, such as the cashier's authority to take payment for merchandise at a checkout counter. **Apparent** or **perceived authority** is that which a third person believes the agent possesses because of the existing circumstances that have been made possible by the principal and upon which the third party is justified in relying. Apparent authority is based on the principle of estoppel. That is, if the principal clothes another with certain vestiges of authority, such as receipt books, application forms, specimen policies, sales literature, and similar items that lead a third party reasonably to believe that an agency relationship exists, the principal will not be allowed later to declare that no agency existed.

State laws require that insurance agents possess certain minimum levels of knowledge about life insurance and, in some cases, a certain amount of training before a license will be granted. Agents are further required by state regulations to observe certain rules of conduct. The insurance company, in turn, may provide additional rules. However, unless such rules are known to the applicant, they may not be binding upon him or her. Insurers are well aware of the powers granted to their agents and of the potential for abuse. Accordingly, they take measures to place third parties on notice of the limitations of the powers granted their agents. These limitations may appear in special notices or lettering in receipt books, applications, or other documents given to the applicant and which the applicant should read.

Powers of the Agent

Two classes of agents exist in law: (1) **general agents** and (2) **special agents.** A general agent's powers are coextensive with those of his or her principal within the limit of the particular business or territory in which the agent operates. A special agent's powers usually are far more limited, extending only to acts necessary to the accomplishment of the particular transaction he or she is engaged to perform. However, the terms "general agent" and "special agent" have other meanings in the insurance industry and vary between non-life insurance (fire, marine, and casualty) and life insurance. In the former, a "general agent" has wide authority to enter into insurance contracts, whereas in the life insurance field, a general agent almost always has very limited authority. Thus, the person who is designated as a general agent for life insurance solicitation purposes is really a special agent in the eyes of the law. But this designation can be even more confusing since the term "special agent" is also used to identify a person who acts as a solicitating agent and who works for a "general agent." Such a "special agent" has even less authority than his or her "general agent" but, like the "general agent," is considered legally to be a special agent in the eyes of the law.

Agents acting within the actual or apparent scope of their authority make their principal—the insurance company—liable for their wrongful or fraudulent acts, omissions, and misrepresentations. Provided that the policy or application contains no restrictions on the agent's authority, the acts and knowledge of the agent in relation to anything pertaining to the application or policy generally are held by the courts to be the acts and knowledge of the company. This estoppes it from taking advantage of any forfeiture occasioned by the agent's errors or fraudulent acts.

A large amount of litigation has arisen from what may be termed as the overenthusiasm of the agent. It takes time to complete an application, take premium payments, and give receipts. Meanwhile, the agent usually engages in general conversation with remarks such as "you have a good deal," "you're covered," and others. They may be unrelated to any questions posed by the applicant. When problems develop later, it becomes extremely difficult to determine what was said as well as what conversation was related to the subject. To guard against this, most insurers try to call attention to the limitations of the authority of the agent by use of a larger type size or use of color in receipts or other documents and literature that are provided to the applicant. If the applicant fails to read such

warnings, he or she may have difficulty claiming that he or she was misled.

Although there is no unanimity in the decisions, the weight of authority is to the effect that, in the absence of restrictions, the company is liable not only for the acts of its agents, but also for the acts and knowledge of the subagents and employees to whom the agent has delegated authority. In insurance, it is a common practice and is frequently found necessary for agents to employ others to assist them in their work, and since authority has been delegated to them, the courts have regarded it as "just and reasonable that insurance companies should be held responsible not only for acts of their agents, but also for the acts of the subagents employed within the scope of their agents' authority." Although it may be argued that the company has not authorized its agents to delegate their authority to others and that it would therefore be an unreasonable extension of the company's liability, it must be remembered that agents are employed by the companies in accordance with the usages and necessities of the business.

Policy Limitations

As a general rule, life insurance companies insert a provision in their policies or application forms prohibiting their agents from altering the contract in any way. Although the wording of such clauses is not uniform, the following may be regarded as representative of the usual provision:

> A change in this policy is valid only if it is approved by an officer of the Company. The company may require that the policy be sent to it for endorsement to show a change. No agent has the authority to change the policy or to waive any of its terms.

Despite the apparent reasonableness of such policy provisions, various court decisions dealing with the matter are by no means in harmony, and, as a result, various rules have been formulated.[37]

[37]George James Couch, *Couch Cyclopedia of Insurance Law,* 2nd ed. (Rochester, N.Y.: Lawyers Co-operative Publishing Co., 1959–1968), §26:82.

One such rule is to the effect that policy limitations upon any agent's authority operate as notice to the proposed insured of the limited extent of the agent's powers and thus protect the company.[38] In another group of cases, the courts have adopted an attitude more favorable to the policyowner/insured, by holding that such policy restrictions upon an agent's authority are not conclusive as to those matters involved before the contract is completed, but relate only "to the exercise of the agent's authority in matters concerning the policy after its delivery and acceptance, the theory in the main being that no presumption can reasonably attach that the insured was cognizant of such provisions or could anticipate that they would be incorporated into the policy."[39] Still another rule holds, in effect, that restrictions in the policy relate only to acts before a loss has occurred.[40]

Perhaps the rule having the most support at present is one prohibiting the company from rescinding the insurance in case of policy violation (1) where the company or any agent clothed with actual or apparent authority has waived, either orally or in writing, any provision of the policy, or (2) where the company, because of some knowledge or act on its part or on the part of its agent, is estopped from setting up as a defense the violation of the terms of the contract.[41] Courts generally are reluctant to allow parol (oral) evidence to vary a written document. However, whether the courts rely on an oral waiver of policy provisons or upon the doctrine of estoppel,[42] the company is held bound. This holds even though some provision of the contract has been violated and the policy contains a provision limiting the agent's power to make policy changes.

Doctrine of Reasonable Expectations

When one makes a payment, the normal expectation is that one has purchased something for value given. To suggest that this is not true strikes a discordant note. Courts have used strong langauge to condemn restrictive language in policies, receipts, and other literature given to the applicant as well as aggressive sales promotions to acquire new customers. One court pointed out that in such a situation, the confusion existing was the creation of the insurer and that the **reasonable expectations** of the policyowner would not be frustrated.[43] Judge Learned Hand, dealing with conditional receipts, in another case said: "An underwriter might so understand the phrase, when read in its context, but the application was not to be submitted to underwriters: it was to go to persons utterly unacquainted with the niceties of life insurance, who would read it colloquially. It is the understanding of such persons which counts. To demand that persons wholly unfamiliar with insurance shall spell all this out in the very teeth of the language used is unpardonable."[44] Still other courts, while not specifically overruling the prohibitions against oral contracts as stated by the Supreme Court, utilize the doctrines of waiver, estoppel, or election to prevent forfeiture of coverage.[45]

In the course of their daily business, agents are frequently asked to express opinions on the meaning of policy provisions. It is of the utmost importance that a clear understanding should exist between the company and its agents as regards the expression of such opinions. What, then, is the legal effect of the agent's opinion? Early law was extremely legalistic. A person was required to read and know what he or she had signed. Thus, the *mere opinion* of an *agent* could not change the clear meaning of a written contract. To suggest such action was to strike at the very heart of contract law, particularly where the actual authority of the agent was limited. This response ignored the realities of insurance practices.

The insurance industry has worked hard in

[38]*Ibid.,* §26.83.

[39]*Ibid.,* §26.86.

[40]*Ibid.,* §26.88.

[41]*Ibid.,* §26.90.

[42]For a discussion of this point, see W. R. Vance and B. M. Anderson, *Handbook of the Law of Insurance,* 3rd ed. (St. Paul, Minn.: West Publishing Co., 1951), Chaps. VIII and IX; Keeton, *Insurance Law, Basic Text,* pp. 341–347.

[43]*Allen v. Metropolitan Life Ins. Co.,* 208 A. 2d 638, 44 N.J. 294 (1965).

[44]*Garnet v. John Hancock Mutual Life Insurance Co.,* Conn., 160 F 2nd 599 at 601 (1947) quoted by dissent in *Morgan v. State Farm Life Insurance Co.,* 400 P. 2nd 223, 240, One. 113 (1965).

[45]*McGowan v. Prudential Ins. Co. of America,* D.C. Pa., 253 F. Supp. 415, reversed 372 F. 2d 39 (1966); *Fesmire v. MFA Mut. Ins. Co.,* D.C. Tenn., 293 F. Supp. 1214 (1968).

the past 50 years to improve the image of the insurance agent. Advertisements proclaim the expertise and professionalism of the insurance agent. The prospective applicant is told of the reliability and dependability of the insurer if only the applicant will submit to the tender ministration of the insurance agent. State insurance departments insist on minimum educational qualifications and insurers spend enormous sums of money in agent training to support professionalism. Therefore, it should not come as a surprise that the courts have taken the insurers at their advertised word. In the field of automobile sales, courts have decided that automobile manufacturers should not be permitted to advertise the virtues of their product and at the same time insist on standing on the terms of the sales contract disclaiming warranties. For the same reason, neither should an insurer be allowed to advertise the expertise of its agency force and then deny these very qualities after the product has been purchased. The concern is that to ignore the disparity of the bargaining positions between the average insurance purchaser and the relatively well-educated insurance agent is to invite overreaching on the part of the insurers. Accordingly, when an insurance agent renders an opinion that is contrary to the written contract and the proposed policyowner relies on such an opinion, it is possible that the insurer may be bound.[46] The courts will, in effect, apply the principles of estoppel, implicitly even if not explicit.

Agent's Liability to Principal for Misconduct

The relation of the agent to his or her principal is such that the agent should never further his or her own personal interests by disobeying or exceeding the principal's instructions. Any misconduct of the agent makes him or her personally liable to the principal for the damage occasioned. This responsibility is based on the law of agency. Any loss or damage to the principal must be indemnified by the agent. Examples of agent's misconduct are exceeding specific authority,

binding unacceptable risks, failure to transmit information concerning risks, collusion with the applicant, incorrect statements concerning the proposed insured, failure to transmit funds collected on behalf of the principal, and failure to follow explicit instructions issued by the principal. In practice, however, most cases involving serious violation of agency agreements are resolved by the agents' being discharged and a revocation of license.

Insurer's Liability for Delay, Improper Rejection, or Failure to Act

Many courts have held that when an insurer is holding an applicant's premium but has not issued the insurance policy, it is elementary justice to either hold that a contract of insurance is in existence or else hold the company liable for damages caused because of its failure to insure or for delay in accepting the application if the proposed insured's position is changed by death or otherwise. The liability of the insurer may fall under contract because of a receipt or otherwise, or it may be in tort for damages generally. In most cases these damages will be the face amount of the proposed policy. The theories that allow the applicant to recover from the insurer are several:[47] (1) that there is an implied agreement to act promptly, particularly since the insurer holds the premium;[48] (2) that there is a constructive or implied acceptance of the application because of a lack of a timely acceptance or rejection of the application;[49] (3) that the court will construe the terms of the receipt against the insurer and liberally in favor of the applicant and

---

[46]*Farly v. United Pac. Ins. Co.,* 525 P. 2d 1003, 269 Ore. 549 (1974); *Harr v. Allstate Ins. Co.,* 255 A. 2d 208, 54 N.J. 287 (1969); Keeton, *Insurance Law, Basic Text,* Chap. 6; Appleman, *Insurance Law and Practice,* §7307.

[47]Keeton, *Insurance Law, Basic Text,* pp. 46ff.; Appleman, *Insurance Law and Practice,* §§7221–7233.

[48]*Peddicord v. Prudential Ins. Co. of America,* 498 P. 2d 1388, Okla. (1972); *Gorham v. Peerless Life Ins. Co.,* 118 N.W. 2d 306, 368b Mich, 335 (1962).

[49]*Harvey v. United Ins. Co.,* 245 P. 2d 1185, 173 Kan. 227 (1952); *Wadsworth v. New York Life Ins. Co.,* 84 N.W. 2d 513, 349 Mich. 240 (1957); *National Bank of Commerce v. Royal Exchange Assur. of America, Inc.,* 455 F. 2d 8792, C.A. Tenn. (1972) (the failure to act promptly on the application led the insured to believe that the insurance had been accepted and therefore there was an implied acceptance of insurance).

provide interim insurance;[50] (4) that the long delay or other mishandling misleads the applicant to his or her detriment and estoppes the insurer from denying the existence of insurance;[51] (5) that the applicant has the choice of suing the insurer under contract of implied promise to act promptly or in tort for failure to act within a reasonable time;[52] (6) that the insurance company has a duty to the applicant to act promptly and when it fails to perform this duty it is negligent and liable to the policyowner or his or her beneficiaries;[53] and (7) that the taking of an application, acceptance of the first premium, and issuance of a receipt provide an interim policy of insurance irrespective of any contrary provisions in the application or receipt.[54]

The tort or negligence action is the majority view. But other conduct by the insurer may provide coverage. For example, the failure to return the premium promptly with the rejection has been held to be unconscionable and thus provides interim coverage.[55] In other cases, the courts have not been concerned with the relationship between the insurance company and its agents. Instead, it has viewed the company and its agent from the standpoint of the applicant. This had given rise to the concept of reasonable expectations discussed earlier. The conduct of some insurers has been judged to be in bad faith and coverage reinstated.[56] The amount of delay that may be involved varies with the circumstances. Often, either the agent or the company, or both, may be aware of circumstances that require an acceptance or rejection within a definite time limit. One example of this involved a case where an individual made an application for insurance with the intention of replacing existing insurance. It was clear to the court that the insurer should have recognized the need for a decision before the existing policy was allowed to lapse. This was particularly true in the eyes of the court in cases where the individual insured was no longer insurable.[57]

There are many other cases not involving receipts where the agent, in his or her desire and enthusiasm to secure business, oversteps the authority granted, and in accordance with established principles, the courts are inclined to render decisions in favor of the insured-applicant. The companies often accept the obligations imposed upon them by the misconduct of the agent rather than to submit the matter to ligitation. They accept it as a cost of doing business. They may take other steps to prevent such future misconduct by the agent, but this will not involve the policyowner.

PROVISIONS PROTECTING THE POLICYOWNER

A life insurance policy is a piece of property. The owner of the policy may be the individual on whose life the policy is written, it may be the beneficiary, or it may be someone else. In most cases, the insured is also the owner of the policy. The person designated as the owner has vested privileges of ownership, including the right to assign the policy as collateral, receive cash values and dividends, borrow against the policy, designate a new owner, and change the beneficiary (unless subject to restrictions—see below). At the death of the insured, the beneficiary becomes the owner of the proceeds and other rights under the policy. There

[50] *Jones v. John Hancock Mut. Life Ins. Co.,* 289 F. Supp. 930, affirmed 416 F. 2d 829, Mich. (1968); *Service v. Pyramid Life Ins. Co.,* 440 P.2d 944, Kan. (1968); *Metropolitan Life Ins. Co. v. Grant,* 268 F. 2d 307, C.A. Cal. (1959).

[51] *Barnes v. Atlantic & Pacific Life Ins. Co. of America,* 530 F. 2d 98, C.A. Ala. (1976).

[52] *Moore v. Palmetto State Life Ins. Co.,* 73 S.E. 2d 688, 222 S.C. 492 (1952).

[53] *Peddicord v. Prudential Ins. Co. of America,* 498 P. 2d 1388, Okla. (1972); *Werthman v. Catholic Order of Foresters,* 133 N.W. 2d 104, 257 Iowa 483 (1965); *Hinds v. United Ins. Co. of America,* 149 S.E. 2d 771, 248 S.C. 285 (1966); *Mann v. Policyholder Life Ins. Co.,* 51 N.W. 2d 853, 78 N.D. 724 (1952) (life insurance company has solicited and received application and premiums and thus has duty to act promptly).

[54] *Trip v. Reliable Life Ins. Co.,* 449 P. 2d 1155, 210 Kan. 33 (1972).
[55] *Smith v. Westland Life Ins. Co.,* 115 Cal. Rptr. 750 (1974).
[56] *Life Ins. Co. of Southwest v. Nims,* 512 S.W. 2d 712, Tex. Civ. App. (1974).

[57] *Prince v. Western Empire Life Ins. Co.,* 428 P. 2d 163, 19 Utah 174 (1967) (application to replace $80,000 of existing insurance which the insured applicant allowed to lapse; insured killed in the meantime).

are a number of policy provisions intended to protect the owner of the policy.

Entire Contract Clause

The **entire contract clause** provides that the policy itself and the application, if a copy is attached to the policy, legally constitute the entire contract between the parties. This clause protects the policyowner in that the company cannot, merely by reference, include within the policy its procedural rules, the application (unless a copy is attached to the policy), or statements made to the medical examiner. This fact means that the company cannot assert misrepresentation by the applicant unless the application is attached to the policy. The clause also protects the company in that the application, if made part of the contract (which it normally is), becomes part of the consideration for the contract and material misrepresentations made by the applicant can be used by the company in denying liability (but see following section on the incontestable clause) or seeking reformation or rescission of the contract.[58]

Incontestable Clause

The **incontestable clause** was introduced by life insurance companies on a voluntary basis to provide greater assurance to the public that relatively innocent misstatements by applicants would not be the cause of a claim being denied. A typical policy provision consistent with the simplified language utilized in current contracts would read as follows:

> Except for accidental death and disability premium payment benefits, we cannot contest this policy after it has been in force for two years while the insured is alive.

[58]A **reformation** is an equitable remedy wherein a contract is reformed (i.e., redrafted) to conform to the original intention of the parties. This remedy is often used where a mistake has been made by one or both of the parties in drafting a contract (e.g., misspelled name).

A **rescission,** also an equitable remedy, typically involves more serious contentiousness and involves a cancellation or avoidance of a contract. This remedy is frequently used where fraud or other material misrepresentation is involved.

The clause has been given a broad interpretation. It prevents a life insurance company from voiding a life insurance contract after the passage of the specified time—typically two years (assuming that the insured survives that long)—even on grounds of material misrepresentation or fraud in the application for the contract. The rationale for this broad interpretation is the protection of beneficiaries. From the standpoint of the owner and the beneficiary, the incontestable clause removes the fear of lawsuits, especially at a time— namely, after the death of the insured—when it may be difficult for the beneficiary, successfully, to combat with competent testimony a company's charge of misrepresentation. This could be particularly difficult in view of the fact that the insured individual who made the representations that form the basis of the contract is no longer alive to present his or her side of the case.

From the standpoint of public policy, it is undesirable to have dependents subject to a forfeiture for violations that might remain unknown for many years and, at the death of the insured, leave the dependents without protection—the basic purpose of the life insurance contract. Moreover, if a policy is contested, the issue is typically resolved in the courts. This involves delay in claim settlement at the very time when the need for speedy payment is greatest. The law grants insurers only the first two policy years in which to initiate this process. Thereafter, they are barred from contesting the validity of the contract unless the insured dies before the two years have expired; then there is generally no time limit on such a contest.

The incontestable clause is similar to a short statute of limitations. By inserting the policy provision, the company undertakes to make all necessary investigations concerning the good faith and all other circumstances surrounding the application within the time limit stipulated in the clause. It limits the period of time the insurer can use the defense of fraud, concealment, or material misrepresentation to defeat the contract. The company agrees not to resist claim payment if premiums have been paid and if no violation of the contract has come to light during the stipulated time limit following the issuance of the policy and if, during the time, the company has taken no action to rescind the contract.[59]

Grace Period

The usual **grace period** provision permits premiums to be paid for up to 30 or 31 days after the due date and, importantly, during this period, the policy remains in effect. Many companies are now including 60- or 61-day grace periods, especially on universal life policies. If the insured dies during the grace period, the company is permitted to deduct the overdue premium plus interest from the settlement with the beneficiary. The purpose of this provision is to protect the policyowner against "unintentional lapse." If it were not for this provision and the payment were even one day late, evidence of insurability could be required to reinstate the policy.

Although companies are permitted under the law to charge interest, they rarely do so because of the small amounts involved and the expense of collection. It should also be noted that since the company collects a premium only in the event of death within the grace period, most of those who lapse pay no share of the cost of insurance for that period, in essence receiving a month's protection free.

Nonforfeiture Provision

In the early days, life insurance policies had no cash values. If a policy lapsed, the policyowner "forfeited" any "excess" contributions. **Standard Nonforfeiture Laws** now prohibit such forfeitures.

Under Standard Nonforfeiture Laws, policies must contain a statement of the mortality table and rate of interest used in calculating the non-forfeiture values provided by the policy, as well as a description of the method used in calculating the values. In addition, a table is required showing the cash surrender and other nonfor-

[59]There have been a few cases in which the fraud associated with the issuance of the policies has been so outrageous that policies were allowed to be voided from their inception even though the period of contestability had expired. See Joseph M. Belth, ed., *The Insurance Forum,* Vol. 12, No. 9 (September 1985), p. 84.

feiture options for each of the first 20 years. These options are discussed in Chapter 9. Nonforfeiture values must be equal to or greater than those required by the law.

Much misunderstanding surrounds cash value calculations for traditional policies and the stated interest rate. The rate is sometimes mistakenly thought to be a policy's rate of return. This misunderstanding does not apply to the same extent with policies such as universal life (UL) and current assumption whole life (CAWL), wherein cash values are derived using the so-called retrospective approach (see Chapter 20 for details). Traditional policies use the prospective approach.

The prospective method utilizes a discount approach and derives a present value figure as the cash value. Thus, the *higher* the interest rate stated in the prospective-based cash value (i.e., traditional) policy, the *lower* will be the cash value, other things being the same. Conversely, the *lower* the interest rate used, the *higher* will be the policy's cash values, other things equal. Hence, if two traditional whole life policies were identical in every way except that one carried a cash value interest rate of 3 percent and the other a 5 percent interest rate, the policy with the 3 percent rate would have the higher cash values. As a practical matter, of course, things are rarely "equal." Usually—but not always—a policy with a higher cash value has a higher premium, lower dividends, or both. Even if the "equal" assumption is relaxed, one cannot judge the effective rate of return on cash value policies by reference to this nonforfeiture policy interest provision.

Some persons who do not understand life insurance fundamentals often seize on this low-stated cash value interest rate and assert that this is the policy's rate of return. This is incorrect. It is merely a conservative discount rate used to derive cash values on a prospective basis.

In contrast to the situation that exists with traditional policies, UL and CAWL policies' stated interest rates—either guaranteed or current—are not used to derive cash values on a discount basis. These interest rates are simply applied to add amounts to an already (usually) existing cash value; that is, they are used in interest compounding, not discounting. Thus, the *higher* the interest rate used, the *higher* are the resultant cash values, and vice versa, other things equal. Again, other things rarely are "equal." As illustrated in preceding chapters, one policy may credit a higher interest rate than another, yet have higher loading charges assessed against the cash values, with the result that the total value is less on the higher-interest contract.

Reinstatement Provision

Another standard provision relates to **reinstatement.** The term refers to the situation where (1) the premium has not been paid within the grace period or, with respect to UL and CAWL policies, the policy has insufficient cash value to pay the monthly mortality and expense charges; (2) the policy, therefore, has lapsed; and (3) the policyowner desires to reactivate the policy.

Nature of Provision. One of the conditions relating to reinstatement is that the insured must furnish evidence of insurability satisfactory to the company. Otherwise, insureds in poor health would routinely apply for reinstatement and there would be **selection against the company.** Experience shows that the impaired are more apt to seek reinstatement than are the unimpaired.

Most unintentional lapses are followed within a short period (two to four weeks) by an application for reinstatement. The insurer usually takes a liberal view in such cases, since the chance of adverse selection is minimal. Companies have the contractual right to require a medical examination and other evidence of insurability, but in practice, only limited evidence usually is required for recent lapses. The longer the period since the lapse, the more closely the requirements coincide with those imposed for new applications.

The term "evidence of insurability" is broader than "good health." Insurability connotes standards with regard to such subjects as occupation, travel, other insurance, and financial conditions, as well as the physical characteristics or health status of the insured. The classic example of the distinction between "good health" and "insurability" is the case of a criminal condemned

to death—he or she may be in perfect health, but hardly insurable.[60]

The term "satisfactory to the company" has generally been held to allow the insurer to require evidence that would be satisfactory to a reasonable insurer.[61] It should be remembered that an insurer is in business to accept, not to decline applications, and if the person is insurable, the presumption must be that he or she will be accepted.

A second condition that must be met for reinstatement is the payment of past-due premiums or, with respect to UL policies, past-due monthly deductions, with interest thereon. The usual terms require payment of the overdue amounts, less any dividends that would have been paid, usually with interest at 6 or 8 percent. Any outstanding policy loan also must be either repaid or reinstated through payment of past-due interest.

The reinstatement provision was originally included voluntarily by companies to safeguard accumulated policy values. Under such older contracts, if the premium was not paid when due, not only did the policy lapse, but the values that had accumulated under the policy were forfeited.

The standard provision for reinstatement does not require that reinstatement be permitted if the policy has been either surrendered for its cash value or continued as extended term insurance and the full period of coverage has expired. Many companies include this restriction in their contracts.

The Pros and Cons of Reinstatement. Although company practice is liberal, reinstatement is seldom permitted by companies or required by law more than five years after lapse, due to the high costs involved. The reasons that reinstatement of a recently lapsed policy may be to the policyowner's advantage relative to the purchase of a new one include:

1. The old policy may have a lower premium rate per $1,000 since it may have been issued at a younger age.

---

[60] *Kallman v. Equitable Life Assurance Society,* 248 App. Div. 146, 288 N.Y. Supp. 1032 (1st Dept. 1936): affirmed, 272 N.Y. 648, 5 N.E.2d 375 (1936).

[61] 18 Cal.2d 635, 117 P.2d at 7 (1941).

2. The incontestable and suicide periods of the older policy may have expired or be closer to expiration.[62]

3. The owner usually will incur front-end loads again on the purchase of a new policy, whereas these amounts may already have been paid under the old policy.

4. Initial cash value increases under new policies usually are less than those found with older policies, other things being equal.

5. The older policy may contain provisions that are more liberal (e.g., lower policy loan rate or more attractive settlement option rates) than those found in new policies.

6. The insurer for the older policy may be more disposed to reactivate the old policy (by imposing a lower standard of insurability) than the issuer of a new policy.

On the other hand, the preceding arguments could prove to be unpersuasive for one or more of the following reasons:

1. The new policy may, in fact, have a lower premium rate per $1,000 even at the higher issue age since competition has driven rates to new lows, and with respect to pure term policies, payment of back premiums rarely makes sound economic sense.

2. In the absence of an insured who intends to misrepresent information, the fact that a new incontestable period may be incurred can be of little importance.

3. In the absence of an insured who intends to commit or has tendencies toward committing suicide, the fact that a new suicide period may be incurred can be of little importance.

4. Some policies today have little or no front-end load, and even with the payment of a new front-

end load, a new policy may be superior from a cost standpoint to the older one.

5. Similar to reason 4, initial cash value increases on a new policy could be equal to or greater than those of an older policy.

6. The newer policy may contain provisions that are more liberal (e.g., premium payment flexibility, greater participation in the insurer's investment experience) than those of the older policy.

7. The amount of money necessary to be paid in interest and back charges may be more profitably used to fund the purchase of additional insurance or to lower the effective cost of the new policy.[63]

Therefore, as is often the case in life insurance, there is no clear-cut "yes" or "no" answer as to whether policyowners would be better off financially by reinstating an older policy or purchasing a new one. It can be stated that currently, if the old policy is a guaranteed-cost, nonparticipating contract that was issued some years ago, it frequently is advantageous to purchase a new contract rather than seek reinstatement. Knowledgeable and conscientious agents can be invaluable in helping clients evaluate and make this decision.[64]

Misstatement of Age or Sex

The laws of most states require that policies include a provision that if the age of the insured is found to have been misstated, the amount of insurance shall be adjusted to be that which would have been purchased by the premium had the correct age been known. For example, consider an ordinary life policy for $50,000 issued at age 35 at an annual premium of $900. Assume that when the death claim was filed, the true age at issue was found to be 36 and $50,000 of coverage at this age would have required a premium of $960. The amount payable by the company would then be 900/960 of $50,000, or $46,875. Although not a standard provision, the amount payable would be

---

[62]The law is not entirely clear, but the majority view is that the incontestable clause is reinstated, making the policy contestable again but only with respect to statements made in connection with the reinstatement application. A second view is that the original contestable period is effective, while a third and very minority view holds that the original contestable period is effective with respect to the policy as a whole but the reinstatement itself is a separate agreement that has no incontestable period and can be contested for fraud at any time. See William F. Myer, *Life and Health Insurance Law* (Rochester, N.Y.: The Lawyers Co-operative Publishing Co., 1972), §8:17. In contrast, the courts have been virtually unanimous in holding that the suicide clause does not run again. *Ibid.,* §10:1.

[63]Some companies by practice—rarely by contract—permit a lapsed policy to be reinstated through a procedure that does not involve payment of all back premiums. It involves a redating and reissuance of the policy and is referred to as **reinstatement by redating.**

[64]However, it must be acknowledged that an agent may have a vested interest in selling a new policy since he or she will receive a commission.

adjusted in a similar manner if a misstatement of sex has been made on the application.[65]

In the event that the error in age is discovered while the policy is still in force, the procedure followed depends upon whether the age has been under- or overstated. If the age has been understated, the insured is usually given the option of paying the difference in premiums with interest or of having the policy reissued for the reduced amount. In the case of overstatement of age, a refund is usually made by paying the difference in reserves. This provision, originally included in policies voluntarily by many insurers, is intended to deal contractually with the potential problem of having a misstatement of age being considered a material misrepresentation, thus being the basis for policy avoidance.

PROVISIONS PROTECTING THE COMPANY

A number of provisions in life insurance contracts primarily protect the life insurance company against adverse selection. These include the suicide clause, the delay clause, and certain hazard restriction clauses permitted by law.

Suicide Clauses

At one time, life insurance contracts excluded the risk of suicide entirely. This was unfortunate since the very purpose for which the policy was purchased—to protect dependents—could be defeated. In addition, it was not necessary to exclude suicide completely to protect the company. Suicide is one of the causes of death that make up the total mortality rate, and such deaths can be and are included in the mortality tables upon which premiums are based. It is necessary, however, for the company to protect itself against cases where insurance is purchased in contemplation of suicide. Adequate protection against this selection against the company can be obtained by

excluding the risk of suicide for the first one or two policy years. It is worthwhile noting that this provision protects the policyowner also in that it helps assure other policyowners that they will not pay more than their equitable share of the cost of insurance.

The clause is intended to protect against adverse selection, not to exclude the risk of suicide as such. Most state laws permit an exclusion of up to two years, and this is the usual practice. A number of companies, however, use a one-year exclusion. A typical **suicide clause** reads as follows:

> For the first two full years from the original application date, we will not pay if the insured commits suicide (while sane or insane). We will terminate the policy and give back the premiums paid to us less any loan.

The question of whether a death is suicide or due to other causes is almost always left to a jury. There is a legal presumption that a person will not take his or her own life. This fact, plus the tendency of courts to seek ways of ruling for dependents, often make it exceedingly difficult to prove suicide. For example, some courts have held that an "insane" person, by definition, cannot commit "suicide," since suicide requires a knowledge of right and wrong. This result has emerged even in the face of the "while sane or insane" policy language of the provision. Thus, under this interpretation, an insane person who takes his or her own life has not committed suicide, and the company would be required to honor the death claim. Where death is in fact determined to be by suicide and within the period of exclusion, the company will refund the premiums paid, with or without interest, depending on the contract.

Delay Clause

Life insurance policies must contain a provision granting the company the right to defer payment of any cash value or making of a policy loan (except for purposes of paying premiums) up to six months after request is made for it. This provision is intended to protect the company against "runs," where investments might have to be liquidated under adverse circumstances. Only

[65]Proposals are under consideration in Congress and several state legislatures to eliminate sex as a rating factor in all lines of insurance. Montana currently prohibits the use of gender as a rating factor. See Chapter 24.

Misstatements of sex are not common and usually occur as a result of simple transcribing error; not because the proposed insured was unsure of his or her gender.

one company is known to have invoked this clause in the last several decades and, at that, received criticism for having done so. It is intended to be used only under dire circumstances.

Hazard Restrictions

The life insurance policy is an "all-risk" contract, with the law permitting the use of only limited exclusions. One, the **aviation exclusion,** denies coverage in case of death from aviation. It is included in life insurance contracts today only under certain exceptional circumstances. All companies cover fare-paying passengers on regularly scheduled airlines. Similarly, anticipated flights on unscheduled airlines usually do not result in any policy restrictions or an increased rate. Even private pilots and the pilots and crews of commercial airlines are being insured standard or with only slight extra rates. The major area where aviation restrictions are still strictly applied is the case of military aircraft. It is important to note that virtually all restrictions as to coverage can be eliminated if the insured is willing to pay an extra premium.

Companies usually insert so-called **war clauses** in their contracts during periods of impending or actual war, particularly for policies issued to young men of draft age. The clauses normally provide for a return of all premiums paid with interest or a refund equal to the reserve element of the policy if death occurs under conditions excluded in the policy. War clauses are canceled at the end of the war period.

The major purpose of war clauses is to control *adverse selection* on the part of buyers of insurance. Those entering military service would be a larger proportion than normal of individuals buying insurance, and they would also be inclined to buy larger policies than they would in peace-time. The experience of many companies after World Wars I and II showed that they could have covered the war risk without extra premium. Without such clauses, however, the potential adverse selection involved could have significantly impacted the overall mortality experience.

In general, there are two types of war clauses: (1) the status type and (2) the results type. Under the **status** type of clause, the policy will not pay for the death of an insured while he or she is in the military service, regardless of the cause of death. Some companies liberalize this clause by excluding only death outside the "home area," as defined in the clause. Usually, this home area is defined as the United States and Canada, but other definitions are not infrequent. Under the **results** type of clause, there is no coverage if the death is a result of war. The basic distinction between clauses is the significance of the cause of death: Under the status clause, if the insured is in military service, the cause of death is immaterial, and even if one slipped on a bar of soap while taking a bath at home and death resulted, there would be no coverage. Under the results clause, the cause of death would have to be related to military activity.[66]

The validity of war clauses has not been the subject of much litigation, but the interpretation of the clauses has given rise to a large volume of cases. Much litigation has revolved around the question of whether a particular clause is a status clause or a results clause. Other litigation has related to the nature of death and over the existence of war itself.[67]

---

[66]*Hazle v. Liberty Life Ins. Co.,* 186 S.E. 2d 245, 257 S.C. 456 (1972).

[67]See *Berley v. Pennsylvania Mutual Life Insurance Company,* 373 Pa. 231, 95 A.2d 202 (pa. 1953); *Stucker v. College Life Insurance Co. of America,* 208 N.E. 2d 731 (Ind. 1965).

Chapter 9

The Life Insurance Contract: II

PROVISIONS PROVIDING POLICYOWNER FLEXIBILITY

Life insurance policies have always been flexible financial instruments and are becoming even more so. A thorough understanding of the provisions that provide this flexibility is essential for the agent or financial advisor to provide competent professional counseling to clients.

Policy Loan Clause

Laws in all states require inclusion of policy loan provisions in policies with cash values. The provision usually provides, in effect, that (1) the company will lend an amount not to exceed the policy cash value less interest to the next policy anniversary; (2) interest is payable annually at a rate specified in the policy; (3) interest that is not paid when due will be paid automatically by establishing a further loan against the policy to the extent of the amount of interest due; (4) if the total indebtedness equals or exceeds the cash value, the policy will terminate, subject to 31 days' notice to the policyowner; and (5) the policyowner may repay the loan either in whole or in part at any time. Policy loans are a significant source of

flexibility to the policyowner. Also, no one must approve the loan and it is confidential.

The amount of loan available usually includes the cash value of any paid-up additions.[1] A policy loan is not actually due and repayable until either the policy itself matures or the total indebtedness, including unpaid interest, equals the cash value. The automatic continuation of the loan is one of the unique features of policy loans.

Policy Loan Interest Rate. The policy loan interest rate is required to be specified in the policy. When market rates are significantly above the maximum contractual policy loan rate, massive use of policy loans results as individuals borrow at the lower rate. As a result, money that could otherwise be invested at high yields has to be made available to policyowners in the form of policy loans. On many older policies in force, the fixed policy loan rate is 5 or 6 percent, well below current rates. In an effort to rectify the imbalance, the NAIC adopted a new **Model Policy Loan Interest Rate Bill** in December 1980. This new model permits variable-interest-rate policy loans.

---

[1]See "Dividend Options" later in this chapter.

This bill, or one comparable, has now been enacted into law in all states.

Under the Model Law, companies can change the policy loan interest rate up to four times in any given year. Companies are required to evaluate the need for a policy loan interest rate change at least once each year. The rate is not permitted to exceed Moody's Composite Yield on seasoned corporate bonds two months prior to the determination date. The insurance company is not permitted to increase the applicable policy loan interest rate unless the defined ceiling permits a change of at least one-half of 1 percent upward. The bill does not require the insurance company to increase the policy loan rate whenever it would be permissible under the statute. On the other hand, when interest rates are declining, the legislation requires that the insurance company reduce the variable loan interest rate whenever the ceiling rate has declined to at least one-half of 1 percent below the rate currently being charged on policy loans. This assures that the applicable interest rate will decline as market interest rates decline.

Some jurisdictions also have provisions requiring that certain representations be given to the state insurance department for interest rates in excess of 6 percent. Most of them concern a showing that the policyowners will benefit through higher dividends, lower premiums, or both. One state, Arkansas, retains a 10 percent statutory limit on life insurance policy loan interest.

Enactment of the NAIC model bill does not make variable interest rates applicable to policy loans on existing policies. It is applicable only to new policies issued with the variable-interest-rate provision. As discussed in Chapter 5, a number of companies have made offers to their policyowners to accept the variable loan interest rate provision in exchange for more liberal dividends. It will take many years before a substantial amount of the total available cash values of insurance in force would be represented by newer policies containing the newly permitted provision.

Automatic Premium Loan. Although not usually required, many companies include a provision for an **automatic premium loan** (APL). It provides that if a premium is unpaid at the end of the grace period, and if the policy has a sufficient cash value, the amount of the premium due will be advanced automatically as a loan against the policy.[2] Because of the nature of universal life (UL) policies, they have no APL-type provision.

In some states the policyowner must specifically elect to make the provision operative. The purpose of the APL provision is protection against unintentional lapse, as where a premium payment is simply overlooked. If the policy were allowed to lapse, the nonforfeiture options would be effective, but if the policyowner wanted to reinstate the policy, the insured would have to furnish evidence of insurability satisfactory to the company. With the APL, the policyowner need only repay the loan, and the original policy death benefit continues. The major disadvantage of the APL is that it may tend to encourage laxity in payment of premiums and result in indebtedness exceeding the cash value. This problem will be recognized as the same type of concern as that which exists with UL policies, where mortality and expense charges are deducted from the cash value.

Policy loans have sometimes been used as a part of an organized plan to finance the premiums due on certain cash value policies. Under these plans, each year the policyowner borrows, subject to certain restrictions, that year's cash value increase from the insurance company and applies it toward payment of the premium due. The policyowner pays only the difference between the premium due and the amount borrowed, plus interest on the outstanding loan. Prior to enactment of TRA '86 and subject to certain guidelines, loan interest was tax deductible. Hence, this plan could be attractive to policyowners in high marginal tax brackets. This method of financing life insurance policies is discussed in more detail later.[3]

Borrowing Your Own Money? The appropriate operation of the policy loan feature of cash value insurance policies has been the subject of

---

[2]Rhode Island requires that all new policies issued in that state contain an automatic premium loan provision unless the policyowner elects otherwise. Maryland requires it to be offered. It is not a statutory requirement in other states.

[3]See Chapter 13.

considerable misunderstanding and misinformation. Some persons contend that the insurance company should not charge interest on policy loans since "you're borrowing your own money." This view is incorrect and demonstrates a lack of understanding of life insurance fundamentals.

There are two reasons why policy loan interest must be charged. First, in calculating premiums to be charged the public, life insurers assume in their computations that the assets generated by blocks of policies will be invested and will earn interest.[4] The company discounts (lowers) premiums in advance for these anticipated interest earnings. If the policyowner removes—via a policy loan—his or her proportionate share of these assets, and if the insurer charged no interest on this loan, the company's assumptions regarding future earnings on these assets would not be realized. If the insurer did not charge interest for loans, it logically also should not discount premiums in anticipation of future investment earnings. The net result would be that premiums would be significantly higher, but the policyowners would not have to pay interest "to borrow their own money."

The second reason that it is appropriate to charge interest on policy loans relates to a fundamental misunderstanding on the part of critics as to the nature of the cash value. A policy's cash value is not the "policyowner's money" in the usual sense of the word. The cash values of an insurance policy result from the prefunding of future mortality costs. They are not a "savings account" in the usual sense of the term. In fact, the policyowner does not have legal title to the specific assets backing the cash value. The insurance company owns the assets backing all policy liabilities. The policyowner has title to a right (policy surrender) which, when exercised, results in the cash value being paid to the policyowner. In finance terms, the policyowner owns a "call." He or she can either (1) surrender the policy, obtain the cash value, and give up insurance coverage, or (2) continue the policy and obtain the right to have the face amount paid to the beneficiary. Both rights cannot be exercised simultaneously. They are mutually exclusive. Therefore, policyowners do not borrow "their own money." Rather, they have a right to request a policy loan using the policy's cash value as full security to back the loan—akin to the popular revolving home equity loans.

The Beneficiary Clause

The **beneficiary clause** in a life insurance contract provides another significant element of flexibility to the policyowner. The clause permits him or her to have the proceeds of the policy distributed to whom and in the form he or she wishes. The policyowner can prepare a plan of distribution in advance which accomplishes his or her personal objectives, allowing appropriately for future contingencies.

Nature of Designation. The rights of the policyowner and the beneficiary depend upon whether a beneficiary designation is revocable or irrevocable. There may be situations, mostly involving divorce settlements and creditors, where a policyowner will not want to retain the right to change beneficiaries. In these situations, the designation is said to be **irrevocable** and the beneficiary is held to have a vested right in the policy. This vested right is so complete that neither the policyowner nor his or her creditors can impair it without the beneficiary's consent.[5]

Thus, in the case of an irrevocable beneficiary designation, unless there is some specific policy provision authorizing the policyowner to make policy loans, surrender the policy, or exercise other specific prematurity rights or privileges, he or she may not take any action that will in any way diminish or affect the right of the beneficiary to receive the full amount of insurance at the death of the insured. In the usual case, the practical effect of an irrevocable designation is as if the beneficiary and the policyowner were joint owners of the policy. The policyowner cannot act without the consent of the irrevocable beneficiary.

Today, virtually all policies contain a provision reserving to the policyowner the power to change the beneficiary or beneficiaries at will

---

[4]See Chapter 2.

[5]*Condon v. New York Life,* Iowa 658, 166 N.W. 452 (1983).

contingent beneficiaries, will prevent the proceeds from falling into the probate estate of either an owner/insured or the original beneficiary. Another provision sometimes utilized is a direction that the proceeds are payable to the beneficiary only if he or she is alive at the time of payment. The latter provision, with the proper use of the income settlement options, will also avoid most of the problems mentioned above.

Assignment Provision

Ownership rights in life insurance policies, like other types of property, can be transferred by the current owner to another person. Such transfers are referred to as **assignments.** Assignments are of two types: **absolute** and **collateral.**

Absolute Assignments. An absolute life insurance policy assignment is the irrevocable transfer to another person by the existing policyowner of *all* of his or her rights in the policy. In other words, it is a change of ownership. In the case of a *gift,* the assignment is a voluntary property transfer involving no monetary consideration. Gifts of life insurance policies are frequently made among family members for both personal and tax reasons.[12]

From time to time, a life insurance policy is *sold* for a valuable consideration. For example, a policy owned by a corporation on the life of a key employee may be sold for an amount equal to its cash value to the employee upon employment termination. As with a gift, such transactions are accomplished through an absolute assignment of policy rights, typically using an absolute assignment form furnished by the insurer.

As pointed out earlier, an irrevocable beneficiary must consent to an assignment of the policy since he or she is, in effect, a joint owner. In the case of a revocable beneficiary, many courts have held that an absolute assignment, by itself, does not change the beneficiary.[13] Other courts have ruled the opposite. The new owner, of course, can change the beneficiary by following the customary procedures.

Collateral Assignments. A collateral assignment is a partial and temporary transfer of policy ownership rights to another. Collateral assignments are ordinarily used as collateral security for loans from banks or other lending institutions (or persons). Such assignments are partial in the sense that only *some*—not *all* as in an absolute assignment—policy rights are transferred, and they are temporary in the sense that the transferred partial rights revert back to the policyowner upon repayment of the debt.

The vast majority of life insurance policy collateral assignments use the American Bankers Association (ABA) Collateral Assignment Form No. 10. The form was developed jointly by the American Bankers Association and the Association of Life Insurance Counsel. The ABA Form 10 attempts to provide adequate protection to the lender but at the same time to permit the policyowner to retain certain rights under the policy. Thus the assignee (e.g., the lending institution) gets the right to (1) collect the proceeds at maturity, (2) surrender the policy pursuant to its terms, (3) obtain policy loans, (4) receive dividends, and (5) exercise and receive benefits of nonforfeiture rights. On the other hand, the policyowner retains the right to (1) collect any disability benefits, (2) change the beneficiary (subject to the assignment), and (3) elect optional modes of settlement (subject to the assignment). Under the form, the assignee also agrees (1) to pay over to the beneficiary any proceeds in excess of the policyowner's debt; (2) not to surrender or obtain a loan from the insurance company (except for paying premiums) unless there is default on the debt or premium payments, and then not until 20 days after notification to the policyowner; and (3) to forward the policy to the company for endorsement of any change of beneficiary or election of settlement option.

Policy Provision Concerning Assignment. Although policies are assignable in the absence of policy assignment provisions, life insurance companies today include in their policies an **assignment clause** of some kind. Although much

---

[12]See Chapter 14.

[13]*Continental Assur. Co. v. Connoy,* 209 F.2d 539 (3rd Cir. 1954); *Rountree v. Frazee,* 282 Ala. 142, 209 So.2d 424 (1968).

beneficiary at the same time as the primary beneficiary is designated.

Change of Beneficiary. In the absence of an irrevocable beneficiary designation, the policyowner may change the designation at will. The policy provides the method for accomplishing this and although companies usually require that this method be followed carefully, in the majority of cases a beneficiary change is a routine matter.

However, where the policyowner has done all that he or she could to effect a beneficiary change, but because of factors beyond his or her control the procedure was not followed, a beneficiary change will be deemed to have been accomplished notwithstanding the failure to comply fully with the policy requirements. The courts reached this result by use of the **doctrine of substantial compliance.**[7] Thus, where a policyowner signed the change of beneficiary form and sent it to his wife to deliver to the company agent but was killed before the delivery to the agent, the change of beneficiary was effective.[8] In another case, the policyowner/insured requested change of beneficiary forms, signed them, but delayed forwarding them to the company, although there was ample time and opportuntiy. The forms were mailed after the death of insured, but it was held to be an ineffective change of beneficiary.[9]

Common Disaster. The right of a beneficiary to receive the proceeds of a life insurance policy is usually conditioned on his or her surviving the insured. Usually, there is no problem of survivorship, but where the insured and the beneficiary die in the same accident and there is no evidence to show who died first, the question arises as to whom the proceeds are payable. There is no common-law presumption based on age or sex as to which died first.[10] Although there

has been much diversity of decisions, courts in states that have not adopted the Uniform Simultaneous Death Act (see below) have awarded the proceeds to the insured's estate in the absence of a contingent beneficiary, particularly where the insured has reserved the right to change the beneficiary.

However, most states have enacted the **Uniform Simultaneous Death Act.** This act, which is not confined to insurance, provides in a section on insurance that "where the insured and beneficiary in a policy of life or accident insurance have died and there is not sufficient evidence that they have died otherwise than simultaneously, the proceeds of the policy shall be distributed as if the insured had survived the beneficiary." This, of course, resolves the question of survival in those states where the act is effective, but it does not solve the main problems facing policyowners and insurance companies. Specifically, if the proceeds are payable in a lump sum, and no contingent beneficiary is named, no matter who is determined to have survived, the proceeds will be paid into the probate estate of the insured or the beneficiary. This possibly will subject the proceeds to depletion through unnecessary probate and related costs, additional taxes, and the claims of creditors.

Related to this situation are the much more frequent short-term survivorship situations, where the beneficiary survives the insured by a very short period of time. Here there is no question of survivorship, but similar problems exist. In addition, there is a possibility of shrinkage in the proceeds because of prior election of a life income settlement option, under which the entire proceeds are considered fully earned even though the beneficiary lived to receive only one or a few installments.[11]

In approaching this problem, many companies use a so-called **survivorship clause** or **time clause** that provides that the beneficiary must survive the insured by a fixed period after the insured's death to be entitled to the proceeds. This clause, in conjunction with the naming of

[7]Vernon's A.T.C. Insurance Code, §3.48; *Pena v. Salinas,* 536 S.W. 2d 671, Tex. Civ. App. (1976).

[8]*Pabst v. Hesse,* 173 N.W. 2d 925, 286 Minn. 33 (1970).

[9]*Magruder v. Northwestern Mut. Life Ins. Co.,* 512 F.2d 507, C.A. Tenn. (1975).

[10]W. R. Vance, and B. M. Anderson, *Handbook of the Law of Insurance,* 3rd ed. (St. Paul, Minn.: West Publishing Co., 1951), p. 724.

[11]If a minimum number of installments were guaranteed, installments equal to the guarantee number would be paid.

contingent beneficiaries, will prevent the proceeds from falling into the probate estate of either an owner/insured or the original beneficiary. Another provision sometimes utilized is a direction that the proceeds are payable to the beneficiary only if he or she is alive at the time of payment. The latter provision, with the proper use of the income settlement options, will also avoid most of the problems mentioned above.

Assignment Provision

Ownership rights in life insurance policies, like other types of property, can be transferred by the current owner to another person. Such transfers are referred to as **assignments.** Assignments are of two types: **absolute** and **collateral.**

Absolute Assignments. An absolute life insurance policy assignment is the irrevocable transfer to another person by the existing policyowner of *all* of his or her rights in the policy. In other words, it is a change of ownership. In the case of a *gift,* the assignment is a voluntary property transfer involving no monetary consideration. Gifts of life insurance policies are frequently made among family members for both personal and tax reasons.[12]

From time to time, a life insurance policy is *sold* for a valuable consideration. For example, a policy owned by a corporation on the life of a key employee may be sold for an amount equal to its cash value to the employee upon employment termination. As with a gift, such transactions are accomplished through an absolute assignment of policy rights, typically using an absolute assignment form furnished by the insurer.

As pointed out earlier, an irrevocable beneficiary must consent to an assignment of the policy since he or she is, in effect, a joint owner. In the case of a revocable beneficiary, many courts have held that an absolute assignment, by itself, does not change the beneficiary.[13] Other courts have ruled the opposite. The new owner, of course, can change the beneficiary by following the customary procedures.

Collateral Assignments. A collateral assignment is a partial and temporary transfer of policy ownership rights to another. Collateral assignments are ordinarily used as collateral security for loans from banks or other lending institutions (or persons). Such assignments are partial in the sense that only *some*—not *all* as in an absolute assignment—policy rights are transferred, and they are temporary in the sense that the transferred partial rights revert back to the policyowner upon repayment of the debt.

The vast majority of life insurance policy collateral assignments use the American Bankers Association (ABA) Collateral Assignment Form No. 10. The form was developed jointly by the American Bankers Association and the Association of Life Insurance Counsel. The ABA Form 10 attempts to provide adequate protection to the lender but at the same time to permit the policyowner to retain certain rights under the policy. Thus the assignee (e.g., the lending institution) gets the right to (1) collect the proceeds at maturity, (2) surrender the policy pursuant to its terms, (3) obtain policy loans, (4) receive dividends, and (5) exercise and receive benefits of nonforfeiture rights. On the other hand, the policyowner retains the right to (1) collect any disability benefits, (2) change the beneficiary (subject to the assignment), and (3) elect optional modes of settlement (subject to the assignment). Under the form, the assignee also agrees (1) to pay over to the beneficiary any proceeds in excess of the policyowner's debt; (2) not to surrender or obtain a loan from the insurance company (except for paying premiums) unless there is default on the debt or premium payments, and then not until 20 days after notification to the policyowner; and (3) to forward the policy to the company for endorsement of any change of beneficiary or election of settlement option.

Policy Provision Concerning Assignment. Although policies are assignable in the absence of policy assignment provisions, life insurance companies today include in their policies an **assignment clause** of some kind. Although much

---

[12]See Chapter 14.

[13]*Continental Assur. Co. v. Connoy,* 209 F.26 539 (3rd Cir. 1954); *Rountree v. Frazee,* 282 Ala. 142, 209 So.2d 424 (1968).

considerable misunderstanding and misinformation. Some persons contend that the insurance company should not charge interest on policy loans since "you're borrowing your own money." This view is incorrect and demonstrates a lack of understanding of life insurance fundamentals.

There are two reasons why policy loan interest must be charged. First, in calculating premiums to be charged the public, life insurers assume in their computations that the assets generated by blocks of policies will be invested and will earn interest.[4] The company discounts (lowers) premiums in advance for these anticipated interest earnings. If the policyowner removes—via a policy loan—his or her proportionate share of these assets, and if the insurer charged no interest on this loan, the company's assumptions regarding future earnings on these assets would not be realized. If the insurer did not charge interest for loans, it logically also should not discount premiums in anticipation of future investment earnings. The net result would be that premiums would be significantly higher, but the policyowners would not have to pay interest "to borrow their own money."

The second reason that it is appropriate to charge interest on policy loans relates to a fundamental misunderstanding on the part of critics as to the nature of the cash value. A policy's cash value is not the "policyowner's money" in the usual sense of the word. The cash values of an insurance policy result from the prefunding of future mortality costs. They are not a "savings account" in the usual sense of the term. In fact, the policyowner does not have legal title to the specific assets backing the cash value. The insurance company owns the assets backing all policy liabilities. The policyowner has title to a right (policy surrender) which, when exercised, results in the cash value being paid to the policyowner. In finance terms, the policyowner owns a "call." He or she can either (1) surrender the policy, obtain the cash value, and give up insurance coverage, or (2) continue the policy and obtain the right to have the face amount paid to the beneficiary. Both rights cannot be exercised simultaneously. They are mutually exclusive. Therefore, policyowners do not borrow "their own money." Rather, they have a right to request a policy loan using the policy's cash value as full security to back the loan—akin to the popular revolving home equity loans.

The Beneficiary Clause

The **beneficiary clause** in a life insurance contract provides another significant element of flexibility to the policyowner. The clause permits him or her to have the proceeds of the policy distributed to whom and in the form he or she wishes. The policyowner can prepare a plan of distribution in advance which accomplishes his or her personal objectives, allowing appropriately for future contingencies.

Nature of Designation. The rights of the policyowner and the beneficiary depend upon whether a beneficiary designation is revocable or irrevocable. There may be situations, mostly involving divorce settlements and creditors, where a policyowner will not want to retain the right to change beneficiaries. In these situations, the designation is said to be **irrevocable** and the beneficiary is held to have a vested right in the policy. This vested right is so complete that neither the policyowner nor his or her creditors can impair it without the beneficiary's consent.[5]

Thus, in the case of an irrevocable beneficiary designation, unless there is some specific policy provision authorizing the policyowner to make policy loans, surrender the policy, or exercise other specific prematurity rights or privileges, he or she may not take any action that will in any way diminish or affect the right of the beneficiary to receive the full amount of insurance at the death of the insured. In the usual case, the practical effect of an irrevocable designation is as if the beneficiary and the policyowner were joint owners of the policy. The policyowner cannot act without the consent of the irrevocable beneficiary.

Today, virtually all policies contain a provision reserving to the policyowner the power to change the beneficiary or beneficiaries at will

---

[4]See Chapter 2.

[5]*Condon v. New York Life,* Iowa 658, 166 N.W. 452 (1983).

while the policy is in force. When this right is reserved—so-called **revocable** designations—the named beneficiary obtains no vested rights in the policy or in its proceeds but possesses only a "mere expectancy until after the maturity of the contract." Thus, where the policyowner reserves the right to change the beneficiary, he or she is regarded, in the absence of any other assignment of policy rights, as the complete owner of the policy.

Designating the Beneficiary. The importance of being careful in the setting up of the beneficiary designation cannot be overemphasized. If the policyowner's intentions are to be carried out effectively, the language must be precise and unambiguous.

Numerous illustrations may be cited for the need to use care in describing beneficiaries. Consider some class designations. Designations that relate to children have invited misunderstanding and litigation. The policyowner who designates "my minor children" is not thinking about the fact that eventually children will reach adulthood. Where a husband's policy was payable to "the insured's children," the term included those by a former wife but not his wife's children by a former husband.

Adopted children are included in the term "children," whereas stepchildren may not be so included. The term "dependents" is limited to those actually dependent upon the policyowner for support. Illegitimate children, if acknowledged by the policyowner, are generally included in the designation "children." However, if the policyowner fails to legitimize them, generally, they will not be included in such a designation.

The term "relatives" has been held to include "those by marriages as well as by blood, but not an illegitimate child"; the term "heirs" refers to "those who take under the status of descent and distribution."[6] Even if the "correct" person ends up receiving the policy proceeds, litigation and delay can erode policy proceeds and the sheer

[6]For the manner in which the courts have interpreted the various terms that are commonly used in designating beneficiaries in life insurance policies, see 44 Am. Jr. 2d, Insurance §§1727–1790.

human aggravation itself fosters ill-will and invites family discord. Too often, this most important aspect of policy planning receives far too little care and attention. This is an area where a qualified agent or other financial advisor can be of significant help.

A Minor as Beneficiary. The designation of a minor as beneficiary presents unique problems. For example, if a minor beneficiary is named irrevocably, the policyowner is prevented in the future from exercising any rights under the policy, since the minor must consent, and he or she lacks the capability to do so. It would be necessary to have a guardian appointed, and even then, the guardian very likely would not have the authority to provide the necessary consent to such a change, the reason being that such a change would, in all likelihood, tend to diminish the estate of the minor without any offsetting advantage. A guardian is committed to conserving the minor's estate.

Minor beneficiaries also raise the question of how payment of the proceeds is to be accomplished in the event that the policy matures and becomes payable to such a beneficiary before he or she has reached the age of majority. A minor is not legally competent to receive payment and cannot give a valid release for it. To avoid the possibility of having to pay a second time, insurers generally will not make payment of any substantial amount directly to minor beneficiaries, but will require the appointment of a general guardian. This process is time consuming and can be expensive.

Contingent Beneficiary. The time at which the beneficiary is designated and the time at which the insured dies may be separated by many years. There is no assurance that the primary beneficiary will survive the insured. Often, the primary beneficiary is the spouse who is exposed to the same accident (e.g., automobile) hazards as the insured and may die at the same time as the insured. The policyowner should provide, via the beneficiary designation, for the payment of the policy proceeds in case the primary beneficiary predeceases the insured. This is accomplished through the designation of a **contingent** variation exists in the wording, one company's simplified wording provision reads:

> You can assign this policy. We will not be responsible for the validity of an assignment. We will not be liable for any payments we make or actions we take before notice to us of an assignment.

It should be emphasized that assignment provisions of life insurance policies do not prohibit an assignment without the company's consent, but simply provide that the company need not recognize the assignment until it has received written notice of it, and that it assumes no responsibility as to its validity. The company's major concern is to avoid paying the claim twice.

Change of Plan Provision

Many policies contain a provision granting the policyowner the right to change the policy form. The conversion feature discussed in Chapter 4 on term insurance is an example of a change of plan provision. Most companies limit the change to plans of insurance involving a higher premium rate, although some permit a change to a lower premium rate plan, but only with satisfactory evidence of insurability. Flexible premium policies, in essence, contain a very broad change of plan provision.

In connection with a change to a higher-premium-rate plan of fixed-premium life insurance, the policyowner must usually pay the difference between the then policy reserve on the new form and the policy reserve under the original policy. Changes to plans with higher premium rates do not necessitate evidence of insurability. Companies that do not grant changes to lower-premium plans as a matter of contract right usually will do so as a matter of practice. Since evidence of insurability is required, the incontestability clause is reinstated in the same manner as for a reinstatement. If a change to a lower-premium form is requested, any decrease in reserve or cash value occasioned by the change would be paid by the company to the policyowner.

Change of Insured Provision

Some companies today include a policy provision permitting a change of insureds. This can be particularly useful for corporate-owned life insurance. In the past, when an employee, whose life was insured for the benefit of the corporation, either retired or otherwise terminated employment, the life insurance usually would be surrendered (or sold) and new insurance purchased on the life of the replacement. The change of insured provision, which is subject to insurability requirements, eliminates this necessity and, in effect, also eliminates the front-end load which would otherwise be payable on the newly purchased contract.

Nonforfeiture Options

Another provision of cash value life insurance policies affords the policyowner who chooses to terminate his or her life insurance the option of utilizing the surrender value in several ways. Cash value policies typically stipulate that the surrender value may be taken in one of three forms: (1) cash, (2) a reduced amount of paid-up insurance of the same kind as the original policy, or (3) extended term insurance for the full face amount.

Cash. A policy may be surrendered for the net surrender value shown in the policy as of the date of surrender. Of course, when this option is elected, the protection ceases and the company has no further obligation under the policy. Consequently, even though this can provide a ready source of cash for emergencies and other needs, it should be elected only after careful consideration. Almost the same amount of cash may be obtained through a policy loan, and this may be a better alternative than surrendering the policy.

The available net surrender value is the gross cash value shown in the policy, decreased by any identifiable surrender charges (common in UL policies) and the amount of any policy loan outstanding and increased by the cash value of any paid-up additions, accumulated dividends at interest, and any prepaid premiums.

Besides a complete policy surrender, some policies provide for partial surrenders. As noted in Chapter 6, this is a common feature in universal life policies. Also, traditional participating whole life and endowment policies usually provide that paid-up dividend additions (see "Dividend Options" below) may be surrendered, in whole or in part. Further, as a matter of practice—not by contract guarantee—many companies will permit a partial surrender of traditional cash value policies. However, unlike a UL policy, the face amount is reduced by an amount equal to the proportion by which the cash value is reduced. For example, if $6,000 of a $10,000 cash value is surrendered on a $50,000 ordinary life policy, the face amount would be reduced by 60 percent. This reduction is intended to minimize adverse selection.

Reduced Paid-Up Insurance. A second option permits the policyowner to elect to exchange the net cash surrender value for the equivalent in paid-up insurance of the same type as the original basic policy, exclusive of any term or other rider. All riders and supplementary benefits, such as for disability and accidental death, are terminated, and no further premiums are payable. The exchange is made at rates based on mortality and interest only—not expenses.

Table 9-1 shows that after 10 years, a $56 cash value may be exchanged for $344 of paid-up whole life insurance. This option would be appropriate where a smaller amount of whole life

TABLE 9-1. Minimum nonforfeiture values per $1,000
(1980 CSO mortality table, 7½% interest, ordinary life, male age 35)

End of Year	Cash Value	Paid-Up Insurance	Extended Term Insurance[a]	
			Years	Days
1	$ 0	$ 0	—	—
5	14	112	3	295
10	56	344	10	64
15	108	517	13	28
20	171	646	13	343

[a]Based on the *1980 CET Table.*

insurance would be satisfactory and it was desirable to discontinue premium payments. This option could be attractive, for example, to the policyowner/insured who is approaching retirement, where normally, an individual's income and need for life insurance would be reduced.

The paid-up option may not be available, as such, under UL policies but the same result can be achieved by decreasing the UL face amount to a level that the existing cash value will support indefinitely with no further premium payments.

Extended Term Insurance. The third option permits the policyowner to exchange the cash value for paid-up term insurance for the full face amount.[14] The length of the term insurance period is, in effect, determined by applying the net surrender value as a single term insurance premium, to provide level insurance until the date of expiry.

Referring again to Table 9-1, the tenth-year cash value of $56 may be used to purchase term insurance coverage for the full face amount that will remain in effect for 10 years and 64 days. If the insured does not make a specific election to the contrary, this option is usually the automatic option. This option would be appropriate where the need for the full amount of insurance protection continues, but where the financial capacity to meet premium payments has ceased.

The extended term insurance (ETI) option does not exist as such under UL policies, although the same effect can be accomplished. If the UL policyowner ceases to pay premiums, the policy's face amount is maintained in force for as long as the cash value is sufficient to pay monthly mortality and expense charges. This constitutes the normal operation of the UL policy and therefore need not be viewed as a nonforfeiture option. The end result of this "run-off," however, is similar to that found under the conventional ETI option. Therefore, in effect, ETI is the automatic UL option.

---

[14]If policy loans or paid-up dividend additions are outstanding, both the face amount and cash value are decreased or increased accordingly.

Settlement Options

One of the important things policyowners should consider at the time they purchase life insurance is the manner in which any death proceeds will be paid. Failure to arrange for the proper payment of proceeds may defeat the very purpose for which the insurance was intended. The following section discusses the policy provisions that permit the policyowner (or beneficiary) flexibility in deciding how any death proceeds will be paid: the so-called **settlement options.** Insurers do not make an explicit, separate charge in connection with either the drafting of a settlement agreement or the administration of its terms and conditions. It should be noted that most insurers also permit cash values to be paid out under one or more settlement options. This can be particularly valuable at retirement when the policyowner no longer needs the insurance protection and desires to annuitize the policy's cash value as a retirement benefit.

Legal Nature. Following the insured's death, a contractual relationship exists between the insurance company and the beneficiary—whether the proceeds are payable in a lump sum or under a settlement option. If the policyowner, during the insured's lifetime, sets up the settlement arrangement, performance of that agreement after the insured's death is regarded merely as a continuation of the third-party beneficiary arrangement. If, on the other hand, a beneficiary, entitled to a lump-sum settlement, elects to receive the proceeds under one of the settlement options, some courts have held that a new direct contractual relationship exists between the company and the beneficiary. In either case, however, as a party to a direct contractual relationship or as a third-party beneficiary, the beneficiary may enforce his or her rights under the life insurance contract or subsequent settlement agreement.

Types of Options. Settlement options are usually designated in the contract and most contracts provide a choice from among one or more of the options discussed below. Although most companies permit arrangements not specifically granted by contract, virtually all companies are more liberal respecting income settlement plans adopted by the policyowner before death than for those requested by the beneficiary. It should be noted that the policyowner in designating any settlement option may give the beneficiary as much or as little flexibility as the policyowner desires. Thus, with all the options discussed below, a policyowner could totally "lock in" the manner in which proceeds would be paid to the beneficiary, with neither the insurer nor the beneficiary having any right to alter the arrangement at the insured's death. Alternatively, the policyowner could design a settlement agreement which, on the death of the insured, gave the beneficiary total freedom to alter its terms, but in the absence of a change by the beneficiary, the policyowner's wishes would be followed by the company. Also, of course, there exists a "flexibility" continuum between these two extremes. Insurers will work closely with the financial advisor and policyowner to provide for the desired degree of flexibility to the beneficiary.

1. *Cash or lump sum.* In a strict sense, a "lump-sum" settlement is not an "option," because life insurance contracts usually provide for lump-sum settlement in the *absence* of any other direction by the policyowner or beneficiary.

In deciding whether to have proceeds paid to the beneficiary in a lump sum, the agent or other financial advisor will want to remember that such a settlement usually affords no protection against the creditors of the beneficiary. Such protection usually can be arranged in connection with the income options, but only if elected before the insured's death.[15]

Many policies provide for interest to be paid from the date of death, even if a settlement option had not been elected. Indeed, several states have recently enacted laws requiring the payment of such interest.

Although there are circumstances where a

---

[15]See "Creditor Rights in Life Insurance" later in this chapter.

lump-sum settlement may be indicated, the interest option, discussed next, is very flexible and permits adjustments to be made in light of changing economic, health, and other circumstances.

    2. *Interest option.* Under the interest option, the proceeds remain with the company and only the interest earned thereon is paid to the beneficiary. A minimum interest rate is guaranteed in the contract, although most, if not all companies credit a rate higher than the guaranteed minimum. In most companies, the interest cannot be left to accumulate and compound, but must be paid out monthly, quarterly, semiannually, or annually. Since there are legal limits to the length of time a principal sum may be kept intact (see below), companies frequently limit the time that they will hold a principal sum under this option to the lifetime of the primary beneficiary or 30 years, whichever is longer.

    The interest option is one of the most widely used options. The main advantage of the interest option is that it assures the beneficiary freedom from investment worries, while guaranteeing both principal and a minimum rate of return. In addition, however, depending upon individual company rules and state laws, the primary beneficiary may be given:

1. The right to name who is to receive any balance at his or her death, or the right to change the contingent beneficiaries previously designated by the policyowner.
2. The right to make withdrawals of all or part of the principal, subject to the limitations prescribed by the policyowner in the settlement agreement. Most companies will permit any reasonable combination of limiting factors (so much per year, at certain ages, and so on), or the proceeds may be held without any withdrawal privileges.
3. The right to elect to change to another settlement option at a later time, when circumstances may have changed. For example, the proceeds may be left under the interest option with the right in the primary beneficiary to change to any other option, including the life income option (see below), at a later date.
4. Protection from most creditors, under a spendthrift clause included in the policy.

The right of withdrawal and the right to change to another option are the sources of flexibility in the interest option, and it is usually the foundation upon which most comprehensive settlement agreements are formulated.

    3. *Fixed-period option.* This is one of the two options based on the concept of systematically liquidating principal and interest over a period of years, *without reference to life contingencies.* The other is the fixed-amount option, discussed below.

    The fixed-period option, as its name indicates, provides for the payment of the proceeds in installments over a definite period of months or years, usually not longer than 25 or 30 years. The amount of proceeds, the period of time, the guaranteed minimum rate of interest, and the frequency of payments determines the amount of each installment. Any interest in excess of the guaranteed rate is usually credited at the end of each year.

    The fixed-period option is valuable where the most important consideration is to provide income for a definite period, as in the case of a readjustment period following the insured's death or while children are in school. Most companies permit policyowners to give the beneficiary the right to commute, or discount, all remaining installments and receive a lump sum, and some companies will permit the beneficiary to select the date when payments are to begin. However, aside from these options, the fixed-period option is not very flexible.

    Since the basic characteristic of this option is the period of time selected, a policy loan that is outstanding at the insured's death will reduce the amount of each installment but will not affect the number of installments. For the same reason, any dividend accumulations or paid-up additions payable with the proceeds will operate to increase the beneficiary's income, the number of installments remaining the same.

    4. *Fixed-amount option.* Under the fixed-amount option, the amount of income is the primary consideration rather than the period of time over which the proceeds and interest are to be liquidated. Here a specified amount of income is designated, such as $500 per month, and payments are continued until the principal and interest thereon are exhausted.

In most situations, the fixed-amount option is more advantageous than the fixed-period option, because it is more flexible. Most companies permit the policyowner to specify varying amounts of income at different times, and the beneficiary may be given the right of withdrawal in whole or in part, or the right to withdraw up to a certain sum in any one year on a cumulative or noncumulative basis. In the case of both the fixed-period and fixed-amount options, the commencement of these installments can be deferred to a particular time by holding the proceeds under the interest option until that time. As in the case of the interest option, most companies will permit a beneficiary to direct that any unpaid balance be placed under some other option (usually the life income option).

Since the amount of each installment is the controlling factor under this option, dividend accumulations or additions payable with the proceeds, together with any excess interest earned while installments are being paid, increase the number of installments but do not affect the amount of each installment. Conversely, loans outstanding at the insured's death or withdrawals of principal by the beneficiary serve to decrease the number of installments.

There is usually a special rule governing minimum installments under the fixed-amount option. Usually, at least $50 per year or a minimum of a stated amount per month is required to be paid out for each $1,000 of proceeds. The rule is in keeping with the purpose of the option; that is, to exhaust the principal and interest within some reasonable length of time.

It should be noted that the fixed-amount and fixed-period options basically represent the same idea expressed in different ways. Both systematically liquidate principal and interest over a period of years, without reference to a life contingency. For this reason, the guaranteed interest factor is usually the same for both options in a given contract.

5. *Single life income options.* The several forms of single life income options represent the other broad class of settlement options—those liquidating principal and interest *with reference to life contingencies.* These options are unique to life insurance companies. No other financial institution can make such an arrangement with its clients. Single life income options are, in reality, forms of life annuities and thus serve the same economic functions.

The amount of each installment depends on the type of life income (annuity) selected, the amount of the proceeds, the rate of interest being credited, the age of the beneficiary when the income commences, and the sex of the beneficiary (where permitted). The most common forms of life income options are (1) the pure life income option, (2) the refund life income option, and (3) the life income option with "period certain" or "installments guaranteed."

In the **pure life income option,** installments are payable only for as long as the primary beneficiary (the income recipient) lives. In other words, no further payments are made to anyone when the primary beneficiary dies. Since no refunds or further payments are made at the beneficiary's death, the pure life income option provides the largest life income per $1,000 of proceeds for a given beneficiary. However, most persons hesitate to take the risk of forfeiting a large part of the principal in the event of an early death. This is particularly true where there are relatives to whom they wish to leave funds that they do not need for themselves. For example, this form probably would be inappropriate for a widow with young children, as it affords no protection to the children in the case of early death of their mother.

The **refund life income option** may take the form of a **cash refund annuity** or an **installment refund annuity.** It will be remembered that both annuities guarantee the return of an amount equal to the principal sum less the total payments already made. The difference in the two forms is that under the cash refund option, a lump-sum settlement is made following the death of the primary beneficiary instead of continuing the installment payments.

Under the **life income option with period**

certain, the most widely used life income option, installments are payable for as long as the primary beneficiary lives, but should this beneficiary die before a predetermined number of years, the company will continue the installments to a second beneficiary until the end of the designated period. The usual contract contains two or three alternative periods, the most popular being 10 and 20 years, but others may be obtained on request. This option is frequently useful where a widow or widower and minor children are concerned, since it assures the desired income for life while still guaranteeing that the income will last until the children are grown, regardless of the date of death of the parent.

Table 7–1 showed three forms of single life income options. It can be observed that the longer the guarantee period, the less the monthly proceeds. Moreover, as expected, the older the beneficiary, the greater the life income. One of the drawbacks of the life income option is that the amount of income to be received by the beneficiary cannot be ascertained prior to the death of the insured since it depends on the age of the beneficiary. The amounts shown in Table 7–1 are calculated based on the insurer's guaranteed minimum rate of interest. Normally, the actual amounts paid would be higher than the minimums guaranteed.

6. *Joint and survivorship life income option.* Under this option, if at the death of the first beneficiary, the second beneficiary is still living, installments are continued during the latter's lifetime. As in the case of joint and survivorship annuities, this option may continue the same income to the surviving beneficiary or reduce the installments to two-thirds ("joint and two-thirds"), three-fourths ("joint and three-fourths"), or one-half ("joint and one-half") of the original amount and continue this reduced amount for the lifetime of the surviving beneficiary. A few companies will grant joint and survivorship options with a period certain of 10 to 20 years.

The joint and survivorship option is most useful in providing for the retirement income of a husband and wife. In such cases, the proceeds of a matured endowment or retirement income policy or the cash value of any form of insurance may be applied under this option.

7. *Other settlement arrangements.* Virtually any desired pattern of income may be obtained by using the various options described above, either singly or in some combination. In many instances, the policyowner may find that he or she can better provide for beneficiaries by selecting a combination of settlement options. Furthermore, he or she may elect options to operate concurrently, successively, or both.

Some companies provide options that are designed to meet a specific need or serve a particular purpose. Actually, these special options are usually a combination of the basic options to fit a particular situation, with an attractive sales title applied to them. For example, a so-called educational plan option provides a fixed dollar income during nine or 10 months of each college year, with a modest "graduation present" in cash after the final installment. This is really a combination of the fixed amount and interest options, with appropriate limitations placed on them to produce the desired effect.

Notwithstanding the wide variety of settlement plans offered by the various options or combinations of options, situations do arise where the standard options do not fit exactly. Upon submission of the facts, the company usually is willing to work out a special settlement plan within reasonable limits.

In those cases where an individual desires greater flexibility than the insurance company will permit, consideration should be given to the use of an individual trustee or the services of a trust company. This is particularly true if discretionary powers are indicated. A life insurance company normally will not accept any arrangement whereby it must exercise discretion in carrying out the terms of the agreement.

Rule against Perpetuities. It is in the public interest to see that property stays in circulation. To this end, rules limit the length of time during which property owners can reserve to themselves enjoyment of property. The common-law **rule against perpetuities** provides that the vesting of the ownership of property cannot be deferred for longer than a life or lives in being and 21 years (plus the period of gestation) thereafter. Simply, this time limit is 21 years after the death of per-

sons living and identified with a given transaction, measured from the date the property is
transferred or the interest in the property is
created.

The common-law rule has been modified
by statute in a few states. Thus, in New York, the
law provides that absolute ownership to personal
property shall not be suspended by any limitation or condition that could extend beyond two
individual lives in being at the date of the instrument creating the limitation or condition.[16]

Although there has been little litigation on
this point,[17] it is generally believed that the rule
against perpetuities is not applicable to settlement
agreements, because such life insurance agreements merely create a debtor–creditor relationship. From a practical point of view, it is
recognized that family needs usually can be met
within these limitations. Consequently, companies usually avoid any possible application of
the rule against perpetuities by prohibiting agreements that would violate such rules.

Rule against Accumulations. The rule
against accumulations prohibits the accumulation
of income for any unreasonable period. In this
connection, all state laws permit such accumulations during the minority of a beneficiary entitled
to the income, but many prohibit such accumulations for an adult. The laws of a few states,
however, will permit the accumulation of income
during some specified period, such as 10 years,
even though the beneficiary is an adult.

In general, since such laws restricting the
accumulation of income are believed to apply to
life insurance settlement options, companies
usually will permit accumulations of interest
under settlement options *only* during the minority
of beneficiaries, regardless of whether the law in
a given state specifically refers to settlement
options. In fact, some companies will not permit
any accumulations.

Provisions Regarding Surplus/Excess Interest Distribution

Virtually all states require that divisible
surplus accumulated on behalf of a given block
of participating policies be distributed annually
to the policyowners. States increasingly are requiring somewhat similar treatment with respect
to excess interest and other earnings on UL and
the newer-type interest-sensitive products.[18] Both
traditional participating and the newer-type
policies are required to have policy provisions
relative to distribution of these excess amounts.
The functioning of such provisions, as applied
to the newer policy types, was discussed in
Chapter 6, so their treatment here will be brief,
with the presentation focusing chiefly on fixed-
premium participating policies. Before discussing the specific nature of the various options
under which surplus is paid, it is important to
understand further details regarding the nature
of the surplus distribution process itself.

Nature of Surplus Distribution. As pointed
out in Chapter 2, surplus under participating
policies is derived from any of three possible
sources: (1) mortality experience being more
favorable than that assumed; (2) expenses being
lower than those assumed; and (3) investment
earnings being greater than those assumed.

In determining how to apportion divisible
surplus (see below), the so-called **contribution
principle** ideally should be followed by the company. The principle holds simply that aggregate
divisible surplus should be distributed among
policies in the same proportion as the policies are
considered to have contributed to surplus.

How the contribution principle is applied
to derive individual policy dividends need not be
discussed here. Although not an exact science,
actuarial techniques have been developed that
capture the intent of the principle,[19] although life
insurance policies themselves are silent on this
point. Some insurers do not follow the principle.
This leads to inequitable treatment of various
classes of policies and can be detrimental to particular policyowners.

---

[16]Section 11, New York Personal Property Law.

[17]In *Holmes v. John Hancock Mutual Life Insurance Company,*
228 N.Y. 106 41 N.E. 2d 909 (1942), the court held that the
New York statute regarding perpetuities did not apply to a
settlement agreement.

[18]See Chapter 6.

[19]See Chapter 21.

An insurance company's board of directors determines, in the aggregate, the amount of surplus to be distributed each year to policyowners. This decision is made in light of the company's financial position, profitability objectives, and other factors. Actuarial advice is provided to management and the board to assist in arriving at this decision. Management, with board approval, decides how to apportion this divisible surplus among the various blocks of policies. Insurance policies are silent as to the proportion of total surplus that is to be distributed among policies. Concern exists that some insurers do not distribute as much surplus, in the aggregate, as they should.[20] This does not relate necessarily to the manner in which divisible surplus is distributed among blocks of participating policies. Rather, it relates to the aggregate amount of surplus declared to be divisible.

Some states limit the aggregate amount of surplus a mutual life insurer can accumulate to a stated percentage of policy reserves (e.g., 10 percent in New York). Some place similar limitations on stock insurers selling participating life insurance, wherein no more than a stated percentage (e.g., 5 percent) of profits flowing from participating insurance can flow to stockholders. However, most insurance codes and almost all policies are silent on these matters.

Even if divisible surplus or excess interest income is reasonable in amount and if the contribution principle is followed, different methods of allocating mortality charges, expenses, and investment income can produce different results. Perhaps the most important element in this respect applies to investment income allocation.

As mentioned in Chapter 6, some insurers follow the so-called **portfolio average method** (PAM) of investment income allocation and some follow the **investment generation method** (IGM). The IGM itself has variations with some insurers including an element of projected earnings, whereas others do not.

The agent or advisor ideally should know on which method a particular company bases its dividend illustrations or excess interest projections.

Again, the policy itself, typically, will not contain information on this question and few state insurance departments require that this information be made available.[21] The use of these methods has been controversial, especially when an insurer changes from one to the other.[22]

The portfolio method develops a more stable dividend pattern than the IGM. In periods of generally rising investment returns, the IGM allows an insurance company to illustrate and pay higher dividends, other things being equal, than can a company that utilizes the PAM. In periods of declining investment returns, the opposite occurs. If investment returns remain stable over several years, results under the two methods tend to converge. State regulation of these practices is inconsistent. Thus, the advisor should be aware that a company could—in theory—change from one method to the other and back again, so as to take advantage of trends in current interest earnings for purposes of having illustrated dividends on new policies be as high as feasible. The problem would be, of course, that older policyowners could suffer from such changes and the advisor should recognize that new policies become old ones after some years. The new NAIC Model Cost Disclosure Regulation attempts to address this potential problem.[23]

Direct Recognition Dividends/Excess Interest. As discussed in Chapter 6, many companies now include in their insurance policies provisions that permit the company to recognize directly in its excess interest or dividend formula the extent of policy loan activity within the policy. These **direct recognition provisions** are exceedingly important, as they have the effect of increasing the effective cost of policy loans and because they result in a higher level of dividends or excess interest paid under nonborrowing policies. In essence, therefore, such provisions link the policy loan and surplus distribution or excess interest provisions, whereas without such provisions, they

---

[20]See, e.g., *Life Insurance Products, Disclosure, and Marketing Practices* (Richmond, Va.: Virginia Bureau of Insurance, October 1981), pp. 22–40.

[21]But see Chapter 10.

[22]See Joseph M. Belth, "Distribution of Surplus on Individual Life Insurance Policyowners," *The Journal of Risk and Insurance,* Vol. XLV (March 1978).

[23]See Chapter 10.

are not *directly* related. This linkage makes loan decisions more complex. Traditional planning techniques must often be modified to evaluate properly the economics of a policy loan.[24]

Dividend Options. With a conceptual understanding of some of the technical aspects of surplus and excess interest distribution, it is now appropriate to discuss the various options available to policyowners in receiving their policies' shares of distributable surplus—the dividends. These options provide policyowners with another potentially important source of flexibility.

The five dividend options found in most policies are: (1) pay in cash, (2) offset part (or all) of the premium payment, (3) purchase paid-up additional insurance, (4) accumulate at interest, and (5) purchase one-year term insurance. These options can be changed at any time under most policies. With the newer interest-sensitive policies, excess interest (and possibly other) earnings are earmarked to be used to increase the policy's cash value or to reduce the level of future premiums, or both.

1. *Cash.* Most states require that the dividend be made available in cash. Under this option, the insurer simply mails a check for the dividend to the policyowner each year. Policyowners usually find one of the other options more attractive. Also, this option is more costly for the company to administer.

2. *Part payment of premium.* Although applying the dividend toward the payment of the next premium under the policy is really the equivalent of cash, a substantial number of policyowners elect this option to reduce their current outlay of funds. They could, of course, take the dividend in cash and remit the full premium, obtaining the same net effect.

3. *Purchase of paid-up additions.* The policyowner may have the dividend applied to the purchase of paid-up additional insurance under the policy. Under this option, the dividend is applied as a net single premium at the insured's attained age to purchase as much paid-up insurance as it will provide of the same type as the basic policy.[25]

The right to purchase a series of paid-up additions at net rates can be attractive. The attractiveness of this option can be further enhanced for an insured whose health has become impaired. Evidence of insurability is not required at the purchase of each additional insurance amount in the future. Paid-up additions themselves may be participating or nonparticipating. If they are participating, the annual dividends on the paid-up additions would further enhance the policy's total cash value and death benefit. Also, most companies permit changes to this option after issue, often without evidence of insurability.

Some individuals do not wish to purchase single premium life insurance and paid-up additions are a type of single premium life insurance, although small in amount. Some consider it wiser to use dividends to reduce current premiums to permit the purchase of additional annual premium insurance. Even so, paid-up additions can be a worthwhile approach to increasing insurance protection, and they offer further flexibility by virtue of there being a cash value available from them. This cash value can be obtained, in whole or in part, by selective surrender of the paid-up additions, without disturbing the basic policy.

4. *Accumulate at interest.* Dividends may be allowed to accumulate in a fund appended to the policy. The company guarantees to pay a minimum rate of interest, although most companies credit rates higher than the guaranteed minimum. These accumulations can be withdrawn at will by the policyowner. If death occurs, the face of the policy is paid plus dividend accumulations, and in the event of surrender, the cash value plus dividend accumulations will be paid.

[24]For one approach to making this evaluation, see Steven Gardiner and Thomas Mahoney, "Policy Loan Planning in the 1980s," *Journal of the American Society of CLU,* Vol. XXXIX (September 1985).

[25]It should be noted that in operation, this option resembles the reduced paid-up insurance option available in connection with surrender values.

5. *Purchase one-year term.* In recent years, many companies have made available an option to apply the dividend to purchase one-year term insurance. This option is sometimes called the "fifth" dividend option, simply because it is fifth in line after the preceding four. The option usually takes one of two forms. One form applies the dividend as a net single premium to purchase as much one-year term insurance protection as it will buy. The other form purchases one-year term insurance equal to the cash value of the policy, with the excess portion of the dividend applied under one of the other dividend options. The latter form is often used in connection with sales presentations involving so-called split dollar life insurance (see Chapter 15). With split dollar insurance, the policy cash value and an amount of the death benefit equal to the cash value are earmarked for the premium payor. The insured names the beneficiary for the balance of the death proceeds. By using dividends to purchase one-year term insurance equal to the cash value, this beneficiary can receive a death payment equal to the full policy face amount.

6. *Other options.* Some companies permit dividends to be used in other ways. One way is to "pay up" the policy earlier than otherwise would be the case. This is also sometimes referred to as the **vanishing premium option.** This means that when the surrender value of the policy (and of any dividend additions) plus any existing dividend accumulations at the end of a policy year equal or exceed the net single premium for the attained age of the insured (according to a given mortality table at a stipulated rate of interest) for an amount of insurance equal to the face amount of the policy, the company, at the request of the policyowner, will endorse the policy as fully paid. Other options are also sometimes found.

CREDITOR RIGHTS IN LIFE INSURANCE

The rights of creditors in claiming life insurance funds are determined by (1) the nature of the beneficiary designation, (2) bankruptcy laws, and (3) exemption statutes. The nature of the beneficiary designation and the change-of-beneficiary clause are critically important as viewed from the standpoint of creditors.

Rights of Creditors of the Policyowner

Treatment of debtors in early times was often extremely harsh. The framers of our Constitution recognized the need for rehabilitation of debtors. Thus, bankruptcy laws were designed to provide an equitable distribution of assets of the debtor, while giving the debtor an opportunity for rehabilitation. A revised **Bankruptcy Reform Act,** effective October 1, 1979, codified all previous laws related to bankruptcy under Title 11 of the U.S. Code.

The statutes and court decisions governing the extent to which cash values and the proceeds of life insurance policies are available to creditors of the policyowner in case of insolvency are of great importance. It is generally accepted by the legislatures and courts that a moderate amount of insurance may be taken for family protection without its being subject to attachment by creditors.

The Federal Bankruptcy Law. Insolvency is not the same as bankruptcy. Insolvency is the inability to pay one's debts. Bankruptcy is the application of bankruptcy laws to a debtor who may or may not be insolvent as that term is defined. One becomes bankrupt when one comes under the protection of the bankruptcy laws.

Title to a bankrupt person's property vests in the trustee, the person appointed by the bankruptcy court to take over the bankrupt's estate. It may include so-called exempt property at the beginning of the proceedings. Exempt property is excluded from the claims of the bankrupt's creditors. The act also refers to state law for determination of what property becomes exempt. Section 522 provides the debtor with a choice of either state or federal exemptions. The act provides, among other provisions, a $7,500 homestead exemption. To avoid discrimination against non-homeowners, the act provides an exemption of other property up to $7,500 in the event that the homestead and certain other exemptions are not used. This special provision may make the federal exemptions more attractive than those provided by the debtor's state, particularly if policy cash values are exempt under the law. Nevertheless, state exemption statutes will be important and must be studied before an intelligent choice can be made.

Where the insured/policyowner has named a beneficiary other than himself or herself, his or her estate, or his or her legal representatives, and has not reserved the right to change such beneficiary, the beneficiary has a vested interest in the policy, and the creditors of the insured/policyowner have no interest in the insurance proceeds.[26] Where the policy is made payable to the insured/policyowner, his or her estate, or legal representatives, it is subject to the claims of creditors in case of bankruptcy except for any other exemptions. If the insured/policyowner names a beneficiary not in the classes listed above, but reserves the unqualified right to change the beneficiary, the policy, if it has a cash surrender value and to the extent of such value, will pass to the trustee in bankruptcy.

Except for the application of either the federal or state exemption statutes, the courts can be expected to interpret a revocable beneficiary designation as giving the trustee in bankruptcy the power to distribute the cash value of a policy among creditors.

Where the policy has no cash surrender value, the courts have held that the trustee has no interest in it. In *Morris v. Dobb, trustee,* a husband took out a policy payable to his legal representatives and subsequently transferred it to his wife four months prior to the filing of a petition in bankruptcy. The policy had no cash value and the court ruled that the trustee had no interest in such a policy.[27]

Cases often arise where shortly following the filing of the petition in bankruptcy, a policy payable to the insured/policyowner or his or her representatives matures through the death of the bankrupt. In that event, are the creditors entitled to the proceeds of the policy? The question was decided by the Supreme Court and incorporated in the Bank-

ruptcy Reform Act.[28] Current law is that the trustee in bankruptcy gets title only to the net surrender value of the policy at the time of the filing of the petition in bankruptcy. It does not extend to any other policy values, such as the protection afforded on the insured's life.

The Bankruptcy Reform Act also reserves to the bankrupt an aggregate interest of $4,000 in life insurance policies on his or her life. Amounts in excess of this are payable to a creditor unless exempted by state laws.

From the standpoint of protection from creditors, whether one should retain the right to change beneficiaries will largely depend on the exemption laws of the state as well as those of the bankruptcy law. Although failure to retain the right to change the beneficiary puts the proceeds and cash values of life insurance policies beyond the reach of creditors, on the whole it greatly limits the usefulness of the insurance policy. The free use of an insurance policy may greatly outweigh the benefit of being secured from protection from creditors. It would seem that when life insurance is only a modest part of a developing estate, the right to change beneficiaries should be reserved in order that the policy of life insurance can be available as an asset with free assignability. As the insured/policyowner begins to expand his or her business activity, the desirability of retaining this feature of the policies can be reviewed. In any event, a change of ownership may be preferred to an irrevocable beneficiary designation.

State Exemption Statutes. From earliest times it has been the policy of Congress to give effect to state exemption statutes. The National Bankruptcy Act of 1898 had a provision to this effect, which has been retained in the new Bankruptcy Reform Act.[29]

State statutes relative to the rights of creditors may be divided into two broad groups, the first exempting proceeds of life insurance

---

[26]*Central National Bank of Washington v. Hume,* 128 U.S. 195 (1888); *Morse v. Commissioner of Internal Revenue,* 100 F.2d 593 (1939).

[27]110 Ga. 606, quoted *In Re Buelow,* 98 Fed. 86 (1900); *Burlingham v. Crouse,* 228 U.S. 459 (1913).

[28]See, e.g., *Burlingham v. Grouse,* 228 U.S. 459 (1913); *United States v. Binham,* 76 F. 2d 573 (1935).

[29]198 U.S. 202 (1905); *Meyer v. U.S.,* 375 U.S. 233, 239 (1963); *In the matter of Marvin M. Summers, Bankrupt,* 253 F.Supp. 113 (1966).

policies payable at the time of the death of the insured, and the second exempting not only the proceeds payable at death, but the cash values as well. The statutes first enacted were of the type of the first group—led by New York in 1840—but since the 1920s, statutes of the second type have predominated, with New York changing its law in 1927. The 1927 New York Act protects the *proceeds and avails* from attachment by the creditors of the insured/policyowner. Cash surrender values and dividends left to accumulate are included in the term proceeds and avails.

It has been held that the right to procure cash surrender values is a right purely personal to the policyowner. It is a condition precedent in the insurance contract whereby the insurance company does not develop any obligations until certain procedures are observed. Accordingly, there is no debt due to the policyowner from the insurance company until the policyowner has created the debt by the exercise of the option.[30] Similarly, the cash surrender value of an endowment life insurance policy is not a vested interest and thus not an asset of the bankrupt debtor.[31] Any payments, however, that have been made to the policyowner, such as cash surrender values or dividends that have been deposited to the debtor's account, are not exempt under a statute such as that of New York because the New York act provides that only "such third person beneficiary, assignee or payee entitled to the proceeds shall be entitled to its proceeds and avails against the creditors and representatives of the owner insured." In interpreting the New York law, it has been held that the assignee may, in fact, be another creditor whose rights will become superior to those of any other creditor. However, this protection would not be extended to the estate of the insured, which for all intents and purposes, is the insured/policyowner.[32]

States other than New York also have life insurance exemption provisions. Many of them are quite brief. For example, Nebraska provides that "all and every benefit accruing under any annuity contract or any other policy...shall be exempt from attachment...and all claims of creditors and of beneficiary if related by blood or marriage."[33]

Under the laws of California, Indiana, Ohio, Maine, New York, Washington, Wisconsin, and others, endowment policies have been included in the exemptions granted to the debtor.[34] However, the cash values of annuities, generally, have not been protected unless expressly provided for by statute. The Bankruptcy Reform Act provides some protection, and other states may move to increase the protection because the exemption granted under the act is comparatively modest. The Bankruptcy Reform Act provides for an evaluation of the cash exemption amounts every six years to keep pace with inflation. As experience develops with the new act, we may see changes in the state exemptions as well, particularly in regard to high-cash-value life insurance and annuity contracts. Where the amounts are relatively modest, it is clear that some protection should be afforded the debtor to avoid pauperization of the debtor and the debtor's family. Yet to determine exactly what is "relatively modest" poses problems in itself. For example, in one case where the creditor has a claim of $52,500 against a debtor who had invested $65,000 in three annuity policies, the purchase of a fourth annuity policy, after notice of the creditor's claim, was held to be a mere continuation of the judgment debtor's investment program and not a payment in defraud of creditors.[35] However, the purchase of a fifth annuity was disallowed because of evidence of intent to defraud creditors.

Some of the laws providing exemption are applicable only where the named beneficiary is of a certain class, such as the individual's spouse or children or a dependent relative. Others are broader in scope. Some enactments limit the

---

[30]R.C.W.A. 48.18.410. *In re Elliott,* 446 P.2d 347, 74 Wash.2d 600 (1968).

[31]*In re Privett,* C.A. Okla., 435 F.2d 261 (1970).

[32]Insurance Law §166, *In re Adas' Will,* 335 N.Y.S.2d 128, 70 Misc.2d 847.

[33]Law of 1933, amended 1941, Sec. 44–37.

[34]30 A.L.R.2d 751 (1952); Am.Jur.2d, Bankruptcy §666.

[35]N.J.S.A. 17:35B–10, 10(a)(1). *O'Niell v. Little,* 258 A.2d 731, 107 N.J. Super. 426 (1969). See Rights of Creditors, 2A, John Appleman, *Insurance Law and Practice* (St. Paul, Minn.: West Publishing Co., 1980), §§1341–1352.

amount of the annual premiums payable for exempt insurance. Under other statutes, the limitation is based on the total amount of insurance proceeds, instead of on the amount of annual premiums paid. For example, South Dakota limits the exemption to proceeds of $20,000, with proceeds in excess of the stipulated figure available to creditors.

Rights of Beneficiary's Creditors

Prior to Maturity. In the absence of a statute exempting the proceeds or cash values of life insurance from the claims of creditors of the beneficiary, the question of whether such creditors can reach the cash values depends upon whether the beneficiary possesses a property right in the policy. If the beneficiary does not possess such a right in the policy, his or her creditors cannot reach the cash values. Remember that a revocable beneficiary has a mere expectancy, and consequently no property right exists to be attached. Even in the case of an irrevocably named beneficiary, creditors of such a beneficiary cannot reach the cash value of the policy, since the beneficiary does not possess the right to obtain the cash value without the consent of the owner.

At Maturity. The rights of a beneficiary, whether designated revocably or irrevocably, vest absolutely upon the death of the insured. In the absence of an exempting statutory provision, the creditors of the beneficiary are entitled to the proceeds of the insurance as soon as that right vests in the beneficiary.[36]

Most of the state laws exempting life insurance proceeds and avails from claims of creditors expressly refer only to creditors of the policyowner/insured. However, some states have very broad statutes that exempt the proceeds of life insurance against the creditors of both the insured

and the beneficiary.[37] State statutes frequently provide that proceeds payable to beneficiaries under fraternal benefit policies are exempt from claims of creditors.

Special Priorities and Constraints

The general rules applying to creditors' rights in life insurance cash values and proceeds do not apply to federal tax liens and situations involving misappropriated funds. Also, most states will permit the use of spendthrift trust clauses to protect life insurance proceeds from creditors of the beneficiary.

Tax Liens. The tax collector takes a dim view of anyone, dead or alive, who fails to pay taxes. Under a federal government tax lien, the government does not have to prove that the debtor or taxpayer is insolvent when it levies on the taxpayer's assets. Where the policyowner/insured retains certain rights under a policy of insurance, these rights can be reached by the government,[38] even in the face of state exemption statutes. Under Federal Tax Lien Law, life insurance companies are required to pay net surrender values as of the time of judgment.

Misappropriation of Funds. Although the rights of beneficiaries in life insurance policies have been greatly enlarged by legislation, it is contrary to public policy to permit life insurance to act as a shelter for assets that equitably belong to another. Thus, where premiums are paid out of misappropriated funds, the right to follow the embezzled funds is not lost merely because such money was used to buy life insurance.

In general, the aggrieved party can follow the wrongfully acquired funds and enforce its rights against the proceeds under the *constructive* or *resulting* trust theory. Under this theory the person holding the funds does so as a trustee for the other party. There is no uniformity as to the

[36]*Murray v. Wells,* 53 Iowa 256 (1880); §640; 57 A.L.R. 692. In the case of *Holmes, appellant v. Marshall,* 145 Cal. 777 (1905), the court held that under certain conditions, the exemption extends "not only against the debts of the person whose life was insured, and who paid the premiums, but also to the debts of the beneficiary to whom it is payable after the death of the insured." See also S. Dak. L. Ch. 58-12-4 (1966).

[37]Appleman, *Insurance Law and Practice,* §§1348, 1374.

[38]26 U.S.C.A. (I.R.C. 1954), §7403; *U.S. v. Sterkowicz,* 266 F. Supp. 703 (1967); Appleman, *Insurance Law and Practice,* §10905.

amount of recovery. In some cases, the premiums paid by the policyowner following his or her insolvency were obtainable by the aggrieved party, and in others, they obtained the insurance money in the proportion that the premiums paid subsequent to the insolvency bore to the sum total of the premiums paid on the policy. Thus, when a policyowner's clear intention is to defraud his or her creditors by taking out insurance or by assigning it, the beneficiary is not protected against claims of the policyowner's creditors.

Spendthrift Trust Clauses. In addition to the few broad statutes that exempt life insurance proceeds from the claims of the creditors of both the insured and the beneficiary, a majority of states have laws permitting the policyowner to include in the policy installment settlement provisions a so-called **spendthrift trust clause,** which will protect the proceeds from claims of the beneficiary's creditors.

The clause can be attached to a policy in the form of an endorsement or rider and becomes a part of the policy. Under the clause, the beneficiary has no power to assign, transfer, or otherwise encumber the payments that are payable. The payments are not subject to any legal process, execution, garnishment, or attachment proceedings. In a majority of states, the provisions extend only to beneficiaries other than the policyowner. Otherwise, such a device could be used by a policyowner to defraud creditors.

If the mode of settlement is selected by the beneficiary, the payments that are received are not secure from the claims of the beneficiary's creditors as is the case of the spendthrift trust arrangement. The spendthrift clause protects only the money being held by the insurance company. Once money is paid to the beneficiary, it loses its distinction as unpaid life insurance proceeds. The outstanding characteristic of spendthrift statutes is the permissive nature of the exemption. The company and someone else must agree on the exemption before it can become operative. Practically, this means that the *policyowner* must provide for the clause in the installment settlement provisions of the policy. It should be recognized, however, that such clauses severely restrict the beneficiary's prerogatives under the settlement payout. The spendthrift trust clause should be used only after appropriate consideration of other planning objectives.

In the majority of those states where no statute exists, the courts have upheld the use of spendthrift trust clauses. Such clauses are not valid in only a few states, and even in these, a discretionary trust may be used to accomplish the same thing.[39]

---

[39]For a comprehensive review of creditors' rights in life insurance, as well as a digest of state insurance exemption laws, see *Advanced Underwriting Service* (Indianapolis, Ind.: The Research and Review Service of America, Inc.), §10.

Chapter 10

Cost Analysis of Life Insurance and Annuities

The two preceding chapters have discussed the legal and operational aspects of life insurance contracts, an understanding of which is essential to sound policy evaluation. This chapter continues the policy evaluation theme but considers life insurance contracts from a cost standpoint. It presents some of the common techniques for comparing policy prices and reviews the various state regulations that require cost and other disclosures.

THE LIFE INSURANCE PURCHASE DECISION

Many individuals (typically with the help of agents) shop carefully before deciding on the type of life insurance they should buy and from whom they should buy it. Others, for a variety of reasons, do little or no comparison shopping and may make unsound decisions regarding the particular type or amount of life insurance to buy or the insurance company from which to buy it. Often just a little knowledge can result in substantial savings over a lifetime.

Making a wise life insurance purchase decision is not easy. One must first decide whether *any* life insurance is needed. If some life insurance is

appropriate, the amount must be decided on next. These two issues are analyzed in Chapter 12.

Questions must also be answered as to the kind of insurance to buy and from whom to buy it. This typically involves discussions with one or more life insurance agents and a determination as to how much to spend for life insurance as well as an assessment of the cost of the life insurance being considered. Consumers, and to a lesser extent, agents and other financial advisors, have great difficulty determining the estimated cost of life insurance.

The buyer should not necessarily seek that mirage called "the best buy." Rather, the buyer should seek a policy that is reasonably priced in relation to other policies available from other sound life insurance companies.

LIFE INSURANCE POLICY COST ANALYSIS

The Need for Cost Comparisons

Life insurance policy costs can vary greatly. Cost variations result from differences in company operational efficiency, investment performance, underwriting policy, profit objectives, the costs associated with marketing, and a host of other variables. A higher-cost policy may reflect either better value for the purchaser or simply an expensive policy with little or no justifiably offsetting benefits.

Many life insurance purchasers do not attain the goal of procuring a relatively low cost policy because:

1. They are unaware of cost differences,
2. They have difficulty estimating costs, and/or
3. They engage in little or no comparison shopping either because of personal circumstances or individual values.

Surveys support reasons 1 and 2. Respondents often erroneously equate a policy's premium to its cost, indicating a basic ignorance concerning the other factors entering into cost determination. The premium is a measure of the annual outlay for a policy, not its cost. Cost includes all elements of a policy (premiums, death benefits, cash values, dividends, etc.), not just premiums.

Common Methods for Comparing Policy Costs

The major objective of any method used to compare the cost of one life insurance policy with another is to create a means of guiding a prospective policyowner to a competitively priced policy or group of policies. In reality, the cost of life insurance to any individual is dependent on that particular individual's unique circumstances and the actual cash flows experienced under the policy. This can be determined only after the contract has been terminated by death, maturity, or surrender and then only in terms of the time value of money to the individual. Even so, attempts to estimate costs prospectively are useful and desirable.

No known method of comparing life insurance costs takes into consideration all possible factors that a consumer should consider in the purchase decision. It is important to supplement "cost" information with "benefit" and other information. However, the reader needs to start

with an appreciation for some of the more common cost comparison methods.

Seven cost comparison methods are discussed in this chapter. Other cost comparison methods exist but are not covered here.[1] With one exception, the methods can prove useful in appropriate circumstances as an aid in life insurance policy cost evaluation. A summary table at the end of this section highlights the main characteristics of each method.

Traditional Net Cost Method. The **traditional net cost** (TNC) method, in use for years, is the easiest cost comparison method to understand and calculate but also can be the most misleading. To arrive at a cost under the TNC method, one adds together the illustrated premiums over a stated time period (usually 10 or 20 years) and subtracts from this figure the sum of the policy's illustrated dividends, if any, taken to the end of the period. From this result is subtracted the policy's illustrated cash value (and terminal dividends, if any) at the end of the period chosen. Dividing by the face amount (in thousands) and the number of years in the stated time period yields the TNC per thousand per year.[2]

The TNC method was, and sometimes still is, used to compare the costs of two or more life insurance policies. Although the traditional method can be helpful for determining income tax liabilities[3] under a single life insurance policy, its results are misleading when used to measure policy costs. By ignoring the time value of money, it fails to weigh fairly the various funds flows associated with life insurance policies. Moreover, the TNC can be manipulated easily by lowering dividends or cash values on policies in their early years and increasing them in later years, thus appearing to lower policy cost. Use of this method for comparing policy costs is now illegal in most states.

A variation of the TNC method is often used in policy illustrations. Many insurance com-

---

[1]See, for example, *Analysis of Life Insurance Cost Comparison Index Methods,* (Society of Actuaries, 1974).

[2]See formula 1 in the chapter appendix for the TNC formula.

[3]See Chapter 13.

panies and agents include in their illustrations a column that shows the policy's annual increase in cash value netted against that particular year's net premium (i.e., gross premium less illustrated dividend). Some agents will state or imply that the year's increase in cash value is due solely or chiefly to that year's premium payment. Of course, this is not true, as the increase may be due chiefly to interest credited to the cash value, not the premium payment.

Interest Adjusted Net Cost Method. The **interest adjusted net cost** (IANC) method was developed to correct for the omission within the TNC method of the time value of money. The IANC analysis, like the TNC analysis, is conducted over a set time period (typically, 10 and 20 years) and considers a policy's premiums, death benefits, cash values, and dividends in much the same manner as the TNC method, except that interest is recognized.

To calculate the IANC (also called the **surrender cost index**), the policy's premiums and dividends are accumulated at some assumed interest rate over a selected period. The accumulated dividends are subtracted from the accumulated premiums. From this figure is subtracted the cash value (and terminal dividend, if any) at the end of the time period. The result of this calculation is then divided by the accumulated value of one per year at the assumed interest rate and for the time period and by the face amount in thousands.[4] If the interest rate assumed in the IANC analysis were zero, note that you would simply obtain the policy's TNC.

The NAIC Model Life Insurance Solicitation Regulation (see below) requires two interest-adjusted cost indices for a policy—a surrender cost index and a **net payment cost index.** The payment index is an estimate of the average annual "out-of-pocket" net premium outlay (premium less annual dividend), adjusted by interest to reflect the point in time when premiums and dividends are paid during a 10- or 20-year period. The surrender cost index is the payment index less the annualized equivalent of the cash

value available to the policyowner at the end of the 10- or 20-year period, adjusted for interest. Interest-adjusted indices are of value to show the relative estimated price positions of two or more similar policies.

The IANC method should be used to compare similar policies only, since a fair comparison would require approximately equal outlays.[5] The IANC method has other drawbacks, too. For example, the method is subject to manipulation in much the same way, although to a lesser extent, as the TNC method. Like other methods, it provides an accurate measure of cost only over the time period chosen and then only if all assumptions prove to be fact.

IANC indices (both surrender and net payment) are often shown on both a guaranteed basis and an illustrated (or projected) basis. In fact, as mentioned below, this is required under the 1983 NAIC model disclosure regulation. The previous NAIC model regulation effectively requires the same thing. It mandates that an **equivalent level annual dividend** (ELAD) be shown. The ELAD is interpreted as that portion of the pricing of a participating policy that is not guaranteed. It represents the average annual illustrated dividend, weighted for the time value of money. It is calculated by accumulating the annual illustrated dividends at interest and dividing the result by the appropriate interest factor to obtain a level annual equivalent to the (nonlevel) illustrated dividends.[6]

Table 10–1 shows IANC figures at 5 percent for policies whose gross premiums per $1,000 appeared in Table 5–2. Observe that (1) little relationship exists between premiums charged and net costs, and (2) net costs vary greatly among these similar policies.

---

[4]See formula 2 in the chapter appendix for the IANC formula.

[5]If outlays were held approximately equal for two policies, one of which had a significantly lower premium than the other (i.e., they were "dissimilar"), some form of "side fund" arrangement would be necessary under the lower-premium policy. If a fair comparison were to be made, this, in turn, would necessitate an adjustment downward in the lower-premium policy's face amount to maintain approximately equal total death benefits under each plan. See the discussion later in this chapter of the cash accumulation method for further details.

[6]See formula 4 in the chapter appendix.

TABLE 10-1. Interest adjusted net cost figures for selected ordinary life policies
(from Table 5-2—age 35, male, $25,000 policy basis)

Type of Policy	Company	Gross Premium per $1,000	20-Year IANC per $1,000
Participating	A	$13.64	$ 2.61
	B	14.31	0.15
	C	14.88	2.65
	D	16.16	−2.60
	E	17.11	2.65
	F	17.90	3.16
	G	23.69	8.41
Nonparticipating	H	12.02	5.80
	I	12.33	5.42
	J	13.45	6.68
	K	13.52	6.41
	L	14.04	6.06
	M	18.05	8.40
	N	18.90	9.00

Policy A's gross premium is $13.64 per $1,000 of insurance and its 20-year IANC is $2.61 per $1,000. This $2.61 index can be interpreted as follows. If a 35-year-old male bought this ordinary life policy and paid the stipulated premium for 20 years and at that time surrendered the policy, the policyowner's average annual cost per $1,000 of insurance would have been $2.61, *assuming* that dividends were paid exactly as illustrated and assuming further that the policyowner valued money at 5 percent per year (the interest rate specified by most states' life insurance cost disclosure regulations). "Cost" here means simply the average annual amount estimated to be retained by the insurer to cover its death benefit payments, expenses, and profit.

An understanding of the interest adjusted method is important because its indices are required to be provided to prospective life insurance purchasers in the majority of states in the United States, and even in those states without a requirement, many insurers routinely provide the indices on their policy illustrations. More is said on this point later in this chapter.

The method is not commonly used by agents and financial consultants when they are preparing their own cost comparisons between two or more policies. Other methods, some of which are discussed below, are usually found to be better suited for this purpose. This is especially true when dissimilar policies are being compared.

Equal Outlay Method.[7] One method used by some planners to compare the costs of two or more policies is the equal outlay method (EOM). This method assumes that equal amounts of money are expended under each of two proposed insurance arrangements. This method can be used to compare both similar and dissimilar policies, although not without some problems. When both policies have flexible premium payments, it is a simple matter to set premiums and face amounts at the same levels, thereby examining the respective surrender values and total death benefits at specific future points. Other things being the same, the policy with the larger illustrated future values probably would be preferred.

Table 10-2 illustrates this approach. Cash value buildups on two universal life (UL) policies are shown on three bases: (1) guaranteed assumptions, (2) intermediate assumptions, and (3) current assumptions. The planned annual outlay is illustrated as $1,000 per year for both policies and death benefits are set at $100,000 per year. Both policies guarantee a minimum interest rate of 4 percent. Policy A is currently crediting 10.75 percent and policy B is currently crediting 11.3 percent to cash values. Intermediate values are shown on a 9 percent assumption. On all three bases, policy B illustrates greater values at every duration. Thus, other things being the same (e.g., contract provisions, agent service, company quality, etc.), policy B would be preferred to policy A.

The EOM is also used to compare the costs of two or more policies when one is a fixed-premium contract. The premium level and face amount of the flexible contract can be set equal to those of the fixed-premium contract.[8] Future cash values then can be compared as under the previous example. Table 10-3 illustrates a comparison between the UL policy B shown in Table 10-2 and the Table 5-3 ordinary life policy.

The premiums for the UL policy are set to those for the ordinary life policy. The UL premium pattern could be assumed to track exactly either

---

[7]This term is that of the authors and is not necessarily used generally.
[8]This is feasible only if the minimum required premium for the flexible contract is no greater than that of the fixed-premium contract; otherwise, the procedure should follow that outlined for two fixed-premium contracts discussed later.

TABLE 10-2. Equal outlay method: two universal life policies
(male, age 35, nonsmoker)

| Year | Policies A and B | | Cash Values | | | | | |
| | Planned Annual Premium | Annual Death Benefits | Guar. Basis | | Intermediate Basis | | Current Basis | |
			Policy A (4%)	Policy B (4%)	Policy A (9%)	Policy B (9%)	Policy A (10.75%)	Policy B (11.3%)
1	$1,000	$100,000	$ 123	$ 718	$ 125	$ 789	$ 125	$ 808
2	1,000	100,000	798	1,493	950	1,714	958	1,773
3	1,000	100,000	1,485	2,249	1,844	2,720	1,976	2,845
4	1,000	100,000	2,181	3,018	2,813	3,807	2,887	4,029
5	1,000	100,000	2,888	3,796	3,862	4,988	3,999	5,336
6	1,000	100,000	3,588	4,581	4,996	6,253	5,221	6,782
7	1,000	100,000	4,294	5,367	6,221	7,686	6,564	8,380
8	1,000	100,000	4,999	6,157	7,543	9,116	8,038	10,151
9	1,000	100,000	5,700	6,944	8,971	10,788	9,658	12,112
10	1,000	100,000	6,396	7,739	10,513	12,479	11,438	14,289
11	1,000	100,000	7,098	8,510	12,179	14,359	13,396	16,686
12	1,000	100,000	7,755	9,882	13,982	16,394	15,552	19,341
13	1,000	100,000	8,409	10,038	15,936	18,595	17,929	22,282
14	1,000	100,000	9,039	10,778	18,058	20,979	20,552	25,544
15	1,000	100,000	9,638	11,488	20,349	23,548	23,447	29,151
16	1,000	100,000	10,201	12,159	22,839	26,338	26,644	33,161
17	1,000	100,000	10,719	12,795	25,542	29,361	30,177	37,617
18	1,000	100,000	11,185	13,385	28,479	32,644	34,087	42,573
19	1,000	100,000	11,590	13,922	31,671	36,807	38,414	48,089
20	1,000	100,000	11,926	14,396	35,141	40,079	43,206	54,234

the ordinary life policy gross premium ($1,446) or net premium (yearly premium less dividend) pattern. Also, projected UL policy death benefits could be set equal to the ordinary life policy death benefits, even when dividends are used to purchase paid up additional insurance. The latter assumption presumes that the insured could meet any future insurability requirements that may be imposed.

As a practical matter, such comparisons are only rarely made on the basis that both future premium and death benefit patterns are held constant. The usual way is to hold outlays constant and set only *initial* policy death benefits approximately equal. The comparison in Table 10-3 assumes that the ordinary life policy's dividends are used to purchase paid-up additional insurance, thus producing an increasing yearly total death benefit. One could attempt to obtain a close match of subsequent death benefit amounts by using the UL option B death benefit pattern.

Table 10-3 shows values for each policy on the basis of current illustrations and projections. If future results followed exactly those implicit in the illustrated and projected values, one would prefer the UL policy to the ordinary life policy, assuming that the customer would otherwise find either policy suitable. However, the likelihood of actual future values tracking those implicit in the illustrated and projected values is slight.

This UL policy's projected values are based on **new money** assumptions, while this ordinary life policy's illustrated future values are based on the insurer's current **portfolio rate of return.** Thus, if one believed that new money rates were likely to remain at this current high level, the UL projections could be realized as shown. However, if this occurred, presumably dividends actually paid under the ordinary life policy would be higher than illustrated. No cost comparison method can adequately address this problem of incompatability, which really relates to the assumptions that underlie illustrative pricing rather than the specific comparison method chosen.

The equal outlay method also can be used to compare two or more fixed-premium policies or a flexible-premium and a fixed-premium contract where the fixed contract's premium was below the minimum required for the flexible contract. The procedure is often used by agents in

TABLE 10-3. Equal outlay method: universal life and ordinary life policies
(from Tables 10-2 and 5-3)

Year	Annual Premiums for Both Policies	Cash Values		Death Benefits	
		Illustrated Ord. Life	Projected U. Life	Illustrated Ord. Life	Projected U. Life
1	$1,446	$ 3	$ 1,282	$100,011	$101,282
2	1,446	177	2,763	100,112	102,763
3	1,446	1,685	4,414	100,311	104,414
4	1,446	3,334	6,237	100,852	106,237
5	1,446	5,193	8,252	101,823	108,252
6	1,446	7,244	10,487	103,235	110,487
7	1,446	9,523	12,954	105,113	112,954
8	1,446	12,052	15,689	107,470	115,689
9	1,446	14,853	18,716	110,328	118,716
10	1,446	17,957	22,074	113,712	122,074
11	1,446	21,389	25,773	117,637	125,773
12	1,446	25,161	29,864	122,088	129,864
13	1,446	39,311	34,400	127,101	134,400
14	1,446	33,875	39,413	132,708	139,413
15	1,446	38,889	44,900	138,947	144,900
16	1,446	44,403	51,095	145,866	151,095
17	1,446	50,459	57,819	153,504	157,819
18	1,446	57,113	65,290	161,909	165,290
19	1,446	64,426	73,596	171,146	173,596
20	1,446	72,462	82,827	181,267	182,827

making "term versus whole life" comparisons and "term versus universal life" comparisons. The method can be used for any two policies, one of which has a higher premium than the other. It can be far simpler than techniques discussed below but also can result in unfair comparisons, as will be explained.

To illustrate, assume that our trusty 35-year-old male, nonsmoker is interested in comparing a YRT policy to an ordinary life policy. We will use the aggregate YRT premiums shown in Table 4-2 and the ordinary life premiums and values from Table 5-3. The equal outlay procedure assumes that the outlays for the two plans are held equal. This is accomplished by assuming that annual differences between the higher-premium policy and the lower-premium policy are accumulated each year at some reasonable after-tax rate of return. The outlays for the two "plans" are thus held equal.

Table 10-4 illustrates this procedure assuming that dividends on the ordinary life policy are used to purchase paid-up additional insurance. The ordinary life's annual premium is $1,446 and the initial premium for the YRT policy is $145.

The difference is $1,301. This difference is accumulated at an assumed after-tax earnings rate of 7 percent. The difference in the second year's premium is $1,298. This difference is added to that of the previous year's fund balance ($1,301 plus interest of $91) to yield a beginning fund balance for policy year 2 of $2,690 (not shown). This procedure is continued for several more years.

Table 10-4 shows that side fund values are projected to be greater than those of the whole life policy through policy year 10. From policy year 11 forward, the whole life's illustrated cash values are greater than the side fund's projected balance.

The analysis is not unbiased since the YRT arrangement provides a higher death benefit in the early years for the same outlay. To have a fair comparison, *total* death benefits should also be held equal. One could then simply compare the future estimated values, as in the case of the two UL policies. If this were done, one would illustrate either an increase in the face amount of the higher premium policy to that of the term plus side fund death benefit *or* a decrease in the term policy face amount. Both approaches would result

TABLE 10-4. Equal outlay method: ordinary life and YRT
(from Tables 4-2 and 5-3)

(1)	(2)	(3)	(4)	(5)	(6)	(7)	(8)
				Plan Values		Death Benefits	
Year	Ordinary Life Premium	YRT Premium	Difference between Premiums	Difference Compounded at 7%	Ordinary Life Surrender Value[a]	YRT Plus Side Fund[b]	Ordinary Life with Paid Up Additions
1	$1,446	$145	$1,301	$ 1,392	$ 3	$101,392	$100,011
2	1,446	148	1,298	2,878	177	102,878	100,112
3	1,446	154	1,292	4,462	1,686	104,462	100,311
4	1,446	162	1,284	6,149	3,345	106,149	100,852
5	1,446	172	1,274	6,942	5,193	107,942	101,823
6	1,446	185	1,261	9,847	7,245	109,847	103,236
7	1,446	200	1,246	11,870	9,523	111,870	105,113
8	1,446	219	1,227	14,014	12,052	114,014	107,470
9	1,446	242	1,204	16,283	14,854	116,283	110,328
10	1,446	268	1,178	18,683	17,958	118,683	113,712
11	1,446	299	1,147	21,218	21,389	121,218	117,637
12	1,446	333	1,113	23,894	25,162	123,894	122,088
13	1,446	373	1,073	26,715	29,312	126,715	127,101
14	1,446	417	1,029	29,686	33,875	129,686	132,708
15	1,446	466	980	32,813	38,890	132,813	138,947
16	1,446	521	925	36,100	44,404	136,100	145,866
17	1,446	581	865	39,552	50,459	139,552	153,504
18	1,446	646	800	43,177	57,113	143,177	161,909
19	1,446	716	730	46,980	64,427	146,980	171,146
20	1,446	791	655	50,970	72,462	150,970	181,267

[a]Guaranteed cash value plus illustrated cash value of paid-up additional insurance.
[b]$100,000 YRT face amount plus column 5.

in slightly more money being credited to the side fund.[9]

However, an attempt is made to maintain only approximate equality of death benefits. This is usually accomplished by assuming that dividends under participating policies purchase paid-up additions or one-year term insurance equal to the policy's cash value. This could also be handled by attaching a cost-of-living feature to the policy.

The term arrangement's total projected death benefits exceed those of the ordinary life policy through policy year 12 and, like the side fund balance, exceeds the ordinary life figures by substnatial amounts in the early policy years. The ordinary life's illustrated death benefits become

substantially greater than those under the YRT arrangement in later years.

Where does this type of analysis leave us? First, if the need for insurance is, say, 10 years or less, the YRT arrangement is clearly superior from a purely financial standpoint based on the stated assumptions. This result is expected and would be found with most forms of whole life versus term comparisons. Whole life and universal life policies usually have low early surrender values because of the high acquisition and other first-year charges.

On the other hand, this ordinary life policy's relative cost position appears to improve continuously (based on these assumptions) as time passes. However, an unequivocal endorsement of the ordinary life policy could not be made even if the planning horizon were longer than 10 or 11 years. This is because the equal outlay method is incapable of rendering a totally fair comparison if the level of total death benefits cross at any point in the analysis. It is possible that the additional

[9]In the first instance, the whole life premium would need to be raised to support the higher face amount, which would mean more money for the side fund. In the second instance, the term premium would be lowered to support the lower face amount—thus resulitng in the premium savings being placed into the side fund.

amounts contributed to the side fund by causing the early death benefits to be equal would more than make up for the later inferior position of the YRT arrangement.

In such ambiguous cases, the analyst may be compelled to use the cash accumulation or other methods that adjust for unequal death benefits (see below). However, the other methods require a computer. This method does not.

As with all cost comparison methods, the EOM is no better than the assumptions that underlie the calculations. The assumptions used here will be reasonable for some persons but not for many others. Further, this method, like others, is only one tool available for use in making the purchase decision. Other important quantitative and qualitative factors also should be considered, such as the quality of the agent, the reputation of the company, contractual provisions, and so on.

It should also be noted that the analyses above and elsewhere do not actually require an individual to save the difference in premiums. Whether a given individual chooses actually to create a "side fund" is a human decision not a costing decision.

Cash Accumulation Method. The **cash accumulation method** (CAM) is a more sophisticated cost comparison method than the equal outlay method.[10] As alluded to above, it functions in the same way in that (1) outlays for the two (or more) plans being compared are set at equal levels, (2) the annual premium differences are accumulated at some assumed interest rate, and (3) one simply observes the cash value/side fund differences over time in an effort to draw meaningful cost-based conclusions. However, the CAM corrects for the unequal death benefits bias of the equal outlay method. The face amount of the lower premium (e.g., term) policy is hypothetically adjusted each year such that the sum of the "side fund" and the new face amount exactly equals the face amount of the higher premium (e.g., whole life) policy. In the early policy years, at least, this

often means that the lower premium policy's face amount will be declining.[11]

Table 10–5 illustrates the CAM applied to the same two Table 10–4 policies. The 7 percent after-tax interest assumption is maintained. The outlays are held at the same level by accumulating the annual differences at interest, as are the total illustrated death benefits (columns 8 and 9). This eliminates the Table 10–4 bias against the YRT plan that existed in the early policy years.[12] As a result of being able to lower the YRT face amount, and therefore the YRT premium in the early years, the accumulated differences are larger than formerly.

Under this CAM comparison, one observes that the illustrated cash surrender value of the ordinary life policy first exceeds the projected side fund balance in policy year 11 and by policy year 20, the difference between the two values has continued to widen, reaching $22,016 ($72,462 – $50,446). Although not shown here, post–year 20 differences track a similar pattern.

In the early policy years, a clear cost advantage exists for the term arrangement and, as expected, an even greater advantage than existed under the equal outlay method. Since the death benefits under each plan are held equal, one can focus on the fund versus cash value differences.

Which plan is the better buy? The best answer is: "It depends." If the prospective purchaser is more interested in short-to-medium-term results, the term arrangement appears superior *based on the stated assumptions and with other things being the same.* If a longer-term view is taken, the ordinary life plan may be the preferred approach *based on the stated assumptions and with other things being equal.* It should be remembered that in all cost

---

[10]See Michael L. Murray, "Analyzing the Investment Value of Cash Value Life Insurance, *The Journal of Risk and Insurance,* Vol. XLIII (March 1976), pp. 121–128.

[11]This decline sometimes reverses. The direction and magnitude of the face amount change is a function of the relative costliness of the policies being compared.

[12]Although not a problem with this analysis since dividends are earmarked to purchase paid-up additional insurance, any dividends that would be paid in cash or accumulated at interest should be included as a part of the total death benefit if the company would pay such dividends upon death. Similarly, any terminal dividends to be paid on death should be included. Any regular or terminal dividends paid on policy surrender also should be included as a part of the surrender value.

TABLE 10-5. Cash accumulation method: ordinary life and YRT
(from Tables 4–2 and 5–3)

(1)	(2)	(3)	(4)	(5)	(6)	(7)	(8)	(9)
				Plan Values			Death Benefits	
Year	Ordinary Life Premum	YRT Premium	Difference between Premiums	Difference compounded at 7%[a]	Ordinary Life Surrender Value[b]	YRT Face Amount	YRT Plus Side Fund[c]	Ordinary Life with Paid-Up Additions
1	$1,446	$ 143	$1,303	$ 1,394	$ 3	$ 98,617	$100,011	$100,011
2	1,446	144	1,302	2,885	177	97,227	100,112	100,112
3	1,446	148	1,298	4,476	1,685	95,835	100,311	100,311
4	1,446	153	1,293	6,173	3,344	94,679	100,852	100,852
5	1,446	161	1,285	7,979	5,193	93,844	101,823	101,823
6	1,446	173	1,273	9,900	7,244	93,336	103,236	103,236
7	1,446	186	1,260	11,941	9,523	93,172	105,113	105,113
8	1,446	204	1,242	14,106	12,052	93,364	107,470	107,470
9	1,446	227	1,219	16,397	14,853	93,931	110,328	110,328
10	1,446	254	1,192	18,820	17,957	94,892	113,712	113,712
11	1,446	277	1,169	21,388	21,389	96,249	117,637	117,637
12	1,446	326	1,120	24,083	25,161	98,005	122,088	122,088
13	1,446	374	1,072	26,916	29,311	100,185	127,101	127,101
14	1,446	429	1,017	29,889	33,875	102,819	132,708	132,708
15	1,446	494	952	33,000	38,889	105,947	138,947	138,947
16	1,446	571	875	36,246	44,403	109,620	145,866	145,866
17	1,446	662	784	39,623	50,459	113,881	153,504	153,504
18	1,446	767	679	43,122	57,113	118,787	161,909	161,909
19	1,446	891	555	46,735	64,426	124,411	171,146	171,146
20	1,446	1,035	411	50,446	72,462	130,821	181,267	181,267

[a](Column 4 plus column 5 for the previous year) × 1.07.
[b]Guaranteed cash value plus illustrated cash value of paid-up additional insurance.
[c]Column 5 plus column 7.

analyses the benefits surrounding the policies being compared are assumed to be the same. This is rarely the case.

The interest rate assumed in the analysis can be of crucial importance. Table 10–6 shows 10- and 20-year figures for the Table 10–5 column 5 (accumulated differences) and column 6 (ordinary life cash surrender) values at various interest rates. The variations in values can be great. At an after-tax interest rate between 9 and 10 percent over the 20-year period, the benefit swings in favor of the term arrangement.

A comment should be made about the process of equalizing death benefits. In actual fact, few, if any, purchasers of term insurance would actually cancel (or add) portions of term coverage each year so as to match exactly the side fund change. This would be not only inconvenient but could result in the policy face amount falling below the required company minimum amount. The CAM does not actually *require* that the term policy's

face amount be changed each year, or any year. As a cost comparison method, it is not intended to dictate how a policy is or should be structured. This is a separate decision. Its utility is in showing the agent and prospective purchaser how relative costs and values vary by imposing a hypothetical equality requirement over outlays and death benefits.[13]

As discussed in Chapter 13, death benefits under a life policy and those from other sources might not be treated the same from a tax and other standpoints. For example, some states do not impose an inheritance tax on life insurance death proceeds paid to certain specified beneficiaries (e.g., family members). However, the tax is imposed on other assets that pass at death.

---

[13]The CAM used here equalizes end-of-year death benefits. Beginning-of-year death benefits could have been used. Ideally, midyear figures would be used, but this adjustment complicates the analysis and adds little to precision.

TABLE 10-6. Cash accumulation method: effect of changing interest assumptions

(Table 10-5 policy values)

(1) Duration (years)	(2) After-Tax Interest Rate Assumed (%)	(3) Accumulated Premium Differences	(4) Ord. Life Surrender Value	(5) Excess of (3) over (4)
10	3	$14,954	$17,957	$ −3,003
	4	15,835	17,957	−2,122
	5	16,770	17,957	−1,187
	6	17,764	17,957	−193
	7	18,820	17,957	823
	8	19,942	17,957	1,985
	9	21,133	17,957	3,176
	10	22,398	17,957	4,441
	11	23,742	17,957	5,785
	12	25,169	17,957	7,212
20	3	$29,759	$72,462	$ −42,703
	4	33,913	72,462	−38,549
	5	38,679	72,462	−33,783
	6	44,169	72,462	−28,293
	7	50,446	72,462	−22,016
	8	57,650	72,462	−14,812
	9	65,917	72,462	−6,545
	10	75,401	72,462	2,939
	11	86,283	72,462	13,821
	12	98,764	72,462	26,302

Thus, this (usually) 6 percent tax would mean that it would take $100,000 of other accumulated assets to be worth a $94,000 life insurance policy, even ignoring all other factors.

Also, life insurance death proceeds may enjoy certain protection from creditors claims (see Chapter 9), which in some cases is an advantage that should be considered. These and other considerations should enter into any analysis when insurance is being compared with noninsurance financial instruments.

Comparative Interest Rate Method. Another popular method used to compare the relative costs of two policies is the **comparative interest rate** (CIR) method.[14] The CIR method is a

[14]The CIR is more commonly known in the life insurance industry as the **Linton Yield** method. It is named for the distinguished actuary, M. A. Linton of the Provident Mutual Life Insurance Company, who devised and used the method. See Joseph M. Belth, "The Rate of Return on the Savings Element in Cash-Value Life Insurance," *The Journal of Risk and Insurance,* Vol. XXXV (December 1968), pp. 569–581; and Stuart Schwarzschild, "Rates of Return on the Investment Differentials between Life Insurance Policies," *The Journal of Risk and Insurance,* Vol. XXXV (December 1968), pp. 583–595.

special case of the CAM. It differs only in that it solves for the interest rate that causes the accumulated value of the annual differences in policy premiums (the "side fund") to be equal to the higher premium policy's surrender value at the end of the period of analysis. Stated differently, the CIR is the rate of return that must be earned on a hypothetical (or real) side fund in a "buy term invest the difference" plan so that the value of the side fund will be equal exactly to the surrender value of the higher premium policy at a designated point in time. The higher the CIR, the less expensive the higher premium (e.g., whole life) policy relative to the alternative plan (e.g., term plus side fund). Like the CAM, outlays and death benefits are held equal. The CIR method requires a computer as the solution interest rate is found by an iterative process through trial and error.

Table 10–6 showed that at some interest rate between 9 and 10 percent, the 20-year figures switched from favoring the ordinary life plan to favoring the YRT arrangement. In fact, at 9.70 percent, the 20-year accumulated differences exactly equal the 20-year surrender value. Thus,

9.70 percent is the 20-year comparative interest rate for the illustrated ordinary life policy compared to the YRT policy and based on the stated assumptions.

The CIR method can be used to compare any two dissimilar policies, and if a standard set of term rates is used, CIRs of similar policies can be compared easily. Any ranking of *similar* policies based on IANC figures closely parallels a ranking based on the CIR method.

The CIR figure is sensitive to the level of the lower-premium-policy's rates. If one wanted to make a cash value policy "look good" relative to a term policy, one need only select a high-cost term policy to use in the analysis to present an attractive CIR. The opposite result could be obtained by reversing the bias.

A comparative interest rate has meaning to an agent, other financial advisor, or the careful shopper as an interest rate that can be imputed to a policy. The CIR can be contrasted with the rate earned on other financial instruments, although the shortcomings in doing so should be understood. Cash values and other savings are not the same. For example, cash value life insurance policies may enjoy certain advantages (e.g., favorable tax treatment, premium waiver features, etc.) not found in other financial instruments. These advantages are not considered in the CIR calculation. Moreover, the CIR is an imputed rate of return and although analogous to an internal rate of return as that concept is understood in finance, it is not identical to it. As such, it *does not* represent the "true" rate of return that the company is crediting to the policy.

It must be remembered that rarely should an evaluation of any two financial instruments be made based solely on interest rates. For example, the interest rate credited to a passbook savings account should not be compared without qualification to the percentage yield on a share of stock.

Yearly Rate of Return Method. The **yearly rate of return** (YROR) method[15] can be especially useful in analyzing cash value policies. It solves for the rate of return to make benefits available

[15]See Joseph M. Belth, *Life Insurance: A Consumer's Handbook,* 2nd ed. (Bloomington, Ill.: Indiana University Press, 1985), pp. 89–91.

at the end of a particular policy year equal the investment in the policy for that year. The "benefits" under a cash value life insurance policy are the cash value and dividend at the end of the policy year being analyzed plus the value of the net death benefit for that year. The "investment" for a particular policy year is the premium paid that year plus the cash value at the beginning of the year. The YROR is derived by dividing the annual policy "benefits" by the corresponding year's "investment" and subtracting 1 from the quotient.

Because of this method's potential usefulness in policy analysis, the reader should be familiar with its details. The formula is

$$YROR = \frac{policy \text{ "benefits"}}{policy \text{ "investment"}} \text{ minus } 1$$

An analogy might prove helpful. Assume that you invested $1,000 in a no-load stock mutual fund that developed a value (benefit) of $1,080 at the end of the first year. Assume that another $1,000 was invested at the beginning of the second year and that the total value at the end of the second year was $2,330. The first year's rate of return would be calculated as follows:

$$YROR_1 = \frac{benefits}{investment} - 1$$

$$= \frac{\$1,080}{\$1,000} - 1$$

$$= 0.08$$

The second year's return would be

$$YROR_2 = \frac{\$2,330}{\$1,000 + \$1,080} - 1$$

$$= 0.12$$

In other words, the effective first year return on the fund was 8 percent. The second year's return was 12 percent. Note that the second year's "investment" includes the $1,080 together with the additional payment of $1,000, since leaving the $1,080 stock value to remain intact is, for analysis purposes, equivalent to investing $1,080.

TABLE 10-7. Yearly rate of return (YROR): universal life, current assumptions $100,000 face amount
(using Table 4-2 YRT rate as price of protection)

(1) Policy Year	(2) Planned Premium	(3) Beg. Year Investment [(2) + (4) prev.]	(4) Year End Surrender Value	(5) Price of Protection per $1,000	(6) Total Price of Protection[a]	(7) Yearly Rate of Return (%)
1	$1,000	$ 1,000	$ 808	$1.45	$144	-4.82
2	1,000	1,808	1,773	1.48	145	6.10
3	1,000	2,773	2,845	1.54	150	7.99
4	1,000	3,845	4,029	1.62	155	8.83
5	1,000	5,029	5,336	1.72	163	9.34
6	1,000	6,336	6,782	1.85	172	9.76
7	1,000	7,782	8,380	2.00	183	10.04
8	1,000	9,380	10,151	2.19	197	10.32
9	1,000	11,151	12,112	2.42	213	10.53
10	1,000	13,112	14,289	2.68	230	10.73
11	1,000	15,289	16,686	2.99	240	10.77
12	1,000	17,686	19,341	3.33	269	10.88
13	1,000	20,341	22,282	3.73	290	10.97
14	1,000	23,282	25,544	4.17	310	11.05
15	1,000	26,544	29,151	4.66	330	11.07
16	1,000	30,151	33,161	5.21	348	11.14
17	1,000	34,161	37,617	5.81	362	11.18
18	1,000	38,617	42,573	6.46	371	11.20
19	1,000	43,573	48,089	7.16	372	11.22
20	1,000	49,089	54,234	7.91	362	11.22

[a]($100,000 − column 4) × (column 5) × (0.001).

A similar procedure is followed for life insurance YROR computations. A key difference is that cash value life insurance policies provide savings *and* death protection. The value of this death protection benefit must be included in the calculation. The YROR formula for a cash value life insurance policy is

$$\text{YROR} = \frac{CV_t + D_t + (YP_t)(F_t - CV_t)(0.001)}{P_t + CV_{t-1}} - 1$$

where CV_t = illustrated cash value at the end of policy year t

D_t = illustrated dividend or other nonguaranteed premium credit at end of policy year t, if not already included in the premium, P_t

YP_t = assumed yearly price of insurance per $1,000 of protection in policy year t

F_t = illustrated death benefit at end of policy year t

P_t = illustrated premium at beginning of policy year t

Table 10-7 illustrates a YROR calculation using the Table 4-2 YRT premiums and the lower-cost Table 10-2 UL policy. Values shown are based on *current* assumptions only.

To aid understanding, let us "walk through" a particular year's calculation. Assume that we desired to determine the implicit rate of return for the UL policy for the ninth policy year. The ninth year's "benefits" are

Ninth year illustrated surrender value	$12,112
Ninth year price of protection	213
Total value of ninth year's "benefits"	$12,325

The $213 price of insurance is based on the policy's net amount at risk and is calculated as follows:

$$(YP_9)(F_9 - CV_9)(0.001) =$$

$$(\$2.42)(100,000 - 12,112)(0.001) = \$213$$

The ninth year's "investment" is

Ninth year premium payment	$ 1,000
Eighth year (beginning of ninth year) surrender value	10,151
Total ninth year "investment"	$11,151

Thus,

$$YROR_9 = \frac{\text{benefits}}{\text{investment}} - 1 = \frac{\$12,325}{\$11,151} - 1 = 1.1053 - 1 = 0.1053 = 10.53\%$$

This may be compared to the ninth-year figure shown in column 7 of Table 10-7. Other years' computations are calculated in a similar fashion.

The YROR gives a *year-by-year* rate of return for a cash value policy, while the CIR gives an *average* rate of return. The YROR calculations can be made without a computer, but can be time consuming if many years' figures are desired. Yearly "prices of protection" are needed for both methods.

The YROR can be helpful in those situations where a person is deciding whether to retain a policy for another year or where it is of interest to observe how a policy performs on a year-to-year basis. This method should be used only for policies with cash values and the results should be interpreted cautiously when the cash values are small.

Yearly Price of Protection Method. Whereas the YROR assumes a mortality cost (or price of protection) and derives a rate of return figure, the **yearly price of protection** (YPP) method assumes a rate of return and derives a yearly price of protection figure. The resultant figure represents an estimate of the price, in a given year, of the net protection (death benefit less cash value) provided under a policy. The beginning-of-year policy "investment" (i.e., the end-of-previous year's cash value plus current premium) is first accumulated at interest to the end of the year. From this result is subtracted the end-of-year policy surrender value (i.e., cash value plus dividend). The resultant figure is then divided by the year's net amount at risk in thousands to arrive at a measure of the policy's yearly price.[16]

The YPP gives year-by-year costs for a life insurance policy, while the IANC method gives an *average* cost. Use of a computer is not necessary to derive YPP figures, although if several years' figures are desired, the calculation can be tedious. Advantages of the YPP method are the same as those of the YROR method, although the result-

ing YPP figures have no intrinsic meaning by themselves.[17] However, when compared to a set of yearly renewable term premiums, one can easily obtain an idea of the costliness of the policy's protection element.[18]

While the YROR method is to be used only with policies that have cash values, the YPP method may be used fairly with both term and cash value policies. However, the YPP method should not be used with policies whose cash values approach or exceed their face amounts as the small net amount at risk can cause wide (and not very meaningful) fluctuations.

Cost Analyses of Existing Policies

The preceding cost comparison methods, when adjusted, can be used to compare an existing, older policy with a new one. Such comparisons are often necessary to help determine whether an existing policy should be replaced with a new one.

The *interest adjusted method* can be used to compare an existing policy with a proposed one provided they are of the same type. However, adjustments are necessary in the calculation and they can cause more confusion than clarity. In any event, the method is rarely used in replacement evaluations.[19]

The *equal outlay method* is often used in comparing an existing to a proposed policy. If the proposed policy is a flexible premium contract, the

---

[16]See formula 6 in the chapter appendix for the formula.

[17]One authority believes this method to be of great importance in the life insurance purchase decision. His book on buying life insurance provides "benchmark" yearly prices as guidelines. See Belth, *Life Insurance: A Consumer's Handbook*.

[18]A technical adjustment to the YRT term premiums would be required to permit a fair, direct comparison. Because the formula develops an end-of-year figure and YRT premiums are for the begininning of the year, it is necessary to add one year's interest to each YRT premium.

[19]The necessary formulas can be found in Harold Skipper, Jr., "Cost Disclosure in Life Insurance Replacement," *The Journal of the American Society of Chartered Life Underwriters*, Vol. XXXIV (October 1980), pp. 48–49.

analysis is simple. The only change that must be made is to assume some appropriate disposition of the cash value of the existing policy. This potential surrender value could be paid into the proposed policy or it could be maintained outside the insurance program.[20]

If the cash value is assumed to be paid into the new policy, no other special adjustments are necessary for a reasonably fair analysis, assuming that the death benefits of the two polices are held roughly equal. One simply illustrates future values of the two policies and compares results. If, however, the released cash value is not paid into the new policy and if the amount involved is not inconsequential, two adjustments should be made to have a reasonably fair analysis. First, the death benefits should be made approximately equal, and second, the time value associated with the released cash value should be recognized.

An example may clarify the concepts involved. Assume that a consumer is contemplating replacing a 10-year-old guaranteed cost, nonpar ordinary life policy with a new universal life policy. Selected data on the two policies are shown in Table 10–8. Outlays are held equal, as are death benefits, except for later years, during which the UL death benefit would have to increase to comply with the current tax-law definition of life insurance. The existing policy's current cash surrender value is shown as $10,000. If the ordinary life policy is replaced, this $10,000 is assumed to be paid into the UL policy.

To simplify the concepts involved, assume that (1) no significant differences in policy provisions exist between the existing and proposed policies, (2) no policy loans are outstanding, (3) the minimum deposit technique is not beneficial to this consumer, and (4) the consumer is insurable at nonsmoker rates. Assume also that the suicide and contestable periods being incurred again are of little personal significance.[21]

Based on guaranteed minimum values, the UL policy cash values are generally inferior to the future values of the older nonparticipating policy. At the intermediate rate of 9 percent, the UL policy values exceed those of the older policy from year 5, with the difference becoming significant by year 20. Naturally, at the current rate of 12 percent, the benefit in favor of UL is even greater. Again the older policy values are superior during the first couple of years, due to the UL policy's initial surrender charges.

This comparison is not totally unbiased since the UL policy death benefit exceeds $100,000 beginning at year 11 (12 percent assumption) and at year 13 (9 percent assumption). All other things being the same and with the assumptions used here, one might conclude that replacement would be in this consumer's best interest financially.

A comparison between two *fixed-premium policies* can be made using the equal outlay method if adjustments are made to minimize bias. However, results frequently are still ambiguous. A cost-based decision can be made using these results *if* the policy against which the method is biased proves superior.

In exploring the replacement alternative under this approach, the surrender value realized under the existing insurance must be recognized. This can be done in either of two ways. First, it can be assumed that the released surrender value is invested. Thus, the total death benefit of the proposed arrangement would be the proposed policy's face amount plus the side fund composed of the released surrender value. To compare similar death benefits, therefore, one should use a face amount for the proposed policy that was equal to the net amount at risk of the existing policy. The released cash value should also be shown, at interest, as being available to augment the total value available on surrender under the proposed arrangement. One then equalizes outlays by accumulating the differences, as before.

As an alternative, the analysis under the equal outlay method can be made by assuming that a maximum policy loan will be made from the existing policy. In essence, this enables the analyst to ignore the surrender value of the existing policy since it would be available for out-

[20]The potential income tax implications of maintaining the values outside the program should be considered carefully. See Chapter 13.

[21]Some companies will waive these periods under replacement cases to the extent that they had expired under the replaced policy, even if the replaced policy is with another company.

TABLE 10-8 Replacement evaluation

	Existing Policy	Proposed Policy
Policy type:	Ordinary life, nonpar	Universal life
Issue date:	10 years ago	Now
Issue age:	25	35
Face amount:	$100,000	$100,000
Annual premium:	$1,200	$1,200

		Interest Rate Basis		
Time		Guaranteed (4½%)	Intermediate (9%)	Current (12%)
		Surrender Values		
Now	$ 10,000	$ 10,000	$ 10,000	$ 10,000
1 year	11,800	10,084	10,530	10,830
5 years	19,000	15,890	19,734	22,289
10 years	29,000	24,303	36,508	46,089
20 years	45,000	45,579	101,021	159,184
		Death Benefits		
Now	$100,000	$100,000	$100,000	$100,000
1 year	100,000	100,000	100,000	100,000
5 years	100,000	100,000	100,000	100,000
10 years	100,000	100,000	100,000	102,318
20 years	100,000	100,000	158,603	249,919

side investment under either the existing or the proposed arrangement. Also, it results in an automatic adjustment within the existing policy to permit a fairer comparison. The net death benefit of the existing arrangement would be the face amount less the loan. The death benefit of the proposed plan should be set at this same level. This, of course, results in a lower outlay for that policy than otherwise. Also, the existing policy's future surrender values should be lowered by the loan amount *and* the policy loan interest payment (after taxes, if deductible) should be included as a part of the existing policy's yearly outlay.

The latter approach is, in many ways, easier to follow and also implicitly takes into consideration the possible advantage accruing to the existing policy from a low policy loan interest rate. After making the necessary adjustments, one then proceeds as before, equalizing outlays under the two arrangements by accumulating the differences.

Under this method, an older term policy could be similarly compared to a new term or cash value policy, and an older cash value policy could be compared to a new term or other cash

value policy. The procedure is essentially the same. However, whenever fixed premium contracts are involved, results often are not as clear as might be desired. An accepted premise with respect to possible policy replacement is: *If in doubt, don't replace.*

The ambiguous results of the equal outlay method, as a technique for comparing existing and proposed policies, can usually be avoided through use of the *cash accumulation* or *comparative interest rate methods*. An essential adjustment in using both of these methods, however, is to treat the present surrender value of the existing policy as an additional first-year payment under that policy or to recalculate its outlays and values, assuming a maximum policy loan. This permits a fair analysis. Other than this adjustment, however, the analysis is conducted as before and interpreted accordingly.

The *YROR* method can be particularly instructive in replacement evaluation if the existing policy is a cash value contract that is proposed to be replaced by a term policy. One derives YROR figures that have meaning in themselves if the term rates used are realistic. If the consumer finds the figures to be too low, a replacement may be in order. For example, YROR figures for the older nonpar policy shown in Table 10–8 compared with the Table 4–2 YRT policy result in the following:

Policy Year	Yearly Rate of Return (%)
1	6.5
5	4.0
10	3.5
15	1.9
20	1.9

Similarly, the *YPP* method can be used to compare an existing term policy to a proposed cash value policy. The YPP figures for the cash value policy only need be compared directly to the term rates.[22] At times, however, the results can be ambiguous under this method also.

Cost Comparison Limitations/Summary

Cost comparison methods yield precise figures. This precision can lend an unwarranted aura of authenticity and creditability to results. All cost comparison methods have limitations. Many were discussed above. One particularly important limitation is that *all methods rely on policy dividend illustrations or projections of nonguaranteed policy values.* Since such values are not guaranteed, cost comparisons among participating or other policies containing nonguaranteed elements or between such policies and guaranteed cost, nonparticipating policies should be interpreted cautiously. This is not to say that such comparisons are invalid, but rather that relatively small cost differences are not significant.

Companies use different methods to allocate investment earnings. Some use the portfolio average method; others use a new money approach. The problems associated with comparisons between policies using different methods were discussed earlier.

The prospective purchaser and his or her advisor should recognize that values projected or illustrated for many years into the future are highly

uncertain. In general, the use of shorter planning horizons is probably more appropriate today due to recent volatility in interest rates. On the other hand, the long run should not be ignored—particularly where major differences exist.

Another limitation of cost comparison methods is that they usually are *predicated on annual premiums* charged by insurers. However, only about 20 percent of policyowners pay premiums annually. Insurers incur extra expenses on policies for which premiums are paid monthly, quarterly, or semiannually and also lose the use of the funds. Since expenses and lost interest can vary considerably, a consumer could be misled into purchasing a policy whose cost is relatively low when based on annual premiums but whose cost is uncompetitive when based on the actual mode of premium payment.[23]

Implicit carrying charges associated with nonannual premiums can be determined with the results factored into the purchase decision. These simple formulas may be used to calculate the implicit carrying charges in life insurance premiums.

Mode	*Formula*
Monthly	$\dfrac{36\,(12M - A)}{13A + 42M}$
Quarterly	$\dfrac{12\,(4Q - A)}{5A - 2Q}$
Semiannually	$\dfrac{2\,(2S - A)}{A - S}$

M is the monthly premium, Q is the quarterly premium, S is the semiannual premium, and A is the annual premium.[24] A simple example: Assume that a \$1,000 annual premium policy has a monthly premium of \$90. The implicit carrying charge, using the first formula above, is

$$\frac{36(12 \times 90 - 1,000)}{13(1,000) + 42(90)} = \frac{36(80)}{16,780} = 17.2\%$$

[23]See Harold Skipper, Jr., "The Effect of Premium Payment Frequency on Life Insurance Cost Rankings," *The Journal of Risk and Insurance*, Vol. XLVII (June 1980).

[24]Joseph M. Belth, "A Note on the Cost of Fractional Premiums," *The Journal of Risk and Insurance*, Vol. XLV (December 1978).

[22]But see footnote 18.

Another potential shortcoming of cost comparisons is that they often exclude supplementary benefits that may be purchased, such as premium waiver or family coverage. This omission is appropriate if the benefit is not included in both policies. Otherwise, the policy comparisons should be based on the entire package. An insurer may have a reasonably attractive basic life policy but charge excessively for the "options," not unlike the situation that exists when purchasing an automobile.

Other potential limitations include the fact that some cost comparison methods can be used fairly to compare similar policies only. Further, some methods focus on one or two policy years only, possibly ignoring other equally important years. All methods must make some arbitrary assumptions to derive costs. These assumptions may not be appropriate for the buyer. All methods ignore the potential income tax implications of policy termination and potential estate and inheritance taxation of death proceeds. Finally, and of great importance, no method is capable of factoring into the cost formula the quality and integrity of the advisor and insurer.

Table 10–9 provides a summary of the key characteristics of the cost comparison methods discussed in this chapter. The table is intended only to highlight points and, as with all such summaries, is subject to numerous qualifications.

ANNUITY CONTRACT COST ANALYSIS

As discussed in Chapter 7, annuities sold today can offer exceptional value. During their accumulation phases, annuities have little or no element of pure life insurance protection. Annuity cost comparisons are, therefore, simpler than life insurance cost comparisons.

Although annuity cost comparisons are less complex, they are no less essential. If an annuity provides for a front-end load, a back-end load, or both, one should not attempt to assess its competitiveness based on the advertised rate of return. Rather, an effective yield based on gross contributions should be calculated.

Table 10–10 provides an illustration of the importance of this concept. The purchaser is assumed to contribute $1,000 per year to this flexible-premium deferred annuity. The insurer currently credits 10.25 percent to the net cash value. Projected surrender values for selected future years are shown in the third column. The purchaser might be shown these values and advised that the current accumulation rate was 10.25 percent. This rate is based on contributions net of expenses and is not representative of the annuity's effective yield.

The final column gives the effective average yields for selected periods. The impact of the loads is obvious. If the insurer credited 10.25 percent to the net contribution, and if the annuity were terminated at the end of the fifth year, the effective yield would be 3.69 percent, not 10.25 percent.

The calculation to derive the effective yield is the same as the internal rate of return (IRR) calculation in finance. It is simply the interest rate that causes a stream of payments to equal a stipulated future value. It should be based on *gross contributions* and on the contract surrender value, net of all surrender charges.

An easy way to estimate an annuity's IRR— if it provides for level premium payments—is first to divide the gross premium into the accrued net surrender value for the point of analysis. This gives an annuity factor for which a corresponding interest rate can be found. A compound interest table (that shows the accumulated value of 1 per year paid at the beginning of each year) is entered at the selected number of years and the annuity factor closest to the calculated factor is located. One has then but to observe the interest rate applicable to that factor. The same approach can be followed for a single-premium deferred annuity by using a compound interest table showing accumulations of a single principal payment of 1.

For nonlevel contributions, a computer is usually necessary. Annuity projections also may be based on portfolio rates or new money rates. Again, this difference should be recognized.

COST AND BENEFIT DISCLOSURE REGULATION

Most states require that certain information be provided to a prospective policyowner about the

TABLE 10-9. Summary of key points of common cost comparison methods

	Traditional Net Cost	Interest Adjusted Net Cost	Equal Outlay	Cash Accumulation	Comparative Interest Rate	Yearly Rate of Return	Yearly Price
Technique	Sum premiums less CV and dividends; ignores interest	Sum premiums at interest less sum dividends at interest and CV	Accumulate premium differences at interest	Accumulate premium differences at interest while holding death benefits equal	Accumulate premium differences at interest rate that causes equal future values and equal death benefits	Ratio of policy "benefits" to "investment"	Policy "investment" less "benefits"
Solves for:	"Net cost"	Average net cost	Surrender value and death benefit differences	Surrender value differences	Average rate of return that causes equality	Yearly rate of return	Yearly price of protection
Assumptions needed	Money has no time value	Rate of return	(1) Rate of return (2) Equal outlay	(1) Rate of return (2) Equal outlay (3) Equal death benefits	(1) YRT rates (2) Equal outlay (3) Equal death benefits	YRT rates	Rate of return
Compares similar policies?	No	Yes	Yes, but often ambiguous results	Yes	Yes, if common YRT rates used	Yes, if common YRT rates used	Yes
Compares dissimilar policies?	No	No	Yes, but results often ambiguous	Yes	Yes	Yes	Yes
Requires computer?	No	No, but time consuming	No but time consuming	Yes	Yes	No	No
Good for replacement evaluation?	No	No	Yes, with modification	Yes, with modification	Yes, with modification	Yes, but results often ambiguous	Yes, but results often ambiguous

TABLE 10-10. Illustrative annuity yields

Year	Annual Contribution	Surrender Value	Advertised Yield (%) (Based on Net Contribution)	Effective Yield[a] (%) (Based on Gross Contribution)
1	$1,000	$ 717	10.25	−28.26
2	1,000	1,761	10.25	−8.22
3	1,000	2,912	10.25	−1.50
4	1,000	4,181	10.25	1.78
5	1,000	5,580	10.25	3.69
10	1,000	15,514	10.25	7.85
15	1,000	31,900	10.25	8.96
20	1,000	58,591	10.25	9.41
25	1,000	102,067	10.25	9.63
30	1,000	172,885	10.25	9.77

[a]From date of issue to year indicated.

policy that he or she is considering purchasing. Special disclosure requirements apply to existing policies where a replacement is being proposed and also to flexible premium policies.

Background of Disclosure Issue

Although recommendations for improving cost disclosure were made as early as 1908 by the Wisconsin insurance commissioner, significant activity on the issue did not occur until the 1960s, beginning with the actions of the late Senator Philip A. Hart. Following Hart's threat of federal legislation, an industry study committee was appointed and it concluded in 1970 that the most suitable cost comparison method was the interest adjusted cost method.[25]

The NAIC adopted an interim model life insurance disclosure regulation in mid-1973 and a final version in 1976. The final version, the NAIC **Life Insurance Solicitation Model Regulation,** incorporates an expanded version of the interest adjusted method for cost comparisons. Its details are discussed later.

Important congressional subcommittee hearings on life insurance marketing and cost disclosure were held in 1973 and 1978,[26] both of which raised questions about existing disclosure and marketing practices.

The Federal Trade Commission (FTC) staff was also investigating marketing problems in the life insurance business at this time and released its report in 1979.[27] This report identified several "consumer problems" in life insurance marketing and cited several reasons for those problems. The report presented detailed recommendations by the FTC staff as to how they believed these problems could be remedied. The FTC staff believed significant changes should be made in the NAIC approach to cost disclosure. The FTC staff report caused much turmoil within the life insurance industry. The industry testified vigorously against the report.

The NAIC had been mindful of the criticisms of its solicitation regulation. As a result, it formed a Cost Disclosure Task Force in 1979 to solicit comments on the issues involved and to evaluate the regulation. The Task Force's 1980 report encountered strong opposition and was shelved.

The Virginia Bureau of Insurance released a report in 1981 on some problems and issues associated with life insurance and annuity products and their marketing.[28] An alternative disclosure

[25]*Report of the Joint Special Committee on Life Insurance Costs* (1970).

[26]*The Life Insurance Industry,* Parts 1, 2, and 3 (Washington, D.C.: U.S. Government Printing Office, 1973) and Part 4 (1974) and *Life Insurance Marketing and Cost Disclosure* (Washington, D.C.: U.S. Government Printing Office, 1978).

[27]*Life Insurance Cost Disclosure* (Washington, D.C.: 1979).

[28]*Life Insurance Products, Disclosure and Marketing Practices* (Richmond, Va.: Virginia Bureau of Insurance, 1981).

approach to the NAIC was recommended which relied on the comparative interest rate method for cash value policies and on a disclosure system that permitted the individual to control the quantity of data he or she received. The Virginia report also recommended the substitution of a single comprehensive life insurance and annuity disclosure regulation for several separate NAIC regulations.

The NAIC adopted new disclosure regulations in 1983, some details of which are discussed below. As this book was going to press, the NAIC had under consideration the possibility of requiring disclosure of a "yield index" figure for certain cash value products. This index, similar to the CIR, is calculated using a policy's net amount at risk rather than the hypothetical side fund as with the CIR.

NAIC Cost Disclosure Requirements

Over 35 states require cost and benefit disclosure to prospective life insurance purchasers as recommended in the NAIC 1976 Model Life Insurance Solicitation Regulation. The regulation requires that the prospective purchaser be supplied with (1) a **Buyer Guide's** that contains an explanation of life insurance products and how to shop for them, and (2) a **Policy Summary** containing pertinent data about the particular policy the prospect is considering. The regulation does not apply to annuities, credit life insurance, group life insurance, variable life insurance, and life insurance policies issued in connection with pension and welfare plans.

Disclosure Requirements. In general, the insurance company is required to provide, to all prospective purchasers, a Buyer's Guide and a Policy Summary prior to accepting the applicant's initial premium or premium deposit. There are two exceptions: If the policy for which application is made contains an unconditional refund provision of at least 10 days or if the Policy Summary contains such an unconditional refund offer. In these cases, the Buyer's Guide and Policy Summary may be delivered with or prior to delivery of the policy. Most states now mandate a 10-day

"free look" requirement. The insurer is also required to provide a Buyer's Guide and a Policy Summary to any prospective purchaser upon request.[29]

The Buyer's Guide. The Buyer's Guide is a document that is intended to help prospective purchasers (1) decide how much life insurance to buy, (2) decide what kind of policy to buy, and (3) compare the costs of similar life insurance policies. The language of the Guide is mandated by the regulation.

The suggestion in the Buyer's Guide for choosing an amount of life insurance to buy is general, advising the consumer "to figure how much cash and income your dependents would need if you die." The Guide explains briefly three types of life insurance—term, whole life, and endowment—pointing out positive and negative aspects of each. Next, the consumer is advised that "your chances of finding a good buy are better if you use two types of index numbers. . . ." The consumer is admonished: "Look for Policies with Low Index Numbers." These index numbers are contained in the Policy Summary.

The Buyer's Guide explains the distinction between participating and nonparticipating life insurance and includes a general description of the Life Insurance Surrender Cost Index (the name used by the NAIC for the IANC) and the Life Insurance Net Payment Cost Index and advice on how to use them.

The Policy Summary. The Policy Summary is a document containing the disclosure information on the specific policy being considered by the consumer. The name and address of the insurance agent (if any) and the insurance company must appear on the Summary, together with the generic name of the insurance policy (e.g., "whole life insurance").

The Policy Summary must contain certain policy data (premiums, death benefits, cash values, dividends, etc.) for the first five policy years and

---

[29]In the case of policies whose equivalent-level death benefit does not exceed $5,000, a somewhat modified Policy Summary must be provided.

for representative policy years thereafter, sufficient to illustrate clearly the pattern of premiums and benefits. These years must include the tenth and twentieth years, plus data for "at least one age from 60 through 65 or, if earlier, policy maturity."

In addition to the foregoing policy data, the effective policy loan interest rate must be stated and 10- and 20-year surrender cost and net payment cost indices provided. The procedure to calculate the indices is mandated by the regulation. A 5 percent interest assumption is to be used. If the policy is participating, the Equivalent Level Annual Dividend (ELAD) must be disclosed. Each of these figures was discussed earlier in the chapter.

The Solicitation Regulation requires an agent to inform any prospective purchaser of the full name of the company for which he or she is acting as a life insurance agent. The salesperson is prohibited from using terms such as financial planner, investment advisor, financial consultant, or financial counseling in such a way as to imply the agent is generally engaged in a fee-for-service advisory business unless that is actually the case. The use of the TNC method of cost comparison is prohibited except to show a policy's cash flow pattern.

The 1983 Modifications. In late 1983, the NAIC adopted revisions in its 1976 model solicitation regulation. The revised regulation, the **Life Insurance Disclosure Model Regulation,** had not been adopted by any state at the time this book was going to press. It would eliminate the use of ELAD and substitute for it a requirement that two sets of surrender and payment indexes be calculated, one on a guaranteed basis alone and the other based on illustrated or projected values. It also would provide that an existing policyowner had the right to obtain certain policy data. The 1976 model did not require this, although Alabama and Georgia have such provisions in their regulations.

The new model would require the method of investment income allocation (i.e., new money or portfolio average) to be shown on the Policy Summary issued by mutual insurers and, if the mutual insurer did not follow the contribution

principle, a statement to that effect must also be included. Any change from one investment income allocation method to the other would require that affected policyowners of a mutual company be notified.[30]

Other changes were made also. The Buyer's Guide was updated to include information on newer policy forms and a "discontinuity index" had to be calculated (but not provided to the consumer) in an effort to detect any policy that had "manipulated" values.

Universal Life Disclosure Regulation

The NAIC also adopted a **Universal Life Insurance Model Regulation.** This regulation establishes minimum valuation and nonforfeiture standards for UL and current assumption whole life policies and mandates certain policy provisions. It also supplements, to an extent, disclosure requirements of the 1976 and 1983 disclosure regulations. For example, it requires that a policyowner must receive, at least annually, a report that summarizes the recent activity in the policy, including full policy values. As of 1986, at least 10 states had adopted this regulation, and a number of other states impose some of the regulation requirements. Also, as a practical matter, most companies voluntarily comply with the regulation anyway.

Annuity Disclosure Regulation

The NAIC **Model Annuity and Deposit Fund Disclosure Regulation** requires the disclosure of the effective yield of annuities on a gross contribution basis. It is similar to the 1983 life insurance disclosure regulation in terms of its general requirements. A Contract Summary must be provided, as must a Buyer's Guide to Annuities. Variations of this model exist in only a few states.

---

[30]None of these requirements would apply to stock companies selling participating insurance. Those who already own or may purchase a participating policy from a stock insurer arguably should be entitled to the same protections and disclosures as those who purchase a participating policy from a mutual insurer. At the time this book was going to press, there was some movement to suggest that this deficiency is being addressed.

LIFE INSURANCE POLICY REPLACEMENT REGULATION

The very mention of the word "replacement" evokes strong opinions and emotions from many within the life insurance business. Replacement activity has been and remains at a high level. Some insurance executives and agents have expressed alarm over this trend, arguing that life insurance consumers are losing millions of dollars by switching policies. Others argue that replacement is usually in the consumer's interest, that an existing life insurance policy should be no more sacred or immune to replacement than any other consumer purchase, and that today's new products are superior to older policies. Some agents and insurers have a marketing strategy based on replacement of existing insurance.

The 1970 and 1979 NAIC Model Replacement Regulations

In 1970, the NAIC adopted its first **Model Replacement Regulation.** This regulation, still in effect in two states, requires an insurer (or agent) to provide the consumer contemplating a replacement with (1) a notice and (2) a Comparison Statement. The notice points out that "as a general rule, it is not advantageous to drop or change existing life insurance in favor of a new policy." The Comparison Statement is to be completed by the replacing agent. It is to provide the consumer with comparative data on the existing and proposed policies to assist the consumer in his or her decision as to whether to replace.

The NAIC adopted a revised replacement regulation at its December 1978 meeting. This regulation represented an improvement over the previous regulation. Several states' replacement regulations are patterned after this version.

Under this regulation, the agent proposing a replacement must provide the insured with a **Replacement Notice** and a completed **Comparative Information Form.** The agent is to leave with the applicant copies of all sales materials used and to send to the replacing insurer signed copies

of the Notice and the Comparative Information Form plus copies of all sales proposals. An agent attempting a conservation effort must leave with the consumer a copy of all materials used in connection with that effort and must submit to his or her own company a copy of such materials.

The replacing insurer is to send to the existing insurer a verified copy of the Comparative Information Form within three days of receipt of the insurance application. Further, the replacing insurer must either delay issuance of the new policy for 20 days or provide a 20-day unconditional refund offer with the replacing policy.

If the existing insurer undertakes a conservation effort, it must either complete, correct, and send to the consumer the Comparative Information Form it received from the replacing insurer or send the consumer a Policy Summary completed in compliance with the solicitation regulation if the state has adopted it. Cost comparison information need not be included in the Policy Summary. The existing insurer is, in turn, to provide to the replacing insurer a copy of the materials it sent the consumer in its efforts to conserve the policy.[31]

Both the older and newer versions of the regulations have shortcomings. Critics claimed that the regulations constituted a road map as to how to replace. On the other hand, claims were made that the regulations discouraged many justifiable replacements because of the time-consuming task of compliance. Others pointed out that the disclosure form provided much policy data, the usefulness of which was, at best, questionable and, at worst, counterproductive.[32]

The 1984 NAIC Model Replacement Regulation

In 1984, the NAIC adopted its latest replacement regulation, the **1984 NAIC Model**

---

[31]Contrary to the stated belief of some of the authors' students, the U.S. Postal Service did *not* draft this regulation.

[32]The regulations were critized for other reasons as well. See *Virginia Report, op. cit.,* pp. 85–93; and especially, James W. Newman and Harold Skipper, Jr., "Regulating Life Insurance Replacement Activity," *Journal of Insurance Regulation,* Vol. 1 (September 1982).

Replacement Regulation. This model is patterned, in key parts, after the replacement regulation adopted by Virginia in 1982. The Virginia regulation resulted from the criticisms contained in the report cited earlier and itself benefited from some pioneering work in this respect by Alabama. Several states' regulations are similar to this latest model.

The new regulation retains much from its predecessors but eliminates totally the requirement that a comparison form be used. The applicant is to be provided a notice, but it is far simpler than earlier notices and puts more of the burden on the consumer to protect his or her own interests. Other differences in procedure are required. Although acknowledged to be an improvement over earlier model regulations, the 1984 model is still considered by some to be less than desired.

The Replacement Debate

Arguments as to whether replacements are "good" or "bad" provide the individual buyer and agent or other financial advisor little or no guidance. The question is whether a *particular* proposed replacement is in the policyowner's best interest. Generalizations are of no help in attempting to answer this question.

Many replacements are, no doubt, contrary to the policyowner's best interests. No less doubtful is that many other replacements are justified. The policyowner considering replacement should consider several factors. For example, most cash value life insurance policies have their initial costs charged, one way or another, against early cash values. These initial high costs would already have been met under an older policy. However, a cost analysis will determine whether this argument is persuasive, just as a cost analysis will reveal whether a higher premium rate for a new policy is justified financially.

Most persons who replace life insurance believe that they are benefiting financially by the move. Figure 10–1 shows results of a 1984 survey of why policyowners replaced their policies. In many cases, the replacement was related to changing individual needs, not to perceived cost advantages.

The fact that incontestable and suicide clauses begin anew under new policies should always be considered, but this is rarely found to be persuasive enough by itself to forestall a replacement. Moreover, some companies will waive these clauses on new policies to the extent that they had elapsed under the older policy.

It is often said that existing policies may have more favorable provisions than new policies and that cost analyses alone do not reveal this. This can be correct. The opposite can also be true. In any event, the importance of evaluating policy contractual provisions should again be mentioned as a key element in policy evaluation.[33]

If an older policy is not perceived as serving the consumer's needs, it may be that the existing insurer can make an internal exchange on more beneficial terms than that which a new insurer may be willing. It also can be the case that an older policy, through changes in dividend options or through policy loans and other features, could be adjusted to meet new circumstances.

In any event, a policyowner should never discontinue existing coverage before the new coverage is approved for issuance by the replacing company and is in effect.

The agent or other financial advisor should approach a proposed policy replacement with no prejudices either for or against replacement. Replacement is neither "good" nor "evil." It is a neutral activity. A sound, fair analysis will help determine whether in a given situation, replacement should be undertaken. As a general rule, if results of the analysis do not provide a reasonably clear decision in favor of replacement, the policyowner probably should not replace.

---

[33]See Chapters 8 and 9.

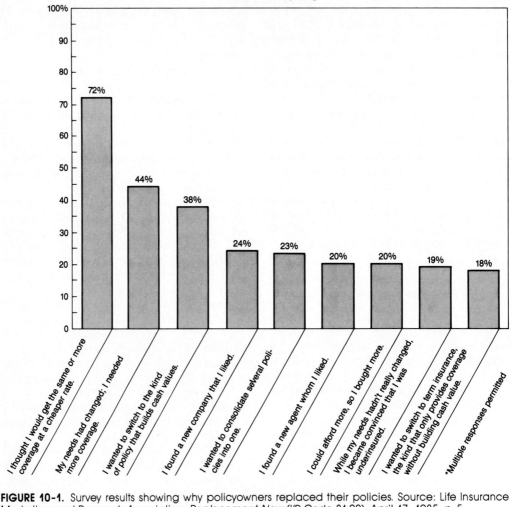

FIGURE 10-1. Survey results showing why policyowners replaced their policies. Source: Life Insurance Marketing and Research Association, *Replacement Now* (I/R Code 81.00), April 17, 1985, p. 5.

APPENDIX

Formulas for Selected Cost Comparison Methods

Symbols used in the formulas below are:

n = number of years

P_t = illustrated premium at beginning of policy year t

D_t = illustrated dividend (or other nonguaranteed premium credit if not included in P_t) at the end of policy year t

CV_n = illustrated cash value plus terminal dividend at the end of policy year n

F_t = illustrated death benefit at end of policy year t

i = assumed interest rate

YP_t = assumed yearly price of insurance per \$1,000 in policy year t

DB_t = illustrated death benefit at the beginning of policy year t

Traditional Net Cost Method

The formula for the traditional net cost for a period of n years is

$$TNC_n = \frac{\sum_{t=1}^{n} P_t - \sum_{t=1}^{n} D_t - CV_n}{(F_n)(0.001)(n)} \qquad (1)$$

Interest Adjusted Net Cost Method

The formula for the interest adjusted net cost for a period of n years is

$$IANC_n = \qquad (2)$$

$$\frac{\sum_{t=1}^{n} P_t(1+i)^{n-t+1} - \sum_{t=1}^{n} D_t(1+i)^{n-t} - CV_n}{(F_n)(0.001)\left[\sum_{t=1}^{n}(1+i)^{t}\right]}$$

If the policy death benefit is not constant over the period of evaluation, an *equivalent-level death benefit*

may be calculated as follows and substituted for F_n above:

$$ELDB_n = \frac{\sum_{t=1}^{n} DB_t(1+i)^{n-t+1}}{\sum_{t=1}^{n}(1+i)^{t}} \qquad (3)$$

The net payment index formula is identical to (2) above *except* that the cash value (CV_n) term is omitted.

Equivalent-Level Annual Dividend

The formula for the equivalent-level annual dividend for a period of n years is

$$ELAD_n = \frac{\sum_{t=1}^{n} D_t(1+i)^{n-t}}{(F_n)(0.001)\left[\sum_{t=1}^{n}(1+i)^{t}\right]} \qquad (4)$$

Yearly Rate of Return Method

The formula for the yearly rate of return for policy year t is

$$YROR_t = \qquad (5)$$

$$\frac{CV_t + D_t + (YP_t)(F_t - CV_t)(0.001)}{P_t + CV_{t-1}} - 1$$

Yearly Price of Protection Method

The formula for the yearly price of protection method for policy year t is

$$YPP_t = \frac{(1+i)(P_t + CV_{t-1}) - (CV_t + D_t)}{(F_t - CV_t)(0.001)} \qquad (6)$$

Chapter 11

Insurance Advisor and Company Evaluation

The three preceding chapters discussed various contractual and cost analyses that can be undertaken to evaluate life insurance policies. However, as mentioned before, it can be of little value to obtain a low-cost, well-designed policy whose provisions are favorable to the buyer if the insurance company backing the contract is of less than desired quality. Moreover, even if both the policy and the insurer backing the contract are of high quality, the advice received and followed in connection with the purchase could have been ill-conceived or not well suited to the buyer's needs. The results could be a high-quality policy (backed by a high-quality company) that would not accomplish the desired personal financial planning objectives. Clearly, the agent's or other insurance advisor's advice and recommendations can be key elements, particularly if the client's needs are for more than a basic life insurance program.

INSURANCE ADVISOR EVALUATION

Selecting a qualified advisor should be a first priority for most persons who are in need of specialized services. Even if an inexperienced, well-motivated advisor recommends a decision that he or she believes best for the buyer's objec-

tives, the decision may not be in the best interest of the prospect or client. Regrettably, some agents and other insurance advisors, although well intentioned, simply are not well informed. Too often, the state examination to become a licensed agent is not sufficiently rigorous to separate out those with too little knowledge. Moreover, in most states, persons, including professionals in other areas, who give advice about life insurance and who are not life insurance agents, are not required by the state to demonstrate any level of professional competence in life insurance matters. For the vast majority of persons the most judicious method of buying life insurance is probably to find a good agent or other advisor who has the qualifications needed for the buyer's particular needs.

From the buyer's standpoint, a good agent or other advisor is one who:[1]

1. Places the interest of the client first
2. Has up-to-date knowledge of the business, including product and market availability
3. Gives clients continuing service—that is, periodically reviews the client's needs and makes recom-

[1] *How to Pick a Life Insurance Agent* (Washington, D.C.: National Association of Life Underwriters, 1978).

mendations necessary to keep each client's life and health insurance program current and effective

How does one find such a person? It is not easy. Helpful sources of information can include local business and professional persons, existing clients, and advisors themselves, although this word-of-mouth approach is far from foolproof. The value of the opinions of business and professional persons depends on their knowledge of life insurance and their experience with a prospective advisor. The advisor's clients may be limited in their perspective by lack of experience with other advisors; they may not know what services to expect. On the other hand, if an individual is pleased with an advisor and his or her service, this can be important.

A potenial proxy for client satisfaction for agents who have been in the business for at least a few years is whether the agent has qualified for the National Quality Award (NQA). Preferably, the agent would have qualified for the NQA for many consecutive years. The NQA is awarded each year only to those agents whose lapse ratios for business written in the previous year are very low. This suggests that their clients are pleased with their purchases.

Most individuals do not have the opportunity or inclination to investigate a prospective advisor carefully. There are, however, several additional inquiries that can be made with relatively little effort.[2]

First, what education and training does he or she possess? As with all business persons, the greater the education and training within their fields of expertise, the better, other things being the same. Of course, this should not necessarily automatically be used as a criterion to exclude those without undergraduate or graduate college degrees.

In this connection, one might prefer to deal with those persons holding a recognized professional designation. Literally dozens of insurance and financial planning-related designations exist today that can be appended to the advisor's name. Many are highly specialized and may not have the desired relevance to life insurance in financial planning. Others must be considered as not yet having proven themselves as to durability and/or professional content. Three designations worthy of consideration by the buyer are: (1) Chartered Life Underwriter (CLU), (2) Chartered Financial Consultant (ChFC), and (3) Certified Financial Planner (CFP).

The CLU designation program is the oldest and best known of the three. To obtain and use the CLU designation, which is granted by The American College (formerly known as The American College of Life Underwriters), the student is required to pass 10 examinations that are administered by the S. S. Huebner School of CLU Studies and to meet certain character and experience requirements. The examinations relate to the traditional areas of economics, finance, and accounting as well as insurance law, employee benefit planning, life product and market understanding, business, estate, and personal uses of life and health insurance, and selected areas of noninsurance investments. A recently introduced CLU track permits candidates to focus more on multiline insurance applications.

The ChFC and CFP professional programs are broader in scope than, but do not cover life insurance matters in as much depth as, the CLU program. The CFP program, which predates the ChFC program, requires candidates to pass six comprehensive examinations. To obtain and use the ChFC designation, the student is required to pass 10 examinations, some of which will be waived for a person holding a CLU designation. Both CFP and ChFC examinations test students' understanding of the broad concepts and applications of personal financial planning. The successful candidate in each program also must meet certain character and experience requirements. The ChFC designation is granted by The American College.[3] The CFP professional designation program is administered by the College for Financial Planning.[4]

---

[2]See James L. Athearn, *It Pays to Shop for Life Insurance* (Cincinnati, Ohio: National Underwriter Co., 1977), Chap. 8.

[3]For further information regarding the CLU and ChFC programs, contact The American College, 270 Bryn Mawr Avenue, Bryn Mawr, PA 19010.

[4]For further information regarding the CFP Program, contact the College for Financial Planning, 9725 Hampden Avenue, Denver, CO 80231.

Although only the CLU designation is oriented specifically toward life insurance and its many uses, both the CFP and ChFC programs help ensure that the individual is well versed in life insurance fundamentals and its applications. Individuals who hold one or more of these professional designations should be regarded as knowledgeable professionals. Of course, one finds many capable non-designation-holding persons who provide quality advice. As with any professional designation, it is no guarantee of competence or trustworthiness. However, from a buyer's perspective, the burden of proof should be on those not holding a recognized professional designation.

A *second* inquiry relates to whether the agent has the freedom to place business with more than one company and to sell any type of life insurance and annuity contract. If an agent does not hold an NASD license, he or she cannot offer the variable-type products. Some agents represent only one company and cannot place business with other companies. In some markets this may not be a problem, depending on the quality of the company represented and its products. For more specialized needs, this could pose difficulty for the client, as no one company is best in everything.

Third, has the advisor been involved with the life insurance business long enough to acquire the knowledge and skill needed to provide professional service to the buyer? Some writers recommend five years as the minimum service, other things being equal, necessary to assure professional qualifications. However, it is important to note that even a relatively new advisor may have support services that will provide reasonable assurance that his or her relative lack of experience will not be detrimental. Also, every individual's situation does not require the most highly trained person who might specialize in intricate estate planning or tax work. Relatively new, younger agents frequently relate well to young men and women who are just starting their families and careers. Moreover, there is something to be said for having an agent of approximately the same age as the client so their working life spans may closely coincide.

Fourth, is the agent a career, full-time insurance agent? Persons who are part-time insurance or financial advisors are usually best avoided in the absence of exceptional circumstances.

Fifth, how does the agent or advisor maintain current knowledge in his or her field? When was the last time he or she attended an advanced education or training program or seminar? Toward what professional designations is the person working? What exams have been passed?

Sixth, the buyer needs to ask himself or herself how he or she "feels" about a particular prospective advisor. Irrespective of the individual's competence, professional designations, and so on, does he or she seem to be the type of person with whom one will feel comfortable in discussing personal matters and in whom one can place trust? Intuition pays an important and worthy role here.

A buyer who is successful in selecting a good advisor will minimize the chances of purchasing insurance at unfavorable prices and terms, from low-quality companies, or that is not well matched to needs. Since one cannot be certain that a particular advisor is "good," it is prudent for the buyer to become familiar with insurance concepts generally, including methods designed to facilitate policy-cost and other comparisons, as discussed in Chapters 8 to 10.

LIFE INSURANCE COMPANY EVALUATION

In evaluating a life insurance company, the advisor (and the buyer) should consider several factors and should understand the pecularities of the various types of entities that provide life insurance coverage.

Organizations Providing Life Insurance

Several different types of organizations offer life insurance, five of which are presented here. Government-provided life insurance coverage under social insurance programs is discussed in Chapter 25.

Commercial Life Insurance Companies. Commercial life insurers are either stocks or mutuals. A **stock life insurance company** is one that is organized and incorporated under a state's laws for the purpose of making a profit for its stockholders. Policyowners have no ownership interest in stock companies.

A **life insurance mutual company** also is organized and incorporated under a state's laws but has no stockholders. The policyowner is the customer and, in effect, an owner, in contrast to the stock company, where the policyowner is a customer only.

The number of commercial life insurance companies in the United States at the end of 1983 totaled an estimated 2,082. At year-end 1982, 194 of these companies had been writing life insurance for more than 50 years and 31 were at least a century old.

Of the companies in business at mid-1984, at least two were domiciled in each state with the exception of Alaska, which had one. Arizona had the largest number (561), followed by Texas (261) and Louisiana (108).

Stock companies comprise 94 percent of the total, with mutuals accounting for the balance. Mutual companies, which are generally older and larger than the stock companies, had 53.0 percent of the assets of all U.S. commercial life companies and accounted for 41.5 percent of life insurance in force. In the past 18 years, five companies have converted from the status of a mutual company to a stock company and two stock companies have converted to mutuals. Figure 11–1

compares mutual and stock life insurance companies in the United States by number, assets, and life insurance in force.

Comparisons are often made between stock and mutual insurers. A few of the arguments for each are examined here.

1. *Control.* Since a stock company is owned by the stockholders, the directors and officers answer to them and not directly to the policyowners. As in all stock corporations, control legally lies with the holders of the majority of the stock. However, just as with other large corporations, a stock company with a large number of widely scattered stockholders is controlled by its management group through proxy arrangements. In such cases, the effective control is, in fact, not in the hands of the stockholders or the policyowners but in the hands of the management group operating the company. The likelihood that management will ignore the interests of policyowners, however, is slim with substantial and well-established stock life companies, because of competition and insurance regulatory oversight. In some cases, limited management participation by policyowners is permitted. For example, policyowners may be given the right to elect several directors, although a minority.

In a mutual company, policyowners theoretically own the company and control the management. In practice, this is true only to a limited

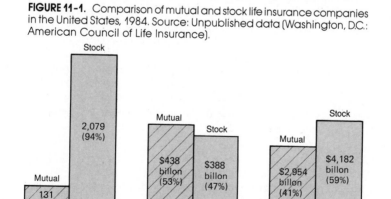

FIGURE 11-1. Comparison of mutual and stock life insurance companies in the United States, 1984. Source: Unpublished data (Washington, D.C.: American Council of Life Insurance).

extent. The limited effectiveness of policyowners' control of a mutual company is due to the facts that (1) policyowners do not perceive themselves as owners of the company but rather as customers, (2) they are numerous and widely scattered geographically, (3) they have little capacity or inclination for intercommunication, (4) the stake of each policyowner in the company is proportionately small, and (5) many policyowners do not understand the nature of a mutual company or know that they have a right to vote at elections of directors. As in the case of a well-established stock company, a well-established mutual company is controlled by its management group through proxy arrangements. Again, lack of control by the policyowners usually is not a serious problem.

2. *Security.* Another long-debated aspect of the stock versus mutual issue relates to which is the more secure. In the initial development period of a stock company, its capital and surplus are a significant factor in its guarantee of payment. Later when it has accumulated substantial surplus, this element of security becomes much less important. Over the years, a contingency fund, still necessary to absorb unfavorable fluctuations and losses, will be composed primarily of surplus earnings and accumulated profits. A mutual company's contingency fund will be made up entirely of surplus earnings. All the assets and earnings are held by the mutual company for the benefit and protection of its policyowners. These earnings are available to reduce the cost of insurance or may be added to the company's surplus for additional safety.

The relative security of stock and mutual companies is largely an academic question. Both customarily use conservative assumptions in their premium computations and this affords an additional element of security, often more significant than the capital of stock companies. The basic issues underlying security are sound and efficient management and adequate supervision and control by government authorities. Incompetent management can be disastrous to policyowners of either stock or a mutual, but this seldom occurs.

3. *Cost.* Another dimension of the issue

has been the question of relative cost of products. Proponents of mutual companies have argued that since favorable financial results flow to policyowners, their policies will be less costly than those sold by stock companies, where stockholders benefit from favorable results. Proponents of stock companies argue that stock companies have more incentives toward efficiency that more than make up to policyowners for the profits paid stockholders.

Generalizations on the question of cost are dangerous. Some mutual companies are more efficiently run than some stock companies, and vice versa. Even if a given company is efficiently operated, there remains no guarantee that policyowners—either in a mutual or stock company—will receive the benefit. Stock companies may pay out good profits to stockholders. Mutual companies may use them to build even more surplus.

Whether a particular policy is low cost is usually not a function of organizational form but of insurer efficiency and the extent to which the insurer passes to policyowners the resulting efficiency gains. As was clear from earlier chapters, variations are great.

Fraternal Benefit Societies. **Fraternal benefit societies** in the United States and Canada had over $104 billion of life insurance in force at year-end 1985. There are over 200 such societies in the United States, although most have little or no life insurance business in force. As fraternals have several unique features and they are not discussed elsewhere in this book, their operations will be covered here.

1. *Background.* Fraternal life insurance made its appearance about the same time as industrial life insurance, and in answer to the same needs—those of low-income persons. The volume of life insurance written by fraternals grew rapidly, particularly during the 1880s and 1890s. In fact, during a part of this period, the amount of fraternal life insurance in force exceeded the ordinary insurance in force in all commercial companies.

Between 1919 and 1940, fraternal life insurance in force showed a steady decline, but since 1940 it has gradually increased. Even so, it now accounts for a far smaller share of total life insurance in force than formerly. The prime reasons for this relative decrease were the relentless compounding of difficulties by a fundamentally defective product design—the assessment plan of insurance and, to a lesser extent, the introduction of group life insurance by commercial companies.

A **pure assessment system** requires premium payments from members only when one dies. Such aggregate payments are used to pay the death benefits promised to the insured. No advance premium payments are collected and no advanced funding is involved. Fundamental to the assessment system is the assumption that an annual influx of new, younger members would tend to maintain the same age distribution for the whole group, which, it was thought, would prevent the cost of insurance from increasing. The inequity of equal assessments, irrespective of age, eventually became apparent and had an adverse effect on the ability to secure and retain new members at the younger ages. But even if the average age had been maintained, the assessment would have increased as the original members reached older ages, because of the higher mortality cost at these older ages.

The defects of the pure-assessment system led to the adoption of the **graded-assessment system,** under which assessments were graded upward by age at entry. This modification still failed to recognize the basic fact that the cost of insurance on a year-to-year basis depends on the current age. A few of the societies, realizing this fact, followed the YRT plan for assessments. This was a financially sound plan, but as commercial companies had discovered, prohibitive costs developed at the older ages.

Gradually, many societies realized that life insurance benefits must be based either on an adequate YRT plan or, if whole life insurance was to be provided, on the level-premium plan with attendant reserves. The ultimate transition to a sound actuarial basis, which has been accomplished by all fraternal societies of consequence, was aided by legislation initiated by the fraternals themselves through the National Fraternal Congress of America and the Associated Fraternities of America.

2. *Nature.* Fraternal benefit societies have existed in this country for over 100 years. The early fraternal societies were formed on a localized basis, purely for social and benevolent purposes. Members and their families were provided various forms of assistance during sickness and unemployment and at death, on an informal basis. In many societies, eligibility for membership depended on such factors as nationality, language, membership in some religious denomination or sect, or occupation.

Many societies today accept members without regard to such factors, but most retain membership prerequisites such as those enumerated. Some societies have both "social" and "beneficial" members, with only the latter participating in the insurance benefits.

Numerous charitable, institutional, recreational, health, educational, religious, and membership activities and benefits are provided by fraternal benefit societies. In addition, countless hours of service are devoted to the public in the form of community activities.

Fraternal benefit societies are defined and their supervision provided for in all the states and the District of Columbia by special sections or chapters of the respective state insurance codes. Except for the minimum reserve requirements, the provisions and requirements are somewhat less comprehensive than those pertaining to commercial companies.

Fraternals are often required by law to have a "representative form of government." This connotes a controlling body, composed of representatives elected either directly by the members or by the delegates from the local lodges or intermediate bodies chosen in accordance with the society's constitution or bylaws. Proxy voting is prohibited, thus minimizing this device as a means of perpetuating a management group.

3. *The fraternal insurance contract.* Fraternal benefit societies use a so-called **open contract.** Under this contract, the society's constitution and bylaws, and any future change therein, are, by reference, made a part of the contract with the member. In the "closed contracts of commercial companies, the terms of the life insurance contract and the application constitute the entire agreement between the company and the policyowner.

The merits of the open contract have been much debated. The open contract permits assessments, but these would be permitted only in the event of insolvency. Should this occur, the board of directors or the governing body may levy an assessment on each member in an amount equal to an equitable proportion of the deficiency. The member may pay the assessment, in which case all is well. But if he or she does not pay it, two alternatives appear. At the member's option, unpaid assessments may become an interest-bearing lien against the certificate, or he or she may accept a certificate with a reduced benefit, free of any lien, the present value of the reduction being equal to the assessment levied.

İt should be pointed out that if a commercial insurer becomes insolvent, a court will permit the establishment of liens and related alternatives no different in effect from those established by the board of directors or governing body of an impaired fraternal benefit society. Thus, in New York, only in the case of insolvency could a society exercise the open contract feature to reduce in any way the benefits guaranteed by the contract. In other states, the approval of the insurance commissioner would undoubtedly be necessary before such a move could be taken.

The leading fraternals offer all common insurance plans. For the most part, they have not issued annuities, except in connection with settlement arrangements. However, many of the larger societies do issue annuities, some are issuing health insurance contracts, and at least one has set up a mutual fund outlet.

4. *Tax-exempt status.* Fraternal benefit societies are exempt from premium taxation. Exemption for fraternals under the tax laws of most states has been justified by arguing that fraternals engage in community endeavors and charitable enterprises for their members, in addition to providing insurance benefits.

Fraternals differ in fulfilling the "fraternal" nature of their obligations. In many cases, the insurance operations of fraternals have more importance than have their various member and community service activities. Some fraternals place emphasis on the "fraternal" aspect of their service to members. Statutes provide latitude for such expression to enable members through a representative form of government to fashion an organization responsive to member needs and preferences.

Savings Banks as Insurers. Three states—Connecticut, Massachusetts, and New York—permit mutual savings banks to sell life insurance. At year-end 1985, such insurance amounted to $16.4 billion, a 4.9 percent increase over 1984. A great part of this total was in Massachusetts and New York. The amount in force in Massachusetts ($4,776 million) and in New York ($9,617 million) had been growing at a steady rate, while the growth in Connecticut (currently $1,959 million) remains relatively slow at least in part because of the relatively small amount of life insurance permitted on one life under state law. Since 1981, however, New York has experienced no growth. Admitted asets as of December 31, 1985 totaled $1,333 million, of which $559 million were in Massachusetts, $672 million in New York, and $92 million in Connecticut.

These figures indicate that although the business and assets of savings-bank life insurance are substantial, they are relatively insignificant when compared with the aggregate figures for commercial life insurance companies. Just as with fraternal life insurance, a somewhat detailed discussion is presented here on savings bank life insurance, as they are not touched upon elsewhere in this volume.

1. *Background.* Massachusetts, in 1907, became the first state to empower its mutual savings banks to establish life insurance departments for the purpose of providing life insurance and annuity benefits to residents and those working in the state. Similar laws were enacted in New York in 1938 and in Connecticut in 1941.

The Massachusetts law was the result of proposals made by Louis D. Brandeis following the Armstrong investigation in New York.[5] The

[5]This was an investigation by the state of New York, in 1905, into many phases of life insurance company operations. Louis D. Brandeis acted as counsel for the Policyholders Protective Committee, which had been formed as a result of the investigation.

testimony taken in the investigation had emphasized the excessive amounts spent by some companies at that time for commissions on new business and also had brought out the comparatively high cost of weekly premium industrial insurance and the high rate of lapse.

The purpose of the Massachusetts law was to provide low-cost, over-the-counter insurance to all residents of the commonwealth who wanted it. The reduction in cost under the savings-bank system depended primarily on the elimination of the sales costs incurred by commercial companies, chiefly through eliminating commissions to soliciting agents, and the benefit of a lower rate of lapse.

Bills for the establishment of savings-bank life insurance have been introduced in a number of other states, where savings banks are not as strong and numerous, but since the Connecticut bill in 1941, no new enabling legislation has passed. Quite naturally, the most active opposition to savings-bank life insurance has come from life insurance agents' organizations, which consider savings-bank life insurance an unfair threat to their means of livelihood. In the past, commercial life insurance companies opposed such bills mainly on the ground that they were discriminatory, in that the insurance departments of the banks were not made subject to the same conditions and requirements as the commercial insurance companies. Recent legislation has generally provided for the same requirements and conditions as apply to commercial companies.

2. *Nature.* Savings-bank life insurance is transacted on an over-the-counter basis or by mail and without the use of soliciting agents. This is a type of **direct response** marketing.[6] This normally results in considerable savings in expense, fewer lapses, and a low cost to policyowners.

Since a savings bank is not equipped to handle many of the technical details of the administration of a life insurance business, each state has a central organization that furnishes the actuarial, medical, and certain other services for the banks. The central organization computes the premium

[6]See Chapter 30.

rates, which are the same for all issuing banks in a given state, and also prepares policy forms, application blanks, and so on. Thus, in some ways the savings-bank life insurance system is similar to a single life insurance company, with the central organization serving as the "home office" and the individual banks the "branches." Each issuing bank, however, is an independent unit, issues its own contracts, maintains records, and retains and invests the assets of its own insurance department.

The surplus funds belonging to the insurance department of a bank are available only to the policyowners of that bank. In addition, the assets of the banking and insurance departments of a given issuing bank are kept separate from each other, and the assets of one are not available for the liabilities of the other. Further, an equitable allocation of expenses between the savings department and the life insurance department is required. The central organization, however, maintains a contingency or guaranty fund, established by the contributions of the insurance banks, that is available to protect policyowners of all participating banks.

An important feature of savings-bank life insurance, which lends stability to the system, is the **unification of mortality.** In view of the relatively small amounts of insurance issued and in force in many of the banks, the mortality experience of individual banks is subject to relatively large yearly fluctuations. To lend stability to the individual banks, mortality costs for all participating banks in a given state are pooled, and in effect, each bank experiences proportionately the same mortality cost. By this process, death losses are unified.

The banks have authority to sell the usual types of ordinary policies, annuities, and group insurance. Sales of term insurance, especially decreasing term insurance to cover the unpaid balance of a mortgage, have been proportionately higher than in commercial companies. Waiver of premium benefits are available in all three states. Disability income benefits are not available under the ordinary forms of policies issued, and only New York permits the accidental death benefit to be issued on ordinary policies.

The terms of the contracts are similar to

those of commercial companies, and all contracts are participating. Cash and loan values and non-forfeiture options are available after one year[7] and, in the early years, are on a more liberal basis than in the usual commercial-company contract. These favorable values reflect the much lower first-year expense due to the absence of agents' commissions and other agency expenses and low overhead costs.

The amount of insurance obtainable from any one bank by any one applicant is limited by law in each state. The limit in Massachusetts is $15,000, subject to an aggregate limit of insurance in force at any time on any one life in all savings banks of $1,000 times the number of banks: currently a $60,000 limit.

The New York limit is $50,000. In Connecticut, the limit of insurance obtainable by one applicant is $25,000 for individual coverage and $50,000 for group coverage. Effective January 1, 1986 the individual and group limit increases were tied to the CPI.[8] The minimum policy in Connecticut is $500; in Massachusetts, $1,000; and in New York, $2,000.

Savings-bank life insurance is available only to residents of or workers in the state, but of course, remains in force if the policyowner should leave the state.

Wisconsin State Fund. Wisconsin is the only state wherein the government is authorized to sell life insurance. The Wisconsin State (Life) Fund, established in 1911, permits certain designated government officials and state banks to sell life insurance coverage through the state fund but only within the state. All applications are processed and supervised through the Insurance Commissioner's office and administered by the state treasury department.

The fund engages in no advertising and employs no agents. Insurance costs are low. The total amount of insurance in force is small.

The U.S. Government. The U.S. federal government is a major seller of individual policy life insurance coverage. Government life insurance

in this country was started to provide life insurance protection to military personnel. Again, because these programs are not covered elsewhere in this volume, they will be discussed here in some detail. Four major programs are discussed.

1. *United States Government Life Insurance.* The oldest of the government life insurance programs, **United States Government Life Insurance** (USGLI), was established by Congress in 1919. It granted renewable term insurance, up to a maximum of $10,000, to those in the military services, for the benefit of selected beneficiaries only. Later, the right of conversion to cash value policy plans was accorded. By the War Veterans' Act of 1924, USGLI was extended to all members of the armed forces, and in 1928 a special disability income rider was made available. Sales of USGLI were terminated in 1951 and the total amount in force today under this program is small. *All* USGLI policies were declared paid up as of January 1983.

2. *National Service Life Insurance.* The second of these programs, **National Service Life Insurance** (NSLI), was established by the National Service Life Insurance Act of 1940. After passage of this act, USGLI could only be obtained by persons entering service between 1921 and 1940 or upon such persons' reenlistment. During World War II, the NSLI program became the largest single life insurance operation in history, with a peak of over $121 billion of life insurance in force. Following World War II, the insurance in force declined as only a small percentage of insureds renewed their term insurance or converted to certain cash value forms of life insurance made available to them.

Under NSLI, the face amount of the insurance issued ranged from a minimum of $1,000 to a maximum of $10,000, in muiltiples of $500. Even though some individuals might have had both NSLI and USGLI in force, the maximum government life insurance permitted under all plans combined is $10,000. In addition to a five-year term policy, NSLI made available five whole life policy forms and three endowment forms.

NSLI is participating, and dividends declared by the Administrator of Veterans Affairs may be used in the traditional ways. NSLI dividends have been very liberal, and the net cost of

---

[7]In Connecticut, the cash value is available after six months' premiums have been paid.

[8]Public Act #81–345, state of Connecticut.

such policies has been exceedingly favorable. The U.S. government absorbs *all* administrative expenses and reimburses the NSLI Trust Fund for certain service-connected deaths. The purchase of the coverage was voluntary and was paid for by the buyer.

In view of the far-reaching extent of this particular government insurance program, many feared that NSLI would interfere seriously with commercial insurance sales. Such fears proved largely unfounded, partly because the government's system made the younger generation more life insurance-minded, partly because a maximum of $10,000 insurance is relatively small, and partly because only a small proportion of service personnel retained their government insurance after discharge.

3. Gratuitous-indemnity program. The Servicemen's Indemnity Act of 1950, passed after a long series of investigations into the operation, cost, and justification of the entire government life insurance program, essentially ended the sale of new NSLI to those in service. It automatically insured persons on active duty between 1950 and 1956 for $10,000, less the amount of any NSLI and USGLI maintaned in force.

The **gratuitous-indemnity benefit** was payable only in monthly installments for 10 years, and only to a restricted group of beneficiaries. Following discharge from service, the veteran had the right to apply for NSLI. Owners of regular NSLI and USGLI in active service were permitted either to cancel their old policies and come under the gratuitous-indemnity plan (reacquiring them after discharge) or to continue NSLI or USGLI in force, with the pure insurance risk part of the premium waived by the government. The law also provided two new types of insurance for veterans: **Veterans Special Term Insurance,** available through 1956, and **Service Disabled Veterans Insurance,** the latter being the only government life insurance program still open to new business.

The Servicemen's and Veterans' Survivor Benefit Act of 1956 made sweeping changes in the entire program. The act, with minor exceptions, terminated the gratuitous-indemnity program as of January 1, 1957. Social Security

benefits were extended to service members and dependents on a full contributory basis. With this action, the extension of government life insurance benefits to *new* personnel was terminated. There is still, however, a considerable amount of government life insurance in force, particularly under the NSLI program.

4. Servicemen's Group Life Insurance. **Servicemen's Group Life Insurance,** established in 1965, provides members of the uniformed services on active duty with group insurance written by commercial life insurance companies. Similar in concept to the Federal Employees Group Life Insurance plan, the program is administered through a "primary insurer" licensed in all states. Other companies may participate as reinsurers even though not so widely licensed, subject to Veterans Administration approval of the criteria for selecting such companies. Approved companies may elect to participate in converting SGLI to individual policies, irrespective of whether they act as reinsurers of the group plan.

Premiums paid by service personnel cover normal peacetime mortality costs and administration expenses. All costs attributable to the extra hazards of military service are paid by the federal government.

Insurance is provided automatically to full-time active-duty persons in the uniformed services. The insurance remains in effect during active duty and for 120 days after separation from service, unless terminated earlier at the insured's request and unless the insured is totally disabled at the time of separation or release from active duty.

Each eligible person is covered automatically for $35,000 of group term insurance without evidence of insurability, unless he or she takes affirmative action in writing to elect either (1) to have no insurance at all under the program, or (2) to be covered for $5,000, $10,000, $15,000, $20,000, $25,000, or $30,000. There are no other choices.

The Veterans Insurance Act of 1974, amended effective October 17, 1981, established a postseparation insurance program that provides for conversion of SGLI at reasonable rates, to a five-year, nonrenewable term policy known as

Veterans Group Life Insurance (VGLI). At the end of the term period, the insured has the right to convert the insurance to an individual, cash value policy with any of the participating companies. A list of eligible companies is furnished by the Office of SGLI. The new policy is issued at standard rates regardless of health and for not more than the amount of VGLI. The conversion privilege is identical to that which existed under the prior law and applies to all VGLI coverage.

Evaluating Life Insurance Companies

It is clear that many organizations provide life insurance, although for practical purposes stock and mutual insurance companies and to a lesser extent, fraternal benefit societies, are the only suppliers of individual life insurance to the general population. Further discussion will therefore focus on these insurers.

Many factors enter into an evaluation of an insurer. This section reviews some of these factors, attempting to discriminate between those that are meaningful and those that are not. As will be seen, the proper evaluation of an insurer can be complex. Factors to be considered below are (1) product availability, (2) service, (3) security, (4) fairness to policyowners, and (5) operational performance.

Product Availability. Individual life insurance companies usually do not attempt to serve all markets. Many companies specialize in one or a few areas only. Organizational structure, service facilities, and cost of operation differ widely, depending on the insurer's target markets.

Individual companies vary considerably in the quality and types of policies made available. For example, some high-quality companies choose not to offer a full range of individual life and health insurance products to all markets. Thus, even if a given company were judged to be otherwise acceptable, its product offerings might eliminate it from consideration by a potential customer or agent.

Another factor of significance relates to the company's underwriting practices. Many companies issue substandard business, and companies differ as to what constitutes a "standard" risk. Some companies are much more liberal than others in the flexibility permitted in utilizing settlement options. It is axiomatic that, other things being equal, greater liberality in company practices implies more service and possibly higher costs to the purchaser.

Service. Service is a term with a variety of meanings. Variations in service are primarily a matter of management philosophy rather than company type.[9] In some companies, a request for information, a policy loan, processing a death claim, or other aspects of a life insurance service are handled much more efficiently than in other companies. The service aspect of life insurance has become much more important with the advent of more flexible policies. Other things being equal, this greater service implies greater cost.

Great variation exists in the level of service rendered by agents. Some companies place great emphasis on the training of agents and spend large sums to keep them informed as regards legal, tax, and other changes that affect the service a given agent is capable of rendering. A separate question, in regard to the amount and adequacy of service from any agent, is his or her *desire* to serve, and the service incentives in the agent's compensation plan.

Security. The most important element in company evaluation is security. If a company's financial solidity is questionable, all other aspects can be meaningless.

1. *Importance of security.* Life insurance involves a long-term financial guarantee. The life insurance promise differs from those on other consumer products in at least two important respects. First, in life insurance the promise *is* the product. There is no inherent value in the pieces of paper called a life insurance policy. Only the promise embodied in the policy has value. Second, the duration of the life insurance promise is potentially much longer than most others. The company states, essentially, that it plans to fulfill all its obligations under a life insurance policy whenever it is called upon to do so—tomorrow or 50 years from

[9]See Robert A. Marshall, Bruce A. Palmer, and Steven N. Weisbart, *Services to the Life Insurance Policyowner/Consumer* (Atlanta, Ga.: Education Foundation, Inc., 1976).

now. For these two basic reasons, the financial strength and integrity of a life insurance company is more vital to its customers than would be true of most other companies.

2. *Measures of strength.* It is difficult to establish general rules as to what makes a company safe. Many companies point to their large amounts of insurance in force, implying that this connotes safety. Others might focus on their total assets or policy reserves, suggesting that high levels mean correspondingly high security.

The task is further complicated because of the traditional practice of relying on the financial information supplied by insurers to state insurance regulators. This information may not accurately reflect a company's true financial position, because of the unique accounting convention required. Financial statements prepared on the basis of generally accepted accounting principles ideally should be used.[10]

The size of a company in terms of assets has little to do with safety. Assets are accumulated from premiums and investment income and stand behind the policy liabilities that represent the minimum amounts required by law to meet contract obligations as they fall due. Whether a company maintains reserve liabilities in excess of the minimums is a function of management philosophy and is influenced by federal income tax laws.[11]

Although the entire financial picture, as measured by assets, liabilities, insurance in force, level of premiums, mortality experience, and so on, can be informative in appraising a life insurance company, surplus—derived on the basis of a fair valuation of assets and liabilities—is the most useful item for assessing the strength of a company. Surplus is the excess of assets over liabilities. Total surplus (including special surplus funds as well as unassigned surplus) is often compared with the corresponding figure for the preceding year. Any significant change from one year to the next should be analyzed as to cause. A suitable analysis is particularly important if surplus has decreased.

As an absolute figure, the amount of surplus has relatively little meaning. The adequacy of a given amount of surplus can be determined only in relation to some measuring rod. In this connection, two ratios are commonly used.

1. Surplus as a percentage of liabilities
2. Surplus per $1,000 of insurance in force

The ratio of surplus to liabilities has received the quasi approval of regulatory authorities as a basis for evaluating a particular insurer's surplus position. Nevertheless, this ratio is not completely satisfactory, because the surplus needed in relation to particular liabilities varies by type of business. In the case of group and health insurance, for example, reserves are usually quite small in relation to the amounts at risk. On the other hand, the types of business that do not involve mortality or morbidity contingencies, such as funds held under interest options or dividends left to accumulate, would require very little surplus. In such cases, a comparatively small surplus in relation to the liability might be entirely satisfactory.

The ratio of surplus to liabilities, expressed as a percentage, makes no allowance for the proportions of the various types of liabilities and is less than satisfactory for comparing companies that differ significantly in the composition of their business. Despite these limitations, this ratio is probably the most nearly satisfactory simple measure of the financial strength of a company.

The second measure of a company's surplus position, surplus per $1,000 of insurance in force, affords greater weight to group insurance than does the ratio of surplus to liabilities. But surplus per $1,000 of insurance in force also has disadvantages. In fact, this ratio probably gives too much weight to group insurance. Also, it gives no weight to annuities, supplementary contracts, health insurance, and the minor types of liabilities, all of which need surplus held for them.

To a certain extent, these two ratios complement each other. Probably a more accurate picture can be obtained by comparing companies on the basis of both figures than by comparing them on the basis of either ratio alone.

[10]See Chapter 32.
[11]See Chapter 33.

Two other ratios that are used at times as measures of company strength involve the substitution of "assets" for surplus in the ratios discussed above. These ratios are (1) assets as a percentage of liabilities, and (2) assets per $1,000 of insurance in force.

Since assets equal liabilities plus surplus, the figure for assets as a percentage of liabilities is simply 100 percent more than the figure for surplus as a percentage of liabilities. Therefore, a comparison of companies on the ratio of surplus to liabilities or the ratio of assets to liabilities will produce similar results.

In contrast, the amount of assets per $1,000 of insurance in force is almost completely meaningless as a measure of the strength of a company. This figure, rather than measuring the strength of a company, reflects the age and composition of the company's business. A company with large reserves for annuities and supplementary contracts could conceivably have assets of over $1,000 per $1,000 insurance in force and yet be in serious financial difficulty.

It also should be noted that life insurer solvency cannot necessarily be assessed easily without reference to the quality of the insurer's investments and, importantly, the relationship between anticipated investment returns and contractual obligations. These aspects of insurer security pose particularly difficult assessment problems.

Clearly, the factor of safety is not subject to absolute objective measurement. If it were, state insurance departments would be able to guarantee absolute safety, which in fact they have not been able to do through present modes of regulation.[12]

3. *Best's insurance ratings.* A.M. Best Company, Inc., publishes a volume annually that con-

tains comprehensive statistical data and comments about the history and operation of virtually every important U.S. and Canadian life insurance company. *Best's Insurance Reports* also include a policyholders' rating assigned by Best's analysts for most insurance companies. The policyholders' rating classifications are:

A +, A	Excellent
B +	Very good
B	Good
C +	Fairly good
C	Fair

Ratings are omitted altogether for many companies. In the words of *Best's Reports,* these ratings "reflect our opinion of the relative strengths of each institution compared with others, based upon averages within the life/health insurance industry." If a rating institution gives a low or no rating to a company, this is worthy of serious consideration. On the other hand, a high rating by an organization is not conclusive in terms of safety, but should be viewed favorably.

Other life insurer ratings services exist, although they are not widely used. In general, one is probably well advised to rely on *Best's* ratings, in the absence of more concrete information.

Fairness to Policyowners. A buyer will want to purchase insurance from, and the conscientious agent will want to sell insurance for, only those companies that treat policyowners fairly. Fairness extends to all aspects of insurance company operations from underwriting and pricing, to service, to claims.

A key element of fairness deals with the insurer's actual or implicit promise to permit owners of participating policies or current assumptions nonparticipating policies to share equitably in the insurer's favorable experience. As illustrated in Chapter 5 and elsewhere, this does not always happen, although it probably is correct to state that the majority of life insurers genuinely strive toward fairness.

Determining whether a particular insurer will deal fairly with its policyowners is not easy. To an extent, regulatory oversight can ensure some degree of fairness, but the latitude enjoyed

---

[12]The National Association of Insurance Commissioners (NAIC) operates an early warning system that is intended to assist state insurance regulators in overseeing the financial condition of insurers operating in their states. This **Insurance Regulatory Information System** (IRIS), a computer-linked network, provides various financial ratios and other information to regulators. Regrettably, the resulting information is not available to financial advisors or to the public. See Chapter 33.

by company management in terms of reasonable surplus and other allocations among policyowners is great.

For companies selling participating insurance, one can get a hint of the company's philosophy by comparing its past dividend illustrations to dividends actually paid.[13] Frozen or below-illustrated actual dividend payments should be viewed with suspicion, although based on current pricing techniques, one cannot be certain that future payments will equal past illustrations.

Insurer Operational Performance. Companies differ widely in the composition of their business, in accounting practices, and in methods of reporting operational results. Unless allowance is made for such differences, operational comparisons between companies have little, if any, validity. Unfortunately, sufficient information is usually not available to permit such adjustments. As a practical matter, however, such comparisons are made, and it is important to be acquainted with the limitations of such comparisons. They often center around interest income, mortality experience, and expenses as well as lapse rates, rates of growth, and dividends for policyowners.

1. *Interest.* The rate of interest earned on an insurer's total asset portfolio is usually calculated by the formula specified to be used in the annual statement filed with the state insurance departments. Interest rates based on this method for the past year are often referred to as "earned" rates. They are likely to be reported based on (1) gross investment income (i.e, before deducting any investment expenses or taxes); (2) net income before income taxes (but after deducting investment expenses and depreciation); or (3) net after federal income tax (i.e., gross investment income minus all investment expenses and all investment taxes, *including* a portion of the federal income tax). The current federal law on life insurance company income taxation is based on a unified approach that aggregates both net investment income and net "underwriting income." Some companies treat

part or all of the federal income tax as a tax on insurance operations and not as a tax on investment income.

Because of the diversity of practice with regard to treating federal income tax as an investment or insurance expense and the lack of a sound theoretical basis for making such an allocation, net interest rates of various companies *after* federal income tax simply are not comparable. Moreover, with the significant variations in expense rates for various types of investments, comparisons of the *gross* rates for companies with different asset distributions are not reliable indicators of how the more significant *net* rates would compare.[14]

Net rates *before* federal income tax, as given in annual reports, are a sounder basis for comparison and represent one of the more satisfactory measures of the success of a life insurance company's overall investment performance. The rate of interest on this basis for 1985 for U.S. life insurance companies was 9.63 percent (9.87 percent, excluding separate accounts). Even this measure of investment results does not reflect the tax advantages of tax-exempt securities and of stocks, since this net interest rate is *before* tax.

Total investment income may be related only to those assets that back liabilities that are assumed to be credited yearly with interest at a specified rate, the so-called **interest-bearing liabilities.** An interest rate computed on the basis of this restricted group of assets would naturally be higher than one based on total assets.

Although of doubtful value because of the differences in reserve bases, the investment operation results of life insurance companies are sometimes measured by comparing net investment income with the *interest required* to be earned on the interest-bearing liabilities. Thus, the actual rate earned on the total assets may be compared

---

[13]Information on this is available in publications such as Best's *Flitcraft Compend* (Oldwick, N.J.: A.M. Best Co., annual) and selected issues of *Best's Review*.

[14]The ratio of investment expenses to mean assets is sometimes quoted as a measure of investment expense. However, variations in this ratio from company to company may be caused solely by differences in the composition of the investment portfolio, not by actual differences in the rates of investment expense on each asset classification. Also, since a large part of investment expense is incurred in making new investments, such a ratio could be unduly influenced by the amount of new investment in the year in relation to total invested assets.

with the average rate required to maintain the interest-bearing liabilities.

Normally, neither realized nor unrealized capital gains and losses enter directly into the determination of any of the interest rates discussed above, although they can have a considerable effect on the success of a company's investment program. In periods of general growth or decline, this can be an especially important omission.

It should be noted that in light of the more volatile interest rate environment and the introduction of interest-sensitive and variable products, the overall rate of return is not as important as it once was. The spread between the actual return and the amount credited on a particular line (product) or the performance of a separate account can be the critical performance measures.[15]

A company's **dividend scale interest rate** is more commonly quoted today than in times past. Usually, this rate includes realized capital gains and losses and if the policies contain a direct recognition feature, will normally be quoted as if no policy loans were outstanding. From a buyer's and agent's point of view, this figure can be quite meaningful.

For example, one well-known company's portfolio-based net income before income taxes is 7.88 percent. If the net income from policy loans is omitted—as it should be with the company's direct recognition feature—the net interest rate rises to 9.23 percent. Including realized capital gains and losses raises the rate to 10.75 percent; the rate credited by the company through its dividend formula.

2. *Mortality.* No really satisfactory basis is available for comparing the mortality experience of different companies. Theoretically, the mortality experience on life insurance can be measured by comparing the ratio of the "actual" mortality experienced to the "expected" (or "tabular") mortality according to a given table of mortality. Misleading ratios may result, however, unless the table being used as the basis for the expected mortality shows about the same pattern of mortality, according to age and according to the number of years the policy has been in force, as does the actual mortality experience. Moreover, the same table must be used by the companies being compared, and the same assumptions regarding the influence of gender on mortality must be made.

The rate of growth and stage of development of individual companies can mitigate against valid mortality comparisons. A relatively new company, with most of its business still in the select period (five to 15 years), would show a much lower actual rate of mortality and hence a lower rate of actual to expected mortality than many other companies. In some cases, such a situation might actually hide poor underwriting performance.

Still another reason why the aggregate ratio of actual to expected mortality for one company should not be compared with the aggregate ratio for another company is that both the actual mortality rates experienced and the expected mortality rates assumed are likely to be considerably different for each of the four main classes of business—ordinary, group, credit, and industrial.

Mortality ratios also are affected by the proportions of medically examined and nonmedical business and the proportions of males and females insured. Thus, a company that writes a significant proportion of its business on a nonmedical basis would expect to experience higher mortality rates than another company that writes a relatively insignificant proportion of nonmedical business. The additional mortality costs on nonmedical business usually are offset by the savings in expense through eliminating the medical examination and additional underwriting costs, and this fact would have to be taken into account to make a valid comparison. A similar situation exists in connection with the relative proportions of male and female business. Male mortality is higher than female mortality.

In view of these and other complicating factors, the ratio of actual to expected mortality for a company rarely is reported either in annual reports or in trade publications and usually should not form the basis for comparing companies.

3. *Expenses.* The dollars spent for expenses by a life insurance company may be obtained from its annual report or from trade publications, but it is practically impossible to find a suitable

---

[15]See Chapter 31.

standard to ascertain whether the rate of expenses is high or low. Standards sometimes used for purposes of comparison are the ratio of expenses to (1) the amount of insurance in force, (2) premiums received, and (3) total income. None of these is entirely satisfactory. Many factors influence expenses. For example, the variations between first-year expenses and renewal-year expenses are so significant that they must be considered. First-year expenses are usually many times those incurred in a renewal year. Expense rates also vary significantly among various lines of business.

Table 11–1 shows expense ratios based on the three measuring rods mentioned above and indicates the weaknesses of each ratio. The aggregate rate of expense of a company is a poor indicator as to the expense rate that will be charged against various classes of policies in calculating dividends or other policy credits. Expense rates published in trade publications are of relatively little value for purposes of comparison. Annual reports of life insurance companies usually convey little or no real information about the level of expenses. Most references to expense rates deal with the expense question in only the most general terms.

4. *Lapse rates.* In view of the incidence of expense problem, lapse rates are frequently shown in annual reports and trade publication. Lapse rates are generally high in the first policy year, lower in the second, and then decrease gradually until they level off between the fifth or tenth year. Lapse rates also tend to vary with issue age, sex, plan of insurance, and mode of premium payment. In general, lapse rates are low at juvenile ages and high at the younger adult ages, decreasing gradually at the middle and higher ages as the age at issue increases. It usually is considerably higher on term plans than on whole life or other cash value plans.

TABLE 11-1. Evaluation of various expense ratios

Ratio	Comments
Expenses / Amount of insurance in force	1. It gives no weight to annuities, supplementary contracts, health insurance, and disability and accidental-death benefits.
	2. It gives no weight to miscellaneous operations that are usually conducted on a self-supporting basis. Examples of such operations are handling dividend accumulations and prepaid premiums.
	3. It makes no allowance for the difference between first-year and renewal-year expenses, unless some arbitrary adjustment is introduced, such as multiplying the amount of new business by a factor of, say, 5 or 10.
	4. It makes no allowance for the difference between expenses on ordinary, group, credit, and industrial business, unless some arbitrary weighting of the categories is introduced.
	5. It makes no allowance for variations in expenses with age, sex, and plan of insurance.
	6. It makes no allowance for differences in methods of operation. For example, a company doing little or no nonmedical business might have a high expense rate, but this would presumably be offset at least in part by more favorable mortality experience.
Expenses / Premiums received	1. Comments 2, 3, 4, and 6 of first grouping.
	2. It gives some weight (but not necessarily the proper weight) to annuities, health insurance, and disability and accidental-death benefits.
	3. It gives *no* weight to supplementary contracts.
Expenses / Total income	1. Comments 3, 4, and 6 of first grouping.
	2. It gives weight to supplementary contracts.
	3. It raises questions about handling of investment expenses.

Because of the several variable factors, any comparison of the overall lapse rates of companies can be misleading unless the composition of the business of each company is similar. In any event, a clear separation should be made between first-year lapse rates and renewal lapse rates. First-year lapse rates higher than the industry average, irrespective of the cause, should cause the company to be viewed with caution.

5. *Rate of growth.* Most companies take pride in their growth, and annual reports and other sources usually present a record of the company's growth over the previous five or 10 years. If the growth rate of a company is less than the average for the industry, it may be an indication of poor management or high costs. On the other hand, it may also be an indication that management is satisfied that the company is growing at an efficient rate and believes that money spent to increase the rate of expansion might not be justified. A very rapid rate of growth may indicate undue expansion without regard to costs, or it may indicate a vigorous and capable management. Small, recently established companies would be expected to grow at faster percentage rates than older, larger companies.

Items most frequently used in measuring growth are increases in (1) amount of new insurance paid for, (2) insurance in force, (3) premium income, and (4) assets. Considerable analysis is desirable before drawing any conclusions from the comparative growth rates of companies. However, in the absence of a reasonable justification, a decrease in amount in force, premium income, or assets should be interpreted as a warning signal.

6. *Dividends to policyowners.* The annual reports and marketing information of companies issuing participating insurance virtually always report the amount set aside for dividends in the coming year and how it compares with dividends in the past year. This is particularly so if the dividend scale has been increased for the coming year.

While reports of dividend *scale* increases are worthy of note, reports of overall dividend payout increases alone are of little significance as a measure of insurer operational performance. Generally, it is to be expected that total dividends paid out each year should increase as more participating insurance is sold and as existing policies' dividends should normally increase over time. Buyers and agents should rely on comparisons between dividends actually paid and dividends illustrated, on an individual policy basis, rather than gross dividend payments.

Chapter 12

The Life Insurance Planning Process

Chapter 1 presented an overview of the personal financial planning process and elements common to such plans. It suggested, generally, how life and health insurance can be useful in financial planning. Subsequent chapters should have helped the reader develop an understanding of (1) life insurance fundamentals, (2) the various types of life insurance products, and (3) aspects of sound evaluation of life insurance and annuity products, agents and companies. This chapter begins a process of examining, in more detail, some of the ways that life insurance can fit into individual financial plans.

The main purpose served by life insurance—protection against the financial consequences of death—is covered in this chapter. Chapter 13 examines the income, estate, and gift taxation of life insurance and some of the ways that life insurance can be used to optimum tax advantage. Chapter 14 introduces the reader to estate planning and suggests how life insurance often fills a critical void in such planning. It also covers the use of life insurance as a savings vehicle, including preparation for retirement. The business uses of life insurance are discussed in Chapter 15.

The nature and role of health insurance in financial planning are discussed in Chapters 16–17.

INTRODUCTION

Life insurance is the most effective and efficient means of planning for the adverse financial consequences of death for the average family. Indeed, for most persons in need of additional financial resources at death, life insurance often is the *only* feasible alternative.

In the majority of situations, life insurance is intended to substitute for the individual—either totally or partially—as an income producer for the family (or business). Just as a business might purchase insurance to reimburse itself for earnings lost because of fire that forces the business to cease operations, so might an individual purchase life insurance to replace earnings lost because of death terminiating his or her income earning power.

This concept of **human life value** views lost earnings from the perspective of those who benefit from the individual's earnings. It differs from that espoused by others, but for purposes of individual life insurance evaluation, seems more useful and logical.[1]

RISK MANAGEMENT AND LIFE INSURANCE PLANNING

The financial consequences of premature death is one of the personal loss exposures faced by all individuals (see Chapter 1). As such, the risk management (or financial planning) process can provide an excellent framework for its evaluation and treatment.

Other approaches also are sometimes followed to measure the financial impact of death on the family (or others) and therefore the need for life insurance. Unless the approach incorporates all steps of the risk management process, any resulting plan may be faulty in one or more respects. For example, life insurance equal to five, six, or seven times annual salary sometimes is suggested as appropriate for the average family. This and other such simple approaches ignore potentially vital aspects of sound risk management.

[1]The human life value (HLV) concept has been associated with determining life insurance needs for perhaps 100 years. Its use in law predates its use in life insurance by a considerable margin. Its principal use today is in litigation involving wrongful death cases where an attempt is made to place a value on a deceased's life for purposes of seeking financial recovery from the wrongdoer. See Philip Eden, *Estimating Human Life Values: A Source Book for Attorneys, Financial Planners, Economists, Human Statisticians and Career Counselors,* 2nd ed. (Berkeley, Calif.: Technipress International, 1985).

The late S. S. Huebner proposed and popularized the human life value concept as a philosophical framework for the analysis of economic risks faced by individuals. A somewhat modified version of this concept is implicit in the discussion herein. The general approach to deriving a measure for HLV is to calculate the present value for an individual's future projected earnings but subtracting self-maintenance costs. This approach views HLV from the individual's perspective since it does not consider those who receive financial benefit from the individual's continued life. For details, see Louis J. Dublin and Alfred J. Lotka, *The Money Value of a Man,* rev. ed. (New York: The Ronald Press Company, 1946). See also Juan B. Aponte and Herbert S. Denenberg, "A New Concept of the Economics of Life Value and Human Life Value," *The Journal of Risk and Insurance,* Vol. XXXV (September 1968), pp. 337–356.

The term **life insurance programming** has been used for decades to describe the risk management process applied to life insurance planning. Regrettably, in many presentations on programming, the need for and the role of each step in the risk management process is not always made clear and one or more steps may be overlooked. The risk management approach provides an analysis matrix and maximizes the likelihood that all elements will be considered.

The reader may recall the six-step risk management process:

1. Gather information.
2. Establish objectives.
3. Analyze information.
4. Develop plan.
5. Implement the plan.
6. Monitor and revise plan periodically.

The process helps determine whether any life insurance is needed and, if some is needed, the amount. A judgment as to the most suitable type of life insurance and as to the company from which to purchase it also should result from the process. The process, ideally, should not take a static view of individuals' needs but rather should be capable of factoring into the analysis the possibility of changing financial requirements over time.

Gather Information

The first step is the gathering of the relevant quantitative and qualitative information on the individual to permit a sound identification of financial loss exposures arising from his or her death. As mentioned in Chapter 1, this involves identification and valuation of the individual's assets and liabilities as well as information on the person's income and expenditures. The information is often gathered through a fact-finding questionnaire.[2]

Assets. Assets normally are divided into two categories: **liquid assets** and **nonliquid assets.**

[2]See, Chapter 1, p. 2, and footnote 4.

Liquid assets are those that are available to be liquidated with reasonable price certainty on the individual's death. This normally includes stocks, bonds, money market and savings accounts, mutual funds, amounts available on death in pension, profit-sharing, or individual retirement accounts, and any other such assets. All assets should be assessed at current market value. If real estate is to be sold, its value should be included, as would any interest to be sold in a closely held business. The latter assets, however, may be difficult to sell quickly at their market value under the circumstances following the owner's death.

Nonliquid assets might include the family's house, automobiles, personal effects such as clothing, jewelry, and so on, and household goods. These assets are usually passed to heirs intact. However, the realizable value of any of these items to be sold on death should be included as a liquid asset.

The net death benefit of any life insurance (gross death benefit less policy loans) payable to or for the benefit of the family should be included as a liquid asset for life insurance planning purposes. This is appropriate, as one is attempting to estimate the resources and liabilities of an individual assuming that he or she just died.

Life insurance cash values are not normally shown as separate assets for death planning purposes. They are subsumed in life insurance death proceeds. If an important part of one's savings program is funded via insurance cash values, it can be more revealing and helpful to list net cash values as assets available on death. An advantage of this approach is that the personal balance sheet can be used for death, retirement, and other savings and investment planning programs. If this is done, life insurance death proceeds should be shown on a net amount at risk basis. The result is the same irrespective of approach followed.

Liabilities. Review of the individual's liabilities will show those to be paid at death and those to be transferred to heirs. Most liabilities must be paid at death. Some liabilities may be assumable by others (e.g., some mortgage loans) or may be in more than one person's name.

Typical liabilities to be paid on death include outstanding balances on credit and charge cards, tax obligations, personal loans and notes, auto loans, and loans from family members. If the home mortgage loan is to be paid off, its outstanding balance would be included. If it is not to be paid off, it should be excluded but its monthly payment recognized as a possible income need (see below).

Income. The information gathering process will show total family income. For a *single-parent family,* this income usually is derived primarily or solely from the parent's salary. A single-parent family unit is more likely to have income from outside the unit than is a two-parent family. Thus, a divorced individual may be receiving alimony or child support payments. A divorced person sometimes receives financial support from parents or grandparents, and a widowed spouse may be receiving income from the deceased spouse's employer, insurance, or government sources.

Since the single parent's salary is usually the most important income source, the parent's death could have a financially (not to mention emotionally) devastating impact on the children. This potential income loss should be clearly recognized and dealt with.

The divorced single parent could have his or her income disrupted by the death or disability of the former spouse, who provides child support or other financial assistance. Similarly, a parent's or relative's voluntary financial support to a single-parent family could cease on the donor's death. Both situations should be identified as potential loss exposures and addressed to the extent feasible.

The income of a *dual-wage earner family* could be materially affected by the death of either wage earner. This should be factored into the analysis (see below) just as one would consider the impact on a *two parent, single-wage earner family.*

In this case a family member may earn little or no income, yet his or her death still have an adverse financial effect on the family. Consider the spouse who earns little or no outside income, but maintains the household. The death of such a non-wage earner can result in major increases in family expense. If the surviving spouse and children cannot or will not perform the necessary household functions formerly performed by the decreased spouse, the family may be forced to secure outside household services (e.g., a housekeeper) and/or to rely increasingly on service businesses (e.g., dry cleaners, restaurants, auto service firms, baby sitters, etc.). Total household expenses could rise significantly. Also, postmorten expenses (see below) can be significant. The potential loss exposures often are overlooked.

Savings and Investment Programs. The death of a parent usually causes a disruption in savings. Perhaps the most common concern in this respect is disruption of saving to fund college education for children. An otherwise soundly conceived plan to accumulate funds to finance education can be completely disrupted by death of a parent. As a result, most parents consider the contingency of disruption of planned savings and investment programs as falling properly into the loss exposure category.

Postmortem Expenses. Remember that the purpose for gathering data on the individual's financial situation is to help identify loss exposures. Death itself creates expenses—so-called **postmortem expenses.** For example, probate costs will be incurred. **Probate** is the process of filing, validating, and executing a will by a court.[3] Probate costs vary significantly from state to state and as a function of the estate size. However, costs commonly range from 2 to 5 percent of the gross estate, but can be much higher.

Postmortem expenses include estimated final illness expenses. Of course, a well-designed and implemented financial plan would provide for medical insurance or other means of meeting these expenses. Also, funeral expenses, which today average around $5,000, should be recognized in the financial plan.

Estate and inheritance taxes can constitute a major postmortem expense for those whose net worth is large (see Chapter 13). Inheritance taxes vary from state to state and in the manner of their application. They often range from 1 to 14 percent of the value of the property inherited, with exemptions for the surviving spouse and children.

Inheritance and federal estate taxes should be estimated and included as a postmortem expense to be met on death.

The Spouse. The preceding discussion has generally assumed that information gathering and loss exposure identification has been on one spouse only—the chief family income earner. However, the same information gathering/loss identification process should be followed for the spouse as well. Good risk management principles consider the financial consequences of all possible loss combinations. A dual-wage-earner family often requires the income from both persons. The death of either or both could be financially devastating for the family unit. As suggested above, even if the spouse is not a wage earner, his or her death could create financial hardships. This should be analyzed. The fact remains, however, that the first priority is the principal wage earner. Although the probability is low, there is also the possibility of simultaneous death, a loss combination with additional financial consequences.

Establish Objectives

As discussed in Chapter 1, a family should establish not only overall financial objectives but specific subobjectives as well. For life insurance planning purposes, this usually means that the individual, often along with his or her spouse, must determine the income levels desired for the survivor on the death of either spouse. This process can be difficult. There is no "correct" answer.

A commonly stated objective is for the survivor to be able to maintain his or her current living standard after the death of his or her spouse. This may translate into a survivor income need of at least 60 percent of the predeath family income. The amount would be less than the current total family income as the deceased spouse's self-maintenance expenses would end. For a family with children, self-maintenance expenses normally are considerably less than one-half total family income.

Postdeath income objectives are often predicated on the human life value concept. The idea is to estimate the financial impact on income

---

[3]See Chapter 15.

recipients of the death of the main income earner and to replace that amount of lost income—in other words, to replace (financially) the deceased person as a source of earnings. This is the same as maintaining the current living standard.

One must also establish objectives regarding such things as:

- Liabilities to be paid off on death
- The amount of money to be provided to cover post-mortem expenses
- The amount of money (if any) to be established as a family emergency fund
- The amount of money (if any) to be established as a fund to finance education
- The amount of money (if any) to be left to friends, relatives, and associates and to charitable or other institutions

The professional financial advisor assists the client in establishing these and other objectives. Merely to conclude that a certain amount of money would be desirable for a particular purpose is not sufficient. One often also must decide how to provide the money and over what time period. For example, if an education fund is to be established, this goal-setting exercise should address the issue of how the money will be paid (e.g., as a lump sum, annually, monthly, etc.).

The objective setting process usually takes place as part of information gathering. The advisor mentally "walks" the client through a loss exposure identification/objective setting exercise, providing guidance, yet being careful not to impose his or her own values.

Objectives often are changed or adjusted as costs of their implementation become clearer. These costs emerge from the next two steps in the risk management process.

Analyze Information

The third step in the personal financial planning/risk management process is to analyze the relevant data and loss exposures in light of the individual's stated objectives. In risk management terms, this step involves an attempt to measure the financial consequences of the losses.

The Chapter 1 discussion mentioned that loss analysis has two dimensions: frequency and severity. For life insurance planning purposes, loss frequency (i.e., probabilities of death) information has no utility to the individual. The individual will either live or die. Sound risk management analysis presumes that the potential loss will occur and attempts to measure its potential financial consequences. A plan of action is then developed (next step) to deal with the potential loss in case it does, in fact, occur.

Applied to life insurance planning, this means that the analysis of the financial consequences of death should *assume that death is about to occur.* The analysis yields a measure of the potential loss severity (i.e., the consequences of death) from a financial point of view. Thus, this step's function really is to estimate loss severity only.

The needed analysis usually is neither simple nor precise. This is because the analysis necessarily involves assumptions concerning the future, and actual results will invariably differ from assumptions. Even so, the exercise has merit. If done properly, it provides an idea of the possible range of the family's financial loss caused by an individual's death as well as the extent of disruption to present plans that would occur.

Although this and the next step (plan development) are presented here separately, they are often accomplished together. The agent or other financial advisor customarily *both* analyzes the information *and* simultaneously develops a suggested plan of action.

Several avenues can be followed in measuring the financial consequences to a family (or to a business or others) of the death of one of its members. In all cases, however, the basic approach is the same. The family (or others) will have certain resources from which to meet—in whole or in part—its objectives. To the extent existing resources do not meet the objectives fully or fail to provide a good match, the individual will be faced with three choices: (1) revise the financial objectives downward or otherwise acknowledge that a gap exists between resources and objectives, (2) ensure that additional resources will be available on death, or (3) a combination of (1) and (2).

The postdeath financial objectives established by individuals usually fall into two categories: (1) cash and (2) income.

Cash Objectives. Cash objectives (or needs) require a single-sum cash amount to fulfill. They are the easiest to estimate. Typical cash needs arise from the need or desire to pay off outstanding liabilities such as auto and personal loans, charge card balances, incurred income tax liabilities, and so on. If an objective is to pay off an outstanding mortgage loan balance, this too would be included.

Cash needs also might arise from a desire to establish or augment an educational fund. Postmortem expenses, for the most part, also fall into this category. Each of these cash needs will have been identified in the information-gathering/objective-setting stages.

Income Objectives. While cash needs usually are subject to fairly precise estimation, quantifying income objectives (needs) requires assumptions that render figures that are approximations only.

Deriving a measure of a family's (or other's) postdeath income needs involves first, a determination of the annual net amount needed, taking into consideration all important variables, such as likely income resources (e.g., Social Security), changing family responsibilities, and inflation. Second, these annual net income amounts are converted to a single-sum (present value) equivalent. This involves future interest rate assumptions.

The process sounds simple and is in concept. However, what is the "best" set of assumptions as to future inflation and interest rates is open to debate. In addition, several methods can be used to derive the needed figure. Some aspects of these important elements are reviewed below.

1. *The method used.* Several methods exist to analyze income needs. The two most common are (1) the **capital liquidation** and (2) the **capital retention** approaches. The capital liquidation approach assumes that both principal (capital) and interest are liquidated over the relevant time period to provide the desired income. The capital retention approach assumes the desired income is provided only from the investment earnings of the principal and that no part of the desired income is made from capital. In other words, the capital is retained undiminished, even after death.

Each method has advantages and drawbacks. The liquidation approach requires a smaller capital sum to provide a given income level than the retention approach. The retention approach permits a capital sum to be passed on to the family's next generation (or to whomever is designated). It is considered more conservative since in an emergency, capital could be invaded.

Where the need for income is for the whole of life, the capital liquidation method can be approached in one of two ways. *First,* the future desired lifetime income can be funded through the purchase of a life annuity from a life insurance company. The annuitant cannot outlive the income, but for reasons examined in Chapter 7, the purchase probably should not be made before age 60, 65, or 70. Income needed prior to this time could be provided from life insurance through the fixed-period settlement option or from other sources.

The *second* way of funding lifetime income is to assume a maximum age beyond which the income recipient is unlikely to live and provide for the complete liquidation of principal and interest between the present and that age. Some analysts use age 80 as the terminal age. This approach to funding "lifetime" income can be through the fixed-period settlement option or through other means.

Each of these capital liquidation approaches has advantages and drawbacks. The critical decision variable in the second approach is the maximum age. If the terminal age is set too low, the income recipient may outlive the income. This result could be disasterous. The higher the age, the higher the principal sum required to fund the income.

Other things being the same, the life annuity will generate a higher income than the other liquidation approach (assuming a high terminal age), as each payment contains an element of survivorship benefit. Also, of course, with the life annuity, the income recipient cannot outlive the income.

Most annuities sold today—both as individual products and as policy settlement options—permit only level payouts or have the payout vary with current investment performance (which may not track inflation). The approach of establishing a fixed maximum age, if properly funded, permits an income stream that can be increased with inflation but simultaneously will reduce the age to which income will be payable.

The decision to follow the capital retention or one of the capital liquidation methods is not an "all or nothing" proposition. One need not either pay out *all* capital or retain *all* capital. A continuum exists between the two extremes.

2. Inflation assumptions. The effects of inflation on anticipated future income needs and resources and other relevant areas should be factored into the analysis. Future inflation rates are difficult to predict. Inflation rates since the 1970s have ranged from 3 to 14 percent. Although near-term expected inflation rates are low by 1970s/ early 1980s standards, long-term prospects remain cloudy.

The agent or other financial advisor should help the client estimate anticipated inflation in light of current and expected economic conditions. To perform this function well, the advisor should be familiar with broad economic trends.

The best approach to factoring inflation into any analysis is to select a range of inflation rates and determine the sensitivity of results to changing inflation assumptions. However, unless presented in a clear, simple manner to the client, this type of sensitivity analysis can obscure the analysis' broader purpose. Care must be taken to avoid this result.

3. Interest assumptions. The interest rate selected for discounting can greatly influence results, especially when sums are discounted over many years. The interest rate(s) used will affect both needs and resources, as each will be subject to discount. The interest rate selected normally is that which can be earned after taxes in the present economic environment on long-term, secure, fairly liquid investments—a conservative rate. Speculative investments are not generally advised for such family financial planning.

Figure 12-1 shows interest rates credited on 10-year Treasury securities over the past several years. Such stated rates are referred to as **nominal interest rates.** Interest rates tend to follow infla-

FIGURE 12-1. Yearly changes in the Consumer Price Index and 10-Year Treasury security yields, 1960–1985. Sources: Federal Reserve Bank of St. Louis, *Review,* Vol. 66 (December 1984), p. 20; and *Statistical Abstract of the United States, 1985,* 105th ed. (Washington, D.C.:), U.S. Department of Commerce, p. 467. *Note:* Treasury security rate based on semiannual data. CPI rate based on annual data.

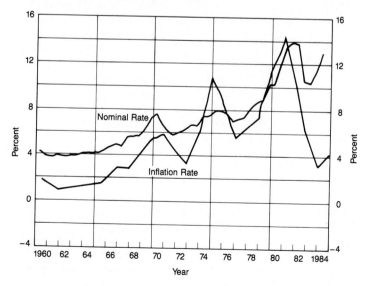

tion rates and over time, nominal interest rates have been about 1 to 3 percent higher than the inflation rates, as shown in Figure 12-1. The difference between the nominal interest rate and the inflation rate is referred to as the **real interest rate.**

Thus, the real rate of interest usually falls within the range 1 to 3 percent. This suggests that the advisor and client probably should select an interest rate 1 to 3 percent higher than the selected inflation rate. As illustrated in Figure 12-1, real interest rates have been higher in the 1980s than during past periods. Many economists believe that high real interest rates will not persist for long. However, the advisor and client must select the inflation and interest assumptions believed most realistic for the client.

As with inflation, a range of interest rates ideally should be applied to the analysis to determine results under changing conditions. Again, however, care is needed to avoid having the procedure and its details overshadow the purpose of the analysis.

To simplify tax considerations, the interest rate selected can be an after-tax rate. This requires an estimation of the income recipient's marginal income tax bracket. This should not be difficult. Thus, if a gross taxable investment return of 10 percent is expected and if the income recipient is expected to be in a 35 percent combined federal and state marginal marginal tax bracket, the effective after-tax return is 6.5 percent.[4] If investment returns are expected to be tax exempt, the after tax return would be the gross return.

4. *The interaction of inflation and interest.* The interaction between the assumed inflation rate and the assumed discount (interest) rate should be understood. Consider, for example, that a $10,000 per year income is desired for five years and that an after-tax discount rate of 8 percent is judged reasonable. Ignoring inflation, the present value of five $10,000 per year payments at 8 percent interest, with the first payment made now, is $43,120.[5]

[4] The formula is (gross rate of return) × (1 − tax rate) = (0.10) × (1 − 0.35) = 0.065.

[5] $$\$10,000 \times \left[\sum_{t=1}^{5} \left(\frac{1}{1 + i} \right)^{t-1} \right] =$$

$$\$10,000 \times 4.312 = \$43,120.$$

A non-level-payment stream—like that developed if inflation is considered—requires a different approach. (In fact, any plan that provides for a level income stream in an inflationary environment, in reality, provides a steadily decreasing "real" income.) Assume the same five $10,000 per year payments and 8 percent after-tax interest rate as before. However, assume also that inflation is estimated to be 5 percent annually over the payout period and that it is desired to provide the equivalent purchasing power of today's $10,000 for each payment.

Table 12-1 illustrates the calculation for this inflation-adjusted income stream. It shows that $47,298 invested to earn 8 percent after taxes will just be sufficient to provide a yearly income whose purchasing power remains constant in the face of a 5 percent inflation rate. As expected, this sum is greater than that needed if one ignores inflation.

Sometimes a reasonable approximation for the present value of an inflated income series can be obtained at the real interest rate; that is, the difference between the nominal interest rate and the assumed inflation rate. For example, the present value of the five $10,000 annual payments at three percent (8 percent–5 percent) is $47,171 rather than $47,298. The difference is not significant. If the time period involved is not great and if only a good approximation is sought—which is usually the case in such planning—this approach can suffice. The true present value, however, will always be understated where both the nominal and real rates are positive—the usual situation.

The preceding example assumed capital liquidation over a fixed period. What if a lifetime income is needed? To derive the needed present value, one can calculate the present value of income payments to a certain advanced age (e.g., 65), then add to that figure the present value of the purchase price at that time of a life annuity.

An example will illustrate the concepts involved. Assume that $10,000 after-tax annual income is desired for the full lifetime of a 35-year-old. Assume 8 percent to be a reasonable after-tax return and inflation at 5 percent.

The problem can be approached in stages. First, assume that a life annuity will be purchased at some advanced age (e.g., age 70) to fund the post-70 lifetime income need and that income

TABLE 12-1. Present value of $10,000 per year with inflation of 5 percent
(first payment now)

(1) Year	(2) Annual Payment in Today's Dollars	(3) Annual Payment in Inflated (5%) Dollars [(2) × 1.05ⁱ]	×	(4) Present Value Factor at 8%	=	(5) Present Value at 8% of Inflated Payments
0 (Now)	$10,000	$10,000		1.0000		$10,000
1	10,000	10,500		0.9259		9,722
2	10,000	11,025		0.8573		9,452
3	10,000	11,576		0.7938		9,190
4	10,000	12,155		0.7350		8,934
				Total present value		$47,298

prior to then will be provided from a fund established for that purpose, such as the fixed-period annuity option.

The amount of money needed to fund the inflated payments from age 35 to age 70 is $225,510, derived using the procedure illustrated in Table 12–1. To determine the value today of the purchase price of the annuity that begins at age 70, the amount of the (inflated) annual income at age 70 must be known. While the purchasing power is to be $10,000, the nominal value would be $55,160.[6] In other words, at 5 percent inflation, $55,160 in 35 years would have the same purchasing power as $10,000 today.

At age 70, a decision would be required as to the best type of annuity to be purchased. An analysis of the pros and cons of variable annuities, indexed annuities, and flexible premium deferred annuities could be conducted at present under various payout assumptions designed to hedge the inflation risk. Realistically, however, the annuity (and other investment) products available many years from now may bear little resemblence to those products that exist today. Thus, unless the income recipient were now within a short time period of purchasing a life annuity, any detailed analysis as to the most appropriate annuity type and how best to structure the annuity payout would be largely wasted effort.

Hence, for long-term income planning, the agent or other financial advisor probably should merely estimate an annuity purchase price for the projected (inflated) income. This price should be based on current guaranteed purchase rates.

These long-term guaranteed rates typically will be based on a 2½ to 4 percent interest assumption, with the insurer actually crediting contemporary rates of return. By using the guaranteed rates, however, implicit allowance is made for inflation.

In the example, an insurance company would charge a 70-year-old between $600 and $900 for each $100 of annual income desired, with the income starting at age 70. Thus, for an income of over $55,000, the purchase price at age 70 might be (with rounding) between $330,000 and $500,000. Using the lower figure, one has but to calculate the value at age 35 of the $330,000 sum needed at age 70. Discounting at 8 percent yields a present value of $22,308.[7] Stated differently, $22,308 today will grow to $330,000 in 35 years at an after-tax earnings rate of 8 percent.

Therefore, the total amount of money estimated to be needed now (at the income recipient's age 35) to provide annually $10,000 for life in constant purchasing power is $247,818, the sum of the two present value figures ($225,510 + $22,308 = $247,818).

This precise-appearing number should be recognized for what it is: our best guess. It is based on numerous assumptions, a change in any one of which could affect results significantly. For example, if all other assumptions remained the same but the actual after-tax return were 7 instead of 8 percent, the sum needed today to fund the $10,000 income stream would be increased to $289,527. In cases such as those investigated here,

---

[6]$10,000 \times (1.05)^{35} = \$10,000 \times 5.516 = \$55,160.$

[7]$\$330,000 \times \left(\frac{1}{1.08}\right)^{35} = (\$330,000)(0.0676) = \$22,308.$

liberal rounding would be the norm. Thus, the $247,818 figure might become $250,000 (a typical premium banding amount) and $289,527 might become $300,000.

If a lifetime income is desired but without using a life annuity, one can utilize either (1) the capital liquidation approach that requires the establishment of a maximum age beyond which the income recipient would be highly unlikely to live, or (2) the capital retention approach.

Under the capital liquidation approach *not* involving a life annuity, we perform a calculation for an income stream that is to cease only at an advanced age, such that the income recipient is highly unlikely to outlive it. This procedure follows that used to derive present values in Table 12–1. Continuing the same example, assume that income were desired to age 85; that is, $10,000 of *real* income would be needed for 50 years. The present value of this stream would be $232,112.[8]

Under the capital retention approach and using the same interest and other assumptions as before, but ignoring inflation for now, one would ask the question: What amount of money must be on hand now, the income alone from which would provide $10,000 per year? The answer is obtained by dividing the interest rate into the desired annual income. The result, $125,000, is verified easily by multiplying $125,000 by the 8 percent earnings assumption to show that it produces the needed $10,000.[9]

To ignore inflation in the capital retention approach can be as foolish as doing so under the capital liquidation approaches. Our hypothetical

income recipient would want to receive $10,000 this year, $10,500 next year, and so on. The capital sum necessary to provide such inflated income payments is $360,000.[10]

In deriving a measure of the financial consequences of death, it often proves easiest to net expected future income resources against future expected income needs, and then to derive a present value for the annual differences. This is often more convenient than calculating present value figures for each income stream separately, then netting the present value of the resource stream against the present value of the needs stream.

Difference between Resources and Objectives.
The final step in the analysis process is to net the resources available against the established needs for cash and net income to derive a figure for the shortfall (or overage) of resources to meet needs. This figure represents a measure of the net financial consequences of death (the loss) to the family based on the objectives identified earlier. Ideally, a range of figures would be developed based on various interest, inflation, and other relevant assumptions to provide a "feel" for the sensitivity of the results to the assumptions.

Static versus Dynamic Analysis. The range of values developed above for the financial consequences of death is valid for the year of analysis only. That is, the measure represents the financial consequences of death assuming that death occurs at the present. However, the financial analysis is not complete unless some idea can be obtained as to probable future figures.

The financial consequences of death can be expected to vary with time. It may either increase or decrease. The professional agent or other financial advisor will estimate how this future pattern may evolve, based on current in-

---

[8]This figure can be found by use of a shortcut formula for the present value of a series of n steadily increasing (or decreasing) payments. It is

$$A = P \left[\frac{1 - e^n}{1 - e} \right]$$

where A = present value figure sought
P = initial payment

$e = \dfrac{1 + r}{1 + i}$

r = assumed inflation rate
i = assumed discount rate

[9]Note, however, that the $125,000 would generate the $10,000 at the *end* of the year. If it were desired to have the first payment made now, $10,000 should be added to the $125,000 principle, to yield a needed amount of $135,000.

[10]A shortcut formula for deriving the capital sum (C) needed to provide a steadily increasing income stream in perpetuity is

$$C = \frac{P}{1 - e}$$

where e and P are as defined in footnote 8 and e is between 0 and 1. If e is greater than 1, there is no shortcut formula. If e is 1 (i.e., $i = r$), the value is undefined.

formation and client objectives, as well as on reasonable assumptions as to future events.

If net needs are estimated to decrease over time, the death benefit of a policy purchased to fill the gap should also decrease. If needs are expected to increase, the policy purchased to help meet the needs should be flexible enough to track future anticipated increases.

The procedure to convert from the traditional static planning approach to a dynamic approach is conceptually simple. One simply plays a "what if" game as to the future. The traditional static approach to planning asks the question: What if the individual were to die today? An answer is then sought, the purpose of which is to derive a quantitative measure for the adverse financial consequences of death.

The dynamic approach to planning asks the same question but it is repeated for each succeeding year; thus,

- What if the individual were to die today?
- What if the individual were to die next year?
- What if the individual were to die two years from now?
- What if the individual were to die three years from now? etc.

To answer each question, future resources must be estimated. The future needs already would have been estimated, but a revised present value calculation would be necessary. The estimation of future resources and needs is not easy. It requires assumptions as to future savings and investment habits, future income earnings, as well as a host of others.[11] The process can be exceedingly complex. This should be avoided. The objective is to obtain some idea of the likely *pattern* of future resources and needs, and to avoid becoming bogged down in details.

If a broad, integrated financial plan of the type discussed in Chapter 1 has been developed, it will contain projections as to future savings, investments, earnings, and other aspects of

[11]See Joseph M. Belth, "Dynamic Life Insurance Programming," *The Journal of Risk and Insurance,* Vol. XXXI (December 1964); and Terry Rose and Robert I. Mehr, "Flexible Income Programming," *The Journal of Risk and Insurance,* Vol. XLVII (March 1980).

"resources." If reasonable, these figures can be used to estimate the financial consequences of death occurring in future years. If no overall financial plan exists from which to draw these projections/estimates, the agent or other financial advisor ideally should, with the advice of the client, develop his or her own measures.

Because of the highly subjective nature of the needed assumptions, one should not be too concerned with precision or with insignificant details. But since future investment, savings, and other goals sometimes are not met, the projections should be conservative.

Plan Development

The next step in the personal financial planning/risk management process is to develop a plan to accomplish the stated objectives, based on the analysis of the financial consequences of death. This plan should evolve only after the various alternative means of treating the loss exposure have been explored. The plan usually emerges as the agent/planner is analyzing the relevant information in light of the client's objectives.

In considering client alternatives, the planning time frame can be separated into short-run and long-run periods. The possible alternatives available to the individual over the short run usually are exceedingly limited, with more emerging over the long run.

Possible short-run alternatives are those that can be adopted now and in the near future to fill the financial gap created by the client's death. In the short run, insufficient time exists to increase savings or investments meaningfully, and the client has little or no control over the level of other (e.g., Social Security benefits) resources.

The longer term affords more alternatives. Sufficient time exists to implement an enhanced savings/investment program to fill a financial void. One may choose to enhance savings through life insurance policy cash values, through an annuity, or through savings outside the insurance mechanism. As discussed below, an insurance-funded savings program can offer several important advantages over other savings media, although the benefits of diversification should be kept in mind.

The dynamic analysis results should suggest

a pattern of future needs. An increasing, decreasing, constant, or fluctuating future need pattern may be revealed. Ideally, the insurance purchased to fill this need should track or be capable of tracking the estimated future pattern. Also, since actual results rarely follow estimations exactly, the plan (insurance) should be sufficiently flexible to adapt to unanticipated changes.

The prior information-analysis step should include a review of existing life insurance policies and annuities from a cost as well as a structure viewpoint. If existing policies are not well suited to current needs or not competitively priced, replacement should be considered. If replacement is justified, an alternative to the existing policy should emerge at this plan development stage. If the existing policy is judged suitable and cost-effective, any recommended change in the beneficiary designation(s), ownership, settlement option(s), or other area is a part of plan development.

In developing a recommended plan, the agent/planner should identify one or more low-cost life insurance policies from high-quality companies that are suitable in light of the client's characteristics, objectives, and current financial condition. How the policy is to be structured (settlement options, beneficiary designations, dividend options, loans, etc.) and paid for should be included in the plan.

The plan should not evolve in isolation from other death planning needs such as establishment or revision of wills and trusts.[12] A comprehensive plan includes more than taking care of legal necessities. A sound plan established before death should help guide the survivors (and executor) through this most traumatic of life's events.[13] Most agents and financial planners are not qualified to develop and implement all aspects of the needed plan. A team approach is needed.

The developed plan would be presented to the client for his or her consideration. Based on further goal clarification and on existing constraints, changes may be made.

[12]See Chapter 14 on estate planning.
[13]It is beyond the scope of this book to examine the other dimensions of predeath planning.

Plan Implementation

Once a plan is developed and agreed to by the client, the program must be implemented. Plan implementation usually means, among other things, taking the necessary life insurance application from the client and securing funds to pay the first premium. If changes are needed in existing policies or if they are to be replaced, the necessary forms must be secured, completed, and furnished to the appropriate company(ies).

The life insurance dimension of the plan is not fully implemented until the policy sought is issued on a basis acceptable to the client and structured in line with earlier established goals. The necessity for clarity in all areas of the contract, especially the beneficiary designation, was made clear earlier.

Plan Monitoring and Revision

If the individual's future evolved exactly as had been estimated, *if* assumptions as to future inflation rates, interest rates, and other areas proved to be fact, *if* no important tax law or other changes were made, and *if* no better life insurance or other financial products were available in the future marketplace, no plan revision would be needed. Clearly, this will not happen. The professional agent or other advisor monitors program performance and client circumstances as well as the tax, legal, and market environment. Deviations in actual from estimated results should be examined to determine their impact on the program and appropriate revisions made.

Important "life events" such as marriage, divorce, important business undertakings, home buying, birth of children, children attaining financial independence, and so on, should trigger an automatic reevaluation of the program. In general, program evaluation should take place every one to three years, irrespective of the happening of life events.

Any significant changes in "environmental factors" should also trigger reevaluation. New insurance and other financial products can render older products obsolete. Changes in Social Security, inflation rates, interest rates, employee benefit programs, tax laws, and a whole host of other variables can cause a program to go off its mark.

Both the individual and the advisor should be attuned to changes—environmental and personal—that can have an impact on the implemented program. Ideally, the insurance products selected to implement the program would be sufficiently flexible to adapt to changes. A policy that provides for experience participation contains an automatic mechanism for at least partially adapting to changing economic conditions. The guaranteed right to purchase additional insurance without evidence of insurability, either by increasing the existing policy's face amount or by purchase of a new policy, can be another mechanism permitting flexibility. Universal life and other policies that permit premium payment flexibility and policy death benefit adjustability can be particularly well adapted to changing life-cycle needs.

ILLUSTRATION

An illustration should be helpful in bringing together the concepts discussed above. For reasons of space, the presentation focuses on the analysis and plan design steps.

Relevant Information/Objectives

Steve and Debbie Williams, both age 35, have two children, Philip, age 7 and Gwen, age 2. Steve is the manager of a clothing store and Debbie is a grammar school teacher. The total annual before-tax family income is $100,000, which translates to $70,000 after taxes. Steve earns $63,000 ($45,000 after taxes); Debbie earns $37,000 ($25,000 after taxes).[14] Other relevant financial information is summarized on the following page.

Steve and Debbie, with the counsel of their agent, have determined that their overall objective is for each to be able to maintain his or her standard of living if the other died. As shown

[14]The analysis could have assumed Steve earned $37,000 and Debbie earned $63,000. Since earnings of the average female worker are lower than the earnings of the average male worker, Steve is shown with the higher figure. This in no way should be interpreted as suggesting that average earnings for females should be lower.

	If Steve Dies First	If Debbie Dies First
Nonliquid assets		
Home	$130,000	$130,000
Autos	13,000	13,000
Household / personal effects	37,000	37,000
	$180,000	$180,000
Liquid assets available on death		
Individual life insurance	$ 50,000	$ 0
Group life insurance	25,000	50,000
Pension plan death benefit	10,000	0
Savings / investments	20,000	20,000
Checking account balance	2,000	2,000
	$107,000	$ 72,000
Cash needs on death based on objectives		
Mortgage loan balance	$110,000	$110,000
Auto loan balance	10,000	10,000
Establish emergency fund	20,000	20,000
Establish educational fund	50,000	50,000
Charge-card balances	3,000	3,000
Funeral expenses	5,000	5,000
Probate / admin. expenses	3,000	3,000
	$201,000	$201,000

(continued)

Annual income objectives / resources
  Desired after-tax family income on death

With both children at home / in college	$ 45,000	$ 45,000
With one child at home / in college	43,000	43,000
With no child at home	40,000	40,000

Social Security Survivor Benefits[15]

Both children under 18 or, if in college, under 22	$ 13,050	$ 9,360
One child under 18 or, if in college, under 22	6,525	4,680
At survivor's age 65	8,700	6,420

above, they estimate that $45,000 per year after taxes would be needed by the survivor while both children were at home, that $43,000 would be needed while only Gwen was at home, with $40,000 needed thereafter. These income objectives assume the mortgage loan and other debts are paid off, a desired objective. They also desire to establish an educational fund of $50,000 for the children's education and to have an emergency fund of $20,000.

Static Analysis

In conducting a static analysis, several assumptions are necessary. The key ones here are:

Reasonable after-tax earnings (discount) rate	7%
Average annual inflation rate	4%
Average annual wage increase rate	5%

Moreover, it is assumed that a life annuity will be purchased at age 70 to fund needed lifetime income from that age and that the annual income objective as well as Social Security benefits increase each year with the inflation rate.

Table 12–2 illustrates the derivation of the present value of net income needs, assuming that Steve dies first. Column 2 shows the annual income objective in today's dollars and column 3 shows the equivalent in inflated dollars. Column 4 shows the estimated annual Social Security survivor benefit, inflated at 4 percent, that would be payable. Debbie's annual income is shown in column 5. These figures are increased by 5 percent per year. The column 6 figures are the amounts by which Social Security and Debbie's income fall short of the desired objective.

The amounts become significant but the purchasing power is the relevant concern, not the absolute size of the numbers. Thus, if inflation averaged 4 percent, the $101,518 age-65-income shortage would have the same purchasing power as $31,300 today [the $31,300 being the difference between the income objective ($40,000) and the noninflated Social Security benefit ($8,700)].

The present value of each column 6 figure is shown in column 7. The discount rate used is 7 percent. Adding the column 7 figures yields $193,144, the present value of the entire income stream to age 70.

In other words, if all assumptions actually materialized as fact in the future, $193,144 would be exactly sufficient to provide an annual (inflated) income to precisely fill the income gap revealed in column 6. Table 12–3 demonstrates this fact through a cash flow analysis.

The preceding provides income only through age 69. If a lifetime income is desired, provision should be made for income beyond this period.

At age 70, the needed (real) income of $40,000 would require a nominal income then of $157,840. Social Security benefits are estimated to be $34,330, thus leaving an age 70 shortfall of $123,510. If the capital liquidation approach is used wherein an annuity would be purchased at age 70 to fund this and future income shortfalls, its estimated purchase price at age 70 would be $741,060.[16] The value today of this needed amount is about $70,000.[17]

The following, therefore, is a summary of the net life insurance needed:

---

[15]Social Security survivor benefits are based on the "insured status" and past earnings record of the worker. See Chapter 25.

[16]Using a purchase price of $600 per $100 of annual income.

[17]$741,060 × (1/1.07)^{35} = $69,437.

TABLE 12-2. Present value of net income needs

		(1)	(2)	(3)	(4)	(5)	(6)	(7)
Year	Debbie's Age	Debbie's Income Objective	Annual Income Objective (at 4%)	−	Annual Social Security Benefit (at 4%)	−	Debbie's Annual Earnings (at 5%) =	Annual Income Shortage	Value Today of Inflated Income Shortages
1	35	$45,000	$ 45,000		$13,050		$ 25,000	$ 6,950	$ 6,950
2	36	45,000	46,800		13,572		26,250	6,978	6,521
3	37	45,000	48,672		14,115		27,562	6,995	6,109
4	38	45,000	50,619		14,679		28,941	6,999	5,713
5	39	45,000	52,644		15,267		30,388	6,989	5,332
6	40	45,000	54,749		15,877		31,907	6,965	4,966
7	41	45,000	56,939		16,512		33,502	6,925	4,614
8	42	45,000	59,217		17,173		35,177	6,867	4,276
9	43	45,000	61,586		17,860		36,936	6,789	3,951
10	44	45,000	64,049		18,574		38,783	6,692	3,640
11	45	45,000	66,611		19,317		40,722	6,571	3,341
12	46	45,000	69,275		20,090		42,758	6,427	3,053
13	47	45,000	72,046		20,893		44,896	6,257	2,778
14	48	45,000	74,928		21,729		47,141	6,058	2,514
15	49	45,000	77,925		22,598		49,498	5,829	2,261
16	50	43,000	77,441		11,751		51,973	13,716	4,971
17	51	43,000	80,538		12,221		54,572	13,745	4,656
18	52	43,000	83,760		12,710		57,300	13,749	4,353
19	53	43,000	87,110		13,218		60,165	13,726	4,061
20	54	43,000	90,594		13,747		63,174	13,674	3,781
21	55	40,000	87,645		0		66,332	21,313	5,508
22	56	40,000	91,151		0		69,649	21,502	5,193
23	57	40,000	94,797		0		73,131	21,665	4,890
24	58	40,000	98,589		0		76,788	21,801	4,599
25	59	40,000	102,532		0		80,627	21,905	4,318
26	60	40,000	106,633		0		84,659	21,975	4,049
27	61	40,000	110,899		0		88,892	22,007	3,790
28	62	40,000	115,335		0		93,336	21,998	3,540
29	63	40,000	119,948		0		98,003	21,945	3,301
30	64	40,000	124,746		0		102,903	21,843	3,070
31	65	40,000	129,736		28,218		0	101,518	13,336
32	66	40,000	134,925		29,346		0	105,579	12,962
33	67	40,000	140,322		30,520		0	109,802	12,599
34	68	40,000	145,935		31,741		0	114,194	12,246
35	69	40,000	151,773		33,011		0	118,762	11,902

Present value of column 7 $193,144

Present value of income stream to age 70	$193,144
+ Present value of age 70 annuity	70,000
+ Cash needs objectives	201,000
= Total needed to fulfill objectives	$464,144
− Existing resources	107,000
= Shortage of resources over needs	$354,144

The analysis therefore reveals that if the stated objectives are not modified and are to be met, Steve needs an additional $357,000 life insurance on his life.

The result is influenced by the interest and inflation assumptions. Table 12–4 shows how the net result varies at different inflation and interest rate assumptions. The level of these assumptions greatly influences results. Since results are so sensitive to the assumptions, any resulting net figure over such long time periods is, at best, an educated guess. The appearance of scientific precision should not obscure this simple truth.

The same analysis should be conducted assuming that Debbie died first. Recall that the family's income and other objectives apply ir-

TABLE 12-3. Cash flow analysis

Year	(1) Assets at Start of Year	−	(2) Annual Income Supplement	+	(3) Interest at 7.0%	=	(4) Assets at End of Year
1	$193,144		$ 6,950		$13,034		$199,228
2	199,228		6,978		13,457		205,707
3	205,707		6,995		13,910		212,622
4	212,622		6,999		14,394		220,017
5	220,017		6,989		14,912		227,940
6	227,940		6,965		15,468		236,443
7	236,443		6,925		16,066		245,585
8	245,585		6,867		16,710		255,429
9	255,429		6,789		17,405		266,044
10	266,044		6,692		18,155		277,507
11	277,507		6,571		18,965		289,901
12	289,901		6,427		19,843		303,317
13	303,317		6,257		20,794		317,855
14	317,855		6,058		21,826		333,623
15	333,623		5,829		22,946		350,739
16	350,739		13,716		23,592		360,615
17	360,615		13,745		24,281		371,151
18	371,151		13,749		25,018		382,419
19	382,419		13,726		25,809		394,502
20	394,502		13,674		26,658		407,486
21	407,486		21,313		27,032		413,206
22	413,206		21,502		27,419		419,123
23	419,123		21,665		27,822		425,280
24	425,280		21,801		28,244		431,723
25	431,723		21,905		28,687		438,505
26	438,505		21,975		29,157		445,688
27	445,688		22,007		29,658		453,338
28	453,338		21,998		30,194		461,534
29	461,534		21,945		30,771		470,360
30	470,360		21,843		31,396		479,913
31	479,913		101,518		26,488		404,883
32	404,883		105,579		20,951		320,255
33	320,255		109,802		14,732		225,184
34	225,184		114,194		7,769		118,759
35	118,759		118,759		0		0

TABLE 12-4. Variability of results with changing inflation and interest assumptions
(assumes Steve dies first—static analysis)

Interest Assumption (%)	Inflation Assumption (%)				
	0	2	4	6	8
0	$1,184,000	$1,399,000	$1,772,000	$2,414,000	$3,522,000
1	896,000	1,059,000	1,339,000	1,819,000	2,643,000
3	543,000	639,000	800,000	1,073,000	1,536,000
5	360,000	418,000	513,000	672,000	938,000
7	261,000	298,000	357,000	451,000	608,000
9	207,000	231,000	268,000	327,000	421,000
11	176,000	192,000	216,000	254,000	313,000

respective of who dies first and that the same financial and income information applies as before. The only exceptions are that Steve's life insurance (total of $75,000) and pension death benefit ($10,000) must be excluded as liquid resources and the Social Security survivor benefit would be based on Debbie's (lower) earnings and are different. Also, Debbie's employer provides $50,000 of group term coverage. The cash needs are the same as for the analysis with Steve (i.e., $201,000). Existing resources are $72,000, showing an initial deficit of $129,000.

Steve earns more than the desired income objective. The present value of the excess of his after-tax income plus Social Security over the desired income is more than the $129,000 deficit.

If, therefore, it were decided not to pay off the mortgage and other debts, but rather to continue to make payments from current income, there probably is no need for additional life insurance on Debbie's life. If it is desired to pay off the mortgage, the amount of life insurance needed would be around $129,000.

Dynamic Analysis

The preceding analysis developed a life insurance amount figure assuming that death occurred at present. However, would $357,000 be the amount needed assuming that death occurred next year? What about in two years? three years? etc.? The answer to this series of questions can be

TABLE 12-5. Estimated annual values of future liquid assets

Assuming Death Occurred in Year	Pension Plan Death Benefits (at 15.0%)	+	Savings and Invest Balances (at 10.0%)	+	Checking Account Balances (at 4.0%)	+	Total Life Insurance Assuming No Change	=	Annual Projected Liquid Asset Values
1	$ 10,000		$ 20,000		$2,000		$75,000		$ 107,000
2	11,500		22,000		2,080		75,000		110,580
3	13,225		24,200		2,163		75,000		114,588
4	15,209		26,620		2,250		75,000		119,078
5	17,490		29,282		2,340		75,000		124,112
6	20,114		32,210		2,433		75,000		129,757
7	23,131		35,431		2,531		75,000		136,092
8	26,600		38,974		2,632		75,000		143,206
9	30,590		42,872		2,737		75,000		151,199
10	35,179		47,159		2,847		75,000		160,184
11	40,456		51,875		2,960		75,000		170,291
12	46,524		57,062		3,079		75,000		181,665
13	53,503		62,769		3,202		75,000		194,473
14	61,528		69,045		3,330		75,000		208,903
15	70,757		75,950		3,463		75,000		225,170
16	81,371		83,545		3,602		75,000		243,517
17	93,576		91,899		3,746		75,000		264,222
18	107,613		101,089		3,896		75,000		287,598
19	123,755		111,198		4,052		75,000		314,005
20	142,318		122,318		4,214		75,000		343,850
21	163,665		134,550		4,382		75,000		377,598
22	188,215		148,005		4,558		75,000		415,778
23	216,447		162,806		4,740		75,000		458,993
24	248,915		179,086		4,929		75,000		507,930
25	286,252		196,995		5,127		75,000		563,373
26	329,190		216,694		5,332		75,000		626,215
27	378,568		238,364		5,545		75,000		697,477
28	435,353		262,200		5,767		75,000		778,320
29	500,656		288,420		5,997		75,000		870,074
30	575,755		317,262		6,237		75,000		974,254
31	662,118		248,988		6,487		75,000		1,092,593
32	761,436		383,887		6,746		75,000		1,227,069
33	875,651		422,276		7,016		75,000		1,379,943
34	1,006,998		464,503		7,297		75,000		1,553,798
35	1,158,048		510,954		7,589		75,000		1,751,590

exceedingly important. At $357,000, Steve could be either grossly overinsured or underinsured in later years.

The dynamic approach requires assumptions as to future liquid assets and cash needs. Thus, the declining outstanding mortgage will lessen future cash needs. However, inflation likely will drive up credit-card balances and probable funeral and probate costs. If the emergency fund is to maintain its purchasing power, it must also increase with inflation. The value of savings and investments might be expected to rise as would employer-provided pension plan death benefits. In sum, *all* elements of Steve and Debbie's pro forma financial situation are dynamic, over time.

Accumulated resources, income sources, cash, and income needs all change as Steve and Debbie move through their family life cycle.

To illustrate the process, assume that the pension plan death benefit increases 15 percent annually and that the value of savings and investments increases 10 percent annually. These rates of increase are assumed to include both reinvestment of earnings and additional contributions. Also, assume that checking account balances, charge-card balances, postmortem expenses, and desired emergency fund balances increase with the inflation rate.

Tables 12-5 and 12-6 summarize these figures, over time, based on the same assumptions

TABLE 12-6.

(1) Assuming Death Occurs in Year	(2) Annual Mortgage Loan Balance	+	(3) Annual Balances on Other Debts (at 4%)	+	(4) Annual Emergency Fund (at 4%)	+	(5) Annual Educational Fund Balances (at 7%)	+	(6) Annual Post-mortem Expenses (at 4%)	+
1	$110,000		$13,000		$20,000		$50,000		$ 8,000	
2	109,366		13,520		20,800		53,500		8,320	
3	108,651		14,061		21,632		57,245		8,653	
4	107,846		14,623		22,497		61,252		8,999	
5	106,939		15,208		23,397		65,540		9,359	
6	105,916		15,816		24,333		70,128		9,733	
7	104,764		16,449		25,306		75,037		10,123	
8	103,466		17,107		26,319		80,289		10,527	
9	102,003		17,791		27,371		85,909		10,949	
10	100,355		18,503		28,466		91,923		11,386	
11	98,498		19,243		29,605		98,358		11,842	
12	96,405		20,013		30,789		52,621		12,316	
13	94,047		20,813		32,021		56,305		12,808	
14	91,389		21,646		33,301		60,246		13,321	
15	88,395		22,512		34,634		64,463		13,853	
16	85,020		23,412		36,019		68,976		14,408	
17	81,218		24,349		37,460		0		14,984	
18	76,934		25,323		38,958		0		15,583	
19	72,106		26,336		40,516		0		16,207	
20	66,666		27,389		42,137		0		16,855	
21	60,536		28,485		43,822		0		17,529	
22	53,629		29,624		45,575		0		18,230	
23	45,845		30,809		47,398		0		18,959	
24	37,075		32,041		49,294		0		19,718	
25	27,192		33,323		51,266		0		20,506	
26	16,056		34,656		53,317		0		21,327	
27	3,507		36,042		55,449		0		22,180	
28	0		37,484		57,667		0		23,067	
29	0		38,983		59,974		0		23,990	
30	0		40,542		62,373		0		24,949	
31	0		42,164		64,868		0		25,947	
32	0		43,851		67,463		0		26,985	
33	0		45,605		70,161		0		28,064	
34	0		47,429		72,968		0		29,187	
35	0		49,326		75,886		0		30,355	

and information used in the static analysis plus the additional stated assumptions. Estimated future liquid asset values available if Steve were to die in each year are shown in Table 12–5. For example, if Steve died in year 7, it is estimated that the total liquid asset value in that year would be about $136,092, composed of a $23,131 pension plan death benefit, $35,431 in then current investments and savings, a $2,531 checking account balance, and the $75,000 of life insurance. No change is assumed in the life insurance as this is the value sought.

Table 12–6 follows the same approach but based on liabilities and objectives. Thus, if Steve were to die six years from the present (year 7),

the then outstanding mortgage balance would be $104,764. Charge-card and personal loan balances, estimated to grow at the inflation rate, might be around $16,449 six years from now. At that time, $25,306 would be required to maintain the same $20,000 emergency fund purchasing power, based on the inflation assumption of 4 percent.

Continuing across the table, the value needed to fund the college education then would be $75,037. This deserves comment. Steve and Debbie want a $50,000 educational fund established if either Steve or Debbie died at present. At a 7 percent assumed earnings rate, this means that they believe they will need $98,358 by year

(7) Cash Needed in Year of Death to Purchase Annuity at Age 70	=	(8) Annual Total Cash Needs	+	(9) Present Value in Year of Death of Income Shortage to Age 70	−	(10) Total Estimated Resources	=	(11) Additional Life Insurance Needed in Year of Death
$ 70,000		$271,000		$193,144		$ 107,000		$ 357,144
74,900		280,406		199,228		110,580		369,054
80,143		290,385		205,707		114,588		381,504
85,753		300,971		212,622		119,078		394,515
91,756		312,199		220,017		124,112		408,104
98,179		324,105		227,940		129,757		422,288
105,051		336,730		236,443		136,092		437,081
112,405		350,113		245,585		143,206		452,482
120,273		364,297		255,429		151,199		468,527
128,692		379,326		266,044		160,184		485,186
137,701		395,246		277,507		170,291		502,462
147,340		359,484		289,901		181,665		467,720
157,654		373,647		303,317		194,473		482,492
168,689		388,592		317,855		208,903		497,544
180,498		404,354		333,623		225,170		512,807
193,132		420,967		350,740		243,517		528,190
206,652		364,662		360,615		264,222		461,056
221,117		377,915		371,151		287,598		461,468
236,595		391,760		382,420		314,005		460,175
253,157		406,204		394,502		343,850		456,857
270,878		421,250		407,487		377,598		451,139
289,840		436,898		413,206		415,778		434,326
310,128		453,140		419,124		458,993		413,272
331,837		469,966		425,281		507,930		387,316
355,066		487,353		431,724		563,373		355,704
379,921		505,276		438,507		626,215		317,567
406,515		523,693		445,689		697,477		271,906
434,971		553,189		453,340		778,320		228,209
465,419		588,366		461,535		870,074		179,828
497,999		625,863		470,362		974,254		121,971
532,859		665,838		479,915		1,092,593		53,160
570,159		708,457		404,885		1,227,069		−113,727
610,070		753,900		320,257		1,379,943		−305,785
652,775		802,358		225,187		1,553,798		−526,253
698,469		854,036		118,762		1,751,590		−778,792

11 (Philip's age 17). Thus, the amounts necessary in the intervening years must be such as to grow to $98,358 by year 11.

The simplifying assumption is made that one-half the fund balance is paid to Philip at his age 18 and the balance, accumulated at interest, is paid five years later when Gwen enters college at her age 18. Thus, no educational fund is shown as needed beyond her age 18. If, in fact, both Steve and Debbie survived to this point, they presumably would have already made provision for their children's education.

Continuing across the table at year 7, an estimated $10,123 would be needed at that time to cover postmortem expenses. Column 7 shows the estimated cash amount needed, $105,051 in year 7, to fund the purchase, at age 70, of the life annuity referred to earlier.

Column 8 is the simple sum of columns 2 through 7. It shows the amount required to fund

all cash needs each year, if death were to occur in that year. Hence, if death were to occur in year 7, an estimated $336,730 would be required to fund fully all of the column 2 through 7 needs.

The present value of the income stream necessary to fill the income gap to age 70 appears in column 9. The yearly shortage figures were shown in Table 12-2. Their present value was $193,144—the figure shown for the first year in column 9. If death occurs in year 2, not in year 1, the amount needed to fund the income shortages as from year 2 is estimated to be $199,228; from year 3, $205,707, and so on. Thus, if death were to occur in year 7, an estimated $236,443 would be required *at that time* to fund the Table 12-2 income shortages from the seventh year to age 70.

Total projected annual resources (column 10) are then netted against the sum of yearly cash and income needs to derive yearly figures that represent the total projected annual shortages of

FIGURE 12-2. Life insurance needs (i = 4%, r = 7%)

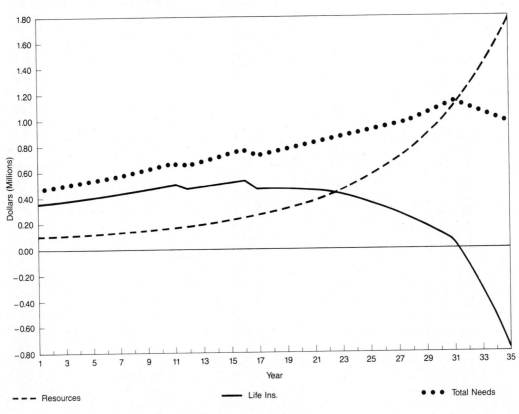

resources to meet needs (column 11). If the assumptions used to derive these figures actually materialized as fact in the future, the column 11 figures would represent the amounts of life insurance that Steve should have in force on his life in each year.

As shown in Figure 12–2, the estimated needed amounts increase through year 11. The needed amount then decreases because one child (Philip) is considered "out of the nest." Projected needs begin to increase again but decline in year 17—when Gwen has left the "nest." Amounts thereafter remain in the $400,000 range for several years then drop preciptiously as total estimated resources reach high levels. If all assumptions were realized, the need for life insurance protection is estimated to cease at about age 65. However, this assumes a constant savings pattern as well as large employer-provided funding. Whether these will be realized in fact is always questionable and a financial plan should be flexible enough to adapt to unrealized hopes.

A note of caution is in order here. Again, the precise-appearing numbers can lend an unwarranted aura of authenticity to these types of analyses. Column 11 figures shown for many years into the future should be regarded more as educated guesses than anything else. Credence should be given to the general level of the first five or perhaps 10 years' values, but beyond that one would be well advised to look at trends only. The intent of this exercise is to show how future death patterns can be estimated and to highlight the great importance of selecting a policy that can adjust to the future pattern.

Chapter 13

Tax Aspects
of Life Insurance

Because of their socially worthwhile role, certain tax benefits are accorded life insurance and annuity contracts, provided that they are used in a manner consistent with their purpose. Poor planning can result in adverse tax treatment. This chapter introduces the reader to the federal income, estate, and gift tax treatment of life insurance and annuities and suggests ways of avoiding adverse tax consequences. Because, important tax code revisions were pending as this book was going to press, the reader is urged to check the information presented below against completely up-to-date sources.

INCOME TAX TREATMENT
OF LIFE INSURANCE

In examining the income tax treatment of life insurance, it will prove convenient to examine the tax treatment by component of the life insurance policy.

Premiums

Premiums paid for individual life insurance policies are considered a personal expense and are not deductible for income tax purposes.[1] This applies to government life insurance as well as life insurance issued by commercial insurers and fraternal benefit societies.

Of course, premiums paid to fund life insurance that is payable to a charity may be deductible as charitable contributions and premiums paid for life insurance under an alimony agreement may be deductible as alimony payments. Moreover, premiums paid by employers for life insurance protection that benefits employees are deductible as a business expense.

Death Proceeds

IRC Section 101(a)(1) Treatment. The general rule is that life insurance death proceeds *are not* includable in the beneficiary's (or anyone else's) gross income for federal income tax purposes.[2] Thus, if an insured under a $100,000 life insurance policy died after premiums of $3,000 had been paid, the general rule would hold that the entire $100,000 would be received income tax

---

[1] In perhaps the majority of countries in the world, premiums paid for life insurance policies are tax deductible.

[2] Internal Revenue Code (IRC), Section 101(a)(1).

free by the named beneficiary, irrespective of the amount of cash value or of past premiums paid and irrespective of who occupied the position of policyowner, insured, beneficiary, or premium payor. "Death proceeds" include not only the policy face amount but any additional insurance amounts paid by reason of the death of the insured, such as accidental death benefits and the face amount of any paid-up additional insurance or any term rider. Death proceeds paid under an annuity contract are not considered life insurance death proceeds and do not enjoy exemption under this section.

Exceptions to Section 101(a)(1) Treatment. The general rule is simple, but regrettably, has complicating exceptions. These exceptions are discussed below briefly.

1. *Transfer for value rule.* If a life insurance policy or any interest in a policy is transferred to another person for a valuable consideration, the death proceeds lose their income-tax-exempt status, in whole or in part.[3] The amount of the consideration paid plus all net premiums paid by the transferee (the person to whom the policy or interest was transferred) may be recovered income tax free on death. The excess of the gross death proceeds over the consideration paid plus net premiums paid would be taxable to the beneficiary as ordinary income. Thus, if Barbara sold her $100,000 policy to Heather (i.e., changed ownership) for $3,000 and if Barbara died 10 years later with Heather having paid $12,000 in premiums (net of dividends), the beneficiary would receive $15,000 tax free ($3,000 consideration plus $12,000 premiums paid), but the $85,000 balance would be ordinary income for tax purposes.

This **transfer for value rule** applies to any transfer, for a valuable consideration, of a right to receive all or a part of the death proceeds of a life insurance policy. The most common situation where the rule is invoked involves sales of policies, but the rule is not limited to sales only; it applies to any transfer involving a valuable consideration.

[3]IRC Section 101(a)(2).

Certain transactions are exempt from the transfer for value rule. They are:

1. Where the transfer (by sale or otherwise) is to the insured. (For example, a corporation sells a key person policy that it owned to the insured/key employee when the employee resigned.)
2. When the transfer (by sale or otherwise) is to
   (a) A partner of the insured;
   (b) A partnership in which the insured is a partner; or
   (c) A corporation in which the insured is an officer or shareholder.
3. Certain transfers that do not involve a tax-basis change, including
   (a) A tax-free corporate organization or reorganization; or
   (b) A bona fide gift.

Thus, irrespective of any earlier transfers for value, if ownership of the policy is acquired by the insured, death proceeds are income tax exempt (item 1 above). Similarly, any transfer in connection with the business applications noted in items 2 or 3(a) results in death proceeds being accorded Internal Revenue Code (IRC) Section 101(a)(1) treatment (i.e., income tax exempt). Finally, where a policy is transferred, *not* for a valuable consideration, but as a gift, death proceeds remain income tax exempt. Thus, a gift of a policy on one spouse's life to the other spouse through an absolute assignment (i.e., change of ownership) normally would fall outside the transfer for value rule.

2. *Failure to meet IRC definition of life insurance.* IRC Section 7702 contains a definition of life insurance for purposes of determining whether a policy qualifies for favorable tax treatment. This definition is important for many reasons and is discussed in detail below.

In general, however, the definition attempts to limit the Code's favorable life insurance tax treatment to policies whose savings element (cash values) do not predominate over the protection aspect. Two tests are prescribed to make this determination (see below). If the policy fails to meet one of these two tests, the policy is treated, for tax purposes, as if it were a combination of

(1) pure term life insurance equal to the policy's net amount at risk, and (2) a taxable fund that is equal to the policy cash value. The pure term portion is subject to Section 101(a)(1) treatment (i.e., income tax exempt). The cash value portion does not receive Section 101 treatment, instead being taxed in a manner similar to any other investment (i.e., any gain over its basis would be subject to ordinary income taxation). Its basis would be measured as discussed below but would also include any amounts on which income taxes had already been paid.

3. *Other.* Other highly specific reasons can cause life insurance death proceeds to be taxed, wholly or partly. It appears that a lack of insurable interest at the time of a life insurance policy's issuance will cause the contract to be considered a wager and, therefore, death proceeds received in excess of premiums paid (net of dividend credits) would be taxable as ordinary income.[4] Whether an insurable interest existed would be determined under the applicable state law. Also, the state law would determine whether *any* proceeds would be paid. Recall that to have a valid contract, an insurable interest need exist at policy inception only, not at time of claim.[5] Other situations that can invite income tax treatment include:

- Proceeds received by a creditor from life insurance on the debtor/insured's life
- Proceeds received as corporate dividends (see Rev. Rul. 61–134)
- Proceeds received as alimony

Tax Treatment of Settlement Options. Life insurance death proceeds can be paid out under one or more of the settlement options.[6] The favorable income tax treatment of the policy (lump-sum) death proceeds is unaffected by election of a settlement option, although income taxes may be due on any *interest paid* on the death proceeds.

Under the **interest option,** interest received

by the beneficiary is taxable as ordinary income. Interest retained by the company also is taxable unless the beneficiary cannot withdraw either principal or interest for a stated time period. At the end of the time period, all previously accrued untaxed interest would be taxable.

Under the **installment and life income settlement options,** each payment is deemed to be composed of part principal and part interest. The portion that is deemed to be a return of principal is not taxed. The procedure for deriving this portion is to calculate an **amount held by the insurer** (usually, the single-sum amount payable at the insured's death) and pro rate this amount over the actual or expected payment period.

Amounts in excess of the annual prorated principal are treated as interest and are treated as taxable income to any recipient other than the surviving spouse of an insured who died before October 23, 1986. Such a surviving spouse is entitled to exclude up to $1,000 of interest annually in addition to the prorated tax-free return of principal.[7] The Tax Reform Act of 1986 (TRA '86) eliminated the $1,000 per year spousal exclusion for deaths occurring after October 22, 1986.

To derive the prorated amount excludable as a return of principal under the **fixed-period option,** the amount held by the insurer is divided by the number of installments within the fixed period. The excess of each payment over this amount is deemed interest income. Thus, if $100,000 of death proceeds is to be paid over a 10-year fixed period and the payments are $15,000 per year, $10,000 ($100,000 divided by 10 years) is excluded from yearly taxable income as being a return of principal. An additional $1,000 may be excluded if the recipient is the surviving spouse of an insured who died before October 23, 1986.

The procedure to arrive at the excludable amount of each payment under the **fixed-amount option** is to divide the amount held by the insurer by the number of payments required to exhaust the principal at the *guaranteed* interest rate. The amount of each payment in excess of this figure is deemed to be interest, and if the recipient is the insured's surviving spouse, the $1,000 additional exclusion applies for deaths before

---

[4]See, for example, *Atlantic Oil Co. v. Patterson,* 331F.2d 516 (5th Cir. 1964).

[5]See Chapter 8.

[6]See Chapter 9.

[7]IRC Section 101(d)(1)(B).

October 23, 1986. Payments made beyond the guaranteed period are considered to be interest only, and therefore no exclusion for return of principal is allowed on these excess payments.

The amount to be excluded from taxable income of each payment under one of the **life income settlement options** is determined by reference to the recipient's life expectancy. The amount held by the insurer is divided by the recipient's life expectancy to derive the excludable portion of each payment. For deaths occurring before October 23, 1986, the recipient's life expectancy is determined by reference to the mortality table used by the insurer. For deaths after October 22, 1986, IRS-prescribed tables must be used. If the life income option contains a refund feature or guaranteed minimum number of installments, the amount held by the insurer is reduced by a factor intended to represent the actuarial value of the refund or guarantee feature. The insurer furnishes this figure.

For example, assume that the insured died prior to October 23, 1986 and that the $100,000 death proceeds are to be paid under the life income option with a 10-year period certain. The beneficiary is a 60-year-old male with a life expectancy, according to the insurer's mortality table, of 22 years. The insurer advises that the actuarial value of the 10-year period certain feature is 8 percent of the amount held by the insurer. Stated differently, the contingent beneficiary's interest in the payouts is valued at 8 percent of the total, since there is a chance that the primary beneficiary might die before the 10-year period. Thus, the $100,000 proceeds would be reduced by 8 percent to $92,000, which, when divided by the 22-year life expectancy yields $4,091, the amount excludable annually as return of principal. If the recipient is the deceased's spouse, an additional $1,000 exclusion is available. The same exclusion amounts apply as long as payments are made to the primary beneficiary, even beyond the individual's life expectancy.

Living Proceeds

IRC Section 72 governs the income taxation of proceeds received under a life insurance policy during the insured's lifetime—so-called living proceeds.[8] Living proceeds include policy dividends, single-sum cash surrender payments, and matured endowments. Each of these is discussed below.

Policy Dividends. Dividends under participating life insurance policies are considered a return of investment or basis and therefore are tax exempt. This result is uneffected by the option selected. If dividends are left to accumulate at interest, the interest credited on the accumulation is, of course, taxable. In general, excess interest earnings or other cash value or premium credits on universal life and other current assumption policies are treated like dividends for tax purposes and are also, therefore, tax exempt.

Two exceptions exist to this general rule. First, if the total of the *dividends received* exceeds the total of the premiums paid, all dividend amounts received in excess of the sum of premiums paid constitute ordinary income. Second, dividends (or other credits) paid under certain high-cash-value life insurance and endowment policies may attract adverse tax treatment "when the amount at risk . . . is sufficiently minimal that the contract should be treated as an annuity."[9] In such cases, the life policy will be treated as an annuity for tax purposes. As discussed below, annuity dividend treatment is not as favorable as that for life insurance policies.

Cash Surrender Payments. The general rule for taxation of lump-sum cash value payments made on surrender of life insurance policies is the **cost recovery rule.** Under the cost recovery rule, the amount included in the policyowner's gross income upon policy surrender is the excess of the gross proceeds received over the **cost basis.** The cost basis of a life insurance contract normally is the sum of the premiums paid less the sum of any dividends received in cash or credited against the premiums. When dividends have been used to purchase paid-up additional insurance or left to accumulate at interest, the cash value of the addi-

---

[8] Income taxation of annuities is also addressed under this Code Section. See later in this chapter.

[9] U.S. Senate Report 97–494, Vol. 1, p. 351.

tions and the value of the accumulations would be includable in the gross proceeds.

Premiums paid for supplementary benefits such as the premium waiver and accidental death benefit features are not a part of the basis. Premiums waived under the premium waiver feature, logically, should be included in the basis.[10] If policy loans are outstanding on surrender, the net surrender value (cash value less loan) would constitute the gross proceeds, but the loan amounts previously received lower the basis.

For example, assume that the owner of the $100,000 ordinary life policy illustrated in Table 5-3 surrendered the policy for its cash value at the end of 20 years and that dividends were paid in cash exactly as illustrated in that table (an unrealistic assumption). The amount subject to ordinary income tax treatment would be calculated as follows:

	Sum of premiums paid	$28,920
Less:	Sum of dividends received	−22,279
Equals:	Cost basis	$ 6,641

	Gross proceeds	$32,180 (cash value)
Less:	Cost basis	−6,641
Equals:	Taxable gain	$25,539

The cost basis of a life insurance policy includes the pure cost of insurance. Arguably, yearly mortality charges should be excluded from the basis as representing current expenditure and not an investment. Thus, to the extent these mortality charges are included in the basis, tax income to the policyowner technically is understated by that amount.

Losses on surrender of a life insurance policy normally cannot be recognized for income tax purposes. The theory for not allowing a deductible loss is that the method for computing taxable gain (and loss) makes no allowance for the cost of pure insurance protection, and therefore any loss is composed, in whole or in part, of such mortality costs.

Gain on policy surrender can be avoided if the surrender involves a Section 1035 exchange. This is discussed further below.

The cost recovery rule seems also to apply to life insurance policy cash value withdrawals and partial surrenders. An exception to this cost recovery treatment occurs for cash distributions received as a result of certain policyowner-initiated reductions in policy benefits. In such situations, the distribution will be taxed as ordinary income to the extent there is untaxed income in the contract and subject to certain ceiling amounts.[11]

Matured Endowments. Living proceeds received from a matured endowment are taxed in the same manner as proceeds received on policy surrender. The basis is subtracted from the gross proceeds to derive taxable income.

Policy Loans

General Treatment. Policyowners can secure loans under their cash value policies up to the amount of and on the security of the then cash value of the policy. The interest rate charged or the method used to derive the interest rate to be charged on such loans is stated in the contract.

As a general rule and subject to important exceptions noted below, policyowners could take income tax deductions for interest paid on policy loans for tax years 1986 and before. For tax years beginning after 1986, the extent of any permissible deduction depends on the particular year.

Prior to TRA '86, personal interest not incurred in a trade or business was generally fully deductible by the individual taxpayer. TRA '86 reversed this treatment so that, beginning in 1987, the deduction for personal interest is to be phased out. For tax years beginning after 1990, no deduction for personal (also called "consumer") interest will be allowed. During the phase-out period, the following percentages of aggregate personal interest will be deductible: 65 percent for 1987; 40 percent for 1988; 20 percent for 1989; and 10 percent for 1990.[12] Policy loan interest in connection with personally-owned (as opposed to business-owned) life insurance is considered "personal interest" and, therefore, subject to the preceding limitations.

Policy loan interest paid on policies owned

[10] However, in *Estate of Wong Wing Non,* 18 TC 204 (1952), the tax court did not follow this logic.

[11] IRC Section 7702(7)(B).
[12] *1987 Tax Facts,* Vol. 1 (Cincinatti, Ohio: The National Underwriter Co., 1987), p. 516.

by a business and covering the lives of officers, employees or other persons financially interested in the policyowner's business is deductible, subject to certain constraints. TRA '86 provides that, for such policies purchased after June 20, 1986, an interest deduction is allowed only on policy loans of less than $50,000 per individual insured. The $50,000 limitations does not apply to policies purchased prior to June 21, 1986.

To obtain any deduction, the interest actually must be paid. If added to the existing loan or deducted by the insurer from the proceeds of a new loan, it is not deductible. In the two latter cases, a deduction will be allowed if and when the interest is actually paid, including paid by deduction on policy surrender or maturity.

Financed ("Minimum Deposit") Insurance. The preceding business-related deduction does not hold when policy loans are used to finance life insurance under a systematic plan of borrowing. Thus, interest due on loans to finance the purchase of single premium life insurance policies (after March 1, 1954) is not tax deductible.[13] A single premium policy is defined as one under which substantially all of the premiums due on the policy are paid within the first four policy years, or a substantial number of future premiums is deposited with the insurer in the first year.[14]

IRC Section 264(a)(3) further provides that a deduction is denied for interest paid on an indebtedness "incurred or continued to purchase or carry a life insurance, endowment, or annuity contract . . . pursuant to a plan of purchase which contemplates the systematic direct or indirect borrowing of [sic] part or all of the increases in the cash value of such contract (either from the insurer or otherwise)." This rule applies only to contracts purchased after August 6, 1963 and contains four exceptions.[15] If a financing plan meets at least one of these exceptions, interest is deductible subject to the TRA '86 constraints. The four exceptions are discussed below.

Most financed insurance qualifies for the deductibility of interest (if at all, in the future)

under the **four-in-seven exception.** It provides that a deduction is allowed if no part of (at least) four of the first seven annual premiums due on a policy is paid through borrowing, either from the policy or elsewhere. A new seven-year period begins if a "substantial increase" in premiums occurs.

If borrowing in any year exceeds the premium for that year, the excess is considered to be borrowings used to finance the previous year's premium. Thus, the four-in-seven test is violated if policyowner borrowings during the seven-year period exceed an amount equal to three years' premiums, irrespective of when the borrowing takes place during the period.

The four premiums can be paid in any order. Also, it appears that once the seven-year requirement had been satisfied, borrowing beyond that period can be at any level.[16]

The second of the four exceptions holds that irrespective of whether a systemic plan of borrowing exists, if the interest paid on borrowings to pay premiums does not exceed $100 during a taxable year, the interest is deductible, again, subject to the TRA '86 constraints regarding personal interest. However, if interest exceeds $100, the entire amount is subject to the general rule.

The third exception is that an interest deduction will not be denied if indebtedness is "incurred because of an unforeseen substantial loss of income or unforeseen substantial increase in . . . financial obligations."[17]

The final exception states simply that an interest deduction on indebtedness will not be denied "if such indebtedness was incurred in connection with [a] . . . trade or business."[18] This exception is not as broad as may appear. It is intended to be used where loan proceeds are applied to finance usual business or commercial activities, such as business expansion. It does not provide an exception for life insurance financed to fund key person, split-dollar, deferred compensation, and other such plans.[19] The four-in-seven exception normally is used in these business situations.

---

[13]IRC Section 264(a)(2). See Rev. Rul. 79–41.
[14]IRC Section 264(b).
[15]IRC Section 264(c).

[16]See *Tax Facts,* pp. 383–384.
[17]IRC Section 264(c)(3).
[18]IRC Section 264(c)(4).
[19]Reg. Sec. 1.264-4(d)(4). See Chapter 15.

Illustration. Use of the four-in-seven exception to finance cash value life insurance policies has been widespread practice for many years. TRA '86 has significantly diminished the attractiveness of financing insurance, except for business situations. Using policy (or other) loans to pay life insurance premiums still can be advantageous in certain circumstances..

The process of financing life insurance in this manner commonly is referred to as **minimum deposit.** Of course, this refers to the method of financing, not to a type of policy. Table 13–1 illustrates a possible minimum deposit scheme, assuming a 45-year-old insured and dividends are used to purchase paid-up additional insurance. A 50 percent combined federal/state marginal income tax bracket is assumed.

Under this arrangement, the policyowner pays the first, second, sixth and seventh premiums in full with no portions paid from loans. The third, fourth, and fifth premiums are paid from policy loans, with the loans being for the amount of each premium and no greater sum. Interest is assumed to be paid in cash, with no portion paid from borrowing during policy years 1 to 7. Under this scheme, all policy loan interest paid on this financed, level-premium policy should qualify under the four-in-seven rule as an income tax deduction provided the policy meets the TRA '86 business-related exception and, with respect to loan amounts of $50,000 and over, provided the policy was purchased prior to June 21, 1986.

As of policy year 8, the four-in-seven rule would have been satisfied, and therefore the policyowner presumably may undertake whatever borrowings are desired—including exercising a maximum loan under the policy—without jeopardizing the policy's tax status. The illustration shows a so-called "zero pay" approach for payments after year 7. This approach strives to obtain a zero *after-tax* outlay in each year after year 7. This is accomplished by the policyowner (1) paying each year's interest charges in cash (to obtain the income tax deduction), then (2) exercising a loan to pay both the premium *and* the after-tax cost of the interest payment. In the example, the policyowner's marginal income tax bracket is assumed to be 50 percent; thus, the after-tax interest cost is one-half the actual interest payment; the amount borrowed in excess of the year's premium payment. With the

policy and financing arrangement shown here, it is clear that both the death benefit and the net surrender value generally increase over time, even in the face of the increasing loan balance.

Administration of a minimum deposit plan is complex. It requires a major service commitment from the agent or other advisor. The policyowner must be advised each year as to how much, if any, to borrow under the policy, and the loan transaction must be completed. Annual interest should be paid faithfully each year if the plan is to take optimum advantage of tax leverage. In later policy years, the absolute amount of the interest payment can be great, demanding a substantial policyowner cash flow.

Minimum deposit insurance arrangements can constitute an unexpected "tax trap" for the ill-informed or just unlucky. The cost basis for a minimum deposited policy can be negative by a large amount. Recall that policy loans reduce the policy basis. After many years of financing a life insurance policy, cumulative loans typically will exceed premiums paid by a substantial amount. The net cash value (cash value less loans) of such policies typically is small. Upon surrender of such a policy, the owner would receive a check for the small net surrender value but at the same time, have caused the cost recovery rule to be invoked. The result of the highly negative cost basis would be that the owner potentially could be facing a monumental tax bill for surrendering a policy that contained virtually no net surrender value. This pitfall can be especially cruel if the surrender occurs because of financial reverses.

These potential pitfalls suggest that financing life insurance should be approached only with the greatest of care. Even then, it is risky and subject to factors beyond the insurer's and policyowner's control. Enactment of TRA '86 should remind life insurance buyers that tax laws change, and the tax-motivated buyer can be left in an unenviable position.

Section 1035 Policy Exchanges

An important, although formerly largely ignored section of the IRC has attracted great interest lately as a result of extensive replacement activity. This section, entitled "Certain Exchanges of Insurance Policies," applies when a

TABLE 13-1. Illustration of minimum deposit plan
($100,000 ordinary life, male, age 45 50% marginal tax bracket, dividends to purchase paid-up additions)

	(1)	(2)	(3)	(4)	(5)	(6)	(7)	(8)	(9)	(10)
					Annual After-Tax Outlay [(1) − (2) + (3) − (4)] − .50(3)	Total Cash Value[b]			Year-End Totals after Loan	
Year	Premium Paid in Cash	Premium Paid by Loan	Interest Paid in Cash	Additional Policy Loan[a]			Total Insurance[c]	Total Loan	Cash [(6) − (8)]	Insurance [(7) − (8)]
1	$2,584	$0	$0	$0	$2,584	$49	$100,128	$0	$49	100,128
2	2,584	0	0	0	2,584	1,987	101,083	0	1,987	101,083
3	0	2,584	0	0	0	4,432	102,192	2,584	1,745	99,505
4	0	2,584	207	0	103	7,034	103,528	5,168	1,660	98,153
5	0	2,584	413	0	207	9,311	105,117	7,752	1,749	97,055
6	2,584	0	620	0	2,894	12,864	107,169	7,752	4,802	99,107
7	2,584	0	620	0	2,894	16,241	109,753	7,752	8,779	101,691
8	0	2,584	620	310	0	19,851	112,633	10,646	8,779	101,561
9	0	2,584	852	426	0	23,723	115,841	13,656	9,520	101,639
10	0	2,584	1,092	546	0	27,871	119,388	16,786	10,413	101,930
11	0	2,584	1,343	671	0	32,255	123,286	20,042	11,411	102,443
12	0	2,584	1,603	802	0	36,929	127,506	23,427	12,564	103,142
13	0	2,584	1,874	937	0	41,908	132,062	26,948	13,882	104,036
14	0	2,584	2,156	1,078	0	47,209	136,955	30,610	15,374	105,120
15	0	2,584	2,449	1,224	0	52,846	142,201	34,419	17,050	106,406
20	0	2,584	4,099	2,050	0	86,805	174,302	55,871	28,699	116,196
@70	0	2,584	6,107	3,053	0	132,957	218,865	81,972	47,706	133,614
@75	0	2,584	8,549	4,275	0	195,314	279,718	113,727	77,038	161,442
@80	0	2,584	11,521	5,761	0	278,764	359,944	152,362	120,328	201,487
@85	0	2,584	15,137	7,569	0	390,163	467,053	199,368	182,820	259,710

[a] Equal to after-tax cost of interest paid in cash.
[b] Guaranteed cash value + cash value of paid-up additions.
[c] $100,000 + face amount of paid-up additions.

person "exchanges" an existing policy for a new one *and* does so in conformity with the section's requirements. If this is done, no gain need be recognized on the exchange (replacement). The adjusted basis of the old policy is carried over to the new contract. This can be an advantageous way of effecting a replacement when a surrender would otherwise result in a taxable event.

The mechanics of a Section 1035 Exchange can be complicated and time consuming but rewarding. The details are not presented here but involve assigning the existing policy to the new insurer and having the new insurer effect the surrender. Other procedures also have been suggested.[20]

IRC Definition of Life Insurance[21]

Background. During the mid-1970s, the design of life insurance products, which had been relatively stable for several decades, began to change. Some of the new insurance products functioned more like short-term investments than as vehicles for protection against premature death or accumulation of long-term retirement funds. Consequently, these new products raised significant questions as to the appropriateness of certain tax benefits that had been provided for traditional types of life insurance policies.

In response to the issues raised by these new products, the Tax Equity and Fiscal Responsibility Act of 1982 (TEFRA) provided a definition of life insurance for flexible premium (universal life) products. Moreoever, the taxation of annuities was modified to reduce incentives for their use as short-term investment vehicles.

The Deficit Reduction Act of 1984 greatly expanded and refined the provisions enacted by TEFRA. Specifically, tne new law added Section 7702 to the IRC, which provided, for the first time a federal, statutory definition of life insurance for

all life insurance products. It also modified the annuity taxation rules enacted by TEFRA to inhibit further the use of annuities as short-term investment vehicles. Failure of a policy to meet the definition results in the policy being treated as a combination of term insurance and a taxable side fund.

Traditional whole life policies generally contain an established actuarial relationship among premiums, reserve, cash value, and death benefits. The policy reserve is defined as the amount which, when added to the present value of future premiums payable under the policy, will equal the net single premium at the policyowner's attained age. Policy cash values generally are either slightly less than or equal to the policy reserve.

With the development of flexible premium policies, these relationships became more complex. Most early universal life policies were designed simply with a required **corridor** of pure life insurance protection between the policy's cash value and the face amount, rather than incorporating a specific actuarial relationship between the two. The corridor was established to ensure that the policy contained at least some element of pure life insurance protection. As a result, some universal life policies were established with cash values substantially in excess of the amount actuarially required to prefund future mortality charges. Congress was concerned that the excess premiums paid into these types of policies were more in the nature of an investment than a premium required to support an insurance benefit.

To address this situation, Congress mandated that life insurance policies must meet one of two tests specified in the new IRC Section 7702. Whichever test is chosen, that test must be met for the entire life of the contract.

Description of Alternative Tests. To qualify as a life insurance contract, the contract must meet the criteria of *either* of the following tests.

The first test, the **cash value accumulation test,** is intended to apply mainly to traditional cash value policies. This test requires that, by the terms of the contract, the cash surrender value cannot at any time exceed the net single premium required to fund future contract benefits. The net single premium is calculated assuming an interest rate equal to the greater of 4 percent or the rate

---

[20]See T. P. Manno and R. T. Nolan, "Internal Revenue Code §1035 and the Other Side of Exchange Programs," *The Journal of the American Society of Chartered Life Underwriters,* Vol. XXXIX (November 1985); and J. Timothy Lynch, "Exchange of Insurance Policies under Internal Revenue Code Section 1035," *The Journal of the American Society of Chartered Life Underwriters,* Vol. XXXVII (October 1983).

[21]This section draws from Arthur Andersen & Co., *The 1984 Tax Reform Act: Impact on the Insurance Industry* (1985), pp. 39–41; and Ernst & Whinney, "Qualification as a Life Insurance Contract," No. K 58236, December 21, 1984.

guaranteed in the contract. The mortality charges are based on those specified in the contract or, if not specified, the mortality charges used in determining statutory reserves for that contract.

The second test, intended for universal life and related policies, requires that both a guideline premium and a death benefit requirement be met:

- The **guideline premium requirement** is met if the cumulative premiums paid under the contract do not exceed, at any time, the greater of the "guideline single premium" or the sum of the "guideline level premiums" at that time. The guideline single premium is computed using interest at the greater of 6 percent or the rate guaranteed in the contract. Mortality charges are based on those specified in the contract or, if not specified, the mortality charges used in determining statutory reserves for that contract. The guideline level premium is computed in a manner similar to the guideline single premium except that the minimum interest rate is 4 percent rather than 6 percent.

- The **death benefit requirement** is met if death benefits exceed 250 percent of the cash value for an insured of attained age up to age 40, grading down to 100 percent of the cash value at attained age 95. Table 13–2 shows applicable percentages for various ages. Thus, if a 35-year old owns a cash value policy whose cash value is $10,000, the policy death benefit must be at least $25,000 ($10,000 × 250%) for the policy to meet the death benefit requirement.

TABLE 13-2. IRC Section 7702 "corridor" requirements of selected ages

Age	Factor (%)
0–40	250
45	215
50	185
55	150
60	130
65	120
70	115
75	105
90	105
95	100

Computational Rules. The law provides several significant rules for calculations related to the qualification tests above. For one, any future net amount at risk cannot exceed the net amount at risk existing when the policy was issued. In addition, when future policy benefits are changed

(e.g., a scheduled change in death benefits or the purchase of paid-up additions), a new calculation must be made to determine whether the policy continues to qualify as life insurance.

The 1984 Act requires that, for purposes of the definitional tests, the policy maturity age must be assumed to be between ages 95 and 100. This rule generally prevents policies endowing before age 95 from qualifying as life insurance. The new definition of life insurance generally applies to policies issued after December 31, 1984.

If the policy fails to meet the definitional tests, a part of the increase in the net surrender value (cash value less surrender charges) during a year can be subjected to ordinary income taxation. A taxable amount will result if the "benefits" received under a life insurance policy exceed the premium paid for the year. "Benefits" are the sum of (1) increase in net surrender value, (2) cost of pure life insurance protection, and (3) dividends received. The cost of the pure insurance protection is the lesser of the cost determined by multiplying the net amount at risk by (1) the applicable IRS uniform premium rate or (2) the mortality charge, if any, stated in the contract.

If a life insurance policy meets the definitional requirements originally but later does not do so, all prior years' deferred income is to be included in the taxpayer's/policyowner's gross income. Obviously, both the agent (or other planner) and the policyowner must rely heavily on the life insurance company to ensure that the policy does not inadvertently fail to meet the IRC definition. Companies are and should be capable of providing such guidance.

Failure to meet the IRC definition also excludes the cash value portion of any life insurance policy from the favorable IRC Section 101(a)(1) treatment; i.e., the cash value portion is not treated as "death proceeds." The net amount at risk of such policies would, however, qualify for Section 101(a)(1) treatment.

INCOME TAX TREATEMENT OF ANNUITIES

Tax rules on annuities have changed over the past few years in an attempt to discourage the use of annuities as short-term tax deferred investments rather than as long-term retirement funding vehicles.

Tax Treatment during Accumulation Period

Pre-TRA '86 law provided, in general, that interest credited to annuity cash values accumulated on a tax-deferred basis. TRA '86 maintained this treatment for *personally-owned* annuities but changed the tax treatment for annuity contracts owned by corporations and other entities. With some exceptions, interest credited on contributions made after February 28, 1986 to such a corporate-owned (or similarly-owned) annuity contract is taxable to the contract owner. This new rule does not apply to such entity-owned annuities that are held under tax qualified retirement plans and certain other situations (IRC Section 72(u)). Thus with the exceptions noted below, the owner of a personal annuity will not have to include this interest income in his or her gross income until such time as annuity liquidation begins.

However, any dividends paid, cash value withdrawals, loans, and amounts received on partial surrender of an annuity will be taxable as ordinary income to the extent that the contract cash value exceeds the cost basis (usually, the premiums paid). The balance is received as a recovery of investment and is tax free. This rule is different from that which applies to qualified life insurance contracts. This rule applies to contracts effective and contributions made after August 13, 1982.

Amounts received on contracts effective before August 14, 1982 are taxed under the cost recovery rule, whereby the owner/taxpayer can recover tax free an amount equal to his or her investment in the contract. Only after full recovery of the basis are further withdrawals taxable. Much of the former tax abuse through annuities centered around this favorable rule.

Not only must post-1982 annuities and contributions follow the interest first rule, a further 10 percent penalty may be imposed on taxable payments received in taxable years beginning after December 31, 1986 under an annuity.[22] The penalty does not apply to (1) a series of substantially equal periodic lifetime payments, (2) any payments made to the contract owner (or annuitant) who is at least 59½ years old, or (3) any

payments under a "qualified" retirement plan. Also, withdrawals because of death or disability do not incur the penalty.

Tax Treatment during Liquidation Period

The income tax rules for taxation of annuity payouts are identical in principle to those discussed earlier with respect to life insurance settlement options. Therefore, emphasis will be placed here only on the differences in treatment.

An **exclusion ratio** must be derived. This is the ratio of the **investment in the contract** to the **expected return** under the contract. The resulting ratio, when multiplied by the amount of each guaranteed payment, represents the amount of each annuity payment that can be excluded from gross income. The balance of the payment is taxable income.

TRA '86 changed the applicability of the exclusion ratio. If the annuity liquidation period begins *before* January 1, 1987, the exclusion ratio applies to *all* payments received throughout the entire payment period, even after the annuitant has recovered an amount equal to his or her investment. This treatment is identical in principle to that of settlement options.

However, if the annuity liquidation period begins *after* December 31, 1986, the exclusion ratio applies only to payments received until an amount equal to the investment in the contract is received. Payments received after recovery of the contract investment are fully taxable (IRC Section 72(b)).

The investment in the contract normally is the premium cost, net of dividends *received* and not previously taxed. Under settlement options, the death proceeds constitute the contract investment. The expected return of the contract is, in general, the total amount the annuitant can expect to receive under the contract.

The tax treatment of the fixed period and fixed amount annuity payout options is the same as the equivalent settlement option. The tax treatment of the life income options is the equivalent to the life income settlement options, with two exceptions. First, the $1,000 per year surviving spouse exclusion does not apply. Second, instead of using life expectancy and other mortality information supplied by the insurer, the annuitant

---

[22] A 5 percent penalty is imposed on certain other withdrawals. See *Tax Facts*, pp. 6–8.

must use the special IRS tables designed for this purpose.[23]

ESTATE TAX TREATMENT OF LIFE INSURANCE AND ANNUITIES

Life insurance and annuity death proceeds often are subject to federal estate taxation. To understand how estate taxation applies to these death proceeds, a basic understanding of the mechanics of the federal estate tax law is necessary. Moreover, and often of greater importance, it is important to understand how life insurance can be a creative and flexible financial tool in the overall estate planning process. This section introduces the reader to the details of estate taxation. The following chapter examines estate planning and some of the uses of life insurance in estate planning.

Overview of Federal Estate Tax

The federal estate tax is a tax on a person's right to transfer property on his or her death. Although not a tax on the property itself, it is calculated on the value of such property. The tax, introduced at a modest level in 1916, can be of great importance in relatively large estates. Generally, anyone who dies in 1987 or later leaving a gross estate of greater than $600,000 must file a federal estate tax return (Form 706). Amounts are lower for deaths occurring before 1987.

The federal estate tax is a graduated tax, starting at 18 percent, building to a 55 percent marginal rate for amounts over $2.5 million. As of 1988, the highest marginal rate will be 50 percent. The maximum rate formerly was 70 percent, but since 1981, a scaling down of rates has occurred.

The first step in calculating the federal estate tax owed is to measure the value of the decedent's **gross estate.** The gross estate is, roughly, the value of all property or interests in property owned or controlled by the deceased person.

Next, **allowable deductions** are subtracted from the gross estate. The result is the **taxable estate.** Allowable deductions include funeral and administration expenses, debts of the decedent, as well as bequests to charities and the surviving spouse.[24]

To the taxable estate is added **adjusted taxable gifts,** which are gifts made after 1976. The sum is referred to here as the **computational tax base.** The reason for this addition is that the current estate tax law is a so-called "unified" transfer tax law that applies to both transfers made at death and transfers made during life. It is necessary to add the value of lifetime transfers (gifts) back to the tax base to arrive at the appropriate marginal tax bracket. As will be seen, however, a credit can be taken for prior gift taxes paid.

The appropriate **tax rate** is then applied to the computational tax base to derive the **tentative federal estate tax.** This figure is only "tentative," as from it may be subtracted certain **credits** for gift and other taxes paid as well as the so-called **unified credit.** The unified credit is available by law to everyone and, as of 1987 and later, can offset up to $192,000 of transfer (both estate and gift) taxes. The practical effect of this unified credit is to eliminate all taxes on estates whose computational tax base is $600,000 or less.

After applying all applicable credits against the tentative federal estate tax, one arrives at the amount of **federal estate taxes owed.** The federal government expects to receive this amount of money within nine months of the decedent's death. An extension of up to 12 additional months can be granted by the IRS in unusual circumstances. Table 13–3 summarizes the preceding steps. Under each major category are found the relevant items that compose the category together with the applicable IRC section. The balance of this section will present somewhat more detailed information regarding the federal estate tax, starting with an elaboration of the composition of the gross estate.

---

[23]See, generally, IRS Reg. Section 1.72.

[24]The gross estate less all allowable deductions *except* bequests to the surviving spouse and to charities is referred to as the **adjusted gross estate.**

TABLE 13-3. Federal estate tax computation

Gross Estate	−	Allowable Deductions	=	Taxable Estate	+	Adjusted Taxable Gifts	=	Computational Tax Base	×	Tax Rate	=	Tentative FET	−	Credits	=	Federal Estate Tax
Owned Property (Sec. 2033)		Funeral Expenses [Sec. 2053(a)(1)]				Gifts made after 1976 that are not otherwise includable in the gross estate, net of annual exclusions taken [Sec. 2011(b)]				See Table 13–4 [Sec. 2001(c)]				Unified Credit (Sec. 2010)		
Dower and Curtesy Interests (Sec. 2034)		Administration Expenses [Sec. 2053(a)(2)]												State Death Taxes Paid (Sec. 2011) See Table 13–5		
Gifts within 3 Years of Death (Sec. 2035)		Claims against Estate [Sec. 2053(a)(3)]												Gift Taxes Paid (Sec. 2012)		
Gifts with Life Interest Retained (Sec. 2036)		Mortgages and Other Debts [Sec. 2053(a)(4)]												Previous FET Paid (Sec. 2013)		
Gifts Taking Effect at Death (Sec. 2037)		Unreimbursed Casualty and Theft Losses (Sec. 2054)												Foreign Death Taxes Paid (Sec. 2014)		
Revocable Gifts (Sec. 2038)		Charitable, Public, and Religious Bequests (Sec. 2055)														
Annuities (Sec. 2039)		Bequests to Surviving Spouse (Sec. 2056)														
Joint Interests (Sec. 2040)																
Powers of Appointment (Sec. 2041)																
Life Insurance Death Proceeds (Sec. 2042)																
Transfers for Insufficient Consideration (Sec. 2043)																
Certain Marital Deduction Property (Sec. 2044)																

Gross Estate

The gross estate, the starting point for estate tax computation, is composed of the value of the decedent's interest in all property. Outright ownership of property is not required for its value to be includable in the gross estate.

The value for estate tax purposes is the **fair market value** of the property at the date of death or, if a lower estate value would result (because of investment losses, etc.), six months after death—the so-called **alternate valuation date.** A penalty of from 10 to 30 percent of the amount of tax owed can be imposed by the IRS for undervaluation. Special valuation rules are available for property used for farming purposes and for closely held businesses.[25]

The gross estate is derived by summing the values of each of the categories shown under Gross Estate in Table 13-3. Some are reviewed briefly below.

Property Owned by the Decedent (Section 2033). This category includes all property of the decedent passing by will or by the state's intestacy laws if the decedent died without a valid will. Thus, the value of all personal property, such as personal effects, automobiles, jewelry, and so on, and of real property, such as one's home, vacant land, business, and so on, are included within this category. For most persons, this is the largest single category of the gross estate. If the decedent had owned a life insurance policy *on someone else's life* (i.e., the decedent was not the insured), the policy *cash value* would be included in the decedent's gross estate under this section.

Certain Gifts. The IRC provides that the value of certain classes of gifts also must be included in the gross estate. They fall into four categories.

First, certain gifts (IRC Section 2035) made by the decedent within three years of his or her death are to be "brought back" into the gross estate. These include transfers in which the donor/decedent had retained certain interest in or power over the gifted property and gifts of life insurance policies.[26] Gift taxation is discussed below.

Second, gifts with a life interest retained (Section 2036) are brought back into the gross estate. Such gifts are those where the decedent had gifted property to someone else but had retained for life the right to receive income from the property, the right to use the property, or the right to designate who ultimately would receive the property or income. For example, assume that a mother gave her house to her children but had retained the right to live in the house for the rest of her life. Section 2036 of the IRC would require that the value of the house must be included in the mother's gross estate.

Third, gifts taking effect at death (Section 2037) may be includable in the gross estate. A gift taking effect at death occurs when property is given to someone (in trust or otherwise) but with the stipulation that they may take possession or enjoyment of it only upon the donor's death. If the likelihood of the gift reverting to the donor immediately before death is greater than 5 percent, the entire value is includable in the gross estate. For example, assume that a grandfather established a trust for his granddaughter with the trust corpus (assets) to be paid to her on his death, but if she predeceased him, the corpus is to revert to him. If just before the grandfather died, there had been a greater than 5 percent chance that he would have survived the granddaughter, the value of the entire gift would be includable in his gross estate.

Fourth, gifts made by the decedent wherein he or she retained the power to alter, amend, revoke, or terminate the gift are revocable gifts (Section 2038) and are includable in the gross estate.

Annuities (Section 2039). If a decedent was receiving annuity payments at his or her death—either from purchase of an annuity or under a life insurance policy settlement option—and if those payments ceased at the annuitant's death, there is no property interest to include in the gross estate. Annuity and settlement option payouts often provide for a refund or guaranteed

---

[25]IRC Section 2032A.

[26]See *Tax Facts,* pp. 547–548.

income feature and many are of the joint and survivor type.[27] If income (or other) payments are to be made to another person on the annuitant's death, the present value of those survivor benefits might be includable in the estate.

A **premium payment test** is applied to determine the extent to which such survivor benefits are to be included in the decedent's gross estate. If the decedent paid no part of the contract purchase price, the entire value of the survivor benefits is *excluded* from the gross estate. If the decedent paid the full contract purchase price, the opposite result occurs. If the decedent paid only a part of the purchase price, that proportionate share of the survivor benefit is included in the gross estate.

For example, assume that the decedent contributed the full $50,000 toward the purchase of a joint and last survivor annuity and the value of the survivor benefit on the decedent's death was determined to be $40,000.[28] The entire $40,000 would be includable in the decedent's estate. If the decedent had paid one-fourth of the purchase price, $10,000 would be includable, and if the full purchase price had been contributed by the survivor, no part of the survivor benefit would be included in the decedent's gross estate.

The cash value of an annuity *during its accumulation period* would be includable in the decedent's estate under this Code section if, and to the extent that, the decedent had made contributions toward its purchase. As of the 1984 tax law changes, the value of any *qualified* retirement annuity is now included in the gross estate. Formerly, its value up to a maximum of $100,000 could be excluded.

Joint Interest Property (Section 2040). Property owned jointly by the deceased person and someone else, referred to as **joint interest property** under the IRC, is includable, in whole or in part, in the decedent's gross estate. The extent to which such property is includable is a function of the nature of the ownership interest.

Although state variations are great, in general, four types of joint ownership are found.

Property is held in **joint tenancy** when it is owned by two or more persons and, on the death of any one of the owners, his or her ownership interest passes automatically to the surviving owners. Ownership is not considered as vested in the individuals but as vested in the owners as a group. As such, 100 percent of the property's value is includable in the decedent's gross estate, *except* for the extent to which the survivors contributed to the property's purchase. Thus, if the decedent's estate, on whom the burden rests, can prove survivors contributed $80,000 toward a $100,000 property purchase price, only 20 percent of the property's current value would be includable in the decedent's estate. Under a joint tenancy, the decedent's heirs have no claims against the property; the surviving owners continue to be the sole owners but as a group. Ownership interest arising from a joint tenancy is not and cannot be passed by will.

A **tenancy by the entirety** is a joint ownership of property between spouses. Like the joint tenancy, it provides a right of survivorship. Unlike the joint tenancy, however, the property is deemed to be owned 50 percent by each spouse, irrespective of who contributed the purchase price. Thus, 50 percent of the then property value is includable in the gross estate of the first spouse to die. Ownership interest does not pass by will but rather by the nature of the ownership.

A **tenancy in common** is a joint-ownership arrangement wherein each member owns his or her share outright—not as a member of the group—and wherein his or her ownership interest can be passed to heirs by will. On the death of a member of a tenancy in common, his or her proportionate share is includable in the gross estate.

Eight states in the United States have **community property** laws.[29] These laws establish that property acquired during marriage is the property of the marriage "community" and, as such, on the death of one spouse, one-half of the value is includable automatically in the decedent's estate,

---

[27]See Chapters 7 and 9.

[28]Measured by determining the amount that the same insurance company would charge the survivor, based on his or her attained age, for a single life annuity.

[29]The community property states are Arizona, California, Idaho, Louisiana, Nevada, New Mexico, Texas, and Washington.

irrespective of the proportions of the purchase price paid by the decedent.

Power of Appointment (Section 2041). If a decedent held a **general power of appointment** over property on his or her death, the value of the property is includable in the gross estate. A general power of appointment exists when the individual has the right to dispose of the property that he or she does not own *and* could make the disposition in favor of himself or herself. For example, a beneficiary may be receiving a lifetime income under a trust and have the power to withdraw all or a portion of the trust corpus during his or her lifetime. This right to "invade" the trust corpus is a general power of appointment and will cause the entire value of the trust to be includable in the beneficiary's gross estate on death, even though the beneficiary may never have actually exercised the withdrawal right.

A **special power of appointment,** wherein the individual has the power to appoint anyone *other than* himself or herself or his or her estate to receive property, does not cause property to be includable in the gross estate. Also, property over which an individual has a general power of appointment will not be includable in the gross estate if the holder's right to consume or invade the property is limited by defined standards relating to his or her health, maintenance, education or support.

Life Insurance (Section 2042). IRC Section 2042 provides that life insurance death proceeds are includable in a decedent/insured's gross estate for federal estate tax purposes where (1) the proceeds are payable to or for the benefit of the decedent's estate, or (2) the insured possessed, at death, any incidents of ownership in the policy.[30]

Thus, even if the insured did not own the policy, the death proceeds would be includable in his or her gross estate if it received the proceeds, either because it was named beneficiary or because no named beneficiary was eligible (e.g., all named beneficiaries predeceased the in-

sured). Also, proceeds payable, not "to" but "for" the benefit of the decedent's estate are includable in the gross estate. For example, assume that Glen is the owner and beneficiary of a $250,000 policy on Thelma's (his wife) life and that he collaterally assigns the policy to a bank to cover her loan of $100,000. If she dies, the $100,000 debt—which would be includable as an estate liability—would be paid off. The $100,000 death proceeds utilized to extinguish the estate's debt is therefore includable in the wife's estate even though the husband was both owner and beneficiary of the policy.

If the deceased insured possessed no incidents of ownership in the policy and if proceeds are not payable to or for the benefit of the estate, proceeds escape inclusion in the gross estate. Incidents of ownership include the right to change the beneficiary, the right to surrender or otherwise terminate the policy, the right to assign the policy, the right to obtain a policy loan, or, in general, the ability to exercise any important right of the policy. Complete policy ownership certainly will cause death proceeds to be includable in the estate but possession of only one important policy right—even without total ownership—normally will also cause the entire proceeds to be includable in the gross estate.

A policy can be removed from the gross estate even though the insured was the owner if it is given to someone else via absolute assignment (and provided that proceeds are not payable to or for the benefit of the estate). However, if the ownership transfer occurs within three years of the date of death, the policy proceeds, in whole or in part, will be includable in the gross estate as a gift made within three years of death (IRC Section 2035). If the donor (previous owner) continues to pay premiums on the policy, the entire death proceeds would be includable. If the donee (new owner) pays premiums after transfer, proceeds equal to the ratio of premiums paid by the donee to total premiums paid would be excluded from the decedent's gross estate.[31]

---

[30]The reader is reminded that IRC Section 101(a)(1) exempts life insurance death proceeds from *income* taxation. IRC Section 2042 concerns *estate* taxation.

[31]This area can become complex. See *Tax Facts,* pp. 430–438. Also, policy proceeds can be includable in the gross estate if the transfer falls within one of the rules of IRC Sections 2035, 2038, or 2041.

Miscellaneous. Certain other interests are includable in the gross estate: (1) dower and curtesy interests (Section 2034), (2) transfers for insufficient consideration (Section 2043), and (3) certain marital deduction property (Section 2044). A dower (for the wife) or a curtesy (for the husband) is a statutory requirement directing that a surviving spouse must receive at least a certain minimum proportion of the estate of the deceased spouse. Transfers for insufficient considerations are those wherein the amount paid for property was below fair value (e.g., Bettie sold her business to deAnn, her daughter, for below fair market value). The excess of the fair market value over the consideration received is includable in the gross estate.

The Taxable Estate

After arriving at a value for the gross estate, the next step is to derive a value for the taxable estate. The taxable estate is the gross estate less allowable deductions. IRC Sections 2053–2056 define these deductions. Each of these four sections is discussed below.

Expenses, Debts, and Claims (Section 2053). Deductions are permitted for the cost of the decedent's funeral and for the expenses associated with the administration of the estate. The latter expenses include appraisal fees, attorney's fees, executor's commissions, and the like.

Claims against the estate—such as those arising from unpaid property, income, and other taxes owed prior to death—are deductible. Indebtedness of the decedent can be deducted provided that the asset (if any) to which the indebtedness applies is included in the estate. Thus, mortgage and auto loan balances at time of death are deductible. Other debts, such as those arising from consumer loans and charge card balances, are also deductible provided that the decedent is legally responsible for the payment.

Unreimbursed Losses (Section 2054). Casualty and theft losses incurred during estate settlement are deductible from the gross estate. If the loss is indemnified by insurance or otherwise, only the net loss is deductible.

Charitable and Related Bequests (Section 2055). Property left to qualified religious, charitable, scientific, literary, and educational organizations as well as property left to foster amateur sports competition and the prevention of cruelty to children or animals is deductible. Additionally, bequests to qualified veterans' organizations are deductible.

Bequests to Surviving Spouse (Section 2056). For most families, the deduction permitted for property left to a surviving spouse is the most important permissible deduction. This **marital deduction** permits a deduction from the gross estate of any property passing to the surviving spouse.[32] Thus, if all net estate assets are left to the surviving spouse, the taxable estate is zero.

Certain property may not qualify for the marital deduction even though it is left for the spouse's benefit. For example, if a wife's will provides that the surviving husband will receive income from a business for as long as he lives but that upon his death, the entire business passes to her daughter, the property is considered **terminable interest property** and, as such, does not qualify for the marital deduction. In general, a property interest that passes to a surviving spouse but which would not be includable in the spouse's estate is terminable interest property and fails to qualify for the marital deduction.

Certain qualified terminable interest property does, however, qualify. In general, such property is that which passes to the surviving spouse and (1) the surviving spouse is entitled to a lifetime income payable at least annually from the property, and (2) no one (including the spouse) has the power to appoint any part of the property to anyone other than the spouse during the spouse's lifetime.

Computational Tax Base

To the taxable estate is then added the value of adjusted taxable gifts to derive a computational

---

[32]Prior to 1982, the marital deduction was limited to one-half of the adjusted gross estate. The adjusted gross estate is the gross estate less deductions *other than* those for charitable and spousal bequests. This 50 percent test no longer applies.

tax base. Adjusted taxable gifts are those made after 1976 for which a gift tax return was filed, which are not otherwise includable in the decedent's gross estate, and net of permitted exclusions.

As mentioned earlier, the current estate tax law is a transfer tax law in that it applies to both living and testamentary (i.e., death) transfers. This "unified" approach means that it is necessary to add back for estate tax purposes the value of property transferred during life. This permits the calculation of a tax based on all transfers, both living and testamentary. A credit is permitted—as discussed below—for previous gift taxes paid, but since the unified transfer tax is a progressive tax, a recalculation is necessary.

Individuals are permitted to give away annually up to $10,000 per donee (gift recipient) and not pay any gift tax or even file a return. If a spouse joins in the gift, up to $20,000 per donee annually may be given without incurring any gift tax. Moreover, one spouse may give the other any amount and incur no transfer tax liability as the marital deduction is available for such gifts.

The value of adjusted taxable gifts is the sum of all post-1976 gifts, net of exclusions and deductions. Also, unlike the incomplete gifts includable in the gross estate, gift taxes paid on these adjusted gifts may be excluded from the gross estate. The value included in the computational tax base is the property value at the time of the gift, not its current value.

Tentative Federal Estate Tax

To the computational tax base is applied the appropriate federal estate tax rate to derive the tentative federal estate tax. Table 13-4 gives these transfer tax rates by bracket for the year 1988 and later. For transfers occurring in 1984–1987, the marginal tax rate is 53 percent (rather than 50 percent) for amounts between $2.5 million and $3.0 million and 55 percent for amounts over $3.0 million. Otherwise, the tax brackets and rates are as shown in Table 13-4.

Federal Estate Tax Owed

The actual federal estate tax owed is obtained by netting certain permissible credits against the tentative federal estate tax.

Unified Transfer Tax Credit (Section 2010). Tax law permits a substantial "unified" credit to be applied against estate (and gift) taxes otherwise due. This unified credit is applied on a cumulative basis to all lifetime and testamentary

TABLE 13-4. Estate and gift tax rate schedule effective 1988

If Computational Tax Base		The Tentative Tax Is:		
Is More Than:	But Does Not Exceed:			
$ 0	$ 10,000	18 percent		
10,000	20,000	$1,800	plus 20% of the excess over	$10,000
20,000	40,000	$3,800	plus 22% of the excess over	$20,000
40,000	60,000	$8,200	plus 24% of the excess over	$40,000
60,000	80,000	$13,000	plus 26% of the excess over	$60,000
80,000	100,000	$18,200	plus 28% of the excess over	$80,000
100,000	150,000	$23,800	plus 30% of the excess over	$100,000
150,000	250,000	$38,800	plus 32% of the excess over	$150,000
250,000	500,000	$70,800	plus 34% of the excess over	$250,000
500,000	750,000	$155,800	plus 37% of the excess over	$50,000
750,000	1,000,000	$248,300	plus 39% of the excess over	$750,000
1,000,000	1,250,000	$345,800	plus 41% of the excess over	$1,000,000
1,250,000	1,500,000	$448,300	plus 43% of the excess over	$1,250,000
1,500,000	2,000,000	$555,800	plus 45% of the excess over	$1,500,000
2,000,000	2,500,000	$780,800	plus 49% of the excess over	$2,000,000
2,500,000	No limit	$1,025,800	plus 50% of the excess over	$2,500,000

transfers. It applies as a dollar-for-dollar offset against the tax. Table 13-5 shows that for tax years 1987 and later, the unified transfer credit will be $192,800. The credit is sufficient to avoid all estate taxes on a computational tax base of $600,000.

TABLE 13-5. Unified transfer credits and equivalent exemption amounts

Year	Tax Credit	Equivalent Exemption Amount
1983	$ 79,300	$275,000
1984	96,300	325,000
1985	121,800	400,000
1986	155,800	500,000
1987 and later	192,800	600,000

Credit for State Death Taxes Paid (Section 2011). States levy their own forms of death taxes. The state tax may be on an heir's right to receive property (an **inheritance tax**) or one on a decedent's right to transfer property (an **estate tax**). Whatever form the tax takes, federal law permits a credit against the federal estate tax for death taxes paid to states, subject to a maximum credit. Table 13-6 shows maximum permissible

credits.[33] Those states whose laws would not otherwise develop a tax as high as the permissible federal credit often utilize a **credit estate tax.** These laws stipulate that the state death tax will be the greater of (1) the tax developed by applying the state's computational tax rules, or (2) the maximum credit permitted for state death taxes in federal law.

Credit for Gift Taxes Paid (Section 2012). Previous gift taxes paid can be taken as a credit against the estate tax. This treatment is appropriate since the value of previous gifts is added back into the estate.

Other Credits. Two final credits are permitted. First, to prevent double taxation, a credit is allowable for death taxes paid to a foreign country or U.S. possession if (1) the value of the pro-

[33]The actual IRC table shows figures based on the *adjusted taxable estate* rather than the taxable estate, as shown in Table 13-6. The adjusted taxable estate is the taxable estate reduced by $60,000. This $60,000 adjustment has been included in Table 13-6 to simplify the presentation. Results are unaffected.

TABLE 13-6. Maximum credits for state death taxes

If Taxable Estate Is More Than:	But Does Not Exceed:	The Maximum Credit Is:
$ 0	$ 100,000	0
100,000	150,000	0.8%
150,000	200,000	$400 plus 1.6% of the excess over $150,000
200,000	300,000	$1,200 plus 2.4% of the excess over $200,000
300,000	500,000	$3,600 plus 3.2% of the excess over $300,000
500,000	700,000	$10,000 plus 4% of the excess over $500,000
700,000	900,000	$18,000 plus 4.8% of the excess over $700,000
900,000	1,100,000	$27,600 plus 5.6% of the excess over $900,000
1,100,000	1,600,000	$38,800 plus 6.4% of the excess over $1,100,000
1,600,000	2,100,000	$70,800 plus 7.2% of the excess over $1,600,000
2,100,000	2,600,000	$106,800 plus 8% of the excess over $2,100,000
2,600,000	3,100,000	$146,800 plus 8.8% of the excess over $2,600,000
3,100,000	3,600,000	$190,800 plus 9.6% of the excess over $3,100,000
3,600,000	4,100,000	$238,800 plus 10.4% of the excess over $3,600,000
4,100,000	5,100,000	$290,800 plus 11.2% of the excess over $4,100,000
5,100,000	6,100,000	$402,800 plus 12% of the excess over $5,100,000
6,100,000	7,100,000	$522,800 plus 12.8% of the excess over $6,100,000
7,100,000	8,100,000	$650,800 plus 13.6% of the excess over $7,100,000
8,100,000	9,100,000	$786,800 plus 14.4% of the excess over $8,100,000
9,100,000	10,100,000	$930,800 plus 15.2% of the excess over $9,100,000
10,100,000	No limit	$1,082,800 plus 16% of the excess over $10,100,000

perty is includable in the gross estate, and (2) the property is situated in that foreign country or possession.

Second, it sometimes happens that one person leaves property to another and the second dies within a short time of the first person's death. If estate tax was paid by the first decedent on the property left to the second decedent, part or all of that tax may be available as a credit against the estate tax bill of the second decedent. The permissible credit, a function of the time elapsed between the deaths, is a decreasing percentage of the estate tax paid on the first death transfer:

- 100% if deaths occur within two years
- 80% if deaths occur within three or four years
- 60% if deaths occur within five or six years
- 40% if deaths occur within seven or eight years
- 20% if deaths occur within nine or 10 years
- 0% if deaths occur 10 or more years apart

Illustration

An illustration will be used to try to "unify" the preceding points. Assume Mike Magnus, age 48 and a resident of Georgia, dies in 1988, leaving behind his wife, Dawn, and their two children, Lexi and Cary, both adults.

Table 13–7 shows the personal balance sheet for Mike and Dawn prepared with the help of their agent, just before Mike's death. The current market values and the nature of the ownership interests are given. Dawn is named as beneficiary under the annuity.

In addition to the assets shown in Table 13–7, Mike was the insured and owner of $100,000 of group life insurance. Dawn is beneficiary. Only two years earlier, Mike had transferred ownership of a $500,000 term life policy to his daughter, Lexi, and she promptly named herself beneficiary. Mike continued to pay premiums on the policy. Four years ago, Mike and Dawn had given their son, Cary, $200,000 to help him start a landscaping business.

Mike's will provides that Dawn should receive the $300,000 in common stock, the autos, and Mike's personal effects. It also provides that the entire mortgage loan is to be paid off. The real estate investment (a $1,000,000 office complex) is to be held in trust for the children with Dawn receiving the income from the investment for her lifetime. She is given no rights to alter this

TABLE 13-7. Personal balance sheet of Mike and Dawn Magnus

	Market Value	Nature of Ownership/Liability
Assets		
Residence	$ 200,000	Tenants by the entirety
Common stock	300,000	Mike
Corporate bonds	200,000	Mike
Vacant land	300,000	Dawn
Real estate investments	1,000,000	Mike
Annuity cash values	300,000	Mike
Personal effects	50,000	Dawn
Personal effects	50,000	Mike
Checking and savings account	40,000	Tenants by the entirety
Autos	40,000	Mike
Total assets	$2,480,000	
Liabilities		
Home mortgage	$ 100,000	Tenants by the entirety
Charge-card balance	5,000	Dawn
Charge-card balance	5,000	Mike
Auto loans	20,000	Mike
Total liabilities	$ 130,000	
Net worth (assets less liabilities)	$2,350,000	

trust arrangement. He stipulated that Georgia State University was to receive $10,000 for its music program. The balance of the estate is to be divided equally between his two children.

The value of items includable in Mike's gross estate is summarized as follows:

Item	Value	Justification
Residence	$ 100,000	Dawn considered as owning 50% of value (Section 2040)
Common stock	300,000	Ownership (Section 2033)
Corporate bonds	200,000	Ownership (Section 2033)
Real estate investment	1,000,000	Ownership (Section 2033)
Annuity cash value	300,000	Annuity (Section 2039)
Personal effects	50,000	Ownership (Section 2033)
Checking/savings account	20,000	Dawn considered as owning 50% of value (Section 2040)
Autos	40,000	Ownership (Section 2033)
Group life insurance	100,000	Life insurance with incidents of ownership by insured (Section 2042)
Personal life insurance	500,000	Gift made within three years of death (Section 2035)
	$2,610,000	

Allowable deductions would be as follows:

Item		Amount	Justification
Funeral expenses		$ 5,000	IRC Section 2053(a)(1)
Administration expenses		90,000	IRC Section 2053(a)(2)
Claims against estate		10,000	Income and property taxes, IRC Section 2053(a)(3)
Debts		125,000	Mortgage plus $5,000 charge balance and $20,000 auto loan. IRC Section 2053(a)(4)
Charitable bequests		10,000	IRC Section 2055
Marital deduction	300,000		Common stock
	40,000		Autos
	50,000		Personal effects
	100,000		His share of residence
	20,000		His share of checking/savings
	100,000		Group life insurance
		$610,000	Total: IRC Section 2056
Total		$850,000	

Thus, the taxable estate is:

Gross estate	$2,610,000
Less: Allowable deductions	850,000
Taxable estate	$1,760,000

To the taxable estate of $1,760,000 would be added the value of adjusted taxable gifts. The $500,000 term policy given to the daughter does not fall within this category. The $200,000 given jointly by Mike and Dawn to Cary is includable as an adjusted taxable gift but only to the extent of one-half of the value of the gift (because it was a joint gift) and only after taking the $10,000 annual gift exclusion.

Thus, the computational tax base is:

Taxable estate	$1,760,000
Plus: Adjusted taxable gifts	90,000
Computational tax base	$1,850,000

We now use the $1.5–2 million bracket of Table 13–4 to determine that the tentative federal estate tax is (1) $555,800 plus (2) 45 percent of the excess of $1,500,000 (the $350,000) or $157,500, for a total of $713,300.

Credits available to offset the tentative tax are (1) the unified transfer credit and (2) the state death tax credit. The gift tax credit is not available, as no gift taxes actually were paid on the earlier gifts.

Using Table 13-5, we determine the maximum unified credit to be $192,800 and from Table 13-6, the maximum state death tax credit to be $70,800 (first $1.6 million) plus 7.2 percent of the excess of the *taxable* estate, or $11,520 ($160,003 ×7.2%) for a total of $82,320.

Thus, the federal estate tax actually owed would be calculated as follows:

Tentative federal estate tax	$ 713,300
Less: Unified credit	−192,800
Less: State death tax credit	−82,320
Federal estate tax owed	$438,180

It is instructive, at this point, to summarize the cash needs of Mike's estate. They derive from amounts needed to:

Pay off mortgage	$100,000
Pay off Mike's charge-card balance	5,000
Pay off auto loans	20,000
Pay funeral expenses	5,000
Pay administration expenses	90,000
Settle estate claims	10,000
Charitable bequests	10,000
Pay state death taxes	82,320
Pay federal estate taxes	438,180
Total liquid needs	$760,500

This amount must be paid by Mike's executor from estate resources. Even though the estate net worth is considerable, the estate's liquidity is not as great as might have been desired. Assuming that the property distribution directed by his will is to be followed, the only remaining liquid assets in the estate are the corporate bonds of $200,000, clearly insufficient to cover the $760,500 cash needs. This means that other assets must be liquidated to settle the estate's obligations and the estate's obligations must be met *before* distribution of property to the heirs. It should be noted that the *entire* estate tax obligation could have been eliminated had Mike's will directed that optimum advantage be taken of the marital deduction. This oversight could be an example of poor planning. This and other problems are discussed more fully in Chapter 14.

THE GIFT TAX TREATMENT OF LIFE INSURANCE AND ANNUITIES[34]

The federal gift tax, like the federal estate tax, is imposed upon the right of transferring property to another. The estate tax reaches those transfers that take place when a property owner dies, whereas the gift tax reaches those transfers that take place during the property owner's lifetime.

Despite the imposition of this tax, there can be certain advantages to making gifts. Since life insurance policies often are the subject of gifts, the planner should be aware of the gift tax ramifications. To understand these, an overview of the general provisions of the gift tax law will be presented. There follows an examination of the gift tax treatment of life insurance in particular. Chapter 14 examines the planning aspects of gifts in more detail.

Overview of Federal Gift Tax Law

A lifetime gift to an individual incurs a federal gift tax generally at the same rate as the federal estate tax. The unified rate schedule in Table 13-4 shows the tentative tax relating both to taxable estate transfers and to taxable gifts. Similar to the estate tax situation just covered, the unified credit shown in Table 13-5 is applied directly to reduce the tentative gift tax shown.

The amount of gift tax payable in a specific taxable period is determined by a four-step process:

1. Add all of the donor's lifetime taxable gifts, including prior gifts and current gifts. Taxable gifts do not include the $10,000 per year per donee exclusion.

2. Apply the unified rate schedule to the total taxable gifts to reach the tentative tax.

3. Subtract the taxes actually paid on the lifetime transfers made for past taxable periods, based on the unified rate schedule.

4. Subtract the unified estate and gift tax credit. The result is the gift tax payable in the current period.

[34]This section draws from "Taxation of Life Insurance," *A Survey of Advanced Sales* (Indianapolis, Ind.: The Research and Review Service of America, Inc., 1981), pp. 19-23.

At the time the unified rate schedule replaced the prior gift tax law, certain transitional rules had the effect of reducing the unified credit on certain prior gifts. For purposes of discussion here, it can be stated that generally, the unified credit shown in Table 13–5 will apply to the majority of cases encountered.

Gift Tax Exclusion. The federal gift tax law is not aimed at the usual exchange of gifts associated with birthdays, holidays, and similar occasions. Therefore, the law permits the donor to make this type of gift, beginning in 1982, without tax by excluding the first $10,000 of outright gifts in any one year to any one recipient.

This annual $10,000 exclusion applies to gifts made to each recipient, no matter how many are included in the donor's plans each year. Moreover, it is available year after year. This means that an individual could give $10,000 each to an infinite number of recipients each year without incurring any gift tax liability.

The exclusion is applied to each donee individually, and if a donee receives less than $10,000, the exclusion is limited to the actual amount of the gift. So if Bill gives $9,000 to Beverly and $11,000 to Peggy, Bill can exclude only $19,000 ($9,000 for Beverly and $10,000 for Peggy) and would have $1,000 in taxable gifts for the year.

The annual exclusion is available only where the gift is one of a **present interest** in property. This means that the donee must have possession or enjoyment of the property immediately rather than at some future date. The exclusion is not available in connection with gifts of **future interests** in property. This term covers any interest in property that does not pass into the donee's possession or enjoyment until some future date.

The "Gift-Splitting" Privilege. When married residents of community property states make a gift, the gift is usually considered as being one-half from each spouse. This is, of course, because each usually is considered the owner of a one-half interest in the community property. In accord with the general plan of equalizing the tax treatment in community and noncommunity property states, the gift tax law contains a provision allowing married couples to "split" their gifts. Thus, where a married individual makes a gift of personal property to someone other than a spouse, it may be regarded as made one-half by each spouse. This privilege of "splitting" a gift when made to a third party is extended only to property given away by a husband or wife. If the property was owned by the husband, for instance, his gift tax return will show the total gift, and then subtract one-half thereof as a gift made by his spouse. This, in effect, gives the taxpayer the advantage of doubling the annual exclusion. Therefore, a married individual can make gifts of $20,000 per year to any one beneficiary without incurring any gift tax liability if the spouse consents to splitting the gift.

Deductions. Like the federal estate tax marital deduction, the **gift tax marital deduction** permits tax-free transfers between spouses. This deduction is available without limit.

Just as with the federal estate tax, the gift tax law permits full deduction for gifts to qualified charities. Such charitable organizations generally are of the same type as those mentioned previously in the discussion of the estate tax charitable deduction. Gifts to private individuals can never qualify for the charitable deduction, no matter how needy or deserving the beneficiaries may be.

Gifts of Life Insurance

Life insurance is often the subject of gifts. In fact, a life insurance policy is especially well suited for gifts. The general subject of gifts of life insurance includes gifts of the policy itself, gifts of premium payments, and gifts of policy proceeds. Each of these will be dealt with individually, since the valuation of each differs.

Gift of Life Insurance Contract. If an insured purchases a life insurance policy and retains no ownership interest in the policy whatsoever, the insured has made a gift of the policy. Similarly, a policyowner who irrevocably assigns all of his or her rights in an existing policy has made a gift of the policy.

If a donor takes out a new policy (either annual premium or single premium) and has it

issued initially in the name of a donee, the value of the gift equals the gross premium that the donor has paid. If the policy is an annual premium contract and the donor continues to make premium payments, each premium the donor pays thereafter will be a gift in that amount.

If a donor gives a donee a single premium or paid-up life insurance policy which was issued in a prior year, the value of the gift equals the **replacement cost** of the policy. The replacement cost of a policy is equal to the single premium that an insurance company would charge for a comparable contract issued at the insured's attained age.

If a donor gives a donee a life insurance policy that was issued in some previous year, and upon which premiums remain to be paid, the replacement cost of the policy may be difficult to ascertain. Thus, government regulations provide that the value of the gift will be equal to the policy's **interpolated terminal reserve** (the policy reserve interpolated to the date of the gift), plus the value of unearned premiums and any accumulated dividends, and less any indebtedness against the policy. The reserve value, not the cash surrender value, is considered, although the difference often is negligible except in the early years of a policy. The following example illustrates the computation of a policy's interpolated terminal reserve.

Assume that a gift is made today of a policy whose issue date is 10 years, eight months ago. This year's annual premium of $1,800 was paid on its due date, eight months ago. The tenth and eleventh years' terminal reserves are shown below, together with the computation.

	Eleventh-year terminal reserve	$16,000
Less:	Tenth-year terminal reserve	−13,900
	Increase in reserve	$ 2,100

Thus, the value of the gift will be composed of three parts:

| 1. | Pro rata reserve increase (8/12 of increase of $2,100) | $ 1,400 |

2.	Pro rata annual premium paid (4/12 of premium of $1,800)	600
3.	Beginning year reserve	13,900
	Total gift value	$15,900

Gift of Premiums. When an individual makes premium payments on a life insurance policy that he or she neither owns nor is the insured, the individual has made a taxable gift to the policyowner in an amount equal to the premium paid, subject to the $10,000 annual exclusion. So if John makes a premium payment on a policy owned by Charlotte, and under which Bettie is the beneficiary, John has made a gift to Charlotte in the amount of the premium payment.

On the other hand, premiums paid by an insured are gifts if the insured has no incidents of ownership in the policy and the proceeds of the policy are payable to a beneficiary other than his or her estate. Premiums paid by a beneficiary on a policy he or she also owns are not gifts.

Gift of Insurance Proceeds. Under normal circumstances there is no gift when life insurance proceeds are paid to a beneficiary. However, in some extraordinary instances there may be a taxable gift.

Where one person owns a policy, a second is the insured, and a third is the beneficiary, a gift can be considered as occurring from the policyowner to the beneficiary. The amount of the gift equals the full amount of the insurance proceeds.

Say Nan owns a policy of life insurance on her husband's life, with their children named as revocable beneficiaries. Nan will be deemed to have made a gift to the children in the full amount of the proceeds when they are paid at her husband's death. There is no real intent to make a gift in the literal sense—but a taxable gift has been made nevertheless.

A gift of endowment insurance proceeds also occurs when, upon the maturity of an endowment insurance policy, the proceeds are paid to a revocable beneficiary who is someone other than the owner.

Chapter 14

Life Insurance
in Estate, Retirement,
and Savings Planning

A common misconception is that an estate is only the property that one leaves at death. The term "estate planning" in its broadest sense encompasses the accumulation, conservation, and distribution of an estate. The overall purpose of the estate planning process is to develop a plan that will enhance and maintain the financial security of individuals and their families. Estate planning has come to include lifetime financial planning that may lead to increases in the individual's estate as well as the conservation of existing assets. Estate planning should make provision for financial security during the retirement years as well as the intended and orderly disposition of one's property at death.

Previous chapters have suggested some ways in which life insurance can be useful as a savings instrument and in estate planning. This chapter expands these discussions. Estate planning is discussed first. This includes the nature of the estate planning "team" and the various tools used in estate planning, including life insurance. Retirement planning and uses of life insurance as a savings instrument are discussed next.

ESTATE PLANNING

Impediments to a Well-Planned Estate [1]

Most individuals do not realize that even if they have not created an estate plan and executed the appropriate documents to implement their plans, a plan has been created for them. The plan will be created and imposed on them by the state in which they reside. Each state has its own statutory scheme for the disposition of its citizens' property at death if the resident dies either without a valid will or having made an incomplete disposition of property.

These **intestate succession statutes** are based on degrees of consanguinity (blood relationship) to the decedent rather than on the distribution of property according to the intentions and desires of the deceased individual. Without a will, one may not leave property to

[1]This and the next two sections draw heavily on Susan M. Harmon and Gwenda L. Cannon, "Estate Planning: An Overview," in Susan M. Harmon, ed., *Readings in Estate and Gift Tax Planning,* 2nd ed. (Bryn Mawr, Pa.: The American College, 1983). Used with permission.

charity. Neither may an unrelated friend inherit any property from the deceased. If no relatives exist, the property will be distributed to the state. The property is said to have **escheated** to the state.

A current valid will is essential to having an updated estate plan, and the will should be reviewed periodically to assure that a property owner's most recent intentions are honored at death. If family circumstances or laws have changed dramatically since the will was written, the will's provisions may be seriously out of touch with the property owner's current wishes, but the existing will is the one that will be followed until and unless it is replaced with a later valid will. This situation can produce disturbing results.

The potential estate and gift tax relief that the current federal estate and gift tax laws appear to provide may make many individuals believe that they no longer have a need for a carefully planned estate. The truth is in direct contradiction to this viewpoint—only by utilizing the tax laws to maximum advantage can property owners carry out their postdeath intentions and prevent the unnecessary erosion of their estates due to taxes. For example, the unlimited marital deduction that allows an individual to pass an entire estate to a surviving spouse free of federal gift and estate taxes appears to offer relief from taxation. In reality, use of the unlimited marital deduction may be enormously expensive since property will pass to others unprotected by the marital deduction at the death of the second spouse.

While important tax planning options can be utilized in estate planning, tax relief should not be the primary objective of estate planning. The best estate plan is one that accurately reflects the individual's wishes, needs, and objectives in a manner that minimizes the potential tax liability to the lowest level consistent with the client's aims. This means that various tax options as well as their "cost" in rigidity, loss of control over assets, tax liability, and so on, should be explained to clients to allow them to understand both the costs and benefits of these options and to choose those that reflect their desires and intentions. An estate plan that reduces the estate tax liability to zero is a poor plan if the cost is the perversion of the client's wishes.

Estate tax liability often is predetermined by the form of ownership in which the asset is held prior to the owner's death. An example of an asset that frequently is owned or positioned improperly is life insurance. If the insured retains any incidents of ownership in life insurance, the proceeds are includable in his or her gross estate. This could subject proceeds to unnecessary taxation, although the unlimited marital deduction could make a transfer less necessary. Proper ownership of assets, including life insurance, must be analyzed on a case-by-case basis. Also, there is a danger in transfer if the marriage is less than solid.

Another form of property ownership that can be problematic in estate planning is joint tenancy with right of survivorship. If insufficient thought is given to the way in which assets are titled, all or most property may be owned in this form. This could mean that the surviving spouse would inherit too much of the property relative to the children, possibly resulting in excessive estate tax liabilities at the second death.

Another impediment to effective planning relates to inadequate health insurance. The cost of a protracted period of disability may so erode an otherwise adequate estate that the estate owner leaves nothing to the beneficiaries at death except a burdensome amount of debt. The ownership of adequate health insurance protection is an important consideration in planning any estate. Disability protection, in particular, often is ignored or misunderstood despite the fact that there is a greater likelihood of a significant period of disability before retirement age than there is of an early death.

Still another impediment that should not be underestimated is inflation. At the very least, continuing inflation necessitates periodic reviews of existing estate plans to keep abreast of projected estate tax liabilities, as these can be affected by inflation through "bracket creep" even though the real value of assets has not increased materially. It is also necessary to review asset valuations, projected income from assets held, and amounts of life insurance in terms of constant dollars to assure that the estate owner's family would continue to be adequately protected.

Inadequate liquidity may be a major problem in an otherwise well-planned estate. Three factors are particularly important in assessing liquidity needs in estate planning: (1) the amount and terms of debt of the estate owner, (2) the projected estate tax liability, and (3) the types of assets that comprise the estate.

At the time of an estate owner's death, the amount and terms of debt for which a decedent is personally responsible may dramatically reduce either the actual assets or the net income stream that would be available to the beneficiaries. The same is true of estate tax liabilities.

The type of assets owned at the time of death also will affect the cash available to the beneficiaries for their income needs. For example, when a closely held business is the primary estate asset and has been the principal source of income to the decedent and family through the decedent's salary and bonuses, there is frequently an immediate family cash shortage when salary and bonuses cease. This results in financial stress to a family trying to deal with the death of a family member. Furthermore, if no advance planning is done, assets, including the family business, may have to be sold under disadvantageous market conditions at greatly reduced prices to pay estate bills or taxes. Such situations should be considered prior to their occurrence, and both the estate owner and the family should make appropriate plans to avoid these problems. If the business is to be sold, the arrangements for the sale should be reduced to legally enforceable agreements. Liquidity may be available from retirement plans or life insurance proceeds. Also, salary continuation plans are a possible way to soften the financial shock of a breadwinner's death.

The Estate Planning Process

The estate planning process is identical in principle to the overall financial planning process. First, data must be obtained and objectives established. This would normally be done as a part of the fact finding for the overall personal financial plan. The existing estate plan must be evaluated for potential impairments. Then a plan is designed for, presented to, and approved by the client. After the client reviews and approves the plan, it must be implemented, including the ex-

ecution of any necessary legal documents and transfer of property. Finally, the client should be made aware that there should be a periodic review of the plan to determine if changes in financial positions, family relationships, goals, tax laws, or other circumstances necessitate changes in the plan.

The creation of a comprehensive and creative estate plan is a highly rewarding experience for the estate planning practitioner regardless of the discipline from which he or she emerges. Although the emphasis placed on certain aspects of estate plans will vary depending on the knowledge and background of the practitioner, the primary objective of a good planner should be to effectuate and implement the desires and objectives of the individual for whom the plan is created in an efficient and effective means. The client is the director of the plan. The professionals are the producers. An estate plan reflects the personality of the client. It may evidence his or her cares and concerns for other human beings as well as for himself or herself. Or the plan may reflect his or her own self-interest, grievances, and grudges. Much will be revealed about the client's character, philosophy of life, and attitudes by the types of planning options selected and the reasons for which he or she selects them.

The Estate Planning Team

Individuals from more than one professional discipline are qualified to assist clients in estate planning. The greatest benefit and the best results for a client can be obtained from an approach that enlists a variety of advisors to assist in total financial planning, including estate planning. If, however, the client is interested only in estate planning or only in death planning, the estate planner should perform these tasks. Perhaps the client will become interested in more complete planning through a successful relationship.

The estate planning team has traditionally consisted of an attorney, an insurance specialist, a bank trust officer, an accountant, and an investment counselor. A newer member of the team, who also may be one of the preceding specialists, is the financial planner. It is frequently

the financial planner or the insurance specialist who made the first contact with the client, sensitized him or her to the need for estate planning, and motivated him or her to become involved in the process. This person often acts as coordinator for the entire plan, although any other capable member of the team might fill this role.

The accountant is the advisor most likely to have annual contact with the client through preparation of the client's tax returns. This gives him or her the opportunity to be familiar with the size, amount, and nature of the client's estate. The accountant may be the person who can most easily provide a valuation for any asset in the estate where it is not easily ascertainable. Valuation is particularly crucial if one recommendation in the estate plan is a buy–sell agreement to provide for a transfer of a business interest upon death or disability.[2] The accountant also may be of help in preparing a final estate tax return.

The trust officer may be the person to whom the client initially turned for information and for estate planning services if professional management were desired in the administration of trusts. A good trust officer will be familiar with estate planning and the various estate planning tools that can be used. As executors or trustees, trust officers have primary responsibility for gathering and safeguarding the assets, settling the estate, investing estate assets during the administration period, and making distribution, as necessary, to the estate or trust beneficiaries. The bank trust department may also be responsible for filing estate and fiduciary income tax returns.

The life insurance specialist plays an important role on the estate planning team because he or she can provide products that will give the estate the necessary cash to pay the estate tax and other liabilities as well as to fund the income needs of the surviving family. Life insurance is the primary asset of many estates, and consequently, the major source for family income after an estate owner dies. Life insurance agents who have become CLUs should be knowledgeable in the fields of insurance as well as estate planning and taxation and can provide an invaluable service as a knowledgeable member of the team.

The attorney is a crucial member because plans usually cannot be executed properly without knowledge of the law. The attorney is responsible for assuring that the intentions of the client are expressed in legally enforceable documents that will serve as the basis for carrying out the client's postmortem plan. These documents virtually always include wills and may include trusts, buy–sell agreements, and other documents if a sophisticated estate plan is elected.

Estate planning has become vastly more complicated and challenging as a field of practice. The effective estate planner is familiar with the applicable local and federal law and has a good working knowledge of subject matter pertaining to property, probate, wills and trusts, federal and state taxation, corporations, partnerships, business, insurance, and divorce. An estate planner must be able to explain relevant portions of these subjects to the client in plain language. The client who is spoken down to or expected to deal with technical jargon will not feel confident and may well abandon the project. A client has an absolute need to understand fully his or her options and make his or her own decisions. At the same time, the planner must take care to avoid the unauthorized practice of law or any other profession not his or her own.

Estate Planning Tools[3]

Tools available for estate planning should be used to ensure that (1) assets are sufficient to meet objectives, (2) beneficiaries receive assets in the proportion and manner desired, (3) the minimum in income, estate, gift, and state death taxes and other transfer costs is paid subject to accomplishing the desired objectives, and (4) sufficient liquidity exists to cover transfer costs. Several estate planning tools are examined below with the foregoing objectives in mind.

Wills. A will is a legal declaration of an indivdiual's wishes as to the disposition to be made of his or her property on death. It is the

---

[2]See Chapter 15.

[3]This section draws from Fred A. Tillman and Jack Rice, *Who's Next Please?* (Indianapolis, Ind.: Russell R. Muller Retail Hardware Research Foundation, 1982). Chap. 9.

principal means by which an estate plan is implemented. Like the estate plan, it must be kept up to date and reviewed frequently so that it meets objectives.

A will affords the opportunity not only to declare beneficiaries, but also permits the implementation of plans to save income, estate, and gift taxes; name an appropriate executor; arrange for the payment of obligations; and establish trusts, among other things.

A will is an **ambulatory** instrument, meaning that it does not take effect until the death of the **testator** (the person making the will). Therefore, it can be changed at any time during life. A new will can expressly revoke any prior wills. A **codicil** changes the part of the will with which it is inconsistent. A will can be physically destroyed or mutilated with the intent of revoking it.

Wills also may be modified by state law. For example, a bequest to a former spouse executed prior to divorce typically is invalid. Some states even declare the entire will invalid upon divorce. Generally, a beneficiary is prohibited from obtaining a share under the will if the beneficiary murdered the testator.

Children born or adopted after a will is executed might be permitted to share in the estate, even though they were not mentioned in the will. In at least one state, however, the failure to contemplate after-born children renders the entire will invalid.

Since only the original will is valid, it is important that it be kept in a safe place and that others know where it is located. Generally, a safe-deposit box is *not* a good place to keep a will. Invariably, when this is done, the testator dies on Friday night, and it may be impossible to obtain the will until at least Monday. There might be a need to read the will immediately to be certain that all the testator's instructions are carried out.

It generally is not a good idea to distribute a large number of copies of a will. The estate planner, the attorney, or perhaps the executor could keep the original and probably should have copies, but too many additional copies would be hard to collect and destroy should a change be made in the will. If copies of old wills are left in the hands of others, it is entirely possible that

someone with a copy will not know that changes have been made and may attempt, in good faith, to begin carrying out instructions that are no longer valid.

A will must meet technical and legal requirements. First, the testator must be of proper age. In most states this is the age of majority, but some states will allow a younger person to make a will. The testator must be competent to make a valid will. Competency means that the testator understands that he or she is making a will, knows the extent and nature of the property being disposed of, and knows the natural objects of his or her bounty. The will must be free from fraud and undue influence.

The will also must be in writing and properly executed, according to applicable state law. Oral wills generally are not valid, with some exceptions. The will must be signed, indicating intent to make a will, and attested to by the appropriate number of witnesses (which varies from state to state).

In many states, a surviving spouse is entitled to what is called a statutory or forced-heir share of the deceased spouse's property. This usually amounts to a one-third share. If the decedent has made a will leaving a lesser amount to the surviving spouse, the survivor can *elect against the will* and receive the same amount that would have been received had the testator died without a will. In some states, the right to elect against the will extends to children as well.

Gifts. A gift is the transfer of property ownership for less than an adequate consideration. The difference between market value and the sales price constitutes a gift.

For a gift to be complete, the **donor** (gift giver) and **donee** (gift recepient) both must be competent, and the donor must have a clear intent to make a gift. Furthermore, the donor must give up ownership and control, and the gift must be delivered and accepted by the donee. A gift is not considered complete for tax purposes if it is delivered and then borrowed back for an indefinite period of time.

As mentioned in Chapter 13, $10,000 can be given away in property or cash each year to any one person, regardless of relationship, without incurring gift tax liability. Also, a gift can be "split" between husband and wife, irrespective of which one owns the property. The total amount that can be excluded from gift tax consequences can be increased to $20,000 per year per person by using the split gift.

By making gifts (in property or cash) within the annual exclusion, the value effectively is taken out of the estate for tax purposes. In other words, $10,000 per year can be given to any one person, no gift tax liability incurred, and the gifted property removed from the estate. If a gifting program is started early and continued, a series of annual exclusion gifts can substantially reduce the taxes on the estate.

If a gift of more than $10,000 ($20,000 split gift) is made to any one person during the calendar year, a taxable gift has been made. A federal gift tax return should be filed, and gift tax will be assessed according to the tax rate schedule. It is not necessary actually to pay gift tax to the federal government until the unified tax credit amounts have been exhausted.

What are the advantages of making taxable gifts, particularly since these gifts are added back to the estate for estate tax purposes under current law?

1. Individual gifts, up to the amount of the annual exclusion, are not added back to the estate for purposes of calculating federal estate tax. Thus, the estate is reduced by the amount of the annual exclusion.

2. A credit is allowed against any federal estate tax due equal to the amount of any gift tax paid during lifetime. That is, taxes are not paid twice on the same transfer.

3. There is no federal estate tax on the appreciation of the value of the gift from the date of gift to the date of death. For example, suppose that Judy gave her daughter, Kerrie, property valued at $100,000 in 1982. The property increases in value to $200,000 by 1987, the year of Judy's death. The market value at the date of gift, less the annual exclusion, is $90,000 ($100,000 minus $10,000). This amount will be added back to Judy's estate. Thus, the appreciation from the date of gift to the date of death ($100,000) will not be included in the estate for federal estate tax purposes.

4. If a gift is made to someone other than the spouse, federal income tax can be saved if the property transferred would have otherwise produced taxable income to the donor. For example, should Mosella give her son income-producing property, he will pay the income tax on amounts earned, rather than her. If the son is in a lower tax bracket, both will realize a savings in federal income tax.

There are many reasons for making gifts other than just to save taxes. The principal reasons are listed below.

1. People derive satisfaction from giving to others.
2. The expense of administration and other costs associated with processing the estate can be minimized or avoided by giving the property away during lifetime. (However, avoiding this expense may negate primary planning objectives.)
3. Anyone can review the public records of a probate court. By making a gift, the property is removed from probate and privacy retained.
4. By giving the property away, management responsibilities are shifted to other persons—the new owners.
5. Should one feel that he or she is no longer able to manage assets properly, the assets might be given away to protect their value. Unfortunately, most persons are unable to recognize when they are no longer competent to make the appropriate decisions.
6. Making gifts to children can provide them the opportunity to learn how to manage money or property.
7. If an individual has assets that he or she wishes to go to a particular individual and anticipates the possibility of family disharmony, making a gift during lifetime can be extremely important to meet the objective. If a will does not exist or is declared invalid because of a will contest, property that passes through the estate could wind up in the hands of the wrong people. By giving the property away, this risk is eliminated.

A life insurance policy typically is an excellent type of property to use for a gift. The value of the gift is the sum of the unearned premium and the interpolated terminal reserves, as discussed earlier.[4] But if the policy were included in

---

[4]See Chapter 13.

the estate at the time of death, the estate tax value would be the amount of the death proceeds. If the face amount of the policy was $100,000 and the value for gift purposes was no more than $10,000, the policy could be transferred by gift within the annual exclusion, and there would be no gift tax consequences. In addition, the donor must live more than three years from the date of the gift to avoid inclusion of the proceeds of the policy in his or her estate under IRC Section 2035.

Greatly appreciated property may make an appropriate gift. If sale of the property is anticipated, a gift to a person who is in a lower income tax bracket can make good financial sense. The donee would then sell the property and pay less taxes on the gain. The gift tax consequences should be compared with income tax consequences to determine whether taxes in the overall transactions are lessened.

If it is contemplated that the property will be sold after death, it often should be retained rather than given away. This is because of the "stepped-up basis." If property is given away and the donee sells it, income tax must be paid on the gain. If the property is retained and its value included in the estate, an estate tax must be paid on the market value of the property. However, the value of the property included in the gross estate becomes the new basis to be used by the beneficiaries or the estate for income tax purposes.

Suppose that Larry owned only one piece of property. He paid $10,000 for it and it is now worth $200,000. If he gives the property away and the donee sells it, income tax must be paid by the donee on the full gain. If he does not give away the property but retains it until his death, naming the person to whom he would have given it during lifetime as the beneficiary, the value of the property ($200,000) would be included in his estate for estate tax purposes. The $200,000 value becomes the new income tax basis for the beneficiary. If the property were sold for the $200,000 market value, there would be no gain and no income tax would have to be paid by the beneficiary. Thus, the income tax is forgiven.

As can be seen, it might be better for tax purposes to keep property rather than give it away. Of course, one must determine in each case whether a tax savings would take place. The addi-

tional costs associated with probate should not be overlooked. These might be sufficient to offset any tax savings.

Joint Ownership of Property. The various types of joint ownerships, presented earlier, need not be discussed again except to point out that joint ownership can be a means of bypassing the probate estate and thus avoiding probate costs. This can be helpful in some situations.

A potential disadvantage of joint ownership should be noted. Under a tenancy by the entirety (right of survivorship between husband and wife), the tax law requires that only 50 percent of the market value of the property be included in the gross estate of the first joint tenant to die. Although this avoids estate tax on one-half of the total property value in the first estate, 100 percent of the market value at the time of the death of the surviving spouse would be included in his or her estate. This is true because he or she would receive the first decedent's interest through survivor's rights. (This, of course, assumes that the surviving spouse does not sell or give away the property during his or her lifetime.)

Since only 50 percent of the value of the property was included in the first spouse's estate, the stepped-up basis for income tax purposes will apply only to that part of the total value. The excluded 50 percent will not get the stepped-up basis. If the property might be sold during the surviving spouse's lifetime, this area should be examined carefully. It might be better to have the entire property value includable in the gross estate to obtain a stepped-up basis on the total value of the property.

Trusts. A trust is a legal arrangement whereby one party transfers property to someone else who holds the legal title and manages the trust property for the benefit of others. The person who establishes the trust is called the **grantor** (or settlor). The person who receives the legal title and manages the property is called the **trustee,** and the person for whose benefit the property is held is the **beneficiary.** As the word trust implies, faith and confidence are placed in the trustee to act solely on the beneficiary's behalf. Legally, the trustee has a fiduciary responsibility to act in accordance with the law and the provisions of the trust instrument.

Trusts are effective estate planning tools. They often supply elements that are impossible to obtain through a direct gift. Income, estate, and gift tax savings also can be effected through the use of trusts. Trusts can eliminate the need for guardianship of property. One can provide a life income for family members, with the principal of the trust distributed to charity. Assets can be protected from creditors through the use of a trust.

There are many types of trusts, each designed to meet specific objectives. A trust can be created during lifetime, called an **inter vivos** or **living trust,** or through your will, called a **testamentary trust.** Thus, one can transfer property to a living trust or retain ownership until death and then pass the property to a trust by will. The living trust can be **revocable** or **irrevocable;** that is, the grantor can terminate the trust at will and regain ownership of the property, or he or she can give up ownership and control permanently.

1. *Revocable trusts.* A revocable trust might be desirable as a device to transfer assets directly to beneficiaries outside the probate estate. This avoids probate costs in estate settlement. Because the property is outside probate, the business of the trust can continue on an uninterrupted, confidential basis, or the trust can be terminated and assets distributed to the beneficiaries confidentially and without administrative delay.

A revocable trust might be a better vehicle than a will for making certain that particular individuals receive specific property. If property is transferred to a revocable trust during lifetime, it is difficult to argue that the donor's real intention was not being carried out by the trust. On the contrary, the will could be attacked for any number of reasons, including incompetence, the undue influence of others, and so on. An irrevocable trust could be used for the foregoing purpose, but the grantor could not regain control and ownership if circumstances should change.

A revocable trust is not without disadvantages. No income, estate, or gift tax savings exist under a revocable trust. The transfer into the trust does not constitute a completed gift; therefore, no gift tax is assessed. Since a complete gift is not made effective, ownership of the property is retained for tax purposes. Thus, the trust property will be included in the taxable estate, and trust income is taxable to the grantor. Administration and management charges must be paid under a trust arrangement. These charges serve to offset savings generated from the use of a trust.

2. *Irrevocable trusts.* Control and ownership are relinquished over property placed in an irrevocable trust. This loss of flexibility could be a high price to pay should conditions change.

When property is placed in an irrevocable trust, generally a complete gift has been made that may have gift tax consequences. Of course, income and estate tax savings that are applicable to any gift of property or cash may also result.

3. *The marital deduction and two-trust will.* The marital deduction can be an important estate planning device. The marital deduction provisions of the IRC provide for an unlimited deduction for property left to the surviving spouse. It is, therefore, possible to leave everything to the surviving spouse and incur no federal estate tax. To do so, however, might actually result in a higher total estate tax liability when the taxes on the estates of both spouses are taken into consideration.

Suppose that after deductions for expenses, debts, and losses, Len's estate has a value of $2,000,000. If the entire value were left to his surviving spouse, Becky, and not dissipated or given away under the annual exclusion during her lifetime, an estate tax of $561,000 would be imposed upon Becky's subsequent death (provided that death occurs in 1987 or later) and probate cost probably would be at least $60,000 (3 percent of probate estate). This would result in $1,379,000 being left ultimately to the children ($2,000,000 – $561,000 – $60,000).

There are better ways to provide for the surviving spouse. Assuming that Len died in 1987 or later, he could have left Becky $1,400,000 under the marital deduction. This amount would not be taxed in Len's estate. The $600,000 balance, which could be left to the children or others, is equal to the exemption equivalent, and the unified credit would equal the amount of tax assessed against the estate. Thus, no estate tax would be payable.

Assuming that Becky owns no other assets and does not dissipate or give away the $1,400,000 received from Len, her estate would pay estate taxes of $301,940, after application of the unified credit (and estimated postmorten costs of $42,000). The other $600,000 escapes all estate taxation on Becky's death.

Trust arrangements typically are used as a vehicle to effect the above plan through what is known as a **two-trust will.** Testamentary trusts are established to permit the surviving spouse to have substantial enjoyment of all the estate owner's property during his or her lifetime, bypass the surviving spouse's estate as to the property that will eventually go to others, and qualify an optimal amount of the assets for the estate tax marital deduction.

First, a **marital trust** is established to receive property that qualifies for the marital deduction when the first spouse dies. When the surviving spouse dies, any amounts not consumed or given to others will be taxed in his or her estate. Although it is not necessary to establish a trust for the marital deduction property, it may prove convenient to provide management for the assets. If the surviving spouse has the experience, ability, and time to manage these assets, a trust is unnecessary.

Generally, the marital trust must provide that the surviving spouse has the right to consume or give away the principal of the trust. This general power of appointment gives the spouse the right to invade principal whenever desired and permits it to qualify for the marital deduction. The trust must provide for the distribution of income to the spouse at least annually. If the trust remains intact and the surviving spouse does not exercise the power of appointment, either during lifetime or through his or her will, the property of the trust can be distributed to beneficiaries as designated in the will.

Property that is not left to the surviving spouse in the marital trust or not used to pay expenses, taxes, other bequests, and so on, is placed in a second trust, known as the nonmarital or **residuary trust.** The surviving spouse has the right to the income for life from the residuary trust property and has a limited power of invasion of the principal. The income from the residuary trust would supplement the income provided by the marital trust and the principal could also be available, if needed, subject to certain restrictions. On the death of the surviving spouse, all right to income from the residuary trust is terminated, and the trust property would not be taxed in his or her estate. This gives the surviving spouse the effective use of all the decedent's property during his or her lifetime, without having the residual trust included in that spouse's estate for federal estate tax purposes.

Figure 14–1 compares (1) the simple will approach whereby Len's $2,000,000 net estate is left outright to Becky, and (2) the two-trust arrangement whereby the $2,000,000 estate is divided between the marital and residuary trusts. The residuary trust receives property equivalent in value to that necessary to utilize fully the unified credit (i.e., $600,000). As a trust, no probate costs are assessed against its value on the beneficiary's death and, since the beneficiary does not own the trust, it is excludable from her estate. These two sources constitute the savings of $277,060 of the trust arrangement over the simple will arrangement. As a result of the use of the marital deduction and the two-trust will, the deceased couple's children and other beneficiaries would receive a significantly larger share of the estate than if it were necessary to pay estate tax.

4. *The "Kiddie Tax."* As noted earlier, while a living trust must be irrevocable to obtain tax advantages, the requirement that one give up all interest and control in the property constitutes a high price. Until enactment of TRA '86, a *Clifford Trust* (also called a *short-term trust*) offered an acceptable alternative to this dilemma for some persons. The pre-TRA '86 rules still apply to transfers to Clifford Trusts made before March 2, 1986, and therefore, such trusts will still be found in many persons' estate plans. These older rules provided that the trust must have had a term of more than 10 years (or the lifetime of the beneficiary, whichever ends first). When the trust ends, the principal is to be returned to the grantor. Income tax liability during the term of the trust was shifted from the grantor to either the trust or the trust beneficiary and usually from higher to a

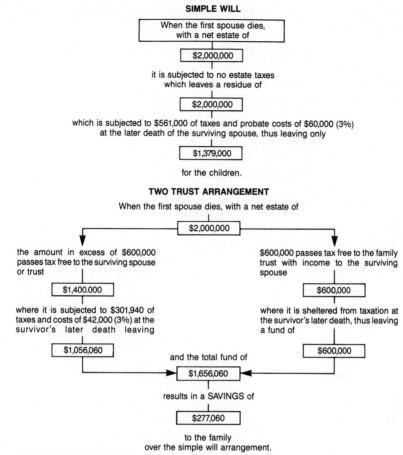

FIGURE 14-1. Simple will versus two-trust arrangement. Source: Modified from illustration from *Advanced Sales Course*, 8th ed. (Washington, DC.: Life Underwriter Training Council, 1985), Vol. 9, p. 170.

lower tax bracket, provided that the beneficiary had the right to income generated from the trust property. (But, see below.)

TRA '86 repealed IRC Section 673—the section permitting traditional Clifford Trusts. Thus, for transfers made in trust after March 1, 1986, the Clifford Trust is probably an ineffective income-shifting device for most persons. As alluded to above, however, such pre-March 2, 1986 trusts are grandfathered, although trust income may be subject to the so-called "kiddie tax."

Under pre-TRA '86 law, a minor child paid tax on his or her earned (generally, compensation for personal services rendered) or unearned (generally, income derived from other than personal services rendered) income based on the child's own tax rate. Ordinarily, this meant a lower total family tax bill if income could be shifted from a parent's typically higher tax rate to the child's typically lower tax rate.

TRA '86 provides, in effect, that the *unearned* income (over $1,000) of children *under age 14* will be taxed at the parents' (typically higher) marginal tax rate. This rule is effective for tax years beginning in 1987 and later . This so-called **kiddie tax** applies to unearned income from all sources, including existing custodial accounts and income distributed from existing trusts, even irrevocable trusts.

The kiddie tax law clearly diminishes the attractiveness of income-shifting devices for younger children. On the other hand, the tax arguably enhances the attractiveness of savings through life insurance and annuities.

5. *Trusts for minor children.* Many persons make gifts from time to time to their minor children to accumulate a substantial fund for education or other use when they are old enough to handle the responsibility. A trust can be useful in such situations.

The tax code, however, will not allow an annual exclusion for a gift of a future interest. Unless the beneficiary has the right to the present possession and enjoyment of the property, the annual exclusion will not be allowed. Thus, the annual exclusion would not be available for a gift to a minor in trust where the funds were not presently available to that minor.

One way to avoid this problem is to establish the trust for minors known as a **Section 2503(c) Trust.** By meeting the requirements for this trust, a gift can be made to minors without the loss of the $10,000 annual gift tax exclusion. To qualify for the annual exclusion, the trust must contain provisions wherein (1) the trustee has the discretion to distribute both principal and income, (2) the beneficiaries are entitled to receive the principal of the trust when they reach age 21, and (3) should any of the beneficiaries die before reaching maturity, his or her share of the assets would pass through his or her estate.

By meeting the requirements of the trust, income can be accumulated until the minor reaches age 21 and the $10,000 annual exclusion per beneficiary can be used. This type of trust for minors is a popular device. It is often used by grandparents who wish to establish an educational fund for their grandchildren. A provision could be contained wherein the trust could be continued beyond age 21, provided that the beneficiaries agree to this continuation.

Another form of the trust for minors is called a **Section 2503(b) Trust.** It differs from the "c"

trust in that the income must be distributed to the beneficiaries annually. Furthermore, there is no requirement that the principal be distributed to the beneficiaries at any particular time or age, if ever. The annual exclusion is available for gifts made to this type of trust.

Gifts also can be made to minors under the **Uniform Gifts to Minors Act.** Under this act, an adult is named custodian for the minor and manages the property through a custodian account. The property is distributed to the minor at age 18.

6. *Crummey trusts.* A more recent trust innovation is called the **Crummey Trust.** In spite of its misleading name (which came from the name of the litigant who fought and won the battle with the IRS), the Crummey Trust is a very useful device. The annual exclusion is available for gifts made to the trust, provided that the beneficiaries have a reasonable opportunity to demand amounts contributed to the trust. If the reasonable period for the demand expires without such a request having been made, the gift amounts cannot later be taken down by the beneficiaries and are eligible for the annual exclusion.

An irrevocable life insurance trust with a "Crummey" provision can be an effective estate planning tool. A gift to such a trust qualifies as a present interest gift and therefore for the $10,000 per year annual exclusion. The trustee can use such gifts to pay the premiums on a life insurance policy on the life of the donor and the policy death proceeds should not be includable in the donor's gross estate on his or her death.

7. *Life insurance trusts.* As noted earlier, the value of a life insurance policy for gift tax purposes is the interpolated terminal reserve plus unearned premium rather than the face amount. This makes the gift of the life insurance policy a popular tax-saving device. Many persons use a **life insurance trust.** Under this arrangement, an insurance policy on the grantor's life is placed in trust with the policy proceeds payable to the trust as beneficiary. Generally, should the grantor live more than three years from the date the trust is established, and if all incidents of ownership in the policy are relinquished, the proceeds will not be a part of the grantor's taxable estate.[5]

Death proceeds can be invested or distributed to trust beneficiaries through arrangements that are not available under life insurance policy settlement options. Therefore, it generally is more desirable to have policy proceeds paid in a single sum to the trust rather than have the insurance company pay the proceeds on an installment basis with interest. Of course, there is no guarantee that the trustee will make wise investments, and there are no guarantees with the trust as under an insurance contract.

The planner should be certain that there is a need for an insurance trust rather than an outright gift of life insurance. The $10,000 annual exclusion can be made available for the outright gift of a life insurance policy, as well as for the premiums paid on a policy by the donor. However, when a policy is assigned to such a trust or when premiums are paid on policies held in such a trust, the $10,000 annual exclusion may not be available unless a "Crummey" provision is included in the trust instrument. Therefore, the gift of a policy in trust and the future premium payments can be fully taxable gifts that are later added back to the estate for estate tax purposes. Also, there are no income tax savings for an insurance trust if the policy insures either the donor or his or her spouse. If the trust were sufficiently funded so that the income to the trust were adequate to pay the premiums, the trust income would still be taxed to the grantor.

Life Insurance for Estate Liquidity[6]

Life insurance is often the best way to provide liquidity needed for estate clearance. Even so, several questions remain to be answered. In particular, what products should be purchased? Who should be the owner of the policy? How should the beneficiary designation be structured? How can the insurance be structured to get liquidity into the hands of the person who must pay estate costs?

Since the marital deduction coupled with the unified credit may eliminate or greatly reduce estate taxes at the death of the first spouse, the focus for liquidity to meet estate taxes often centers on the second spouse's death. Assuming that life insurance is the best way to provide this, several ways are available to provide the cash economically. One way would be to use individual policies insuring both lives in a sufficient amount to meet the projected need. A second approach would be to use a joint-life policy providing for payment of the face amount at the first death. A third approach would be to use a joint life policy that pays the face amount when the second insured dies rather than the first.

Finally, only one spouse might be insured. If the insured is the first to die, the proceeds can be retained for ultimate liquidity needs. This may be the only solution if one spouse is uninsurable and may not be a bad idea even if both are insurable and the proceeds provide adequate liquidity for both estates. Furthermore, the surviving spouse could invest the proceeds to supplement income.

Formerly, third-party ownership of life insurance was not uncommon. The obvious reason was to keep the insurance proceeds out of the estate of the insured. The spouse of the insured generally was the owner. With the unlimited marital deduction, less need exists for insurance to be owned by the spouse.

In large estates and with large amounts of insurance, it may be appropriate to have the insurance owned by a party other than the insured or spouse. A trust is one alternate owner. A child may be another. Use of an irrevocable trust as owner may be especially wise if the insurance is not to be used at the first death, but retained for meeting estate liquidity needs on the second death. As noted earlier, gifts to the trust—which can be used by the trust to pay life insurance premiums—can qualify for the $10,000 annual gift tax exclusion if the trust contains a "Crummey" provision.

Special care should be taken in designating ownership of joint policies. If either spouse/insured

---

[5]If the policy is applied for and owned by the trustee from its inception, the policy death proceeds may be excluded from the gross estate even if death occurs within the first three years.

[6]This section draws from *Advanced Sales Course,* 8th ed. (Washington, D.C.: Life Underwriter Training Council, 1985), Vol. 9, pp. 156–157 and 166–167.

is owner of a second death policy, the proceeds will be included in the estate of the second to die. With a first death policy, the survivor may be able to transfer the proceeds before being subjected to tax.

Can it be assumed that if insurance is payable to the surviving spouse or to the children of the estate owner, it will somehow get into the hands of the executor, who generally pays the estate clearance costs? Probably not.

The alternatives for getting the insurance proceeds into the executor's hands include:

1. Having the insurance payable to the estate
2. Relying on the beneficiary to lend money to the estate
3. Relying on the beneficiary to buy assets from the estate

The first alternative has several disadvantages:

1. Proceeds will be includable in the estate and subject to tax, although the marital deduction could negate this tax.
2. In most states administration costs will be increased, since they are a percentage of probate assets.
3. Proceeds become subject to the claims of estate creditors.
4. State death tax exemption for insurance proceeds may be lost.

The likelihood of alternative 2 or 3 working as planned depends on who is named beneficiary. The greatest likelihood of the estate owner's plans being carried out is when the insurance is payable to a trust, with the trustee authorized to either lend money to the estate or purchase assets from the estate. To be effective, trust provisions cannot require the trustee to loan money or purchase assets from the estate without jeopardizing the tax advantages of using a trust. They merely give the trustee the power to do so at the trustee's discretion. It is difficult to imagine a case wherein a trustee would not loan money or purchase assets should the need arise and the trust instrument has authorized (but not required) such action.

It is common to have insurance purchased for estate liquidity owned by and payable to an irrevocable, inter-vivos trust with trust income payable to the spouse for life and corpus payable to the children at the spouse's death. This follows the two-trust arrangement discussed earlier. In fact, the will of the insured estate owner often pours the nonmarital share of the estate into the irrevocable insurance trust.

A gift is created when life insurance is placed in an irrevocable trust. Unless certain provisions are included in the trust, the gift would be a gift of a future interest and would result in gift taxes on the death proceeds being required of the grantor. Use of a Crummey Trust can avoid this problem by creating a gift of a present interest at the time of premium payment.

RETIREMENT PLANNING

The retirement planning process conceptually is identical to that followed in death planning. The nature of the "loss"—"excessive" longevity—is, of course, different. Even so, the procedure followed is the same.

Gather Information

Both death-related and retirement-related information typically would be gathered at the same time. The needed information includes existing liquid assets that could be used to provide retirement income and information concerning employer-sponsored retirement, profit-sharing, and/or other such sources of retirement income.

Information regarding probable retirement benefits provided under the Social Security program also should be obtained, as should eligibility for other government benefits. Estimations are necessary in most cases. If the time to retirement is great, estimates will, at best, be gross approximations only.

Establish Objectives

Retirement income objectives usually are couched in general terms, such as being able to maintain one's current standard of living during retirement. Quantifying this general objective is desirable but not easy.

Analyze Information

With objectives established, one must then analyze relevant information gathered earlier to measure the financial consequences of retirement. The present value of future income needs should be netted against the present value of future estimated resources. The result is a measure of the net present value of the shortage of resources to meet the desired income objective.

Interest rates should be reasonable in light of historical and current trends, as should projected inflation rates. Utilizing the assumed inflation rate, one would determine the (inflated) level of income desired at retirement age, based on a projection of the current-day equivalent. Next, the expected annual income resources would be netted against the desired annual income needs. Three classes of common resources are: (1) employer-sponsored income, (2) government-provided income, and (3) income from personal resources.

Some planners ignore government-provided benefits because of a perceived uncertainty as to their reliability. While the Social Security system's future benefits may be modified, their being materially curtailed seems unlikely. The possibility of the system being abandoned altogether seems so remote as to be safely ignored.

The same Social Security estimation quandary exists for retirement planning and predeath planning, although it is more complex here. No resolution will be perfect. The additional complexity comes about because the Social Security *survivor* benefit is, for the present, a known, calculable product, and near-term projections probably are reasonable. However, for those not near retirement, projecting Social Security benefit levels several decades from the present is speculative. As a result, such calculations should be viewed as providing gross estimates only. In any event, Social Security retirement benefits should be netted against the retirement income need to derive annual deficit figures.

Employer-sponsored retirement benefits can be equally, if not more, troublesome to estimate. People change employers. Even if one remained with the same employer until retirement, no guarantee exists that the benefit plan would remain the same. Plans are changed. Even if neither the employer nor the plan were changed, obtaining reliable estimates for future benefits can be difficult. As discussed in Chapter 28, retirement benefits provided under an employer-sponsored pension, profit-sharing, or other such plan are a function of the plan benefit formula and future employer funding levels.

Even so, an attempt should be made to establish a *conservative* estimate for retirement income from employer-sponsored sources. One approach is to determine from the employer the employee's projected benefit level to determine what is believed to be the expected **wage replacement ratio** at retirement. The wage replacement ratio is the fraction found by dividing (1) the postretirement, employer-sponsored retirement income by (2) the preretirement annual wage.

Thus, if the employer-sponsored retirement income is expected to be 40 percent of the preretirement wage level, and, if the retirement income need is equal to the preretirement wage level, one need examine only a 60 percent net retirement income level from nonemployer sources. If the retirement income need is less than the preretirement wage, appropriate adjustments are made. Projected personal savings and investments also should be netted against the retirement income need.

Using either the capital retention or one of the two capital liquidation approaches, one then derives an inflation- and interest-adjusted figure for the present value of the future income stream as of the planned retirement age.[7]

Develop Plan

Next, the alternative means of accumulating the needed sum should be explored. For example, eligible persons can establish a tax-qualified individual retirement annuity (IRA) making level, increasing or some other pattern of annual contributions. Other means whereby the amount could be accumulated might include:

• Purchase non-tax-qualified flexible premium deferred annuity.

[7]See Chapter 12.

- Establish non-tax-qualified savings and/or investment program.
- Establish nonqualified deferred compensation plan with employer, if feasible.[8]
- Establish 401(k) arrangement with employer, if feasible.[9]
- Establish tax-sheltered annuity plan with employer, if feasible.[10]
- Utilize cash values of needed life insurance protection.
- Find a rich, generous friend or relative.
- Combinations of the above.

One or several of these arrangements usually proves feasible. Ideally, contributions would be income tax deductible and earnings would accumulate on a tax-deferred basis. The advantages of annuities and life insurance cash values in this regard were noted earlier.

Implement Plan

After the plan alternatives have been considered and a plan developed and agreed to by the client, the plan should be implemented. This may entail applying for an annuity, following through with the paperwork to establish an IRA or other tax-qualified plan, or making other commitments.

The key to sound plan implementation is less the paperwork mechanics and more a firm commitment by the client to make the necessary contributions regularly. More individually crafted retirement plans fail from lack of commitment than for any other reason.

Monitor and Revise Plan

As with predeath planning, actual results under one's retirement plan are highly unlikely to track precisely those assumed for the future. This necessitates periodic fine-tuning and, occasionally, a complete overhaul. Again, important life events and environmental changes can affect results materially.

[8]See Chapter 15.
[9]See Chapter 28.
[10]See Chapter 28.

SAVINGS AND INVESTMENT PLANNING

The common reasons for establishing a savings/investment program were presented in Chapter 1. The establishment and implementation of a savings/investment program should follow the usual steps in the financial planning process. Life insurance and annuities can be important in such a program.

Life Insurance as a Savings Instrument

In accumulating a savings plan, an individual is subject to five significant perils: (1) the danger of not living long enough to complete the savings/investment fund; (2) the danger of becoming disabled and not being able to make the deposits necessary to build the fund; (3) the possible lack of industry, initiative, or opportunity to earn sufficient income to make the deposits; (4) the possible lack of willpower to continue the arrangement for a long period of time; and (5) the inability, through faulty investment, to keep what may have been saved. Life insurance is, of course, useful in item 1 and health insurance in item 2. Life insurance, because of its quasi-compulsory nature, can also be helpful to some persons who have difficulty disciplining themselves to save regularly. Life insurance also provides safety of principal not present in many other individual investments.

In evaluating life insurance as a savings/investment vehicle, a number of standards can be used. Four—security, yield, liquidity, and convenience—are examined below. By any of them, carefully purchased life insurance can be a reasonable, sound accumulation vehicle.

Of the various attributes of an ideal investment, safety of principal usually is the most important. More people learned that lesson during the Great Depression of the 1930s than probably ever before. Life insurance, despite the thousands of depository institution bankruptcies during that depression, weathered the period admirably. McCahan's detailed investigation, covering the 23-year period to 1932 (the time of the investigation), showed that "the average annual loss to policyowners during those 23 years did not exceed

29 cents for every $1,000 of net reserve."[11] Even with respect to companies that suspended operations during the depression years of 1930–1932, he concludes:

> If the depression period (1930–32) be taken by itself, the average losses from companies failing during these three years will not exceed 91 cents for every $1,000 of average net reserve held by all life insurance companies in this country. Thus, it may truthfully be said that the institution was 99.9 percent safe throughout a period of extraordinary financial strain.[12]

Life insurance company portfolios represent an accumulation of purchases over a long period of time. Even if interest rates declined, most life insurance companies' portfolios would be slower to feel the decline than many other portfolios. A large part of the portfolio consists of bonds bought advantageously over a period of many years and having a long time to run before maturity.

In view of the high degree of security of life insurance investments, the rates of interest earned by the companies are high. At the present time, life insurance companies earn an average of 9.87 percent, which is as high as, or higher than, any other institutions of comparable safety. The careful life insurance or annuity purchaser can procure a contract whose implicit rate of return is easily competitive with other savings media of comparable safety, although increasingly the newer product forms shift much of the investment risk to the policyowner.

Life insurance and annuity contracts are liquid investments. Whenever desired, the policyowner may surrender (sell) to the insurance company his or her cross section of the company's investment portfolio at the "price" stipulated in the cash value table. As explained in Chapter 9, an amount equal to the cash value in life insurance

policies may nearly always be borrowed without delay or publicity at a fair, guaranteed rate of interest. The loan really is made against the policyowner's potential claim against the company for either a surrender or a death benefit.

Whereas safety of principal and reasonable rate of return are the first considerations of a good investment, avoidance of managerial care is an important factor to most. The insurance company gives the policyowner the benefit of its experience and skill with respect to inquiry, analysis, and appraisal, its judgment of trends, its understanding and application of fundamental principles of investment, and its willingness to assume all routine cares.

The policy term may be made short or long in accordance with the policyowner's desire. Many persons prefer to have the investment extend over considerable periods of time. The investment period may be made to coincide with the anticipated working period or any other desired period. The investment period may run to any one of numerous maturity dates or be completely flexible. In the meantime, the cash value is readily obtainable for the promised amount, thus enabling the policyowner to terminate the investment prior to the maturity date of the contract.

There are other advantageous aspects about life insurance. Life insurance companies are subjected by the states to special taxes, but from the policyowner's standpoint, the disadvantage can be balanced by advantages extended to life and health insurance in the fields of income and inheritance taxation.[13]

In the majority of states, life insurance policies payable to dependent relatives are protected under exemption laws against the claims of creditors of the policyowner. Often, the amount of insurance declared exempt from creditors' claims is limited to some reasonable amount. Various states, however, have made their exemption acts relate to all policies without respect to amount and without regard to the fact that the

---

[11]S. S. Huebner and David McCahan, "The Solvency Record of Life Insurance," Chap. 7 in *Life Insurance as an Investment* (New York: Appleton-Century-Crofts, 1933).

[12]*Ibid.*

[13]See Chapter 13.

right to change the beneficiary has been reserved by policyowner.[14]

ment. On the other hand, calculation of the rate of return on cash value insurance is not simple.[15]

Life Insurance and Other Investments

In selecting life insurance as a savings medium, a decision often is made between buying cash value life insurance or "buying term and investing the difference." In comparing the alternatives, the amount of death protection and the amount of annual outlay should be held approximately equal between the plans. In general, the "buy term and invest the difference" alternative will be preferred only if its accumulated savings value (or rate of return) significantly exceeds that of the cash value life insurance alternative. What constitutes a "significant difference" depends on the value the buyer places on the several favorable attributes of cash value life insurance as a savings medium that are independent of the rate of return.

The buyer may also compare cash value life insurance as a savings medium to buying term and investing the difference by comparing the imputed rate of return on the "savings portion" of the cash value life insurance with the return on alternative savings plans. In this connection, comparison of risky to nonrisky investments solely on the basis of expected rate of return is inappropriate. The greater the investment risk, the greater the probability that the investment fund will not be available for its intended purpose. Similarly, the taxation of individual investments and the buyer's income tax bracket should be taken into consideration.

The estimation of the current after-tax rate of return on a relatively safe non-life insurance investment usually can be made with little difficulty. The problem is more complex looking forward for 20 years or more because of uncertainties about taxes and rates of return on future reinvest-

FAMILY FINANCIAL PLANNING AND TRA '86

The numerous references throughout Chapters 13 and 14 (and elsewhere in this volume) to the changes brought about by TRA '86 should serve as a clear signal as to the need to review family financial plans carefully. The changes, the most comprehensive since 1954, affect virtually every taxpayer. The full impact of these changes on financial plans and planning still is not known.

The new law eliminated many popular tax shelter techniques. Individual tax rates were lowered, and personal exemptions and standard deductions were raised. Corporate tax rates also were lowered, but the closing of certain "loopholes" is intended to result in corporations paying higher income taxes.

Besides the direct impact on financial planning brought about by TRA '86, more general lessons should emerge. First, it graphically illustrates the need for plan monitoring and revision. What was a "smart" financial plan for 1986 and earlier tax years, could easily slip into the opposite category for 1987 and later tax years, if no plan changes were made.

Second, enactment of the law should remind agents, financial planners, and others that long-term financial planning that is tax-driven can be fraught with problems. Tax considerations will always be important in financial plans but, often, they have unduly influenced decision-making, resulting in a corruption of the means of accomplishing clients' objectives and also enormous client dissatisfaction when the tax rules change—as they did with TRA '86.

[14]See Chapter 8.

[15]See Chapter 10.

Chapter 15

Business Uses
of Life Insurance

Life insurance is most often used for family or other personal reasons. The preceding chapters emphasized this fact. However, life insurance serves important business purposes as well. This chapter discusses these uses.

The business uses of life insurance are numerous. Most uses can be classified into one or more of the following categories:

1. Key employee indemnification
2. Credit protection
3. Business continuation arrangements
4. Special employee compensation plans

KEY EMPLOYEE INDEMNIFICATION

The purpose of key employee insurance is to indemnify a business firm for the loss of earnings brought about by the death (or disability) of a key officer or other employee. Many business firms have been built around a single individual whose capital, energy, technical knowledge, experience, or power to plan and execute make him or her a most valuable asset of the organization and a necessity to its successful operation. Numerous examples illustrate the dependence of a successful business upon the personal equation. Thus, a cor-

poration or firm may be vitally interested in one of its officers, whose financial worth as an endorser, or ability as an executive, may be the basis of its general credit rating. A manufacturing or mining enterprise may be dependent on someone who alone possesses the chemical or engineering knowledge necessary to the concern. A publishing house may have engaged someone who alone can be the author of a proposed work and may be obliged to incur considerable outlay before it is written. The sales manager of a large business establishment may have made himself or herself indispensable through his or her ability to organize an efficient body of salespeople, to employ the most effective methods of selling, and to develop profitable markets.

These are only a few illustrations of the many that might be given to show the importance of a human life as an asset to the successful operation of a business. This importance was recognized in a well-known 1951 tax court case. The court stated:

What business purpose could be considered more essential than key man [or woman] insurance? The business that insures its building and machinery and automobiles from every possible hazard can hardly be expected to exercise less care in protecting itself against the loss of two of its most vital assets—managerial skill and experience.[1]

Economic losses due to death or disability may be guarded against by making the business itself the beneficiary of appropriate policies on the lives of the officers or other employees under consideration. In the event of death or disability, the business will be indemnified promptly for the loss of the services of the deceased or disabled employee, and the proceeds received will enable it to bridge the period necessary to secure the services of a worthy successor or substitute.

In any specific case, it is difficult to determine accurately the economic loss that would be suffered by the business concern in the event of the key person's death or disability. The problem of estimating the loss may be approached by estimating the present value of lost earnings or measured by the additional compensation necessary to secure an experienced replacement. In either case, consideration should be given to the question of whether the loss is a temporary or permanent one. The degree of accuracy with which the value of the economic loss produced by the death or disability of a key person can be determined varies according to the type of business, particular function of the key person, and other circumstances.

Procedurally, the business entity—be it a corporation, partnership, or sole proprietorship—generally is the applicant, owner, beneficiary, and premium payor. The policy type should be selected in light of the expected need duration and with respect to the possible desire to have cash values available for other purposes (e.g., as loan collateral, to indirectly fund a deferred compensation arrangement, etc.). Whole life and universal life policies are most often used for key employee indemnification. However, if the need is relatively short term or if it is desired to accumulate funds outside the life insurance policy, term life insurance policies may be preferable.

The income tax treatment of key employee life insurance usually is straightforward, being similar to that for personally-owned insurance.[2] Unless the business would be subject to the alternative minimum tax (see below), taxable income does not arise from either cash value increases or receipt of policy death proceeds. Premiums paid are not tax deductible.[3]

Policy death proceeds will not be includable in the key employee/insured's gross estate for federal estate tax purposes if the insured possessed no incidents of ownership in the policy and if the proceeds are not payable to or for the benefit of the insured's estate. However, if the insured had an ownership interest in the business, the death proceeds payable to the business could be considered in deriving the value of the business for estate tax purposes.

ENHANCEMENT OF CREDIT

Anything that stabilizes the financial position of a firm improves its general credit rating. Life insurance can serve to enhance the credit of a business organization by indemnifying for the loss of a key person and/or assuring the continuation of the firm as a going concern in the event of the death of the owner(s). Insuring the lives of key persons assures banks and other lending institutions as well as suppliers that the business will have a financial cushion in the event of the death or disability of one or more key personnel. In addition, if a cash value form of life insurance is used, the liquidity of the firm is improved through the accumulation of cash values that are available at all times. The cash values are shown on the firm's balance sheet as assets. Similarly, if prospective lenders or other creditors are assured of the continuation of the firm as a going concern in the event of the death or disability of the owner(s), the firm will not only be able to obtain a larger line of credit, but usually will be able to obtain it on better terms.

In addition to the general improvement of a firm's credit rating, a life insurance contract may be pledged as collateral. The cash value of life insurance is pledged to a lender via a collateral assignment form. Under such an arrangement,

---

[1] *The Emeloid Co., Inc. v. Commissioner,* 189 Fed.2d 230 (1951).
[2] See Chapter 13.

[3] An argument can be made that an economic value at least equal to the yearly price of protection (see Chapter 10) should be deductible by the business in the same way that a business can deduct premiums paid for property and liability insurance.

the basic security for the loan lies in the savings element of the contract, and the amount of the loan is covered by the cash value of the policy. If the borrower dies before the loan is repaid, the lender simply deducts the borrower's obligation from the proceeds, the excess being paid to the designated beneficiary. If the borrower is unwilling or unable to repay the loan at maturity, the lender can recover its funds either by surrendering the policy for cash or by exercising the policy loan privilege. In the normal course of events, the loan is repaid at maturity and the policy reverts to the borrower. Policyowners frequently borrow directly from the insurance company by utilizing the policy loan privilege. The concept of the loan is the same, however, with the policy being assigned to the insurance company instead of a bank or other lender. It should be noted that the rate of interest charged on policy loans usually is more favorable than that charged by lending institutions although limits apply.

A policy may also be pledged as collateral with a different purpose in mind. Its purpose may be to protect the lender against loss arising only out of the death of a key person or the borrower. Thus, life (and health) insurance may be used advantageously in that large number of instances where a business person, already established in business, may need more credit for its proper development, but where the banker feels that the business does not warrant further loans. To the banker, the individual at the head of the business is a very important asset. The bank may feel that while the business itself does not warrant another loan, the business plus the individual who manages it would justify the extension of further credit. Here, however, the contingency of early death or disability must be provided for. In other words, a life and/or health insurance policy in favor of the creditor is a hedge against the contingency of the loss of the value of the life upon which the repayment of the loan is primarily dependent.

In this case, the loan is not made against the cash value of the policy itself. In fact, it is new life insurance taken for credit purposes and, therefore, normally would not as yet have a cash value. The real security behind the loan is the demonstrated business ability of the borrower.

In addition to short-term credit situations, life insurance may be used as collateral in connection with bond issues. Thus, assume that a firm raises $500,000 on bonds that mature in 20 years, and that the nature and organization of the business are such as to make it chiefly dependent for its credit and successful operation upon the life of one individual. Under such circumstances, the unexpected death of this individual might impair the concern to such an extent that the liquidation of its assets might not prove sufficient for the full redemption of the bonds. Thus, life insurance can be the means of assuring creditors that the bonds will be redeemed upon maturity, thus helping to reduce the use of any severe restrictions and the interest rate charged.

BUSINESS CONTINUATION ARRANGEMENTS

In the case of a sole proprietorship, partnership, or close corporation,[4] the problems of business stability and continuation following the death or disability of one or more of its owners are critically important to both the family of the deceased owner and the surviving owners and employees. To understand the vital role life and health insurance can play in this regard, it will be necessary to review briefly the effects that the death or disability of an owner can have on the stability and continuation of a business.

Partnership

The partnership form of business organization has a number of advantages, but it is subject to the general rule of law that any change in the membership of the partnership causes its dissolution. The law provides that upon the death of a general partner, the partnership is dissolved and the surviving partners become liquidating trustees, charged with the responsibility of immediately winding up the business and paying over to the

---

[4] A close or closely held corporation is characterized as one wherein a small number of persons are stockholders who typically control the company as directors and run its affairs as officers. Closely held stock usually is traded privately and is not bought and sold in any organized stock market.

estate of the deceased a fair share of the liquidated value of the business. Liquidation of a business, which involves the "forced sale" of assets, almost invariably results in severe asset shrinkage. Under such conditions, accounts receivable might bring only a fraction of their normal value; inventory and plant must be disposed of, often at sacrifice prices; and goodwill is lost completely. From the viewpont of the survivors, liquidation not only produces losses to them by shrinkage in asset values but more important, destroys their very means of earning a living.

The seriousness of the consequences often leads survivors to attempt to continue the business by buying out the interest of the deceased partner and reorganizing the partnership. This procedure usually is not practicable, however, for two reasons. First, in most cases, it is not possible to raise the necessary cash. Second, even if the surviving partners can raise the cash to purchase the interest of the deceased, they have to prove that the price paid for the interest is fair. Their fiduciary status makes this impracticable. In fact, in some states, they are not permitted to purchase the interest, since it in effect involves a trustee purchasing trust property.

In the usual case, it is also impracticable for an heir who has not already been involved in the business to become a member of the reorganized partnership or to purchase the interests of the surviving partners. The record of litigation clearly indicates that in the absence of *advance* agreement among the partners, attempts to continue the business are fraught with legal and practical complications.[5]

It is increasingly common for the members of a partnership to enter into a so-called **buy-and-sell agreement,** which binds the surviving partners to purchase the partnership interest of the first partner to die, at a prearranged price set forth in the agreement, and obligates the estate of the deceased partner to sell such interest to the surviving partners. The value of the various partnership interests is determined at the time the agreement is entered into and periodically revalued, or a formula for value determination is included in the agreement.

Partnership buy–sell agreements are of two types: **entity** and **cross-purchase.** Under the entity approach the partnership is obligated to buy out the ownership interest of any deceased partner, with each partner having bound his or her estate to sell if he or she were the first to die.

Under the cross-purchase approach, the agreement is among the partners themselves, not between the partnership and the partners. Each partner binds his or her estate to sell his or her partnership interest to the surviving partners and each surviving partner would have bound himself or herself via the agreement to buy the interest of the deceased partner.

Life insurance commonly is used to fund such agreements. Under the entity approach the partnerhsip itself applies for, owns, and is beneficiary of a life insurance policy on each partner's life. The face amount of each policy usually is equal to the value of the insured partner's interest in the partnership. Under the cross-purchase approach each partner applies for, owns, and is beneficiary of a life insurance policy on each of the other partners' lives. The face amount of each policy usually is equal to the agreed-upon value of the interest that the surviving partner/policyowner would purchase from the deceased partner's estate.

Upon the first death among the partners, the operation of the plan is simple. The life insurance proceeds are used by the partnership or surviving partners, as the case may be, to purchase the interest of the deceased from his or her estate. The partnership is reorganized by the surviving partners and continued in operation, and the heirs of the deceased receive in cash the "going-concern" value of the involved partnership interest. All parties benefit by the arrangement, and the problems of liquidation are obviated. The surviving partners can enter into a new buy-and-sell agreement or amend the original agreement to account for changes in the value of their respective interests.

The business continuation arrangement of a personal-service partnership (e.g., lawyers, doctors, and the like) usually differs from that dis-

[5]For an excellent and thorough treatment of the problems of business continuation and the use of life and health insurance in solving the problems, see Edwin H. White and Herbert Chasman, *Business Insurance,* 5th ed. (Englewood Cliffs, N.J.: Prentice-Hall, Inc., 1980).

cussed above. Provision usually is made for a continuation of income to the deceased partner's estate or heirs for a specified time period, with the income amount possibly based on a profit-sharing agreement. A separate agreement might provide for the purchase (and sale) of the deceased partner's tangible business assets.

When a partner is totally disabled, his or her special talents, knowledge, and ability may be no longer available to the partnership. Instead, the disabled partner becomes a drain on the business financially, and the nondisabled partner(s) must assume the disabled partner's responsibilities and duties without adequate compensation. The non-disabled partners are faced with the problem of earning sufficient money to provide for their usual shares of the partnership profits as well as those of the disabled partner. If they hire a capable replacement for the disabled partner, it is even more difficult to maintain the disabled partner's salary. On the other hand, if a replacement is not hired, the burden on the nondisabled partners may become unbearable, particularly if the disability lasts very long.

As in the case of death, the alternative of taking in family members not already active in the business is fraught with dangers and problems. Similarly, liquidation is not a proper solution. Over and above the possible losses brought about by the forced sale of the business, the nondisabled partners must start all over again in building their careers. Here again, as in the case of the death of a partner, the ideal solution is a properly drawn buy-and-sell agreement that binds the nondisabled partners to purchase the partnership interest of the disabled partner at a prearranged price set forth in the agreement and obligates the disabled partner to sell that interest to the nondisabled partners. The agreement can be funded by disability income insurance policies. Also, disability buyout policies exist that provide a lump-sum payment on total disability (see Chapter 16).

The income tax treatment of partnership buy/sell life insurance is the same as that for personal insurance. That is, premiums are not deductible whether paid by the partnership or a partner. Death proceeds receive IRC section 101(a) treatment (i.e., normally income tax free). The cost basis of each surviving partner is increased by the proceeds received by the partnership in the case of the entity plan and by the amount paid for the deceased partner's interest under the cross-purchase plan.

Life insurance death proceeds are excluded from the gross estate of the insured unless the insured possessed any incidents of ownership or the proceeds are payable to or for the benefit of the insured's estate. Any death proceeds payable to the partnership normally would increase the value of the partnership for estate tax purposes, unless the buy–sell agreement firmly establishes the partnership value, in which case the agreement value will control.[6]

Close Corporation

Although the death of a stockholder does not legally dissolve a corporation, the nature of a close corporation leads to practical problems that often make retirement of the deceased's interest desirable. The practical difficulties encountered in attempting to continue the closely held business in operation following the death of a stockholder stem from the facts that (1) the stockholders of a close corporation also are its officers, (2) earnings are distributed primarily in the form of salaries, and (3) there is no ready market for the stock. Close corporations are so similar to partnerships in basic operation that they have been described as "incorporated partnerships." Consequently, a prearranged plan to retire a stockholder's interest following death or total disability can be vital for the stockholders in a close corporation.

Upon the death of a majority stockholder in a close corporation, the surviving stockholders have four alternatives: (1) to accept an adult heir of the deceased into the actual management of the firm; (2) to pay dividends, approximately equivalent to the salary of the deceased stockholder,

---

[6]The agreement value may not establish firmly the value for IRS estate taxation purposes unless three conditions are met: (1) the estate of the deceased partner is obligated to sell the partnership interest on death, (2) the deceased partner must have been prohibited during life from selling his or her partnership interest without first offering to sell it to the partnership or other partner, and (3) the sale price must have been fair and adequate at the time the agreement was made. See *Advanced Sales Reference Service* (Cincinnati, Ohio: The National Underwriter Co., 1986), Sections 40–43.

to the heir or heirs with little or no participation in management on their part; (3) to admit into active management of the firm outside interests to whom the stock of the deceased may have been sold; or (4) to purchase the stock from the estate of the deceased.

All of these may prove undesirable or impracticable. In the first case, an adult heir normally would be able to contribute little to the management of the business and might well be a constant source of disruption in its operation. The second alternative probably would be unpalatable to the survivors, since they would be bearing all the burdens of management but would be sharing the fruits of their labor equally with another who is contributing nothing but capital to the firm. If the survivors chose to pay less in dividends than the approximate salary of their former associate, this could lead to dissatisfaction on the part of the heir and other complications. The entrance of outsiders into the management of the firm could well be very unsatisfactory. Associates in a close corporation, as in a partnership, join forces because they work well together and each has a certain contribution that, taken together, produces a vigorous, profitable combination. In many cases, the outsiders may not be acceptable and lead to a disruption of the business or, in extreme cases, even to liquidation of the firm. More important, if the outsiders' stock constituted a majority interest, the survivors would be at the mercy of the new owners, who would control such matters as compensation and dividend policy. The final alternative may not be practicable because the survivors may not be able to raise the cash, agreement may not be possible as to a fair price, or the heirs may simply refuse to sell.

The minority stockholder situation poses potential problems no less formidable. The minority stockholder's heirs, while they may not be able to exercise control, nonetheless can render life miserable for the survivors. All stockholders have rights, such as being entitled to a proportionate share of dividends, to examine the corporate records (within reason), and generally to participate in all stockholder activities. Lawsuits by disgruntled minority stockholders are not uncommon.

The majority stockholder's heirs can enforce their wills on the surviving stockholders; minority stockholder's heirs generally cannot. However, this distinction might be more apparent than real. In the first instance, the surviving minority stockholders may decide to abandon the business altogether; starting out afresh on their own. The heirs of the deceased majority shareholder may be at the mercy of the minority stockholders since the minority stockholders are the ones who typically would understand the business best and would be most likely to continue it as a successful going concern.

Clearly, however, the heirs of a deceased minority stockholder are in an unenviable position. They own stock (that was possibly subject to federal and state death taxes) that has little or no marketability (who would buy a minority interest in a closely held corporation?) and for which they receive no income (closely held stock rarely pays dividends).

From the viewpoint of the heirs of a deceased majority stockholder, they face the possibility of trying to sell the stock either to the surviving stockholders or to outsiders, neither of whom would normally be inclined to offer a reasonable price. Indeed, the surviving stockholder/officers probably would not have the resources to buy out the majority interest, and even if they did, they may prefer to take this amount of money and start a new business. Outsiders would purchase a majority interest only with the greatest of caution since the principal value of the business probably would be the remaining employees, who could leave. Alternatively, the heirs could demand an active role in the business or demand cash dividends, either course probably leading to ruin.

These and other difficulties can be avoided by a properly drawn buy-and-sell agreement financed by life insurance. Such agreements may be of the **entity** (usually called **stock-redemption**) or **cross-purchase** type. The agreement binds the surviving stockholders (cross-purchase) or corporation (entity), as the case may be, to purchase the stock of the deceased stockholder at a prearranged price set forth in the agreement and obligates the estate of the deceased stockholder to sell his or her stock to the surviving stockholders (cross-purchase) or the corporation (entity). As in the case of the partnership agreement, each stockholder's interest is valued at the time the agreement is drawn up and should be revalued periodically and the agreement amended to incorporate the new values.

Each stockholder is insured for the value of the stock interest owned, the insurance being owned by either the corporation or the other stockholders. Upon the first death among the stockholders, the life insurance proceeds are used by the corporation or surviving stockholders, as the case may be, to purchase or retire the stock of the deceased from his or her estate. Thus, the business future of the survivors is assured and the heir receives cash instead of a speculative interest.

The stockholders of a close corporation, who are active in the business, are in a position similar to that of partners in a partnership. Consequently, the possibility of a working owner becoming disabled over a long period is a serious risk for the business. The basic problems and available solutions are discussed in Chapter 16. The best available solution lies in funding a properly drawn buy-and-sell agreement with appropriate amounts of disability insurance.

The Tax Aspects of Life Insurance to Fund Corporate Buy–Sell Agreements. Premiums paid for life insurance to fund corporate buy/sell agreements are not income tax deductible under either the entity or cross-purchase approach. Death proceeds and cash value increases do not give rise to taxable income, in the absence of an alternative minimum tax problem (see below).

It is possible to fall into the transfer for value "trap" with life insurance purchased to fund an entity stock buy-out agreement.[7] If life insurance is owned by a corporation to fund an entity buy-out agreement and it is decided later to change to a cross-purchase agreement, the corporate-owned policies could not be transferred directly to the relevant stockholder (i.e., to someone other than the insured) without activating the transfer for value rule. The rule allows exceptions for transfers between partners and the partnership but not from corporations to stockholders.

As with the partnership entity buy–sell agreement, life insurance policy death proceeds will not be includable in a deceased stockholder's estate unless the stockholder held one or more incidents of ownership or unless the proceeds were payable to or for the benefit of the stockholder's estate. Death proceeds payable to the corporation may, however, cause the deceased stockholder's stock value to rise, unless the buy–sell agreement firmly established that value.[8]

Another consideration in using corporate-owned life insurance to fund such agreements is whether life insurance cash value increases and/or policy death proceed payments would invoke the new **alternative minimum tax** (AMT).

The Tax Reform Act of 1986 (TRA '86) provided for imposition of an AMT with respect to so-called "tax preference items."[9] Subject to various adjustments, the AMT rate is 20 percent and, in principle, is invoked if application of the AMT procedure produces a greater tax than that produced by application of regular tax law. Tax preference items are, in general, amounts that accrue to the corporation but are not includable in its taxable income.[10] A new preference item added by TRA '86 could mean that the AMT could apply where (1) a policy's yearly cash value increase exceeds that year's net premium, or (2) death proceeds paid exceed the policy's cash value.

Under most cash value life insurance contracts sold today, the yearly cash value increases, after the first few policy years, exceed the net annual premium. Also, death proceeds will exceed a policy's cash value with virtually all life insurance policies (i.e., policies will have a positive net amount at risk). Either or both instances could trigger the AMT depending upon the details of the particular corporation.

If corporate ownership of a life insurance policy would trigger the AMT, consideration should be given to the cross-purchase approach wherein the corporation is neither the owner nor the beneficiary of the policies. Note also that the

---

[7] Recall that a life insurance policy transferred to another person for a valuable consideration can cause a portion of the death proceeds to be treated as ordinary income to the beneficiary. See Chapter 13.

[8] The agreement will be held to establish the value if certain conditions are met. See footnote 6.

[9] IRC Sections 55–59.

[10] IRC Section 57.

AMT, in concept, could be triggered by key person life insurance as well as other situations of corporate-owned life insurance (see below).

Factors to Consider When Choosing a Buy–Sell Agreement.[11]

There are many factors—both financial and otherwise—to be considered when choosing the type of corporate buy/sell agreement, several of which are summarized below.

1. *Tax factor.* Closely held corporations often are taxed at lower rates than their stockholders. When this is the case, the entity (stock redemption) plan may be more attractive than the cross-purchase plan because the corporation will need fewer before-tax dollars to generate premium payments. If the stockholders are in a lower tax bracket than the corporation, a cross-purchase plan may be advisable. Also, as mentioned above, the AMT situation should be evaluated.

2. *Ease of administration.* In any stock purchase plan, the creation of a sinking or insurance fund is essential. With only two stockholders, there is little difference in the ease of administration with either a stock redemption or cross-purchase plan. Each requires the purchase of only two insurance policies—either by the corporation for a redemption or the stockholders themselves for a cross-purchase.

When the number of stockholders increases, the situation becomes more complicated. Under a stock redemption plan the corporation need purchase only one policy per stockholder. Under a cross-purchase, however, each stockholder generally would purchase a policy on each of the other stockholders. The total number of policies would equal $n (n - 1)$, where n is the number of stockholders. If there are five shareholders, for example, 20 policies would be needed.

By using a trust, it is possible to have a cross-purchase plan with only one policy needed per stockholder. Under a cross-purchase plan utilizing a trusteed agreement, the trustee applies for and owns the policies purchased to fund the underlying buy–sell agreement. Each stockholder contributes to the trust his or her share—determined in one of several ways—of the total premium. When a stockholder dies, the trustee collects the insurance proceeds, purchases the decedent's stock from the estate, and distributes the shares to the survivors in accordance with the underlying agreement. The trustee also often holds the stock for all the stockholders.

3. *Effect upon basis in the corporation.* In a stock redemption plan, the corporation purchases stock from the selling stockholder or estate. Since the other stockholders are not involved in the sale, they will retain their original stock with no increase in cost basis, even though they will now own a larger percentage of the shares outstanding and thus a larger percentage of the corporation. Since their basis has remained the same while their control and ownership have increased, upon subsequent sale these two factors should serve to increase their taxable gain. In a cross-purchase plan, the remaining stockholders purchase stock with their own funds, thereby acquiring an increase in basis equal to the purchase price for the new shares. Upon any subsequent sale, this new basis should serve to reduce the amount of any taxable gain realized by the selling stockholder.

To demonstrate the effect of both plans on an individual's cost basis, assume that the ABC Corporation has a current value of $150,000. Each of three equal owners has an investment of $10,000 in the business. Thus, the value of each owner's share is $50,000 (and each is insured for this amount) and each owner's cost basis is $10,000. Assume that a stockholder dies and subsequently a second owner retires and sells to the third.

Impact of death and later sale under a stock redemption plan

- Assume that A dies, whereupon the corporation collects $50,000 in death proceeds and redeems A's stock.
- The business value remains $150,000, so

  B's value = $75,000 and the cost basis remains $10,000

  C's value = $75,000 and the cost basis remains $10,000

[11]This area draws from "Stock Redemption/Cross-Purchase," *Advanced Sales Course* (Washington, D.C.: Life Underwriter Training Council, 1985), Vol. 9, pp. 109–113.

- When B subsequently retires and sells to C (a living buyout), assuming no change in value, the result is a $65,000 taxable gain for B ($75,000 – $10,000).

Impact of death and later sale under a cross-purchase plan

- Assume that A dies, whereupon B and C each collect $25,000 proceeds and buy A's stock.
- The business value remains $150,000, so

B's value = $75,000 but the cost basis is $10,000 + $25,000 = $35,000

C's value = $75,000 but the cost basis is $10,000 + $25,000 = $35,000

- The result is:

Sale price	$75,000
Less: Cost basis	35,000
Taxable gain	$40,000

This can be an important consideration if one or more stockholders is likely to sell his or her share during life. If the shareholder is likely to retain the stock until death, the stock will obtain a step up in basis to its then current market price on the death of the stockholder. The result, therefore, would be the same irrespective of whether the ownership interest had increased through a cross-purchase or entity agreement.

4. *Accumulated earnings problem.* The IRC imposes a tax if a corporation accumulates earnings beyond its reasonable needs. A stock redemption plan conceivably could aggravate an accumulated earnings problem, since the corporation owns the cash values of the insurance policies or the assets of the funding vehicle. In a cross-purchase plan, since the shareholders own the life insurance policies, an accumulated earnings problem will not arise as a result of this ownership.

5. *Corporate creditors.* Under a stock redemption plan, the corporation is the owner and beneficiary of the life insurance policies funding the arrangement. It would be possible for creditors of the corporation to attach these policies and their proceeds as general corporate assets. This problem would not be encountered under a cross-purchase setup.

6. *State law restrictions.* The laws of most states provide that corporate redemptions can be made only from available corporate surplus. Thus, no surplus—no redemption. Insurance proceeds and contributions to capital can help alleviate this problem, which would not be faced under cross-purchase buy-outs.

7. *Loan limitations.* Many close corporations operate on credit. In the normal course of business, this presents no problems. However, the loan agreements used by most banks contain a restriction prohibiting the payment of dividends or redemption of stock without the prior consent of the bank. What this means is that if credit is likely to be an important aspect of the business, a stock redemption agreement could fail unless it were fully funded and the indebtedness satisfied, so that creditors would not object to a redemption.

8. *Attribution rules.* As a general rule, a complete redemption of a shareholder's stock by a corporation will result in a normal taxable gain [IRC Section 302(b)(3)]. However, a redemption of only a portion of a shareholder's stock will invoke dividend treatment—an undesirable result. Hence, most stock redemption buy-out plans involve the *complete* redemption of stock.

However, IRC Section 318 contains so-called **attribution rules,** the effect of which can be to *attribute* the stock owned by family members or estate beneficiaries to a decendent. Thus, if Nancy owns 100 shares of stock in Nancy's Fancy Books and her husband, Ed, also owns 100 shares, Ed's ownership interest will be attributed to Nancy on her death. Thus, a "complete" redemption of Nancy's 100 shares will be deemed a partial redemption and therefore invoke unfavorable dividend treatment. There are means available in some cases to avoid the harsh operation of these rules, but their discussion is beyond the scope of this volume.

Section 303 Redemption. Many estates are comprised largely of stock in a closely held business. Such estates often have liquidity problems. These problems can cause a forced, disadvantageous sale of estate assets or even business liquidation. Congress enacted IRC Section 303 to help alleviate such problems.

Specifically, a tax-free redemption can be effected for an amount to cover federal and state death taxes, funeral expenses, and estate administration expenses, provided that certain conditions are met. This tax-free redemption can be important since normally a partial redemption of stock would be treated as a taxable dividend to the redeeming stockholder.

To qualify for a Section 303 redemption, the value of the stock must be includable in the decedent's gross estate, must represent at least 35 percent of the adjusted gross estate, and redemption must be made within three years and 90 days after the estate tax return is filed. Other stipulations also apply.

This technique clearly can be useful when the stockholder's business ownership represents a major portion of the total estate assets. It should be equally clear that life insurance is a natural funding vehicle. The corporation would apply for, own, and be beneficiary of a policy whose face amount was sufficient to provide the corporate funds needed to effect the redemption. The income tax treatment of such insurance would be the same as key employee insurance.

SPECIAL EMPLOYEE COMPENSATION PLANS

Individual life insurance often is used to provide supplementary benefits to selected employees. The employees are those whose skills, talents, and experience render them valuable assets to the business. Through these supplementary plans, the employer can provide benefits beyond those offered to rank-and-file employees. The objective, of course, is to attract and retain these talented employees by rewarding them in special ways.

These plans are typically **nonqualified.** This means simply that the employer makes no effort to meet the qualification requirements of the IRC for tax-favored treatment of the plan costs or benefits. A qualified plan must meet certain nondiscrimination and a host of other requirements.[12] In a qualified plan, the employer's

---

contributions are immediately tax deductible, and the employee enjoys certain tax advantages as well. However, the very purpose of a special compensation plan is to discriminate in favor of a select few employees whose contributions to business' success are vital. Hence, such plans usually are nonqualified.

This section discusses two of the most commonly found types of life insurance-funded, nonqualified employee compensation plans: deferred compensation plans and split-dollar life insurance plans.

Nonqualified Deferred Compensation Plans

A nonqualified deferred compensation plan is a contractual arrangement under which compensation for services rendered is postponed, usually until retirement. If properly arranged, the employee will not pay tax on these deferred amounts until they are actually received (e.g., subsequent to retirement), when, presumably, the individual would be in a lower marginal income tax bracket. The employer does not obtain an income tax deduction for such payments until such time as they actually are made available to the employee.

Types of Plans. Nonqualified deferred compensation plans are often divided into two types. The first type, often referred to as a **pure deferred compensation plan,** usually is employee-initiated. It provides for the employee to give up some portion of present compensation or forgo raises or bonuses in return for which the employer agrees to pay a deferred income at some future time. The employee desires to avoid additional current income—which presumably is not needed presently—and current taxation on that income.

The second type, often referred to as a **salary continuation plan,** usually is employer-initiated. Under this arrangement, the employer also agrees to pay a deferred income at some future time but the employer provides the plan as an additional incentive for key employees to remain with the business. It involves no reduction in current income, instead serving as a benefit supplementary to others provided to rank-and-file employees.

---

[12]See Chapter 28.

In tax and other respects, the two types are the same. The difference involves motivations.

Funded and Unfunded Plans. Nonqualified deferred compensation plans may be funded or unfunded. A plan is **funded** when the employer establishes and transfers assets to an escrow account or a trust fund as security for its promise to make future deferred compensation payments. The employee is said to have a beneficial interest in such plan assets.

An **unfunded** nonqualified deferred compensation plan exists when the employer has not formally earmarked assets to fund the plan or, stated differently, when the employee must rely exclusively on the employer's unsecured promise to make deferred compensation payments. A plan is not considered "funded" merely because the employer establishes a reserve fund to meet future obligations under the plan, provided that the fund is not formally linked to the obligation and remains a general asset of the business.

Employer contributions to a funded nonqualified plan will be taxable to the employee unless the employee's rights in the funds are subject to a "substantial risk of forfeiture." Whether a substantial risk of forfeiture exists is not easily determinable. Because of these and other tax uncertainties, nonqualified *funded* plans are used only in exceptional circumstances. As a result, further discussion will be limited to unfunded plans.

Income Tax Treatment. Nonqualified deferred compensation plans have income tax implications to both employers and employees. Each is discussed below.

Generally, the employer will not be entitled to an income tax deduction until such time as amounts are actually or constructively received by the employee. Thus, premium payments or other contributions to fund a deferred compensation plan informally are not deductible currently to the employer. However, when payments are made to the employee, typically subsequent to retirement (or to his or her designated beneficiary on death), the employer may take a deduction for the payments, provided that they are not deemed by the

IRS to constitute unreasonable compensation.[13]

If the employee dies, and as a result, payments are made under a deferred compensation arrangement to a designated beneficiary, such payments normally would be deductible by the employer in the year the payment was made.

A properly drafted deferred compensation plan should result in no income tax obligations to the employee during the deferral period. Payments will be treated as ordinary income to the employee when they are actually or constructively received by the employee. Income is considered **constructively received** if it is made available to the employee or otherwise set aside for him or her. Income is not constructively received if it is subject to substantial risk of forfeiture or if the employer's promise to pay future benefits is unsecured. The employer's purchasing a life insurance policy or annuity (or other investment) to fund the obligation informally does not constitute a secured promise provided that the employee has no interest in the policy or annuity.

Many deferred compensation agreements provide survivor benefits. The IRC generally permits up to $5,000 to be paid income-tax-free as an employee death benefit to a deceased employee's beneficiary.[14] Thus, deferred compensation survivor benefits would be received income tax free to the extent of $5,000, provided that the deceased employee did not possess a nonforfeitable right to receive the payments immediately before death. If the agreement provides for a risk of forfeiture (e.g., via a noncompete clause or nontermination clause), the $5,000 exclusion should apply. Amounts in excess of $5,000 would be subject to ordinary income taxation in the hands of the beneficiary, but only as the amounts were received.

---

[13]Generally, this would not be a problem. It can be a problem where the employee also is a substantial stockholder. In such cases, the IRS often argues that the compensation really is a disguised dividend and therefore not tax deductible to the corporation.

[14]IRC section 101(b). Group life insurance is not considered to be an "employee death benefit" under this code section, and group term life death proceeds are normally received income tax free. See Chapter 26.

Estate Tax Treatment. If an employee were receiving deferred compensation payments at his or her death and if the agreement provided that such payments were to be continued after death, the present value of the remaining payments normally would be includable in the decedent's gross estate.[15] If payments ceased on death, there obviously would be nothing to include in the gross estate.

If death occurred during the deferral period, the present value of the future payments would be includable in the decedant's gross estate if the deceased employee had an enforceable right in the future to receive postemployment benefits. If the plan did not provide such postemployment benefits, any payments made to the named beneficiary may not be included in the gross estate. Such death-benefit-only (DBO) plans have been the subject of considerable litigation.

Life Insurance in Deferred Compensation Plans.[16] Informal funding through life insurance can be especially attractive where the plan provides for the payment of death benefits. When a reserve is established through investment in assets other than life insurance, and the employee dies shortly after the plan is started, the size of the fund may be inadequate to meet the employer's obligation. Where life insurance is used as an informal funding device, the premature death of the employee will not only give rise to the employer's obligation to pay death benefits, but also will create the funds with which to meet that obligation.

Another factor that enhances the attractiveness of life insurance as an informal funding device can be the income-tax-preferred status of the cash value buildup in the policy during the accumulation period. Earnings on most other forms of assets that might be used to accumulate a reserve will be currently taxable to the employer.

With the enactment of TRA '86, corporate-owned annuities lost much of their attractiveness as informal funding media since their cash value increases are no longer tax deferred. Also, with respect to life insurance funding, the corporation's AMT situation should be kept in mind.[17]

An additional advantage of life insurance funding is the option it gives to the employer at the time the employee reaches retirement age. The employer may either use the cash values of the policy to meet its obligation to pay retirement benefits or if other assets are available for that purpose, keep the policy in force and at the death of the employee collect the death proceeds.

Life insurance funding also makes available the waiver of premium benefit. This will relieve the employer's obligation to pay premiums if the insured employee becomes permanently and totally disabled. The dollars that are no longer needed to pay premiums can be used to either provide disability income to the employee or reduce the employer's costs under the plan.

Where life insurance is used in an informally funded deferred compensation plan, the employer normally will be the policyowner, premium payor, and beneficiary of the policy on the employee's life.

The availability of settlement options, especially where the deferred compensation plan requires the employer to pay a life income to the employee, is another reason for informal funding through life insurance. By electing a life income option, the employer can pass on to the insurance company the risk of the employee living beyond his or her normal life expectancy. Where a settlement option is used, care should be taken not to designate the employee or his or her beneficiary as the direct beneficiary under the terms of the life insurance policy. This is to avoid the conclusion that the policy has, in effect, been distributed to the employee or his or her beneficiary so that the full value of the policy would be taxable to the recipient all in one year. To avoid this result, the employer should designate itself as beneficiary under the terms of the settlement option. The employer will then receive the installment pay-

---

[15]IRC section 2039(a). See *Advanced Sales Reference Service,* Section 63 for a discussion of this point.

[16]This area draws from White and Chasman, *Business Insurance,* pp. 553–555.

[17]With life insurance funded nonqualified deferred compensation plans, the AMT situation will be less crucial than with other forms of corporate-owned life insurance. An additional, offsetting item—deferred compensation expense—can be netted against cash value increases and death proceed payments. This item is not tax deductible but is a valid expense for book purposes.

ments from the insurance company and in turn pay the employee out of its funds.

Split-Dollar Life Insurance Plans[18]

Split-dollar life insurance is a funding method, not a life insurance policy. It is an arrangement to provide funding for individual cash value life insurance. The arrangement divides or "splits" the death benefit, the living benefits, and possibly the premium between two parties—hence the name "split dollar."

The objective of split-dollar plans is to join together the *needs* of one person with the *premium-paying ability* of another. Often this means cooperation between an employee and his or her employer, but the concept can be applied to an infinite variety of other relationships: child-parent, stockholder-corporation, buyer-seller, and so on.

The split-dollar plan may provide employees substantial amounts of life insurance protection, generally at an outlay well below that which they would pay for the same policy individually. The employer is free to discriminate among employees benefitted by this plan. The employee also can be allowed to purchase the policy from the employer at termination or retirement. This can provide the employee with a supplemental retirement benefit.

When used as a fringe benefit, split-dollar insurance proceeds are usually intended as (1) a death benefit to the employee's beneficiary, and (2) a reimbursement to the employer for its share of premiums paid. This same concept in recent years has gained added significance for the stockholder-employee.

The Classical Split-Dollar Plan. Although many variations of split-dollar plans exist, an understanding of the classical split-dollar plan will be helpful.[19] Under this arrangement, the employer

and employee join in the purchase of a cash value insurance contract on the employee's life. The employer provides the funds to pay that part of each annual premium equal to the annual increase in the cash value. The employee pays the balance. The employer is entitled to receive death proceeds from the policy equal to the cash value, or at least a sufficient part thereof to equal its total premium payments. The employee names the beneficiary for the balance of any proceeds.

Although the employee's share of annual premiums may be substantial in the early years, it will decrease each year as the annual increases in cash value grow progressively larger. In many cases, the employee's share reaches zero after a relatively short time. As the employer takes over more of the obligation to pay premiums, its share of the death proceeds increases. Nevertheless, through the appropriate use of dividend or other options, the employee's share of the death benefit often can be maintained at an approximately constant amount.

Split-Dollar Systems. Two major systems have been developed for the establishment of a split-dollar life insurance plan: the **endorsement system** and the **collateral assignment system.**

1. *Endorsement system.* Where a split-dollar plan is established under the endorsement system, insurance on the life of an employee is applied for and owned by the employer. The employer is primarily responsible for premium payments. However, in the classical split-dollar arrangement, the employee agrees to reimburse the employer for the portion of each premium payment that exceeds the annual increase in the cash value of the policy. The employer is named the beneficiary for that portion of the proceeds equal to the cash value. The employee designates a personal beneficiary to receive the remainder of the proceeds. The employee's rights are protected by an endorsement on the policy that modifies the employer's rights as policyowner. This endorsement provides that the designation of the employee's personal beneficiary to receive the proceeds in excess of the cash value cannot be changed without the consent of the insured employee.

Some life insurance companies have

---

[18]This section draws from White and Chasman, *Business Insurance,* pp. 560–585, and *Split Dollar Life Insurance* (Bryn Mawr, Pa.: American Society of Chartered Life Underwriters, 1982).

[19]Although the classical plan is much discussed and is the plan dealt with in the IRC, relatively few split-dollar plans are arranged in this manner. See "Variations of the Classical Split-Dollar Plan" later in this section.

adopted a slightly different approach to the endorsement system of split-dollar plan. These companies permit the ownership of policy rights to be split, with the insured employee designated as owner of that portion of the death proceeds in excess of the cash value and the employer designated as owner of all the other rights and benefits under the policy.

If the split-dollar plan is terminated prior to the death of the insured employee, the employer recovers its premium outlay directly from the cash value that it controls as owner of the policy. This may be accomplished by surrendering the policy or giving the insured employee the option to purchase it for an amount equal to its cash surrender value.

2. *Collateral assignment system.* When a classical split-dollar insurance plan is established under the collateral assignment system, the insured employee applies for and owns the policy. He or she then designates his or her own personal beneficiary. The insured employee is primarily liable for premium payment. However, in a separate agreement, the employer obligates itself to "lend" the employee an amount of money each year equal to the annual increase in the cash value. Generally, this loan is made interest-free. Thus, the employee's out-of-pocket cost will be limited to that portion of each annual premium that exceeds the annual increase in cash value. To protect the employer, the employee collaterally assigns the policy to the employer as security for the amount of the loan. At the insured employee's death, the employer recovers the amount of its loan from the death proceeds, not as a beneficiary of the policy, but as a collateral assignee.[20]

3. *Factors bearing on choice of split-dollar systems.* Several factors help determine which split-dollar system should be used. One factor to consider is whether the employer wants the cash value available for use in its business during the term of the split-dollar plan. If it does, the endorsement system or split-ownership variation is preferable. Under the collateral assignment system, the policy cash value generally will not be available to the

employer. Under the endorsement system, the employer, as owner of the policy, is free to borrow from the policy at any time and for any reason.

Where the parties intend to use the policy to fund a nonqualified deferred compensation arrangement, the endorsement method should be used. This is especially true when the insured employee is *not* a stockholder or officer of the corporation. Under the endorsement method, the employer owns the policy and the cash value. At the retirement of the insured employee, the employer can elect to receive the cash value under a settlement option or continue to pay the premiums on the policy until the death of the employee. In the latter case, the death proceeds could be used to offset the benefit paid under the deferred compensation agreement. If the collateral assignment system is used, the insured employee is owner of the policy. If the policy is to be used to fund a deferred compensation plan, it will have to be transferred to the corporation. This would involve a transfer for value that would not come under the exceptions to the transfer for value rule for income tax purposes unless the insured employee was a stockholder or officer of the corporation.[21] This would subject a portion of the death proceeds to ordinary income tax treatment.

If a policy already in force and personally owned by the insured employee is to be used to establish a split-dollar plan, it will be simpler to adopt the collateral assignment system. However, if the policy is a key person policy owned by the employer, the simpler approach would be to utilize the endorsement system.

Income Tax Consequences of Split-Dollar Plans. Split-dollar plans give rise to income tax consequences to both employees and employers.

1. *Income tax treatment of employees.* Under a 1964 IRS ruling, the typical split-dollar plan is considered to result in a taxable **economic benefit** to the employee represented by the amount of the annual premium cost that the employee should bear and of which he or she is relieved.[22] The value of the benefit, to be included annually in the

---

[20]See Chapter 9 under "Assignment Provision."

[21]IRC Section 101(a)(2). See Chapter 13 under "Transfer for Value Rule."

[22]Rev. Rul 64–328, 1964–2 CB 11.

employee's taxable income, is an amount equal to the one-year term cost of the life insurance protection that the employee is entitled to from year to year, less any portion of the premium provided by the employee. In arriving at the annual economic benefit to the employee, the one-year term insurance rates contained in the government's so-called **PS-58 Rate Table** should be used. Table 15–1 gives these rates.[23] If the issuer of the insurance policy publishes rates for individual, initial issue, one-year term policies available to all standard risks, such rates may be used in place of the PS-58 rates.[24] Many companies have such term rates that are significantly lower than the PS-58 rates. Using the lower rates decreases the amount of taxable income imputed to the employee.

An example of how the economic benefit to the employee is determined should be helpful. At this point, policy dividends will be ignored.

[23]This table reflects one-year term costs based on Table 38, U.S. Life & Actuarial Tables, and 2½% interest. These rates also are used to determine the economic benefit that is taxable to an employee because of death benefits provided under a pension plan. See Chapter 28.

[24]Rev. Rul. 66–110, 1966–1 CB 12.

Assume that a $100,000 ordinary life policy with an annual premium of $2,000 is purchased under a classical split-dollar plan. In the year in question the annual increase in cash value, and thus the employer's contribution toward the premium, is $1,800. The employee must, therefore, pay $200 ($2,000 – $1,800). Further, assume that if the employee dies during the year, the portion of the death proceeds payable to the employer is $10,000 (the total of its premium contributions) with the remaining $90,000 of death proceeds payable to the insured employee's personal beneficiary.

To determine the amount the employee must include in his or her taxable income as a result of the economic benefit he or she receives, the first step is to calculate the term cost of the insurance protection provided to his or her personal beneficiary. Assume that the employee's attained age is 42. Based on the PS-58 Rate Table, the term cost of insurance protection is $5.07 per $1,000. Since $90,000 would be payable to the employee's personal beneficiary, the total cost of the insurance protection is $456 ($90,000 × $5.07/$1,000). However, the employee contributed $200 toward the premium payment. Hence, the value of the net economic benefit and the amount included in his or her taxable income is $256 ($456 – $200).

TABLE 15-1. PS-58 rates: one-year term premiums, for $1,000 of life insurance protection

Age	Premium	Age	Premium	Age	Premium
15	$1.27	37	$ 3.63	59	$ 19.08
16	1.38	38	3.87	60	20.73
17	1.48	39	4.14	61	22.53
18	1.52	40	4.42	62	24.50
19	1.56	41	4.73	63	26.63
20	1.61	42	5.07	64	28.98
21	1.67	43	5.44	65	31.51
22	1.73	44	5.85	66	34.28
23	1.79	45	6.30	67	37.31
24	1.86	46	6.78	68	40.59
25	1.93	47	7.32	69	44.17
26	2.02	48	7.89	70	48.06
27	2.11	49	8.53	71	52.29
28	2.20	50	9.22	72	56.89
29	2.31	51	9.97	73	61.89
30	2.43	52	10.79	74	67.33
31	2.57	53	11.69	75	73.23
32	2.70	54	12.67	76	79.63
33	2.86	55	13.74	77	86.57
34	3.02	56	14.91	78	94.09
35	3.21	57	16.18	79	102.23
36	3.41	58	17.56	80	111.04
				81	120.57

Each year the amount included in the employee's taxable income will vary because the term rate and protection amount will be different.[25]

The value of any policy dividends used to benefit the employee also will be includable in his or her taxable income. As with the economic benefit treatment, the tax implications of any additional benefits received by the employee on account of policy dividends under a split-dollar plan will be the same whether the endorsement system or the collateral assignment system is used.[26]

2. *Income tax treatment of employer.* Premiums paid by an employer on insurance covering the life of an employee where the employer is directly or indirectly a beneficiary under the policy are not deductible.[27] As a result, the employer is not allowed a tax deduction for its share of premiums under a split-dollar plan. In the absence of an AMT problem, cash value increases do not invoke income tax treatment.

3. *Income tax treatment of death proceeds.* The income tax treatment of any death proceeds payable under a split-dollar plan will be governed by IRC Section 101(a).[28] Thus, in the absence of a IRC Section 7702 (definition of life insurance) or a transfer for value problem or of an AMT problem, both the employer and the personal beneficiary of the employee will receive their share of the proceeds income-tax-free.

Estate Tax Treatment of Split-Dollar Plans. The IRC provides that death proceeds of insurance are includable in the gross estate of a decedent/insured if he or she possessed any of the incidents of ownership in the policy or if proceeds are payable to or for the benefit of the decedent/insured's estate.

Under the usual endorsement system the employer will be the sole owner of the life insurance policy used to fund a split-dollar plan.

However, to protect the insured employee's rights under the agreement, the ownership rights of the employer are modified by endorsement which provides that the insured employee's personal beneficiary cannot be changed without the consent of the insured employee. This is an incident of ownership. This ownership right might be avoided if the agreement provided that the beneficiary cannot be changed without the consent of the beneficiary, rather than the insured. In any event, with the current unlimited marital deduction available, the question of ownership may not be as important as it was previously, unless the beneficiary is someone other than the spouse of the insured.

Under the collateral assignment system, the insured employee generally is the owner of the policy. As such, he or she can exercise all the incidents of ownership. Therefore, the death proceeds should be includable in his or her gross estate for federal estate tax purposes.[29] The estate tax value of the proceeds should be the full proceeds less the amount which must be paid to the employer in satisfaction of the debt owed to it under the split-dollar agreement.[30]

Where the collateral assignment system is used and the insured employee wants to keep the proceeds out of his or her gross estate, the beneficiary for the insured employee's share of the proceeds should initially apply for and own the life insurance policy. The owner of the policy should then enter into the collateral assignment split-dollar agreement with the insured's employer. Under this arrangement, the insured employee has no incidents of ownership in the policy, and presumably the proceeds should be excludable from his or her gross estate.

Where a split-dollar plan (regardless of the system under which it is established) is instituted between a corporation and a majority stockholder-employee, the portion of the proceeds payable to a beneficiary other than the corporation may be includable in the gross estate of the insured majority stockholder-employee even where the necessary steps have been taken to eliminate the possession of any incidents of ownership in the

---

[25]Only policies purchased under split-dollar arrangements or utilized to establish such arrangements *after* November 13, 1964 are treated as giving rise to a taxable economic benefit to the employee.

[26]Rev. Rul. 66–110, 1966–1 CB 12.

[27]IRC Sec. 264(a)(1).

[28]Rev. Rul. 64–328, 1964–2 CB 11.

[29]IRC Sec. 2042(2).

[30]Reg. Sec. 20.2053–7.

policy held *directly* by the insured. This result is based on an estate tax regulation that attributes the incidents of ownership possessed by a corporation in an insurance policy on the life of a majority stockholder to the majority stockholder to the extent the proceeds are *not* payable to or for the benefit of the corporation.[31]

Variations of the Classical Split-Dollar Plan.

Under the classical split-dollar plan, the employer contributes an amount equal to the annual increase in cash value each year and the insured employee contributes the balance of the annual premium due, if any. In the first few years of the plan, the financial burden on the insured employee could be substantial. Also, where the employee's premium contribution exceeds the economic benefit, no carryover of the excess contribution to future years is allowed. Primarily as a result of these difficulties, several variations of the classical split-dollar approach have evolved, a few of which are discussed below.

1. *Averaging.* Under the averaging approach, the employer pays a level amount each year that is equal to a specified fraction of the policy's cash value after a specified number of years. For example, the employer might pay each year ½₀ of the twentieth-year cash value. The employee would pay the balance of each premium. Thus, the employee's contribution is leveled out to ease his or her burden in the early policy years. Over the specified period (say, 20 years), aggregate contributions by both the employer and employee are the same as under the classical plan.

2. *PS-58 costs.* Under the PS–58 cost approach, the employee pays an amount each year equal to that year's PS-58 cost. (Depending on the use of dividends, the death benefit may vary from year to year.) The employer pays the balance, if any, of each premium. It is worth noting that a policy issued at a young age eventually may generate a PS-58 cost substantially larger than the gross annual premium.

3. *Employer pays all.* Under this variation,

the employer pays the full premium each year. The employee makes no contribution to the premium and merely reports taxable income on the value of the economic benefit received each year.

4. *Bonus and double bonus.* The so-called bonus and double-bonus plans are merely minor adaptations that combine aspects of the PS-58 and employer-pay-all approaches. The employer is willing to pay the entire cost of the plan. However, cognizant of the fact that its expenditure on behalf of the employee's economic benefit is not deductible, the employer instead adopts a PS-58 cost plan and pays the employee a bonus sufficient to enable the employee to pay the PS-58 costs. The employer's expenditure is precisely the same as with the employer-pay-all approach, but a portion of it (equal to the PS-58 measured bonus) is presumably deductible as compensation. The employee now pays tax on the bonus rather than on PS-58 costs. So the employee is in the same position with a *bonus* as with employer-pay-all plan.

The double bonus is a PS-58 cost plan, supplemented by a bonus each year in an amount equal to twice the PS-58 cost. Hence, in the past, if the employee were in a 50 percent tax bracket, half the bonus would be used to pay tax on the bonus. The other half becomes the employer's contribution to the split-dollar plan.

5. *Allocation of death proceeds.* The classical split-dollar plan allocates a death benefit to the employer equal to the sum of its aggregate contributions. Another approach is to allocate to the employer a portion of the death proceeds equal to the employer's contributions accumulated at some specified rate of interest. This reflects the time value of money. An interest rate equal to the after-tax policy loan rate often is used, since premiums for split-dollar plans often are financed through policy loans.[32]

"Unsplitting" the Policy.

Because of the insured's advancing age, and hence increasing PS-58 costs, a time may come when the split-dollar arrangement is no longer attractive. (Of

---

[31]Reg. Sec. 20.2042–1(c)(6). See Rev. Rul. 82–145.

[32]But see Chapter 13.

course, other considerations sometime may lead to a similar conclusion.) Three alternatives are commonplace in "unsplitting" split-dollar plans: (1) convert to key person insurance, (2) a rollout, and (3) a spinout.

1. *Convert to key person insurance.* Under this approach, the insured (or third-party owner) releases his or her interest in the policy to the corporation. This normally would be an undesirable solution *unless* the insured is an officer or stockholder of the corporation, since it would appear to constitute a transfer-for-value. If the insured is a principal stockholder, he or she may prefer to have the corporation retain the policy death proceeds to be used in a Section 303 redemption or a postdeath total liquidation of the corporation.

2. *Rollouts.* A rollout occurs when the corporation makes a maximum policy loan, followed by a transfer of its remaining ownership rights in the policy to the insured. The employer probably would sell the policy to the insured for the difference between the gross cash surrender value and the policy loan, if any.

The insured would have a continuing interest obligation on the policy loan. Since the corporation has recoverd an amount equal to the cash value and no longer has any commitment under the split-dollar agreement, it can (if it wishes) give the insured employee annual bonuses equal to the interest payable.

3. *Spinouts.* Another approach is referred to as a spinout. Rather than taking a policy loan, the corporation merely transfers its interest in the policy as a bonus to the insured. Any transfer to a third-party owner should be a separate subsequent event, with the insured gifting the policy to the third-party owner to avoid a transfer-for-value.

Under a spinout, the insured would be taxed on the value of the policy. If the insured chooses to do so, he or she could borrow against the policy to pay the tax. This leaves the insured with a considerably smaller policy loan than is the case with the rollout. Again, the corporation may see fit to give the insured employee annual bonuses equal to the interest payable on this (smaller) loan.

4. *Caveat.* Each of the foregoing "unsplitting" techniques works nicely for a classical split-dollar plan. Under such a plan, the corporation's contributions have precisely equaled the policy's cash value. However, with more ambitious plans (i.e., plans where the corporate contributions have exceeded the increase in cash value), it is necessary to reckon with the excess of total corporate contributions over total cash value. This excess was, presumably, in the nature of a loan to the employee. A release or discharge of this indebtedness generates taxable income to the individual who is so enriched. The solution may be to undertake "unsplitting" only in a policy year when the cash value is as large as (or, at least, not much smaller than) the corporation's cumulative contributions. This will eliminate (or, at least, minimize) the problem of discharge of an indebtedness.

Other Uses of Split-Dollar Insurance Plans. In the typical employer-employee split-dollar plan, insurance is purchased on the life of the employee. However, an employee may need insurance protection on the life of someone else. Split-dollar plans can be useful in these cases also.

1. *Sole proprietor buy-out.* An individual who is the sole owner of a business, whether incorporated or not, may not have any family members to whom he or she wants to leave the business at death. It may be difficult to sell the business to an outsider at a fair price. In such a situation, it is not unusual for the business owner to seek out a key employee of the firm and offer to sell the business to him or her at the business owner's death. Although the employee may be eager to accept the offer, one major stumbling block often is the lack of funds with which to make the purchase. An obvious solution would be insurance on the life of the employer owned by the employee. However, the employee may not be able to afford the premium payments. To solve this problem, the employer may enter into a split-dollar insurance plan with the employee. In this case, the insurance is on the life of the employer rather than the employee.

2. *Split-dollar in a cross-purchase buy–sell agree-*

ment. One drawback to the use of a cross-purchase buy–sell agreement is that the stockholders are personally responsible for the payment of premiums on insurance used to fund the plan. However, the corporation can help to finance the purchase of the needed insurance through the use of a split-dollar plan. Where a split-dollar plan is entered into for this purpose, the collateral assignment system generally is used. Each stockholder will apply for and own a policy on the life of his or her co-stockholder(s). Each stockholder then collaterally assigns the policy he or she owns on his or her co-stockholder's life to the corporation as security for the corporation's premium payments.

If a split-dollar plan used to fund a cross-purchase buy/sell agreement is arranged under the endorsement system, it could result in a transfer-for-value problem. Under this system, normally the corporation will apply for and own the life insurance. It then transfers the right to receive a portion of the policy proceeds on the life of each stockholder to his or her co-stockholder. This is a transfer-for-value (the consideration being services rendered to the corporation) to a co-stockholder of the insured. Such a transfer does not come within any of the exceptions to the transfer-for-value rule and would thus subject the proceeds to income taxation. Some companies believe that this potential problem can be avoided by setting up the ownership and beneficiary arrangement at policy inception and thereby avoid any "transfer."

Where one of the parties to the cross-purchase buy/sell agreement is a majority stockholder-employee, the use of a split-dollar plan to help fund the agreement could create a serious estate tax trap. This is because the incidents of ownership in the life insurance policy on his or her life possessed by the corporation will be attributed to the majority stockholder-insured if they extend to the proceeds of the policy *not* payable to the corporation.[33] The result could be that the value of the stock in the corporation and the insurance proceeds received by the co-stockholder

and used to purchase the stock will both be includable in his or her gross estate.[34]

3. *Family split-dollar plan.* It is not necessary to have an employer-employee relationship to take advantage of the benefits that can be provided by a split-dollar insurance plan. For example, a parent may be concerned about the lack of insurance protection for his or her married child in the event that the child's spouse should die. The parent may be willing to assist the spouse financially in the purchase of insurance on his or her life but does not want to do so at the expense of the share of his or her estate that would go eventually to his or her spouse and other children. In this circumstance, the parents can enter into a split-dollar plan with their child's spouse by the terms of which the parents will receive back from the proceeds an amount equal to the premiums they paid. The child will then be protected by insurance on his or her spouse's life at a minimal cost to them. Since this is not an employer-employee arrangement, there should be no taxable income. However, the value of the economic benefit received as a result of the arrangement may be treated as a taxable gift from the parents. In most cases, however, a gift tax will not be payable since the economic benefit will not exceed the $10,000 annual exclusion.

4. *Other uses.* There are obviously many other situations where the split-dollar concept can be put to good use between family members. The possible uses to which a split-dollar insurance plan can be put have by no means been exhausted. Any time one party has a need for insurance protection and another party can be found who is willing to assist in the purchase of the insurance needed, the elements are present for the adoption of a split-dollar insurance plan.

---

[33]Reg. Sec. 20.2042–1(c)(6).

[34]However, case law has held that no double inclusion will result if the buy-sell agreement is properly drafted, binding the use of the insurance. See *Advanced Sales Reference Service,* Section 54.

Chapter 16

Individual Health Insurance Contracts

INTRODUCTION[1]

Public and private spending for medical care in the United States totals more than $355 billion a year or $1,459 per person, an increase of almost 700 percent within the last two decades. Corporate spending on employee health has doubled since 1978, to $77 billion a year. Doctors' fees, hospital bills, and related medical expenses account for more than one of every $10 spent in the economy. The federal government predicts that these costs will continue to escalate at a rate of $50 billion a year. In response to these growing costs of health care, private health insurance premiums have necessarily also been increasing—*an average of 25 percent annually.*[2] It is not surprising to find the current concentration on cost containment[3] and alternative health care delivery systems.[4]

This chapter provides an overview of the providers of health insurance and the broad types of coverage available. Since almost 90 percent of all medical expense coverage provided by life and health insurers is delivered through the group mechanism,[5] the treatment of individual medical expense insurance in this and the next chapter will not be detailed. A detailed treatment is reserved for the discussion on employee benefits.[6] In contrast, disability income insurance protection often is provided by individual policies, and hence the discussion of disability income insurance and its uses will be more comprehensive.

Broad Types of Coverage

Health insurance, among other names, is called accident and health insurance, accident and sickness insurance, or in the laws of about a dozen

[1]Chapter prepared substantively by Robert I. Damon, Assistant Vice President, Health Insurance, The Guardian Life Insurance Company of America.

[2]Rob La Rue, "Financial Incentives in Group Health Insurance," *Journal of Insurance Regulation,* Vol. 4 (September 1985), p. 40.

[3]See Charles C. Phelps, *Health Care Costs: The Consequences of Cost Sharing* (Santa Monica, Calif.: The Rand Corporation, 1982). See also Robert A. Cooper, *Health Care Cost Management: Issues, Strategies, and Current Practices* (Brookfield,

Wisc.: International Foundation of Employee Benefit Plans, 1984).

[4]See "Buyers Forcing Revolution in Health Care Delivery," *Business Insurance,* July 22, 1985.

[5]*Source Book of Health Insurance Data, 1984–1985* (Washington, D.C.: Health Insurance Association of America), p. 25. Unless specifically noted otherwise, all statistical data presented in this chapter are from this source.

[6]See Chapter 27.

states, simply disability insurance. These various titles are a broad reference to two very different categories of insurance, known separately as **medical expense** insurance and **disability income** insurance. Each major category contains various distinctive plans of coverage to protect the insured against specific financial losses from injury or disease.

Sometimes known as "health care" insurance, medical expense insurance provides a broad range of benefits that can cover virtually all expenses connected with hospital and medical care and related services for the insured and covered family members. Plans may be limited to basic benefits for specific kinds of medical services or may be expanded to provide comprehensive benefits for all major medical expenses associated with a severe injury or long-term illness. Benefits are usually paid as reimbursement of the actual expenses that an insured incurs. Some benefits, however, are paid as fixed indemnities without regard to the actual cost of care.

Disability income insurance, often called "loss of time" or "loss of income" insurance, provides periodic payments when an insured is unable to work because of injury or sickness. Coverage is related, at least in part, directly to the insured's occupational duties and earnings. Benefits are usually paid monthly as fixed indemnities while the insured is disabled, although certain plans of business insurance may provide reimbursement-type coverage.

Both medical expense and disability income insurance are available on either a *group* or *individual* basis, although as pointed out above, most medical expense insurance, other than supplemental coverages, is now sold on a group basis, particularly among the commercial insurance companies. The distinctions between group and individual insurance arise primarily in the ways in which they are marketed and the manner in which coverage is finally issued and administered.[7]

Individual versus Group Coverage

Group health insurance refers to arrangements in which coverage is provided for groups

[7]See Chapters 26 and 30.

of individuals under a single master contract issued to a group policyowner. The policyowner may be an employer, an association, a labor union, a trust, or any other legitimate entity that was not organized solely for the purpose of obtaining insurance. Members of larger groups generally obtain coverage without having to furnish evidence of insurability, but such evidence usually is required for groups of less than 10 lives. Group medical expense plans generally cover the group member, his or her spouse, and any dependent children.

Each member receives a certificate of insurance that describes briefly the major provisions of the master contract. The policyowner may pay the entire premium or require a partial contribution from each member, who remains covered while the master contract is in force and he or she maintains a valid relationship with the policyowner. Because of reduced marketing and administrative costs, group insurance generally costs less than an individual plan with comparable coverages.

Individual health insurance, on the other hand, is an arrangement in which coverage is provided to a specific individual under a policy that is issued solely to that individual. Except in mass marketing techniques, the insured must furnish evidence of insurability before a policy will be issued. Companies maintain separate records for each policy and conduct all transactions, including premium collection, on a direct basis with each insured. As in group insurance, individual medical expense policies generally include family coverage.

HEALTH INSURANCE PROVIDERS

In a 1979 study, the Health Insurance Association of America, a national trade organization, identified 42 separate systems of disability income protection that are available to disabled persons in the United States. These compensation systems include individual and group insurance plans and "entitlement" programs of the federal government for disabled persons who are protected under various social insurance laws. The following is a representative sampling of these systems:

Federal disability compensation systems

- Primary Social Security Disability Benefits
- Dependents' Social Security Disability Benefits
- Veterans Administration Disability Benefits
- Civil Service Disability Benefits
- Railroad Retirement Act
- Longshoremen's and Harbor Workers' Compensation Act

State and local government compensation systems

- Workers' Compensation
- State Temporary Disability Benefits
- Supplemental Security Income
- Aid to Families with Dependent Children
- Food Stamps

Insurance industry compensation systems

- Disability Income
- Hospital Indemnity
- General and Individual Liability
- Business Overhead Expense
- Creditor Disability Income
- Disability Buy/Sell

A comparable listing could be made for medical expense benefit systems. By the end of 1983, in fact, the U.S. Census Bureau estimated that 85 percent of the population was covered by either government or private health insurance. Health insurance in the United States is available under varying qualifications from six principal sources: (1) commercial insurance companies, (2) Blue Cross and Blue Shield organizations, (3) Health Maintenance Organizations (HMOs), (4) Preferred Provider Organizations (PPOs), (5) self-insured plans, and (6) federal or state governments.[8] Each is discussed briefly below. It is important to remember that this brief discussion of health insurance providers contemplates both individual *and* group insurance. Some providers are involved in both lines, but, for example, HMOs and PPOs are essentially group arrangements.

---

[8]For a thorough analysis of health insurance providers, see Burton T. Beam, Jr., and John J. McFadden, *Employee Benefits* (Homewood, Ill.: Richard D. Irwin, Inc., 1985), Chap. 8.

Commercial Insurance Companies

More than 800 commercial insurance companies were writing some form of health insurance at the end of 1983.[9] These stock and mutual corporations are organized as life, casualty, or health insurance companies to provide medical expense and disability income insurance on a group or individual basis. Private insurers write virtually all of the disability income insurance available in the United States, with the exception of various government income replacement programs.

The insurance policies of commercial insurers generally provide for payment of benefits directly to the insured, unless the insured has specifically assigned payment to a designated provider of medical services. At the end of 1983, nearly 111 million persons were covered under policies issued by commercial insurance companies.

Blue Cross and Blue Shield Plans

The Blue Cross and Blue Shield Association coordinates the 90 Blue Cross and Blue Shield plans that operate statewide or regionally across the nation as nonprofit hospital and medical service corporations. These plans dominate the market for basic medical expense coverage in many geographic areas, primarily because of lower premiums from a favored tax status and close ties to the hospitals and organized medical societies in the localities that they serve. Major medical and group dental insurance are often available from Blue Cross and Blue Shield plans. At the end of 1983, more than 81 million persons were covered under Blue Cross and Blue Shield plans.

Blue Cross plans are nonprofit hospital expense prepayment plans. Most plans were organized by hospitals in the area served by the plan. Historically, member hospitals usually elected the board of directors, which normally included members from the public and the medical profession, as well as hospital administrators. Today, the composition of the boards has changed significantly to reflect more business and consumer representation.

---

[9]Because of the more detailed treatment of commercial insurers in Chapter 11, this discussion is brief.

The plans provide for hospital care on a "service-type" basis, by which Blue Cross enters into contracts separately with member hospitals for certain types and amounts of hospital services and then reimburses the hospital directly for those covered services rendered to plan subscribers. The subscriber, the "Blues" term for insured, is billed only for those services not covered by the Blue Cross certificate, and unlike commercial health insurance, there usually is no direct payment to the person covered.

Basic Blue Cross coverage usually provides for full hospital services up to 365 days in semiprivate accommodations and for a wide range of miscellaneous hospital services, including laboratory and x-ray testing, use of the operating room, medications and supplies, and general floor nursing. Most plans cover some outpatient services for accidental injury, for minor surgery, and for certain diagnostic laboratory or x-ray tests that can be performed in advance of actual hospital admission (preadmission testing). In addition, most Blue Cross plans offer supplementary or extended benefits beyond the basic certificate, to include nursing home care, care in the home after hospitalization, dental treatment, prescription drugs, and coverage for catastrophic illness.

Subscribers of one Blue Cross plan who move into the area of another plan are entitled to transfer membership to the new home area. To provide service to national or multistate accounts, the Blue Cross and Blue Shield Association was brought into existence in 1948, and its responsibilities have enlarged continuously. The Association plays an important coordination and standard-setting role since Blue Cross plans are separate nonprofit corporations in separate jurisdictions, each plan having its own contracts and its own schedule of rates and benefits.

Blue Cross subscribers normally go to a hospital that cooperates with the plan in their area. In the event that a subscriber is hospitalized in a nonplan hospital, a special benefit is allowed, often less liberal than that normally provided. If a subscriber is hospitalized outside the area of the plan to which he or she belongs, the Inter-Plan Service Benefit Bank enables him or her to be treated temporarily as a member of the Blue Cross plan of the area where he or she is then hospitalized and to receive the benefit of that local plan.

The majority of Blue Cross plans are coordinated with Blue Shield plans. **Blue Shield** plans are nonprofit organizations offering prepayment coverage for surgical and medical services performed by a physician. Independently organized on a state or regional basis within a state, these plans are members of the National Association of Blue Cross and Blue Shield Plans and are now commonly controlled locally by a board of directors representing both the consumer and the medical profession. As in the case of Blue Cross, each plan operates autonomously, but the National Association has developed a set of comprehensive contract definitions to assure common administration from plan to plan for subscribers in large national or multistate groups. It should be noted, however, that in recent years there has been a consolidation of more than half of the Blue Cross and Blue Shield plans. In some cases, this has involved a complete merger; in others, the consolidation has been partial with a single staff but separate governing boards.

The typical Blue Shield plan provides benefits similar in nature to those provided under the surgical and physicians' expense-benefit provisions of the commercial health insurance policy. In most plans, Blue Shield has completed contractual agreements with area physicians to provide the care promised under the plan. However, since it is much more difficult to negotiate fee schedules with several hundred doctors, in contrast to a handful of hospitals in the area, Blue Shield has not been able to adopt the same full-service philosophy of Blue Cross. In an effort to resolve the fee problem, most plans have established an income ceiling, typically $6,500 for an individual and $9,500 for a family. If a subscriber's income is below this level, he or she is entitled to full service without any additional fee for various surgical and medical procedures of a physician. If his or her income is above the income ceiling, the subscriber remains responsible for the difference between the Blue Shield reimbursement and the physician's usual fee. Most Blue Shield plans now offer surgical benefits without specific schedules and provide coverage for "reasonable and customary" charges, often making direct reimbursement to the subscriber rather than the physician.

Blue Cross/Blue Shield major medical coverage is available on both a group and an individual basis. These plans generally are superimposed on basic plans that are in effect under both cooperating organizations.[10] The major medical plans offered resemble those of commercial insurers. A deductible is involved and the subscriber usually must pay a 20 percent coinsurance fee until out-of-pocket expenses reach a certain amount, often $2,000, after which no coinsurance applies. The benefit maximum for major medical expense may be $250,000 or more. Many, if not most Blue Cross/Blue Shield plans offer comprehensive major medical for their local groups. In addition, the Blue Cross and Blue Shield Association has adopted (as a condition of plan membership) a so-called "Meta Matrix" as the basis for multistate accounts. The matrix is organized by benefit types (i.e., services) and scope (limits/maximums on days, visits, dollar limits, etc.). It allows for the service benefit as well as comprehensive major medical.

The distinct advantage enjoyed by Blue Cross/Blue Shield has been the favorable tax treatment given these organizations. Whereas commercial insurance companies have long been subjected to federal income taxes, a variety of state taxes—including a significant tax on premiums received—and even certain local taxes, Blue Cross/ Blue Shield organizations traditionally have been virtually immune to significant state taxes. Blue Cross/Blue Shield plans also are afforded favorable treatment under the federal income tax laws. Recently, some states have withdrawn their nonprofit status, and legislation has been proposed that would eliminate their federal income tax exemption.

Health Maintenance Organizations

Perhaps the most significant recent development in the financing and delivery of prepaid physician and hospital care has been the rapid growth of **health maintenance organizations**

(HMOs).[11] An HMO provides a wide range of comprehensive health care services for members who are enrolled on a group basis and who pay a fixed periodic premium in advance for the services of participating physicans and cooperating hospitals. HMOs differ from traditional insurance plans in that they are both the financing *and* servicing mechanism. They emphasize preventive medicine and early treatment through prepaid routine physical examination and diagnostic screening techniques. At the same time, they provide complete hospital and medical care for sickness and injury.

The 1973 federal legislation, and later amendments in 1976, essentially provided for substantial government funding through grant arrangements to encourage the establishment of Health Maintenance Organizations. But the most important support for development of HMOs came from the fact that the law allows HMOs to require that any employer with 25 or more employees that provides health care benefits must offer enrollment in an HMO as an alternative to traditional forms of insurance, unless no such cooperative plan is located nearby (no HMO crosses state lines). HMOs have become a significant factor in the health industry. By early 1985, the various types of HMOs had grown to 337 operational units serving approximately 17 million people.

Health maintenance organizations are basically prepaid group practice plans that have an agreement with one or more hospitals for admission of enrolled members on a service-type basis. A group of physicians is organized into a cooperative to provide complete office and hospital care. They may (1) practice in a clinic setting as salaried staff of the HMO, (2) provide individual care in their own offices, or (3) operate in a full group practice for salary or on a per capita basis. Over two-thirds of existing HMOs are organized as full group practices in the latter arrangement. Most HMOs accept enrollment only from clearly designated groups, such as employees of any of several employers, or residents of a particular

---

[10]See Chapter 27 on major medical expense insurance.

[11]See Charles Ostheimer, "Shifting the Risks: Growth of the HMO Market," *The National Underwriter*, Life/Health ed., January 4, 1986.

locality, although some may permit enrollment from the general population on an individual basis.

HMOs can be sponsored by government, medical schools, hospitals, employees, labor unions, consumer groups, insurance companies, and hospital-medical service plans. When a life insurance company is involved, the company or service plan contracts to pay in advance for the full range of health services to which the insured is entitled under the terms of the health insurance contract. These services include hospitalization, surgery, and routine physical care.

Preferred Provider Organizations

Preferred provider organizations or arrangements, called either PPOs or PPAs, are emerging as cost-containment mechanisms intended to lower the cost of medical care and the insurance that funds it. Employers and insurance companies have begun to view PPOs as a significant factor in their efforts to control rapidly rising medical care costs.[12]

PPOs have developed rapidly because of their low startup costs and the fact that employees have freedom to choose from what can be a long list of providers. In essence, they are a compromise between the traditional fee-for-service system, in which employees have virtually complete freedom to choose providers, and HMOs, in which employees are usually locked into one group of providers for their health care needs.

Under the usual PPO arrangement, an employer, union, or insurer obtains price discounts or special services from health care providers in return for channeling employees or members to them. The third-party payor contracts with a group of medical care providers, who furnish services at lower-than-usual fees in return for prompt payment and a certain volume of patients. Although PPOs can be organized by insurance companies, unions, or groups of employers, they are frequently organized by the providers themselves. The contractual arrangement

may accommodate either group or individual practices; it also defines the scope of medical services to be provided. There is no "standard" contractual relationship.

In contrast to HMOs, practitioner participants in a PPO are paid on a fee-for-service basis as their services are used but under a schedule that is the same for all participating practitioners. Some PPOs also attempt to control utilization through bonus arrangements provided participating practitioners.

As pointed out above, employees are not required to use the PPO facilities. Employees are offered incentives to do so, however. The plan may pay 100 percent of the charges of a PPO and only 80 percent of the charges of a nonpreferred provider. The plan may also include favorable deductibles and coinsurance payments. Nevertheless, the employee may choose health care services outside the PPO.

Despite the rapid growth in the numbers of PPOs, not everyone is convinced that all PPOs will help control costs. In contrast to insurers, which are regulated by the states, and HMOs, which have to meet certain standards to be federally qualified, any entity can call itself a PPO. Some industry observers believe there will be a shakeout period and that the market will eliminate PPOs that cannot deliver on their promise to cut costs.[13]

Hospital Systems

Although not a specific alternative delivery system, some hospital systems, caught in a crunch of declining occupancy rates, are trying to preserve their market share by underwriting group health insurance. By selling group health insurance products, the hospital systems hope to fill their empty beds by encouraging employees to use certain hospitals through cost incentives.

A number of the nation's major multihospital systems have already purchased (or plan to acquire soon) an established life insurance company through which they can offer group health insurance products to employers. Still

---

[12]See "PPOs Seen Grabbing 25% of Health Care Market by 1995," *The National Underwriter,* Life/Health ed., January 4, 1986.

[13]Jerry Geisel, "Buyers Forcing Revolution in Health Care Delivery," *Business Insurance,* July 22, 1985, pp. 3–7.

other hospital systems are forming partnerships with insurers that give the health care institutions the marketing abilities of an insurer without having to buy one.

Among the products that are being offered to employers by such hospital systems are traditional fee-for-service health plans, preferred provider organizations, health maintenance organizations, and even group life insurance products. The plans offered by hospital systems often guarantee that employers' costs will not rise over a certain aggregate amount each year. In return for the guaranteed rates, the hospital systems are hoping to attract more business to their hospitals. The guaranteed rates to employers offered by the systems give them some leverage when competing for group health business with commercial insurers, Blue Cross and Blue Shield plans, and unaffiliated HMOs and PPOs. Some systems admit that they do not anticipate making a profit on their insurance underwriting activities but are entering the market to increase utilization at their facilities.

Self-Insured Plans

Both medical expense and disability income insurance are made available through self-insured or self-funded plans of employers, labor unions, and fraternal or cooperative groups. These plans may require enrolled members to share in the funding through dues or contributions. The benefits provided under these plans are similar to those of commercial group insurance contracts, but usually are the amount desired and affordable by a specific group of individuals.

Larger employers, particularly those with employees in more than one state, are likely to provide benefits through a trust governed by the Employees Retirement Income Security Act of 1974 (ERISA). Since ERISA preempts state insurance laws under certain conditions, employers who use a trust arrangement do not have to provide the specific insurance benefits that are mandated in a number of states. The excessive costs of providing mandatory benefits, which often differ from state to state, have led to an increase in self-insured groups.

Insurance companies may service these groups under administrative service only arrangements (ASOs) or by minimum premium plans (MPPs). Under ASOs, the insurance companies are paid a fee by the self-insured group to process the claims and benefits paperwork. The insurance companies perform similar administrative functions under MPPs, but also provide insurance against a certain level of large, unpredictable claims.[14]

Federal and State Governments

Nearly $149 billion, approximately 42 percent of national health care expenditures in 1984, were spent at all levels of government for health and medical programs, including funding for research projects and construction of medical facilities. Expenditures of the federal government were more than double those at the state and local level.

The majority of federal spending for health services is directed to six major groups: persons eligible for Medicaid, persons eligible for Medicare, military personnel and their dependents, veterans, federal civilian employees, and native Americans. The major part of state spending for health services is paid toward workers' compensation medical expenses, state contributions to Medicaid, and the public health programs of the nation's 53 official state health agencies.

In addition, the federal government covers nearly 107 million workers under the disability provisions of the Social Security Act and finances disability income programs for members of the armed forces, veterans, federal employees, railroad employees, coal miners, longshoremen, and harbor workers. All states have passed workers' compensation laws to require employer-paid benefits for work-related disability, and six states require comparable benefits for disability that is not job related.

Although most of the government programs are directed toward the indigent or to selectively defined groups, several important programs apply to the general public. These are the benefits

[14]See Chapter 27.

available from Medicare for medical expenses, from Social Security for disability, from workers' compensation, and, in six states, from so-called "cash sickness" plans.

Medicare.[15] Medicare is a two-part program of federal health insurance for persons age 65 and older. Part A is a compulsory hospital insurance benefits plan in which all eligible persons are enrolled without charge. Part B is a voluntary supplementary medical insurance plan that provides for reimbursement of physician fees and for which persons who choose to enroll must pay a monthly premium.

Individuals who are entitled to Social Security retirement benefits are automatically enrolled in Part A at age 65, except that employer-provided group insurance remains primary (i.e., pays first) for employed persons between ages 65 and 70. Medicare is also provided to younger persons who have been disabled for at least two years under the Social Security or Railroad Retirement Acts and to persons with severe chronic kidney disease.

Part A benefits are paid directly to participating hospitals. Part B benefits are paid directly to the beneficiary or, on assignment, to the providers of the service. An agency of the federal government establishes guidelines for payment of all benefits, which are then paid by fiscal intermediaries, primarily commercial insurers or Blue Cross and Blue Shield organizations that are under contract with the agency to provide administrative services.

Both parts of Medicare make the beneficiary responsible for a fixed amount of initial expenses— a deductible—and for a proportionate amount of other expenses—coinsurance. The deductible and coinsurance for Part A are adjusted each year according to a formula in the Medicare law and have increased each year since the program began in 1966. The Part B deductible has changed less frequently and the coinsurance percentage has never been adjusted.

Except for a deductible that applies on the first day of admission, Part A pays all hospital charges for semiprivate care during the first 60 days of confinement in a benefit period. After that, it pays all charges, except for a daily coinsurance amount, from the sixty-first through ninetieth days. An additional 60 days of coinsured benefits, known as the Lifetime Reserve, are available for hospital care after the ninetieth day. Except for used Lifetime Reserve days, all benefits are restored at the end of any period of 60 days in which the beneficiary has not been confined in a hospital or a skilled nursing facility.

After a calendar-year deductible, Part B pays 80 percent of all "reasonable" charges for physican's services and the cost of certain other services during that year. The beneficiary is responsible for the deductible and coinsurance plus any difference between the provider's actual charge and the amount that Medicare has determined is a reasonable charge. The "reasonable" or allowable charge of Medicare is always the *lowest* of (1) the doctor's *actual* charge, (2) the *customary* charge that the doctor most frequently makes for the same service, or (3) the *prevailing* charge, which is a charge no higher than the customary charges of 75 percent of the doctors in a specified area. Annual increases in prevailing charges in a locality are limited to an amount justified by the economic index.

Social Security Disability Benefits.[16] At the end of 1984, approximately 2.6 million individuals were receiving monthly benefits from Social Security for total disability. Persons are eligible for federal disability benefits if they are "fully insured" for Social Security and, for claimants age 31 and older, if they have worked at least five out of 10 years in covered employment before becoming disabled. Younger claimants have lesser requirements. A person is fully insured for Social Security if he or she has worked in covered employement for 40 quarters or 10 years.

A worker is entitled to disability benefits at the end of five completed months of disability if he or she is under age 65 and is unable "to engage in substantial gainful activity by reason of any medically determinable physical or mental impair-

[15]See Chapter 25 for a more detailed treatment of Medicare.

[16]See Chapter 25.

ment that can be expected to result in death or last for a continuous period of not less than 12 months." This is a restrictive definition of disability since the individual must be unable to engage in any kind of substantial work that exists in the national economy. It is immaterial under the law whether such work exists in the immediate area, whether a specific job vacancy exists, or whether the individual would be hired if he or she applied for work.

The disabled worker's monthly benefit, known as the **primary insurance amount** (PIA), is based on **average indexed monthly earnings** (AIME), each of which is calculated by formula from the worker's taxable earnings. PIAs currently range from $300 to $900 and are increased each July 1 for disabled persons to reflect increases in the Consumer Price Index. Qualified family members of a disabled worker are entitled to a monthly benefit that is 50 percent of the PIA, subject to certain overall family limits. Both the primary and dependent benefits are reduced by the amount of any workers' compensation disability income benefits. Disability benefits end at age 65 and automatically convert to retirement benefits.

Workers' Compensation. All states have enacted workers' compensation laws that hold employers responsible for the costs of work-related injuries or sickness. Disabled workers do not have to prove that the employer was negligent to receive benefits. Instead, the laws establish a schedule of benefits to be paid for each type of disabling injury or sickness. Most states allow employers to purchase insurance from commercial insurers. Twelve states permit a choice between a competitive state fund and private insurance companies. Six states, however, require employers to insure in a monopolistic state fund.

Usually, all employees of a covered employer are eligible for benefits if they become disabled because of a job-related injury or sickness. Workers' compensation provides full coverage for hospital and medical costs for duration of need. A rehabilitation benefit is often available to encourage return to a prior occupation or to retrain the disabled worker for a new occupation.

Disability income benefits are determined

by law in each state and vary widely, but generally are two-thirds of the average weekly wage before disability began. These benefits normally are subject to a maximum weekly payment and may be subject to maximum durations.

State Temporary Disability Benefits. Most employees in California, Hawaii, New Jersey, New York, Rhode Island, and Puerto Rico are covered under temporary disability laws providing coverage for nonoccupational injury or illness. Weekly indemnity ranges from 50 percent to 66⅔ percent of average weekly earnings, subject to maximum limits. In general, benefits become payable after the employee has been disabled for at least seven days and continue for a maximum period of from 26 to 52 weeks. Except in Rhode Island, which requires use of a state fund, employers may insure with either private insurance companies or competitive state funds.

HEALTH INSURANCE BENEFITS

Medical Expense Insurance

Medical expense insurance provides reimbursement for the costs of medical care required in the treatment of injury or sickness. Most individuals in the United States obtain this coverage as group insurance through employer-sponsored programs insured by commercial insurance companies, by Blue Cross and Blue Shield organizations, or by HMOs. However, several major commercial insurers, the Blues, and many small private companies continue to offer individual health care insurance.

Individual medical expense insurance has many of the characteristics of group insurance, except that benefit amounts generally are lower and premium costs often are considerably higher than comparable group coverage. In both group and individual insurance, however, the term "medical expense" covers a wide range of care, including the services of medical practitioners, nurses, hospitals, and outpatient facilities, as well as medicines, medical equipment, and supplies.

Group medical expense insurance is discussed in detail in Chapter 27. The following summaries of the important subdivisions of medical expense coverage will serve as an introduction to this category of health insurance and identify the types of benefits that are sold as individual insurance. Coverage that is limited primarily to one or two kinds of medical expense is referred to as basic coverage. Broader plans of insurance that cover a full range of medical services and supplies are called major medical expense or comprehensive coverage plans.

Individual insurance policies may vary from state to state to meet specific requirements of law for mandated benefits or to meet minimum benefit levels for a specific category of coverage in those states that have adopted a version of the Model Regulation to Implement the Individual Accident and Sickness Insurance Minimum Standards Act of the National Association of Insurance Commissioners.

Basic Hospital Expense. Basic hospital expense provides benefits for each day of hospital confinement to cover room and board, general nursing care and special diets, and miscellaneous hospital expenses such as laboratory and x-ray services, medicines and other supplies, and the use of operating or treatment rooms. The policy usually will have a specified reimbursable limit for hospital room and board charges, set either at the hospital's daily semiprivate rate or at a specific dollar amount in a range $85 to $200 for each day in a period of continuous confinement for from 90 days to one year. The benefit for miscellaneous hospital expenses is usually set as a separate limit based on a multiple of 15 or 20 times the daily room limit or an amount between $1,500 and $10,000 for all such expenses during one period of confinement.

Basic Surgical Expense. Basic surgical expense coverage provides benefits for surgical services of physicians in or out of hospital. The policy typically includes a surgical schedule that establishes a specific benefit amount for each surgical operation and a maximum limit on all related operations. The maximum limit generally is set at the highest reimbursable amount that will be paid for the most severe operation and generally ranges from $600 to $3,600.

Physician's Nonsurgical Expense. This coverage provides benefits for the nonsurgical services of physicians for medical treatment of injury or sickness in or out of hospital, often at a specific rate for each visit for treatment up to a maximum limit on the number of treatments or physician visits in a given period. Typically, the benefit ranges between $20 and $50 per visit for up to 60 visits in a year. This basic benefit is often combined with basic surgical coverage in the same policy, but separate limits apply for each type of coverage.

Hospital Confinement Indemnity. In contrast to basic hospital expense that is provided on a reimbursement basis, hospital confinement indemnity coverage pays a fixed sum on an **indemnity basis** for each day of hospital confinement. The benefit is most commonly sold as monthly indemnity in amounts between $1,000 and $6,000 for continuous confinement of up to one year or more. The monthly indemnity shown in this way actually is an aggregate of potential daily payments in any 30-day period of hospitalization. Thus, a policy providing $1,500 monthly indemnity would pay $50 for each day in a hospital.

Major Medical Expense. Major medical expense coverage provides a broad range of coverage for virtually all kinds of expenses associated with a serious illness or injury. The insured usually is responsible for a fixed amount of initial expenses—the deductible—that is the greater of a fixed-dollar amount, such as $2,000, or the amount of benefits paid for the same illness or injury by all other medical insurance in force for the insured. Individual insurance deductibles that coordinate with other benefits are known as **variable deductibles.** The insured is also responsible for a proportionate amount of the medical expenses incurred—coinsurance—up to a specific total of out-of-pocket expenses, after which the policy usually pays 100 percent of all further charges for a specified period of time.

When issued on a **calendar-year basis,** major medical policies cover all medical expenses of a covered person in excess of the deductible for all illnesses or injuries in a given year. The benefit period is one year and a new deductible is required each year before benefits are paid. Variable calendar-year deductibles often are under $500. Total benefits for all medical expenses of each covered person usually are limited to a lifetime aggregate of between $250,000 and $1 million in individual policies.

When issued on a **per cause basis,** the policies will cover only those medical expenses in excess of the deductible that apply to a specific illness or injury of each covered person. The benefit period is usually three years for per cause coverage, and separate deductibles apply to the medical expenses for each unrelated health condition. The variable deductible is usually between $1,000 and $5,000. Generally, individual policies of this type provide a lifetime maximum benefit of between $50,000 and $1 million for each separate illness or injury of each covered person.

There is also a "short-term" version of major medical coverage on the market, **temporary major medical,** that is intended to cover an individual whose employment is temporarily interrupted. It usually runs for three or six months and is nonrenewable or renewable for only one term if the coverage is on a three-month basis. This restriction is consistent with the purpose of the coverage.

Comprehensive Major Medical Expense. Comprehensive coverage combines the important features of basic hospital and surgical expense coverage with major medical expense coverage in a single policy. Usually, the insured is required to satisfy a very low deductible after payment of the basic benefits and before the major medical coverage takes effect. Coinsurance applies to the major medical benefits up to a specific amount of out-of-pocket expense. Benefit maximums generally are set at $1 million, either as an aggregate for all expenses under calendar-year plans or as a lifetime maximum for each unrelated condition in per cause plans.

A version of comprehensive coverage, known as **stop-loss** insurance, is sold on an individual basis with a very high variable deductible in the range $25,000 to $50,000 or more to provide coverage upon exhaustion of other basic or major medical expense coverage. Such policies may provide an unlimited amount of benefits in

excess of the deductible for benefit periods of up to five years, but generally do not begin to pay benefits until the insured has recovered payments from all other medical insurance available to him or her.

Medicare Supplement.[17] In all states, the term "Medicare Supplement" may apply only to a policy that meets specific minimum standards set out in insurance law or regulation. The trend in the insurance industry has been away from policies that supplement only portions of the Medicare program and toward two basic types of policies: (1) the Medicare Wraparound policy and (2) the Comprehensive Medicare Supplement policy.

The **Medicare Wraparound** policy usually provides benefits that correspond directly to the deductible and copayment that are imposed on the insured by current Medicare provisions. Such policies may continue to pay benefits after Medicare benefits are exhausted for hospital and nursing home confinement. Coverage is limited through the application of maximum benefit limits.

The **Comprehensive Medicare Supplement** policy is best described as a Medicare Wraparound policy that has significantly higher maximum benefit limits or is unlimited with respect to the duration of confinement in a hospital or skilled nursing home. It may pay benefits toward Medicare Part B expenses that exceed the amount deemed "reasonable" by Medicare (the insurer pays claims on a "usual and customary" basis). It also may provide benefits for a variety of health care expenses that are not covered at all by the Medicare program. The Comprehensive Medicare Supplement contract employs the principles of major medical insurance.

Specified Disease Coverage. So-called "dread disease" coverage refers to individual medical expense insurance that pays a variety of benefits up to substantial maximums solely for the treatment of a disease named in the policy, most typically

[17]This section is based on *A Course in Individual Health Insurance, Part A* (Washington, D.C.: Health Insurance Association of America, 1983), pp. 64–66.

cancer or heart disease. Benefits usually are paid as scheduled amounts of indemnity for designated events, such as hospital confinement, or for specific medical procedures, such as chemotherapy. Because insurance is limited to medical expenses associated with a single devastating disease, *this coverage should be used only to supplement other health insurance.*

Disability Income Insurance

Disability income insurance is sold in a variety of plans to meet personal and business needs when the insured is unable to work and suffers a loss of income as a result of sickness or injury. Personal insurance is available from commercial insurance companies, on either a group or an individual basis. Most business disability income insurance is sold only on an individual basis.

Personal disability income insurance provides a periodic payment of indemnity on an "occupational" basis when the insured is unable to perform specific job-related duties or on a "residual" basis when he or she is at work at reduced earnings. Group insurance more commonly uses an occupational definition of disability, whereas individual insurance will use either an occupational or loss-of-income concept, frequently combining both in a single policy.

Group insurance is more likely to coordinate with other income replacement programs at the time of the claim so that group benefits are reduced or "offset" by amounts paid under workers' compensation or Social Security. Individual insurance, on the other hand, does not coordinate with other sources of disability income. It pays irrespective of other payments. Companies selling disability income coverage take all other sources of disability payments into account at the time they underwrite the policy. As a result, insurers limit the amount of disability income coverage that they will sell to an individual to an amount that is judged to bear a reasonable relationship to the individual's potential net income loss. Thus, insurers typically will sell an amount of coverage no greater than the individual's gross income *less* income and Social Security taxes and other sources of disability payments.

In group insurance, plans with benefit durations of two years or less usually are referred to as **temporary disability insurance,** while those with longer durations are usually called **long-term disability** (LTD) **insurance.** Individual policies with benefit durations of five years or less are sometimes called "short term" and those with longer durations are sometimes called "long term."

Group disability income insurance is discussed in Chapter 27. Chapter 17 will analyze the individual disability income policy in detail and will explore the supplemental coverages that generally are available as optional benefits for personal use. The balance of this chapter will examine other uses of individual disability income policies.

BUSINESS USES OF DISABILITY INCOME INSURANCE

Most major companies have adapted the total disability benefit provisions of the personal disability income policy to meet specialized business needs. The following will serve as an overview of the variety of coverages that are now in use as individual disability insurance for business purposes. Except as otherwise noted, the policy provisions and the definitions of disability are identical to those of the personal contract (see Chapter 17).

The uses of health insurance to provide employee benefits for all employees, including key employees, are covered in the chapters on group insurance. It should be noted, however, that in companies where little or no health insurance is provided employees on a group basis, employers can use individual health plans to attract and/or retain key employees.

The basic need to offset the loss arising out of the disabilities of a key employee or owner (sole proprietor, partner, or stockholder) of a business firm were explained in Chapter 15. Thus, key employee indemnification and funding business continuation arrangements are important uses for individual disability income insurance. In addition, overhead expense insurance and a variety of special salary continuation plans constitute the other major business uses of individual disability income insurance products.

It is important to remember that the risk of a prolonged disability often is an even more serious threat than death at any age. The comparison of disability and death rates presented in Chapter 1 makes it clear that the chance of a serious disability is substantial.

Overhead Expense Insurance

Overhead expense insurance covers the monthly business expenses of business owners and professionals in private practice when they are disabled. A reimbursement-type benefit is paid during total disability that is uniformly defined in occupational terms. The policies usually begin benefits at the end of 30 or 60 days of disability and pay up to a specified amount of benefits each month, while disability continues until an aggregate benefit amount has been paid. The aggregate amount generally is a multiple of 12, 18, or 24 times the monthly benefit rather than a specifically limited duration of months. The basic policy waives any premium due during disability.

Most companies allow insureds to purchase optional benefits that provide coverage during periods of partial or residual disability or that give the insured the right to purchase additional insurance at a future time without evidence of good health. These items are discussed in detail in Chapter 17.

Covered expenses usually are those that the Internal Revenue Service accepts as deductible business expenses for federal income tax purposes. They include rent or mortgage payments for the business premises, employee salaries, installment payments for equipment (but usually not inventory), utility and laundry costs, business insurance premiums that are not waived during disability, and any other recurring expenses that the insured normally incurs in the conduct of his or her business or professional practice. The major insurers pay benefits on a cumulative basis, so that if the full monthly benefit has not been paid in a given month because of lower than expected covered expenses, any unpaid benefit is carried forward and is available to be paid in any

month in which expenses exceed the designated monthly benefit. Benefits generally are available to insure up to $10,000 a month of covered expenses.

Disability Buy-out Insurance

The use of disability income insurance in funding business continuation arrangements is the second most common form of business disability income insurance, although it is offered by a handful of major companies only. The policies provide cash funds to a business or professional partnership or small corporation to purchase the business interests of a totally disabled partner or stockholder. Policies are arranged so that benefits are not payable until after 12, 18, or 24 months of disability. That duration is chosen to correspond to a "trigger point," which is the date designated in the formal buy–sell agreement at which the healthy persons must buy out the totally disabled insured/owner.

Insureds generally are considered totally disabled if, because of sickness or injury, they are not able to perform the major duties of their regular occupations and are not actively at work on behalf of the business or practice with which they were associated. Benefits may be paid as monthly indemnity to a trustee, who then releases the total payment at the trigger point. More commonly, benefits are paid as a lump sum or under a periodic settlement arrangement in reimbursement of the actual amount paid by the buyers to purchase the disabled insured's interest.

The maximum benefits of buy-out policies are established at the time of underwriting and are based on the value of the business entity as determined by one or more generally accepted accounting methods. Under so-called **indemnity-type policies,** insurers must pay the maximum amount specified in the policy regardless of the actual value of the business at time of claim. Under **reimbursement policies,** on the other hand, insurers can reduce the benefit so that it does not exceed the actual value of the business at the time the buy–sell occurs. For this reason, indemnity policies rarely provide a maximum above $350,000 for any one insured, while reimbursement policies may be available with maximums up to $1,000,000 on any one individual.

Key Employee Disability Income Insurance

Key employee disability insurance provides for payment of a monthly indemnity to a business entity during the total disability of an essential employee who is the named insured under the policy. Benefits begin after a specified period of disability, called the elimination period, and continue while the insured is disabled for up to 12 or 24 months.

The amount of indemnity typically is high to reflect the value of the employee to the business and generally is, and should be, issued independently of any limits that the insurance company may have set for personal insurance. Although the payment of benefits depends on the disabled status of the insured, the policy itself is owned by the business entity and all benefits are paid directly to the business. The business firm may then use the indemnity to pay the salary of a temporary or permanent replacement. The funds also may be used to shore up credit, offset any loss of expected profit, or otherwise contribute to the solvency of the business until a replacement is recruited and trained. The maximum limits vary among commercial insurers but can reach in excess of $15,000 a month.

Salary Continuation Plan

Salary continuation plan (SCP) is a generic term for a variety of marketing arrangements that provide disability income insurance on a personal basis for multiple employees of a single employer. The plan may be a formal or informal arrangement to replace salary or wages of a disabled employee. Ordinarily, the insurance company will use its regular personal disability income policy forms, but allows a premium discount because of multiple lives and also may guarantee a certain level of coverage that will be issued to each employee without evidence of good health.

At time of renewal, policies are list-billed to the common employer, who often is shown as owner of each employee's policy. The employees may contribute all or part of the premium, although many plans are "employer pay all" arrangements. When insureds leave employment, they have the right to continue the policies in force, but the premiums that they must pay personally on renewal will no longer be discounted.

SCPs are classed as business insurance since under certain circumstances the employer may deduct premiums for tax purposes, in which case benefits of the policy become ordinary taxable income for the covered employee. Because the plans are employment related, they are affected by a number of federal and state employment laws that prohibit discrimination because of sex or age and that protect employees' benefit rights.

TAX TREATMENT OF INDIVIDUAL HEALTH INSURANCE

The income tax treatment of individual health insurance generally is straightforward and simple. Premiums paid for personal individual medical expense insurance coverage are deductible as unreimbursed medical expenses on an individual's federal income tax return, provided that the individual itemizes deductions, but only to the extent that all other unreimbursed medical expenses exceed 7.5 percent of the taxpayer's adjusted gross income. Premiums for personal individual disability income insurance protection are not deductible. Benefits received from personal medical expense and disability income insurance policies are received free of income tax.[18]

The income tax treatment of key employee disability income insurance and disability buy-out insurance is the same as that for personal coverage; that is, premiums are not deductible and benefits are received income tax free.[19] Premiums paid for overhead expense insurance ordinarily will be deductible by the business as a necessary business expense.[20] Benefits received will be taken into income but may be offset in whole or in part by the business expenses that the policy benefits are designed to cover.

[18] For the income tax treatment of group health isurance, see Chapter 27.

[19] Rev. Rul. 66–262, 1966–2 CB 105.

[20] Rev. Rul. 55–264, 1955–1 CB 11. However, this ruling relates only to self-employed individuals.

Chapter 17

Evaluating Health Insurance Contracts

THE HEALTH INSURANCE CONTRACT [1]

Health and life insurance policies share the common elements of general contract law and resemble each other in overall structure. However, individual health insurance contracts are more complex than those used in life insurance, since more than one loss may occur while the policy is in force, a more varied spectrum of losses is present, and the cause of loss is more often subjective. As a result, health insurance contracts require a much larger number of technical definitions and provide a far greater range of optional coverages.[2]

Of all insurance lines, disability income policies are the least amenable to generalized analysis and comparison. Such contracts are designed to permit flexible adaptation to the individual needs of the insured through a broad range of interrrelated benefit patterns and optional coverages. Probably no other type of insurance relies as heavily on subtle distinctions in benefits and the language used to describe them.

Contract design and language differ from company to company and often from policy to policy within the same company. Intense competitive pressures force companies to find that unique provision or that more precise definition that will distinguish their policies in the marketplace. Companies constantly change contracts as they restate old concepts in new ways and introduce innovative coverages for the disability risk.

Nonetheless, there are basic criteria for thoughtful analysis and evaluation of all individual health insurance contracts. Although they are designed to meet markedly different needs in financial planning, both medical expense and disability income insurance policies share some general characteristics that distinguish them from other types of insurance.

Regulatory Constraints

The insurance laws of all states govern the form and content of the individual health insurance contract. Almost every form in use must

---

[1] Chapter prepared substantively by Robert I. Damon, Assistant Vice President, Health Insurance, The Guardian Life Insurance Company of America.

[2] For an excellent review of all aspects of health insurance, see *A Course in Individual Health Insurance A and B* (Washington, D.C.: Health Insurance Association of America, 1983). See also *A Course in Group Life and Health Insurance, Part A, Part B,* and *Part C* (Washington, D.C.: Health Insurance Association of America, 1985, 1985, and 1984). HIAA course materials may be obtained from the association's office, 1025 Connecticut Avenue, Washington, DC 20036.

be filed for approval of the insurance department in the state where it will be issued or delivered. In general, an insurance department can disapprove a form if it contains any provision that is judged deceptive, inequitable, or misleading; or if the benefits provided are unreasonable in relation to the premiums charged.

All states have adopted some version of the **NAIC Model Uniform Policy Provisions Law,** which covers matters as diverse as the size of type in which a form may be printed and the wording of certain provisions that must appear in the policy. Many states mandate specific benefits that must be included in medical expense policies. About two dozen states have regulations to standardize policy content, to prohibit uneconomic coverages, and to establish minimum standards for benefit amounts, definitions, and limitations in health insurance contracts.

Over half of the states have laws that require companies to write insurance contracts in simplified language that is accessible to anyone with the equivalent of a tenth-grade education. At the time each form is filed with the insurance department, the company must certify that the form is readable on the basis of certain standard tests of written material.

As an adjunct to the state insurance laws, the decisions of various state and federal courts have an important effect on the way that health insurance contracts are written. These judicial opinions may give new interpretations to prevailing insurance principles or may restate existing insurance law. To a more limited degree, the structure of the health insurance contract is influenced by federal laws on social insurance programs, human rights, and employment benefits.

The Contractual Agreement

The health insurance contract is a financial agreement between the insured and the company. It is a conditional promise of the company, made in exchange for the insured's premiums, to pay benefits at some future time when the insured suffers a covered loss. The policy describes in detail the rights and obligations of both the insured and the company.

For a loss to be paid, the insured must have kept the policy in force through the timely payment of premiums, and the insured must have suffered an economic or physical loss of the kind defined in the policy. Timely notice and satisfactory proof of loss must be furnished when there is a claim. If the insured meets all of these conditions, the company must renew the policy according to its terms; must provide prompt service to help the insured file claims; and must pay benefits when a valid loss occurs.

Basic Elements

Six basic elements are common to all individual health insurance policies. These are (1) the insuring clause; (2) the consideration clause; (3) the renewal provisions; (4) the exclusion provisions; (5) the general provisions; and (6) the benefit provisions.

All states require that the renewal provision, or a summary of it, be printed on the first page of the policy. In most states the first page must also include a "free look" provision that usually allows the insured a period of 10 days from receipt of the policy in which to review it and, if desired, return it for a full refund of premiums paid.

With these two exceptions, companies are permitted to arrange the contract in whatever manner they choose as long as the overall appearance does not give undue prominence to any part of the text or create a misleading document. Most companies draft a single policy to meet the requirements of the majority of states in which they operate and will attach riders to modify the contract for use in other states with special requirements.

PROVISIONS IN HEALTH INSURANCE CONTRACTS

The Insuring Clause

The insuring clause contains the company's promise to pay benefits. It also may describe the types of losses that the policy will cover, or it may simply tie the promise to all the terms and limitations of the policy. The clause appears on the first page above the facsimile signatures of the secretary and president of the company.

Over the years, the insuring clause has evolved from a cumbersome provision, filled with complicated definitions and exclusions, to a reasonably simple and straightforward statement of the company's agreement to provide insurance. The following examples are from disability income contracts of four leading companies and display the various forms that the insuring clause may take.

In the first example, the company specifies the types of loss against which insurance is provided and defines the two causes from which loss must result.

> Subject to all the provisions of this policy, we insure you against disability or other loss resulting from:
> - *Sickness,* which first makes itself known while this policy is in force; or
> - *Injury,* which is accidental bodily injury that occurs while this policy is in force

The second company includes the same elements as the first, but merely identifies the causes of loss, which are then defined elsewhere in the policy.

> We will pay for Total Disability or other covered loss resulting from Injuries or Sickness subject to the definitions, exclusions and other provisions of this policy. Loss must begin while this policy is in force.

A third insurer uses only a simple sentence to promise insurance for loss that results from two specific causes.

> The Company will pay the benefits provided in this Policy for loss due to Injury or Sickness.

In the final example, the company embraces the entire policy without otherwise identifying the kinds of loss or their causes.

> The Company hereby furnishes insurance to the extent set out in this policy. All of the provisions on this and the pages which follow are part of this policy.

The Consideration Clause

The consideration clause summarizes the factors that led the company to issue the policy and represents the insured's part of the insurance agreement. It is generally a simple statement that the insured has completed an application and paid a premium in exchange for the company's promise to provide insurance. The clause usually appears in or near the general provisions of the policy, although several major companies now omit it entirely from their current contracts.

In the past, the consideration clause was often combined with the insuring clause or appeared in close conjunction with it. But regardless of where they are found in the policy, the two clauses together reflect the underlying principle of contract law—that two parties have agreed in a "meeting of the minds."

Most companies will use the consideration clause to make the application a part of the policy. Unless a copy of the application is included in the policy, the company cannot later contest the insurance contract because of any misstatements or misrepresentations made by the insured in answer to questions in the application. The following example from a disability income policy is typical of the consideration clause.

> We have issued this policy in consideration of the representations in your application and payment of the first term premium. A copy of your application is attached and is a part of this policy.

Renewal Provisions

The renewal provision describes the renewal and premium arrangements of the policy. Individual health insurance contracts are classified according to their renewal rights, of which the most common are (1) noncancellable, (2) guaranteed renewable, or (3) conditionally renewable.

Renewal rights carry differing costs. **Noncancellable** policies have guaranteed premiums and are likely to be more expensive than those that are guaranteed renewable and in which premiums can be changed. Policies that the company can refuse to renew under certain conditions and in which premiums can change generally are the least expensive forms of individual health insurance.

The various state insurance laws and regulations are not uniform in defining these renewal categories. Some states will allow termination of guaranteed renewal rights in disability income policies at age 60, or earlier, or at the time the insured qualifies for retirement benefits under the Social Security Act. The definitions that follow are those in common use for each category in policies offered by the leading disability income companies.

Noncancellable Contracts. A noncancellable policy gives the insured the right to renew the policy to age 65 by timely payment of a premium rate at the end of each term. A guaranteed premium rate is set forth in the contract and may not be changed by the insurer. During that period, the company cannot cancel the policy or make any unilateral change in its benefits. This renewal category is generally limited to disability income insurance.

Guaranteed Renewable Contracts. A guaranteed renewable policy gives the insured the right to renew the policy to age 65 by timely payment of the premium rate in effect at the end of each term. During that period, the company has the right to change the premiums for all insureds of the same class at their original insuring ages, but cannot cancel the policy or make any unilateral change in its benefits. This renewal category is used for both medical expense and disability income insurance.

Conditionally Renewable Contracts. A conditionally renewable policy gives the insured a limited right to renew the policy to age 65, or some later age, by timely payment of the premium rate in effect at the end of each term. The company has the right to refuse to renew coverage only for reasons stated in the policy by giving written notice to the insured 30 days in advance of the premium due date. The company will usually retain the right to change premiums and benefits for all insureds of the same class. This renewal category

is used for both medical expense and disability income insurance.

The stated reasons for nonrenewal vary according to the type of insurance, but the company cannot refuse to renew coverage solely because of a change in the insured's health after the policy has been issued. The company may refuse to renew a specific class of insureds or may discontinue a policy series for all insureds in a single state. On an individual basis, the company may refuse to renew when the insured changes to a more hazardous occupation, when the economic need for the policy ends, or when the insured becomes overinsured through purchase of other insurance that will provide benefits in excess of the expected loss.

This provision is used in most specialized business disability income forms other than overhead expense insurance. In such policies, the company retains the right to nonrenew on an individual basis when the covered business risk no longer exists or when other specified events occur. The company may also have the right to change benefits, but usually will guarantee that the premium rates cannot change.

The conditional renewal provision appears uniformly in noncancellable and guaranteed renewable disability income policies to provide continuous coverage from age 65 to age 75 while the insured remains employed on a full-time basis. During this period, the insured pays a renewal premium at the rates then in effect for persons of the same attained age and class of risk. Monthly indemnity is rarely reduced, but the benefit period usually is limited to two years during the conditional renewal period.

Exclusion Provisions

Most of the limitations in disability income contracts occur through operation of various definitions related to the benefit provisions. It is also a common practice to attach a rider or waiver to the policy of an individual insured to exclude benefits for a specific health condition that was named in the application. However, all health insurance policies will contain a general exclusion provision to exclude loss for certain unpredictable or uncontrollable events.

The most common exclusion in disability income contracts provides that the policy will not cover loss that begins in the first two policy years from a *preexisting condition*. As a general concept, a preexisting condition is an undisclosed health condition that was present within a specified number of years before the policy was issued and required medical attention or caused symptoms for which a prudent person would have sought medical care.

The precise definition of a preexisting condition differs among the states. Some limit the period of treatment or symptoms to five years before the date of application. In others, it is held to one or two years, and two major states will not allow use of the prudent person test. The preexisting condition exclusion applies only to health conditions that the insured did not reveal in the application. Health conditions that were fully disclosed on the application are covered unless the company has attached a rider to exclude a condition by specific name or description.

Companies may also exclude loss caused *by war or act of war* and *by intentionally self-inflicted injury.* Until recent years, all individual disability income contracts used an exclusion for normal uncomplicated pregnancy and childbirth. The major companies are now omitting the pregnancy exclusion in disability income policies intended for their most favorable occupational classes. Individual medical expense policies contain more numerous exclusions, similar to those of group insurance.[3]

A final important limitation, which is no longer part of the exclusion provision, appears in the general provisions of the policy to suspend coverage while the insured is on active duty in the military service of any country or international authority. This *military suspense provision* allows the insured to place the policy back in force without evidence of good health when active duty ends.

General Provisions

The general provisions deal with premium matters, claims administration, and various legal rights of the insured and company. Most of them are prescribed in the **NAIC Model Uniform In-** **dividual Accident and Sickness Policy Provisions Law,** known as the UPPL, that has been adopted in some version in all states. A company must use language at least as favorable as the law's 12 required and 11 optional provisions, although it may omit any provisions that are inconsistent with the coverage of the policy.

Required Provisions. The three most significant of the required provisions allow a *grace period* of 31 days for payment of premiums, permit *reinstatement* under specific conditions if the policy has lapsed, and make the policy *incontestable* after two years so that the company cannot use misstatements in the application to void the policy or deny claim. The remaining mandatory provisions deal primarily with payment of claims and the periods of time within which the insured must give notice of claim and proof of loss. The required provisions are used uniformly among all insurers in both medical expense and disability income policies.

Optional Provisions. Most major insurers now use only those optional provisions of the UPPL that allow for a benefit adjustment because of *misstatement of age* and that amend the contract to the minimum requirements of state law in *conformity with state statutes.* The remaining optional provisions generally are inappropriate for and not used with noncancellable or guaranteed renewable policies since they deal with various benefit reductions or exclusions because of other insurance or changes in the insured's occupation or earnings after the date of policy issue.

Benefit Provisions

The benefit provisions are the central element of all health insurance contracts and describe in detail the conditions for benefit payment. The balance of this chapter will analyze the various components of the benefit provisions in personal disability income policies. The comparable provisions of individual medical expense policies are in most respects identical to those for group health insurance discussed later and will not be duplicated here.[4]

[3]See Chapter 27.

[4]See Chapter 27.

DISABILITY INCOME BENEFITS

Individual disability income policies are designed to provide monthly benefits to replace lost income when the insured is disabled as the result of sickness or injury. The primary benefits of the policy usually are clustered together in the contract under a prominent heading, and any supplemental or optional benefits will appear in rider forms attached to the policy. A number of companies now use sophisticated electronic systems to integrate basic and optional coverages within a computer-printed policy without the need for attachable riders.

The **basic benefit arrangement** in the policies of the major insurers consists of a monthly benefit for total disability and a waiver of premium benefit. The **supplemental coverages** most commonly include a monthly benefit for residual or partial disability; a monthly benefit that is paid when certain social insurance programs are not providing benefits; a cost-of-living benefit; and a guarantee for purchase of additional insurance at a later date. These provisions are augmented by a **policy schedule,** which summarizes the available benefits, and by a series of technical definitions, which control and limit the way in which benefits are administered.

The policy schedule is a computer-printed summary of the principal benefits of the insurance policy, including any supplemental coverages, and usually appears immediately after the cover page of the policy. The schedule shows the effective date of insurance, identifies the insured and policyowner (if different), and displays the benefit amounts and the premiums charged for them.

Important Definitions

The technical definitions may be included in the benefit provisons, but more typically they form a separate part of the policy to define terms that apply to evaluate loss and control payment of benefits. Among the most important of these are the definitions of injury, sickness, preexisting conditions, and disability.

The major insurance companies uniformly define **injury** to mean *accidental bodily injury* that occurs while the policy is in force. This definition employs "results" language and has replaced an older provision which was known as an accidental means clause. The distinction between the two definitions is important since not all accidental bodily injuries result from accidental means.

Under the accidental means clause, a bodily injury has to meet two tests in order to be a covered loss: both the *cause* of the injury and the *result* (the injury itself) have to be unforeseen or unexpected. For example, a person who deliberately jumps from a wall and breaks a leg would not have a covered loss under the accidental means clause. Although the result—a broken leg—was unexpected, the cause—a voluntary leap—was not. On the other hand, loss would be covered under the accidental bodily injury definition since the broken leg was an unexpected result even though the precipitating act was intentional. Most states now prohibit use of the accidental means clause in health insurance contracts.

Most of the leading companies define **sickness** to mean sickness or disease that *first manifests* itself while the policy is in force. Some insurers use a modification of the "first manifest" language so that sickness means a sickness or disease that is *first diagnosed and treated* while the policy is in force. In either case, the intention is to cover only sickness that is first contracted after the policy takes effect.

It is customary to use a **preexisting condition** limitation in policies that contain a "first manifest" or "first diagnosed" definition of sickness. That limitation applies in the first two policy years to exclude benefits for any loss that results from a medical condition that the insured misrepresented or failed to disclose in the application for insurance. Although the limitation may vary from state to state, the following is typical of how a preexisting condition is defined:

> Preexisting condition means a medical condition which exists on the Effective Date and during the past five years either:
>
> 1. Caused you to receive medical advice or treatment; or
> 2. Caused symptoms for which an ordinarily prudent person would seek medical advice or treatment.

Defining Disability

Traditionally, individual disability income policies have been called "loss of time" insurance because of the occupational definitions used to qualify the insured as disabled. A disabled person under these types of policies is presumed to have suffered a loss of income because he or she cannot be present in the workplace. The definitions of **total disability** and **partial disability** are premised on the inability of the insured to perform certain occupational tasks. Within the past decade, a new generation of disability policies has emerged as "income loss" insurance, in which **residual disability** is defined in terms of lost income or a reduced capacity to earn income.

Total Disability. Essentially, there are two different ways in which insurance companies define total disability. One is a **gainful occupation** definition, which is popularly, if somewhat inaccurately, called "any occ." The other is a **regular occupation** definition, usually referred to as "your occ."

Under a gainful occupation clause, insureds are considered totally disabled when they cannot perform the major duties of any gainful occupation for which they are reasonably suited because of education, training, or experience.[5] Since the insured may be able to work at any of several suitable occupations even though incapable of working at his or her regular job, this clause is a more restrictive definition of disability than the regular occupation definition. It can limit recovery of benefits under the policy.

On the other hand, a regular occupation clause deems insureds to be totally disabled when they cannot perform the major duties of their regular occupations. A regular occupation is the one in which the insured was engaged at the time disability began. Under this definition, insureds can be at work in some other capacity and still be entitled to policy benefits as long as they cannot perform the important tasks of their usual occupations in the usual way.

The most common variation of the regular occupation definition is one that deems insureds to be totally disabled as long as they (1) cannot perform the major duties of their regular occupation, and (2) are not at work in any other occupation. If an insured is disabled for his or her regular job, the insurance company can terminate disability benefits only if the insured voluntarily has chosen to work at some other job. If this provision is used, the company cannot insist that the insured go to work in some other suitable occupation.

Since several states require a regular occupation definition for at least the first year of claim, the leading disability writers often will combine both occupation clauses in the same policy form to provide a regular occupation definition for a specified period of time and a gainful occupation definition after that. The specified period will vary between two and 10 years in the policies of the major insurers. Many companies allow regular occupational coverage to age 65 for their most favorable classes of risk.

The following example is taken from a leading company's "loss of time" policy that is available to its next-to-most-favorable rating class:

Total Disability, before age 55 or before benefits have been paid for five years for a period of disability, whichever is later, means that due to Injuries or Sickness:

1. You are unable to perform the duties of your occupation; and
2. You are under the care and attendance of a physician.

After you attain age 55 or after benefits have been paid for five years for a period of disability, whichever is later, Total Disability means that due to Injuries or Sickness:

1. You are unable to engage in any gainful occupation in which you might reasonably be expected to engage because of education, training or experience, with due regard to your vocation and earnings at the start of disability; and
2. You are under the care and attendance of a physician.

---

[5]Although not common today, except in limited benefit policies, at one time some policies provided that insureds were considered totally disabled only if they were unable to engage in *any* occupation. This exceedingly narrow definition generally has been supplanted by the newer "any occ" definition because of company practice and law.

Almost all insurers specify in the definition of disability, or in a separate policy provision, that an insured must be under the care and attendance of a physician to qualify for disability benefits. Most companies do not interpret the medical care requirement literally, since common sense and various court decisions dictate that an insurer cannot deny benefits under this provision if medical care is not essential to the disabled insured's well-being or recovery. The company cannot insist that an insured maintain a physician-patient relationship for the sole purpose of certifying disability.

It is common to include a definition of **presumptive disability** in policies that provide benefits for total disability. Under the presumptive clause, an insured is always considered totally disabled, even if he or she is at work, if sickness or injury results in the loss of the sight of both eyes, the hearing of both ears, the power of speech, or the use of any two limbs. Usually, the company will begin benefits immediately upon the date of loss and will waive the medical care requirement. The insured can be at work in any occupation, and full benefits will be paid while loss continues to the end of the policy's benefit period.

Partial Disability. The partial disability provision has been the traditional method for paying a reduced amount of benefits to an insured who has returned to work in a limited capacity. Partial disability customarily is defined in occupational terms with reference to "time and duties." The following is typical of this definition:

> Partial disability means that you are at work, but because of sickness or injury:
>
> 1. You are unable to perform one or more but not all of the major duties of your occupation; or
> 2. You are not able to be present at work for more than one half of the time required in your usual work week.

Residual Disability. In recent years, the concept of residual disability has replaced the partial disability provision as a means for paying proportionate benefits to an insured who is at work at reduced earnings as a result of sickness or in-

jury. The residual concept differs from conventional "loss of time" principles since it emphasizes protection of income rather than protection of occupational performance.

The most common definition of residual disability employs a "time and duties" test, combining both occupational and income considerations, as follows:

> Residual disability means that due to Injuries or Sickness:
>
> 1. You are not able to do one or more of your important daily business duties or you are not able to do your usual daily business duties for as much time as it would normally take for you to do them;
> 2. Your Loss of Monthly Income is at least 25 percent of your Prior Monthly Income; and
> 3. You are under the care and attendance of a physician.

An alternative definition of residual disability is referred to as a "pure income" test and rests solely on loss of earnings:

> Residual disability means that you are engaged in your regular or another occupation and your Income is reduced due to Accident or Sickness by at least 20 percent of your Prior Income.

Either of these definitions also must be supported by additional definitions that specifically define prior and current income and the technical methods by which the company will determine the amount of lost income. As a practical matter, most companies will consider a loss of more than 75 or 80 percent of prior income to be a loss of 100 percent, which, in effect, is a presumptive determination of residual disability.

Basic Components of the Benefit Provision

Three basic components establish the premium cost and define the payment of benefits under disability income policies. These are (1) the elimination period, (2) the benefit period, and (3) the amount of monthly indemnity. All other parts of the policy relate to these common elements to limit or expand their value in meeting the specific needs of the insured at time of loss. The strength of a particular disability income plan lies in how liberally the insurance company permits these elements to operate within the provisions of the policy and through its own administrative practices.

The Elimination Period. The elimination period, sometimes called the waiting period, is the number of days at the start of disability for which no benefits are paid. It is a limitation on benefits somewhat like the deductible used in medical expense insurance. It is meant to exclude the inconsequential illness or injury that disables the insured for only a few days and that is more economically met from personal funds.

In general, companies make available elimination periods of 30 days, two months, three months, six months, and one year. Since indemnities of the policy are paid at the end of each month of continuing disability, a three-month elimination period usually will mean that a disabled insured will not receive benefits for at least 120 days from the time that sickness began or injury occurred. Premiums are lower for policies with longer elimination periods. Most companies require that the elimination period be the same for sickness and injury.

The major insurers allow for a break in the elimination period so that the insured will not be penalized by any brief attempt to return to work before the elimination period has expired at the start of disability. The brief recovery generally is limited to six months, or if less, the length of the elimination period. If the insured is then again disabled from the same or a different cause after the interruption, the company will combine the two periods of disability to satisfy the elimination period.

The Benefit Period. The maximum benefit period is the longest period of time for which benefits will be paid under the disability policy. The benefit period usually is the same for sickness and injury and is available for durations of two years, five years, to age 65, and for life if continuous, total disability begins before age 55 or age 60.

Most disabilities are of short duration.

Roughly 98 percent of all disabled persons recover before one year has elapsed, and most disabled individuals recover within six months of the time disability began. On the other hand, if disability lasts beyond 12 months, chances of a return to productive work diminish markedly, particularly at older ages. The effect of extended disability can be financially devastating. The longer maximum benefit periods are more consistent with sound personal risk management principles.

All companies include a provision that is related to the benefit period and that deals with consecutive or recurrent episodes of disability and identifies whether the company is dealing with a new or continuing claim. The typical provision states that the company will consider **recurrent periods of disability** from the same cause to be one continuous period of disability unless each period is separated by a recovery of six months or more.

This recurrence language protects the insured from multiple elimination periods so that benefits for recurring loss from the same cause become payable immediately for the unused portion of the original benefit period. Conversely, the provision allows for a new benefit period, and a new elimination period, if loss results from a different cause at any time after an earlier disability or if loss recurs from the same cause more than six months after recovery.

The Benefit Amount. The benefit of the personal disability income policy is almost always payable as a fixed amount of **monthly indemnity.** The indemnity for total disability generally is written on a **valued basis,** which means that the stated policy benefit is presumed to equal the actual monetary loss sustained by the disabled insured. This valued amount is not adjusted to the insured's earnings or other insurance payments at time of claim for total or partial disability. During a period of residual disability, however, indemnity may be reduced in proportion to lost earnings of the insured.

Companies limit the amount of disability income coverage they will sell to an applicant so that the total of all monthly indemnity does not exceed about 85 percent of earned income for insureds with low annual incomes, grading downward to about 65 percent or less for those in the highest income brackets. These limits take into account other compensation that may be available to the disabled insured (e.g., employer sick pay plans, government programs, and other personal or group insurance). Insurers may also reduce these limits for individuals with significant unearned income or for those with net worth exceeding $3,000,000.

These limits are intended to avoid overinsurance, which occurs when benefits equal or exceed a disabled insured's predisability income. Insurers agree that overinsurance provides little incentive for a disabled insured to return to work, and as a result, recovery is delayed or does not occur at all. The existing insurance laws do not provide an effective mechanism for controlling overinsurance at point of claim, so that companies must rely almost entirely on issue limits at the time of underwriting to avoid its effects.

Nevertheless, under the regular limits of the leading disability writers for personal insurance, an insured with adequate income in the more favorable risk classifications may acquire up to a maximum of $11,000 in monthly indemnity for total disability. This amount generally is separate from indemnity limits established for special business insurance policies, such as overhead expense insurance.

Basic Benefit Arrangements

The basic benefit arrangement of a noncancellable disability income insurance policy consists of the benefit for total disability and a benefit for waiver of premium. These two components are common to all insurers, regardless of any additional coverages that may be included directly in the policy form. The benefit provision usually describes the circumstances of loss, the way in which the company will pay benefits, and at what point benefits may end.

Total Disability Benefit. The following is typical of the benefit provision for total disability:

When you are totally disabled, we will pay the monthly indemnity as follows:

- You must become totally disabled while this policy is in force.

- You must remain so to the end of the elimination period. No indemnity is payable during that period.
- After that, monthly indemnity will be payable at the end of each month while you are totally disabled.
- Monthly indemnity will stop at the end of the benefit period or, if earlier, on the date you are not longer totally disabled.

Waiver-of-Premium Benefit. The waiver-of-premium benefit characteristically will waive any premiums that fall due after the insured has been totally disabled for 90 days and will allow for refund of any premiums paid during those 90 days. Further premiums will be waived while the insured remains disabled until age 65. Some companies also may waive premiums that fall due within 90 days after recovery. The premium waiver feature invariably terminates when the insured becomes age 65.

Other Benefits in the Basic Provision. The basic benefit provision often contains a number of minor but competitively necessary provisions that are not appropriate as optional benefit riders since they do not carry a significant premium consideration. These supplemental benefit provisions include a transplant benefit, a rehabilitation benefit, a non-disabling injury benefit, and a capital sum benefit.

The **transplant benefit** provides that if the insured is totally disabled because of the transplant of an organ from his or her body to the body of another individual, the company will deem him or her to be disabled as a result of sickness.

The **rehabilitation benefit** generally allows a specific sum, often 12 times the sum of the monthly indemnity and any supplemental indemnities, to cover costs not paid by other insurance or public funding when the insured enrolls in a formal retraining program that will help him or her return to work. The **nondisabling injury benefit** pays up to a specific sum, usually one-fourth of the monthly indemnity, to reimburse the insured for medical expenses incurred for treatment of an injury that did not result in total disability.

The **capital sum benefit** pays a lump sum, usually 12 times the sum of the monthly indemnity and any supplemental indemnities, if sickness or injury results in dismemberment or loss of sight and the insured survives the loss for 30 days. The lump sum is in addition to any other indemnity payable under the policy and is payable for two such losses in the insured's lifetime. A "capital loss" usually is limited to the irrecoverable loss of the sight of one eye or the complete loss of a hand or foot through severance above the wrist or ankle.

Supplemental or Optional Benefit Arrangements

Among the leading insurers, the most common supplemental benefits are (1) a social insurance supplement, (2) a residual disability benefit, (3) a partial disability benefit, (4) a cost-of-living benefit, and (5) a guarantee of future insurability. Although some insurers may include one or more of these benefits in the basic benefit provision, they are more frequently available for an additional premium as optional benefit riders that are attached to the policy. The benefits and the premiums of each optional rider generally are shown on the schedule page.

Social Insurance Supplement. The social insurance supplement (SIS), or social insurance substitute, responds to the underwriting problem that is created by the existence of substantial benefits potentially available for disability under workers' compensation or for disability or retirement under the Social Security Act. Most insurance companies take these substantial benefits into account and, to avoid overinsurance at a later time, sharply limit the amount of conventional disability income insurance that will be issued to applicants with incomes below $35,000.

However, the insured may not always qualify for the anticipated benefits of the social insurance plans. He or she may suffer a loss that is not covered by workers' compensation or that does not meet the restrictive definitions of Social Security for total and permanent disability. If the insurance company has limited the amount of personal insurance, the individual will be under-

insured each month by several hundred dollars or more.

The SIS benefit, as it is popularly called, was developed to meet this potential coverage gap. The supplemental benefit provides an amount of monthly indemnity that approximates the amount the insured might reasonably expect to receive from Social Security for total disability. The SIS benefit is paid, under the conditions of the policy for total disability, when the insured is not receiving benefits from any social insurance plan. The SIS benefit is payable either as a fixed amount of indemnity that ceases when the insured begins to receive any income from a social insurance plan or may be reduced by a dollar-for-dollar offset of the benefit actually paid under the social insurance plan. If the offset method is used, the company will usually specify a floor amount below which the SIS benefit will not be reduced while total disability continues.

Most companies define social insurance plans in terms of workers' compensation and Social Security. A few insurers include the non-occupational disability coverage required under the laws of California, Hawaii, New Jersey, New York, Rhode Island, and Puerto Rico. This supplemental benefit is not renewable after the insured becomes age 65 or, if earlier, after he or she retires under Social Security.

Residual Disability Benefit. The residual disability benefit provides reduced monthly indemnity in proportion to the insured's loss of income when he or she has returned to work at reduced earnings. In policies that provide for a regular occupational definition of total disability, the residual benefit is payable only when the insured has returned to work in his or her usual occupation. Most companies allow the insured to be either totally or residually disabled to satisfy the elimination period of the policy and to qualify for waiver of premium.

The provisions for residual disability resemble those used for total disability, but are accompanied by a series of technical definitions to define prior and current income and to describe the formula that will be employed to compute the proportionate benefits. The customary formula is as follows:

$$\text{residual indemnity} = \frac{\text{loss of income}}{\text{prior income}} \times \text{monthly indemnity amount}$$

In this formula, **loss of income** means the difference between the insured's *prior income* and *current income*. Usually, loss of income in excess of 75 or 80 percent of prior income is considered to be 100 percent loss. In all cases, income refers only to earned income and excludes unearned income from savings, investments, or real property.

Prior income is usually defined as the average monthly income for the tax year with the highest earnings in the two or three years immediately before the date on which the insured became disabled. Most companies will index prior income at the end of each year of claim to adjust for increases in the cost of living.

Current income means the insured's earned income in each month while he or she is residually disabled. Insurers differ in their treatment of current income, but it will be valued either on the basis of cash actually received or on an accrual method to exclude income that was earned but not collected before disability began.

For example, assume that Jerry, who is residually disabled, is receiving current income of $800 per month but had a prior income of $2,000 per month. Assume also the monthly indemnity to be $1,000. Jerry could collect $600 under the residual benefit, calculated as follows:

$$\text{residual indemnity} = \frac{2,000 - 800}{2,000} \times 1,000 = \$600$$

Some companies will apply the residual benefit formula strictly throughout the benefit period. Several companies will use the exact rate of current income to compute benefits for the first six months of payment and then will average current income at six-month intervals for the remainder of the claim. Other companies will guarantee a minimum benefit during the first six months of a residual claim by providing the greater of the residual indemnity from the formula or 50 percent of the monthly indemnity for total disability. The residual benefit is payable for the duration of the benefit period of the policy or until loss of income is less than 20 or 25 percent of prior income. Companies usually will not renew disability provisions after the insured becomes age 65.

Partial Disability Benefit. The residual concept generally has replaced the partial disability benefit. Many companies, however, provide a partial disability provision as an optional benefit for their less favorable occupational risks. The typical partial indemnity is 50 percent of the monthly indemnity for total disability. It is payable for up to six months or, if less, for the remainder of the benefit period of the policy when the insured has returned to work on a limited basis after a period of compensable total disability that results from either sickness or injury.

Cost-of-Living Benefit. The cost-of-living adjustment benefit, often referred to as COLA, provides for adjustments of benefits each year during a long-term claim to reflect changes in the cost of living from the time that claim began. Adjustments are computed by the rate of change shown in the Consumer Price Index for All Urban Consumers (CPI-U) as published by the U.S. Department of Labor.

The method of adjustment is relatively complex, but generally calls for a comparison of the CPI-U for the current claim year with the CPI-U for the year in which claim began. If the CPI-U has gone up or down since the start of claim, benefits for the next 12 months are adjusted by the percentage change in the CPI-U. The percentage change is limited to a specified rate of inflation, generally ranging between 5 and 10 percent compounded annually.

The adjusted benefits of the policy may go up or down each year as the CPI-U rises or falls, but the benefits cannot be reduced below the level specified in the policy on the date of issue. Some companies apply a cap to limit increased benefits to a maximum of two or three times the original indemnities. In others, the adjusted benefits can rise without limit on the maximum increase before the insured is age 65.

When the insured recovers, the adjusted benefits generally are reduced to the level of those in force on the date of issue. A few companies will allow the recovered insured to retain the adjusted benefits in the last year of claim permanently upon payment of any required premium.

Guarantee of Future Insurability. The guarantee of future insurability, or the future increase option, allows an insured to purchase additional disability income insurance in future years despite any change in health. The total increase option that the insured may exercise under this benefit varies among companies but most often cannot exceed two times the monthly indemnity that the insured has in force in all companies on the original policy's date of issue.

The insured may exercise purchase options once a year until age 50 or so. The amount of additional monthly indemnity that the insured can purchase each year will be subject to the company's limits for insurance in relation to earned income and in some companies may be further limited to a specific amount, typically $500. In other companies, the insured can purchase all or part of the total increase option on any option date before age 45. After that, increases each year may not exceed one-third of the original total.

If the insured is disabled on an option date, he or she can purchase additional monthly indemnity, but the additional amounts usually will not apply to the current claim. At least one major insurer, however, will allow the disabled insured to purchase more insurance under this benefit and will apply up to $600 of the additional indemnity to the open claim. Other companies can be expected to follow this liberal approach.

Chapter 18

Fundamentals of Life Insurance Mathematics

The student of life insurance cannot truly understand life and health insurance until he or she has developed a sound appreciation for the underlying mathematics of life and health insurance. Chapter 2 provided an overview. This chapter begins a more detailed treatment. It presents a discussion of the raw materials—probability, mortality, and interest concepts—of life insurance mathematics and applicable principles. Chapter 19 applies these principles to develop net premiums. With an understanding of net premiums, Chapter 20 examines the concepts and state regulations regarding life insurance reserves and surrender values. Chapter 21 then examines the computation of a gross premium rate structure and delves into several dimensions of nonguaranteed life insurance policy cost and benefit elements. Finally, Chapter 22 presents various aspects of rate-making, reserving, and surplus distribution as relates to health insurance.

MEASUREMENT OF RISK IN LIFE INSURANCE

Some means of scientifically measuring risk is necessary if insurance is to be priced properly. This measurement of risk lies at the foundation of any system of insurance and is possible through the application of the laws of probability.

The Laws of Probability

Three probability laws are used in life and health insurance: (1) the law of certainty, (2) the law of simple probability, and (3) the law of compound probability. The use of these principles facilitates the mathematical description of risk. The three laws may be stated as follows:

1. Certainty may be expressed by unity, or 1.
2. Simple probability, or the probability or chance that an event will happen, may be expressed by a fraction, which may take a value of from 0 to 1.
3. Compound probability, or the chance that two independent events will happen, is the product of the separate probabilities that the events, taken separately, will happen.[1]

A general statement of the method for determining **simple probabilities** is: The *denominator* equals the total number of possible events or ex-

[1]There are laws of compound probability where the separate events are dependent, but they do not enter into the present discussion.

posures (e.g., lives) and the *numerator* is composed of only those instances that satisfy some stipulated condition (e.g., deaths).

The corollary that *the sum of all the separate probabilities equals 1* is based on the assumption that the events are **mutually exclusive.** Events are mutually exclusive if the occurrence of one of the events precludes the possibility of the occurrence of the other. For example, if a person dies at age 35, he or she clearly cannot die at age 36 or some other age.

The **compound probability** that both of two independent events will happen is equal to the product of the simple probabilities that the events taken separately will happen. Suppose that two coins are tossed up, and it is desired to know the chance that both will fall heads up. Since it is known that the chance is ½ that each separate coin will fall heads up, the probability that *both* will fall heads up is ¼ (½ × ½).

According to the law of compound probabilities, only when two events are **independent** will the product of simple probabilities equal the probability that both events will happen. For the two events to be independent, the happening of the one must have no effect on the occurrence or nonoccurrence of the other.

The Use of Probability to Forecast Future Events

These three laws of probability are useful in estimating the likelihood of future events. Future events can be foretold in one of two ways: (1) by **deductive reasoning** and (2) by **inductive reasoning.** The validity of deductive reasoning depends on the completeness with which all the causes of work in the determination of any phenomenon are known. In the coin-toss example above, we knew by our powers of observation that the chance of a coin falling heads up was ½. We *deduced* this. The limitations of the human mind are such that deductive reasoning does not furnish a sound basis for insurance purposes. We cannot yet estimate loss probabilities (i.e., probability of death) deductively. We can, however, estimate such probabilities inductively. Such logic flows from the

assumption that what has happened in the past will happen again in the future, if the same conditions are present. Reasoning inductively does not require an analysis of the causes of phenomena to be able to predict future events.

Inductive reasoning is applied in life insurance. From data showing ages at death in the past, probabilities of death and of survival in the future are estimated. This prediction is based on the assumption that a *law of mortality* exists. This law holds that certain causes are in operation which determine that out of a large group of persons, a set proportion will die each year until all have died. It is assumed that the impact of the law of mortality would be subject to precise measurement if only the causes at work were known. However, it is not necessary to know all the operating causes to predict fairly accurately the rate of mortality in a group of persons. By studying the rate of death within any group (if it is sufficiently large) and noting all the circumstances that might, according to our best knowledge, affect that rate, it is possible to anticipate that any future group of persons surrounded with approximately the same set of circumstances can expect approximately the same rate of death. Thus, a working basis is available for predicting future rates of death. Mortality statistics are necessary to develop a scientific plan of life insurance.

The Law of Large Numbers

The accuracy with which the theoretical estimates approximate actual experience has important bearings on the success of any method of insuring lives. This accuracy depends on two factors: (1) the accuracy of the statistics underlying the estimates and (2) the number of units or trials taken.

With reference to the first factor, it should be obvious that accurate data are fundamental if an accurate measure of the law of mortality is to be obtained. Mortality statistics, from whatever source, should be scrutinized carefully to detect inaccuracies in the original data.

The second factor that determines accuracy of the estimates is the number of units or trials

taken. As the number of trials is increased, the relative variation of actual from the true "probable" experience decreases, and if a very great number of trials were taken, actual and probable experience would virtually coincide. This generalization is called the **law of large numbers.**[2] It is fundamental to all insurance. For example, if a coin were flipped 10 million times and the chances were exactly ½ that each flip would produce heads, the actual results would be so near 50 percent heads that the relative difference would be negligible.

Premium rates are based on estimates of future probabilities of loss. These estimates will not be valid representations of future experience unless a sufficiently large number of cases exists to guarantee that large fluctuations in results will be minimized. Prediction of future mortality rates in life insurance based on what has happened in the past can be made for a large group of persons. It cannot be made for a single individual or even a relatively small number of persons (such as 1,000). When a mortality table shows that persons of a certain age die at the rate of seven per 1,000 per year, that does not mean that out of a group of 1,000 exactly seven will die within a year, but that out of a large group, containing many thousands, the deaths will occur approximately at the rate of seven per 1,000.

With reference to the prediction of future mortality rates, the law of large numbers has a double application: (1) to the data base from which the statistics were drawn, and (2) to the population to which the rates will be applied. Future mortality is estimated on the basis of past mortality data. But the statistics used for this purpose must include a sufficiently large group of representative individuals to ensure the operation of the law of large numbers. Assuming that the collected data are accurate and based on a large enough sample, they may be used to estimate future mortality. Then, in applying these mortality rates, a large enough number of individuals must be involved if the actual experience in the future is to be reasonably close to the anticipated experience.

[2]See also the discussion in Chapter 2. In mathematical terminology, this statistical principle is known as Bernoulli's theorem.

Distribution of Life Insurance Claims

Suppose that a hypothetical life insurance company insures the lives of a certain number of persons in a single year and that the probability that any one of the insureds will die that year is 2/100. The insurance company will expect a certain number of claims (2 percent of all the insureds), but its actual claims may be more or less than the expected number. According to the law of large numbers, if the number of insureds is large enough, the actual claims will very likely show only a small relative deviation from the expected claims. Using probability theory, one can calculate the probabilities of various deviations from the expected claims, depending on the number of insureds.

Figure 18–1 shows the probability of various deviations where the number of lives insured is 1,000, 5,000, 25,000 and 50,000. In particular, the figure shows that the probability of actual claims being within 5 percent of expected claims is 18.2 percent if 1,000 lives are being insured, 39.0 percent if 5,000 lives are insured, 74.2 percent if 25,000 lives are insured, and 89.0 percent if 50,000 lives are insured. Although not shown in the chart, the probability of actual claims being within 5 percent of expected claims is greater than 99.99 percent if 1,000,000 lives were insured.

Mortality Statistics

The establishment of any plan of insuring against death requires some means of giving mathematical values to the probabilities of death. The preceding discussion of the laws of probability demonstrated that this can be accomplished through the application of the laws of probability to mortality statistics. Mortality tables are presentations of such data organized in a form to be usable in estimating the course of future deaths.

The two basic sources of mortality statistics are:

1. Population statistics derived from census enumerations and the returns of deaths from registration offices; and

2. Statistics derived from insured lives.

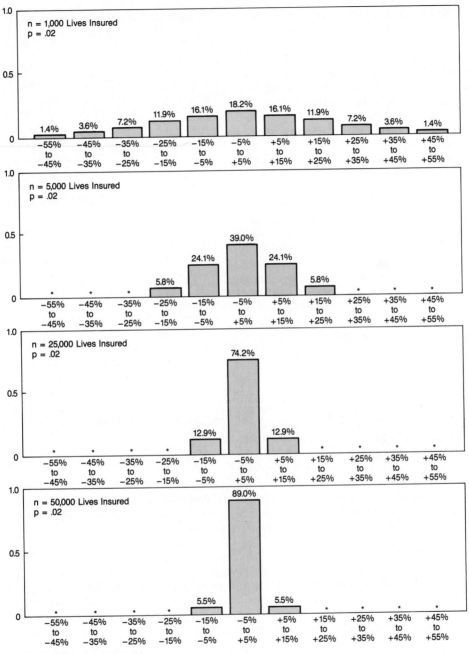

*Probabilities are less than 1%

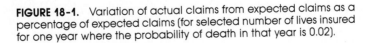

FIGURE 18-1. Variation of actual claims from expected claims as a percentage of expected claims (for selected number of lives insured for one year where the probability of death in that year is 0.02).

Both census enumerations and death registration records contain significant error. Census data, collected by a large number of individuals through personal interviews, are particularly susceptible to error. Misclassification of information is frequent, some individuals are omitted, inaccurate information is provided by the respondents either willfully or inadvertently, tabulation errors creep in, and not infrequently, ages are reported as unknown. Records of death provided to the National Office of Vital Statistics are frequently incomplete and inaccurate.[3]

On the other hand, the mortality statistics of insured lives tend to be quite accurate. The nature of the insurance process leads to a careful recording of the date of birth, sex, and date of death of insured individuals. This facilitates derivation of accurate death rates for the various age and sex classifications.

The mortality experienced among insured lives is significantly different from that of the general population because most insured lives have been subjected to the underwriting process of the insurance company. Virtually all mortality tables used today for life insurance are based on the experience of insured lives.

Mortality Table Construction

The theory of probability is applied in life insurance through the use of a mathematical model known as a mortality table. It reflects assumed mortality rates or a record of mortality observed in the past and is arranged in a form to show the probabilities of death and survival at each separate age. It shows a hypothetical group of individuals beginning a certain age and traces the history of the entire group year by year until all have died. Since any description will best be understood by reference to an actual table, the **Commissioners 1980 Standard Ordinary Table of Mortality** (*1980 CSO Table*) for males is presented in Table 18-1.

Overview. The heart of the table is the column of "yearly probability of dying," with the yearly probability of surviving, being simply 1 minus the probability of dying. The other essential features of a mortality table are the two columns of the "number living" and the "number dying" at designated ages.

It will prove helpful to introduce the reader to some standard actuarial notation. This will simplify later discussion. These include:

x = age

q_x = probability of dying during age x
    = $d_x \div l_x$

p_x = probability of an individual age x surviving one year
    = $l_{x+1} \div l_x$

l_x = number living at age x
    = $l_{x-1} - d_{x-1}$

d_x = number dying during age x
    = $l_x - l_{x+1}$

A person of any age will either die or survive that year. Thus, it can be seen for any age,

$$q_x + p_x = 1 \qquad (1)$$

Moreover, it should be noted that each d_x and l_x is related as follows:

$$l_{x+1} = l_x - d_x \qquad (2)$$

In words, the number of persons living at any age $x + 1$ (l_{x+1}) can be found simply by subtracting the number dying (d_x) in the year previous from the number who were alive at the beginning of the previous year (l_x).

In the case of the *1980 CSO Table*, it is assumed that a group of 10,000,000 males (l_0) come under observation at exactly the same moment as they begin the first year of life (age 0).[4] Of this group, 41,800 die (d_0 =10,000,000 × 0.00418) dur-

---

[3]Ample evidence of this is the fact that qualification for recognition as a "registration area" requires the recording of only 90 percent of the probable deaths in an area.

[4]The *1980 CSO Table* has separate tables for male and female lives. The illustrations throughout the mathematical discussion are based on males lives, but the reader should note that a distinction by sex is made in the actuarial processes employed by most companies.

TABLE 18-1. **Commissioners 1980 standard ordinary (CSO) table of mortality**
Male Lives

Age (x) at Beginning of Year	Number Living at Beginning of Designated Year (l_x)	Number Dying during Designated Year (d_x)	Yearly Probability of Dying (q_x)	Yearly Probability of Surviving (p_x)
0	10,000,000	41,800	0.004180	0.995820
1	9,958,200	10,655	0.001070	0.998930
2	9,947 545	9,848	0.000990	0.999010
3	9,937,697	9,739	0.000980	0.999020
4	9,927,958	9,432	0.000950	0.999050
5	9,918,526	8,927	0.000900	0.999100
6	9,909,599	8,522	0.000860	0.999140
7	9,901,077	7,921	0.000800	0.999200
8	9,893,156	7,519	0.000760	0.999240
9	9,885,637	7,315	0.000740	0.999260
10	9,878,322	7,211	0.000730	0.999270
11	9,871,111	7,601	0.000770	0.999230
12	9,863,510	8,384	0.000850	0.999150
13	9,855,126	9,757	0.000990	0.999010
14	9,845,369	11,322	0.001150	0.998850
15	9,834,047	13,079	0.001330	0.998670
16	9,820,968	14,830	0.001510	0.998490
17	9,806,138	16,376	0.001670	0.998330
18	9,789,762	17,426	0.001780	0.998220
19	9,772,336	18,177	0.001860	0.998140
20	9,754,159	18,533	0.001900	0.998100
21	9,735,626	18,595	0.001910	0.998090
22	9,717,031	18,365	0.001890	0.998110
23	9,698,666	18,040	0.001860	0.998140
24	9,680,626	17,619	0.001820	0.998180
25	9,663,007	17,104	0.001770	0.998230
26	9,645,903	16,687	0.001730	0.998270
27	9,629,216	16,466	0.001710	0.998290
28	9,612,750	16,342	0.001700	0.998300
29	9,596,408	16,410	0.001710	0.998290
30	9,579,998	16,573	0.001730	0.998270
31	9,563,425	17,023	0.001780	0.998220
32	9,546,402	17,470	0.001830	0.998170
33	9,328,932	18,200	0.001910	0.998090
34	9,510,732	19,021	0.002000	0.998000
35	9,491,711	20,028	0.002110	0.997890
36	9,471,683	21,217	0.002240	0.997760
37	9,450,466	22,681	0.002400	0.997600
38	9,427,785	24,324	0.002580	0.997420
39	9,403,461	26,236	0.002790	0.997210
40	9,377,225	28,319	0.003020	0.996980
41	9,348,906	30,758	0.003290	0.996710
42	9,318,148	33,173	0.003560	0.996440
43	9,284,975	35,933	0.003870	0.996130
44	9,249,042	38,753	0.004190	0.995810
45	9,210,289	41,907	0.004550	0.995450
46	9,168,382	45,108	0.004920	0.995080
47	9,123,274	48,536	0.005320	0.994680
48	9,074,738	52,089	0.005740	0.994260
49	9,022,649	56,031	0.006210	0.993790
50	8,966,618	60,166	0.006710	0.993290

Age (x) at Beginning of Year	Number Living at Beginning of Designated Year (l_x)	Number Dying during Designated Year (d_x)	Yearly Probability of Dying (q_x)	Yearly Probability of Surviving (p_x)
51	8,906,452	65,017	0.007300	0.992700
52	8,841,435	70,378	0.007960	0.992040
53	8,771,057	76,396	0.008710	0.991290
54	8,694,661	83,121	0.009560	0.990440
55	8,611,540	90,163	0.010470	0.989530
56	8,521,377	97,655	0.011460	0.988540
57	8,423,722	105,212	0.012490	0.987510
58	8,318,510	113,049	0.013590	0.986410
59	8,205,461	121,195	0.014770	0.985230
60	8,084,266	129,995	0.016080	0.983920
61	7,954,271	139,518	0.017540	0.982460
62	7,814,753	149,965	0.019190	0.980810
63	7,664,788	161,420	0.021060	0.978940
64	7,503,368	173,628	0.023140	0.976860
65	7,329,740	186,322	0.025420	0.974580
66	7,143,418	198,944	0.027850	0.972150
67	6,944,474	211,390	0.030440	0.969560
68	6,773,084	223,471	0.033190	0.966810
69	6,509,613	235,453	0.036170	0.963830
70	6,274,160	247,892	0.039510	0.960490
71	6,026,268	260,937	0.043300	0.956700
72	5,765,331	274,718	0.047650	0.952350
73	5,490,613	289,026	0.052640	0.947360
74	5,201,587	302,680	0.058190	0.941810
75	4,898,907	314,461	0.064190	0.935810
76	4,584,446	323,341	0.070530	0.929470
77	4,261,105	328,616	0.077120	0.922880
78	3,932,489	329,936	0.083900	0.916100
79	3,602,553	328,012	0.091050	0.908950
80	3,274,541	323,656	0.098840	0.901160
81	2,950,885	317,161	0.107480	0.892520
82	2,633,724	308,804	0.117250	0.882750
83	2,324,920	298,194	0.128260	0.871740
84	2,026,726	284,248	0.140250	0.859750
85	1,742,478	266,512	0.152950	0.847050
86	1,475,966	245,143	0.166090	0.833910
87	1,230,823	220,994	0.179550	0.820450
88	1,009,829	195,170	0.193270	0.806730
89	814,659	168,871	0.207290	0.792710
90	645,788	143,216	0.221770	0.778230
91	502,572	119,100	0.236980	0.763020
92	383,472	97,191	0.253450	0.746550
93	286,281	77,900	0.272110	0.727890
94	208,381	61,660	0.295900	0.704100
95	146,721	48,412	0.329960	0.670040
96	98,309	37,805	0.384550	0.615450
97	60,504	29,054	0.480200	0.519800
98	31,450	20,693	0.657980	0.342020
99	10,757	10,757	1.000000	0.000000

ing the year, leaving 9,958,200 lives (l_1) to begin the second year.[5] The table proceeds in this manner to record the number dying each year of life and the number living at the beginning of each succeeding year, until only 10,757 of the original group are found to be alive by age 99, and these 10,757 die during that year.

Derivation of Death Rates. It is impossible for any insurance company to insure a group of several million persons of exactly the same age and at exactly the same time. It is equally impossible to keep any such group under observation until all have died. Insurance policies are written at all times of the year and on lives at various ages. It is possible, however, for one company or a group of companies to keep a record of all insured lives, showing at each age the number of persons under observation and the number that die. If a sufficient volume of data is collected showing (1) the ages at which persons come under observation and (2) the number of each sex dying at each age, a mortality table may be constructed.

Suppose, for illustration, that the following data have been collected for male lives:

Age	Number of Life-Years Observed	Number Dying during Year
0 to 1	10,000	80
1 to 2	30,000	90
2 to 3	150,000	600
3 to 4	80,000	360

From these figures, death rates may be computed for the respective ages in the following manner:[6]

Age	Rate of Death Expressed as a Fraction	Rate of Death Expressed as a Decimal
0	$\dfrac{80}{10,000}$	0.0080
1	$\dfrac{90}{30,000}$	0.0030
2	$\dfrac{600}{150,000}$	0.0040
3	$\dfrac{360}{80,000}$	0.0045

The rate of mortality (q_x) at any given age is the quotient of the number of deaths and the corresponding exposure for the period of study.[7] The rate represents the probability that a person who has just attained a given age will die before he attains the next age. The rate of mortality is usually expressed in terms of the number of deaths per thousand.

The mortality table may be constructed by using an arbitrary number of persons, known as the **radix,** assumed to be alive at the youngest age for which death rates are assumed. Successively, the mortality rates are applied at each age until the initial assumed number of lives is extinguished. Applying the death rates developed above to an arbitrary radix of 10,000,000 will illustrate the process (see the chart at the top of page 317).

Since the probability of dying at age 0 is taken as 0.0080, 80,000 deaths will occur during the year among the 10,000,000 starting at age 0. This leaves 9,920,000 of the group to begin age 1. These die at the rate of three per thousand (0.0030), making 29,760 deaths during the year. In this way, the original 10,000,000 are reduced in number by deaths year after year until all have died. This is the basis of the statement that the

---

[5]Applying formula 2, one finds that $l_0 - d_0 = l_1$ or 10,000,000 $- 41,800 = 9,958,200$.

[6]If the period of observation is more than one year, which it usually is, the number under observation is adjusted to reflect this fact. Thus, if the period of observation were five years, one individual under observation would be observed at five successive ages, unless he died or lapsed his policy during the period. The deaths occurring at each age are compared with the total "exposure" at that age.

[7]The distinction between "mortality rates," as the rates above are called by actuaries, and "probabilities of death" is one of the preciseness of attained age. For purposes of simplification here, death rates and probabilities of death are assumed to be identical. For the construction of a mortality table, probabilities of death are necessary; they have reference to rates of dying among a group of persons who have just attained a certain age of life.

(1)	(2)	(3)	(4)	(5)
Age (x)	Number Living at Given Age (l_x)	Mortality Rate For Given Age (q_x)	Number of Deaths before Next Age (d_x) [(2) × (3)]	Number Living at Next Age (l_{x+1}) [(2) − (4)]
0	10,000,000	0.0080	80,000	9,920,000
1	9,920,000	0.0030	29,760	9,890,240
2	9,890,240	0.0040	39,561	9,850,679
3	9,850,679	0.0045	44,328	9,806,351

mortality table represents "a (hypothetical) generation of individuals passing through time."

Since the radix of the table (l_0) is arbitrary, the numbers in the columns headed "number living" and "number of deaths" are not significant in and of themselves.[8] They simply reflect the series of death rates, the real heart of a mortality table.

Sometimes a mortality table has an additional column showing the "expectation of life" or "life expectancy" at each age. The figure in this column opposite any age is the *average* number of years of life lived after attaining that age by all who reach that age. Expectation of life can be a misleading term, since it has no significance for any individual. The probable future lifetime of any person depends on many factors, including his or her state of health, and may be more or less than average. It is commonly supposed that life insurance companies make premium rate calculations on the assumption that everyone will live for the period of his or her "life expectancy." This is not the case, as explained in Chapters 19 and 21.

Adjustments to Mortality Data. A mortality table used by a life insurance company in calculating premium rates, reserves, and cash values does not reflect the precise mortality rates developed from the basic mortality data. Because the volume of experience is not uniform at all ages and is insufficient to provide completely credible or reliable statistics, two types of adjustments may

be made to the derived rates: (1) the rates are "smoothed" into a curve (the process is known as **graduation**), and (2) a **margin** may be added to the rates in the derived curve.

Graduation is performed to eliminate the irregularities in the observed data that are believed not to be true characteristics of the universe from which the sample experience was extracted. One of the several methods of graduation is used, depending on the data involved and the purpose of the computation. The objective in all cases, however, is to introduce smoothness and regularity while preserving the basic characteristics of the observed values.

The addition of a margin to the derived rates is done where the rates will be used as a **valuation table** and is in the interest of safety.[9] In a life insurance mortality table used to value policy liabilities, this means showing higher death rates than those actually expected. In an annuity valuation table it means showing lower rates of mortality than those expected. Thus, the *1980 CSO Table* is a life insurance valuation table and had margins added to the underlying mortality rates. Margins may also be provided by adjusting the underlying data prior to the derivation of the basic rates themselves. In any case, the insertion of such margins enhances the security behind life insurance contracts and is considered a sound practice. It should be noted, however, that where the actual experience of a company is being analyzed, such as in gross-premium and asset-share studies, a **basic experience table,** representing the most probable level of mortality, is needed, and no margins for conservatism are added.[10]

[8]For the *American Experience Table,* the radix was 100,000 at age 10; for the *1941 CSO Table,* it was 1,000,000 at age 1; for the *1958 CSO Table,* 10,000,000 at age 0; and for the *1980 CSO Table,* it is 10,000,000 at age 0.

[9]See Chapter 20.

[10]See Chapter 21.

Types of Mortality Tables

Select, Ultimate, and Aggregate Tables. Mortality tables may be classified as select, ultimate, and aggregate. These terms have reference to whether the table reflects the effects of the underwriting process. As discussed in Chapter 4, insured lives, having passed the necessary requirements before becoming insured, show a lower rate of mortality than do lives not subject to such scrutiny. Thus, the number of deaths occurring among 10,000 insureds aged 40 who have just passed a medical examination can be expected to be fewer than among 10,000 persons aged 40 who were first insured at age 30 and have been so insured for 10 years. So it is important for a company in estimating the probable mortality to know whether it has a large number of newly selected lives.

A **select mortality table** is based on data of recently insured lives only. An **ultimate table** excludes these early data, usually the first five to 15 years following entry, and is based on the ultimate mortality among insured lives. The *1980 CSO Table* is an ultimate table. **Aggregate tables** include all the mortality data, the early years following entry as well as the later ones. Since companies are usually interested in establishing conservative reserve estimates, it is generally considered safer for a company to compute reserve liabilities on the basis of the mortality among risks for whom the benefits of fresh medical selection have passed.

A select mortality table shows rates of mortality by both age and duration of insurance. Since the greatest effect of selection generally wears off in five to 15 years, the mortality rates are usually differentiated by duration only for such a period. An example of a select mortality table is presented in Table 18-2. The blocked ages show how the mortality rates vary by duration even though each is age 30. The rates shown in column "6 and over" represent the ultimate mortality level and constitute an ultimate mortality table. Accordingly, this table is a **select and ultimate table.**

Select tables are used for purposes of analysis and comparison. The basic tables prepared and published by the Mortality Committee of the Society of Actuaries from data supplied by a group of established companies are constructed to show both select and ultimate mortality, since their primary purpose is to reflect mortality trends.

The mortality tables used in expressing participating life insurance premiums usually are ultimate tables. Select mortality is used frequently in asset share calculations, in dividend and other nonguaranteed element calculations, and in the calculation of nonparticipating gross premiums.

Mortality Tables for Annuities. A mortality table based on life insurance experience is not suitable for use in connection with annuities, for several reasons. One reason is that annuities generally are not purchased by individuals in poor health. At the higher ages (particularly in the case of annuity contracts purchased by single premiums for immediate income), the rates of mortality experienced among annuitants generally are lower than among insureds under life insurance policies. A life insurance mortality table would overstate expected mortality rates.

Another important reason is that the

TABLE 18-2. Select and ultimate mortality table
(rates per 1,000)

Age at Issue	Year of Insurance					6 and Over	Attained Age
	1	2	3	4	5		
25	0.71	0.82	0.88	0.93	0.97	1.01	30
26	0.72	0.82	0.89	0.96	1.00	1.06	31
27	0.73	0.83	0.92	0.99	1.05	1.12	32
28	0.74	0.84	0.93	1.03	1.11	1.21	33
29	0.74	0.84	0.97	1.08	1.20	1.32	34
30	0.74	0.86	1.02	1.16	1.31	1.44	35

gradual improvement in mortality rates as time goes on provides a gradually increasing margin of safety for life insurance but has the opposite result for annuities. In fact, it is recognized that no annuity mortality table based on past experience can be used safely. What is needed is a table that shows the (lower) rates of mortality anticipated in the future rather than the rates that have been experienced in the past. Such a table is known as a **table with projection.**

Static Tables versus Tables with Projection. All life insurance mortality tables in use today are **static tables,** in that they do not provide for changes in their rates depending on the calendar year to which they apply. As the secular trend toward mortality improvement has continued, these static tables have been replaced periodically by other static tables based on more recent experience. The improvement in mortality has led to increasing margins of life insurance premiums during the period in which a mortality table is used with adjustment, since the "postponement" in death payments enables the companies to earn additional interest on their invested funds and to collect additional premiums. However, in participating policies as well as indeterminate premium and current assumption nonparticipating policies, these gains can be credited to policyowners via enhanced dividends or other nonguaranteed payments or benefits.

The situation has been just the reverse in connection with annuity contracts where improving mortality has led to smaller margins. Postponements of death have led to additional payments. To avoid the large expense of constructing new static tables frequently, the traditional practice was to make an allowance for the decrease in mortality rates by using age "setbacks." That is, the static table was continued in use, but the rates shown in the table were assumed to be those that apply to lower actual ages.[11] Setbacks of from one to four years are used by many companies. Annuity tables used today usually contain projection factors on different bases that can be applied to the basic table to make allowance for future reductions in mortality rates. The construction of such projected tables is too technical to be discussed here. The importance of providing for mortality improvement in annuity mortality tables can be seen in the fact that annuity business constitutes a significant and growing proportion of most life insurance companies' total business.[12]

Published Tables in Use Today. A multitude of mortality tables are in use today. The ones discussed below are used chiefly for purposes of valuing companies' policy reserves and establishing minimum acceptable surrender values, not for ratemaking.

1. *Life insurance tables.* The **Commissioners 1941 Standard Ordinary Table of Mortality** (*1941 CSO Table*) was used extensively for policies issued between 1948 and 1966. The *1941 CSO Table* is still important because much outstanding insurance is based on this table. For many years prior to the advent of the *1941 CSO Table*, the **American Experience Table of Mortality** was widely used.[13]

The **Commissioners 1958 Standard Ordinary Mortality Table** (*1958 CSO Table*) was developed by the Society of Actuaries from the combined ultimate mortality experience of 15 large insurers between 1950 and 1954. The *1958 CSO Table* was at one time required to be used as the basis for minimum reserves and nonforfeiture values for newly-issued policies in all states.[14] As of the mid-1980s, the *1980 CSO Table* (see below) had effectively replaced the *1958 CSO Table* as the mandatory table.[15]

---

[11]For example, a person who actually is 65 is assumed, for purposes of premium calculations, to be subject to the mortality rates of a person of 64 or 63, thus increasing the premium for a given amount of annuity income.

[12]Annuity business includes, in addition to individual annuities, group annuities and settlement option arrangements.

[13]Although it is of little practical significance, it is historically important to note that the *Actuaries'* or *Seventeen Offices Table,* which in large measure preceded the *American Experience Table,* was of British origin and introduced into the United States by Elizur Wright as the standard for the valuation of policies in Massachusetts.

[14]See Chapter 22.

[15]Most states have until 1989 to change to the *1980 CSO Table.*

TABLE 18-3. Selected mortality tables
(deaths per 1,000 at ages indicated)

Age	American Experience	1941 CSO	1958 CSO	1980 CSO Male	1980 CSO Female	1983 Table a Male	1983 Table a Female
0	154.70	22.58	7.08	4.18	2.89	—	—
5	13.60	2.76	1.35	0.90	0.76	0.38	0.19
15	7.63	2.15	1.46	1.33	0.85	0.44	0.19
25	8.06	2.88	1.93	1.77	1.16	0.62	0.35
35	8.95	4.59	2.51	2.11	1.65	0.92	0.55
45	11.16	8.61	5.35	4.55	3.56	2.40	1.12
55	18.57	17.98	13.00	10.47	7.09	5.99	2.89
65	40.13	39.64	31.75	25.42	14.59	12.85	7.34
75	94.37	88.64	73.37	64.19	38.24	35.05	20.13
85	235.55	194.13	161.14	152.95	116.10	90.99	65.52

The newest ordinary life tables are the **Commissioners 1980 Standard Ordinary Mortality Tables** *(1980 CSO Tables)*, with separate versions for males and females.[16] These tables reflect a decline in mortality rates at most ages from those in the *1958 CSO Table*. However, the *1980 CSO Table* reflects a "spurt" in male mortality rates in the late teenage years. This spurt results in higher 1980 male mortality rates at some ages, relative to the 1958 rates. The increases in male mortality rates during the late teenage years result in *declining* male mortality rates between ages 21 and 28 in the *1980 CSO Table*. By contrast, the 1980 female mortality rates always increase with age after about age 10, as is true in most other mortality tables.

The newest mortality table for industrial insurance is the **1961 Commissioners Standard Industrial (CSI) Mortality Table.** Use of the *1961 CSI Table* is mandatory for computing minimum reserves and nonforfeiture values for industrial policies after 1967. There also is a table for use with group life insurance, the **Commissioners 1960 Standard Group Mortality Table.** Table 18-3 compares the death rates for a selected group of ordinary life tables and for a modern annuity table, the *1983 Table a.*

4. *Annuity tables.* Five individual annuity tables are in use today in the United States: the 1937 Standard Annuity Mortality Table, the Annuity Table for 1949, the 1955 American Annuity Table, the 1971 Individual Annuity Mortality Table, and the 1983 Annuity Mortality Table. Also, three group annuity tables are in use today: the Group Annuity Table for 1951, the 1971 Group Annuity Mortality Table, and the 1983 Group Annuity Mortality Table.

The **1937 Standard Annuity Table** formerly was used extensively for individual annuity business. The steady improvement in mortality led to the development of the **Annuity Table for 1949,** which introduced projection factors to reflect continued improvement in mortality rates. The **1955 American Annuity Table** was developed to provide reasonable rates for annual premium deferred annuities and life income settlement options. The **Group Annuity Table for 1951** was the first table based on the experience of group annuitants and was widely used in computing rates and reserves for group annuities.

When interest rates increased to levels substantially higher than the level used in determining minimum reserves, new annuity business created a surplus drain for life insurance companies. Use of older annuity mortality tables gave partial relief from the strain caused by these low

---

[16]Other *1980 CSO Tables* exist. Because of the need to comply with a United States Supreme Court decision regarding gender-neutral insurance in certain employment related situations, there are various "merged gender" tables. Also, a 10-year select *1980 CSO Table* exists as well as a table for extended term insurance (the *1980 CET Table*). The CSO select table is based on the same underlying ultimate data as the regular *1980 CSO Tables*. However, the mortality rates vary not only with age and sex, but also with the number of elapsed years since the policy was issued. Finally, there is also a set of nonsmoker/smoker *1980 CSO Tables*. These tables can be used in states that permit reserving and surrender value differences between smokers and nonsmokers.

valuation interest rate ceilings, but more accurate reserves needed up-to-date mortality and interest bases. Thus, two new mortality tables, the **1971 Group Annuity Table** and the **1971 Individual Annuity Table,** were developed to be used with higher interest rates in setting reserves. Two new projection scales for males and one for females were also designed for use with the 1971 Group Annuity Table.

Two further annuity mortality tables were adopted by the NAIC in 1983 and are now being adopted by the states. At the publication date of this book, over 37 states had adopted these new tables. One is for reserve and nonforfeiture purposes on individual annuity business (the so-called **1983 Table a**) and the other applies to group business (the **1983 GAM Table**).

Other Considerations

Application of the Laws of Probabilities to Mortality. The statement was made earlier in this chapter that risk in life insurance is measured by the application of the laws of probability to the mortality table. Now that these laws are understood and the mortality table has been explained, a few simple illustrations may be used to show this application. Suppose that it is desired to estimate the probability of a man's death within one, two, or five years of age 35. This probability, according to the laws explained earlier, will be determined according to a chosen mortality table and will be a fraction, of which the denominator equals the number living at age 35 and the numerator is the number that have died during the one, two, or five years, respectively, following that age. According to the *1980 CSO Table,* 9,491,711 men are living at age 35 and 20,028 die before the end of the year. Hence, the probability of death within one year is

$$q_{35} = \frac{d_{35}}{l_{35}} = \frac{20,028}{9,491,711} = 0.00211$$

During the two years following the stated age, there are $20,028 + 21,217$ deaths, for a total of 41,245. Therefore, the probability of dying within two years (represented by $_2q_{35}$) is

$$_2q_{35} = \frac{d_{35} + d_{36}}{l_{35}} = \frac{41,245}{9,491,711} = 0.00435$$

Similarly, the total number of deaths within five years is $20,028 + 21,217 + 22,681 + 24,324 + 26,236$. Thus, the probability that a man entering age 35 will die within five years ($_5q_{35}$) is

$$_5q_{35} = \frac{d_{35} + d_{36} + d_{37} + d_{38} + d_{39}}{l_{35}} = \frac{114,486}{9,491,711} = 0.0121$$

Note that this last expression could be simplified as follows:

$$_5q_{35} = \frac{l_{35} - l_{40}}{l_{35}}$$

where the difference between the number living at age 35 (l_{35}) and living at age 40 (l_{40}) equals the number who died during this five-year interval.

Probabilities of survival can also be expressed by the table. The chance of living one year following age 35 (p_{35}) will be a fraction, of which the demoninator is the number living at age 35 and the numerator is the number that have lived one year following the specified age (i.e., to age 36). Thus,

$$p_{35} = \frac{l_{36}}{l_{35}} = \frac{9,471,683}{9,491,711} = 0.99789$$

Use of Mortality Tables in Ratemaking. The discussion in the following chapters utilizes the *1980 CSO Table* in illustrating the principles involved in ratemaking. As emphasized in Chapter 2, the *1980 CSO Table* is not, however, used by life insurance companies as the primary basis for establishing premium rates. They use tables reflecting up-to-date experience (often based on the company's own most recent experience) in establishing premium rates. The *1980 CSO Table* is used for reserve valuation and nonforfeiture-value purposes.

UNDERLYING PRINCIPLES

Interest

As pointed out in Chapter 2, prefunding for life insurance protection via either a fixed, level premium or a flexible premium can lead to the accumulation of large sums of money, which are often held by insurers for many years before being used to pay benefits. The funds are invested in income-producing assets, the earnings on which permit life insurance companies to charge lower premiums than otherwise would be the case. Because interest plays such a vital role in the actuarial calculations and the actual operations of a life insurance company, it is essential to consider some of the more important concepts.

Basic Terminology. **Interest** may be defined as the price paid for the use of money. The original investment, referred to as the **principal amount** or simply **principal,** accumulates by the end of a specified term to a sum referred to as the **accumulated amount.** The amount earned for this particular period is the difference between the accumulated amount and the principal.

Abbreviations are commonly used in dealing with interest. Some are:

I = interest amount

S = accumulated amount

A = principal amount

i = interest rate

n = number of compounding periods, often expressed in years

By use of these abbreviations, the statement that an accumulated amount is equal to the principal amount plus interest may be expressed as $S=A+I$. The statement that the interest earned in one year is equal to the principal times the rate per annum may be expressed as $I=Ai$. By rewriting the statement for accumulated amount, one obtains $S=A+Ai$, or $S=A(1+i)$. The equation $S=A(1+i)$ states that the amount to which principal will accumulate in one year at a given rate is equal to the principal multiplied by the sum of 1 plus the interest rate.

Interest that is credited or paid only on the original principal is described as **simple interest.** In many cases, as is the case for life insurance calculations, interest earnings will be left with the original principal to themselves earn interest.

When interest is not distributed but used to earn additional funds, the interest earned on it is described as **compound interest.**

Basic Compound Interest Functions. Four basic compound interest functions are used in insurance mathematics. An understanding of these functions is important for anyone interested in insurance or any other area of finance.

Accumulated Value of 1. The amount to which a principal will accumulate in one year at a given rate per annum has been expressed as $S_1=A(1+i)$. If this amount were invested for an additional year, the interest for the second year would be i times S_1. The amount at the end of the second year could then be expressed as

$$S_2 = S_1 + iS_1$$
$$= S_1(1+i)$$
$$= A(1+i)^2$$

By continuing to use simple algebra, it may be shown that the accumulated value of A at the end of n years may be expressed as $S=A(1+i)^n$. Since interest tables show the value for a principal of 1, the values $(1+i)^n$ may be found in the appropriate interest table and multiplied by the principal amount to determine the future value. Table 18A–1 in the chapter appendix provides such compound interest factors at various interest rates.

Present Value of 1. In all financial areas, it is often necessary to provide a set amount of money at the end of a specified period. To achieve this goal, a sum of money is invested today. The principal that must be invested now to accomplish some objective in the future is referred to as the **present value.**

Since $S=A(1+i)^n$, it is only necessary to divide both sides of this equation by $(1+i)^n$ to determine the expression $A=S/(1+i)^n$. To determine the present value of the amount—that is, the principal—it is only necessary to divide the amount S by $(1+i)^n$.

Of course, $S/(1+i)^n$ is equivalent to

$$S \times \left(\frac{1}{1+i}\right)^n$$

The symbol v is commonly used for $1/(1+i)$. Thus

$$\left(\frac{1}{1+i}\right)^n$$

is abbreviated as v^n. Tables for the value v^n at various interest rates are available. Table 18A–2 in the chapter appendix is such a table. The figures given in such tables are commonly referred to as the present value of 1 rather than $1/(1+i)^n$ or v^n. Present value tables were developed so that multiplication rather than division could be performed to obtain present value results.

Accumulated Value of 1 per Year. Suppose that an investment of $1 is made at the beginning of each year for three years. To determine the accumulated amount at the end of three years, it is only necessary to add the amounts to which each of the payments will grow. The first $1 will grow to an amount of $(1 + i)^3$. The second $1 will grow to an amount of $(1 + i)^2$, and the third $1 will grow to an amount of $(1 + i)$. The total amount at the end of three years may be expressed as

$$\ddot{s}_{\overline{3}|} = (1 + i) + (1 + i)^2 + (1 + i)^3$$

where $\ddot{s}_{\overline{n}|}$ is the symbol for the accumulated value at the end of n years of 1 invested at the *beginning* of each year for n years.[17] In general,

$$\ddot{s}_{\overline{n}|} = (1 + i) + (1 + i)^2 + \cdots + (1 + i)^{n-1} + (1 + i)^n$$

Table 18A–3 in the chapter appendix gives tables of $\ddot{s}_{\overline{n}|}$ at various interest rates.

Present Value of 1 per Year. Another common compound interest problem is to determine what principal (i.e., present value) should be invested now that will be sufficient to provide equal annual payments at the *end* of each year for the next n years. The total present value of the payments may be computed by summing the present value of each payment. For example, suppose that we wish to find the present value of $1 payable at the *end* of each year for three years. The present values of the first, second, and third payments are v^1, v^2, and v^3, respectively. The total present value may be expressed as $a_{\overline{3}|} = v^1 + v^2 + v^3$, where $a_{\overline{n}|}$ is the symbol for the present value of 1 paid at the end of each year for the next n years.[18] In general, then,

$$a_{\overline{n}|} = v + v^2 + \cdots + v^{n-1} + v^n$$

Table 18A–4 in the chapter appendix gives tables of $a_{\overline{n}|}$ at various interest rates.

Annuities

An **annuity** is simply a series of payments (or receipts).[19] Usually, the payment is a constant amount, and the intervals are regular, as, for example, $100 payable at the end of each month for 10 years, or $5000 payable at the end of each year for 20 years. The annuity payment may be payable under all circumstances or may be contingent on a particular person being alive. The former are called **annuities certain.** The latter are called **life annuities.** A life annuity payable in no event for more than a set term of years (but terminating if and when the individual dies during the set term) is called a **temporary life annuity.**

In cases where the annuity payments are assumed to be made at the *beginning* of each period, the annuity is referred to as an **annuity due.** Its symbol is $\ddot{a}_{\overline{n}|}$. In cases where the annuity payments are assumed to be made at the *end* of each period, the annuity is referred to as an **annuity immediate.** Its symbol is $a_{\overline{n}|}$. Annuity theory plays an important role in actuarial calculations because premium payments *to* a life insurance company by a policyowner constitute an *annuity due to the company.*

---

[17] The notation $\ddot{s}_{\overline{n}|}$ is commonly read as "*s* double-dot angle *n*." The two dots above the *s* mean that payments are made at the beginning of each period. An *s* without the two dots means that the payments are made at the end of each period.

[18] The $a_{\overline{n}|}$ notation is commonly read as "*a* angle *n*." The absence of the two dots above the *a* indicates that payments are made at the end of each period. See footnote 17.

[19] What is a series of payments to the payor is a series of receipts to the recipient.

Assumptions underlying Rate Computations

When the problem of life insurance rate computation is approached, several questions arise at once. The answers will directly influence the results obtained. For instance, how often will the premium be paid? Annually, semiannually, or otherwise? How many premiums will be paid? For five, 10, or 20 years or for life? Additional questions: What will be done with the money between the time it is received and the time it is paid out? How will mortality rates be determined for periods of less than one year's duration in case, for instance, monthly premiums are decided upon (standard mortality tables give nothing less than yearly rates of mortality)? How much time will elapse between death and payment of the death claim? Clearly, these and many other questions must be answered before the computation of rates is begun.

Premiums may be paid in a single cash sum, called a single premium, which pays for the entire risk incurred during the life of the policy, or they may be paid equally over the life of the contract in periods ranging from one week to one year. Many policies are purchased by an annual premium. In this connection, two simplifying assumptions are made here: (1) premiums are paid at the beginning of each policy year, and (2) matured claims are paid at the end of the policy year in which the policy matures.[20] Accordingly, if a policy is purchased by a single premium, this sum is to be paid at the inception of the risk. In the case of level annual premiums, the first payment is to be made on the date of issue of the policy, and equal amounts are then paid annually thereafter on the anniversary of this date.

It is evident in the case of single premiums, and it is true only to a lesser degree with level annual premiums, that the company will have the money on hand for some time before being called upon to pay matured claims. Amounts in excess of that needed to meet current expenses and other policy obligations are invested and earn interest while in the company's possession. These interest earnings are an important source of the funds available to pay claims. But since the company does not know the rates of interest to be earned in the future, it is necessary to assume a rate that is reasonably certain of being earned each year throughout the potentially long life of a policy.[21] Since much of the premium money received by the company often is held for a number of years before being paid out in the form of matured claims, it will be possible to earn interest on interest.

In determining the interest rate to be assumed in computing guaranteed maximum premiums (or in choosing a guaranteed minimum interest-credit rate or rates under a universal life policy), it is necesary to select a rate that the company is *sure* of earning on the average over a long period of years. The assumption that 9 or 10 percent could be earned might be disastrous, for although the company might earn that rate in prosperous years, the rate might decrease. If the company failed to earn the assumed 9 or 10 percent rate, it could be called upon to replenish its inadequate earnings from surplus built up in previous years or, in the absence of the latter, might be forced into bankruptcy. Companies issuing participating or any of the newer current assumption nonparticipating insurance policies will generally select a conservative interest rate, with the intention and expectation of returning to the policyowner, through dividends or otherwise, earnings in excess of the rate selected. A typical rate used by companies for original rate computations might be 5 percent. The rate chosen may make little difference (other things being the same) as long as it is not too high (which could endanger solvency) or too low (which could produce an uncompetitively high premium), since much of the excess earnings under most cash value policies sold today eventually will be paid or credited to policyowners.

The second assumption was that matured claims are assumed to be paid at the end of each

---

[20]Of course, companies do not actually wait to pay death claims until the end of the policy year. They are paid promptly. However, the assumption that they are paid at the end of the year simplifies the analysis while not doing harm to the concepts.

[21]Amounts actually earned in excess of those assumed can be credited to the policyowner via dividends under participating policies, via lower premiums on indeterminate premium policies, and via higher cash value interest credits on universal life and other current assumption policies.

policy year. If there is a fairly even distribution of deaths through the policy year (roughly equivalent to all deaths at the middle of year), the payment of claims would occur on the average six months after death.[22] Thus, the assumption of paying death claims at the end of the year is too generous, to the extent of six months' interest in discounting claims. If premium rates are computed at 5 percent, this would mean a loss to the company of $250 on a $10,000 policy. Even so, many companies calculate net premiums on the assumption that claims are paid at the end of the year. The error introduced typically is corrected by an adjustment in the expense-loading formula or in the timing of interest credits.

The assumption of when in the policy year deaths occur is of financial importance to insurance companies primarily in the case of policies with premiums payable at intervals more frequently than once a year. In the case of monthly premiums, if only one-twelfth of the annual premium has been collected in the first month, but one-sixth of the year's total mortality costs occur during the first month, the company will have overestimated the funds on hand to pay losses. With some mortality tables, this situation occurs during the first 10 years of life and during the twenties, when the mortality rate is decreasing and proportionately more deaths occur at the beginning of the year than toward the end of the year. At other ages, the mortality rate generally increases, and the discrepancy between the assumption of uniform deaths and the actual situation is favorable to the company.

In addition to these assumptions, the following must be known to compute premium rates in life insurance:

1. The age of the insured
2. The sex of the insured (where this is permitted as a factor)
3. The benefits to be provided
4. The mortality table to be used (possibly involves separate tables for smokers and nonsmokers, etc.)
5. A rate of interest
6. The amount to cover the company's expenses of operation, profits, and a margin for contingencies

Also, an estimate is needed as to the proportion of policyowners whose contracts terminate each year for reasons other than death or maturity of the policy. Together, all of these assumptions are used to test the tentative gross premiums through asset-share studies—discussed in Chapter 21.

Interaction of Probability, Mortality, and Interest Concepts

As pointed out earlier, the process of obtaining the present value of a dollar payable at a specified time in the future is referred to as **discounting.** Assuming that the payment of the dollar in the future is not a certainty but is contingent on some insured individuals' being alive, it is necessary to reduce the *present value* of the future dollar still further, reflecting the probability that the individual will be alive to pay it. The process of "discounting" for probability is referred to as taking an **expected value.**

For example, assume that it is desired to know the value today of a promise to pay $1,000 in 20 years if a male now aged 30 is alive at that time. Assume that money is valued at 7½ percent and the *1980 CSO* mortality rates apply. From Table 18A-2, we know that the value today of $1,000 to be paid in 20 years—ignoring the survival probability—is found by multiplying the present value factor (at 7½ percent and 20 years) by $1,000. Thus, $1,000 × 0.235 = $235.

The probability that a male aged 30 will live for 20 years, symbolized as $_{20}p_{30}$, is found by the ratio of the number living at age 50 (l_{50}) to the number living at age 30 (l_{30}) (i.e., l_{50}/l_{30}), or, from Table 18–1, 8,966,618 ÷ 9,579,998, which equals 0.936. Thus, the present *expected* value of the $1,000 to be paid at age 50 is found by taking the product of the present value and the expected value (i.e., $235 × 0.936 = $220). This would

TABLE 18-4. $1,000 ordinary life policy, male, age 80

(*1980 CSO Table*, 6% interest)

	Premiums				Benefits			
	(1)	(2)	(3)	(4)	(5)	(6)	(7)	(8)
Attained Age (x)	Level Annual Premium	Interest Discount Factor (v^{t-1})	Probability of Survival $(_tp_{80})$	Present Expected Value of Premium $[(1) \times (2) \times (3)]$	Death Benefit	Interest Discount Factor (v^t)	Probability of Death (d_x/l_{80})	Present Expected Value of Benefit $[(5) \times (6) \times (7)]$
80	$131.42	1.0000	1.0000	$131.42	$1,000.00	0.9434	0.0988	$ 93.25
81	131.42	0.9434	0.9012	111.72	1,000.00	0.8900	0.0969	86.20
82	131.42	0.8900	0.8043	94.07	1,000.00	0.8396	0.0943	79.18
83	131.42	0.8396	0.7100	78.34	1,000.00	0.7921	0.0911	72.13
84	131.42	0.7921	0.6189	64.43	1,000.00	0.7473	0.0868	64.87
85	131.42	0.7473	0.5321	52.26	1,000.00	0.7050	0.0814	57.38
86	131.42	0.7050	0.4507	41.76	1,000.00	0.6651	0.0749	49.79
87	131.42	0.6651	0.3759	32.85	1,000.00	0.6274	0.0675	42.34
88	131.42	0.6274	0.3084	25.43	1,000.00	0.5919	0.0596	35.28
89	131.42	0.5919	0.2488	19.35	1,000.00	0.5584	0.0516	28.80
90	131.42	0.5584	0.1972	14.47	1,000.00	0.5268	0.0437	23.04
91	131.42	0.5268	0.1535	10.63	1,000.00	0.4970	0.0364	18.08
92	131.42	0.4970	0.1171	7.65	1,000.00	0.4688	0.0297	13.92
93	131.42	0.4688	0.0874	5.39	1,000.00	0.4423	0.0238	10.52
94	131.42	0.4423	0.0636	3.70	1,000.00	0.4173	0.0188	7.86
95	131.42	0.4173	0.0448	2.46	1,000.00	0.3936	0.0148	5.82
96	131.42	0.3936	0.0300	1.55	1,000.00	0.3714	0.0115	4.29
97	131.42	0.3714	0.0185	0.90	1,000.00	0.3503	0.0089	3.11
98	131.42	0.3503	0.0096	0.44	1,000.00	0.3305	0.0063	2.09
99	131.42	0.3305	0.0033	0.14	1,000.00	0.3118	0.0033	1.02
				$698.96				$698.96

represent the value of the promise, based on the stated assumptions.

If expenses are ignored and the net premium rate for a life insurance policy is calculated, at date of issue, the present value of all future expected premiums must be equal to the present value of all future expected benefits, where values are "discounted" for both interest and mortality. In word form, therefore, we observe that at issue date for any life insurance policy:

present value of future premiums (PVFP) = present value of future benefits (PVFB)

This relationship is illustrated in Table 18–4 for a hypothetical $1,000 ordinary life policy issued at male age 80. Column 1 shows the net level annual premium that hypothetically would be paid at the beginning of each year if the insured were alive then. Column 2 shows present value factors, where the factor for the first year is 1 since the premium is paid now. Column 3 shows the probability of survival to each attained age shown.

Column 4 lists the present expected value of each premium payment. The $698.96 total at the bottom on column 4 is the total present expected value of all future premiums.

Column 5 shows yearly death benefits payable. The figures in column 6, the discounts for interest, are smaller than the corresponding figures in column 2 because death benefits are assumed to be paid at the end of the year, whereas premiums are paid at the beginning of the year. Hence, death benefits are discounted for one more year than premiums. Whereas column 3 shows the probability of survival to pay the premium at each age, column 7 shows the probability of dying and therefore the likelihood of payment of the death benefit at each age. Column 8 shows the present expected value of each future benefit. The total of $698.96 at the bottom of column 8 is the total present expected value of all future death benefits and is the same as the present expected value of all future premiums. Thus, at date of issue, we see that PVFP = PVFB.

Table 18-4 reflects the interaction of probability, mortality, and money concepts. Each of these elements has been included in its proper place and has been combined with the other elements according to a precise mathematical blend. The result is that based on the given assumptions as to mortality and interest, an insurance contract represents an equal exchange of value between the policyowner and the company. The policyowner pays the premiums. The insurer agrees to pay the stated death benefits and the present expected values are equal. The following chapters will consider premium calculations in detail. It is important not to lose sight of this basic goal in all insurance contracts: the exchange of equal *expected* values at date of issue.

APPENDIX
Interest Tables

TABLE 18A-1. Accumulated value of 1, at various interest rates

$(1 + i)^n$

Years n	3%	5%	6%	7%	7.5%	9%	12%
1	1.030	1.050	1.060	1.070	1.075	1.090	1.120
2	1.061	1.102	1.124	1.145	1.156	1.188	1.254
3	1.093	1.158	1.191	1.225	1.242	1.295	1.405
4	1.126	1.216	1.262	1.311	1.335	1.412	1.574
5	1.159	1.276	1.338	1.403	1.436	1.539	1.762
6	1.194	1.340	1.419	1.501	1.543	1.677	1.974
7	1.230	1.407	1.504	1.606	1.659	1.828	2.211
8	1.267	1.477	1.594	1.718	1.783	1.993	2.476
9	1.305	1.551	1.689	1.838	1.917	2.172	2.773
10	1.344	1.629	1.791	1.967	2.061	2.367	3.106
11	1.384	1.710	1.898	2.105	2.216	2.580	3.479
12	1.426	1.796	2.012	2.252	2.382	2.813	3.896
13	1.469	1.886	2.133	2.410	2.560	3.066	4.363
14	1.513	1.980	2.261	2.579	2.752	3.342	4.887
15	1.558	2.079	2.397	2.759	2.959	3.642	5.474
16	1.605	2.183	2.540	2.952	3.181	3.970	6.130
17	1.653	2.292	2.693	3.159	3.419	4.328	6.866
18	1.702	2.407	2.854	3.380	3.676	4.717	7.690
19	1.754	2.527	3.026	3.617	3.951	5.142	8.613
20	1.806	2.653	3.207	3.870	4.248	5.604	9.646
21	1.860	2.786	3.400	4.141	4.566	6.109	10.804
22	1.916	2.925	3.604	4.430	4.909	6.659	12.100
23	1.974	3.072	3.820	4.741	5.277	7.258	13.552
24	2.033	3.225	4.049	5.072	5.673	7.911	15.179
25	2.094	3.386	4.292	5.427	6.098	8.623	17.000
26	2.157	3.556	4.549	5.807	6.556	9.399	19.040
27	2.221	3.733	4.822	6.214	7.047	10.245	21.325
28	2.288	3.920	5.112	6.649	7.576	11.167	23.884
29	2.357	4.116	5.418	7.114	8.144	12.172	26.750
30	2.427	4.322	5.743	7.612	8.755	13.268	29.960
31	2.500	4.538	6.088	8.145	9.412	14.462	33.555
32	2.575	4.765	6.453	8.715	10.117	15.763	37.582
33	2.652	5.003	6.841	9.325	10.876	17.182	42.092
34	2.732	5.253	7.251	9.978	11.692	18.728	47.143
35	2.814	5.516	7.686	10.677	12.569	20.414	52.800
36	2.898	5.792	8.147	11.424	13.512	22.251	59.136
37	2.985	6.081	8.636	12.224	14.525	24.254	66.232
38	3.075	6.385	9.154	13.079	15.614	26.437	74.180
39	3.167	6.705	9.703	13.995	16.785	28.816	83.081
40	3.262	7.040	10.286	14.974	18.044	31.409	93.051

TABLE 18A-2. Present value of 1, at various interest rates

Years n	\multicolumn{7}{c}{$(v)^n$}
	3%	5%	6%	7%	7.5%	9%	12%
1	0.971	0.952	0.943	0.935	0.930	0.917	0.893
2	0.943	0.907	0.890	0.873	0.865	0.842	0.797
3	0.915	0.864	0.840	0.816	0.805	0.772	0.712
4	0.888	0.823	0.792	0.763	0.749	0.708	0.636
5	0.863	0.784	0.747	0.713	0.697	0.650	0.567
6	0.837	0.746	0.705	0.666	0.648	0.596	0.507
7	0.813	0.711	0.665	0.623	0.603	0.547	0.452
8	0.789	0.677	0.627	0.582	0.561	0.502	0.404
9	0.766	0.645	0.592	0.544	0.522	0.460	0.361
10	0.744	0.614	0.558	0.508	0.485	0.422	0.322
11	0.722	0.585	0.527	0.475	0.451	0.388	0.287
12	0.701	0.557	0.497	0.444	0.420	0.356	0.257
13	0.681	0.530	0.469	0.415	0.391	0.326	0.229
14	0.661	0.505	0.442	0.388	0.363	0.299	0.205
15	0.642	0.481	0.417	0.362	0.338	0.275	0.183
16	0.623	0.458	0.394	0.339	0.314	0.252	0.163
17	0.605	0.436	0.371	0.317	0.292	0.231	0.146
18	0.587	0.416	0.350	0.296	0.272	0.212	0.130
19	0.570	0.396	0.331	0.277	0.253	0.194	0.116
20	0.554	0.377	0.312	0.258	0.235	0.178	0.104
21	0.538	0.359	0.294	0.242	0.219	0.164	0.093
22	0.522	0.342	0.278	0.226	0.204	0.150	0.083
23	0.507	0.326	0.262	0.211	0.189	0.138	0.074
24	0.492	0.310	0.247	0.197	0.176	0.126	0.066
25	0.478	0.295	0.233	0.184	0.164	0.116	0.059
26	0.464	0.281	0.220	0.172	0.153	0.106	0.053
27	0.450	0.268	0.207	0.161	0.142	0.098	0.047
28	0.437	0.255	0.196	0.150	0.132	0.090	0.042
29	0.424	0.243	0.185	0.141	0.123	0.082	0.037
30	0.412	0.231	0.174	0.131	0.114	0.075	0.033
31	0.400	0.220	0.164	0.123	0.106	0.069	0.030
32	0.388	0.210	0.155	0.115	0.099	0.063	0.027
33	0.377	0.200	0.146	0.107	0.092	0.058	0.024
34	0.366	0.190	0.138	0.100	0.086	0.053	0.021
35	0.355	0.181	0.130	0.094	0.080	0.049	0.019
36	0.345	0.173	0.123	0.088	0.074	0.045	0.017
37	0.335	0.164	0.116	0.082	0.069	0.041	0.015
38	0.325	0.157	0.109	0.076	0.064	0.038	0.013
39	0.316	0.149	0.103	0.071	0.060	0.035	0.012
40	0.307	0.142	0.097	0.067	0.055	0.032	0.011

TABLE 18A-3. Accumulated value of 1 per year, at various interest rates

Years n	3%	5%	6%	7%	7.5%	9%	12%
1	1.030	1.050	1.060	1.070	1.075	1.090	1.120
2	2.091	2.152	2.184	2.215	2.231	2.278	2.374
3	3.184	3.310	3.375	3.440	3.473	3.573	3.779
4	4.309	4.526	4.637	4.751	4.808	4.985	5.353
5	5.468	5.802	5.975	6.153	6.244	6.523	7.115
6	6.662	7.142	7.394	7.654	7.787	8.200	9.089
7	7.892	8.549	8.897	9.260	9.446	10.028	11.300
8	9.159	10.027	10.491	10.978	11.230	12.021	13.776
9	10.464	11.578	12.181	12.816	13.147	14.193	16.549
10	11.808	13.207	13.972	14.784	15.208	16.560	19.655
11	13.192	14.917	15.870	16.888	17.424	19.141	23.133
12	14.618	16.713	17.882	19.141	19.806	21.953	27.029
13	16.086	18.599	20.015	21.550	22.366	25.019	31.393
14	17.599	20.579	22.276	24.129	25.118	28.361	36.280
15	19.157	22.657	24.673	26.888	28.077	32.003	41.753
16	20.762	24.840	27.213	29.840	31.258	35.974	47.884
17	22.414	27.132	29.906	32.999	34.677	40.301	54.750
18	24.117	29.539	32.760	36.379	38.353	45.018	62.440
19	25.870	32.066	35.786	39.996	42.305	50.160	71.052
20	27.676	34.719	38.993	43.865	46.553	55.765	80.699
21	29.537	37.505	42.392	48.006	51.119	61.873	91.503
22	31.453	40.430	45.996	52.436	56.028	68.532	103.603
23	33.426	43.502	49.816	57.177	61.305	75.790	117.155
24	35.459	46.727	53.864	62.249	66.978	83.701	132.334
25	37.553	50.113	58.156	67.677	73.076	92.324	149.334
26	39.710	53.669	62.706	73.484	79.632	101.723	168.374
27	41.931	57.403	67.528	79.698	86.679	111.968	189.699
28	44.219	61.323	72.640	86.347	94.255	123.135	213.583
29	46.575	65.439	78.058	93.461	102.399	135.308	240.333
30	49.003	69.761	83.802	101.073	111.154	148.575	270.293
31	51.503	74.299	89.890	109.218	120.566	163.037	303.848
32	54.078	79.064	96.343	117.934	130.684	178.801	341.429
33	56.730	84.067	103.184	127.259	141.560	195.983	383.521
34	59.462	89.320	110.435	137.237	153.252	214.711	430.663
35	62.276	94.836	118.121	147.914	165.821	235.125	483.463
36	65.174	100.628	126.268	159.338	179.332	257.376	542.599
37	68.159	106.709	134.904	171.561	193.857	281.630	608.830
38	71.234	113.095	144.058	184.641	209.471	308.067	683.010
39	74.401	119.800	153.762	198.635	226.257	336.883	766.091
40	77.663	126.839	164.047	213.610	244.301	368.292	859.142

TABLE 18A-4. Present value of 1 per year, at various interest rates

Years n	$a_{\overline{n}}$						
	3%	5%	6%	7%	7.5%	9%	12%
1	0.971	0.952	0.943	0.935	0.930	0.917	0.893
2	1.913	1.859	1.833	1.808	1.796	1.759	1.690
3	2.829	2.723	2.673	2.624	2.601	2.531	2.402
4	3.717	3.546	3.465	3.387	3.349	3.240	3.037
5	4.580	4.329	4.212	4.100	4.046	3.890	3.605
6	5.417	5.076	4.917	4.767	4.694	4.486	4.111
7	6.230	5.786	5.582	5.389	5.297	5.033	4.564
8	7.020	6.463	6.210	5.971	5.857	5.535	4.968
9	7.786	7.108	6.802	6.515	6.379	5.995	5.328
10	8.530	7.722	7.360	7.024	6.864	6.418	5.650
11	9.253	8.306	7.887	7.499	7.315	6.805	5.938
12	9.954	8.863	8.384	7.943	7.735	7.161	6.194
13	10.635	9.394	8.853	8.358	8.126	7.487	6.424
14	11.296	9.899	9.295	8.745	8.489	7.786	6.628
15	11.938	10.380	9.712	9.108	8.827	8.061	6.811
16	12.561	10.838	10.106	9.447	9.142	8.313	6.974
17	13.166	11.274	10.477	9.763	9.434	8.544	7.120
18	13.754	11.690	10.828	10.059	9.706	8.756	7.250
19	14.324	12.085	11.158	10.336	9.959	8.950	7.366
20	14.877	12.462	11.470	10.594	10.194	9.129	7.469
21	15.415	12.821	11.764	10.836	10.413	9.292	7.562
22	15.937	13.163	12.042	11.061	10.617	9.442	7.645
23	16.444	13.489	12.303	11.272	10.807	9.580	7.718
24	16.936	13.799	12.550	11.469	10.983	9.707	7.784
25	17.413	14.094	12.783	11.654	11.147	9.823	7.843
26	17.877	14.375	13.003	11.826	11.299	9.929	7.896
27	18.327	14.643	13.211	11.987	11.441	10.027	7.943
28	18.764	14.898	13.406	12.137	11.573	10.116	7.984
29	19.188	15.141	13.591	12.278	11.696	10.198	8.022
30	19.600	15.372	13.765	12.409	11.810	10.274	8.055
31	20.000	15.593	13.929	12.532	11.917	10.343	8.085
32	20.389	15.803	14.084	12.647	12.015	10.406	8.112
33	20.766	16.003	14.230	12.754	12.107	10.464	8.135
34	21.132	16.193	14.368	12.854	12.193	10.518	8.157
35	21.487	16.374	14.498	12.948	12.273	10.567	8.176
36	21.832	16.547	14.621	13.035	12.347	10.612	8.192
37	22.167	16.711	14.737	13.117	12.415	10.653	8.208
38	22.492	16.868	14.846	13.193	12.479	10.691	8.221
39	22.808	17.017	14.949	13.265	12.539	10.726	8.233
40	23.115	17.159	15.046	13.332	12.594	10.757	8.244

Chapter 19

Net Premiums

INTRODUCTION

With the preceding life insurance mathematical principles as a base, it is now possible to illustrate one process by which life insurance and annuity premiums are calculated.[1] The process shown includes the calculation of net premiums for term, whole life, endowment, and annuity policies to which amounts to cover expenses, profits, and contingencies are added to develop a gross premium rate structure. Net premiums take into account interest and mortality factors only. This study begins by first determining the **net single premium.** From this, the **net annual premium** can be found. Following this, various methods of loading to ascertain a gross premium rate schedule will be studied.[2]

NET SINGLE PREMIUMS

The Calculation Process

The computation of net premium rates on a life insurance policy generally requires informa-

tion as to (1) the age and sex of the insured, (2) the benefits to be provided, (3) the mortality rates to be used, and (4) the rate of interest assumed. In the computations that follow, mortality will be assumed to be that of the *1980 CSO Table;* the rate of interest assumed will be 5 percent; the face amount of the policy, $1,000; and the insured a male. The age of the insured will be stated in each instance.[3]

Term Insurance

Term life insurance policies cover a specified period and promise to pay the sum insured if the insured dies within this period, nothing being paid if death does not occur during the designated term. Yearly renewable term (YRT) policies are the simplest forms of term life insurance and offer an excellent opportunity to explain the elements of ratemaking.[4]

Suppose that the net single premium is to be ascertained on a one-year term life insurance

---

[1]Another process was illustrated in Chapter 2.

[2]This procedure is not always followed, but in any case, the gross premium is always tested by asset-share studies under realistic assumptions. See Chapter 21.

[3]The reader is reminded that the *1980 CSO Table* usually is not used for ratemaking. It is used for valuing insurance companies' policy liabilities. Most companies use up-to-date mortality experience in deriving premiums to be charged.

[4]For a description of YRT life insurance policies, see Chapter 4.

policy of $1,000 on a male age 45. Immediate use will now be found for two assumptions mentioned in Chapter 18: that premiums are paid at the beginning of each policy year and that matured claims are paid at the close of the policy year. The question is: What amount of money must be paid at the beginning of the year by a policyowner to enable the company to return $1,000 at year-end if the insured dies during the period and the amount is held at interest until the claim is paid? The company is interested in the probability of having to pay the death claim; in other words, the chance of the 45-year-old male dying during the year. This will be determined by means of the mortality table shown in Table 18–1.

Suppose that an insurance company issued 9,210,289 (number living at age 45) one-year term policies to males age 45. If the actual mortality experienced among this group coincided with the experience expected under the mortality table, there would be 41,907 deaths during the year. Since each of these deaths represents a liability of $1,000 to the company, and since the claims are assumed to be payable at the close of the year, the company must have on hand at that time $41,907,000 to pay claims. But this entire amount need not have been collected from the policy-owners, since they were required to pay their premiums at the beginning of the year and the company was able to invest the money at interest for one year at, say, 5 percent. Since $0.9524 accumulated at 5 percent for one year will grow to one dollar at year's end, the company needs to have on hand at the beginning of the year only $39,912,227 (0.9524 × $41,907,000) in order to have at the end of the year sufficient funds to pay $1,000 for each of the 41,907 deaths. To obtain the net single premium each individual should pay, it is only necessary to divide the total fund by the group of 9,210,289 to be insured:

$$\$39,912,227 \div 9,210,289 = \$4.33$$

The net single premium for a one-year term insurance policy at age 45, or the amount of money that must be paid at the beginning of the year to supply each individual's contribution

to the death losses of the group for the year, is therefore $4.33.[5]

The same problem may be approached in a different way and a formula stated for determining costs. An estimated 41,907 males aged 45 will die out of the group of 9,210,289, based on the mortality table used here. This is equivalent to saying that the probability of death during the forty-fifth year (q_{45}) is 41,907/9,210,289, or 0.00455. The expected value of a death claim for an insured is therefore $1,000 × 0.00455, or $4.55. But this value needs to be on hand at the end of the year and money earns 5 percent interest. The amount to be paid by the insured at the beginning of the year will be $4.55 discounted for one year at 5 percent, or $4.55 times 0.9524, which equals $4.33. This may be summarized as follows:

$$\$1,000 \times \frac{41,907}{9,210,289} \times 0.9524 = \$4.33$$

which, in actuarial notation, can be written

$$(1,000)(q_x)(v) = (1,000)\left(\frac{d_{45}}{l_{45}}\right)(v)$$

It must not be assumed from this that an insurance company can insure a single person only. Instead, it must always deal with a group sufficiently large to make certain that the law of large numbers can operate reasonably. But it does not need to insure this entire group with the same kind of policy or at the same age. Results will be satisfactory as long as the entire group of insureds, including all ages and all kinds of policies, is sufficiently large.

If the method used here in determining the premium rate for this insurance is studied carefully, it will be found to embody the following process. Multiply the probability of the occurrence of the event insured against by the amount of the policy, and then multiply by the value of 1 dis-

[5]This method of determining individual net single premiums has been termed the **aggregate approach,** since it emphasizes the total fund necessary to meet death claims as they occur. The alternative approach, which is discussed next, is usually referred to as the **expected value approach.** Either method may be used, but the expected value approach is emphasized here.

counted for one year at the assumed rate of interest. This is a **present expected value.** It is an "expected value" because it is based on mortality probabilities, and it is a "present value" because it is discounted for interest (the time value of money).

To continue, suppose that it is desired to compute the net single premium for a five-year term life insurance policy issued at male age 45; that is, the amount of money that paid in a single sum at age 45 will purchase insurance against death at any time within the next five years. Two facts are apparent: (1) the premium is paid only once, in a single sum at policy inception, and (2) death claims will be paid at the end of the year in which death occurs, not at the end of the five-year period. The latter fact has an important bearing on the interest earned and therefore on the method of computing the cost.

Manifestly, the cost cannot be correctly determined by multiplying the total probability of dying during the five years by the face amount of the policy and discounting this amount in one operation, since some of the money collected will draw interest for only one year, another part will earn interest for two years, and so on. It is necessary to compute each year's mortality costs separately. The probabilities insured against in this case are the chances that a male aged 45 will die during the first year, during the second year, the third year, and so on. In actuarial notation, these probabilities would be found as follows:

$$\frac{d_{45}}{l_{45}} = \frac{41,907}{9,210,289} = 0.00455$$

$$\frac{d_{46}}{l_{45}} = \frac{45,108}{9,210,289} = 0.00490$$

$$\frac{d_{47}}{l_{45}} = \frac{48,536}{9,210,289} = 0.00527$$

$$\frac{d_{48}}{l_{45}} = \frac{52,089}{9,210,289} = 0.00566$$

$$\frac{d_{49}}{l_{45}} = \frac{56,031}{9,210,289} = 0.00608$$

Each of these figures must be multiplied by the amount insured and by the present value of 1 discounted in each instance by the length of time the money is held. The money available for the first year's claims will be held for one year; for the second year's claims, two years; and so on; the funds for the last year's claims being held five years. The relevant discounted values for one, two, three, four, and five years at 5 percent interest are, respectively, 0.9524, 0.9070, 0.8638, 0.8227, and 0.7835. The cost of the five years' of insurance, therefore, can be calculated as follows:

Policy Year (t)	Age (x)	Calculation	Each Year's Cost of Insurance (if paid at inception
1	45	$(\$1,000)\left(\dfrac{d_{45}}{l_{45}}\right)(v)\ = (\$1,000)(0.00455)(0.9524)\ =$	$ 4.33
2	46	$(\$1,000)\left(\dfrac{d_{46}}{l_{45}}\right)(v^2) = (\$1,000)(0.00490)(0.9070)\ =$	4.44
3	47	$(\$1,000)\left(\dfrac{d_{47}}{l_{45}}\right)(v^3) = (\$1,000)(0.00527)(0.8638)\ =$	4.55
4	48	$(\$1,000)\left(\dfrac{d_{48}}{l_{45}}\right)(v^4) = (\$1,000)(0.00566)(0.8227)\ =$	4.66
5	49	$(\$1,000)\left(\dfrac{d_{49}}{l_{45}}\right)(v^5) = (\$1,000)(0.00608)(0.7835)\ =$	4.76
			$22.74

This computation shows that ignoring expenses, taxes, and so on, $22.74 paid to the company by each policyowner and placed at 5 percent interest will furnish enough money to pay all the death claims on this five-year term policy. By simply continuing the process of calculating the cost of insurance on a per year basis, the net single premium for a term insurance contract of any longer durations may be determined.

Whole Life Insurance

A whole life policy provides coverage for the whole of life, promising to pay the face amount whenever death occurs. This policy is like the term contracts just considered, with the exception that instead of being limited to a set number of years, it continues to the end of the mortality table. Since the *1980 CSO Table* assumes that all males die by the end of their one-hundredth year, the maximum possible age for which the cost of insurance

against death needs to be calculated will be 99. The net single premium on a whole life policy issued at male age 45 must, therefore, provide against the possibility that the insured will die during his forty-sixth year, his forty-seventh year, and so on, during every year up to and including his one-hundredth. The separate probabilities insured against will be 55 in number—that is, for ages 45 to 99 inclusive.

The chance of dying in each separate year (d_{x+t-1}/l_x) will be multiplied by the face amount of the policy ($1,000) and this amount discounted for the number of years between the issue of the policy (i.e., the payment of the single premium) and the payment of death losses. Thus,

Policy Year (t)	Age (x)	Calculation			Each Year's Cost of Insurance (If paid at Inception)
1	45	$(\$1,000)\left(\dfrac{d_{45}}{l_{45}}\right)(v)$	$= (\$1,000)\,(0.00455)\,(0.9524)$	$=$	$ 4.33
2	46	$(\$1,000)\left(\dfrac{d_{46}}{l_{45}}\right)(v^2)$	$= (\$1,000)\,(0.00490)\,(0.9070)$	$=$	4.44
3	47	$(\$1,000)\left(\dfrac{d_{47}}{l_{45}}\right)(v^3)$	$= (\$1,000)\,(0.00527)\,(0.8638)$	$=$	4.55
$\vdots$	$\vdots$	$\vdots$	$\vdots$		$\vdots$
53	97	$(\$1,000)\left(\dfrac{d_{97}}{l_{45}}\right)(v^{53})$	$= (\$1,000)\left(\dfrac{29,054}{9,210,289}\right)(0.0753)$	$=$	0.24
54	98	$(\$1,000)\left(\dfrac{d_{98}}{l_{45}}\right)(v^{54})$	$= (\$1,000)\left(\dfrac{20,693}{9,210,289}\right)(0.0717)$	$=$	0.16
55	99	$(\$1,000)\left(\dfrac{d_{99}}{l_{45}}\right)(v^{55})$	$= (\$1,000)\left(\dfrac{10,757}{9,210,289}\right)(0.0683)$	$=$	0.08
					$270.84

This $270.84 is the present expected value of this policy's share of all the death claims payable from age 45. It is therefore the net single premium that will purchase a whole life policy issued at age 45, based on the stated assumptions. It is true that a few men outlive their one-hundredth year, but since the computations assume that the insured will not have survived this age, and since sufficient money will have been accumulated to pay the claim at the close of the one-hundredth year of life, the policy may be surrendered for its full face amount at that time.

A couple of other comments are in order here. Note that the probabilities of death used in the net single premium calculation are not the same as the yearly death probabilities shown in Table 18–1. An understanding of this difference is crucial. The death probabilities shown in column 3 of Table 18–1 give the probabilities of death for a person *who has attained the stipulated age,* whereas the death probabilities used in the calculation above give the probabilities that a person *now age 45 will die in various future years.*

An examination of the two death probabilities at age 99 will illustrate this important difference. The probability of a 99-year-old male dying within his next year of life is shown as 1—a certainty—in Table 18–1. In other words, a person who has attained age 99 is, according to this mortality table, certain to die during the next year. On the other hand, the probability of a 45-year-old dying during his age 99 is d_{99}/l_{45} or 10,757 ÷ 9,210,189, or 0.00117—a small likelihood. This suggests that our 45-year-old male is highly *unlikely* to die during his ninety-ninth year. Why? It is highly unlikely that he will live to attain such an advanced age in the first instance. (The only way that he could die during his ninety-ninth year is if he survived to age 99!)

The net single premium calculation for a whole life policy, in essence, apportions the probability of dying (a certainty) over the various years remaining in one's life. Thus, if the death probabilities in the foregoing whole life net single premium computation are summed, they would equal 1. On the contrary, a summation of the Table 18–1 yearly death probabilities would have no meaning.[6]

Endowments

Endowment insurance is not very popular today in the United States.[7] Even so, several important life insurance principles are illustrated in endowments. For this reason, an understanding of their functioning mathematically is important.

Pure Endowments. A pure endowment promises to pay the face amount if and only if the insured survives a specified period. Thus, a five-year pure endowment would pay the policy amount if the insured is living five years from the date of issue. Table 18–1 shows, for example, that of the 9,210,289 males living at age 45, 8,966,618

[6]Indeed, they would sum to greater than 1! This is also the reason why a comparison of YRT rates to age 100 and the level premium for an ordinary life policy is not meaningful mathematically without adjustment of the YRT premiums for the probabilities of survival. See Robert E. Cooper, "The Level Premium Concept: A Closer Look," *Journal of the American Society of Chartered Life Underwriters,* Vol. 30 (July 1976).

[7]See Chapter 4. The new tax-law definition of life insurance has further decreased endowment popularity. See Chapter 13.

are still living at age 50. Thus, the probability of a male age 45 surviving for five years, symbolized $_5p_{45}$, is

$$_5p_{45} = \frac{l_{50}}{l_{45}} = \frac{8,966,618}{9,210,289} = 0.97354$$

Stated differently, the probability of the occurrence of the event insured against is 0.97354. Since the money paid as a single premium will be held five years before the policy matures, the formula for determining the net single premium for a $1,000 policy (at 5 percent interest) is

$$\text{NSP} = (\$1,000)(_5p_{45})(v^5) =$$
$$(\$1,000)(0.97354)(0.7835) = \$762.77$$

A clear distinction must be made between a pure endowment and a savings account that is left to accumulate at an agreed rate of interest. The insured cannot obtain possession of the money invested in a pure endowment before the expiration of the endowment period. Nothing is returned if the insured should die during this period. It remains in the fund needed to pay the survivors. A bank savings account, on the other hand, is not lost through death of the investor. This fact makes it possible to divide the $1,000 that will be paid *in case of survival through the endowment period* into two funds, one of which might be called an investment fund and the other a **benefit of survivorship** fund. The investment fund element of our five-year pure endowment will equal $762.77 plus interest compounded for five years at 5 percent. Using the formula for the accumulated value of 1 per year, this results in

$$S = (A)(1.05)^5 = (\$762.77)(1.2763) = \$973.52$$

This $973.52 is the amount that would be obtained by investing the net single premium of this pure endowment policy at 5 percent interest for five years. The remainder of the $1,000, or $26.48, comprises the survivor's share of the amounts left by those insureds who died before their policies matured—benefit of survivorship. The possibility of losing the entire amount of one's investment by death before the endowment period has expired makes the pure endowment a policy that finds little favor with the insuring public.[8] For this reason, it is combined with, or constitutes a feature of, some other kind of policy. It is interesting to note that a life annuity is merely a series of pure endowments (see below).

Endowment Insurance. An endowment promises to pay a certain sum in case the insured dies within the term of the policy, or (usually) a like sum at the end of the term in case of survival. This contract includes the pure endowment feature just discussed and, in addition, insurance against death during the term of the endowment. Thus, a five-year endowment insurance policy issued at male age 45 will pay the face amount if the insured dies during the first, second, third, fourth, or fifth years, or it will pay the same sum at the end of the endowment period. The net single premium for these two promises can be found by adding the net single premium for five years of term life insurance coverage and the net single premium for a five-year pure endowment. Based on our assumptions, the net single premium for the five-year pure endowment is $762.77 and for the five-year term is $22.75 for a total of $785.22.

Other types of endowment contracts— partial endowments, semiendowments, and double endowments—are sometimes issued. They differ from the policy just explained only in that the amount due on survival (i.e., the pure endowment element) differs from the amount paid on death.[9]

The contracts illustrated here have involved only one life. Life insurance companies, however, issue policies covering risks on two or more lives— joint life and survivorship life policies are examples.[10] But the computation of premium rates on risks involving more than one life would carry us more deeply into actuarial science than is appropriate here. The purpose of our premium analyses is merely to give an adequate idea of the principles involved in the more common types of policies and the impact of interest and survivorship on the cost of insurance.[11]

Life Annuities

The remaining class of contracts to be analyzed is known as life annuities.[12] Life annuities promise to pay the possessor a stated income at intervals of one year, or more frequently, during the annuitant's lifetime. It will be seen, therefore, that they furnish a type of investment whereby the recipient can be assured of an income for life.

Annuities covering a single life are ordinarily of two kinds, **immediate** and **deferred.** Annuities may be temporary—that is, limited to a term of years during the lifetime of the annuitant—or may continue for the whole of life, or may promise a minimum number of payments irrespective of whether the annuitant is living. The cost of each of these contracts will be considered in turn.

Immediate Life Annuities. An immediate temporary life annuity of $100, purchased, say, at age 70 and continuing for a period of 10 years will promise to pay the annuitant $100 one year from date of purchase, if he or she is then living, and $100 at each anniversary of that date, if still living, until 10 payments have been made. The cost of this contract will be the net single premium (present expected value) at age 70 for the payments of the sums promised to the annuitant. Since a payment is made to the annuitant at the end of each year, the cost for each year must be determined separately and these amounts added to obtain the net single premium. Such an annuity is equivalent to a series of 10 pure endowments, the first maturing in one year from date of purchase, the second in two years, the third in three years, and so on, until the 10 payments have been made.

Although the formulas are equivalent to

---

[8]In some jurisdictions, pure endowment contracts are prohibited by law.

[9]Note that the so-called "deposit" term life insurance policy discussed in Chapter 4 is, in reality, a term policy with a modest pure endowment feature.

[10]See Chapter 5.

[11]The computation of net premiums for joint life contracts is effected by the application to the mortality table of the law of compound probabilities in determining the probability that joint lives will fail, that they will survive and so on.

[12]This discussion will relate only to single life annuities. As pointed out earlier, however, annuities may be issued on any number of lives.

those for insurance, the mortality table used is different, since insurance companies find that annuity mortality experience produces lower mortality rates than does insurance mortality experience. The **1983 NAIC Individual Annuity Mortality Table for Males** (*1983 Table a*), without projection, shown in Table 19–1, is widely used for annuity valuation.[13] According to this table, the probability that the first of our 10 annuity payments will be made equals the probability that

a man aged 70 will survive one year (p_{70}), or, expressed in the form of a fraction, l_{71}/l_{70}, which equals 7,747,883/7,917,079. The $100 paid in case of survival is paid one year from the date of purchase of the annuity, and therefore the net cost of the first payment will be the value of this sum discounted for one year at 5 percent and multiplied by the probability of survival. The process is continued through the second, third, etc., year as follows:

Policy Year (t)	Age (x)	Calculation				Cost of Year's Annuity Payment
1	70	($100) $\left(\dfrac{l_{71}}{l_{70}}\right)(v)$	= (100)	$\left(\dfrac{7,747,883}{7,917,079}\right)$	(0.9524) =	$ 93.20
2	71	($100) $\left(\dfrac{l_{72}}{l_{70}}\right)(v^2)$	= (100)	$\left(\dfrac{7,564,669}{7,917,079}\right)$	(0.9070) =	86.67
3	72	($100) $\left(\dfrac{l_{73}}{l_{70}}\right)(v^3)$	= (100)	$\left(\dfrac{7,366,997}{7,917,079}\right)$	(0.8638) =	80.38
$\vdots$	$\vdots$	$\vdots$	$\vdots$			$\vdots$
8	77	($100) $\left(\dfrac{l_{78}}{l_{70}}\right)(v^8)$	= (100)	$\left(\dfrac{6,152,440}{7,917,079}\right)$	(0.6768) =	52.50
9	78	($100) $\left(\dfrac{l_{79}}{l_{70}}\right)(v^9)$	= (100)	$\left(\dfrac{5,863,577}{7,917,079}\right)$	(0.6446) =	47.74
10	79	($100) $\left(\dfrac{l_{80}}{l_{70}}\right)(v^{10})$	= (100)	$\left(\dfrac{5,560,108}{7,917,079}\right)$	(0.6139) =	43.11
						$667.29

If the contract issued at male age 70 promises to pay an annuity for the whole of life, the computations must continue throughout the annuity mortality table, which in the case of the *1983 Table a*, is through age 115. The computation of the cost of this whole life annuity is shown in the chart at the top of page 340 (the first 10 years being the same as for the term annuity just computed):

[13]The authors have computed this table complete with l_x, d_x, and p_x values, using a radix of 10,000,000 lives at age 5.

TABLE 19-1. 1983 individual annuity mortality table
(male lives)

Age (x) at Beginning of Year	Number Living at Beginning of Year (l_x)	Number Dying during Year (d_x)	Yearly Probability of Dying (q_x)	Yearly Probability of Surviving (p_x)
5	10,000,000	3,770	0.000377	0.999623
6	9,996,230	3,499	0.000350	0.999650
7	9,992,731	3,328	0.000333	0.999667
8	9,989,403	3,516	0.000352	0.999648
9	9,985,887	3,675	0.000368	0.999632
10	9,982,212	3,813	0.000382	0.999618
11	9,978,399	3,931	0.000394	0.999606
12	9,974,468	4,040	0.000405	0.999595
13	9,970,428	4,138	0.000415	0.999585
14	9,966,290	4,236	0.000425	0.999575
15	9,962,054	4,333	0.000435	0.999565
16	9,957,721	4,441	0.000446	0.999554
17	9,953,280	4,559	0.000458	0.999542
18	9,948,721	4,696	0.000472	0.999528
19	9,944,025	4,853	0.000488	0.999512
20	9,939,172	5,019	0.000505	0.999495
21	9,934,153	5,215	0.000525	0.999475
22	9,928,938	5,421	0.000546	0.999454
23	9,923,517	5,656	0.000570	0.999430
24	9,917,861	5,911	0.000596	0.999404
25	9,911,950	6,165	0.000622	0.999378
26	9,905,785	6,439	0.000650	0.999350
27	9,899,346	6,702	0.000677	0.999323
28	9,892,644	6,964	0.000704	0.999296
29	9,885,680	7,226	0.000731	0.999269
30	9,878,454	7,498	0.000759	0.999241
31	9,870,956	7,759	0.000786	0.999214
32	9,863,197	8,029	0.000814	0.999186
33	9,855,168	8,308	0.000843	0.999157
34	9,846,860	8,626	0.000876	0.999124
35	9,838,234	9,022	0.000917	0.999083
36	9,829,212	9,515	0.000968	0.999032
37	9,819,697	10,134	0.001032	0.998968
38	9,809,563	10,928	0.001114	0.998886
39	9,798,635	11,915	0.001216	0.998784
40	9,786,720	13,124	0.001341	0.998659
41	9,773,596	14,582	0.001492	0.998508
42	9,759,014	16,327	0.001673	0.998327
43	9,742,687	18,375	0.001886	0.998114
44	9,724,312	20,703	0.002129	0.997871
45	9,703,609	23,279	0.002399	0.997601
46	9,680,330	26,069	0.002693	0.997307
47	9,654,261	29,050	0.003009	0.996991
48	9,625,211	32,177	0.003343	0.996657
49	9,593,034	35,437	0.003694	0.996306
50	9,557,597	38,775	0.004057	0.995943
51	9,518,822	42,178	0.004431	0.995569
52	9,476,644	45,602	0.004812	0.995188
53	9,431,042	49,023	0.005198	0.994802
54	9,382,019	52,455	0.005591	0.994409
55	9,329,564	55,921	0.005994	0.994006
56	9,273,643	59,435	0.006409	0.993591
57	9,214,208	63,016	0.006839	0.993161
58	9,151,192	66,712	0.007290	0.992710
59	9,084,480	70,695	0.007782	0.992218
60	9,013,785	75,157	0.008338	0.991662

TABLE 19-1. (continued)

Age (x) at Beginning of Year	Number Living at Beginning of Year (l_x)	Number Dying during Year (d_x)	Yearly Probability of Dying (q_x)	Yearly Probability of Surviving (p_x)
61	8,938,628	80,296	0.008983	0.991017
62	8,858,332	86,280	0.009740	0.990260
63	8,772,052	93,247	0.010630	0.989370
64	8,678,805	101,230	0.011664	0.988336
65	8,577,575	110,230	0.012851	0.987149
66	8,467,345	120,228	0.014199	0.985801
67	8,347,117	131,192	0.015717	0.984283
68	8,215,925	143,072	0.017414	0.982586
69	8,072,853	155,774	0.019296	0.980704
70	7,917,079	169,196	0.021371	0.978629
71	7,747,883	183,214	0.023647	0.976353
72	7,564,669	197,672	0.026131	0.973869
73	7,366,997	212,427	0.028835	0.971165
74	7,154,570	227,472	0.031794	0.968206
75	6,927,098	242,767	0.035046	0.964954
76	6,684,331	258,222	0.038631	0.961369
77	6,426,109	273,669	0.042587	0.957413
78	6,152,440	288,863	0.046951	0.953049
79	5,863,577	303,469	0.051755	0.948245
80	5,560,108	317,071	0.057026	0.942974
81	5,243,037	329,216	0.062791	0.937209
82	4,913,821	339,452	0.069081	0.930919
83	4,574,369	347,231	0.075908	0.924092
84	4,227,138	351,825	0.083230	0.916770
85	3,875,313	352,603	0.090987	0.909013
86	3,522,710	349,178	0.099122	0.900878
87	3,173,532	341,399	0.107577	0.892423
88	2,832,133	329,422	0.116316	0.883684
89	2,502,711	313,825	0.125394	0.874606
90	2,188,886	295,252	0.134887	0.865113
91	1,893,634	274,336	0.144873	0.855127
92	1,619,298	251,686	0.155429	0.844571
93	1,367,612	227,884	0.166629	0.833371
94	1,139,728	203,484	0.178537	0.821463
95	936,244	179,023	0.191214	0.808786
96	757,221	155,019	0.204721	0.795279
97	602,202	131,955	0.219120	0.780880
98	470,247	110,383	0.234735	0.765265
99	359,864	90,646	0.251889	0.748111
100	269,218	72,933	0.270906	0.729094
101	196,285	57,337	0.292111	0.707889
102	138,948	43,883	0.315826	0.684174
103	95,065	32,548	0.342377	0.657623
104	62,517	23,262	0.372086	0.627914
105	39,255	15,909	0.405278	0.594722
106	23,346	10,325	0.442277	0.557723
107	13,021	6,294	0.483406	0.516594
108	6,727	3,559	0.528989	0.471011
109	3,168	1,835	0.579351	0.420649
110	1,333	846	0.634814	0.365186
111	487	339	0.695704	0.304296
112	148	113	0.762343	0.237657
113	35	29	0.835056	0.164944
114	6	5	0.914167	0.085833
115	1	1	1.000000	0.000000

Policy Year (t)	Age (x)	Calculation			Cost of Year's Annuity Payment
1	70	$(\$100)\left(\dfrac{l_{71}}{l_{70}}\right)(v)$	$= (\$100)\left(\dfrac{7{,}747{,}883}{7{,}917{,}079}\right)(0.9524)$	$=$	\$ 93.20
2	71	$(\$100)\left(\dfrac{l_{72}}{l_{70}}\right)(v^2)$	$= (\$100)\left(\dfrac{7{,}564{,}669}{7{,}917{,}079}\right)(0.9070)$	$=$	86.67
3	72	$(\$100)\left(\dfrac{l_{73}}{l_{70}}\right)(v^3)$	$= (\$100)\left(\dfrac{7{,}366{,}997}{7{,}917{,}079}\right)(0.8638)$	$=$	80.38
•	•	•	•		•
•	•	•	•		•
•	•	•	•		•
43	112	$(\$100)\left(\dfrac{l_{113}}{l_{70}}\right)(v^{43})$	$= (\$100)\left(\dfrac{35}{7{,}917{,}079}\right)(0.1227)$	$=$	0.00ª
44	113	$(\$100)\left(\dfrac{l_{114}}{l_{70}}\right)(v^{44})$	$= (\$100)\left(\dfrac{6}{7{,}917{,}079}\right)(0.1169)$	$=$	0.00ª
45	114	$(\$100)\left(\dfrac{l_{115}}{l_{70}}\right)(v^{45})$	$= (\$100)\left(\dfrac{1}{7{,}917{,}079}\right)(0.1113)$	$=$	0.00ª
					\$936.18

ªLess than 0.0005.

If this same annuity guaranteed that the first five payments were to be certain—that is, not affected by the death of the annuitant before their completion—this fact would have to be taken into consideration in computing the net cost. The distinction would lie in the fact that these five payments would not be affected by death, or to put it in actuarial terms, the probability of payment would be a certainty, or 1. Therefore, the first five payments would be discounted only for interest. The sixth and all subsequent payments would be dependent on the probability of survival, and their net cost would therefore be computed in the same manner as above for the pure life annuity.

Deferred Life Annuities. Immediate life annuities are usually purchased by persons of advanced age and contemplate the payment of benefits at periodic intervals following the date of issue. Some persons are interested in an annuity contract that can be purchased by annual sums paid during their wage-earning years. The deferred life annuity offers this opportunity. It bears a close resemblance to private pension plans, under which money is accumulated year by year in small amounts from the wages of the employees and contributions by the employer, and is paid

periodically during the lifetime of the employee after he or she has attained retirement age.

The traditional deferred life annuity was usually purchased by an annual premium. Of course, flexible-premium deferred annuities may be paid for with most any desired, reasonable premium pattern. It is also possible to pay for such a contract by a single premium paid at the date of purchase of the contract.

If it is desired to find the net single premium payable for a man, for example, at age 40 that will purchase the right to receive a whole life annuity of $100 beginning at age 70, there are two possible ways of approaching the problem. First, it may be asked: What is the amount of money that must have been accumulated by the company by the time the annuity begins? This is equivalent to asking how much money must be on hand at age 70 to furnish $100 annually during life, the first payment to be made when the annuitant reaches age 70. The problem at this point is therefore identical with that of the immediate whole life annuity just discussed, with the single exception that here the first $100 payment is made at age 70, whereas in the former case, the first payment was made at age 71. Therefore, the insurance company must have on hand at the time the annuitant becomes 70 years of age the amount of money necessary to purchase an immediate life annuity, the first payment being at age 70. Taking the figures from our previous computations, we find a new net single premium of $936.18 + $100.00, or $1,036.18. This amount may be considered as the net cost *at age 70* of a whole life annuity *due,* the first payment of which is made to the annuitant at that age.

The amount payable by a man at age 40 that will furnish this sum at age 70 ($1,036.18) will be the present value of this sum discounted for 30 years at the assumed rate:

$$A = (S) \times (v^{30}) = \$1.036.18 \times 0.2314 = \$239.77$$

A deferred annuity is almost always purchased on a basis whereby payments—single or periodic—made during during the accumulation period are not forfeited in the event of death. The calculation made above is based on this premise. If the cost of this contract taken out at age 40 had been computed on the assumption that the single premium paid at age 40 or the level annual premiums paid from ages 40 to 70 were forfeitable (i.e., the purchaser relinquished any right to his or her contributions in case he or she failed to survive to age 70), the calculation would have further discounted the $239.77 figure for the probability of survival from age 40 to 70.

NET LEVEL PREMIUMS

The Level-Premium System

Insurance policies may be purchased by a single cash sum or by periodic payments made monthly, quarterly, semiannually, or annually, and with some flexible premium contracts, on an irregular basis. Policies ordinarily are purchased by periodic premiums. However, with traditional forms of life insurance, the determination of level premiums is often made only after the single premium has been ascertained.

If policyowners are given the choice of payment for insurance by single or annual premiums, the amounts of the latter must be determined on such a basis that the company will receive the equivalent value under each method of payment.

Since the manner of computing the net single premium is known, the problem can be solved by finding a series of net annual level premiums that is actuarially equivalent to the net single premium. Such premiums will be paid during the life of the insured or for a limited number of years, but *cease upon his or her death.* Note that this is the same definition as a life annuity.

It can be helpful to consider annual premiums as being "annuities." However, they differ in four important respects from the annuities thus far considered. First, they are paid *by* the policyowner *to* the company, whereas regular annuities are paid *by* the company *to* the annuitant. Second, annuities are ordinarily purchased by single or annual premiums. If annual premiums are analogous to annuities, what does the company offer for the series of annuity (premium) payments? It pays for them *with the policy,* which promises a cash payment upon the happening of the insured event.

Third, annuitant mortality was shown to be considerably lower than life insurance mortality. This consideration, however, does not apply to the "annuities" represented by the annual level life insurance premiums, and regular life insurance mortality is used in the calculations regarding life insurance annual level premiums. Obviously, life insurance purchasers will have the mortality experience of insureds, not that of annuitants.

Fourth, the time when annual level premiums and annuity payments begin is different. The immediate life annuity pays the first annual income installment one year from the date of issue of the contract. In practice, the first annual premium is payable *when the policy is issued,* not one year later as is the case with annuities. Thus, the series of premium payments is a life annuity *due.*

The net level premium cannot be obtained simply by dividing the net single premium by the number of installments agreed upon. The net single premium is a discounted expected value, and the net annual level premium must reflect (1) the possibility that the insured may die and not pay future premiums, and (2) the smaller sum that will be invested at compound interest, with the resultant loss of interest earnings to the company.

The problem stated previously may now be restated in the following terms: The series of net annual level premiums will be a life annuity due equivalent in value to the net single premium for the policy benefits.

Computation of the Net Annual Level Premium

Term Insurance. In computing net annual level premiums, one can start by ascertaining the net single premium for the policy benefits. The second step would be to define the *premium payment period* over which the annual premium is to be paid and for which the *life annuity due* is to be ascertained.

An example will help clarify the issues. Assume that we are seeking the net annual level premium to purchase a five-year term insurance policy of $1,000 at male age 45 using the *1980 CSO Table* and 5 percent interest. It was found

earlier that the net single premium on this policy was $22.74. Begininng at date of issue, the annual level premium will be paid over a five-year period, or until prior death, and is therefore a *five-year temporary life annuity due.*

Since the amount of the annual level premium is the unknown quantity, it will be impossible to proceed directly to the computation of its present value, but it is feasible to take any assumed premium, such as $1, and compute the present value of an annuity due for this amount. An annuity due of $1 on the policy in question will be equal to a temporary immediate annuity for four years plus $1 paid initially (making it an annuity due). Note that the *1980 CSO Table,* not the *1983 Table a* would be used, because the calculation is required for a life insurance policy.

Thus, the calculation for the present value of the five-year life annuity due would be as follows:

Policy Year (t)	Age (x)	Calculation			Each Year's Present Expected Value
1	45	1 due immediately			1.000
2	46	$\left(\frac{l_{46}}{l_{45}}\right)(v) = \left(\frac{9,168,382}{9,210,289}\right)$	(0.9524)	=	0.948
3	47	$\left(\frac{l_{47}}{l_{45}}\right)(v^2) = \left(\frac{9,123,274}{9,210,289}\right)$	(0.9070)	=	0.898
4	48	$\left(\frac{l_{48}}{l_{45}}\right)(v^3) = \left(\frac{9,074,738}{9,210,289}\right)$	(0.8638)	=	0.851
5	49	$\left(\frac{l_{49}}{l_{45}}\right)(v^4) = \left(\frac{9,022,649}{9,210,289}\right)$	(0.8227)	=	0.806
					4.504

This 4.504 is the present expected value equivalent of 1 per year for five years. Thus, an annual premium of $1.00 for this period would purchase any policy the net single premium of which was equal to $4.504. But the net single premium on the policy in question was found to be $22.74. If the present value of the annuity due is divided into the net single premium on this policy, the resultant factor would show how many times the annual level premium of $1 must be taken to obtain an annual level premium, the present value of which will equal the net single premium. From this analysis it is possible to state a general rule for ascertaining the net annual level premium on

any policy: *Divide the net single premium by the present value of a temporary life annuity due of 1 for the premium-paying period.* Thus,

$$\text{NLP} = \frac{\text{NSP}}{\text{PVLAD of 1 for PPP}}$$

The net annual level premium on a five-year term insurance policy of $1,000 issued at age 45 is thus $5.05, computed as follows:

$$\text{NLP} = \frac{\text{NSP}}{\text{PVLAD of 1 for PPP}} = \frac{\$22.74}{4.504} = \$5.05$$

Ordinary Life Insurance. The net single premium for a whole life policy of $1,000 issued at age 45 is $270.84, according to the earlier figures. To find the net annual level premium for an ordinary life policy, this sum must be divided by the present value of a life annuity due of 1 for the whole of life, since premiums are paid annually through the life of this policy. The method of ascertaining the present value of the life annuity due of 1 is as follows:

The net annual level premium for an ordinary life policy of $1,000 issued at male age 45, *1980 CSO Table,* 5 percent basis, is therefore $17.69, found as follows:

$$\frac{\$270.84}{15.312} = \$17.69$$

Limited Payment Whole Life Insurance. If it is desired to pay for the whole life policy above

Policy Year (*t*)	Age (*x*)	Calculation			Each Year's Present Expected Value
1	45	1 due immediately			1.000
2	46	$\left(\frac{l_{46}}{l_{45}}\right)(v) = \left(\frac{9,168,382}{9,210,289}\right)$	(0.9524)	=	0.948
3	47	$\left(\frac{l_{47}}{l_{45}}\right)(v^2) = \left(\frac{9,123,274}{9,210,289}\right)$	(0.9070)	=	0.898
•	•	•	•		•
•	•	•	•		•
•	•	•	•		•
53	97	$\left(\frac{l_{97}}{l_{45}}\right)(v^{52}) = \left(\frac{60,504}{9,210,289}\right)$	(0.0791)	=	0.001
54	98	$\left(\frac{l_{98}}{l_{45}}\right)(v^{53}) = \left(\frac{31,450}{9,210,289}\right)$	(0.0753)	=	0.000ᵃ
55	99	$\left(\frac{l_{99}}{l_{45}}\right)(v^{54}) = \left(\frac{10,757}{9,210,289}\right)$	(0.0717)	=	0.000ᵃ
					15.312

ᵃLess than 0.0005.

in 20 annual payments instead of allowing them to continue throughout life, it is necessary to compute the annual level premium that continued for 20 years or ceasing upon prior death, will purchase this policy. In accordance with our formula, the annual level premium in this case will be found by dividing into the net single premium the present value of a *temporary* life annuity due for a term of 20 years following age 45. The calculation of the present value of this life annuity due at male age 45 for 20 years would be as shown in the chart at the top of page 344.

The net annual level premium, therefore, for a 20-payment whole life policy issued at male age 45 is $270.84 + 12.333, or $21.96.

It should be noticed that in all cases, the net single premium for the whole life policy (the

numerator in the formula) is the same regardless of the premium-paying period selected. In the case of a 30-payment whole life or a life paid-up-at-65 policy, the same principle would be followed, dividing the net single premium ($270.84 at male age 45) by the present value of a life annuity due for the appropriate premium-paying period.

Deferred Annuity. Fixed-premium deferred annuities are ordinarily paid for by means of annual rather than single premiums, and the premium may, in theory, continue through the entire period of deferment or, as in the case of the whole life policy above, may be limited to a stated number of years. As with premiums on insurances, the annual level premium on these contracts is paid only while alive. If, therefore, the

Policy Year (t)	Age (x)	Calculation	Each Year's Present Expected Value
1	45	1 due immediately	1.000
2	46	$\left(\dfrac{l_{46}}{l_{45}}\right)(v) = \left(\dfrac{9,168,382}{9,210,289}\right)(0.9524)\quad=$	0.948
3	47	$\left(\dfrac{l_{47}}{l_{45}}\right)(v^2) = \left(\dfrac{9,123,274}{9,210,289}\right)(0.9070)\quad=$	0.898
•	•	• •	•
•	•	• •	•
•	•	• •	•
18	62	$\left(\dfrac{l_{62}}{l_{45}}\right)(v^{17}) = \left(\dfrac{7,814,753}{9,210,289}\right)(0.4363)\quad=$	0.370
19	63	$\left(\dfrac{l_{63}}{l_{45}}\right)(v^{18}) = \left(\dfrac{7,664,788}{9,210,289}\right)(0.4155)\quad=$	0.346
20	64	$\left(\dfrac{l_{64}}{l_{45}}\right)(v^{19}) = \left(\dfrac{7,503,368}{9,210,289}\right)(0.3957)\quad=$	0.322
			12.333

deferred annuity issued at age 40 begins the payment of an annual income of $100 at age 70 and if the net single premium for it is $239.77 (see above), the annual premium on this policy may be paid until one year prior to the beginning of the annuity (until the holder of the contract is 69). In this case, the series of annual premiums becomes a temporary life annuity due for a term of 30 years—ages 40 to 69 inclusive. The amount of this net annual premium would be found, therefore, by dividing the net single premium by the present value of a life annuity due of 1 computed for the 30-year term stated. Since this is an annuity premium, it is necessary to use the same annuity mortality table used in calculating the net single premium for the policy.[14]

The present value of the 30-year life annuity due is 15.505, the present expected value of an annual level premium of $1 paid over the same term as the premiums on the deferred annuity. This figure divided into the net single premium for the deferred annuity gives a net annual level premium:

$$\frac{\$239.77}{15.505} = \$15.46$$

[14]No detailed example of this calculation is given. The procedure is the same as illustrated for the 20-payment whole life policy but with the use of 30 years instead of 20 and with the use of an appropriate annuity mortality table.

Chapter 20

Life Insurance Reserves and Surrender Values

One of the most difficult subjects for the layperson to appreciate in connection with the administration of a life insurance company is the need for the existence of the enormous assets possessed by the companies. The fact is that the great majority of these assets are required as backing against the liabilities of the company to its policyowners. Without these assets accumulated to assure payment of the companies' liabilities to policyowners, the security of life insurance protection as we know it would not be possible. The chief such liability is known as the policy reserve. As discussed briefly in Chapter 2, surrender values are related to reserves in that they represent the claim against the assets by policyowners who discontinue their policies. This chapter discusses both reserves and surrender values in more detail.

RESERVES

Financial Importance

The *Life Insurance Fact Book for 1986* shows that U.S. life insurance companies held, on December 31, 1985, total admitted assets amounting to $825.9 billion and of this sum, $665.3 billion, or 80.5 percent is required as backing against policy reserve liabilities. In other words, over four-fifths of the total funds held by life insurance companies represent funds held to support their reserve liabilities. Such vast resources justify a careful analysis of the nature and purposes of the reserve liabilities.

The Origin and Definition of the Reserve

Previously, it was stated that life insurance policies may be purchased by a single payment, by fixed annual premiums paid over a period of years, or by flexible premiums. It was also pointed out that mortality rates generally increase with increasing age. Thus, in the early policy years, fixed-level premiums and (often) flexible premiums paid exceed the annual cost of insurance. The excess premium funds not used immediately to pay policy claims and expenses must be recognized by the company and preserved for the benefit of policyowners until needed at some future date. In like manner, when a policy is purchased by a single premium, this premium becomes the total contribution toward claims to be paid and costs to be incurred under contracts of the class, and a large share of this single premium must be held by the company to meet these future obligations.

The simplest way to define the statutory reserve is to say that it is the amount that, together with future net premiums and interest, will be sufficient, according to the valuation assumptions, to pay future claims. This is the prospective definition of the reserve. Statutory reserve calculations effectively ignore company expenses and lapse rates, instead being based solely on state-sanctioned mortality and interest assumptions and on the nature of policy benefits and method of calculation. Another way of looking at the reserve is the retrospective view under which the reserve is considered as the difference between the accumulation at interest of the net premiums received in the past and the claims paid.

Reserve calculations (valuations) of policy liabilities require use of a mortality table and an interest rate. It is then necessary to calculate the net premium, on the basis of the table and rate selected and in the manner that has been described in Chapter 19.[1] Then, if the policy duration for which the reserve is needed is selected, the calculation may proceed, using either the prospective or retrospective method. The retrospective and prospective reserves always are exactly equal to each other, assuming the same set of actuarial assumptions.

It is important to realize that the retrospective (and therefore the prospective) reserve has nothing to do with a company's actual past experience. It is always calculated on the assumption that experience has been in accordance with the mortality table selected and interest rate assumed. The term "reserve" has come to have a technical meaning in life insurance because most states have passed minimum reserve standards establishing definite methods of valuing policy liabilities.[2]

Reserve Is a Liability

The word "reserve" is somewhat misleading. It does not have the same use here as in the usual commercial dealings, where "reserve" is often synonymous with "surplus." The policy reserve of a life insurance company is a liability. It represents a measure of the value of obligations to policyowners. As will be brought out in the following discussion, if the company does not maintain the proper policy reserves, it eventually may be unable to pay claims. The policy reserve is the most important of a life insurance company's liabilities.

Methods of Calculation

Restrospective Reserve. The retrospective method may be explained in terms of either an individual policy or a group approach.

1. *Group approach.* The reserve arises out of the payment of a net (valuation) premium in excess of that needed to meet current mortality costs. Under this approach, premiums in the early policy years usually are more than sufficient to pay the death claims that are assumed, creating a fund that can be used in later policy years, when death rates rise sharply and premiums alone may be insufficient to meet the then current claims. The retrospective reserve can be thought of as an unearned net premium reserve, representing the provision in early premiums for advance funding of the benefits of surviving insureds, and is shown on the company's financial statement as a liability item.[3]

2. *Individual approach.* The retrospective reserve valuation method also may be illustrated with reference to an individual policy. The retrospective terminal reserve for any particular policy year can be obtained by adding the *net premium* for the year in question to the *terminal reserve* of the preceding year, increasing the combined sum (called the *initial reserve*) by one year's interest at the assumed rate, deducting the *cost of insurance* for the current year, utilizing the assumed mortality table.

Consideration of the process by which this reserve is built involves an understanding of the

---

[1] It is also necessary to select a specific valuation method. See "Other Aspects" later in this chapter.

[2] See "Regulation of Reserves and Surrender Values" later in this chapter.

[3] A simplified example was given in Chapter 2.

cost of insurance concept. Reference was made in previous chapters to the **net amount at risk,** which is the death benefit minus the terminal reserve at the end of the policy year.[4] When an insured dies, the reserve held for the policy is no longer required. Under this approach, the value of assets corresponding to that reserve is considered to be freed to help pay the claim. The balance of the claim (the amount at risk) is paid through charges against all policies in the group, including those that mature as a death claim.

The contribution each insured must make as his or her pro rata share of death claims in any particular year is determined by multiplying the net amount at risk at the end of such year by the tabular probability of death during such year. This procedure, of course, is identical in concept to the manner in which the mortality charge of a universal life (UL) policy is determined.[5]

Prospective Reserve. Although the retrospective method of computation provides a clear exposition of the origin and purpose of the reserve, it typically is not used. The prospective method is more commonly used.

As mentioned earlier, the reserve is the balancing factor in the basic insurance equation; that is, in prospective terms, the reserve is the difference between the present expected value of future benefits and the present expected value of future net premiums.[6]

At the inception of a contract, the present value of future benefits (PVFB) is exactly equal to the present value of the future net premiums (PVFP): thus,

$$PVFB = PVFP \quad \text{(at date of issue)}$$

But as soon as the contract goes in force and one premium has been paid, the present value of future benefits almost always exceeds the present

value of future net premiums.[7] This should be apparent since fewer premiums (or no premiums) remain to be paid and the present value of future benefits is greater because the policy is nearer to maturity. The difference between these two is a reserve obligation of the company: thus,

net level terminal reserve (age of valuation)	=	PVFB (age of valuation)	–	PVFP (age of valuation)

It has already been shown that the net single premium (NSP) for a given policy is equal to the present value of future benefits, so the equation above may be written

net level terminal reserve (age of valuation)	=	NSP (age of valuation)	–	PVFP (age of valuation)

Also, the present value of future net premiums necessarily must be equal to the net level annual premium (NLP) for the contract under consideration, multiplied by the present value of a life annuity due (PVLAD) of 1 for the remaining premium-paying period. Finally, then, the equation may be written in word form as follows:

Net level terminal reserve (age of valuation)	=	NSP (age of valuation)	–	NLP (age of issue)	×	PVLAD of 1 for remaining premium-paying period

This same approach may be illustrated somewhat more analytically and concisely as follows:

$$_tV_x = 1{,}000\, A_{x+t} - P_x \cdot \ddot{a}_{\overline{x+t}}$$

where $_tV_x$ is the net level terminal reserve for an ordinary life policy issued at age x at the end of any number of years t, and the other variables have the same meaning as in Chapter 19.

---

[4]See Chapter 2.

[5]See Chapter 6.

[6]For word economy, the word "expected" will be dropped from further references. The reader should understand, however, that all such calculations are *expected value* calculations.

[7]This is true in general of ordinary life polices, but for issue age 0 on the *1958 CSO Table* ordinary life, the first-year terminal reserve was negative. The statement also is often not true for decreasing term insurance if premiums are level for the duration of the term.

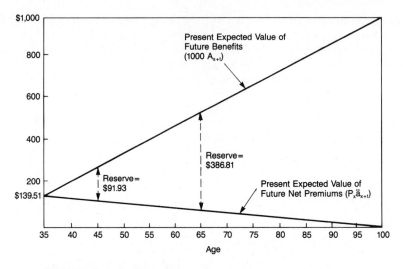

FIGURE 20-1. Derivation of the reserve: prospective method for ordinary life policy (age 35, *1980 CSO Table*, 6% interest, net level premium reserves).

The manner in which the present value of future benefits and the present value of future net premiums diverge to create the necessity for a reserve is illustrated in Figure 20-1 (not drawn to scale).

Considering the equation, the computation of the twentieth-year net level reserve on a 15-payment whole life policy issued at age 35 is

$$\text{net level terminal reserve }_{55} = \text{NSP}_{55} - (\text{NLP}_{35} \times 0) = \text{NSP } 55$$

or

$$_{20}V_{35} = 1{,}000A_{35+20} - P_{35}(0) = 1000A_{55}$$

The result illustrates the principle that on a paid-up policy, there are no future premiums; consequently, the reserve must be equal to the present value of future benefits, which can be measured by the net single premium of the given policy at the attained age of valuation. The principle is even more graphically illustrated by the single-premium policy, which is paid up after the payment of the first premium. Thus, a single-premium whole life policy issued at male age 35 would produce an identical twentieth-year reserve and be equal to the net single premium for a whole life policy at male age 55. The reserves at a given attained age

on all paid-up policies of the same type and amount and calculated under the same assumptions are, at the age of valuation, equal to each other, and all equal the net single premium for that generic type of policy.

Considering a policy that is not fully paid up, the computation of the present value of future net premiums involves the determination of the original net level annual premium applicable to the contract, which is multiplied by the present value of a temporary life annuity due of 1 for the remaining premium-paying period. Thus, the twentieth-year net level reserve on an ordinary life policy issued at age 25 would be

$$\text{net level terminal reserve }_{45} = \text{NSP}_{45} - \text{NLP}_{25} \times \begin{array}{c}\text{PVLAD of}\\ \text{1 for life}_{45}\end{array}$$

The tenth-year net level reserve on a 20-payment whole life policy issued at age 25 would be

$$\text{net level terminal reserve }_{35} = \text{NSP}_{35} - \text{NLP}_{25} \times \begin{array}{c}\text{PVLAD of 1}\\ \text{for 10 years}_{35}\end{array}$$

Table 20-1 shows the actual computation of these reserves, utilizing the principles developed here and in Chapter 19.

TABLE 20-1. Computation of prospective net level reserves
(1980 CSO Table, 6% interest)

Age	Net Single Premium per $1,000			Present Value of Life Annuity Due of 1		
	Whole Life	20-Year Endowment	10-Year Endowment	Life	20 Years	10 Years
25	$ 89.49	$321.72	$561.47	16.086	11.983	7.747
35	139.51	328.95	562.89	15.202	11.855	7.722
45	218.61	349.54	568.24	13.805	11.491	7.628
55	330.34	396.30	581.12	11.831	10.665	7.400

$$\begin{array}{c} \text{Net level} \\ \text{terminal reserve} \\ \text{(age of valuation)} \end{array} = \begin{array}{c} \text{NSP} \\ \text{(age of} \\ \text{valuation)} \end{array} - \begin{array}{c} \text{NLP} \\ \text{(age of} \\ \text{issue)} \end{array} \times \begin{array}{c} \text{PVLAD for 1 for} \\ \text{remaining premium-} \\ \text{paying period} \end{array}$$

Computation

1. Twentieth-year net level terminal reserve, ordinary life issued at age 25:

net level reserve $_{45}$ = NSP$_{45}$ − (NLP$_{25}$ × PVLAD of 1 for life$_{45}$)

$$= \$218.61 - \frac{\$89.49}{16.086} \times 13.805$$

$$= \$141.81$$

2. Tenth-year net level terminal reserve, 20-payment life issued at age 25:

net level reserve $_{35}$ = NSP$_{35}$ − (NLP$_{25}$ × PVLAD of 1 for 10 years$_{35}$)

$$= \$139.51 - \frac{\$89.49}{11.98} \times 7.722$$

$$= \$ 81.84$$

3. Tenth-year net level terminal reserve, 20-year endowment issued at age 25:

net level reserve $_{35}$ = NSP$_{35}$ − (NLP$_{25}$ × PVLAD of 1 for 10 years$_{35}$)

$$= \$562.89 - \frac{\$321.72}{11.983} \times 7.722$$

$$= \$355.57$$

Significance of Actuarial Assumptions

In measuring or valuing its liabilities under outstanding contracts, a life insurance company must make assumptions as to the rate of mortality among its insureds and the rate of earnings on the assets standing behind the reserves. These assumptions are reflected in the mortality table and rate of interest assumed in making the valuation, which are themselves limited by state and federal (tax) laws. The preceding discussion assumed the *1980 CSO Table* and 6 percent interest. Other assumptions, however, can be and are used in reserve valuations. It is important, therefore, to consider the impact on reserves of the choice of the mortality table and interest rate used.

Mortality. In practice, it frequently is impossible to determine which of two mortality tables will result in larger reserves at a given age and duration simply by reviewing the mortality rates. A change in mortality not only affects the number of deaths at a given age, but also affects the number surviving at subsequent ages. Under the net level premium method, the effect of a change in mortality is somewhat spread over the premium-paying period. Because the impact of a change in mortality is not uniform from age to age and duration to duration, it may result in

TABLE 20-2. Net level terminal reserves per $1,000, different mortality tables
(1941, 1958 and 1980 CSO mortality tables, 6% interest, issued at male age 35

Duration	Ordinary Life			Endowment at Age 65		
	1941	1958	1980	1941	1958	1980
1	$ 9.44	$ 8.48	$ 7.63	$ 14.47	$ 14.20	$ 13.91
10	110.57	102.36	91.93	179.29	179.24	176.17
20	256.80	242.74	221.77	467.52	471.70	469.47
30	428.58	411.53	386.81	1,000.00	1,000.00	1,000.00
50	747.75	726.02	724.36			
60	858.58	854.21	852.84			

either an increase or a decrease in reserve at any given age and duration. With the computer facilities currently available, the simplest way to analyze the effect of a change in mortality is to calculate the reserves on both mortality bases for representative plans and issue ages. Without actually calculating the reserves, the determination of the effect on reserves of a change in mortality assumptions is a complex mathematical problem and is beyond the scope of this volume.[8] Table 20-2 shows a comparison of reserves under the *1941 CSO Table,* the *1958 CSO Table,* and the *1980 CSO Table,* assuming an interest rate of 6% in each case.

Interest. The impact on reserves of a change in the interest assumption can easily be visualized. Thus, if the rate of interest assumed is decreased, the result will be an increase in reserves. This may be explained simply by the fact that the smaller anticipated earnings must be offset by a larger reserve at any point in time. The impact of a change in interest assumptions on the reserves of an individual contract utilizing the *1980 CSO Table* is presented in Table 20-3.

An explanation of the impact of the change in interest assumption in terms of the conventional prospective and retrospective methods of calculation is not as easily grasped. Such an explanation is complicated by the fact that both the earnings on assets backing the reserve and the net premiums are affected by the change, and the net effect of these modifications leads to the final reserve level.

[8]See C. Wallace Jordan, Jr., *Life Contingencies,* 2nd ed. (Chicago: Society of Actuaries, 1967), pp. 118–123.

TABLE 20-3. Net level terminal reserves per $1,000, varying rates of interest
(ordinary life, *1980 CSO Table,* male age 35)

Duration	Rate of Interest		
	3%	4.5%	6%
1	$ 13.32	$ 10.04	$ 7.63
10	145.56	115.41	91.93
20	315.30	264.27	221.77
30	496.89	438.58	386.81
50	799.91	761.82	724.36
60	898.60	876.01	852.84

Plan of Insurance. The relative net level reserves for various plans of whole life insurance based on the indicated assumptions are illustrated in Table 20-4. The table demonstrates the fact that all limited payment policies, assuming the same age of issue, amount, and underlying assumptions, have the same reserve as a single-premium policy after they have been fully paid. In terms of the formula discussed earlier, the temporary life annuity due becomes zero after all premiums have been paid, and the reserve becomes the net single premium in question at the insured's attained age.

Modified Reserves

Loading and the Incidence of Expense. Ideally each class of policies should pay its own cost. From the standpoint of the company, however, the problem of meeting the expense when it occurs is of greater immediate importance. The primary difficulty is that the expenses of the first policy year greatly exceed those of any subsequent

TABLE 20-4. Net level terminal reserves, various whole life policies
($1,000, male age 35, *1980 CSO Table,* 6% interest)

Duration	Ordinary Life	Life Paid Up at 65	20-Pay Life	10-Pay Life
1	$ 7.63	$ 8.51	$ 10.39	$ 17.08
2	15.61	17.42	21.29	35.09
3	23.94	26.73	32.72	54.07
4	32.60	36.45	44.69	74.08
5	41.61	46.58	57.22	95.15
10	91.93	103.68	128.61	218.61
20	221.77	256.33	330.34	330.34
30	386.81	472.36	472.36	472.36
40	567.82	628.12	628.12	628.12
50	724.36	762.81	762.81	762.81
60	852.84	873.37	873.37	873.37
65	1,000.00	1,000.00	1,000.00	1,000.00

year and, in fact, frequently exceed the entire premium. That first-year expenses will be high can be seen by considering that selling expenses, such as agents' commissions, and expenses of medical examinations, of approving applications, and of preparing policies for issue, as well as the expenses of setting up records for new policies, are all incurred in the first policy year.

Thus, the major problem of the incidence of expense is that policies typically cannot pay their first-year expenses from the amount available from the first premium. These expenses must be met when incurred, yet the company faces the necessity of maintaining a reasonable premium level, of paying death claims during the year, and of holding in reserve the remainder of the net premium.

Consider, for example, an ordinary life policy whose gross premium per $1,000 is $13.39 at age 35. Its net premium, $9.18 (using *1980 CSO Table* and 6 percent), would be increased at 6 percent interest to $9.73 at the close of the policy year. Of this amount, $2.10 is necessary to pay the *estimated* cost of insurance for the year. Thus, $7.63 ($9.73 − 2.10) constitutes the terminal reserve that should be held in anticipation of future claims against the policy. The balance of $4.21 ($13.39 − 9.18) is the only portion of the first premium that is available to pay the first year's expenses, and this would be insufficient.

These first-year costs must be provided from some outside source, or some modifications of the system of level reserve valuation must be made. For an old and well-established company with a large surplus, the solution to the problem is comparatively simple, for it can pay expenses of new business from surplus and depend on replacing the amount from margins in the loadings of the later premiums. This, however, is not possible for new and small companies, for they have relatively little surplus from which to borrow to supply the demands of a rapidly increasing business.

There exists the further possibility of dealing with this problem through some modification of the system of valuing reserves, whereby the policy reserve of the first year or of the first few years can be reduced. Two important methods of modifying full net level terminal reserves used in the United States today are known, respectively, as the **full preliminary term method** and the **Commissioners' Reserve Valuation Method.**

Full Preliminary Term Method. The germ of the full preliminary term concept was introduced into the United States from Europe. The technique is to treat the first year of insurance as term insurance, irrespective of the type of contract actually involved, and to assume that the original contract goes into effect at the beginning of the second policy year. Hence, the title "preliminary term" is a logical one.

This method of valuation provides that the

first year's premium under any form of policy pays for term insurance for one year and that the regular policy, for reserve purposes, is to come into operation one year later than the age of issue, and will be for a one-year-shorter premium-payment period. By this means, the company is relieved of the necessity of establishing a terminal reserve against the policy for the first year, and the entire premium becomes available for payment of current claims and expenses. Since the amount required for first-year claims is the net premium for 1-year term insurance, the total amount available for expenses is the excess of the gross premium for the particular plan over the net 1-year term rate.

For example, the net level premium on an ordinary life policy at male age 35 (using the *1980 CSO Table* and interest at 6 percent) is $9.18. The net premium for one-year term insurance at age 35 is $2.11 ($1,000 ×0.00211). Thus, the excess amount released to help defray first-year expenses would be $7.07 ($9.18 – $2.11). On the 20-payment whole life plan at the same age, the corresponding excess is $9.66, whereas on an endowment at age 65 plan, it is $12.98. The net premium for the later years of the policy is then increased, and correspondingly, the difference between the gross and net premium is reduced, since the gross premium paid by the policyowner does not change. The net premium becomes the net premium for insurance issued at an age one year higher, at a date one year later, and for a term one year shorter.

The reserves held on the policy for the second and later years are the reserves based on this new net premium. Thus, an ordinary life policy's reserve at the end of the first year would be zero. The reserve at the end of the *second* year would be equal to that of the *first*-year terminal reserve for an ordinary life policy issued at *age 36*. The renewal (age 36) net premium is equal to the net level premium for age 36, and it is sufficient to provide benefits for an ordinary life policy with level net premiums issued at age 36. The remainder of the gross premium is available each renewal year for expenses.

The effect of the full preliminary term method, compared to the net level method, is to defer funding the first-year reserve and amortize this amount over the remaining premium-paying period of the contract. It is important to note that this method of valuation makes no distinction between various types of cash value contracts.

For most low-premium policies written by a typical life insurance company, the additional amounts made available by treating the first year of insurance as term insurance is not adequate in relation to heavy first-year expenses. The remainder of the amount needed must be drawn from its surplus assets. Thus, it is possible for a rapidly growing company to have a "capacity" problem, despite the fact that it is using the preliminary term plan.

On higher-premium plans, on the other hand, the first-year reserve "borrowed" is correspondingly greater, since the cost of one-year term insurance remains the same. The logic of this position has led regulatory authorities to prescribe the use of some modification of the full preliminary term method of valuation, the most important of which is known as the Commissioners' Reserve Valuation Method.

Commissioners' Reserve Valuation Method. The Commissioners' Reserve Valuation Method (CRVM) in effect makes the 20-payment whole life policy the maximum basis on which deferred reserve funding is permitted, and in doing so, divides policies into two groups:

1. The full preliminary term method described above is used if the net premium for the second and subsequent years for the plan in question does not exceed the corresponding modified net premium for a 20-payment whole life plan.

2. For plans with higher premiums, the additional amount for expenses is limited to approximately the same amount as is permitted under the preliminary term method for a 20-payment whole life policy. It is not exactly the same as the 20-payment life amount in the case of policies that require more or less than 20 years' premiums, because the amount "borrowed" is "repaid" by a level premium payable for each year of the premium-paying period, including the first.

For example, for ordinary life at male age

TABLE 20-5. Terminal reserves per $1,000, various methods of valuation
(1980 CSO Table, 6% interest, male age 35)

Plan	Policy Year	Full Preliminary Term Method	Commissioners' Reserve Valuation Method	Net Level-Premium Method
Ordinary life	1	—	—	$ 7.63
	5	$ 34.24	$ 34.24	41.61
	10	84.95	84.95	91.93
	15	145.27	145.27	151.79
	20	215.79	215.79	221.77
20-payment life	1	—	—	10.39
	5	48.18	48.18	57.22
	10	121.98	121.98	128.85
	15	214.33	214.33	218.30
	20	330.34	330.34	330.34
At age 65 endowment	1	—	3.38	13.91
	5	64.19	67.36	77.21
	10	164.55	167.37	176.17
	15	293.70	296.09	303.53
	20	461.98	463.80	469.47

35, the CRVM calls for the full preliminary term method, because the net premium at male age 36 is less than the corresponding 20-payment life preliminary-term-basis premium for the second and subsequent years of $12.67 (i.e., the 19-payment life rate at male age 36).

However, in the case of the endowment at age 65 issued at male age 35, the modified method applies, since the rate at male age 36 for an endowment at age 65 of $15.85 exceeds the 19-payment life rate at male age 36 of $12.67. Following the method of paragraph 2, the additional amount available for expenses is found to be $9.66, which is equal to the amount given earlier for the 20-payment life plan under the preliminary-term plan. However, where the premium-paying period differs from 20 years, the result will be slightly different. Table 20–5 presents terminal reserve values under the several methods of valuation discussed above using 6 percent interest.

Terminal, Initial, and Mean Reserves

Depending on the point of time within the policy year when valuation occurs, reserves may be classified as terminal, initial, and mean. The calculations illustrated earlier have been concerned primarily with the **terminal reserve**— that is, the reserve at the end of any given policy year. The **initial reserve,** the reserve at the beginning of the policy year, is equal to the terminal reserve for the preceding year, increased by the net level annual premium (if any) for the current year. The **mean reserve** is the arithmetic average of the initial reserve and the terminal reserve for any year of valuation.

As discussed in Chapter 21, the initial reserve is used principally in connection with the determination of dividends under participating policies. The initial reserve generally is selected as the basis for allocation of interest earnings in excess of those assumed in the reserve.

The terminal reserve also is used in connection with dividend distributions, since mortality savings are allocated on the basis of the net amount at risk, and the terminal reserve is used to determine the net amount at risk. The terminal-reserve concept also is used to determine nonforfeiture values, although since 1948, a so-called adjusted premium is rather than the net level premium in such determination.[9] The terminal reserve also is used in connection with the form of reinsurance that is based on yearly renewable term insurance for the net amount at risk.[10]

The mean reserve is used in connection with the annual statements of life insurance companies.

[9] See later in this chapter.
[10] See Chapter 24.

Since policies are written at different points throughout the year and company annual statements are prepared as of December 31, it could be complicated and expensive to attempt a precise calculation for each individual policy. Consequently, for purposes of the annual statement, it is generally assumed that the policy anniversaries are uniformly distributed throughout the calendar year of issue, and the mean reserve is used for such valuation purposes.

Other Reserves

Deficiency Reserves. In the past, if gross premiums charged by a life insurance company for a particular class of policies were less than the valuation net premiums, the company was required to maintain a supplemental reserve, called a **deficiency reserve.** Valuation net premiums historically have been considerably less than gross premiums. In recent years, however, continued improvement in mortality and increasing price competition brought gross premium levels down to or even below valuation net premiums. This was particularly a problem for smaller companies with limited surplus available to establish such supplemental reserves.

Deficiency-reserve requirements (or their equivalent) are founded on the theory that the use, in the prospective reserve formula, of a valuation net level premium larger than the actual gross premium overstates the present expected value of future premiums and consequently understates the amount of the reserve. The deficiency is represented by the present expected value of the excess of the valuation net premium over the gross annual premium. In contrast to regular policy reserves, which under whole life policies increase with duration, deficiency reserves for a given class of policies decrease over time, disappearing altogether at the end of the premium-paying period.

In 1976, the NAIC changed the computation of reserves for policies that had previously been subject to deficiency reserve requirements. These changes were carried over into the 1980 valuation law. The law defines the minimum re-

quired reserve on such a policy as the present expected value of future benefits less the present expected value of future valuation net premiums calculated by the method (commissioners' or net level) actually used in computing the reserve for that policy but using the minimum valuation standards of mortality and rate of interest. However, the gross premium on the policy is to be substituted in this reserve calculation at each contract year in which it is less than the valuation net premium described above. If the reserve calculated in this way is larger than the reserve otherwise required, it would become the minimum reserve for that policy. The new provision does not use the term "deficiency reserve"; instead, it defines a new minimum reserve. In practice, however, the term "deficiency reserve" is still used to connote these special situations.

Reserves for Individual Deferred Annuities. There are three basic forms of annuity policies: the flexible- or fixed-premium deferred annuity, the single-premium deferred annuity, and the single-premium immediate annuity. When any annuity becomes income paying, it is reserved on the basis of a legally recognized mortality table and interest rate using the annuitant's attained age and the monthly income, taking into account any minimum benefit guarantees. The mortality standard generally used is more conservative than that used for life valuation. (Of course, "conservative" for life insurance means higher mortality rates, while "conservative" for annuities means lower mortality rates.)

Annual premium deferred annuities are policies where the owner pays annual premiums during an accumulation period until such time as the annuitant begins to receive income. These annual premiums may be a specified amount or may be subject to the discretion of the owner under flexible premium annuities. At income commencement, an annuitant receives the monthly income based on the cash value of the policy at that time and the annuity factor used by the company for the annuitant's attained age.

Individual deferred annuities have been reserved on the basis of net premiums that were accumulated at an interest rate that was limited to a maximum rate specified in the state laws. In 1976, the Commissioners' Annuity Reserve Valuation Method was defined to clarify the intent of the existing statute. This method requires the comparison of the present value of future guaranteed benefits at each duration with the present value of future required premiums to that duration. The greatest excess revealed by these comparisons would be the minimum reserve for the contract.

Supplementary contracts involving life contingencies are generally valued according to the mortality and interest basis on which the payments were calculated.

Reserves for Paid-Up Contracts. Under contracts where no further premiums will be received, reserves are merely "valuation net premiums" (i.e., the present value of future benefits). This would include (1) single-premium life and endowment contracts, (2) immediate life annuities, (3) paid-up life and endowment policies, and (4) supplementary contracts issued to beneficiaries in lieu of a lump-sum payment.

Reserves for Substandard Policies. In the case of substandard policies, an additional reserve liability is recognized to anticipate the additional mortality risk over that expected for a standard policy. There are numerous methods by which this reserve is calculated, and the approach followed varies from company to company.

Similarly, the adverse selection reflected in the mortality experience under group and term conversions may be recognized by establishing an additional reserve for the extra mortality experienced. Again, reserving for these items is not uniform.

Reserves for Special Benefits. The law requires that a minimum reserve liability be maintained for accidental death and waiver of premium benefits, and an appropriate liability for supplementary contracts without life contingencies, dividend accumulations, and similar benefits.

Accidental death benefit minimum reserves are determined in a similar manner to ordinary policy reserves, using a mortality table (currently, the *1959 Accidental Death Benefits Table*) based on accidental death.

Reserves for waiver of premium and other disability benefits are, of course, based on appropriate morbidity and mortality tables. These form the basis for predicting the joint probability of dying or becoming disabled and, assuming that the waiver of premium annuity has been entered upon, the joint probability of death or recovery.

Supplementary contracts without life contingencies, dividend accumulations, premiums paid in advance, and similar benefits are easily valued, involving only compound interest calculations.

Voluntary Reserves. In addition to the specific policy/benefit reserves (legal and voluntary) that are held to meet specific policy obligations, life insurance companies set aside various voluntary reserves that really represent earmarking of surplus for particular purposes, and may or may not be liabilities.

SURRENDER VALUES

Whether the reserve derives from a level-premium type of policy or a flexible-premium contract, the result is the same—prefunded mortality charges. What is an appropriate and fair disposition of these prefunded charges if the policyowner surrenders his or her policy? It is clear that under such circumstances, the company, since its future liability under the policy ceases, no longer requires the assets standing behind the reserve liability for the purpose originally intended. Experience has shown that it is not necessary for the protection of the company or other policyowners to insist that the policyowner forfeit the entire reserve value of the policy. It has therefore become a universal practice to permit the policyowner who surrenders his or her policy to receive a surrender value.

Although the practice of allowing a surrender value in some form is an old one, for many years the matter was entirely optional with companies. Some companies voluntarily granted cash surrender values and others did not. All states today have "nonforfeiture laws" that define the minimum amount that must be returned upon surrender of a policy.[11] Today, many companies provide surrender values in excess of the minimums required by law.

In determination of the proper value to be granted discontinuing policyowners, company practice is based on certain principles. Before examining the Standard Nonforfeiture Law, these principles are considered briefly.

Concepts of Equity

The actual treatment of withdrawing policyowners generally can be based on any one of three possible concepts of equity. One view is that the policyowner should receive nothing, on the grounds that the sole function of a life insurance contract is to provide certain designated benefits in the event of the death of the insured or survival to the maturity date of an endowment policy. Premiums could be discounted for anticipated surrenders (dividends could also be increased in a participating contract), and thus the forfeiture could be reflected in a reduction in the cost of insurance. In the early days of the business, this view generally was accepted and applied, in many cases without an adjustment in the premium for the contract. Such practices led to the introduction of nonforfeiture legislation, and this approach probably would be difficult to sell today in the absence of complete and effective disclosure. Discussions on this matter are being held.[12]

At the other extreme, the withdrawing policyowner might be considered as being entitled to the return of all premiums paid (less dividends), plus interest at the contractual rate, less a pro rata share of assumed death claims and average expenses of the company, that is, almost the full reserve under the contract, irrespective of the policy year in which the surrender occurs. This

view, of course, ignores the question of the incidence of expense and assumes that unamortized acquisition expenses under policies surrendered during the early years after issue would be borne by existing policyowners or charged to the general surplus of the company.

Proponents of this philosophy argue that the healthy growth of a company is essential for the welfare of all policyowners, and consequently, the loss resulting from terminations at the early durations should be a charge on all policies and not specifically assessed against new policies. The strict application of this view would provide a surrender value just slightly less than the full reserve even at the end of the first policy year. A modified form of this approach would have the acquisition expenses due to early terminations borne partially by the continuing policyowners and partially by the new policies, resulting in a surrender value something less than the full reserve and more than the asset share (see below), until the acquisition expenses had been fully amortized, after which it would equal the full reserve.

The third concept of equity is that the withdrawing policyowner should receive a surrender value as nearly as possible equivalent to his or her contribution to the funds of the company, less the cost of protection received, and less any expenses incurred by the company in establishing and handling the policy. This view has as its objective that the withdrawal of a policyowner should neither benefit nor harm continuing policyowners. Under this concept, the amount received by the withdrawing policyowner would be based on the pro rata share of the assets accumulated by the company on behalf of the classification of policies to which his or her policy belongs—that is, the so-called asset share.

Reasons Justifying Paying Less Than the Asset Share

It will be remembered (Chapter 2) that the asset-share value is equal to the pro rata share of the assets accumulated by the company on behalf of the block of policies to which a particular policy belongs. This value reflects the incidence of expense and its relationship to policy duration.

[11]Under the leadership of Elizur Wright, the state of Massachusetts enacted the first such law on May 10, 1861.

[12]See various post-1980 issues of the *Record* of the Society of Actuaries.

The surrender benefit may be justifiably less, for several reasons, including (1) adverse financial selection, (2) adverse mortality selection, (3) contribution to a contingency reserve or profits, and (4) cost of surrendering the policy.

Adverse Financial Selection. A reason advanced for not allowing the terminating policyowner to obtain the full asset share is the possibility that during periods of financial stringency, policyowners may surrender their policies to such an extent that the company may be greatly weakened financially to the detriment of remaining policyowners. In normal times, life insurance companies have an excess of income over expenditures that is more than sufficient to meet demands for loans and cash values. During difficult economic times, however, demands by policyowners may be so great that it becomes necessary to liquidate valuable assets at depressed prices. The right of the policyowner to demand the surrender value of the policy at any time also necessitates a more liquid investment policy than would otherwise be required.[13] Many companies believe that those policyowners who surrender their policies should be charged with the loss of investment earnings, including capital losses, arising from their action, and they take this into account in fixing the amount of the surrender value.

Adverse Mortality Selection. A further argument advanced in favor of granting a surrender value less than the full asset share— although some writers question its correctness or importance—refers to the "adverse mortality selection" that is assumed to be brought about by the allowance of liberal surrender values. The position taken by the supporters of this view is as follows. A life insurance policy is a unilateral contract, to which the company must always adhere but which the policyowner may terminate at any time. Whenever, therefore, the payment of premiums seems a hardship, the healthy

policyowner, not feeling the immediate need for insurance, may have no hesitancy in discontinuing coverage. Insureds in poor health, on the contrary, will appreciate fully the value of their insurance and will exert themselves to the utmost to pay the premium. Hence, according to this view, policies on the good risks are likely to lapse on a larger scale if surrender values are liberal, while impaired risks will stay with the company. The result is a reduction in the average vitality of the insureds remaining with the company. It is therefore argued that retiring policyowners should receive less than the pro rata share of their policies in order to provide a fund to meet the higher death rate among the poorer risks that remain. Although seemingly logical, this tendency has been difficult to substantiate statistically.

Other Reasons. Another reason advanced for paying a smaller surrender value relates to the principle followed by some companies that each contract should make a contribution to the company's general contingency reserve or surplus. This is needed to absorb adverse fluctuations produced by occasional catastrophes, such as wars and epidemics, that may occur only once in several decades. To the extent that such a "permanent" contribution is required, the surrender allowance should be reduced.

In a stock company, an adjustment may be made in the surrender allowance to account for that policy's contribution to profits, which is in recognition of the risk borne by stockholders' investments. Finally, a certain amount of expense is incurred in processing the surrender of a policy. Some companies adjust the surrender allowance to reflect this factor, rather than taking it into account in their premium loading formula.

Company Liberality

A major factor affecting a company's practices with regard to surrender allowances is competition. In recent years, a significant number of companies have allowed surrender values far in excess of the minimums required by law. In the event of the termination of such contracts prior to the point where the asset share equals the full

---

[13]Companies have the legal right to postpone payment of the cash surrender value for a period of six months. From a practical standpoint, however, this right should be invoked only under the most severe financial circumstances.

cash value, the unamortized acquisition expenses must of necessity be borne by persisting policy-owners. If the amount is large, this would appear to be straining the argument that "new business is vital to the sound management of a life insurance company." As long as the values are equal to or greater than the minimum values required by law, the only question involved is the equity between terminating and persisting policyowners. The question of what constitutes "equity" in this case is a matter of company judgment.

REGULATION OF RESERVES AND SURRENDER VALUES

All states in the United States have laws that stipulate the requirements that insurers must meet in calculating reserves and surrender values. These laws have the effect of establishing minimum values below which insurers may not venture in setting up reserves and surrender values. The **Standard Valuation Law,** in effect, defines the minimum reserves for life insurance and annuity contracts. The **Standard Nonforfeiture Law,** in effect, defines minimum surrender values. Insurers are free to maintain reserves at a level higher than those required by the valuation laws and may have surrender values higher than those required by the nonforfeiture laws, but they cannot be lower. Most states' laws are patterned closely after the 1980 NAIC model laws, which are discussed below.

The basis for both reserve and surrender value computation is stated in terms of the mortality table to be used, the maximum rate of interest to be assumed, and the method to be applied. The requirements differ as between life insurance and annuities and as between ordinary, group, and industrial life insurance. Supplementary agreements relating to proceeds left with the insurance company are subject to special rules.

Background

Early nonforfeiture laws were enacted to prevent the forfeiture of equities built up in level premium policies, and early valuation laws were designed to ensure company solvency. Tradi-

tionally, the surrender values required to be returned have been called **nonforfeiture values,** and the form in which these values may be taken are referred to as nonforfeiture options.[14] Except in reference to legislation, the term "surrender value" increasingly has been substituted because of its simplicity and better connotation.

Prior to 1948, the legal minimum standard in most states for computing reserves and surrender values for ordinary insurance was the *American Experience Table* and 3½ percent interest. The minimum basis (mortality table) for valuing reserves and surrender values for newly issued ordinary policies was changed in 1948 to the *1941 CSO Table.* Previously, nonforfeiture benefits were linked directly to reserves, whereas under the 1948 law, this close tie-in was obviated, with the result that greater equity could be maintained between insureds at different ages and also with respect to different plans of insurance. The elimination of the former linkage recognized that reserves are an aggregate measure of future liabilities, whereas nonforfeiture values are an approximate measure of accumulated policyowner equity in a particular contract. The 1948 law also established a new method of calculating nonforfeiture values. Variations of this method have been used since that time.

The *1958 CSO Table* and 3½ percent interest were established as the minimum standards for reserves on ordinary policies issued on or after January 1, 1966. The interest rate was changed to 4 and later to 4½ percent.

Minimum *surrender* values could be based on 5½ percent interest for annual premium policies and on either 5½ or 6½ percent for single-premium policies. In addition, changes in 1972 updated the valuation mortality tables for both group and individual annuities. Under 1976 amendments, the maximum nonforfeiture interest rate that could be used was 1 percent higher than the statutory interest rate specified for determining minimum reserves.

In spite of the seemingly continual process of updating the earlier valuation and nonforfeiture laws, the need for further changes appeared to be

[14]See Chapter 9.

constant. Each time a change in mortality tables or interest rates was necessary, an amendment was necessary in every state's valuation and nonforfeiture laws. This was both a time-consuming and expensive process. It was widely recognized that the *1958 CSO Table* was out of date and that, with interest rate volatility, it was likely that further changes would be needed in the interest rate assumptions.

The 1980 Valuation and Nonforfeiture Laws

In response to these converging problems, a new Model Standard Valuation Law and a new Model Standard Nonforfeiture Law were adopted by the NAIC at its December 1980 meeting, the effects of which were intended to introduce greater flexibility into the laws and to render them more suitable for current conditions. All jurisdictions in the United States have now adopted the new NAIC models or close variations thereof.

The new laws have no effect on existing life insurance policies and individual annuity contracts. The new laws do not affect the reserves that have already been set up on existing group annuity-type contracts, but the future growth of these reserves could be affected.

Changes from Earlier Laws. Three important aspects of the new laws deserve comment: (1) dynamic maximum interest rates, (2) new mortality bases, and (3) certain technical changes.

1. *Dynamic interest rates.* The new laws define the maximum interest rates that can be used to calculate reserves and nonforfeiture benefits on a "dynamic" basis. The maximum permitted interest rate automatically is adjusted if a recalculation produces a significant change. The laws make use of the Moody's Corporate Bond Yield Average-Monthly Average Corporates, as published by Moody's Investors Service, Inc., as the applicable index. However, the maximum interest rates themselves depend on the type of insurance contract, and they may be much smaller than this Composite Yield Rate. These maximum interest rates are recalculated at 12-month intervals. It should be noted that the maximum interest rate

for a particular life insurance policy or individual annuity contract is fixed at its date of issue. A change in the maximum interest rate could apply to newly issued life insurance policies or individual annuity contracts, but not to ones already in force.

The "dynamic" interest basis appears to be a great improvement in that it automatically can adjust maximum interest rates to current conditions without the need for legislative action. Of course, the laws permit an insurance company to use lower interest rates than the permitted maximums if the company wishes to do this.

2. *New mortality rates.* The laws make use of new mortality tables for individual life insurance, which were developed by a Society of Actuaries' Committee. All these tables are constructed separately for males and females. These new tables are styled as the *Commissioners 1980 Standard Ordinary Mortality Tables,* the *Commissioners 1980 Standard Ordinary Mortality Table with Ten Year Select Mortality Factors,* and the *Commissioners 1980 Extended Term Insurance Tables.*[15] The new tables are based on a study of data on insured lives, exposed to death during the years 1970 to 1975. These new tables reflect the substantial improvement in mortality rates that has occurred since the preparation of the mortality tables specified in the old model laws.

The laws also contain a procedure whereby new mortality tables developed in the future can become effective in a state, without being specifically named in the text of the laws. First, the NAIC must adopt any such new tables. Then they have to be approved by regulation promulgated by the Commissioner of Insurance for that state. The new mortality tables can be tables for individual life insurance or tables for other classes of contracts described in the laws.

3. *Certain technical changes.* The laws contain many technical changes, although the fundamental calculation processes remained unchanged. This summary identifies only a few of the changes.

The laws changed the formula for the expense allowance used in the Standard Nonfor-

---

[15]Other specialized *1980 CSO Tables* exist. See f. 16, p. 320.

feiture Law for life insurance, so as to reflect more accurately current patterns of expenses. The laws allow the Commissioner of Insurance for a state to promulgate regulations describing appropriate minimum reserves and minimum nonforfeiture benefits for certain new or complex plans of life insurance that were not contemplated when the model laws were originally written. The laws also cause the minimum reserves and minimum non-forfeiture benefits for some life insurance policies in the early policy years to be increased over what they would be otherwise, in certain cases where the plan provides relatively high guaranteed benefits or cash values in one or more of the later policy years.

Current Requirements. As mentioned earlier, valuation and nonforfeiture laws stipulate (1) the mortality table to be used, (2) the *maximum* interest rate to be assumed, and (3) the method to be applied. The *1980 CSO Tables* may be used now and are the *required* to be used for both reserve and surrender value calculations as of 1989.

The maximum interest rates permitted vary as between annuities and life insurance and within each of these categories, based on duration and plan types. The possible choices are great and need not be presented here except in summary form. Thus, for life insurance policies, permissible maximum interest rates are:

Guaranteed Duration	Maximum Permissible Valuation Interest Rate (%)	Maximum Permissible Nonforfeiture Interest Rate (%)
10 years or less	7.25	9.00
More than 10 but less than 20 years	6.75	8.50
20 years or more	6.00	7.50

These rates apply to policies issued during the period 1983–1986 (latest available date) and were derived from the Moody's Composite Index mentioned earlier. Thus, for life insurance policies with a guaranteed duration of 20 years or more, companies may use up to 6 percent to calculate reserves and up to 7½ percent to derive surrender values. The prospective method generally is required in these laws.

For single-premium immediate annuities

and certain settlement options, the maximum permissible valuation rate for 1985 issues (latest date available) was 11 percent. Maximum rates for previous years were 11.25 percent for 1983 and 1984 issues. Maximum permissible valuation interest rates for other annuities range from 6.25 to 12.50 percent, depending on annuity duration, whether there exists any future interest guarantee, the basis of fund valuation, and the exact type of plan.

The nonforfeiture law stipulates that the nonforfeiture interest rate cannot exceed 125 percent of the reserve interest rate. Of course, insurance companies are free to use rates lower than the maximum permitted in law and many do so in the interest of conservation.

The valuation laws stipulate that the method used for calculating minimum reserves can be the CRVM (discussed earlier). The net-level-premium method, in other words, is not required but may be used as it develops higher reserves than the CRVM.

The minimum nonforfeiture value at any policy duration is the present value at that time of the future benefits under the policy less the present value of future *adjusted* premiums. This is essentially the prospective-reserve formula utilizing an adjusted premium in lieu of the valuation net level premium. The adjusted premium is the level premium necessary to pay the benefits guaranteed by the policy (the net level premium) *plus* the level equivalent of a certain defined special *first-year expense allowance.*

Under the pre-1980 laws, the maximum allowance for special first-year expenses was defined as a constant of $20 per $1,000 of insurance, plus a percentage (40 percent) of the adjusted premium for the policy, and a percentage (25 percent) of either the adjusted premium for the policy or the adjusted premium for a whole life policy issued at the same age for the same amount of insurance, whichever was less. According to the previous legislation, the first-year expense allowance could not exceed a maximum of $46 per $1,000 of insurance. Note that with this old formula, the percentage allowance was of the adjusted premium—the item being sought.

This "circularity" was removed by the 1980 changes to make the formula a function of the *net premium* rather than the *adjusted premium.* Thus, under current law, the maximum allowance is defined as being 125 percent of the lesser of (1) the nonforfeiture net level premium or (2) $40 per $1,000; plus a constant of $10 per $1,000 of insurance. This new approach greatly simplified the calculation. It can be seen that the maximum first-year expense allowance is now $60 (1.25 × $40 + $10).

Illustration of Adjusted-Premium Method.

The first step in deriving surrender values under the Standard Nonforfeiture Law is to determine the special first-year expense allowance. This may be based on the company's expense situation, competitive pressures, or other considerations, but is limited by the maximum amount permitted under the law.

The second step in the process is to calculate the adjusted premium. This may be approached from two standpoints. It may be regarded as the net annual level premium required to amortize a principal sum equal to the present value of the benefits under the policy and the special first-year expense allowance. Thus, the present value of future benefits (PVFB) for an ordinary life policy issued at male age 35 (based on the *1980 CSO Table* and interest at the permitted maximum of 7½ percent) is equal to the net single premium for such a policy, $96.19. The net level premium is $7.42. The maximum special first-year expense allowance

for such a policy is, therefore, $19.28[16] The total of $96.19 and $19.28 yields a principal sum of $115.47. The net annual level premmium that will amortize this sum may be obtained by dividing $115.47 by 12.955, the present value of a life annuity due of 1 as of age 35. The result, $8.91, is the adjusted premium.

The second way of looking at the adjusted premium is that it is the sum obtained by adding to the regular net annual level premium the annual amount needed to amortize the special acquisition expenses over the premium-paying period. Thus, by dividing $19.28 (maximum special first-year expense allowance) by the present value of a life annuity due of 1 for the premium-paying period, 12.955, the annual amount of $1.488 is obtained, which, when added to the net level premium for an ordinary life policy issued at male age 35, $7.42, gives $8.91 the same adjusted premium determined above.

The final step in determining the minimum surrender value is to substitute the adjusted premium for the regular net level premium in the formula employed in the computation of prospective reserves. The following summary of the calculation of the tenth-year minimum non-forfeiture value for an ordinary life policy issued at male age 35 (*1980 CSO Table,* 7½ percent) will illustrate the application of the principles developed here:

[16] $1.25 \times 7.42 + \$10 = \$19.28.$

$$\text{NFV (age of valuation)} = \text{present value of benefits} - \text{present value of future adjusted premiums}$$

$$\text{NFV (age of valuation)} = \text{NSP (age of valuation)} - \frac{\text{NSP (original age)} + \text{special expense allowance}}{\text{PVLAD of 1 PPP}} \times \text{PVLAD of 1 for remaining premium paying period}$$

$$\text{NFV}_{45} = \text{NSP}_{45} - \frac{\text{NSP}_{35} + \text{special expense allowance}}{\text{PVLAD of 1 PPP}} \times \text{PVLAD of 1 for life at age 45}$$

$$= \$162.95 - \frac{\$96.19 + \$19.28}{12.955} \times 11.998$$

$$= \$56.02$$

It should be noted that the only difference between this formula and the minimum reserve formula utilized earlier is the addition of the expense factor to the original net single premium, resulting in a net level adjusted premium. Thus, in prospective terms, the nonforfeiture value is the present value of future benefits less the present value of future adjusted premiums.

Modifications of the Adjusted-Premium Method. The illustration above demonstrates the calculation of minimum surrender values under a 7½ percent interest assumption. As mentioned earlier, many companies provide surrender values in excess of the minimums of the law. This may be accomplished by (1) assuming lower first-year expenses than the maximum permitted, (2) assuming the maximum expenses and amortizing them over a shorter period or at an uneven rate over the premium-paying period, (3) assuming a rate of interest lower than that permitted by law, or (4) a combination of the above.

If lower first-year expenses are assumed, the adjusted premium will be smaller, making the present value of future adjusted premiums smaller and resulting in larger surrender values. Similarly, in the case of amortizing the maximum permitted excess first-year expense allowance over a shorter period or at an uneven rate, the adjusted premium is itself "adjusted," resulting in appropriately modified surrender values. In those cases where the premium is adjusted to produce higher surrender values, the modified adjusted premium is known as a **nonforfeiture factor**. Similarly, the term **adjusted-premium method** refers to the derivation of minimum values only. Where larger values are derived through the use of nonforfeiture factor(s), the term **standard nonforfeiture-value method** is applied. It is important to remember that the law requires only that values no less than those derived by the adjusted-premium method be provided.

Table 20–6 illustrates the variation in surrender values with changes in the interest assumption only, holding the mortality and expense allowances constant. It is clear from this table that the interest assumption is of great importance in determining the level of surrender values, especially at early policy durations.

TABLE 20-6. Effect of interest rate assumption on surrender values
(ordinary life, male, age 35, $1,000 basis); based on 1980 NAIC model law

End of Policy Year	Interest Rate:			
	3%	5%	7½%	9%
1	$ 0	$ 0	$ 0	$ 0
2	0	0	0	0
3	13.33	5.78	0	0
4	27.92	16.20	6.70	2.89
5	42.79	26.97	14.04	8.81
10	121.05	86.02	56.02	43.04
15	205.63	154.21	108.01	87.82
20	295.66	231.63	171.28	143.81
25	388.53	316.33	245.01	211.21
30	482.45	407.03	329.03	290.58

Table 20–7 shows how different mortality tables produce different results, with each using the 1980 adjusted premium method and interest at 5 percent.

TABLE 20-7. Effect of mortality assumption on surrender values
(ordinary life, male, age 35, $1,000 basis;) interest at 5 % based on 1980 NAIC model law

End of Policy Year	1941 CSO	1958 CSO	1980 CSO
1	$ 0	$ 0	$ 0
2	0	0	0
3	6.51	7.22	5.78
4	18.90	18.73	16.20
5	31.64	30.62	26.97
10	100.64	95.60	86.02
15	178.05	169.71	154.21
20	262.63	251.62	231.63
25	352.29	339.45	316.33
30	444.11	429.98	407.03

Requirements for Nontraditional Products[17]

The new valuation and nonforfeiture laws permit state insurance commissioners to promulgate special reserve and surrender requirements for policies whose cost and benefit structures do not fit easily into the classical mold.

[17]This section draws from Society of Actuaries, "N.A.I.C. Update," *Record,* Vol. 10, No. 2 (1984), pp. 961–965.

Commissioners increasingly have been taking advantage of this legislative opportunity by stipulating special requirements for universal life (UL) and current assumption whole life (CAWL) insurance plans. These special requirements usually are patterned after the NAIC Universal Life Model Regulation, so discussion will center on this model.

In viewing reserve and surrender value requirements for UL policies, it should be recognized that the UL account value mechanism is the cost structure of the policy, and only that. The guarantees of interest, mortality, and expense charges take the place of the premium rate in a more traditional form of insurance. It is this premium rate that is unbundled and not the valuation structure. Understanding this subtle point is necessary. It brings about an entirely different approach toward valuation and nonforfeiture compliance.

Some individuals have supported restricting one or more of these UL pricing elements to the standards used for deriving reserve and surrender values. Arguably, any such restrictions are unnecessary and unfair. Any restrictions on these UL items are analogous to stipulating the maximum premium rates on traditional whole life insurance. The account value, therefore, is not necessarily a good representation of either the minimum surrender value or reserve.

Consider the CAWL policy. The Standard Nonforfeiture Law defines a minimum cash value in terms of future *guaranteed* benefits and premiums. With CAWL policies, all of the information required to calculate a minimum surrender value is available. The future guaranteed benefits are known as are the premiums, on a guaranteed basis. With these two pieces of information, the minimum surrender value is completely defined.

The NAIC Model Regulation recognizes this fact. The section specifying surrender values for CAWL plans basically is a restatement of the Standard Nonforfeiture Law, with a bit of explanation as to how future guaranteed benefits are to be found. Quoting from the regulation:

Future guaranteed benefits are determined by (1) projecting the policy value, taking into account future premiums, if any, and using all

guarantees of interests, mortality, expense deductions, etc., contained in the policy or declared by the insurer; and (2) taking into account any benefits guaranteed in the policy or by declaration which do not depend on the policy value.

The last term, referring to benefits guaranteed which do not depend on the policy value, may seem odd. Policies may have guarantees that exist in addition to those of the account value, and these secondary guarantees are as much a part of future benefits as projected death and endowment benefits. Several policies on the market utilize such a guarantee. It is usually present in policies where the account value will not support whole life benefits on a guaranteed basis. The policy form will contain an additional guarantee that the policy will turn out to be at least whole life, regardless of the performance of the account value. Obviously, if the guaranteed plan of insurance is whole life, the minimum surrender values must be those of whole life. With these secondary guarantee forms, there may be cases where the minimum surrender value is greater than the full account value.

A markedly different approach is taken in defining minimum surrender values for UL plans. Because of the multitude of problems in any application of the prospective method, the retrospective method was adopted. It was believed that the policyowner would be most interested in the relationship between the account value and the **surrender value.** The difference between the account value and the policy surrender value—the surrender charge—is the quantity regulated by the Model. Basically, the surrender charge can be no bigger than the unused unamortized portion of the special expense allowance prescribed by the Standard Nonforfeiture Law. The Model Regulation specifies that the expense allowance shall be that for level-premium, level-death-benefit endowment insurance at the maturity date. The rationale for choosing a "whole life" expense allowance is that most UL is sold as a substitute for traditional forms of whole life insurance. In addition, the expenses incurred in writing a UL policy are comparable to plans where the whole life expense allowance is permitted. Any expense allowance smaller than that for whole life would leave UL plans at an unfair disadvantage in comparison with traditional plans of insurance.

In general, using the retrospective approach outlined in the Model Regulation, minimum surrender values are higher than those for comparable traditional plans. To explain this, it is necessary to analyze surrender charges implicit in traditional plans.

Current law, in essence, permits two forms of "surrender charges" to bring the reserve down to the level of the surrender value. The first type is the unamortized expense allowance. This can be considered as a type of "surrender charge" that is allowed in traditional plans. In addition, however, the surrender value often is calculated using a rate of interest higher than that used in calculating the reserve. This second form of "surrender charge," the "interest differential," is the amount lost when using a retrospective approach to UL nonforfeiture values. This sacrifice was made in the interest of simplicity and workability.

The UL *reserve* methodology is merely an interpretation of the Standard Valuation Law, not a reworking of it. The method for calculating minimum reserves is the same for both CAWL and UL plans of insurance and is prospective in nature. The procedure is exceedingly complex and beyond the scope of this text. In general, it requires an assumption as to future premiums and contains an adjustment mechanism when premiums actually paid do not meet the assumed premium. Even this approach was under review by the NAIC at the time this book was going to press, and modifications were expected.

Chapter 21

Gross Premium Rate Structures and Nonguaranteed Policy Elements

The concept of the net premium was analyzed in the preceding chapters. A company must, however, collect premiums that, supplemented by interest, will enable it to meet *all* costs under the contract, including the policy's share of the company's operating expenses and perhaps a contribution to surplus. The charges intended to meet these multiple objectives are referred to as the gross premium rate structure. From this rate structure is determined the premiums actually paid by policyowners.

One should not examine gross premium rate structures without also recognizing that most cash value policies sold today in the United States provide a mechanism for lowering the effective cost of policies below that based on the guaranteed assumptions. Historically, the payment of dividends under participating policies has served this function. Of course, today other techniques exist, such as excess interest credits and indeterminate premium rate structures.

GENERAL CONSIDERATIONS IN DERIVING GROSS PREMIUMS

A gross premium may be regarded as either (1)

the valuation net premium increased by an amount called loading, or (2) a sum derived independently of the valuation net premium and based on all factors that enter into a gross premium computation (i.e., mortality, interest, expenses, lapse rates, contingency allowance, and an allowance for a contribution to surplus and/or profit). The gross premiums of mutual companies historically were arrived at by the former method, whereas the premiums of stock companies typically were derived by the latter method. In recent years there has been a trend toward use of the second approach by both stocks and mutuals, and the second approach typically is followed in establishing the structure of charges and credits under universal life (UL) policies. This trend toward selecting a gross premium level first and then working back from that to design a policy that can be supported by that premium level reflects the increasing importance of competitive forces in deriving gross premiums.

It should be noted that the combination of mortality, expense, and surrender charges and interest credits *is* a UL policy's rate structure. The only difference, conceptually, between the UL and traditional forms is that the structure is "unbundled" under UL and other similar policies and "bundled" under the more traditional forms. For purposes of discussion, it should be understood that for UL and similar unbundled policies, the account value mechanism serves the same function as and, in effect, is the same as the gross premium rate structure under more traditional forms of life insurance.

Basic Criteria and Parameters

In developing a gross premium rate structure for a block of policies, considerations such as adequacy, equity, legal limitations, competition, and specific company objectives all enter into the process. Adequacy clearly is the most important requirement of a gross premium rate structure, because company solvency can be jeopardized by inadequate premiums. Equity in a premium structure primarily is for the benefit of the policyowners, although a practical limit exists to the degree of equity that can be attained. Charges must not be in conflict with any law.[1] Deficiency reserve statutes or their equivalent indirectly may influence premium charges for practical reasons.[2] Competition will obviously affect a company's premium rates. In setting growth and profit goals, other objectives, such as markets selected, products emphasized, or compensation philosophy, can all affect the gross premium rate structure finally adopted.

Nature of Insurance Company Expenses

Insurance company expenses may be divided into **investment expenses** and **insurance expenses.** The former class includes the costs of making, handling, and protecting investments, and since they are related directly to the production of investment income by the company, they are deducted from the gross income on investments. They are, therefore, taken into account in determining the net rates of interest to be used in calculating premiums or excess interest credits.

Insurance expenses are those of a noninvestment nature and may be classified in various ways. The costs of procuring, underwriting, and issuing new business, including commissions attributable to the first year's premiums, are regarded as **first-year expenses.** The various costs of maintaining and servicing outstanding policies, as well as renewal commissions, are regarded as **renewal expenses. Claims expenses** include claim litigation costs and appropriate amounts for salaries, rent, utilities, and so on, attributable to the claim department. Finally, there is what can be called **administrative expenses,** which include expenses such as salaries, rent, utilities, and so on attributable to the non-claim, non-underwriting executive (e.g., president's salary) and administrative functions.

For purposes of determining a proper expense allocation, these various insurance expenses may be analyzed further and assigned to three major groups:

1. Expenses that vary with the amount of premiums: for example, agent's commissions and premium taxes

2. Expenses that vary with the amount of insurance: for example, underwriting costs tend to vary with the size of the policy

3. Expenses that vary with the number of policies: for example, the cost of preparing policies for issue, establishing the necessary accounting records, sending of premium notices, and so on.

There are two major problems associated with reflecting expenses in the premium rate structure. These problems are (1) the equitable distribution of expenses among different classes of policies and among policyowners at different ages—the problem of making each class of policy pay its own cost, and (2) the recognition of when expense is incurred. The solution to these problems is complicated by the objective of living up to statutory requirements, of maintaining a consistent policy regarding surrender values and dividends, of accomodating those expenses that do not fall neatly into one of these groups, and of meeting the competition of other companies. The problems may be complicated further by the desired premium-payment pattern. For example,

---

[1] For example, Wisconsin currently limits gross premiums directly by specifying in the law the maximum premium that may be charged. Wisconsin is the only state presently with such a statute.

[2] See Chapters 4 and 20.

with UL policies, the front-end or back-end loads or other implicit charges (e.g., mortality and/or interest margins) are not likely to track the actual incidence of expense. On the other hand, UL and other unbundled products can facilitate the matching of expense charges to expenses incurred. The UL premium rate structure, unlike that of more traditional policies, is not constrained to a fixed, level premium pattern, thus potentially easing the incidence of expense matching problem.

Because the objectives of adequacy and equity are sometimes in conflict with the objective of maintaining or improving the competitive position of the company, the final gross premium rate structure normally represents a compromise. Nevertheless, in the aggregate, adequacy must be maintained.

Nature of Loading

A truly equitable system of loading for expenses would result in every policyowner paying the expenses properly attributable to his or her policy. The foregoing analysis of insurance company expenses suggests that loading may consist partly of a percentage of premium charge, partly of a charge for each $1,000 of insurance, and partly of a charge for each policy. In fact, the expense charges of many UL and other unbundled products are structured in this tripartite manner. Many unbundled products, however, omit one or more of the three elements in their expense charges, with some having no identifiable expense charges. In the latter situation, the company's expenses must be met from margins built into the mortality charges and into the interest credits.

The expense loading formulas of more traditional forms of life insurance often will convert the "per policy" expense element to a "per $1,000" charge by relating it to the average-size policy issued. To meet competition and to provide greater equity between classes of policies where the average-size policy issued varies considerably, most companies assume a separate average-size policy for each policy band or for the principal plans of insurance and age groups in their premium calculations.

The loading formula includes, in addition

to an allowance for expenses, a provision for contingencies and a margin for contribution to surplus or profits. With the per policy expenses converted to an "amount per $1,000 basis," the hypothetical expense loading formula may be reduced to two factors: (1) a percentage of the premium and (2) a constant per $1,000.

DEVELOPING TENTATIVE GROSS PREMIUM RATE STRUCTURE

Although the gross premium rate may be viewed as a net premium augmented by an amount called loading, it is more frequently regarded as an amount derived independently of the valuation net premium, based on all the factors that enter into the gross premium. The five elements basic to the calculation are (1) the expected amount and incidence of claims, (2) an appropriate rate of investment return, (3) withdrawal rates and amounts withdrawn, (4) amounts and incidence of expenses and (5) a factor to provide a margin for contributions to surplus or profit. Under traditional policy forms, assumptions as to each of these elements can be selected, a formula embodying all of them derived, and a premium rate calculated. Under unbundled product forms, assumptions are still required, but the possibility of offsetting one element (e.g., decreased expense charges) with another (increased mortality charges) complicates the analysis. In any event, with both bundled and unbundled product forms, the tentative gross premium rate structure is tested by asset-share studies to be certain it is consistent with company objectives. Therefore, its method of development is not critical.

The determination of unit expense rates involves both the amount of expense incurred, as shown by cost evaluations, and the time of its occurrence. Although the derivation of the individual unit expense rates is beyond the scope of this volume, a few additional comments might be appropriate. Claim expenses and the costs of paying surrender values, dispensing policy loans, and processing beneficiary changes may be accounted for separately and treated as additional benefits. The cost of writing the policy and establishing records would be assessed on a per-policy basis; valuation fees paid the state insurance department would be on a per-$1,000 basis; and underwriting expenses would be split two ways, with one part on a per-$1,000 basis and one part on a per policy basis. Salaries would be allocated on the basis of the nature of the work done, using time studies or other appropriate measures. Utilities usually follow the salary distributions.

Once all unit expenses are developed, they are then combined to give a pattern of (1) per-policy, (2) per $1,000, and (3) percentage expenses separately for the first year and renewal years. The unit expense rates developed on the basis of careful cost evaluations can be tested for accuracy by applying them to appropriate company functions. If such application results in total expenses approximating those actually incurred, it may be presumed that they do, in fact, represent the operating costs of the company. Judgment modifications can be made, of course, depending on management's optimism or pessimism regarding the future.

Having determined the present value of all expenses and spread them over the premium-paying period, it is only necessary to include a margin for profit and contingencies and—in the case of some participating policies—dividends, to produce the tentative gross premium. Table 21–1 presents a set of hypothetical expense factors reflecting the principles discussed.

For participating insurance, an additional allowance may be included for the specific purpose of creating a surplus from which dividends can be paid or such dividends may be implicit in the contingency margins. Such decisions involve broad managerial policy and vary from company to company. A moderate provision might be 5 percent of the gross premium, or alternatively, the equivalent amount expressed per premium dollar and per $1,000. The loading formula for participating business is usually expressed in terms of the tabular (the reserve basis) net premium.

TESTING THE TENTATIVE GROSS PREMIUM RATE STRUCTURE

A gross premium rate structure derived by applying a loading formula to a set of net premiums commonly is tentative only and is *tested*, at a minimum, at various pivotal issue ages, such as 0, 15, 25, 35, 45, and 55. The purpose is to see whether under realistic assumptions as to mortality, investment earnings, expenses, and terminations, the rate structure would develop sufficiently high asset accumulations to provide the surrender values and death and other benefits promised under the contract, and to meet the legal requirements and to assure that the resulting net costs are competitive, reasonable, and consistent.

TABLE 21-1. Hypothetical expenses

Expense Item	First Year			Renewal				
						Percent Premium by Duration (years)		
	Per Policy	Per $1,000	Percent Premium	Per Policy	Per $1,000	2-9	10-15	16-20
State taxes			2.0			2.0	2.0	2.0
Commissions			60.0			7.3	5.0	3.0
Expense allowance			20.0			2.7	1.8	1.1
Medical and inspection	$22.15	$0.90						
Acquisition	20.93	0.21	14.0					
Maintenance	22.12	0.05	—	$22.12	$0.05	—	—	—
	$65.20	$1.16	96.0	$22.12	$0.05	12.0	8.8	6.1
Claim expense:	$32.25 per policy plus $0.20 per $1,000							

Asset-Share Calculations

It will be recalled from Chapter 2 that such tests are based on the asset-share model. The purpose is to determine, for any block or class of policies (same plan and ratebook), the expected fund per $1,000 of insurance held by the company at the end of each policy year after payment of all policy benefits and expenses, taking into consideration all premiums paid and expected (realistic) interest earnings. Each year's accumulated fund, divided by the number of surviving and persisting insureds, produces the **asset share.** Asset-share studies are really simulations of expected experience[3] for blocks of policies using the best estimates of anticipated operating experience. The purpose of such an asset-share calculation is to see if the individual elements of the policy are well balanced and will produce acceptable results for both the insurance company and policyowners. The gross premium rate structure is only one of the many factors being evaluated.

By comparing the asset share at each duration with the comparable surrender value and reserve, the company can evaluate the adequacy and equity of the tentative gross premium structure. From an accounting standpoint, the amount taken from surplus to cover excess first-year expenses for a given block or class of policies is not fully recovered until the asset share equals the reserve. Up to that point, funds must be "borrowed" from surplus. The extent of the strain on statutory surplus may be mitigated through a modified reserve system.[4] Determination of the duration at which the full policy reserve is to be accumulated (when the asset share equals or exceeds the reserve) is a management decision influenced by the competitive situation. The length of time over which this takes place (where the company has a "book" loss on the block of policies) is known as the **validation period.** The shorter the period, the larger must be the gross premium or the lower must be policy benefits or margins for contingencies and/or profit.

It is not unusual for a well-established company to take eight to 12 years to amortize the acquisition expenses of a particular class of policies. Companies with a large volume of new business relative to their total volume in force or companies that expect termination rates to be high may amortize their acquisition expense within a period of five years or less.

Most companies expect policies to make some permanent contribution to surplus, the extent being a management decision limited by considerations of safety, equity, and competition.[5] The actual contribution as opposed to the "book" contribution of a block of policies (negative or positive) depends on the relationship between the asset share and the surrender value of the policy. When a policy is terminated by surrender, the reserves are released because, of course, the company is not required to maintain a reserve liability on its balance sheet for policies that are no longer in force. If the asset share exceeds the surrender payment, the company has a real gain. This typically occurs after the first few (e.g., three to 10) policy years. The asset share commonly is less than the surrender value in the early policy years, so the company has a real loss from surrenders during this period. Determining the point at which the asset share for a block of policies should equal or exceed the surrender value is an important management decision. Once a surrender has occurred, the impact of that policy on the company's gain or loss is fixed.

If the asset shares produced by the tentative gross premium rate structure are deficient in the light of company objectives, the premiums may be increased in some fashion or some specific item of expense or outgo (i.e., dividends, cash values, etc.) decreased. If the fund accumulation appears excessive, premiums can be reduced or benefits increased.

---

[3] Asset-share studies are also made using historical data. Such asset-share research is an integral part of monitoring developing experience and (for companies writing participating insurance) evaluating the adequacy and appropriateness of current dividend scales.

[4] See "Modified Reserve Systems," Chapter 20.

[5] The state of New York regulates the contribution that participating policies can make to surplus in the aggregate.

Selection of Most Probable Assumptions

If the asset-share calculations are to be a reasonable test of premium adequacy and equity between blocks of policies, the factors entering into the calculation must be chosen with great care. The assumptions underlying any mathematical model are critical to its effectiveness as a predictive device.

Mortality. Selection of the most probable assumption as to mortality is complicated by the secular trend toward mortality improvement. It might be argued that the asset-share study should reflect anticipated improvement in future mortality. The vast majority of companies do not reflect such anticipated improvement in their computations but do test under varying mortality scenarios. Regardless of this feature, all companies utilize the latest available experience.

The best source of information on current trends, incidence, and levels of mortality among ordinary insureds has been the *Reports* of the Committee on Mortality under Ordinary Insurance and Annuities, published annually by the Society of Actuaries. These data are compiled by the Committee from statistics supplied by a number of the largest life insurance companies. The experience is published on a select and ultimate basis. The death rates generally are shown for all ages on juvenile lives, but only at quinquennial age groups with respect to adult lives. Periodically, the committee publishes a graduated mortality table based on these data. Most larger companies use mortality from their own experience.

Interest. Determining the rates of interest to be used in asset-share calculations involves estimates of investment returns over the next 20 or more years. These estimates must be made with knowledge that the long-range impact of interest on life insurance is great. From the standpoint of the shareholder in a stock company, the leverage based on the margin between actual and assumed interest rates is enormous.

The rates selected normally will fall within a range of possible rates, the upper limit of which (during a period when interest rates are increas-

ing) is the rate being earned on new investments, and the lower limit the valuation rate of interest for policies currently being issued. For both mutual and stock companies, allowance is made in selecting these rates for the impact of U.S. federal income taxes. Furthermore, recognition can be given to the possibility of changes in earned interest rates in future years. For example, 9 or 10 percent might be assumed for years 1 to 10, with 7 percent thereafter.

Operating Expenses. Both mutual and stock companies develop their expense rates in a similar manner. The average size of new policies is computed by plan and age at issue, and applied to the constant expense per policy to permit the expression of expense rates in terms of a percentage of the premium plus a number of dollars per $1,000 of insurance. Since the expense factors are based on the average collection frequency of the company's business, the expenses within the asset-share study must be adjusted to reflect the estimated proportions of the types of premium payment frequency. If the tentative gross premium rate schedule was based on a detailed analysis of current expenses, these same expense rates could be used as a basis for estimating future expense. Otherwise, a detailed cost study must precede the asset-share calculation.

Termination Rates. Predicting future lapse (termination) rates is a difficult task. The difficulty is caused by the extreme fluctuations over the years, largely as a result of economic conditions. Although lapse rates generally are not as important to the adequacy test as the other three factors, for small companies with extremely high lapse rates during the early policy years, the financial implications can be quite significant.

As in the case of the other factors, it is customary to test over a range of termination rates based on the company's individual experience, although published studies naturally provide a guide.[6] Termination rates are influenced by many

[6]See M. A. Linton, *The Record of the American Institute of Actuaries*, Vol. XIII (1924), pp. 283–316; see also C.F.B. Richardson and John M. Hartwell, *Transactions of the Society of Actuaries*, Vol. III (1951), pp. 338–372; and Ernest J. Moorhead, "The Construction of Persistency Tables," *Transactions of the Society of Actuaries*, Vol. XII (1960), pp. 545–563.

factors, including the quality of the agency force, age at issue, amount of premium, frequency and method of premium payment, and others. In practice, termination rates usually are differentiated by the plan of insurance, age at issue, and frequency and method of premium payment. Under most plans, termination rates are highest the first two years and lower thereafter.

Termination rates are necessary in premium calculations only because of the disparity between surrender values and the asset shares available for distribution to withdrawing policyowners. If surrender values were exactly equal to each year's actual asset share, lapse rates could be ignored.

Sample Asset-Share Calculation

The process by which a gross premium rate schedule is tested was illustrated with an example in Table 2–6. That table is reproduced below as Table 21–2. It may be recalled that the gross premium for the ordinary life policy being tested was $15.50 per $1,000 and that cash values (column 7) were calculated on the minimum permitted bases (*1980 CSO* and 7½ percent) and that net level reserves (column 18) were used (at 6 percent and *1980 CSO*).

Other needed assumptions included expected death (column 3) and withdrawal rates (column 4), expected expenses (column 5), and illustrated dividends (column 8). A net investment earnings rate of 9 percent was assumed to be reasonable over the next 20 years. Column 17 gives the yearly asset shares for the hypothetical policy being tested, with column 19 providing the anticipated net surplus position of the company for this policy.[7]

The assumptions used in an asset-share calculation are supposed to represent the best estimates of what the actual experience will turn out to be. Invariably, however, actual results will deviate from those assumed. Companies expect

this. As a result, they will conduct several asset-share calculations with various underlying assumptions. This enables the actuary to judge the sensitivity of the results under varying possible future conditions.

Tables 21–3 through 21–10 present an indication of the sensitivity of the hypothetical asset-share calculation illustrated in Table 21–2 to change by showing the impact of the following changes in assumptions and benefits:

1. Decrease interest rates from 9 percent to 7 percent (policy never validates)
2. Increase mortality by 10 percent
3. Increase expenses by $1 the first year and $0.28 each subsequent year
4. Increase gross premium from $15.50 to $16.00
5. Reduce dividends by $0.50 each year except the first
6. Increase cash values above legal minimum
7. Change reserve basis from net level to Commissioners' Reserve Valuation Method (CRVM)
8. Increase withdrawal rates by 50 percent

In examining these tables, it is instructive to note the impact on the validation period in each case (see column 19). Similarly, note the point at which the block of policies would "be in the black" from a profit and loss standpoint (i.e., the time at which the **surrender contribution**[8] turns positive, the asset share having exceeded the surrender value).

Practically, of course, more than one factor may be adjusted simultaneously to examine the effects of the combined changes. Where a combination of adjustments is made, the strength and direction of change in asset-share values cannot always be determined intuitively. As mentioned earlier, computers permit a wide range of experimentation in finding a combination of factors that are compatible with the objectives of the company.

---

[7]No further discussion of the example based on the stated assumptions is presented here. See Chapter 2 for such a discussion.

[8]The term "surrender contribution" was coined by William H. Rabel of the Life Office Management Association.

TABLE 21-2. Asset-share calculation, $1,000 ordinary life issued at male age 35 ($15.50 rate per $1,000)

(1) Policy Year	(2) Number Paying Premiums at Beginning of Year	(3) Number Dying[a]	(4) Number Withdrawing[b]	(5) Number Alive at End of Year after Withdrawals [(2)−(3)−(4)]	(6) Expense Rate per $1,000	(7) Cash Value per $1,000 on Withdrawal[c]	(8) Dividend per $1,000
1	100,000	88	20,000	79,912	27.00	0.00	0.00
2	79,912	81	8,630	71,201	3.00	0.00	0.50
3	71,201	85	5,696	65,420	3.00	0.00	1.00
4	65,420	91	4,056	61,273	3.00	6.70	1.50
5	61,273	94	2,941	58,238	3.00	14.04	2.00
6	58,238	105	2,096	56,037	3.00	21.72	2.50
7	56,037	113	1,793	54,131	3.00	29.73	3.10
8	54,131	121	1,569	52,441	3.00	38.12	3.70
9	52,441	130	1,415	50,896	3.00	46.87	4.30
10	50,896	139	1,272	49,485	3.00	56.02	5.90
11	49,485	157	1,187	48,141	3.00	65.55	6.60
12	48,141	168	1,107	46,866	3.00	75.50	7.30
13	46,866	179	1,031	45,656	3.00	85.88	8.00
14	45,656	191	958	44,507	3.00	96.71	8.70
15	44,507	203	890	43,414	3.00	108.01	9.40
16	43,414	217	868	42,329	3.00	119.79	10.20
17	42,329	233	846	41,250	3.00	132.02	11.00
18	41,250	250	825	40,175	3.00	144.69	11.80
19	40,175	270	803	39,102	3.00	157.79	12.70
20	39,102	292	782	38,028	3.00	171.28	13.60

TABLE 21.2. (Continued)

Policy Year	(9) Fund at Beginning of Year [(16) Prior Year]	(10) Premium Income [($15.50)×(2)]	(11) Expense Disbursements [(2)×(6)]	(12) Death Claims [$1,000×(3)]	(13) Amount Paid on Surrender [(4)×(7)]	(14) Total Dividends Paid [(5)×(8)]
1	0	1,550,000	2,700,000	88,000	0	0
2	-1,345,460	1,238,636	239,736	81,000	0	35,601
3	-497,996	1,103,616	213,603	85,000	0	65,420
4	273,053	1,014,010	196,260	91,000	27,186	91,910
5	974,785	949,732	183,819	94,000	41,281	116,476
6	1,641,374	902,689	174,714	105,000	45,517	140,093
7	2,287,256	868,574	168,111	113,000	53,314	167,806
8	2,917,408	839,031	162,393	121,000	59,813	194,032
9	3,537,220	812,836	157,323	130,000	66,327	218,853
10	4,149,049	788,888	152,688	139,000	71,252	291,962
11	4,707,452	767,018	148,455	157,000	77,804	317,731
12	5,245,756	746,186	144,423	168,000	83,574	342,122
13	5,772,539	726,423	140,598	179,000	88,539	365,248
14	6,289,774	707,668	136,968	191,000	92,652	387,211
15	6,798,458	689,859	133,521	203,000	96,129	408,092
16	7,300,371	672,917	130,242	217,000	103,975	431,756
17	7,786,424	656,100	126,987	233,000	111,686	453,750
18	8,255,015	639,375	123,750	250,000	119,370	474,065
19	8,705,313	622,713	120,525	270,000	126,704	496,595
20	9,130,727	606,081	117,306	292,000	133,942	517,181

TABLE 21-2. (Continued)

Policy Year	(15) Interest Earned during Year {0.09 [(9)+(10)−(11)−½ (12)]}	(16) Fund at End of Year [(9)+(10)−(11)−(12)−(13)−(14)+(15)]	(17) Asset Share at End of Year: [(16)÷(5)]	(18) Reserve[d] at End of Year	(19) Surplus per $1,000 at End of Year [(17)−(18)]
1	−107,460	−1,345,460	−16.84	7.63	−24.47
2	−34,835	−497,996	−6.99	15.61	−22.61
3	31,456	273,053	4.17	23.94	−19.76
4	94,077	974,785	15.91	32.60	−16.69
5	152,433	1,641,374	28.18	41.61	−13.43
6	208,516	2,287,256	40.82	50.97	−10.15
7	263,810	2,917,408	53.90	60.67	−6.77
8	318,019	3,537,220	67.45	70.73	−3.27
9	371,496	4,149,049	81.52	81.14	0.38
10	424,417	4,707,452	95.13	91.93	3.20
11	472,276	5,245,756	108.97	103.09	5.87
12	518,717	5,772,539	123.17	114.65	8.52
13	564,198	6,289,774	137.76	126.61	11.15
14	608,848	6,798,458	152.75	138.99	13.76
15	652,797	7,300,371	168.16	151.79	16.36
16	696,109	7,786,424	183.95	165.03	18.92
17	737,913	8,255,015	200.12	178.66	21.46
18	778,108	8,705,313	216.68	192.68	24.01
19	816,525	9,130,727	233.51	207.06	26.45
20	852,615	9,528,994	250.58	221.77	28.81

[a]Deaths based on select and ultimate experience mortality table. Deaths assumed to occur in middle of policy year on the average.

[b]Withdrawals based on Linton BA lapse rates. Assumed to occur on anniversary at end of policy year.

[c]Minimum required cash values; 7½ percent interest assumption.

[d]Net-level-premium reserves, 1980 CSO Table, 6%.

TABLE 21-3. Asset-share calculation with 7 percent interest rate instead of 9 percent

(1) Policy Year	(17) Asset Share at End of Year	(18) Reserve at End of Year	(19) Surplus per $1,000 at End of Year [(17) − (18)]	(20) Surrender Contribution per $1,000 at End of Year [(17) − (7)]
1	$ − 16.54	$ 7.63	$ − 24.17	$ − 16.54
2	− 6.53	15.61	− 22.14	− 6.53
3	4.61	23.94	− 19.32	4.61
4	16.07	32.60	− 16.54	9.36
5	27.78	41.61	− 13.83	13.74
6	39.54	50.97	− 11.43	17.83
7	51.40	60.67	− 9.27	21.67
8	63.35	70.73	− 7.38	25.23
9	75.37	81.14	− 5.77	28.50
10	86.46	91.93	− 5.47	30.44
11	97.25	103.09	− 5.84	31.70
12	107.83	114.65	− 6.82	32.34
13	118.17	126.61	− 8.44	32.30
14	128.21	138.99	− 10.79	31.49
15	137.89	151.79	− 13.90	29.88
16	147.08	165.03	− 17.94	27.30
17	155.67	178.66	− 22.99	23.65
18	163.54	192.68	− 29.14	18.85
19	170.45	207.06	− 36.62	12.66
20	176.21	221.77	− 45.56	4.93

TABLE 21-4. Asset-share calculation with a 10 percent increase in mortality

(1) Policy Year	(17) Asset Share at End of Year	(18) Reserve at End of Year	(19) Surplus per $1,000 at End of Year [(17) − (18)]	(20) Surrender Contribution per $1,000 at End of Year [(17) − (7)]
1	$ − 16.96	$ 7.63	$ − 24.59	$ − 16.96
2	− 7.27	15.61	− 22.89	− 7.27
3	3.71	23.94	− 20.22	3.71
4	15.22	32.60	− 17.38	8.52
5	27.22	41.61	− 14.39	13.19
6	39.53	50.97	− 11.44	17.81
7	52.24	60.67	− 8.43	22.50
8	65.36	70.73	− 5.36	27.24
9	78.92	81.14	− 2.22	32.05
10	91.95	91.93	0.01	35.93
11	105.08	103.09	1.99	39.54
12	118.50	114.65	3.85	43.01
13	132.17	126.61	5.56	46.30
14	146.13	138.99	7.13	49.41
15	160.34	151.79	8.54	52.33
16	174.76	165.03	9.74	54.98
17	189.37	178.66	10.71	57.35
18	204.13	192.68	11.45	59.44
19	218.87	207.06	11.81	61.09
20	233.57	221.77	11.79	62.28

TABLE 21-5. Asset-share calculation with expenses increased by $1 the first year and $0.28 each subsequent year

(1) Policy Year	(17) Asset Share at End of Year	(18) Reserve at End of Year	(19) Surplus per $1,000 at End of Year [(17) − (18)]	(20) Surrender Contribution per $1,000 at End of Year [(17) − (7)]
1	$ − 18.20	$ 7.63	$ − 25.83	$ − 18.20
2	− 9.01	15.61	− 24.62	− 9.01
3	1.46	23.94	− 22.48	1.46
4	12.42	32.60	− 20.18	5.72
5	23.86	41.61	− 17.75	9.83
6	35.60	50.97	− 15.37	13.89
7	47.70	60.67	− 12.97	17.96
8	60.16	70.73	− 10.56	22.04
9	73.02	81.14	− 8.12	26.14
10	85.28	91.93	− 6.65	29.27
11	97.62	103.09	− 5.47	32.08
12	110.16	114.65	− 4.50	34.66
13	122.89	126.61	− 3.72	37.01
14	135.80	138.99	− 3.19	39.09
15	148.91	151.79	− 2.89	40.90
16	162.12	165.03	− 2.91	42.33
17	175.39	178.66	− 3.27	43.37
18	188.69	192.68	− 3.99	44.00
19	201.85	207.06	− 5.21	44.06
20	214.78	221.77	− 7.00	43.49

TABLE 21-6. Asset-share calculation with gross premium increased to $16.00

(1) Policy Year	(17) Asset Share at End of Year	(18) Reserve at End of Year	(19) Surplus per $1,000 at End of Year [(17) − (18)]	(20) Surrender Contribution per $1,000 at End of Year [(17) − (7)]
1	$ − 16.15	$ 7.63	$ − 23.79	$ − 16.15
2	− 5.55	15.61	− 21.16	− 5.55
3	6.48	23.94	− 17.45	6.48
4	19.18	32.60	− 13.43	12.47
5	32.51	41.61	− 9.11	18.47
6	46.28	50.97	− 4.69	24.56
7	60.62	60.67	− 0.04	30.89
8	75.58	70.73	4.86	37.46
9	91.21	81.14	10.07	44.34
10	106.56	91.93	14.63	50.54
11	122.33	103.09	19.24	56.78
12	138.70	114.65	24.04	63.20
13	155.69	126.61	29.08	69.82
14	173.36	138.99	34.36	76.64
15	191.74	151.79	39.95	83.73
16	210.88	165.03	45.85	91.09
17	230.80	178.66	52.14	98.78
18	251.58	192.68	58.90	106.89
19	273.15	207.06	66.09	115.36
20	295.56	221.77	73.79	124.28

TABLE 21-7. Asset-share calculation with dividends reduced by $0.50 each year except the first

(1) Policy Year	(17) Asset Share at End of Year	(18) Reserve at End of Year	(19) Surplus per $1,000 at End of Year [(17) − (18)]	(20) Surrender Contribution per $1,000 at End of Year [(17) − (7)]
1	$ − 16.84	$ 7.63	$ − 24.47	$ − 16.84
2	− 6.49	15.61	− 22.11	− 6.49
3	5.27	23.94	− 18.67	5.27
4	17.68	32.60	− 14.92	10.98
5	30.72	41.61	− 10.90	16.68
6	44.19	50.97	− 6.79	22.47
7	58.20	60.67	− 2.47	28.46
8	72.79	70.73	2.06	34.67
9	88.02	81.14	6.88	41.14
10	102.91	91.93	10.98	46.90
11	118.19	103.09	15.09	52.64
12	133.99	114.65	19.34	58.50
13	150.37	126.61	23.76	64.50
14	167.35	138.99	28.36	70.64
15	184.97	151.79	33.18	76.96
16	203.25	165.03	38.22	83.46
17	222.21	178.66	43.55	90.19
18	241.90	192.68	49.22	97.21
19	262.25	207.06	55.19	104.46
20	283.29	221.77	61.52	112.01

TABLE 21-8. Asset-share calculation with cash values increased above legal minimun

(1) Policy Year	(17) Asset Share at End of Year	(18) Reserve at End of Year	(19) Surplus per $1,000 at End of Year [(17) − (18)]	(20) Surrender Contribution per $1,000 at End of Year [(17) − (7)]
1	$ − 16.84	$ 7.63	$ − 24.47	$ − 16.84
2	− 6.99	15.61	− 22.61	− 6.99
3	3.91	23.94	− 20.02	0.94
4	15.27	32.60	− 17.34	3.44
5	27.09	41.61	− 14.52	6.06
6	39.25	50.97	− 11.72	8.66
7	51.77	60.67	− 8.89	11.27
8	64.68	70.73	− 6.04	13.91
9	78.01	81.14	− 3.13	16.60
10	90.77	91.93	− 1.16	18.33
11	103.63	103.09	0.54	19.79
12	116.72	114.65	2.07	21.08
13	130.05	126.61	3.44	22.19
14	143.61	138.99	4.62	23.11
15	157.42	151.79	5.63	23.84
16	171.39	165.03	6.36	24.29
17	185.48	178.66	6.82	24.45
18	199.67	192.68	6.99	24.32
19	213.79	207.06	6.73	23.75
20	227.78	221.77	6.01	22.72

TABLE 21-9. Asset-share calculation with modified reserves

(1) Policy Year	(17) Asset Share at End of Year	(18) Reserve at End of Year	(19) Surplus per $1,000 at End of Year [(17) − (18)]	(20) Surrender Contribution per $1,000 at End of Year [(17) − (7)]
1	$ − 16.84	$ 0.00	$ − 16.84	$ − 16.84
2	− 6.99	8.04	− 15.03	− 6.99
3	4.17	16.43	− 12.26	4.17
4	15.91	25.16	− 9.25	9.21
5	28.18	34.24	− 6.06	14.15
6	40.82	43.67	− 2.85	19.10
7	53.90	53.44	0.46	24.16
8	67.45	63.58	3.87	29.33
9	81.52	74.07	7.45	34.65
10	95.13	84.95	10.18	39.11
11	108.97	96.19	12.78	43.42
12	123.17	107.84	15.33	47.67
13	137.76	119.89	17.87	51.89
14	152.75	132.37	20.38	56.04
15	168.16	145.27	22.89	60.15
16	183.95	158.60	25.35	64.16
17	200.12	172.34	27.78	68.11
18	216.68	186.47	30.21	71.99
19	233.51	200.96	32.55	75.72
20	250.58	215.79	34.79	79.30

TABLE 21-10. Asset-share calculation with withdrawal rate increased 50 percent

(1) Policy Year	(17) Asset Share at End of Year	(18) Reserve at End of Year	(19) Surplus per $1,000 at End of Year [(17) − (18)]	(20) Surrender Contribution per $1,000 at End of Year [(17) − (7)]
1	$ − 19.25	$ 7.63	$ − 26.88	$ − 19.25
2	− 10.55	15.61	− 26.17	− 10.55
3	− 0.11	23.94	− 23.94	− 0.01
4	11.26	32.60	− 21.35	4.55
5	23.11	41.61	− 18.50	9.08
6	35.37	50.97	− 15.60	13.66
7	48.11	60.67	− 12.56	18.38
8	61.36	70.73	− 9.37	23.24
9	75.15	81.14	− 5.99	28.27
10	88.46	91.93	− 3.47	32.45
11	102.02	103.09	− 1.08	36.47
12	115.95	114.65	1.30	40.45
13	130.27	126.61	3.65	44.39
14	144.99	138.99	6.00	48.28
15	160.11	151.79	8.32	52.10
16	175.65	165.03	10.62	55.86
17	191.57	178.66	12.92	59.56
18	207.88	192.68	15.20	63.19
19	224.44	207.06	17.38	66.66
20	241.29	221.77	19.52	70.01

OTHER ASPECTS

Premiums Paid at Intervals of Less Than 1 Year

The calculations earlier in this text illustrate the determination of an annual premium. It would be possible to follow the same principles for any unit of time, but the mortality tables in existence are not graded for periods of less than a year. When the policyowner pays other than annually, a "carrying charge" is added to the "fractional premiums" based on the company's experience.

The purpose of the carrying charge is to reimburse the insurance company for the additional expense associated with more frequent premium collection, to offset the loss of interest stemming from the deferment of part of the year's premium, and to compensate for the higher lapse rates that may arise when premiums are paid other than annually. In addition, the carrying charge should be viewed as including an element of life insurance, because companies do not collect any remaining fractional premiums in the year of death.

A fractional premium often is calculated by multiplying the annual premium by a specified factor and, sometimes, adding to the result a flat dollar amount. Common factors for semiannual premiums are 0.51, 0.515, and 0.52; for quarterly premiums, 0.26, 0.2625, and 0.265; and for monthly premiums, 0.083, 0.0875, and 0.09.

Return of Premium Policies

Policies sometimes include a provision whereby on the death of the insured, an additional death benefit equal to the sum of the premiums paid will be paid to the beneficiary if death occurs within a stipulated time period. In actuality, of course, the company does not "return" the paid premiums. It simply calculates its premiums on the basis that the amount of life insurance protection each year equals the policy face amount plus an additional death benefit equal to the then sum of the premiums paid to date.

Premium Rates Graded by Size of Policy

It was pointed out earlier that certain expenses vary with the number of policies. If the premium formula were to incorporate a constant for this element that did not vary by amount of insurance, the premium rate per $1,000 would decline as the face of the policy increased.

In the case where multiple size classifications are being used, two quantity discount systems have developed in practice.[9] Each is discussed below separately. It should be noted, however, that most insurers use *both* systems.

Under the **band system,** a number of "size bands," usually four or five, is established, with different premium rates applying within each class. The following would be a typical arrangement under this sytem:

Size Band	Premium per $1,000 for a Particular Plan and Age
$ 10,000– 49,999	$16.00
50,000– 99,999	15.00
100,000–249,999	14.50
250,000–499,999	14.25
500,000 and over	14.00

Under the **policy fee system,** the premium for a policy is expressed as the product of the amount of the policy and a "basic" rate per $1,000, plus a flat amount (known as the **policy fee**). For a particular plan and age, the premium might be $25 plus $16.50 per $1,000. This would work out to $355 for a $20,000 policy, for example; $850 for a $50,000 policy; $1,675 for a $100,000 policy; and so on.

With both systems, the loading formula is modified so that the amount of expense that is deemed to be independent of size is treated accordingly in determining the premium. It should be remembered, however, that the total amount necessary to cover expenses is not changed by such gradations, and the lower-amount policies must of necessity pay a higher rate to offset the "discount" granted to the larger-amount policies.

[9]Elgin G. Fassell, "Premium Rates Varying by Policy Size," *Transactions of the Society of Actuaries,* Vol. VIII (November 1956).

SURPLUS AND ITS DISTRIBUTION

The earlier chapters made clear that life insurance policies sold today often contain elements that are not wholly guaranteed. Participating life insurance policies, of course, always have been characterized for their nonguaranteed aspect—dividends. However, with the advent of indeterminate premiums and charges and of excess interest credits—all on nonparticipating policies—the entire area of nonguaranteed policy elements has assumed greater prominence than formerly. The actuarial aspects of how companies determine excess interest and other credits on such policies is not well defined at this time, and the standards to be applied are not yet agreed upon . Since earlier chapters have already discussed such policies[10] and because of the great uncertainties concerning acceptable actuarial standards and practices that may ultimately be applicable to this area, no additional discussion of these policies will be presented in this section. Rather, the emphasis will be on surplus distribution for participating policies.

Nature of Surplus

Guaranteed life insurance premiums are calculated conservatively. This is essential if an insurer is not to jeopardize its long-term viability. Consequently, it is expected that over time companies normally will show a gain from operations. The immediate result of a gain is to increase the surplus position of the company. The size and disposition of this gain will depend, in addition to other factors, on whether the business written by the company is on a participating basis; a guaranteed cost, nonparticipating basis; or one of the current assumption nonparticipating bases.

In the aggregate, statutory surplus will develop only if a company accumulates funds in excess of those needed to establish policy reserves and other liabilities.[11] Surplus arises out of favorable deviations from the assumed experience as to mortality, interest, and loading contained in

the gross premium. These constitute the primary sources of additions to surplus and usually are designated as **mortality savings, excess interest,** and **loading savings.** The word "savings" is used here to connote both the residue arising from operations that were more efficient and economical than anticipated and margins intentionally provided in fixing the gross premium rate schedule. It is important to remember that even though participating premiums usually are made conservative, capable management can make a significant difference in the yearly amounts added to surplus.

The statutory surplus of a company arising from a given block of policies consists of the sum of the excess interest, mortality savings, and savings from loading, plus gains from minor sources. For some policies, ages at issue, and durations, some or all of the three gains could be negative. In particular, it is almost always the case for the savings from loading to be negative in the first policy year, when the company's expenses are high.

Gains from Investment Earnings. Since life insurance policies often are written for a long term of years, it is essential that companies assume a conservative rate of interest for their net premium and reserve computations to assure its being earned throughout the life of the contract. If a company has based its reserves on the assumption that it will earn 5 percent but actually earns 7 percent, that difference of 2 percent represents the excess of investment earnings over the return necessary to maintain reserve liabilities of the company and, if considered advisable, may be returned to the policyowners who contributed it.

Gains from Mortality. This gain arises because life insurance companies in the United States do not experience, normally, as heavy a mortality as is indicated by the mortality table employed by them in reserve calculations. In view

---

[10]See Chapters 2, 6, and 9.

[11]Insurers' decisions regarding surplus distribution to policyowners are heavily influenced by the statutory accounting procedures required by state insurance regulators. As a result,

this decision focuses on *statutory* surplus as opposed to surplus as would be measured by a realistic assessment of the company's cash flows. The difference in approaches should not affect the ultimate amount of surplus generated by a block of policies; only the timing of the recognition.

of the fact that the reserve mortality table deliberately is made conservative, it is natural that a surplus gain normally results from operations. It is important not to place too much reliance on one year's mortality experience, since it tends to fluctuate from year to year. In the interest of stability and safety, therefore, most companies average mortality experience over a period of years. It is important to remember that a surplus gain does not necessarily mean that the block of policies is profitable. The surplus gain or loss relates actual experience to the reserve liability value which usually is very conservative.

Gains from Loading. Sound insurance company management dictates that the gross premium should be more than sufficient to meet normal requirements, so that the company and its policyowners may be protected against exceptional conditions. In fact, as pointed out earlier, the loading on a participating policy frequently includes an amount for dividends to the policyowner together with the surplus gains from other sources. Competitive conditions, especially in the matter of agents' commissions, as well as inflationary pressures on expenses, have at times caused expenses to exceed loadings in the aggregate. In recent years, utilizing increasingly sophisticated computer systems, life insurance companies have made a marked effort toward economical management.

Gains from Surrenders. Surrender values, as explained previously, normally are less than policy reserves. The difference between (1) reserves released as a result of surrender and (2) surrender values allowed constitutes another source of statement surplus. Such a gain frequently represents, in whole or in part, amounts returned to surplus that originally were taken from it to establish the reserves. In general, a surplus gain from surrenders will be a "paper" gain—a repayment of previously borrowed surplus—where the asset share is less than the policy surrender value. The gain will be a "real" gain where the asset share is greater than the surrender value. "Real" gains derived from this source are usually treated as

an offset to expenses when calculations are made to apportion divisible surplus to policyowners.[12]

Distribution of Surplus

Divisible Surplus. Following each year's operations, a company must determine how much of the total surplus (previously existing plus additions for the year) should be retained as a contingency fund or other special surplus appropriation and how much should be distributed to policyowners. No fixed relationship may exist between the surplus gain in a particular calendar year and the dividends distributed to policyowners on the next policy anniversaries. The directors or trustees of the company, as a matter of business judgment, make the decision. The amount earmarked for distribution is designated as **divisible surplus,** and once set aside by action of the directors or trustees, loses its identity as surplus and becomes a liability of the company.

In deciding what portion of the total surplus should be retained as contingency funds, a balance must be maintained between the need for a general contingency fund and the competitive advantages of a liberal dividend scale. When the surplus earned for any given year is not sufficient to permit the company to maintain its current dividend scale, the management may decide to use a portion of the general contingency fund for this purpose.[13] On the other hand, if during a temporary period, additions to surplus are more than adequate to support the existing dividend scale, the excess will usually be added to the general contingency fund to avoid the expense and complications involved in changing the scale. If the excess is substantial and is expected to continue over a reasonable period, competitive con-

---

[12]In the apportionment of surplus, as will be explained in a later section, it has been found that it is more practical to treat all surpluses as coming from the three main sources mentioned previously: loading, interest earnings, and mortality. Surplus from other sources, such as forfeitures and appreciation in the value of assets is therefore not treated separately, but considered in connection with expenses and interest earnings respectively.

[13]A given company may earmark a special fund for "dividend fluctuations," but the principle is the same.

siderations will usually lead to a change in the scale.

In the interest of security of the benefits and good management, life insurance companies maintain surplus and general contingency funds that bear a reasonable relationship to liabilities. As policy reserves increase through new business and the natural accretion under old policies, surplus and general contingency funds should also increase. With many companies, each policy is expected to make a permanent contribution to the surplus of the company. These contributions enable companies to fulfill their contractual obligations even in the face of a severe catastrophe of the type that may occur only once in several decades. Thus, over the entire lifetime of a class of policies, aggregate dividend distributions[14] made often will be somewhat less than the contributions of the class to surplus. On the other hand, some companies have a dividend practice that results in substantially complete liquidation of each generation's contributions to surplus by the time that generation of policies is eliminated from the books.

Although companies may, in the absence of legislation, use their discretion in determining the amount of surplus to be distributed, some states regulate this matter by statute. New York limits the amount of surplus a company can retain on its participating business to an amount not exceeding $850,000, or 10 percent of its policy reserves and other policy liabilities, whichever is greater. The purpose of this legislation is to prevent companies from retaining more surplus than is judged necessary to offset factors such as fluctuations in the mortality rate and interest earnings that may interfere with the payment of stable dividends.

Frequency of Distribution. Dividends on practically all participating policies sold in the United States at the present time are paid annually. In many states this is required by statute. A few policies are still in existence on which deferred dividends are paid.

Deferred dividends are those that are not

payable until the close of a stipulated number of years, such as five, 10, 15, or 20. Policies providing for payment of dividends in this manner commonly are called deferred-dividend, accumulation, distribution, or semi-tontine policies. The underlying principle of the plan is that those policyowners who fail to continue premium payments to the end of the designated period—because of death, surrender, or lapse—lose the dividends they would have received under the annual-dividend plan. The lost dividends revert to those policyowners who continue their premium payments throughout the deferred-dividend period.

The deferred-dividend plan lost favor with the public, and as stated before, it has been almost wholly superseded by the annual-distribution system. The latter plan, it is argued, is well adapted to the policyowner who wishes to keep his or her annual net outlay to the lowest possible figures and also serves to encourage managerial economy, since extravagance could be revealed by a reduction in the annual-dividend distribution.

The deferred system in a modified form is still used to some extent in Canada. Under Canadian law, dividend distributions may be made every five years, but the amount of surplus set aside for deferred dividends during a five-year period must be carried as a liability until it is paid. Most Canadian companies pay an interim dividend in the event of death during the period, but not in the event of lapse or surrender.

The Contribution Principle. The allocation of divisible surplus among policyowners is a complex matter: Equity is the theoretical objective, but consideration must be given to competition, flexibility, and simplicity. That the allocation must be competitive is obvious. Flexibility can be viewed as a facet of equity, since adaptability to changing circumstances is essential if equity is to be attained. Simplicity is desirable both from an expense viewpoint and from the viewpoint of understanding by agents and policyowners. The earlier discussion of the sources of surplus would suggest that one way of obtaining reasonable equity would be *to return to each class of policyowners a share of the divisible surplus proportionate to the contribution of the class to the surplus.*

[14]This includes, in addition to the usual dividends distributed annually, extra dividends and terminal dividends. See below.

This concept is known as the **contribution principle.** It should be noted that the principle does not require the return of all contributions to surplus. It merely requires that the divisible surplus be allotted to the policyowners in the approximate proportion in which they contributed to it. This principle underlies the equity implicit in participating insurance.

The Three-Factor Contribution Method.
The contribution principle provides the underlying philosophical base for surplus distribution. The most widely used approach for applying the principle is referred to as the three-factor contribution method.[15]

The three-factor contribution method is based on an analysis of the sources of surplus and develops dividends that vary with the plan of insurance, age of issue, and duration of the policy. In the interest of simplicity, consideration is usually limited to the three major sources of surplus: excess interest, mortality savings, and loading savings. Where special benefits are involved, such as disability and accidental death, an additional factor is sometimes included for these features.

1. *The formula.*[16] The three-factor contribution method may be expressed generally as

$$D_t = I_t + M_t + E_t$$

where D_t = dividend per \$1,000 payable at the end of policy year t

I_t = excess interest factor for policy year t

M_t = mortality savings factor for policy year t

E_t = expense savings factor for policy year t

Each of the three factors, in turn, can be determined by the following formulas:

$$I_t = (i_t' - i_t)(_{t-1}V_x + _tP_x)$$

$$M_t = (q_{x+t-1} - q_{x+t-1}')(1,000 - _tV_x)$$

$$E_t = (_tG_x - _tP_x - _te_x)(1 + i_t')$$

where x = age of issue

i_t' = dividend interest rate in policy year t

i_t = reserve interest rate in policy year t

$_tV_x$ = t^{th} policy year's terminal reserve per \$1,000 for a policy issued at age x

$_tP_x$ = t^{th} policy year's valuation annual premium per \$1,000 for a policy issued at age x

q_x = reserve mortality rate at age x

q_x' = dividend mortality rate at age x

$_tG_x$ = t^{th} policy year's gross annual premium per \$1,000 for a policy issued at age x

$_te_x$ = t^{th} policy year's expense charge per \$1,000 for a policy issued at age x

The following sections will consider briefly the operation of the preceding formula. The discussion of each factor will include a sample calculation for that factor. The sample will be based on a hypothetical \$10,000 ordinary life policy issued 15 years ago to a male *then* age 25. The gross annual premium is \$170.00 (\$17.00 per \$1,000). Net-level-premium reserves are assumed to be calculated on the *1958 CSO Table,* with interest of 3 percent. The valuation net annual premium calculated on these assumptions is \$11.28 per \$1,000. Policy reserves per \$1,000 face amount at the end of the fourteenth and fifteenth policy years are \$162.97 and \$176.80, respectively.

2. *Interest factor.* The interest factor (I_t) is the simplest element of the dividend, consisting of the excess interest on, usually, the initial reserve for the policy period at the end of which the dividend is payable.[17] Recall that the initial reserve

[15] Another method of computing dividends is the so-called experience-premium method, which is used by a number of companies in this country. Its purpose is to avoid decreases in dividends on any plan, even with a very low excess-interest factor. See Joseph B. Maclean, *Life Insurance,* 9th ed. (New York: McGraw-Hill Book Company, 1962) pp. 159–160.

[16] See Joseph M. Belth, ''Distribution of Surplus to Individual Life Insurance Policy Owners,'' *The Journal of Risk and Insurance,* Vol. XLV (March 1978), pp. 10–11.

[17] Many companies utilize the mean reserve on premium-paying policies and the initial reserve on policies where premiums have been fully paid.

is the previous year's terminal reserve $(_{t-1}V_x)$ plus the valuation net level premium $(_tP_x)$.

Assume that the dividend interest rate is 8 percent for this policy.[18] Under such circumstances, the rate of excess interest $(i_t' - i_t)$ would be 5 percent. Thus, on the $10,000 ordinary life policy issued at male age 25 that had been in force 15 years, the per $1,000 interest factor of the dividend would be as follows:

$$I_t = (i_t' - i_t)(_{t-1}V_x + _tP_x)$$

$$I_{15} = (i_{15}' - i_{15})(_{14}V_{25} + _{15}P_{25})$$

$$= (0.08 - 0.03)(\$162.97 + \$11.28)$$

$$= (0.05)\ (\$174.25)$$

$$= \$8.71$$

The interest factor has a strong influence on the dividend, particularly at long durations where the reserve is large.

Although the interest factor is simple in concept, several complications arise in application. Several bases are used to compute the rate of investment yield.[19] For purposes of asset-share studies underlying the dividend formula, it is common to use a base consisting of the interest-bearing liabilities and surplus. Interest-bearing liabilities include policy reserves, funds held under settlement agreements, dividend accumulations, and advance premiums.[20] Where certain items, such as dividend accumulations, have a minimum guarantee, some companies credit such items only with the guaranteed rate and increase the net effective rate for regular policy dividend purposes. The final rate utilized in the dividend formula may well be less than the rate used in the asset-share studies. This results in a contribution to the assets backing general contingency reserves, part of which ultimately may be distributed as a termination dividend (see below). With many companies, the excess-interest factor reflects the general trend of the company's investment earnings and would be set at a level that, according to the best judgment of the company, should be appropriate for a number of years. For short periods of time, the factor could be based on a higher rate than is actually being earned.

Some companies vary the dividend interest rate by the length of time the policy has been in force. Such companies artificially segregate policies into different "generations" and use a dividend interest rate for each generation that is based on the investment return on the assets accumulated on behalf of that generation. Thus, different generations easily could be credited with different interest rates. This **investment generation method** of investment income allocation tends to produce a dividend pattern that can change rapidly as earnings change.

Other insurers base their dividend interest rate on the average investment return of their entire asset portfolio. This **portfolio average method** does not segregate policies into generations, instead using the same dividend interest rate for all participating policies. This method produces a more stable dividend pattern than one based on the investment generation method. Both of these methods of investment income allocation, as discussed in earlier chapters, have been subject to considerable discussion and debate, and render cost comparisons between such policies more difficult.[21] Questions have been raised about possible incomplete disclosure and the possibility of a company switching from one method to the other, depending on market rate changes.[22]

Many companies also tie their dividend interest rate directly or indirectly to the policy loan rate or activity. Thus, under the **direct recognition** approach discussed earlier, the excess interest rate will be based directly on the policy loan activity and rate.[23] If a policyowner borrows heavily under his or her policy at a favorable in-

---

[18]Actual dividend interest rates can vary significantly from company to company.

[19]For example, the base logically could be ledger assets, admitted assets, or invested funds.

[20]Most companies will permit policyowners to prepay premiums by discounting them at a given rate of interest. The discounted premiums so paid are applied as of the appropriate premium due dates. In the event of the death of the insured, all unapplied premiums (less unearned discount) are returned to the beneficiary.

[21]See Chapters 6, 9, and 10.

[22]The 1984 NAIC Model Life Insurance Disclosure Regulation would require mutual insurers to disclose their practices in this regard.

[23]See Chapters 6 and 9.

terest rate relative to the market rate, this could have the effect of lowering dividends.

The treatment of capital gains and losses on assets other than stocks and bonds also can vary between companies. Some companies take these into account in fixing the dividend interest rate when they reflect actual market transactions as opposed to unrealized gains or losses arising out of adjustments in book value. The more common practice, however, is to transfer such gains and losses to an investment fluctuation fund or to a general contingency reserve, where over a period of time the gains and losses tend to offset each other. This stabilizes net interest earnings.

Companies also differ in the treatment of investment expenses. They particularly differ in their treatment of general overhead expenses and federal income taxes. This can make a significant difference, and although this should not affect the aggregate amount of surplus distributed, it does affect the pattern of distribution as between blocks of policies.

Under the three-factor contribution approach, the correct base to apply the dividend interest rate is the initial reserve *less* one-half a year's cost of insurance. The difference between this theoretically correct base and the mean reserve is small. Although the mean reserve would be a more accurate measure of the policy funds available for investment, the difference in results is so insignificant that most companies continue to use the initial reserve without the adjustment for one-half year's cost of insurance.

With a constant dividend interest rate, the excess-interest contribution increases with duration if reserves increase. At all ages of issue and durations, it is larger for higher-premium forms than for lower-premium policies. Thus, assuming the same duration and age of issue, excess interest makes a greater contribution to the dividend of a 20-year endowment policy than of an ordinary life policy, particularly at longer durations.

3. *Mortality factor.* The mortality factor in the three-factor formula can be derived by multiplying (1) the difference between the mortality rate used for reserve computation (q_x) and the (usually) lower rate to be used for dividend purposes (q_x') by (2) the year's net amount at risk

$(1,000 - {}_tV_x)$. Continuing with the earlier example, the mortality savings for the 15-year-old ordinary life policy, with reserves based on the *1958 CSO Table* and 3 percent interest, would be calculated as follows (assuming $q_{39}' = 0.00225$):

$$M_t = (q_{x+t-1} - q_{x+t-1}')(1,000 - {}_tV_x)$$

$$M_{15} = (q_{39} - q_{39}')(1,000 - {}_{15}V_{25})$$

$$= (0.00325 - 0.00225)(\$1,000 - \$176.80)$$

$$= (0.001)(\$823.20)$$

$$= \$0.82$$

Thus, the mortality savings factor for our example policy in year 15 is $0.82 per $1,000. Adding this $0.82 to the excess interest factor of $8.71, yields a total of $9.53 as that portion of the fifteenth year's policy dividend attributable to mortality savings (M_t) and excess interest (I_t). There remains but to add to this sum the loading savings factor (see below).

Many companies will express the mortality savings factor as a percentage of the assumed "cost of insurance."[24] The percentage for any block of policies generally depends only on the attained age of the insured and the company's experience among all insureds at that age and duration. The mortality factor of the formula normally takes the form of a scale of percentages of the assumed cost of insurance, decreasing with attained age, and reflecting the company's actual mortality experience age by age as compared with the rates shown in the mortality table assumed in calculating reserves. The scale of percentages may range from a high of 40 to 50 percent at the younger ages to a low of 5 to 10 percent at the older ages. Since mortality experience under term policies is often considerably different age by age from that of cash value plans, a separate scale of mortality savings often would be applied to such classes of policies.

The percentage utilized in the final dividend calculation normally is based on the ultimate mortality experience, although the select experience is utilized in the asset share underlying the development of the dividend distributions. Otherwise, a decreasing dividend scale by duration could

[24]See Chapter 20.

result because of large mortality savings at early durations. The savings from the effect of selection are assumed to be applied toward the payment of excess first-year expenses and hence are distributed indirectly in accordance with the method used to assess expenses to the various blocks of policies.

The mortality contribution normally is smallest on the higher-premium plans and higher ages of issue since the net amounts at risk are smaller. With advancing duration, a declining percentage factor is applied to a steadily smaller net amount at risk and hence in the usual case, a smaller cost of insurance. The higher the premium (because of plan or age at issue), the more pronounced is the decline in mortality savings. This is not invariably so, however. The cost of insurance actually increases at the higher ages under certain types of policies. In these cases, the increase in the rate of mortality more than offsets the decrease in the net amount at risk, resulting in an increased mortality cost for the year. In general, however, the mortality factor results in a decreasing contribution with greater durations.

In contrast to the interest factor, the mortality contribution is highly significant for term insurance policies. The percentage factor is applied to a larger net amount at risk, and hence cost of insurance, resulting in a relatively greater proportionate contribution to the dividends distributable to term policies.

4. Loading factor. The loading factor (E_t) of the dividend consists of the difference between (1) the gross premium and (2) the valuation net premium and an expense charge, with the difference taken as a year-end figure by increasing the amount for a year's interest at the dividend interest rate. Recall that in our example, the gross premium per $1,000 was $17.00 and the valuation net annual premium was $11.28. Assume the fifteenth year's expense charge to be $5.00. The loading savings factor for the example would therefore be calculated as follows:

$$E_t = ({}_tG_x - {}_tP_x - {}_te_x)(1 + i_t')$$

$$E_{15} = ({}_{15}G_{25} - {}_{15}P_{25} - {}_{15}e_{25})(1 + i_{15}')$$

$$= (\$17.00 - \$11.28 - \$5.00)(1 + 0.08)$$

$$= (\$0.72)(1.08)$$

$$= \$0.78$$

Thus, the loading factor for our example for policy year 15 is $0.78. The fifteenth year's dividend per $1,000 face amount for our hypothetical policy is therefore

$$D_t = I_t + M_t + E_t$$

$$D_{15} = I_{15} + M_{15} + E_{15}$$

$$= \$8.71 + \$0.82 + \$0.78$$

$$= \$10.31$$

The assessment of expenses probably presents one of the greatest difficulties connected with the distribution of surplus, as discussed earlier in this chapter. In general, the expense charge frequently is in the form of "a percentage and a constant"—that is, a percentage of the premium and a constant of so many dollars and cents per $1,000 of face amount. The constant may vary to allow for differences in the average amount of policy by plan of insurance. The percentage element of the expense charge usually is on a decreasing basis, at least for the first few years, to reflect the lower expenses after the first two years. There are wide differences among companies, both in gross premiums charged and in the manner of computing the expense charge. Consequently, the importance of the loading factor will vary considerably, the amount being much higher in a company with "high" gross premiums than in a company utilizing "low" gross premiums. The pattern in most cases, however, is for the loading contribution to increase for the first few years and thereafter to increase slightly or remain roughly constant.

5. Dividend pattern. For most plans of whole life insurance, the annual dividend under the contribution plan usually will increase with duration. This is entirely aside from an increase in the scale itself. The normal increase of dividends with duration is due to the fact that the interest factor normally increases with duration. In the usual case, this more than offsets the tendency for the mortality and loading factors to decrease with duration, but this is not always so. An unfavorable investment market may well cause just the opposite to occur, as happened in the 1940s, when the average rate of return dropped below 3 percent. Also, the fact that many insurers have switched to the investment generation method of interest allocation renders dividend patterns far less stable.

Special Forms of Surplus Distribution. Some companies pay extra dividends or terminal dividends in addition to the regular annual dividends. An **extra dividend** may consist either of a single payment made after a policy has been in force a specified number of years or of a payment made periodically at stated intervals. The single-payment extra dividend is usually used where no first-year dividend is paid, the extra dividend serving as a substitute. This practice has the practical advantage of reducing the strain of initial expenses and also may have a tendency to reduce the first-year lapse rate. This procedure has the effect of assessing a larger share of first-year expense against those policies that terminate prior to the time when the extra dividend is paid.

Extra dividends paid periodically (say, at every fifth year) have little justification in theory unless it is that regular dividends have been calculated on an extremely conservative basis and equity insists that extra dividends be paid periodically to the policyowners as the experience develops. A practical advantage, however, lies in the fact that illustrative net costs over a period of years are reduced by these extra amounts; only those policies remaining in force get the additional payments. This is particularly true of an extra dividend payable only at the end of the twentieth year.

Some companies pay a **terminal dividend** in the event that a policy terminates by maturity, death, or surrender. In most cases, such dividends are payable only if the policy has been in force for a minimum length of time. Terminal dividends, in theory, have the purpose of returning to terminating policyowners part of the general surplus to which they have contributed, or adjusting for a guaranteed cash value that is something less than

the asset share. Some companies, however, in effect use terminal dividends as a means of making their policies appear more attractive from a cost standpoint than they really are. This occurs when a company uses particularly high terminal dividends only at the duration required for cost index calculation purposes.[25]

It is important to note the distinction between a postmortem or mortuary dividend and a terminal dividend payable at death. A **postmortem dividend** is payable at death but either is paid in proportion to the part of the policy year of death for which premiums have been paid or represents a one-time distribution of surplus, mainly on term insurance, in lieu of dividends on each policy anniversary while the insured was living.

Practical Considerations. In establishing a scale of dividends, a number of practical considerations impinge on the decisions made. For example, the dividend scale should be satisfactory to existing policyowners. They have been conditioned by the existing scale to a pattern of dividends and significant changes, as a practical matter, normally would be accomplished by a series of adjustments. Also, the net cost position of the company under a proposed scale must be checked against those of competitors both to avoid dissatisfaction among the agency force and to assure a competitive product from the buyer's viewpoint. Similarly, the administrative cost of developing and implementing a new scale must be considered. At some point, the increased cost of greater theoretical equity outweighs the benefit involved. These and other practical considerations are an integral part of the process of establishing a scale of dividends for participating contracts.

The various options under which dividends may be taken were discussed in Chapter 9. Chapters 6 and 9 discuss some of the problems connected with "frozen" dividend scales and the comparability of dividend scales.

---

[25]See Chapter 10.

Chapter 22

The Mathematics of Health Insurance

Premiums for individual health insurance policies are affected by many factors, such as the rates of morbidity, interest, expense, and lapse. However, other factors, such as the method of selling employed, the underwriting philosophy, and the claims administration policy, as well as the overall philosophy and objectives of the insuring company, may result in a different experience by several companies issuing similar types of coverage. Similarly, changes and variations in hospital administration and medical practice, both geographically and from time to time in the same locality, and the impact of varying regulatory, economic, and business conditions make it difficult to predict reliably the future net annual claim costs.

BASIC PRINCIPLES OF RATEMAKING

The Rating Process

Ratemaking involves the analysis of available data and the development for the various classifications of insureds of premium rates that are *adequate, reasonable,* and *equitable.* Thus, in pricing benefits, companies classify insureds according to characteristics such as age, sex, geographic area, and occupation, depending on the type of

benefit involved and any legal or competitive constraints. Such classifications are considered necessary if reasonable equity between policyowners is to be realized.

If an average premium rate were charged all insureds regardless of the loss exposure presented by a particular individual, serious antiselection by those with a high exposure would result, and individuals with a lower loss exposure would not purchase the insurance. There are, however, practical limitations on the process of refining classifications in the interest of equity. As in life insurance, the parameters are established by the increasing administrative expense of dealing with multiple classes and the need to have a sufficient volume of business within a class to provide reliable experience and stability in the rate structure.

Competition usually will keep premium rates reasonable in relation to the benefits provided, but this is not always the case. Some states require filing of health insurance rates, and an increasing number of states require approval of premium rates on individual policies.

Adequacy is the most important criterion against which a premium rate should be measured. Where a new type of coverage is being introduced with unreliable experience, the margin of safety built into the premium is larger than in an established type of coverage with its own body of experience. As discussed below, companies normally test the level of their premiums with asset-share studies, utilizing various assumptions as to expense rates, lapses, morbidity, mortality, and interest. The ready availability of computers has permitted significant refinements in developing and testing gross or net premiums.

It also should be noted that in addition to developing premium rates for new policies, there is the problem of revising rates on existing individual policies where they are issued on an adjustable-premium, guaranteed-renewable basis.

Measures of Morbidity Experience

In establishing premium rates for any type of health insurance coverage, it is necessary to begin by providing a measure of the expected net annual claim cost per policy.

Unit Benefit Costs. The net annual claim cost of any benefit is the product of the frequency of occurrence and the amount of the average claim (severity). The unit benefit cost method entails calculation of the cost of providing a unit benefit, so that the net annual claim cost of benefits actually provided can be determined by multiplying the unit benefit cost by the appropriate benefit amount.

The unit of exposure may be $1 of daily hospital benefit, $1 of monthly income disability benefit, a standard maximum surgical schedule, or other suitable units selected. Unit costs can be broken down to reflect the combination of age, sex, occupation, geographic location, and so on.

It is possible to obtain the net annual claim cost without separately determining the frequency and average amount of claim for the benefit under consideration.[1] For example, all hospital miscellaneous benefits paid during the year under policies providing the same maximum benefit can be divided by the appropriate exposure to determine the net annual claim cost per life. In like manner, if interest is ignored, the net annual claim cost per

dollar of monthly income, under disability income insurance with a particular elimination period and maximum benefit limit, may be determined by dividing the value of total incurred claims at each age of disablement by the total monthly idemnity exposed. The result will be the same as the rate of disability (frequency) multiplied by the value of the disabled life annuity, computed without interest (average amount of claim).

Continuance Tables. The determination of (1) the expected claim frequency among insured lives, and (2) the average claim value are two important problems that confront the actuary. The mathematical measurement of the effect on claims cost of various elimination periods usually is handled by developing a continuance table, which shows the probabilities of claim continuance for various durations or amounts.[2]

Hospital confinement, for example, may be expressed as the number of patients remaining in the hospital at the end of t days out of an assumed initial number of patients confined to a hospital, such as 10,000. Figure 22–1 reflects a study of the probability of continuance of hospital confinement among 10,000 lives confined (adult males).

In disability income insurance, the elimination period has a dramatic effect on the rate level required. Figure 22–2 reflects a study of the probability of continuance of disability among 10,000 lives disabled at age 40.

In like manner, a major medical continuance table could express the probability that the claim experience will equal or exceed t dollars, from which the effect of varying deductibles and varying maximum amounts can be determined.

Continuance tables are helpful in computing the average-size claim. Such average claim values, in combination with the expected claim frequency (rate of claims), produce the expected net annual claim cost for the pattern of benefits under consideration. The method is easy to apply in practice where a single benefit, such as a monthly disability income benefit, is being considered. When benefits are combined in various ways with

---

[1]It can be done the other way, however, using one body of data for *frequency* and another for *claim size.*

[2]For an explanation of the development and utilization of continuance tables, see Edwin L. Bartleson et al., *Health Insurance,* 2nd ed. (Chicago: Society of Actuaries, 1968), pp. 192-196.

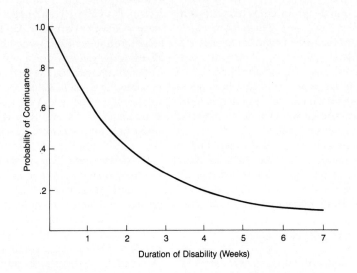

FIGURE 22-1. Probability of continuation of hospital confinement among 10,000 lives confined (adult males).

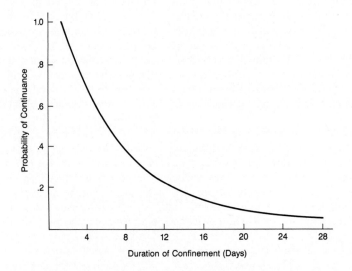

FIGURE 22-2. Probability of continuation of disability among 10,000 lives disabled at age 40 (adult males).

different elimination periods and different maximum benefit limitations, the problem of measuring the expected net annual claim cost becomes exceedingly complex.

Net Level Premiums. The net level premium for a disability income contract, as in the case of life insurance, is the level annual payment needed to pay benefits if (1) future claims exactly follow the average claim amounts assumed, as well as the frequency rates shown in the morbidity tables adopted; (2) deaths among persons insured occur at the rates given by the assumed mortality table; and (3) the rate of interest earned is that assumed in the rate basis. Thus, the net level premium at date of issue is found as follows:

$$NLP = \frac{\text{present value of future net annual claim costs}}{\text{present value of a life annuity due of 1 per annum for the premium-paying period}}$$

The present value of future net annual claim costs is the value at date of issue of all benefits that are expected to be paid until the termination date of the contract, appropriately discounted with interest. Table 22-1 illustrates the calculation of a net level premium for a five-year term, guaranteed-renewable hospital expense policy issued to a male aged 60.

Loss Ratios. This method of establishing the level of morbidity costs is based on the ratio of benefits incurred to premiums earned. It is an acceptable method for developing premium rates on business issued on a one-year term basis, but not for business issued on a level-premium basis. The loss-ratio method should be used with great caution when comparing morbidity costs between different companies. Such comparisons can be meaningless because of differences in (1) premium levels for the same types of benefits, (2) types of policies with varying benefits, (3) reserve requirements, (4) lapse rates, or (5) rates of company growth.[3]

Gross Premiums

The gross premium must provide for benefits, expenses, and contingency margins in the event that claims and expenses are higher than anticipated.[4] Gross premiums are usually calculated on the assumption that they will be paid annually, but they may be paid semiannual, quarterly, or

[3]See John B. Cumming, "Regulatory Monitoring of Individual Health Insurance Policy Experience," *Transactions of the Society of Actuaries*, Vol. 34 (1982), pp. 617-634.

[4]This section draws on *A Course in Individual Health Insurance, Part A*, pp. 105-120, and *Part B* (Washington, D.C.: Health Insurance Association of America, 1983).

TABLE 22-1. Illustrative calculation of net level premium five-year guaranteed-renewable hospital expense policy

(male, age 60)

(1) Attained Age	(2) Annual Claim Cost during Year Following Attained Age	(3) Average Period from Date of Issue of Contract to Commencement of Claim (Years)	(4) Proportion of Those Insured Who Will Survive Average Period	(5) Amount of 1 Discounted at 4½% per Annum for Average Period	(6) Present Expected Value of Claim Cost [(2) × (4) × (5)]
60	$18.10	0.5	0.9898	0.9302	$16.665
61	18.70	1.5	0.9688	0.8653	15.676
62	19.32	2.5	0.9462	0.8050	14.716
63	19.96	3.5	0.9222	0.7488	13.783
64	20.62	4.5	0.8965	0.6966	12.877

Total of column 6, present value of future annual claim costs $73.717

Present value of a five-year temporary life annuity due of 1 at
age 60 (1980 CSO Table, 4½%) 4.436

Net level premium = $\frac{\$73.717}{4.436} = \$16.62$

monthly. Gross premiums on individual health insurance policies usually are paid on a level basis, which means that the same premium is payable each year, from the date of issue to the end of the term period of the policy, such as to age 65. Gross premiums also may be developed on a one-year term basis or a step-rate basis. A number of companies issue comprehensive major medical benefits where the premiums increase each year to keep pace with annual increases in medical costs.

Factors Affecting the Premium. The premium rates for a particular benefit depend on such factors as (1) morbidity, (2) expenses, (3) persistency, (4) interest, and (5) contingency margins.

1. *Morbidity.* As we have seen in dealing with mortality rates, the only element considered is the number of deaths during a year compared with the total number of persons exposed in the class. In contrast, in the measurement of morbidity, the annual claim cost for a given age-sex-occupational class is the product of (a) the annual frequency of a particular event and (b) the average claim when such an event occurs. For example, the annual frequency of hospitalization for a given age and sex might be 10 percent, the average duration of hospital stay might be seven days, and therefore the annual claim cost for a $100 daily hospital benefit would be $70 (0.1 × 7 × 100).

In health insurance, although mortality is a consideration, the primary consideration is the morbidity cost. Annual claim costs may vary, depending on the kind and amount of benefits, according to such factors as age, sex, occupational class, and geographical area. Inasmuch as most policies contain more than one benefit, it is necessary to obtain separate annual claim costs for each type of benefit.

Most morbidity tables used to calculate net annual claim costs of disability income benefits exclude the experience during the calendar year that a policy is issued. Attempts to identify the influence of underwriting on experience by policy year— select experience—have not been too successful, in contrast to the success of the practice for life insurance. The pattern of select experience under disability insurance is quite different from that for mortality under individual life policies. At ages 40

and under, the benefits of selection in the early policy years are almost negligible. This probably is due to the fact that for ages below 40, sickness costs tend to increase by policy duration, but accident costs tend to decrease by policy duration.

Also, and for many companies of even greater importance, there is apparently important selection against the company by those applying for disability income policies whose elimination periods and maximum durations are relatively short. Studies show that at ages 50 to 65, there is a substantial increase in morbidity by policy duration that continues until the coverage terminates. Applicants who become insured in their 20s and 30s develop a higher level of morbidity after age 50 than those applicants who become insured after age 50. Furthermore, the experience varies considerably, depending on the type of benefit under consideration. The experience is further complicated in the case of medical expense insurance by the continuing inflation in the cost of medical services, and in the case of disability insurance, by the U.S. economy.

Obviously, consideration should be given to the relationship of select to ultimate experience in establishing gross premiums, in order that the premiums for insurance issued at advanced ages properly may reflect the savings from selection.

2. *Expenses.* To obtain suitable expense rates for the determination of premium rates, it is necessary to make detailed cost studies in which all the various expense items are expressed as (a) a percentage of the premium, which is called a per-premium type of expense (e.g., premium taxes and agents' commissions); (b) an amount per policy, which is called a per-policy type of expense (e.g., cost of underwriting and issuing a policy); or (c) an amount per claim paid (e.g., cost of investigating and verifying a claim). The per-premium types of expenses, because of the nonlevel commission rates, are usually larger in the first policy year, decrease during the next few policy years, and then are level for the remaining duration of the policy. The per-policy types of expenses are much larger in the first policy year, to reflect the cost of underwriting and issuing the policy. The per-policy type of expense after the first policy year is relatively

constant, except for the impact resulting from inflation.

3. *Persistency.* The persistency rate for a group of policies is defined as the ratio of the number of policies that continue coverage on a premium due date to the number of policies that were in force as of the preceding due date. Thus, if out of 100 policies that are issued, 75 policies are in force on the first policy anniversary, the first year annual persistency rate is 75 percent. The persistency rate usually improves with policy duration, and for some types of coverage, the annual persistency rate will be 95 percent or higher after the fifth policy year. Naturally, other factors affect persistency rates. In general, persistency rates usually are higher at the older issue ages and better for the less hazardous occupations. Persistency usually is better in connection with major medical expense and disability income coverages than on basic hospital expense coverages.

Lapses are important in health insurance rating for two reasons. First, expenses are higher during the first year than in subsequent years because of the expenses of issuing the policy or certificate and because of the typically higher first-year commission rate. Also, claim rates under health insurance tend to increase as the age of the insured increases. In view of these factors, which vary by age at issue and policy duration, the premium-rate level will depend on the rate of lapse.

4. *Interest.* When a level premium is used, the company will have, after the first few policy years, an accumulation of funds arising from the excess of premium income over the amounts paid for claims and expenses. As in level-premium life insurance, the funds accumulated during the early policy years will be needed in the later policy years, when the premium income is not sufficient to pay claims and expenses. In computing premium rates, therefore, it is necessary to assume a suitable interest rate to reflect the investment earnings on these accumulations.

Interest rates are of less significance in the calculation of health insurance premiums than in calculating life insurance premiums. The ratio of claims to premiums under health insurance dur-

ing the early policy years is substantially greater than under level-premium life insurance. Accordingly, more of the premium is used for claim payments soon after it is received by the insurance company and is therefore not available for investment and the accumulation of substantial reserves, such as is true of level-premium life insurance. It is important to consider interest in measuring the average claim cost under long-term disability income coverage. The value of the disability annuity can be significantly reduced because of the interest discount.

5. *Contingency Margins.* As in the case of life insurance premium rates, it is necessary to introduce a margin for contingencies into the premium-rate calculation. One method of doing so is to calculate a premium on the basis of most probable assumptions and then increase the premium by a percentage to provide some margin for contingencies. Another method is to introduce conservative morbidity, expense, persistency, and interest assumptions and determine a premium on that basis. Both approaches can produce approximately the same aggregate results.

Derivation of the Gross Premium. Having determined for a particular type and amount of benefit all the assumptions for a given issue age, sex, occupational class, area, and so on, as to morbidity, expenses, persistency, and interest rate, the actuary estimates what the gross premium will be. This tentative gross premium is tested against realistic expense, claim, persistency, and interest assumptions over an arbitrary period, commonly 20 years. If the tentative gross premium produces a fund accumulation that is too high or too low at the end of the projected period of coverage, an appropriate adjustment is made in the tentative premium to establish the appropriate gross-premium level needed to support the particular policy under consideration.[5] In the case of par-

---

[5]It also is possible to solve the asset-share formula, with the appropriate assumptions and parameters, with the gross premium as the unknown and thus arrive at the appropriate gross premium directly. For a detailed description of how asset shares are used to determine premium rates, see *A Course in Individual Health Insurance, Part A* (Washington, D.C.: Health Insurance Association of America, 1983), pp. 105–129.

ticipating policies, if it is subsequently determined that the accumulated fund at any time, together with future premiums, is in excess of the amount needed to pay future claims and expenses, dividends may be paid. Similarly, if the policies are nonparticipating, the company will realize a profit that it is entitled to for insuring the risk. In general, the margins in the premium rates are smaller on nonparticipating policies than on participating policies. Margins should be larger on noncancellable policies because premiums cannot be increased.

Gross premiums usually are not derived for every age by the method described above but possibly for every decennial age, such as ages 20, 30, 40, 50, and 60. Premiums for intervening ages can then be derived by fitting a curve through the premiums for these ages. Another approach utilized by some companies is to determine for each plan the net level premiums (based only on morbidity, mortality, and an interest rate) for each age and to find a loading formula, usually in the form of a constant plus a percentage of the net level premium, that will approximately reproduce the gross premiums that are obtained for decennial ages.

Significance of Judgment. The morbidity statistics used by an actuary who is assigned the job of computing the health insurance rates for a company about to enter the business may come from several sources and may involve several modifications of the basic data based on experience and judgment. In veiw of the lack of reliable data and the multiplicity of factors producing variable cost levels, informed judgment plays an important part in health insurance rate making. A comparison of the gross premiums charged by other companies for similar benefits can help a company determine whether the premiums it contemplates charging are competitive.

ANNUAL CLAIM COSTS

The net annual claim cost can be viewed as the product of the claim frequency and the average claim value. Since many types of benefits with varying claim values are issued in the field of health insurance, it is necessary to consider each type of benefit separately in developing the necessary formulas and in applying the appropriate morbidity data for ratemaking purposes.

Accidental Death and Dismemberment

If r_x represents the accidental-death rate at age x, if the principal-sum death and dismemberment benefit provided is $1,000, and if we let k equal the percentage of total claims that are dismemberment claims, we can write an equation that expresses the pure annual premium P_x for accidental death and dismemberment as

$$(1-k)P_x = \$1,000r_x$$
$$P_x = \frac{\$1,000r_x}{1-k}$$

Dismemberment claims usually represent about 10 percent of total accidental death and dismemberment claims. In such a case, $k = 10$ percent and

$$P_x = \frac{\$1,000r_x}{0.90}$$

Since accidental-death rates vary only slightly with age at most ages at which this benefit is issued, it is usual to charge the same premium at all issue ages. Another method used is to charge the same premium rate for all issue ages less than age 45. For higher issue ages, premiums would increase with issue age.

Medical Expense Benefits

Hospital Room and Board Benefits. The average net annual claim cost varies considerably with the type of hospital benefit, the level of benefits provided, the maximum duration of hospitalization benefits, and the age and sex of the insured. Separate net annual claim costs may be developed from available statistics for males, females, and children, on the basis of $1 of hospital benefits payable for varying maximum durations. Occupational hazards and variations in claim costs by geographic area may be taken care of by adjusting the net annual claim cost. This method might be used on individual health insurance. In the case of group insurance, adjustment factors might be applied to the gross premiums.

Hospital Miscellaneous Expense Benefits. The hospital miscellaneous expense benefit is intended to provide coverage for hospital services not covered by the room-and-board benefit. Net annual claim costs may be developed from available statistics. Such claim costs would vary by age and sex for adults but not for children.

Hospital room and board and miscellaneous expense benefits, until recently, were determined without regard to geographic location. Since on regular hospital and surgical coverage, an individual buys so many dollars of daily benefit, he or she tends to buy what is needed for his or her area, and geography is not usually too important. There is now a trend toward using net annual claim costs for miscellaneous hospital coverages that vary by geographic location. This trend has developed since the introduction of major medical coverage, where experience studies have confirmed the necessity for such refinement to establish equity among various policyowners, both for individual and group coverages.

Maternity Benefits. Maternity benefits normally are handled separately, since they have a separate cost pattern. Under individual policies, if the maternity benefit is included as an optional benefit that may be removed by the policyowner at any time, a gross annual premium of as much as $30 per $100 of maternity benefit may be considered appropriate.

Surgical Benefits. The surgical benefit schedules in common use are fairly standard, and the costs of providing these standard benefits are fairly well established. In addition, the relative frequencies of certain procedures have been recorded on a basis unrelated to the benefit schedule. It is possible, therefore, to develop rates for varying surgical benefits quite reliably. The process includes examining enough claims to determine the expected average claim cost under the new schedule as compared with the standard schedule, and adjusting the rate used for the standard

schedule by multiplying it by the ratio of the average net annual claim cost under the new schedule to the average net annual claim cost under the original schedule. Such cost variations are usually determined separately for adult males, adult females, and children for nonmaternity surgical benefits. The additional cost for obstetrical claims is determined separately.

Major Medical Benefits. The most difficult part of determining realistic rates for major medical coverage, whether on an individual or a group basis, has been the problem of adjusting available morbidity statistics, many of which have been developed from base-plan coverages, to the types of benefits provided under major medical coverage. Factors other than the age and sex of covered persons that influence the cost of benefits include:

1. The effect of inflation, increased utilization, and better technology on medical care costs (by far the most important item).
2. The effect on benefit costs of increased earnings of the insured.
3. The effect of geographic area on benefit costs for both employee and dependent coverages.
4. The effect on benefit costs of various recognized deductibles and percentage participation (coinsurance) factors.
5. The difference in the level of cost between ''per-illness'' plans and ''all-cause'' plans.
6. The effect on benefit costs of inside limits, such as (a) a maximum hospital daily room and board benefit or (b) a maximum surgical fee schedule. Such limits tend to affect the utilization of private-room facilities in the hospital as well as the amount payable for standard surgical procedures, where the charges for such items may vary greatly depending on the geographical location and the nature of the individual hospital confinement or surgical procedure required.

Cost Variations by Benefit Type. The cost variations according to the type of benefit are illustrated in the tables that follow, which show annual claim costs for hospital and surgical, maternity, major medical, and disability income benefits.

Table 22–2 shows that the annual claim costs for hospital and surgical benefits generally increase by age. The annual claim costs for females are

TABLE 22-2. Annual claim costs for certain hospital and surgical benefits

Attained Age	$10 Daily Hospital Benefit, Maximum Benefit Period 90 Days		Miscellaneous Hospital Expense Benefit, $200 Maximum Benefit		$100 of Maximum Surgical Benefit Standard Schedule	
	Male	Female	Male	Female	Male	Female
20–24	$ 3.77	$ 5.68	$ 8.87	$64.85	$ .94	$1.79
25–29	4.60	7.67	10.87	15.14	1.11	2.61
30–34	5.72	9.76	12.95	20.24	1.32	3.31
35–39	7.07	11.56	15.20	25.09	1.59	3.77
40–44	8.66	13.13	17.80	29.45	1.92	3.94
45–49	10.65	13.89	20.72	32.03	2.33	3.88
50–54	13.93	14.29	24.34	33.88	2.84	3.71
55–59	16.61	14.95	28.53	33.64	3.49	3.56
60–64	21.50	16.65	33.01	32.53	4.29	3.56
	Child		Child		Child	
All ages	$3.21		$40.78		$1.20	

Source: *Transactions of the Society of Actuaries—1979 Reports*, pp. 245, 247, 256.

quite a bit higher at the younger ages than for males; with increasing age, however, they become lower for females than for males. Usually, no distinction is made by sex or age in deriving the annual claim costs for children.

Table 22-3 shows annual claim costs for a $100 maternity benefit. The cost of maternity benefits decreases by age. The cost of the benefits during the first policy year will be low because of the effect of the maternity waiting period (usually 10 months). The maternity claim rates at the younger ages are much greater than at the older ages, and therefore the cost of the maternity benefits is higher at the younger ages. However, if the maternity benefit is included on an optional basis, there is likely to be selection by the insured, and therefore the claim cost probably will not vary by the age of the insured.

TABLE 22-3. Annual claim costs for $100 maternity benefit

Attained Age	Annual Claim Costs
20–24	$23.50
25–29	18.30
30–34	8.70
35–39	3.00
40–44	0.70
45–49	0.10

Source: *Transactions of the Society of Actuaries—1979 Reports*, p. 262.

Table 22-4 shows the annual claim costs for one plan of major medical benefits. The costs of

the benefits increase with age, but the increase by age is much greater for major medical benefits than for the basic hospital and surgical benefits shown in Table 22-2. As indicated in the heading for Table 22-4, the costs shown are for a particular plan. They will be different for other plans, depending on their specifications.

It must be kept in mind that studies of morbidity experience are based on experience that is already out of date, and since morbidity costs applicable to the future are needed, it is necessary for the actuary, particularly for major medical coverages, to use projection or trend factors.

TABLE 22-4. Annual claim costs—major medical expense benefits
($500 deductible amount, $10,000 maximum amount, 75% coinsurance, no hospital room and board limit, calendar duration 3 and later)

Attained Age	Annual Claim Costs		
	Male	Female	Child (All Ages)
35–39	$ 86.82	$ 71.59	$27.42
40–45	94.09	113.54	
45–49	116.86	152.16	
50–54	165.37	163.00	
55–59	220.94	190.05	
60–64	272.18	249.06	
65–69	303.96	326.74	

Source: *Transactions of the Society of Actuaries—1979 Reports*, p. 367.

There is a variation in the cost of medical care by geographical area. Under hospital and surgical expense coverages, benefits usually are subject to a daily hospital benefit limit and to a surgical schedule, and therefore there usually is no need to vary premium rates by area. In the case of major medical expense coverages, however, the cost of the benefits will be higher in high-cost areas. To a certain extent, this can be controlled by using so-called inside limits for room and board benefits and by the use of a surgical schedule. If inside limits are not used, premium rates often are varied by geographical area. For a major medical policy providing comprehensive medical expense benefits, with no inside limits, the cost of the benefits in the highest-cost areas of the United States is about three times higher than in the lowest-cost areas.

Disability Income

The annual claim costs for a disability income benefit vary significantly by occupational class. Table 22–5 shows the annual claim costs

TABLE 22–5. Annual claim costs per $100 of monthly disability income benefit
(maximum benefit period, one year; seven-day elimination period)

Attained Age	Annual Claim Costs		
	Accident	Sickness	Accident and Sickness
Male—Occupation Group I			
Under 30	$10.30	$13.10	$23.40
30–39	8.90	10.80	19.70
40–49	8.20	15.70	23.90
50–59	6.40	24.90	31.30
60–69	5.20	42.00	47.20
Male—Occupation Group II			
Under 30	$12.40	$10.90	$23.30
30–39	14.30	11.40	25.70
40–49	13.30	19.30	32.60
50–59	10.80	32.20	43.00
60–69	11.70	49.00	60.70
Female—Occupation Group I			
Under 30	$ 5.30	$14.10	$19.40
30–39	6.40	19.40	25.80
40–49	7.10	25.40	32.50
50–59	9.40	30.10	39.50
60–69	6.70	31.20	37.90

Source: *Transactions of the Society of Actuaries—1979 Reports*, pp. 294, 295, 296.

for one particular disability income plan. The costs will vary according to age, sex, occupational class, elimination period, and maximum duration of benefits. If the elimination period and maximum duration of benefits are different for sickness benefits than for accident benefits, it is necessary to develop separate costs for accident and for sickness. Occupation Group I shown in the table covers white-collar types of occupation classes, and Occupation Group II covers blue-collar types of occupation classes.

PREMIUM-RATE VARIABLES

The inability to work because of accident or sickness is subjective in nature and involves an attitude as well as a physical or mental impairment. Since disability is at least partially a state of mind, experience is subject to many factors including the level of unemployment, the attitude of insureds, people's work ethics and their attitudes toward retirement, and the attitudes of physicians who certify disability. In an attempt to cope with these problems, insurers underwrite health insurance coverage carefully and use several risk classification factors, as discussed below.

Age and Sex Classifications

Age is of major importance in almost all forms of health coverage, as discussed previously. The premium rates for females for hospital, surgical, and medical expense benefits and disability income benefits are higher than for males, at the younger ages. With increased age, however, the costs become lower for females. For group, but not for individual insurance, the relationship also varies between employed females and dependent females. Female group rates may be calculated as a percentage increase over the male rate or may be based on an analysis of actual experience on female lives.

Disability income benefits usually are issued to regularly employed persons only. The rates for females generally range from 1½ to 2 times the male rate.

Occupational Classifications

Most hospital and surgical plans do not pay benefits for work-related illness or injury that would be payable under workers' compensation. Since this exclusion eliminates much of the adverse effect of hazardous occupations, it is customary to charge the same premium for hospital and surgical benefits regardless of occupation. Industry loadings are, however, used for group insurance.

Accidental death and dismemberment benefits and disability income benefits may be issued on an occupational basis. In such cases, it is customary to subdivide the various occupations into at least three classes with appropriate extra premiums depending on the degree of extra morbidity expected. Some occupations may be eliminated entirely because of the extreme occupational hazard.

Geographical-Area Classifications

Within the United States, the location of the insured individual is rarely a factor for determining premium rates for disability income or accidental-death insurance. However, there are indications that there are cost variations by area on disability income. Therefore, the actuary often will determine whether the variations are significant enough to introduce them into the premium structure. Geography is more significant in major medical insurance costs mainly because of wide variation in hospital rates and other medical care expenditures. Variations in claim frequency also occur in some areas.

Elimination Periods

The elimination of income benefits for varying periods (such as seven, 14, 30, 60, 90, 120, 180, or 365 days) is a method used to provide benefits that suit the various income-replacement needs of insureds in the event of disability. Many persons have underlying employer-provided or other disability plans that cover the first several weeks of disability. The cost of benefits decreases as the elimination period increases.

If a continuance table is used for disability income benefits, it is easy to make the necessary adjustments in rates for various elimination periods. Ideally, however, there should be a continuance table for each elimination period, since the experience for policies with different elimination periods differs.

Major medical policies often provide, through the use of a deductible, for the elimination of the first dollars of hospital or medical expenses incurred. The amount of the deductible depends on the type of plan being offered. In group insurance, major medical coverage often provides for payment of all covered physicians' hospital charges (usually at semiprivate room rate) at a rate of 80 percent, but with a maximum "out-of-pocket cap" on the insured's payment of $1,000. After the insured has incurred such out-of-pocket expenses, the insurer pays 100 percent of all further covered expenses. Benefits would be subject to a deductible of $50 to $250 or more. It is customary to provide a fixed maximum benefit of $500,000, $1,000,000 or more, except for certain inside limits. A few companies are issuing comprehensive major medical benefits on individual policies with benefits similar to those described above for group insurance, although, in general, benefits provided under individual policies tend to be less liberal than those provided under group plans.

Recently, there is a trend toward unisex rating. The results of a 1984 study of 25 companies are shown below.

	Number of Companies
Full sex rating	8
Unisex on top occupational classes	12
Unisex on high salaries only	1
Full unisex rating	4
	25

Source: "Underwriting of Individually-Issued Accident and Health Products," *Record of the Society of Actuaries*, Vol. 10 (1984), p. 1847.

Smoking

A recent survey showed that many companies have adopted premium differentials for smokers and nonsmokers. The differential ranges from 6 to 10 percent.

Dependent Classifications

For individual insurance, it is customary to charge a rate for each child rather than a rate for all children, as is done in group.[6] The premium for children varies by type of plan but not by age or sex. The hospital stay usually is short for most surgical procedures performed on children; therefore, the level of miscellaneous benefits provided by the plan affects the claim cost most dramatically and may vary the relationship between the cost of coverage for adults and for children.

The premium rate for dependent coverage under group insurance depends on the age of the employee and may or may not be independent of industry, depending on the insurer. For group coverages, as opposed to individual, there is no additional charge for children after the first, whether the plan is basic hospital and surgical or major medical. Although charging for each additional child would produce greater equity, it complicates administrative procedures. Since a portion of the premium normally is paid by the employer, the insured employees still receive equitable treatment under a properly designed group plan covering their dependents.

Other Premium Classifications

Increasingly, companies are issuing individual noncancellable disability income or guaranteed-renewable medical expense policies to impaired risks, subject to the payment of an extra premium. Numerical morbidity ratings have been established for each insurable impairment, varying from approximately 125 to 300 percent. Two ratings are required for each impairment—one for accident-only policies and another for accident and sickness, including hospital and surgical and major medical. Some impairments are standard for accident only but are rated for accident and sickness coverage.

It should be noted that some relatively undesirable hospital and surgical risks can be accepted for disability income coverage if there is, say, at least a 30-day elimination period. On the other hand, there are some poor disability income risks that are acceptable hospital risks.

HEALTH INSURANCE RESERVES AND LIABILITIES

In health insurance, as in life insurance, it is important that proper provision be made in the company liabilities for all the obligations assumed by the company under its contracts, irrespective of whether it is required by law. Liability accounts are established for present or future claims against the company's assets that must come from the premiums already received. Reserve is the term used to refer to the amount of the liability of the company to fulfill future contingencies and unpaid liabilities already incurred.

Health insurance reserves and other liabilities may be classified broadly as follows:

1. **Policy reserves** include those amounts necessary for the fulfillment of contract obligations as to future claims, which include pro rata unearned premium reserves and additional reserves for level premium policies.
2. **Claim reserves and liabilities** include those amounts necessary to cover payments on claims already incurred.
3. **Expense liabilities** include those amounts necessary to pay expenses and taxes under obligations incurred by the company from operations prior to the annual statement date.

Table 22–6 shows a hypothetical company statement illustrating the various health insurance reserves and liabilities that are discussed below.[7]

Policy Reserves

Unearned Premium Reserves. In determining the amount of the unearned premium reserve

---

[6]On major medical, it is feasible to use an all-children rate on individual insurance because of the cost-reduction effect of a large deductible. This effect is lacking on basic individual coverages, and hence a per-child rate usually is considered necessary.

[7]In the Life Insurance Company Annual Statement Form, provision is made for a breakdown of health insurance reserves in Exhibit 9, and liability for policy and contract claims in Exhibit 11. See Chapter 32.

TABLE 22-6. XYZ Insurance company annual statement of financial condition December 31, 1986

Assets:	
Cash	$ 170,000
Bonds	675,000
Stocks	
Preferred	75,000
Common	25,000
Real estate owned	40,000
First-mortgage loans	316,000
Premiums due and unpaid	43,000
Total assets	$1,344,000
Liabilities, capital, and surplus:	
Unearned premium reserve	$ 320,000
Net-level-premium reserves	
(additional reserve for	
noncancellable policies)	35,000
Premiums paid in advance	40,000
Liability for claims in course of settlement	140,000
Liability for claims incurred	
but unreported	50,000
Present value of future amounts	
due on claims	110,000
Reserve for future contingent benefits	20,000
Liability for dividends declared	20,000
Liability for expenses and taxes due	
and accrued	85,000
Mandatory security valuation reserve	36,000
Capital	250,000
Unassigned surplus	238,000
Total liabilities, capital, and surplus	$1,344,000

to be included in the annual statement, the pro rata portion of the full gross premium from the statement date to the end of the period for which premiums have been paid on the policy is required to be set up as a reserve regardless of the renewal provisions of the policy. In establishing the appropriate amount to be set up, approximation methods often are used. It is often assumed that premium due dates are distributed uniformly over the year so that, on the average, one-half of the total premiums in force, regardless of the mode of premium payment are unearned as of the end of the year. This normally is the largest item among the policy reserves, unless the company has large amounts of noncancellable or guaranteed-renewable business.

The unearned gross-premium reserve automatically provides a reserve allowance for the payment of expenses that will be incurred after the statement date, as well as for the benefit payments that will be incurred and must be paid

out of the premiums already received by the company. Premiums paid on or before the statement date but due after the statement date are classified separately as premiums paid in advance.[8]

Additional Reserves for Noncancellable and Guaranteed-Renewable Policies. Noncancellable and guaranteed-renewable health insurance policies usually provide coverage to a specified age, such as 60 or 65, and often are issued on the basis of a level premium payable each year after the date of issue. Because of increasing morbidity costs as the age increases and the use of a level premium, excess funds are accumulated in the early years (measured by the reserve liability), which eventually are consumed through increased claim costs by the expiration date of the benefits in much the same manner as reserves on term-to-age-65 life insurance policies are built up in the early years and later decrease to zero at age 65. As in life insurance, the so-called active life reserve, calculated prospectively, is equal to the difference between the present value of future benefits and the present value of future premiums.

The **1985 Commissioners Disability Tables,** adopted by the National Association of Insurance Commissioners in 1985, are the minimum standard for the valuation of disability income benefits due to accident and sickness for policies issued on or after January 1, 1987. Their use in 1986 is optional, provided, of course, the individual state has adopted the NAIC model. For accidental-death benefits, the minimum standard is the **1959 Accidental Death Benefit Table.**

As in the case of life insurance, to establish a minimum standard for reserves, state regulatory authorities specify particular morbidity and mortality tables and a maximum rate of interest. For health insurance benefits, companies are permitted to use as an interest assumption the maximum rate currently permitted by law for the valuation of new life contracts, and for mortality, any table permitted by law in the valuation of cur-

[8]Advance premiums are not a part of the unearned premium reserve but appear as a separate liability, because the premiums paid are not yet due. The insured may change his or her mind and request the return of the premium, and sound accounting practice indicates separate treatment.

rently issued life insurance. Companies may use a net-level, or a one- or two-year preliminary-term method of valuation for active-life reserves. Although the additional reserve is required only on noncancellable or guaranteed-renewable policies or policies where the right of nonrenewal is limited, the need for such reserve exists on any level-premium type of coverage where the incidence of cost increases with advancing age.

Reserve for Future Contingent Benefits. If a hospital policy, whether individual or group, creates a contingent liability for pregnancies that exist at the time of termination of the policy by the company, it is necessary to set up the value of such contingent liability. There are a number of acceptable methods of estimating such liability.[9] This reserve may be carried as either an active-life reserve or a claim reserve or a claim liability. If carried as either an active-life reserve or a claim reserve, it is segregated and designated as the reserve for future contingent benefits.

Claim Reserves and Liabilities

There are many acceptable methods of estimating the liability of the company for outstanding claims that have not been paid in full on the date the annual statement is being prepared. Any method selected to determine the amount of outstanding claim liability should be one that will assure adequacy and fairly reflect the actual liability, which will later be developed after sufficient time has passed to permit the company to tabulate the actual results that occur subsequent to the statement date.

Present Value of Amounts Not Yet Due on Claims. Disability income benefits, with the problem of determining the reserve liability for disabled lives, provide the best example of the complicated nature of this claim-liability item. The rate of recovery decreases with increasing duration of disability, so that the value of the

[9]See New York State Insurance Department, *Examination of Insurance Companies,* Vol. 3, and the N.A.I.C. instructions that accompany the Annual Statement Blank. See also Bartleson et al., *Health Insurance,* pp. 157–158.

claim annuity for a long-duration benefit period normally increases as the duration of any particular disability becomes greater, until the value of the claim annuity reaches a peak and then gradually decreases to the end of the period for which benefits are payable. In estimating this liability item as of the valuation date, it is, therefore, desirable to show for each claim the age at date of disability, the number of months or years the claimant has been disabled, and the number of years of benefit remaining, in order to be able to apply the appropriate claim annuity factor to the amount of the monthly benefit being provided. If the monthly income is not payable for more than one year, the claim annuity valuation factors may be based on an average age and on average durations that vary with the type of benefit being considered.

Hospital, surgical, and medical expense benefits are usually settled in a single sum, and it is not practical to obtain the claim liability for each claim. Instead, by making a reconciliation of previous years' claims, a factor can be developed such that by applying the factor to the cash claims payable during the calendar year, a good estimate can be made of the claim liability at the end of the year.

Claims Due and Unpaid. This item normally is small or nonexistent for health insurance claims. Most companies will pay any amount due on a claim as soon as the amount can be determined and the claim approved.

Claims in the Course of Settlement. The liability shown for this item will be based on claims on which notice of claim has been received but on which all the proofs of loss or other papers have not been received, so that the claim cannot be approved on the statement date. Some companies examine each claim individually and prepare a list showing each item involved. Others use approximate methods in various ways. One method is to add the total amount of outstanding claims and apply to it a factor obtained from the experience on previous valuation dates. Another method is to analyze a sample of claims and determine a percentage factor that is applied to

the total liability for claims, including both accrued and unaccrued amounts.

Claims Incurred but Not Reported. Experience will show that many claims that were
actually incurred prior to the statement date are
paid after that date each year, because the company had no knowledge of the claim until after
such statement date. It is usual to tabulate such
claims each year and relate the amount to some
base, such as volume of business in force or
earned premiums on the type of coverage involved. The total liability for incurred but unreported
claims is divided into two parts: **accrued** and **contingent.** The accrued liability is reported as "incurred but unreported" as part of the policy claim
liability. The contingent liability accruing *after* the
valuation data is included under "Present Value
of Amounts Not Yet Due on Claims."

Liability for Expenses

It is necessary to provide in the company
liabilities on the statement date a reasonable
estimate of the claim expenses that will be paid
on unpaid losses incurred prior to the statement
date. Such liability may be computed as a cost per
claim or as a percent of the liabilities for claims
incurred, or as a combination of both. In major
medical coverage, where the cost of settling claims
may be much higher per claim than under base-
plan coverage, it is usually necessary to develop
separate factors for each type of coverage, based
on actual studies of handling the various types of
claims.

The reserve for expenses, other than claim
expenses, may be accounted for in the unearned
gross-premium reserve, or if such reserve is not
adequate, an additional amount may be set up in
the expense liability. This might be true during
the first year if unpaid commissions or other expenses will be greater than the loading provided
in that year's premium calculation.

Group Reserves and Liabilities

A company's liabilities under group health
contracts create the need for the same types of
policy and claim reserves as do individual health

insurance contracts. The amounts of the reserves,
however, usually are smaller. In general, premiums
are paid monthly under group health contracts,
and the company reserves the right to adjust
premium rates on any policy anniversary. Nevertheless, it is important to keep the level of
premiums and therefore the insured's costs on a
stable basis.

Other Reserves and Liabilities

Liability for Dividends Payable. On the
statement date, participating health insurance
policies will have dividends declared that will not
be payable until after the statement date. The
liability for such payments should be set up as
a liability on the statement date.

Surplus and Contingency Reserves. Contingency reserves, which are *not* liabilities, are
sometimes established on a voluntary basis to
allow for the possibility of an upward trend in
claim costs or an unusual occurrence. In state
disability plans, they may be established as an
offset to decreasing premiums without a corresponding decrease in liability, where premiums
are paid on current wages, while benefits depend
on wages during a base period. Some states require the accumulation of a contingency reserve
for group health business.

SURPLUS DISTRIBUTION

Individual health insurance policies are issued on
both a nonparticipating and a participating basis.
However, overall experience—except for some disability income policies—has not been too good,
and therefore dividends either have not been
payable at all or have been relatively small. Group
health insurance policies are virtually always "participating" through a variety of experience-rating
devices. The concepts underlying both dividends
and experience rating are similar, but may differ
somewhat in basic philosophy. In any case, the
process should take into consideration the surplus
position of the policyowner or class, the extent to
which losses are pooled (averaged) among cases,

the expenses incurred as between policyowners or classes, and the total surplus available for distribution.

For the larger group health cases, it is practicable to develop the appropriate dividend or premium refund through the use of fund accounts. As in the case of life insurance, this involves the accumulation from date of issue of the premiums paid, increased in some cases by interest earnings. From this amount, losses incurred, accumulated expenses incurred directly or allocated to the case, and allowances for contingencies and profit are deducted. From this net accumulation, total dividends paid previously are deducted, and the result is the surplus amount *available* for distribution.

Individual Policies

In the case of individual policies, funds are accumulated separately for each class of policy (sometimes referred to as policy form). In this way, the amount of surplus accumulated for any dividend class is ascertainable. The dividend formula used is usually simple, taking into account only broad equities. For example, for policies that have been in force for, say three years, a specified percentage of the premiums, varied in some companies by duration, may be returned as a dividend. In connection with dividends, the asset share calculation is used principally as a test of the adequacy of the accumulation for any dividend class. As pointed out earlier, the adequacy of the company's contingency reserve for this type of business will affect the proportion of current

earnings that is added to the contingency reserve for a particular class of policies.

Group Policies

An approach similar to that used for individual classes is used in dealing with small group cases. Here, groups are classified and surplus distribution is determined through the use of fund accounts for each class of groups. Again, only a limited number of variables is considered. In small cases, morbidity experience must be averaged, because of the low credibility of the individual case's experience. Expenses are relatively high, but because of the smaller discounts granted such cases, they may develop reasonable dividend distributions over a period of time.

In the case of large groups, the fund-account approach is applied to each group. The chief problems involve the development of unit expense charges for indirect expense items, the determination of the period of amortization of acquisition expenses, and the individual case contribution to contingencies and/or profits. In all but the largest cases, it is necessary to establish a limit on the maximum level of losses that will be considered in the experience-rating formula. This usually is achieved by imposing a limit on an aggregate basis or, in some cases, an aggregate limit and a maximum for a single claim during a given experience period.

In all cases, the experience-rating formula will give consideration to (1) premiums paid, (2) incurred losses (modified by loss limits and credibility), (3) direct and allocated expenses, and (4) allowances for contingencies and/or profits.

Chapter 23

Life and Health Insurance Underwriting: I

THE PURPOSE OF UNDERWRITING

In any insurance plan, each insured person contributes to a common fund from which amounts are paid to or on behalf of the unfortunate ones who suffer covered losses. To maintain equity among insureds, each should contribute according to the loss probabilities he or she transfers to the common fund. If one person is allowed to pay less than his or her share, it will necessitate an overcharge against other persons. In each instance, therefore, the insurance company should determine the loss expense presented to it by the insured and charge a fair premium for it. This cannot be accomplished without careful selection and classification of risks.

In any group of average individuals of the same age, some are near death, some have impaired health, some are exposed to unusual risks of overall death because of occupation or other activity, the great majority are in good health, and some few are free of even the slightest impairment. Knowledge and understanding of the way the various factors influence mortality enables the company to classify insureds into groups that will give relative mortality rates close to those that are anticipated.[1] Those groups subject to a higher-than-average mortality are said to be **substandard.**

Two views of anticipated relative mortality are depicted in Figures 23-1 and 23-2. Both figures show insurers' perceptions of distribution of relative mortality for a randomly selected group of persons of the same age and sex. In each case, 100 percent represents average mortality for the group.

Figure 23-1 gives a more traditional view of insurers' anticipated mortality as implicit in their pricing structure and underwriting practices. No segregation is made in pricing or underwriting between persons who smoke cigarettes and those who do not smoke.

Figure 23-2, on the other hand, depicts a more contemporary view of insurers' anticipated relative mortality as implicit in their pricing and underwriting. Here the classification scheme employed recognizes differences in anticipated mortality between smokers and nonsmokers.

The figures portray the wide range of anticipated future mortality for a group of persons.

[1]Pearce Shephard and Andrew C. Webster, *Selection of Risks* (Chicago: The Society of Actuaries, 1957), p. 2.

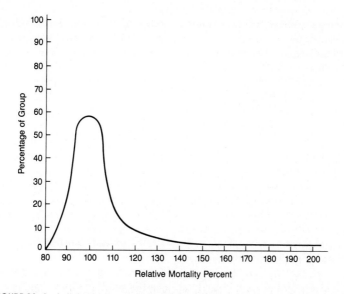

FIGURE 23-1. Anticipated mortality based on risk characteristics *excluding smoking* represented in a randomly selected group of the same age and sex, with 100 percent representing average mortality for group.

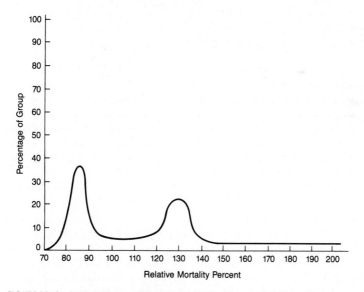

FIGURE 23-2. Anticipated mortality based on risk characteristics *including smoking* represented in a randomly selected group of the same age and sex, with 100 percent representing average mortality for group.

Clearly, all should not be offered insurance on the same terms. Life insurance companies must establish ranges of mortality expectations within which proposed insureds would be regarded as average, and hence insurable at standard premium rates, or conversely, the limits beyond which they would be considered substandard and subject to higher rates or policy restrictions or denied insurance altogether.

The development of the bimodal distribution in current experience, as shown in Figure 23–2, is intended to reflect current practice as relating to the need for two "standard" classifications. Those who smoke exhibit higher mortality, age by age, than those who do not smoke. As the body of mortality experience has developed, more and more companies are implementing two standard classifications, one for smokers and one for nonsmokers (see below). Some companies have established "super standard" or preferred classifications that permit them to charge rates based on better-than-average anticipated mortality. In addition to establishing the limits for the various classes of risk, the company must adopt procedures that permit proposed insureds to be properly classified.

The process is complicated by the fact that persons applying for life insurance do not constitute a randomly selected group as depicted in Figure 23–1. An individual's decision with regard to insurance may be based on his or her knowing or suspecting more about his or her health than the company does. It is only natural for the individual to "decide" on the most favorable basis to him- or herself. This tendency, known as **adverse selection** or **selection against the company,** appears whenever an individual has freedom to buy or not to buy, to choose the amount or plan of insurance, and to persist or to discontinue as an insured. In addition to separating and classifying risks, a major purpose of underwriting is to protect the company against such adverse selection.

More broadly stated, the purpose of underwriting is to ensure that insurance is issued on such terms and conditions and at such a premium that the degree of risk presented to the insurer is fairly reflected in the terms, conditions, and premiums.

The term underwriting, commonly used throughout the insurance business, actually incorporates implicitly two essential elements: (1) *selection* and (2) *classification.* Selection is the process whereby an insurance company decides whether to provide *any* insurance coverage. Classification is the process whereby an insurer decides on the terms, conditions, and price at which the insurance will be issued. The principles and factors underlying a given company's underwriting philosophy are outlined in the following section.

UNDERWRITING PHILOSOPHY

Certain fundamental principles and factors govern sound selection and classification procedures. Some are mutually inconsistent, but they must be considered in the formulation of an underwriting philosophy. The life insurance company's philosophy directly reflects the resultant balance among these opposing principles and considerations.

The Standard Group—Nonsmokers and Smokers

An accepted principle is that the standard group—those regarded as average and insurable at standard rates—should be broad enough to encompass the greatest percentage of insureds. Evidence of this in practice is the fact that currently, 94 percent of the applications for ordinary insurance are accepted at standard rates.[2]

Overexacting standards and procedures could result in an excessive number of rejections and rated cases. This could undermine the morale of salespersons, tend to increase the cost of operation, and involve public relations considerations. Appraisal of an individual's expected mortality cannot be exact in any case. Apart from the practical considerations mentioned, the broader the

---

[2]Of the remaining 6 percent, only 2 percent are declined, with the remaining 4 percent being offered substandard rates. See *1986 Life Insurance Fact Book,* (Washington, D.C.: American Council of Life Insurance, 1986), p. 102.

base of standard risks, the more stable will be the mortality or morbidity experience of the standard group. The extension of this principle is limited by considerations of equity and competition.

While an important underwriting objective is to have the majority of insureds fall within the standard group, change is continuing to split the standard group into two classes, as illustrated in Figure 23-2. This split has been caused by a recognition within many companies' pricing structures and underwriting procedures of the higher mortality of smokers. This has led, in effect, to the establishment of two standard classes.

The Substandard Groups

The substandard classes or gradations of risk to be recognized in a company's premium-rate structure are a function of the balance between the need to minimize the number of classifications for the purposes of obtaining sufficient mortality and morbidity data and administrative considerations, on the one hand, and, on the other, the need to maximize the number of classifications to avoid competitive disadvantages and to achieve reasonable equity. Naturally, the size of the company, marketing objectives, product type, and other company policies are involved in the decision to provide substandard insurance and in the classifications to be established. This question is addressed more fully in Chapter 24. It should be emphasized that when a given risk factor leads to a significantly large "substandard" group (e.g., smokers), creation of two "standard" classifications is considered desirable by many companies.

Balance within Each Class

Having defined its risk classifications, a company should maintain a reasonable balance among the insureds accepted in each classification. If the overall mortality experience within each classification is to approximate the predicted average for the group, every insured within that class whose mortality experience is expected to be higher than average must be offset by one

whose experience is expected to be lower than average.

Maintaining the proper balance within a standard classification is a difficult task. In considering a borderline application, a home office underwriter, is tempted, by reasons of agency pressures, desire for business, and human nature, to approve the application for the lowest possible rating. This is evidenced by the fact that studies consistently show that the distribution of risks within each substandard classification is skewed toward the top limit of the class. This fact is considered, of course, in establishing the premium rate for the class, but it demonstrates the human element in the underwriting process.

Emphasis on the Major Risks

The underwriting process is concerned primarily with significant risk exposures that are not common to all persons seeking insurance. Risk exposures that are common to the applying group operate to increase the mortality among all lives and are reflected in the general mortality levels assumed.

Airline travel is so widespread that the accidental deaths or disabilities that result are regarded as a part of the general hazards of life and provided for in the general mortality levels underlying the rate structures. Relatively fewer persons, however, are airplane pilots, and it is the additional airtime of engaging in piloting a plane that would be of concern from an underwriting standpoint. Underwriters do ignore factors that produce some extra mortality, but none of these (e.g., extensive driving, moderate overweight, or moderately elevated blood pressure) produce extra mortality sufficient to be rated substandard. These same factors, however, cannot be ignored if the problem is severe (poor driving record, marked overweight, or significantly elevated blood pressure). In sum, the process of underwriting constantly strives to ascertain significant risk factors that set a given proposed insured apart from the normal members of a group. Where a given risk factor (e.g., smoking) is identified as setting a substantial proportion of the group apart from other members of the group, a separate standard classification often is indicated.[3]

Equity Among Insureds

The manner in which insureds are rated must recognize the principle of equity. Some grouping of insureds is desirable to have a reasonable volume of experience within a given classification and due to expense considerations. On the other hand, to be satisfactory to the proposed insured and the company, the spread between the worst and best risks within a classification should not be so broad as to produce significant inequity or hinder a company in competition. In practice, the width of rating classes tends to vary directly with the degree of accuracy with which it is believed that the extra mortality can be appraised. Hence, class widths are to some extent a function of the dependability of the available mortality data on impaired lives. Differences between companies, in practice, are the result of different judgments as to what is the best overall policy.

Recognition of Underlying Mortality Assumptions

Risk classification reflects the mortality levels assumed in determining the premium rate applied. If the proposed insured is to be considered at standard rates, the expected mortality experience must be comparable to that used in determining these rates.

In practice, some companies, especially large ones, continually study their mortality experience and evaluate their classification rules. They review their experience on lives accepted standard and compare their experience on impaired lives with the standard experience. Based on such study and analyses, each company adjusts its classification rules where indicated. The

basic objective is to assure reasonable equity within a given classification.

Since insured experience is made up of selected lives, at least as effective underwriting must be exercised in the future as in the past if mortality is to be similar to that provided for in the premium rate structure. But a situation of generally improving mortality might permit acceptance of some impaired lives without exceeding the mortality assumed in the premium calculations. Such action, however, would adversely affect the company's competitive position if other companies continued to accept only "standard" risks at their standard rates.[4]

FACTORS AFFECTING THE RISK

In deciding whether to issue life insurance (selection) and, if so, on what terms and conditions and at what price (classification), life insurance companies usually examine several factors. This is necessary not only to ensure that policyowners are treated equitably, but also to guard against them being charged either excessive or inadequate rates for the insurance coverage. Underwriting is therefore, an essential link through which the three objectives of ratemaking—that rates are adequate, equitable, and not excessive—are attained. This section reviews the chief factors examined by life insurers in underwriting (1) life insurance and (2) health insurance.

The Life Insurance Risk

Age. Expected future mortality of an individual is clearly related to that person's age. The older the person, other things being the same, the higher the likelihood of death and therefore the higher should be the premium rate. Equity in underwriting individual cases demands this.

Age is therefore a key factor in determining the rate to be charged an individual for life insurance. Age is rarely a *selection* factor, however, except for individuals who are of advanced age or, with some types of insurance, very young age. Some insurers may use age alone to deny some

---

[3]Separate standard classifications within one company are not new. Companies writing industrial and ordinary insurance have traditionally used different "standard" pricing, reflecting the significant differences in anticipated mortality between the two life and health insurance markets. Similarly, except where legislation prohibits differentiation in pricing on the basis of sex, there are, in effect, two standard classes based on this risk factor.

[4]Shepherd and Webster, *Selection of Risks,* p. 3.

types of insurance to older (e.g., past age 70 or 75) persons. This may occur because the insurer may believe its statistical base to be too small to permit proper rating, the insurer may have insufficient confidence in its underwriting process for advanced ages, and/or the insurer believes the premium rate it would be required to charge to be too high for marketing purposes.

The applicant is not required to furnish proof of age at the time that he or she applies for insurance, since (1) such a requirement could cause delay, (2) few persons misstate their age, (3) such proof is usually easily obtained if needed, and (4) the misstatement-of-age clause handles those situations where the age was misstated.[5] In the case of an immediate annuity, under which it would not be practical to adjust the amount of the benefits if a misstatement of age is discovered at the time of the annuitant's death, proof of age usually is required at the time of annuity purchase.

Sex. The proposed insured's gender, like age, is rarely used as a selection factor but is routinely used as a classification (rate-setting) factor with respect to individual life insurance. Yearly probabilities of death of females are less than the yearly probabilities of death of similarly situated males. As a result, most insurers in most states charge lower life insurance premium rates and higher annuity rates for females than for males. This was not always true, with insurers several decades ago charging women the same or higher rates than men because of "the frailty of women and the hazards of childbirth." Increasingly accurate statistics, competition, and a widening mortality gap between the two sexes caused insurers to alter this practice.

While mortality statistics clearly show a difference in death rates between men and women and can therefore be used *statistically* to justify charging different rates for men and women, other important considerations have arisen. The question now being debated is: Is it *socially* acceptable to charge men and women different rates for life insurance (and annuities)? The state of Montana has concluded that it is *not* socially acceptable and has banned the use of gender as a rating factor.

Legislation has been introduced in other states to accomplish this same objective, although to date no other state has followed Montana's lead. The issue is one of statistical relevance versus social policy.[6]

Physical Condition. The physical condition of a proposed insured is of basic significance in underwriting. One of the determinants of physical condition is build.[7] Build includes height, weight, and distribution of the weight. Experience has shown that overweight increases the mortality at all ages. Although moderate overweight may not, in and of itself, have a ratable effect, it can magnify the significance of other physical ailments, such as cardiac conditions.

Most companies use a table showing average weights, and expected extra mortality is shown as a percentage of standard. At the "best" weights—less than the average—the tables indicate a better-than-average mortality rate.

Other aspects of a proposed insured's physical condition are also important. Companies seek to determine a proposed insured's overall physical condition. Companies know from experience that future mortality experience will depend, in varying degrees, on abnormalities present in one or more of the important systems of the body—nervous, digestive, cardiovascular, respiratory, genitourinary, and glands of internal secretion. The defects and disabilities that may be found in the organs of the body and the methods of ascertaining them are necessarily medical in character. No attempt is made to explain them here. However, some of the more common of these that usually increase the risk may be mentioned. Thus,

---

[5]See Chapter 8.

[6]See Mary W. Gray, "The Case for Nondiscrimination in Insurance," *Journal of Insurance Regulation*, Vol. 2 (September 1983), pp. 3–10; and Barbara J. Lautzenheiser, Jo Conway Roberts, and Mavis A. Walters, "H.R.100/S.372: Are They Necessary?," *ibid.*, pp. 11–19.

[7]The first comprehensive statistical study of the relationship between build and mortality covered the experience on policies issued by the principal companies from 1885 through 1908 and was published in 1913 as the *Medico-Actuarial Mortality Investigation*. The most recent investigation was made by the Society of Actuaries and the Association of Life Insurance Medical Directors of America, encompassing the ordinary issues of 25 companies for the years 1954 to 1972 and published in 1979 in a study entitled, *Build and Blood Pressure Study, 1979.*

an examination of the circulatory system may reveal elevated blood pressure, a heart murmur, or a high or intermittent heart rate. An analysis of the urine may disclose the presence of albumin, sugar, or red blood cells. When there are indications of any of these or similar conditions, further examination may be necessary before the application can be accepted on terms satisfactory to both parties.

Coronary risk factors are used by many companies in their overall assessment of expected mortality. Factors such as low blood cholesterol, optimal blood pressure, and non-cigarette smoking contribute significantly toward improved mortality from heart disease.

Acquired immune deficiency syndrome (AIDS) is becoming increasingly important to life and health insurers because of its rapid spread and (to date) always fatal effect. Insurers desire to treat AIDS like any other medical condition for individual underwriting purposes. This means being able—if they wish—to have proposed insureds tested for the presence of the AIDS virus antibodies indicating past exposure to the virus. Many, however, oppose the use by insurers of such tests, with some jurisdictions prohibiting their use altogether. Concern exists about unfair discrimination and test result confidentiality. A National Association of Insurance Commissioners (NAIC) Advisory Committee was examining the issues surrounding AIDS and insurance at the time this book was going to press.

Smoking. Whether an individual smokes cigarettes is today an important risk factor by itself. In the past, smoking was considered but only rarely as a factor of importance by itself. For example, if a person had a respiratory problem and smoked, the underwriting decision might be less favorable than if an otherwise similarly situated individual had the same medical problem and did not smoke. However, smoking unaccompanied by any other negative factor was not normally a cause of a less favorable rating.

Insurers now understand that smoking, even in the absence of any other negative factor, causes future mortality to be worse than average and, the degree of variation is of such significance

as to warrant separate classification. So important is this factor that at some ages the average female *smoker* can be expected to exhibit higher mortality than the average *nonsmoking* male of the same age. Younger smokers (e.g., age 35) will exhibit higher mortality than many older (e.g., age 42) nonsmokers. Smoking aggravates many other health problems. As a result, most insurers now have separate rates for smokers and nonsmokers and factor smoking habits into overall risk assessment.

Information regarding smoking habits is elicited on the application and verified through medical and nonmedical (e.g., consumer reporting agency) sources. Verification has proven difficult, with many persons misrepresenting the fact that they smoke.

Current experience has led most companies to subdivide the *standard group* into about 70 percent nonsmokers, who experience about 85 percent relative mortality, and 30 percent smokers, who experience about 135 percent relative mortality. This differential is a rough approximation that varies by age. Some have suggested that cigarette smokers experience twice the mortality of nonsmokers.

A few companies still call their nonsmoker class "preferred" and require some additional criteria such as build be met. However, it is still essentially a nonsmoker group and not a "super standard" group. Assuming a continuing decline in the proportion of the population smoking, the nonsmoker class should become *the* standard class, with smoking becoming a risk factor leading to a substandard classification.

Personal History. Insurance companies inquire into facets of the proposed insured's background that could have a bearing on his or her expected mortality. This investigation may include the individual's health record, habits, driving violations, amount of insurance already owned, and so on.

The health record is usually the most important of the personal-history factors. If the individual has in the past suffered a serious illness or accident, an appraisal of its probable effects on future life will be made. The appraisal frequently will require that, in addition to the medical history given by the proposed insured, reports be obtained from personal physicians and hospitals.

Insurance history is important. The proposed insured may have been refused life insurance by some company or offered insurance under special terms. If so, this fact may imply an extra hazard that existed formerly and may still be present and should be investigated. There are legal restrictions in some states that prohibit the basing of an adverse action solely on information of any previous such action by another company. In any event, sound underwriting practice dictates that the company make every effort to establish for itself the proposed insured's insurability. Also, the individual may have such a large amount of insurance already in force on his or her life that a request for more may be indicative of speculation if not justified by present income and finances.

Family History. Family history is considered important by some companies because of the transmission of certain characteristics by heredity. If the history shows that most members of the family have lived to old age and have been free to an advanced age from heart disease, cancer, diabetes, and similar diseases, it may be inferred that the proposed insured will be less susceptible to such diseases. In many companies, however, family history is not used directly in classification unless it reveals a characteristic that appears in some form also in the proposed insured. For example, two or more deaths below age 60 because of cardiovascular disease in the family may suggest a need for a sizable additional debit[8] in the case of an individual with elevated blood pressure or only a small debit in the absence of elevated blood pressure or other impairments of the cardiovascular system.

Occupation. Occupational hazards are not as important today as in the past, although in certain cases they can be. Occupational hazards may increase the risk in at least three different ways. First, the occupation may present an environmental hazard, such as exposure to violence, irregular

[8]See pp. 418–419.

living, or a temptation to experiment with drugs or overindulge in alcohol. Second, the physical conditions surrounding an occupation can have a decided bearing upon health and longevity, as with persons who work in close, dusty, or poorly ventilated quarters or are exposed to chemical toxins. Finally, there is the risk from accident, such as is faced by professional auto racers, crop dusters, and professional divers.

An individual who has recently changed from a hazardous occupation to a safer form of employment may be underwritten carefully, since he or she may still retain ill effects from the earlier employment. In some cases, the change may have been prompted by a health factor. Also, there is a greater possibility of a return to the former occupation than is a person without such a history. Usual practice is to ignore prior occupation if the individual has been removed from it for a period of one or more years. Because of increased attention to job safety and working conditions, ratings have been reduced or eliminated for many occupations.

Aviation. It is usual to ask in the application if the proposed insured engages in aviation activities. Flights as a fare-paying passenger on regularly scheduled airlines are not sufficiently hazardous to affect the risk, particularly since such travel has become so widespread. But where there may be a definite aviation hazard involving commercial, private, or military flying, the proposed insured may be requested to fill out a supplementary questionnaire devoted entirely to this subject. The company may then charge an extra premium to compensate for the aviation hazard, or, infrequently, this cause of death may be excluded from the policy entirely. If the risk is excluded and if death occurs from aviation activities, the company is liable only for a return of premiums paid or the reserve accumulated on the policy, and sometimes whichever of the two produces the larger figure.

Alcohol and Drugs. Information is usually sought regarding the proposed insured's use of habit-forming drugs and intoxicating beverages. If it is found that the individual uses alcoholic beverages in large amounts, he or she may be declined or offered substandard insurance, depending on the degree of use. Use of alcohol in moderation is considered normal. Use of drugs not prescribed by a physician or drug abuse may call for a declination depending on the type of drug. A history of misuse or unsupervised use may require an extra rating, depending on the length of time since the drug or drugs were used.

Hazardous Sports and Avocations. With a high standard of living and a search by many persons for new ways to spend their leisure time, hobbies and avocations are becoming important underwriting factors. Such activities as scuba diving, mountain climbing, competitive racing, hang gliding, and sky diving clearly can involve a significant additional hazard to be considered in the underwriting process. If there is a hazard causing increased expected mortality and the individual is insurable on some basis, he or she is usually charged a flat extra premium commensurate with the risk. In states where it is permitted, a rider excluding death from participation in the hazardous activity may be employed occasionally.

Antiselection and Speculation. Some few applicants misrepresent information when applying for insurance. Companies therefore inquire into the character and financial standing of all applicants. Information sought about character includes business as well as personal activities. The applicant's reputation for meeting obligations and fairness in dealings may indicate the type of moral risk involved. Financial status, as represented by personal net worth, size and sources of income, and permanency of the income, is probably as important as any factor. Even where the amount of insurance applied for is not large, if the applicant appears to have sufficient protection already, the case will bear close investigation.

Speculation must be avoided, not only when the insured takes out insurance on his or her own life, but when one person wishes to insure the life of another. Although the law gives an individual an unlimited insurable interest in his or her own life, the need for insurance, as determined from such factors as financial status and dependents, largely governs the maximum amount the com-

pany will sell to an individual. Where the insurance is applied for by one person on the life of another, companies also want to know about the insurable interest and the extent of the economic loss that the death of the insured will cause the applicant. Applications for life insurance for speculative purposes are rare when compared with total insurance sold, but the cases are frequent enough to be of importance. Individual cases have involved millions of dollars. Also, a company has a legal responsibility to protect against speculation by an individual who does not have an insurable interest in the life of another, because it could be sued for damages if the amount of insurance was possibly a contributing factor to the insured's death.

Today, most companies will insure children at birth. The mortality experience for this class of business has been excellent. Some companies will issue whatever amounts are reasonable on a child's life provided that the parents (if insurable) have a suitable insurance program and provided that all children in the family are insured for comparable amounts. The underwriting problem is to guard against one child being selected for insurance.

Comparatively few persons at advanced ages can qualify as good risks. The earning power of such individuals usually has decreased or ceased, thus reducing the insurable value and the need for protection. Companies insure older persons only after careful underwriting and then usually to provide liquidity to meet estate taxes and other cash needs following the death of a person with substantial property holdings. Insurance of older persons by those on whom they are dependent is often speculative, whether intentional or not, and is approached with caution.

Military Service. In the absence of hostilities, contracts are issued to military personnel with no exclusions or limitations. The adverse selection involved with individuals engaged in or facing military service during a period of armed conflict can constitute an underwriting problem. Underwriting action taken in the past has been either outright declination, a limitation on the amount of insurance issued, or the attachment of a so-called "war clause," which may limit the insurer's obligation to the refund of premiums paid with interest, depending on the cause of death.[9] The war clause was used extensively during World War II in policies issued to military personnel. The clause was also used during the Korean conflict, primarily on military personnel who were under orders to go to Korea or were members of particularly hazardous combat forces. They generally were not used during the Vietnam war. In any event, when hostilities cease, war clauses are routinely cancelled and may not be reactivated.

Residence. The mortality rate in most developing countries is higher than in the United States and Canada, mostly because of inadequate nutrition and medical care and poor living conditions. Individuals moving to the United States and Canada from such a country may already have been adversely affected by those conditions. When a U.S. or Canadian proposed insured intends to reside in a developing country, the possible increased hazards of disease, poor living conditions, and political unrest must be considered. A flat extra premium rate may be charged.

Another concern in underwriting individuals residing, or who have resided, in foreign countries is the inability to develop the full extent of underwriting information. It is difficult, generally, to obtain investigative reports, attending physician statements, and other underwriting information on a timely basis.

The Health Insurance Risk

In underwriting of individual health insurance—just as in life insurance—the hazards that affect the probability of loss must be evaluated. In contrast to life insurance, the multiplicity of benefit types has an important bearing on the evaluation of the hazards. The claim rates and the average severity of the claims are affected by many of the same factors as those discussed for the life risk, but their significance varies. To avoid duplication, the following dissussion on selection and classification in health insurance attempts to con-

centrate on the unique aspects of individual health insurance underwriting.[10]

Age. Age affects annual claim costs differently, depending on the type of benefit involved, although both frequency and severity of claim increase with advancing age for all types of benefits. In the case of long-term disability, the increase in risk can be as rapid as that found in death rates. For medical expense coverages and short-term disability income contracts, the increase is not marked until about age 55. Thus, guaranteed-renewable and noncancellable disability income policies and life insurance disability riders are usually issued with premiums graded according to age of issue. Other types of policies, such as those that are optionally renewable by the insurance company, sometimes utilize a flat premium from, say, ages 18 to 55, with sharply higher rates for renewals or new issues at higher ages. In the past, policies have not been available at ages much beyond 60, although in recent years medical care expense coverage has been extended increasingly to these older ages. There is normally little need for income-replacement coverage at advanced ages, since some form of retirement income is available to most insureds. Currently, some modern disability policies provide for continuance to age 70 or 72, subject only to full-time employment.

Adverse selection is a severe problem at older ages, but considerable medical expense protection is provided for retiring persons under group policies and under federal Medicare coverage. Most individual policies currently available are limited as to amount and type of coverage after a certain age, such as 65 or 70, although some companies have made lifetime coverage available. Most companies now offer Medicare supplement policies that pay those expenses not covered by Medicare.

Sex. Sex, as in the case of life insurance policies, is of considerable significance in health

---

[10] See *A Course in Individual Health Insurance—Part A* (Washington, D.C.: Health Insurance Association of America, 1983), pp. 167–210; and Charles A. Will, *Life Company Underwriting* (New York: Life Office Management Association, 1974).

[9]See Chapter 8.

insurance underwriting. Females show higher disability rates than males at all but the upper ages (e.g., 55 and older) in most studies. This is true even for policies that exclude coverage of maternity expenses. In the past, underwriters believed that these higher rates were due to a greater hazard of malingering in connection with women, since they were not normally the breadwinners. Also, companies were reluctant to issue disability income coverage to working women because their employment traditionally was viewed as temporary and intermittent. Where issued, such coverage was frequently limited to shorter benefit periods and lower benefits than were offered to men. Life insurance disability income riders and long-term noncancellable disability income policies were seldom issued to women. For all types of policies, women were usually charged a higher rate than men, even if the maternity risk was excluded. Where such coverage was included, rates for the childbearing ages were even higher. These practices, based on the higher rates of disability actually experienced, were almost universal. Currently, however, as a result of legislation and regulation in the area of civil rights, sex has virtually ceased to be a selection determinant. Most companies now offer the same policy benefits and provisions to men and to women, although often at a higher premium rate and often with an exclusion for normal pregnancy.

Medical Aspects. To evaluate a proposed insured for health insurance, it is necessary to consider both his or her *health history* and *current physical condition.* This evaluation is done primarily by estimating the probable influence of current impairments and previous medical histories on future claims.

1. *Medical history.* The importance the underwriter attaches to a history of past illness or accident will vary, depending on the nature of the condition and its severity, the frequency of attacks, the degree of permanent impairment, and the length of time that has elapsed since recovery. This is important for both accidental injury and sickness coverages. For example, a history of epilepsy or vertigo would increase the probability of accident, and diabetes, overweight, or cardiovascular con-

ditions would increase the duration of disability from injury or sickness.

Particular attention is paid to chronic conditions where the probability of recurrence is high. Less attention is necessary for acute conditions, even if quite serious, if recovery has been good, permanent impairment is not evident, and a reasonable time has elapsed without recurrence. Thus, a chronic condition such as asthma will be regarded more seriously than a history of kidney stones or gallbladder trouble. Naturally, conditions that are both chronic and serious, such as heart disease, hypertension, and cancer, will be underwritten very carefully and may require declination if coverage on an extra premium basis cannot be offered.

2. *Physical condition.* Obviously, the present and potential physical condition of the proposed insured is important. The present physical condition and past health record must be evaluated to predict the probability of future disability. Naturally, an individual who is currently disabled or undergoing medical treatment for a significant ailment at the time of application is not eligible for insurance against losses resulting from the currently existing impairment.

Fitness, as evidenced by blood pressure and pulse as well as weight, is of considerable significance. Thus, whereas overweight and elevated blood pressure are not disabling of themselves, they are considered indicators of a higher future incidence of cardiovascular impairment. Overweight can also complicate any future surgical procedures or disabilities from any cause and can increase the time needed for recovery.

Underweight, especially if marked, is also an underwriting consideration that should be viewed in the light of the proposed insured's history—as in the case of ulcer, bronchitis, frequently recurring colds or pneumonia, colitis, and so on. It could also be an indication of an undiagnosed condition that would call for a medical examination by the company. However, underweight of and by itself is usually not significant. As in the case of life insurance, cigarette smoking also is recognized as a significant underwriting factor. Many companies use separate health insurance premium rates for smokers and nonsmokers.

3. *Family history.* The health history of the family sometimes is taken into account in underwriting health insurance. The application may request information on the age and health status of living parents, brothers, and sisters, and on age at death and cause of death for those deceased. Family history is usually of little significance in underwriting health insurance.

Financial Status. The financial status of the proposed insured can be a prime underwriting consideration for individual health insurance coverages.

1. *Plan of insurance.* One of the most important factors affecting actual claim rates is the type of policy and the type and amount of benefit. In this regard, the definition of disability itself is important (e.g., "own occupation," "any occupation," or "any reasonable occupation").[11] In medical expense coverages, the definition of claim eligibility may be in terms of admission to a hospital, treatment by a physician, and/or the incurring of an expense. The length of the elimination period, the benefit period, the amount of the deductible, and the extent of percentage participation (coinsurance) can be major factors in determining claim rates for disabilities of short duration.

Over and above the differences in rates due to different definitions of covered events, differences in types and amounts of benefits will produce different claim rates. This is possibly a reflection of moral hazard. Under exactly the same definition of disability and elimination period, for example, higher claim rates result for a disability income benefit than for a waiver-of-premium benefit. In general, the greater the prospective benefit in terms of both amount and duration, the greater will be the claim rate, other things being equal. Naturally, where the potential benefit exceeds the loss, particular difficulties arise. In such a case, the insured can make a profit from disability, and the motivation for malingering and a slow recovery are greatest.

The underwriter's primary concern with differences in disability definition is to be careful to apply appropriate criteria to specific types of

[11]See Chapter 17.

insurance. When a policy or life insurance disability rider is noncancellable, stricter standards are usually applied in initial underwriting. There can be no renewal underwriting, as can be done with optionally renewable individual health insurance. More conservative standards must also be applied to contracts providing high benefits in terms of amount or duration, or both. Similarly, stricter standards are applied for policies covering sickness than for those covering accidental injury only.

In practice, the strictest underwriting standards are applied to the long-term, noncancellable disability income policies and to life insurance disability riders. In the case of medical expense coverage, similar high standards are applied to major medical expense contracts. Disability income contracts and medical expense contracts renewable at the option of the company are underwritten more liberally. The most lenient underwriting standards are applied to industrial and limited policies, where benefit amounts are small and durations are short.

It should be noted, however, that there is a growing conviction that proper standards must be applied to all plans regardless of renewability provision, since the main claim problem is the large continuing claim rather than repeat claims. Once an insured is on claim status, it really does not matter if the contract is noncancellable or optionally renewable.

2. *Relation of insurance to loss.* The most significant underwriting safeguard against moral hazard is a reasonable relationship between the insurance benefit and the amount of potential loss. Underwriters believe that the insured should share in the loss to some extent. This may be accomplished by limited benefit periods, limitations on the amount of insurance issued, and policy provisions limiting the amount that may be collected in relation to the loss.

In medical expense coverages, for example, the amount of benefit for each type of expense usually is limited and stated in the contract. Also, some policies exclude such expenses as nurses' fees, drugs, appliances, prosthetics, and blood plasma.

In major medical expense policies, such items as dental services, services in government hospitals, and services primarily for rest or diagnosis usually are not covered. Such contracts also commonly include deductible and percentage participation (coinsurance) provisions. The deductible serves mainly to avoid duplication with underlying basic policies, but the coinsurance provision causes the insured to participate directly (20 to 25 percent) in loss payments above the deductible.

In disability income contracts, the main reliance is on limiting the amount of benefit in relation to earned income. Companies will not issue coverage for more than a portion of the proposed insured's earned income. This portion may be a straight percentage of earned income or a percentage plus or minus a stated amount. It was not uncommon in the past to insure as much as 75 or 80 percent of the insured's earned income, but with disability benefits offered by the federal and some state governments, and the effect of taxes on take-home pay, this percentage has rapidly decreased.

In addition to an amount limit based on percentage of income, most life insurance companies establish a maximum issue and participation limit—the overall maximum amount of disability coverage they will participate in writing on any one individual regardless of income. This usually varies by class. Some companies have a maximum limit as high as $10,000 per month on the best class of risks.

Most companies also will test the need and incentive to return to work by scrutinizing the individual's unearned income and net worth. This financial analysis can be very important when application is made for sizable amounts of disability insurance.

For those with higher incomes and coverages involving long benefit durations, noncancellable or guaranteed-renewable features, and life insurance disability income riders, even stricter standards are applied. In noncancellable policies, the **average earnings clause** is sometimes used, particularly where the benefit duration is long. Since many companies do not use the clause, and since it takes no account of take-home pay, it is of limited value. Benefit prorating provisions are rarely found in medical expense policies, and there is no protection against duplication of benefits in the usual policy. State laws often prohibit in-

dividually issued medical expense policies from having coordination-of-benefit clauses. Rising health insurance claims and the rising level of disability claims under Social Security have directed attention to the underwriting problems in these areas, and safeguards against such situations are being sought.

Occupation. The probability of disablement is materially affected by occupation, particularly as regards the peril of accidental injury. Certain occupations, such as heavy-construction workers, loggers, miners, and the like are normally uninsurable on an individual basis. The duties of an occupation will also affect a claimant's ability to work, and this, as well as the accident peril, is a basis for classifying and rating occupations. For example, after becoming disabled by a lower-back condition, it would be easier for a desk clerk than, say, a construction worker to return to work. Experience has indicated that the incentive to malinger is greater among certain lower-paid occupations where the work is repetitive and unchallenging than among business owners and professionals. This factor is of significance mostly in connection with disability income coverage.

For disability income, insurable occupations are classified into broad groups of about the same average claim cost, with appropriate scales of premium rates applying to each class. The number of classes may vary from four to six, depending on the type of company and the types of coverage provided. There is some diversity among companies in this regard.

The complexity of occupational classifications is greatest in the noncancellable policies. Limited and industrial contracts are usually sold at a uniform rate for all occupations with some being excluded by policy provisions. Some companies restrict sales of noncancellable policies to occupations with relatively favorable experiences. Some companies, having no such restriction, will at times have limitations as to benefit periods and amounts available to the less favorable occupations.

Antiselection and Speculation. Antiselection and speculation are particularly serious problems in health insurance. The subjective nature of the disability status and the difficulties in defining the insured events complicate the problem considerably. In underwriting a disability application, the underwriter must make subjective evaluations that take into consideration such nebulous factors as motivation to work, occupational stability, and the financial situation of the proposed insured. For example, the owner of a profitable small business, who knows that continued profitability depends on his or her being on the job every day, may have much stronger motivation to return to work than an individual whose business may be on the verge of collapsing. The underwriter must make a subjective evaluation of which individual will be disabled longer in the event of an accident or sickness and which one will be more inclined to malinger and take unfair advantage of any benefit provisions.

The character of the insured is one of the important determinants of claim rates. Insurers must contend with such conditions as psychosomatic illness, accident proneness, and hypochondria, as well as deliberate malingering. The underwriter must be careful to avoid **overinsurance.** In addition to the basic safeguard of limiting the amount of benefit to something less than the insured's take-home pay and avoiding duplicate hospital coverages, companies scrutinize all aspects of the underwriting process for evidence of moral hazard.

An applicant who voluntarily approaches a company for insurance requires careful consideration. Experience has indicated that there is a better-than-average chance that he or she has knowledge of some condition that will make the insurance particularly valuable to him or her (i.e., there exists **selection against the insurer**). In most cases where the occupation is characterized by unstable earnings, work performed at home (particularly where both spouses are involved), irregular or seasonal work, or any connection with illegal or dubious activities, underwriters will be hesitant to approve the appplication. Any evidence of fraud or misrepresentation in the application will also be considered significant.

Other Factors. Other factors that affect physical hazard to some degree include foreign travel or residence, habits, and avocations. Foreign travel or residence is considered in underwriting health risks because of the difficulty in claim administration and in obtaining underwriting data. Drug addiction or excessive use of alcohol are, of course, quite significant. These affect both the physical and moral hazard and normally lead to rejection. Exclusion riders are usually used for individuals who participate in particularly hazardous sports. Private aviation activities are excluded by policy wording from some disability contracts where an accidental-death benefit has been automatically included in the contract. For those companies granting unrestricted aviation coverage, such activities, including the type and frequency of flying, become an underwriting consideration.

UNDERWRITING SUBSTANDARD RISKS

In the issuance of substandard life and health insurance, provision must be made for higher than standard mortality or morbidity. This may be done by charging an extra premium in addition to the standard premium or other methods. These are discussed below, first with reference to life insurance, then health insurance.

Life Insurance on Substandard Risks

Statistical information on past experience is essential to develop an equitable basis for providing insurance on lives subject to different impairments. Companies have accumulated considerable statistics on impairments that aids them in estimating their influence on mortality. Similarly, the wide experience of reinsurers, especially with substandard-risk appraisal, has assisted direct-writing companies in establishing sound underwriting systems.

Companies use two types of statistics on past experience. Experience under life insurance policies is useful but often is not available in sufficient quantity, particularly on impairments that occur infrequently or that have mortality so high that insurance is unobtainable at a reasonable price. Articles in medical journals are useful to underwriters in providing data on impairments for which insurance is not available or for which insurance experience is not sufficiently current to reflect the results of new medical developments.

Some companies use reinsurance extensively to seek standard insurance on risks that are substandard by their own underwriting standards. Some reinsurance companies pursue this business aggressively. They are willing to assume risks that a direct writing company, concerned about maintaining competitive pricing for standard risks, is not willing to assume.

Methods of Classification. Once underwriting information about a proposed insured has been assembled, it must be evaluated and a decision reached as to whether the individual is to be accepted at preferred or standard rates, treated as a substandard but acceptable risk, or rejected entirely. Occasionally, a risk is postponed for a period of time until the effect of a condition or impairment is resolved. For instance, if the proposed insured is expecting imminent surgery, a decision could be postponed until after the surgery. Ideally, the selection and classification system used by a company should (1) measure accurately the effect of each factor affecting the risk; (2) assess the combined impact of interrelated factors, including those in conflict; (3) produce equitable results; and (4) be relatively simple and inexpensive to operate. Two basic systems have been in use in the United States over the years in an effort to accommodate those concerns: the judgment method and the numerical rating system.

1. *The judgment method of rating.* Originally and for many years companies used the judgment method of rating. Under this method, the company depended on the combined judgment of those in the medical, actuarial, and other departments who were qualified for this work. The judgment method of rating functions effectively when there is only one unfavorable factor to consider or where the decision is simply one of accepting the proposed insured at standard rates or rejecting him or her entirely. Where multiple factors (some possibly in conflict) were involved or a proper substandard classification was needed, it left something to be desired. Moreover, it required the use of highly skilled personnel to achieve proper risk appraisal with consistency of treatment. To overcome the weakness of the judgment

method of rating, the life insurance business developed the so-called numerical rating system.[12]

2. *The numerical rating system.* The numerical rating system is based on the principle that a large number of factors enters into the composition of a risk and that the impact of each of these factors on longevity can be determined by a statistical study of lives possessing that factor. Under this plan, 100 percent represents a normal or standard risk—one that is physically, morally, and financially sound, and has a need for the insurance.

Each of the factors that might influence a risk in an unusual way is considered a debit or a credit. Values are assigned to the individual factors. For example, if the mortality of a group of insured lives reflecting a certain degree of overweight, or a certain degree of elevated blood pressure, has been found to be 150 percent of standard risks, a debit (addition) of 50 percentage points will be assigned to such degree of overweight or blood pressure.

Judgment still enters into the operation of the numerical system, primarily in the assignment of numerical values to each factor and, when it occurs, in determining the effect of two or more factors that are related to each other in some way. When two factors are so related that one affects the other, judgment and past experience may dictate an addition that is greater or smaller than the mere addition of the numerical factors. For example, if family history shows several early deaths from heart disease, this adverse factor may be nullified somewhat by a good physical condition, good build, normal electrocardiograms, and similar favorable factors. On the other hand, such a family history plus findings of overweight or elevated blood pressure will probably warrant a larger debit than the sum of the two adverse factors.

The system in practice is applied with common sense and has the advantages of greater consistency of treatment and of permitting lay underwriters to process all applications other than

[12]See Arthur H. Hunter and Oscar H. Rogers, "The Numerical Method of Determining the Value of Risks for Insurance," *Transactions of the Actuarial Society of America,* Vol. XX, Part II (1919).

those requiring detailed medical analysis. This reduced reliance on physicians in underwriting helps minimize the expense of the underwriting process.

A hypothetical illustration will help make clear the operation of the numerical rating system. Suppose that an attorney, age 35, applies for a universal life policy. Information obtained by the company reveals the following facts: height, 5 feet, 9 inches; weight, 205 pounds; family history, better than average; habits, good; personal history shows medical attention for slightly elevated blood pressure. A paramedical examination is requested and the individual's blood pressure is found to be 150/90. From tables developed for this purpose, the company will first ascertain the basic rating for this individual. This depends on the build. In this case, the basic rating according to the company's table is 125, because the individual is overweight. In other words, the overweight in such cases is expected to result in mortality that equals 125 percent of average. To this basic figure, 50 is added for elevated blood pressure. The total is 175. On the other hand, a credit of 10 may be allowed for a favorable family history. The net result, 165, represents an expected mortality 65 percent greater than that expected for standard risks. The analysis is summarized as follows:

Factor	Debits	Credits
Base = 100		
Build: overweight	25	
Physical condition: blood pressure	50	
Family history		10
	75	10
Rating = 165		

The ratings obtained by this method range in most companies from a low of 75 to a high of 500 or more. In most companies, the ratings that fall between 75 and 125 are classified as standard. Some companies may broaden the standard category to include ratings up to 130 or 140, particularly at the younger ages. Proposed insureds that produce a rate in excess of the standard limit are either assigned to appropriate substandard classes or declined.

The scale of ratings produced by the numerical rating system might be classified in a particular company as follows:

Standard				Substandard		
75 85 100 115			125	135 145 155		

	Uninsurable
485 500	

Some companies will issue ratings as high as 1000 percent. Generally, ratings over 500 percent are referred to as experimental underwriting.

Wide differences in underwriting decisions can exist among competing life insurance companies. This can be explained in two ways. First, the size of the numerical debits in their impairment manuals may differ. Second, their judgment in assessing debits and credits may differ. In addition, some numerical measures of impairments or variations of impairments do not appear in the manuals.

3. Use of the computer in underwriting. For some years, managers of life insurance underwriting departments have utilized the computer to relieve the underwriter of many clerical operations associated with application screening. Certain application data, including answers to underwriting questions, can be input by personnel at agency offices that process applications received from agents. The computer can be programmed to identify answers that raise possible underwriting problems. The computer, in effect, underwrites the application and eliminates the need for a normal underwriting review unless problems are identified.

The percentage of applications that can be computer rated depends on the amount of data input and the sophistication of the computer program in identifying and even rating adverse data. At a minimum, the computer can identify "yes" or "no" answers. If the answers are all "no," the application can be approved. At the other extreme, the computer can calculate the mortality debits for build, blood pressure, and other numerical measurements, and show on a screen the details to a "yes" answer so that the underwriter does not need to await receipt of the written application before completing underwriting action.

Incidence of Extra Mortality. Although a number of factors may cause a proposed insured to be rated substandard, more than 75 percent are rated because of various physical impairments such as heart murmurs, overweight, diabetes, and elevated blood pressure.[13] However, a rating system cannot be constructed for substandard insurance that follows over time precisely the pattern of extra mortality of each impairment. This would be prohibitively expensive and is impracticable because knowledge of substandard mortality is insufficiently developed. Absolute equity is an objective to be sought. It is not attainable.

The majority of companies therefore categorize substandard insureds into three broad groups: (1) a group in which extra deaths remain approximately the same in all years following the issue of the policy, (2) a group in which the extra deaths increase as insureds grow older, and (3) a group in which extra deaths decrease with time. Examples of the constant type of extra deaths would be hazardous avocation or occupation. An example of increasing extra mortality would be a person with diabetes, whereas a person who had just undergone a supposedly successful operation would be representative of the decreasing category. Such a classification permits companies to assess premiums according to the incidence of the extra deaths. If companies expect the same number of extra deaths to occur in two groups over a particular period of time, but also expect the timing to be different, different types of extra premiums will be needed for the extra mortality in the group where the extra deaths occur early

("decreasing") from those where the deaths occur later ("increasing").

Methods of Rating. Several methods exist for rating impaired lives. In general, an effort is made to adapt the method to the type of exposure represented by the impaired individual, but departures from theoretically correct treatment are made for practical reasons. The objectives in establishing an extra-premium structure are that it be (1) equitable between impairments and between classes, (2) easy to administer, and (3) easily understood by agents and the consumer public. Several such premium structures are discussed below.

1. *Multiple table extra.* By far the most common method used for substandard insurance is the multiple table extra method. Substandard risks are divided into broad groups according to their numerical ratings, and premium rates, or mortality charges in the case of universal life policies, are based on mortality rates corresponding to the average numerical ratings in each class. Most companies use the same nonforfeiture values and dividends as for standard risks. Some companies do not permit the extended term insurance option with higher-rated cases.

Generally, numerical ratings up to about 125 are considered standard and such policyowners pay the same premium rates. The procedure in setting up a substandard class is identical, except that the average rating of each additional substandard class is progressively higher than that for the standard class. Companies usually provide for at least four and sometimes as many as six or seven substandard classes when special nonforfeiture values are used, and as many as 16 classifications when standard values are used. Proposed insureds are then placed in the appropriate class (standard or substandard) in accordance with their numerical ratings. The average numerical rating within these classes may range from about 125 to 500 or even higher. An example of a scale of substandard classifications is shown in Table 23–1.

Under this method, a special mortality table is developed for each substandard classification, reflecting the experience of each, and a set of gross-

[13]Based on a recent study of ordinary insurance, the reasons for extra ratings showed the following distribution: cardiovascular renal disease or its symptoms, 33 percent; weight problem, 14 percent; other medical reasons, 26 percent; occupation and other reasons, 27 percent. See *Life Insurance Fact Book, 1986* (Washington, D.C.: American Council of Life Insurance), p. 103.

TABLE 23-1. Illustrative scale of substandard mortality classifications

Table	Mortality (%)	Numerical Rating
1	125	120–135
2	150	140–160
3	175	165–185
4	200	190–210
5	225	215–235
6	250	240–260
7	275	265–285
8	300	290–325
10	350	330–380
12	400	385–450
16	500	455–550
—	—	Over 550

premium rates is computed for the classification. Table 23–2 shows illustrative gross-premium rates for an ordinary life contract under different scales of substandard mortality classifications. The standard rates are also shown for purposes of comparison.

These rates are not necessarily representative of the rates charged by any company but show the relationship between rates for different substandard classes. Companies also vary premium rates for substandard risks by plan, with the extra charges being lower for the higher cash value plans, other things being equal. Universal life extra premiums are based on the net amount at risk and, depending on plan design, could either be equivalent to term or to ordinary life extra premiums.

Substandard premiums do not increase in proportion to the degree of extra mortality in-

volved. This is due to the fact that the loading does not increase in proportion to the degree of extra mortality involved.

Multiple table extra ratings do not differentiate among the various types of substandard risks with different incidences of extra mortality (i.e., increasing, decreasing, or constant). The assumption of a constant percentage of the standard mortality rates implies a number of extra deaths per thousand that increases with age for all types of cases rated on this basis. Although theoretically this method may not exactly reflect, then, the incidence of extra risk, this procedure is justified on an expense basis, and on the average is reasonably accurate. Many companies use the multiple table extra method for some impairments and flat (see below) extras for others.

Notwithstanding the fact that many companies write insurance on persons subject to 500 percent of standard mortality, there is a point beyond which the degree of extra mortality is so high and the number of similar risks so limited that companies do not wish to insure them. As the ratings increase, fewer applicants are normally willing to pay the necessarily higher premiums, and the ones who are willing may know, somehow, that they are even worse risks than the company has estimated. As the premium is increased for a policy of individual insurance, the likelihood of adverse selection increases markedly.

2. *Flat extra premium.* This method is used where the extra mortality, measured in additional deaths per thousand, is expected to be constant,

TABLE 23-2. Illustrative participating gross premium rates, ordinary life, male, nonsmoker

Age	Rates for Standard Risks	Table 1: 120–135%	Table 2: 140–160%	Table 3: 165–185%	Table 4: 190–210%
15	$ 8.19	$ 8.94	$ 9.69	$10.44	$11.19
20	9.12	10.02	10.92	11.81	12.72
25	10.46	11.49	12.51	13.54	14.56
30	12.45	13.75	15.15	16.45	17.65
35	14.82	16.45	18.07	19.70	21.32
40	18.08	20.01	21.93	23.86	25.78
45	22.25	24.70	27.15	29.60	32.05
50	28.43	31.46	34.48	37.51	40.53
55	36.48	40.23	43.98	47.73	51.48
60	47.22	51.80	56.37	60.95	65.52
65	62.05	67.25	72.45	77.65	82.85

either for a temporary period or permanently, and largely independent of age. Under this method, a regular policy is issued, but a constant extra premium is charged to provide for the additional expected mortality. The policy is treated as standard for the purpose of dividends and nonforfeiture values.

The method is appropriate for most hazardous occupations and avocations, since much of the extra mortality is of an accidental nature and independent of age. The method is also appropriate to cover temporary extra mortality (for a specified period) where most of the extra risk falls in the early years after an operation.

3. *Lien plan.* One of the first problems encountered in the sale of substandard insurance was the difficulty of convincing the applicant that provision must be made for the extra mortality. To meet this problem, companies in some cases offered to issue a regular policy at standard rates with a lien against it, to be deducted in the event of the death of the insured. In theory, the term and amount of a lien can be calculated to be the actuarial equivalent of the extra mortality involved. The amount of the lien can be kept constant or the method refined to provide for a lien that reduces over time. The method was best adapted to a decreasing risk, however, and it was used chiefly for this class of risks.

The method had some advantages. It appealed to many insureds because it was easily understood. Many were willing to accept the lien against their insurance because of their optimism regarding the future; and often, the agent would sell additional insurance to cover the lien. On the other hand, the method had such serious defects that it has never been used extensively in this country and is, in fact, illegal in some states. In most instances, the amount of the lien, of necessity, was large compared with the face of the policy, and the insured often did not understand or realize that his or her protection was smaller than the face of the policy. Furthermore, in the case of decreasing risks, to which it usually was applied, the lien reduced the protection at the time the insured needed it most—during the early years following the issuance of the policy, when the need usually is the greatest. In fact, its overall use in the United States is negligible today except in some individual-policy pension trust plans.[14]

4. *Other methods.* In addition to the methods already discussed, another method of treating substandard insureds is to provide a limited death benefit equal to a refund of premiums if death occurs in the first few years (typically first two years). This, together with a higher standard premium, is used by some companies, particularly at older ages (over 50), who offer insurance by mail with little or no underwriting.

Companies sometimes have been willing to treat certain proposed insureds, who would have been substandard, as standard risks if the policy applied for was of a relatively high premium variety. Such a policy would have a higher reserve than lower-premium forms, thus lessening the risk assumed by the insurer. It is assumed that there is less antiselection with high-premium plans. Some companies refuse to issue term plans at high ratings, such as above 250 or 300 percent, primarily because of concern about adverse selection, particularly at each premium due date when the better risks in the group have less incentive to continue the policy.

Improvement in Expected Mortality. After a policy has been issued substandard under the permanent flat-extra-premium or multiple table extra method, the insured may become eligible to purchase insurance at standard rates, or under better terms than those governing the rated policy. Under such circumstances, insureds expect reconsideration. Many are automatic, in the sense that the rating is reduced in conjunction with the new underwriting evidence on a repeat sale that has a lower or no rating. Many companies enclose a notice with the policy that they will consider reducing or removing the rating on or after a specific anniversary, and some also enclose a reminder in the premium mailing on that anniversary. Most reconsiderations are noncompetitive, but some may be triggered by an offer of standard insurance made by another company.

To prevent insured persons from withdraw-

---

[14]The lien system, however, is used extensively in the United Kingdom and Canada.

ing, companies generally make some provision for handling such improvements. For the company to remove the extra charge without loss to itself, the extra charge in the first instance must have been computed with data from which the improved lives were eliminated at the point where their ratings were removed. If the extra premium for the impairment was calculated from data that included lives that had improved, the company theoretically should not remove the extra charge. In the latter case, some of the insureds would no doubt improve, but others will grow worse, and since the company could not increase the charges against those that deteriorate, it should not reduce charges to those that improve. As a practical matter, however, most companies anticipate such withdrawals and will reduce the premium if they received evidence that the risk has improved, or remove the rating if standard.

When an apparent reduction in expected mortality is due to a change in residence, occupation, or avocation, some companies require a probationary period of one or two years prior to rating removal. At the end of this period, the company makes a retroactive refund of the extra premium dating from the time the change occurred. This protects the company against the possibility that the insured will return to the former occupation, avocation, or residence. Some companies, for practical reasons, however, make the change without such a probationary period.

Health Insurance on Substandard Risks

As in the case of life insurance, the health insurance company can either reject an application, accept it at standard rates on a regular policy form, accept it on a restricted policy form, or accept it on a regular policy form with an extra premium. In recent years, there have been significant advances in the underwriting of impaired risks for health insurance, so that today only a small proportion of such risks are ineligible for insurance on some basis. Techniques for handling impaired risks include (1) exclusion riders, (2) extra premiums, (3) limitations on policy benefits, and (4) a combination of any of the above.

Exclusions. In contrast to life insurance, ex-

clusions are a common method of handling physical impairments in health insurance. An exclusion rider is an endorsement attached to a policy that excludes from coverage any loss arising from a named disease or physical impairment. With such losses excluded and other aspects of the case normal, full coverage can be issued for other types of losses at standard rates. The exclusion may be somewhat broader than the condition that leads to its use. For example, a proposed insured with a history of kidney stones might be offered a policy excluding all diseases of the kidneys or genitourinary tract. Such an approach is considered essential because a kidney-stone condition might aggravate another related disease, and it also avoids possible problems in the event that a claim based on a slightly different manifestation of the same condition is filed.

Although it is true that a broad exclusion rider impairs the value of the coverage, it is usually far preferable to the alternative. The only alternative often is declination if the condition is one that would be impossible to price accurately (such as a highly subjective condition). Furthermore, from the company's standpoint, the existence of the impairment can often produce disability even from unrelated ailments. Circumstances that commonly require waivers include back injuries, appendicitis, hernias, and optionally elective surgical procedures.

Extra Premiums. Most companies offer full coverage to certain impaired risks at an extra premium. There are several variations. Some companies offer coverage with an extra premium only on selected impairments or selected plans; others offer on all bases. Some reduce benefits and/or increase the elimination period for certain impairments and charge an extra premium in addition. Companies void the preexisting condition exclusion in the policy with respect to an impairment for which an extra premium is charged.

There are a multitude of problems in obtaining morbidity statistics that accurately reflect increased expected morbidity. Yet the prospect of offering broad coverage for preexisting conditions that could cause disability or hospitalization has encouraged many companies to change their underwriting practices and grant more complete coverage for an extra premium. Many impairments that cannot be satisfactorily excluded because they either are too broad in scope (such as psychoneurosis) or have too many systemic complications (such as many heart conditions or diabetes) can now be covered with an extra premium rather than declined. However, the use of the extra-premium approach does not eliminate the need for exclusions. Although exclusions are probably resorted to less frequently, there are still problems in granting unrestricted coverage in all instances.

Modification of Type of Coverage. The third major method of handling impaired health risks is to modify the type of policy. In the case of borderline applications, health insurance underwriters frequently settle the problem by offering a different and more limited form of coverage. This limitation may be a lower amount, a shorter benefit period, or a longer elimination period. This last device is particularly useful for cases where the medical history involves short-term disabilities only.

Renewal Underwriting. Renewal underwriting is concerned with the health history of the insured, and also changes in occupation, income, residence, or habits, all of which may have made him or her an undesirable risk. With optionally renewable policies, the company has an opportunity to reevaluate its insureds periodically. Some companies do not avail themselves of their right to reunderwrite optionally renewable policies unless or until the loss ratio for that particular group of policies reaches a point where action must be taken. Cancellation and reunderwriting seem unfair to some persons. It is said that the insured often does not fully understand the terms of the contract or, if he or she understands them, does not appreciate their full importance. This is one reason so many companies, especially life insurance companies, are now charging more and guaranteeing renewal of their policies to a specified age, rather than emphasizing one-year term plans.

Chapter 24

Life and Health Insurance Underwriting: II

SPECIAL UNDERWRITING PRACTICES

Normal underwriting standards are relaxed or create special underwriting concerns in several areas. The following discussion is intended to explain how reasonable results can be obtained in these areas.

Nonmedical Life Insurance

A substantial proportion of all new life insurance is written without the benefit of a medical or paramedical examination. Besides group life insurance, an increasing proportion of ordinary life insurance is sold without a medical or paramedical examination.[1] The expression **nonmedical life insurance** normally refers to ordinary insurance sold in this manner.

In one sense, the use of the term is unfortunate, as it sometimes conveys the (erroneous) idea that the insurance is issued without *any* medical information. Of course, this is not the case. Medical information is still sought but it is gathered from the proposed insured by the agent seeking answers to the application questions (and possibly from attending physician statements and other sources). The term "nonmedical" should be understood to be synonomous with "no physical examination required."

For many years, the medical examination was considered a necessity. Toward the end of the nineteenth century, life insurance companies in England began to experiment with nonmedical underwriting on a limited basis. Not until 1921, however, did several Canadian companies begin to experiment with nonmedical as it is practiced today. The motivation for the development was a shortage of medical examiners, particularly in the rural areas, and the desire to reduce the expense rate on the predominantly small policies issued at that time. The practice spread to U.S. companies about four years later and is firmly entrenched today in both Canada and the United States.

While nonmedical underwriting lessens the demands on the medical profession and facilitates the sale and processing of an application, the primary justification lies in the savings in expense. As long as the expenses saved by elimination of the medical examination are greater than the cost of any extra mortality incurred because

---

[1]About two out of every three policies of ordinary insurance are currently being written on a nonmedical basis. These policies account for approximately one-third of the amount of new ordinary insurance written.

of its elimination, it is economically sound. Actuarial studies underlie the nonmedical rules utilized by life insurance companies. Modifications are made in these rules from time to time as indicated by emerging experience, including the increasing costs of medical examinations in recent years.

Perhaps the most important safeguard built into the nonmedical underwriting rules is a *limit on the amount* available on any one insured. In the early days, this limit was $1,000. When the experience proved to be more favorable than anticipated, the limits were gradually raised. During the 1970s, many companies provided up to $100,000 or higher on a nonmedical basis, subject to age limitations, and virtually all would issue $50,000 on that basis.

Nonmedical limits have "exploded" in recent years. Some companies have limits as high as $500,000 at the younger ages (through age 30) and at least one company has a $1,000,000 maximum. The maximum age still generally holds at 40 or 45. The reasons for this dramatic change are the effects of inflation on underwriting expenses, continuing reduction in deaths from natural causes at the younger ages, and high interest rates that have decreased substantially the present value of the extra mortality from not obtaining a medical exam.

A second safeguard built into nonmedical rules is a *limit on the ages* at which the insurance will be issued. Nonmedical insurance is not regularly available beyond age 40 or 45, except in special situations, such as salary savings groups, where the age limits might be higher. Most companies impose no lower age limit, offering it down to age zero.

Other safeguards include the general limitation of nonmedical insurance to *medically standard* risks. Companies will usually consider occupations where the extra hazard is largely accidental and all aviation and avocation exposures on a nonmedical basis. Some companies offer nonmedical coverage to higher ages or for larger amounts if the proposed insured has completed a comprehensive physical within the past six months or one year and the results are available from the attending physician. In addition to the expansion of nonmedical underwriting, there has also been expanded use of *simplified underwriting* in which only a few medical history questions are asked.

The application form used for nonmedical insurance contains the questions that would normally be asked by the medical examiner as well as the usual questions completed by the agent under a medical application. In those cases where adverse medical information is developed from these or other sources, the company may require a complete medical examination. It has been estimated that this occurs in about 10 percent of the nonmedical applications.

Guaranteed Issue Insurance

One of the important contractual arrangements under which retirement benefits are provided to employees is the individual contract pension trust. Under this arrangement, benefits are provided through retirement annuity or retirement income contracts purchased by the employer, through a trustee, for each of the employees eligible to participate in the pension plan. Traditionally, if retirement income contracts were used, each employee had to furnish evidence of insurability in the form of a satisfactory medical examination. Many companies today underwrite such plans on a nonmedical basis. In fact, the arrangement goes beyond the conventional concepts of nonmedical insurance. If the *group* is acceptable, the insurance company dispenses with individual underwriting and agrees in advance to accept applications for insurance on all employees who are actively at work. This practice is known as **guaranteed issue.** There is no underwriting beyond a screening of the group.

The mortality experience on these arrangements is higher than normal mortality, as would be expected. To offset the anticipated extra mortality under guaranteed issue plans, many companies pay lower commissions, and either charge a higher premium or separately classify the policies for dividend purposes.

Reinstatements and Policy Changes

When a life insurance policy lapses for nonpayment of the premium within the grace period, the policyowner has the contractual right to apply for policy reinstatement.[2] The owner must pay back premiums plus provide evidence of insurability satisfactory to the insurer. Evidence of insurability is typically provided via a reinstatement application. This application is a shortened version of the original application and is completed with minimal effort and time. Underwriting requirements commonly are less strict for recently lapsed policies and the entire process streamlined. For policies that have been lapsed for a longer time period and for which reinstatement is sought, the underwriting procedure more closely resembles that for a new insurance policy.

Underwriting also may be required in connection with certain policy changes. In general, an insurer will require evidence of insurability on any policy change that *increases* the policy's net amount at risk, except of course, when the change is one guaranteed by the contract (e.g., automatic face amount increases under a cost of living rider). Thus, if a policyowner wishes to increase the policy face amount under a universal life or other policy, evidence of insurability ordinarily will be required.

Also, if it is desired to add additional benefits—such as premium waiver, accidental death benefit, or guaranteed insurability option—to an existing policy, the insurer typically will require evidence of insurability. In each case, the essential purpose is to avoid adverse selection.

Highly Impaired Risks

In some cases, individuals with significant impairments have opportunities to obtain insurance at a cost they can afford even though the original application may have been declined by one or more companies. These opportunities can be found in companies that specialize in this market.

Specialist brokers often have arrangements with a large number of these specialist companies and can readily identify the company likely to make the best offer for a specific impairment. Often companies have a business arrangement with substandard specialist companies or brokers so that they can assist their agents in obtaining coverage through an alternate source. A proposed

insured should not be unduly discouraged by a declination from one company since considerable variation in underwriting judgment can exist even among companies specializing in highly impaired risks.

SOURCES OF INFORMATION CONCERNING LIFE AND HEALTH INSURANCE RISKS

A company may utilize several sources in obtaining information about a proposed insured, including (1) the applicant, (2) a physical examination, (3) the agent, (4) attending physicians, (5) consumer reporting agencies, and (6) the Medical Information Bureau. The data from these sources overlap. The "double check" is justified by experience. The federal Fair Credit Reporting Act of 1970 and individual state Fair Insurance Information Practices laws have established procedures for the collection and disclosure of certain underwriting information to ensure fairness and equitable treatment of the consumer with regard to confidentiality, accuracy, disclosure, and proper use.

The Application

Although application forms are by no means uniform in their content or arrangement, they generally consist of two parts. Part I of *life insurance* applications contains questions requesting nonmedical information. Thus, the proposed insured usually must give information regarding the following: name, present and past home and business addresses, occupation, sex, date of birth, name and relationship of beneficiary, amount and kind of insurance for which application is made, amount of life insurance already carried, driving record, modifications or refusal to issue insurance, past and contemplated aviation activities, avocations, and plans for foreign residence. In addition, the company will ask if the life insurance applied for is intended to replace insurance in force. This is required by most states over the applicant's signature.

Part I of the *health insurance* application consists of the proposed insured's statement of certain information about him- or herself and members

---

[2]See Chapter 8.

of his or her family, if applicable, and a description of the policy for which application is being made. The application form is usually quite detailed and complete for noncancellable, guaranteed renewable, and optionally renewable insurance but less so for industrial and limited policies. In its most complete form, it will include the individual's name, address, sex, date of birth, occupation, business, and employer. Normally, the application will also call for information as to present earnings and health insurance carried in all companies, including the one to which application is being made. At times, life insurance in force must be listed, particularly if any disability income riders are involved. Such coverages must, in many cases, be described completely, including any applicable waiting periods and deductibles. The applicant is required to state whether any life or health company has ever rejected or modified his or her application, canceled or refused to renew a policy, or refused payment of a claim as well as the reason for any such treatment.

Part II consists of medical history, furnished by the proposed insured to the medical or paramedical examiner, or if the policy is applied for on a nonmedical basis, to the agent, in response to questions that the latter is instructed to ask. Thus, questions are asked regarding the illnesses, diseases, injuries, and surgical operations experienced in the last 10 years, and regarding every physician or practitioner consultation in the past five (or some other number of) years. Other questions relate to the present physical condition. For example, questions are asked about the state of health. Because of their importance, all companies ask questions relating to the proposed insured's use of alcohol, cigarettes, and drugs. Finally, questions are asked about the individual's parents and siblings, including the number now living, their present health condition, and the date and cause of any deaths that have occurred.

Recently, some companies have also introduced "simplified underwriting" where at younger ages and for smaller amounts, which have a lesser mortality risk, and in order to save the time of the applicant, agent, and underwriter, only a few questions of a nonmedical nature are asked. This process is similar to that of a regular Part I application, but the medical history questions, which usually make up Part II, are condensed into only a few, less detailed questions. This can be done because medical history at younger ages, where simplified underwriting is primarily used, is generally not very extensive or significant.

The Medical (or Paramedical) Examination

If a physical examination is called for, the proposed insured's answers to the Part II medical history questions are recorded by the physician or paramedic. Also, the physician or paramedic reports the findings of his or her own medical examination. The examination by a paramedic might include height and weight measurements, pulse and blood pressure readings, and chest and abdomen measurements, as well as the collection of a urine sample. A physician might include all of these items plus examine the condition of the heart, lungs, and nervous system. In the case of life and disability policies, more detailed examinations involving blood chemistry studies, chest x-rays, and electrocardiograms are often used, and a second medical examination may be required.

The medical examination is not foolproof. Medical science is far from perfect and impairments unknown to both the proposed insured and physician can pass undetected. Also, some individuals go to considerable effort to appear at their best through rest and diet and may deliberately or unintentionally not disclose important items of health history. Through the use of available information from all sources, an underwriter tries to create an accurate "picture" of the individual and arrive at a fair decision.

Insurance companies increasingly are using paraprofessionals in lieu of physicians. Paramedical-type centers operate in many areas of the country, although the vast majority of paramedical examinations are made in the proposed insured's home or office. Technicians will take the individual's medical history and administer tests as mentioned above. For an additional charge, an electrocardiogram and a blood test may also be given. In addition, some centers have medical doctors available. The principal reason for the increasing popularity of paramedical facilities is a combination of cost and shortage of physicians to administer insurance exams. Most insurance companies availing themselves of this service use it with policies not exceeding a certain size but beyond the company's nonmedical limits, or in lieu of a second medical exam when one is required.

In health insurance, a medical examination is used regularly in applications for large amounts of long-term disability income coverage and life insurance disability income riders, and sometimes for major medical coverage at the older ages. In most other types of health insurance, it is used in doubtful cases. In the case of limited policies, it is virtually never used. In general, the frequency of use of the medical examination and the detail involved are not as great for health insurance applications as for life cases because of expense considerations.

The Agent's Report

Most companies include on the back of the Part I application certain questions the agent is to answer. Companies will usually ask the agent for how long he or she has known the proposed insured and whether he or she knows of any adverse information about him or her. The agent may also be asked to express an opinion about his or her knowledge of the individual's financial standing, character, and environment.

When a company does not require an agent's report, it relies on its general instructions to its agents to prevent them from writing applications on persons who are not acceptable risks. If the agent believes the risk is doubtful, he or she may be instructed to submit a preliminary inquiry. If the individual has ever been refused insurance by any company, the agent may be instructed to report this fact to the company.

Attending Physician Statements

The attending physician statement (APS) is used where the individual application and/or the medical examiner's report reveals conditions or situations, past or present, about which more information is desired. It may reveal additional health conditions or the names of additional physicians not reported in the application.

Because professional ethics prevent a physi-

cian from divulging such information without the consent of the patient, the consent of the individual is always obtained. The applicant or proposed insured almost always signs an authorization at the time of application, and a copy of this is sent to the physician with the request for the additional information. Standards exist in some states for these authorizations as well as the extent to which information obtained with them may be disclosed to others.[3] The APS is considered by many as the single most important source of underwriting information.

Consumer Reports

Life insurance companies obtain consumer reports or investigative consumer reports on all persons who apply for relatively large amounts of insurance. In the case of modest amounts (say $100,000 and less) and at the younger ages, many companies do not routinely obtain such reports. These reports can provide information bearing on the insurability of the proposed insured. Most companies use the services of **consumer reporting agencies** that maintain a staff to make such reports for these and other (e.g., employment) purposes.

A **consumer report** is defined by the federal Fair Credit Reporting Act (FCRA) to be a written, oral, or other communication of any information by a consumer reporting agency that has a bearing on the consumer's credit worthiness, credit standing, credit capacity, character, general reputation, personal characteristics, or mode of living and which is expected to be used in whole or in part to establish eligibility for insurance.[4] An **investigative consumer report** is a consumer report for which information was obtained from personal interviews with neighbors, friends, associates, or others acquainted with the consumer.[5]

When the company receives an application, if the company's rules call for a consumer report, one is promptly ordered, giving the applicant's name, age, sex, occupation, and places of residence

---

[3]See pp. 435–436.

[4]F.C.R.A., Section 603(b). Consumer reports are also used for credit and employment purposes.

[5]F.C.R.A., Section 603(e).

and business. In some companies, the request for the report is made by the agency. The report is sent directly to the home office. The FCRA requires the applicant to be notified that such a consumer report may or will be made. This notification may be part of the application form or it may be a separate notice.

When the amount of insurance is not particularly large, the investigator will make a rather general inquiry into the habits, character, financial condition, occupation, avocations, and health of the applicant. If the amount of insurance is large or if concern exists about possible adverse selection, a more careful and detailed report is often obtained, particularly regarding financial information, and more informants contacted. To obtain the necessary information for an investigative report, the investigator may interview the applicant's employer, neighbors, banker, accountant, business associates, and others who may be able to contribute the information desired, and often the applicant him- or herself. The investigator will also check public records.

The Medical Information Bureau

Another source of information regarding insurability is the Medical Information Bureau (MIB). A membership association of virtually all U.S. life insurance companies, it acts as a clearinghouse for confidential data, primarily of a medical nature, on individuals who apply for life or health insurance to member companies.

Member companies are required to code and report to the MIB certain medical impairments covering a broad spectrum of health conditions found during the underwriting process. Only data obtained from a medical source or directly from the applicant are to be reported as medical codes. No information obtained in connection with life, health, and disability claims is to be reported to the MIB. A limited number of nonmedical codes exists, such as for reckless driving, aviation, and hazardous sport activities, which are reportable because they may be of significance to home-office underwriters. Member companies do not indicate in their reports to the MIB their

underwriting decisions, nor do they state the amount or type of insurance applied for.

Member companies screen proposed insureds against the MIB computer data files. If an impairment code is found, the company attempts to substantiate the code through its own investigation. If it fails to substantiate the recorded condition, it can submit a request for details through the MIB to the original reporting company. The original reporting company furnishes whatever details (if any) it wishes. MIB rules and many state laws stipulate that a member may not take any unfavorable underwriting action wholly or in part on the basis of MIB information. Such information is to serve only as an "alert" to the member. The member, through other sources, is to substantiate any unfavorable underwriting action by corroborating favorable data regarding a particular condition.

A service provided by MIB of special interest to health insurers is the Disability Income Record System (DIRS). The purpose of this system is to provide information about applications for disability income insurance that will assist insurers in recognizing situations involving potential overinsurance.

The DIRS employs a central file that records certain nonmedical information about disability applications processed by the subscribing companies. When a member receives an application for disability income insurance involving a monthly disability income benefit of $300 or more with a benefit period of at least 12 months, it sends this information to the DIRS file. This information, which is retained in file for five years, is made available to any other member company to which an individual may apply for disability income insurance.

The various state insurance-related privacy laws require that an individual be informed in writing, before completing the application for insurance, that the company may report information to the MIB. The applicant is also advised how to obtain disclosure of his or her MIB file and dispute its accuracy. An authorization is signed permitting an inquiry to MIB. MIB disclosure and disputed accuracy procedures are those of the federal Fair Credit Reporting Act and state privacy requirements.

REINSURANCE OF LIFE INSURANCE RISKS

Reinsurance may be defined as a device by which a life insurance company transfers all or a portion of its exposure under a life insurance policy to another company. It is insurance for the insurer. The company that issued the policy originally is known as the **direct-writing** or **ceding company.** The company to which the risk is transferred is the **reinsurer** or **assuming company.**

Purposes of Reinsurance

Although the primary purpose of reinsurance is to avoid too large a risk concentration within one company, it also may be used to take advantage of the underwriting judgment of the reinsurer, to transfer all or certain classes of substandard business,[6] to reduce the drain on surplus caused by writing new business, to stabilize the overall mortality experience of the ceding company, or, in the case of newly organized companies, to obtain advice and counsel on underwriting procedures, rates, and forms. A company also must provide competitive facilities to its agency force and accept the large majority of the cases written by its agents, regardless of the amounts involved.

Reinsurance also is used regularly by most companies as a means to obtain better underwriting offers for proposed insureds who do not qualify for a standard or a moderately substandard offer under their own underwriting standards. Some reinsurers with liberal underwriting philosophies aggressively seek this type of

---

[6]Life reinsurance also may be undertaken to transfer all or a specific portion of a company's existing liabilities to the reinsuring company, including the administration of these policies directly with policyowners. This is known as **assumption reinsurance** and might be utilized where a company wishes to withdraw from business entirely or from a particular territory. Alternatively, specified blocks of business may be reinsured under **portfolio reinsurance.**

business. Typically, the ceding company will retain only a small or no portion of the risk.

The Concept of Retention

A life insurance company deals with a type of risk that in the aggregate may be measured and predicted with a remarkable degree of accuracy, the closeness of the approximation depending on the number and homogeneity of the individuals in the group. On the other hand, the exposure of one individual may be $300,000 and the exposure of another $25,000. The probability of death for each may be the same, but the impact on the surplus of a company because of death clearly would be much greater in the case of the $300,000 policy.

In the case of a recently organized or small company, the need for a maximum limit on the amount of insurance it will retain for its own account on any individual life should be obvious. In companies with a relatively small total number of insureds, mortality experience can fluctuate widely from year to year. In such companies, the surplus funds available to absorb unusual losses usually are small, and a single large death claim or several significant claims might have a marked effect on operations for the year. As a company increases in size, with an increasing total volume of insurance in force, and increasingly large surplus funds, the chance of significant fluctuations in its overall mortality experience will decrease (thanks to the law of large numbers), and the company's ability to absorb unusual losses will increase. Thus, it can gradually and safely increase its maximum retention on any one life.

There is no simple formula for fixing a retention limit, since it depends on a number of factors peculiar to a company's economic position and manner of operation. Such factors include (1) the size of the company's unallocated surplus, (2) the quality of its agency force, (3) the quality of the home-office underwriting staff, (4) the distribution of insurance in force (by amount, number of policies, sex and age, proportion substandard, etc.), and (5) the probable distribution of new business and average amount per policy. In general, the smaller the group of units exposed to loss and the less homogeneous they are, the sharper and more sudden can be the fluctuations and therefore the lower should be a company's limit of retention. Limits range from $10,000 in small, recently established companies to $5,000,000 or more in the largest companies. There may be various limits within a given company, depending on age at issue, substandard classification, and sometimes, plan.

Reinsurance Arrangements

The traditional plans of reinsurance developed to deal with individual risks may be broadly described as **proportional reinsurance. Nonproportional reinsurance** plans are also available, with the objective of stabilizing the overall mortality experience of the ceding company. Nonproportional reinsurance usually takes one of three forms: stop-loss reinsurance, catastrophic reinsurance, or spread-loss reinsurance.[7] The basic characteristic that differentiates them from traditional proportional reinsurance plans is that they relate the reinsurer's liability to some measure of overall experience on all or specified "blocks" of the ceding company's business, rather than to individual or specific policies of insurance. In addition, the proportion in which the ceding company and the reinsurer will share losses under nonproportional reinsurance is not determinable in advance. These forms are adaptions of property and liability reinsurance and are not widely utilized in the life field. In view of the predominance of proportional reinsurance, the remainder of this discussion relates to that form.

Agreements. Reinsurance may be arranged on a **facultative** or an **automatic** basis. Under the facultative plan, each application is under-

[7]**Stop-loss reinsurance** becomes payable if and when the aggregate death claims experienced by the ceding company in a year exceed some predetermined level. **Catastrophic reinsurance** covers multiple insured deaths arising from a single accident or other occurrence. Under **spread-loss reinsurance,** excess claims in a year are covered by the reinsurer, which is then, in effect, reimbursed over a period of time, allowing the ceding company to spread its loss over several years.

written separately by the reinsurer. When the direct writing company receives an application for a policy for more than the amount it wishes to assume, it negotiates with one or more reinsurers for a transfer of the part of the insurance that is in excess of its own retention. Copies of the ceding company's application papers are sent to the reinsurer(s) for evaluation. The reinsurer(s) then makes its (their) own underwriting judgment and advises the ceding company.

The facultative method has certain advantages. It is flexible, and questions about the underwriting information developed can be discussed in the reinsurance negotiations. The original insurer also obtains the advice of the reinsurer with whom it negotiates. The major disadvantages are the additional time required for completing the transaction, which may result in loss of business to competitors, and a higher administrative cost per $1,000 for such coverage.

The automatic plan provides that the direct writing company *must* transfer an agreed amount of each applicable insurance policy to the reinsuring company immediately upon payment of premium and the issuance of the policy. The reinsurer *must* accept the transfer that falls within the scope of the treaty. The agreement always provides that not more than a certain amount per policy may be transferred to the reinsurance company, and the automatic agreement may provide for a distribution of the excess to more than one reinsuring company. The usual "split account" system is based on the first letter of the insured's surname (reinsurer 1 gets letters A–K and reinsurer 2 gets L–Z). When an application exceeds the limits of automatic treaties, facultative reinsurance is secured.

The original insured is not a legal party to any reinsurance contracts that may result. He or she must look solely to the direct-writing company for any payments to which he or she is entitled under the policy, and the direct-writing company is liable for such payments regardless of the existence and terms of any reinsurance contracts to which it may be a party.

Plans. Two general methods exist for defining a reinsurer's liability in case of a loss under either facultative or automatic agreements. One of these is the **coinsurance plan,** under which the reinsurer assumes a proportionate share of any liability arising under the terms that govern the original policy. If a loss occurs, the reinsurer is liable for a part thereof, determined according to the size of the insurance assumed in relation to the amount of original insurance. Thus, if the reinsurer has accepted one-half the original insurance, it becomes liable for one-half of any loss. In return for this guarantee, the reinsurer receives a pro rata share of the original premium less a ceding commission and allowance, the purpose of which is to reimburse the direct-writing company for an appropriate share of the agent's commissions, premium taxes paid to the state of domicile of the insured, and a portion of the other expenses attributable to the reinsured policy. Similarly, the reinsurer reimburses for a proportionate share of dividends paid. In general, the reinsurance contract is, in essence, a reduced copy of that entered into by the original company with the insured.

Another plan of reinsurance is the **yearly renewable term plan.** This plan is particularly appropriate for smaller ceding companies, as it results in larger assets for these companies and is simpler to administer than the coinsurance plan. Under this plan, the reinsurer assumes the reinsured policy's net amount at risk for that amount in excess of the ceding company's retention. The ceding company pays premiums on a yearly renewable term basis. Thus, for policies with declining net amounts at risk, a decreasing amount of reinsurance is purchased each year. If a loss occurs, the reinsurer is liable for the amount that it has assumed that year, and the ceding insurer is liable for its retention plus the full reserve on the reinsured portion of the policy.

In the interest of permitting a company to retain control over the funds arising out of its own policies, a **modified coinsurance plan** has been developed. Under this arrangement, the ceding company pays the reinsurer a proportionate part of the gross premium, as under the conventional coinsurance plan, less commissions and whatever allowances have been arranged for, premium taxes, and overhead allocable to reinsured policies. At the end of each policy year, the reinsurer pays to the ceding company a reserve adjustment equal to the net increase in the reserve during the year,

less one year's interest on the total reserve held at the beginning of the year. The net effect of the plan is to return to the ceding company the bulk of the funds developed by its policies.

Modified coinsurance can be considered as yearly renewable term on a calendar-year basis as the reinsurer, after paying the reserve adjustment, cash surrender values, and commissions and allowances, is left with only a risk premium. Aside from the reserve adjustment, the modified coinsurance plan follows that of the regular coinsurance plan.[8] Table 24–1 provides a comparative analysis of the three basic reinsurance plans.

Source of Funds

Table 24–2 includes an example of the distribution of liability between a direct-writing company and a reinsurer with respect to a $100,000 ordinary life policy issued to a 35-year-old male reinsured under the coinsurance, yearly renewable term, and modified coinsurance plans. In each case, a retention of $25,000 is assumed.

REINSURANCE OF HEALTH INSURANCE RISKS

Some health insurance coverages involve substantial liability. As in the case of life insurance, reinsurance is utilized to avoid disruptive fluctuations in experience and company operating results. Reinsurance is also used for experimental coverages or for the writing of unusual lines where the spread of risk is not expected to be adequate.

Proportional Reinsurance[9]

As pointed out above, reinsurance methods involve sharing the risk on either a proportional

---

[8]Due to a special provision in the 1959 Federal Life Insurance Company Tax Act, modified coinsurance plans were widely utilized in recent years by companies to avoid major amounts of federal income tax. The loophole was closed by the 1982 Tax Equity and Financial Responsibility Act.

[9]This and the following section draws from *Individual Health Insurance* (Washington, D.C.: Health Insurance Association of America, 1983), pp. 206–209.

TABLE 24-1. Comparative analysis of reinsurance plans

Plan	Amount of Reinsurer's Liability in Case of Death	Responsibilities of Reinsurer	Allocation of Premium	Advantages
Yearly renewable term	Net amount at risk on portion of original policy reinsured[a] (reinsured amount tracks policy's net amount at risk above retention)	Reserves: YRT reserves only Nonforfeiture values: none Dividends: none	Premium to reinsurer equals net amount at risk times yearly renewable term rate for attained age (first-year rate may be 50% of renewal or less, to recognize insurer's high, first-year expenses)	Preferred by majority of companies; allows greater amount of asset retention and more premium for investment Ceding insurer retains investment profits Simplicity, inexpensive to administer Ceding insurer retains investments backing policy reserves
Coinsurance	Face amount on portion of original policy reinsured[a] (reinsured amount tracks policy's face amount in excess of retention)	Reserves: pro rata share Nonforfeiture values: pro rata share (reinsurer usually does not participate in policy loans) Dividends: pro rata as expense reimbursement	Premium to reinsurer equals pro rata share of gross premium less allowances	Preferred by companies with high acquisition costs for their term plans Reinsurer shares in surplus drain of new business Reinsurer shares reserve liability pro rata
Modified coinsurance	Same as coinsurance	Reserves: none; however, at end of policy year, reinsurer pays to ceding company net amount of increase in reserves during year, less growth due to required interest Nonforfeiture values: none, because reserves are held by ceding company Dividends: pro rata as expense reimbursement	Premium to reinsurer equals pro rata share of gross premium less allowances	Same as coinsurance above, but also cash value plans return to ceding company the bulk of funds developed by policies Original insurer's assets not diminished

[a]In most cases, the portion of the original policy reinsured equals the face amount of the original policy minus the ceding company's retention limit. In some cases under facultative agreements, however, the ceding company might retain less than its usual retention limit.

TABLE 24-2. Source of funds for paying a death claim under the coinsurance, yearly renewable term, and modified coinsurance plans[a]

(ordinary life, male age 35, policy amount $100,000, $25,000 retention)

Year	Direct Writer		Reinsurer		Total
	Reserve	Surplus	Reserve	Surplus	
		Coinsurance			
1	$ 228.50	$24,771.50	$ 685.50	$74,314.50	$100,000
2	466.25	24,533.75	1,398.75	73,601.25	100,000
3	712.25	24,287.75	2,136.75	72,863.25	100,000
4	966.75	24,033.25	2,900.25	72,099.75	100,000
5	1,230.00	23,770.00	3,690.00	71,310.00	100,000
10	2,672.50	22,327.50	8,017.50	66,982.50	100,000
20	6,229.50	18,770.50	18,688.50	56,311.50	100,000
		Yearly Renewable Term			
1	$ 914.00	$24,771.50	$ 0.00	$74,314.50	$100,000
2	1,865.00	24,533.75	0.00	73,601.25	100,000
3	2,849.00	24,287.75	0.00	72,863.25	100,000
4	3,867.00	24,033.25	0.00	72,099.75	100,000
5	4,920.00	23,770.00	0.00	71,310.00	100,000
10	10,690.00	22,327.50	0.00	66,982.50	100,000
20	24,918.00	18,770.50	0.00	56,311.50	100,000
		Modified Coinsurance			
1	$ 228.50	$24,771.50	$ 685.50	$74,314.50	$100,000
2	1,186.02	24,533.75	678.98	73,601.25	100,000
3	2,180.94	24,287.75	668.06	72,863.25	100,000
4	3,210.34	24,033.25	656.66	72,099.75	100,000
5	4,275.25	23,770.00	644.74	71,310.00	100,000
10	10,127.76	22,327.50	562.24	66,982.50	100,000
20	24,612.90	18,770.50	305.10	56,311.50	100,000

[a]Assumes the *1980 CSO Table*, 5%, NLP reserve method, and claim paid on last day of policy year prior to any reserve payment from the reinsurer to the direct writer.

or nonproportional basis. Proportional reinsurance can be expressed either as **quota share** or **surplus share.** Under the quota-share method, the reinsurer participates in a predetermined proportion of every risk in a specified category. Thus, a company might reinsure 40 percent of every risk written on a certain policy form or forms, regardless of the size of the risk. This basis also could apply to the company's entire health insurance portfolio or to one specific benefit among several benefits offered. In certain cases (e.g., experimental coverage), the ceding company might want the reinsurer to participate in a relatively large share of the risk.

In surplus-share reinsurance, the reinsurer assumes the liability above a predetermined dollar amount called the ceding company's **retention.** Here, for example, a ceding company might retain up to $100,000 of accidental death benefit on any one life. Amounts in excess of this retention would be reinsured. When a disability income policy is involved, a company might retain $2,000 a month. Once the retention is selected, the reinsurer shares proportionately in the risk. Thus, if a disability policy is issued for $4,000 a month and the retention is $2,000 a month, 50 percent of all payments are reinsured. Similarly, if the policy is for $8,000 a month, 75 percent of all payments would be reinsured.

This method of reinsurance perhaps is the best means of leveling out marked or chance fluctuations in experience, especially when an insurer does not have the proper spread of risk on larger cases. A relatively small portion of an insurer's business is reinsured, with this portion made up of the larger risks that are potentially less desirable, especially for disability income and accidental death. The larger the risk, generally speaking, the greater the hazard of antiselection and malingering, and greater care is exercised in handling the claim.

Excess-of-Loss Reinsurance

With excess reinsurance, a reinsurer reimburses a portion of the claim payments by the ceding insurer, but only after the ceding insurer has made payments for a specified number of months of total disability or after its retention, expressed in dollars, is exceeded. In excess-of-time (extended wait) reinsurance, the extended-wait period extends beyond the elimination period found in the policy itself. The extended-wait period can be one, two, five, or even 10 years under this plan before the reinsurer becomes responsible for payment. The reinsurer's share of such claim payments after the extended-wait period may be 70 or 80 percent of the monthly benefit. This reinsurance covers total disability benefits only and does not cover any other benefit of the policy, such as partial disability. It is not unusual to combine extended-wait with other types of reinsurance, such as surplus-share.

As in the case of life reinsurance, an *automatic* treaty may have all the cases ceded automatically, or it may be a combination of automatic and facultative segments. The latter is most common. A *facultative* treaty would have no automatic provision, and each case would be underwritten by the reinsurer.

LAWS AFFECTING UNDERWRITING

As discussed above, the underwriting process involves the collection and use of personal information concerning individuals who apply for life and health insurance. This fact has led to public concern about how insurers use this information as well as the confidentiality with which it is maintained. The federal **Fair Credit Reporting Act** of 1970, discussed earlier, was one of the first federal laws that addressed these concerns. Other federal and state laws and regulations place limits on insurers' freedoms with respect to the collection, maintenance, use, and disclosure of personally identifiable information on consumers. Each of the more important ones is discussed below.

The Fair Credit Reporting Act

The federal FCRA was one of the first important laws affecting life insurance companies' information practices. The FCRA requires users of investigative consumer reports to notify the individual who is the subject of such a report that the report will be or has been requested. The user—in this case, the insurer—must also advise the consumer that he or she has the right to request disclosure of the nature and scope of the investigation.

A second requirement of the FCRA imposes a duty on the user of *any* consumer report to supply the subject consumer with the name and address of the consumer reporting agency if any action is taken to the consumer's detriment *and* the report contributed in whole or in part to the decision. This requirement applies whenever insurance (or credit) is denied or the charge increased because of information contained in the report. The consumer has the right then to request disclosure.

In general, every **Consumer Reporting Agency** (CRA), when requested, must disclose to the consumer the nature and substance of all information (except medical) contained in his or her file. Not only must the information itself be disclosed, but the CRA must also advise the consumer of the CRA's sources, except it need not disclose sources used solely to compile an investigative consumer report. Although the FCRA does not give consumers the right to see and obtain copies of the report (only to learn the "nature and substance" thereof), in practice, however, CRAs routinely permit the consumer to see and to obtain actual copies of the report.

If the consumer disputes the completeness or accuracy of an item of information in his or her file, the CRA must reinvestigate within a "reasonable period of time" to ascertain the accuracy of the disputed information. If the reinvestigation proves the file information inaccurate or if it cannot be substantiated, the disputed data must be deleted. If, on the other hand, the in-

vestigation fails to resolve the dispute, the consumer has the right to have filed a statement of up to 100 words presenting his or her side of the contested matter. Thereafter, the statement or a clear summary thereof must accompany the consumer report.

Several states have Fair Credit Reporting Acts. Generally, they track the federal law except for extending certain additional rights to consumers or for limiting CRA's actions in some ways.

The NAIC Model Privacy Act[10]

In 1979, the National Association of Insurance Commissioners adopted the **NAIC Insurance Information and Privacy Protection Model Act** (NAIC Model Privacy Act). It was revised in 1980 and again in 1981 and has since been adopted by nine states. However, its importance extends beyond these states' borders, as most insurers commonly comply with the Act's requirements even in those states that have not enacted the law.

The NAIC Model Privacy Act is both a lengthy and a complex document. As a result, space permits only an overview of its significant provisions.[11] The Act clearly and purposely is patterned after the insurance recommendations contained in the Privacy Protection Study Commission's (PPSC) Report.[12]

The Act may be divided arbitrarily into

three areas. The first (Sections 1 and 2) stipulates the scope of the Act and gives key definitions. The second (Sections 3 to 13) contains the Act's operative provisions wherein the obligations imposed upon insurers, agents, and insurance-support organizations and the rights given to insurance consumers are stipulated. The third area (Sections 14 to 24) contains the NAIC Model Privacy Act's enforcement and immunity provisions.

Thus, within the first area, the Act establishes that with respect to life/health insurance, the residency of the individual determines the applicable state law. The Task Force that drafted the Act hoped that this approach would avoid any conflict of laws problem.

Within the second major area of the Act (the operative Sections 3 to 13) are found, in some form, most of the insurance recommendations of the PPSC. Thus, the NAIC Model Privacy Act prohibits the use of pretext interviews except in certain claim situations. The Act requires that a notice of an insurer's information practices be given to applicants and to certain policyowners.

The Act mandates that insurers and agents identify clearly to an individual inquiries that elicit information that is desired solely for marketing, research, or other purposes not directly related to the insurance transaction at hand. The Act mandates minimum standards for disclosure authorization forms used by insurance institutions, agents, and insurance-support organizations.

Individuals are given the right under the Act to be interviewed in connection with the preparation of any investigative consumer report. Certain persons are given a right of access to personal information on them maintained by insurers, agents, and insurance-support organizations. A corresponding right to request correction also is provided.

The Act requires insurers to advise individuals of the reasons for any adverse underwriting decision affecting them and, if requested, to provide individuals with the information upon which the decision was based. The Model Act further stipulates that no insurer or agent may base an adverse underwriting decision on the mere fact of a previous adverse underwriting decision. It also provides that no insurer should base an adverse

---

[10]This section draws from Harold Skipper, Jr., "An Analysis of the NAIC Model Privacy Act," *Best's Review,* Vol. 80 (March 1980).

[11]See James W. Newman, Jr., "A Description and Explanation of the NAIC Insurance Information and Privacy Protection Model Act," *Journal of Insurance Regulation,* Vol. 1 (March 1983), pp. 352–377, for a more complete discussion of the Act.

[12]Privacy Protection Study Commission, *Personal Privacy in an Information Society* (Washington, D.C.: U.S. Government Printing Office, 1977), pp. 188–222. For a summary of the PPSC recommendations, see Harold Skipper, Jr., "Recommendations of the Privacy Protection Study Commission of Importance to Life and Health Insurers," *Best's Review,* Life/Health ed., (August 1977); and Harold Skipper, Jr., "Recommendations of the Privacy Protection Study Commission of Importance to Property/Casualty Insurers," *Best's Review,* Property/Casualty ed., (October 1977).

underwriting decision on personal information received from an insurance-support organization whose primary source of information is insurance institutions (i.e., the MIB).

Section 13, dealing with disclosure limitations and conditions, is the most complex section of the Act. This section specifies the circumstances under which insurers, agents, and insurance-support organizations may disclose information about an individual without the individual's specific consent.

The third major area specifies the power given the insurance commissioner under the Act and the remedies available to him or her. This area also provides that any person subject to an order of the commissioner has the right to obtain a review of such order through the appropriate county court. Violations of cease and desist orders are punishable by fine and/or suspension or revocation of an insurer's or agent's license.

Regulations and Laws Related to Unfair Discrimination

In addition to the limitations on a life insurance company's freedom to contract discussed earlier, various prohibitions exist in state laws against discrimination among persons applying for insurance. Many states have laws that provide that life insurance companies may not discriminate unfairly between individuals of the same class and of equal expectation of life in premiums, policy terms, benefits, or dividends. State laws also prohibit unfair discrimination because of sex, marital status, race, religion, or national origin. Some states prohibit discrimination because of sexual preference, as well.

Concerns about unfair discrimination led California to ban the use in underwriting of the results of a screening test for detecting the presence of AIDS antibodies. Wisconsin has a similar, although less stringent prohibition and other states are considering parallel legislation. The District of Columbia has prohibited insurers from using AIDS-related tests for a period of five years. These types of prohibitions flow from concerns about stigmitization, unfair discrimination, and confidentiality, especially since most AIDS' victims

are homosexual. The insurance industry has argued strongly against such prohibitions as being an unprecedented departure from an insurer's ability to underwrite with access to all pertinent medical information about the proposed insured. With the rapid spread of AIDS, these and other AIDS-related issues (e.g., how to pay AIDS-related health care costs) will pose a challenge to insurers, lawmakers, and insurance regulators. For its part, the National Association of Insurance Commissioners (NAIC) appointed an advisory committee of representatives from the insurance industry, academia, and the gay rights community to recommend appropriate public policy compromises on the several AIDS-related insurance issues. At the time this book was going to press, the committee had not been able to resolve the testing or confidentiality issues, but had made progress on the issue of unfair discrimination. It recommended that "sexual preferences" not be used in underwriting and that insurers not make inquiries about a person's sexual preferences.

The issue of unfair discrimination based on sex continues to be important to the insurance business. The implications of the U.S. Supreme Court's decision in the *Norris* case—prohibiting the use of sex-distinct mortality tables in an employer's voluntary deferred compensation plan—remains unclear, except for employer-sponsored plans.[13]

Montana became the first (and at this writing, the only) state to prohibit the use of sex as a rating factor in individual insurance, including individual life and health insurance. Similar legislation has been introduced in several other states, but to date, none has received sufficient support for enactment. However, efforts continue by those who oppose use of sex as a rating factor, in the federal and state legislatures and courts, to proscribe its use.

The argument by opponents of sex-based pricing is that it is unfair, from a social standpoint, just as the use of race as a rating factor would be considered unfair socially, irrespective of statistics.

---

[13]*Arizona Governing Committee v. Norris,* 77, L.Ed.2d 1236, (July 1983).

The insurance industry and others contend that use of sex-based pricing is not only justified—actuarially, women as a group live longer than men as a group—but that *to fail* to recognize a price difference would itself be unfair discrimination.

The NAIC adopted a **Model Regulation to Eliminate Unfair Sex Discrimination** in 1976 and the majority of states have regulations or other requirements similar to those embodied in this NAIC model regulation. The regulation does not prohibit use of sex-based pricing; rather, it prohibits the denial of insurance coverage or benefits on the basis of sex or marital status.

The NAIC also adopted a **Model Regulation on Unfair Discrimination in Life and Health Insurance on the Basis of Physical or Mental Impairment.** The regulation prohibits refusal or limitation of coverage or rate differentials based solely on physical or mental impairment unless the refusal, limitation, or rate differential is based on sound actuarial principles or actual or reasonably anticipated experience. Several states have adopted regulations or passed laws in this area.

A companion regulation—the NAIC **Model Regulation on Unfair Discrimination on the Basis of Blindness or Partial Blindness**—has been adopted, in one form or another, in most states. The regulation stipulates that the refusal to insure or to continue to insure, or the limitation on the amount, extent or kind of coverage available to an individual or the charging of a different rate, solely on the basis of blindness or partial blindness, constitutes an unfair discrimination under the state's Unfair Trade Practices Act. The regulation enjoys strong insurance industry support. Its wide adoption may deter similar federal legislation.

Chapter 25

Social Insurance

This chapter begins a four-chapter discussion on employee benefit plans, with an emphasis on insured plans. This chapter presents a brief overview of employee benefit plans followed by a discussion of the various social insurance programs in existence today in the United States. Chapters 26 and 27 follow, with each addressing various aspects of group life and health insurance. Chapter 28's discussion on retirement plans completes the employee benefit plan presentation.

INTRODUCTION TO EMPLOYEE BENEFIT PLANS

Today, government, employers and individuals all play a role in the economic security of American families and individuals. Employee benefit plans have a very important place in this process of providing financial security.[1] Employee benefit plans generally are employer-sponsored plans that provide benefits if employees die, become sick or disabled, or lose their earnings as a result of retirement or unemployment. Such benefits have become a significantly increasing part of the

system of total compensation provided by employers in the United States. Such employee benefits, together with other elements of a company's compensation system, should be effectively planned, coordinated, and balanced to help meet the objectives of both employees and the employer.

According to the latest available U.S. Chamber of Commerce survey results, its members' average payment for employee benefits was 36.6 percent of payroll in 1984, about the same percentage that employers paid the previous year.[2] However, the cost per employee grew from $7,582 in 1983 to $7,842 in 1984. Insurance costs rose by the largest amount, from 7 percent to 7.4 percent of payroll. Significantly, however, the Chamber estimates that 88 percent went to pay for health insurance. The cost of all employer-paid health care—including insurance, a portion of employer-paid Social Security taxes, disability costs, and sick leave—averaged $2,385 per employee and amounted to 30.4 percent of all benefit costs and 11.1 percent of payroll. Retirement benefits were most costly at $2,419 per employee. Of this, Social Security costs were $1,408, or 6.6 percent of

---

[1]For an excellent study of employee benefit plans, see Burton T. Beam, Jr., and John J. McFadden, *Employee Benefits* (Homewood, Ill.: Richard D. Irwin, Inc., 1985).

[2]Chamber of Commerce of the United States, *Employee Benefits 1985.* This study is updated annually.

payroll, and pension costs were $1,011, or 4.7 percent of payroll. In addition to the results of its survey, the Chamber of Commerce also estimated that the costs of providing employee benefits for *all* employees within the United States amounted to $610 billion in 1984, up from $550 billion the year before.

There are many definitions of the term employee benefits.[3] This volume, however, will deal only with (1) income maintenance during periods when regular earnings are interrupted because of death, disability, retirement, or unemployment and (2) benefits to meet medical expenses associated with illness or injury.

SOCIAL INSURANCE PLANS

As suggested above, government plays an important role in providing economic security to families and individuals. Social insurance programs develop primarily in response to a perceived need by society for certain types of economic security measures for which neither individuals themselves nor private insurers can (or will) provide adequate coverage. Since the introduction of the Social Security program in 1935, many Americans have come to expect the government to provide at least a minimum level of protection against the financial consequences of premature death, old age, disability, and unemployment.

Social insurance programs in the United States may be classified into four categories:

1. Old-age, survivors, disability and health insurance
2. Unemployment insurance
3. Workers' compensation insurance
4. Temporary disability insurance

The emphasis in this text is on private employee benefit programs. Social Security, however, is so significant, both in terms of its own benefit structure and its impact on private plan design, that a reasonably detailed overview of this program seems essential. A brief overview of the other social insurance programs is also included.

[3] See Beam and McFadden, *Employee Benefits,* p. 4.

OLD-AGE, SURVIVORS, DISABILITY AND HEALTH INSURANCE PROGRAM

The Social Security Act of 1935, motivated largely by the severe business depression of 1930–1936, gave to this nation an old-age benefit system for the first time.[4] This depression highlighted the reasons why such a government plan of protection was needed; to wit: (1) the transformation of the national economy from an extended family, self-sufficiency basis, where the aged contributed to family support, to a complex urban system under which the self-sufficiency of the nuclear family largely ceased; (2) the increasing need, under the new urban system, for the old to have money for room and board without their having the opportunity to earn a living; (3) the increasing specialization and efficiency of industrial establishments, which made it difficult for the old to retain their jobs and next to impossible for them to secure new jobs if the old ones were lost; and (4) the rapid increase, both absolutely and relatively, in the number of old persons in the population. At first, benefits were available only to the worker, but in 1939, the system was enlarged to provide insurance protection to the worker's family. The new enlarged system then assumed the name of Old-Age and Survivors Insurance (OASI).

Several amendments were made in the 1940s and 1950s, the effects of which were to expand the system and increase benefits. Amendments in 1956 made disability income part of the bundle of benefits provided in the act (changing the name to Old-Age, Survivors, and Disability Insurance—OADSI).

Further amendments and benefit increases were made throughout the 1960s and 1970s. The

[4] The 1935 Social Security Act was a broad attack on the problems of financial insecurity. In addition to old-age insurance benefits, the act covered other areas, including aid to the blind, orphans, and aged, and unemployment insurance. This discussion will be concerned only with the present system. For an extensive study of Social Security, see Robert J. Myers, *Social Security* (Homewood, Ill.: Richard D. Irwin, Inc., 1985). See also *History of the Provisions of Old-Age, Survivors, Disability, and Health Insurance, 1935–1983,* U.S. Department of Health and Human Services, Social Security Administration, Office of the Actuary, April 1984.

1965 amendments introduced, among other things, a new Title XVIII to the Social Security Act. This title initiated a health insurance program for the aged, popularly referred to as Medicare, thus changing the name to the Old-Age, Survivors, Disability, and Health Insurance (OASDHI) program—its current name.

Coverage

Coverage for Old-Age, Survivors, and Disability Insurance (OASDI) is conditioned on attachment to the labor market. The program is not based on the principle of universal coverage of all residents in the country, but rather, aims to cover all those gainfully employed.

Virtually all occupations are covered today, although certain occupations are subject to special eligibility rules because of administrative or constitutional reasons. Covered on an elective basis are state and local government employees and ministers. At the present time, about 95 percent of the gainfully employed are covered under OASDI.

Eligibility for Benefits

The benefits derived from OASDI depend on the **insured status** of the individual worker. There are three types of insured status: (1) fully insured, (2) currently insured, and (3) disability insured. Determination of an individual's insured status depends on his or her number of *quarters of coverage* and when they were earned.

For 1986, a quarter of coverage is given for each full $440 unit of annual earnings on which Social Security taxes are paid, up to a maximum of four quarters per year. This earnings amount is adjusted annually according to changes in the general earnings level.

Fully Insured Status. An individual can attain fully insured status by being credited with either (1) 40 quarters of coverage earned at any time after 1936 or (2) at least one quarter of coverage (whenever earned) for every calendar year elapsing after 1950 (or after the year in which the worker attains age 21, if later), up to the year in which he or she reaches age 62, dies, or becomes

disabled. A worker who fulfills the first requirement remains fully insured even if he or she spends no further time in covered employment. A minimum of six quarters of coverage is required in any case. Subject to certain requirements set forth in law, a year during which a worker is disabled does not adversely affect his or her eligibility for fully insured status.

Currently Insured Status. An individual can attain currently insured status by being credited with a minimum of six quarters of coverage during the 13-quarter period ending with the quarter in which he or she dies. Note that fully insured status is related to the length of attachment and currently insured status to the recentcy of attachment to the labor market.

Disability Insured Status. An individual worker is eligible for cash disability benefits if he or she (1) is fully insured, (2) has at least 20 quarters of coverage out of the last 40 quarters prior to disability, and (3) has been disabled for at least five months by a disability that is so serious that it prevents him or her from engaging in "any substantial gainful activity" and that has lasted or may be expected to last at least 12 months or to result in death. For persons under age 31, the coverage requirements are reduced. The disabled individual must also be willing to accept state vocational rehabilitation services.

Benefit Amounts[5]

To understand the Social Security benefit structure, one must understand certain key concepts and terms in the law that determine benefit amounts.

Primary Insurance Amount. All monthly income benefits are based on the worker's primary insurance amount (PIA), which is the monthly amount paid to a retired worker at age 65 or to a disabled worker. The primary insurance amount, in turn, is based on the worker's average indexed monthly earnings (AIME).

[5]This section draws on George E. Rejda, *Social Security and Economic Security,* 2nd ed. (Englewood Cliffs, N.J.: Prentice Hall, Inc., 1984), pp. 103–108.

Average Indexed Monthly Earnings. Prior to the 1977 amendments to the Social Security Act, a technical flaw existed in the provision for computing benefits. The way the original legislation was written, covered workers benefited twice during a period of inflation. First, the benefit scale was adjusted upward to reflect the price inflation. Second, since wages tended to increase during inflationary periods, higher wages would also produce still higher future benefits. The result was that workers retiring in the future could receive retirement benefits exceeding 100 percent of their earnings in the year prior to retirement. Naturally, long-run costs would have increased significantly. The AIME basis for determining benefits was developed in response to this unintended result of the earlier legislation.

This wage-indexing method is designed to ensure that monthly cash benefits will reflect changes in wage levels over the worker's lifetime so that the benefits paid will have a relatively constant relationship to the worker's earnings before retirement, disability, or death. The result is that workers who retire today and workers who will be retiring in the future will have about the same proportion of their earnings replaced by Social Security retirement benefits.

Earnings are indexed by multiplying the actual earnings subject to Social Security taxation for the year being indexed by the ratio of (1) average wages in the second year before the worker reaches age 62, becomes disabled, or dies to (2) average wages in the year being indexed. For example, assume that George retired at age 62 in 1986. The significant year for setting the index factor is the second year before he attained age 62 (1984). If George's actual taxable wages were $4,000 in 1956, this amount is multiplied by the ratio of the average annual wage in 1984 to the average annual wage in 1956. Thus, George's indexed earnings for 1956 would be calculated as follows:

$$\underset{\substack{\text{(actual} \\ \text{earnings} \\ \text{in 1956)}}}{\$4,000} \times \frac{\underset{\substack{\text{(average annual} \\ \text{wages in 1984)}}}{\$16,773.10}}{\underset{\substack{\text{(average annual} \\ \text{wages in 1956)}}}{\$3,532.36}} = \underset{\substack{\text{(indexed} \\ \text{earnings} \\ \text{for 1986)}}}{\$19,943.33}$$

A similar calculation is carried out for each year in the measuring period, except that earnings for and after the indexing year are counted in actual dollar amounts. The adjusted earnings then are used to determine the worker's primary insurance amount.

To obtain the AIME, one must first calculate the number of years elapsing between (1) the first day of the year in which the insured reached age 22 or January 1, 1951, if later, and (2) the year before the insured becomes 62, dies, or becomes disabled. Five is arbitrarily subtracted from this result.[6] This further result is converted from years into months.

The worker's indexed covered earnings are then calculated for the relevant time period, following the procedure illustrated above. These earnings are subject to year-by-year maximums, shown in Table 25-1. The years with the highest indexed earnings are used, but if the individual does not have as many years with earnings as must be used, zeros must be used for the remaining years. Those periods during which an insured individual is totally disabled are to be omitted in the calculation of the number of years used in determining the average indexed monthly earnings. The effect of the "dropout" and "disability freeze" provisions is to increase the average indexed monthly earnings and consequently, the benefits to be provided. In retirement cases, the

TABLE 25-1. Maximum covered earnings to be used in calculating average indexed monthly earnings

Period	Amount	Period	Amount
1937–1950	$ 3,000	1977	$16,500
1951–1954	3,600	1978	17,700
1955–1958	4,200	1979	22,900
1959–1965	4,800	1980	25,900
1966–1967	6,600	1981	29,700
1968–1971	7,800	1982	33,400
1972	9,000	1983	35,700
1973	10,800	1984	37,800
1974	13,200	1985	39,700
1975	14,100	1986	42,000
1976	15,300	1987	43,800

[6]For persons disabled before age 47, the number of dropout years is four for ages 42–46, three for ages 37–41, two for ages 32–36, one for ages 27–31, and none for ages under 27.

number of years used cannot be less than five. Earnings in any years after 1950 can be used, including years before age 22 and years after age 61.

PIA Formula. After the worker's AIME is established, a weighted formula is used to determine the primary insurance amount. Based on the 1986 benefit formula, which is applicable to persons who attain age 62 in 1986 (or workers under age 62 who die or become disabled in 1986), the PIA is determined as follows:

90 percent of the first $297 of AIME

+

32 percent of the next $1,493 of AIME

+

15 percent of the AIME in excess of $1,790

The formula "break points" are adjusted annually to reflect changes in average wages in the national economy. In addition, the benefit amount resulting from application of the formula is subject to the automatic cost-of-living provisions (see below) for the year of attainment of age 62 (or prior death or disability).

As is evident, the benefit formula is heavily weighted in favor of the low-income worker. Table 25–2 further illustrates this point.

Automatic Cost-of-Living Adjustment. Monthly cash benefits automatically are adjusted for specified changes whenever the Consumer Price Index (CPI) increases by at least 3 percent during the measuring period. Benefits are increased by this same percentage, provided that Congress has not enacted a general benefit increase (and the stabilizer provisions[7] are not operative). If the cost-of-living adjustment is made, the taxable wage base and earnings test (discussed below) are also automatically adjusted.[8]

The cost-of-living provision is valuable, since the real purchasing power of the cash benefits tends to be maintained during inflationary periods. Recognizing the political sensitivity of Social Security benefits, it is not surprising to note that in the event of a decline in the CPI during the measuring period, the benefits are not changed.

Maximum Family Benefits. There is a limit on the maximum monthly benefits that will be paid to a family based on the earnings record of

[7]To protect the trust funds during adverse economic conditions, a financial stabilizer has been built into the system. See Rejda, *Social Security and Economic Security,* p. 106.

[8]The maximum wage base is adjusted annually based on changes in average wages in the national economy if benefits are increased according to the automatic cost-of-living provisions. *Ibid.,* p. 120.

TABLE 25-2. Illustrative primary insurance amounts and maximum family benefits for persons attaining age 62 as of early 1986 (or dying or becoming disabled before age 62 in early 1986)

Insured Worker's Average Indexed Monthly Earnings	Primary Insurance Amount[a]	Maximum Family Benefit	
		Retirement or Survivor	Disability
$ 100	$ 90.00	$ 135.00	$ 90.00
200	180.00	270.00	180.00
400	300.20	450.30	340.00
600	364.20	546.30	510.00
800	428.20	702.30	642.30
1,000	492.20	876.40	738.30
1,500	652.20	1,167.80	978.30
2,078[b]	788.20	1,380.40	1,182.30
3,225[c]	960.30	1,681.60	1,440.40

[a]Monthly benefit for retired worker at age 65 or disabled worker at any age.
[b]Maximum AIME for person attaining age 62 in 1986 (who has not had a disability freeze).
[c]Maximum AIME for person dying in early 1986 (with less than $37,800 in earnings in 1986).

one person. For persons disabled in 1983 and later, the maximum family benefit is the *lower* of (1) 85 percent of the worker's AIME (or actual PIA if higher) or (2) 150 percent of the PIA. The maximum family benefit for persons who reach age 62 in 1986 or who die before age 62 in 1986 is based on the following formula:

150 percent of the first $379 of PIA

+

272 percent of the next $169

+

134 percent of the next $166

+

175 percent of the PIA in excess of $714

Whenever the total monthly benefits payable to all beneficiaries on the basis of one worker's earnings record exceed the maximum allowed, each dependent's or survivor's benefit is reduced proportionately (but not the worker's benefit) to bring the total within the maximum. Table 25-2 presents illustrative primary insurance amounts and corresponding maximum monthly family benefits for persons attaining age 62 in early 1986, or dying or becoming disabled before age 62.

Nature of Benefits

The OASDI program provides retirement, survivorship, and disability benefits. As pointed out above, all benefits are based on the insured worker's primary insurance amount.

Retirement Benefits. The insured worker's retirement benefit, a life income, is referred to as the **old-age insurance benefit** and is equal to 100 percent of the worker's PIA for retirement at the **normal retirement age** (NRA). NRA is 65 until 2003. It slowly increases then until it is 67 in 2027.[9]

The spouse of a retired worker is entitled to a benefit (**wife's/husband's benefit**) equal to 50 percent of the worker's PIA if he or she is at the NRA or older at time of claim,[10] or regardless of age, if the retired worker has under his or her care a dependent and unmarried child of the worker under age 16, or regardless of age if the child is disabled before age 22. In addition, each unmarried child under 18 or disabled before 22 is entitled to a benefit (**child's benefit**) equal to 50 percent of the worker's PIA. Of course, the total benefits payable to a retired individual and his or her dependents are subject to the overall family maximums. Retirement benefits are available only to fully insured workers.

Survivorship Benefits. The unremarried spouse of a deceased, fully insured worker can be entitled to survivor benefits as early as age 60. He or she is entitled to 100 percent of the deceased worker's PIA if he or she waits until the NRA or later to receive benefits. **Widow's/widower's benefits** between ages 60 and the NRA are reduced proportionately. The NRA for widows and widowers increases beyond age 65 for those attaining age 60 in 2000 and gradually rises to 67 for those attaining age 60 in 2022 (i.e., becoming 67 in 2029). If the widow/widower is aged 50–59 and also disabled, she or he can be entitled to a disability benefit. Regardless of age, if a widow/widower has under her or his care a dependent and unmarried child under age 16 of a worker or a child disabled since before age 22, he or she is entitled to a benefit equal to 75 percent of the PIA (**mother's/father's benefit**). In addition, a dependent and unmarried child under 18 (or under 19 if attending a primary or secondary educational institution on a full-time basis), or regardless of age if disabled before age 22, is entitled to a benefit equal to 75 percent of the primary insurance amount (**child's benefit**). Dependent parents 62 and over are each entitled to a benefit equal to 75

---

[9]A man or woman who retires as a worker when the NRA is 65 can elect to retire at age 62 with a permanently reduced benefit equal to 80 percent of his or her full benefit (PIA). When the NRA increases above 65, the reduction for early retirement increases (and the factor for age 62 is 70 percent when the NRA is 67). Benefits are prorated for retirement between ages 62 and the NRA.

[10]The spouse of a retired worker, when the NRA is 65, may qualify for benefits as early as age 62, but with a reduced benefit; 75 percent of the full benefit is payable at age 62, and proportionately more if benefits are first claimed between ages 62 and 65. When the NRA increases above 65, the reduction for early retirement increases (and the factor for age 62 is 65 percent, when the NRA is 67).

percent of the PIA (**parent's benefit**).[11] The same maximum family benefit applies as in retirement cases. In addition to the income benefits, on the death of the worker who was living with a spouse or who leaves a spouse or child immediately entitled to monthly benefits, a lump-sum benefit of $255 is paid (**death benefit**).

All these survivorship benefits are available to the dependents of a fully insured worker. The dependents of a currently insured worker are eligible only for (1) the mother's (father's) benefits, (2) the survivor child's benefit, and (3) the lump-sum death benefit.

Disability Benefits. The **disability income benefit** is equal to 100 percent of the primary insurance amount, but it continues only as long as disability exists. The determination of disability is made by state agencies, with the right of review by the Social Security Administration. The determination of continuance of disability is made by the Social Security Administration.

Monthly payments are payable to the dependents of persons receiving disability insurance benefits. The dependents eligible for these benefits are the same as the ones who would qualify as dependents of persons receiving retirement benefits. Following legislation in 1980, a lower family maximum benefit applies in disability cases than in retirement and survivor cases (namely, the lower of 150 percent of PIA or 85 percent of Average Indexed Monthly Earnings but not less than the PIA). See Table 25–2.

The 1980 amendments accented the importance of rehabilitation in the disability program. Thus, a disabled beneficiary who performs services despite severe handicaps can continue to receive benefits for 12 months. In addition, the law also provides a three-month period of adjustment for beneficiaries who medically recover from their disabilities.

An unmarried child of a deceased, disabled, or retired worker, disabled prior to age 22, is eligible for a cash disability benefit at age 18 or after. The child's disability benefits are payable as long as the disability continues and are the same as the

benefit received by a dependent child of a deceased or retired worker. There is also a mother's/father's benefit, payable to the parent who has in his or her care a disabled child receiving benefits. This applies if he or she is a spouse of a disabled, retired, or deceased worker. The rehabilitation features of the disability program also apply to a disabled child. Blind persons are eligible for disability benefits even if only fully insured.

Reductions and Other Benefit Changes

A Social Security beneficiary can totally lose, or be subject to a reduction in, benefits under certain situations.

Earnings Test. If an eligible person is, in 1986, aged 65 to 69 and receives earnings of more than $7,800 a year[12] from covered or noncovered employment, some or all benefits will be lost for that year. There is no loss of benefits for earnings of $7,800 or less. There is a loss of $1 in benefits for every $2 of earnings on the portion of earnings over $7,800. However, no benefits are lost for any month in the first year of retirement in which the individual neither earns more than $\frac{1}{12}$ of the annual exempt amount in wages nor renders substantial services in self-employment. The earnings test applies to all beneficiaries under age 70, except disabled beneficiaries.

The earnings of a person who is receiving benefits as a dependent or as a survivor affect only his or her own benefits and not payments to other members of his or her family. Thus, if the wife of a deceased worker loses her benefit because of the earnings test, her children (under age 18, disabled since age 18 or to age 19 if they meet the school-attendance requirement) will continue to receive their benefits.

Dual Eligibility. A person eligible for more than one benefit will receive in effect the highest benefit for which application has been made. Thus, a wife, eligible in her own right as an insured worker, can draw benefits under her hus-

---

[11]If only one parent is entitled to this benefit, the benefit is 82½ percent of the deceased's primary insurance amount.

[12]For beneficiaries who are under 65 in 1986, the limit is $5,700. This amount increases automatically in accordance with changes in the general level of wages.

band's insured status only to the extent that they exceed the amount of her old-age benefit. Also, the benefits for a spouse of a retired, disabled, or deceased insured worker are reduced by any pension that such spouse earned from a retirement system for government employees that was not coordinated with Social Security.

Delayed Retirement. A worker receives a special increase in his or her old-age benefits for each month that he or she delays retirement between the NRA and age 70 ($\frac{1}{12}$ of 1 percent per month for persons who attain age 62 before 1979 and $\frac{1}{4}$ of 1 percent for persons who attain age 62 in 1979–1986; such rates will rise for later attainments until it is $\frac{2}{3}$ of 1 percent for those who become 62 in 2003 and after).

Changes in Family Status. Social Security benefits are terminated when changes in family status, such as marriage or divorce, alter the conditions under which payments are made. For example, payments to a nondisabled child stop when he or she reaches age 18, or 19 if attending high school, and payments to a widow/widower generally stop if she/he remarries (but not if at age 60 or over).

Other. *Failure to file* for benefits after eligibility may deprive a person of benefits for a period of time. The act grants monthly benefits retroactively for a period of six months (12 months for disability cases). The individual also has a responsibility, periodically, to check into the accuracy of the Social Security Administration's records relating to his or her account. Errors must be corrected within three years, three months, and 15 days, except under conditions specifically noted in the law.[13] Benefits also may be lost because of certain *work outside the United States* and if the individual is convicted of *certain subversive crimes.*

Taxation of Social Security Benefits. As a result of 1983 amendments, part of the Social Security benefits is now subject to federal income

taxation. Beginning in 1984, up to one-half of the Social Security benefits will be included in the gross income of beneficiaries whose modified adjusted gross income exceeds certain base amounts. The base amounts are $25,000 for a single taxpayer, $32,000 for married taxpayers filing jointly, and zero for married taxpayers filing separately.

Medicare Program

The 1965 amendments in the Social Security Act added Title XVIII, initiating a health insurance program for the aged. Medicare represents one of the most sweeping changes ever made in the history of the Social Security Act.[14]

Medicare is, in general, a two-part program of federal health insurance. Under *Part A,* the Hospital Insurance Plan, essentially all persons aged 65 or over and all persons who have been receiving Social Security disability benefits for at least two years are covered for extensive hospitalization benefits.[15] *Part B,* which is optional, provides a supplementary program of surgical and physician's care, and certain other benefits, for persons over age 65 and all persons who have been receiving Social Security disability benefits for at least two years. For 1986, eligible persons must pay a monthly premium of $15.50 for this coverage.

Medicare is secondary in payment to private group health insurance or liability insurance in some cases [e.g., to liability insurance under automobile policies, to group health insurance for chronic renal disease for the first 12 months, and to group health insurance for persons actively at work (and their spouses) for employers with 20 or more employees].

The Basic Plan—Hospital Insurance. The basic hospital-plan benefits include the following:

[14]The 1972 amendments extended Medicare to persons under 65 who receive Social Security or railroad retirement benefits based on long-term disability or who have chronic renal disease and require hemodialysis or a kidney transplant.

[15] All persons who are eligible to receive Social Security benefits because of being at least age 65, as a worker (even if not actually retired), a spouse, or a survivor or because of receiving benefits based on disability for at least 24 months are automatically eligible for health insurance benefits. All other persons (with minor exceptions) can buy this protection by paying premiums ($214 per month in 1986).

[13]See *Social Security Handbook,* 8th ed. (Washington, D.C.: U.S. Department of Health and Human Services, 1984), pp. 209–212.

1. *Inpatient hospital services* for up to 90 days in each *benefit period.* There also is a provision for a lifetime reserve of 60 days that can be used after the 90 days in a *spell of illness.* In 1986, the patient pays a deductible amount of $492 for the first 60 days, plus a deductible of $123 a day for the next 30 days for each spell of illness, plus a deductible of $246 a day for the lifetime-reserve days. Hospital services include all those ordinarily furnished by a hospital to its inpatients. However, payment is not made for private-duty nursing or for the hospital services of physicians except by medical or dental interns or residents in training under approved teaching programs. Inpatient psychiatric hospital service is included, but a lifetime limitation of 190 days is imposed.

2. *Posthospital skilled nursing care* (in a facility having an arrangement with a hospital for the timely transfer of patients and for furnishing medical information about patients) after a patient is transferred from a hospital (after at least a three-day stay) for up to 100 days in a benefit period. But in 1986, after the first 20 days, patients pay a deductible of $61.50 a day for the remaining days of care in a spell of illness.

3. *Posthospital home health services* on an unlimited visit basis. The recipient must be in the care of a physician and under a plan established by a physician within 30 days of discharge calling for such services. These services include intermittent nursing care, therapy, and the part-time services of a home health aide. The patient must be homebound, except that when certain equipment is used, the individual can be taken to a hospital, extended-care facility, or rehabilitation center to receive some of these covered home health services in order to receive the advantage of the necessary equipment.

A **benefit period** is considered to begin when the individual enters a hospital and ends when he or she has not been an inpatient of a hospital or skilled nursing facility for 60 consecutive days.

The deductible amounts for inpatient hospital care will be increased to keep pace with increases in hospital costs. The daily coinsurance amounts for longstay hospital and extended-care facility benefits will be adjusted correspondingly.

Supplementary Medical Insurance Plan. The supplementary plan provides, subject to a $75 annual deductible and a 20 percent participa-

tion (coinsurance) above the deductible, the following benefits:

1. *Physicians' and surgeons' services,* whether furnished in a hospital, clinic, office, home, or elsewhere.

2. *Home health services,* without limit (identical to those covered under hospital insurance), are available and are not subject to the costsharing provisions.

3. *Medical and health services,* including diagnostic x-ray, diagnositc laboratory tests, and other diagnostic tests; x-ray, radium, and radioactive-isotope therapy; ambulance services; surgical dressings and splints, casts, and other devices for reduction of fractures and dislocations; rental of durable medical equipment, such as iron lungs, oxygen tents, hospital beds, and wheelchairs used in the patient's home; prosthetic devices (other than dental) that replace all or part of an internal body organ; braces and artificial legs, arms, and eyes; physical therapy treatments; and so on. In some instances, certain services are not subject to the deductible and coinsurance provisions (e.g., diagnostic laboratory tests under some circumstances and ambulatory surgical centers).

4. *Psychiatric care,* subject to a special limitation on outside-the-hospital treatment of mental, psychoneurotic, and personality disorders. Payment for such treatment during any calendar year is limited, in effect, to $250 or 50 percent of the expenses, whichever is smaller.

The program recognizes only the so-called "reasonable charges" for services. Thus, not all of physician charges may be reimbursable under the program. If any of the services outlined above are covered under the basic plan, they are excluded from coverage under the supplementary plan. The law provides for special rules regarding enrollment periods and the time when coverage commences.

Financing OASDHI

The Old-Age, Survivors, and Disability Insurance system and the Hospital Insurance Plan are financed on a contributory basis, shared equally by employee and employer.[16] The employee

---

[16]The Federal Insurance Contributions Act (FICA), Chap. 21, Internal Revenue Code.

pays a tax on the wages that he or she receives, and the employer pays a tax on its payroll. The 1986 rate of contribution is 7.15 percent of covered wages and of payroll, for a total contribution of 14.3 percent of covered payroll. The tax in 1987 is calculated on the first $43,800 of wages paid to an employee. The tax rate is scheduled to rise to 15.02 percent in 1988 and 15.3 percent in 1990 (and the maximum taxable earnings will rise with earnings trends). The employer withholds the employee's tax from his or her pay and remits the employee's tax and its own tax to the U.S. District Director of Internal Revenue for that district.

The tax pattern is somewhat different for the self-employed covered under the act. To finance this phase of the program, the self-employed pay a tax equal to the combined employer/employee rate, but with a tax credit that decreases the rate somewhat below this level (until 1990). This tax, 12.3 percent in 1986, is imposed on self-employment income up to the same maximum amount as in the employer/employee tax. The tax rate is scheduled to rise to 13.02 percent in 1988. The self-employed person pays his or her tax on the basis of a special schedule attached to the federal income tax return.

The cost for the Supplementary Medical Insurance is paid by the enrollee and the federal government. Currently, the enrollee premium rate meets only 25 percent of the cost for the aged and about 19 percent for the disabled, with general revenues meeting the remainder. Premiums are at a rate determined by the Secretary of Health and Human Services. A higher rate is paid by those enrolling late, after their initial point of eligibility—10 percent additional for each full year of delay. As of January 1, 1986, a standard premium rate of $15.50 is applicable.

When paid, the funds collected for the several programs are allocated to the Old-Age and Survivors Insurance Trust Fund, the Disability Insurance Trust Fund, the Hospital Insurance Trust Fund, and the Supplementary Medical Insurance Trust Fund. They are managed by boards of trustees consisting of the Secretaries of the Treasury, of Labor, and of Health and Human Services, and two public trustees. The Secretary of the Treasury is known as the Managing Trustee and has wide powers of management over the trust

funds. The funds must be invested in securities that are the direct obligation of or guaranteed by the U.S. government. Funds are disbursed from these accounts to cover benefit payments and administrative expenses.

The complete Social Security law now comprises several hundred pages. In a condensed digest of this nature, it obviously is impossible to cover the many hundreds of potential circumstances and situations that might arise. Individuals should always contact their local Social Security office for information on any point that concerns them.

Current Financial Condition of Social Security and Medicare

A serious short-range financing crisis confronted the OASDI program in the early 1980s, largely as a result of the adverse economic conditions then (and the financing under the 1977 Act being based on moderately optimistic assumptions as to economic conditions). The 1983 amendments (which were based largely on the recommendations of the bipartisan National Commission on Social Security Reform) probably established the program on a sound financial basis at least for the 1980s, and probably for the next 20 to 30 years as well. Further, the long-range financing (up to the mid-2000s) seems to be reasonably well in hand. These amendments made many changes in order to accomplish this result—extending coverage to almost all categories not covered previously, delaying the cost-of-living adjustments of benefits for six months each year, making up to 50 percent of benefits being subject to income tax for high-income persons, raising the normal retirement age, and advancing some of the previously scheduled increases in the tax rates.

Many believe that the hospital insurance portion of Medicare will have a financing crisis confronting it at some time in the next 15 years. The reason for this is primarily that its tax rate is scheduled to be level after 1986, but hospital costs probably will increase more rapidly than the general earnings level (on which taxes are based). In the last few years, much of the steeply upward trend of hospital costs has lessened, but still a problem exists in this area for both the Medicare program and the health insurance programs for the working population and dependents.

The Supplementary Medical Insurance portion of Medicare has no financing problems because it is financed on a one-year term basis (other than, of course, that the cost to the enrollees and to the General Treasury will increase steadily and significantly over the years).

National Health Insurance

In the 1970s, considerable attention was directed toward the development of a comprehensive National Health Insurance plan. Among the most crucial problems faced by a family seeking medical care were high and rapidly rising costs, a chronic shortage of physicians and nurses, and unevenly distributed health facilities, which result in some communities and even entire counties having neither physicians nor hospitals. A number of comprehensive solutions to the nation's health care crisis was under consideration. Since then costs have continued to rise, but efforts at cost control have increased significantly. Currently, no significant legislative proposals relating to national health programs are under consideration, although President Reagan's administration seems to support some form of catastropic health insurance protection. He has called for a report on how the private and government sectors might work together toward such an end.

Whatever direction is taken in connection with health care proposals and other recommended modifications of the overall Social Security program, the Social Security Act marks a milestone in the evolution of American life. Its influence on the economic security of the American people is significant and pervasive.

OTHER SOCIAL INSURANCE PLANS

This section provides a brief overview of (1) unemployment insurance, (2) workers' compensation insurance, and (3) temporary disability insurance. Whereas unemployment insurance is a joint federal-state program, workers' compen-

sation insurance and temporary disability laws are individual state programs.

Unemployment Insurance

In contrast to OASDHI, unemployment insurance is not financed or administered primarily by the federal government, but by the states with some federal participation. The Social Security Act of 1935 provided for a payroll tax to be levied on covered employers in all states. The act was intended to motivate the individual states to establish unemployment insurance programs under guidelines issued by the federal government. This was accomplished by granting a credit against up to 90 percent of the federal tax *if* a state established an acceptable program based on the federal guidelines. All states now have such unemployment insurance programs.[17]

Unemployment insurance programs have several objectives: (1) to provide periodic cash income to workers during temporary periods of involuntary unemployment, (2) to help the unemployed find jobs, (3) to encourage employers to stabilize employment, and (4) to help stabilize the economy during recessionary periods.

Coverage and Benefits. Although the detailed requirements vary from state to state, the pattern of requirements that must be met to be eligible to receive unemployment benefits include: (1) have a recent, prior attachment to the labor force (usually 52 weeks or four quarters), (2) be able to work and be available for work, (3) be actively seeking work, (4) be free from disqualification (e.g., discharge for misconduct), and (5) satisfy any prescribed waiting period (usually one week). Unemployed workers are required to register at local unemployment offices, and officials of the U.S. Employment Service provide assistance in finding suitable jobs.

In most states, regular unemployment insurance benefits are paid for a maximum of 26 weeks. The basis for determining the amount of

---

[17]For a comprehensive discussion of this subject, see Rejda, *Social Insurance and Economic Security,* Chap. 14.

the weekly benefit payment varies, but in one way or the other, it reflects the individual compensation during a base period just prior to unemployment. Benefits in all states are subject to minimum and maximum amounts.[18]

During periods of high unemployment, some workers exhaust their regular unemployment benefits. A federal–state program of **extended benefits** has been established that pays additional benefits to such workers. The state must extend the benefit duration by 50 percent, up to a maximum of 13 weeks. The costs of the extended benefits are shared equally by the federal government and the states.

Financing of Benefits. State unemployment insurance programs are financed largely by payroll taxes paid by employers on the covered wages of employees.[19] All tax contributions are deposited into a Federal Unemployment Trust Fund administered by the Secretary of the Treasury. Each state has a separate account that is credited with the unemployment-tax contributions and the state's share of investment income. Unemployment benefits are paid out of each state's account.

As of January 1986, each covered employer must pay a federal payroll tax of 6.2 percent on the first $7,000 of annual wages paid to each covered employee. The employers can credit toward the federal tax any state contributions paid under an approved unemployment insurance program and any tax savings under an approved experience-rating plan. The maximum credit is 5.4 percent, leaving 0.8 percent being paid to the federal government. Many jurisdictions use a taxable wage base in excess of the $7,000 federal standard.

All states use a method of **experience rating** whereby an employer whose employment record is volatile will have a higher tax rate than an employer whose employment record has been stable. The theoretical basis for using experience rating is to provide a financial incentive to employers to stabilize their employment. Many cyclical and seasonal firms, however, have little control over their employment and see little financial incentive for them to stabilize employment.

Workers' Compensation Insurance

Workers' compensation is based on the fundamental principle of liability without fault.[20] The employer is held absolutely liable for the occupational injuries or diseases suffered by the workers regardless of who is at fault. Disabled workers are paid for their injuries according to a schedule of benefits established by law. Employees are not required to sue their employers to collect benefits. The full cost of providing workers' compensation benefits normally is borne by the employer. In theory, this cost will be included in the cost of production and passed on to the consumer. In practice, the ultimate burden of the cost will be a function of the elasticity of demand for the employer's product or service.

Coverage and Benefits. The key criterion for coverage under workers' compensation laws is that accidental occupational injuries or death must arise out of and be in the course of covered employment. Self-inflicted injuries and accidents resulting from an employee's intoxication or willful disregard of safety rules usually are excluded. Illnesses resulting from occupational diseases are covered in all states. Some states, however, cover only those diseases that are specifically listed in the law. Workers' compensation laws provide (1) medical care reimbursement, (2) disability income, (3) death benefits, and (4) rehabilitation benefits. Benefit levels vary significantly from state to state.

Financing. Employers can comply with the law by purchasing a workers' compensation policy,

---

[18]As of January 1985, the maximum weekly benefit ranged from $84 ($141 with dependents) in Indiana to $294 (including dependents) in Massachusetts.

[19]In four states, Alabama, Alaska, New Jersey, and Pennsylvania, employees must also contribute.

[20]For a comprehensive discussion of this subject, see S. S. Huebner, Kenneth Black, Jr., and Robert S. Cline, *Property and Liability Insurance,* 2nd ed. (Englewood Cliffs, N.J.: Prentice Hall, Inc., 1982), Chaps. 28 and 29.

by self-insuring, or by obtaining insurance from a monopoly or competitive state fund. Most employers purchase workers' compensation policies from private insurance companies. The policy guarantees the benefits that must legally be provided to workers who are occupationally disabled.

Self-insurance is allowed in most states. Many large firms prefer to self-insure their workers' compensation losses and avoid the administrative costs associated with workers' compensation contracts. In such cases, the employer must obtain administrative approval and usually is required to post a bond or other security.

Workers' compensation insurance can be purchased from a state fund in 19 states. In six of these states, covered employers must purchase the workers' compensation insurance from a monopolistic state fund. In the other 13 states, the insurance may be purchased either from the state fund or private insurers.

Workers' compensation premiums are calculated as a percentage of payroll and are based on the occupational classes of their workers. Larger employers with workers' compensation premiums above a specified amount are subject to experience rating. Under experience rating, employers are encouraged to take an active interest in employee safety since injuries and fatalities directly affect their workers' compensation premiums.

Temporary Disability Insurance

As noted in Chapter 17, temporary disability benefit plans have been enacted in five states—California, Hawaii, New Jersey, New York, and Rhode Island—and Puerto Rico. Under these laws, employees can collect disability income benefits regardless of whether their disability begins while they are employed. Such benefits are not provided for disabilities covered under workers' compensation laws. From a benefit standpoint, these laws, except in New York, generally are patterned after the state unemployment insurance law.

Employees contribute to the cost of the plans in all six jurisdictions. In two of them, California and Rhode Island, *only* employees contribute. Except for Rhode Island, which has a monopolistic state fund, an employer may obtain coverage from either a competitive state fund or private insurers. The laws require that private coverage must provide benefits at least as liberal as those prescribed under the law. In effect, these plans are compulsory group health plans similar to the voluntary plans in effect in many businesses. Self-insurance generally is permitted.

Chapter 26

Group Insurance Plans: I

Group insurance is a plan of insurance that provides coverage to a number of persons under one contract who have a specific relationship to the policyowner. Originating in the early years of this century to provide life insurance benefits, the group approach has been applied to an increasing variety and number of groups and is now utilized to provide a wide range of employee benefits.

Group insurance is the youngest but fastest-growing branch of the life insurance business. As of the end of 1985, approximately 668,000 plans of group life insurance were in force in U.S. life insurance companies, covering more than 152 million persons and providing over $2,730 billion of protection.[1] These figures do not reflect the tremendous developments of the other group areas, especially group health insurance and group annuities. Taken in the aggregate, the group business has become a major segment of the life insurance operations.

GROUP INSURANCE FUNDAMENTALS

Group insurance is a means through which groups of persons who have a specific relationship to the policyowner are provided coverage under a single contract. The accepted meaning of group insurance is not as elementary as this definition might suggest. What is considered group insurance today might not have been considered group insurance several decades ago. Over time, innovative underwriting techniques of group insurers and regulatory actions have had the effect of defining the product more specifically and assigning certain characteristics to it.

A sound understanding of group insurance and the vast scope of group products can be acquired only through a discussion of its origin, its unique characteristics, its differences from and similarities to other forms of insurance, and a reasonably detailed examination of each of its components. Achieving such a comprehension of group life insurance and group health insurance is the objective of this chapter and Chapter 27.

Distinguishing Characteristics

In a comparison of group insurance with other forms of insurance underwritten by a life

---

[1] Unless noted to the contrary, all statistical aggregates used in this section are taken from *Life Insurance Fact Book* (Washington, D.C.: American Council of Life Insurance, 1986).

insurance company, a number of unique features is evident: (1) the substitution of group underwriting for individual underwriting, (2) the use of a master contract, (3) low administrative cost, (4) flexibility in contract design, and (5) the use of experience rating.[2]

Group Underwriting. Probably the most significant distinguishing characteristic of group insurance is the substitution of group underwriting for individual underwriting. In group cases, no individual evidence of insurability is usually required, and benefit levels can be substantial, with few, if any, important limitations.[3]

Group underwriting normally is not concerned with the health, morals, or habits of any particular individual. Instead, it is aimed at obtaining a group of individual lives or, what is even more important, an aggregation of such groups of lives that will yield a certain predictable rate of mortality or morbidity. If a sufficient number of groups of lives is obtained, and if these groups are reasonably homogeneous in nature, the mortality or morbidity rate is predictable. The point is that the group becomes the unit of underwriting, and insurance principles may be applied to it just as in the case of the individual. To assure that the groups obtained will be reasonably homogeneous, the underwriting process in group insurance is aimed at avoiding adverse selection by entire groups or a large proportion of the individuals within a given group.

In underwriting group insurance, then, certain essential features must be present that either are inherent in the nature of the group itself or may be applied in a positive way to avoid serious adverse selection. These are reviewed below.

[2]For a comprehensive study of group insurance, see Burton T. Beam, Jr., and John J. McFadden, *Employee Benefits* (Homewood, Ill.: Richard D. Irwin, Inc., 1985). See also *A Course in Group Life and Health Insurance, Part A* and *Part B* (Washington, D.C.: Health Insurance Association of America, 1985).

[3]In recent years, there has been a trend toward large amounts of group life coverage on individual lives, with a consequent reintroduction of evidence of insurability, as in the case of ordinary insurance. Another exception is the underwriting of very small groups (fewer than 10 lives). Some form of individual evidence of insurability usually is required for these groups. These cases are treated later in this chapter.

1. *Insurance incidental to group.* The insurance must be incidental to the group; that is, the members of the group must have come together for some other purpose than to obtain insurance. For example, group insurance furnished the employees of a given employer would not be the feature motivating the formation and existence of the group.

2. *Flow of persons through group.* There should be a steady flow of persons through the group; that is, there must be an influx of new young lives into the group and a flow out of the group of the aged and impaired lives. In the case of groups of actively working employees, it may be assumed that they are in average health. In fact, some employers impose preemployment physical examinations, which provide another screening device. In the case of nonworking groups, the latter inherent features would not be present. Use of age rating will help offset this requirement for some groups.

3. *Automatic determination of benefits.* Group insurance underwriting requirements commonly insist on an automatic basis for determining the amount of benefits on individual lives, beyond the control of the employer or employees. If the amount of benefits taken were completely optional, it would be possible to select against the insurer, since those in poor health would tend to insure heavily and the healthy ones might tend to elect minimum coverage.

It should be noted, however, that as the group mechanism has evolved, insurance companies have responded to demands of the marketplace, particularly larger employers, for more flexibility in the selection of benefits. This flexibility typically is expressed in optional amounts of life insurance in excess of basic coverage provided by the employer and in extra health insurance benefits in excess of the employer's basic program.

Also, the popular concept of **cafeteria plans** allows participating employees to select among an array of benefits sponsored by the employer. Using a predetermined allowance of employer funds, the individual may select, subject to certain basic coverages being required, a combination of benefits which best meets his or her individual needs.

4. *Minimum participation by the group.* Another underwriting control is bound up in the requirement that substantially all eligible persons in a given group be covered by insurance. In contributory plans, generally at least 75 percent of the eligible employees should join the plan if coverage is to be effective. In the case of noncontributory plans, 100 percent participation is required.[4] By covering a large proportion of a given group, the insurance company gains a positive safeguard against an undue proportion of substandard lives.

5. *Third-party sharing of cost.* A portion of the cost of a group plan ideally should be borne by the employer or some other third party, such as a labor union or trade association. The noncontributory plan is simple, and it gives the employer full control over the plan. It provides for insurance on all eligible employees and thus eliminates any difficulties involved in connection with obtaining the consent of a sufficient number of employees in order to meet the minimum participation requirement. Also, there is no problem of distributing the cost among the various employees as in the contributory plan.

The contributory plan is usually designed to be less costly to the employer. Hence, with employee contributions, the employer is likely to arrange for more adequate protection for the employees. It can also be argued that if the employee contributes toward his or her insurance, he or she will be more impressed with its value and will appreciate it more. On the other hand, the contributory plan has a number of disadvantages. It is more complicated in operation, at times increasing administrative costs considerably. Each employee must consent to contribute toward his or her insurance, and as stated before, a minimum percentage of the eligible group must consent to enter the arrangement. New employees entering the business must be informed of their insurance privilege. If the plan is contributory, the employee

---

[4]In those cases where employees refuse the insurance for religious or other such legitimate reasons, which do not involve any elements of "selection," this rule is relaxed.

may not be entitled to the insurance until he or she has been with the company for a period of time (e.g., one month). If he or she does not agree to be covered by the plan within a period of 31 days, he or she must provide satisfactory evidence of insurability to become eligible. Some noncontributory plans also have such probationary periods.

6. *Efficient administrative organization.* There should be a single administrative organization able and willing to act on behalf of the insured group. In the usual case, this is the employer. In the case of a contributory plan, there must be a reasonably simple method, such as payroll deduction, by which the master policyowner can collect premiums. An automatic method is desirable from both an administrative and an underwriting standpoint.

There are, of course, a number of miscellaneous controls typically used in group insurance plans that are of underwriting significance, but the discussion above will permit an appreciation of the theory of group underwriting. The discussion applies to groups with a large number of employees. It should be noted, however, that a majority of the groups are not of large size. The size of a group is a significant factor in the underwriting process. In smaller plans, more restrictive underwriting practices relating to adverse selection are used. These include less liberal contractual provisions, and in some cases, individual underwriting of group members.

Master Contract. A second unique characteristic of group insurance is the use of a master contract, with or without certificates of insurance, in lieu of individual policies. Such certificates are the insured person's evidence of insurance coverage. Use of certificates and a master contract are, of course, one of the sources of economy under the group approach. The master contract is a detailed document carefully setting forth the contractual relationship between the group policyowner and the insurance company. The insured persons under the contract, usually employees and their beneficiaries, are not actually parties to the contract, although they may enforce their rights as third-party beneficiaries. The four-party relationship (employer, insurer, employee, and beneficiaries) found in a group insurance plan is unique, and it serves to create a number of interesting and unusual problems common only to group insurance.

Low Cost. A third feature of group insurance is that it essentially is low-cost protection. The very nature of the group approach permits the use of mass-distribution and mass-administration methods that afford group insurance important economies of operation not available in individual insurance. Such economies are more significant in larger cases. In some smaller-group cases, administrative unit expenses could conceivably approach those of individual insurance.

Probably the most significant savings in the cost of marketing group life insurance lies in the fact that group commissions absorb a much smaller proportion of net income than commissions for individual contracts. Because the marketing system relieves the agent (or broker) of many of the duties, responsibilities, and expenses normally connected with selling and servicing individual insurance, and also because of the large premiums involved in many group insurance cases, the commission rate is considerably lower than for individual contracts. In addition to being lower, the commission rates are usually graded downward as the size of the premium developed by the case increases.

In the case of large-group insurance buyers, many deal directly with insurance companies and commissions are nearly eliminated for all practical purposes. In such cases, however, fees frequently are paid to consultants involved.

The nature of the administrative procedures permits simplified accounting techniques. The mechanics of premium collection are less involved, and experience refund procedures are much simplified, because there is only one party with which to deal—the master policyowner. Of course, the issuance of a large number of individual contracts is avoided, and because of the nature of group selection, the cost of medical examinations and inspection reports is minimized. Finally, administrative procedures are simplified on group term life, as a large proportion of group coverage is on a term basis as opposed to a cash value form, which requires special records for reserve and nonforfeiture-value purposes.

Flexibility. In contrast to the individual contract, which must be taken essentially as written, the larger policyowner may have a voice in the design and preparation of the group insurance contract. While the contracts follow a pattern and include certain standard provisions, considerably more flexibility exists here than in individual contracts. The degree of flexibility permitted is, of course, a function of the size of the group involved. The group insurance program is usually an integral part of an employee welfare program, and in most cases, the contract can be molded to meet the objectives of the policyowner as long as the requests do not entail complicated administrative procedures, open the way to possible serious adverse selection, or violate legal requirements.

Experience Rating. Another special feature of group insurance lies in the fact that premiums often are subject to experience rating. The experience of the individual group may have an important bearing on dividends or premium-rate adjustments. The larger the group, and hence the more reliable the experience of the individual group, the greater the weight attached to its own experience in any single year. The possibility that premiums may be increased or reduced by dividends or premium-rate adjustments because of an employer's own experience gives the employer a vested interest in maintaining a favorable loss and expense record. It is most important to keep this factor in mind in understanding group insurance practices.

Some insurers experience-rate based on the class or type of industry or even based on the type of contract. For small groups, most insurance companies use **pooled rates** under which a uniform rate is applied to all such groups. The point at which a group is large enough to be eligible for experience rating varies from company to company based on that insurer's book of business and experience.

Advantages and Limitations of Group Mechanism

Advantages. The group insurance mechanism has proved to be a remarkably effective solution to the need for employee security benefits, for a number of reasons. The utilization of mass-distribution techniques has extended protection to large numbers of persons with little or no life or health insurance. The increasing complexity of our industrial/service economy has brought increasingly large numbers of persons together, and the group mechanism has enabled the life insurance industry to reach vast numbers of individuals within a relatively short period and at low cost. Group insurance also has extended protection to a large number of uninsurable people. Equally important has been the fact that the employer usually pays a large share of the cost.

Another factor of significance, and one of the more cogent motivations for the rapid development of group insurance, has been the continuing federal encroachment in this area. The federal Old-Age, Survivors, Disability and Health Insurance program has expanded rapidly, but many competent observers believe that had not group insurance provided substantial sums of life insurance, health insurance, and old-age protection, the social insurance plan would have developed even more rapidly.

Limitations. From the viewpoint of the employee, group insurance has one great limitation—the temporary nature of the coverage. Unless an employee converts his or her coverage to an individual policy (which is more expensive), the employee loses his or her insurance protection in the event the group plan is terminated, in the event of termination of employment, and often also, at retirement. Most employees shift jobs at one time or another, and many fail to take advantage of their privilege to convert their group coverage. Naturally, this is no problem if they attain similar coverage in a new group.

Group life and health protection is continued after retirement in an increasingly large proportion of cases today, often, however, at levels reduced from those available to the employed worker. Where such continued protection is not available, however, the temporary nature of the coverage is a serious limitation. It should be noted that group health insurance may often be continued as a supplement to Medicare.

Another problem of significance involves individuals, especially supervisory and top-management employees, who may be lulled into complacency concerning their life insurance programs by having large amounts of group life insurance during their working years. Many of these persons fail to recognize the need for, or are unwilling to face the cost of, individual life insurance. Perhaps of even greater significance is the fact that the flexibility of the group approach is limited to the design of the master policy and does not extend to the individual covered employees. Further, it fails to provide any analysis of the financial problems of the individual, a service normally furnished by the agent or other advisor. However, many agents discuss group insurance coverage with individuals as a foundation for discussing the need for additional amounts of individual life insurance.

Types of Eligible Groups [5]

The types of groups eligible for group insurance coverage have broadened significantly over the years. This wider eligibility is reflected in both statutory regulations and in the underwriting philosophy of group writing insurers. Group insurance is permitted today for types of groups that did not even exist in the early days of its development, and written on some types of groups whose applications would not have been even given consideration when the product was first introduced. The NAIC model bill permits coverage on four specific categories of groups. Many states permit coverage on additional types of groups not even identified in the NAIC model bill.

Employees of a Single Employer. The employees of a single employer is the first category

[5]This section draws from Robert W. Batten, George H. Hider, et al., *Group Life and Health Insurance,* Vol. 1 (Atlanta, Ga.: Life Office Management Association, 1979), pp. 36–38.

mentioned in the NAIC model bill. An "employer" may be interpreted as a sole proprietorship, a partnership, or a corporation. Also, "employees" may be not only the immediate employees of the employer, but several other categories as well. The single employer group is by far the dominant type of group provided group insurance coverage.

Debtor–Creditor Groups. Group credit insurance (life and disability income) has grown rapidly, reflecting our credit-oriented society. The policyowner in such plans is a creditor, such as a bank, a small-loan company, credit union, or any business that has significant accounts receivables, including those relying heavily on credit-card customers. The insurance benefits are payable to the master policyowner rather than to the individuals insured or their beneficiaries. In the event of the debtor's death, the life insurance proceeds generally cancel the indebtedness that provided the basis for the coverage. Debtors usually must be under a binding, irrevocable obligation to repay the indebtedness for coverage to be effected.

Labor Union Groups. Members of labor unions may be covered under a group contract issued to the union itself. The insurance must be for the benefit of persons other than the union or its officials. In theory and generally in practice, it is not permissible for the entire premium to be paid directly by member contributions. It is common, however, for payment to be made from funds partially contributed to the union by members specifically for their insurance and partially by the union from its own funds. In some cases, the union pays the total premium from its own funds.

Group contracts often are written on multiple-employer groups and issued to the trustees of a fund created through collective bargaining processes. Such an arrangement is typically established by two or more employers in the same or a related industry, by one or more labor unions, or even jointly by employers and labor unions. The Taft-Hartley Act prohibits employers from turning over funds for employee welfare plans directly to a union—hence the need for trustees for the fund.

Multiple-Employer Trusts. A relatively new type of eligible group, organized to overcome restrictions on the availability of group insurance in some states, is the multiple-employer trust (MET). METs may be sponsored by life insurance companies or independent administrators, and they may be insured or self-insured. The sponsor designs the plan, selects the employers (or other groups) that will be permitted to participate, and usually handles the administration. Each such trust also must have a trustee, usually the trust department of a bank.

All financial transactions flow through and are accounted for by the trust. If the MET is uninsured, the member employers pay premiums to the supporting organization that uses the money to purchase a group contract. The entire group of employers is experience rated, permitting greater credibility to be given the groups' own experience. It also permits very small groups to buy group insurance in those states prohibiting the sale of group insurance to groups with fewer than 10 lives.

Self-insured METs assume the responsibility of making claim payments through a third-party administrator. They should assess adequate premiums (contributions) and maintain appropriate reserves. In the early development of METs this was not always done properly, and several METs have become bankrupt.[6] These early failures of uninsured trusts led Congress to amend legislation so as to require self-insured METs to meet state insurance regulations concerning the adequacies of contributions and reserve levels.

Miscellaneous Groups. As suggested earlier, there are many other types of groups, not specifically identified in the NAIC model bill, that are eligible for group insurance through company underwriting practice and enabling state laws. These include trade associations, professional

[6]Life Underwriter Training Council, "Group Insurance," *Advanced Sales Course,* Vol. 9, p. 35.

associations, college alumni associations, veteran associations, customers of large retail chains, and savings account depositors, among many others. States permit coverage of dependents of covered workers as well.

GROUP LIFE INSURANCE

Group life insurance is one of the most common forms of employee benefit plans offered in the United States. At year-end 1984, almost 40 percent of all life insurance in force (by face amount) was on a group basis. The average amount of group life insurance in force per employee was over $15,000. Almost 90 percent of group life coverage is accounted for by employer-employee groups.

Nature of Coverage

In addition to the eligibility of the group itself, other criteria are involved in coverage under a group life insurance contract. Since the individual-employer group is by far the most important type of group being provided group life insurance benefits, the remainder of this discussion of group life insurance is directed principally toward this type of group.

Minimum Size and Proportion. Many years ago, insurers believed that a minimum of 50 lives was necessary to qualify for group life coverage and state law confirmed this. Today, states permit groups to be insured with 10 or fewer lives. State laws also stipulate the minimum proportion of the eligible employees that should be insured under a group life contract.

Requirements of this nature are desirable. They assure the maintenance of a reasonable average age with a view to preventing a rise in total premiums from year to year, and also protect the insurance company against the group becoming substandard through adverse selection. Also, the larger the group, the less the expense per person insured. It is for these reasons that insurance com-

panies usually prescribe a minimum number of employees to be covered for group life insurance. In general, for employer-pay-all (noncontributory) plans, insurers usually require that all employees or all of any class thereof, determined by the conditions of employment, must be insured. Where employees contribute a portion of the premium (i.e., a contributory plan), at least 75 percent of the employees must be included under the plan.[7]

Individual Eligibility Requirements. In general, only regular, active, full-time employees are eligible for group life insurance. All such employees, or all such employees in certain classes determined by conditions pertaining to their employment (e.g., "all salaried employees" or "all hourly paid employees"), must be included in the group as eligibles.

Another individual eligibility requirement for coverage is that an employee must be actively at work and must work no fewer than the normal number of hours in a work week at his or her job on the date when he or she becomes eligible for coverage. The requirement, of course, assures a reasonable minimum of health and physical well-being and protects the insurer against serious adverse selection.

A waiting or **probationary period** is often applied to new employees (usually one to six months) before they become eligible for insurance. The probationary period minimizes the record-keeping and administrative expenses involved in setting up records for employees who remain with the employer for a very short period, although with the widespread use of computers, this is less important than formerly.

After the completion of probationary period, the employee is automatically covered

---

[7]As the types and sizes of groups covered have expanded, the minimum participation requirements have become a function of size, legal requirement, and rate basis. So-called association cases commonly insure less than 75 percent of the eligible individuals, reflecting a rate basis somewhat higher than normally used on employer groups. Similarly, in the 10- to 25-life range, many companies require a participation of 85 percent.

under a noncontributory plan. Under a contributory plan, the employee is given a period of time, known as the **eligibility period,** during which he or she is entitled to apply for insurance without submitting evidence of insurability. This period is limited, usually to 31 days, to minimize selection against the company by the employee. For the same reason, it is customary to require evidence of insurability from employees who have discontinued their coverage and desire to rejoin the plan, or who did not enroll during the eligibility period. In the event the plan is written on a noncontributory basis, these rules do not apply, since all employees (or all employees within the designated classes) are covered automatically unless they specifically decline coverage.

Duration of Coverage. Once the insurance becomes effective for a particular employee, the protection continues as long as he or she remains in the service of the employer (assuming, of course, that the employer maintains the plan in force). The master contract usually gives the employer the right to continue premium payments for employees temporarily off the job, provided that the employer does so on a basis that precludes individual selection. Upon permanent termination of service, the employee's coverage continues for 31 days beyond the date of termination. During this extension of coverage, the employee has an opportunity to replace the expiring protection with individual insurance, to obtain employment with another firm with group insurance, or to convert the expiring term insurance to a cash value form of insurance. Some states now require a longer extension of coverage in the event of termination of employment.

An increasing proportion of plans continue coverage after retirement, providing at least enough insurance to cover the employee's last illness and funeral expenses. In the past, many plans continued full benefits on retired lives, with no special provision for prefunding the rapidly rising costs as the number of covered retired employees increased. The cost of providing such life insurance coverage can be very high. (See "Postretirement Coverage" below.)

Benefits

Traditional Approaches to Benefit Amounts. To minimize adverse selection, the amount of group life insurance for which an employee is eligible is usually determined by a system that precludes the employee from selecting the coverage amount. Generally, this system uses one or more of four bases for determining the amount of group coverage: (1) a set dollar amount to all employees; (2) a function of employee compensation; (3) a function of employees' position; and/or (4) a function of each employee's length of service. Any life insurance benefit schedule that tends to discriminate in favor of highly compensated or managerial employees can cause the loss of important tax benefits (see below).

1. *Fixed amount.* The use of a fixed-amount benefit plan places all employees in one category. It has the advantage of simplicity, but it also has the important disadvantage of placing all employees on an equal level. If group insurance is to serve as a means of rewarding workers in the interest of stabilized labor, and this is one of the strong arguments, it seems neither wise nor fair that low-paid or new employees should obtain the same benefits as those who are skilled or have served the employer for years. However, the fixed-amount plan greatly minimizes adverse selection and stabilizes cost. This type of benefit has been used principally for union welfare funds.

2. *Amount of compensation.* Most group life plans base the amount of insurance on employees' earnings. A simplified scale utilizing earnings classes might be as follows:

Annual Earnings	Insurance Amount
Less than $20,000	$20,000
$20,000 or more, but less than $40,000	40,000
$40,000 and over	50,000

The plan could be based on any common earnings unit. This approach has the advantage, in a contributory plan, of relating cost to ability to pay and also recognizes, to some extent, the increase in human life value represented by increases in compensation. The schedule established frequently attempts to replace lost earnings for 1 or 1½ years. More recently, there has been a tendency to adopt a benefit formula that is a multiple of earnings, usually rounded to the nearest $1,000. Multiples of 1, 1½, and 2 times earnings are common.

3. *Position.* When the salary or wage is difficult to determine in advance, as in the case of pieceworkers or salespersons, the insurance may be set according to the position held by the employee. Thus, officers, superintendents, and managers may receive $50,000 each; foremen and salespersons $30,000 each; and all other employees $20,000 each. This approach is used frequently and tends to reflect ability to pay and need.

4. *Service.* Under the so-called service plan, the amount of protection is increased in accordance with the length of time that the employee has been in the employer's service. Service plans have declined in popularity in recent years because of cost implications and the fact that the amounts of insurance grow inversely in relation to the needs of most lower-paid employees. As the plan provides increasing amounts of insurance based on length of service, it tends to result in progressively higher premium costs.

5. *Combination.* To benefit its most valuable employees, an employer may adopt a plan in which amounts of group term life insurance are determined on the basis of both salary and length of service. A typical plan would determine the amount of insurance an employee is entitled to by multiplying the employee's annual salary by the product of the appropriate salary and years of service factors.

Minimum and Maximum Amounts. Regardless of the plan used, some provision is always made to keep the amounts of insurance extended to executives and others with high salaries in line with the total amount of protection extended to the whole group. Thus, insurance companies usually will not write less than $500 or $1,000 on any one insured, nor more than a certain maximum amount, determined by both the number of persons insured and the average amount of insurance per employee. In the past, state-mandated maximums were common. Today only the state of Texas retains such a maximum.

Underwriting limitations on amounts are necessary in smaller groups to minimize adverse selection. In larger groups, where the group's individual experience has a strong effect on the level of dividends, a maximum is highly desirable to avoid undue fluctuations in cost from year to year.[8]

Virtually any company will write as much as $40,000 on an individual life under proper underwriting circumstances, and in some cases, as high as $1,000,000 and over is being provided on individual lives. Many insurance companies will permit individual amounts in excess of their normal maximums, provided that evidence of insurability is submitted for the excess amounts or that other safeguards are established to protect against severe adverse selection.[9]

The willingness of some insurance companies to superimpose a schedule of life insurance benefits on an already existing plan provided by another company has led to the writing of amounts of group life insurance on a single life far beyond what one company's underwriting rules will permit. The question of how much group life insurance should be provided on a single life has been a point of controversy in the life insurance field.[10]

---

[8]In many cases, companies will place a maximum on the amount of coverage on a single life that will be charged to the experience of the individual case, with any excess coverage being pooled among cases.

[9]Other safeguards include inspection reports on one or more individuals, extra premiums charged on the case, excess amounts reinsured, special reserves built for the case, and excess-amount risks pooled for experience purposes.

[10]See Batten, Hider, et al., *Group Life and Health Insurance,* pp. 68–69.

Conversion Privilege. An insured employee has the privilege of converting the face amount of his or her group insurance protection to an individual policy of cash value insurance under certain conditions. Normally, the employee may convert, within 31 days after termination of employment or cessation of membership in an eligible classification, to one of the company's regular cash value forms at standard rates for his or her attained age. The most significant advantage to the employee lies in the fact that no evidence of insurability is required.[11]

The death benefit provided under a group life insurance contract is continued during the conversion period (usually 31 days) after an employee withdraws from the eligible group. In the event of the employee's death during this period, a death benefit is paid under the group policy.

Waiver of Premium Benefits. A waiver of premium clause commonly is used in group life contracts. As long as the insured proves his or her disability periodically, this clause provides that coverage will continue indefinitely with no payment of premium from the employer or, if contributory, from the employee.

Plans of Insurance

Yearly Renewable Term Insurance. The basic plan of insurance under which group life insurance is provided is yearly renewable term insurance. This insurance coverage has many of the characteristics of that provided through individual policies. With respect to any covered employees, the protection expires at the end of each year but is renewed automatically without evidence of insurability. As in the case of individual coverage, the premium rate per $1,000 of protection increases at an increasing rate from year to year. Despite this, however, the employee's contribution

(if the plan is contributory) usually remains at the same level regardless of his or her attained age. The level contribution by the employee is practicable because the employer absorbs the portion of the cost in excess of the employee's annual contribution. Thus, the employer's contribution for any individual employee usually increases year by year. On the other hand, the employer's total contribution to the plan may well remain stable or even decline, depending on the benefit formula, the age and sex composition of the group, and the experience of the plan.

The simplest way to comprehend the relative roles of the employer and employees in financing a term plan is through the calculation of the average annual premium for a hypothetical plan. This is presented in Table 26-1 for the first year of group term insurance. Each employee is assumed to be a male and have insurance equal to two years' salary, subject to a maximum of $100,000.

The first step in calculating the average annual premium is to determine the total premium payable at each age represented by the group of covered employees. The sum of these values, as shown in Table 26-1, is $81,448.50. To this sum must be added a so-called policy constant, which is $2.40 per year per $1,000 but is applied only to the first $40,000 of insurance. This recognizes the minimum expenses associated with any group. The total aggregate annual premium, then, is $81,544.50, and it is only necessary to apply an advance expense adjustment factor to derive the initial annual premium. In this instance, the group qualifies for a 35 percent discount, and the initial annual premium is $53,003.92. The final step in deriving the average annual premium per $1,000 simply involves dividing $53,003.92 by the number of $1,000 units of insurance—namely, 7,550—which gives $7.02. Assuming that the employees' contributions are $3.50 per $1,000, the employer must bear the difference of $3.52 per $1,000, or $26,500.50. In practice, these premiums and contributions normally would be converted to a monthly basis.[12]

---

[11]A conversion privilege is also available on the termination of the master contract, but under far more restrictive conditions. See *ibid.,* pp. 69-70. In view of the importance of group insurance as a factor in the security of most employees, some liberalization of the conversion privilege would be desirable. Although adverse selection is a problem, the improved service to insured employees would appear to justify a continuing effort to liberalize the conversion privilege.

[12]Not all companies calculate group life rates exactly as presented. Many companies would in fact find premiums based on Table 26-1 to be uncompetitive in today's market.

TABLE 26-1. Calculation of average annual premium per $1,000 of group term life insurance

Attained Age	Number of Employees	Insurance per Employee	Total Amount of Insurance	Annual Premium per $1,000[a]	Total Premium
20	5	$ 15,000	$ 75,000	$ 2.75	$ 206.25
25	5	35,000	175,000	2.97	519.75
30	10	45,000	450,000	3.15	1,417.50
35	10	55,000	550,000	3.74	2,057.00
40	20	70,000	1,400,000	5.28	7,392.00
45	20	80,000	1,600,000	8.08	12,928.00
50	20	90,000	1,800,000	12.51	22,518.00
55	10	100,000	1,000,000	19.55	19,550.00
60	5	100,000	500,000	29.72	14,860.00
	105		$7,550,000		$81,448.50

Total Annual Premium	$81,448.50
Addition for "policy constant" (40 × $2.40)	96.00
Aggregate annual premium	81,544.50
Advance expense adjustment (35%)	−28,540.58
Initial annual premium	53,003.92
Average annual premium per $1,000	
($53,003.92 ÷ 7,550)	$7.02

[a]The 1961 Standard Group Life Insurance Premium Rates (1960 Commissioners Standard Group Table of Mortality at 3%, loaded by basic loading percentage).

If the experience under a pooling arrangement of small-size employers is favorable, the dividend or retroactive rate adjustment will reduce the employer's cost. Under some plans, the dividend might equal and occasionally exceed the employer's contribution. In the latter instance, the excess of the dividend is at times applied in some manner for the benefit of the employees. This is required by law in some states.

Group insurance premiums are paid by the employer monthly. Annual, semiannual, and quarterly modes are possible but are used with small groups only. All adjustments in the amount of insurance during the year, arising out of new employees, terminations, and reclassifications, are made on the basis of the average-monthly-premium rate, regardless of the actual ages of the employees involved. At the end of each policy year, a new average monthly premium is computed.

Yearly renewable term insurance rates are guaranteed for one year only. From a practical standpoint, companies try to avoid rate increases, because they are disturbing to the contractholder, and where possible, prefer to make adjustments in cost through the experience-rating process.

Where group term life plans are on a contributory basis, employee contributions frequently are at a uniform rate per $1,000 regardless of age. In regard to setting the level of contributions, the important principle is to see that the cost of the employee is such that the insurance is an attractive buy in comparison with insurance available to him or her under individual policies.

New York and Michigan set a maximum limit (60 cents per month per $1,000) on the amount of employee contributions. Limitations also arise in other situations, depending on company underwriting philosophy.

Cash Value Life Insurance. Several different types of group life plans provide cash value insurance. The basic purpose of these and of retired lives reserve approaches is to fund postretirement life insurance. These are discussed in detail below.

Companies use a variety of factors to load or reduce their rates: male-female mix, average amount of insurance, whether insurance is noncontributory, and the type of industry.

Taxation of Group Life Insurance [13]

While the tax treatment of group insurance premiums paid by an employer is relatively straightforward, the income tax treatment to covered employees is more complex. In general, premiums paid for employees' group insurance are deductible by the employer. Premiums paid by sole proprietors and partners for group insurance on their own lives, however, are not deductible since they are not considered employees.

Employee Income Taxation. Under current law, the cost of the first $50,000 of group term life coverage is income tax exempt to the employee. Amounts in excess of $50,000 may invoke taxable income. If the employee contributes toward the cost of the insurance, all of his or her contributions are allocable to the coverage provided in excess of $50,000. This is advantageous since it serves to reduce or even eliminate any income tax consequences to the employee for having group coverage in excess of $50,000.

The economic benefit flowing to employees who enjoy coverage in excess of $50,000 is calculated on a monthly basis. The following procedural outline illustrates both the calculations of the amount taxable to the employee and the offset of any employee contributions:

1. Find the total amount of group term life insurance coverage for the employee in each calendar month of a taxable year.
2. Subtract $50,000 from each month's coverage.
3. Apply the appropriate rate from the Uniform Premium Table (Table 26–2) to any balance for each month.
4. From the sum of the monthly cost, subtract total employee contributions for the year.

An example will illustrate the application of this approach. Assume that John, age 56, is provided $150,000 of group term life insurance coverage throughout the year by his employer and that John contributes $15 per month ($.10 per $1,000) toward this coverage. The procedure to

TABLE 26-2. Uniform premium rates for $1,000 of group term life insurance protection[a]

Under 30	$0.08
30 to 34	0.09
35 to 39	0.11
40 to 44	0.17
45 to 49	0.29
50 to 54	0.48
55 to 59	0.75
60 and over	1.17

[a]IRS Reg. & 1.79–3(d)(2). The employee's age for purposes of the Uniform Premium Table is his or her attained age on the last day of the taxable year.

derive John's taxable income from the employer providing this protection would be as follows:

Amount of coverage	$150,000
Less: Exempt amount	– 50,000
Equals: Excess over exempt amount	$100,000
Excess over exempt amount	$100,000
Times: Uniform premium table rate	× 0.75 per $1,000
Tentative monthly taxable income	75.00
Times: Months of coverage	× 12
Equals: Tentative yearly taxable income	$900.00
Tentative yearly taxable income	$900.00
Less: Employee contributions ($15/month × 12 months)	– 180.00
Equals: Taxable economic benefit	$720.00

The tax treatment above assumes that certain conditions specified by Section 79 of the Internal Revenue Code (IRC) and related regulations have been met. In designing a plan to meet these requirements, there are two areas of special concern: (1) those groups covering fewer than 10 employees, and (2) the nondiscrimination rules of Code Section 79(d).

Under 10 Lives/10 or More Lives. Where a group has fewer than 10 lives, underwriting and amounts of insurance are both limited by IRC Regulation 1.79-1(c), which requires that all full-time employees who provide required satisfactory evidence of insurability must be included unless they explicitly state their intention not to participate. The formula for determining the amount of life insurance is prescribed, and underwriting is

[13]This section draws on LUTC, "Group Insurance," pp. 42–43.

restricted to a medical questionnaire. No physical examination is permitted.

Where 10 or more lives are involved, the basic rule is that regular underwriting is permissible and the amount of insurance for each employee can be computed under any formula that precludes individual selection.

Nondiscrimination Rules. The Tax Reform Act of 1986 (TRA '86) imposed additional rules regarding nondiscrimination for all group life plans. Under the law,[14] the exemption from income taxation of the cost of the first $50,000 of group term life insurance is not available (or only partially so) to highly compensated individuals if the plan discriminates in their favor or if benefits are not distributed broadly among the rank-and-file employees. Under TRA '86, group term must meet both three eligibility tests and a benefits test or a single alternative test, which requires that the plan benefit at least 80 percent of the employer's nonhighly compensated employees. These new comprehensive nondiscrimination rules for statutory employee benefit plans are applicable to all group insurance programs.

Other Tax Aspects. The employer may deduct the portion of the premium credited to any retired lives reserve fund (see below) for continuing coverage on retired employees. However, the amount added to the retired lives reserve must be no greater than the amount required to allocate the cost over the working lives of the employees, and the policyowner must have no right to capture any portion of the reserve as long as any active or retired employees remain alive. Similarly, a corporation's nonrefundable contributions to an employee's trust to provide group health and group term life insurance for both active and retired employees is deductible under Code Section 162. Contributions by the employer that are applied toward the savings portions of group cash value plans (see below) are deductible by the employer but taxable currently to the employee.

Death proceeds payable under group life insurance, as with individual coverage, are received income tax free whether received from term or cash value group insurance.[15] The general rules for including life insurance proceeds in the gross estate for federal estate tax purposes apply.[16] An employee can assign all incidents of ownership in group life insurance as long as both the master policy and applicable state law permit it.

Postretirement Coverage

Three general approaches have been used to provide life insurance protection to retired employees: (1) continuation of a portion of the term life insurance; (2) retired lives reserve (RLR); and (3) cash value life insurance. Continuation of a portion of the group term life insurance is straightforward. Unless the original amount of coverage is very modest, the coverage to be continued often is a flat dollar amount, such as $5,000 or $10,000, or it varies from a minimum of 25 percent to a maximum of 50 percent of the former coverage. The other two approaches deserve further consideration.

Retired Lives Reserve.[17] A retired lives reserve (RLR) is a group product with the basic objective of providing continuing life insurance beyond retirement. RLR consists of two basic elements: (1) term insurance (usually annually renewable to age 100) that qualifies as group term insurance under IRC Section 79, and (2) a reserve that will be accumulated, prior to retirement, to be used to pay premiums on the term insurance after retirement. Under a properly designed plan, an employer can make tax-deductible contributions to the fund on behalf of employees and the contributions are not taxable income to the employees. The fund may be administered through a trust or by a life insurance company. As long as any employees under the plan are alive, the reserve cannot revert to the employer. If the employee dies or quits before retirement, the reserve value is used to fund future costs for others in the plan.

[15] IRC Section 101(a). See Chapter 13.

[16] See Chapter 13.

[17] LUTC, "Group Insurance," p. 37. For a comprehensive discussion of RLR, see Beam and McFadden, *Employee Benefits,* pp. 102–107.

[14] Section 79(d).

The Tax Reform Act of 1984 introduced additional constraints on the use of retired lives reserves that have materially reduced interest in and utilization of retired lives reserves. The law makes deduction for contributions on behalf of key employees contingent on the plan being nondiscriminatory under Section 79 (see taxation discussion above) and generally limits the amount of coverage to $50,000.

Cash Value Life Insurance. Postretirement life insurance coverage is also funded through the use of various cash value life insurance plans. These plans fall into three categories.

1. *Group paid up.* At one time, the group term plus paid-up approach was the most popular plan for providing postretirement life insurance coverage.[18] This plan is a combination of accumulating units of single-premium whole life insurance and decreasing units of group term life insurance. The combination provides the same death benefits as regular employer group term plans. Each paid premium consists of the individual employee's contribution and the employer's contribution. Employee contributions usually are applied to purchase increments of paid-up single-premium whole life insurance, the amount of which is determined by the individual employee's attained age and the contribution amount. The employer's contribution is applied to provide an amount of decreasing term insurance, which when added to the accumulated face amounts of the paid-up whole life insurance purchased by the employee, equals the total amount for which he or she is eligible.

Ordinarily, at retirement the portion of the insurance that is still on a term basis will be discontinued, the paid-up insurance remaining in force for the balance of the employee's lifetime. The employee may have the right to convert the term portion. When an employee terminates employment prior to retirement, similar provisions apply. He or she may withdraw the surrender value in cash if he or she wishes to terminate the insurance

entirely. There is relatively little interest in this coverage today.

2. *Group ordinary.* There is no typical group ordinary insurance product. Rather, the terminology is used to describe any product (except group paid-up insurance) that provides cash value life insurance to a group of employees and that will qualify for favorable income tax treatment under IRC Section 79.[19] The cost of the term portion of the coverage is paid by the employer and the cash value portion, which the employee may be able to decline, generally is paid by the employee.

In general, federal income tax treatment of the term life insurance portion of group paid-up insurance and group ordinary insurance is essentially the same as for group term life insurance. The portion of any employer contributions paying for the cash value portion of the insurance is taxable to the employee as additional compensation. The sale of this type of coverage has been minimal in recent years.

3. *Group universal life.* Recently, a number of companies have begun marketing a group universal life product (GULP).[20] These products include the typical guaranteed interest rate, the usual death benefit and loan options, and the flexibility and potential high returns associated with new interest-sensitive life products.[21] Universal life may be particularly attractive right now in light of regulations proposed by the Financial Accounting Standards Board, which could mandate that corporations report the liability of future postretirement life insurance benefits making prefunding programs a necessity. To the extent employers can shift the responsibility of providing postretirement life insurance coverage to their employees, they can also minimize the need to

---

[18]This plan is also known by the designations *group life with paid-up values, group paid-up and decreasing term,* and *group paid-up.*

[19]Beam and McFadden, *Employee Benefits,* p. 109.

[20]See, for example, "Metropolitan Unveils Group Universal Life," *National Underwriter,* Life/Health ed. (July 27, 1985) and LIMRA, "Introducing Group Universal Life," *Market-Facts,* Vol. 4 (November, 1985), pp. 17–20. See also. Burton T. Beam, Jr. and Edward E. Graves, "Group Universal Life Insurance As An Employee Benefit," *Benefits Quarterly,* Vol. 2, No. 3 (Third Quarter 1986).

[21]See Chapter 6 for a discussion of universal life insurance.

show any potential liability on their financial statements.

Overall, GULP works much the same way as individual universal life. But as a group program, it does differ in certain ways.[22]

1. Coverage generally is issued up to some limit without evidence of insurabilty. Although limits do vary (depending on specific plan provisions, the size of the participating group and the insurer's underwriting standards), such coverage usually is high enough to meet most employees' needs.
2. Policies typically are available on a low-commission basis.
3. Administrative charges should be lower than those assessed for individual coverage.

Another (less positive) difference is that the use of group underwriting standards to limit adverse selection may cut into GULP's flexibilty to some extent. Active employment, for example, is likely to be a prerequisite for participation, and minimum and maximum amounts of coverage (e.g., from one to four times pay) usually are prescribed. Some proof of insurability also may be required for very large amounts of insurance. The plans typically are employee-pay-all. Nevertheless, overall plan design remains highly flexible.

GULP has a great deal to offer employees. It can be an inexpensive and convenient way to purchase cash value life insurance. And employees have a chance to invest—at attractive interest rates—in a tax-favored vehicle.

Terms of Policies and Certificates

Various important features of group life insurance policies have already been discussed. In connection with the term of the contract and renewal, where the policy is issued on the yearly renewable term plan, the insurance company cannot refuse to renew each year if the employer wishes to continue the contract and pays the premiums. However, the premium rates may be increased to such an extent that for all practical purposes, the right to renew may not be of any value.

[22]*TPF&C Letter,* Issue 233 (March 12, 1986).

The master policy also provides that if at any time the number of employees does not equal the required number (e.g., 10), or if the plan is contributory and the required minimum percentage (e.g., 75 percent) of employees is not under the plan, the policy may be canceled.

Also, the laws in most states require certain standard provisions. Thus, the employer must deliver to the employee a certificate showing the amount of insurance and the name of the beneficiary, and containing a conversion clause. Another required clause provides for an adjustment in premiums and insurance in case the age of an employee has been misstated. If the age has been overstated, the employer will receive a refund. If the age has been understated, the employer will be required to pay the amount by which past premiums have been deficient. Note that this method of adjusting policies for misstated ages differs from the adjustment made in individual life policies.

Group life insurance policies also contain an incontestable clause, although it is of less significance than in individual insurance. In addition, the policy usually provides for (1) a grace period of 31 days in connection with premium payments; (2) a right to have death proceeds paid in installments; (3) the necessity for making claims within one year following the last premium payment for the employee in question; (4) continued insurance, for the period provided by the contract, on laid-off employees, provided that the employer continues to pay the necessary premium; and (5) extension of the insurance to employees who are eligible but have been erroneously reported ineligible.

Supplemental Coverages

Supplemental benefits may be added to group term life insurance contracts through the use of riders. These riders may include (1) supplemental life insurance, (2) accidental death and dismemberment insurance, (3) survivor income benefits, and (4) dependent life insurance. With the exception of dependent life insurance, these coverages may also be written as separate contracts.

Supplemental Life Insurance. To provide flexibility to employees in tailoring group life insurance protection to their needs, supplemental life insurance is sometimes made available as part of a group life insurance plan. The supplemental coverage is normally contributory, with the number of options available based on the underwriting requirements of the life insurance company, the wishes of the employer, and applicable statutory requirements. The term **voluntary life insurance** is frequently used to denominate plans where each employee can choose an amount of additional insurance in increments up to a maximum based on the employee's earnings (e.g., three times salary).

Accidental Death and Dismemberment Insurance. Many group life insurance contracts provide accidental death and dismemberment (AD&D) coverage. AD&D insurance provides a benefit if an employee dies, loses the sight of one or both eyes, or loses a hand or a foot, directly and solely as a result of an accidental bodily injury. Although it can be written on a nonoccupational basis only, AD&D insurance usually is written as 24-hour coverage.

The benefit structure of AD&D coverage is based on an amount called the **principal sum**—typically equal to the coverage under the basic group life insurance contract. In the event of accidental death, the benefit is equal to the principal sum. In addition to this accidental death benefit, a benefit schedule is provided in the contract relating types of injuries to the principal sum. For example, in the case of loss of both hands, both feet, or both eyes, the principal sum is payable. Similarly, one-half the principal sum is payable for the loss of one hand, foot, or eye.

The amount of insurance is usually payable in a lump sum (installment payments may be requested) to the designated beneficiary. For other losses, payment is made to the employee. Accidental death and dismemberment benefits normally cease at retirement even if the basic life insurance coverage continues.

Under some plans, an elective benefit that is not part of a regular group life insurance program is available, called **voluntary AD&D.** Employees usually pay all or almost all of the premium, and the employer's payroll deduction facilities are used for collecting the employee's contributions. The benefits of voluntary AD&D are essentially the same as those of basic AD&D, the most significant differences being in the substantial amounts of coverage available and the employee's privilege of selecting the amount of coverage.

Survivor Income Benefits. Survivor income benefits are a form of monthly income that become payable upon the death of an employee who may be covered under either a pension plan[23] or a group life insurance plan. There are three characteristics that distinguish true survivor benefits from the more traditional types of group life insurance: (1) the proceeds are payable in the form of monthly income only; (2) the covered employee does not name his or her beneficiary, as benefits are payable only to specified beneficiaries; and (3) benefits are usually payable only as long as there is a living survivor beneficiary and in some cases may cease on remarriage.

Although specific provisions vary from company to company, the survivor benefits product is designed around the foregoing three characteristics, with special features aimed at meeting the needs of employees with the greatest family responsibilities. One company markets the following survivor benefits product:

1. Single employees are not eligible for survivor benefits.

2. Permissible beneficiaries include only an employee's spouse and/or children.

3. Benefits are normally expressed as a percentage of the employee's predeath earnings and are payable in two forms: a spouse benefit and a children benefit. The most common spouse-benefit percentage is between 20 and 40 percent of an employee's predeath earnings, and the children-benefit percentage is usually significantly lower.

4. The spouse benefit normally is payable until the spouse reaches age 62 or 65. The children benefit is payable until the youngest unmarried child reaches age 19 or, alternatively, age 23, if in school.

[23]See Chapter 28.

5.   The benefit ceases if the spouse remarries or dies before the end of the benefit period. When the youngest unmarried child reaches the limiting age for children, the children benefit ceases.

Life insurance protection for the average American family provides the equivalent of less than two years of income continuance following a wage earner's death. Proponents of survivor benefits believe that they can play an important role in augmenting the amount of insurance protection for the American family.

Dependent Life Insurance.   It is common for group life insurance contracts to provide coverage on the lives of employees' dependents. The law in most jurisdictions permits employers to extend group term life insurance to the employee's spouse and eligible children. The amounts of dependent life insurance usually are small in relation to the amount of insurance on employees. The definition of dependents usually includes an employee's unmarried dependent children who are over, say, 14 days of age but under some specified age, such as 19. The employee is automatically the beneficiary under the coverage.

Many states limit life insurance benefits on dependents. These limits usually restrict the amount of insurance on the spouse to a maximum amount and frequently provide that in no event will the spouse receive more than 50 percent of the benefit provided the employee. Children's benefits are also restricted in many jurisdictions.

Group Credit Life Insurance

Group credit life insurance is a special form of group term insurance issued to a creditor covering the lives of his or her debtors in the amount of their outstanding loans. The insurance is payable to the creditor should the insured debtor die before the loans are repaid. Group credit life insurance has shown a prodigious growth during recent years. Except for the modifications[24] necessary to account for the fact that credit life insurance is designed for one specific objective, the contract and pattern of operation essentially are the same as other group coverages.

---

[24] These modifications are important, however. For example, no conversion privilege is provided, minimum rates may be quoted independent of age, maximum rates may be regulated, the policyowner legally may be the beneficiary, and in some states, there are substantially lower legal-amount maximums.

Chapter 27

Group Insurance Plans: II

GROUP HEALTH INSURANCE[1]

The basic theory of group underwriting and group administration applies to group health insurance just as it applies to group life insurance. Much of the earlier discussion of individual health insurance also applies to group health insurance.[2] In contrast to disability income coverage, most of which is provided under *individual* plans, the vast majority of medical expense coverage is delivered through the *group* mechanism. Consequently, the emphasis in this discussion will be on medical expense insurance.

In contrast to individual health insurance policies, group coverage usually provides benefits for occupational accidents and illnesses only. This is because occupational disabilities normally are covered under state workers' compensation laws. The standard provisions for individual health insurance contracts are not applicable to group health insurance. In general, insurance company practices under group contracts are considerably

more liberal than under individual contracts. However, some states require the inclusion of certain standard provisions in group contracts.

The insurance company may have a right to refuse to renew the master group health insurance contract, but no individual participant may be cancelled or denied renewal except by termination of the entire group. There are, of course, other minor differences, but basically, group health insurance benefits follow the pattern of individual health insurance benefits, with some modification to recognize the principles of group underwriting and group administration.

Group insurance can be written to provide virtually any combination of health insurance benefits. As with individual policies, group health insurance benefits may be broadly classified as (1) disability income and (2) medical expense.

GROUP DISABILITY INCOME INSURANCE

There are essentially two approaches to the provision of disability income benefits, which can be described as short-term disability and long-term disability benefits.[3]

---

[1]This chapter is based on *A Course in Group Life and Health Insurance, Part A* (Washington, D.C.: 1985). HIAA course materials may be obtained from the association's office, 1025 Connecticut Avenue, Washington, D.C. 20036.

[2]See Chapters 16 and 17.

[3]See Chapters 16 and 17 for more details on disability income insurance.

470

Short-Term Disability

This coverage is intended as income replacement for a relatively short period of time, more often payable from the first day of disability resulting from an accident and from the eighth day when resulting from sickness. Many other combinations of waiting periods are utilized. Income benefits for both accident and sickness usually are payable for up to 13, 26, or 52 weeks. Federal law requires that pregnancy be treated the same as a sickness under all fringe-benefit plans for employers with 15 or more employees. Many states have requirements that are more or less strict than the federal requirement. The cost impact of these laws can be severe.

Long-Term Disability

Benefits are provided here in recognition of the continuing need of income for the duration of a long-term disability arising from either accident or sickness and without regard to whether it is job connected. The definition of disability usually does not require total and permanent disability. Many companies include a **residual disability benefit** and a **presumptive disability** clause in their contracts. Under the residual benefit clause, the insured does not have to be totally disabled to qualify for benefits. If disability reduces an insured's income by at least 20 percent, the plan pays a proportionate benefit (20 percent or higher) for as long as two years. This residual disability benefit is consistent with the increasing emphasis on rehabilitation services as part of plan benefits. Under the presumptive benefit provision, the total loss of sight, speech, hearing, or two or more limbs automatically qualifies the individual for long-term disability benefits. The usual elimination period is waived.

Benefits normally are not provided until the expiration of an elimination period, which may run from seven days to six months. The duration of benefits, assuming the continuation of disability, usually is until age 65, but alternative approaches, such as lifetime accident, are not uncommon. The size of the group is a most important underwriting consideration. With large groups, considerable latitude in underwriting is prevalent. Another important underwriting consideration for long-term

disability is the nature of work performed by the group. "Blue-collar" groups are underwritten with considerable caution.

GROUP MEDICAL EXPENSE INSURANCE[4]

Group medical expense insurance coverages are available to provide full or partial reimbursement for a wide range of health care expenses incurred by insured employees and their eligible dependents. The coverages provided are in a continuous process of change and expansion, responding to changes in demand and in technology. The more common coverages are discussed below.

Hospital Expense Benefits

As in the case of individual insurance, group hospital expense insurance normally treats separately the expense of room and board charges and the expenses for other hospital services. With regard to the **daily room and board charge,** many plans are underwritten on the basis of paying the actual charges up to a specified maximum. Other plans provide a benefit that is indefinite as to amount, being equal to the hospital's actual charge but not to exceed the charge for a room in a specified classification, such as semiprivate. The daily room-and-board benefit for a single confinement is payable under basic medical expense plans up to a maximum number of days, such as 31, 70, or 120, and occasionally, 365.

The **hospital miscellaneous expense benefit** may be written on an unscheduled basis up to a maximum of 15, 20, or more times the daily room and board rate, or it may be written on a scheduled basis with dollar limits. Some plans afford miscellaneous hospital expense benefits without dollar limits.

The 1978 Civil Rights Act requires that maternity benefits be the same as nonmaternity benefits for employers with 15 or more employees. This additional risk may be self-insured or covered by the group plan. Most employers choose to provide only for complications under the group plan.

Traditionally, a person due to have surgery would be admitted to the hospital one or, at times,

[4]HIAA, *A Course in Group Life and Health Insurance,* pp. 50–74.

two days prior to enable the hospital to perform necessary tests, such as blood analyses and x-rays. These tests usually can be done on an outpatient basis, thus eliminating unnecessary and expensive confinement. This use of **preadmission testing** has developed as part of a series of efforts to hold down medical care costs.

Surgical Expense Benefits

Surgical insurance provides reimbursement for the charges made by physicians for surgical procedures. Surgical expense benefits may be provided on a scheduled or nonscheduled basis. Under a **scheduled plan,** a specific allowance for each surgical procedure is listed on a schedule developed by the company. Differences among company schedules are based on: (1) the amount that they allow for each procedure; (2) the overall maximum benefit for multiple procedures; and (3) the relative or proportionate value of the procedures listed in the schedule to each other. A typical published schedule may include 100 different operations that cover each of the important categories of surgical procedures. Reimbursement for unlisted procedures is based on a scale proportionate to the listed procedures.

Under a **nonscheduled plan,** instead of a specific allowance, reimbursement of the surgeon's fees, and usually the anesthetist's fee, are based on the usual and customary charge for the procedure performed. A usual and customary charge is defined by each company based on the charges normally made by a physican for a similar service and the amount usually charged by physicians in the specific geographic area where the service is provided.

In the case of multiple operations, the benefit paid usually varies depending on whether the two or more operations involve separate incisions, are in different operative fields, or are separated in time.

Interest in the use of **second surgical opinions** remains high. Medical expense plans not specifically providing second surgical opinion coverage may provide the benefit. Many major medical plans (see below) consider second surgical opinions as a covered medical expense and reimburse such charges on a usual and customary

basis, subject, of course, to deductible and coinsurance provisions.

Some plans *require* second surgical opinions before *elective* surgery. Under this mandatory approach, surgical benefits would be reduced (e.g., 60 percent of the scheduled benefit or of the usual and customary charge) if the patient had elective surgery without seeking a second opinion. This provision would also apply if the patient chose to have elective surgery when the second opinion (or the third opinion where there was a difference between the first two opinions), did not confirm the need for surgery.

Major Medical Expense Insurance

Major medical expense insurance plans cover a wide range of medical care charges with few internal limits and a high overall maximum benefit. Reimbursement for covered expenses may be provided in one of two ways:

1. By first covering certain expenses with a basic plan of medical benefits, supplementing the basic plan with major medical coverage.
2. By using one reimbursement formula for the total covered expenses without distinguishing between those expenses that would otherwise be covered under a basic plan and those expenses to be covered as major medical expense benefits.

The major medical coverage under the first approach is usually referred to as *supplemental* major medical expense insurance. The second approach is known as *comprehensive* major medical expense insurance.

Supplemental Major Medical Expense Benefits. A supplemental major medical expense insurance plan is superimposed on the insurer's own basic group medical expense benefit or a basic plan provided by another company, such as Blue Cross/Blue Shield. An insured individual is reimbursed first for hospital and surgical charges, fees for physician's visits, or any other charges covered by specific reimbursement formulas in the basic plan. All covered expenses not reimbursed under the basic plan (due to limitations or maximums in the basic plan formula or because the expenses involved were outside the scope of the basic plan) are subject to a so-called **corridor deductible.** After this deductible amount has been satisfied, the supplemental major medical plan usually pays a percentage, such as 80 percent, of the remaining covered expenses. The total cost to the claimant, therefore, is the amount of the deductible plus the percentage of expenses not reimbursed as a result of the coinsurance provision under the major medical formula. A typical supplemental major medical plan is illustrated in Figure 27–1.

Comprehensive Major Medical Expense Benefits. Comprehensive major medical expense in-

surance covers virtually all types of medical care services and supplies. The reimbursement formula applies to the total covered expenses subject to a deductible. The deductible is sometimes referred to as an **initial deductible** since it applies before major medical benefits come into play. Thus, a simple comprehensive plan could provide for the reimbursement of 80 percent of all combined covered expenses in a calendar year after a deductible of $300, up to a lifetime maximum of $1,000,000. The main advantages of comprehensive major medical plans are simple plan design and avoidance of duplicate coverage and frequent plan revisions.

FIGURE 27-1 Major medical expense benefits. Source: *A Course in Group Life and Health Insurance, Part A* (Washington, D.C.: Health Insurance Association of America, 1985), p. 82.

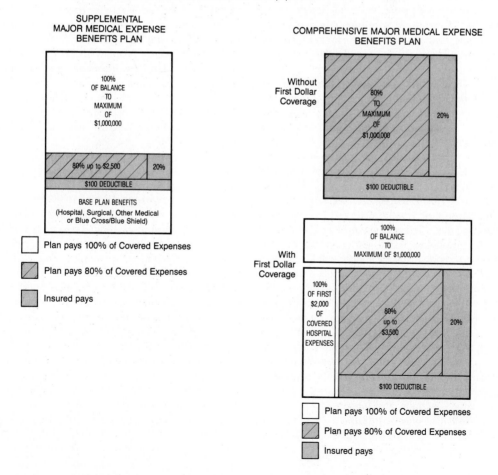

Some plans provide for first-dollar coverage. In some plans, certain types of expenses are not subject to a deductible, such as hospital expenses, and no coinsuranace is used on the initial hospital expenses, such as the first $2,000 or $5,000. Surgeons' fees may be treated similarly, subject to a usual and customary fee limitation. It is possible to waive or modify the deductible and coinsurance features for other services, such as physicians' hospital visits and diagnostic tests, thus further matching the basic plus supplemental major medical concept. Many plans today provide a $1,000 or $2,000 maximum annual out-of-pocket cap on expenses. The elements of a particular plan—the size, type, and application of the deductible, full coverage on certain coverages, and a dollar limit on out-of-pocket expenses to be borne by the insured—reflect both the desires of the policyowner and the underwriting practices of the insurer. Diagrams of a comprehensive plan both with and without first-dollar coverage are presented in Figure 27.1.

Features of Major Medical Plans. Supplemental and comprehensive major medical have common provisions, such as deductibles, coinsurance, overall maximum benefits, and covered expenses.

1. *Deductible.* The primary purpose of the deductible is to lower premium costs. This is accomplished by avoiding unnecessary utilization and eliminating small claims and the expense of handling them. In meeting the deductible amount, an accumulation period feature is included as a device to assure further that only significant claims will be covered. The **accumulation period provision** defines the period of time during which incurred medical care expenses may be accumulated to satisfy the deductible. A variety of deductible provisions exists. The type and amount of the deductible and the way it operates are design aspects of the plan reflecting the policyowner's desires and the underwriting requirements of the insurer. Deductibles can be classified as: all-cause, per cause, corridor, and integrated.

(a) **All-cause deductible.** Under this type of deductible, all expenses incurred, regardless of

the number of illnesses or accidents giving rise to the expenses, are accumulated to satisfy the deductible. The calendar year is almost universally used for both the accumulation period and the benefit period. Assuming a $100 deductible, it applies to each calendar-year benefit period and must be satisfied between January 1 and December 31. Thus, the all-cause deductible is often referred to as a calendar-year deductible. Benefits are paid, following the satisfaction of the calendar-year deductible, for expenses incurred during the remainder of the calendar year.

In view of the fact that some insureds incur expenses early in the year and others incur expenses late in the year, a **carryover provision** is usually included for the latter. Under such a provision, expenses incurred in the last three months of a calendar year (which accumulate toward satisfaction of the deductible for that year) may be carried over to be used toward satisfying the deductible for the next calendar year.

To reduce the financial impact of the deductible on large families, if several members have major expenses in one year, a **family deductible** provision is usually included, which waives the deductible for all family members after any two or three of them individually have satisfied their deductibles in the same year.

The all-cause approach is simple to administer and easy to understand. This can be an important advantage in plan design.

(b) **Per cause deductible.** In the case of the per cause deductible, all expenses incurred because of the same or related causes are accumulated to satisfy the deductible after which benefits begin. The unique characteristic of the per cause deductible is that the benefit period for *each* cause starts with the first expense that is used to satisfy the deductible and normally ends one or two years after the date it starts. In other cases, the benefit period ends two years from the date the deductible was satisfied. When benefit periods longer than one year are provided, it is common to include an alternate basis for terminating the benefit period. The benefit period might be cut off at the end of a period of 60 or 90 days, during which less than a certain amount of expenses (e.g., the deductible amount) is incurred. Once a benefit period has ended, the deductible must be satisfied again to start a new one. An individual could have to satisfy two or more deductibles in a given 12-month period, but this would be a rare occurrence.

The chief advantage of the per cause approach is that claims for minor, unrelated illnesses are eliminated. This approach, however, can cause administrative problems. With advancing age, it often is difficult to distinguish among causes of diseases. It is not surprising that the per cause deductible approach is not very popular today.

(c) **Corridor deductible.** The most common method of applying an all-cause (calendar-year) or per cause deductible in supplemental major medical plans involves the use of a corridor deductible. This deductible is called a corridor deductible because it applies after the basic plan benefits have been exhausted and must be satisfied by additional expenses incurred before the supplemental major medical benefits are payable. Thus, medical expenses that exceed the amounts covered in the basic plan are covered under the supplemental major medical coverage only *after* the corridor deductible is satisfied. The amount of the deductible typically is $100 or $150.

(d) **Integrated deductible.** The integrated deductible involves a "corridor" that is the greater of (1) a fairly high amount, such as $500, or (2) the basic plan benefits. For example, if the basic plan paid $625 and the stated value of the integrated deductible was $500, the deductible would be deemed to be $625 and supplemental major medical benefits would be payable. However, if the basic plan only paid $300, $200 additional expenses would be needed to satisfy the $500 deductible before supplemental major medical benefits would be payable.

(e) **Common accident provision.** A common accident provision, included in many major medical plans, provides that only *one* deductible will have to be satisfied when two or more insured persons *in the same family* are injured in a common accident. A carryover feature in a calendar year type plan may also be included. In such cases, only one deductible applies to the total covered medical care expenses incurred as a result of the accident both in the calendar year in which the common accident occurred and in the following calendar year.

2. *Coinsurance.* The term **coinsurance** refers to the percentage of covered expenses paid by a medical expense plan. Thus, a plan with 80 percent coinsurance will pay 80 percent of covered expenses, while a person who receives benefits under the plan must pay the remaining 20 percent. The term **percentage participation** is used in some plans.

The coinsurance or percentage participation provision has two objectives. It serves both to keep plan costs down and to retain the insured's financial interest in the cost of services, thereby helping to minimize unnecessary utilization of services. Under the usual provision, for covered expenses incurred beyond the deductible, the insured is required to pay 20 percent. Many plans apply a dollar limit to the coinsurance amount to be borne by the insured, by eliminating coinsurance for the balance of the calendar year after the insured has incurred, for example, $2,500 in coinsured expenses.

3. *Overall maximum benefit.* Unless specifically identified as coverage limitations, usual and customary charges for all eligible expenses are covered by the plan provisions up to the overall maximum benefit of the plan. As with the application of the deductible, the overall maximum benefit may be written on a lifetime or a per cause basis.

(a) **Lifetime.** The lifetime (all-cause) maximum benefit applies to all covered expenses during the entire period of coverage. A reinstatement provision usually is included to avoid penalizing insureds who either have partially or wholly exhausted their benefits, but have recovered to the extent of again being acceptable insurance risks. A typical reinstatement provision provides that the maximum may be reinstated, after say, $5,000 or $10,000 in benefits are used, by submitting evidence of insurability satisfactory to the insurance company. It is also common to provide some form of *automatic reinstatement.* For example, a set amount (e.g., $5,000 or $10,000) or set percentage (e.g., 10 percent of the full maximum) of benefits paid each year will be reinstated automatically as of each

January 1. Still another approach reinstates some or all of the maximum if the insured does not incur medical care expenses of more than a specified amount during a given period (e.g., $500 during a six-month period). Since it is not uncommon today to find maximums as high as $1,000,000, and even unlimited benefits, the reinstatement provision has lost much of its significance.

(b) **Per cause.** The per cause overall maximum benefit applies to each cause. Under such a provision, an insured who is receiving benefits under a per cause plan for the treatment of both diabetes and a heart condition, would have a separate overall maximum benefit apply to each illness. A typical per cause reinstatement provision states that when a covered person has received benefits for any one accidental injury or any one sickness equal to the overall maximum benefit, benefits for such injury or sickness will terminate unless evidence of insurability satisfactory to the insurer is submitted. At the same time, coverage for other unrelated injuries or sickness continues to be effective.

4. *Covered expenses.* Major medical plans cover usual and customary charges incurred for most medical care services, supplies, and treatments prescribed as necessary or performed by a physician. Exact eligible charges and their description vary from plan to plan, but the scope of covered expenses usually includes:

- Professional services of doctors of medicine and osteopathy, and other recognized medical practitioners
- Hospital charges for semiprivate room and board and other necessary services and supplies
- Services of registered nurses and, in some cases, licensed practical nurses
- Physiotherapy
- Anesthetics and their administration
- X-rays and other diagnostic laboratory procedures
- Oxygen and other gases and their administration
- Blood transfusions, including the cost of blood where charged
- Drugs and medicines requiring a prescription
- Specified ambulance services
- Rental of durable mechanical equipment required for therapeutic use

- Artificial limbs or other prosthetic appliances, except replacement of such appliances
- Cast, splints, trusses, braces, and crutches
- Rental of a wheelchair or hospital-type bed

As pointed out earlier, plans also may provide coverage for confinements in skilled nursing facilities as well as home health care expense and hospice care expense benefits.

Dental Expense Insurance

One of the fastest-growing health coverages is dental expense insurance. The contracts of some insurance companies have been written on a comprehensive medical basis, with all types of dental expenses, above a deductible, covered on a percentage participation (coinsurance) basis up to a maximum dollar amount. Often, the deductible does not apply to routine oral examinations. Companies believe that such examinations are a sound investment to keep overall costs down. Many companies make available a basic dental expense program, as contrasted with the comprehensive or major medical approach. These programs represent first-dollar coverage with scheduled limits.

In most plans, the coinsurance feature follows the pattern of major medical, with the percentage being set at 75 or 80 percent. Reduced coinsurance percentages, typically 50 percent, are applied to orthodontia and certain restorative work, usually involving the use of gold or other precious metals. A maximum amount of benefits is payable under the program to any one covered person. This maximum amount and how it is applied varies. For example, one type of plan provides benefits for covered expenses up to $1,000 or $2,500 in any calendar year, or $50,000 in any lifetime. Another provides a maximum of $1,000, but not more than $500 in any one calendar year applied separately to each covered member of the family. As mentioned above, orthodontia typically is handled separately, with a separate maximum and increased participation in cost by member (frequently, 50 percent participation).

This dental expense coverage may or may not be packaged with other health insurance benefits. Also, the low average claim and high claim frequency have forced companies to develop automated claim-processing systems. As a result, dental plans that are separate from other medical coverages are simpler to manage in the special system. When dental coverage is packaged with other benefits, the deductible may be applied on the total of dental and medical expenses (**integrated deductible**), or dental expenses may be subject to a separate deductible. Because of administrative complexity, many companies avoid the integrated-deductible approach. In underwriting these cases, insurance companies have been very selective, and early underwriting rules often required a minimum participation of 100 and a minimum contribution of 50 percent on the part of the policyowner. However, there is a trend toward reducing these requirements.

This coverage represents an important development in the group health field. It should be noted that these initial plans were developed in close cooperation with the American Dental Association, whose active interest in this coverage continues.

Skilled Nursing Facility Expense Benefits

Skilled nursing facility expense coverage provides reimbursement for medical expenses incurred when an insured individual is confined in an extended-care facility and requires ongoing active medical and skilled nursing care. The coverage enables a patient to be transferred by a physician from a hospital room to a less expensive extended-care facility when medical needs relate almost exclusively to continued skill nursing care.

The *definition* of an extended-care facility is of extreme importance. The coverage does *not* intend to provide custodial care in institutions with little or no medical care facilities. Many companies limit the coverage only to those institutions approved by Medicare as skilled nursing facilities. Other companies specifically define the services that must be provided.

The amount and extent of benefits available varies. Thus, there may be a total dollar limit for each day of confinement in an extended-care facility or a specific dollar limit for room and board and for necessary services and supplies (similar to a typical hospital expense insurance plan). A daily limit that is expressed as a percentage (usually 50 percent) of the hospital room and board benefit available under hospital and/or major medical expense insurance coverages is used by some companies.

Plans are available ranging from 30 to 200 days per confinement in an extended-care facility. Interestingly, at times the maximum number of days is reduced by two days for each day the insured individual was confined in a hospital for the same disability.

Coverage is limited to those individuals (1) requiring supervised medical treatment, (2) confined in an extended-care facility at the recommendation of a physician, and (3) under a physician's care while confined. Although there are some exceptions, it is common to require hospitalization for a minimum period of three to five days prior to confinement in an extended-care facility. In addition, many plans require that the extended-care facility confinement begin within a specific period (e.g., seven to 14 days) from the date of discharge from the hospital for the same cause of disability.

Home Health Care Expense Benefits

Home health care benefits are usually provided as a supplement to hospital expense or major medical expense insurance. The coverage provides reimbursement for cost of a variety of types of skilled care. The objective is to minimize institutional confinement when the services required by the patient can be provided more comfortably and less expensively at the patient's home.

Plans typically provide reimbursement for home health care charges such as:

1. Care by a physical, occupational, or speech therapist
2. Nursing care, part-time or intermittent, provided under the supervision of a registered nurse
3. Services of a home health aide, part-time or intermittent
4. Medical social services provided under the direct supervision of a physician

5. Care provided by a hospital intern or resident in training under an approved hospital teaching program

The charges may be made by a hospital or by a home health care agency. Covered charges begin within a specific number of days following hospitalization or confinement in an extended-care facility for the same or a related disability. There is a trend, however, toward making these benefits available with hospitalization if it might otherwise be required.

Medical care and treatment expenses are covered provided that they are:

1. Prescribed by a physician in lieu of hospitalizing the patient
2. Furnished under a plan established and periodically reviewed by a physician
3. Furnished on a visiting basis in the patient's home or in the outpatient department of a hospital, skilled nursing facility, or rehabilitation center

Home health care plans usually include a coinsurance provision and a maximum number of covered home health care visits, such as 40 in a calendar year.

As implied above, this coverage will not pay for any services provided when the insured individual is not under the regular care and treatment of a physician; services rendered by a person who ordinarily resides in the insured's home or who is a member of the insured's immediate family; and services covered under any other plan. Specific exclusions include expenses for custodial care, meals, general housekeeping services, and personal comfort items.

Other Medical Expense Benefits

A variety of different plans is available to cover other types of medical expenses. For example, some plans provide for the cost of **diagnostic x-ray examinations** and **laboratory tests** when these services are rendered in a physician's office or to an outpatient at a hospital. Such plans may take several forms. One fairly typical arrangement is to establish an annual maximum benefit such as $50. Within that maximum, benefits often are limited by type of service according to a prescribed schedule (e.g., x-ray, $25).

Many plans provide reimbursement of **physicians' nonsurgical fees.** Such coverage usually is written on an "in-hospital" basis. However, it can be written "while totally disabled" or on a comprehensive basis regardless of the nature of the disability, covering the physician's visits at home or in his or her office, subject to a maximum per call and a maximum total either in dollars or in duration of time. Usually, the first two or three calls are excluded (a deductible provision) except when calls result from an accident.

Recently, **vision-care expense coverage** has been made available generally. Basic and major medical expense coverages long have covered expenses for diagnosis and treatment of an illness or injury of the eye. Vision-care expense insurance plans, on the other hand, provide reimbursement for the cost of eye examinations to determine whether the individual needs glasses and, if so, for the cost of required frames and lenses. Single-vision, bifocal, and trifocal lenses usually are covered, as are contact lenses and other aids for subnormal vision. To minimize overutilization, coverage is usually limited to one examination and one pair of lenses only in any 12 consecutive months and one pair of frames every two years. Medical or surgical treatment, vision training, sunglasses, safety glasses, and duplication of existing lenses or frames because of breakage or loss are commonly excluded.

Prescription drug expense insurance covers drugs with very little, if any, cost to the insured individual. Streamlined approaches to administration and claims processing are essential under this coverage because of the large number of small claims involved.

One of the most recent developments in medical care expense insurance coverages is **hospice care expense benefits.** A hospice is a program of care for the terminally ill patient and his or her family. The focus is on palliative care and social support services rather than the normal curative approach to medicine. Hospice teams are composed of trained medical personnel, homemakers, and counselors who help the patient and the family cope with the social and psychological as well as the physical stresses of death and bereavement.

Benefits are provided for usual and customary charges made by the hospice. The **benefit period** starts when the attending physician certifies that the patient has a life expectancy of six months or less. It ends when the patient dies or at the end of a specified period, such as six or 12 months, whichever happens first. A new benefit period may be established by recertification if the patient is still living at the end of a benefit period. A defined **period of bereavement** begins when the patient dies and typically ends six or 12 months after the date of death. Benefits are usually limited to a specified number of counselling sessions for the surviving dependents. A dollar maximum per session is usually applicable. Benefits for services that have not been recommended by an attending physician or for those that an insured would not legally have had to pay in the absence of insurance are excluded. Although there is increasing interest in hospice coverage, it is not widely written. The major obstacle to its development has been the lack of accreditation standards for hospice services, but progress is being made.

Finally, note should be taken of some special plans that provide a substantial level of benefits in cases of severe illness. In this category are various kinds of so-called **dread-disease insurance.** In such cases, the frequency of illness is quite low but may well involve substantial costs. Because of the low frequency, cost appears to be low, and where major medical expense insurance is not available, this coverage serves a need. It should be noted, however, that such coverage may be misleading and lull employees into believing they have broader coverage than they really have—when major medical is what they really need. This type of coverage has fallen into disfavor with some regulatory authorities.

TAXATION OF GROUP HEALTH INSURANCE

Disability Income Benefits

As with all types of health insurance benefits, premiums (or other employer contributions) paid by an employer for disability income insurance for employees are tax deductible by the employer and are not taxable income to the

employee for federal income tax purposes. Employee contributions, on the other hand, are not tax deductible by the employee. Consistent with these two rules, the payment of benefits under an insured plan or a noninsured salary continuation plan will result in the receipt of taxable income by the employee to the extent the benefits received are attributable to *employer* contributions. Thus, if the employer pays 75 percent of the monthly premium and the employee pays 25 percent, 25 percent of any benefits received will be tax-free and 75 percent taxable.[5]

Medical Expense Benefits

In contrast to employer-financed disability income benefits, medical expense benefits received by an employee are not taxable to an employee unless they exceed the medical expenses incurred. The Tax Reform Act of 1986 revised the nondiscrimination rules for self-insured medical reimbursement plans and extended them to insured plans. The nondiscrimination rules are the same as those applicable to group life insurance.[6]

ALTERNATIVES FOR GROUP BENEFIT PLAN FUNDING[7]

Introduction

During the 1960s, with rare exceptions, the traditional group insurance contract was the arrangement under which group benefit plans were funded. In the 1970s many corporations experienced reduced profits and cash flow problems. At the same time, benefit programs became more liberal with accompanying premium increases. Escalating inflation and greater utilization increased the cost of providing health insurance benefits. During the same time period, the cost of borrowing money for corporate pur-

---

[5]IRC Section 37 provides a tax *credit* for persons who are disabled and have modest taxable income. See, Burton T. Beam, Jr., and John J. McFadden, *Employee Benefits* (Homewood, Ill.: Richard D. Irwin, Inc., 1985), pp. 128–129.
[6]For a discussion of the tax treatment of self-funded plans, see *ibid.,* pp. 195–196.
[7]HIAA, *A Course in Group Life and Health Insurance,* pp. 257–262.

poses rose to historic highs. These developments gave risk managers and other financial officers a reason to investigate alternate financing mechanisms for their benefit programs.

Generally, employers were (and are) interested in examining alternative methods of financing benefit programs for one or both of the following reasons:

1. To control and use reserve funds that would normally be available to the insurance company under a conventional fully insured plan, and/or
2. To reduce or eliminate payment of state premium taxes and risk, profit, and contingency charges, which normally are part of the cost under a conventional fully insured plan.

In response to these developments, a number of techniques have been developed by insurers that modify conventional methods of funding group insurance but offer a reasonable guarantee of comparable benefits. They are described briefly below.

Fully Insured Plans

Retrospective Premium Arrangement. Under a retrospective premium arrangement, premiums are set realistically to cover expected claims and expenses without the margin for contingencies usually included to cover higher than expected levels of either. In lieu of the premium margin is an agreement under which the insurer reserves the right to collect additional premiums at the end of the policy year if claims and expenses are higher than the premiums paid. The additional premium is usually limited so that the amount paid will not be greater than that which would have been required under the company's standard premium schedule.

Cost-Plus. Cost-plus funding offers the employer another funding alternative for group benefits. By assuming a portion of the risk normally assumed by an insurance company, the employer may achieve certain economies with the insurance company remaining the guarantor of benefits. Approximately two-thirds of the money normally held in reserves by the company can be held by the employer, increasing the options for use of money. Cash flow should be improved since the employer has use of the insurance company's money expended in claims until approximately 45 days following the end of the month in which claims are actually paid. Money, which in a conventionally insured plan would have been returned as a dividend, is never paid out by the employer.

Through a cost-plus plan the employer assumes the cost of the benefit payments and administrative expenses of the plan on a month-to-month basis up to specified annual deferred and stop-loss limits. In using this funding method, certain values of a conventionally insured plan are lost. Monthly budgeting is more difficult with the loss of a fixed, level premium, and cash flow will be less predictable in the short run. Upward claim fluctuations may mean a greater plan cost in some years that would have been true on an insured, guaranteed plan. Also, financial responsibility for terminal (runoff) claim liability beyond a minimum reserve established is assumed by the employer.

Extended Grace Period. Another way of increasing the cash flow for the policyowner is to extend the usual 31-day grace period for the payment of premiums by an additional 30 or 60 days. This permits the policyholder to retain the use of two or three months' premium, thus permitting the employer, effectively, to retain a substantial portion of the reserves normally held by the insurer.

Release of Reserves. An insurer, on request, may agree to release to the policyowner the reserves it is holding on the employer's contracts. Since liability for benefits due after termination of the contract remains with the insurer, the insurer will usually require a letter of credit from the policyholder in the amount of the reserves released.

Flexible Funding Life Insurance. Flexible funding is a cost-plus approach to funding life insurance. Under such an arrangement, the policyholder's monthly premium is equal to the claims paid in the previous month plus reserve adjustments, premium taxes, and the insurer's expense charges. Although the policyholder may accept liability for all claims, most plans are designed to limit the policyholder's liability to what the premium would have been under a conventional fully insured arrangement.

Alternatives to Fully Insured Plans

The concept of an employer self-funding a medical care benefit plan as an alternative to an insured plan really is not a new one. Initially, health benefit programs were self-funded, and self-funding also has been a common vehicle used by employers for workers' compensation benefits. Many employers perceive that self-funding will save premium taxes, improve cash flow through the use of money otherwise held by the insurer as reserves, and will permit them to avoid providing certain state-mandated benefits. Other employers see self-funding as a way to take advantage of their own good claims experience rather than participating in an averaging process.

In evaluating whether to adopt self-funding, the *size of the group* is of primary importance. In considering the cost of self-funding versus insurance, the financial manager weighs the advantages above against the cost of additional management and administrative resources required and loss of insurance company expertise in such areas as claims payment and cost containment. Also, the importance of current cash flow to the company, the additional risk under some cash flow arrangements, and employee reaction to self-funding must all be factored into the analysis.

Minimum Premium Plans. Minimum premium plans (MPPs) create a partially self-funded arrangement that has premium tax savings for the employer as its primary objective. Under an MPP the policyholder assumes liability for claims up to a specified amount, such as 90 percent, of estimated monthly claims.

An **individual stop-loss** arrangement, which is part of such plans, limits the policyholder's liability for any insured individual's claims within a specific period to a predetermined dollar maximum. Amounts over this maximum

(the individual stop-loss limit) do not count toward the 90 percent. Premiums to cover losses over the 90 percent level, to maintain reserves, and to cover operating costs are paid to the insurance company.

Under an MPP, the employer/policyholder, as needed, deposits funds to a special bank account to cover claims up to the 90 percent estimated amount. The insurer, acting as agent of the policyholder, pays claims out of the special account first. When claim payments exceed the 90 percent amount (on either a monthly or annual basis), the insurer makes payments from its own funds. The insurance company continues to provide the same services, assumes the same risks, and unless some special arrangement is made, holds essentially the same claim reserves as those under a conventional fully insured plan. The reserves must be maintained since, on termination of the group plan, the insurer is still responsible, as under a fully insured plan, to pay all covered outstanding claims. In some minimum premium plans, however, the policyholder agrees to assume responsibility for all outstanding claims upon discontinuance of the plan. In such cases, the need for the insurer to maintain reserves is eliminated.

Most states assess premium taxes only on premiums received by the insurance company for payment of claims under an insurance contract. Thus, by channeling 90 percent of the claim funds directly from the policyholder to the covered individuals, premium taxes are avoided on that portion of the medical care costs.

Administrative Services Only. Under an Administrative Services Only (ASO) arrangement, the insurer reviews claims and makes payment from the employer's funds, providing claim administration services. In the usual case, full administrative, underwriting, and actuarial services are provided as well. There is, however, no insurance and, therefore, no insurance contract is involved. The ASO agreement is a service contract between the insurer as administrator and the employer as buyer. It specifies the services to be provided by the insurer, the rights and obligations of both parties, and the administrative fees involved.

As protection against the risk of catastrophic

losses, the employer who chooses ASO frequently purchases stop-loss insurance on medical care expenses from an insurance company. **Aggregate stop-loss** indemnifies the employer for the accumulation of claims that exceeds a predetermined limit within a specified period of time.

In lieu of protection against an accumulation of losses under the overall plan, a maximum can be set on claims per individual (individual stop-loss), above which the insurance company is responsible. Both the aggregate and individual forms of stop-loss insurance may be written on the same account.

Letters of Credit. Although a letter of credit is not itself a cash flow option, it is sometimes required as a security measure to protect the insurance company because of the risk inherent in several alternate funding arrangements. It is a document issued by a bank to the insurance company to guarantee the policyholder's promise to pay monies due under such funding arrangements. The bank receives a fee for this credit guarantee service.

Table 27-1 shows various funding methods available and summarizes the handling of the key cost components under each.

TABLE 27-1. Group benefit funding methods

	Premium Rates	Reserves	Risk	Retention
Insured conventional	Established and guaranteed for a stated period	Established and held until plan ceases	Assumed by insurer above premium income	Commissions, administrative expense, risk charge, and taxes
Insured retrospective premium rating	Established at a level lower than conventional, with provision for lump-sum additional payment	Established and held until plan ceases	Assumed by insurer above premium income, including retrospective limit	Commissions, administrative expense, risk charge, interest loss, and taxes
Insured cost-plus	None or only for first year; premium is equal to paid claims plus insurer charges	Established, perhaps in the form of a deposit, and held until plan ceases	Assumed by insurer in excess of a generally conservative stop-loss point	Commissions, administrative expense, lower risk charge, interest loss, and taxes
Partially self-funded minimum premium plan	Covers all charges by the insurer; includes amounts needed to fund the insured part of the risk, reserve charges, insurer administrative expense and taxes on premium received by the insurer	Established on both the insured and self-funded portions of the plan; these reserves are held by either the insurer or the policyholder until the plan ceases	Assumed by insurer for amounts in excess of pre-determined premium and plan contributions; in event of termination of the plan, the run out claims are insured by the insurer or self-funded by the policyholder	Commissions, administrative expense, risk charge, and taxes on only the premium received by the insurer where permitted by state law
Self-funded with administrative services only	None or used only for cost analysis	None or used entirely by employer for cost accounting and tax purposes	Assumed by employer	Administrative expense; consultant fees may be borne separately by employer

Chapter 28

Retirement Plans

Each individual has the primary responsibility for his or her own welfare—or so our society decrees. Personal thrift has played and probably always will play a major role in providing for old-age security. Government efforts for the most part have been directed toward providing a basic minimum benefit, as a matter of right, through various forms of social insurance. With assurance of a minimum benefit, the employee, through his or her own individual effort and supplemented by any benefits his or her employer may provide, can seek to raise his or her old-age income to an "adequate" level. This has been augmented in recent years, through federal income tax legislation that permits individuals to accumulate tax-favored savings for retirement purposes.

INTRODUCTION

One of private industry's most significant contributions toward old-age security lies in the development of private pension plans. Every established firm must eventually face the problem of superannuated workers and at that point must choose among three alternatives: (1) discharge them without a retirement income, (2) leave them on the payroll, or (3) grant them a retirement in-come. For business and ethical reasons, the first choice is deemed impracticable; and the second procedure obscures retirement costs in the payroll. Because its flexibility permits the private pension system to meet the particular needs of various industries, a well-planned program of an employer for a company's employees is the most efficient way to take care of superannuated workers.

In making the decision to install a pension plan, an employer naturally considers the value of the increased efficiency and production arising from its installation against the cost of such a program. Because of favorable tax treatment for "qualified" plans, the cost of a pension program to employers has been relatively low. This has been a significant factor in the rapid development of private pension plans.

The rapid growth of private pension plans serves as evidence not only of the employee's interest in, but also of industry's acceptance of, the desirability of a planned pension program. As of December 31, 1985, it was estimated that 40.0 million individuals were participants in private pension plans with life insurance companies.[1]

[1] *1986 Life Insurance Fact Book* (Washington, D.C.: American Council of Life Insurance), p. 55.

CONCEPTS OF PENSION PLAN DESIGN AND OPERATION

Impact of Federal Legislation

Income Tax Law. The federal income tax law relating to *qualified* pension plans is extremely favorable to the establishment of a pension program. This is because (1) employer contributions are considered an ordinary and necessary business expense, which are currently deductible from corporate income in determining the income tax; (2) the earnings of a qualified pension plan are exempt from income taxation; (3) employer contributions are not taxable to the employees as income in the years in which contributed, but rather at such time as they are received in the form of benefits (usually after retirement, at what would normally be a lower tax rate, usually with double exemptions). If the full benefit is received in a single year, it may be eligible for special favorable "lump-sum" income taxation. As a practical matter, very few funded plans that have been installed have not been qualified within the meaning of the tax law.

The general requirements of a qualified plan may be summarized as follows: (1) a *written, legally binding arrangement* must exist and must be *communicated* to the employees; (2) the plan must be for the *exclusive benefit* of the employees or their beneficiaries; (3) it must be impossible for the principal or income of the trust to be diverted from these benefits to any other purpose until all liabilities have been satisfied; (4) the plan must benefit a broad class of employees, and not discriminate in favor of officers, stockholders, or highly paid employees; (5) the plan must meet certain *minimum requirements on participation and vesting* (nonforfeitability), as discussed below; (6) the plan must provide that in the event of a plan merger, a participant's benefit under the resulting plan will be at least equal to that benefit to which he or she would have been entitled prior to the merger, determined as if both plans had terminated at the time of the merger; (7) the plan must provide that a participant's benefits under the plan may not be assigned or alienated; (8) the plan must stipulate when benefit payments will commence (and this time is subject to certain

stipulated maximums); (9) if the participant is married, the plan must, under certain circumstances, provide for a joint and survivor or survivor annuity, as discussed below; (10) the plan must provide for limitations in maximum benefits, as discussed below; (11) the plan must provide that benefits to a participant or beneficiary who is already receiving benefits, or who has terminated service, may not be decreased by reason of later increases in Social Security benefits; and (12) the plan must provide for a claims review procedure if the claim of a participant or beneficiary is disallowed.

Employee Retirement Income Security Act of 1974. In addition to the federal income tax law, the Employee Retirement Income Security Act of 1974 (ERISA) is an exceedingly important piece of legislation. The provisions of ERISA pertaining to participation, vesting, and funding influence virtually every aspect of retirement plan design.

1. *Limitations on contributions and benefits.* Contributions to and benefits received under qualified plans are limited by ERISA. With respect to **defined-benefit plans** (see below), the plan must provide that the annual benefit may not exceed the lesser of (1) $90,000[2] or (2) 100 percent of the participant's highest average compensation for three consecutive years. Notwithstanding this limitation, however, ERISA permits an annual benefit of at least $10,000 for an employee if he or she has not participated in a defined-contribution plan (see below). Under the Tax Reform Act of 1986 (TRA '86), the defined benefit maximums remain the same except that the full $90,000 benefit will be permitted only at *Social Security Retirement Age* rather than at age 62.

With respect to **defined-contribution plans,** the annual addition to a participant's account may not exceed the lesser of (1) $30,000[3] of (2) 25 percent of the participant's compensation for the year. For purposes of the limitation,

---

[2]For plans years after 1987, this amount will be adjusted for increases in the cost of living (and at ages below 65).

[3]For plans years after 1987, this amount will be adjusted for increases in the cost of living.

annual additions to an employee's account include employer contributions, forfeitures, and for years beginning after December 31, 1986, 100 percent of after-tax employee contributions. If an employee participates in both a defined-benefit and a defined-contribution plan, special rules apply. The 1986 Tax Reform Act froze the defined contribution limit (25% or $30,000) until the indexed dollar limit for defined benefit plans reaches $120,000. After this, the defined contribution dollar limit will remain ¼ of the defined benefit dollar limit.

2. *Prohibited transactions and fiduciary responsibility.* ERISA imposes certain excise taxes on **prohibited transactions** between the trust and disqualified persons. Prohibited transactions include the sale, exchange, leasing, loaning (except for certain loans to the participant), furnishing of goods or services, and so on, between the plan and a related party. A **related party** includes the employer, participant, trustee, and substantial owners of the organization. The tax is initially 5 percent of the amount involved in the transaction and is imposed on the disqualified person. The failure of the disqualified person to correct the transaction within the prescribed time will result in an additional tax of 100 percent of the amount involved in the prohibited transaction. However, the Department of Labor is authorized to provide exemptions from the prohibited transaction restrictions and has done so in many cases.

ERISA also requires that a plan fiduciary discharge its duties solely in the interest of the plan participants and their beneficiaries. In regard to its conduct, the fiduciary is held to a strict, prudent-person standard. In addition, a fiduciary is personally liable for breaches by a cofiduciary that it (1) knowingly participates in or conceals, (2) enables to occur by failure to comply with its own duties, and/or (3) fails to make reasonable effort to rectify. ERISA also provides limitations with respect to (1) the investment of fund assets in employer securities or employer real property, (2) plan termination insurance, and (3) reporting and disclosure requirements. Provision also is made for judicial review of an adverse decision by the Internal Revenue Service (IRS) with respect to a plan qualification.

The legal and tax details of pension plans are highly complex, and a complete discussion is beyond the scope of this text.[4] Because these laws and regulations play such a major role in every aspect of the creation, design, and operation of a pension plan, several general aspects are nonetheless covered below.

Pension-Plan Design

Eligibility. A qualified pension plan must set forth rules to determine who will be covered by the plan. Relatively few plans cover all employees. For example, employees who always work fewer than 1,000 hours per year are almost always excluded from coverage. Coverage may also be restricted to employees of a given plant or division or to unionized or nonunion employees. In addition to determining the class or classes of employees to be covered, pension plans may make coverage for the individual employee contingent upon a minimum length of service (waiting period) and/or attainment of a certain minimum or maximum age. Numerous variations of service and age requirements for coverage may be designed, but one way or another, all are intended to reduce cost by eliminating certain groups of employees that show a record of high turnover and those hired close to retirement and by simplifying administration of the plan.[5] In any case, the eligibility provisions must be drawn carefully to meet the objectives intended, taking into account the nondiscrimination requirements of the Internal Revenue Code; the Civil Rights Act of 1964, which has been interpreted to require nondiscrim-

---

[4]See Dan M. McGill, *Fundamentals of Private Pensions,* 5th ed. (Homewood, Ill.: Richard D. Irwin, Inc., 1984); Everett T. Allen, Jr., Joseph J. Melone, and Jerry S. Rosenbloom, *Pension Planning* (Homewood, Ill.: Richard D. Irwin, Inc., 1984); and Burton T. Beam, Jr., and John J. McFadden, *Employee Benefits* (Homewood, Ill.: Richard D. Irwin, Inc., 1985).

[5]The purpose of eliminating employees who are hired close to retirement is to hold down the cost of a defined benefit pension program. The cost of providing a defined benefit pension increases with the age of the employee. In addition, an employer normally feels less responsibility for the retirement needs of a person who was in his or her service for only a few years before retirement.

inatory provisions for male and female employees; and the Age Discrimination in Employment Act.[6]

A plan may not require as a condition of participation a period of service longer than one year or a minimum age of more than 21 years. However, a plan may require two years of service if it provides for a full and immediate vesting of all participants upon entry into the plan. No maximum age for participation is permitted, except in the case of target benefit or defined benefit plans, which may exclude those who commence employment within five years of normal retirement age. Employees of all corporations, partnerships, and other businesses that are members of a controlled group are treated as if they were employees of a single employer.

Normal Retirement Age. Every pension plan has a normal retirement age. This is necessary because a fixed age or schedule of ages for retirement is fundamental in estimating costs, determining the appropriate rate of accumulating funds for retirement benefits, and as important, to permit organization and planning for the retirement of employees.[7] Virtually all pension plans make provision for "early" or "deferred" retirement, subject to certain conditions.

Benefit Formula. Since an employee's standard of living normally is related to his or her earnings, it is important that retirement benefits bear a reasonable relationship to those earnings.[8] For an employee to have an adequate income at

the time he or she retires, it generally has been considered necessary to have, including Social Security, an income that is approximately 50 to 70 percent of his or her average compensation in the five to 10 years immediately preceding retirement. Because of inflation and the fixed nature of most pension arrangements, a problem that also receives attention is maintaining the adequacy of income after retirement. Some possible approaches to this problem are (1) "cost-of-living" or "wage'indexed" benefits, and (2) periodic increases in benefits for retired employees on an ad hoc basis.[9]

Traditionally, benefit formulas have been classified into two broad categories: (1) defined benefit and (2) defined contribution. Under a **defined benefit** type of formula, the benefit developed by the formula is fixed, and the cost will depend on the age and sex distribution of eligible employees and the operating experience (i.e., mortality, turnover, investment return, expenses, etc.) of the plan. A **defined contribution plan** establishes a rate or method of contribution by the employer only (noncontributory) or employee and employer jointly (contributory), and the amount of benefit provided for each employee will vary depending on the age, sex, and length of covered service prior to actual retirement age and the operating experience of the plan.

The main differentiating characteristic between the defined benefit and the defined contribution types of plans is the fact that in the defined benefit formula, the benefit is fixed and the contribution varies, while in the defined contribution approach, the employer's contribution is fixed by formula (or may be determined annually in the case of a profit-sharing or stock bonus plan) and the benefit varies.

A plan using a defined contribution formula provides an individual account for each participant and bases the employee's benefits solely on the amount contributed to the participant's account and any expense, investment return, and forfeitures allocated to such participant's account. Since the definition of the basis for contribution(s) is completely flexible, a number of qualified plans has evolved with the dual objectives of provision

---

[6]Generally, the Age Discrimination in Employment Act will not prohibit age provisions normally included in a qualified retirement plan, although there are some exceptions.

[7]It is possible, of course, to establish a range of ages at which employees may retire, such as 62 or 65. In such cases, an assumption is made, in estimating costs, as to the distribution of employees retiring at each age. Many negotiated pension plans do not explicitly state one specific "normal" retirement age. This, of course, is applicable only to defined-benefit plans. Defined contribution plans by their nature do not face such problems.

[8]It is important to note that while the great majority of union-negotiated plans provide benefits that are tied to length of service rather than earnings, it is assumed that the duration of employment within the collective-bargaining unit is such that the average employee will have a retirement benefit that is comparable, as a percentage of earnings, to that of salaried employees.

[9]See McGill, *Fundamentals of Private Pensions,* Chap. 11.

of retirement income and deferral of current taxable income. These include money purchase pension plans, profit-sharing plans, stock bonus plans, and also voluntary employee contributions. When a participant becomes eligible to receive a benefit, his or her benefit equals the amount that can be provided by the fund balance.

In addition to the defined benefit and defined contribution formulas, there is also a hybrid plan, often referred to as a **target-benefit plan.** Under a target-benefit plan, the projected benefit to be provided the participant is determined as if the plan were a defined benefit plan. The contributions necessary to fund this plan are then determined, based on assumed interest and mortality factors. Once the amount of the contribution, stated as a percentage of the participant's compensation, is determined, the plan then operates as a defined contribution plan, in that the participant is entitled upon his or her retirement to the benefits that can be purchased by the amount in his or her account, rather than the "target benefit" used to establish the amount of the employer's contribution to be made on his or her behalf.

Because of the increasing popularity of benefit formulas based on "final pay," the "fixed benefit" nature of a defined benefit plan has lost some of its significance. Although the so-called defined benefit formula may produce a fixed amount of benefit for a given year of service, the final retirement benefit is a function of the employee's compensation in his or her final years of service prior to retirement. Thus, the "defined" benefit is not really definite as to dollar amount until it has been recomputed based on the employee's "final pay," which frequently is based on the average of his or her last five years of credited service prior to retirement. It is true, of course, that the employer must increase his or her contributions on behalf of the employees as the salary increases.

Many collective-bargaining agreements involved defined contributions but with distinct characteristics. These so-called **Taft-Hartley plans** really are not defined contribution plans; the benefit is defined as well as the contribution. This is an actuarial anomaly, since only by sheer coincidence could these two fixed functions re-

main in balance over any time period. Practically, the anomaly is resolved through periodic adjustments of either the benefit scale, the contribution rate, or both. Such plans are considered defined benefit plans for purposes of ERISA.[10]

Defined benefit formulas may be a flat dollar amount or may be related to earnings, to service, or to a combination of earnings and service. Thus, a given formula may provide a retirement benefit of $300 a month regardless of earnings or service, 30 percent of "final average pay," 1½ percent of annual pay for each year of credited service, or others. In any case, where appropriate, earnings and service are carefully defined. Defined benefit formulas based on earnings frequently are integrated with Social Security benefits. An integrated benefit may provide a larger benefit on earnings in excess of the Social Security wage base per annum,[11] to offset the fact that Social Security benefits are weighted in favor of the lower-income groups. Instead, it may reduce plan benefits by taking into consideration Social Security received by a participant. The extent of the differential in benefits permitted in excess of the Social Security wage base is prescribed by the IRS.

Benefit formulas based on service normally give credit for both *past service*—that is, service prior to the installation of the plan—and *future service*. Generally, the sum-total cost of the credits granted for past service represents the *initial past-service liability* at the date of the installation of the plan. Credit for past service is sometimes limited, by counting service after a given age only, such as 35 or 40, or by limiting the number of years' credit for past service to, say, 15 or 20. In any case, an employee's retirement benefit is the total of past- and future-service credits under the pension plan at retirement.

Maximum Benefits. Before ERISA, it was not customary for plans to impose an upper limit

---

[10]*Ibid.,* pp. 103–104.

[11]A larger benefit can be provided on benefits below the Social Security wage base as well. For example, a money purchase plan (type of defined contribution plan) could provide that all participants will receive an employer contribution of 3 percent of compensation, plus an amount equal to 6 percent of compensation for all amounts in excess of $10,000 per annum.

on the benefits that would be payable (other than that implicit in a flat benefit formula). As mentioned earlier, ERISA and later amendments imposed a limit on the benefits that can be provided under a defined benefit plan and a limit on the contributions that can be made under a defined contribution plan.

Additional requirements apply to contributions and benefits under a top-heavy plan.[12] A **top-heavy plan** is a plan under which the value of accrued benefits for **key employees** (certain officers and owners) and their beneficiaries exceeds 60 percent of the value of accrued benefits for all employees and their beneficiaries. Most small plans are top-heavy. Whether a plan is top-heavy is determined each plan year.

If a plan is top-heavy, it is subject to adjustments in the maximum limits on contributions and benefits, a maximum limit on recognizable compensation, more rapid vesting, and for nonkey employees, minimum benefits or contributions. A top-heavy plan must provide at least minimum benefits or contributions for all participants who are not key employees. As a practical matter, when the requirement applies, most plans usually apply it to all employees.

A top-heavy plan (applies to all plans starting in 1989) may not take account of compensation in excess of $200,000 in determining benefits or contributions. This $200,000 will be subject to cost-of-living adjustments after 1985 in the same manner as the dollar limits under Section 415.

Supplemental Benefits. In addition to a retirement income, many pension programs include death, withdrawal, disability, or other supplemental benefits during the preretirement period. Although it is important that such supplemental benefits not be included at the expense of an adequate retirement income, they can form an important part of a well-designed employee benefit program. Naturally, what supplemental benefits are provided will depend on the personnel policy, finances, and other individual circumstances of the employer. Supplemental death benefits will be subject to limitations imposed by

IRS regulations on both death and disability benefits. The most commonly provide supplemental benefits are based on death or disability.

The portion of the supplemental benefits to be provided under the retirement plan and the portion to be provided under a separate group insurance program are other decisions for the individual employer, with the help or guidance from an independent consultant, the insurance company, or both. Management has come to recognize that to the maximum extent possible, there must be a coordination of all sources of income available to the employee from both employer and government plans. Such coordination is challenging because supplemental benefits may be provided in a number of ways. It should be noted, however, that historically, coordination of all forms of employee benefits with government programs has been rather poor.

The Retirement Equity Act of 1984 provides for automatic death benefits for all vested participants, whether they be active or terminated or retired, under any pension plan. A death benefit in the form of a joint and survivor annuity may be waived in writing by both the participant and the spouse.

The survivor benefit can be provided by the purchase of an annuity from the funds that are held under a deposit administration contract.[13] Substantial supplemental death benefits can be subject to wide cost variations unless a special insurance arrangement is used. Normally, the plan provides these benefits directly out of an unallocated fund. Regardless of the funding used, how large a pension the surviving spouse should receive is a matter calling for serious consideration on the part of the employer. As in any employee benefit plan, it should be simple and easy for the employee to understand.

Employee Contributions. Pension plans may be contributory or noncontributory. Under a contributory plan, the employee provides part of the funds necessary to purchase his or her benefits, with the employer assuming the remain-

---

[12]This discussion draws on McGill, *Fundamentals of Private Pensions,* pp. 107–108.

[13]See "Deposit Administration Contracts" later in this chapter.

ing cost.[14] Under a noncontributory plan, the employer bears the total cost of the program. Today about 80 percent of all defined benefit plans are noncontributory. For many years, the majority of plans that were not the result of collective bargaining were written on a contributory basis. In many cases, such contributions permit the installation of a plan where the employer's financial position is such that unless they are utilized, no plan would be installed at all. In other cases, employee contributions are used to enlarge the benefits provided, or are used on the theory that employees' appreciation will be greater if they bear part of the cost of their benefits.

Although most employees are covered under noncontributory plans, the current trend in pension plans appears to be toward contributory plans. The theoretical case for noncontributory plans rests largely on the deferred-wage concept.[15] If retirement benefits can be regarded as deferred wages, the argument that the employer should assume the total cost of such benefits is logical. On the other hand, if they are not considered deferred wages, the rationale for unilateral financing tends to fail. But apart from the philosophical aspects of the question, there are strong practical arguments in favor of a noncontributory approach to financing. For example, a significant reason lies in the fact that employer contributions to a qualified pension plan are deductible for income tax purposes. Employees' contributions (except to the extent that such contributions qualify for the limited retirement-savings deduction provided by IRC Sections 219 or 220) must be made from after-tax income. A special plan, referred to as a Section 401(k) plan, provides that employees may make limited pretax contributions to a defined contribution plan (see below). This privilege does not apply to employee contributions to defined benefit pension plans.

Vesting. It is a well-established principle of pension planning that an employee must be permitted to recover his or her contributions, with

interest (or adjusted for earning experience) if he or she withdraws from employment. An employee's rights in that portion of accrued benefits derived from his or her own contributions are nonforfeitable. The employee's vested or nonforfeitable percentage of the employer contributions may vary from 0 to 100 percent, depending on the vesting schedule in the plan and the length of service, and in some cases, age of the participant.

The vesting provisions of pension plans can be classified on at least four different bases: the *kinds* of benefits vested, the point in *time* when the eligible benefits vest, the *rate* at which the accrued benefits vest, and the *form* in which the benefits may be taken.[16] As to the *kinds* of benefits vested, retirement, death, and total disability are all vested when they enter a payment status. Except for this status, however, the traditional approach has been to vest the basic retirement benefit only. As to *time*, employer contributions may become vested in the employee immediately, or as usually is the case, the vesting may be deferred until certain age and/or service requirements have been met.

As to the *rate* at which benefits vest, the employer's contribution may vest in full or only in part, although eventually it will have to be 100 percent vested. A graded vesting provision, which provides an increasing percentage of vesting based on service up to 100 percent, is in reality partly a time and partly an amount classification. Complete vesting is required upon a participant's attaining normal retirement age.

A qualified plan must provide vesting of accrued benefits in accordance with one of the following alternatives: (1) full vesting after 10 years of service, with no graded vesting during the 10-year period; (2) full vesting on a ratable basis after 15 years of service (at least 25 percent at five years, increasing 5 percent per year for the next five years, and 10 percent per year for the remaining years); or (3) full vesting under the Rule of 45. Under this rule, an employee who has completed five full years of service must have a vested and nonforfeitable right to at least 50 percent of his or her accrued benefits under the plan when the sum of his or her age and the number of years of service totals 45. For each following

---

[14]Sometimes a plan is referred to as contributory only if the participant is required to make contributions; not if the contributions are voluntary.

[15]McGill, *Fundamentals of Private Pensions*, pp. 15–20.

[16]*Ibid.*, pp. 135–140.

year, an additional 10 percent of accrued benefit must be vested. Under the Rule of 45, an alternative vesting of 50 percent after 10 years of service, with an additional 10 percent for each further year of service, is required. (This rule repealed in 1989 by 1986 Tax Reform Act.)

The *form* of the vested benefits depends to some extent on the contractual instrument used to fund the benefits. If the plan is funded through a trust, the vested terminated employee generally retains a deferred claim against the trust fund in the amount of his or her vested benefits. If the plan is funded through a contract with a life insurance company, the vested benefits may take the form of a paid-up insurance or annuity contract or a deferred claim against the plan.

The term **portable pensions** has found some acceptance in pension literature to describe vested pension benefits that would follow the employee and be put into any new plan under which he or she is covered, or vested benefits that would be transferred to some central pension clearinghouse. Portability of pensions has, at least to a limited extent, become a reality with the enactment of ERISA, which provides for rollover contributions to an individual retirement account and to other qualified retirement plans.

Under ERISA, an individual may avoid taxation on a distribution of money or property from an individual retirement account (IRA) or qualified plan by reinvesting the money or property received, within 60 days, in another qualified IRA or plan for his or her benefit.[17] To qualify for this reinvestment, a **rollover contribution** from a qualified-plan distribution must be reduced by that portion of the distribution attributable to the employee's after-tax contributions, as all amounts in an IRA are to have a zero tax basis. Amounts from a disqualified retirement annuity and excess contributions to an IRA may not be rolled over into an IRA. Furthermore, an individual may roll over amounts between IRAs only once each year, even though he or she may roll over amounts from a qualified plan into an IRA more than once within a one-year period.

Methods of Distribution. As pointed out above, a plan may be required to distribute bene-

fits in the form of a joint and survivor annuity or a survivor annuity. Other common methods of distribution are payments in equal periodic installments for a certain term (i.e., monthly for 10 years) or in a lump sum. Lump-sum distributions are usually eligible for favorable 10-year (5-years after 1986) income-averaging treatment, or they can be rolled over into an IRA or another qualified plan to defer income taxes.

METHODS OF FINANCING

Funding Procedure

Once the basic features of a pension plan have been determined, consideration must be given to the various techniques used to measure the accrual of costs and liabilities under a pension plan. These techniques are usually referred to as **actuarial cost methods.**

An actuarial cost method is a particular technique for establishing the amount and incidence of the annual actuarial cost accrued for pension plan benefits, or benefits and expenses, and the related actuarial liability. The legal instruments, such as pension contracts issued by insurance companies, under which the actuarial cost arrangements operate, are referred to as **funding media** or **funding vehicles.** Pension contracts issued by insurance companies may incorporate both the *actuarial cost method* and the pension *plan,* although there is a technical distinction. A given pension plan might have one document relating to the plan, and a separate legal instrument under which the funding method operates, the plan being incorporated only by reference. With separate documents, it is possible to amend the plan and not alter in any way the funding method or vehicle being employed. The essence of the funding process is the accumulation of assets to offset the liabilities arising under the pension plan as measured by the actuarial method utilized.

Prior to the enactment of ERISA, only a few plans operated on the pay-as-you-go basis.[18] Under this arrangement, retirement benefits

[17] IRC Sec. 408(d)(3).

[18] Under *Opinion 8,* issued in 1966 by the Accounting Principles Board of the American Institute of Certified Public

were paid as a "supplementary payroll." Payments were taken out of current operating revenue and were charged to operating costs.[19] No funds were set aside in advance for the payment of pension obligations even at retirement. This type of arrangement furnished the smallest degree of security to the employee, since neither the active nor the retired employees could look to a segregated fund or a third-party guarantee for satisfaction of the pension claims.[20] In contrast to pay-as-you-go, advance funding is the conventional financing technique used in pension plans today. The several patterns of advanced funding may be broadly classified as (1) benefit-allocation and (2) cost-allocation methods.[21] Although given pension benefits can be funded by several methods, usually one or the other will be more appropriate, depending on the benefit formula and other characteristics of the plan.

Benefit Allocation. This method of funding, also known as the "accrued benefit" or "single-premium" method, involves the setting aside, in one sum, of the amount of money needed to fund in full one unit of benefit. In practice, this unit of benefit is almost always related to a year of service—that is, it is the benefit earned during one year of service. Thus, if an employee earns currently an annual benefit at age 65 of $35, a paid-up annuity in that amount would be funded for that employee. Thereafter, this particular employee would have a paid-up annuity in the appropriate amount funded each year at an increasing cost per dollar of benefit based on his or her attained age at the time of each purchase. At retirement, this employee's income would be the total

of each of these annual increments of benefits.

The benefit-allocation method assumes that the normal cost[22] of a pension plan for any particular year is precisely equal to the present value of the benefits credited to the employee participants for service during that year. Thus, a funding policy geared to this cost method funds future-service benefits fully as they accrue. Past-service benefits are funded according to a schedule adopted by the employer, usually over a period of years.[23] The benefit-allocation method of funding is virtually always used in connection with group deferred-annuity contracts[24] and may be used with other types of plans.

Cost Allocation. The other category of funding patterns, known as cost allocation methods, can be used with any type of benefit formula but are especially adaptable to the type of formula that provides a composite benefit as opposed to a series of unit benefits.

1. Individual level-cost methods. The individual level-cost method, *without supplemental liability* (see below), is one under which the total benefits to be paid to an employee are estimated and the sum required to provide the benefits is accumulated through level amounts contributed over the remaining years of service. The most familiar form of the individual level-cost method is the individual level-premium method, which is employed in connection with individual and group cash value insurance contracts.[25] This funding method provides the benefits that would be payable to the employee if his or her rate of compensation remained unchanged to normal retirement age. The premium is a function of the entering age of the employee. In the event that the rate of compensation and benefits increases, an adjustment in the amount of insurance is made, and the funding of the increase in benefits is accomplished by a separate and additional level premium, payable from the date of increase and based on the age at that time. Contracts funded by this method are written in amounts designed

Accountants, neither pay-as-you-go nor terminal funding is an accepted principle of accounting for the cost of pension plans in financial statements.

[19]This is the way that Social Security benefits are funded.
[20]Dan M. McGill, "Public and Private Pension Plans," in *Pensions: Problems and Trends* (Homewood, Ill.: Richard D. Irwin, Inc., 1955), p. 39.
[21]McGill, *Fundamentals of Private Pensions,* pp. 262–271.
[22]The normal cost under any actuarial cost method is the cost that would be attributable to the current year of a plan's operations if, from the earliest date of credited service, the plan had been in effect and costs had been accrued in accordance with the particular actuarial cost method. See *ibid.,* p. 354.

[23]See *ibid.,* pp. 382–383.
[24]See *ibid.,* p. 518.
[25]*Ibid.,* p. 518.

to provide benefits for the entire period of credited service, and consequently, no distinction is made between past- and current-service costs; that is, the supplemental liability for past service is not determined and handled separately.

The individual level-cost method *with supplemental liability* (past-service liability determined separately) serves as the funding guide for many trust fund plans and deposit administration contracts.[26] The rationale here is that benefits are funded at a level-amount basis over the employee participant's *entire* working lifetime. The supplemental liability for past-service benefits is separately ascertained. It may be viewed as the accumulated value, with the benefit of both interest and survivorship in service, of the normal cost contributions assumed to have been made in respect of all participants with credited past service at the time the plan is installed. Widely known as the **entry-age normal method,** this funding method permits a flexible policy with regard to funding the past-service or so-called supplemental liability.

2. *Aggregate level-cost methods.* The aggregate-cost methods are analogous to the individual level-cost methods, except for the calculation of costs and contributions on a collective rather than individual basis. As in the case of the individual level-cost methods, the annual cost accruals may be determined with or without the past service supplemental liability determined separately.

Under this method, without supplemental liability, the total employer cost of all future benefits for present employees, less employer funds on hand, is expressed as a level percentage of future payroll of present employees. Each year, as new employees enter, the "level" percentage must be recalculated. The actual calculation is made by dividing the present value of the future compensation of the employees entering into the funding calculations, or the present value of the appropriate portion thereof, into the present value of the estimated amount of benefits, less any employer funds on hand. This determines what is generally called the accrual rate, or aggregate-cost ratio. The cost is determined by multiplying the compensation, or appropriate portion thereof, paid during the year to employees entering into the funding calculations, by the accrual rate. In contrast to this, the actuary can create a supplemental liability (determine the past service liability separately) to provide greater funding flexibility.

Aggregate-cost methods are most widely used in trusteed (noninsured) plans, although they are equally adaptable to group deposit administration and immediate participation guarantee contracts.[27]

Funding Requirements. ERISA imposed certain funding requirements that are generally limited to pension plans. Profit-sharing and stock-bonus plans are excluded from the funding requirements, as are certain defined-benefit pension plans funded on a current basis solely with individual or allocated group insurance contracts. With respect to money purchase plans, which are defined contribution plans, an employer is required to make contributions in accordance with the plan's contribution formula. Required contributions under defined-benefit plans are more complex and basically require funding sufficient to meet normal service costs and to amortize past-service costs and experience losses. Unless eligible to elect the alternative minimum funding account, plans must meet the requirements of the minimum funding standard account, which requires that unfunded past-service liability on the effective date of the plan be amortized over a 40-year period with respect to plans in existence on January 1, 1974, and over a 30-year period for plans not in existence on that date. Furthermore, increases in unfunded past-service liability arising from plan amendments and changes in liabilities resulting from a change in actuarial assumptions are to be amortized over a period of 30 years, whereas experience gains and losses are to be amortized over a 15-year period. Notwithstanding the foregoing rules, the employer's required contribution is limited to the amount necessary to make the plan fully funded—that is, the contribution necessary to make the value of the plan assets equal to the accrued liabilities

[26]*Ibid.,* p. 519.

[27]*Ibid.,* pp. 519–520.

under the plan, computed on a going-concern basis.

An employer's failure to meet the minimum funding requirements will result in a nondeductible 5 percent excise tax. This tax is imposed on an annual basis on the accumulated funding deficiency. Furthermore, failure to fund the deficiency within 90 days, plus extensions, after the mailing of the deficiency notice with respect to the 5 percent tax will result in an additional tax equal to 100 percent of the funding deficiency. In hardship cases, the Secretary of the Treasury may waive the funding requirements, but the amounts so waived must be amortized over a period not to exceed 15 years.

Pension Costs

Advance funding involves the setting aside of funds for the payment of pension benefits in advance of their due date. In the case of defined benefit plans, the cost of providing the benefits must be estimated years in advance. In estimating pension costs, some of the factors that may be taken into account include (1) mortality, (2) interest, (3) expense of operations, (4) turnover, (5) age of retirement, and (6) changes in compensation. It should be clear that these factors will vary considerably over time and that the use of the word "estimating" is appropriate. The ultimate cost of a pension plan is equal to the benefits paid out, plus the cost of administration, less the earnings (including capital gains and losses) on any funds set aside for the payment of benefits.[28] This is not, however, the true cost to the employer. In order for the true cost of a plan to be obtained, this cost or net financial outlay must be adjusted for such factors as reduced labor turnover, retirement of inefficient employees, improved morale, and others. Because these factors are difficult to evaluate, the net financial outlay generally is assumed to represent the cost of the plan. It is important to remember that a pension plan is a long-range venture, and ultimate costs cannot be

determined accurately in advance. This is true even in an insured pension plan, since contracts are experience rated,[29] and the employer's own experience will have a marked effect on the level of dividends or experience-rate credits.

Financing Vehicles

Broadly speaking, there are three financing vehicles for funding pension plans: (1) the fully insured plan, (2) the noninsured plan, and (3) the split-funded plan. Noninsured plans are often referred to loosely as **self-administrered** or **trusteed.** A trust is virtually always used in noninsured plans, with a trustee or investment manager being responsible for the investment and management of the funds accumulated under the plan. On the other hand, where separate insurance policies on the lives of the covered individuals are used as a funding medium, the contracts are also often held in trusts. To avoid confusion in terminology, the original distinction of "insured" and "noninsured" is used in this discussion.

Noninsured Plan. The noninsured plan usually involves the establishment of a trust for the benefit of the employees. Under such defined benefit plans, an enrolled actuary is employed to make estimates of the sums that should be put into the trust. A bank or insurance company invests the funds so deposited, and when an employee retires, the bank or insurance company pays out a monthly check or a lump sum to the retired employee on the direction of the employer. The employer assumes all the risks—investment, mortality, and expense—under the trusteed defined benefit plan. The enrolled actuary takes no responsibility for investment and mortality results, but uses reasonable actuarial assumptions in estimating pension costs. Similarly, the trustee takes no responsibility except to invest the money in accordance with the law and its best judgment or at the direction of the employer (depending on the trust indenture).

The employer is in a sense a self-insurer. But

[28]Some authors would include an item for "pooling gains and losses," arising out of the fact that investment and mortality results under many insured plans and some noninsured plans involve some averaging of results.

[29]Plans employing individual life insurance contracts under a pension trust are not experience-rated, but are treated like other individual life insurance policies. See "Level-Premium Annuity Contracts" below.

it should be noted that under a noninsured plan, the employer or, in the event of insolvency of the employer, the employee assumes risks that may be assumed by the insurance company under an insured plan. The plan provisions usually limit the employer's liability to whatever monies are in the trust. The benefits promised by a defined benefit pension plan usually will be insured at least in part by the Pension Benefit Guaranty Corporation (PBGC). Since the noninsured plan is a self-insured plan, such an approach has the least risk for large companies (or groups of companies) with sufficient spread of risk to permit predictable results and to keep administrative costs reasonable. Further protection has been provided participants by the minimum-funding requirements under ERISA, discussed earlier.

The trusteed approach may have advantages for those corporations large enough to self-insure the pension risk. The advantages include (1) economy of operation, (2) greater flexibility in both funding and plan provisions, and (3) the possibility of better investment results because of greater investment freedom. Although trusteed plans are noninsured in the sense that no guarantees are provided to covered individuals, the use of insurance company services is not precluded. Several insurance companies have developed contracts that permit the use of the insurance company's investment services and, if desired, its administrative and actuarial services, but do not involve irrevocable guarantees to individuals. Investment of funds with insurance companies at a minimum guaranteed rate of return is also increasingly popular. Even though such contracts do not fall within the traditional definition of insured pension plans, these arrangements have proven to be an increasingly important source of business for insurance companies.

Combination Plan. There are pension programs in which two or more types of contracts are combined or an employer makes use of an insurance contract in conjunction with a noninsured trusteed arrangement. All such variations are called **split-funding contracts.** Frequently, a bank is used to hold and invest a part of the monies in the active life fund, and monies may be moved from the bank to the life insurance company to provide guaranteed annuities as employees retire. If the life insurance company does not hold any of the monies prior to retirement and receives money only as employees retire to purchase the guaranteed annuities, the arrangement is called a **maturity funding contract.** In another version, a portion of the contribution is invested in cash value life insurance policies, with the remainder of the fund held and invested by the trustee.

Noninsured pension arrangements are worthy of more comprehensive treatment, but in view of the nature of this text, the remaining discussion is concerned primarily with insured pension plans.

INSURED PENSION CONTRACTS

Life insurance companies offer considerable flexibility in tailoring a funding vehicle appropriate to meet individual employer needs. This flexibility makes it difficult to describe the available arrangements in simple terms. In this discussion, names are attached to various types of insured pension arrangements, but it should be understood that the contracts can be modified to fit particular requirements.

Life insurance companies are in the business of accepting risks, so they are willing to underwrite several different risks associated with pension plans and to underwrite them to varying degrees, depending on the employer's wishes. Some of these risks are as follows:

1. More individuals may live to retire than the mortality tables used anticipated.
2. Those who retire may live longer than the mortality tables used anticipated.
3. The rate of interest earned on investments may fall below the anticipated level.
4. There may be defaults in the investment portfolio, or it may be necessary to sell particular investments at a loss.
5. Expenses of handling the plan may be higher than anticipated.[30]

[30]It should be noted than in a well-designed employee benefit program, which provides death, disability, and retirement benefits with reasonably comparable values, the actuarial experience will not be significantly different whether more

Life insurance companies are also in the position of providing a variety of services, many of which may be varied to suit the employer's wishes. Except for certain benefit guarantees, the services provided by a life insurance company can be provided by consultants and other organizations specializing in providing services in the pension field.

Single-Premium Annuity Contract

Probably the insurance company rises to its maximum usefulness in the rather unusual situation where the employer determines the benefit that will ultimately be payable to each of its employees and makes a *single payment* to an insurance company to guarantee that all these benefits will be paid as they become due. Such an arrangement is used frequently for a body of employees who have already retired. It is unusual with respect to employees who are still working, except in the situation where an uninsured trusteed arrangement is terminated for one reason or another, or there is a recovery of plan surplus, and the monies in the trust are used to purchase deferred annuities for the employees covered by the trust. The insurance contracts written under these circumstances are commonly referred to as **single-premium group annuity contracts.**

Level-Premium Annuity Contracts

Sometimes an employer makes an estimate of the amount of pension that will be payable when the employee reaches his or her normal retirement age, and the insurance company is asked to quote a *level-amount payment* for each employee that can be guaranteed to provide the estimated amount of pension. The insurance company guarantees that if the indicated premium is paid each year until the employee retires, the insurance company will pay the indicated amount of benefit.

---

employees become disabled, more die, or more live and retire. However, if just one function, such as death, is isolated, obviously a higher or lower rate than expected can significantly change the experience with respect to that one plan. As companies develop more sophisticated benefit programs, the effect of risk becomes less significant.

An arrangement of this type can be provided either through separate policies issued on the lives of the individual employees or through a master group annuity contract issued to the employer with certificates of coverage given to the employees. In either event, it is quite common to provide a life insurance feature during the period prior to retirement. Where separate policies are issued on the lives of the employees, the policies generally are issued to and held by a trustee, and the arrangement is called an **individual policy pension trust.** Where a group vehicle is used, it may be called a **group permanent contract,** a **level-premium group annuity contract,** or a **level-premium contract with lifetime guarantees.** Under this type of arrangement, the insurance company assumes all the risks and provides all the services, and, in particular, guarantees a price structure.

Single-Premium Deferred Annuities

Under **group deferred annuity contracts,** the employee's pension is separated into pieces that are associated with years of employment. Thus, for each year of service, the employee might be entitled to an annual pension at retirement of 2 percent of his or her year's salary, or he or she might be entitled to a flat amount, such as $50 of monthly income for each year's service. Each year, the employer then purchases a single-premium unit of deferred annuity, which will become payable when the employee reaches his or her normal retirement age. The employee's pension is the sum of the units that were purchased for him or her. Once the annuity has been purchased, the insurance company assumes all the risks and provides all the services. Although the company's risk with respect to any individual may extend for 40, 50, or 60 years with respect to the premium it *has received,* the life insurance company has not guaranteed the price it will charge for additional units *to be purchased* several years in the future. It is customary, however, for the insurance company to guarantee its rate structure with respect to the first five years of the contract.

A basic characteristic of all the insurance arrangements described is that each employee can be told with certainty that a benefit has been purchased or is being purchased for him or her, and the life insurance company guarantees that it will be paid. The employer is in the secure position of knowing that he or she is not placing on future management the risk that the promised benefits will turn out to have been inadequately funded, and the responsibility of making up a deficiency or incurring employee dissatisfaction by reducing the promised benefits.

It is characteristic of this type of arrangement that monies are set aside to provide pensions for some employees who will not stay with the employer until they have satisfied the vesting provisions, and furthermore, the employer must meet each year's pension obligation (based on current service) in full. Many employers indicated a desire for some method by which the employer could have greater latitude in the determination of its annual payments into the pension fund, by discounting its payments to allow for the probability that some of its employees will not persist in employment, and augmenting its payments to anticipate future pay increases. For these and other reasons, both level-premium and single-premium deferred annuities are less popular today, with the deposit administration contract concept being developed in response to these shortcomings.

Deposit Administration Contracts

Under the **deposit administration contract,** the life insurance company takes all the risks and provides all services, but *only with respect to employees who have retired.* With respect to those employees who have not yet reached their retirment dates, the life insurance company provides no direct guarantees with regard to employer contributions for employees, except that pensions will be provided to the extent that monies are available at the time the employees retire. An enrolled actuary supplies the employer with estimates of the amount of money that should be set aside each year to make reasonably certain that sufficient funds will be on hand to purchase annuities for employees as they retire. These monies are turned over to the life insurance company for safekeep-

ing and investment. The life insurance company guarantees that there will be no capital impairment and that at least a specified minimum rate of interest will be earned on the funds. It also guarantees that a particular price structure will be used to establish annuities for the employees as they retire.

The deposit administration contract sets out a schedule of annuity purchase rates and a rate of interest (both conservative) at which the monies in the contractual fund (the active life fund) will be accumulated, both being guaranteed, usually, for the first five years. These guarantees can be changed from year to year as to *future* contributions. The minimum rate of interest and the rate schedules in effect at the time a dollar is paid to the insurer apply to that dollar regardless of when it is withdrawn from the active life fund to provide an annuity. Currently, some companies guarantee purchase rates for five or 10 years of *retirements,* with a right to change the annuity purchase basis for new retirees after that. Following the change, another five- or 10-year period may be applicable. The volatility of investment results has caused many companies to avoid the standard types of long-term guarantees.

The life insurance company has not assumed the risk of the number of persons who will stay with the employer until retirement, but has assumed all the other risks listed above. The insurance company may not provide all services, since the employer or its consultant may maintain employee records, determine the amounts to be paid into the plan, and evaluate the adequacy of funds to provide for future retirements.

Immediate Participation Guarantee Contract

Another popular form of contract is referred to as an **immediate participation guarantee contract** (IPG). These contracts are similar to deposit administration contracts in that the employer's contributions are placed in an unallocated fund and the life insurance company guarantees that the annuities for retired employees will be paid in full. They differ from deposit administration contracts in the extent to which, and the time at which, the insurance company assumes mortality, invest-

ment, and expense risks with respect to retired lives. The IPG contract may be said to have two stages of existence. The first or active stage continues for as long as the employer makes contributions sufficient to keep the amount in the fund above the amount required to meet the life insurance company's price to provide guaranteed annuities for employees who have retired. The contract enters its second stage if the amount in the fund falls to the so-called critical level.

In the active stage, the contract fund is charged directly with the contract's share of the life insurance company's expense and credited directly with its share of investment income (minus a small risk charge). The fund is also credited or charged directly with the contract's share of the company's capital gains and losses and the investment and expense experience with respect to retired employees. If the employer allows the fund to fall to the critical level and the contract enters the second stage, the amount in the fund is used to establish fully guaranteed annuities, and the fund itself ceases to exist.

Under an IPG contract, as long as the employer's contributions are sufficient to maintain the contract in active status, the life insurance company is relieved of investment, mortality, and expense risks with respect to all employees, both active and retired. If and when the contract enters the second stage, all these risks will be assumed by the insurance company. Of course, the company is under a substantial risk during the active status of the contract, since it has provided a guaranteed price structure that the employer can unilaterally decide to take advantage of at any time that it feels the probable future course of investment, mortality, and expense risks will be such that it will be to its advantage to shift the risk to the life insurance company.

Recently, some IPG contracts have been modified, eliminating the guaranteed annuity rates; rather, they provide a certificate stating that nonguaranteed payments will be made until the fund is exhausted. Under this arrangement the employer is responsible for the adequacy of funding, and employees have no assurance from the life insurance company that their benefit payments will continue until death.

Special Investment Arrangements

Separate Accounts. During the 1960s, insurance companies secured authority to set up separate accounts. Such accounts are held separately from the other assets of the company and are not subject to the usual investment restrictions on insurance companies. The insurance company issues contracts under which the investment results credited directly reflect the investment results of the separate account.

During the 1970s, the most common form of separate account was one in which the funds of many contract holders were pooled for investment in common stocks. Today, however, insurance companies have pooled accounts invested in stocks, bonds, mortgages, real estate, and other assets. Also, a large contract holder, who does not wish to participate in a pooled separate account, may request the insurance company to establish a separate account for the company's exclusive use.

Separate accounts also may be used to provide variable annuity benefits. Amounts placed in the account usually are converted into units, and the amount of each employee's benefit is measured in terms of units. The amount of each monthly annuity payment is equal to the product of the number of units to which the employee is entitled and the unit value for the month.

Investment Year Method of Crediting Interest. Virtually all life insurance companies now use the investment year or new money method of determining the rate of investment income to be credited to a given pension plan. For many years, it was standard practice to credit the account with the net rate of interest earned on the insurer's total investment portfolio—the average or portfolio rate. When interest rates were rising rapidly in the 1950s, the average life insurance company portfolio rate of return lagged the new money investment rates considerably, placing life insurers at a competitive disadvantage with banks for pension business. The investment year method was adopted in the early 1960s to minimize the adverse selection involved and to meet the competition of the banks for pension funds.

Under the investment year or new money, approach, assets acquired during a particular calendar year are treated as a separate cell or component of the general asset account. The net investment income, including realized capital gains and losses, derived from the assets in that calendar-year cell is credited to the cell. The asset composition of the cell changes annually due to maturities, repayments, redemptions, sales, and exchanges. Naturally, this affects the rate of return credited to the cell.

Guaranteed Investment Contracts. Under Guaranteed Investment Contracts (GICs), the insurance company accepts from a qualified retirement plan a specific amount of money, usually $100,000 or more, and agrees to refund the money at a fixed date some one to 15 years in the future. Interest is guaranteed for the life of the contract, usually at rates competitive with other long-term fixed-income investments. The interest may be paid at fixed intervals or held to compound until the termination date of the contract.

Since the fixed term of the contract is one of its key features, substantial penalties are usually imposed for premature withdrawal (if allowed at all). Expenses of the insurance company are often expressed as a small subtraction from the gross interest rate quoted. In general, GICs in their various forms are a preferred investment vehicle for pension plans today.

OTHER RETIREMENT PLANS

Profit Sharing

Profit-sharing plans are a type of defined contribution plan. Profit-sharing plans intended for retirement income purposes present a problem, since the amount available to provide an income at retirement is usually not known before retirement. Annually, each employee is allocated a *share* of the amount contributed to the profit-sharing plan. Each employee's share is usually handled in a manner similar to employee contributions, although the return of the amount in an employee's account in the event of termina-

tion of employment may be dependent on a vesting provision. Although relatively rare, the amounts of money made available each year may be used as single premiums to purchase whatever amounts of annuity can be provided on the basis of a price structure guaranteed by an insurance company.

Where the share allocated to each employee is placed in an individual account for him or her under a noninsured trust, his or her accumulation at retirement may be used to purchase a guaranteed annuity under an arrangement similar to the maturity funding contract described earlier. Many insurance companies have developed contracts, both group and individual, that function during the accumulation phase something like the noninsured trust—and at retirement as a maturity funding contract.

Keogh Plans

For many years, there were restrictions on the participation of partners and proprietors in qualified retirement programs. Special plans called **Keogh** or **HR-10 plans** were used to cover partners or proprietors—self-employed individuals. After 20 years of the campaign for parity between self-employed and corporate retirement plans, the Tax Equity and Fiscal Responsibility of 1982 (TEFRA) finally granted such parity to all new and old retirement plans established by self-employed businesses. With that parity came the ability of self-employed businesses to maintain the same types of defined benefit and defined contribution plans as were available previously only to corporations. Existing Keogh plans were amended to comply with the new law and became essentially regular pension and profit-sharing plans. In time, the need for the term *Keogh plan* will disappear.

Individual Retirement Accounts (IRAs)

Individual retirement accounts (IRAs) were created by ERISA to encourage retirement savings by persons who were not actually participating in qualified pension, profit-sharing, or Keogh plans. Until 1987, anyone can set up an IRA irrespective of whether he or she is covered by a qualified plan. After 1986, individuals covered by a qualified plan may make a tax deductible IRA contribution only if he or she has adjusted gross income of less than $40,000, $25,000 for single returns). IRA contributions are deductible from current taxable income, and investment earnings on contributions accumulate tax free until distributed.

Types of IRAs. A **regular IRA** is one established by an individual to provide retirement income for himself or herself. For taxable years after December 31, 1981, any qualified person under age 70½ can contribute 100 percent of annual *earned* income to a regular IRA up to a maximum contribution of $2,000 year. Since the primary purpose of IRAs is to provide income during retirement, there are significant penalties for withdrawal of funds prior to that time. The minimum age at which distribution can be made without penalities is 59½. However, if death occurs prior to that age, the IRA can be distributed to the survivors without any penalty for early withdrawal.

The Tax Reform Act of 1976 enlarged the scope of the IRA provisions by allowing working employees eligible for regular IRAs to establish **spousal IRAs** for their *nonworking* spouses.[31] If an individual establishes *both* a regular and a spousal IRA, the total *combined* contribution is limited to $2,250 per year. No more than $2,000 a year can be placed in any one account.

IRA Funding Instruments. ERISA authorized three different funding instruments for IRAs: (1) individual retirement accounts, (2) individual retirement annuities, and (3) individual U.S. retirement bonds. The third type (IRA bond) was based on a special issue of government savings bonds originally authorized but not offered since April 30, 1982. The bonds were discontinued, primarily due to a lack of interest on the part of investors.

Of the two presently available types of IRA funding instruments, **individual retirement accounts** are by far the most popular. At the present time, more than 90 percent of all IRAs are invested in some form of individual retirement account. This particular type of IRA takes one of three distinct forms. One form is a **trust** or **custodial acocunt,** whereby investments generally are made exclusively in mutual fund shares, usually within a specific family of funds. A second form is a **bank trust** or **custodial account,** whereby contributions are usually invested in one or more of the bank's interest-bearing instruments or, in some cases, self-directed accounts. This form of IRA generally is offered by commercial banks, mutual savings banks, credit unions, and savings and loan associations. The third form is a trust arrangement, offered by stockbrokers, called a **self-directed account.** Under this form of IRA, the owner is permitted to select and manage his or her own individual investments from the wide range of stocks, bonds, mutual funds, and direct participation programs that are available from the investment dealer.

The other type of IRA authorized is the **individual retirement annuity.** Individual retirement annuities generally are either fixed- or variable-annuity contracts that are issued by insurance companies. These contracts are flexible-premium deferred annuities. That means that a series of equal or differing investments may be made periodically under the contract.

Since these insurance contracts are endorsed specially and nontransferrable to meet the necessary IRA requirements, no trustee or custodian is required. When the participant or beneficiary reaches retirement age, the contract may then be used to provide a regular income payment by one of several methods provided for in the terms of its settlement-option provisions. Because the laws governing IRAs specifically prohibit IRA investment in life insurance, such policies may not be used for any type of IRA.

Rollover IRAs. Individuals wishing to change the funding instruments under which their IRAs are invested can do so by utilizing a rollover IRA. The annual contribution limits for regular and spousal IRAs do not apply to rollover IRAs, but to avoid taxation as a premature withdrawal, the rollover must be completed within 60

---

[31]The maximum of $2,000 or 100 percent of annual *earned* income of the working spouse applies as in the case of the regular IRA.

days. As pointed out earlier, each individual is allowed only one rollover per year between IRAs.

Simplified Employee Pension Plans (SEPs)

An employer can establish a simplified employee pension (SEP). Basically, a SEP is a written plan that requires the employer to make contributions, based on a formula contained in the plan, for all employees who have attained the age of 21 and who have performed service for the employer during at least three of the preceding five calendar years. Funds contributed to the SEP by the employer are allocated directly into IRAs maintained for each plan participant. The amount of contribution that can be made to each employee covered by the plan is the lesser of 15 percent of the employee's compensation or $30,000, compared to a maximum of $2,000 with an IRA. TRA '86 considerably broadened the possibilities for participation by employees in smaller SEPs by providing an elective salary reduction option up to $7,000 annually. Beginning in 1988, the $7,000 is indexed to reflect cost-of-living increases.[32] SEPs were developed with the intention of simplifying the administration and reporting requirements for the employer.

Employees of Charitable Organizations, Educational Institutions, and Other Public Bodies (403(b))

Employees of a charitable organization described in Section 501(c)(3) of the Internal Revenue Code, which is exempt from tax under Section 501(a), and employees of a public educational institution, and certain other public bodies, are entitled to special tax treatment on monies used by their employer to purchase an annuity for them. Federal tax law and regulations provide that such an employer may agree with the employee to have a portion of the money that would otherwise be part of his or her pay set aside by the employer in an annuity contract for him or her. These funds eventually will be subject to tax, but not until the money, with accumulated interest, is actually received, either as a cash withdrawal or as annuity payments. Such funds are commonly called 403(b) annuities (from the applicable section of the Internal Revenue Code) or **tax-sheltered annuities** (TSAs) or **tax-deferred annuities** (TDAs).

The regulations governing the maximum amount of money that may be set aside each year on behalf of an employee are quite complex; however, in general, the maximum contribution payable on behalf of an employee is equal to 20 percent of his or her current year's total compensation, times the total period of employment with his or her employer (expressed in years and fractions thereof), less the sum of prior contributions and certain other tax-deferred employer contributions on his or her behalf. Various types of insurance contracts, individual and group, are used as the funding vehicle for such annuities, which have proven to be a substantial source of business for many insurance companies.[33]

Employees of other public bodies, such as states, counties, and municipalities, enjoy a similar device referred to as a **Section 457 deferred compensation arrangement.** Under this arrangement, the employer agrees with each employee to reduce his or her pay by a specified amount and to invest the deferrals in one or more investment outlets that may include insurance products. The amount so deferred, plus investment earnings, will be distributed to the employee on death, retirement, or other termination of employment. The principal difference between Section 457 plans and 403(b) plans is that the investments in a Section 457 plan are owned by the employer. The employee looks to the public entity for satisfaction of his or her benefit claim, not the insurance company or other investment outlet. Deferred annuities, which may be fixed or variable, are popular in these deferred compensation plans.

Employee Savings Plan

In recent years many companies have introduced one or more types of employee savings plans

---

[32]The $7,000 limit is reduced by any salary deferral made to a 401(k) or TSA 403(b) plan.

[33]Elective deferrals will be limited to $9,500 annually under 1986 TRA.

to supplement other existing retirement plans. A savings plan is a defined contribution plan under which employees have separate accounts. Usually, qualified savings plans are designed as profit-sharing plans because only a profit-sharing plan permits account withdrawals during employment, and this is an important feature of the plan if the plan is to be a flexible savings medium for employees. Thus, in general, a savings plan can be viewed as a contributory profit-sharing plan. Two forms of such employee savings arrangements are known as thrift plans and 401(k) plans.

Thrift Plans. A thrift plan is designed to encourage savings by employees from *after-tax* income. An employee, for example, might be permitted to contribute up to 10 percent of his or her salary to the plan. All investment earnings accumulate tax free until distribution, although the employee contribution itself is *not* tax deductible. Withdrawals from thrift plans are permitted under conditions specified in the plan by the employer. The conditions will usually reflect the employer's view of the plan as a long-term savings program.

Most thrift plans provide for partial matching of employee contributions by employers. The employer will usually contribute 50 cents for each dollar of employee contributions, although other matching arrangements are used. Most plans, however, will not provide for matching of contributions in excess of 6 percent of an employee's salary. Employees frequently are given some choice about how the funds in their thrift plans accounts are invested, employees usually allocating their accounts among various types of investment funds (e.g., money market, corporate bond, or stock). Many thrift plans are being changed to 401(k) plans to permit employee *pre-tax* contributions (see below).

401(k) Plans. Another employee savings plan, usually referred to as a 401(k) plan, also allows for partial matching of employee contributions by employers.[34] A major difference between the two plans, however, is that a 401(k) plan provides *current* as well as future tax savings for employees. Under a 401(k) plan, employees agree to defer a percentage of pretax income. The money arising from this decision reduces current (taxable) salary and is placed directly in the 401(k) plan by the employer. The 401(k) contribution is considered to have been made by the employer and is therefore generally not treated as part of an employee's taxable income for federal income tax purposes.[35] As in the case of a thrift plan, all investment income earned under a 401(k) plan accumulates tax free until distributed. Furthermore, upon distribution (which is as a lump sum), present law permits employees to use the favorable 10-year (5-year effective in 1987) income-averaging rule.

The 401(k) arrangement has become very popular as an employee benefit since both employees and employers benefit therefrom. TRA '86 revised the nondiscrimination test for 401(k) elective deferrals providing a new definition of highly compensated employees. In addition, the IRS has established stricter rules for 401(k) plans, the withdrawal provisions, in particular, being very stringent. No withdrawals from 401(k) plans are allowed before age 59½ except for participants who die, become disabled, retire, change jobs, or suffer financial hardships. Under TRA '86, withdrawals also are allowed prior to age 59½ where the plan terminates or the company is sold. Some 401(k) plans permit loans to employees, but with the passage of TEFRA, loans were limited to the lesser of $50,000 or 50 percent of the vested value of an employee's account.

[34]As in the case of SEPs, elective deferrals will be limited to $7,000 annually under 1986 TRA.

[35]Although 401(k) contributions are not subject to federal income taxes, a few states and municipalities do tax them. Also, effective January 1, 1984, 401(k) contributions are subject to Social Security taxes. The provisions of the Tax Reform Act of 1986 further limits their attractiveness.

experience. Thus, in a mutual company, the policyowner pays a typically fixed premium stated in his or her policy (usually higher than the premium for a similar nonparticipating contract in a stock company), but the actual or net cost to the policyowner will depend on the dividends allocated to his or her policy each year by the board of directors. The fixed premium stated in the contract is the initial outlay and represents the maximum, but the final actual net outlay is less by the amount of dividends paid on the contract.

Normally, mutual companies issue only *participating* policies. Sometimes, they also issue *nonparticipating* policies, but these policyowners, as with policyowners of stock companies, are simply customers of the mutual company. As suggested earlier, the traditional emphasis on participation versus nonparticipation as a characteristic distinguishing a mutual from a stock company is no longer valid.

The organization of a new mutual company presents some serious practical problems. As in the case of a stock company, funds are needed to cover the expenses of operation, make the required deposits with the state insurance department, and provide a surplus or contingency fund to meet any unusual fluctuations in experience before the company has had time to accumulate such funds from its operations.

In the case of a stock company, funds for all these purposes are obtained from the sale of stock; but in a mutual company, the only sources of funds at the beginning are the first premiums paid in by the original member-policyowners or funds borrowed to get the company going. The lack of profit incentive undoubtedly is a significant factor in explaining why relatively few mutual companies are formed, but in addition, the statutory requirements for the formation of a new mutual life insurance company are exceedingly stringent. For instance, the state of New York requires that a mutual company cannot *begin* operation as a going concern unless it has applications for not less than $1,000 each from 1,000 persons, with the full amount of one annual premium for an aggregate of $25,000, *plus* an initial surplus of $150,000 in cash. It should be apparent that there would be great difficulty in finding a large number of individuals who are insurable and who are willing to apply for insurance in, and to pay the first premium to, a company that is not yet in existence and not yet able to issue policies.

These difficulties of organization of a new mutual life insurance company are so great that none has been organized for many years, and no new mutual company is likely to be formed. The only practical way of organizing a new life insurance company is on a stock basis. A stock company, after it has been fully established and has attained adequate financial stability, can be converted into a mutual company.[7]

Procedure

In general, the procedure in organizing a new life insurance company is the same for both stock and mutual companies. Both types of companies are corporations and must be organized in accordance with the provisions of the state laws applying to corporations generally, or as is usually the case, in accordance with special insurance laws regulating the organization of insurance corporations.[8]

The various state laws as regards the organization of insurance companies are similar, and the pattern prescribed by the law of New York is representative of the general procedure. In that state, the incorporators (at least 13 persons) first apply to the state for a charter setting forth the name of the company, its location, the type of business to be transacted, its powers and how they will be exercised, the method of internal control, the amount of capital (if a stock company), and

---

[7]Many of the large mutual companies in existence today (e.g., Metropolitan, Prudential, and Equitable of New York) were, in fact, originally stock companies that were "mutualized." At one time, some states provided for a guaranty capital put up temporarily by those persons interested in forming a mutual company. This guaranty capital was to be retired as soon as the mutual company's operations stabilized financially. Sometimes the stock remained outstanding for some period while the company operated on the mutual idea. But this would hardly justify a separate classification as a type of company.

[8]At one time, insurance companies were organized by a special act of the legislature, which became the "charter" of the company.

LIFE INSURANCE COMPANY FORMATION

Although it is theoretically possible for the life insurance business to be undertaken by an individual or by a partnership, the form of organization should be one that will provide both permanence and a high degree of security of payment. Only a corporation has the inherent characteristics to meet these requirements, and under the various state insurance laws, that is the only form of business organization permitted to undertake the life insurance business.

Thus, from a practical and legal viewpoint the operation of the life insurance business requires the formation of a corporation. Both stock companies and mutual companies are organized as corporations.

Stock Company

A stock life insurance company is one that is organized for the purpose of making profits for its shareholders. Traditionally, stock companies issued **guaranteed-cost, nonparticipating policies,** where the policyowners shared neither in any savings or profits nor in any losses that might arise in the operation of the business. Every policy element was fixed at issue. Stock companies sometimes issued **participating policies,** on which dividends could be paid to policyowners. When stock companies issue participating policies, some states impose limitations on the extent to which the shareholders of the company may benefit from the participating business.[5] The majority of states, however, impose no special regulation on the participating insurance sold by stock companies.

With the introduction of the various forms of **current assumption, nonparticipating policies,** the distinction between stock and mutual companies on the basis of participation has become even less relevant. Virtually all individual cash value policies "participate" one way or another. Corporate coverage product lines (e.g., group insurance and pensions) of stock companies

have also been indistinguishable from those of mutual companies for some time.

The life insurance business is highly specialized and is subject in every state to special *insurance laws.* As in other respects, the formation of a life insurance corporation is regulated by these insurance laws. Under the state insurance laws, a company must have a minimum amount of capital and surplus before it can secure a license to operate as a life insurance company. For instance, under New York state law, a stock life insurance company must have a minimum of $1 million capital and an initial surplus of 200 percent of the initial capital. These minimum capital requirements are intended to ensure that the new company can make the deposits required to become licensed,[6] has sufficient funds for normal operations, and has a "contingency fund" to meet any adverse fluctuations in experience that occur during the initial development period. Once the stock has been subscribed and the various state requirements met, the company can be organized by the shareholders and begin business.

Mutual Company

A mutual life insurance company is also a corporation, but it has no capital stock and no shareholders. The policyowner in a mutual company is both a customer *and* in a sense, an owner of the company, in contrast to the policyowner in a stock company, who is a customer only. The policyowner in a mutual company is a member of the company and has the right to vote in the election of the board of directors or trustees.

Technically, the assets and income of a mutual company are owned by the company. The policyowners are usually considered to be contractual creditors, with the right to vote for directors as provided for by law. The company is administered, and its assets are held, for the benefit and protection of the policyowners and beneficiaries and either are held for their benefit and protection as reserves, surplus, or contingency funds or are distributed to them as dividends to the extent that management deems such action warranted as a result of the company's

[5] For example, the state of New York provides that profits on participating policies and contracts are limited to the larger of (1) 10 percent of such profits, or (2) 50 cents per year per $1,000 of participating business. See Sec. 216, New York Insurance Law.

[6] See Chapter 33.

experience. Thus, in a mutual company, the policyowner pays a typically fixed premium stated in his or her policy (usually higher than the premium for a similar nonparticipating contract in a stock company), but the actual or net cost to the policyowner will depend on the dividends allocated to his or her policy each year by the board of directors. The fixed premium stated in the contract is the initial outlay and represents the maximum, but the final actual net outlay is less by the amount of dividends paid on the contract.

Normally, mutual companies issue only *participating* policies. Sometimes, they also issue *nonparticipating* policies, but these policyowners, as with policyowners of stock companies, are simply customers of the mutual company. As suggested earlier, the traditional emphasis on participation versus nonparticipation as a characteristic distinguishing a mutual from a stock company is no longer valid.

The organization of a new mutual company presents some serious practical problems. As in the case of a stock company, funds are needed to cover the expenses of operation, make the required deposits with the state insurance department, and provide a surplus or contingency fund to meet any unusual fluctuations in experience before the company has had time to accumulate such funds from its operations.

In the case of a stock company, funds for all these purposes are obtained from the sale of stock; but in a mutual company, the only sources of funds at the beginning are the first premiums paid in by the original member-policyowners or funds borrowed to get the company going. The lack of profit incentive undoubtedly is a significant factor in explaining why relatively few mutual companies are formed, but in addition, the statutory requirements for the formation of a new mutual life insurance company are exceedingly stringent. For instance, the state of New York requires that a mutual company cannot *begin* operation as a going concern unless it has applications for not less than $1,000 each from 1,000 persons, with the full amount of one annual premium for an aggregate of $25,000, *plus* an initial surplus of $150,000 in cash. It should be apparent that there would be great difficulty in

finding a large number of individuals who are insurable and who are willing to apply for insurance in, and to pay the first premium to, a company that is not yet in existence and not yet able to issue policies.

These difficulties of organization of a new mutual life insurance company are so great that none has been organized for many years, and no new mutual company is likely to be formed. The only practical way of organizing a new life insurance company is on a stock basis. A stock company, after it has been fully established and has attained adequate financial stability, can be converted into a mutual company.[7]

Procedure

In general, the procedure in organizing a new life insurance company is the same for both stock and mutual companies. Both types of companies are corporations and must be organized in accordance with the provisions of the state laws applying to corporations generally, or as is usually the case, in accordance with special insurance laws regulating the organization of insurance corporations.[8]

The various state laws as regards the organization of insurance companies are similar, and the pattern prescribed by the law of New York is representative of the general procedure. In that state, the incorporators (at least 13 persons) first apply to the state for a charter setting forth the name of the company, its location, the type of business to be transacted, its powers and how they will be exercised, the method of internal control, the amount of capital (if a stock company), and

---

[7]Many of the large mutual companies in existence today (e.g., Metropolitan, Prudential, and Equitable of New York) were, in fact, originally stock companies that were "mutualized." At one time, some states provided for a guaranty capital put up temporarily by those persons interested in forming a mutual company. This guaranty capital was to be retired as soon as the mutual company's operations stabilized financially. Sometimes the stock remained outstanding for some period while the company operated on the mutual idea. But this would hardly justify a separate classification as a type of company.

[8]At one time, insurance companies were organized by a special act of the legislature, which became the "charter" of the company.

to supplement other existing retirement plans. A savings plan is a defined contribution plan under which employees have separate accounts. Usually, qualified savings plans are designed as profit-sharing plans because only a profit-sharing plan permits account withdrawals during employment, and this is an important feature of the plan if the plan is to be a flexible savings medium for employees. Thus, in general, a savings plan can be viewed as a contributory profit-sharing plan. Two forms of such employee savings arrangements are known as thrift plans and 401(k) plans.

Thrift Plans. A thrift plan is designed to encourage savings by employees from *after-tax* income. An employee, for example, might be permitted to contribute up to 10 percent of his or her salary to the plan. All investment earnings accumulate tax free until distribution, although the employee contribution itself is *not* tax deductible. Withdrawals from thrift plans are permitted under conditions specified in the plan by the employer. The conditions will usually reflect the employer's view of the plan as a long-term savings program.

Most thrift plans provide for partial matching of employee contributions by employers. The employer will usually contribute 50 cents for each dollar of employee contributions, although other matching arrangements are used. Most plans, however, will not provide for matching of contributions in excess of 6 percent of an employee's salary. Employees frequently are given some choice about how the funds in their thrift plans accounts are invested, employees usually allocating their accounts among various types of investment funds (e.g., money market, corporate bond, or stock). Many thrift plans are being changed to 401(k) plans to permit employee *pre-tax* contributions (see below).

401(k) Plans. Another employee savings plan, usually referred to as a 401(k) plan, also allows for partial matching of employee contributions by employers.[34] A major difference between the two plans, however, is that a 401(k) plan provides *current* as well as future tax savings for employees. Under a 401(k) plan, employees agree to defer a percentage of pretax income. The money arising from this decision reduces current (taxable) salary and is placed directly in the 401(k) plan by the employer. The 401(k) contribution is considered to have been made by the employer and is therefore generally not treated as part of an employee's taxable income for federal income tax purposes.[35] As in the case of a thrift plan, all investment income earned under a 401(k) plan accumulates tax free until distributed. Furthermore, upon distribution (which is as a lump sum), present law permits employees to use the favorable 10-year (5-year effective in 1987) income-averaging rule.

The 401(k) arrangement has become very popular as an employee benefit since both employees and employers benefit therefrom. TRA '86 revised the nondiscrimination test for 401(k) elective deferrals providing a new definition of highly compensated employees. In addition, the IRS has established stricter rules for 401(k) plans, the withdrawal provisions, in particular, being very stringent. No withdrawals from 401(k) plans are allowed before age 59½ except for participants who die, become disabled, retire, change jobs, or suffer financial hardships. Under TRA '86, withdrawals also are allowed prior to age 59½ where the plan terminates or the company is sold. Some 401(k) plans permit loans to employees, but with the passage of TEFRA, loans were limited to the lesser of $50,000 or 50 percent of the vested value of an employee's account.

[34]As in the case of SEPs, elective deferrals will be limited to $7,000 annually under 1986 TRA.

[35]Although 401(k) contributions are not subject to federal income taxes, a few states and municipalities do tax them. Also, effective January 1, 1984, 401(k) contributions are subject to Social Security taxes. The provisions of the Tax Reform Act of 1986 further limits their attractiveness.

Chapter 29

Life Insurance Company Organization and Management

Organizations providing life and health insurance may be classified broadly as (1) commercial, (2) government, and (3) other. The characteristics of government, savings bank, fraternal and certain nonprofit organizations providing death, accident, sickness, and retirement benefits have been presented throughout this text.[1] The majority of the life and health insurance in force in the private sector of the U.S. economy has been issued by commercial life insurance companies, several aspects of which were discussed in Chapter 11. Just as the greatest portion of this volume has been concerned with the contracts, coverages, and practices of commercial life insurance companies, so this chapter is devoted primarily to a discussion of the organizational, financial, and management characteristics of this class of companies.

Commercial life insurance companies commonly are classified as **stock** or **mutual.** The distinguishing characteristic of a stock company is its shareholders. If a company has shareholders,

it is a stock company. If the policyowners own the company, it is a mutual company, irrespective of the kinds of policies it issues.[2]

Mutual insurers generally are older and larger than stock life insurers. Until recently, they were dominant with respect to life insurance in force, their share having declined from 62 percent in 1960 to 42.7 percent in 1983. During this period, the number of stock insurers increased from 1,273 in 1960 to 1,950 in 1984, changing both the market share of stock and mutual insurers but perhaps more important, changing the life insurance industry's ability to respond to the deregulation of the financial services marketplace.[3] In fact, organizational form has become an important issue, with considerable interest and discussion surrounding the question of demutualization (see below).[4]

---

[1] See Chapter 11 for a discussion of fraternals, savings banks, the Wisconsin State Fund, and various government plans as providers of life insurance; see Chapter 16 for a discussion of Blue Cross/Blue Shield, health maintenance organizations, and preferred provider organizations; and Chapter 25 for a discussion of government as a provider of Social Security benefits.

[2] One author believes the criterion ought to be voting rights, and recommends "mixed company" for companies in which both shareholders and participating policyowners have voting rights. See Joseph M. Belth, "Types of Life Insurance Companies," in Dan M. McGill, *Life Insurance,* rev. ed. (Homewood, Ill.: Richard D. Irwin, Inc., 1967), p. 790.

[3] See "Stocks Outstrip Mutuals: GAO Study," *The National Underwriter,* Life/Health ed. (December 21, 1985), p. 3.

[4] See Richard E. Stewart, "The Great Debate," *Best's Review,* Life/Health ed., Vol. 85 (January 1985).

any other essential particulars. In addition to advertising in a prescribed manner their plan to incorporate themselves as an insurance company, the organizers file a "certificate of intention" and a copy of the charter with the superintendent of insurance before they become a corporation. They then receive subscriptions to the capital if the company is to be a stock company, or receive applications for insurance and the premiums therefor if the company is to be a mutual. It is important to note that they may still not issue policies. When the legal minimum capital has been subscribed, or when the premiums on the necessary minimum amount of insurance, in the case of a mutual company, have been paid in, and when the statutory deposit has been made with the superintendent, the organization may be completed.

At this point, the subscribing shareholders or initial applicants for insurance elect the directors, who in turn authorize the issuance of the stock or the policies, as the case may be. At this organizational meeting, the owners adopt bylaws covering such matters as the duties of officers and committees, regulations on investments, maximum amount of insurance to be written on a single life, the territory in which business is to be transacted, and so on. The newly elected directors then meet to elect officers and set up committees of the board to take charge of particular departments of the general administration of the company, delegating powers appropriately. At this point, assuming that the company's application for a license to do business in the state has been approved by the state insurance department, staff, supplies, and equipment may be secured and business begun formally.

HOME-OFFICE ORGANIZATION

Fundamentally, the organization of a life insurance company home office follows the pattern of other corporations that are concerned with the collection, investment and disbursement of funds. Organization in general has three main elements: (1) levels of authority, (2) departmentalization, and (3) functionalization. Each of these elements plays an important role in establishing an efficient

organizational structure and in ensuring efficient coordination of effort within that structure.

The organization of a life insurance company is no different in its possession of these elements. In terms of total organizational structure, life insurance companies are most frequently *line-staff-functional* organizations. Individual segments of a life insurance company, however, may be organized on a line basis, with all operations directly under the control of the manager. The agency department, on the other hand, is normally organized on a *line and staff* basis, where the agency vice-president is supported by the line assistants (directors of agencies) and also staff assistants (e.g., directors of research and training).

Companies differ widely by size, fields of operation, objectives, and other factors. Their actual organizational patterns also differ, since many companies' organizational pattern develops as a matter of evolution. Subject to this limitation, it is the purpose of this section to outline the more important official positions, committees, and departments of the average well-established life insurance company and to describe briefly their respective functions and duties.

Levels of Authority

There usually are four levels of authority in a life insurance organization. The board of directors and its various committees are, of course, the top or *directorial* level of authority. The president and senior officers of the company are found at the *executive* level. In addition to serving as part of the executive management team, the senior executive officers are given authority and responsibility for particular functions. Each of the vice-presidents has subordinate officers at the *managerial* level who are responsible for the day-to-day functions of their departments. These subordinate officers, who may serve in line, staff, or functional relationships, make decisions on all matters within the limits of authority delegated to them. Finally, the supervisors in charge of subdivisions of the departments are found at the *supervisory* level of authority.

The Board of Directors. The board of directors and the several committees of the board constitute the top level of authority in a life insurance company. In a mutual company, the directors typically are elected by the policyowners from among their own number, whereas in a stock company, they are elected by the shareholders and, in order to qualify, must be the owners of a designated number of shares. But whatever the method of election, the board possesses complete supervisory powers over those who manage the company. It is empowered not only to select the president and other principal officers, but to delegate to them such powers as it sees fit. It also meets at stated intervals to approve or disapprove the recommendations of officials and the findings of committees, and to consider and pass judgment on all important matters concerning the general business conduct of the company. Since the transactions of a life insurance company assume a great variety of forms, it is usually considered desirable that the directorate be composed of individuals who possess varying and wide experience.

To expedite the proper fulfillment of its functions and to bring its members into close touch with the business affairs of the company, the board divides itself into a number of standing committees. In many companies, the president and other officers are members of the board of directors and hence are entitled to membership on important committees. Where the executive officers are not directors, they are invited to various meetings in an advisory capacity. These committees vary in the different companies but usually include an *executive* or *insurance committee,* a *finance committee,* a *claims committee,* and an *audit committee.* The executive committee, consisting of the president and certain members of the board, considers such matters as bear a vital relation to the general business policy of the company. For example, the committee determines the kinds of insurance contracts the company will sell, the provisions of the contracts, the premium rates, the territory in which the company will operate, and so on. The finance committee, consisting of the president, the chief investment officer, and treasurer of the company and a certain number of the directors, exercises supervisory control over the company's investment policy and practices. In larger companies, it is quite common to have a separate committee to deal with real estate and mortgage loans. The claims committee has general control over the payment of claims and, in particular, determines policy in regard to doubtful or contestable claims. The audit committee maintains general supervision over the company's accounting system and records. Its objective is to give additional assurance regarding the integrity of (a) financial information used by the board in making decisions, and (b) financial information distributed to outsiders. In the case of stock companies, it has become a widespread practice also to establish a compensation committee to oversee the company's compensation policies and to approve specifically the compensation of senior management.

In general, the officers of the company who carry on its active management initiate action, the function of the directors being to approve or disapprove the recommendations made. For the most part, directors' committees will be guided by the recommendations of the officers of the company who are directly concerned. This is particularly true in the case of committees dealing with technical details of the business.

Executive Officers. The executive officers are responsible for carrying out the policies determined by the board of directors and for the general management of the business. These officers usually comprise the president; one or more vice presidents, each of whom has charge of a department; and the treasurer. The president is usually entrusted by the board of directors with broad executive powers, and ideally should be well versed in financial matters and have broad life insurance experience so as to interpret properly the results attained in the respective departments of the company, advise the board of directors in supervising the general business conduct of the company, determine the best policy for it to pursue, and direct the work of subordinate officials. He or she also is entrusted with the duty of selecting subordinate officials and department heads. The several vice-presidents, each of whom usually has charge of a department of the company, must also keep up with the general business operations of the company, so as to be in a position to assist the president in his or her duties, to assume the president's responsibilities (or those of a ranking vice-president) during his or her absence, and to be prepared to assume the office in the event of promotion.

Departmentalization

The operations of life insurance companies involve three basic functions: to sell, to service, and to invest. For a company to carry out these functions properly, it must have high-quality professional actuarial, legal, underwriting, and accounting advice. Consequently, most companies operate within seven major functional areas: actuarial, agency, accounting and auditing, investments, law, underwriting, and administration.

Departmentalization simply means the division of work to be performed into logical sections or assignments. Business organizations normally are departmentalized on either a *functional,* a *geographical,* or a *product* basis. Examples of all three types of departmentalization are found in many life insurance companies. Thus, the actuarial department is established on the basis of function, a southern department follows from a geographical viewpont, and the ordinary or group departments are established on the basis of product. In any case, a given company usually will follow an individual pattern. The following discussion of functional departmentalization will illustrate the internal organization and activities of a life insurance company.

The **actuarial department** establishes the company's premium rates, establishes reserve liabilities and nonforfeiture values, and generally handles all the mathematical operations of the company. This department is also responsible for analyzing earnings and furnishing the data from which annual dividend scales and excess interest and other credits are established. The actuarial staff designs new policies and forms and is responsible for filing them with the various state insurance departments. The department also makes mortality studies and often supervises the underwriting practices of the company. It works closely with the marketing department in considering policy design and other factors that affect the competitive position of the company's agency force. Finally, because of the importance of the technical actuarial element in group insurance and group

annuities, this department frequently handles the administration of such business or exercises a considerable degree of functional responsibility over it. The role of the actuary is vital to the operation of a life insurance company. In many smaller companies, the actuary will in effect serve as executive vice-president and exercise considerable influence over all areas of operations.

The **marketing department** is responsible for the sale of new business, conservation of existing business, and certain types of service to policyowners. This department supervises the activities of the company's agents and is responsible for advertising; sales promotion; market analysis; recruiting, selection , and training of agents; and controlling agency costs.

The **accounting and auditing department,** under the direction of the vice-president and comptroller, is responsible for establishing and supervising the company's accounting and control procedures. Auditing, at both the agent and home office levels, is done by an independent unit of this department. The actual preparation of the annual statement is handled here, although the actuarial department exercises considerable functional control in this regrad. The accounting department is, of course, responsible for matters concerning federal, state, and local tax laws and regulations. It is also responsible for expense analysis and other operational statistics not handled by the actuarial department.

The **investment department,** usually under the direction of an investment vice-president, handles the company's investment program under policies laid down by the board of directors. The department, besides passing on the merits of the company's investments prepartory to presenting them to the finance committee for final approval, usually is the custodian of the bonds, stocks, and other investments held by the company, and is entrusted with the duty of collecting the interest and dividends earned on them. To invest the company's money in securities that are safe and yet will yield a return higher than the rate assumed for premium and reserve computations requires a skill and a wide knowledge of the various classes of investments in which life insurance companies are permitted to invest their funds. The volatile interest rates experienced in recent years, coupled with innovative new products and increased competition, has enhanced the importance of highly competent investment management.

The **legal department** is charged with the responsibility of handling all the company's legal matters. These include, among other things, the conduct of court cases growing out of contested claims, foreclosure proceedings, and imperfect titles; the sufficiency and correctness of policy forms, agency contracts, bonds, and notes; the inspection of titles to property purchased by the company or upon which it has granted loans; and the analysis and interpretation for the benefit of the company of the statutory and court law governing life insurance in the states where the company operates.

The **underwriting department** is responsible for establishing standards of selection and for passing judgment on applicants for insurance. In some companies, the **medical department** is given separate status. The medical director supervises the company's medical examiners and may be the final authority to pass upon the insurability of applicants. In some instances, however, general underwriting control may rest in the hands of a vice-president who is not a physician. The department makes use of many underwriting specialists who are not physicians. Many underwriting decisions do not depend on a physician's opinion, since "insurability" connotes more than "good health."

The **administration department,** often headed by the secretary, is responsible for providing home office service to the company's agents and policyowners. This usually includes the issuance of new policies, premium and commission accounting, claims, loans, surrenders, policy changes, and similar transactions. This department is also responsible for personnel administration and home-office planning. The secretary has charge of the company's correspondence, the minutes of the board of directors and its various committees, and the company's records. It should be noted that many companies also departmentalize on the basis of product, having separate departments for *ordinary, industrial, health,* and *group* insurance, depending on the lines they write.

In addition to committees of the board of directors, a number of interdepartmental commit-

tees may be appointed by the executive officers to coordinate the efforts of the various departments. These committees normally report their findings to the officer responsible for their appointment. Some of the interdepartmental committees that might be appointed are an insurance committee, a budget committee, a public relations or advertising committee, a human resources and employee-benefit committee, a research committee, and a personnel and management training committee.

Although this description of home-office organization is representative, it may not actually fit any particular company. It is presented merely to illustrate one possible type of home-office organization.

LIFE INSURANCE COMPANY MANAGEMENT

As implied earlier, the activities performed in the operation of a life insurance company may be classified into one of three major functional areas: marketing, investments, or administration. The degree to which a life insurance company succeeds reflects the consolidated effort of all the activities of the organization.

Establishing Company Objectives

The first step in providing a foundation for guiding departmental decision-making and goal setting is for top management to define the company-wide or overall objectives of the firm. After establishing company-wide objectives, management must define its marketing and investment objectives and the means for attaining them within this framework. Procedures must be established for communication and understanding of objectives and policies by those responsible for implementing them and the evaluation of actual results in light of the objectives. Each home-office department must be made aware of its role in the attainment of objectives.

These principles really must become a management platform on which all departments can base their activities and bring to bear their respective talents toward the achievement of the objectives. They help familiarize key members of each department with overall company policies, so that they can relate their own activities more closely to central objectives. By giving each department a better understanding of the policies of all other departments, better coordination of interdepartmental activities is promoted. They also provide an orderly process for policies to be changed from time to time to meet changing conditions, needs, and objectives.

Holding Companies

In recent years, the use of holding companies has been the central theme of the intercorporate reorganizations that have occurred in managements' attempts to help their organizations improve their earnings and long-term growth possibilities through diversification. The deregulation of the financial services area has materially enhanced this development. For the most part, the holding companies are financial corporations owning or controlling one or more insurers, mutual-fund broker-dealer organizations, mutual-fund management investment research companies, consumer finance companies, and other financially related corporations. Some stock life insurance companies are owned or controlled by nonfinancial holding companies and conglomerates that group together in unrelated fields.

The latter development was viewed with alarm by some. A Special Committee on Insurance Holding Companies, appointed by the Superintendent of Insurance of the State of New York, concluded:

> The holding company device, when it involves affiliation with noninsurance enterprises, jeopardizes the interest of both the public and the policyholder, and especially will do so if its development is indiscriminate and without benefit of close regulatory supervision.[9]

The committee went on to recommend the relaxation of some restraints, traditional in insurance practice and insurance law, that they believed had added unnecessarily to the pressures to organize noninsurance holding companies. These recommended changes related to the for-

mation and acquisition of subsidiaries, disclosure of intercorporate relationships among parents and subsidiaries and their affiliates to the superintendent of insurance, the liberalization of investment regulations, and greater freedom in raising capital through the sale of senior securities and securities convertible into equities.

The relationship of mutual insurance companies to the holding-company device is different from that of the stock insurance company. Holding companies formed by one or more stock companies are commonly called **upstream holding companies.** The holding company sits at the top of the intercorporate structure. It is owned by the shareholders, and, in turn, it owns subsidiaries. A **downstream holding company** is usually formed by a mutual insurance company.[10] It sits in the middle of the intercorporate structure. It is owned wholly or in part by the mutual that sits at the top, and it owns subsidiaries. The significance of the distinction is that the downstream holding company presents few regulatory problems to state insurance departments, because the parent mutual is directly subject to insurance regulations. As a consequence, a downstream holding company is a feasible device only if the parent mutual has a very strong surplus position, and under present laws, it can never have the flexibility available to an upstream holding company.

The large mutual life insurance company with a significant surplus position is capable of diversification through acquisition or otherwise by simple management decision, provided that the activity is permitted by the state insurance department. The state of New York enacted legislation similar to that recommended by the Special Committee regulating insurance-related holding companies in 1969.[11] The greater flexibility provided by this legislation minimized the need, at that time, for large mutual insurers to create holding companies. The inexorable deregulation of the financial services marketplace, however, has continued to raise concerns over most mutual companies' ability to compete effectively in the new environment where access to equity capital and related financing alternatives is becoming increas-

[9] *Report of the Special Committtee on Insurance Holding Companies,* State of New York Insurance Department, 1968, p. 7.

[10] Downstream holding companies may be formed by a stock company also.

[11] See New York Insurance Law, Chapter 190, Sec. 6.

ingly important. Since mutual life insurance companies have no stock outstanding to exchange for stock in a holding company or for a holding company or conglomerate to acquire, the problems of upstream diversification and control of mutual insurers by holding companies cannot occur. In addition, although mutual life insurance companies can engage in downstream diversification (by purchasing a holding company), restrictive insurance laws in many states make this impractical.[12] As discussed below, this situation, in face of the greatly increased competition both within and from outside the traditional life insurance business, has created interest in demutualization.

Corporate Governance

Corporate governance has developed into a vital issue affecting American insurers generally. In this connection, the SEC adopted a sweeping and important series of amendments to its proxy rules. The amendments called for additional disclosure to shareholders concerning the structure, composition, and function of corporate boards of directors and their committees. In particular, companies were required to disclose sufficient details concerning director and nominee relationships with the company and its customers and suppliers to enable shareholders to assess meaningfully director independence. Expanded disclosure was required concerning (1) standing audit, compensation, and/or nominating committees; (2) director attendance at meetings; (3) director resignations; (4) shareholder proposals; and (5) settlement of election contests. The purpose of these changes was to improve the information available to shareholders and thereby enable them to assess more accurately the performance of their directors and facilitate informed voting.

Although the actions of the SEC directly affect only stock life insurance companies that file reports with the SEC and those mutual companies marketing equity products through registered separate accounts, other initiatives in the corporate governance arena have been directed specifically at mutual life insurance companies. A number of

difficult, sensitive issues concerning mutual companies have surfaced at hearings, including, for example, whether policyowners have proprietary interests in the company and whether disclosure should be required of dividend distribution policies.

Organization for Performance [13]

The first job of any company is to earn a profit. Profits are needed by a life insurance company so that it can build its capital base, assure its ability to grow, and mature its insurance contracts. Profits are also needed so that the company can pay a satisfactory return to its owners, whether they be shareholders in the case of a stock company, or policyowners who stand in the position of owners in the case of a mutual company.

The key objective of the company must be to seek to obtain a profit level that represents an adequate return on the capital deployed—at least equal to the cost of that capital. If this result is achieved, the company is creating value for its shareholders and policyowners. If it is not achieved, the company is destroying value of the shareholders and policyowners. This is the ultimate test of management accomplishment. The return that the market dictates on equity capital is, depending on conditions, commonly in the range 15 to 18 percent. This can be considered as being the measure of the minimum result that must be achieved if management is doing its job and creating value.

Obviously, this measurement is a difficult one for a mutual company, because policyowner dividends potentially combine both price adjustment and owner return elements. If management is to be assured that it is creating value, it needs to have the ability to measure return on equity (ROE), in the aggregate and for the several business lines or segments. Furthermore, it is a driving force in the development of corporate strategy. Some strategy options consistent with the creation of value are (1) the abandonment of

---

[12]With downstream diversification, the parent company (whether mutual or stock) would be subject to direct control by insurance regulatory authorities.

[13]This section draws on Harry D. Garber "Organization for Performance: Profit Centers," *1984 Financial Officers' Forum-Selected Proceedings* (Atlanta, Ga.: Life Office Management Association, 1984), pp. 22–24.

businesses that are not now earning a satisfactory return and that cannot be fixed in one way or another to achieve this return level, (2) downsizing a business to a niche of the market where it can achieve a superior return, or (3) making a deliberate decision to grow a business in which a company has a competitive advantage. There are others.

Many companies believe that the best way of obtaining a satisfactory overall return on equity is to establish the financial goals for all or most profit centers in terms of ROE. Also, this approach can help ensure that the amount of capital retained in support of each business is appropriate. The use of ROE-based goals for profit centers is not essential, but it is helpful in achieving the overall ROE objective.

In competitive businesses, the financial results depend ultimately on the success of the company in achieving a unique or predominant position in those segments of the market that it chooses to serve. This position may stem from a low cost structure, a unique sales operation, a special underwriting or investment skill, and so on, each of which importantly enhances profit. The key to the success for the company is to assure that these unique positions continue and that changes in other elements of the cost or pricing structure do not negate these positions.

In all areas of organization there are no simple or "correct" answers. There are different choices, each with its own advantages and disadvantages. The choice will often depend more on the company's history, its current circumstances, or sometimes on the easy availability of information, than on the merits one can determine on balance of a particular approach.

CONVERSION FROM ONE TYPE OF COMPANY TO ANOTHER

Mutualization of Stock Companies

Some stock companies have been converted from stock form into mutual form through a procedure that is called **mutualization.** In essence, mutualization involves the retirement of the outstanding capital stock of the company, coupled with the transfer of control of the company from the shareholders to the policyowners. The motivations for such a move vary widely, including, for example, a desire to prevent control of the company from falling into undesirable hands through a change in stock ownership.

The officers of the company usually initiate mutualization proceedings by submitting a proposal to the board of directors. The key factor is, of course, the price to be paid for each share of stock and the manner of payment. The price must be attractive enough from the viewpoint of the shareholders to induce them to relinquish their rights of ownership and control. On the other hand, from a company's viewpoint, the price must be limited practically by the fact that the remaining surplus, after mutualization, must be adequate to permit sound operation of the company. Sometimes, it is quite important that the payment for the shares be spread over a long period of time so as not to impose an undue burden on current surplus.

If the plan, including the price to be offered to the shareholders, is approved by the board of directors, the plan must be submitted to the state insurance department for the approval of the commissioner of insurance. Assuming that the proposed plan is approved, it will then be submitted to the policyowners and shareholders in accordance with the requirements of the applicable state insurance law.

In executing a mutualization plan approved by the necessary majorities, the company takes up the stock to the extent feasible. Some of the stockholders may object to the plan for one reason or another, and the process of taking up stock will usually require some time. As the stock is bought up, it is not canceled but transferred to trustees for the policyowners, who vote the stock in their behalf. Normally, a substantial majority of the total stock can be purchased immediately, so that effective ownership and control are obtained by the policyowners. Ultimately, when all the shares of stock have been purchased, the stock may be canceled and the company becomes fully mutualized.[14]

---

[14]For a study of mutualizations, see Linda Pickthorne Fletcher, "Mutualization of Stock Life Insurance Companies" (Ph.D. dissertation, University of Pennsylvania, 1964).

Conversion of a Mutual Company to a Stock Company

Although relatively rare, a few mutual life insurance companies have been converted to stock companies.[15] For a period of months, **demutualization,** the conversion of a mutual life insurance company into a stock life insurance company, was one of the hottest topics in the life insurance industry. One company announced a decision to demutualize.[16] Most of the larger mutual life insurance companies said they were considering the possibility, and the topic of demutualization was discussed in articles in the trade press, major newspapers, and business magazines. Recently, interest appears to have diminished. Many major mutual life insurance companies have issued public statements indicating a lack of interest in demutualization, and articles in the press on this subject are less frequent. Even so, as deregulation of the financial services business continues, this question likely will continue to be a critical part of the long-term corporate strategy for many mutual life insurance companies. Thus, a somewhat detailed discussion of demutualization is presented.[17]

In a conversion action, the mutual life insurance company literally is transformed into a shareholder-owned enterprise through a process in which policyowner membership rights are exchanged for valuable consideration (i.e., cash, additional benefits, and/or possibly, common stock in the resulting stock company). If the company wishes to raise new equity capital (which is one of the principal reasons for a conversion action), that step may be taken at the time of conversion or at some later date. If new capital is raised on the conversion date, ownership of the company will be shared between the former policyowner-members and the new shareholders. If no new capital is raised, the former policyowner-members initially will own all the shares of the company.

In some cases, the conversion action may be taken so that the converted mutual company may be acquired by another company. In this case the consideration to policyowner-members will usually be in the form or cash of additional benefits.

The converting mutual company may wish to go through a restructuring in which an upstream holding company is created. The parent holding company would own all the shares of the converted insurance company, the policyowner-members would receive shares of the holding company, and the shares sold to the public would also be shares of the holding company.

Steps in the demutualization process involve three distinct approval phases. The first is the decision by the board of directors of the company that a conversion is important to the company's future progress *and* that the conversion plan is in the interest of policyowners. Although state legal requirements vary, the board's action usually will require approval of a super-majority of the directors.

The second approval required will usually be that of the insurance commissioner of the company's domiciliary state. The purpose is to assure that the proposed conversion plan meets the various requirements of state law, including, but not limited to, the provision for future policyowner dividends, the fairness of the total amount of the consideration to policyowners in exchange for their membership rights, the allocation of that amount among policyowners, the fairness of the amounts paid by nonpolicyowner shareholders (particularly in the case of a proposed acquisition of the company by another entity), and limitations on acquisitions of stock by officers and directors. The insurance department will probably employ actuarial, legal, investment banking, and accounting consultants to review the conversion plan and to advise the commissioner. Almost always there will be a public hearing to permit interested parties to present concurring and opposing views with respect to the proposed plan. After the hearing, the commissioner will approve the conversion plan as submitted, approve the plan with amendments, or reject the plan. Approval or at least a "nonobjection" basis by insurance regulatory authorities in other states in which the company is licensed may also be required.

---

[15]See, for example, "Memo Explaining How Mutual Life Company Switched to Stock," *The National Underwriter,* Life ed., March 27, 1965.

[16]See "Union Mutual Takes the Plunge,' *Best's Review,* Life/Health ed., Vol. 89 (January 1985), p. 30.

[17]This discussion is based on Harry D. Garber, "Demutualization—Wave of the Future or a Passing Fad?" *The Journal of the American Society of CLU,* Vol. XL (March 1986).

Once the company and the insurance commissioner have agreed on a conversion plan, it is submitted to policyowners for their approval. The degree of support required depends on state law, but a typical requirement is that two-thirds of those voting must approve the conversion plan. Before voting, all policyowners receive a comprehensive set of material describing the conversion plan and presenting the specific dollar amount of consideration, or the number of shares (or the basis on which this number would be determined) that the policyowner will receive in exchange for the surrender of his or her membership rights. If a favorable vote is received, the mutual life insurance company can then proceed with the conversion action.

A key question concerning demutualization action is how it will affect the insurance coverages of persons with participating policies. This is a complex question. It is sufficient to state that the conversion action should not have a materially adverse impact on the company's ability either to meet the policy guarantees or to pay policyowner dividends on a scale comparable to those that would have been paid in the absence of demutualization.

The primary reason a mutual life insurance company would consider demutualization is to obtain access to equity capital and related financing alternatives (convertible debentures, warrants, preferred stock). This is becoming increasingly important. As the integration of the financial services industry accelerates, the requirements for capital growth and capital investments multiply. Major capital investments must be made in (1) computer systems equipment and facilities, (2) the growth of sales and distribution capabilities, and (3) acquisitions that broaden product offerings, increase scale, bring access to new customers and new markets, and so on. Without such investments, some mutual companies could find that they would be unable to keep pace and would suffer an inevitable decline in competitive position and vitality, to the detriment of the policyowner-members.

For mutual and stock life insurance companies, the main source of equity capital has been and will continue to be retained earnings from their insurance operations. To the extent that re-

tained earnings cannot provide all the capital required (and today's competitive markets place limits on the amount of retained earnings available from existing business), companies must access the capital markets for new equity or debt funds. Stock companies have available the full range of public market financing options. Mutual companies today can obtain capital funds through debt but have very limited access to equity capital. For some mutual companies, this limited access may not be sufficient.

A second interest in demutualization could stem from the enhanced corporate structure flexibility it would permit. A basic structural advantage of the stock life insurance company form is that it permits formation of an upstream holding company. Through this mechanism the company can (1) limit the impact of insurance regulatory controls and restrictions on noninsurance operations, and (2) permit acquisitions of insurance companies to be made without diminution of statutory surplus.

The latter benefit, which may be particularly important in the present industry consolidation phase, requires a brief explanation. If a life insurance company acquires another insurance company, the excess of the purchase price over the acquired company's statutory surplus must be charged immediately to the statutory surplus of the acquiring company. If the acquisition is made by an upstream holding corporation, however, there is no charge to the statutory capital of either insurance company. As the market values of most stock life insurance companies are well in excess of their respective statutory book values, this requirement places severe limitations on the ability of mutual life insurance companies to make necessary acquisitions of stock insurance companies (both life as well as property and liability).

These are the two key reasons for a mutual company to consider demutualization. There are three other oft-mentioned reasons, which for most companies will be less important. First, stock companies report their financial results on a GAAP basis. Converting mutual companies would be able to use a comparable financial reporting basis and one that may conform much more closely to their internal management reporting basis. Second, the newly adopted federal income tax law for life insurance companies includes for mutual companies an "add on" tax element that can constitute a major share of the company's total tax. Although the federal tax savings from conversion could be significant, the converted company will probably have to pay cash dividends to shareholders that could consume all or a major part of these tax savings. Finally, availability of common stock increases compensation flexibility and permits acquisition to be done for stock and without tax consequences to the seller.

As the inexorable consolidation of the financial services industry proceeds, mutual life insurance companies will be subject to increasing competitive pressure. In anticipation of times of even greater competition, mutual companies naturally focus on those legal or structural matters that might offer significant advantages to their nonmutual competitors, and prominent among these advantages is the ability to raise equity capital and to form an upstream noninsurance holding company. It is this concern about the ability of mutual entities to compete on equal terms in the future with shareholder-owned companies that underlies the active interest of some mutual life companies in having demutualization legislation enacted. Most companies are not sure that they will ever seek to convert to stock company status, but they want to have the option available if, and when it is needed.

Having legislation on the books is one thing, deciding to demutualize is quite another. The determination of whether a company should seek to convert will be an individual company decision based on the company's position in the market, its business goals, its capital position and needs, and the likelihood and ability to achieve these goals without undertaking the wrenching course of demutualization. The analysis work required for such a decision is burdensome and ordinarily will not be undertaken unless it is believed to be necessary.

If, as expected, future developments in the financial services marketplace tighten competition further and increase capital demands, more mutual life insurance companies will be required to consider seriously whether conversion represents a necessary strategic action.

LIFE INSURERS IN THE FINANCIAL SERVICES INDUSTRY [18]

The financial services industry consists of those organizations involved in saving, lending, managing, or transferring money. Insurance companies are included in this industry. Life insurance company pricing principles have caused the industry, almost by accident, to be in the savings business.

As a result of its accidental participation in the financial services marketplace, most life insurance companies have only recently considered themselves in competition with other sectors of the financial services industry. Given the fact that the marketplace may appear to be more rational and orderly than it actually is, and given that the insurance industry is a relatively new participant in the financial services industry, what impact will this have on the marketing of life and health insurance?

The insurance business has been changing rapidly despite the rigidity of its regulatory structure. Other financial industries have been able to compete with the insurance companies in risk management, even though they are prohibited from entering the insurance market directly.

While some noninsurance financial service companies have entered the insurance business through acquisitions, for the most part this has been done through marketing arrangements or partnerships. This is due partly to regulatory restrictions, but it also can make good business sense, since the jury is still out as to whether some of these arrangements really make sense. Partnerships—whether product supply arrangements or shared compensation arrangements for referrals—are easier to enter and exit than full-fledged acquisitions and tend to involve heavy elements of variable rather than fixed costs.

Insurance company experimentation with other channels of distribution, whether financial service companies or others, involve either product supply arrangements or some form of shared compensation arrangement. Product supply arrange-

---

[18]This overview draws from Robert Carlson, "The Evolving Life Industry," in *The Emerging Financial Industry,* Arnold W. Sametz, ed. (Lexington, Mass.: Lexington Books, D. C. Heath and Company, 1984), pp. 29–32.

ments are proliferating. Stockbrokerage sales of annuities and single-premium life are the only clear successes to date. But considerable experimentation is taking place with banks, thrifts, and retailers, and even with real estate brokers and other entities using their own sales representatives to sell certain—mostly demand-oriented—insurance products. In other instances, where the partner is either unable to sell the insurance product directly for regulatory reasons or does not wish to build its own agency force, various compensation arrangements have evolved, such as customer list purchase fees, agent-in-lobby rentals, shared commissions in return for referrals, and so on. Such arrangements presume that the sponsorship of the outside party will so enhance the insurance agent's ability to prospect that additional aggregate compensation will be sufficient to compensate the partner and still add to the agent's income.

Some believe that insurance companies are on the verge of vast change because, in effect, all financial business today deals with the management of risk and many established companies plan to offer all products/services to cope with both pure and speculative risk. Given the basic risk management expertise, asset size, and relative stability of its cash flows, some believe that the average insurance company is more capable

of successful evolution in these directions than is the average bank or securities firm. A diversified insurance company might be able to offer many banking and security services without handling customer deposits or securities per se. One expert concluded: "The insurance industry. . .lagged behind other entrants in the financial market wars of the 1970s. However, like the battleship, once it comes about and gets on course, it will prove to be a formidable competitor in all financial service markets."[19]

Others have a somewhat different perspective. They suggest that to the extent that the largest life and health insurance companies broaden their portfolio and become full-service financial service institutions, there is a legitimate question as to their ability to manage the kind of diversity that will emerge as organizations begin owning widely different kinds of companies. It will be interesting to observe the changing financial services scene in the next few years.[20]

[19]Henry Kaufman, "The New Financial Environment," in *The Emerging Financial Industry,* pp. 18–19.

[20]For an excellent review of the changing financial services marketplace, see Alan Gart, *Banks, Thrifts, and Insurance Companies—Surviving the 1980's* (Lexington, Mass.: Lexington Books, D. C. Heath and Company, 1985).

Chapter 30

Marketing Life and Health Insurance

The degree to which a life insurance company succeeds reflects the consolidated effort of all the activities of the organization. As was pointed out in Chapter 29, these activities may be classified into three major functional areas: marketing, investment, and administration. Of these three major areas, marketing is the largest in terms of both personnel requirements and costs. Effective marketing, that is, the provision of appropriate products to consumers through an effective distribution system, is critical to the well-being of a life insurance company. It assures an adequate volume of new business at reasonable cost.[1]

If a company's effort is to be successful, however, management must see that a proper relationship exists among all home-office functions. Each home-office executive who is responsible for a particular functional department must understand the role of his or her department in the marketing process and its contribution to the objectives of marketing as overall company goals.

DEVELOPING AND MAINTAINING A MARKETING PROGRAM

The development and maintenance of a realistic marketing program is the primary responsibility of senior marketing executives. Each company has its own unique definition of desired markets, distribution systems, and products. The elements of a marketing program include an analysis of the markets available to or desired by the company, identification of the nature of the perceived competition, and determination of the distribution techniques to be used by the company.[2] A marketing plan must also include the design of a sales compensation system, a basic pricing strategy, and the special administrative systems and support needed by particular market segments or products. For example, universal life (UL) and variable life (VL) are computer-intensive products demanding systems development far beyond normal administrative systems. The marketing plan is then utilized to develop a product portfolio and project future production by product and amount.

---

[1] Richard T. Mauer, et al., "In Search of Marketing Excellence," *MarketFacts*, Vol. 2 (October 1983), pp. 8–23.

[2] Richard L. Hall, "Blueprint for Marketing Research," *MarketFacts*, Vol. 3 (November 1984), pp. 6–11.

Once the company marketing plan is initially documented, management must evaluate the company's basic goals with respect to growth and profit and the capabilities of the home office and marketing operations. If there were no limit to the availability of capital, manpower, and expertise, management could simply decide what to achieve and proceed to do it. In reality, however, the marketing plan must reflect the realistic growth and profit objectives of the company and the capabilities of the home office and marketing support organizations. The marketing plan should reflect a realistic assessment of the particular strengths and weaknesses of the organization in relation to those factors considered critical to the success of the marketing plan. It is this assessment that leads to broad or narrow product portfolios, different distribution system structures, geographic concentration, and so on—the search for competitive advantages. It also should be noted that with the current emphasis on rates of return and separate account business such as variable life, close coordination with the investment function is essential.[3]

The results of this planning and development activity will be a quantification of what the company wants to achieve, reflecting a balance between long-term and short-term goals. With priorities established, specific goals set down, and a product portfolio established, the stage is set, theoretically, for selecting and utilizing one or more distribution systems to deliver the products developed. Typically, however, the distribution system comes first and the tentative decisions regarding distribution systems significantly influence the process of developing a product portfolio.

The management of the distribution system(s) selected (or those already in place) traditionally has constituted the major operational responsibility of senior marketing management. In some large companies today, however, the distribution and manufacturing functions are being separated, with each being run as a profit center under a senior marketing officer.

Most students of the industry agree that marketing systems utilizing career agents have been responsible for the widespread acceptance of life insurance.[4] Career agents have been and are a vital force in the development of the industry. Per capita coverages in various countries suggest that those that have emphasized career agent systems excell others by a large margin. Japan, the United States, and Canada lead the world in relative life insurance in force and are leaders in employing forms of career systems.[5]

In part because of the success of those systems utilizing career agents, competing systems have developed. In fact, a number of systems might not be feasible unless the basic career agency system survives and flourishes. Some systems serve special markets or provide special products. Others provide portfolios to almost everyone. Indeed, there are many systems for distributing life and health insurance—surprisingly many. Before examining the distribution management process, it might be helpful to review the various distribution systems extant in the life insurance industry today.

DISTRIBUTION SYSTEMS

The individual life and health insurance business in the United States has two distinct distribution systems: (1) agency and (2) direct response.[6] Figure 30–1 shows these two systems, along with the various subsystems.

Direct response marketing is a broad term for the practice of contacting potential customers without the use of a salesperson. In a direct response sale, no commissions are paid to an agent, since the buyer responds directly to the company because of solicitation via mail, broad-

---

[3]The matching of assets and liabilities is a critical element of the investment process today. See Chapter 31.

[4]See, for example, J. O. Stalson, *Marketing Life Insurance: Its History in America* (Cambridge, Mass.: Harvard University Press, 1942).

[5]See Chapter 3.

[6]This overview is based on Archer L. Edgar, "Distribution Systems," *Marketing for Actuaries—Individual Life and Health, SOA Part 9 Study Note* (Hartford, Conn.: LIMRA, 1984), pp. VIIII-1 to VIII-6.

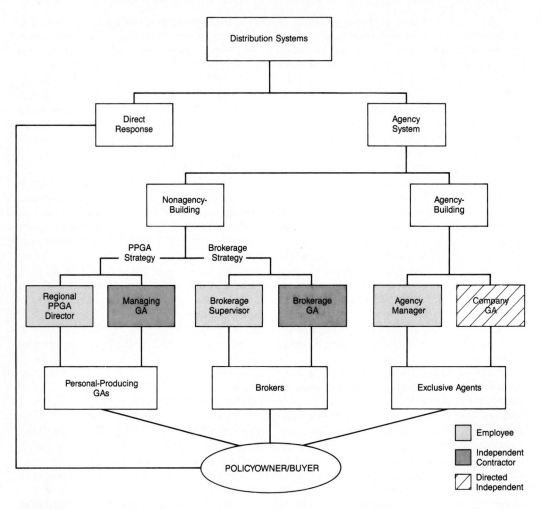

FIGURE 30-1. Source: *Marketing for Actuaries—Individual Life and Health* (Hartford, Conn.: LIMRA, 1984), pp. viii-2.

cast media, coupons, and so on.[7] Although direct response marketing is growing rapidly, it is still estimated to account for only 2 percent of life insurance sales and slightly more of health insurance sales.

The **agency system** may be viewed as comprising two types: (1) agency-building companies and (2) nonagency-building companies. It includes the network of agents or producers that include:

[7]In certain states, under existing counter-signature laws, an agent is involved in direct response insurance transactions.

1. Life-only agents (exclusive, full-time agents and independent, full-time personal producers who represent more than one company)

2. Property and liability agents who also write life insurance (exclusive agents and independents representing more than one company)

3. Life agents who also write property and liability insurance

4. Other entities that utilize client relationships to sell life insurance-related products (e.g., real estate agency offering mortgage protection insurance, automobile dealer offering credit life and

health insurance, or a stock brokerage firm offering annuity or life products)

Independent life insurance agents, independent property and liability agents, stockbrokers, realtors, and similar producers are commonly known as "brokers." The term "broker," as loosely used in the U.S. lexicon of life insurance distribution, describes a relationship between the producers and the insurer and not the producer-client relationship as in non-life insurance, where the broker usually represents the client rather than any insurer.

Within each of the primary distribution systems, a variety of selling techniques is employed. For example, companies have attempted to reach large numbers of prospects at the workplace through payroll deduction plans. More recently, experiments to make the agent more accessible, such as being located in supermarkets and retail stores, have attempted to capture walk-in trade. Similarly, a number of companies have made arrangements to offer their products at banking locations. In all these cases, a salesperson of some kind, compensated either by salary or by commissions, is involved in the sale.

A given company's distribution strategy may involve direct response, agency system, or both. Within the agency system, the company may distribute its products through producers with whom it has an "exclusive" selling agreement, or it may offer its products through any available producers without them being required to represent that company exclusively.

Companies using the agency-building strategy (also referred to as exclusive-agent or career-agent companies) recruit, finance, train, and house agents to represent them, often on an exclusive basis. Those using the nonagency-building strategies usually do not finance, train, or house the agents who represent them. Instead, they provide products to round out the portfolios of other companies' exclusive agents and of other independent producing outlets. Consequently, marketing strategy in nonagency-building companies involves gaining access to and maintaining relationships with producers whose primary affiliations and sometimes occupations are with others.

Agency-Building Subsystems [8]

Two well-recognized marketing structures are used within the agency-building system: **general agencies** and **branch offices.** General agencies are headed by individuals referred to as general agents (GAs) who are appointed by the home office and have a status akin to that of independent contractors. Usually, expense allowances are paid to cover such items as rent, clerical help, travel, postage, telephone, and the general agent is responsible for the financial management of the agency. Under the branch office structure, agencies are headed by agency managers—employees who carry out the assignments of the home office and are directly supervised by the home office in the financial management of the agency.

The General Agency System. The general agency system, which in its pure form is only theoretical today, is the oldest of the systems and aims to accomplish through general agents what the managerial system is designed to do through branch offices. The company-appointed general agent represented it within a designated territory over which he or she was given control, and by contract, the company agreed to pay the agency a stipulated commission on the first year's premiums plus a renewal on subsequent premiums. In return, the general agent agreed to build the company's business in a given territory. The general agent might pay his or her agents all of the agency's first year's commission plus a renewal somewhat smaller than the one he or she received from the company, or the general agent might pay all the commission on the first year's premium and retain the renewals, or again, he or she might retain a portion of the commission on both the first year's premium and the renewals. The difference between what the general agent received from the company and the amount paid to agents was (and still is) known as an override or overriding commission.

Although formerly the case, today the general agent no longer is directly responsible for

[8]See George G. Joseph and Archer L. Edgar, "No Funeral for the Agency System," *MarketFacts,* Vol. 2 (May 1983), pp. 18–21.

the collection of premiums and interest on loans, the receipt of loan applications and proofs of loss, and other clerical work that arises naturally in connection with insurance sold in his or her territory. Routine matters of this nature usually are handled by a separate group of persons, located in the general agent's office or in separate offices throughout the country, directly responsible to the home office. An arrangement of this nature relieves the general agent of details not directly related to production and at the same time offers the advantages that accrue from close contacts with such matters. It is also now common for the company to pay the office rent directly. This is done to discourage the closing of the office, leaving the company without representation. In addition, companies now make payment of substantial nonvouchered amounts titled "expense reimbursement allowances." These and other changes discussed below have led to GAs being called "directed independents."

It should also be noted that while agents' contracts formerly were made with the general agent and not with the company, this is no longer the case. Even in the pure general agency contract, where the company, theoretically, has no control over the appointment of agents, the company usually specifies the form of contract to be used and reserves the right to reject agency appointments.

Two classes of general agencies exist: (1) those in which the general agent relies chiefly on personal business for his or her main profit and considers the income derived from subagents of minor importance,[9] and (2) those in which the general agent subordinates his or her personal business and aims to develop a large force of subagents, with a view to deriving his or her chief profit from the commission overrides on the business of these agents. In the first class, the general agent will consider personal business of greatest importance and will select only those prospective applicants that he or she can handle with minimal supervision and support. Needless to say, such an agency is not as advantageous to subagents as the second class, where although the general agent

may obtain some personal business, he or she will nevertheless promote the welfare of his or her agents in preference to personal business.

The Managerial System. As contrasted with the general agency system, the managerial system is utilized by the largest companies. It is characterized by branch offices in various locations, each headed by an agency manager. The agency manager, who is a company employee, is usually selected because of his or her success as an agent, is charged with the responsibility of securing and directing agents within a given territory, and of instructing and otherwise helping and encouraging them in their work as solicitors.

As in the case of home-office employees, the agency manager, cashiers, and clerks at the branch office are paid by salary. The agency manager's compensation is composed of a base salary, which usually is relatively small, and an incentive element based on his or her performance. Much of the incentive portion is related to the amount of new production; these are additional payments (bonuses) for desirable performance, such as increasing the volume of business through his or her office, for adding to the number of productive agents, for maintaining good persistency, or for operating in a cost-effective manner.

Agency managers may be assisted by assistant managers, supervisors, specialists, unit managers, or district managers. Assistants are responsible for specific functions or for units of agents or may provide overall assistance to the head of the agency.

The cashier or office manager is particularly important in the branch office system. He or she is expected to keep all office records; to look after all correspondence in connection with applications and policies; to assist in filing proofs of loss, applications for policy loans, and payment of cash values on surrenders; to answer all communications from policyowners that are not of sufficient importance to be referred to the home office; and to supervise the clerical staff.

Agency-building systems, either general agency or managerial, are also used by *fraternal* organizations that offer life and health insurance to their members. The agents of such religious or social groups offer individual policies to the members of the association.

---

[9]This type of arrangement is really a nonagency-building strategy and has evolved into a separate, significant marketing system. See p. 522.

Two additional subsets of the agency-building system are multiple-line exclusive agent and combination operations. Agents in **multiple-line exclusive-agent** operations sell only the life and health and property and liability insurance products of one group of affiliated companies. Historically, most of these companies were rural operations that grew out of state farm bureaus. As contrasted with other career systems, agencies within this system normally are one-person operations with only clerical support supplementing the agent's personal sales effort.

Combination or **home service systems** also have been known as "industrial" and "debit" operations.[10] The unique characteristic of this operation is the assignment of a definite geographic territory to agents. At one time agents also collected renewal premiums on business in force in the territory, but the collection aspect is being deemphasized by some companies today.

Originally, much of this business was industrial insurance with weekly home collections. Today, an increasing proportion of the business sold is ordinary insurance (hence "combination") and is on a monthly or less frequent basis. The territory is becoming a sales territory, as less of the business requires collection of premiums by the agent. The activities of agents in this system usually are more closely supervised than in the others.

Nonagency-Building Subsystems

The two most common subsets of the nonagency building subsystem are (1) brokerage and (2) personal-producing general agents (PPGAs). As pointed out above, companies that market through nonexclusive-agent strategies provide products or services to agents who are already engaged in life insurance selling. Thus, the key to this strategy is to gain access to the producer. Retaining the producer's loyalty is accomplished by service, compensation, and personal relationships. The method of access to the producer, compensation agreements, and marketing philosophy differ between brokerage and PPGA companies.

Brokerage. Brokerage companies gain access to producers through a company employee, a **brokerage supervisor,** who acts as a "manufacturer's representative," or through an independent **brokerage general agent,** who performs the same function. Both of these individuals are authorized to appoint brokers on behalf of the company. Direct contracting in response to trade press advertising is also used.

Brokerage has many variations, depending on the orientation of the company. Some life companies seek surplus or rated business from the agents of other companies; some find product niches; others seek life business from independent life producers. Some life affiliates of property and liability companies sell life insurance through independent insurance agencies associated with the property and liability parent. Still others sell through financial institutions, stockbrokers, realtors, automobile dealers, and financial consultants. Since all of these producers may represent several companies, the sale to the producing agency precedes the product sale. Here the company's brokerage supervisor plays the key role.

At one time, companies utilizing a brokerage strategy and selling through independent life agents and representatives of other companies specialized in term and substandard business. Today, the range of products for which companies using the brokerage strategy compete has broadened to include almost all lines of insurance. Innovative products, pricing, commissions and service are the competitive tools involved.

This full-product-line orientation has encouraged a separation between *manufacturing* and *distribution* and has spawned a variation of brokerage in which an exclusive-agent company formally acts as distributor for a product of another company, the manufacturer. In this home-office-to-home-office arrangement, the distributing company acts as a brokerage general agent and its agents act as brokers for the manufacturing company in product lines where the distributing company may either be noncompetitive or simply not wish to offer a particular product.

[10]Bruce C. Dalzell, "Unlocking the Future of Combination Company Business," *MarketFacts,* Vol. 4 (July 1985), pp. 18–27. See also Robert A. Marshall, "Home Service Marketing," in *Marketing Life and Health Insurance,* Nancy E. Strickler, ed., (Atlanta, Ga: Life Office Management Association, 1981), pp. 321–351.

Another variation of this strategy has been the development of the noncompany affiliated "marketing organization" that is both independent and virtually totally self-supporting. Under its contracts, it receives maximum compensation with virtually no market support services. Such organizations are true independent marketing organizations.

Personal-Producing General Agent (PPGA).

PPGA companies gain access to producers through an organizational structure parallel to the one in brokerage companies: (1) company-employed regional directors of PPGAs, (2) independent contractors—managing general agents, and (3) direct contracting with individuals identified through trade press advertising. Both regional directors and managing general agents are authorized to appoint PPGAs.

The PPGA strategy has gained in importance in recent years.[11] In the more traditional regional director approach, experienced life agents are hired under contracts that provide both direct and overriding commissions plus some type of expense allowance. For this, the PPGAs supply their own office facilities and receive technical assistance in the form of computer services and advanced sales support. It is not uncommon for personal-producing general agents to have contracts with more than one company. The managing general agent approach typically specializes in single products, such as universal life or disability income, and is essentially franchised to appoint PPGAs for the company in a territory.

Although there are philosophical differences in approach, the clear difference at the producer level between the independent contractor brokerage strategy and the independent contractor PPGA strategy is in the commission schedule. The former resembles an agent contract and the latter has elements of a general agent contract. It is important to note that both strategies can operate simultaneously in the same company along with others.

Direct Response System[12]

A growing proportion of life and health insurance sales is made without the use of an agent. Although aggregate sales are still relatively small, interest in this strategy is increasing. Few insurance companies market their products solely by direct response methods, but many utilize both the agency marketing system and the direct response marketing system. These companies may offer some of the same coverages through both marketing systems. The principal differences to the consumer for certain products can be one of cost and service. The same level of coverage sold through an agent may sometimes cost more than when sold through an efficient direct response marketing program, but, of course, the potential exists for greater personal service if an agent is involved in the transaction.

The life and health insurance sold by direct response marketing is usually not sold as basic coverage, but essentially is supplemental in nature (i.e., it helps to fill the gaps in basic coverages). The products are not complex. They normally are easy to understand, require relatively small premium outlays, and are serviced through the economies of computerized solicitation, issuance, and administration. Comprehensive life and health insurance protection, annuities, estate planning, and so on, do not readily lend themselves to direct response marketing methods, and generally require the services of a professional agent. It should be noted, however, that where direct response marketing effort is directed to a select group of consumers under a *sponsored arrangement,* it can offer a broader range of relatively complex products. At least one company sells automobile insurance, cash value life insurance, and even tax shelters to its customer base very effectively.

Regardless of how the sale has been completed, by an agent or direct response marketing, from that point on the client frequently deals with the company on a direct basis. The premium

[11]Paul H. McClain, "The State of the PPGA Union," *Market-Facts,* Vol. 3 (August 1984), pp. 14–18; see also Archer L. Edgar, *U.S. PPGA and Brokerage Distribution Strategies: An Overview* (Hartford, Conn.: LIMRA, 1984).

[12]This section draws from Gerald F. Bevan and Colin S. Braybrooks, "The Sale of Insurance through the Mail," *Journal of the American Society of Chartered Life Underwriters,* Vol. XXXVI (January 1982), pp. 18–26. See also Kenneth C. Otis, II, and William J. Ruth, Jr., "Direct Response Marketing," in *Marketing Life and Health Insurance,* pp. 352–376.

notices are sent by mail. The premiums are paid by mail, and at times, claims often are filed and benefit checks delivered by mail. In this sense the direct response concept—whereby the company deals directly with the consumer—is not restricted to a few direct response specialty companies, but is a concept common to all elements of the business of insurance.

Direct mail is the oldest and probably the best known method of direct response marketing. It is dependent on the availability of mailing lists that may be rented from a large number of sources. As this method has been refined through the years with the aid of computerization, lists can be created that are very specific as to the demographics of the individuals who make up the lists.

Newspaper, magazine, and broadcast (radio/TV) advertising reach large numbers of consumers, but only on a very broad basis. In terms of total numbers reached, broadcast advertising surpasses all other media. Direct response marketing use of television, utilizing well-known personalities as sponsors, is growing each year, for two reasons. First, the audience is staggering in its potential. Second, direct response specialists have learned how to reach, on an efficient basis, specialized groups of viewers. Despite this interface, however, no way has yet been devised to have an application completed and thus the sales transaction finalized.

The key to understanding the direct response system of marketing lies in a knowledge of the specialized advertising techniques used in this marketing method. The NAIC identified three broad types or categories of health insurance advertisements in its 1974 Accident and Sickness Advertising Model Rules and Guidelines that provide a helpful framework for understanding these advertising approaches. As defined in the NAIC Guidelines, these categories are as follows:

1. *Institutional advertisement:* "an advertisement having as its purpose the promotion of the reader's or viewer's interest in the concept of (accident and sickness) insurance, or the promotion of the insurer."

2. *Invitation to inquire:* "an advertisement having as its objective the creation of a desire to inquire fur-

ther about the product and which is limited to a brief description of the loss for which the benefit is payable." Such an advertisement may include the amount of benefit payable, and/or the period of time during which the benefit is payable. It may not refer to the cost of the coverage. It is obvious that this is the type of advertisement that is most suited to broadcast advertising, wherein the listener or viewer is encouraged to seek from the company further information about the product.

3. *Invitation to contract:* "an advertisement which is neither an invitation to inquire nor an institutional advertisement." Such an advertisement will contain all the information necessary to make a decision to purchase—including an application form—so that the consumer can make and carry out the decision to purchase the insurance product.

The NAIC advertising rules and regulations provide very detailed stipulations as to the content of the advertisements, particularly those that are invitations to contract. Limitations and exclusions must be clearly set forth, and deceptive words or phrases may not be used. Some states require approval of every advertisement prior to use.

The prevalent direct response media in use today (direct mail, print, and broadcast) have begun to make greater use of the emerging medium of *telemarketing*—the use of the telephone to improve life and health insurance sales. The importance of this medium is evidenced by the proliferation of toll-free numbers. Telemarketing is a high-unit-cost medium. However, justification for this higher cost is found in relatively high response rates. Telemarketing is also personal once a consumer makes the initial phone call. Personalization and mass marketing are combined in telemarketing, improving marketing effectiveness.

Advocates of direct response marketing believe that direct response insurance marketing and the traditional agency system are compatible. They point out that they complement each other by making available a maximum amount of insurance coverage to a maximum number of people. Each system tends to concentrate on different segments of the marketplace—direct response reaching essentially the supplemental market and agents servicing the more complex markets.

Group Insurance Distribution

The group department of a typical company markets its products through its general agencies or branch offices and through brokers and employee benefit consultants. The sales department is headed by an executive officer (group sales vice-president) responsible for the sale and service of the product. While some group insurance, usually the smaller cases, is sold by a company's own career agents, group sales more commonly follow the brokerage model with group representatives calling on independent benefit consultants, national brokerage houses, independent property and liability agencies, and agents of other companies. Sales to the larger-case employer-employee and association markets tend to be made through specialized brokers or, in some instances, written directly with the employer. Many of the recent developments in distribution systems reflect a continuing effort to find more effective ways to deliver insurance products to larger numbers of customers.

In addition to group insurance, per se, various forms of **mass marketing** have developed, frequently involving an agent. Association group, credit-card solicitations, and payroll deduction efforts are good examples. While association group and credit-card solicitations are direct response techniques, generally an agent is involved in the association group business. Supplementary coverage like payroll deduction (salary allotment) is a form of mass marketing, sponsored by the employer. Just as innovations in products continue (leveraged by the financial environment and changing technology) marketing distribution systems will respond interactively with all present and evolving systems. This process should become even more innovative as distribution increasingly is separated from manufacturing and made a specific profit center.[13]

AGENCY MANAGEMENT [14]

As pointed out earlier, the agency system is the most widely used distribution system and accounts for the bulk of the premium income generated by the insurance industry. Distribution outlets exist in at least all of the major cities in which a company operates. These outlets, headed by an agency manager (general agent or branch manager), represent the life insurance industry's main contact with consumers. Effective field management is essential to those systems employing an agency force.

The Agency Manager

An agency head's basic responsibility is to manage resources to achieve the common objectives of the agency and the company. In terms of activities, the duties of the agency head consist of (1) manpower development, including product and sales skills training; (2) supervision of the field force; (3) motivation of agents and staff; (4) business management activities (e.g., office duties, public relations activities, interpreting company policy, and expense control); and (5) personal production.

Personal production by the agency head has a *very low priority* in agency-building companies. Although it is permitted, the need for growth and the design of the agency manager's compensation formula both mitigate against significant activity of this type.

Agency Development.[15] Recruiting is the process by which the number of full-time career agents in the individual agencies is not only maintained but expanded. Recruiting is not one activity but a process, the steps of which include (1) finding sources of prospective agents, (2) determining acceptable qualifications, (3) approaching prospective agents, (4) using selection tools, (5) interviewing the candidate, and (6) contracting with qualified individuals. The manager usually attempts to locate a number (three to five) of pros-

---

[13]See Chapters 26 and 27 for a comprehensive discussion of group insurance.

[14]This section draws on Phillip R. Pepper, "Field Management," in *Marketing Life and Health Insurance*, pp. 399–424.

[15]See Steven M. Brown, "State-of-the-Art Agent Selection," *MarketFacts*, Vol. 2 (April 1983), pp. 6–11.

pective agents at one time. Since there is always fallout in the selection process, the group technique usually allows some recruits to be added to the agency from each recruiting effort. Recruiting a group rather than one agent at a time is also a more efficient use of a field manager's time.

Considerable effort has been made in raising the standards for new agents and in increasing their productivity. Most companies have become increasingly careful in their selection of new agents. They also devote much attention to the training of their agents in the nature and uses of life and health insurance and sales methods.

In view of the broad range of interest-sensitive and traditional products on the market today, the agency manager has a significant challenge in training an agency force adequately. Agency managers do, however, have access to a wealth of training materials. In addition to that made available by the agency manager's own company, a wide array of material is available from industry associations and commercial publishers. The agency manager must also maintain an appropriate and effective continuing education program for all agents, both those recently established and those who are experienced professionals.

Supervision of the Agency Force. The level of supervision provided for agents is a function of the agent's experience and length of service. Close supervision is particularly helpful to a new agent until he or she develops good work habits and feels comfortable in the working relationship with the supervisor. Experience has shown that agents react positively to supervision where they (1) are told what to expect at the outset, (2) view the supervision as helpful in improving their performance, and (3) help set the objectives against which they will be measured. Most agency managers have a practice of having some form of communication with each of their agents every day. The relationship that develops between an agent and the manager (supervisor) is an important factor in the success or failure of a new agent.

In the sales management process, an agency manager provides the stimulus to make an agent feel motivated to take action that results in sales and related goals. Agency managers demonstrate personal interest in each agent, use formal in-depth reviews and group meetings, encourage attendance at industry organization meetings, provide special office privileges, and conduct sales contests, all to create an environment in which agents will feel motivated. Each of these motivational activities is intended to demonstrate to and cause each agent to perceive the concern of the agency manager for his or her welfare and thus stimulate the agent to higher production.

Business Management. In addition to these basic activities, the agency manager also must carry out a number of normal business management activities, including office duties, public relations activities, expense control, and interpreting company policy. Whether the agency is a "scratch" agency or an established one, the agency manager must be or quickly become a highly organized person because the job is so unstructured. As the agency grows, the agency manager must develop second-line management and must delegate those functions for which his or her personal involvement is not essential. Otherwise, the agency manager will be unable to give adequate personal attention to those matters that are critical to the success of the agency.

Management Compensation

Basic Approach. The agency manager is compensated for services according to the terms and conditions of a written compensation contract. In general agency companies, the typical agreement provides for a scale of commissions (sometimes called first-year override) based on the first-year premiums for new business and a separate scale or scales to be applied to premiums paid in the second and subsequent policy years (a renewal override). In addition, the general agent receives expense reimbursement allowances based on first-year premiums and, in many cases, a renewal expense allowance.

In managerial companies, the compensation typically is an annual salary based on an incentive compensation formula applied to the previous (sometimes current) year's agency production. Most companies design their formula to achieve specific objectives. For example, some companies pay extra compensation to the agency manager based on the production of each new career agent for that agent's first two or three years, and others pay a bonus for new gains in manpower. Some companies pay a bonus when annual production exceeds that of the previous year. Still others offer bonuses based on persistency targets or improvements in agency persistency. Regardless of the particular contract that a company may offer to an agency manager, the job of building a "career shop" is such that the contracts differ only in the emphasis that is placed on individual elements of the job. Normally, expense experience is reflected specifically as an aspect of managerial compensation.

Current Developments. A number of interesting developments are taking place in management compensation. First, a minimum agency size, or the ability to attain some optimum or cost-effective stage is becoming a standard requirement. This is vital to a successful agency operation, but arriving at that effective stage depends on a number of unrelated events. However, it is important to recognize that size per se will not ensure agency success. Sufficient capitalization and sound business judgment and management are also major facets of business life today.

The margins available to provide management compensation and/or expense absorption are shrinking. The per unit payment on products delivered has been steadily declining, and this can be offset only by increased productivity. There is also a need to invest in technological advances to improve cost performance and provide needed agent support. High utilization is essential to permit recovery of technology costs. An agency must be able to afford to purchase technology and must be large enough to make its use profitable.

Managerial companies almost always absorb expenses through an expense management formula. This formula credits or charges the manager, based on the relationship between actual costs and a standard tied to production. These are often capped or limited, but the net impact on the manager's income can be significant. Efforts are now under way to link compensation directly to agency profitability (e.g., penalize agency head compensation for loans on in-force business).

Traditionally, a distinguishing characteristic of a general agency operation has been the value of future renewal commissions built up as deferred compensation either as a retirement program or a factor contributing toward a retirement program. This feature of a general agent's contract has been almost sacred. It is being reconsidered in light of changing conditions. The fact is that the renewals can be wiped out by the replacement of existing business either now, with newer products paying less or nothing, or later, when nothing can be done to offset their disappearance. In the long run, the answer may well be a formal retirement program.

As the field office administers a broader range of financial products, the agency head must provide increasing management support and expertise. The traditional line organization is being replaced by a *functional emphasis.* Thus, an agency might have a brokerage specialist, specialists in various product lines, or technical support persons in specialized areas. This meets a number of current needs but also creates problems for the agency and the company.

A functional manager can be effective and can provide a return on investment more quickly than a line supervisor. The training time is virtually nonexistent, since the individual is employed because expertise is already present. In addition, functional managers are less likely to be sought after by other companies and thus are less likely to want to leave.

Functional management does, however, create company problems. Functional management is specialization management. Companies need a pool of potential managers for future growth, and functional management does not produce additional first-line supervisors and agency managers. The transition from specialization to generalization is needed to satisfy the company's need for new and additional managers; this is relatively more difficult than in the typical line organization.

Agent Compensation

Basic Approach. Agents are hired and compensated by the company. A significant portion of the agent's contract is devoted to the compensation that he or she is to receive.[16] Agents' compensation is usually on a commission basis, calling for a high commission on the first year's premium and a much smaller commission on future premiums. The contract provides for the **vesting** of renewal commissions if the agent achieves certain levels of production or completes a minimum period of service, such as five, 10, 15, or perhaps 20 years.[17]

In recognition of the service an agent is called on to give long after the renewal commissions have expired, many companies pay a **service fee,** which commences after renewals stop and continues as long as the agent remains with the company and the policy stays in force. The service fee is a small percentage, usually 2 or 3 percent, and almost never vests in the agent.

Many companies also pay additional commissions or bonuses based on satisfactory production (commissions, premiums, or volume) or persistency, or a combination of both. The presence and nature of such additional compensation vary widely and is a function of the philosophy of the company involved. In addition to direct compensation, fringe benefits such as retirement, life, health, and disability insurance benefits are provided by many companies.

Typically, life insurance companies that are licensed to do business in New York State pay agents' compensation equal to 100 percent of a level annual premium, which is divided into a first-year commission of 50 to 55 percent, with the total of renewal commissions equaling the balance. The renewals may be equal in amount or concentrated into three or four unequal installments. If the company does not do business in New York State, total agents' compensation is usually larger.

Under a straight-commission contract, the agent earns nothing until he or she makes sales. As a result, a new agent has to draw on another source of income until his or her commissions build to a reasonable level. It has become common today for companies to finance a new agent's first months or years in the business.[18] Financing plans differ widely but may be illustrated in general terms. For example, the **drawing-account approach** simply means that the new agent is extended credit by the company on a stipulated weekly or monthly basis, or as he or she needs it. In most cases, the agent must pay the money back as he or she is able, and usually even if he or she terminates his or her contract. In some contracts, however, part of the advance is considered a subsidy.

Many companies agree to provide a stipulated salary against which any commissions earned are credited. Subject, usually, to certain minimum production or validation requirements, the agent may continue under this plan for a period up to, say, three years. In most companies, he or she may go off the plan at any time he or she chooses. If the agent leaves the company, he or she is usually not responsible for any debit balance outstanding. Other financing plans provide decreasing salary and pay part or all of the commissions from the beginning. The variations are almost infinite. But in any case, it should be remembered that regardless of the financing plan, an agent must sell life insurance to make a living selling life insurance.

The agent's contract may contain provisions regulating the territory in which the agent must operate (usually only in combination or home service companies); his or her duties in the collection of premiums; his or her authority to alter or change the insurance contract; the maintenance and ownership of books or records; and numerous other provisions relating to the various things that might arise while the agent is devoting time and energy to the sale of life and health insurance.

Current Developments. [19] Compensation plans increasingly include *minimum production* com-

---

[16]For a survey of research by the Life Insurance Agency Management Association relating to field compensation, see *1985 LIMRA Research* (Hartford, Conn.: LIMRA, 1985). See also Paul D. Laporte, "Fees for Services: Fiction?" *Market-Facts,* Vol. 2 (May 1983), pp. 6–17.

[17]Vesting refers to the ownership of the renewals. Practically, vested renewals means that the agent's renewals will continue to be paid even if he or she terminates his or her connection with the company.

[18]Losses are usually shared to varying degrees by the company and the general agent or manager. See Paul D. Laporte, "Financing the New Agent," *Marketing for Actuaries—Individual Life and Health,* pp. XII-1 to XII-10.

[19]Richard B. Hopkins, "Field Compensation: Where Are We Headed?" *MarketFacts,* Vol. 2 (March 1983), pp. 18–21.

ponents. Today, neither the company nor the individual agency can afford to provide support and service to producers who do not sell enough business. There is increasing recognition that the rising costs of the traditional support areas plus the significant price of new technology needed to deliver today's products require acceptable production levels. Small agencies and small producers often cannot be supported in light of current competitive conditions and the cost of benefit programs.

More and more companies are imposing minimum production requirements as a requisite to receive certain defined supports, such as housing or clerical assistance or even retention of the contract itself with attendant benefit programs. Some companies are even correlating the benefits available to the level of production.

Life insurance companies and agency managers recognize an obligation to provide reasonably competitive products if they are to expect an agent to place all or most all of his or her business through the agency and with the company. High levels of individual performance make a producer very profitable to the company. This profit can—and increasingly is—shared with successful producers through **bonus arrangements.** There are restraints on bonuses, especially for those companies operating in New York State, but significant and meaningful bonuses can be developed even within New York regulatory limitations.[20]

Another area of current interest in agent compensation is the **leveling of commissions.** This approach can minimize the loss incurred on business not in force for a long enough period of time. Level commissions also can compensate the agent more in line with the long-term service requirements of new types of products. An increase in the use of level commissions is anticipated with some of the new products (e.g., universal life) that readily lend themselves to this approach. This leveling would have particular impact on agents and brokers who specialize in such level commissioned products.

In connection with the use of level commissions, ongoing service requirements cause two concerns. First, there is the need, with attendant cost, to provide for transferability of the level renewals (or part of them) to a new, assigned agent. Ongoing service is considered a key requirement for some newer products. Second, there is increasing discussion of separating policy service and client service. There are no clear definitions of what these functions mean to the agent and more important, to the client. This whole area is acknowledged to be a difficult administrative problem.[21]

Agent financing plans are used to augment the early earnings shortfall in the compensation system. Level commission plans could materially increase financing subsidies. This situation can be compounded by an inability with flexible products to arrive at any meaningfully acceptable measure of net annualized commissions. Still another factor influencing the length of the financing period is the growing emphasis on financial counseling. There is a real question as to how a company can accomplish the necessary training and development in face of the high financing validation requirements that are necessary to attract individuals required to sell current products and services.

Despite the significant investment by a company, an agent, once financed and trained, tends to feel that he or she is free to operate independently. Given the extremely high developmental costs and the potential that the successful agent may "go to the highest bidder," some thought is being given to an amortization of developmental costs as a contractual obligation of the agent. Naturally, this is a sensitive issue, but reality may insist that something be done to deal with the cost question.

Still another development of current interest is the establishment of agent-owned reinsurance companies. Some companies have helped establish such facilities to provide an incentive for high-volume agents to place a large proportion of their best-quality business with the sponsoring company so that the agents will then participate in the good experience of their high-quality production. Essentially, it is a joint venture between a company and outstanding producers, with the result that both the direct writing company and the agent-owned

[20] *Ibid.*   [21] *Ibid.*

reinsurer make additional profits. Agents' increased profits flow from their ownership of the reinsurance company, where reinsurance on the business is placed by the direct writing company.

Although there is a great deal of discussion of **fees for services,** the concept is new and evolving. For agencies specializing in financial counseling, there is, potentially, a large opportunity in selling services and advice as well as products. The industry has experience in the pension field, where pension services for fees are provided to clients. There is a major difference, however, between the marketing of pensions and the marketing of individual life and health insurance.

Support to an agent who does financial counseling for a fee is crucial. Shifting from a commission-based system to one employing fees for services is a major change with significant implications for costs, individuals, and organizations. The entire area of compensation design is in a state of flux.

Compensation of Brokers and Independent Agents

Brokers.[22] Since most brokers are, from a legal standpoint, agents, the commissions offered to these individuals vary as greatly as they do for agents.[23] If the brokering agent in question is not a general agent or is not entitled to override commissions, compensation will be paid as provided in the agent contract. If the brokering agent is also a general agent, overrides equal to an additional 30 or 40 percent may be paid. These overrides may also apply to all renewal commissions. In addition to these commissions, renewals, and overrides, general agents may be eligible for office and expense subsidies and production bonuses.

There is also a wide range of employee benefits and other rewards for production paid to brokers. It is necessary to look at the form of contract under which the brokering agent works.

If the amount of business placed with a given company is large, the broker will participate in all bonuses offered by the company. A general agent who acts as a broker for any given company will usually receive the same fringe benefits and bonus arrangements that are available to general agents of that other company. If individual agents of the general agent provide a large volume of business to a particular company, those particular agents will usually receive extra bonuses and be invited to special sales conferences as a reward.

It is common practice in the life insurance industry to annualize commission payments. Regardless of the mode of payment chosen by the applicant, the company assumes that all (or most) of the year's premium is received at the time the policy is issued. Assuming a 55 percent commission rate, 55 percent of the full year's premium will be paid the agent as soon as the policy is issued. In many cases, brokerage companies do not have the close relationship that normally exists with exclusive agents. As a result, some do not annualize commissions, since it is sometimes difficult to retrieve unearned commissions when contracts lapse. Brokers who do business with a given company infrequently receive extra benefits or bonuses. On the other hand, large brokerage producers tend to be treated as well as exclusive agents, and this treatment can even include a full range of employee benefits.

Most life insurance agency contracts include a service fee allowance. Such service fees usually begin at the end of all renewal commission payments. This allowance, which varies from 2 to 5 percent and is seldom vested, continues for the lifetime of the contract. Although there are exceptions, most agents receive no service fee allowance on brokered business.

Independent Agents.[24] The intense competition for the life production of independent property and liability agents has caused the total compensation package typically made available to independent agents to be similar to that granted career agents. Comparable commission

[22]This section draws from Richard E. Johnson, "The Brokerage Distribution System," in *Marketing Life and Health Insurance,* pp. 260–262.

[23]Most states require individuals selling life and health insurance to be licensed as an agent regardless of the number of companies with which they place business.

[24]This section draws from Bruce A. Palmer, "All-Lines Agents," in *Marketing Life and Health Insurance,* pp. 297–298.

rates and expense allowances generally are included in the total package. In addition, the independent agent is normally provided the opportunity to qualify for sales contests, trips, awards, and other special prizes. The agreement between the company and the agent (agency) may also provide for persistency and/or production bonuses, fully vested renewal commissions, service fees payable after expiration of renewal commissions, and commission overrides if the agency possesses a general agent (usually PPGA) contract. A significant difference between the contracts offered to independent property and liability (P&L) agents and those offered to exclusive life agents pertains to agent financing plans, which are not made available to independent P&L agents.

PRODUCT DEVELOPMENT[25]

Only after a life and health insurance company has developed a marketing plan should it consider the products it will develop to meet the needs of the markets it has chosen to address. In practice, of course, this order is often reversed: that is, define a target market, determine products, and then consider how best to market them. In any case, products will play a critical role in the company's efforts to achieve market penetration. In the case of established companies, the process of constantly evaluating and upgrading the product portfolio is necessary to respond to a changing external environment and revised company objectives.

The External Environment

Product development, of necessity, must reflect the changing social, economic, legal, and competitive environment. Ideally, a company's market research function will monitor the external environment continuously and forecast trends so that the company can develop products to take advantage of new opportunities and respond to needed adjustments to its current portfolio.

Competiton in life and health insurance comes from both other insurance companies and other industries.[26] Competition from other companies can have a significant impact on product design. Competition may relate to that for agents and brokers, or to price, product design, underwriting, and/or policyowner service. A company must respond to the actions of its major competitors when they develop a product that threatens its market share. Pressure on product designers is also created when a competitor develops an exciting new product, thus creating an innovative image for itself. A company's sales force may demand a similar product, and the product designers may have to respond with a product so that the company does not appear to be falling behind.

One critical management decision in product development is evaluating whether to respond quickly to competition or wait to see how the market will respond to a competitor's new product. In particular, where high startup costs or development expenses for administrative systems are involved, the company may well decide to wait to see the response to a competitor's product before committing resources to such a product.

Some major companies have a specific philosophy of always staying just behind the leading edge on any new product. They let another company introduce a new product, obtain regulatory approval, and educate agents and the public about the virtues of the new product. In those cases where the product turns out to be successful, such companies then move to bring out an improved version of it as quickly as possible. This strategy is feasible since companies cannot patent or copyright their new ideas.

The external environment provides a complex, difficult array of influences. Many factors in that environment interact and are synergistic, but all impinge on the product design process.

---

[25]This section draws from R. C. Dowsett and R. G. Boeckner, "Product Development," in *Marketing Life and Health Insurance*, pp. 101–133; and Robert D. Shapiro, "The Process of Premium Formulation," *SOA Part 7 Study Note* (Itasca, Ill.: Society of Actuaries, 1982). See also Francois Genest, "Product Development: Easy as Pie," *MarketFacts*, Vol. 2 (June 1983), pp. 6–12; and Allen D. Booth and Robert D. Shapiro, "The Product Development Program for Insurance Companies," *SOA Part 9 Study Note* (Itasca, Ill.: Society of Actuaries, 1982).

[26]E. J. Moorhead, "Competition," *Marketing for Actuaries— Individual Life and Health Insurance*, pp. V-1 to V-9.

Despite the uncertainties and the complexity of monitoring the environment and forecasting trends, the process of product design is critically dependent on the quality of this effort.

The Process of Product Design

Once a marketing strategy has been established that is consistent with the company's corporate objectives and perception of the external environment, the broad guidelines are in place for the product design process to begin and decisions about the product portfolio to be made. The company's marketing strategy will usually be developed by the senior marketing officers and then approved by senior management. Establishment of product design objectives that are consistent with the marketing strategy is a joint effort of the marketing department and the product design actuaries.

The product design function is usually handled as a staff function. Changes in the product mix may be essential if the company is to survive. Particular lines of business may have to be eliminated because they are no longer growing and profitable. Such decisions are best initiated by staff who have no vested interest, as line personnel might, in continuing to offer unprofitable existing products. In addition, the design of innovative products usually requires extensive research, which is best performed as a staff function.

The Process of Premium Formulation

The premium formulation function can have meaning only in the context of the total insurance company management plan. In practice, premium rates cannot be set simply by "building in" profit together with the other assumptions as to mortality, morbidity, persistency, expenses, and other expected characteristics of the business. Instead, premium rates must be established to balance the various, often conflicting requirements of management, shareholders, and policyowners (both present and future), within the overall constraints resulting from the need to preserve company solvency.

Most companies develop their rates on "best-estimate" actuarial assumptions, building in a specific desired margin for profit. By developing the premium scale utilizing realistic actuarial assumptions (including an explicit profit margin), the management of the results is made easier. The assumptions underlying the asset share studies can then function as performance standards for the company. The development of projections based on realistic gross premium assumptions provides a base against which to monitor future experience, thus facilitating decision making.

Price management requires systematic comparison of actual to expected results, with action taken wherever possible to rectify any significant deviations from expected results. Thus, a rate increase on a block of individual health business, a revision in a dividend scale, or a new ratebook might be indicated. The projections described above provide a basis for creating the *expected results*. A good price management system will include a periodic *comparison* of these results with the *emerging actual experience*.

When significant deviations occur, the *reason* for the deviations must be determined. Additional studies often are needed. Where indicated changes cannot be made without creating other unacceptable results (e.g., required premium increase would price the company out of particular critical markets), there may be a need for complete reassessment of the company's basic pricing plan.

Once the deviations are defined and appropriate corrective action implemented, the process continues to its next sequence. It is a dynamic circle of planning, product review, and experience analysis. Findings may suggest that existing products or services have entered into the maturity or even decline stages of the product life cycle (see below.)

Marketing Implications of New Products

In marketing theory, the **product life cycle** is a theoretical construct that attempts to describe the key turning points and stages in the life of a product from introduction to decline. Like any generalization, it does not perfectly describe every product's life; however, it does represent a powerful analytical tool that marketers use to set strategy.[27]

The four stages of the product life cycle are: introduction, growth, maturity, and decline. These stages are represented in Figure 30-2, a graph that displays the values of hypothetical sales and profits throughout the four stages.

During the **introduction stage** for a new product, sales are low and profits are negative because of the investment in startup costs. In this stage, the typical promotion strategy is to convince consumers of the utility and value of the product itself rather than focusing on a particular brand or make. Since there are usually few competitors, pricing is not a major concern.

As the product moves into the **growth stage,** sales and profits increase dramatically. Eventually, profit per unit sold declines. This is because new competitors enter the market and some of these new entrants may use price cutting as a strategy to increase market share and catch up to already established competitors. Promotion focuses on distinguishing the advantages of one brand over another.

In the **maturity stage,** sales level off and total profits being to decline. There are few new entrants because existing competitors keep profit margins low. Some competitors may even withdraw because of the limited profit potential.

In the **decline stage,** sales and profits continue to slide. There is a general "shake out" of the market. Unprofitable distribution channels are eliminated. Competitors generally sacrifice market share to maintain profit margins.

The product life cycle is a useful concept because it can help predict how the market is likely to work in different phases. For example, a company entering the market during the growth stage would be well advised to build unique and valuable features into its version of the product because consumers will begin to make choices based on individual features once the value of the generic product is well established.

With a couple of key additions, the product life cycle can be adapted as a useful tool for describing the evolution of traditional and nontraditional life insurance products. One key addition is the regulatory environment for the new product. Another key addition is tax law. Because nontraditional products are so dependent on tax efficiencies for their marketability, changes in tax rulings and laws can have a major impact on their development.

MARKETING TRENDS

The marketing scene in the United States is changing at a rate exceeding anything the business

---

[27]This discussion draws on Robert L. Posnak and Charles Carroll, "Overview of Non-traditional Products: Definition, Terminology, Basics," *1983 Financial and Accounting Aspects of Non-traditional Products-Selected Proceedings* (Atlanta, Ga.: Life Office Management Association, 1983).

Figure 30-2

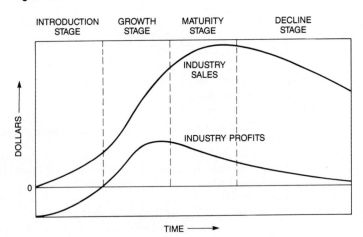

has ever known. The financial services evolution has masked the remarkable changes taking place in the provision of insurance services themselves. Distribution systems and product development are both being influenced significantly by the economic, social, and competitive environment of the 1980s. Changes are so widespread and numerous that it is difficult even to track them. Therefore, the following discussion should be interpreted in light of these changes.

Distribution Systems: 1984 Market Share of Premiums

Life insurance sales in 1984 were up 21 percent over 1983, and that comes on top of a 22 percent increase in 1983. LIMRA estimates that total annualized premium was $8.8 billion in 1984. Also, in 1984, the face amount of life insurance sold was up 13 percent from 1983, with the number of policies sold approximately the same as in 1983. On an industry-wide basis, volume as measured by face amount for 1984 was an estimated $850 billion and the estimated number of policies sold was $17.7 million.[28]

Figure 30–3 indicates the market share of 1983 premiums developed through full-time career agent, brokerage, direct response, personal-producing general agent, multiple-line exclusive agent, and combination companies marketing systems.[29] Direct response marketing has been growing in popularity but still accounts for only a very small proportion of total premiums generated. It is clear that the agency-building systems are still the heart of the life and health insurance marketing effort. Brokerage is also a significant factor, but most brokerage business is written by agents in the agency-building systems.

New agents remain the most important source of the future growth in the insurance industry. Each year insurance companies spend

[28]"1984: A Marketing Wrap-Up," *MarketFacts,* Vol. 4 (April 1985), p. 18.

[29]Irvin W. Goldberg, "New Products—An Overview," *MarketFacts,* Vol. 4 (April 1985), pp. 13–16.

Figure 30-3. 1983 Market share of premiums. Source: *The 1983 Census of Life Insurance Sales Personnel*

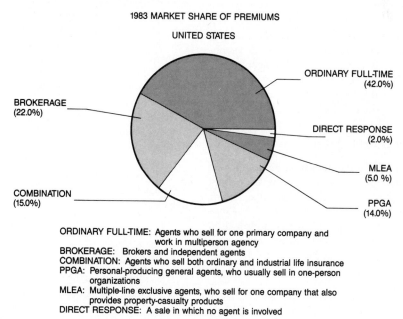

1983 MARKET SHARE OF PREMIUMS

UNITED STATES

ORDINARY FULL-TIME (42.0%)

BROKERAGE (22.0%)

DIRECT RESPONSE (2.0%)

MLEA (5.0 %)

COMBINATION (15.0%)

PPGA (14.0%)

ORDINARY FULL-TIME: Agents who sell for one primary company and work in multiperson agency
BROKERAGE: Brokers and independent agents
COMBINATION: Agents who sell both ordinary and industrial life insurance
PPGA: Personal-producing general agents, who usually sell in one-person organizations
MLEA: Multiple-line exclusive agents, who sell for one company that also provides property-casualty products
DIRECT RESPONSE: A sale in which no agent is involved

large amounts of money to recruit, finance, train, and support new agents. In a new agent's early years, expenditures exceed revenue; the difference is the company's investment. In the later years, when revenue is expected to exceed expenditures, the company hopes to recover the investment.

The size of the company's investment in new agents and the period of time to recover it depend on several factors. Recently, LIMRA completed a study that demonstrated how improvement in certain performance factors can significantly reduce the cost of the company's future growth.[30] Thus,

• Three years after contracting 100 new agents, a company with moderate agent retention and high productivity will have 25 of its recruits remaining, at a net investment of about $120,000 each.

• For a company with low agent retention, the net investment per recruit remaining increases by 60 percent.

• For a company with high agent retention, the net investment decreases by 25 percent.

• The time period to recover these investments ranges from nine years for high retention to 21 years for low retention.

The study concluded that the size of the company's investment in new agents and the period of time to recover it depend on several factors, including productivity, persistency, inflation, and most important, retention. The study demonstrated clearly that while improving agent retention may be far more difficult than improving persistency or productivity, capital spent in this area has the potential for much higher returns.

Major Market Directions

The life insurance industry's natural market remains solid and is expected to grow throughout the next decade. A natural set of consumer needs remains unfulfilled. In fact, there are several fundamental reasons why the real rate of growth in market potential is expected to increase:

[30]LIMRA, *Investing in New Agents: A Cost Blueprint,* I/R Code 33.22, 1985.

1. Baby-boomers, those born between 1945 and 1960, have deferred family formation and the purchase of life insurance.

2. The federal government's reduced inclination to assume full responsibility for individual security has caused individuals to become more concerned about providing independently for their personal financial security.

3. IRA funds are amassing to large dollar amounts. The life insurance industry will find its role in converting these funds to lifetime income streams.

4. Growing proportions of the U.S. population will be senior citizens. They are the most security-conscious demographic segment.

5. Corporations will continue to be more active in assisting employees in achieving a measure of financial security at the employee's expense. One reason for this is that corporations will continue to seek ways to scale back their own fringe-benefit cost increases.

Juxtaposed against a growing market, there are reasons why the providers of services could change, either in identity or in methodology. First, the industry is considered by many to be inefficient in its product delivery. Many companies have spent large sums to retool administrative systems but have not been pricing in support of those costs. The agency system is expensive and driven by the theory that insurance must be sold and will not be demanded.

Second, because of basic inefficiencies, new products with small margins, and competition, industry profit margins are believed by many to be inadequate, at least by historical standards. Third, many companies have focused their efforts on the so-called upscale markets. These markets may be oversold while unmet needs exist in less upscale areas.

As a result, it is likely that the successful company of the future will be larger, more market-focused, and more efficient. This means it is likely that some middle-tier companies will rise to the top via growth coupled with merger or acquisition; that many fringe companies will disappear; and that traditional agency forces will remain feasible, but only in defined niches.

With respect to the upscale market, with its focus on planning and tax (income, estate, and inheritance) implications, relatively little change is expected to occur in the next 10 years. This market will remain an agent-served market, will continue to use a range of life insurance products, and is unlikely to be effectively tapped through alternative distribution systems. Its growth rate probably will not change materially (unless taxed away).

The size of the midscale market will probably grow materially for many of the reasons indicated. The successful competitors will focus on needs and will use alternative distribution systems effectively, including telemarketing, other financial institutions, and other third-party intermediaries. Universal life insurance and its extension, variable universal life insurance, should be featured products, along with basic term insurance. Annuities supported by continued favorable tax treatment could constitute a major new market.

Downscale markets will probably be served by simple security products. The home service business will probably survive the next 10-year period, but will be in a continuing, although not rapid state of contraction. Direct response marketing should continue to play an important role, at least to the extent that it does today, perhaps more so.

It is believed that corporate markets will grow at a rate exceeded only by that of the midscale market. Large corporations can be serviced directly by insurers. Their experience with cost-plus or administrative-services-only group plans taught them that direct contact is possible and cost-effective. An extension of direct corporate purchase of corporate-owned life insurance could be the negotiation of rates and products for distribution directly to corporate employees. Most of these buyers will come from the midscale segment. Advisors and consultants could play a new and important role because of this major trend.

Chapter 31

Life Insurance Company Investment Management

In the aggregate, the magnitude and nature of life insurance company investment activity have established the life insurance business as a significant factor in the capital markets.[1] The cash flow generated from level-premium whole life policies has led to the accumulation of substantial funds available for investment. In addition, the investment returns attained by a life insurer have always been a critically important factor affecting the company's profitability and its competitive position in the marketplace. The investment function has been made even more important from a competitive standpoint with the recent introduction of interest-sensitive products. The marketing of these new products has also made investment management more complex and has affected investment objectives and practice significantly.

THE INVESTMENT PROCESS

Sources of Investable Funds

In a life insurance company, investable funds arise from both insurance and investment operations. The cash flow from insurance operations

[1]See Chapter 3.

arises out of the difference between cash receipts (premiums, annuity considerations, and other deposits) and cash disbursements (benefits and expenses). Cash flow arising out of investment operations consists of current income (earnings from net interest and dividends) earned on existing investments, together with income resulting from maturities, prepayments, redemptions, calls, and sales of specific investments. For most insurers, the magnitude of these cash flows is substantial. In a typical well-established company, annual cash flow available for investment may equal or exceed 20 percent of total assets. The management of these cash flows presents a significant task.

Investment Accounts

The total investment portfolio of a life insurance company can be separated into two types of accounts. The accounts are classified primarily according to the nature of the liabilities or obligations for which the assets are being held and invested. Assets that are used to support contractual obligations providing for guaranteed fixed-dollar benefit payments, normally are held in the company's **general account.** Other invested assets, used to support the liabilities associated with certain products or lines of business (e.g., variable annuities, variable life insurance, and pension products) are generally held in special accounts typically labeled as **separate accounts.**

A separate account generally is established by resolution of the company's board of directors, pursuant to provisions of the insurance law of the state(s) in which it will be marketed. (In many states, it may also be subject to the approval of the commissioner of insurance of the company's state of domicile). The investments of a separate account are segregated from other assets of the company and are selected in accordance with the investment policy for the separate account. The company's obligations under separate account contracts generally vary in value with the investment performance of the accounts, including market value changes and investment income, although that is not true in every case. This is because the separate account contract generally calls for a direct pass-through of the actual investment results to the contract holder.

Industry-wide, the proportion of assets managed in separate accounts can be expected to increase due to the increasing sales of variable annuity, variable life, and pension products. Further, in most states, since separate accounts are relatively free of the qualitative and quantitative restrictions imposed on general accounts (see below), the popularity of separate accounts will probably be further enhanced. Separate accounts equaled 10.7 percent of all assets in 1985 for U.S. life insurers. It should be noted that many insurers, to this point, have chosen not to establish separate accounts.

Special Characteristics of the Investment Process in Life Insurance

Forward Commitments. In view of their substantial premium income, life insurance companies traditionally have had less need for liquidity than other types of financial institutions, and the stability of their cash flow has made it somewhat easier for them to plan ahead over relatively long periods of time. A significant proportion of their investments has involved direct financing of large, productive projects such as factories, utility plants, office buildings, condominiums, shopping malls,

and similar undertakings. Owners/developers planned these projects well in advance and usually arranged their permanent financing long before construction was scheduled to be completed. Because of their strong cash flow positions, life insurance companies frequently were willing to enter into agreements to make investments a year or more in advance of the time when the funds would actually be needed. These contractual arrangements are called **forward commitments.** This special characteristic of the life insurance investment process has made the development of large-scale undertakings far easier and more effective than it would otherwise be. As will be discussed later, changing and more volatile capital markets are making this process less feasible today.

Direct (Private) Placements. Another characteristic of the life insurance investment process has been the emphasis on the direct placement of corporate bonds. **Direct placements** are issues of securities whose terms are negotiated directly between the borrower and the lender, and title to which passes directly from the borrower to the lender.[2]

Life insurance companies played a basic role in the development of the direct-placement market, which in recent years has accounted for one-fifth to nearly one-half of total corporate-bond financing, the balance being offered to the general public through traditional investment and underwriting firms. Direct placements account for about 90 percent of industrial-bond investments of life insurance companies, and life insurance companies account for an estimated 75 to 80 percent of all direct placements. Shrinkage in life insurance company cash flow during tight-money periods normally leads to a decline in the importance of direct placements relative to public issues.

Investment Policies and Objectives

In setting the investment policy and objectives for a company, the board of directors considers the relevant operating and investment risks,

[2]For a fuller description, see Eli Shapiro and Charles R. Wolf, *The Role of Private Placements in Corporate Finance* (Boston: Graduate School of Business Administration, Harvard University, 1972).

the regulatory and other constraints faced by the company, and the investment products available to the investment manager. Recently, there has been a rapid change in each of these areas. As background for examining investment management today, it would appear helpful to review briefly the nature of the investment risks faced by a life insurer.

Investment Risks. The risks involved with investments include (1) business, (2) interest rate, (3) credit, (4) liquidity, and (5) control. **Business risk** is the possibility of losing new business (market share) because the investment activities do not keep up with the development of new products. For example, if the investment department's earnings do not permit competitively priced products, the company could be placed at a competitive disadvantage. The **interest rate risk,** caused by fluctuating interest rates, has increased dramatically as worldwide financial markets are being deregulated. This risk is discussed more fully below. **Credit risk** is the risk of the loss of principal due to default through bankruptcy of the creditor. The rapid growth of "junk bonds"[3] and leveraged buyouts as well as competitive pressure to increase yields are increasing the significance of this exposure. The **liquidity risk** involves having the cash to meet obligations. Managing a company's cash flow is a critical element of its competitive effectiveness and even its survival. With the rapidly expanding financial tools available to investment managers, it is also of critical importance that strong internal **controls** be in place to prevent speculation by investment managers.

The board of directors or its investment committee must also consider the constraints placed on the investment process by state and federal laws and regulations and the accounting rules and guidelines applicable to investments for both statutory and shareholder statement purposes.[4] In addition, with the development of interest-sensititve products and volatile interest rates,[5] it has become imperative that life insurance

companies address the matching of asset and liability cash flow characteristics, giving effect to differing interest rate environments and related product persistency experience. Another major consideration is, of course, whether the investment policy relates to the company's general account (which may be segmented by product or line of business), one of a number of possible separate accounts, or to a subsidiary company established by the life insurer. With the considerations above in mind, the board of directors approves the basic investment policy, objectives, and guidelines for the company's investment operations.

Traditional Objectives. Until the recent development of interest-sensitive products, the liabilities of a life insurance company were composed largely of the policy reserves established on behalf of the outstanding, traditional fixed-premium insurance and annuity contracts. Therefore, the bulk (80 to 90 percent) of a life company's liabilities were considered to represent long-term (on the average), fixed-dollar obligations, and had to be credited periodically with a guaranteed rate of interest. The guaranteed rates were relatively low. Actual earnings in excess of guaranteed rates were reflected in dividend payments for participating policies. In reality, these "long-term" obligations might not be very long term if one recognized the possible effect of the surrender and loan options available to policyowners. Prior to the mid-1970s, market interest rates were relatively low and stable, thus causing life insurance companies few disintermediation problems relating to policy surrenders and loans, and thereby enabling them to behave as if their liabilities were essentially long-term obligations. To maximize their yield, it was normal practice to invest in long-term obligations since the normal yield curve sloped upward; that is, longer maturities tended to produce a greater yield.

Principles of sound financial management dictate that assets be accumulated consistent with the characteristics of the liabilities that a company has assumed. For a life insurance company with long-term obligations, this suggests that a large proportion of assets be long-term, fixed-dollar investments with an overall yield at least equal to the interest rate guaranteed in outstanding con-

---

[3]The term "junk bond" refers to a high-yielding bond of less than investment grade.

[4]See Chapter 32.

[5]During the last 15 years, U.S. Treasury bill rates fluctuated between 3.5 and 17 percent.

tracts. The remainder of the assets generally would be short-term instruments and cash to provide the liquidity necessary to meet current cash flow demands. These objectives generally explained the actions of life companies, as evidenced by the traditional preponderance of investments in long-term, fixed-dollar, interest-bearing bonds and mortgages. This "matching" of assets (investments) and liabilities was perceived to be inherent in the nature of the business.

Liquidity was also not considered a critical factor in investment planning, although its importance could vary from company to company.[6] The cash flow from traditional, level-premium policies was large and, on balance, positive. Until recently, the objective appeared to be the acquisition of the longest maturities compatible with the risk, yield, and liquidity considerations associated with company policy and strategy.

Although from a legal standpoint the insurance transaction creates a debtor-creditor relationship, the traditions of trusteeship and prudent-person responsibility exert a strong influence on investment policy.[7] This traditional, conservative viewpoint, with its heavy emphasis on safety, has been relaxed as relatively greater importance is being attached to higher yields as an investment objective. Even prior to recent high interest rates and the introduction of interest-sensitive products, companies had demonstrated a willingness to sacrifice some safety of principal through the acquisition of investments with slightly higher risk but higher expected returns. Perhaps this exemplified not so much a change in basic investment philosophy as it did increasing competition, more reliance on economic forecasting, and emphasis on *portfolio* rather than *individual* risk. The competitive yield objective has become increasingly important in the life insurance business, which now offers investment-oriented contracts in direct competition with other financial institutions for the saving and investment dollar. The conflict between income and safety is, and will continue to be, however, a fundamental consideration affecting company investment philosophy.

Regulation and Investment Policy

The investment activities of life insurance companies must be conducted within the limitations prescribed by state insurance laws and regulations. Many of the details of these limitations are discussed in a later section of this chapter. At this point it is sufficient to point out that there is a significant degree of uniformity among the several states, due primarily to the role of the National Association of Insurance Commissioners (NAIC) in the formulation of investment regulation. Also, the concentration of many important insurers in a number of leading insurance states makes it possible to emphasize the provisions of a few states and still have the discussion representative of the regulatory environment within which the great majority of investment decisions are made.[8] Nevertheless, individual state statutes and regulations should be examined when specific situations are under consideration.

In general, with respect to general account investments, state laws provide limitations aimed at (1) preserving the safety of the assets standing behind policyowner reserves, and (2) preventing undue risk for the life insurer through disproportionately large investment in one firm, industry or type of security. Thus, investment regulations specify eligible types of investments and the minimum quality criteria for individual investments within the eligible categories. In addition, quantitative limitations are imposed on the amounts that can be placed in eligible investments (see later in this chapter).

Changes in recent years in the regulation of financial institutions, at both the state and federal levels, have had a significant effect on the investment strategies and performance of life insurance companies. At the federal level, the major

---

[6]James E. Walter, *The Investment Process* (Boston: Division of Research, Harvard University, 1962), p. 40.

[7]Robert J. Ferrari, "Life Insurance Company Investments," in Dan M. McGill, *Life Insurance,* rev. ed., (Homewood, Ill.: Richard D. Irwin, Inc., 1967), p. 842.

[8]The New York State Insurance Law is particularly significant because of the extraterritorial provisions that require companies *licensed* to do business in the state to "comply substantially" with New York regulations in all states in which they do business. See *New York Insurance Law,* Sec. 42(5), 90(1).

trend has been toward deregulation of depository institutions (commercial banks and thrifts). This deregulation directly affects the investment strategy and performance of life insurers. The deregulation of depository institutions implies an environment of high and increasing competition for each dollar of savings and the need for insurers to earn a competitive rate of return on their investments to maintain a reasonable share of the savings market. Indeed, their inability to hold share has led, in recent years, to a rising level of cash surrenders and policyowner loans as savers have disintermediated either into money market mutual funds or funds of other financial institutions.

In response to the changing economic and competitive environment, state regulations are being liberalized to permit greater investment flexibility. New financial instruments and investment methods are being developed that can help insurance companies *price* and *manage* the interest-rate (see below) and options risk of their assets and liabilities. The term "options risk" used here refers to contractual provisions in policies and contracts permitting a policyowner or a contractowner to withdraw or deposit funds with the insurer when it is to his or her advantage to do so. Possible financial instruments to assist in managing and pricing options risk include options, futures, interest rate swaps, and call and put bonds. Many of these instruments, particularly the options and futures, are complex instruments for life insurance companies. GAAP and statutory accounting and tax considerations, as well as state regulations, further complicate and limit their practical application to asset/liability management. Although a great many companies are studying the use of futures and options, only a few of the largest companies actually have started to engage in futures or options arrangements.[9]

Strategic Setting

Changing circumstances have led to the elevation of asset/liability management to a position of primary importance in the management of a life insurance company. The onset and persistence of increased interest rate volatility and the rapidly changing financial services marketplace with the consequent proliferation of "investment" as opposed to "insurance" products have made investment performance critical, both to a company's competitive position and to its very survival.

There are several reasons why life insurance companies found themselves greatly exposed to interest rate risk in the early 1980s:[10]

1. Traditional investment practices, geared to a relatively stable financial marketplace and "normal" yield curves, called for investing in very long maturities to obtain high yields and for taking substantial forward commitment positions. In many cases, asset maturities were too long for the company's liability structure.

2. Regulatory constraints, such as limitations on policy loan interest rates and surrender charges and prohibition of the use of financial futures and options, often forced life insurers to offer products that permitted, if not encouraged, investment selection against the company by policyowners and contractholders. Life companies did not have the necessary investment vehicles to control exposure to that risk.

3. Competitive forces have led to the redesign of traditional products to make the investment features more prominent and to provide innovative product features in the form of valuable guarantees and options to policyowners. This has altered the risk/return profile of insurance products to one of greatly reduced *expected* profit margins, with large downside potential if assets and liabilities are not appropriately matched.

4. Life insurance statutory accounting practices, which generally do not require that assets and

[9]James A. Maschoff and Russell W. Swansen, "Savy Investment Strategies," *Best's Review*, Life/Health ed., Vol. 86 (September 1985), p. 140. For a discussion of the applications of special financial instruments, see James A. Tilley, *Risk Control Techniques for Life Insurance Companies* (New York: Morgan Stanley, 1985), pp. 29–37.

[10]James A Tilley, *Asset/Liability Management for Insurance Companies—Risk Control Techniques* (New York: Morgan Stanley, 1983), pp. 1–2. See also Francis H. Schott, "Investment Policy in the New Life Insurance Environment," *LOMA Strategic Planning Seminar*, March 2–4, 1986.

liabilities be valued at market, had masked the deterioration in economic strength caused by increasing interest rates in the early 1980s. In the simplest terms, accounting rules that call for the carrying of fixed-income assets in good standing on the books at cost or amortized value often deter life insurance companies from rebalancing their portfolios to control asset/liability mismatch risk because of the effect that realized capital gains and losses would have on current-year earnings and the surplus position of the company.

5. Finally, some believe that many insurers were not in a position to redress asset/liability imbalances because management information data bases for both assets and liabilities were not in place, techniques to measure the company's "realistic" economic condition were not well developed, and senior management had a lack of experience with this type of problem. Indeed, for many companies, integration of asset and liability management was difficult because the investment managers and product managers were of different "cultures" and had difficulty relating to all aspects of the collective problem even if they wanted to do so.

In recent years, many traditional investment practices have changed, regulatory constraints have been eased or removed, and competitive forces have continued to intensify. Equally important, management understanding of the many dimensions of exposure to interest rate risk has increased.

With the October 1979 change in Federal Reserve policy to one of management of money supply rather than management of interest rates, all financial intermediaries (e.g., banks, insurers, and securities dealers) were thrust into an environment of volatile interest rates. This new interest rate environment, coupled with the introduction of interest-sensitive products, has changed the role of the investment manager from an "investor" to that of "spread manager." The skills needed to manage a business where investment spreads are 4 or 5 percent are radically different from the skills needed to manage a business where a spread of ½ to 1½ percent is more the norm.

Matching the asset cash flows to the liability cash flow needs has materially changed the organization, role, and significance of the investment management of a life insurance company. Many companies within the industry have had difficulty adjusting to these new developments. Complicating matters is the fact that the investment officer of a life company is continually confronted with surplus constraints, tax and accounting rules, and earnings per share pressures. In contrast, pension fund managers and other investment advisors generally are not faced with constraints such as these.

Financial management is a separate discipline within a successfully managed life insurance company. It covers many actuarial and investment considerations—as well as other typical corporate finance, accounting, and cash management functions. In this connection, the American Academy of Actuaries has recommended that a **valuation actuary** be designated for each life insurance company. This individual would be required to certify in the annual statement that the company had matched its assets to its liabilities and had successfully demonstrated that its investment strategy can meet the test of various interest rate scenarios. There has been a suggestion that senior management be required to sign-off with the valuation actuary. Partial implementation of this recommendation was realized in 1986, with 1987 or 1988 the target for full enforcement.[11]

It is important to note that neither the actuaries nor the investment officers in a life insurance company are the *real* chief financial officer. Rather, overall responsibility for understanding the importance of asset and liability management to the profitability and success of the company rests with the chief executive officer.

With this background, it is now appropriate to discuss asset/liability management specifically. Then, in the following section, a brief review of the types and diversification of life insurer investments over recent years will be presented.

---

[11]Andrew M. Jarmel, "The Challenge of Asset/Liability Matching," *National Underwriter*, Life/Health ed. (February 8, 1986), p. 18.

ASSET/LIABILITY MANAGEMENT

Today, a prime investment management responsibility is to participate in the development of a comprehensive program for integrating asset and liability management within the company as it may affect the nature and structure of the general asset account. The ultimate goal of such a program is to support the company's objectives in terms of market share and profitability. The investment manager, of course, must work closely with other key functional officers in support of these company goals. As discussed below, because of the different needs in terms of cash flow and yield, it has become common practice to restructure aggregate asset portfolios into segments that support specific lines of business and within particular lines, specific products. A number of companies have addressed the integration of asset and liability management through this **segmentation** route. The investment manager and a product or line manager work together in seeing that there is an appropriate match between the cash flow needs of the particular product or line of business and the related assets generated by the product line. Essentially, the investment manager becomes a "spread" manager.

This involves managing the spread by product line to ensure that the products are competitive and that an adequate cash flow will be available when needed to meet the cash demands (expenses, loans, surrenders, dividends, etc.) of that as well as all other product lines. This task is complicated by the difficulties in forecasting policy persistency and the volatility of interest rates. The possible introduction of new investment-oriented products and the impact of internal replacements (planned or unplanned) should also be considered. Some of the elements of this task involve making strategic decisions, while others involve developing expertise in both old and new investment technologies.

Interest Rate Risk [12]

The significant increase in interest rates in the early 1980s demonstrated that the image of

the traditional life insurance company product portfolio as requiring a long-term-oriented investment policy was not only untrue, but actually could endanger the solvency of the company.[13] The *demand liability* nature of traditional products was amply demonstrated by the great increase in policy replacements and the concurrent extensive policy loan activity when market interest rates rose to high levels. With the introduction of interest-sensitive products that emphasize the investment-return aspect of life insurance contracts, it has become clear that managing the so-called interest rate risk and the appropriate matching of asset and liability cash flows are critical to the solvency of a life insurance company.[14]

There are two sides to the interest rate risk: the reinvestment risk and the price/liquidity risk. The **reinvestment risk** arises from the possibility of having to reinvest funds when market yields are below levels guaranteed to policyowners and contractholders. It exists because of the tie between a company's asset cash flow and the prevailing interest rate. This tie occurs because of possible repayment options the insurer may have granted to a borrower. If interest rates fall, there will be a tendency for borrowers to repay, thereby *shortening* the asset cash flow in comparison with what it may have been had interest rates remained constant. For example, borrowers holding mortgage loans at 12 percent would seek to refinance (i.e., repay) their loans if prevailing interest rates fall to 9 percent. Similarly, if interest rates rise, one would expect a *lengthening* of asset cash flow, as borrowers who might otherwise repay early are discouraged from doing so.

The **price/liquidity risk** arises from the possibility of having to liquidate assets when market yields are above levels at which the assets were purchased and hence selling assets below cost (i.e., at a discount). There also is a tie between the

---

[12]This discussion draws on James A. Tilley, *Risk Control Techniques for Life Insurance Companies.*

[13]In 1982, the NAIC listed 52 life/health companies in need of immediate "regulatory attention." In 1983, there were 186. In 1984, 229 were listed with still more on the list that were in less immediate financial trouble but that appeared to be targets for attention. John A. Maschoff and Russell W. Swansen, "Savy Investment Strategies," p. 30.

[14]A contingency reserve hedging the effects of interest rate shifts has become known as "C3," a designation given it in a Preliminary Report from the Society of Actuaries Committee on Valuation and Related Problems (March 1, 1979).

cash flow needed for liabilities and prevailing interest rates. When interest rates (especially short-term rates) are high, life insurance policyowners (and the owners of pension or annuity contracts) will tend to choose dollars now over dollars later—using any cash withdrawal or policy loan rights more often, surrendering policies to obtain the cash for alternative investment, or delaying premium payments. This increases cash flow needed currently to meet the liability payments. This has the effect of *shortening* the company's liabilities.

This practice—the withdrawal of policyowner funds in tight-money times—will be recognized as a type of disintermediation. It can have a negative impact on insurers where certain kinds of savings or annuity vehicles—especially those permitting a cash out at book value—are involved. If interest rates fall, disintermediation will be slowed, and liabilities can be expected to *lengthen* (i.e., less cash flow will be needed currently). Companies that write primarily group insurance business or individual life insurance products with little or no cash values would be expected to find that their liability cash flow demands were relatively independent of the interest rate, since policyowners are accorded few, if any, demand options.

Thus, **investment antiselection** by policyowners and contractholders is a source of reinvestment and price/liquidity risk. The antiselection is associated with options that have been written by the life insurer to its clients. **Cash inflow antiselection** arises when policyowners and contractholders have the right to deposit additional funds with the insurer under fixed-rate guarantee arrangements established at some earlier point in time—this right becomes valuable in a falling-interest-rate environment. **Cash outflow antiselection** arises when policyowners and contractowners have the right to withdraw funds under a fixed-rate guarantee from the insurer, subject only to modest redemption penalities not tied to market rates of interest. This right becomes valuable in a rising-interest-rate environment.

These risks have to be related to individual product lines since product design, and therefore cash flow needs, vary significantly. Asset/liability management can be approached through the use of separate accounts or by segmentation of the general asset account. The primary motivation behind **portfolio segmentation** is the need to tailor investment strategies appropriately to the cash flow needs of different lines of business, and within lines, to various products.[15] At one extreme, the investment strategy required to support employee benefits under group life and health insurance coverages is essentially one of optimal cash management because the average time that funds are held before claims are paid tends to be a few years at most, and often under a year. At the other extreme, the investment strategy required to support the stream of pension benefits to a closed group of employees, some of whom have already retired and some of whom have not, involves very long-term fixed-income instruments because the liability stream has a long tail that can extend 50 years or longer.

The asset/liability strategy for a life insurance company is determined with the needs and resources of the *entire* company in mind, although the execution of that strategy can be parceled out to various portfolio and product managers acting on behalf of specific lines of business or products.

The Management of Asset/Liability Imbalance [16]

The first step in asset/liability management usually begins with a careful analysis of the company's liabilities and, in turn, a determination of any mismatches that exist. The second step involves restructuring asset portfolios appropriately. Once the portfolios are corrected, they should be monitored and kept in appropriate balance.

The investment manager should:

1. Know the projected liability structure in order to structure the investment portfolio by maturities, which will then determine yields achievable and hence total yield on the portfolio dedicated to each segment of the company's business.

---

[15] See James A. Tilley, *Risk Control Techniques for Life Insurance Companies;* and James B. Attwood, "Organization for Performance: Assets and Liabilities," *1984 Financial Officers Forum—Selected Proceedings* (Atlanta, Ga.: Life Office Management Association, 1984), pp. 14–21.

[16] James A. Tilley, *Risk Control Techniques for Life Insurance Companies,* p. 4.

2. Know yields available for each segment of the business in order to determne liability structure, since persistency is directly related to competitive yields offered in the market by other insurers.

3. Segment and test scenarios of various levels of interest rates and the persistency that results in order to determine the proper asset structure to match the liability structure.

In order for the actuary to determine the liability structure for a particular line or product, he or she must know the yields involved. Thus, the critical first step is jointly to develop a yield forecast, including the shape of the yield curve. With a given yield forecast, it should be possible to determine a liability structure and, in turn, structure assets to match the cash flow characteristics of the product. This is a complicated task. Typically, with interest-sensitive products, there is no historical experience and hence no concept of persistency (a four- or five-year history is not a credible base of experience). There is no way to judge what effect an interest-sensitive product will have on a company's agents replacing its own business or the impact of replacements by others. In addition, both liabilities and assets are affected differently by rising or falling interest rates. Finally, and most important, interest rates do not rise or fall uniformily along the yield curve. An "inverted" yield curve (short-term interest rates being higher than long-term rates) is a serious threat—even to company solvency.

The real challenge in asset/liability management is to determine the best forecast possible on the liability structure under the most likely interest rate and yield curve forecast and then purposely mismatch investments to obtain the highest yield consistent with acceptable risk. In this process, the company should maintain adequate marketability so that it can change maturities in a hurry if it becomes necessary to do so. The key is to take risk intelligently, earn a return for assuming it, and be able to change strategies quickly if necessary.

Cash flow analysis and forecasting through structured statistical methods have strengthened the hand of the investment manager in responding to the changing economy and product innovations. The rapid development of information technology permitting the development and use of comprehensive data bases, coupled with the development of special financial instruments such as options, futures, and interest rate swaps, has opened up new opportunities for life insurers to attempt to control the interest rate risk. It should be noted, however, that as of early 1986, many states still did not permit insurers domiciled there to use interest rate options and futures. In other states, the degree to which their use is permitted is often very limited, both on a specific basis through narrow definitions of legitimate hedging transactions, and on a general basis through the limitation to a small percentage (usually 2 to 5 percent) of the insurer's general account assets that can be hedged at any one time. As a practical matter, very few life insurance companies have made use of such financial instruments even where they are approved for use.

It is agreed today that investment strategies should be designed to recognize specific corporate objectives, volatile financial markets, and a rapidly evolving product mix. Investment managers recognize that no single strategy can sufficiently meet these demands. Accordingly, they must use an array of strategies in an effort to respond to increased product competition, inflation, and consumer demands for higher current yield and liquidity.[17]

A large portion of the corporate debt purchases made by life insurers are private placements secured by forward commitments (historically up to two years ahead). The same holds true for a large proportion of commercial mortgages. Such commitments usually are legally binding on the supplier of funds (the life insurers), although the borrower retains some flexibility in its decision as to whether the loan (debt issue or mortgage) should be taken down in full or in part at the end of the commitment period. In the current deregulated environment there has been a significant restructuring of investment strategy away from fixed-rate forward commitments in the debt and mortgage markets.

[17]Francis H. Schott, "Investment Policy in the New Life Insurance Environment." See also Anthony Saunders, "The Effect of Changing Regulations on Investment Policy of Life Insurance Companies," in *The Emerging Financial Industry* (Lexington, Mass.: Lexington Books, 1984), Chap. 9, pp. 89–93.

In the place of fixed-rate commitments, some companies have switched to either spot market loans or making more indexed or floating-rate commitments (in which changes in the interest rates are hedged automatically). Because borrowers may react adversely to these more stringent borrowing terms, it should not be surprising to see a continuing fall in the aggregate private debt and mortgage components in the life insurers' portfolios.

The success of group pension funds and variable life insurance and annuities, relative to more traditional life insurance products, should result in a growing importance of *separate accounts* relative to general accounts for many insurers. (Separate account assets were 10.7 percent of all life insurer assets in 1985.) As already noted, separate accounts generally are free of investment restrictions pertaining to general accounts, with cash surrenders and policyowner loans (if any) linked to market values and rates. The relative growth of separate accounts could result in an increasing proportion of equity relative to debt and mortgages in insurers' portfolios. A growing number of companies are offering variable life insurance, in which the policyowner can decide whether his or her premiums will be invested in a relatively conservative stock fund, a medium-traded bond fund, or a money market mutual fund. Approximately 50 percent of the policyowners of one company chose money market mutual funds, 30 percent common stocks, and 20 percent publicly traded bonds.[18] In managing these funds, the life insurer is acting virtually identically to a mutual fund manager whose main preoccupation is with investment results rather than with the provision of traditional life insurance services.

The development of universal life and other new insurance products that emphasize return has raised the problem of restructuring asset portfolios to generate as high a return as possible while ensuring sufficient liquidity in the event of surrender, policyowner loans, or the payment of benefits. As more new product lines are added and with continuing deregulation, life insurance companies will, of course, have to continue to be careful to

ensure that *adequate matching of liability and asset maturities* is achieved for both separate and general accounts. For example, guaranteed investment contracts (GICs) and nonparticipating annuities require a much higher degree of maturity matching than do variable life or variable annuities (with market value adjustments).

Operationally, life insurance companies have to classify insurance products into groups that reflect common cash flow, liquidity, or other shared characteristics. Once this grouping occurs, funds flowing into these product lines (and earned in related investments) are managed separately from other product lines, with different maturity or liquidity characteristics.

A number of possible (and not mutually exclusive) investment strategies to deal with the maturity diversity of new product lines is being utilized. Some companies have created subsidiaries, each specializing in managing the assets relating to a single or group of closely related products. Some life insurers have made extensive use of separate accounts. In lieu of separate accounts, some companies have segmented their general account along product groups. These segmented portfolios have different horizons that approximately match the anticipated cash flow needs for the selected groups of products generating the funds constituting the portfolio.

In sum, a product or line of business provides constraints on the types and maturity of investments that should be funded out of cash flows from that product or line of business. Once these product (line) groupings are defined, the investment manager's task is to select optimal portfolios using conventional modern portfolio theory methods.

The changes necessary to meet the new role of the investment department can be hindered by the influence of inappropriate measures of performance. In more and more companies, past models and measures are being replaced by new organizational structures and new internal measures of performance. It is clear that the overall rate of return is not as important as it once was. The spread between the actual return and the amount credited on a particular line or product is the critical management issue—assuming of course that the actual return is reasonable. It

[18]*Ibid.*

should also be remembered that there has been a deterioration of the credit quality of corporate and municipal debt, which with a volatile bond market, complicates the investment management task even more.

It is worth noting that the recent shift in investment practices has led to a shortening of portfolio maturities in both bonds and mortgages to meet greater needs for liquidity.

PATTERNS OF INVESTMENT

Life insurance company investments may be categorized as follows: (1) government securities, (2) corporate securities, (3) mortgages, (4) real estate, and (5) policy loans and other assets.

Government Securities

All states permit ownership of U.S. government bonds and the bonds of states and their political subdivisions. A few states restrict municipal bond ownership to general obligation bonds. Others permit ownership of limited-liability tax bonds and revenue bonds as well.

Government Bonds. There is probably no better example of the life insurance industry's willingness to adjust itself to the changing capital-demand patterns of the nation than that to be found in an examination of the government-bond account. At the close of 1945, the industry had 45.9 percent of its assets in U.S. government bonds. Subsequent to that year, the demand pattern shifted, and Treasury bonds declined in absolute and relative significance. The 1979 figure for Treasury and federal agency securities was 3.3 percent of assets. The decline was brought about by the ever-increasing capital needs of business and industry in the postwar era, the need for greater investment diversification, and the industry's recognition of a need for a greater yield than that obtainable from U.S. government securities. By 1985 this figure had risen to 15.0 percent. After years of very little attention by life company investors, government bonds have become a major investment outlet. This change resulted both from the fact that short-term governments were pro-

viding yields greater than longer maturities (an "inverted" yield curve) and the need for greater liquidity by the business.

State, Municipal, and Foreign Government Bonds. In view of their federal income tax position, life insurers ownership of state and municipal securities has never been of great relative significance. Currently, this percentage has risen to 1.2 percent. These funds have been used to provide schools, utility systems, and roads to meet the needs of our ever-increasing population.

Foreign bonds are represented largely by Canadian provincial and local government bonds. Foreign government, including international agency, bonds have never represented a significant proportion of life insurance company assets (1.7 percent at the close of 1985).

Corporate Securities

Bonds and stocks of business and industry have, since 1935, constituted the largest single area of investment of life insurance companies, representing 45.4 percent of assets at the close of 1985. Generally speaking, the states permit ownership of the mortgage bonds, debentures, and notes of solvent U.S. and Canadian corporations.[19]

Corporate Bonds. Corporate-bond holdings at the end of 1985 amounted to $296.9 billion and were 36.0 percent of all assets. These investments have remained between 35 and 40 percent as a proportion of all life insurance company assets for the past 25 years. The bulk of corporate-bond holdings at the end of 1985 was invested in U.S. organizations; $14.7 billion was invested in corporations in foreign countries, chiefly Canada.

Corporate bonds include the bonds of railroads, public utilities, and industrial and miscellaneous corporations. Public utility bonds have traditionally been an important medium for life insurance company funds. Such investments have

---

[19]There are restrictions of a statistical nature that vary from state to state. For example, the state of Nebraska requires that an issuing public utility company must have earned the fixed charges on all its debt at least 1 ½ times during the past year.

helped to provide the nation with the power for industrial expansion and the means to distribute it.

Preferred and Common Stocks. Investments in stocks, which account for the other part of corporate securities owned by U.S. life insurance companies, amounted to $77.5 billion at the end of 1985. Common stocks accounted for 86.5 percent of this total. Preferred and common stocks together represented 9.4 percent of total company assets at year-end 1985.

Historically, stocks have been a small percentage of total assets, for reasons rooted both in the investment philosophy of the business and in the laws regulating life insurance. They have not been heavily used as a major investment medium for funds backing life insurance policies, in view of contractual guarantees for specified dollar amounts. Legal restrictions on common stock investments have also discouraged their use to some extent.

Life insurance companies generally have not been restricted in the amount they can invest in preferred stock. Limits exist on the amount of a single issuer's preferred stock that a life insurer can hold. One state's limit is currently 20 percent of the total issued and outstanding stock of any one corporation, not to exceed 2 percent of the admitted assets of the life insurance company. The earnings and dividend requirements are similar to the restrictions on corporate bonds.

Typical restrictions by the states on investment in common stock in this area are the following: limiting total common stock investment to a relatively small percentage of assets of the insurance company or to a percentage of its capital and/or surplus; limiting ownership of the stock of a given company to a very small percentage of that company's outstanding shares; limiting ownership of the stock of a given company to a small percentage of the insurer's admitted assets; and prohibiting ownership of shares that cannot meet a variety of statistical requirements, relating primarily to the issuer's earnings and dividend records. In 1969, New York State raised its limit on common stock to the lower of policyowners' surplus or 10 percent of admitted assets. This, coupled with the growth of separate accounts

without limitation on common stock, led to the increased importance of this type of security. At year-end 1985, common stocks in separate accounts amounted to $33.9 billion or 38.5 percent of total separate account assets, compared with holdings of $6.2 billion or 66.4 percent of separate account assets 11 years earlier.

Mortgages. First mortgages on residential, commercial, and industrial real estate comprise a large area of investment for life insurance companies. The need for funds to finance the building of homes in the 1950s and early 1960s led states to permit virtually unrestricted investment in these loans, which also carried government backing. In the late 1960s, higher yields available on apartments and commercial and industrial real estate slowed the flow of life insurance funds into individual family dwellings. The most general legal restriction on "conventional" (uninsured, nonguaranteed) first-mortgage loans is that the loan must not exceed a percentage of the value of the improved real estate. Some states permit loans in amounts up to 80 percent of value. Many limit the amount to 75 percent.

At year-end 1985, mortgages amounted to $171.8 billion, or 20.8 percent of total life insurance company assets. Seventy-one percent of the mortgage holdings at year-end 1984 were in nonfarm, nonresidential properties; residential loans, on single-family and multifamily properties, represented about 21 percent of the mortgage debt held by life insurance companies, with farm properties the security on the balance. Approximately 5 percent of these loans are either guaranteed by the Veterans Administration or insured by the Federal Housing Administration. Holdings of mortgages guaranteed by the Veterans Administration and the Federal Housing Administration have been declining steadily in recent years.

Real Estate. For many years, investment in real estate for other than operational purposes was forbidden to most life insurance companies. The dynamic nature of the post–World War II economy, however, resulted in an increasing demand for capital from commerce and industry. To remain competitive, a company with a large percentage of its capital tied up in fixed assets often finds itself in need of capital to finance increased plant and inventory requirements. Such circumstances have led to the increased use of the so-called **sale-leaseback** or purchase-leaseback transaction. Here a company builds a plant, warehouse, office, or shopping center and, on completion, sells it to a long-term investor (e.g., a life insurer), at the same time leasing the property back from the purchaser. In reality, this is a financing technique rather than a real estate investment per se.

Typically, companies are allowed to have only a small portion of assets invested in "investment" real estate; 10 percent is a common figure. Many companies increased their real estate **equity investments** in the 1970s and early 1980s in an attempt to protect themselves against the adverse effects of inflation. In the last few years, there has been a surge of new interest in real estate among the larger companies, sometimes taking the form of new development of real property which is wholly owned and operated by the insurance company. In addition, there has been a great deal of joint venture ownership by life insurers in partnership with a real estate management company.

A number of states include a "leeway law" or "basket clause" in their insurance codes, which alleviates, in part, any strain that restrictive statutes may impose on company investment operations. The code of Connecticut includes the following provision: "Any domestic life insurance company may loan or invest its funds to an amount not exceeding in the aggregate eight percent of its total admitted assets in loans or investments not qualifying or not permitted under its charter or under any section of the general statutes."

Policy Loans and Other Assets

Although the policy loan, since it is an income-generating asset, is an "investment," its status in the life insurance company statement is not the normal province of the investment department. As would be expected, the relative significance of these loans as an industry asset fluctuates inversely with the availability of credit from other sources. However, given today's economic environment, policy loans and their corollary, lapses and surrenders, are, and probably will continue to be, a drain on investable cash flow. In contrast to past cycles, policy loans are being utilized by more individuals, affecting substantially smaller policies and more companies than in past cycles. Of deeper concern, however, is that, in contrast to past cycles where market arbitrage was the primary purpose of a policy loan, today more borrowing is being utilized to maintain a standard of living. Thus, the probability of repayment is low. Also, with the possibility that short-term rates could remain above policy loan rates, the historic pattern of loan payback by arbitrageurs may not take place. It should be noted, however, that the rise in policy loans has flattened out since 1982, and in 1985, the outstanding amount actually declined. At year-end 1985 policy loans constituted 6.6 percent of life-company assets.

Cash, due and deferred premiums, collateral loans, joint ventures, and mineral interests constitute the remaining assets of the industry. The first two are obviously not investments, and the others, except for certain joint ventures, have never occupied a position of any prominence in life insurance company investment operations.

Chapter 32

Life Insurance Company Financial Statements

INTRODUCTION

Financial statements and their interpretations are as vitally important to life insurers as they are to any business enterprise. Meaningful statement interpretation is accomplished by a systematic analysis of the statements themselves and by the use of supplemental sources of information.

Life insurance companies file annual financial statements with state insurance commissioners. Those statements are prepared in accordance with state regulatory practices (referred to as statutory accounting practices or SAP) and include extensive data with respect to the insurance company's statutory financial position and results of operations for the year. In addition, many life insurance companies publish annual reports for their shareholders, policyowners, and others. These reports typically include financial statements. However, these financial statements usually are presented in accordance with generally accepted accounting principles (GAAP). This chapter presents a discussion of these types of financial statements as well as of statutory accounting.

STATUTORY ACCOUNTING

The NAIC Annual Statement

The financial condition and management of an insurance company are concerns of state law and are subject to review by state regulatory authorities. For state insurance departments to obtain information that will enable them to evaluate a company's financial condition, each company is required to submit a highly detailed annual statement. These statements are filed with the insurance department in each state and territory in which the company is licensed to do business. In Canada, they are filed with the Dominion Department, which assumes the primary responsibility for the solvency of companies licensed by it.

In 1871, by securing the agreement of the states to adopt a uniform annual financial statement, the National Association of Insurance Commissioners (then known as the National Convention of Insurance Commissioners) rendered one of its most valuable contributions to the insurance business. This so-called **NAIC Blank** is subject to revision annually by a committee of the association, but usually only minor changes are made. Special blanks are prepared by different classes of company (life, property, and so on). The life blank was last revised significantly in 1951. Special reporting blanks have been developed for reporting separate-account business and variable life insurance business.

The Primary Financial Statements. The primary financial statements consist of a **balance sheet** and a **summary of operations.** Each is discussed in more detail below. The balance sheet consists of separate statements of assets and liabilities in summary form. Thus, in the statement of assets, the amount of each main category (such as bonds or common stocks) is shown only in total, and in the statement of liabilities, policy reserves similarly are shown in total for life and health insurance, respectively. Detailed breakdowns of these items are furnished in subsidiary exhibits and schedules (discussed below).

The form of the summary of operations in the NAIC Annual Statement shows the net increase in surplus from all sources, with some exceptions. The excluded items from the summary of operations are shown in the accompanying **capital and surplus account.** The summary of operations statement is accompanied by two supplementary reports: an analysis of **operations by lines of business** and an analysis of **changes in policy reserves** during the year.

The analyis of operations by lines of business is merely an allocation by line of business of the figures shown for all lines combined in the summary of operations mentioned above. It shows how the total net gain for the company, after allocation of dividends to policyowners, is distributed among the different lines of business—life insurance (ordinary, industrial, credit, and group) and supplementary benefits and health insurance (individual, credit, and group). The report relating to changes in policy reserves is a purely technical statement for the use of the actuaries of the state insurance department in verifying certain gains and losses and for other purposes.

Supplementary Exhibits and Schedules. In general, the subsidiary exhibits and schedules provide breakdowns, or further details in regard to some of the items that appear only in total in the primary financial statements.

Among the **Exhibits,** the more important are those furnishing details or classified information about (1) premium income; (2) investment income; (3) capital gains and losses; (4) expenses; (5) taxes; (6) policy reserves; (7) policy and contract claims; (8) life insurance issued, terminated, and in force (the "policy exhibit"); and (9) annuities issued, terminated, and in force (the "annuity exhibit"). A series of general interrogatories follows the exhibits.

The most important **Schedules** found in the NAIC Statement are those relating to real estate, mortgage loans, and securities (bonds and stocks). The schedules for real estate and securities show, in considerable detail, the amounts owned at the end of the year and the purchases and sales during the year. Somewhat similar information is given for mortgage loans, but with less detail. Other important schedules show detailed information regarding (1) individual bank balances, month by month; (2) resisted claims; (3) expenses incurred in connection with legal matters or appearances before legislative bodies, and so on; and (4) proceedings of the last annual election of directors.

A statement of the company's business in the state in which the report is being filed is shown at the end of the statement, following the schedules. The statement shows the numbers and amounts of policies issued, terminated, and in force, together with a statement of premiums collected and policy dividends and benefits paid in the state. Naturally, the necessity of furnishing such information by state requires the insurance company to maintain its records in such a way as to be able to report its business by state.

The NAIC Statement is intended to provide technical information required for proper supervision by the state insurance department of all the financial operations and activities of the company. The nature, detail, and quantity of data required for regulatory purposes make the NAIC Statement a complex and lengthy report.

The Balance Sheet

Nature. The most significant feature of a statutory financial statement probably is the statement of financial condition or **balance sheet.** This consists of a list of the assets and liabilities of the company and its capital and surplus, as of a certain date.

An idea of the capital and surplus available for contingencies can be obtained from the balance sheet, assuming that the assets have been valued properly and that the liabilities have been stated correctly. If the liabilities plus the legal minimum capital and surplus were to exceed the assets, the company would be technically insolvent. Assets virtually always exceed the liabilities by substantial amounts. The excess of the assets over the liabilities consists of capital (in a stock company) and surplus, both earmarked and unassigned.[1] To understand the balance sheet better, it will be helpful to consider briefly certain technical terms that appear in the NAIC Annual Statement as well as the basis of the values that are placed on assets for statutory annual statement purposes.

1. *Technical terms.* **Ledger assets** are those that have been entered on the books (ledgers) of the company. Cash and investments are the main ledger assets.

For practical reasons, some assets are almost never entered onto the ledgers of the company. These are called **nonledger assets.** The most significant of these are (1) overdue investment income (usually small), (2) accrued investment income (earned but not received), (3) net premiums due (or uncollected) on all types of insurance, and (4) deferred premiums on ordinary insurance and annuities. The last class of nonledger assets arises from the fact that policy-reserve liabilities are normally stated on the assumption that premiums are payable annually in advance. This is an overstatement of the reserve liability where policies are payable monthly, quarterly, or semiannually that is adjusted via a deferred premium asset.[2] This last asset offsets the excess reserve liability so that the net effect on the balance sheet is proper.

Assets approved by state regulatory authorities as sound and accepted as such in the NAIC Annual Statement are known as **admitted assets.** Admitted assets are made up of both ledger and nonledger assets. Only the value of admitted assets may be shown on the statutory balance sheet. The values of **nonadmitted assets** may not be included.

Although some nonadmitted assets would be reported in the balance sheets of other businesses, they are not admitted here, in the interest of conservative reporting of a company's financial position. Nonadmitted assets include (1) furniture and equipment,[3] (2) agents' balances (advances to agents), and (3) overdue and accrued interest on mortgages on which the interest is overdue more than a specified period. Companies have some latitude in determining the time period after which such interest will be treated as a nonadmitted asset. Some nonadmitted assets are ledger assets (e.g., agents' balances), and some are nonledger assets (such as overdue interest).

2. *Valuation of assets.* To make clear the basis of the values that are placed on assets for statutory annual statement purposes, it is helpful to classify them broadly as (1) amortizable securities, (2) other securities, and (3) other assets.

(a) Amortizable securities. A substantial proportion of life insurance company assets is invested in securities that are not readily marketable. The problems involved in valuing such investments are significant. Most states provide for

---

[1]As explained earlier, a rough measure of the financial stability of a company is indicated by the relation of the capital and surplus to the liabilities. See Chapter 11.

[2]Assume that a policy is dated September 15, with quarterly premiums paid through the one due September 15. As of December 31, the December 15 premium is due, and its net amount is counted as an asset although it has not yet been paid. The premiums due next March 15 and June 15, required to complete the policy year, are "deferred" premiums, and their net amounts are also counted as assets.

[3]A number of states make an exception for large-scale data-processing equipment, allowing its value after depreciation to be counted as an admitted asset.

a method of valuation of most such securities. The resulting value is independent of current prices in the securities markets.

The law of the state of New York is representative. It provides that (1) no stock or bond that is in default in either principal or interest or that is not amply secured and no "perpetual bond" (one without a maturity date) shall be valued above the market value; and (2) all other bonds— those that are amply secured and not in default— shall be valued on the basis of the purchase price, adjusted so as to bring the value to par at maturity and so as to yield the effective rate of interest at which the purchase was made. The values produced by the method in the second category are known as **amortized values.**

For some years, the Committee on Valuation of Securities, appointed by the NAIC, has supplied specific bases for determining the eligibility of various classes of bonds for amortization. This committee submits an annual report that sets forth these requirements in great detail. Also, it is possible to approach the NAIC Committee on Valuation of Securities and present specific information about a particular situation. If the Committee approves the bond, it is eligible for amortization. The use of the amortized value for a bond is based on the assumptions (1) that the amounts of interest and principal will be paid when due, and (2) that it will not be necessary to sell before maturity.

The expression "amortized value" applies, strictly speaking, only to those bonds bought at a premium (above par), but it is also generally used in connection with bonds bought at a discount (below par). It refers to the adjustments of the original cost (original book value) by which that value is reduced or increased in successive stages until it equals the **par value** on the **maturity date.**

In recent years, where interest rates have fluctuated significantly, market values for such bonds also have fluctuated significantly, complicating the process of maintaining a reasonable balance (match) between the liabilities assumed and the assets standing behind varying types of liabilities. For example, the sale of bonds (with market values well below their maturity values) in order to meet the increased cash flow needs of certain types of liabilities leads to capital losses which directly affect the earnings per share of a company. The sale also complicates the company's tax position. Under the more stable economic environment of the past, where it was not necessary to adjust asset portfolios because of volatile interest rates, and in the absence of interest-sensitive products, amortized values were appropriate. However, the fluctuation in values has become so significant that the state of California (since 1983) requires the disclosure of market values for both preferred stocks and bonds. Many companies provide such information voluntarily. Most companies mark (adjust) their balance sheets to market for internal management purposes, regardless of the statutory or other accounting requirements.

(b) Other securities. Preferred stock in "good standing" generally is valued at cost, a stable value. All common stocks, preferred stocks not in good standing, and bonds not deemed to be amply secured must be valued at or below the market price prescribed by the NAIC. The NAIC publishes these values each year, and these values are used by insurers in preparing their statutory annual statements.

The valuation of nonamortizable bonds poses problems. The only available "nonarbitrary" value, the current price in the market, may be affected temporarily by many factors that have little relation to ongoing value and is, of course, not available for most direct placements. Use of such market values may lead to an apparent loss or gain in surplus that might be completely reversed by *not* doing the same for liabilities. This remains a key area of investigation for life insurance research. A satisfactory solution to the problem will have significant ramifications not only for investment policy, but in terms of product design, the company's ability to supply capital to the economy, and the industry's relative competitive position.

(c) Other assets. Assets other than securities include real estate, transportation equipment, mortgage loans, policy loans, mineral interests, joint ventures, and cash. The value placed on such assets normally is the **book value,** that is, in the case of real estate and transportation equipment, the **cost** (subject to any adjustments, including depreciation, that have taken place), and in the case of loans, the **unpaid principal balance** (less any accrued discounts plus any unamortized premiums).

Real estate may or may not actually be worth the original cost or the present book value. An appraisal could be made periodically as a basis for formally adjusting the book value, but such appraisals are themselves only estimates. Thus, some companies establish an offsetting liability in the form of a special contingency reserve for revaluation of real estate to cover expected losses on sale. On the other hand, if the book values are definitely excessive, they should be written down. The same procedure may be applied to mortgage loans if the security is deemed questionable.

3. *Accrual versus cash basis.* The **cash basis** of accounting (which most individuals use for their personal income tax returns) assumes that reported income and disbursements include only items that have actually been received or disbursed and entered on the books. On the other hand, if items are included that have not actually been received or disbursed but that are attributable to the current accounting period, the income and disbursements are said to be on an **accrual basis.** The summary of operations contained in the NAIC Statement (and in most annual reports) shows income and disbursements on an accrual basis.[4] Examples of income items that have not actually been received are accrued interest and uncollected premiums. Examples of disbursement items that have not actually been disbursed are claims in the course of settlement and taxes payable in the following year on the current year's operations.

Interpreting the Balance Sheet. The sample statutory balance sheet shown in Table 32–1 is that of a hypothetical stock company writing participating insurance. If this were a mutual company, there would be no item for "Capital." Similarly, there would be no items concerned with dividends

to policyowners in a stock company writing only nonparticipating business. On the other hand, an item for dividends to shareholders would exist in stock-company statements.

The assets and liabilities of this company roughly reflect the average distribution of assets and liabilities of all U.S. life insurance companies. To present some concepts for discussion purposes, reasonable assumptions were made as to the breakdown of certain items where the information was not readily available for all companies.

1. *Assets.* The values to be placed on various types of assets are very important in the financial picture presented by the balance sheet. For purposes of the present discussion, assets as shown on a statutory balance sheet may be broadly classified as follows:

1. Cash
2. Investments
3. Net premiums deferred and overdue
4. Interest and rents due and accrued
5. Miscellaneous assets
6. Assets held in separate accounts

(a) Cash. Cash consists of (a) actual cash held at the date of the statement in the company's home office and branch offices, and (b) amounts on deposit in banks. Companies maintain bank accounts in cities throughout the country where they transact business. Part of these deposits may be "at interest." Although "actual cash" is usually of relatively small amounts, cash in banks may amount to as much as ½ to 2 percent of total assets. Since this asset is relatively nonproductive, an unusually large amount of cash would warrant investigation as to its cause. As was pointed out in Chapter 31, a significant problem for life insurance company management is the projection of cash flows to maximize investment income while appropriately matching assets and liabilities.

(b) Investments. The investment portfolio of a life insurance company usually includes (a) bonds, (b) stocks, (c) mortgage loans, (d) real

---

[4]See "The Summary of Operations" below.

TABLE 32-1. Sample statement of statutory financial condition
(balance sheet)

Assets

Bonds[a]		
United States government	$ 4,400,000	
Canadian government (includes political subdivisions)	500,000	
State, county, and municipal	3,900,000	
Public utility	13,000,000	
Railroad	2,600,000	
Industrial and miscellaneous	23,100,000	
Total bonds		$ 47,500,000
Stocks[a]		
Preferred and guaranteed	$ 2,000,000	
Common	7,100,000	
Total stocks		9,100,000
Mortgages		
Insured under Federal Housing Act	$ 8,000,000	
Guaranteed in part by Veterans Administration	5,000,000	
Others (conventional)	15,100,000	
Total mortgages		28,100,000
Real estate and other property		
Home office	$ 735,000	
Real estate held as an investment	2,000,000	
Real estate acquired in satisfaction of debt	55,000	
Transportation equipment	160,000	
Data-processing equipment	50,000	
Total real estate and other property		3,000,000
Other assets		
Loans on policies of the company	$ 8,000,000	
Collateral loans	60,000	
Cash and bank deposits	1,160,000	
Investment income due and accrued	850,000	
Net premiums due and deferred		
(fully covered by policy reserves)	1,800,000	
Miscellaneous assets	430,000	
Total other assets		12,300,000
Total assets		$100,000,000

Liabilities

Reserves for policies and supplementary contracts[b]		
Life insurance	$61,800,000	
Annuities and supplementary contracts		
with life contingencies	17,200,000	
Disability benefits	500,000	
Accidental-death benefit	300,000	
Health insurance	750,000	
Total reserves for policies and supplementary contracts		$ 80,550,000
(this fund, together with future premiums and interest earnings, is to provide for payment of future benefits)		
Supplementary contracts without life contingencies		3,000,000
Policyowner dividends left to accumulate at interest		2,650,000
Policyowner dividends declared for following year		1,600,000
Premiums reserved in advance		1,550,000
Claims in course of settlement (includes amount set aside for claims incurred but unreported)		800,000
Taxes accrued, payable in following year		800,000
Miscellaneous liabilities		1,100,000
Mandatory securities valuation reserve		1,350,000
Total liabilities		$ 93,400,000
Capital		500,000
Special surplus funds		1,100,000
Unassigned surplus		5,000,000
Total liabilities, capital, and surplus		$100,000,000

[a]Bonds subject to amortization according to state laws are carried at their amortized values. Other bonds and all stocks are carried at values prescribed by the National Association of Insurance Commissioners.

[b]In an actual annual report, the reserves for policies and supplementary contracts would probably be shown simply as one lump sum and not broken down as here.

estate, and (e) policy loans.[5] The values placed on each of these classes of investments were explained earlier; that is, bonds, if fully secured and not in default, are included at their amortized values. Other bonds and all stocks are listed at current market values (as determined by the NAIC Committee on Valuation of Securities).[6] Mortgage and policy loans are entered at the amounts of the loans unpaid;[7] and real estate is shown at book or market value, whichever is lower. It is common to write down the book value regularly each year. In some cases, the writedowns may exceed normal depreciation. For many classes of real estate, the book value is lower than the fair market value.

Since the asset page of a statutory report does not reveal the quality of the assets, the most useful information that can be derived from it is some idea of how the distribution of the assets of a particular company compares with the distribution for the life insurance industry as a whole. If the percentage of the assets in each category for a given company approximates that for the industry, the company's investment program is probably somewhere near the middle of the road compared with the programs of other life companies. If, however, significant differences exist, a more thorough investigation of the investment program of the company may be called for. In any such investigation, attention would be given to the specific assets themselves. The comparison of the interest rate earned by the company over a period of time with the average rate for the industry would also be a factor to consider.

In evaluating a company's investment program, it is necessary to consider general business and economic conditions and the effects they might be having on a "prudent" investment program. It should also be remembered that "hind-

sight is better than foresight." Only time can give an accurate appraisal of the soundness of a particular investment program.

U.S. government securities usually do not loom large relative to the industry in a company's statement but this is a function of changing market conditions (at the end of 1985, 15.0 percent).

Corporate bonds, constituting about 36.0 percent of the aggregate assets of all companies, represent, in general, a middle-of-the-road position with respect to security, yield, and liquidity. Tax-exempt bonds (state, county, municipal, and authority issues) represent only a small percentage of assets, but may increase in view of the treatment of earnings from such bonds under current federal income taxation of life insurance companies.

Stocks usually constitute a small percentage of total assets. Preferred and guaranteed stocks make up about 1.3 percent of the total assets of life insurance companies, and common stocks about 8.1 percent. The amount of common stocks, although still relatively small, has increased considerably since the introduction of legislation permitting separate account funding. A significant proportion of assets invested in common stocks that are not invested in separate accounts might indicate an investment program with too little attention to safety. Most state laws limit common-stock investment to a small percentage of the assets, and it would be rare that a national company could or would attain the maximum permitted. A company operating in a limited geographical area with a high percentage of capital and surplus in relation to assets could conceivably approach the legal maximim, but a limiting factor is that the legal maximum is based, not on cost but on current market, and a company would undoubtedly try to leave a safety margin between the amount invested and the amount permitted.

Life insurance obligations have been measured, traditionally, in fixed amounts, and stocks have not been considered satisfactory for extensive investment because their values tend to fluctuate with the market and economic conditions. This leaves the company with the possibility of becoming insolvent during a time of depression, even though it might recover with a substantial surplus when the market price of equities again

---

[5]In most companies, there are other special types of investments, including various types of loans (e.g., "collateral loans") other than mortgage and policy loans, such as partnerships, joint ventures, and so on.

[6]Preferred stocks "in good standing" are shown at their "adjusted values," as determined by the Committee on Valuation of Securities.

[7]Mortgages bought at a premium or discount are shown, in many circumstances, at values that take the premiums or discounts into consideration.

started rising. In sum, equity investments simply do not match companies' traditional fixed amount promises. With the introduction of separate account funding and variable products, interest in stocks will undoubtedly increase.

Mortgages usually constitute the second largest category of investments, representing 20.8 percent of the assets of the life insurance industry in 1985. Mortgages are often regarded as less liquid than bonds, because they usually are not traded as freely. There is, of course, some liquidity through return flows from amortization payments and prepayments. A balance between liquidity and the higher yield available from mortgage investments should be considered in evaluating a company's portfolio. A major consideration, of course, is the percentage of the mortgages that are guaranteed by the Federal Housing Administration (FHA) and the Veterans Administration (VA). These "insured" mortgages typically are more marketable than are conventional mortgages. If investments are made in mortgage loans, it is desirable that they be in significant volume. The higher fixed costs usually involved in servicing residential mortgages make the returns unattractive on a small volume.

Recently, secondary markets for mortgage loans, packaged as securities (referred to as securitization), have become a significant factor in this area. With a secondary market, liquidity is considerably improved, an important need in the current economic environment.

Life insurance company holdings of mortgages guaranteed by the VA and the FHA have been declining steadily in recent years. Also, a large shift has occurred in mortgage portfolios from residential to commercial mortgages. The shift is reflective of current money market conditions.

Investment real estate is a comparatively minor item on the balance sheets of most companies. It is usually judged an unsuitable investment medium for a large proportion of assets because of its special characteristics, including lack of liquidity and instability of value.

The amount of real estate owned that was acquired because of mortgage foreclosure is negligible. In most companies, the home office (land and buildings) also represents only a small proportion of the assets. Occasionally, a small company has a home office that constitutes a significant proportion of assets. This could be an indication of overexpansion or lack of prudent management. There also is a danger that the book value at which such a property is carried may be higher than the amount that could be realized upon sale, especially in times of business depression. It is probably much more common, however, for the book value of a home-office property to be lower than its fair market value. Many companies write down the book value of their home-office property regularly each year to take care of depreciation and obsolescence. "Write-downs" in some cases exceed the actual depreciation.

Transportation equipment in moderate amounts makes a suitable investment medium. The advantages and disadvantages of this type of investment are somewhat similar to those for investment real estate.

Policy loans represented, at year-end 1985, 6.6 percent of life insurance company assets, as compared with a recent peak of 9.3 percent in 1981 and a historical high of 18 percent in 1932 and 1933. As policy loans usually are made only on ordinary insurance, the percentage of policy loans for a particular company might be higher or lower than the industry average, depending partly on the proportion of its policy reserves that represent ordinary insurance and partly on its market.

In general, economic conditions are the major factors affecting the amount of policy loans outstanding. The percentage for a certain company might be considerably higher than the industry average, as the result of factors not of any special significance. On the other hand, a high percentage might be an indication that the company operates in a depressed area and that its business is likely to be more vulnerable to lapse or surrender than the business of an average company. The rise of the market interest rates to levels exceeding the policy loan rate guaranteed in most outstanding contracts has, of course, been the major factor that has led to a higher percentage of policy loans outstanding.

(c) Net premiums deferred and uncollected. As was pointed out earlier, the deferred premium asset is taken to offset the overstatement of the policy-reserve liability brought about by the difference between the assumptions as to premium payments in reserve calculations and the actual modes of paying premiums. In essence, there is an overstatement of both assets and liabilities, resulting in an appropriate net liability. This item also accounts for premiums that are overdue, since the reserve is overstated in this case also.

(d) **Interest and rents due and accrued.** A company statement of assets must include not only assets actually in the possession of the company, but also assets represented by amounts due to the company, whether these actually have become receivable or are merely the accrued part of payments to be received later. In the case of overdue receivables, a sound asset exists only if the payment is secured (the usual case in connection with mortgage and other loans).

Accrued interest (where there has been no default) is a sound asset. In the case of bonds, for example, if the bonds were sold, the sale price would reflect the presence of accrued interest. During normal times, overdue interest likely is very small. It is often reported in combination with the much larger item of accrued interest.[8] In periods of economic depression, overdue interest on mortgages may become sizable. In such periods, its size may be helpful in giving some indication of the quality of the mortgage portfolio. Its usefulness as such an indicator, however, is impaired by the fact that company practices, relative to charging off overdue interest as a nonadmitted asset, vary considerably. It is possible for a company with a portfolio of excellent quality to have proportionately more overdue interest shown on its annual report than has a company with a portfolio of a lesser quality. This could occur if the first company included most of its overdue interest as an admitted asset and the second company treated most of its overdue interest as a nonadmitted asset, perhaps because its ultimate collection was more doubtful than in the case of the first company.

(e) **Miscellaneous assets.** The other assets usually found in a statement are chiefly (a) other amounts due to the company but not yet received

(for instance, reinsurance claim settlements) and (b) collateral loans—neither of which constitute a significant amount in the usual statement. Some companies also include large-scale electronic data-processing equipment in this category. The development of joint ventures, partnerships, and similar relationships brought about through investment activity could be a significant category of assets for a particular company.

(f) **Assets held in separate accounts.** A **separate account** is a fund established by a life insurance company and held separately from all other assets of the company. State laws provide that assets in separate accounts may be invested without regard to the usual restrictions that are placed on the investments of life-company assets. Thus, a separate-account portfolio might be made up of common stocks only, bonds only, mortgages only, or some combination of these or other assets. At the present time, most of the assets held in separate accounts are invested in common stocks and bonds (over 65 percent).

The use of separate accounts has increased substantially since first used in the early 1960s, to the point that aggregate assets in these accounts totaled $88.1 billion at the end of 1985. At that time, the number of life companies filing separate annual statements covering these accounts as required by regulatory agencies had increased to more than 175.

Although separate accounts have been used primarily to handle pension funds, the introduction of variable life insurance and variable universal life has increased the use of separate accounts. Those wishing to have their funds placed in separate accounts accept the investment risks.

A separate account usually holds the funds of many policyowners or annuitants in a combined investment arrangement. This is called a "pooled account." However, an individual separate account may be provided for a large corporate client, holding only its contributions.

2. *Liabilities.* Liabilities as they appear on the usual statutory balance sheet may be classified broadly as follows:

1. Policy reserves
2. Amounts held on deposit

---

[8]No item of overdue interest is carried as an asset on bonds in default, as the market value of such bonds reflects any interest in default.

3. Dividends (to policyowners and shareholders) that have been allocated but are not payable until after the date of the balance sheet
4. Claims incurred but not yet paid
5. Other amounts payable
6. Amounts held for account of others
7. Mandatory securities valuation reserve
8. Special reserves

(a) **Policy reserves.** Policy reserves are amounts that, on the basis of the assumed mortality tables (or other tables) and rates of interest, are needed, together with future net premiums assumed to be received, to provide the benefits included in the company's life, annuity, and health insurance contracts. These include the reserves for the special benefits such as for disability and accidental death benefits, and those for supplementary contracts with life contingencies.

As indicated on the balance sheet in Table 32–1, by far the greatest proportion of the liabilities of a life insurance company is represented by the single category "Policy Reserves." Minimum standards for the calculation of most policy reserves are prescribed by state insurance laws.[9] For the types of coverages for which minimum standards are not prescribed, a company must satisfy the commissioner that the reserve basis used is appropriate. The details of the basis of the policy reserves are reported in the NAIC Statement. A number of insurance departments make a duplicate calculation of most of the policy reserves of domestic companies. The policy reserves shown can usually be assumed to be adequate.

Other things being equal, under the prospective reserve approach (upon which most reserves are calculated), the lower the interest rate used for valuation, the larger the reserve. A low-valuation interest rate is therefore usually regarded as conservative and indicative of a strong basis of valuation. Also, the reserves are larger on a net-level-premium basis than on a preliminary-term or other modified reserve basis, so that, other things being equal, the net-level-premium basis is the more conservative. It should be remembered, however, that a number of other factors—such as the margins in the gross

premiums and the size of surrender granted—should be taken into consideration in appraising the relative conservatism of a valuation basis for policy-reserve liabilities.

(b) **Amounts held on deposit.** This category includes (a) amounts held by the company under supplementary contracts without life contingencies, (b) dividends held under the accumulation option, and (c) premiums paid in advance.

Supplementary contracts include settlements both with and without life contingencies. Those that provide incomes based on life contingencies are life annuities and are included as a part of the policy reserves mentioned above. The remainder—funds held at interest or under the fixed-period and fixed-amount options—are included here.

Policyowner dividends may be accumulated at interest under participating contracts, and in most mutual companies, a large amount is held under this option. The liability shown on the balance sheet will include interest accrued (but not yet payable) to the date of the balance sheet.

Premiums paid in advance do not loom large relative to the policy-reserve liability but can be a significant amount in a particular company. The right to prepay premiums is permitted as a matter of company practice, and most companies will permit limited advanced payments, allowing a moderate discount. The amount of the total liability as shown on the balance sheet is the discounted value of all the premiums so held that have not yet become payable.

(c) **Dividends allocated but not yet payable.** In respect to policyowner's dividends, the generally accepted practice, except on group business, is to set as a liability the estimated amount of dividends to policyowners for the entire following calendar year. This is done on the theory that dividends in a given calendar year should be paid out of surplus actually earned in the preceding calendar year. Some companies, however, do not actually take formal action before December 31 on their dividends for the entire following year. They set as a liability the estimated amount of dividends to policyowners for only part of the following year, such as three months. In

[9]See Chapter 20.

any case, when the directors or trustees take action to allocate a specific sum for dividends, that sum becomes a liability and is shown on the balance sheet as such. In the case of stock companies, dividends to shareholders become a liability at the time they are declared by the board of directors of the company.

(d) Claims incurred but not yet paid. This class of liabilities includes (a) claims due but unpaid, (b) resisted claims, (c) claims in process of being settled, and (d) estimated liability for claims incurred on or before the date of the statement (normally December 31) but not reported to the insurer by that date.

The first two categories are very small, since claims are usually paid as soon as the completed papers are received, and a very small proportion of life and health insurance claims is litigated. The third category is also small and represents those claims that are still under investigation or for which complete papers have not been received. The final category, claims incurred but not yet reported, may be fairly large, especially in connection with health insurance. The amount is estimated on the basis of the experience of prior years.

(e) Other amounts unpaid In addition to unpaid claims, liability will exist for other incurred but unpaid items, such as expenses, taxes, surrender values, and others. An important item in this category is the amount estimated to be payable for federal income tax in the following year on the income of the current year.

(f) Amounts held for account of others. As mentioned earlier, deposits by mortgagors to pay taxes and other like amounts not yet due, amounts due to reinsurance companies, amounts withheld on payroll deductions, and other funds held temporarily must be shown as liabilities.

(g) Mandatory Securities Valuation Reserve. In trying to deal with the problem of valuing securities, regulatory authorities introduced the Mandatory Securities Valuation Reserve (MSVR) in 1951. This reserve serves as a means of preventing undue surplus changes arising from fluctuations in the market value of securities owned. There are two components of the MSVR: (1) the bond and preferred stock component, and (2) the common stock component. In the case of the bonds eligible for amortization

and preferred stocks in good standing, only *realized* capital gains and losses affect the reserve. In contrast, both *realized* and *unrealized* capital gains and losses affect the common stock component since common stocks are carried at market value. Similarly, bonds not eligible for amortization and preferred stocks not in good standing affect the reserve through both *realized* and *unrealized* capital gains and losses.

The amount of the MSVR each year consists of (1) the preceding year's balance, (2) recognized capital gains less capital losses for the current year, and (3) an additional amount added each year in accordance with a formula. A formula determines the maximum amount for the MSVR for each company. Until the maximum is reached, recognized capital gains and losses may be absorbed by the reserve so that they have no effect on surplus. After the maximum is reached, recognized capital *gains* directly increase surplus and recognized capital *losses* can cause the reserve to decrease. Insurers have some discretion in how gains and losses are treated when the MSVR is above zero. If the MSVR balance becomes zero, subsequent recognized capital *losses* would decrease surplus directly.

The maximum MSVR and annual additions to it are calculated by multiplying the admitted values of each of several different types of bonds and stocks by specified percentages. As noted above, however, bonds and preferred stocks are classified as one component, and common stock, including warrants and options, another. The reserve is a requirement only of the general account assets of life insurance companies. Separate account assets typically are carried at market (or estimated market) values.

Since the assets standing behind the MSVR presumably would be available for other purposes if any need or emergency arose, it would seem that they actually should be considered as surplus funds. However, in view of the fact that their amount is determined by regulation and their maintenance is mandatory, they appear in statutory annual statements as a liability.[10]

---

[10]Generally Accepted Accounting Principles (GAAP) would classify the MSRV as an appropriation of surplus rather than a liability account. See later in this chapter.

(h) Special reserves. The distinction between some special reserves that are labeled liabilities by some companies and those that are merely called earmarked surplus by other companies can be a fine one. For example, a special reserve for a particular purpose may be shown by one company as a liability and by another as part of the surplus account.

As a result of the liberal terms of the optional settlements in policies formerly issued, many companies have established a special reserve for unmatured settlement options. This reserve is much more clearly a liability and, in fact, might well be included as a part of the policy reserves. Similarly, the special reserve generally established by companies with group insurance in force to cover the catastrophic risk borders on the nature of a liability. Many companies, however, treat the group insurance reserve as earmarked surplus (see below). The matter of the treatment of special reserves either as liabilities or as surplus is one about which more uniformity would be desirable. The present lack of uniformity tends to make it difficult to compare the statutory balance sheets of particular companies.

Companies occasionally set up other special liability items to cover a variety of special situations where there is greater uncertainty than usual as to whether there actually will be any additional liability. Special items of this type, if small, probably would be included in the term "Miscellaneous Liabilities;" if large, they might be shown separately in the annual report. In either case, they would be shown separately in the NAIC Statement.

It is difficult to appraise such special liabilities for a particular company. If no such liabilities appear on the balance sheet, it could be because the reserve basis is so conservative that no special liabilities need to be set up. On the other hand, it might be because the company's surplus position is not strong enough to permit setting up such special liabilities even though they are badly needed. It would take a thorough actuarial appraisal of the company's structure to enable one to tell which (if either) of these situations was the more likely. Even then, much would depend on the individual judgment of the person making the appraisal. Moreover, where such liability items do appear in a statutory statement, it is virtually im-

possible to determine whether the amount set up is on a conservative basis.

3. *Capital and surplus.* As indicated above, the excess of assets over liabilities consists of capital and surplus.[11] Capital, naturally, appears on the balance sheets of stock companies only. Although the capital item represents an interest of the shareholders in the company, it is nevertheless available for the protection of the policyowners. In the event of financial difficulties, the policyowners' interest comes before that of the shareholders.

Surplus appears in the NAIC Statement in one of two forms:

(a) Special surplus funds. In some companies, part or all of the surplus is earmarked to cover special contingencies. The following examples are illustrative of the types of contingencies covered:

- Voluntary reserve for further strengthening of policy reserves
- Group life insurance reserve for epidemics
- Special reserve for possible loss or fluctuation in the value of investments
- Voluntary reserve for contingencies

Some companies even carry their entire surplus as one special surplus fund to cover all unforeseen contingencies.

(b) Unassigned surplus. This represents either the entire surplus or the part of the surplus that has not been assigned to cover specific or general contingencies. The earmarking of surplus to cover special contingencies can, naturally, be changed from year to year. Thus, a special reserve for investment fluctuation set up at the end of one year could, if necesssary, be used during the following year to absorb mortality fluctuations arising from an epidemic or a war.

[11]There is some tendency in the annual policyowner reports (as opposed to statutory reports) of mutual companies to replace the word "surplus" by some term such as "contingency reserve" or "margin for contingencies." This tendency stems from the possibly unfavorable connotation of "surplus," which implies an excess, or more than is needed. This term might imply to policyowners that a mutual company was retaining larger funds than necessary and paying smaller dividends than it should.

The Summary of Operations

An important feature in the statutory financial statements of many life companies is the **summary of operations** or statement of the operations for the year. A sample summary of operations is shown in Table 32-2. As in the case of the sample balance sheet, the items shown for this hypothetical company are in roughly the same proportions as the corresponding aggregates for all U.S. life companies. The first part of the summary is an analysis of income. The second part is an analysis of the disposition of income.

Income. The income of a life insurance company consists primarily of:

1. Premiums
2. Considerations for supplementary contracts and deposits
3. Investment income
4. Miscellaneous income

    1. *Premiums.* Premium income includes, in addition to regular premiums from policyowners, (a) dividends used by policyowners to purchase paid-up additional insurance and (b) policy proceeds (from death claims, matured endowments, and surrenders) left with the company as consideration for supplementary contracts with life contingencies. When premiums are generated by policy proceeds or dividends, they are treated as

TABLE 32-2. Sample statutory summary of operations
(accrual basis)

Income		
Premiums from policyowners		
Life Insurance	$10,200,000	
Annuities	1,520,000	
Health Insurance	3,080,000	
Total premiums		$14,800,000
Net earnings from investments: interest, dividends,		
and rents less investment expenses and taxes		3,300,000
Funds left with the company: policy proceeds		
placed under supplementary contracts, and		
dividends left to accumulate		1,860,000
Other income		40,000
Total income		$20,000,000
Disposition of income		
Benefits to policyowners and beneficiaries:		
Death benefits	$ 3,000,000	
Matured endowments	600,000	
Annuity benefits	600,000	
Health insurance and disability benefits	1,400,000	
Surrender benefits (insurance)	1,200,000	
Dividend accumulations withdrawn	400,000	
Supplementary contract benefits	800,000	
Dividends to policyowners	1,500,000	
Total benefits		$ 9,500,000
Operating expenses and taxes (excludes investment		
expenses and taxes):		
Agency expenses, including commissions	$ 2,000,000	
Home-office insurance operations	1,500,000	
Premium, payroll, and other insurance taxes	150,000	
Federal income taxes	350,000	
Total expenses and taxes		4,000,000
Increase in required reserves held for the benefit of		
policyowners and beneficiaries		5,500,000
Transfer to surplus account		1,000,000
Total disposition of income		$20,000,000

both disbursements and income in the manner described in the next section on considerations for supplementary contracts and deposits. Premiums constitute the largest source of income.

2. *Considerations for supplementary contracts and deposits.* An important proportion of all policy proceeds from death claims, matured endowments, and surrenders is left with the company under optional settlements without life contingencies. Although no cash payment by the company (other than the first installment) takes place at the time the claim is settled, these amounts are treated as if they were first paid to the policyowner in cash and then immediately repaid to the company. They are therefore entered both as disbursements and as income. Since no cash payment is involved (payment of the first installment being treated as a separate transaction), the total amount of the company's assets is not affected.

The same situation exists with regard to dividends left with the company under the accumulation option. To show the true total amount of dividends "paid," a dividend deposited is included with other dividends among the disbursements and also entered as income.

3. *Investment income.* Investment income comprises (a) interest on bonds and loans, as well as miscellaneous interest such as interest on agents' balances; (b) dividends on stocks; and (c) rents from real estate or transportation equipment owned, including the rent that the company charges itself for occupancy of property owned, such as its home office. The last item is necessary to show a proper yield on the investment.

The amount of "interest" in the case of amortizable bonds normally is not the amount of the coupon but rather the effective interest returned by the bond, including amortization of premium or accrual of discount. The NAIC Statement calls for reporting investment income on both a gross and a net basis—that is, after deducting investment expenses and taxes.

4. *Miscellaneous income.* This is usually quite small in relation to total income. It includes minor items that do not fit clearly into one of the first three categories described above.

Disposition of Income. The second area of the summary of operations covers the disposition of funds received by the company. Major categories include:

1.   Benefits paid to policyowners and beneficiaries
2.   Operating expenses and taxes
3.   Increases in required reserves
4.   Transfers to surplus account

1. *Benefits paid.* Benefit payments include—in addition to regular death, endowment, and annuity payments—cash surrender values, dividends to policyowners, payments under supplementary contracts with and without life contingencies, and waiver-of-premium, disability income, and health insurance benefits.

The full amount of claim payments will be included where the amount is left under a settlement option. This will also be the case where a policy loan is deducted, since the full claim amount equals the cancellation of the asset (policy loan) plus the net cash payment. In the case of disability income benefits (paid in cash) and premiums waived (not paid in cash), both are included in full as disbursements. The waiver of premium is treated as if the premium were first paid to the company and then returned. This procedure is necessary in order to show the proper amount of premium income and benefit payments.

2. *Operating expenses and taxes.* The principal categories of expenses have been discussed previously in connection with gross premium derivation (see Chapter 12). It should be pointed out here, however, that taxes (other than real estate taxes) consist primarily of the federal income tax and state taxes on premiums, both of which are substantial in amount.[12] Other taxes include miscellaneous license fees, Social Security taxes, and the like.

3. *Increases in required reserves.* The amount of funds earmarked to cover the year's increase in total reserves is usually a substantial portion relative to the preceding items. The nature of the various reserve items was discussed earlier.

[12]See Chapter 33.

4. *Transfer to surplus account.* This is the balancing item within the summary of operation. It is the simple difference between the total income and the other dispositions. It customarily is a positive figure but can be negative, especially if the required increases in reserves are substantial, as can happen easily with a fast-growing company.

Changes in Surplus Account

The statutory summary of operations is accompanied by an analysis of the surplus account, which reconciles the surplus at the beginning and end of the year. A sample surplus account is shown in Table 32–3. The basic mechanics of the reconciliation can be explained briefly.

To the unassigned surplus from the previous year add:

1. The net gain from insurance operations
2. Unrealized capital gains
3. Increase in surplus on separate-account business

From the sum of the items above (including previous year's surplus), one then deducts:

1. Dividends to shareholders (recall that dividends to policyowners were deducted in the summary of operations)

2. Realized capital losses
3. Increases in reserves because of a change in the valuation basis
4. Increases in the MSVR
5. Increases in any special reserve fund

The resulting figure is the end-of-year surplus position for the insurer.

GAAP FINANCIAL REPORTING

GAAP accounting, reflecting more faithfully the actual operating condition of insurers, with some modification, is more useful for management planning and control purposes than is SAP. Additionally, GAAP is required in connection with SEC filings and as a condition for listing on the major stock exchanges. This section discusses the key differences between GAAP and SAP and presents some of the recent developments with respect to GAAP.

Differences between GAAP and SAP

The differences between statutory accounting and generally accepted accounting principles are a result of (1) the nature of the life and health

TABLE 32-3. Changes in surplus account

Surplus, December 31, 1985			$5,800,000
Additions			
Transferred from insurance operations	$1,000,000		
Net increase in values of assets	480,000		
Increase in surplus of separate-account business	20,000		
Total additions		$1,500,000	
Deductions			
Dividends to shareholders	$ 100,000		
Net losses on sale of assets	300,000		
Increase in reserves on account of change in valuation basis	200,000		
Increase in Mandatory Securities Valuation Reserve	500,000		
Increase in special surplus funds	100,000		
Total deductions		1,200,000	
Net additions			300,000
Surplus, December 31, 1986			$6,100,000

insurance business, and (2) government regulation. These differences should be examined briefly.[13]

The usually long-term and generally increasing nature of the risks assumed by a life and health insurance company requires that out of the annual premiums, amounts be earmarked each year to ensure the company's ability to pay claims in later years when claim costs may exceed premiums received. These notational claims are discounted values of future benefit payments, minus the discounted values of future premium receipts, and are *liabilities* measured by the *policy reserves.* These reserves change continuously with the passing of time, so that it is not the usual practice to carry them on the formal ledger itself. It is considered appropriate to value these policy reserves only at the time a financial statement is being prepared and to record their amounts directly on the statement without ever recording them in the books of account.

Statutory life insurance accounting, reflecting state government regulation generally and the NAIC Annual Statement specifically, is conditioned by an *emphasis upon solvency,* aimed at ensuring that companies will be able to meet their obligations at any and all times. This emphasis is important because a failure of management to maintain solvency may not be readily discernible before losses have been suffered by policyowners or others. This emphasis on solvency, and the difficulty of ascertaining whether such a state exists, have led to the adoption of more conservative valuation standards than is typical of financial reporting generally in accordance with GAAP.

The usefulness of the NAIC Annual Statement as a measure of year-to-year earnings also is affected by these conservative valuation standards, since they affect both earnings and the change in surplus from one year-end to another. Measurement of the earnings of a life insurance company from one year to another on a basis consistent with general practice in other industries is also made more difficult by the following facts:

1. A relatively long time must pass before it can be determined with reasonable certainty whether the sale of a block of insurance policies has been profitable.

2. The pattern of mortality rates found in *valuation mortality tables* normally is quite different from those found in the individual company *experience tables* used in establishing premium rates.

3. The usual net-level-premium and modified net-level-premium valuation formulas *release expense margins* in premiums in a pattern that may be quite different from the *actual incidence of expenses.*

It should be clear that each of these situations can lead to an actual or potential distortion of the *current earnings* of a stock life insurance company as compared with stock companies of other types.

So it can be seen that significant differences exist between statutory life insurance accounting practices and generally accepted accounting principles. In a more specific sense, SAP differs from GAAP in the following ways:

1. Commissions and other costs of acquiring new business are charged to operations as they are incurred, rather than being deferred and charged to operations as the related income is received. As a result, there is usually a substantial drain on reported surplus for each new life insurance policy sold (particularly if reserves are set up on the net-level-premium basis). Consequently, an increase in the amount of new insurance sold on an apparently profitable basis may produce the anomalous result of a decrease in the reported net gain from operations, and a decrease in the new insurance sold may result in an increase in the net gain from operations.

2. Policy reserves are calculated on either a net-level or modified basis, using conservative interest assumptions and ignoring probability of future lapse rates. The result may be either higher or lower policy reserves under GAAP, depending on the company's book of business.

3. Nonadmitted assets are not counted in the determination of the company's financial condition.

4. The asset values for owned stock of an affiliated company are determined on a relatively conservative basis.

5. The Mandatory Securities Valuation Reserve must be set up to reflect the possibility that bonds may go into default or that stocks' values may decline significantly. However, the amount of the MSVR may not be directly related to the quality and current value of the securities.

[13]See Robert G. Espie, "Financial Statements," in Dan M. McGill, *Life Insurance,* rev. ed. (Homewood, Ill.: Richard D. Irwin, Inc., 1967).

6. Income tax expense is based on income reportable for tax purposes. Deferred taxes are not provided for items that enter into accounting income in one period and taxable income in another period.
7. Realized gains and losses flow directly to surplus rather than through net income.
8. A liability is not generally set up for future income taxes on accrued but unrealized net capital gains.

The impact of changing a stock company statement from a statutory to a GAAP basis is evident in Table 32-4, which shows the adjustments necessary to change ABC's life insurance company's *net income* and *equity* (surplus) from a SAP to a GAAP basis. The significance of the adjustments is apparent.

TABLE 32-4. Adjustments required to move ABC life insurance company financial statements from a SAP to GAAP basis

	Net Income	Equity
Statutory basis	$ 1,000,000	$ 6,600,000
Adjustments		
Deferred acquisition costs	500,000	17,500,000
Future policy benefits	(50,000)	2,500,000
Deferred Federal income taxes	(150,000)	(7,650,000)
Nonadmitted assets	—	1,530,000
Premiums due and deferred	100,000	(750,000)
Mandatory securities valuation reserve	—	1,350,000
Dividends payable	(250,000)	(350,000)
Realized capital loss, net of tax	(300,000)	—
Other	20,000	—
Total adjustments	(130,000)	14,130,000
Generally Accepted Accounting Principle basis	$ 870,000	$20,730,000

Current GAAP Issues

As competition from other financial institutions has forced the life insurance industry to develop products with more competitive investment-oriented characteristics (e.g., interest-sensitive products such as single-premium deferred annuities and universal life insurance), the propriety of using the traditional ordinary life insurance accounting model for these products is being questioned. That model was based principally on a product with level periodic payments over an extended period and fixed benefits. The effect of the model was to provide a periodic profit stream based on a level percent of the premium payments. Today's products can involve single and irregular nonlevel payment streams and variable benefits. Because the industry tends to emphasize the investment characteristics of these products, some believe that an investment-oriented accounting model, such as that used by banks in accounting for customer deposits, would be appropriate. Under this model, for example, profit might be recognized only as interest is earned on invested premiums. Others recommend a blend of the traditional life insurance accounting model and the investment model. The issue is being studied by the Financial Accounting Standards Board (FASB), and the results could significantly modify current accounting practices for these products.

GAAP for Mutual Life Insurance Companies

As noted in this chapter, all insurance companies prepare an annual filing for state regulatory authorities which includes statutory financial statements prepared using accounting practices prescribed or permitted by those regulators. Prior to issuance of the American Institute of Certified Public Accountants (AICPA) Audit Guide for Stock Life Insurance Companies in 1972, no other set of accounting principles existed for the industry. The Audit Guide firmly established a GAAP framework for financial reporting for stock life insurance companies. Since that time, stock life insurance companies generally have prepared their financial statements to shareholders on that basis. That framework was included basically intact in FASB Statement No. 60, Accounting and Reporting by Insurance Enterprises, which was issued in 1982. Like the Audit Guide, Statement 60 excluded mutual life insurance companies from its scope. It is important to remember that Statutory Accounting Principles *are* GAAP for mutuals today.

An AICPA Task Force, established when the Audit Guide was issued, has been studying whether some basis of accounting other than statutory would be appropriate for mutual life insurance company general-purpose financial statements. Although the Task Force has been unable to develop a satisfactory alternative, many mutual life insurance companies are reviewing the possibility of developing some sort of financial reporting framework similar to that of GAAP for stock life insurance companies for internal use. Individual company reasons for wanting such reports vary. The following are among those frequently mentioned:

- To measure more accurately overall and line of business performance.
- To be able to compare company performance with published stock life insurance company financial statements.
- To be prepared for demutualization, should that become desirable. As a stock life insurance company, GAAP financial statement would be necessary.

Because statutory accounting practices often do not satisfy these needs, many mutual life insurance companies are experimenting with financial reports based on accounting principles similar to those used by stock life insurance companies.[14] It should be emphasized that GAAP accounting does *not* affect either the way life insurance companies report to state regulatory authorities or their method of reporting earnings for tax purposes.

REPORTS TO SHAREHOLDERS AND POLICYOWNERS

The NAIC Statement is not intended to be, and is not, a convenient direct source of information for policyowners, shareholders, or the general public. As a result, condensed and simplified financial statements are included in the published **annual reports** issued by companies to their policyowners and/or shareholders. Financial statements to *shareholders* are presented on a GAAP rather than a SAP basis. These statements and the excerpts from the annual reports are also used

by many companies in their advertising and other publicity activities.

Any statutory figures in these reports are prepared, in part, from information in the NAIC Statement. Any financial statements in the annual report are condensed versions of those in the NAIC statement and of those that might be prepared based on GAAP principles.

The scope of annual reports and the kind and detail of the information included in them vary greatly from company to company, and even from year to year for the same company. Most of these reports contain supplementary information on the company's operations, plans, and other matters usually found also in the trade press. Among other things, there frequently is a narrative presentation of a promotional nature. If GAAP financial statements are included, there is also likely to be a reconciliation of the principal GAAP statement items to the corresponding statutory statement items.

In addition to the basic materials described above, additional statistics are usually found in many annual reports. The types of information usually presented include:

1. New business figures, showing amount of insurance and number of policies paid for. Figures may be shown separately for the different lines of insurance (i.e., ordinary, group, industrial, and health insurance). For ordinary insurance, the figures sometimes are broken down into life, endowment, term, and paid-up additions. The average amount of insurance per policy also is often shown.

2. Insurance in force, often according to the subdivisions mentioned above.

3. Benefits paid to policyowners and beneficiaries during the year and total benefits paid since organization.

4. Analysis of death claims during the year according to cause of death.

For each of these items, figures usually are shown for the current year and the preceding year. Frequently, some of them, as well as analyses of the assets by type, also are shown at five-year intervals over a period of years. From the new-business and insurance-in-force figures for prior

[14]See Nelida Garcia, "GAAP: A Trend at Mutual Companies?" *Resources,* Vol. X (September/October 1985), pp. 28–30.

years, some idea of the rate of growth of the company can be obtained. Changes in the distribution of deaths by causes frequently are of interest to policyowners.

The new-business and insurance-in-force figures are usually presented on the same basis as the corresponding information in the NAIC Statement. This leads to duplication in some cases, because the insurance-in-force figures in the NAIC Statement include reinsurance assumed from another company in addition to all directly written business, irrespective of whether any part of it has been ceded to another company as reinsurance. Thus, these figures, if added for all companies, include duplication to the extent that business has been reinsured.

It is common to provide in annual reports a graphical analysis of the "income dollar" for the current year. These charts or graphs differ greatly as to format, but their fundamental features are fairly well standardized. In connection with these charts, it is often pointed out that the money paid to or retained for policyowners and beneficiaries exceeds the funds received from them, because the earnings from investments exceed the operating expenses and taxes. A typical chart is shown in Figure 32–1.

In appraising a company's insurance in force, it is helpful to know the nature of the business being written. One of the more important aspects traditionally was the proportion of term insurance. Because of its low premiums, term insurance ordinarily does not mean as much in the way of permanent growth of a company as does an equal face amount of cash value business.

The average amount of insurance per policy is important. Some expenses depend on the number of policies rather than the amount of insurance, so that the expense rate per $1,000 ordinarily will be somewhat lower on a larger policy than on a small one. Thus, if all other factors are the same, a company with a high average amount of insurance per policy will have a lower expense rate per $1,000 than will a company with a low average amount of insurance per policy. But since all other factors are never the same in two companies, great caution must be exercised in using comparisons of the average amounts of insurance per policy as an indication of relative expense rates.

FIGURE 32-1

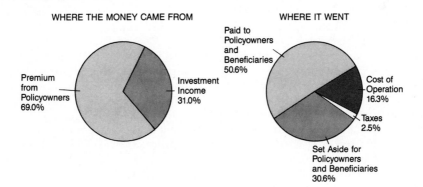

Chapter 33

Regulation and Taxation of Life and Health Insurance Companies

INTRODUCTION

Few business institutions are subjected to as strict and detailed government supervision as life and health insurance companies. The reasons for this become clear when we consider the vital relationship that personal insurance bears to the family and the community. Its mission is security. Millions of individuals rely on it as the principal means of protecting themselves against the financial deprivations caused by death, disability, and the expenses of medical care.

The majority of life insurance contracts, and an increasing number of health insurance contracts, remain in force for many years before maturing or expiring and not infrequently involve obligations by insurers extending for 50 or more years. Huge reserve liabilities are created by these obligations, and the assets underlying these liabilities must be safeguarded adequately. Further, the size of the industry as a financial institution means that it plays a vital role in our national economy.

The nature of the insurance transaction involves the utilization of a technical-legal document that makes a present promise of future performance upon the occurrence of stipulated events. Although much has been done to simplify life in-surance contracts and to enhance their readability, the typical life and health insurance contract remains a technical, complex document. In a non-technical sense, the insurance product is purchased in good faith. These individuals, in many practical ways, rely as much on the integrity of the insurance company and those who act as its representatives as they do on the details of the insurance contract itself.

Despite the almost universal belief in the need for life and health insurance, and its vital importance to all who purchase it, few persons attempt to become acquainted with the management, business policy, and practices of the insurers backing their contracts. Even assuming that a considerable portion of the vast number of policyowners could be induced to take an interest in the condition of their insurers, very few would be sufficiently knowledgeable about insurance matters to ascertain intelligently the true state of affairs. Life and health insurance is necessarily a technical and complicated subject, and, as pointed out in the preceding chapters, the true financial condition of an insurance company can be determined only by expert examination.

Without question, the greatest volume of life and health insurance is sold by reputable companies striving to meet their legal and moral obligations. However, for all the reasons enumerated above, the activities and operations of life and health insurance companies are a fit subject for government regulation designed to protect the public adequately against unjust practices and mismanagement.

The protection of the insuring public is, by far, the most important objective of regulation. Regulation seeks to obtain this objective of policyowner protection through measures focusing on (1) the quality of the insurance products offered, (2) the manner in which they are sold, and (3) the ability of the insurance company to meet its obligations. Other objectives, peculiar to state as opposed to federal regulation, might include raising revenue and retaliation.

Retaliation as an objective of regulatory activities is defensive in nature; thus, retaliatory statutes have been enacted against foreign insurance companies in an effort to protect domestic companies from undue burdens and limitations that might be imposed by other states in which the domestic company desires to do business.[1] Such statutes usually provide that when the laws (usually, tax laws) of another state or foreign country create a greater burden upon a state's domestic insurance companies than that state's domestic laws impose on similar foreign insurers, the commissioner of the state of domicile may impose similar obligations on foreign companies seeking to do business in his or her state. Retaliation as an objective of insurance regulatory legislation is less important today than formerly because of the efforts of the insurance companies, the individual insurance commissioners, and the National Association of Insurance Commissioners (see below) in developing uniform state laws.

It is difficult to understand why **revenue** is listed commonly as an objective of regulation. Life and health insurance companies and their representatives are subject to a variety of license fees, charter fees, and filing fees at the state level, and in some states, municipal license fees. The

principal justification for the taxation of the insurance business is to raise revenue, a small part of which supports regulation. Revenue is not a regulatory device. It is not a reason for regulation.

BACKGROUND OF INSURANCE REGULATION

In the United States, all sovereign powers are vested in the people. The people have created government bodies to serve them and have vested powers in these bodies. The people granted broad general powers to their state governments. In creating a federal government, the people delegated to it certain specific limited authority to act on matters affecting the welfare of the entire nation. Since no provision of the U.S. Constitution specifically limits the authority of the states to legislate on matters over which the federal government was given specific authority, both governments may exercise power in these areas. However, any conflict in legislation or regulation must be resolved by consideration of the fact that the delegation of a specific power to the federal government impliedly limits a general state power. The power of the federal government to act on matters over which it has specific authority is supreme.

Paul versus Virginia

The framers of the Constitution, recognizing that the economic welfare and the safety of the nation would be jeopardized by trade barriers restricting the free flow of trade among the states, incorporated Article 1, Section 8, which gives Congress the exclusive power to regulate commerce with foreign powers and among the states. In general, the right to regulate *intrastate* commerce was reserved for the states. However, Congress, through the commerce clause, has the implied power to regulate matters that affect *interstate* commerce. Since the specifically delegated powers of Congress are supreme to the states' general powers, no state may restrict or impede interstate commerce where Congress has taken action. No state laws are valid that contradict or contravene federal law regarding interstate commerce or matters affecting interstate commerce.

---

[1]A **domestic company** generally is considered to be one domiciled in the state involved. A **foreign company** is an American company whose state of domicile is other than the state involved. An **alien company** is one that is domiciled in a foreign country.

Yet traditionally, insurance has been regulated exclusively by the states. Indeed, until 1944, insurance was not deemed by the U.S. Supreme Court to be commerce within the intent of the Constitution. Some background on this issue will be helpful.

In 1868, in the famous case of **Paul v. Virginia,** the Supreme Court refused to declare an insurance contract an instrumentality of commerce, and asserted the doctrine that there was no doubt of the state power to prohibit foreign insurance companies from doing business within its limits. To quote the Court:

> Issuing a policy of insurance is not a transaction of commerce. . . .These contracts are not articles of commerce in any proper meaning of the word. They are not subject to the trade and barter. . . .They are like other personal contracts between parties which are completed by their signature and the transfer of the consideration. Such contracts are not interstate transactions, though the parties may be domiciled in different states. . . .They are, then, local transactions, and governed by the local law. They do not constitute a part of the commerce between the states.[2]

South-Eastern Underwriters Case

For three quarters of a century following the *Paul v. Virginia* case, accepted practice was to regard the general supervision of all forms of insurance as falling solely within the jurisdiction of the several state governments. The Supreme Court repeatedly reasserted this view. On June 4, 1944, the Supreme Court, in the case of **United States v. The South-Eastern Underwriters Association, et al.,**[3] abandoned the view that insurance was not commerce and therefore was not properly the subject of federal regulation under the terms of the commerce clause of the U.S. Constitution. In holding that insurance was commerce —interstate commerce for the most part—the court swept away the foundations on which the structure of state regulation of insurance had been built. It appeared that insurance was subject to

any regulations Congress desired to impose as well as several existing federal laws that could be construed to apply to the insurance business.

McCarran-Ferguson Act

Congress, in 1945, on the theory that it had the power to redefine the distribution of authority over interstate commerce, and consistent with the granting to other industries of complete or partial protection from antitrust laws, passed **Public Law 15,** commonly known as the **McCarran-Ferguson Act.** The purpose of this act may be found in its title:

> An Act to Express the Intent of the Congress with Reference to the Regulation of the Business of Insurance

In this act, Congress redefined the authority of states and established a plan for cooperative regulation. It seems clear, in retrospect, that Congress desired that there be some amount of collaboration between federal and state governments in a complete system of regulation.

According to the terms of the McCarran-Ferguson Act, the federal government retains exclusive or primary control over certain matters that it deems national in character, that is, matters in which regulation is (or should be) uniform throughout the states. Employer–employee relations (National Labor Relations Act and Employee Retirement Income Security Act) and fair labor standards (Fair Labor Standards Act), as well as agreements for or acts of boycott, coercion, and intimidation (Sherman Act), are deemed by the McCarran-Ferguson Act to be matters of national character and thus subject to the exclusive control of Congress. In effect, certain portions of these laws were related by Congress specifically to insurance.

Further, it is important to note that Congress may expand this area of exclusive or primary control by an act of Congress relating specifically to insurance. Such a federal law would be applicable to the business of insurance and supersede all state statutes in conflict with it. Prior to 1964, the principal acts relating specifically to insurance were limited in application to the District of Col-

---

[2](1868) Wall. (U.S.) 168. See also *New York Life Insurance Co. v. Deer Lodge County,* 231 U.S. 495 (1913).

[3]332 U.S. 533 at 533 (1944).

umbia. In 1964, the Securities and Exchange Act of 1934 was amended to relate specifically to the business of insurance. Since then, other measures have been enacted that assert federal jurisdiction over, and even federal operation of, selected aspects of the insurance business such as flood insurance, crop insurance, and Medicare. Employee health plans were declared a matter for federal jurisdiction by the 1974 Employee Retirement Income Security Act.

Although the McCarran-Ferguson Act declares that the continued regulation of insurance by the states is in the public interest, the law states that certain existing federal statutes (the Sherman Act, the Clayton Act, and the Federal Trade Commission Act), which are general in nature and do not deal with insurance specifically, are made specific to the business of insurance to the extent that "such business is not regulated by state law." Hence, a basic purpose of Public Law 15 was to encourage improved and more uniform state regulation of insurance in the public interest.

State versus Federal Regulation

In the years following the enactment of Public law 15, the National Association of Insurance Commissioners (see below), together with representatives of the insurance industry, undertook to draft model legislation intended to place the regulation of insurance among the several states on a more uniform and adequate basis— that is, to meet the challenge of the **proviso clause** of Public Law 15.

Today, regulation over the insurance industry remains primarily the responsibility of the states. However, Congress retains oversight responsibility with respect to the operation of state insurance regulation. In recent years, the adequacy of state insurance regulation has come under increasing scrutiny. Particular attention has been given to the continued validity of the antitrust exemption now afforded to the insurance business.

In December 1978, the National Commission for the Review of Antitrust Laws and Procedures recommended repeal of the McCarran-Ferguson Act antitrust immunity, primarily to encourage competition among property and liability insurance companies. These recommendations resulted in legislative activity, including hearings and bills in both houses of Congress. As this book was going to press, legislation to amend McCarran-Ferguson was pending in the U.S. Congress.

The debate as to whether the public interest is best served by federal or state regulation is an old one. The controversy could result in (1) the states' continuing to be the primary regulators of insurance, (2) the federal government becoming the primary regulator of the insurance business, or (3) a system of dual regulation, akin to the Canadian approach, under which some types of regulations would be administered by the states and others by the federal government.

Although it is beyond the purpose of this chapter to discuss fully the pros and cons of state versus federal regulation, the following lists provide the reader with an idea of the complexity of the discussion.[4] Some of the arguments made for continuing state regulation include:

- Decentralization of government is a virtue in itself.
- State regulation already exists.
- States can be more responsive to local needs than can the federal government.
- Federal regulation would become cumbersome and perhaps create a rigid, arbitrary bureaucracy.
- Whatever uniformity is necessary has been and continues to be achieved through the NAIC.
- Effects of ill-advised insurance legislation are localized.
- States may serve as "laboratories" for insurance regulation.

On the other hand, arguments given in favor of federal regulation include:

- Lack of uniformity among state insurance codes and conflict in rulings create complications and added expense for insurers operating in several states.
- The expense of having to file financial reports in each state and maintain 51 separate insurance departments is high.

---

[4]See Harold Skipper, Jr., "The Impact of Government Regulation on Insurance Regulation," in *Marketing Life and Health Insurance* (Atlanta, Ga.: Life Office Management Association, 1981), pp. 58–60.

- Ill-advised legislation can be passed easily in states where legislators cannot devote resources to studying legislation as can the U.S. Congress.
- The political nature of the appointment or election of state insurance commissioners may produce poorly qualified regulators who are subject to undue local pressure.
- Conflicts arise between standard federal regulations and state rulings which affect insurer operations.
- Varying state requirements cause insurer inflexibility.
- Most insurers operate in many states, and states find it increasingly difficult to solve regulatory problems involving foreign and alien insurers.
- Insurance commissioners and state legislatures are sometimes overly responsive to domestic insurance companies' pressures to the point of placing extra burdens on nondomestic companies.

THE MECHANISM OF STATE REGULATION

State regulation of the insurance business is conducted by three agencies of government: the courts, the legislature, and the insurance commissioner or other administrative official. In addition, the National Association of Insurance Commissioners (NAIC) performs an increasingly vital role in the development of recommended regulatory law and in the coordination of the activities of the legislatures and commissioners among the various states.

The role of the judiciary in state insurance regulation is threefold. Most obvious to the average insured is the function of deciding cases of conflict between companies and policyowners. The courts further protect the companies and insureds by enforcing criminal penalties against those who violate the insurance law. Finally, insurance companies and their agents may occasionally resort to the courts in an effort to overturn arbitrary or unconstitutional statutes or administrative regulations or orders promulgated by the insurance department.

The role of the court in the regulatory process, although very important to individual and corporate rights, is becoming relatively minor when compared with the role played by the legislature and the insurance commissioner. Within

constitutional limitations, and with the permission of Congress, the state legislatures have the ultimate power to make and amend insurance law. They have enacted insurance codes that establish the broad legal framework and prescribe the general standards governing the activities of the administrative agencies.

The law of a particular jurisdiction usually relates to the requirements, procedures, and/or standards for (1) the organization and operation of the state insurance department, (2) the formation and licensing of the various types of companies for the various kinds of insurance and reinsurance, (3) the licensing of agents and brokers, (4) the filing and sometimes approval of property and liability insurance rates, (5) the filing and approval of policy forms, (6) unauthorized insurers and unfair trade practices, (7) company financial solvency, (8) periodic examination of insurers, (9) complaint handling, and (10) the liquidation and rehabilitation of insurers. Most jurisdictions also incorporate into the insurance law certain standards for the insurance contract, with specific standards for certain lines of insurance—individual life and health insurance, group life and health insurance, industrial insurance, and fire insurance, among others. In addition, the code usually prescribes penalties for the violation of the insurance law.

Administrative Officials

In industrial economies, even highly developed general courts are not equipped to give protection in matters in which only experts can be informed; and legislatures, in addition to their lack of experience, find it impossible and impractical to pass laws involving every phase of a highly technical and rapidly changing industry that might need regulation. Thus, state departments or agencies were created with broad administrative, quasi-legislative, and quasi-judicial powers over the insurance business.

These insurance departments (the first was formed in Massachusetts in 1852) usually are under the direction of a chief official, who may have the title of commissioner, superintendent, or director. In a few states, the responsibility of direction is placed in a commission or board, which, in turn, selects an individual commissioner to carry out established policy. In nearly one-fourth of the states, commissioners are elected; the remainder are appointed, usually by the governor. In many states, the state official who has this responsibility also has other duties, such as state auditor, comptroller, or treasurer; or the departments of insurance is associated with some other department, such as the department of banking or securities.

Since the right to conduct an insurance business, to represent a company in doing insurance business, or to represent the public in placing insurance, is considered to be a privilege, it is limited to those who qualify by obtaining a license. Thus, insurance is brought under the control and supervision of the insurance commissioner by means of the licensing function.

In granting a license, the state has the power to prescribe numerous conditions and limitations that must be observed by companies as a condition precedent to exercising the privilege of doing business within the state. In implementing these various standards, the insurance commissioner is given numerous powers and duties, as discussed below.

National Association of Insurance Commissioners

The National Association of Insurance Commissioners (formerly National Convention of Insurance Commissioners) was organized in 1871. The objectives of the association are (1) maintenance and improvement of state regulation of insurance in a responsive and efficient manner, (2) ensuring reliability of the insurance institution as to financial solidity and guaranty against loss, and (3) fair, just and equitable treatment of policyowners and claimants.

The association has been successful and has served as a unifying and harmonizing force. Some of its more significant accomplishments include (1) the adoption by all states of a uniform blank for companies' annual financial reports; (2) the acceptance by most states of a certificate of sol-

vency by a company's home state, thus eliminating much duplication and expense; (3) acceptance by most states of the principle that a deposit of securities should be required only in a company's home state; (4) adoption of uniform rules for valuation of securities; (5) development of the zone system for the triennial examination of insurance companies; (6) the preparation of new standard mortality tables; (7) the preparation of standard valuation and nonforfeiture laws; and (8) the drafting of many other model laws in the fields of life and health insurance and coordination of liaison activity with the federal government on insurance matters and with other state government associations.

There can be no question of the important role the NAIC has played in the regulation of the insurance industry by the states. In recent years, there appears to have been even more interest in increased cooperative action among the states. As of 1986, the NAIC had recommended more than 150 model laws, regulations, and guidelines applicable to virtually all aspects of state regulation. In addition, the NAIC has undertaken a number of major research projects, and new statistical reporting systems for both testing solvency and measuring profitability have been instituted.

A reasonable degree of uniformity has resulted from the NAIC's efforts in several areas, although uniformity in other areas remains a problem. No state is bound to follow the recommendations of the NAIC. The NAIC has no enforcement power.

Current activities involving the NAIC can be expected to follow the trend of the last few years in the increased number and complexity of issues being addressed. This is particularly true of subjects in which the Congress or various federal agencies have shown an interest, since the natural tendency for the NAIC is to focus attention on issues that are receiving national attention.

Today, such issues include the interaction of antitrust laws with the activities of insurance companies; the problems and alleged abuses in the marketing of particular products, such as Medicare supplement policies and deferred annuities; company solvency; the impact of AIDS on the insurance business; and of course, the continuing discussions of life insurance solicitation and cost disclosure, including regulation of variable and universal life insurance products.

AREAS OF STATE REGULATION

Because of the peculiar nature of the insurance business and the position of public trust that it holds, the authority of the state over the activities of insurance companies is exerted from the moment of birth to the moment of death. The insurance enterprise, whether it be corporation or association, must meet certain requirements in order to be organized and to obtain a license in the various jurisdictions in which it wishes to do business. Its agents and brokers must be licensed, its contract forms approved, and in some instances in the case of health insurance, rates may be scrutinized. Advertising and sales practices are considered and standards of fair competition are established. Company expenses may be regulated. Deposits may be required in various jurisdictions as a guarantee of the willingness of a company to comply with state statutes and to discharge the obligations under its contracts.

The solvency of an insurance company is carefully regulated. There may be limitations on the size of risk that may be accepted by a single company. Specific requirements are established for reserve liabilities, the minimum size of capital and/or surplus, and investments and their proper valuation. Finally, the state presides over the conservation or liquidation of those companies whose solvency is in danger.

Organization and Licensing of Companies

Although the organization of insurance companies is governed to some extent by the law applying to the organization of corporations in general, most states have supplanted most of their general corporation law with special acts pertaining to insurance companies only. State insurance laws describe specifically the requirements for the organization of a life company. Health insurance may be written by either a life, a casualty, or a monoline company specializing in the field. Where

health insurance is written by a life company, the requirements for organization and licensing of a life company usually apply. Generally, a monoline or speciality health company may organize under either the life or casualty sections of the law.

State insurance codes require the drafting of a charter that specifically describes the name and location of the company, the lines of insurance it plans to write, the powers of the organization, and its officers. Frequently, the method of internal organization must be specified. Minimum amounts of paid-in capital and surplus for stock companies are stated, varying from a few hundred thousand to $1 million of capital plus an initial surplus varying from 50 to 200 percent of the minimum paid-in capital for each line of insurance (life or health) to be written. Minimum surplus and participation requirements for mutual insurers also are specified, and increasingly, the minimum surplus requirement is similar to the minimum capital and surplus requirement for stock companies.

Before issuing the certificate of incorporation, a responsible state official will investigate the character of the incorporators of the new firm, its proposed plan of operation and its marketing and financial projections. After meeting these and other requirements, the company is prepared to seek a license to conduct the insurance business.

The requirements for licensing foreign (out-of-state) and alien (non-U.S.) companies may be similar to those for domestic companies—sometimes they are more stringent. All companies (domestic, foreign, and alien) are required to maintain a substantial deposit of securities of a specified quality in trust with the state. To meet this requirement, foreign or alien companies may substitute a certificate from the insurance commissioner of another state in which they are licensed, to the effect that a deposit is being maintained in trust in that state for the purpose of protecting policyowners and/or creditors.

The deposit in trust for alien companies usually is quite substantial, and must be equal in value to its liabilities in the United States, plus a surplus that is at least equal to the minimum capital required for a domestic company licensed to transact the same kinds of business. In addition, several states require a small security deposit with the treasurer of the state for the purpose of protecting the policyowners of that particular state. Also, a foreign or alien company generally must appoint a resident of the state in which it wants to do business as its attorney, for purposes of serving a legal process.

Unauthorized Insurance

One of the more vexatious problems (in the light of the McCarran-Ferguson Act) confronting state insurance regulation involves the question of control over the activities of unauthorized insurance companies. By refusing to apply for a license, the unauthorized insurer may attempt to escape regulation in all states except the state of domicile on the basis that it has no representatives within the state and consequently it is not legally "doing business" within the state. Unauthorized insurers generally make no reports to the state insurance department. They are not subject to examination. Policy forms are not subject to state approval. Since the business often is conducted through the mails, and since interstate mail advertising is not subject to state control, the state commissioner may be powerless to render any service to the policyowner in the adjustment of claims.

At present, seven principal types of regulation are utilized by the states in an effort to control the operations of unauthorized insurers:

1. Under the NAIC Unauthorized Insurers Model Statute, as adopted by most states, the state may prohibit these insurers from "transacting business" within the state without first procuring a license to do so. Similarly, with certain obvious exceptions, no person shall (a) represent an unauthorized insurer in the solicitation, negotiation, or effectuation of insurance, or in any other manner in the transaction of insurance with respect to the subjects of insurance in the state involved; or (b) represent any person in the procuring of insurance in such an unauthorized insurer.

2. Although state unauthorized insurers' acts generally exclude from their scope group life and health policies delivered in other states, the NAIC has recommended that mass-marketed life and health insurance offered by means of direct response solicitation be subject to state advertising and claims settlement practices laws and be required to meet minimum-loss-ratio guidelines that states may have in effect.

3. Several states make such contracts legally voidable by the insured unless during the life of the contract the insurer becomes licensed to transact the class of insurance involved (i.e., life or health insurance).

4. Advertising originating outside the state, and designed to solicit insurance from persons located within the state, may be prohibited. Usually, this prohibition is aimed at the publisher, radio station, and so on, as well as the insurer.

5. Under the NAIC Uniform Unauthorized Insurers Service of Process Act, as adopted by many jurisdictions, the insured may bring a legal action involving a claim against an unauthorized out-of-state insurer by serving process upon the insurance commissioner of his or her home state.

6. The NAIC Non-Admitted Insurers Information Office—a central clearinghouse for the collection of information about insurers not licensed in all jurisdictions—may be used by individual states.

7. A significant number of states have enacted provisions of an NAIC Model assuming jurisdiction of plans providing health care benefits. The purpose of such legislation is to assert jurisdiction over uninsured or partially insured multiple employer or other trusts.

Despite the existence of laws of this type, numerous difficult problems of regulation may be found. They arise largely because the state of domicile does not control adequately the market practices and financial solvency of these companies. The principal problem seems to be the regulation of misleading advertising and solicitation conducted through the mails.

Insurance Company Operations

Once an insurance company is organized and licensed to transact business in the state, almost every phase of its operation is subject to state supervision. Policy forms must be approved, business-getting methods must exclude certain practices, and it must meet the prescribed standard of financial solvency.

Policy Forms. In most lines of insurance—including life and health insurance—policy forms are subjected to some regulation in an effort to protect insureds, policyowners, and beneficiaries against unfair and deceptive provisions and practices.[5] Contract regulation involves (1) the requirement that a policy form may not be used until it is filed with and approved by the state insurance department, and (2) the various requirements or standards for policy form approval.[6]

The insurance commissioner utilizes both general and specific legal standards designed to serve as a guide in his or her effort to determine the appropriateness of forms in the public interest. Much of this statutory and administrative law is based on recommendations of the NAIC. Since the application of general standards creates problems for both the commissioners and the industry, the NAIC and the various commissioners have developed specific standards that are designed to implement the general standard.

1. *Life insurance.* Every jurisdiction requires (or will accept) life insurance contract forms that contain, in substance, certain provisions as prescribed in the laws of most of the states. These statutory provisions, as recommended by the NAIC, include clauses related to the grace period, premium payment, incontestability, entire contract, misstatement of age, annual apportionment of dividends, surrender values and options, policy loans, settlement options, and reinstatement.[7] The required provisions for group life insurance contracts and certificates, as well as those for industrial life insurance contracts, are treated separately.

2. *Health insurance.* In 1946, following the SEUA decision and the passage of the McCarran-Ferguson Act, the NAIC and the All-Industry Committee recommended to the states enactment of an Accident and Health Regulatory Law.

In addition to establishing the requirement that contract forms, classifications, rates, and endorsements must be filed and that forms and endorsements must be approved, this law established the general standard that contracts must not be unjust, ambiguous, unfair, misleading, or encourage misrepresentation. Further, the model law states (although this provision was omitted by some jurisdictions) that forms may be disapproved if "benefits are unreasonable in relation to the premium charged" (see below).

Nearly all jurisdictions have adopted the Uniform Individual Accident and Sickness Policy Provisions Law as recommended by the NAIC in 1950.[8] This law includes specific language for both required and optional provisions and was amended in 1979 by the NAIC to improve readability.[9] As regards both the required and optional standard provisions, the insurer may use wording of its own choosing as long as it is no less favorable to the insured or beneficiary than the provisions as stated in the law.

In addition to the specific language contained in the 1950 law, the insurance commissioner of each jurisdiction has developed numerous specific guidelines by administrative regulation. Requirements are established for the clear labeling of limited policies. Certain types of provisions are prohibited or restricted, and certain practices with respect to the policy contract are controlled. These are too numerous and varied to be considered here.

Increasingly, regulation of health insurance policies is being built upon minimum benefit and disclosure requirements. The NAIC, for example, in 1973 adopted an Individual Accident and Sickness Insurance Minimum Standards Act as well as a regulation in 1974 to implement the act. These regulatory measures separate accident and sickness coverages into nine categories, each of which is subject to particular minimum benefit standards and disclosure rules. This classification of policies, and the public demands for coverages

---

[5] The definition of "approval" varies by jurisdiction. Many jurisdictions require approval of a form prior to its utilization, with the added provision that the form is approved by default at the end of 30 (or 45) days if the commissioner has not taken action.

[6] Much contract regulation actually arises because of undesirable claims, advertising, and other practices surrounding the use of the contract by a few insurers.

[7] See Chapters 8 and 9.

[8] Forty-seven states and the District of Columbia have adopted the Uniform Individual Accident and Sickness Policy Provisions Law. In addition, Georgia, Louisiana, and Alaska have adopted similar statutes.

[9] These required and optional provisions were discussed earlier. See Chapter 17.

that may be compared in the marketplace, can be expected to lead toward increased policy form standardization.

Rates. The supervision of the product involves, in many lines of insurance, the regulation of rates—the product price. The various states regulate rates in most of the property-liability insurance lines. Life (occasionally) and health insurance rates must be filed with the contract forms to which they apply. Generally, they are not subject to approval (see below). They are filed principally to make them a matter of public record for the benefit of those persons who come under the misstatement-of-age and other provisions involving a proration of premium.

1. *Life insurance.* Life insurance rates for individual insurance are regulated only in a most indirect sense. It is believed that competition is an adequate regulator over any tendencies toward rate excessiveness. As a practical matter, rate adequacy may be a problem, and it is believed that minimum reserve requirements (see below) and expense limitations are an adequate safeguard. The states of New York and Wisconsin have complex laws limiting the amount of expenses that can be incurred in the production of new business and the maintenance of old business in force.

The laws of most jurisdictions assume that for stock companies issuing nonparticipating contracts, competition is an adequate guarantor of rate equity among the different classes and generations of insureds. Mutual insurance companies often are prohibited from issuing nonparticipating policies. Where premiums prove to be redundant, equity demands that the excess be returned in the form of a dividend to each class or generation of insureds in proportion to their contributions to the surplus. Most states require that dividends be apportioned and paid (when earned) annually. A few states limit the amount of aggregate surplus that may be accumulated by a mutual insurer. Although announced specific standards do not exist, some commissioners review dividend apportionment formulas from time to time—generally at the time of the examination of the company.

Stock insurance companies issuing par-

ticipating contracts may be required to limit the amount of dividends payable to stockholders in the interest of fairness to insureds under such contracts.

Although life insurance rates are not directly regulated, in recent years there has been widespread state regulation activity designed to improve the quality of information provided to life insurance policyowners and applicants. The most significant price-related development is a requirement in the NAIC Life Insurance Solicitation Model Regulation (in force in almost 40 states) that interest-adjusted cost-comparison and other information be provided to consumers. The FTC has similarly considered the possibility of regulatory price disclosure for life insurance.[10]

2. *Health insurance.* One of the general standards for the approval of health insurance contract forms is basically an attempt to regulate the benefit provisions. It attempts the task by relating benefits to premium. Thus, forms must not be approved (or approval must be withdrawn) if "benefits are unreasonable in relation to the premium charged." This standard, found in the laws of a number of jurisdictions, is general in nature.

Although the distinction is somewhat tenuous, the law appears more nearly to establish standards (the general standard that policies shall be disapproved if benefits are not reasonable in relation to premium) for the approval of policy forms than for rates. It is the policy form that is subject to being disapproved—not the rates—in the event that there is a question about the reasonableness of benefits. However, the specific standard that the NAIC recommended to implement this general standard could provide some degree of surveillance over rates.

Loss-ratio guidelines have recently received renewed interest within the regulatory community as a means for monitoring and controlling pricing activities of health insurers. In 1980, the NAIC adopted and, in 1983, revised guidelines for the filing of rates for individual health insurance forms. The guidelines established loss ratio requirements for medical expense and loss of income coverages, depending on terms of renewal. It is

---

[10]See Chapter 10.

anticipated that heightened regulatory interest in health insurance pricing will continue in the coming years.

Marketing Practices

Broadly interpreted, state regulation of marketing practices includes control over the licensing of agents and brokers and over unfair trade practices.

Licensing of Agents and Brokers. The statutes of nearly all jurisdictions contain provisions for the licensing of resident and nonresident agents and brokers. A few jurisdictions license counselors. No person may act as agent, broker, or counselor within the jurisdiction without first obtaining a license. No company may issue a contract through or remunerate any person (other than on renewal business, or other deferred compensation where the agent has ceased to participate in the development of new business), unless the person holds a valid license.

The procedure that must be followed in obtaining a license is similar for all lines. In addition to the filing of the application by the licensee (in which the licensee must give detailed information regarding his or her character, experience, and general competence), each insurer for which he or she is to be licensed must submit a notice of appointment (or intention of appointment), together with a certificate of trustworthiness and competence signed by a responsible officer of the insurance company. In many states, the new applicant (usually defined as a person who has not held a license in the recent past—two years) meeting these requirements may receive a temporary license, with a permanent license being issued following the successful completion of an examination or such other test of competency in the line for which he or she is seeking a license.[11] Several states require new licensees to undertake a certain minimum number of hours (e.g., 40) of formal training in insurance before they can sit for the state examination. In addition to establishing a minimum standard of competency,

these examinations serve to reduce turnover and thus contribute further to the general upgrading of insurance representatives.

The agent's license may be perpetual until revoked or be subject to renewal at stipulated intervals. Licenses must be renewed through the payment of license and/or appointment fees. The license may be refused, revoked, or suspended by the commissioner, after notice and hearing, on the grounds that the agent willfully violated the law in his or her capacity as an agent, conducted fraudulent or dishonest practices, was proved untrustworthy or incompetent, or made a material misrepresentation in the application for his or her license. In addition, the license is terminated by death or termination of the agent's appointment by the insurance company. In states making provision for brokers, the requirements and procedures for obtaining a broker's license are, in general, similar to those already discussed.

Several states also require agents and brokers to undertake annually specific continuing education in their field. The individual must either demonstrate that he or she has met the minimum number of hours requirement or face nonrenewal of his or her license.

Unfair Trade Practices. Although states have long exercised control over certain unfair practices, especially misrepresentation, twisting, rebating, and unfair discrimination, the impact of the SEUA decision and the McCarran-Ferguson Act led substantially all jurisdictions to adopt the NAIC Model Unfair Trade Practices Act. Although differing in philosophy, the Act was designed to be sufficiently comprehensive to oust the Federal Trade Commission from jurisdiction over these matters. All unfair trade practice acts identify and define certain unfair trade practices. Usually, they give the commissioner the power to investigate and examine, and after notice and hearing, to issue cease and desist orders with penalties for violations. The acts are designed to prevent numerous activities deemed to be unfair, some of which are discussed below.[12]

Rebating is the practice of an agent (or insurer) returning a portion of the premium (e.g.,

---

[11]Controversy over the use of such temporary licenses has resulted in a decrease in their use.

[12]See Skipper, *Marketing Life and Health Insurance,* pp. 53–54.

agent's commission) to an applicant for insurance. Rebating historically has been illegal since it has been considered contrary to the maintenance of fair competition and equity among policyowners. Critics of the rebating prohibition argue that the prohibition is illogical in that it prevents buyers from negotiating fully with the sellers, as is the case with respect to noninsurance commodities and services. The Florida Supreme Court recently found Florida's anti-rebating statute to be unconstitutional as it "unnecessarily limits the bargaining power of the consuming public."[13] Whether other states will follow Florida and the exact impact of the Florida case is unclear at this writing.

Twisting refers to the practice of an agent inducing a policyowner through misrepresentation to discontinue an existing life insurance policy and purchase a new one from the agent. In contrast to simple **replacement,** which is discontinuing one policy to purchase another and is legal, twisting is illegal. The purchase of a life insurance policy, although not a complicated transaction, may involve a complex array of financial data. The consumer easily could be misled, either intentionally or unintentionally, by an agent. In recognition of this fact, several states have promulgated versions of the NAIC Model Replacement Regulations, which require the disclosure of certain information considered pertinent to the proposed replacement decision.[14]

Agents often handle large amounts of their policyowners' money in the form of premium payments, dividend checks, and surrender and loan funds. **Misappropriation** or misuse of these funds even on a temporary basis is illegal. Related to misappropriation is the practice of **comingling** of funds. Agents are not to combine monies belonging to policyowners with their own funds.

In the last few years, the NAIC has developed model regulations to deal with life insurance replacements, sex discrimination, discrimination on the basis of blindness, and discrimination on the basis of physical or mental handicaps. The NAIC is also focusing on the broader subject of classification of risks on sex-based rate differentials in health insurance.

Unfair Advertising Practices. The Federal Trade Commission's "Trade Practices Rules Relating to the Advertising of Mail Order Insurance" promulgated in 1950 represented the first attempt of the commission to regulate the practices of insurance companies (other than actions regarding boycott, coercion, and intimidation) under the proviso clause of the McCarran-Ferguson Act.

To stengthen their contention that advertising was adequately regulated by the state law, the NAIC recommended the Rules Governing Advertisements of Accident and Sickness Insurance with Interpretive Guidelines in December 1955, which were completely revised in 1974. These rules are composed of specific standards designed to serve as a guide to the commissioners in the implementation of the general advertising standards contained in the model Uniform Trade Practices Act.

In 1975, the NAIC recommended Model Rules Governing the Advertising of Life Insurance to the states. A substantial number of states have moved to implement the new rules or to devise other rules designed to regulate life advertising. Some states' regulations have considerably expanded the scope of the NAIC model. The rules recommended by the NAIC regulate the form and content of advertisements, set forth minimum disclosure requirements, and provide for enforcement procedures.

Financial Condition

As indicated previously, the most important objective of regulation relates to the financial soundness of insurance companies. This concern is most obvious in the various statutory and administrative standards and regulations surrounding the financial management of an operating company. Briefly, insurance supervisory authorities desire that an insurance company maintain at all times assets at least equal to its currently due and prospectively estimated liabilities (including minimum capital and/or surplus requirements). Further, in order that the relationship between assets and liabilities will have some meaning, there

[13]Lisa Howard, "Florida Court Strikes Down Anti-rebate Law," *National Underwriter*, Life/Health ed. (June 14, 1986), p. 1.

[14]See Chapter 10.

is a large body of law specifically relating to these items.

Assets. Although there is a decided lack of uniformity in the insurance codes of the various states as they pertain to company assets, all jurisdictions are concerned with the types of investments that are permitted and the techniques of asset valuation. Chapter 31 presented a discussion of the principal aspects of life insurer investment regulation.

It should be noted that nearly all jurisdictions distinguish between capital and reserve investments. New York follows the traditional pattern and requires that funds equivalent to the minimum capital or surplus required by law for the line or lines of insurance being transacted be invested in certain very secure types of investments (cash, government bonds, and mortgages). Life insurance companies may invest all remaining funds in "reserve investments"—"capital investments" plus other permitted investments of second quality.

The law in most jurisdictions requires that no insurance company make any investment or loan unless it is authorized or approved by the company's board of directors, or by a committee authorized by such a board and charged with the supervision or making of such investments. The law further requires that the minutes of any such committee shall be recorded, and that regular reports of the committee shall be submitted to the board of directors. The directors and officers must not have a personal interest in the investments or in their sale to the insurance company.

The valuation of the assets held by an insurer for annual-statement purposes is a complicated and detailed procedure. Most insurance statutes state that the commissioner may specify the rules for determining the value of securities, subject (in some cases) to the limitation that such rules shall not be inconsistent with those established by the NAIC.[15] Through its securities valuation office, the NAIC values on a uniform basis the securities held in portfolios of virtually every insurance company in the United States.

Liabilities. The principal liabilities on insurers' balance sheets are the insurance-policy reserves. An insurance-policy reserve is a balance sheet account established to reflect actual and potential liabilities under expired and outstanding contracts.

1. *Life insurance.* Life insurers are required by law to establish minimum reserves as a liability. In this regard, the Standard Valuation Law and the Standard Nonforfeiture Law, adopted by the NAIC, have been enacted or otherwise made effective in all jurisdictions. Their provisions are applicable, in general, to all policies issued since their enactment or amendment. The valuation of life insurance reserves was discussed earlier.[16] Modified valuation standards and nonforfeiture requirements have been developed by the NAIC for universal life products in the NAIC's Universal Life Insurance Model Regulation adopted in 1983.

2. *Health insurance.* Annual statement health insurance reserves include the unearned premium reserve; the additional reserve (active-life reserve) for policies where the insurer's right of termination is restricted by the terms of the contract or company practice; the reserve for future contingent benefits; the reserve for the present value of amounts not yet due on approved claims; the reserve for claims in the course of settlement; the reserve for incurred but unreported claims; and the claim-expense reserve.

Although the continued financial soundness of an insurer depends on proper investments, together with the correct valuation of all assets, the establishment and proper valuation of reserves is just as important and in the health insurance line, a much more difficult task. In most jurisdictions, the standards utilized in measuring the adequacy of the various health insurance reserves are left to individual company determination, with many companies making this determination in consultation with the actuaries of the respective state insurance departments.[17]

[16]See Chapter 20 for a discussion of the valuation of policy-reserve liabilities.

[15]See Chapter 31 for a discussion of the valuation of assets.

[17]See Chapter 22 for a discussion of health insurance reserves.

Rehabilitation and Liquidation

When, regardless of other regulatory efforts, an insurer is in serious financial or other difficulties, the state insurance department in most jurisdictions has the further responsibility of assuming control over its assets and management, in the case of domestic and alien insurers (where the largest amount of the U.S. assets of the alien insurer are located within the state), or over its assets, in the case of foreign insurers located within the state. The usual procedure requires that when he or she deems it necessary, the insurance commissioner must petition the proper court for a court order appointing him or her (in his or her official capacity) receiver for the purpose of rehabilitation, conservation, or liquidation.

If the commissioner determines that reorganization, consolidation, conversion, reinsurance, merger, or other transformation is appropriate, a specific plan of **rehabilitation** may be prepared. Under a rehabilitation order, the commissioner is granted title to the domestic insurance company's assets and is given the authority to carry on its business until he or she is able to return it to private management after the grounds for issuing the order have been removed. The numerous statutory grounds under which the commissioner may apply for a rehabilitation order include (1) a finding that further transaction of business would be financially hazardous to policyowners, creditors, or the public; (2) a determination that the insurers' officers and/or directors are guilty of certain acts or omissions; and (3) where a substantial transfer of assets, merger, or consolidation is attempted without the prior written consent of the commissioner.

Liquidation of a domestic insurer is the ultimate power of the commissioner under this NAIC model act. When it is found not advisable to attempt rehabilitation, or if rehabilitation becomes impracticable, the commissioner must petition the proper court for a liquidation order. Grounds for liquidation include those listed for rehabilitation and the additional ground that the insurer is insolvent. Under liquidation proceedings, the commissioner is given title to all assets of the insurer wherever located and is directed to take possession of them as soon as possible. Notice is required to be given to other insurance commissioners, guarantee funds, insurance agents, and all persons known or reasonably expected to have claims against the insurer. The act establishes priorities for distribution of assets, with the cost of administration, employee salaries, and policyowner claims receiving highest priorities. Irrespective of whether the ancillary receiverships have been established, the distribution of assets in nondomiciliary states will be controlled by the statutes of the domiciliary state.

In a technical sense, the statutes of several jurisdictions use the term **conservation order** to refer to the court order directing the commissioner to act as receiver for the conservation of assets of a foreign or alien insurance company that is located within the jurisdiction. The grounds forming the basis for the insurance commissioner's request are similar to those for liquidation and rehabilitation. Usually, prior to or concurrent with being named receiver under an order of conservation, the commissioner will revoke or suspend the insurer's license to do business within the state.

The procedure of naming the insurance commissioner (rather than another person) as receiver was developed to reduce the delay and expense associated with the ordinary receivership procedure, thereby speeding the return of a larger payment to the creditors and policyowners of the company. In some cases, it makes possible the rehabilitation of a company, so that there will be little or no loss to those involved. Some jurisdictions still apply the usual procedures utilized in the liquidation of a business firm; that is, the commissioner must petition the proper court for the appointment of a receiver (other than the commissioner), who will then liquidate the company under the direction of the court. Under such circumstances, the possibility of rehabilitation may not exist because of delay, lack of technical ability, and so on.

Life and Health Insurance Guaranty Laws

A development of major import to the life and health insurance business is the increasing number of state enactments of insolvency guaranty laws. This has assumed even greater importance with several recent insolvencies. Generally, these laws provide for the indemnification of losses suffered by policyowners of insolvent companies, through an association that derives funds for this purpose from assessments against solvent companies doing business in the state. In the case of life and health insurance guaranty laws, indemnification may be by payment of claims or cash values or by continuation of the policies of the insolvent company.

The concept underlying guaranty laws first appeared in the early 1900s in state laws (all ultimately repealed) in the field of bank regulation. The first continuing laws that embody the concept are found at the federal level of bank regulation, in the 1933 Federal Deposit Insurance Corporation Act and the 1934 Federal Savings and Loan Insurance Corporation Act, both of which guarantee, up to specified limits, deposits in banks that fail.

Through the early 1940s, the concept spread in scattered enactments in the fields of workers' compensation insurance and public motor vehicle liability insurance. In 1969, the NAIC promulgated a model Guaranty Act for Property and Liability Insurance, which was widely adopted by states in 1969 and 1970. In 1970 the NAIC followed with a similar model guaranty association act applicable to life and health insurance.

From the inception of the idea of insolvency guaranty laws applicable to life and health insurance, the industry took the position that insolvencies should be prevented, because this is one of the primary purposes of state insurance regulation; and that, moreover, guaranty laws were unfair to policyowners of assessed companies, thereby subverting another primary principle of insurance regulation.

Despite these and other objection, the industry, in general, now supports the enactment of state guaranty laws that follow the NAIC model act and contain provisions allowing assessments to be offset against taxes, thus tending to alleviate the unfairness of the law to policyowners of assessed companies. At least 35 states have life and health insurance guaranty laws and additional states are considering such legislation.

Although it is too soon to assess its impact, a revised model guaranty fund bill was adopted by the NAIC at its December 1985 meeting. The new model is intended to strengthen certain weaknesses of its predecessor and would create four separate accounts: one each for life insurance, health insurance, regular annuities, and unallocated annuity contracts. The NAIC is continuing study in this important area, with further action by the NAIC and the states to be expected in the future.

Perhaps the most important factor in the apprehensiveness of the life and health insurance business toward insolvency guaranty laws lies in the felt need for stronger state regulation to prevent insolvencies.[18] The industry has urged the strengthening of state regulation, particularly with regard to improvements in company examinations, more effective minimum capital and surplus requirements and regulatory procedures designed to disclose promptly incipient company financial problems that might lead to insolvency. Several developments in this regard are worthy of mention.

The NAIC Insurance Regulatory Information System (IRIS) has been applied to life and health insurance companies since 1973. It is similar to one applied to casualty companies beginning in 1972. The program consists of a series of ratios calculated from figures shown in company annual statements and other sources and is designed to give a prompt indication of possible financial problems. The tests are not meant to be conclusive as to a company's condition, but are intended simply to furnish state regulators indications of possible financial problems.

McKinsey & Company made a comprehensive study of the convention examination system, the recommendations from which resulted in the preparation of an *NAIC Examiners Handbook*, which is divided into financial condition and market conduct chapters. As implemented by the states, the examination system concentrates on those insurers most likely to be the subject of actual or potential problems. The three key elements for an effective financial examination system are use of the NAIC

---

[18]While agreeing with this view, one former NAIC president has observed that in a private enterprise economy, "insolvencies are going to occur, and the best that regulators can hope to do is to limit their harmful impact." "New NAIC Guaranty Fund Bill Amends Controls on Annuities," *National Underwriter*, December 21, 1985, p. 6.

IRIS tests, implementation of a system for scheduling examinations, and a system for planning and conducting examinations. Scheduling examinations should provide the insurance department with a systematic approach to rank insurers according to priority classifications. The criteria for determining a priority classification include changes in management control, results of the regulatory information tests, results of prior financial condition and market conduct examinations, information from other sources, and the elapsed time since the last examination. Planning of examinations should assign priority to accounts that are most likely to affect solvency. The priority assigned to each account is based upon IRIS test results, previous examinations, and other information.

The New York Insurance Department published a report on the examination of companies and the New York insolvency guaranty law. This scholarly study, two years in the making, suggests radical changes in the examination system in order to focus examination procedures more closely on the prevention of insolvencies.

TAXATION OF LIFE AND HEALTH INSURANCE COMPANIES

Life and health insurance companies are taxed by federal, state, and local governments. The basis for this taxation differs from the basis of taxes levied on other corporations. This difference stems primarily from two factors. First, a large part of life insurance premium income is in the nature of a deposit of funds by policyowners and therefore is not earned income to the life insurance company. Second, the life insurance contract is long term in nature, and the usual approach of annual income taxation is not as appropriate for life insurance companies as for other companies whose contracts usually are completed in a relatively short time.

State Taxation

The most important form of state tax levied on life insurers is the tax on life and health insurance premiums and annuity considerations,

mentioned earlier in connection with the revenue objective of state regulation. Today, all states impose a premium tax of some sort, and the imposition of this tax has developed into a revenue measure rather than a method for financing the regulation of the business. Only about 5 percent of the total premium tax collected is utilized to defray the cost of supervising insurance companies. The tax rates on life and health premiums vary among states from about 1 to 4 percent, the most common rate being 2 percent.

In determining the tax base to which the premium tax rate will apply, it is necessary to include only those direct premiums received from policies insuring risks domiciled in the state. Reinsurance premiums received are not commonly included in the tax base. In two-thirds of the states, annuity considerations are not included in the tax base, and in all but three states that tax annuity considerations, the rate is lower than that applied to life and health premiums. Some states exempt both life insurance premiums and annuity considerations received in connection with qualified retirement plans.

About three-fourths of the states allow dividends paid to policyowners to be deducted from the tax base, except those dividends applied to purchase additional insurance or to shorten the premium-paying or endowment periods of the policies. The remaining states do not allow a deduction for policyowner dividends, but with one exception, none of these states requires dividends applied to purchase additional insurance or to shorten the premium-paying or endowment periods to be included in the base.

About one-fifth of the states allow other taxes, such as ad valorem taxes paid on real estate within the state and state income taxes paid, to be offset against the premium tax. Approximately one-fifth of the states allow a reduction in the premium tax if a designated portion of the company's assets are invested within the state. Such measures are designed to benefit the insurers domiciled in the state. This, together with the fact that some states either do not levy premium taxes on domestic companies or else tax them at a lower rate than that on foreign insurers, means that a majority of states have tax laws favoring domestic companies. In the 1985 case, *Metropolitan Life In-*

surance Company, et al. v. W.G. Ward, Jr., et al., the U.S. Supreme Court stated that a state could not discriminate in favor of its domestic companies in this manner. As a result of this and certain state actions, several states have recently eliminated this tax disparity.[19]

The premium tax laws of most states have a retaliatory feature, as pointed out earlier. These provisions have had the effect of promoting uniformity in the rate of premium taxation among the states by discouraging increases in the tax rate charged by a state on foreign insurers, since such an increase by a state would result in its domestic companies having to pay the same rate in other states.

In the majority of states, the premium tax is in lieu of other specified taxes. In many states, the premium tax is in lieu of all other state and local taxes, except those on real estate and tangible personal property, and license fees.

The premium tax, although administratively simple, has been the object of criticism on the grounds (1) that it constitutes a direct tax on savings applicable only to insurers, (2) that it is a regressive tax in that it hits lower-income persons who purchase life insurance relatively harder than higher-income persons, (3) that it discriminates unfairly against higher-premium (and cash value) forms of life insurance since it is levied on the premium level, and (4) that it discriminates unfairly against those who must pay higher premium rates, such as the elderly and those rated substandard. On the other hand, the tax is viewed by some as a simple substitute for state income taxation.

In most jurisdictions, the states have preempted the taxation of life and health insurance companies as a source of revenue and have not permitted their subdivisions to impose taxes on the companies. Wherever local taxes are permitted and imposed, the maintenance of special records and the filing of reports constitutes a serious administrative burden that is disproportionate to the revenue produced.

Federal Income Taxation[20]

Since the advent of federal income taxation, life insurance company tax formulas have undergone frequent revisions designed to make them acceptable to all segments of the industry and, at the same time, to produce the revenues expected by Congress. To be equitable, a tax formula to be applied to life insurance companies should (1) recognize the long-term nature of the life insurance contract and the difficulty in determining the operating gain in any one year, (2) tax both mutual and stock companies fairly without disrupting the existing competitive balance, and (3) provide an acceptable method for determining the deduction for interest required to maintain policyowner reserves.

From 1913 through 1920, life insurance companies were taxed on their total income under the provisions generally applicable to all business corporations. From 1921 until 1958, life insurance companies were taxed at ordinary corporate rates but only on their net investment income. The Life Insurance Company Tax Act of 1959 changed this yet again by imposing a tax (at ordinary corporate rates) on a life insurance company's "total" income.

The manner in which the 1959 Act derived this total income base, however, was relatively complex and widely misunderstood. The 1959 Act tax base consisted of three parts—an investment income element, an underwriting gain element (which for many companies was only partially taxed on a current basis), and a deferred underwriting gain base—and thus was said to constitute a "three-phase" approach to life insurance company taxation.

In the Deficit Reduction Act of 1984, Congress rewrote the 1959 Act in an effort to correct what it believed were a number of inadequacies.

---

[19]This preferential treatment of domestic insurers is controversial and is not yet settled fully. The Supreme Court in *Metropolitan* was sharply divided on the issue and ruled on two issues only. Others are pending. See "Justices Say State Can't Tax to Favor Local Firms Solely to Promote Industry," *Wall Street Journal,* March 27, 1985. See also Alfred E. Hofflander and Blaine F. Nye, "An Economic Analysis of Discriminatory Premium Taxation," *Journal of Insurance Regulation,* Vol. 3 (September 1984).

[20]This section draws from William B. Harman, Jr. "The Structure of Life Insurance Company Taxation—The New Pattern under the 1984 Act—Parts I and II," *Journal of the American Society of CLU,* Vol. 39 (March 1985) and (May 1985).

These perceived inadequacies related, in part, to the changing nature of life insurance products; to the fluctuating interest rates of recent years, as contrasted with the low and stable interest rates of the 1959 era; to a concern about the overstatement of reserve liabilities and of certain special deductions; and to the partial deferral of tax on underwriting gain. As a result, in the 1984 Act, Congress mandated a conceptually simple tax base that still encompasses a life insurance company's total income, but that does so on a single-phase basis.

Taxable Income. The 1984 Act defines **life insurance company taxable income** (LICTI) to be gross income less applicable deductions. This general approach is the same as that of other corporations, but many of the details necessarily differ, as discussed below.

1. *Life Insurance Gross Income.* The items of receipt, or gross income, of a life insurance company can be divided into five categories:[21]

1. Premiums,
2. Investment income,
3. Capital gains,
4. Decreases in reserves,
5. All other items of gross income

Table 33–1 illustrates the source and magnitude of the gross receipts of U.S. life insurance companies for 1984.

Thus, IRC Section 803(a)(1) includes as an income item of the company, all its *premiums and other considerations* received on its insurance and annuity contracts. According to section 803(b), these receipt items include fees, deposits, assessments, advance or prepaid premiums, reinsurance premiums, and the amount of policyowner dividends reimbursable to the company by a reinsurer with respect to reinsured policies. Also included are premiums or deposits on supplementary contracts or policy proceeds left with the company. A company may reduce its premium receipts includible in gross income by the amount of any returned premiums (e.g., premiums returned

[21]These same items were reflected in "gain from operations" under the 1959 Act.

TABLE 33-1.   1985 income of U.S. life insurance companies

	Amount (000,000 omitted)	Percent of total
Premium receipts		
Life insurance premiums	$ 60,127	26
Annuity considerations	53,899	23
Health insurance premiums	41,837	18
Total premium receipts	$155,863	67
Investment income (net of investment expenses)	67,952	29
Other income (mainly considerations for supplementary contracts	10,212	4
Total income	$234,027	100

Source: 1986 Life Insurance Fact Book (Washington, D.C.: American Council of Life Insurance), p. 59.

because of policy cancellations or errors in determining the premium) and premiums paid to other insurance companies under reinsurance agreements. Based on Table 33–1, approximately 65 percent of a typical life insurance company's gross income will be included under this section.

The other principal source of income of a life insurance company is from its *investment* activities. The investment earnings of a life insurance company consist primarily of interest, dividends, rents, and royalties. As shown in Table 33–1, approximately 29 percent of a typical life insurance company's gross income will consist of investment earnings.[22]

Life insurance companies are taxed on *capital gains* in the same manner as other corporate taxpayers. This includes an alternative tax at a 28 percent rate on any net capital gain (the excess of the net long-term capital gains over the net short-term capital losses).

Any net *decrease in certain insurance reserves* will produce an income item. The reserves in question are those peculiar to life insurance companies

[22]The 1959 Act used an investment income base as one of its three phases. The 1984 Act eliminated this feature of the law, and investment income is now included simply as part of life insurance gross income.

(see below). Life insurance companies are allowed tax deductions when net additions are made to such reserves. Thus, when the reserves are no longer needed and are released, their release or decrease will produce an income item for the company.

Finally, the law contains a catch-all provision that picks up all items of gross income that have not been included under any of the other four categories discussed above. The sum of the five categories described above produces life insurance gross income.

2. *Life Insurance Deductions.* The items of deduction allowed a life insurance company under the 1984 Act can be divided into four categories:

1. General corporate deductions,
2. Deductions peculiar to the insurance business,
3. The special life insurance company deduction,
4. The small life insurance company deduction.

First, a life insurance company is allowed all the deductions allowable to other corporate taxpayers, with certain technical modifications.[23]

Second, life insurance companies are permitted certain deductions that are *peculiar to the insurance business.* Thus, a deduction is allowed for all claims, benefits, and losses incurred on insurance and annuity contracts. These payments are analogous to income tax deductions permitted for a manufacturing organization's cost of raw materials.

A life insurance company is also granted a deduction for any net annual addition to specified insurance reserves that it must maintain with respect to its insurance and annuity contracts. This reserve deduction includes two items: (1) the "savings" element included in premiums or considerations received plus (2) the interest the company must assume to be added each year to the reserve so that it will be sufficient to meet the company's future liabilities. The deductible net increase in reserves is computed by subtracting the opening balance of the reserves (January 1) from the closing balance of the reserves (December 31).

The six insurance reserves taken into account under the 1984 Act are, with only minor exceptions, the same as under the 1959 Act. These reserves are as follows:

1. Life insurance reserves,
2. Unearned premiums and unpaid losses in "total reserves,"
3. Discounted liabilities for insurance or annuity contracts not currently involving life, accident, or health contingencies,
4. Dividend accumulations and other amounts held at interest under insurance or annuity contracts,
5. Advanced premiums and premium deposit fund liabilities,
6. Reasonable special contingency reserves under group contracts for retired lives and premium stabilization.

Under the 1959 Act, the amounts of a life insurance company's reserves at the end of the taxable year generally were the amounts shown on the company's annual statement. The 1984 Act substantially changed the rules for determining life insurance reserves, generally resulting in a considerable *decrease* in such reserves as compared to 1959 Act reserves, particularly in the early years of a policy. The basic rule under the 1984 Act is that the life insurance reserve for any contract shall be the greater of (1) the net surrender value of the contract, or (2) the reserve for the contract as computed under new federally prescribed standards. In no event, however, is this amount permitted to exceed the annual statement figure.

The reserve as computed under the new federal standards is an amount determined in accordance with the methods and assumptions used in calculating the life insurance reserves shown on the company's annual statement, but modified to take account of the following five federal standards.

1. A prescribed tax reserve method. This is the Commissioners' Reserve Valuation Method for life insurance contracts.[24]
2. The "prevailing state assumed interest rate." This rate is the highest assumed interest rate that at least 26 states permit to be used in computing

---

[23]See Harman, "The Structure of Life Insurance Company Taxation" (March 1985), p. 61, for details.

[24]See Chapter 20.

reserves for the particular insurance or annuity contract.[25]

3. The "prevailing commissioners' standard tables." These are the most recent standard tables for mortality and morbidity prescribed by the National Association of Insurance Commissioners that at least 26 states permit to be used in computing reserves for the type of contract involved at the time of issue.[26]

4. The elimination from the reserves of any amount with respect to deferred and uncollected premiums (unless the gross amount of such premiums are included in gross income).[27]

5. The elimination of any reserve in respect of "excess interest" (i.e., interest exceeding the prevailing state assumed interest rate) guaranteed beyond the end of the taxable year.

Using these new federal standards, each life insurance company was required to recompute its life insurance reserves for its first taxable year under the 1984 Act (generally, calendar year 1984) for all contracts in existence at that time. In the absence of special relief, this would have caused virtually all companies to realize income, as the new reserves would be smaller than existing reserves, and the decrease in reserves would produce an item of income. To avoid this result, the 1984 Act provides, as a general rule, a "fresh start" which precludes this from occurring.

Another deduction peculiar to the life insurance business is that permitted for policyowner dividends.[28] This term is defined by Section 808 as any dividend paid or payable to a policyowner in his or her capacity as such, and includes any distribution to a policyowner that is economically equivalent to a dividend. Accordingly, it includes excess interest, premium adjustments, and experience-rated refunds, as well as any amount paid or credited to policyowners (including an increase in benefits) where the amount is not fixed

in the contract but depends on the experience of the company or the discretion of management.

A stock life insurance company is allowed an unlimited deduction for policyowner dividends paid or accrued during the taxable year. A mutual life insurer, however, may be subject to a limitation on the deductibility of its policyowner dividends, as was the case under the 1959 Act (see below).

Besides the general corporate deductions and deductions peculiar to the life insurance business, a **special life insurance company deduction** is allowed equal to 20 percent of the excess of (1) its tentative life insurance company taxable income over (2) the amount (if any) of its small life insurance company deduction (see below). Thus, if a company's tentative LICTI were $100 and its small life insurance company deduction were $60, its special life insurance company deduction would be $8.[29]

The basic reason for the allowance of this special deduction was to avoid any substantial increase in the tax burden on life insurance companies due to the enactment of the 1984 Act, and to tax life insurance companies at an effective tax rate that would allow them to compete with other financial intermediaries. The effect of the deduction is to tax life insurance company income at a maximum effective rate of 36.8 percent, instead of at the 46 percent top corporate rate.[30]

The final major deduction allowed is the **small life insurance company deduction.** This deduction equals 60 percent of the tentative LICTI, up to a maximum of $3,000,000. Thus, the small-company deduction can never exceed $1,800,000 (i.e., 60% × $3,000,000). If a life insurance company's tentative LICTI exceeds $3,000,000, the amount of the small-company deduction is phased out by an amount equal to 15 percent of tentative LICTI in excess of $3,000,000. Thus, for a company with tentative LICTI of $15,000,000 or more, no small-company deduction is allowed. Tentative LICTI is LICTI *before* the two special deductions and excluding

[25]See Chapter 20.

[26]See Chapter 20.

[27]See Chapter 32.

[28]Two other potentially important deductions relate to deductions for assumption reinsurance and for policyowner dividends paid by a reinsurer to the ceding company. See Harman, "The Structure of Life Insurance Company Taxation" (March 1985), pp. 62–63.

[29]($100 − $60) × 0.20 = $8.

[30]46% × (1 − 0.20) = 36.8%.

items attributable to "noninsurance" business.[31]

For example, if a small life insurance company had tentative LICTI of $2,000,000, its small life insurance company deduction would be $1,200,000 (60% × $2,000,000). If, however, the company's tentative LICTI were $5,000,000, its small life insurance company deduction would be $1,500,000, determined as follows:

1. 60% × $3,000,000 = $1,800,000
2. Reduced by 15% ×
   ($5,000,000 –
   $3,000,000)   300,000
                        $1,500,000

The purpose of this deduction was to continue to treat small life insurance companies more favorably than large companies, consistent with the general congressional policy of encouraging small business. The effect of this deduction, when combined with the special life insurance company deduction, is to tax a small company at a maximum effective rate of 14.72 percent, if its tentative LICTI is $3,000,000 or less.[32]

3. *Example.* An example may serve to illustrate both the computation and relevance of tentative LICTI and LICTI. Note that tentative LICTI)1) excludes items attributable to the noninsurance business ($100,000), whereas LICTI includes that $100,000 since it constitutes gain, and (2) tentative LICTI is used to determine the amount of both the small company and special deductions.

Tentative LICTI calculation

Life insurance gross income	$1,000,000
Less:	
General corporate deductions	$300,000

Deductions peculiar to the insurance business	400,000	
Items attributable to noninsurance businesses	100,000	
Total deduction		800,000
Tentative LICTI		$ 200,000

Life insurance deductions

General corporate deductions	$300,000
Deductions peculiar to the insurance business	400,000
Small life insurance company deduction (60% × $200,000)	120,000
Special life insurance company deduction (20% × ($200,000 – $120,000))	16,000
Total Life Insurance Deductions	$836,000

Life insurance company taxable income calculation

Life insurance gross income	$1,000,000
Less: Life insurance deductions	836,000
Life insurance company taxable income (LICTI)	$ 164,000

This illustrates the basic single-phase corporate tax structure that applies to life insurance companies under the 1984 Act. The pattern of taxation has been simplified considerably from the three-phase structure of the 1959 Act. The basic structure is similar to that applicable to other corporate taxpayers. This is particularly true for stock company life insurers. This basic structure also applies to mutual life insurance companies; however, mutual companies have a limitation on the deductibility of their policyowner dividends.

Mutual Company Dividend Treatment. According to current tax-law theory, distributions to customers should be fully deductible by a corporation, whereas distributions to owners of the enterprise should not be deductible. But in the case of a mutual organization, the customers effectively are the owners also.

Mutual companies charge relatively larger premiums and return unneeded excess premiums as dividends to policyowners. This excess generally is conceded to be properly deductible at the corporate level. However, also included in policyowner dividends are some distribution of investment and underwriting earnings of the

---

[31]Congress believed that these two deductions should be allowed only against income arising from the life insurance business. Otherwise, a life insurance company would have a tax advantage in operating a noninsurance business within its corporate framework as compared to a general corporate taxpayer operating the small business but being taxed at a 46 percent corporate tax rate.

[32]46% × (1 – 0.20) = 36.8%, and 36.8% × (1 – 0.60) = 14.72%.

mutual company (since the policyowner is effectively an owner of the company, as well as a purchaser of its services). Many believe that in contrast with the return of excess premiums, these earnings are properly taxable at the corporate level. Congress had to resolve this issue.

Another issue faced by Congress, intertwined with the dividend deductibility issue, was the amount of revenue to be raised from the industry and the way in which it was to be apportioned between stock and mutual companies. For example, a 100 percent policyowner dividend deduction would have permitted mutual companies to pay a very small amount of tax (or perhaps none at all) if they decided to distribute all or substantially all of their earnings to their policyowners. On the other hand, if no deduction were permitted, legitimate payments to policyowners as customers (rather than as owners), which should be deductible under general tax principles, would be denied to mutuals, a result that would be unfair because it would have overtaxed those companies. Thus, it was (and is) crucial to impose appropriate relative tax burdens on each segment—stock and mutual—so that the federal income tax does not favor one segment over the other. Accordingly, in an effort to treat the stock and mutual segments equitably and to raise appropriate revenues from the industry, it was judged necessary to limit the dividend deduction for mutual companies.

The objectives of the 1984 Act's dividend deduction limitation were twofold. First, it was designed to ensure that mutual life insurers did not, through a combination of policyowner dividend distributions and other deductions, reduce their gain from operations after dividends to an amount below a minimum, imputed return on "equity." Second, it was desired to achieve a revenue balance between the stock and mutual segments of the industry. The appropriate segment balance was determined to be 55 percent mutual/45 percent stock for 1984, based on the facts before Congress. It will shift in future years depending on the relative earnings of each segment.

The assumption underlying this portion of the Act is that an appropriate guide to the profitability of mutual life insurers is the profitability on equity of stock life insurers. The mechanics of the limitation on the deductibility of policyowner dividends by a mutual company are complex, involving the determination of a **differential earnings rate** on "equity" between stock and mutual companies.[33] The imputed earnings rate on equity for stock insurers is higher than that for mutual insurers, and this difference is assumed to represent a return to policyowners in mutual companies on their ownership interests in the companies. As such, this amount must be excluded by the mutual company from its dividend deduction (i.e., it is not deductible). The differential earnings rate is recalculated each year.

Preservation of 1959 Act Deferred Tax Base. The 1959 Act permitted stock life insurance companies to defer part of their taxable income. Under the new law, each stock company that had a tax-deferred account on December 31, 1983 is required to continue to maintain this account. Since there are no longer any deferral items, no amount may be added. Amounts in such accounts will be subject to tax under the same rules as those prescribed by the 1959 Act; generally, when amounts are distributed to shareolders or when certain statutory limitations are exceeded. Any such amount is added directly to LICTI.

Proration Concept of the 1984 Act. Over the years, one of the major policy issues in the taxation of life insurance companies has been the treatment of tax-favored income, such as tax-exempt state and municipal bond interest and intercorporate dividends subject to the dividends received deduction. This issue arises because life insurance companies have always been allowed to deduct interest added to insurance reserves, and some part of that reserve interest deduction can be thought of as being derived from tax-favored income. Congress has consistently taken the view that a double deduction would result if a life insurance company were allowed to deduct both interest additions to reserves and also to deduct or exclude the tax-favored income from its tax base. The 1984 Act basically preserved the 1959 Act's treatment of this problem. A deduction is permitted for tax-favored

[33]See Harman, "The Structure of Life Insurance Company Taxation" (May 1985), pp. 77–80 for details.

investments, but it is reduced to prevent it from being counted twice.

This explanation has covered only the main outlines of the life insurance company tax law. Even as this text was going to press, Congress had under consideration a wholesale revision of the entire Internal Revenue Code.[34] One of its professed intentions is to simplify greatly the method

[34]The President signed the Tax Reform Act of 1986 into law on October 22, 1986.

of taxation of individuals and corporations throughout the country. In many ways, the 1984 revision of the life insurance company tax portions of the Code was the first wave of tax simplification. Nevertheless, the proposed legislation, if passed, could make additional changes in the method of taxation of life insurance companies. Obviously, the tax law is a dynamic creature and one that is a major factor in influencing the management of life insurance companies.

Index